lonely planet

South India

Christine Niven
Lindsay Brown
Teresa Cannon
Peter Davis
Paul Greenway
Douglas Streatfeild-James

South India

1st edition

Published by
Lonely Planet Publications
Head Office: PO Box 617, Hawthorn, Vic 3122, Australia
Branches: 150 Linden Street, Oakland, CA 94607, USA
    10a Spring Place, London NW5 3BH, UK
    1 rue du Dahomey, 75011 Paris, France

Printed by
Colorcraft Ltd, Hong Kong

Photographs
All of the images in this guide are available for licensing from Lonely Planet Images.
email: lpi@lonelyplanet.com.au

Front cover: Detail of a painting of the god Ganesh, Mysore (Eddie Gerald, Lonely Planet Image

This Edition
November 1998

Although the authors and publisher have tried to make the information as accurate as possible, they accept no responsibility for any loss, injury or inconvenience sustained by any person using this book.

National Library of Australia Cataloguing in Publication Data

South India

1st ed.
Includes index
ISBN 0 86442 594 5

1. India, South – Guidebooks. I. Niven, Christine, 1954-

915.480452

Christine Niven

Christine set out from New Zealand for the big Overseas Experience at the age of 20 and never really settled down after that. Overlanding from Europe to India was her first long trip and was followed by journeys through China, Japan, South-East Asia and the Middle East. She continues to travel whenever the opportunity arises, probably in defiance of good sense. Christine has also authored *India* and *Sri Lanka* for Lonely Planet.

Lindsay Brown

Lindsay grew up on NSW's south coast and in sunny Melbourne. A promising career in fisheries conservation biology remained just that, and after a brief stint in science publishing he landed a job with Lonely Planet as an editor and resident flora & fauna expert. Lindsay wrote and updated the Kerala chapter and has updated the Tasmania chapter of Lonely Planet's *Australia* guide.

Teresa Cannon

After too many years in a suffocating bureaucracy Teresa Cannon was compelled to escape to the rarefied environment of the Himalaya. There she trekked through century-old forests and traversed the peaks and passes of the western moonscape region. She succumbed to the gentle and continuing welcome *Namaste*, which flowed like a mantra throughout the landscape. She wanted to stay. But visas run out and bank balances diminish. She returned to Australia, but not for long. Her love of travel led her abroad many times. In Asia she gathered material and co-authored a book on Asian elephants which was published in 1995. A children's version was published by Cambridge University Press in April 1998. This is her first work for Lonely Planet.

Peter Davis

Following a brief stint as a cadet photographer Peter lost himself in economics, politics and media at university. His first real job was selling fire extinguishers. He regards this as the start of his extinguished career. He failed at school teaching and drifted into freelance journalism and photography. He has published hundreds of features and photographs from around the world. Elephants play a big part in Peter's life. He is co-author and photographer of *Aliya – Stories of the Elephants of Sri Lanka*. When not chasing a story or an elephant he lectures part time in professional writing at Deakin University and in photojournalism at Photography Studies College in Melbourne.

Paul Greenway

Paul caught his first tropical disease in 1985, and has had the 'travel bug' ever since. Gratefully plucked from the security and blandness of the Australian Public Service, he is now a full-time traveller and writer, who has written a diverse number of Lonely Planet guides, including *Mongolia*, *Madagascar & Comoros* and *Iran*. Paul is based in Adelaide, South Australia, where he supports his beloved Adelaide Crows football club, relaxes to tuneless heavy rock and will do anything (like go to Mongolia and Iran) to avoid settling down.

Douglas Streatfeild-James

Born in Sussex, England, Douglas grew up in Malta, Britain and Canada. In 1986, he backpacked in India and Nepal before going up to Oxford University to read English. During periods of extended vagrancy since then he has canoed 1000km through France, motorcycled across Europe and hiked in Peru and Bolivia. He is the author of the LP guide to *Goa*; he has also written *China by Rail* and *Trekking in the Pyrenees,* and co-written *Silk Route by Rail*.

From the Authors

Christine I would like to thank all the authors who slogged away on this book, and Eddie, who did a great job with the photos. I would particularly like to thank Peter and Teresa for their support and for the huge amount of extra work they did. A big thanks to Venkatesh of the Government of India Tourist Office in Chennai who went out of his way to assist with a never-ending stream of questions, and to Nalini of Giggles Bookshop in Chennai for trusting that the airmail postage on all those books would be repaid, and for the tea and sandwiches and conversation. Many thanks to Professor Robin Jeffrey of La Trobe University in Melbourne for kindly sharing his vast knowledge and his library, and to David Collins, who generously provided all sorts of useful information. Thanks also to Sharan and Sue and to all the editors and designers who hammered this book into shape.

Lindsay I would like to thank PK Antony in Kovalam, Stanley Wilson in Kollam, PJ Vargheese in Kochi, and Helen Robinson in Melbourne. A special thanks goes to Jenny, Patrick and Sinead.

Teresa & Peter Thanks to the many people who gave information, helped with the research, pointed the way to good eating places, tolerated our eccentric behaviour and laughed at our sick humour. Particular thanks go to Mr D Venkatesan at the Government of India Tourist Office in Chennai for whom no request was too difficult; Mr S Shankaran for his humour, generosity and the calm manner in which he responded to our requests; Mr Film News Andaman who knows everyone in the film industry; Mr AS Kumar who seems to know everyone in Tamil Nadu; Mr D Karunanidhi for his generosity and enthusiasm; Mr MM Ansari for his knowledge of Andhra Pradesh and help with translation; Mr Smith in Ooty who understood the nature of our task and steered us in useful directions; Mrs Evam Piljain-Wiedemann for her generosity and information on her tribe – the Todas; Mr K Sanatanan, editor of the Andaman Herald and Mr Asheem Podder, editor of the Daily Telegrams in Port Blair, for their unusual sources and creative ideas. To Corinne & Haillie, thanks for sniffing out the bakery and the late-night cream caramels! We also extend our gratitude to all the auto-rickshaw drivers who gave us hours of entertainment as well as opportunities to hone our negotiating skills; the temple guides, railway officials, hotel and restaurant staff, bookshop proprietors, and thousands of others including fellow travellers who make India such a rich experience.

People in Australia we wish to thank include Aislinn Lalor whose knowledge of the alphabet kept us in order; Michael Davis for his sources on the Andaman & Nicobar Islands; Professor Robin Jeffrey for his sources and his enthusiasm; Liz Branigan who advised on Andhra Pradesh; and Dr Chitra Sudarshan for her ideas and sources; Stuart Hendrix for keeping our house alive. And of course our thanks go to the staff at Lonely Planet, especially Christine, Sharan, Paul, Mark and Carolyn who have given us an opportunity to experience India in such a unique way.

Paul In Chennai, many thanks to K Seshasai and other members of the Madras Naturalists Society; Guiseppe Cassina, for helping to make it all happen so smoothly; Preston Ahimaz of the WWF, for his help and enthusiasm; Mr Venkatesan from the Government of India Tourist Office and Dipankar Ghose, for his hospitality and information. In the Nilgiris, I am grateful to Michael Dawson and Freddie Solomon for their help with trekking information. In Kodagu (Coorg), much appreciation to Brigadier Cariappa, BM Raja Shekar and Ganesh Aiyanna for sharing their insights about local trekking.

Also in India, thanks to Manu K and Sara Jolly for showing me around Kokkre Bellur; Dr Venkatesh and other members of SPARK in Bangalore; Amanda Chalk, in Jog Falls; and Manoj Mishra of TRAFFIC India, Delhi.

At Lonely Planet, my thanks to all the

unsung editors, cartographers and designers, and to Sharan and Christine for their guidance.

Back home in Adelaide, thanks to my family – Mum; Dad & Judy; Gran; and Gill, Graham, Thomas & Amelia – for their support; and to Richard & Janet Allen for being such great friends.

Douglas Thank you to Heather Alden (USA), Ellen Klink (Netherlands) and Dan Hillier (UK). Thanks (again) to Frederick Noronha in Goa for helping with research, and to Kamlesh Amin in Mumbai for clearing up some final details there. In Bangalore special thanks go to Mr Ashok Kumar of the Natyanjali School of Dance for sparing the time to explain the amazing things that they're doing. Thank you, too, to Manjari and Anand Raman from Delhi for putting me in touch with Laccadives and supplying a massive reading list of contemporary Indian literature. Mahesh Nayak and Mr GN Ashoka Vardhana in Mangalore went out of their way to help with local information, and Mr KS Harshavardhana Bhat of the Regional Resources Centre in Udipi spent most of an afternoon letting me look at the archive material held at the centre. In Gokarna, thanks to Diethelm Wertz (Germany) for his encyclopaedic knowledge of Karnataka. Finally, thanks to Simon Mills (UK) for help with the photos, and for assistance with in-depth research on South Indian beer.

This Book

For this first edition of South India, which includes updated information from Lonely Planet's India, Christine Niven coordinated the research and wrote the introductory chapters.

Teresa Cannon and Peter Davis wrote/updated Chennai, Tamil Nadu, Andhra Pradesh and Andaman & Nicobar Islands.

Douglas Streatfeild-James wrote/updated Goa, Karnataka and Lakshadweep.

Lindsay Brown wrote/updated Kerala.

Paul Greenway contributed extra research and several sections, including Flora & Fauna, Ecology & Environment, Nilgiris, Kodagu and Outdoor Activities around Bangalore and Chennai.

From the Publisher

Carolyn Papworth edited this book in Lonely Planet's Melbourne office, with help in editing and proofing from Michelle Coxall, Emily Coles, and Martin Hughes. Mark Germanchis managed the design and mapping, with help from Paul Piaia, Sarah Sloane and Adam McCrow. Quentin Frayne edited and laid out the language chapter. Illustrations are by Ann Jeffree, Sarah Jolly and Tessa King. The cover design is by Simon Bracken. Cups of tea and barrels of laughs by Marty, ta.

Warning & Request

Things change – prices go up, schedules change, good places go bad and bad places go bankrupt – nothing stays the same. So, if you find things better or worse, recently opened or long since closed, please tell us and help make the next edition even more accurate and useful.

We value all of the feedback we receive from travellers. Julie Young coordinates a small team who read and acknowledge every letter, postcard and email, and ensure that every morsel of information finds its way to the appropriate authors, editors and publishers.

Everyone who writes to us will find their name in the next edition of the appropriate guide and will also receive a free subscription to our quarterly newsletter, *Planet Talk*. The very best contributions will be rewarded with a free Lonely Planet guide.

Excerpts from your correspondence may appear in new editions of this guide; in our newsletter, *Planet Talk*; or in updates on our Web site – so please let us know if you don't want your letter published or your name acknowledged.

Contents

Map Legend

BOUNDARIES

.... International Boundary
.... Provincial Boundary
.... Disputed Boundary

ROUTES

..... Freeway, with Route Number
.... Major Road
.... Minor Road
.... Minor Road - Unsealed
.... City Road
.... City Street
.... City Lane
.... Train Route, with Station
.... Metro Route, with Station
.... Cable Car or Chairlift
.... Ferry Route
.... Walking Track

AREA FEATURES

.... Building
.... Cemetery
.... Desert
.... Market
.... Park, Gardens
.... Pedestrian Mall
.... Reef
.... Urban Area

HYDROGRAPHIC FEATURES

.... Canal
.... Coastline
.... Creek, River
.... Lake, Intermittent Lake
.... Rapids, Waterfalls
.... Salt Lake
.... Swamp

SYMBOLS

CAPITAL	.... National Capital		
CAPITAL	...... Provincial Capital		
CITY	.... City		
Town	.... Town		
Village	.... Village		

.... Airport
.... Ancient or City Wall
.... Archaeological Site
.... Bank
.... Beach
.... Bird Sanctuary
.... Buddhist Temple
.... Castle or Fort
.... Cave
.... Church
.... Cliff or Escarpment
.... Dive Site
.... Embassy
.... Golf Course
.... Hindu Temple
.... Hospital
.... Lighthouse
.... Lookout
.... Monument
.... Mosque

.... Place to Stay
.... Camping Ground
.... Caravan Park

.... Place to Eat
.... Pub or Bar

.... Mountain or Hill
.... Museum
.... National Park
.... One Way Street
.... Parking
.... Pass
.... Petrol Station
.... Police Station
.... Post Office
.... Shopping Centre
.... Spring
.... Stately Home
.... Swimming Pool
.... Synagogue
.... Telephone
.... Tomb
.... Tourist Information
.... Transport
.... Zoo

Note: not all symbols displayed above appear in this book

Introduction

To travel to South India is to journey into India's Dravidian heartland. Here, south of the Vindhya Range – the symbolic division between north and south – is a region which cleaves fiercely to its own distinct history, traditions and languages. Indeed, in the mid-1960s when northern politicians attempted to ban English and impose Hindi as the national language, riots broke out across Tamil Nadu; there was talk of Tamil Nadu separating from the rest of India.

More than a quarter of India's population lives in the South Indian states of Andhra Pradesh, Tamil Nadu, Kerala, Goa and Karnataka, and the Union Territories of Pondicherry, the Andaman & Nicobar Islands and Lakshadweep. But to think of South India as one homogenous region is wrong. In fact, it's extraordinarily diverse in terms of landscapes, peoples and cultures, which makes it a rewarding and fascinating destination for travellers – from the temple towns of Tamil Nadu to the dense forests of the Western Ghats and the languid waterways of Kerala.

These days one can fly to Goa and even Kerala on a charter and simply lounge about on the beach – and fly straight back out again. But just behind the beautiful west coast beaches rise the rugged, thickly forested Western Ghats, where you'll find the former British hill stations of Udhagamandalam (Ooty), Kodaikanal (both in Tamil Nadu) and Munnar (in Kerala), with their churches, clubs and playing fields, their bungalows and log fires. Here too, another legacy of colonial days, are tea and coffee

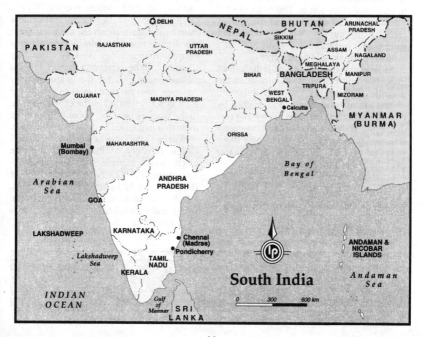

South India

plantations – and endless possibilities for walks with wonderful views.

Back down on the coast, you can tour the World Heritage buildings and cathedrals of the once magnificent Portuguese Empire at Old Goa; cruise along the waterways of Kerala in a converted rice barge or explore the fascinating antique markets of Fort Cochin and the lovely synagogue nearby with its famous blue and white Chinese tiles. Kerala is also famous for its own classical dance form – the theatrical Kathakali – which is steeped in ritual and tradition, and for ayurveda – an ancient system of medicine that uses herbs and massage to treat a range of ailments.

Further north of Kerala, in Karnataka, is Hampi – one-time capital of the wealthy and vibrant Hindu Vijayanagara Empire which so impressed 16th century Portuguese visitor Domingo Paez. Vijayanagara's fine buildings now lie in ruins, but the sprawling site retains a unique atmosphere, one that seems to make travellers linger. The huge, domed mausoleum of Golgumbaz at Bijapur is probably as famous for its 'whispering gallery' as it is for its dome – only St Peter's in Vatican City is said to be larger.

At Sravanabelagola, one of India's most important Jain places of pilgrimage, is the gigantic 10th century statue of Bahubali, carved out of solid granite and reached by climbing 624 rock-cut steps. Every 12 years during the Mahamastakabhisheka ceremony (the next one is in 2005) monks pour thousands of pots of ghee and coconut water over the head of the statue.

Offshore, stretching north of the Maldives, are the pristine coral atolls of Lakshadweep. While not a budget traveller's destination, the islands of Lakshadweep offer a fortunate few the opportunity to experience a truly beautiful and little visited spot in the Indian Ocean, and great diving as a bonus.

Thousands of visitors annually make the pilgrimage to Puttaparthi in Andhra Pradesh to catch a glimpse of Sai Baba, and perhaps to receive sacred ash from his fingertips. But Andhra Pradesh also has fascinating bazaars and the famous Golconda Fort to explore.

Tamil Nadu is virtually synonymous with temples, from the extraordinary Brihadishwara Temple in Thanjavur with its mysterious finial, to the vibrant and intriguing Meenakshi Temple in Madurai with its towering and colourfully ornate *gopurams* (gateways), its patient temple elephants, extraordinary souvenir market and constant activity. But Tamil Nadu is much more than temples. This is the land of the Tamils, cradle of Dravidian culture and one of the oldest classical cultures in existence. Poetry, dance and music flourish – as does the movie industry. Visit Chennai's huge movie studios and you may land a job as an extra.

The vibrancy of Tamil culture is evident even to the least observant traveller; from the *kolam* rice-paste designs that grace household thresholds even in cities like Chennai to the terracotta horses left on village boundaries for the guardian deity Ayyanar, from the great places of pilgrimage such as Kanyakumari in the extreme south, to the serenely peaceful slopes of the sacred mountain Arunachal in the west of the state.

Within Tamil Nadu nestles the small Union Territory of Pondicherry and the world-famous experiment in communal living, Auroville. Offshore in the Bay of Bengal lie the Andaman & Nicobar Islands, which offer some of the best diving in the world, and a chance to experience truly laid-back island life.

Facts about South India

HISTORY

Evidence of human habitation in southern India dates back to Stone Age times; finds include hand axes and, in the case of a recent excavation in the Vindhya Range, a worn limestone statue of a goddess between 25,000 and 15,000 years old. Although archaeologists continue to excavate, for example at Hungsi (Karnataka), nothing has been unearthed so far that parallels the antiquity of the oldest finds on the Indian subcontinent – quartzite pebble tools and flakes from northern Pakistan which are some two million years old.

Over the millennia stone tools diminished in size, a reflection of changing subsistence patterns and the need for new technologies to deal with them. In various parts of the subcontinent, during what is known as the Indian Mesolithic period, hunting and gathering appears to have coexisted with fishing, herding and even small-scale agriculture. But it was in the north that a large and apparently prosperous urban community emerged which continues to fascinate and frustrate those who would seek to unravel its mysteries.

Dubbed the Indus or Harappan civilisation by historians, this community centred on the Indus River Valley and sprawled over a vast area (some 580,000 sq km according to some estimates) that included part of present-day Pakistan. It took about 500 years to reach maturity (in about 2600 BC) and flourished for several hundred more, after which it collapsed, leaving little evidence to indicate exactly why.

Suggestions that the contemporaneous rise in South India of settlements based on cattle herding and agriculture were the result of Harappans moving south have been dismissed by scholars, and it seems more likely that North and South India evolved quite independently of one another at this time. Indeed, excavations in the south, notably in Maharashtra, Tamil Nadu and Karnataka, indicate that agricultural and other patterns that were later to make these regions quite distinct from one another were already being established.

Influences from the North

While the Indus civilisation may not have affected South India, the same cannot be said for the Aryan invasion. The Aryans, who swept down from central Asia between 1500 BC and 200 BC, eventually controlled the whole of northern India as far as the Vindhya Range and pushed the original inhabitants, the Dravidians, south. The *Ramayana* (along with the *Mahabharata*, one of the two great Aryan epics) was written about 300 BC. It is considered by some a poetic expression of this southward thrust.

The Aryanisation of the south was a slow process, but it had a profound effect on the social order of the region and the ethos of its inhabitants. The northerners brought their literature (the four Vedas – a collection of sacred Hindu hymns), their gods (Agni, Varuna, Shiva and Vishnu), their language (Sanskrit) and a social structure that organised people into castes, with Brahmins on top.

Over the centuries other influences flowed from the north, including Buddhism and Jainism. Indeed Sravanabelagola in Karnataka, an important place of pilgrimage to this day, is the spot where more than 2000 years ago the northern ruler Chandragupta Maurya, who had embraced Jainism and renounced his kingdom, came with his guru. Chandragupta died here in the orthodox Jain manner; by deliberate starvation. Jainism was then adopted by the trading community (its tenet of ahimsa, or nonviolence, precluded occupations tainted by the taking of life), and spread through South India by them.

The Emperor Ashoka, a successor of Chandragupta, who ruled for 37 years from about 272 BC, was a major force behind Buddhism's (albeit limited) inroads into the south. Once a campaigning king, his epiphany came in 260 BC. Shocked by the carnage and suffering caused by his campaign against the Kalingas (Orissa), he renounced violence as a means of conquest and embraced Buddhism. He sent Buddhist missionaries far and wide (his son was the first Buddhist missionary to travel to Sri Lanka), and his edicts (carved into rock and incised into specially erected pillars) have been found in Andhra Pradesh and Karnataka. Stupas were also built in southern India under Ashoka's patronage, mostly in Andhra Pradesh although at least one was constructed as far south as Kanchipuram in Tamil Nadu.

The appeal of Jainism and Buddhism, which arose about the same time, was that they rejected the Vedas and condemned the caste system. Buddhism, however, gradually lost touch with the general population and faded as a form of Hinduism, emphasising devotion to a personal god, underwent a revival between 200 and 800 AD. This cult, known as *bhakti*, started in southern India about 500 AD. Bhakti adherents opposed Jainism and Buddhism, and the cult certainly hastened the decline of both in South India. Bhakti was also anti-Vedic, rejecting the notion that priests were required as intermediaries between mortals and gods, and opposing the reliance on ritual with its requisite knowledge of Sanskrit.

Mauryan Empire & Southern Kingdoms

Chandragupta Maurya was the first of a line of Mauryan kings to rule what was effectively the first Indian empire. The empire's capital was in present-day Patna. It was Chandragupta's son, Bindusara, who came to the throne about 300 BC, who extended the empire as far as Karnataka. However, he seems to have stopped there, possibly because the Mauryan Empire was on cordial terms with the southern powers of the day.

The identity and customs of these chiefdoms have been gleaned from various sources, including archaeological remains and ancient Tamil literature (known as *Sangam*). These literary records describe a land known as the 'abode of the Tamils',

within which resided three major ruling families: the Pandyas (Madurai); the Cheras (Malabar Coast); and the Cholas (Thanjavur and the Cauvery Valley). The region described in classical Sangam literature (written between 300 BC and 200 AD) was still relatively insulated from Sanskrit culture, but this was starting to change.

A degree of rivalry characterised relations between the main chiefdoms and the numerous minor chiefdoms, and there were occasional clashes with Sri Lankan rulers. But it seems the concept of kingship was beginning to emerge during this time, and Sangam literature indicates that Sanskrit traditions were establishing a hold. There is also evidence that religious observances included sacrifices to various deities, including Murugan (a son of Shiva). Ultimately, the southern powers all suffered at the hands of the Kalabhras, about whom little is known except that they appeared to have come from somewhere north of the Tamil region, 'and that they were generally regarded as 'evil rulers'.

By this time the Mauryan Empire, which had started to disintegrate soon after the death of the Emperor Ashoka, had been overtaken by a series of rival kingdoms which themselves were subjected to repeated invasions from northerners such as the Bactrian Greeks. Despite this apparent instability, the post-Ashokan era produced at least one line of royalty whose patronage of the arts and ability to maintain a relatively high degree of social cohesion have left an enduring legacy. These were the Satavahanas, and they eventually controlled all of Maharashtra, Madhya Pradesh, Karnataka and Andhra Pradesh. Under their rule, between 200 BC and 200 AD, the arts blossomed: especially literature, sculpture, and philosophy (Buddhism reached a peak in Maharashtra under the Satavahanas).

Most of all, the subcontinent enjoyed a period of considerable prosperity. Overseas trade became especially important in the south because of the region's more limited potential for agricultural development.

Trade & South India

India's trading links with the outside world go back a long way. There is evidence that trade between western Asia and the west coast of India was taking place at least a thousand years before Christ; Hebrew texts refer to the port of Ophir, itself probably located along this same patch of coastline. Indian teak and cedar were used by Babylonian builders as far back as the 7th century BC. But a major breakthrough came with the discovery of the monsoon winds which enabled ships (such as Arab *dhows*) to travel between western Asia and India with relative ease. The extraordinary reach of the Roman Empire during the period of the Pax Romana at the beginning of the Christian era assured the flow of goods between India, West Asia and Europe along two major routes: overland across Persia to North India, and by water (primarily from the Red Sea and the Persian Gulf) to South India – and back.

The anonymous Greek document, *The Periplys Maris Erythraei*, written sometime in the 1st century, describes various ports along the coast of India; and proof that Roman trade was active in South India has turned up over the years in the form of caches of gold coins, Roman pottery and glass. British archaeologist Sir Mortimer Wheeler, digging at Arikkamedu near Pondicherry, uncovered a Roman settlement as well as pieces of pottery that had been manufactured near Rome itself. At Rameswaram, further south, pottery has been uncovered that was in fact made in Tunisia when it was under Roman control. And in central Kerala in 1983, more than 200 gold coins minted in Rome in the 2nd century were discovered by workers excavating clay for bricks. There is also evidence that the Romans had textiles made to order.

Other goods exported from India included ivory, precious stones, pearls, tortoise shells, pepper and aromatic plants. Although Indian luxury goods were coveted by wealthy Romans, not everybody was happy with paying the local traders in bullion. The Roman chronicler Pliny recorded his concern over the impact the trade was having on the Roman treasury, and at one stage an imperial decree went out banning the export of gold.

Indian merchants used trade routes established by the Mauryan Empire and natural corridors such as the Narmada and the Ganges river valleys to move around India. Longer routes traversed vast tracts of Central Asia to link China with the Mediterranean. There is evidence Indian traders were also established in Red Sea ports, and after the decline of the Roman trade, they ventured in the other direction to South-East Asia in search of spices and semi-precious stones.

The Rise of the Cholas

After the Kalabhras suppressed the Tamil chiefdoms, South India split into numerous warring kingdoms. The Cholas virtually disappeared. The Cheras on the west coast appear to have prospered through trading, although little is known about them. It wasn't until the late 6th century when the Kalabhras were overthrown that the political confusion in the region ended. For the next 300 years the history of South India is dominated by the fortunes of the Chalukyas of Badami, the Pallavas of Kanchi and the Pandyas of Madurai.

The Chalukyas were a far-flung family. In addition to their base in Badami, they established themselves in Bijapur, Andhra Pradesh and near the Godavari Delta; the latter branch of the family is commonly referred to as the Eastern Chalukyas of Vengi. It's unclear whether the Pallavas were descended from their namesakes of old; in fact there is evidence they may have emigrated to Kanchi (Kanchipuram) from Andhra Pradesh. After their successful rout of the Kalabhras, the Pallavas extended their territory as far south as the Cauvery River, and by the 7th century were enjoying the full flowering of their reign. They engaged in long-running conflicts with the Pandyas who, in the 8th century, allied themselves with the Gangas of Mysore. This, combined with pressure from the Rashtrakutas (who were challenging the Eastern Chalukyas), had by the 9th century snuffed out any significant Pallava power in the south.

At the same time, a new Chola dynasty was establishing itself and laying the foundations for what was to become the most important empire on the subcontinent in its day. From their base at Thanjavur, the Cholas spread north and absorbed what was left of Pallavas territory and made inroads into the south. But it wasn't until Rajaraja (985-1014) ascended the throne that the Chola kingdom really started to become a great empire. Rajaraja successfully waged war against the Pandyas in the south, the Gangas of Mysore and the Eastern Chalukyas. He also launched a series of naval campaigns that resulted in the capture of the Maldives, the Malabar Coast and northern Sri Lanka, which became a province of the Chola dynasty. These conquests gave the Cholas control over important ports and trading links between India, South-East Asia, Arabia and East Africa. They were therefore in a position to grab a share of the huge profits involved in selling spices to Europe.

Rajaraja's son, Rajendra (1014-44), continued to expand Chola territory, conquering the remainder of Sri Lanka, and campaigning up the east coast as far as Bengal and the Ganges River ('watering their war elephants in the Ganges', as one Tamil poet put it).

Rajendra also launched a campaign in South-East Asia against the Srivijaya kingdom, reinstating trading links that had been interrupted and sending trade missions as far as China.

In addition to its political and economic superiority, the Chola kingdom produced a brilliant legacy in the arts. Sculpture, most notably bronze sculpture, reached astonishing new heights of aesthetic and technical refinement.

Music, dance and literature also flourished, and as a result Tamil culture acquired a more distinct character, enduring in South India long after the Cholas had faded from the picture. Trade wasn't the only thing the Cholas brought to the shores of South-East Asia; they also introduced their culture.

That legacy lives on in Myanmar (Burma), Bali and Cambodia in the dance forms, religion and mythology of the regions.

But the Cholas, eventually weakened by constant campaigning, succumbed to expansionist pressure from the Hoysalas of Halebid (southern Karnataka) and the Pandyas of Madurai, and by the 13th century were finally supplanted by the Pandyas.

The Hoysalas were themselves eclipsed by the Vijayanagar Empire which arose in the 14th century (see below). The Pandyas prospered and their achievements were much admired by Marco Polo when he visited in 1288 and 1293. But their glory was short-lived, as they were unable to resist the Muslim invasion from the north.

Muslim Invasion, Vijayanagar Empire

The Muslim rulers in Delhi campaigned in southern India from 1296, pushing aside a series of local rulers, including the Hoysalas and Pandyas, and by 1323 had reached Madurai in Tamil Nadu.

Muhammad Tughluq rebuilt the fortifications in Daulatabad in Maharashtra to keep control of southern India, but in 1334 he recalled his army in order to wage campaigns elsewhere. As a result local Muslim rulers in Madurai and Daulatabad declared their independence.

At the same time, the foundations of what was to become one of South India's greatest empires, Vijayanagar, were being laid by Hindu chiefs at Hampi (Karnataka).

The Bahmanis, initially from Daulatabad, established their capital at Gulbarga, relocating to Bidar (Karnataka) in the 15th century. Their kingdom eventually included Maharashtra, and parts of northern Karnataka and Andhra Pradesh – and they took pains to protect it.

One of the Bahmani legacies is a series of fortifications (Purandhar, Sholaur, Raichur) constructed to fend off border raids.

The Vijayanagar Empire is generally said to have been founded by two chieftain brothers who, having been captured and taken to Delhi, where they converted to Islam, were sent back south to serve as gov-

EDDIE GERALD

EDDIE GERALD

EDDIE GERALD

EDDIE GERALD

EDDIE GERALD

PAUL BEINSSEN

The people of South India, India's Dravidian heartland, cling fiercely to their unique histories, traditions and languages.

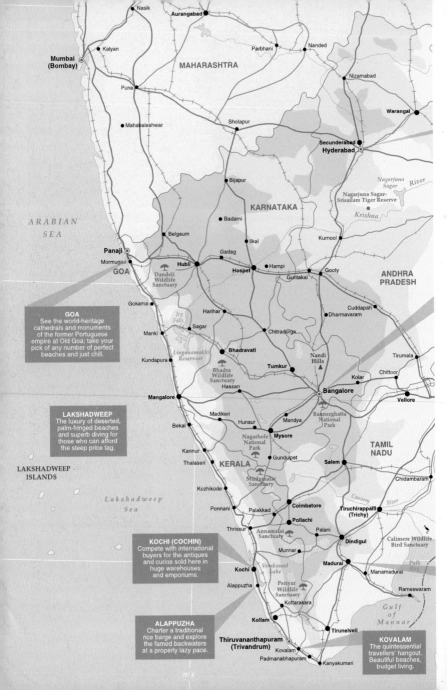

Nasik

Aurangabad

Kalyan

Parbhani

Nanded

MAHARASHTRA

Mumbai
(Bombay)

Nizamabad

Pune

Warangal

Mahabaleshwar

Sholapur

Secunderabad
Hyderabad

Bijapur

*Nagarjuna
Sagar*

River

KARNATAKA

Nagarjuna Sagar-
Srisailam Tiger Reserve

Badami

Krishna

Belgaum

Ilkal

Kurnool

Panaji

Gadag

Mormugao

GOA

Hubli

Hospet

Hampi

Gooty

**ANDHRA
PRADESH**

*ARABIAN
SEA*

Dandeli
Wildlife
Sanctuary

Guntakal

GOA
See the world-heritage
cathedrals and monuments
of the former Portuguese
empire at Old Goa; take your
pick of any number of perfect
beaches and just chill.

Gokarna

Cuddapah

Harihar

Dharmavaram

*Jog
Falls*

Sagar

Manki

Chitradurga

*Linganamakki
Reservoir*

Bhadravati

Kundapura

Nandi
Hills

Tumkur

Tirumala

Bhadra
Wildlife
Sanctuary

Kolar

Chittoor

Hassan

Bangalore

Vellore

Mangalore

Madikeri

LAKSHADWEEP
The luxury of deserted,
palm-fringed beaches
and superb diving for
those who can afford
the steep price tag.

Hunsur

Mandya

Bannerghatta
National
Park

Bekal

Nagarhole
National
Park

Mysore

**TAMIL
NADU**

Kannur

Gundulpet

**LAKSHADWEEP
ISLANDS**

Thalaseri

KERALA

Salem

Chidambaram

Mudumalai
Sanctuary

*Lakshadweep
Sea*

Kozhikode

Cauvery

River

Ponnani

Palakkad

Coimbatore

**Tiruchirappalli
(Trichy)**

Thrissur

Annamalai
Sanctuary

Pollachi

Palani

*Calimere Wildlife
Bird Sanctuary*

KOCHI (COCHIN)
Compete with international
buyers for the antiques
and curios sold here in
huge warehouses
and emporiums.

Munnar

Dindigul

*Pulk
Bay*

Kochi

*Vembanad
Lake*

Madurai

Alappuzha

Manamadurai

Periyar
Wildlife
Sanctuary

Rameswaram

Kottarakara

*Gulf
of
Mannar*

ALAPPUZHA
Charter a traditional
rice barge and explore
the famed backwaters
at a properly lazy pace.

Kollam

Tirunelveli

**Thiruvananthapuram
(Trivandrum)**

Kovalam

Padmanabhapuram

Kanyakumari

KOVALAM
The quintessential
travellers' hangout.
Beautiful beaches,
budget living.

75° E

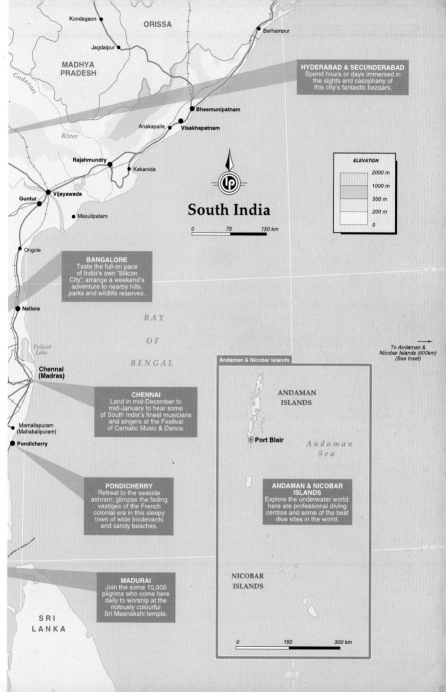

ORISSA

Kondagaon

Jagdalpur

MADHYA
PRADESH

Godavari

River

Berhampur

Bheemunipatnam

Anakapalle • Visakhapatnam

Rajahmundry

Kakanida

Guntur • Vijayawada

• Masulipatam

Ongole

Nellore

Pulicat
Lake

Chennai
(Madras)

Mamallapuram
(Mahabalipuram)

Pondicherry

SRI
LANKA

BAY

OF

BENGAL

South India

0   75   150 km

ELEVATION

2000 m
1000 m
500 m
200 m
0

HYDERABAD & SECUNDERABAD
Spend hours or days immersed in
the sights and cacophany of
this city's fantastic bazaars.

BANGALORE
Taste the full-on pace
of India's own 'Silicon
City'; arrange a weekend's
adventure to nearby hills,
parks and wildlife reserves.

CHENNAI
Land in mid-December to
mid-January to hear some
of South India's finest musicians
and singers at the Festival
of Carnatic Music & Dance.

PONDICHERRY
Retreat to the seaside
ashram; glimpse the fading
vestiges of the French
colonial era in this sleepy
town of wide boulevards
and sandy beaches.

MADURAI
Join the some 10,000
pilgrims who come here
daily to worship at the
riotously colourful
Sri Meenakshi temple.

15° N

To Andaman &
Nicobar Islands (600km)
(See Inset)

Andaman & Nicobar Islands

ANDAMAN
ISLANDS

● Port Blair

Andaman
Sea

**ANDAMAN & NICOBAR
ISLANDS**
Explore the underwater world:
here are professional diving
centres and some of the best
dive sites in the world.

NICOBAR
ISLANDS

10° N

0   150   300 km

85° E

SARA-JANE CLELAND

EDDIE GERALD

GREG ELMS

PAUL BEINSSEN

SARA-JANE CLELAND

EDDIE GERALD

More than a quarter of India's people live in the southern states of Andhra Pradesh, Tamil Nadu, Kerala, Goa and Karnataka, and the Union Territories of Pondicherry, the Andaman & Nicobar Islands and Lakshadweep.

ernors for the sultanate. The brothers, however, had other ideas, reconverted to Hinduism and around 1336 set about establishing a kingdom that was to eventually encompass southern Karnataka, Tamil Nadu and part of Kerala.

Not unnaturally, ongoing rivalry characterised the relationship between the Vijayanagar and the Bahmani empires right up until the 16th century when both went into decline: the Bahmani Empire torn apart by factional fighting; Vijayanagar's vibrant capital laid to waste by Muslim invaders. Much of the conflict centred on control of fertile agricultural land and trading ports; at one stage the Bahmanis wrested control of the important port of Goa from their rivals (although in 1378 the Vijayanagarans wrested it back).

The Vijayanagar Empire is notable for its prosperity, the result of a deliberate policy of giving every encouragement to traders from afar, combined with the development of an efficient administrative system and access to important trading links, including west coast ports. Its capital became quite cosmopolitan, with people from various parts of India as well as from abroad mingling with the crowds in the bazaars.

Portuguese chronicler Domingo Paez arrived here in 1520 and recorded his impressions. He noted the region was generally lacking in water and described how the Vijayanagarans had constructed tanks and irrigated their fields to make the land productive. At one stage he describes how human and animal sacrifices were carried out to propitiate the gods after one of the tanks had burst repeatedly. He describes the fine houses that belonged to wealthy merchants, and the bazaars full of precious stones (rubies, diamonds, emeralds), pearls, textiles including silk, 'and every other sort of thing there is on earth and that you may wish to buy'. He was also impressed by the sheer size of the city; at one point he climbed to the top of a hill to get a better view, but found even then he couldn't take in the entire place as it was built across several ranges. He says its population was extraordinarily large and that the inhabitants enjoyed an unusual abundance of cheap produce.

Paez had arrived in Vijayanagar during the reign of one of its greatest kings, Krishnadevaraya (reigned 1509-29). It was during his rule that Vijayanagar enjoyed a period of unparalleled prosperity and power.

Like the Bahmanis, the Vijayanagar kings invested heavily in protecting their territory and their trading links. Krishnadevaraya employed Portuguese and Muslim mercenaries to man the forts and protect his domains. He also fostered good relations with the Portuguese, upon whom he depended for access to trade goods, especially the Arab horses he needed for his cavalry.

The Coming of the Portuguese

By the time Krishnadevaraya ascended to the throne, the Portuguese were well on the way to establishing a firm foothold in Goa. It was only a few years since they had become the first Europeans to sail across the Indian Ocean from the east coast of Africa to India's shores.

On 20 May 1498 Vasco da Gama dropped anchor near Calicut (Kozhikode). It had taken him 23 days to sail from the east coast of Africa, guided by a pilot sent by the ruler of Malindi. Claims that this pilot was none other than Ibn Majid, arguably the most acclaimed Arab navigator of the 15th century, have been dismissed by scholars as romantic fiction. Still, the identity of this person remains a mystery, although he could well have been a Gujarati, Gujarat's ports being the main centres for India's ocean-going trade at the time.

The Portuguese sought a sea route between Europe and the East that would allow them to trade directly in spices. They also hoped they might find Christians cut off from Europe by Muslim dominance of the Middle East. In India they found spices but no sign of the kingdom of Prester John, the legendary Christian ruler.

Nevertheless, the little party that made its way with Vasco da Gama to a meeting with the Zamorin of Calicut mistook a temple for a church, stopping to pray before an image of 'Our Lady', and receiving a sprinkling of 'holy water' and ash for their foreheads. But at least one of the party noted down later that the church had numerous saints depicted on its walls, some with diadems, others with teeth 'that were so large they came out of their mouths a bit', and still others that had multiple arms.

As for the meeting with the ruler of Calicut, Vasco da Gama sought a private audience to explain himself, and seems to have been well received. Which is more than can be said for the goods he had gathered as presents for the king: some cloth, six hats, a dozen coats, several coral necklaces and six basins, as well as some sugar, butter and honey. As was apparently the custom, these gifts were first inspected by the king's representatives. They were scornful, claiming that da Gama's offerings were hardly worthy of the poorest merchant from Mecca, and they refused to present them to the king. Vasco da Gama requested further audiences with the king, but these were stalled, the ruler of Calicut apparently wary of the person who, although claiming to come from a wealthy land, had failed to produce suitably impressive gifts.

The Portuguese engaged in a limited amount of trading, but became increasingly suspicious that Muslim traders were turning the ruler of Calicut against them, and they resolved to leave, which they did in August. During a hellish three month trip across the western Indian Ocean, 30 of da Gama's men died of scurvy; only about half a dozen sailors on each of the three ships were sufficiently healthy to keep working. One vessel was abandoned and burned off the east African coast. The two remaining boats sailed into Lisbon in July and August 1499.

Dutch, French & British in South India

And so began a new era of European contact with the East. After Vasco da Gama came Francisco de Ameida and Afonse de Albuquerque, who established an eastern Portuguese empire which included Goa (first taken in 1510). Albuquerque waged a constant battle against the local Muslims in Goa, finally defeating them in 1512. But perhaps his greatest achievement lay in playing off two potentially lethal threats – the Vijayanagar Empire (for whom access to Goa's ports was extremely important) and the Bijapuris (who had split from the Bahmanis in the early 16th century and who took control of part of Goa including an important port at Gove).

The Bijapuris and Bahmanis were sworn enemies and Albuquerque skilfully exploited this antipathy by supplying Arab horses – which had to be constantly imported because they died in alarming numbers once on Indian soil. Both kingdoms bought horses from the Portuguese to top up their cavalries, thus keeping Portugal's Goan ports busy and profitable.

The Portuguese also introduced their religion, Roman Catholicism. The arrival of the Inquisition in 1560 marked the beginning of 200 years of brutal suppression and religious terrorism. Not long after, events occurred in Europe that were to have major repercussions for European relations with India. In 1580 Spain annexed Portugal and, until it regained its independence in 1640, Portugal's interests were subservient to Spain's. After the defeat of the Spanish Armada in 1588, therefore, the sea route to the East lay open to the English and the Dutch.

The Dutch got to India first but, unlike the Portuguese, were more interested in trade than they were in religion and empire. They were in fact more interested in Indonesia as a source of spices, and traded with South India primarily for pepper and cardamom. However, the Dutch needed to be able to come up with a viable system that would allow them to trade in various countries without depleting scarce exchange goods (the Indonesians wanted textiles for spices, the Indians and Chinese wanted silver for textiles). They therefore set up the Dutch East India Company which allowed them to maintain a complicated trading structure all the way from the Persian Gulf to Japan.

They set up factories at Surat (Gujarat) and on the Coromandel Coast in South India, and entered into a treaty with the ruler of Calicut. In 1660 they captured Portuguese forts at Cochin (now known as Kochi) and Cranganore.

The English also set up a trading venture, the East India Company, which in 1600 was granted a monopoly. Like the Dutch, the English were at this stage primarily interested in trade, namely spices, and Indonesia was their main goal. But the Dutch proved too strong here and the English turned instead to India, in South India setting up a factory at Madras. The Danes traded off and on at Tranquebar (on the Coromandel Coast) from 1616, and the French acquired Pondicherry in 1674.

Mughals & Marathas

Around this time the Delhi-based Mughals were making inroads into southern India, gaining Bijapur and Golconda (including Hyderabad) before moving into Tamil Nadu. But it was here that Emperor Aurangzeb (who reigned from 1658 to 1707) came up against the Marathas who, in the course of a series of guerrilla-like raids, captured Thanjavur and set up a capital at Gingee near Madras.

Although the Mughal Empire disintegrated following Aurangzeb's death, the Marathas went from strength to strength, and they set their sights on territory to the north. But their aspirations brought them into conflict with the rulers of Hyderabad (the Asaf Jahis), who had entrenched themselves here when Hyderabad separated from Delhi. The Marathas discovered that the French were providing military support to the Hyderabadi rulers in return for trading concessions on the Coromandel Coast. However, by the 1750s Hyderabad had lost much of its power and had become landlocked.

Down in the south, Travancore (Kerala) and Mysore were making a bid to consolidate their power by gaining control of important maritime regions – and therefore access to direct trade links. Martanda Varma

(reigned 1729-58) of Travancore, in southern Kerala, created his own army and sought to keep the local Syrian Christian trading community onside by limiting the activities of European traders in the region. Trade in many goods, with the exception of pepper, became a royal monopoly, especially under Martanda's son Rama Varma (reigned 1758-98).

Mysore started off as a landlocked kingdom, but in 1761 a migrant cavalry officer, Hyder Ali, assumed power and set about acquiring coastal territory. Hyder and his son Tipu Sultan eventually ruled over a kingdom that included Kodagu (Coorg), coastal Karnataka and northern Kerala. Tipu in fact conducted trade directly with the Middle East through the west coast ports he controlled. But Tipu was prevented from gaining access to ports on the eastern seaboard and the fertile hinterland by the English East India Company.

The East India Company at this stage was supposedly only interested in trade, not conquest. But Mysore's rulers proved something of a vexation. In 1780 the Nizam of Hyderabad, Hyder Ali, and the Marathas joined forces to defeat the company's armies and take control of Karnataka. The Treaty of Mangalore, signed by Tipu in 1784, restored the parties to an uneasy truce. But meanwhile, within the company there was a growing body of opinion that only total control of India would really satisfy British trading interests. This was reinforced by fears of a renewed French bid for territory in India following Napoleon's Egyptian expedition of 1798-99. It was the governor general, Lord Wellesley, who launched a strike against Mysore, with the Nizam of Hyderabad as an ally (he was required to disband his French-trained troops and in return gained British protection). Tipu, who may have counted on support from the French, was killed when the British stormed Seringapatam in 1799.

Wellesley restored the old ruling family, the Wodeyars, to half of Tipu's kingdom; the rest went to the Nizam of Hyderabad and the company, and laid the foundations for the formation of the Madras Presidency. Tanjore and Karnataka were also absorbed by the British who, when the rulers of the day died, pensioned off their successors. By 1818 the Marathas, racked by internal strife, had collapsed.

By now most of India was under British influence. In the south the British controlled the Madras Presidency which stretched all the way from present-day Andhra Pradesh in the north to the tip of the subcontinent in the south and from the east coast right across to the Malabar Coast in the west. Kochi, Travancore, Hyderabad and Mysore remained princely states, albeit under the control of a Resident (British de facto ruler).

Post-Independence

After Independence in 1947 the British Residencies and the Madras Presidency were dismantled and South India was reorganised into states along linguistic lines.

The Wodeyars in Mysore, who ruled right up to Independence, were pensioned off. But they were so popular with their subjects that the Maharaja became the first governor of the post-Independence state of Mysore. The boundaries of Mysore state were redrawn on linguistic grounds in 1956 (under the 1956 States Reorganisation Act), and the extended Kannada-speaking state of Greater Mysore was established. This was renamed Karnataka in 1972. In 1996 Kannada-speaking Deve Gowda became India's prime minister.

Goa achieved independence from the Portuguese in 1961, becoming a Union Territory of India. After splitting from Daman and Diu (Gujarat) in 1987, it was officially recognised as the 25th state of the Indian Union. It also won the right to have its own language, Konkani, recognised as one of India's official languages.

Kerala, as it is today, was created in 1956 from Travancore, Cochin and Malabar (formerly part of the Madras Presidency).

The maharajas in both Travancore and Cochin were especially attentive to the provision of basic services and education, and their legacy today is India's most literate state. Kerala also blazed a trail in post-Independence India by becoming the first state in the world to elect a communist government (1957).

Andhra Pradesh was declared a state in 1956, having been created by combining Andhra state (formerly part of the Madras Presidency) with many parts of the Telugu-speaking areas of the old Hyderabadi Nizam's territory.

Tamil Nadu emerged from the old Madras Presidency – although until 1969 Tamil Nadu was known as Madras State. In 1956, in a nation wide reorganisation of states, it lost Malabar district and South Canara to the fledgling state of Kerala. However, it also gained new areas in Trivandrum district, including Kanyakumari. In 1960, 1049 sq km of land in Andhra Pradesh was exchanged for a similar amount of land in Salem and Chengalpattu districts.

The French handed over Pondicherry at Independence in 1947 and it remains a Union Territory of India. Lakshadweep was granted Union Territory status in 1956 (it was, until Independence, controlled by the British). The territory's name was changed from Laccadives to Lakshadweep in 1973. The Andaman & Nicobar Islands, which the British had used as a penal colony, were in 1956 made a Union Territory.

GEOGRAPHY

The Vindhya Range, which stretches nearly the entire width of peninsular India (roughly contiguous with the Tropic of Cancer and for some of its extent with the westward flowing Narmada River), is the symbolic division between the north and south of India. South of the Vindhya Range lies the Deccan Plateau (Deccan comes from the Sanskrit word *dakshina*, meaning south), a triangular-shaped mass of ancient rock (once part of the huge continent known as Gondwanaland) that slopes gently eastward towards the Bay of Bengal. The headwaters of such major southern rivers as the Godavari, the Krishna, and the Cauvery rise in the rain-soaked peaks of the Western Ghats and drain into the bay.

On its western and eastern borders, the

Deccan Plateau is flanked by a series of mountains called ghats (literally, steps).

The Western Ghats (known in Goa and Maharashtra as the Sahyadris) start to rise just north of Mumbai and run parallel to the coast (gaining height as they go; the Nilgiri and Cardamom hills are in fact steep-sided raised blocks within this range) until they reach the tip of the peninsula. Here they merge with the southernmost portion of the Eastern Ghats, a less dramatic chain of low, interrupted ranges that sweep north-east in the direction of Chennai before turning northwards, roughly parallel to the coast bordering the Bay of Bengal.

Anamundi in Kerala is, at 2695m, South India's highest peak. The highest peak in the Eastern Ghats is Armakonda in Andhra Pradesh (1654m). The Western Ghats have an average elevation of 915m and are covered with tropical and temperate evergreen forests and mixed deciduous forest. They harbour a rich array of plant and animal life, including 27% of India's flowering plants.

The western coastal strip between Mumbai and Goa, known as the Konkan Coast, is studded with river estuaries. Further south, the Malabar Coast (which stretches from Goa to Kanyakumari, peninsular India's southernmost point) forms a sedimentary plain (24km to 97km wide) into which are etched the waterways and lagoons that characterise Kerala. The eastern coastline (known as the Coromandel Coast where it tracks through Tamil Nadu) is wider, drier and flatter.

Although politically part of India, the Andaman Nicobar Islands, scattered along the eastern extremity of the Bay of Bengal, are in fact closer physically and geographically to Myanmar and Indonesia respectively, while the coral atolls known as Lakshadweep, situated some 300km west of the Malabar Coast, are in effect a northern extension of the Maldives.

The highest point in the Andamans (there are 300 islands in total) is Saddle Peak (737m) on North Andaman. The dense forests that once covered the Andamans'

hilly interiors are now sparser due to rampant logging. The coasts are fringed with coral and are deeply indented, providing natural harbours and tidal creeks. There are no rivers and few perennial streams. The 19 Nicobar Islands are on the whole flat, and coral-covered. An exception is Great Nicobar which rises to 642m. It has numerous streams and is the only island in this group with plentiful fresh water. Lakshadweep consists of some two dozen islands with a total land area of around 32 sq km. All of the islands but one are coral atolls which slope towards the west, where low-lying lagoons protect the inhabitants from the worst effects of the south-west monsoon.

CLIMATE

South India has distinctly wet and dry seasons but, being tropical, generally lacks the large variations in temperature found in northern India. This is particularly so the further south one goes. On the coast of Kerala, for example, the average mean temperature varies no more than a few degrees, although in the higher regions of the Western Ghats the climate is rather more temperate, with hill stations such as Ooty and Kodaikanal providing a welcome respite from the heat and humidity of the coast during the hottest months. Locals will tell you, however, that even the cool months aren't as cool as they were 30 or more years ago. India's air pollution is often blamed for this, although some say warmer temperatures simply reflect global climate changes.

Kerala is the first place the south-west monsoon strikes (the onset of the monsoon is traditionally regarded as June 1, which is also the date when Keralan schools start their new term after the pre-monsoon break), drenching the state as it sweeps in eastward from the Arabian Sea. As it rises over the Western Ghats it cools and soaks the windward slopes before dropping over the leeward side, parts of which receive only about a quarter of the rainfall dumped to windward. Within about 10 days the monsoon has travelled as far as northern

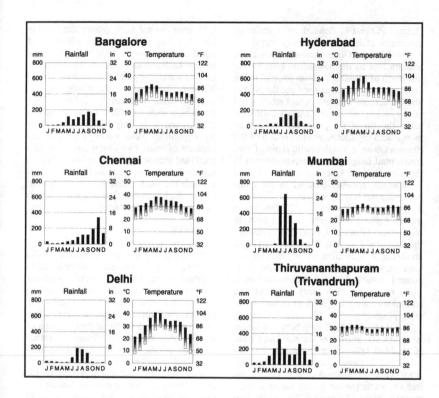

Maharashtra, and by early July it has covered the entire country.

A second soaking occurs in Tamil Nadu and Kerala in November and early December when the retreating monsoon (commonly referred to as the north-east or winter monsoon) blows in from the Bay of Bengal. The coasts of Andhra Pradesh and Tamil Nadu are also occasionally hit by cyclones during these months.

The climate in the Andaman & Nicobar Islands is tropical, with temperatures averaging 29°C, but this is moderated by sea breezes. The islands receive about 3300mm of rain annually, most of it during the south-west monsoon (May to September) and during the cyclonic storms in October and November. Lakshadweep is similarly tropical.

ECOLOGY & ENVIRONMENT

With about 950 million people, and an unrestrained rush to industrialise, India's ecology has been stretched almost to breaking point. It is already one of the most ecologically damaged countries in the world, and with a rising population making ever-increasing demands on dwindling resources, India's crisis has the potential to turn into its catastrophe.

Land Degradation

While India's burgeoning population puts increasing pressure on its natural resources, more than half of its arable land has become infertile through degradation; over six billion tonnes of fertile topsoil are eroded each year; and pollution and degradation results in an annual loss equivalent to about 10% of India's GDP.

An estimated 175 million hectares of land are lost each year, mainly through water erosion as valuable topsoil is swept away by monsoon floods.

Also, from the 1960s, in a desperate bid to increase productivity and feed its population, India introduced large scale chemical fertilising and high-yield grains. Although production was tripled and the people fed, the land was unable to withstand the intensive use. The problem India faces is that to feed the increasing population it will have to resort to more intensive chemical farming and thus exhaust more land.

Deforestation (see the following section) is also a major contributing factor, as is the traditional slash-and-burn method of farming (*jhum*) in which fields are cultivated intensively for a few harvests and then abandoned.

Deforestation

In 1953, the Indian government formulated the National Forest Policy to ensure that 33% of the country would remain under forest cover. Despite this positive step, less than 11% of India is forested today, and much of this is in the far northern regions and in poor condition. Reliable statistics about deforestation are hard to find, but an estimated 8% of India's land has been deforested in the past 15 years. One of the most dramatic examples of deforestation is in the Andaman & Nicobar Islands where forest cover has been slashed from 90% to a shameful 20%.

Perhaps most infuriating for environmentalists is the diversion of forest land for all kinds of development and industrial use since 1985. Statistics from the Ministry of Environment and Forests show that, over the following decade, more than 3500 sq km were deforested in this way.

Part of this process is the policy of 'denotification', the undoing of protected areas for commercial development. In the free market economic conditions of the 1990s, denotification was tantamount to a 'land

The Nilgiri Biosphere Reserve

Of the 14 biosphere reserves in India, the first, and most accessible in South India, is the Nilgiri Biosphere Reserve. It incorporates the national parks of Wynad (Kerala), Mudumalai (Tamil Nadu) and Nagarhole and Bandipur (Karnataka).

Its 5520 sq km protects: eight types of forest, including pristine *shola* forests found mainly in the Nilgiris and Silent Valley; endangered animals, such as Nilgiri langurs, leopards, sloth bears, tigers and Nilgiri tahrs; one of the largest populations in the world of rare Asian elephants; birds, such as cormorants and speckled wood pigeons; various snakes, including monstrous king cobras; and major rivers of South India, the Cauvery, Godavari, Krishna, Kabini and Bhavani.

grab'. Until 1997, state legislatures had the power to denotify any land they pleased. Alarmed by the number of protected areas lost in the early 1990s the Supreme Court ruled that no land could be denotified in this way without the approval of the Indian Board of Wildlife. There is still, however, a continuing battle between developers and conservationists over the best use for this precious land.

There are many other reasons for this drastic deforestation, sadly common to other developing countries:

- increased demand for fuel (about 80% of domestic fuel in rural India is firewood) and building materials
- mining and dams (see following sections)
- encroachment for farm land (especially for coffee, and livestock)
- jhum farming, and the introduction of cash crops, such as cotton and tobacco
- fire
- smuggling – the high price of teak, rosewood and sandalwood ensures that smuggling is big business, especially in Silent Valley, Mudumalai and Bandipur national parks. It thrives because of corrupt forest officers and lack of resources

- introduction of non-native plants (such as parthenium), trees (eg eucalyptus) and animals which upset the ecological balance
- legalised logging, sanctioned by the forest departments, for wood and paper industries

Reforestation Action

Hug a Tree Chipko, an organisation of villagers in the Indian Himalayas concerned about environmental degradation, particularly indiscriminate logging, started over 20 years ago. It captured public attention by hugging trees (Chipko means 'to hug' in Hindi). The Appiko movement (Appiko means 'to hug' in the Kannada language) was started in northern Karnataka in the mid-1980s to protest felling operations sanctioned by the forest department, and has been relatively successful so far.

Adopt a Tree Established in 1988, Tamil Nadu's Annamalai Reforestation Society is replanting thousands of saplings and setting up nurseries and education programmes for local villagers at Mount Arunachala, revered burial place of Sri Ramana Maharishi, among others. The Society is also growing and selling medicinal herbs, with profits ben-

efiting local villages; and promoting new, ecologically-sound methods of agriculture.

Foreigners can assist by partaking in the 'Tree Adoption Scheme': for Rs 2000 you can 'adopt' five saplings. For information and donations, contact the Annamalai Reforestation Society (☎/fax 4175-23645), 60-B/1, ROA Colony, Sri Ramanasramam Post, Tiruvannamalai, 606 603.

Marine Environment

The flora and marine life along the 3000km coastline of South India are under constant threat from pollution, sewage, ports, dams, tourism (especially in Goa), and harmful fishing methods.

Mangroves About 2.5 million hectares of mangroves have been destroyed in India since 1900. Mangroves are home to migratory birds and marine life, are the first defence against soil erosion and help protect the coast from natural disasters such as tidal waves and cyclones. Destruction has been caused by cattle grazing, logging, water pollution, prawn farming (see the following section) and tidal changes caused by the erosion of surrounding land. Only re-

Sacred Groves

Many tribal people, or *adivasis*, regard their local environment as sacred. Some small pockets of forests, and the wildlife inhabiting them, are dedicated to deities which would be angered enough to seek revenge if the forests, or wildlife, are damaged in any way. In some cases, the adivasis will not even gather foliage, fruit or dead wood. In this way these forests, known as sacred groves, remain protected. They can be found throughout India, including Andhra Pradesh and Kerala.

Andhra Pradesh Studies by the WWF suggest there are about 800 sacred groves in this state, of which 100 are of special biological and ecological interest. Most are located near the towns of Cuddapah, Tirupathi and Anantapur (near Gootybailu village, which boasts one of the world's largest banyan trees).

Kerala Kerala's 761 sacred groves or *kavus* protect 720 species of flora. One grove near Alappuzha, contains the Mannarsala Naga Temple and many rare plant species which have medicinal value for leprosy and scabies. At Elanjikal Vallikkavu, near Changannur, the groves are home to threatened species of mongoose, frogs and langurs; and the Ramanthali grove near Payyannur, north of Kannur, is home to banyans and rare white-bellied eagles.

cently have satellite images revealed the full extent of the damage which has been caused.

Prawn Farming The international demand for prawns saw a plethora of prawn farms set up in India, resulting in vast environmental damage to the coastline and birdlife. Mangrove forests are clearcut to build ponds to grow prawns, thus removing a crucial line of defence for coral reefs and habitats for marine life. About 25 million litres of precious fresh water are required to produce one tonne of prawns, and the cost of repairing the damage already exceeds the hundreds of millions of export dollars earned each year. Ironically, prawn production is affected by other environmental damage (eg 40% of prawn farming in Karnataka is affected by the erosion of, and chemicals in, the soil). A ruling by the Indian Supreme Court forced large prawn farms to close, although the Kerala government has been able to supersede the edict from Delhi.

Coral Reefs Three major coral reefs are located around the islands of Lakshadweep and Andaman & Nicobar, and the Gulf of Mannar (near Sri Lanka). Coral is a vital part of the fragile marine ecology, but is under constant threat from over-fishing and bottom-of-the-sea trawling. Other factors contributing to the onslaught against the reefs are shipping, pollution, sewage, poaching and excessive silt caused by deforestation and urban development on the land.

Fisheries India's seas have been overfished to such an extent that stocks are dwindling. Trawlers and factory fishing ships have largely replaced villagers in traditional log boats, and some areas – the coast of Kerala for example – have been overfished, leading to a loss of livelihood for fishing families.

Development
Development projects in India rarely go through the process of preparing an envi-

ronment impact assessment (EIA) before being built, or when they do, EIAs are often flawed or ignored.

Typically, along the Shambvi River in Karnataka, a factory supplying dye for US currency produced an EIA months *after* the factory had been constructed.

Mining Throughout India, many mining rights have been granted without regard for, or requirement to restore, the natural environment. A staggering 15% of Goa is being mined, mostly in the forests bordering the precious Western Ghats of Karnataka. When open pit mines have been fully exploited they are often simply abandoned, scarring the hinterland.

In Goa and other states, heavy rains flush residues from open-cut mines into the rivers and sea, and some seep into the local water table, contaminating drinking water.

Some licences for the mining of gold, silver, platinum and diamonds in Karnataka, and for gold and mica in the Nilgiris, have been granted under dubious circumstances with little or no regard for environmental impact.

Water India's water table is sinking; in places like Goa, the situation is exacerbated by heavy tourism development. For example, regulations that no bore holes be dug within 500m of the high water mark have been ignored to draw water for swimming pools.

Dams are inevitable because of the increase in demand for the already over-stretched supply of water. An estimated 86% of all rainwater runs directly into the sea and monsoons are unreliable. However, dams deliver more than potable water and an energy source; forests are felled, people displaced, agricultural land flooded and marine life destroyed.

The safety, number and cost of dams in India is questionable. Since 1951, Rs 500,000 million has been spent on 246 projects. Almost 35% of these have never been completed, 13 are complete failures and five have breached.

Pollution

India is the 10th most polluted country in the world, and the seventh-largest producer of air pollutants. The effects of pollution are staggering: it costs India at least 4.5% of its annual GDP (according to the World Bank); and 70% of available drinking water is contaminated.

While North India is most heavily affected by pollution, the south is by no means without its share of problems. It's hard to find a river or lake which has not been irreparably polluted with sewage, rubbish and chemical waste. Factories spew chemicals into the sea, rivers and air with little regulative control by undermanned, and sometimes incompetent, local authorities.

Tanneries are often the worst polluters. Some rivers, such as the Noyyal and Bhavani, tributaries of the Cauvery, are now virtually unusable. Pesticides used for cash crops, such as cotton and tobacco, upset the ecology – only about 1% of pesticides (which are often banned in developed countries) actually reach the pests; the rest seeps into the environment.

If that's not bad enough, India actually *imports* pollution, including hazardous industrial waste, toxic chemicals and non-biodegradable batteries. These are dumped into landfills, and water sources, to earn foreign exchange.

Air Pollution Air pollution is a serious problem in India with Delhi, Calcutta and Mumbai among the world's 10 most polluted cities and Chennai and Bangalore not far behind. Just breathing the air in one of India's 23 one-million-plus centres is said to be the equivalent of smoking 20 cigarettes a day.

A major contributing factor is the number of vehicles in India which has trebled since 1990. Most of these are motorbikes and auto-rickshaws which spew out 60 times more pollutants per passengers than a bus. (See also Health, following.)

Health

While the environment is under constant threat, so is the health of the Indian people.

About 65% of diseases in India, such as cholera and dysentery, are avoidable, and mainly caused by polluted water. A rise in malaria in South India, and the resurgence of Japanese B encephalitis in northern Karnataka, has been blamed on deforestation and the building of dams.

At least 40,000 people die prematurely every year from air pollution, 7000 people die of acute asthma, and 40% of children suffer from at least one respiratory illness. The short-term effects for visitors may include wheezing, inflammation of the bronchial tracts, chest pains and shortness of breath. Asthmatics may start suffering immediately and seriously.

The spread of many diseases which are controlled in developed countries, such as tuberculosis (which kills 500,000 Indians each year), certain cancers and polio (India has 60% of the world's polio victims) is a result of the unhealthy environment and, therefore, unavoidable.

Conservation

Considering the wide-scale damage India's ecology has already endured, conservation is perhaps a misnomer and 'damage limitation' a more accurate description. It shouldn't be all doom and gloom, however. There have been some positive developments in recent years which provide hope for the subcontinent's ecological future.

Thankfully, some potentially damaging projects in South India have been stopped, or at least challenged, including:

- the planned extension of the Konkan Railway through the Western Ghats has been stopped. It would have destroyed mangroves, river systems and ancient irrigation systems known as *khazans*.
- the intensive tourist development of Goa, and along the nearby coast, is being actively challenged by many Goan watchdog organisations.
- the building of an 'ecotourism' resort near Nagarhole National Park has been thwarted (see pages 273-75 for details).
- the construction of a 500MW power plant in Kerala is being challenged by a local environment group, because of its potential to harm the ecology of the local lakes.

- construction of the Pooyamkutty hydroelectric project in Kerala was halted because of public opposition.
- the Silent Valley hydroelectric project in Kerala was abandoned because it would have destroyed forests in the pristine Silent Valley.

FLORA & FAUNA

South India has three recognised biogeographic zones: the forested, wet and elevated

Western Ghats that run parallel to the west coast from Mumbai to Kerala; the flat, dry Deccan Plateau that makes up the heart of South India; and the island groups, Andaman & Nicobar (to the east) and Lakshadweep (off the Keralan coast, to the west).

Flora

India boasts 15,000 species of plants and trees (of which 2200 are used in traditional

---

Conservation Contacts

Bombay Natural History Society (☎ 022-284 3869; fax 283 7615), Hornbill House, Shaheed Bhagat Singh Rd, Mumbai, Maharashtra 400 023, is one of the more renowned environmental groups in India.

Centre for Science & Environment (☎ 011-698 1110; fax 698 5879; email cse@sdalt.ernet.in), 41 Tughlakabad Institutional Area, Delhi 110 062, publishes a series of journals on the state of the environment.

Equations (email admin@equation.ilban.ernet.in) 198 2nd Cross, Church Rd, New Thippasandra, Bangalore 560 075, is a tourism pressure group supporting indigenous people.

Madras Naturalists Society (☎ 044-450 813), 36 IV Main Rd, RA Puram, Chennai 600 028, employs the best people to contact in this part of Tamil Nadu.

Merlin Nature Club, 13, 8th Cross, 30th Main, Sarakki ITI Layout, JP Nagar Phase, Bangalore 560 078, is involved in several local ecological projects.

Mysore Amateur Naturalists (☎ 0821-541744), 571, 9th Cross, Anikethana Road, Kuvempu Nagar, Mysore, is involved in Project Pelican.

Society for the Prevention of Cruelty to Animals (☎ 080-286 0205), Kasturba Rd (near the KSTDC Office), Bangalore 560 001, is heavily involved in prevention of cruelty to animal issues.

TRAFFIC International (☎ 01223-277 427; fax 277 237; email traffic@wcmc.org.uk), 219c Huntingdon Rd, Cambridge CB3 0DL, UK, is the international headquarters for the major organisation involved in the prevention of the illegal trade in wildlife. Other offices include **TRAFFIC USA** (☎ 202-293 4800; fax (202) 775 8287; email traffic.us@wwfus.org), 1250 24th St NW, Washington DC 20037, USA; and **TRAFFIC India** (☎ 011-469 8578; fax 462 6837; email traffic@wwfind.ernet.in), 172-B, Lodi Estate, New Delhi 110 003.

Wildlife Association of South India (☎ 080-578 379), 49 Richmond Rd, Bangalore 560 025, is an impressive organisation involved in protecting wildlife.

Wildlife Protection Society of India (☎ 011-621 3864; fax 336 8729; email blue@giasdlol.vsnl.net.in), Thapara House, 124 Janpath, Delhi, is involved in many projects all over India.

WWF is the major NGO working in India: Headquarters (☎ 011-462 7586; fax 462 6837), 172-B Lodi Estate, Max Mueller Marg, New Delhi 110 003. Other regional offices are in Mumbai (☎ 022-207 8105; fax 207 6037), National Insurance Building, 2nd floor, Dr DN Road, Mumbai, Maharashtra 400 001; Goa (☎ 0832-226 020), Hill Side Apartments, Block B, Flat B-2, Ground floor, Fontainhas, Panaji, Goa 403 001; Kerala (☎ 0471-325 183), A/10 Tagore Nagar, TC No 15/989, Vazhutacaud, Thiruvananthapuram, Kerala 695 014; Bangalore (☎ 080-286 3206; fax 286 6685), Kamala Mansion, 143 Infantry Rd, Bangalore 560 001; Chennai (Madras) (☎ 044-434 8064; fax 434 7967), 13 11th St, Nadanam Extension, Chennai, Tamil Nadu 600 035; and Hyderabad, Andhra Pradesh (☎ 040-334 0922), Block 2, Flat 4, Vijayanagar Colony, Hyderabad 500 057.

medicines). A quarter of these are found in the Western Ghats. Forest types include: tropical, wet and semi-evergreen forests in the Andaman & Nicobar Islands and Western Ghats; tropical, moist deciduous forest in the Andamans, southern Karnataka and Kerala; tropical thorn forest, found in much of the drier Deccan Plateau; and montane and wet temperate forests in the higher parts of Tamil Nadu and Kerala. Along the coasts of Tamil Nadu and Kerala, there are also mangroves (aka swamp forests).

Characteristic of the Nilgiri and Anamali hills in the Western Ghats are the patches of moist evergreen forest restricted to valleys and steep, protected slopes. Known as *sholas*, these islands of dark green are surrounded by expansive grasslands covering the more exposed slopes. They provide es-sential shelter and food for animals but their limited size and patchy distribution make sholas vulnerable to natural and man-made disturbances.

Teak, mahogany, rosewood and sandal-wood are common in (and smuggled from) the Western Ghats. You will also see banyan figs; bamboo in the Western Ghats; coconut palms on the islands and along the coastal peninsula; Indian coral tree along the coasts; mangroves in tiny pockets. India is home to 2000 species of orchid – about 10% of those found worldwide. The Nilgiris is one of the finest places to spot orchids such as the (*Calanthe triplicata*).

Fauna

India is home to 340 species of mammals; 80 species of rodents; 560 species of reptiles and amphibians; 200 species of fish;

Medicinal Plants & Trees of South India

About 2200 species of plants and trees growing in India are known to have medicinal value; amazingly, 60% of these can be found in the Western Ghats.

The aquatic, sweet-scented kamala, or lotus, is found in tanks and ponds. Its flowers and filaments are useful in liver complaints, its seeds are used in the treatment of skin diseases, and its fresh leaves mixed with sandalwood make a cooling, soothing balm.

Plant/Part Used	*Distribution*	*Uses*
Amalak/dried fruit	Deccan Peninsula	Dysentery
Ankola/bark	Coastal Karnataka	Antidote for poisons
Foxglove/all	Nilgiris	Heart disease
Lavanga/leaves	Western Ghats	Nausea
Nirgundi/leaves	Konkan Coast	Rheumatism & swelling
Padari/bark	Coastal Karnataka	Scorpion stings
Pooga/unripe nut	Kerala & Karnataka	Laxative
Sarju/resin	Coastal Karnataka	Skin diseases
Shreegandha/wood	Karnataka & Tamil Nadu	Swelling & skin diseases
Suragi/flower buds	Western Ghats	Stimulant
Vishnukranti/all	Western Ghats	Fever & nerve disorders
Kamala/all	Tanks & ponds	Diarrhoea & liver complaints

over 50,000 species of insects; and at least 1200 species of birds. The following is an overview of the more common wildlife found in South India. For more detail, pick up one of the wildlife books listed in the Facts for the Visitor chapter.

Antelopes, Gazelles & Deer You will see plenty of these browsers and grazers in the national parks. The chowsingha or four-horned antelope (*Tetracerus quadricornis*) is the only animal in the world with four horns. It prefers an open forest and grassland habitat, such as found in Bandipur and Nagarhole national parks, where pairs or solo adults are usually seen not far from water. The nilgai (*Boselaphus tragocamelus*), or blue cow, is the largest Asiatic antelope. (Though the nilgai, along with the chowsingha, belong to a separate family from the 'true' antelopes.) It congregates in small herds which can be observed in open forest in parks and reserves in Andhra Pradesh and Karnataka. As it lacks impressive horns it hasn't been a great target for hunters, and its association with the sacred cow has also helped protect it.

Not as lucky is the blackbuck (*Antilope cervicapra*) whose distinctive spiral horns and attractive dark coat make it a prime target for poachers. The blackbuck is one of the few antelopes where males and females differ in coat colour. As the name suggests, dominant males develop dark, almost black, coats (usually dark brown in South India), while the 20 or so females and subordinate males in their herd are fawn in colour. See also the boxed text in the Karnataka chapter.

The slender chinkara or Indian gazelle (*Gazella gazella*), with its light brown coat and white underbelly, prefers the drier foothills and plains. It can be seen in small herds of five or less in national parks and sanctuaries in Karnataka and Andhra Pradesh.

The little mouse deer (*Tragulus meminna*) grows to no more than 30cm. Delicate and shy, its speckled olive-brown/grey coat provides excellent camouflage in the forest understorey. The common sambar (*Cervus unicolour*) is by contrast up to five times as tall. It sheds its impressive horns around the end of April; new ones start growing one month later. This, the largest of the Indian deer, is the favoured prey species of the tiger. The attractive chital (cheetal) or spotted deer (*Axis axis*) is common throughout India and can be seen in most of South India's national parks and sanctuaries, particularly those with wet evergreen forests. This deer is never seen far from water. The barking deer (*Muntiacus muntjak*) is a small deer which bears tushes (elongated canines) as well as small antlers. Its bark is said to sound much like that of a dog but it is a difficult animal to spot in its habitat, the thick forests of Tamil Nadu, Karnataka and Andhra Pradesh.

Tiger The tiger (*Panthera tigris*) is a shy and solitary creature, preferring to live and hunt under the cover of tall grass or forest. It has poor eyesight and smell, but excellent hearing. Tigers prefer deer as their food source, although they will settle for frogs, rodents and fish if deer are scarce or if they are incapacitated by disease or injury; they do not normally attack humans. Tigers live for about 20 years, and can grow to nearly 3m long. While most national parks, including tiger reserves, do contain tigers, you will be very lucky to see one. The best places to try are the Periyar, Nagarjunasagar-Srisaliam and Kalakad-Mundanthurai tiger reserves, and Bandipur and Nagarhole national parks.

Other Cats The leopard (*Panthera pardus*) doesn't stick exclusively to heavy forest cover. Usually leopards are a golden brown with black rosettes, although in the Western Ghats they may be almost entirely black. You may be lucky and see one in the Sanjay Gandhi National Park, near Mumbai or Periyar Wildlife Sanctuary in Kerala.

Leopard-like markings grace the forest-dwelling leopard cat (*Felis bengalensis*), but it is only slightly bigger than an ordinary house cat. It is strictly nocturnal and very rarely seen. Slightly larger than the leopard cat is the widely distributed jungle cat (*Felis chaus*). This bold cat can be seen

Counting Tigers

How many wild tigers roam through India's reserves and forests? This is one of the most frequently asked questions put by travellers to park officials. Unfortunately there is no easy answer. Of the eight subspecies of tiger that were around at the beginning of this century, only five remain. According to both the World Wide Fund for Nature (WWF) and the Environmental Investigation Agency (EIA), the global population of wild tigers does not exceed 5000. Of these, less than 3000 are said to be in India, with around 500 in South India.

Project Tiger is an official agency of the Indian government established in 1973 under the Ministry of Environment and Forests. Its charter is to save the Indian tiger from extinction. Of India's wildlife reserves, 23 are administered by Project Tiger. The main reserves in South India are Bandipur, Nagarjuna Sagar-Srisailam, Namdapha and Kalakad Mundantthyurai.

Within its first few years the efforts of Project Tiger seemed highly successful. Numerous reports were issued stating that tiger numbers had not only stabilised but increased. In Bandipur, for example, the numbers had increased from an estimated 11 in 1972 to 75 in 1997. However in recent years the picture has soured and many environmentalists, both within India and without, question the counting methods used by Project Tiger, as well as claims made by the organisation that the Indian tiger is a long way from extinction.

Global traffic in live animals as well as animal parts is said to be the biggest illegal trade after drugs. INTERPOL claim the value of illegal trade in wildlife is around US$6 billion a year. The tiger forms a significant part of this trade. According to the EIA, the death rate of tigers in India averages one per day. Most of these deaths are from poaching. The demand for tiger is mainly in China and Japan where tiger teeth, nails and bones are used in traditional Chinese medicines and tiger penis soup is a status symbol.

The Indian tiger is listed in Appendix 1 of the Convention on International Trade in Endangered Species (CITES). This means that tiger preservation is to be given a high priority by globally focused environment groups. Although India is a signatory to CITES, it is clear that lucrative profits from tiger poaching and the relatively low risk of detection are clear incentives to flout the CITES agreement. One of the problems has been the liberalisation of the Indian economy. Tiger preser-

hunting in reserves and even in the vicinity of human settlement in broad daylight. Its distinguishing features are a relatively short, thick tail and a fairly uniform grey coat.

Slightly bigger than a house cat, the leopard cat is strictly nocturnal and very rarely seen.

Dog Family The wild dog or dhole (*Cuon alpinus*) is found throughout India. This tawny predator hunts during the day in packs which have been known to bring down animals as large as a buffalo. They are relentless pursuers with an energy-efficient gait, exhausting their prey before the pack attacks.

The Indian wolf (*Canis lupus linnaeus*) has suffered from habitat destruction and hunting. Its coat is fawn with black stipples and it is generally a much leaner looking animal than its European or North American cousins. Though rare in South India, the wolf can be seen in its preferred habitat of dry open forest and scrubland of the Deccan Plateau.

The Indian fox (*Vulpes bengalensis*) has

vation is no longer a high priority when it comes to economic development and resource alloca-tion. Reports of the hopelessly inadequate resources within the Project Tiger reserves are rife. Many staff are without wages. Some don't even have shoes. Vehicles have no spare parts or even fuel and park managers have been given little in the way of training and strategies for conserva-tion. In fact the very attitude within the public service towards postings in wildlife sanctuaries is indicative of the wider problem. Such postings are often regarded as 'punishment positions' and are therefore executed with a degree of reluctance and resentment. This is not to say that there aren't many dedicated individuals on staff who care about the tigers and the ecosystem. The truth is many staff risk their lives for their jobs (every year some are killed in their attempts to stop poachers). But the high level political will necessary to bring about genuine change is regarded by many environment groups as being conspicuously absent.

One example of the extraordinary odds that tigers face can be seen in the Nilgiris Biosphere Reserve in the border region of Tamil Nadu, Karnataka and Kerala. This area, which houses an estimated one-third of India's wild elephant population as well as the Bandipur Tiger Reserve, is undergoing massive transformation because of the Pykara Ultimate Stage Hydro-Electric Project (PUSHEP). This project was started over a decade ago by the Tamil Nadu Electricity Board. In 1996 the highly regarded Bombay Natural History Society reported on the extent of environmental devastation brought about by PUSHEP. Despite reports questioning the economic viability of such a massive project (including one by the central Electricity Authority), the Ministry of Environment & Forests has refused to pull the plug. Meanwhile, local conservationists are seeking court action in order to save the Nilgiris Biosphere Reserve from further destruction.

In 1996 the High Court of India commissioned a special report on the status of the tiger. The recommendations of the report included the granting of statutory authority to the Indian Board for Wildlife (Indian's highest wildlife advisory body, chaired by the prime minister) and the establish-ment of a new Ministry for Natural Resources (Forests and Wildlife). The report noted that the current Ministry of Environment & Forests devotes considerable resources to the evaluation and facilitation of large-scale industrial development projects such as hydro-electric power and mining. As yet the recommendations have not been adopted.

a black-tipped tail and a greyish coat, and because of its appetite for rodents can coexist more comfortably with farming communities than can other carnivores.

Because of its appetite for rodents, the Indian fox coexists peacefully with farmers.

Elephants The Asian elephant (*Elephas maximus*) is smaller than its African cousin, standing on average 2.75m high at the shoulder and weighing up to 5000kg. It is a surprisingly good swimmer, but not agile. With poor eyesight, relying more on smell and hearing to survive, it lives in clans of about 20, normally led by a female. One large male needs up to 200kg of food, and about 200L of water, a day. Elephants can live up to 70 years in the wild and longer in captivity. Male elephants have a yearly period in heat, known as *musth*, which can last several months, and during which time their behaviour tends to be violent and un-predictable.

There are some 27,000 elephants in the wild in India. But although these figures

Elephant Conservation

Poaching The most appalling sight imaginable in the jungles of India is a dead 5000kg elephant, slaughtered for two 10kg ivory tusks. About 100 elephants are killed each year in India for ivory (used for jewellery, chessboards or ornaments) and the number is increasing: the ivory trade has increased five-fold in the last four years. Ivory can also be chipped from live, domesticated elephants, who then regrow their tusks in a few years.

Females do not have tusks, and not all males are 'tuskers' – but most in South India are. The slaughter of only males creates a dangerous imbalance of genders, most noticeable in Periyar Wildlife Sanctuary. After a crop raid, elephants are subject to violent reprisals by villagers (elephants also kill about 40 people in South India each year); and the animals also suffer from a loss of habitat caused by logging, fires, dams, mining and village/urban encroachment.

Project Elephant Also known locally as Gajatme, this conservation movement was started in 1991. It has seen some success in Bandipur, for example: numbers of elephants there rose from 1187 in 1976 to 3271 in 1997. In South India, the project covers several national parks and semi-protected areas:

Anamalai Hills: Indira Gandhi Wildlife Sanctuary
Eastern Ghats: Dharmapuri, Sathyamangalam, Erode and Hosur
Nilgiris: Mudumalai National Park, North Nilgiris, and Gudalur
Western Ghats: Srivilliputhur, Madurai South, Periyar, Tirunelveli and Kanyakumari

One way to avoid poaching is to breed tuskless elephants, known as makhnas, which is being trialled in Periyar. But to ensure the survival of elephants throughout India, there must be: better anti-poaching methods; targeting of traders and dealers in favour of low-level poachers; protection of habitats and natural corridors; minimising the conflict that arises from crop raiding; more

---

may seem quite healthy, tuskers, perennial targets for poachers, are as endangered as tigers. In Periyar Wildlife Sanctuary, which has a sizeable elephant population, there are now 122 females for every male; 20 years ago there were around six females per male. At Periyar, which comes under the auspices of Project Elephant, wildlife experts are testing the breeding of tuskless elephants (known as *makhnas*).

Primates You can't miss these creatures all over South India, whether it's passing through signposted 'Monkey Zones' as you traverse the Western Ghats or fending off over-friendly macaques at temples or as you wait to board a boat at Periyar.

The little pale-faced bonnet macaque (*Macaca radiata*) is named for the 'bonnet'

of dark hair that covers its head, and which is parted neatly in front. These macaques live in highly structured troops where claims on hierarchy are commonly and noisily contested. They are opportunistic feeders: barely a grub, berry or leaf escapes their alert eyes and nimble fingers. The crab-eating macaque (*M. fascicularis*), found in the Nicobar Islands, looks rather like a rhesus or a bonnet macaque, but has a longer, thicker tail. In contrast, the lion-tailed macaque (*M. silenus*) has a thick mane of greyish hair that grows from its temples and cheeks. This endangered macaque is often cited by park advertising material but rarely sighted. Annamalai Wildlife Sanctuary in Tamil Nadu and Silent Valley National Park in Kerala, are important refuges for this primate.

cooperation between state and federal governments; better intelligence about poaching; more training for staff; proper surveys, post-mortems on dead elephants; and improvements in customs procedures.

Elephant Corridors One of the more vital and current conservation issues is the establishment and protection of elephant corridors. These are long passages through forests, jungle and farmland which allow elephants and other wildlife to travel from one protected or remote area to another without hindrance or accident. Importantly, the corridors also allow the inter-breeding of clans.

Predictably, many natural corridors are blocked by roads, power plants, dams and urban developments. This forces some elephants to traverse through farms and villages, resulting in danger to themselves, villagers, domestic animals and crops. For example, in Kodagu (Karnataka) and the Nilgiris (Tamil Nadu), extensive, and expensive, tea and coffee plantations, and to a lesser extent, rice paddies, cover a lot of available flat land, so corridors are under threat.

One elephant corridor, managed by the WWF, is about 10 minutes (on your right) as you leave by train from Mettupalayam towards Ooty, in Tamil Nadu. Other vital corridors are between Moyar and Masinagudi (Tamil Nadu); Kakankote and Bandipur forests (Karnataka); Wynad and Brahmagiri (Kerala); and Kaudinya and Sri Venkateshwara wildlife sanctuaries (Andhra Pradesh).

EDDIE GERALD

Elephant corridors are an essential aspect of the fight to protect the Asian elephant.

Less shy is the common langur (*Presbytis entellus*) or Hanuman monkey, recognisable by its long limbs and black face. India's most hunted primate is the Nilgiri langur (*P. johni*), which inhabits the dense forests of the Western Ghats including the sholas of such ranges as the Nilgiris and Annamalai. This vegetarian monkey is pursued by poachers for the supposed medicinal qualities of its flesh and viscera.

The peculiar-looking slender loris (*Loris tardigradus*) has a soft, woolly brown/grey coat and huge, bush-baby eyes. It is nocturnal, coming down from the trees only to feed, on virtually anything it can find: insects, leaves, berries, lizards, etc. The slender loris is at home in dense rainforest or more open forest, from the coastal plains to the steep mountain valleys. Though not as

obvious as it once was, there is still a trade in South India for live lorises – their eyes are believed by some to be a powerful medicine for human eye diseases as well as a vital ingredient for love potions!

The nocturnal slender loris has huge, bush-baby eyes.

Other Mammals The sloth bear (*Melursus ursinus*) is about 80cm high, and weighs up to 150kg. It has short legs and shaggy black or brown hair, with a touch of white on its chest. It lives in forested areas of the national parks, and in the Nilgiris. It is nocturnal, feeding on termites, honey and fruit, and occasionally carrion. See the Treatment of Animals section for detail on the exploitation of these creatures.

The gaur (*Bos gaurus*), a wild ox (sometimes referred to as the Indian bison), can be seen in the major national parks of Karnataka and Kerala. Up to 2m high, it is born with light-coloured hair, which gets darker as it gets older. With its immense bulk and white-stockinged legs, the gaur is easily recognised. This gentle giant avoids humans where possible and prefers the wet sholas and bamboo thickets in its prime territory, the Western Ghats. Sadly, the large herds of the past are no longer a common sight.

Other furred creatures encountered in South India include: the forest rat (*Rattus rattus*), found in the Nilgiri Hills; common shrew (*Suncus murinus*); giant flying squirrel (*Petaurista petaurista*) and Malabar giant squirrel (*Ratufa indica*), both common in Mudumalai National Park; and porcupine (*Hystrix indica*), found in northern Tamil Nadu.

The gaur is easily recognised by its white stockings and immense bulk.

The common dolphin (*Dolphinus delhis*) is found off either coastlines of the Indian peninsula and dugongs (*Dugong dugong*) have been observed off the Malabar Coast.

Reptiles & Amphibians Of the 32 species of turtles and tortoises in India, you may see the hawksbill, leatherback, green, loggerhead or endangered olive Ridley species in the coastal waters of South India, or the Indian star tortoise (*Geochelone elegans*) waddling along the forest floor in Andhra Pradesh. Three species of crocodiles can be found in India, two of them in South India: the mugger or marsh crocodile (*Crocodylus palustris*) and the saltwater crocodile (*C. porosus*). The latter lives in the Andaman & Nicobar Islands while the mugger is extensively distributed in rivers and freshwater lakes in South India thanks to government breeding programs.

India is home to 155 species of lizards; and 244 species of snakes such as the tiny Perrotet's shield-tail snake (*Plectrurus perroteti*), found in the Western Ghats, and the fearsome 3m-long king cobra (*Ophiophagus hannah*). Frogs and toads are hopping all over the place, including the quaintly named, and pink-thighed, torrent frog (*Micrixalus opisthorodus*), which is endemic to the Western Ghats.

Fish The still pristine luxuriant coral around the islands of Lakshadweep and Nicobar & Andaman supports a diverse marine ecosystem which hosts myriad of tropical fish including the butterfly fish, the parrot fish, the very ugly porcupine fish, and the light-blue surgeon fish. Along the Goan and Malabar coasts, mackerel and sardine are prevalent. Other marine life off the coast of South India includes moray eels, crabs and sea cucumbers. Migratory visitors include the sperm whale (*Physeter catodon*).

In some rivers in the south, you'll see huge mahseer (preferred quarry of the British Raj angler), carp and mully fish.

Invertebrates Leeches are common in the forests, especially during and immediately

Saving the Turtles

The Bhitar-Kanika Sanctuary in Orissa is famous for its efforts to conserve the threatened olive Ridley turtles, but the coast from Elliot Beach, not far south of Chennai, to the tip of Tamil Nadu is also used by turtles for nesting.

Female turtles create 'false nests' to deceive predators (ie dogs, crabs, crows, jackals and humans), and then lay 100 to 200 eggs at one time in a hole. They push the sand tight into the hole by thumping it with their body. Between 45 and 60 days later, the tiny turtles break out of the eggs and, alone, scuttle across the sand to the water.

A Chennai-based youth organisation, Prakruthi, started turtle conservation efforts several years ago with support from the WWF. Together with the Tamil Nadu Forest Department they established hatcheries between Ennore and Mamallapuram. Nesting times along the south-east coast are between November and March, but the best time to view the turtles is from the end of January to early February. The turtles come to the shore and lay their eggs between 9 pm and 5 am. Some of the agencies listed in the Outdoor Activities Around Bangalore section, particularly Sylvan Retreats which serves as a contact point for Prakruthi, organise turtle-viewing trips in season.

---

after the monsoon. South India has some really spectacular butterflies and moths, including the Malabar banded swallowtail (*Papilio liomedon*) and the peacock hairstreak (*Thelca pavi*).

The most magnificent butterflies can be seen in Silent Valley, Kerala, an area little affected by pollution and pesticides.

In the Andaman & Nicobar Islands, you'll certainly come across the huge coconut (or robber) crab (*Birgus latro*), a powerful crustacean easily able to climb coconut palms and rip apart the tough coconut husk.

Treatment of Animals

While religious teaching and tradition gives animals a privileged position of protection in India, you are likely to encounter instances of cruelty to animals during your visit.

The major welfare issue in South India relates to elephant festivals, particularly in Kerala, which the World Society for the Protection of Animals (WSPA) say represent exploitation of an endangered species. They are also concerned about the individual animals; many have welts from constant shackling and some have sores around the head and in the crease of their legs where sharp goads are placed to control them.

There are also a number of festivals which involve the ritual mutilation of wildlife, such as the removal of the fangs of snakes or the mutilation of vultures and foxes. In some cases, animals (mainly livestock) are slaughtered, so be warned.

You may also see the pathetic spectacle of dancing bears, particularly in Karnataka, and WSPA urges travellers not to give money to the bears' nomadic handlers or encourage this exhibition. Sloth bears are an endangered species and more than 100 of them are captured in the wild each year and forced to endure appalling cruelty in their 'training'.

In the Bay of Bengal there is a problem with the capture, sale and slaughter of endangered marine turtle species, particularly olive Ridley and green turtles, and WSPA is targeting these practises through its worldwide Turtle Watch campaign.

In Chennai, and many small cities and towns throughout South India, there are mass euthanasia programmes to control stray dog populations. Despite legislation banning inhumane methods, some authorities still use electrocution and strychnine poisoning to kill the dogs.

For further information on animal welfare issues contact WSPA, 2 Langley Lane, London SW8 1TJ, UK (☎ 0171-793 0540, fax 0171-793 0208; email wspa@wspa.org.uk; internet www.way.net/wspa).

continued on page 42

Birds of South India

The Indian subcontinent is justifiably famous for its birdlife. An immense range of landforms, vegetation and a generally equitable climate support well over 1200 species every bit as diverse and colourful as India's human population. South India hosts a large percentage of the country's birds, and you should be able to see a great variety easily; if you're a keen birdwatcher you will find it a treasure trove. A series of reserves has been set up to protect important biological or scenic sites; some of these are well worth visiting for birdwatching and are mentioned in this section.

The Birds

You will probably notice a few birds about the towns and in the comparative peace of temple grounds, but a trip to one of the many reserves will be particularly rewarding (see National Parks & Wildlife Sanctuaries in the Facts about South India chapter). The Andaman & Nicobar Islands are another attractive option, offering an assortment of endemic species and opportunities to view more widespread species in pleasant surrounds.

A few birds eke out a living even among the bustle and noise of human activity. The house crow is probably the best example. These noisy, gregarious black birds may be seen foraging wherever people leave their scraps. Perhaps no other bird so typifies the settlements and ports of India, and gatherings of crows – known as 'murders' – are a common sight at ghats (literally 'steps' and used by bathers near rivers) and in parks in the early morning. Other, less obtrusive species include the humble house sparrow, which forages for crumbs around dwellings; swallows that dart among buildings after insects; various species of bulbuls that chortle in the trees and bushes; and the ubiquitous mynas that flash their white wing patches when they take off. It seems fitting that so many birds have learned to live in coexistence with India's human inhabitants.

As you travel into the countryside you should see even more birds along the roadside in ponds and fields, patches of bush and on wires. Temple grounds are a good place to enjoy some comparative serenity and watch a few birds. Village ponds can hold a surprising number of birds, from the common sandpiper teetering about on the mud to the Indian pond heron, or paddy bird. Pond herons are common but unobtrusive: they are well camouflaged in greys and browns, and may be almost invisible against the rubble and weeds at the water's edge until they take off, showing their pure white wings.

The blossom-headed parakeet has a more musical call than the squawking of its cousins. It is a luminous green, with a pretty, plum-coloured head and a flash of red on its wings.

No other bird (except perhaps the common myna) so typifies the ports and settlements of India as does the gregarious, ubiquitous house crow.

Waterways are rich in birds. Stalking on long legs at the shallow edge of tanks and estuaries are various species of egrets – graceful white birds with long necks and dagger-like bills; their elegant poise belies the deadly speed with which they spear frogs and fish. The stately great egret is the largest, but smaller egrets can also be sighted; the cattle egret is most commonly seen stalking among livestock for large insects stirred up by passing hooves. Colourful kingfishers wait patiently on overhanging branches before diving for their prey; several species can be seen, including the pied kingfisher, the tiny but colourful common (or river) kingfisher and the striking stork-billed kingfisher, with its massive red bill. The water's edge is also home to smaller and drabber species such as plovers, waterhens and coot, which feed and nest among rank vegetation. The red-wattled and yellow-wattled lapwings are two species of plovers that can be readily recognised by the coloured, fleshy growths on their faces. Lapwings are noisy and territorial birds and they'll soon let you know if you've strayed near their nest!

A flash of colour may turn out to be a bee-eater sallying forth after insects. Pipits and wagtails strut among the stubble of fields, sometimes in large flocks; wagtails can be identified by their habit of wagging their tails up and down. Birds of prey such as harriers and buzzards soar over open spaces looking for unwary birds and small mammals on which they feed.

The white-backed vulture is the most common of its kind in India. It can wheel on thermals for hours on end, scanning the ground for fresh carcasses.

Another bird of prey that can be very much in evidence, especially around rubbish dumps and carcasses, is the black, or pariah kite. Kites and vultures can wheel on thermals for hours on end, the kites constantly twisting their slightly forked tail. Another large hawk, the osprey, feeds almost exclusively on fish, which it seizes with its vicious hooked talons; ospreys patrol large tanks and other waterways.

Although birds are easier to see around waterways, patches of forest often support a richer variety of species. Birds in forests are adapted to feeding in the different layers; thus some pick insects or fruit off the forest floor, and others forage among the branches and leaves. Birds in tropical forests can often be easier to hear than see, and craning your neck to catch a glimpse of what is often just a silhouette among the leaves can be very frustrating!

Among those more often heard than seen are woodpeckers, whose 'drumming' sound is made as they chisel grubs out from under bark. Woodpeckers come in many sizes and colours, from the diminutive piculets to the attractive heart-spotted woodpecker. Their colourful relatives, the barbets, habitually sit at the topmost branches of trees and call incessantly; the crimson-fronted barbet is common in South India. Another family of vocal birds that can be notoriously difficult to catch sight of is the cuckoo. Although the Indian koel is a large, black bird, and surprisingly difficult to see, its loud, piercing cry can be maddening. The malkohas are a colourful group of large, forest-dwelling cuckoos; specialities of the region are blue-faced and Sirkeer malkohas.

Look out for fruiting trees in the forest for they are often a magnet for birds of many species. Fruit-eaters include a number of pigeons and doves, noisy flocks of colourful parrots, the minivets in their splendid red, orange and black plumage, and various cuckoo-shrikes and mynas. Varieties of pigeon include the Nilgiri wood-pigeon and pompadour

The cattle egret goes wherever the herd goes, perching on the backs of cattle and waiting to catch the insects which their hooves stir up.

The koel is a difficult bird to spot, but its cry can be maddening. Male koels are jet black (left); females are speckled greyish-brown and white and have a striped tail (right).

green-pigeon, and two closely related parrots of the region are the Malabar and plum-headed parakeets. Mynas are part of the starling family, and these intelligent, opportunistic birds come in a variety of colours and shapes, among them the hill myna, an all-black bird with a distinctive yellow 'wattle' about the face. Sadly, hill mynas are sought-after as cage birds because they can become quite tame and even learn to talk.

The jewels in the crown for many birdwatchers are the bizarre hornbills, which with their massive down-curved bills resemble the toucans of South America. The largest is the great hornbill, sporting a massive bill and a horny growth on its head (called a casque); the Malabar grey-hornbill is endemic to the region. Hornbills make an impressive and noisy sight as they fly over the canopy trumpeting to each other. At the other end of the spectrum in both size and colour, the iridescent, nectar-feeding sunbirds could be called the jewels in the canopy. A host of smaller birds such as flycatchers, warblers, babblers and the little tailorbird (so-called because it makes a neat little 'purse' of woven grass as a nest) hawk and glean for insects at every layer from the ground up. Sometimes these smaller birds will travel in mixed feeding parties and their antics make a delightful nonstop travelling show.

Where to See Birds in South India
Western Ghats Many birdwatchers head for the portion of the Western Ghats that straddles the border of Kerala and Tamil Nadu. By visiting a couple of reserves in this area one could feasibly see all 23 of southern India's endemic species, plus a swag of others. The Periyar National Park also offers some fine birdwatching. There is accommodation in the park, and boat trips provide a good opportunity to see water birds such as egrets, storks and cormorants, plus large mammals such as elephants, gaur and – with a lot of luck – a tiger. Included in the park's extensive bird list are the stunning great hornbill plus Malabar grey-hornbill, the colourful Malabar trogon and Malabar parakeet. The Indian pitta is a much sought-after speciality and the local example of this colourful family.

Sri Lankamalleswara Wildlife Sanctuary This reserve near Cuddapah, Andhra Pradesh, was established to protect the last known habitat of Jerdon's courser, one of the world's rarest birds. About the size of a large plover, Jerdon's courser is a nocturnal bird that was discovered in the mid-19th century. Even at the time of discovery it was seen only rarely and it disappeared completely in 1900. In 1986 Jerdon's courser was rediscovered when its habitat was being cleared for agriculture and the sanctuary was declared to preserve its last known haunts. It still rates among the world's rarest birds. It is possible to see Jerdon's courser by taking a trip into the reserve at night, but it is essential to obtain permission before a visit. You'll still need a bit of luck to find the courser, but other bird attractions include three species of nightjars – Jerdon's, savanna and Indian – and, during the day, grey francolin, blue-faced malkoha and yellow-wattled lapwing.

Calimere (also known as Kodikkarai) Wildlife Sanctuary Calimere Wildlife Sanctuary is near Vedaranyam on the east coast of Tamil Nadu. By hiring a bike in the village it is possible to spend a pleasant couple of days in the reserve and surrounding lagoons. This is an excellent place for waterbirds, especially the migrant waders. Among the sought-after specialities are spoon-billed and broad-billed sandpipers, the scarce crab plover, both greater and lesser flamingos, and among the larger birds, spot-billed pelican and painted stork.

Dr Salim Ali Bird Sanctuary This sanctuary, 3km from the centre of Panaji, on the south-western tip of the island of Chorao is, at 1.8 sq km, Goa's smallest wildlife reserve. Between October and February it contains an amazingly rich variety of flora and birdlife that will keep the most dedicated birdwatcher happy for days. Residents include kingfishers, eagles, kites, and the pheasant-tailed jacana, to name but a few.

Fruit-eating species of South India include the spotted dove. It has a soft-pink coloured head and breast and a black-and-white spotted 'shawl' at the back of its neck.

Common throughout the South, the pheasant-tailed jacana is a waterbird with an iridescent yellow 'cap', brown feathers, and bright white wings.

Andaman & Nicobar Islands More than 100 bird species are known to breed on the Andamans; through long isolation in the Bay of Bengal 13 unique species have evolved, plus no fewer than 86 distinct island forms of birds also found elsewhere. There are good birdwatching sites close to the capital, Port Blair, and a trip to Mount Harriet will feature a few of the Andaman endemics, plus a good variety of other widespread species. Among the former look out for the imaginatively-named Andaman woodpecker, Andaman wood-pigeon, Andaman serpent-eagle and Andaman treepie. Others not restricted to the islands but eagerly sought are orange-headed thrush, white-rumped shama and forest wagtail.

Corbyn's Cove, south of Port Blair, is a good site for waterbirds and a few to look out for include Indian and Chinese pond-herons; skulkers of the reed beds such as brown coucal, and Baillon's and ruddy-breasted crakes; and songbirds such as reed-warblers and grasshopper-warblers.

Some Tips for Watching Birds

A pair of binoculars will reveal the subtleties of form and plumage not usually detected by the naked eye. Be warned – once you've seen the shimmering colours of a glossy ibis or the brash tones of a bee-eater through binoculars, you may get hooked! Binoculars will also considerably aid identification and help you nut out the subtle – and vexing – differences between the warblers, for example. Basic models can be purchased quite cheaply from duty-free outlets. If you get serious about birdwatching you may want to invest in better quality optics and consider the purchase of a spotting scope. With a magnification usually at least twice that of binoculars, spotting scopes can give stunning views. The drawback is their size (they must be mounted on a tripod for best results). On the other hand, a camera can be attached to some models and a scope then doubles as a telephoto lens.

To help you get the most out of birdwatching, please bear the following in mind:

- Try to get an early start because most birds are generally active during the cooler hours of the day. This is particularly so in arid regions and during hot weather.
- Approach birds slowly and avoid sudden movements or loud talk. Try to dress in drab clothing so as not to stand out. Many species are quite approachable and will allow opportunities for observation and photography. Birds are not usually too concerned about people in a vehicle and stunning views can often be obtained from the roadside.
- Waterbirds and waders respond to tidal movements and are usually best seen on a falling tide as they search for food.
- If you are moved on, be courteous. Always ask permission before birding on private property.
- Do not disturb birds unnecessarily and never handle eggs or young birds in a nest. Adults will readily desert a nest that has been visited, leaving their young to perish.
- Remember that weather and wind can adversely affect viewing conditions and you should not expect to see everything at first attempt.

The graceful, pink-and-white coloured greater flamingo can be seen at the Calimere Wildlife Sanctuary in Tamil Nadu.

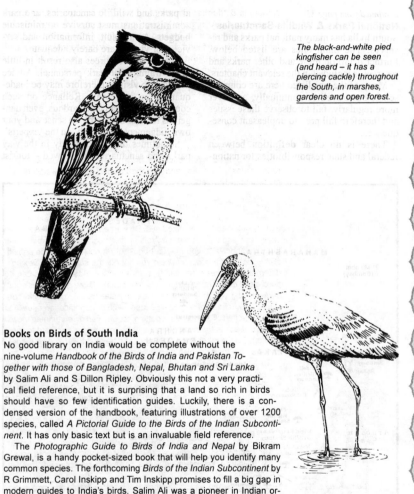

The black-and-white pied kingfisher can be seen (and heard – it has a piercing cackle) throughout the South, in marshes, gardens and open forest.

Books on Birds of South India

No good library on India would be complete without the nine-volume *Handbook of the Birds of India and Pakistan Together with those of Bangladesh, Nepal, Bhutan and Sri Lanka* by Salim Ali and S Dillon Ripley. Obviously this not a very practical field reference, but it is surprising that a land so rich in birds should have so few identification guides. Luckily, there is a condensed version of the handbook, featuring illustrations of over 1200 species, called *A Pictorial Guide to the Birds of the Indian Subcontinent*. It has only basic text but is an invaluable field reference.

The *Photographic Guide to Birds of India and Nepal* by Bikram Grewal, is a handy pocket-sized book that will help you identify many common species. The forthcoming *Birds of the Indian Subcontinent* by R Grimmett, Carol Inskipp and Tim Inskipp promises to fill a big gap in modern guides to India's birds. Salim Ali was a pioneer in Indian ornithology and his autobiography *The Fall of a Sparrow* is a delightful tale of his work in the remote parts of the country during India's move for Independence.

If you'd like to develop your interest in birds further, and also support Indian bird conservation initiatives, consider joining the Oriental Bird Club, c/o- The Lodge, Sandy, Bedfordshire, UK, or the Bombay Natural History Society (Hornbill House, Shahid Bhagat Singh Rd, Mumbai, India 400 023).

David Andrew

The painted stork can be seen at the Calimere Wildlife Sanctuary. Adult birds have a yellow head and beak, pink legs and pink tail feathers.

continued from page 35
National Parks & Wildlife Sanctuaries
South India has many national parks and reserves. The main ones are listed below. Further detail on these and other parks and reserves is included in the relevant chapters.

Many of the tips listed here are common sense, but travellers continually, and ever more regularly, fail to observe these issues and therefore fall prey to unpleasant consequences.

There is no clear definition between federal and state responsibilities for nation-al parks and wildlife sanctuaries, and park administrations must survive on miniscule budgets. As a result, information and services for visitors are barely adequate.

Insufficient resources also result in little or no training for park personnel. Advice provided to visitors therefore may be inadequate, even inaccurate. Reliance on such could therefore lead to hazardous, even dangerous results. Use common sense and your own judgement. Don't rely on the 'experts'.

Sometimes there is disparity in the way parks and sanctuaries are viewed – tourist

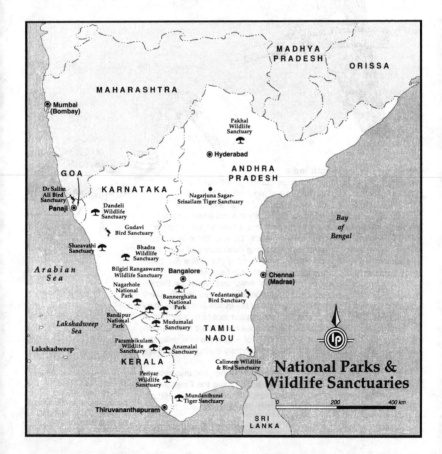

agencies promote them as places for adventure and leisure, while forestry personnel, concerned to protect wildlife, may dissuade tourists. For the visitor, this can result in confusing information, no information and/or critical delays in entry permits.

Usually, but not always, entry to parks for a day visit (from 6 am to 6 pm) requires no permits.

It is on the whole *not* permissible to walk/trek in the parks, or any forested area, without a guide. However finding the right guide may be difficult. Many have little or no training, little knowledge and take no responsibility. Maps generally don't exist. If they do, they are usually inadequate and incorrect. Find the right guide and you are assured of an experience that is educational and rewarding.

Movement in the parks is often confined to very small areas (apparently leaving the bulk of the park as sanctuary for animals). This often results in hordes of people gathering at one site, shattering the peace with loud pop music and unsightly littering.

While parks are generally accessible by public transport many travellers prefer to use their own transport. However private travel within the confines of most parks is not allowed and you may find you've gone to considerable expense only to be advised that you must use an organised tour bus. Such a bus will take you on a one hour trip (about 15km) at a time not conducive to wildlife activity except for the raucous behaviour of your bus companions. So you'll be lucky to see anything.

Walks within the parks are often set to a four-hour maximum.

Most parks have limited accommodation facilities and also limit the length of stay to one night. Some, at a push, will allow up to three nights. Most parks will not allow you to stay unless you have booked your accommodation *in advance*. Some may waive this rule, but rarely. The booking office is always some distance (30km to 50km) away and is often not so accessible, particularly by public transport. In addition to applying for accommodation and undergoing the normal bureaucratic processes, you may also (as at Indira Gandhi Wildlife Sanctuary) be put through a screening process which involves an interview to determine your suitability to enter the park. Such reviews are intended to prohibit undesirable visitors and minimise damage to the environment.

Some travellers prefer to stay in accommodation outside but close to the parks and make day visits. This is possible at some, but not all, of the parks: quite a few of them are too isolated.

At times, your wish to enter a park may simply be denied. The reasons (sometimes real, sometimes fictitious) may be due to circumstances completely outside forestry personnel control – an insurgency group may be using the park as refuge, there may be fires or insufficient water, or the place may have been booked by VIPs. In the latter event, you have no chance!

It seems that the lack of forestry resources has led to a rampant growth in private operators eager to get the tourist dollar but less eager to consider environmental issues and visitor safety. Understandably many travellers, fed up with government red tape, go with the private operators. This is not to say that many private operators do not offer adequate services. However, there are cases where the companies, themselves frustrated by the bureaucracy, break the rules, bribe the officials and trespass into highly sensitive areas.

Parks, Wildlife Sanctuaries & Reserves

State/Territory	Total No.
Andaman & Nicobar Islands	21
Andhra Pradesh	18
Goa	4
Karnataka	27
Kerala	14
Lakshadweep	nil
Tamil Nadu	12

Protected Areas

The term 'protected area' is a generic one used by the Indian government and NGOs to describe an area protected by an order to 'improve, maintain and preserve wildlife and flora'. It can be further divided into the categories listed below. The first national park was established in 1936, and there are now about 400 parks, sanctuaries and reserves – 3.5% of India's total area.

National Park

An area designated to 'develop wildlife', with changes to this designation only possible through state legislation, and a ban on all hunting, exploitation, grazing, logging, mining, development and urban settlements (therefore resulting in some displaced people). National parks often contain a core area which is off limits to all except forest rangers and researchers.

Wildlife Sanctuary

A less important area demanding fewer resources, where permanent settlements are allowed, visitors and tourists are usually permitted, and limited hunting and grazing allowed.

Bird Sanctuary

As for wildlife sanctuaries, above.

Special Reserve

To help protect specific species, mainly tigers and elephants, special reserves have been established, often with the assistance of Indian and foreign NGOs, such as the WWF.

Biosphere Reserves

Large areas of special significance, often marine environments, with international recognition. There are 14 Biosphere Reserves in India, four in South India – Great Nicobar and North Andaman reserves in the Andaman & Nicobar Islands; and the Gulf of Mannar and Nilgiri Biosphere reserves in Tamil Nadu.

The words 'wildlife', 'national park', 'jungle', 'trekking' and 'safari' conjure up exciting ideas in many travellers' minds, especially for those people who have travelled in Nepal, Africa, Australia or North America. In South India it can be quite different. Safari may mean a one hour trip in a jeep through urban areas and a little picnic by a river. A trek may mean just a short walk, again through developed areas. It could also mean the 'real thing'. Take care to ascertain exactly what the tour involves, and ensure that safety standards and environmental issues are respected.

Many of the parks have several names which are used interchangeably depending on the politics, ethnicity, geographical origin and whim of the user. Initially this may be confusing, but can usually be clarified.

It's probably wise to avoid bribery, no matter how strong the coercion or the temptation. There are protocols here. Unless, and even if, you're very aware of them, bribery could get you into serious trouble.

Remember there are several issues at stake here:

• Your safety in the natural environment: there are wild animals out there (or at least the hope is that there are some left). Do you, or your guide have the knowledge and skills to deal with wild animal behaviour? Where will you sleep? Will the lodgings/tents/equipment protect you from the elements and from night wandering animals?

• Your safety with others: travellers are on the whole very safe most of the time. Unfortunately however, there have been some recent tragic reports that once in the isolation of nature, the hired guides became the very antithesis of guides. It must be stressed, such situations are rare, but healthy caution is always recommended.

Environmental damage: The forests of India are screaming for a break. They have been plundered almost to extinction. Little habitat remains. It may be great for you to enter into a pristine environment and experience its beauty and splendour, but what about the environment itself and the animals that inhabit it? It's crucial therefore to observe environmental rules, particularly with waste disposal. Respect areas cordoned off for regeneration. Is your satisfaction at entering a pristine environment worth even more environmental damage?

Finally, in spite of environmental devastation, South India's national parks still provide diverse natural locales with interesting fauna and flora. You'll find most parks and the areas around them, are beautiful, secluded and peaceful – a welcome break from the dust and excitement of the towns. Once you've survived the discombobulating bureaucratic processes, South India's parks will provide space and time for solitude, reflection and restoration.

Bandipur National Park *(Karnataka, pp 254-6)* Bandipur (874 sq km) is one of the parks under the banner of Project Tiger, but you are unlikely to see a tiger: sambar, wild dogs, gaur, flying squirrels, langur, owls, kingfishers and eagles are far more common. No trekking is allowed inside the park, but it's easy enough to organise some scenic day hikes in the region. Visitors can only travel around on an official bus, or on a jeep if you're staying at one particular private lodge. The Forest Department (bookings at Hunsur or Bangalore) has rustic but charming bungalows inside the park; or there are several resorts, hotels and rooms on coffee estates nearby but outside the park.
Best time to see wildlife: April to May
Most comfortable time to visit: November to February

Bhadra Wildlife Sanctuary *(Karnataka, pp 287-8)* Based around the huge Bhadra

Reservoir, this 492 sq km park is between Shimoga and Chikmagalur towns, but not easy to reach or explore. There is a chance to spot sloth bears, wild elephants and panthers, but you are more likely to see wild pigs, gaur and deer. Birdlife includes bluejays, falcons and hornbills. Trekking is allowed within the park, but you must have permission and take a guide. The Forest Department (at Chikmagalur) has bungalows overlooking Bhadra Reservoir, but to explore the park, stay at the Forest Department bungalows at Muthodi.
Best time to visit: October to May
Most comfortable time to visit: October to May

Bilgiri Rangaswamy Wildlife Sanctuary *(Karnataka, pp 253-4)* This remote sanctuary, also known as Bilgiri Temple Sanctuary (after the revered temple in the park), is 540 sq km, and located among remote (and cool) hills in south-east Karnataka. With a bit of luck wild elephants and sloth bear can be seen, but gaur, deer and wild dogs are far more prevalent. There are over 50 species of birds. The Soliga tribal people live inside the sanctuary. The only available accommodation is at an expensive (private) lodge in the park, but the price does include jeep tours. Trekking is possible with permission and a guide (from the lodge or the Forest Department, Chamrajnagar).
Best time to see wildlife: June to October
Most comfortable time to visit: November to May

Dandeli Wildlife Sanctuary *(Karnataka, pp 303-4)* Located in upper Karnataka, near Goa, this 834 sq km park is rarely visited, but worth exploring. As well as deer, gaur and macaques, you can see wolves and wild boar. Partridges, owls and peacocks are some of the birdlife you will see. You can stay in a (private) lodge nearby, a hotel in Dandeli town, or a tent or resthouse inside the park, run by the Forest Department. Alternatively, it's an easy day trip from Dharwad or Hubli. You must hire your own vehicle, with an official guide (from the Forest Department in Dandeli), but this gives you a great chance to explore the park fully and to see wildlife.

There is a useful information centre is at one of the park entrances. The park is closed from June to October.
Best time to visit: December to May

Erivikalum National Park *(Kerala, p 426)* This park stretches over 97 sq km and is located 16km from Munnar, in the tea-growing region of the Western Ghats. There is no organised trekking, but roads and tracks lead to the 2695m peak of Anamudi.

The main attraction is the resident population of extraordinarily tame Nilgiri tahr, often found just inside the entrance to the park proper. It's claimed that this park harbours around half the world's remaining population of this creature – around 1000 individuals.
Best time to visit: November to March
Most comfortable time to visit: November to March

Indira Gandhi Wildlife Sanctuary (Annamalai) *(Tamil Nadu, pp 610-12)* This 958 sq km sanctuary in the Western Ghats contains spectacular scenery and a diverse range of flora and fauna, including elephants and (allegedly) tigers. A number of tribal groups live within the sanctuary. Unfortunately the bureaucracy is also spectacular. Securing permission to enter the sanctuary can exhaust even the most tenacious traveller.
Best time to visit: mid-December to mid-February

Mudumalai National Park *(Tamil Nadu, pp 631-4)* On the border with Karnataka, this park (also referred to as a reserve) forms part of the huge Nilgiri Biosphere Reserve (with the Wynad Wildlife Sanctuary, Kerala, and the Bandipur National Park, Karnataka).

Mudumalai (322 sq km) is primarily a tiger reserve, though you are far more likely to see gaur, deer, wild dogs, langur and Malabar squirrels. Birdlife includes various species of owl, woodpecker and hornbill.

The park is easily accessible from Mysore or Udhagamandalam (Ooty), so it's often overflowing with day-trippers. You can only travel within the park on an official bus or on an elephant ride, which severely limits chances of seeing wildlife, but there are plenty of domesticated elephants to admire and photograph – although you'll probably find the elephant *puja* a bit of a turn-off. The Wildlife Warden's Office (book in Ooty) has several quaint resthouses, or there are a dozen resorts and hotels in nearby villages
Best time to see wildlife: March to April
Most comfortable time to visit: November to February

Nagarhole National Park *(Karnataka, pp 273-5)* Also known as the Rajiv Gandhi National Park, this lovely 643 sq km park is not far from Mysore, Madikeri or Ooty, but not easy to reach, so it's far quieter than other parks. Part of the Nilgiri Biosphere Reserve is in Nagarhole. There is the possibility of seeing tigers and leopards, and you're more likely to see wild elephants here than in other parks in the state. Gaur, deer, langur and jackals are common, and woodpeckers and peacocks are some of the 250 varieties of birds – all easy to spot from watchtowers. Many tribal people live within remote parts of the park.
Best time to visit: October to April

Nagarjuna Sagar-Srisailam Tiger Reserve *(Andhra Pradesh, pp 368-9)* This is a Project Tiger reserve. At 3568 sq km it's by far the largest of any wildlife reserve in Andhra Pradesh. Located 130km south of Hyderabad, the dry deciduous land is divided by the Krishna River, which cuts through the Nallamalai Hills. The authorities claim this sanctuary supports panthers, bears and blackbucks as well as tigers. However, getting permission to enter the park and securing transport within it makes the sighting of wildlife somewhat problematic if not impossible.
Best time to visit: October to June

Pakhal Wildlife Sanctuary *(Andhra Pradesh, p 373)* This is a small sanctuary (879 sq km) 60km south-east of Warangal. The area is mainly dry teak forest and the fauna includes wild boar, sloth bears, wild

dogs and tigers. A number of migratory birds such as ibises, storks and cormorants are also supported by this sanctuary.
Best time to visit: November to June

Parambikulam Wildlife Sanctuary *(Kerala, p 330)* This 285 sq km sanctuary is located in the Annamalai Hills of the Western Ghats, south of the Pallakad Gap and 135km from Palakkad (via Polachi). It stretches around the Parambikulam, Thunakadavu and Peruvaripallam dams, adjacent to the Annamalai Wildlife Sanctuary in Tamil Nadu. The sanctuary is home to elephants, gaur, wild boars, sambar, chital, crocodiles and a few tigers and leopards.

Three tribal groups live within this sanctuary: the Kadas, the Muduvas and the Malai-Malsars. There are also teak and eucalyptus plantations within the sanctuary.
Best time to visit: September to May

Periyar Wildlife Sanctuary *(Kerala, pp 422-5)* This 77,700 hectare sanctuary in the Cardamom Hills encompasses a 26 sq km lake that was created by the British in 1895 as a reservoir for Madurai. Around the lake you will find deciduous forest and grasslands, with evergreen forests elsewhere. You will almost certainly see elephants, and wild boar and sambar are relatively common. You may also see giant Indian squirrels, which are noisy and not too shy.

Birdlife is prolific, but bring binoculars. There is no trekking as such, but you will be able to enter the park on a guided walk. And there are regular boat trips around the lake. There are three state-run hotels inside the park itself, but these should be booked in advance at a state tourist office or hotel. Keen wildlife viewers may want to spend the night at one of the watchtowers. These can be booked at the Wildlife Information Centre.
Best time to visit: September to May

Calimere Wildlife and Bird Sanctuary *(Tamil Nadu, pp 558-9)* Also known as Kodikkarai, this delightful little sanctuary of just under 400 sq km is 90km south-east of Thanjavur. It sits in a wetland jutting out into the Palk Strait, which separates India and Sri Lanka by a distance of only 28km. If you want to see huge flocks of flamingos and other migratory birds, this is the place to come. Dolphins also like this area and in the cooler mornings during December and January they swim close to the shore.
Best time to visit: November to January

Pulicat Bird Sanctuary *(Andhra Pradesh, p 382)* Ninety kilometres from Chennai, this 500 sq km bird sanctuary is a coastal lake on the Bay of Bengal on the border between Andhra Pradesh and Tamil Nadu. Pulicat Lake is teeming with flamingos, pelicans, storks, ducks and a range of other water birds.
Best time to visit: October to March

Sharavathi Wildlife Sanctuary *(Karnataka, p 297)* This 431 sq km sanctuary is based around the enormous Linganmakki Reservoir, not far (by chartered jeep) from Jog Falls.

Commonly seen wildlife includes deer, wild dogs, gaur, langur, porcupines and macaques, though you may also see sloth bears and otters. Many species of birdlife, including cormorants, egrets and teals, are attracted to the reservoir.

Trekking around the sanctuary is possible with permission and a guide. The Forest Department (in Kargal, near Jog Falls) intends to develop the sanctuary for tourists, but currently roads and transport are very limited.

If you have your own equipment, you can camp on the lake and enjoy water sports. It is easy to day trip from Jog Falls.
Best time to visit: October to February
Very heavy rainfall: June to September

Sri Lankamalleswara Sanctuary *(Andhra Pradesh)* Located in the Cuddapah district of southern Andhra Pradesh, this sanctuary of nearly 500 sq km is fairly rugged country. The deep gorges and dry deciduous thorny forest support a range of species including bears, deer, wild boars and panthers. The

sanctuary is also the habitat for the rare and endangered bird called the double-banded or Jerdon's courser (see the Birds of South India section, earlier in this chapter).
Best time to visit: November to March

Vedantangal Bird Sanctuary *(Tamil Nadu, pp 525-6)* This breeding ground for water birds is relaxing, accessible and beautiful. Located 35km south of Chengalpattu and 52km from Mamallapuram, it supports in excess of 30,000 birds in the December/January breeding season. An elevated walking track with lookout towers makes for easy birdwatching.

Bandipur is close to Mysore and Ooty, and borders Mudumalai National Park. Visitors can only travel around on an official tour bus or on the back of an elephant.

You can stay at Forest Department resthouses in the park (book at Mysore or Bangalore), or in hotels, resthouses and resorts in nearby villages.
Best time to see wildlife: March to April. To see elephants migrating from Kerala: November. Most comfortable time to visit: November to February

Wayanad Wildlife Sanctuary *(Kerala, pp 431-6)* This 34,500 hectare sanctuary in the Western Ghats, Kerala, is also known as the Muthanga Wildlife Sanctuary. Wayanad is a remote rainforest reserve connected to the better known Bandipur National Park in Karnataka, and Mudumalai National Park in Tamil Nadu. You will almost certainly see elephants here.

Accommodation is not all that handy: it can be found in the nearest town, Sultan's Battery, 16km west.
Best and most comfortable time to visit: November to February

GOVERNMENT & POLITICS
National Government & Politics
India has a parliamentary system. There are two houses within the parliament: a lower house known as the Lok Sabha (House of the People), and an upper house known as the Rajya Sabha (Council of States).

The lower house has 544 members (excluding the speaker), with all but two elected on a population basis (proportional representation). Elections for the Lok Sabha are held every five years, unless the government calls an earlier election. All Indians over the age of 18 have the right to vote.

Of the 544 seats, 125 are reserved for the Scheduled Castes & Tribes. The upper house has 245 members. The lower house can be dissolved, but the upper house cannot. There is a strict division between the activities handled by the states and by the national government. The police force, education, agriculture and industry are reserved for the state governments. Other areas are jointly administered by both levels of government.

The federal government has the controversial right to assume power in any state if the situation in that state is deemed to be unmanageable. Known as President's Rule, it has been enforced in recent years, either in the event of a security crisis (eg Kashmir in 1990) or because of a political stalemate (a situation that has occurred in Goa, Tamil Nadu and Pondicherry).

The general elections in 1996 produced a fractured mandate, with the long-standing Congress Party winning just 139 seats compared to the 160 seats taken by Bharatya Janata Party (BJP). The fiercely nationalistic BJP government which was subsequently formed lasted only 13 days. It was succeeded in June by the United Front government, a 13 party coalition holding some 130 seats and led by HD Deve Gowda (former chief minister of Karnataka).

Just nine months later, in April 1997, Gowda's government was voted out of office after the Congress Party withdrew its support. A second United Front government was sworn in under the leadership of former foreign minister Inder Kumar Gujral. This too was dissolved at the end of 1997 and India went to the polls in February and March 1998.

Yet again the election failed to produce a party with an absolute majority (273 seats), although the BJP and its allies emerged with the most seats of any single party (264), including Congress (166). After the election, Congress Party president Sitaram Kesri stepped aside to make way for Sonia Gandhi. In late March BJP leader Atal Behari Vajpayee put together a 13 party coalition which included a Tamil regional party led by J Jayalalitha.

The BJP almost instantly followed through on its pledge to make India a formidable world power, detonating a series of nuclear explosions in underground tests in the deserts of Rajasthan in May 1998. The immediate international response to the tests was one of universal condemnation and outrage, but India remained defiant.

State Government & Politics

Each of the states has a governor who is appointed by the president of India for five years, a legislature (elected for five years) and a Council of Ministers under the leadership of a chief minister.

The Union Territories (in South India: Andaman & Nicobar Islands, Pondicherry, Lakshadweep) are administered by lieutenant-governors who are appointed by the President of India. Pondicherry has an elected chief minister and state assembly.

At the time of writing, the majority parties in the South Indian states were: Andhra Pradesh (Telugu Desam Party); Goa (Congress); Karnataka (Janata Dal); Kerala (Communist-led Left Democratic Front); Tamil Nadu (Dravida Munnetra Kazhagam, or DMK).

ECONOMY

India has enjoyed strong economic growth since the reforms which began in 1991. These included lowering market entry barriers, relaxing import licensing for some goods and liberalising the foreign investment policy.

GDP has increased from 0.9% in 1991-2 to around 7% in 1996-7. Growth has primarily come from the industrial sector. State governments have also introduced reforms to encourage foreign investment, especially in infrastructure.

Andhra Pradesh

Sometimes referred to as the granary of India, Andhra Pradesh has a diverse farming base and produces a surplus of grain (10 million tons of rice is harvested annually). Agriculture accounts for half its income and engages about 70% of the population. The state leads all others in the production of tobacco and grows almost all India's virginia tobacco. It ranks fourth of all India's states in industrial production. It is India's largest maritime state, boasting one of the country's largest ports, Vizag, and a second (Kakinada) under development. The Telugu Desam Party has encouraged investment by announcing a new industrial policy in 1995 and establishing a special unit dedicated to clearing investment projects.

Goa

Goa is one of India's wealthiest states, a huge leap from Independence in 1961 when its economy was largely based on fishing, agriculture and the export of primary products such as timber and rubber. Some estimates put its annual growth rate at 6%. While agriculture engages about half the population over the course of a year, it is industry that is largely responsible for the state's income. Mining is also big business; primarily iron ore (mainly exported to Japan), manganese ore and bauxite. Tourism is also a major source of income and employs some 20% of the population (up to 80% of tourists to Goa are domestic). Electronics is slated as a sector for further development. The Konkan Railway will be an important addition to the state's infrastructure and facilitate future development.

Karnataka

One of India's most industrialised states, Karnataka nevertheless derives 49% of its income from agriculture - which employs some 71% of the workforce. It produces 59% of India's coffee and 47% of its *ragi* (a cereal). However, Karnataka is arguably better known for its diverse industrial sector which includes defence-related industries, electronics, telecommunications, steel and textiles. Bangalore is often tagged India's 'silicon city' in recognition of its role as a centre for high tech.

Kerala

The predominance of cash crops in Kerala has resulted in a shortage of food grains (only 23% of the cropped area is devoted to these). However, when it comes to cash crops, Kerala holds its own. It produces 92% of India's rubber, 70% of its coconut, 60% of its tapioca and nearly all its lemongrass oil. It accounts for about 36% of India's marine exports. In comparison to Karnataka, Kerala is relatively unindustrialised; yet its workforce is highly unionised. These two factors are often cited as reasons for Kerala's relatively high unemployment which has fuelled an exodus of skilled labour abroad, mainly to the Gulf states. In 1996 Gulf remittances amounted to 25% of the state's total domestic income. The new international airport at Kochi is India's first private airport. In April 1997 Kerala became the first state in India to install STD/ISD telephones in all its villages.

Tamil Nadu

Tamil Nadu is highly industrialised and produces a wide range of goods including petrochemicals, fertilisers, textiles, cement, steel and cars. It produces 77% of India's finished leather and 60% of its safety matches. It adopts an investor-friendly approach, attracting foreign companies such as Ford and Honda. Agriculture, however, continues to be its mainstay and Tamil Nadu produces impressive yields (2.5 tonnes of rice per hectare – one of the highest in India; 100 tonnes of sugar cane per hectare – a world record). Other crops include tea, coffee and cotton.

Union Territories

Pondicherry's main food crop is rice; cash crops include cotton, sugar cane and oilseed. Agriculture employs 45% of the population. There are 23 large-scale industries and 79 medium-sized ones manufacturing such items as textiles, sugar, cotton yarn, alcohol

and vehicle parts. There are some 5400 small-scale industries. Pondicherry's port is expected to handle some 3.6 million tonnes of cargo by the year 2000.

Fishing is important in the island territories of the Andaman & Nicobar Islands and Lakshadweep. In Lakshadweep the 1993-4 fish catch was around 8000 tonnes. There is a tuna canning factory at Minicoy Island. Lakshadweep also produces the coconut by-product copra and coir (a cottage industry; coir is bartered for rice from the administration which holds a monopoly on the coir trade), and jaggery (palm sugar) and vinegar. Of the 2500 tonnes of coir produced annually, 2000 tonnes are sold in the markets of Mangalore and Kozhikode. A small amount of income is derived from the sale of handicrafts.

In the Andaman & Nicobar Islands, tourism and fishing are viewed as immensely important in the drive for self-sufficiency. The islands' forests have been so depleted that the logging industry is now in decline. Other sources of income include copra, rubber and red oil from palm trees (used as an industrial lubricant). Two major problems facing the islands are the lack of fresh water and electricity (the islands rely on diesel). Desalination plants are being trialled to see if they might provide a viable solution to the water shortage.

POPULATION & PEOPLE

India has a little over 960 million people, according to 1997 UN estimates. Men outnumber women (927 females to 1000 males), with the exception of Kerala which has some 1036 females to every thousand males. After China, India is the second most populous country in the world. Its overall annual growth rate is 1.9%, although this varies quite widely from state to state. Kerala has only a 1.34% growth rate compared to 2.17% in Andhra Pradesh (India's fifth most populous state).

In terms of population density, Lakshadweep weighs in with about 1616 people per sq km (the national average is 273). Kerala, the most densely populated mainland state after West Bengal, has some 800. Population estimates for South India's states for 1998 are (in millions): Andhra Pradesh (76); Goa (1.3); Karnataka (51); Kerala (32); Tamil Nadu (61). South India's Union Territories have a combined population of just over one million.

In South India a large proportion of the population is Dravidian – descendants of the original inhabitants of India. Over the millennia however, invasion, trade and settlement have made South India's population as diverse as anywhere in the country.

Jews settled in what is now Kerala about 2000 years ago. Invaders and traders from the north introduced their cultural traditions (eg Aryan) in various parts of South India over the years. Christians from the Middle East also arrived on Kerala's coast, albeit about 100 AD. Arabs and Chinese came to the Malabar and Coromandel coasts as traders, and were later followed the Portuguese, Danes, French, Dutch and British who ventured even further.

South India also has a small population of tribal peoples, some of whom have managed to preserve their cultural traditions in the face of enormous outside pressures. According to the 1991 national census, some 68 million individuals claim tribal affiliation – about 8% of the total population. In South India most tribal people (*adivasis*) live in remote, hilly, forested regions such as the Western Ghats. Nationally the highest proportion of adivasis to the total state population is in Lakshadweep (94%); the lowest is in Kerala and Tamil Nadu (about 1%). See the boxed text in the Tamil Nadu chapter for more detail.

EDUCATION

India's literacy rate has increased from 18% in 1951 to 52% in 1991. The literacy level is generally lower for women, sometimes considerably so, and is lower in rural areas. However, literacy levels in South India are, with the exception of Andhra Pradesh (45%), well above the national level: Karnataka (56%); Tamil Nadu (63%); Andaman & Nicobar Islands (73%); Pondicherry (75%);

Goa (77%); Lakshadweep (82%); and Kerala (90%). In fact Kerala holds the top spot as India's most literate state. Bihar by contrast is at the other end of the spectrum (38%).

India has 226 universities (every South Indian state has universities), five institutes of technology (including one at Chennai) and four institutes of management (including one at Bangalore). In addition to state-run institutions there are numerous private schools, including those run by churches and Christian missions. Church schools are generally highly regarded and entry to them is eagerly sought, even though fees are relatively expensive. English is the usual teaching medium in these schools. Schooling starts at the age of five and is compulsory and free until the age of 14.

Kerala's high literacy rate is a source of justifiable pride among Keralans, as well as a source of fascination for scholars. Kerala's matrilineal system, which survived until WWII, is often cited as one reason for the phenomenon. Women have traditionally enjoyed a far greater degree of freedom here than in most other parts of India and a part of this freedom has included education. In the late 1950s around 87% of primary-school-age girls attended school. European Christian missionaries who set up schools in Kerala added the stamp of 'respectability' to education for girls. And historically the region has benefited from rulers who were somewhat unusual in their open support of education for the general population.

During British rule, Travancore and Kochi all had higher literacy levels than the neighbouring Madras Presidency. A system of village schools was in place by the 1860s, and before the end of the century, teaching was being conducted in the vernacular – unlike areas under direct British rule where formal education was invariably in English.

Education was seen by Travancore and Kochi rulers as a double blessing: an educated population, they believed, held the key to development; and the maharajas of Travancore firmly believed (maybe naively) that an educated population would be a lot easier to govern than an uneducated one. Since Independence, education has acquired even more importance in the eyes of the people of Kerala, to whom a good qualification is a key to securing a coveted job in the Gulf or elsewhere.

ARTS

(See also the colour section on dance at the end of this chapter.)

Music

South India's own form of classical music, called Carnatic (Hindustani is North India's classical form), traces its origins to Vedic times, some 3000 years ago. Essentially, there are two basic elements in Indian music: the tala and the raga. Tala is the rhythm and is characterised by the number of beats. The raga provides the melody. In Carnatic music both are used for composition and improvisation.

While it has many things in common with its northern counterpart, Carnatic music differs in several important respects – something attributed to the fact that it has been less influenced by Islam. Song, for example, is more important in Carnatic music, and this influences even purely instrumental performances. Visitors may find that Carnatic music sounds a lot more passionate and less restrained than Hindustani. For more information see the boxed text in the Chennai chapter.

Pottery

The potter's art is steeped in mythology. Although there are numerous stories that explain how potters came to be, they all share the notion that a talent for working with clay is a gift from the supreme being, Brahma. This gives potters a very special status; on occasion they act directly as intermediaries between the spiritual world and the temporal one. See the section on local deities under Religion, in this chapter.

The name for the potter caste, *kumbhar*, is taken from the word *kumbha*, or water pot, which is itself an essential component in one version of the story that explains how

potters came upon their calling. And indeed, the water pot is still an indispensable household item throughout India. It is usually narrow-necked but round-based; the shape is quite practical in that women can carry the water-filled pots on their heads with less risk of spillage. The shape is also symbolic of the womb, and thus fertility.

Traditionally every village had its potters' quarter, a convention that endures today. And the division of labour between men and women remains. Women are forbidden to use the wheel, but may create pots using slab or coil techniques. And they may decorate pots once they have been taken off the wheel.

Apart from water pots, potters create a variety of household items, including all manner of storage and cooking pots, dishes, and *jhanvan* – thick, flat pieces of fired clay with one rough side – used for cleaning the feet.

The ephemeral nature of clay-made items

PETER DAVIS

All potters share the notion that a talent for working with clay is a gift from God.

means the potter never wants for work. Potters all over the state of Tamil Nadu are kept especially busy at their wheels thanks to such traditions as the Pongal harvest festival: the day before the festival starts, clay household vessels are smashed and replaced with new ones.

Potters are also called upon to create votive offerings. These include the guardian horse figures (which can be gigantic creations) which stand sentry outside villages in Tamil Nadu (see under Religion, in this chapter); images of deities such as Ganesh (in Karnataka these are created for Ganesh's annual festival in July/August by the *gudigars* who are normally woodcarvers); and other sundry animal effigies. Clay replicas of parts of the human body are sometimes commissioned by those seeking miraculous cures and are intended to be placed before a shrine. Clay toys and beads are also part of a potter's repertoire.

Glazing is rare in South India. One exception is in Tamil Nadu where a blue or green glaze is sometimes used.

Literature

South India's main languages – Tamil, Kannada, Telugu and Malayalam – each have a long literary history. Tamil is generally considered a case apart, not just because of its antiquity (early works can be dated to the 2nd century), but because it evolved independently from Sanskrit. Malayalam actually emerged from Tamil, although Malayalam, Kannada and Telugu (early works date from the 11th to the 9th centuries) all used Sanskrit works as an important source of reference. In all four a distinction is made between formal literary and colloquial language.

Classical Tamil poems provide a literary point of reference for Tamil in the same way that Sanskrit set a standard for the other three languages. In addition, there has been a long tradition of folk literature which has only relatively recently been collected and studied. It seems that, rather than existing as separate entities, the two forms (formal, classical literature and folk literature) matured together and probably influenced one another.

In the 19th century South Indian literature began to reflect the influence of European genres, especially the novel, the short story, the essay and auto/biography. Where once literature had been expressed primarily in verse, now it was quite widely available in prose. Early works to appear in the new styles were mainly translations of English classics (and, to an extent, Bengali). However, by the end of the 19th century South Indian writers were pioneering new forms themselves; and among them Subramania Bharati and VVS Aiyar, who are credited with transforming Tamil into a modern language. Folk ballads (performed by professional balladeers at village temple festivals) and the hymns of the *bhakti* saints, which are still sung in major temples, are two ancient literary genres that have survived into the late 20th century.

Sculpture

Sculpture and architecture are closely related in South India; it is difficult to consider them apart. Sculpture is invariably religious in nature, and not generally an art form through which individuals expressed their own creativity.

Among medieval examples of sculpture, the 7th century relief (Arjuna's Penance) at Mamallapuram is one of the most striking examples. Its fresh, lively touch is reflected in later 9th century Chola shrine sculptures.

Unlike in the north of India, a tradition of South Indian sculpture was able to develop without serious interruption from Muslim invasions. But curiously, despite a high level of technical skill, by the 17th century the work produced appears to lack the life and quality of earlier examples. South India remains, however, famous for its bronze sculptures, particularly those (as with stone) of the 9th and 10th centuries. Artisans employed the lost wax technique to make their pieces, which were usually of Hindu deities such as Vishnu and Shiva and – in the south especially – Shiva in his adored form as Lord of the Dance, Nataraja.

Architecture

Forts A typical South Indian fort is situated on a hill or rocky outcrop with a town nestled at its base, and ringed by moated battlements. Gingee in Tamil Nadu is a good example. Originally built on a hill by the Cholas, it was taken over in 1442 by the Pandya governor of Thanjavur and extended across two neighbouring hills to form a triangle. An outer wall encloses all three hills and a further series of inner walls. To gain access from the outer to the inner walls, one had to pass through a series of 90° turns. A drawbridge slung across a deep chasm near the summit led to a narrow gate, as a final line of defence for the fort's protectors.

Vellore Fort in Tamil Nadu is one of India's best known water forts. Built in the 16th century by a Vijayanagar vassal chief, it was taken over by Muslim rulers and later by Europeans.

Vijayanagar and Bijapur are representative of great metropolitan forts. Bijapur hasn't the natural fortification that Gingee does, but after it was taken over by the Sultan Ismail it was turned into a formidable structure. The city protected by the fort was surrounded by a wall (12m thick and 10m high) made of impacted earth and faced with stone. There were five main gates with double doors clad in iron and set with spikes to deter war elephants.

Palaces The remains of the royal complex at Vijayanagar indicate that local engineers weren't averse to utilising the sound structural techniques and fashions (domes and arches) of their Muslim enemies, the Bahmanis. The eclectic mix of architectural styles also includes conventions employed in Hindu temple design of the time, such as multistoried towers. The Bahmanis, for their part, were influenced by the architecture of Persia and Central Asia, eg the arrangement of living quarters and audience halls. The palace of the Maharajas of Travancore, at Padmanabhapuram, which dates to the 18th century, has private apartments for the king, a zenana, rooms dedicated to public audiences, an armoury, a dance hall

and temples. *(See also the Sacred Architecture section in the Tamil Nadu chapter, pp 574-80.)*

Cinema

India turns out more films than any other country in the world: some 28,000 feature films to date, plus many thousands of shorter ones. In 1996 it produced 683 feature films, with by far the majority of them made in South Indian languages: Telugu (154 films), Tamil (138), Kannada (85) and Malayalam (65). One hundred and twenty six Hindi language films were made in the same year.

South India produced its first feature film in Madras (Chennai) in 1919, six years after the release of India's first truly locally produced film. Since then cinema has become a huge industry in Chennai, overtaking Bollywood (Mumbai by any other name) as India's most prolific film production centre. Ramoji Film City, near Hyderabad in Andhra Pradesh, a four hectare dream factory, can handle the simultaneous production of dozens of films. Chennai's massive MGR studio complex is a good place to gaze at the stars and even to try for a part as an extra (see the boxed text 'The Southern Cinema Invasion' in the Chennai chapter).

South India has thousands of cinemas, to which people flock in their millions. Chennai alone boasts 94 cinemas, many with a seating capacity of 1000.

It's virtually impossible to establish just how much the film industry is worth in the south. However a recent restructuring of India's film industry has meant that, although distributors may reap the benefits of a successful film, they can also claim compensation from the producers if the film flops. Not surprisingly there is now a trend towards lower-budget films costing between Rs 3 million and Rs 6 million.

Films with leading actors, however, can cost in excess of Rs 100 million. One of India's most expensive stars is Rajinikant, a Chennai-based actor with 150 films to his credit. He can command up to Rs 60 million per picture. Female stars earn less than their male counterparts. Khushboo is currently the highest paid, commanding around Rs 3 million per picture.

As with film industries the world over, the film industry in South India is rarely without controversy. Maintaining a balance between artistic integrity and commercialism is an ongoing issue. Cultural representation and political interference is another. For more information on the industry see the boxed text 'The Southern Cinema Invasion' in the Chennai chapter.

SOCIETY & CONDUCT
Traditional Culture
Birth Among Hindus it is still considered preferable to have a boy rather than a girl, and it is considered the privilege of the young wife to go to her parents' house for the confinement. For the first two weeks after birth, mother and child are kept in seclusion, after which, traditionally, a ritual bathing takes place.

There are four important ceremonies that Hindu parents must perform for their newborn child: casting a horoscope (*jatakarma*), name giving (*nama karma*), giving the first solid food (*annaprasana*) and shaving the head (*chaula*).

Chaula takes place when the child is about five years old. An auspicious day is selected by the family priest by consulting the almanac (*panchangam*) and the family priest. The child's father ceremonially cuts the first few strands of hair with a razor and the rest of the job is left in the hands of a skilled barber. In South India it's not uncommon to spot proud parents supervising their child's first (radical) haircut on a visit to one of the Hindu temples.

Among Christians it's the custom to baptise a child about a week after birth – preferably on a Sunday. The child's godparents (or baptism parents, as they are also known) play an important role in the ceremony, and their names are entered with the child's on the baptismal certificate.

Marriage Christian and Hindu communities follow similar processes to procure a

suitable partner for a son or daughter. Discreet inquiries are made among friends and within the community. Desirable attributes in the potential partner include a good job, a good position in society, a respectable family, upstanding character and reasonable looks. In Hindu society horoscopes are drawn up to ensure the prospective couple is compatible, and sometimes the family deity is consulted.

In some Tamil communities, bride price used to be the convention (ie gifts were given to the bride's family), but these days dowries (though illegal) are usually required to be paid by the bride's family, and this can apply to both Hindu and Christian weddings. This custom can either facilitate a match or hinder it; inter-caste marriages become much more acceptable if there's a good dowry, but on the other hand a high-caste girl whose family has no money can find it very difficult to secure a partner from the same sort of background. There is no law against cousins marrying, and in some places a match between a brother's daughter and a sister's son is considered particularly fortunate.

The day before the marriage, the bride puts a number of green bangles (*chuddo*) on her hands. The wedding ceremony itself is a lengthy and noisy affair. Towards the end of the proceedings, the bride and groom join hands in a ritual known as *kanyadana*, while water and silver coins are poured over their clasped hands. The final ritual of the marriage, known as *saptapadi*, takes place when the couple together walk seven steps around the sacred fire, thus making the marriage irrevocable.

Christian weddings are much as they are in the west, although some rituals such as the ritual bathing of the bride before the wedding are borrowed from Hindu tradition.

Divorce & Remarriage In both Christian and Hindu communities, divorce is frowned upon severely, although it is gradually becoming more common. Hindus in particular consider divorce acceptable only in cases where there is no other option – where one of the partners is insane or has an infectious disease such as leprosy. Divorce, traditionally, can also be acceptable if the wife is found to be infertile.

Although the constitution allows for divorcees (and widows) to remarry, few are in a position to do this simply because of the stigma attached to divorce. In some cases a divorced woman's own family will reject her, and there is no social security net to provide for her.

Death Funeral ceremonies in the Hindu community are similar for all the castes. Children below the age of eight are buried, while all others are cremated. In preparation for the cremation, the body is washed, laid on a bier and covered with a shroud. The chief mourner (usually the eldest son) also bathes and then the body is carried by members of the family or friends to the funeral pyre. The son lights the pyre and then walks three times around it with a pot of water, finally standing at the head of the pyre.

On the third day after the cremation the son, accompanied by a few friends and family, collects the ashes, which are then consigned to water – possibly the sea or a stream. Those with enough money will travel north to scatter the ashes on the sacred river Ganges. On the 10th day after the cremation all members of the house take a purifying bath, and on the 11th day a liquid concoction, *panchagavya*, – consisting of, among other things, cow's milk and cow's urine – is sprinkled over the house in a ritual purification.

In the Christian community deaths are followed by burial. The widow may accompany the coffin on to the road outside the house and there break her bangles on it, symbolising the end of her status as a married woman.

Women in Society Women in South India have traditionally enjoyed rather more freedom than their northern sisters. This is especially so in the case of Kerala. Kerala is unique in many ways: it is the most literate state in India; it's the only state where women outnumber men and it is also famous for its tradition of matrilineal kinship.

Back in 1875 a census official for the princely state of Travancore noted that female children were more highly prized than male ones, a sentiment echoed 40 years later. Exactly why the matrilineal-joint family became established in this region is subject to conjecture, although one explanation is that it was in response to ongoing warfare in the 10th and 11th centuries. Young men of the military castes faced an uncertain future as the two warring kingdoms of the Cholas and the Cheras fought for supremacy. With the men absent, women invariably took charge of the household. And the men themselves, it has been argued, would very likely form alliances wherever they found themselves; the children of these unions becoming the responsibility of the mother's family. Whatever the reason, by the 14th century a matrilineal society was firmly established in many communities across Kerala and it lasted pretty much unchallenged until the 20th century.

Although the eldest males managed the household, women were very influential. One 18th century European observer who claimed that a Nair (warrior caste) child never knew the name of his or her father may not have been entirely accurate, but at the time Nair women were considerably more independent than their European counterparts. And a child indeed had little to do with its father. A Nair woman lived in her mother's house, which her father might visit from time to time. She could take many lovers and any resulting children were the responsibility of her household. She inherited the family property. Christian missionaries were horrified. By WWII however, the system had largely disintegrated, probably due to the pressures of a codified legal system and a cash economy.

In other parts of South India such as Tamil Nadu, women also enjoyed more freedom than was the norm elsewhere. Matriarchy was a long-standing tradition within

How to wear a Sari

If you've ever wondered how Indian women manage to keep their saris in position without any fastenings, here's how it's done:

1. With your left hand hold the inside end of the sari material.
2. Tuck the top border of the inner end of the sari into your petticoat, keeping the hem of the sari just above the floor.
3. Keeping the sari at the same height off the floor wind the material round to the front.
4. Make sure the sari is still held firmly – tuck it in a little if necessary.
5. Fold most of the rest of the material into pleats, starting at the right.
6. Hold the pleats firmly making sure the bottom hem is at floor level; tuck in the pleats, letting them fall straight.
7. Wind the remaining material around you and over your left shoulder.

This method of draping a sari is common throughout India and the method increasingly favoured. The sari is worn with a *choli* – a tight, short-sleeved blouse. However, there are many other ways of draping a sari. One researcher has documented more than 100, reflecting tribal and regional variations and even caste differences within regions (see the Books section in the Facts for the Visitor chapter). In some areas saris were (and still are in some places) traditionally worn in two pieces (eg the *mundu* of Kerala, which is still commonly seen), the lower piece more closely resembling a sarong (in the case of the Kerala mundu, it's two to four yards or 1.8m to 3.6m in length, white with little or no border – if there is a border, gold is favoured for special occasions). The style of pleating also shows strong regional variations, eg in Kodagu (Karnataka) the pleats are worn at the back.

The garment typically worn by men in South India is the *dhoti*, a simple piece of cloth knotted around the waist and pulled through between the legs. The *lungi* is also popular. This is a coloured piece of material worn rather like a sarong, but which is sewn from hem to waist so the whole resembles a cloth tube. Then there are garments used only on ceremonial occasions, eg the *jubba* of Kerala which resembles the *kurta* often seen in the north.

When it comes to everyday wear, young people in particular seem increasingly to favour the *salwar kameez*, a garment more commonly associated with the Punjab and North India and comprising pyjama-like drawstring trousers over which is worn a loose, generally long-sleeved, collarless top. This outfit is usually worn with a long scarf, or *dupatta*, which is flung over the shoulder(s) to hang down the back. An ordinary cotton salwar kameez for everyday use costs about Rs 150 to Rs 350 readymade. Of course even the smallest towns have skilled tailors who can whip up a salwar kameez for you cheaply and in no time at all.

1   2   3   4   5   6   7

Tamil communities, and the practise of condoning marriage among cousins meant that young women didn't have to move far away and live among strangers. Dowry deaths and female infanticide were virtually unknown in South India until relatively recent times, but the imposition of consumerism on old customs and conventions has resulted in instances occurring. In recent years Tamil Nadu has recorded an increase in the incidence of female infanticide, and in late 1997 legislation was being mooted that would hold men – not just women – responsible.

Dos & Don'ts

Religious Etiquette Particular care should be taken when attending a religious place (temple, shrine) or event. Dress and behave appropriately; don't wear shorts or sleeveless tops (this applies to men and women) and do not smoke or publicly display affection. Remove your shoes before entering a holy place, and never touch a carving or statue of a deity. In some places such as mosques you will be required to cover your head.

For religious reasons, do not touch local people on the head and similarly never direct the soles of your feet at a person, religious shrine, or image of a deity, as this may cause offence. Never touch another person with your feet. When visiting Buddhist temples and religious sites always walk around them in a clockwise direction.

Photographic Etiquette You should be sensitive about taking photos of people, especially women, who may find it offensive – always ask first. Taking photos at a death ceremony or a religious ceremony or of people bathing (in baths or rivers) will almost certainly cause offence.

Eating & Visiting Don't touch food or cooking utensils that local people will use. You should use your right hand for all social interactions, whether passing money, food or any other item. Eat with your right hand only.

If you are invited to dine with a family, take off your shoes if they do and wash your hands before taking your meal. The hearth is the sacred centre of the home, so never approach it unless you have been invited to do so.

Never enter the kitchen unless you have been invited to do so, and always take your shoes off before you go in. Similarly, never enter the area where drinking water is stored unless you have removed your shoes. Do not touch terracotta vessels in which water is kept – you should always ask your host to serve you.

Swimming & Bathing Nudity is completely unacceptable and a swimsuit must be worn even when bathing in a remote location. In public, at the seaside, Indian women generally prefer to take a dip fully clothed.

RELIGION

Like the rest of the country, South India has a diverse range of religions and religious sects. Most South Indians are Hindu, although given the region's history, there is more mixing and melding than the census figures on religious affiliation would suggest. In Goa, for example, Christians and Hindus often observe the same festivals. In Mapusa, the Church of Our Lady of Miracles was built on the site of an old Hindu temple and the annual feast day sees crowds of Hindus and Christians paying tribute together.

Local and tribal deities have been absorbed into Hinduism over the millennia, although some local deities retain a strong individual presence at village level (see the section on local deities below), and tribal people whom many claim are purely Christian or Hindu, have on occasion preserved their own traditions (see the boxed text on Todas in the Tamil Nadu chapter).

Hinduism

Hinduism is the world's third largest religion after Christianity and Islam but uniquely it has no single founder, no church hierarchy and no central authority. You can't become a Hindu; you must be born one. It's therefore not a proselytising religion because you cannot be converted.

Great Epics

The *Mahabharata* and the *Ramayana* are two great Hindu epics that have been told and retold over the millennia, retaining their potency and popularity to the present day. In the 1980s they were serialised by Indian state television; the *Ramayana* drew an estimated audience of 80 million.

Of the two, the Mahabharata's origins can be traced back the furthest. It is thought to have been composed sometime around the 1st millennium BC and to have been the prerogative of the ruling and warrior classes, focusing as it did on the exploits of their favourite deity, Krishna. By about 500 BC the Mahabharata had evolved into a far more complex creation with substantial additions including the Bhagavad Gita (in which Krishna gives advice to Arjuna before a great battle). It is in fact the world's longest work of literature; eight times longer than the Greek epics the Iliad and the Odyssey combined. The story centres on conflict between the gods – the heroes (the Pandavas) and the demons (the Kauravas). Overseeing events is Krishna (an incarnation of Vishnu) who has taken on human form. Krishna acts as charioteer for the Pandava hero, Arjuna, who eventually triumphs in a great battle with the Kauravas.

The *Ramayana* was composed around the 3rd or 2nd centuries BC and is believed to be largely the work of one poet, Valmiki. Like the *Mahabharata*, it centres on conflict between gods and demons. Basically, the story goes that the childless king of Ayodhya called upon the gods to provide him with a son. His wife duly gave birth to a boy. But this child, named Rama, was in fact an incarnation of Vishnu who had assumed human form to overthrow the demon king of Lanka, Ravana. The adult Rama, who won the hand of the princess Sita in a competition, was chosen by his father to inherit his kingdom. But at the last minute Rama's stepmother intervened and demanded her son take Rama's place. Rama and Sita and Rama's brother Lakshmana were sent into exile and duly went off to the forests, where Rama and Lakshmana battled demons and dark forces. During this time Ravana's sister tried to seduce Rama and his brother, but she was rejected. In revenge, Ravana captured Sita and spirited her away to his palace in Lanka. Rama, assisted by an army of monkeys led by the loyal Hanuman, eventually found the palace, killed Ravana and rescued Sita. All returned victorious to Ayodhya where Rama was crowned king.

The proliferation of deities in the Hindu pantheon (330 million according to some estimates) may be confusing but they are all simply a manifestation of the supreme being.

At the apex of all the millions of lesser gods and goddesses is the trinity of Brahma (the creator), Vishnu (the preserver) and Shiva (the destroyer). Of these three, Vishnu and Shiva have become more important deities. Shiva is especially revered in South India, coupled with worship of the goddess (representing energy or *shakti*). The female aspect, like other Hindu deities, has many forms, is known by many names and may be terrifying or entirely benevolent.

Hinduism's origins go back many thousands of years, with early beliefs apparently centring on fertility and the power of natural forces coupled with the need to placate them. The Aryan invaders enshrined their beliefs (which included gods associated with fire and the sun) in the *Veda* scriptures, which were passed down orally, until they were recorded in Sanskrit some time between 1000 BC and 500 BC. Implicit in the Vedas was the belief in the supreme being, Brahma, creator of the universe.

Alongside the Vedas, and committed to writing at about the same time, were the Dharma Shashtras and the Dharma Shutras. These laid down the parameters of the *varnas*, or in other words, the four social classes that became the foundations for the caste structure: Brahmins (priests, teachers); kshatriyas (rulers, warriors); vaishyas

Gurus & Ashrams

Many people visit South India especially to spend time at an ashram and to receive *darshan* (literally, a glimpse of God) through an audience with a guru. A guru is a spiritual guide; somebody who by example or simply by their presence indicates what path you should follow. The word guru traditionally means either 'the dispeller of darkness' or 'heavy with wisdom'.

Most gurus live in an ashram, which means 'place of striving', a reflection of the Hindu belief that life is a continuous struggle through a series of reincarnations that eventually leads to *moksha* (spiritual salvation). An ashram is established when a guru stays in one place and disciples congregate around him, in time buying land, building facilities and making donations. Most ashrams in India are the legacies of dead gurus.

Ashrams are peppered throughout India – any place of striving can be called an ashram, be it a commercial complex or a person's home, where like-minded people gather to explore their spirituality. Visiting any ashram can be a learning experience and visiting a guru can change your life.

Some ashrams are more reputable than others and, if possible, attend one where a guru resides. The ashrams of living gurus reflect the disposition of the founder and their perception of the needs of their disciples. For example, if you visit Ma Amritanandamayi's ashram in Kerala you will be put to work and at another you might be expected to practice up to four hours meditation per day.

Many ashrams have codes of conduct which can include daily bathing, the avoidance of unnecessary chat or, in the case of Sai Baba's ashrams, when you do talk to do so softly and lovingly. Most ashrams are vegetarian and you may also be asked to abstain from eggs, tobacco, alcohol, and garlic and onions (considered aphrodisiacs). Most people in the ashrams wear white, the colour of purity, and you will feel more comfortable if you don't stand out. Suitable white clothing can be bought or made inexpensively near any ashram.

Most ashrams don't require notice of your arrival but, if you are unsure, check in advance. Talk to locals and other travellers to see which ashram or guru might best suit you. Also many of the gurus sometimes move around without much notice so investigate to avoid disappointment.

The atmosphere surrounding the ashram can have a profound and deeply moving effect on visitors and, although for some this can be a rewarding and unique experience, you are urged to

(trade and businesspeople); sudras (peasants, servants). Untouchables, those who worked in unclean, polluting trades (associated with dirt or death) were considered beneath all others.

In addition to belonging to a varna, people were further classified according to their *jati*, which stipulated their precise occupation (eg cowherd), and this in turn defined their caste. A huge raft of restrictions and obligations attached to the concept of caste and centred on the concept of pollution and purity. Many of these caste concepts survive today. Generally, people marry within their own caste groups.

Whatever one's position in the hierarchy, the common goal was, and remains today, to end the cycle of rebirth (and hence to end suffering in this world) by attaining *moksha* or liberation; negating one's personal identity and merging with the cosmic self. But this is a long, slow process; something that only happens after one has dutifully observed one's social duties.

See the boxed text on p62 for a brief description of some of the major cult deities.

Islam

Islam was introduced to South India from around the 7th century by Arab traders who settled in coastal Kerala and Karnataka. The invading Moghul armies of the 14th century ensured that Islam spread wider and deeper in the south.

use common sense and discernment, as not all ashrams are as sincere in their motives as others.

South India's most high-profile guru, and indeed one of the best-known worldwide, is Sai Baba. His main ashram is at Puttaparthi in Andhra Pradesh (see that chapter for more detail, and for a traveller's impression of an audience with Sai Baba himself, see the boxed text 'A Beeline to Baba' in the Tamil Nadu chapter), where people gather in their thousands to catch a glimpse of Sai Baba and, if they are lucky, to receive sacred ash (*vibhuti*) which appears, magically, to materialise from his fingertips.

Lesser known, but nevertheless someone who has attracted quite a large following in the foreign community, is Ma Amritanandamayi in Kerala. Her ashram is at Amrithapuri and darshan here is quite unlike anything one might have experienced before. Ma Amritanandamayi hugs each and every devotee in turn, and the devotees number many thousands.

The Sri Aurobindo Ashram in Pondicherry (see the Tamil Nadu chapter for detail) is one of the most popular among westerners, and its spiritual tenets represent a synthesis of yoga and modern science.

The Sri Ramanasramam Ashram, at the foot of Annandamalai (see the Tamil Nadu chapter for more information), still draws devotees of Sri Ramana Maharshi who died in 1950. It's a peaceful place where even the monkeys seem contemplative. The ashram has a Web site at: www.rtanet.com/ramana. Also see the Tamil Nadu chapter for information on Swami Dayananda's ashram at Coimbatore.

Bede Griffith's retreat near Trichy is unusual in that it is one of India's few Christian ashrams. Again refer to the Tamil Nadu chapter for more information.

Movement	Place	State	Page
Theosophical Society	Chennai	Tamil Nadu	471
Krishnamurti Foundation	Chennai	Tamil Nadu	471
Ramana Maharishi	Tiruvannamalai	Tamil Nadu	530
Sri Aurobindo	Pondicherry	Tamil Nadu	534
Sai Baba	Whitefield Ashram	Karnataka	234
Sai Baba	Puttaparthi	Andhra Pradesh	382

About 10% of South India's population is Muslim, although this figure is higher in parts of Andhra Pradesh, Karnataka and Kerala. And most are Sunni; the caliph leads the community and is responsible for dispensing justice through the *sharia* (law).

Christianity

Christianity is said to have arrived in South India (specifically the Malabar Coast) with the apostle St Thomas in 52 AD. However scholars say that it's more likely Christianity arrived around the 4th century with a Syrian merchant (Thomas Cana) who set out for Kerala with 400 families to establish what later became a branch of the Nestorian church.

The Nestorian church sect survives today; services are in Armenian and the Patriarch of Baghdad is the sect's head.

Other eastern orthodox sects include the Jacobites, the Canaanites and the orthodox Syrians. Catholicism established a strong presence in South India in the wake of Vasco da Gama's visit in 1498.

Catholic sects which have been active in the region include the Dominicans, Franciscans and Jesuits. Protestantism arrived with the English, the Dutch and the Danish, and their legacy lives on today in the Church of South India.

India has about 16 million Christians; around three-quarters of these live in South India.

South India's Favourite Deities

Vishnu Vishnu preserves the cosmic order. He is considered a redeemer of humanity; a knowable god. Unlike Shiva, Vishnu takes on human form. In fact he is said to have appeared on earth in nine separate incarnations, the most well-known being Rama, Krishna and Buddha. His most famous temple is near Tirupathi in southern Andhra Pradesh. This temple is dedicated to his form as Lord Venkateshwara, one who fulfils wishes.

Shiva Shiva is the agent of death and destruction, but without him growth and rebirth could not take place. At Chidambaram, in Tamil Nadu, he is worshipped as Nataraja, lord of the cosmic dance. Shiva is frequently represented as a *lingam*, a phallic symbol often set in a *yoni*, itself symbolic of the vulva and thus female energy. His guardian is Nandi (the white bull) whose statue can often be seen watching over the main shrine (therefore his master).

Parvati As Shiva's consort, Parvati symbolises the power – *shakti* – embodied in Shiva. The goddess can be benign (this is how Parvati appears), terrifying (eg Durga or Kali), or both (Devi).

Vishnu   Shiva   Parvati

Jainism & Buddhism

South India's small community of Jain people is centred on coastal Karnataka; the 17m-high sculpture of Gomateshvara (one of the world's tallest monoliths) at Sravanabelagola, is at one of Jainism's most important centres of pilgrimage. The Jain religion was founded about the same time as Buddhism (it evolved as a reformist movement against Brahminism) and is centred on the concept of *ahimsa* or nonviolence. There are only about 4.5 million Jains in all of India.

Buddhism developed in India when it was

Murugan Murugan is one of Shiva's sons and a popular deity in South India, especially in Tamil Nadu. He is sometimes identified with another of Shiva's sons, Skanda, who enjoys a strong following in North India. Murugan's main role is that of protector and he is depicted as young and victorious. It is speculated that Murugan may have evolved from an earlier fertility god.

Ayyappan Ayyappan is also one of Shiva's sons identified with the role of protector. His origin is unusual. He is claimed to have been born from the union of Shiva and Vishnu, both male. Vishnu is said to have assumed female form (as *Mohini*) to give birth. He is often depicted riding on a tiger and accompanied by leopards, symbols of his victory over dark forces. Dedicated to Ayyappan, the Sabarimala Temple, on the Kerala/Tamil Nadu border, attracts huge numbers of pilgrims (mainly male; females of menstruating age are prohibited), all hoping to receive a taste of the success, spiritual and temporal, that Ayyappan embodies.

Lakshmi Lakshmi is Vishnu's consort and the goddess of wealth. In Tamil Nadu the rice-paste patterns (*kolams*) that grace the thresholds of homes and temples aim to tempt Lakshmi, and hence prosperity, inside (see the boxed text on kolams in the Tamil Nadu chapter).

Ganesh The chubby and jolly, elephant-headed Ganesh is one of Hinduism's most popular deities. He is the remover of obstacles, the deity whom worshippers first acknowledge when they visit a temple. He is also patron of learning; the broken tusk he holds is the very one he used to write down parts of the *Mahabharata*.

How Ganesh came to have the head of an elephant is explained in various stories. Some say Ganesh was Shiva's son, others that Ganesh was created by the goddess Parvati to guard the door while she bathed. Either way, Shiva, refused entry to Parvati's quarters by Ganesh, lopped off Ganesh's head. When Shiva realised he had killed Parvati's son he sent out attendants with orders to bring back the head of the first creature they encountered. That creature was an elephant. And so Ganesh was restored to life and rewarded for his courage by being made lord of new beginnings and guardian of entrances.

A prayer to Ganesh is invariably accompanied by smashing a coconut, symbolic of smashing the undesirable forces inherent within oneself. Sweetened rice balls, or *modhakam*, are sometimes distributed to children before the deity.

Ganesh

embraced by the Emperor Ashoka. It appears that Buddhist communities were quite influential in Andhra Pradesh between the 2nd and 5th centuries. However, Buddhism's influence waned as Hinduism's waxed in South India, about 1000 years after it was first introduced.

Judaism

South India has a very small population of Jews who can claim to have first settled in the region from the Middle East as far back as the 1st century. Jews became established at Kochi and their legacy continues in the still-standing synagogues and trading houses of Fort Cochin (see the boxed text in the Kerala chapter).

Local & Tribal Deities

Village and tribal people in South India have their own belief systems, but these are far less accessible or obvious to the casual visitor than the temples, ritual and other outward manifestations of the mainstream religions. The village deity may be represented by a stone pillar in a field, a platform under a tree or an iron spear stuck in the ground under a tree.

Village deities are generally seen as less remote and more concerned with the immediate happiness and prosperity of the community; in most cases they are female. In addition to the village deities there are many beliefs about ancestral spirits, especially of those who died violently.

India's tribal peoples have their own myths, deities and rituals; among the best documented are those of the Todas of Tamil Nadu. The Todas have a special affinity with the buffalo. Indeed, the buffalo is such an integral part of their culture and belief system that the ritual surrounding it coexists quite happily with the Christian beliefs and practices many Todas have adopted in relatively recent times. The Todas, who are vegetarian, depend on buffalo milk and the products made from it. But the sustenance the buffalo provides has more than temporal significance. When a Toda dies, a buffalo is killed to accompany that person into the afterlife, making human and beast inseparable in death as in life. For more information on Toda culture refer to the boxed text in the Tamil Nadu chapter.

Dancing
for the Gods

In ancient times dance enjoyed the patronage of kings and temples. Accomplished artists were a source of pride among royals; the quality of their respective dance troupes was at one stage the cause of intense competition between the Maharaja of Mysore and the Maharaja of Travancore. Between the second and eighth centuries trade missions from South India to South-East Asia left a cultural legacy that has endured in the dance forms of countries such as Bali, Cambodia and Myanmar (Burma). These days dance – classical, popular and folk – thrives on city stages, on the cinema screen and in villages throughout South India.

The classical dance forms of South India include Bharata Natyam (Tamil Nadu), Kuchipudi (Andhra Pradesh) and Kathakali (Kerala).

Previous page: Hand-painted Kathakali poster (photograph by Eddie Gerald).

This page: Kerala's famous Kathakali thrives on stage, screen and in temples throughout the South.

EDDIE GERALD

Bharata Natyam

Tamil Nadu's own unique performing art is believed to be India's oldest form of classical dance and remains true to conventions laid down in ancient times. It was originally known as Dasi Attam, a temple art performed by young women called *devadasis*. After the 16th century, however, it fell into disrepute – largely because it became synonymous with prostitution. It was revived in the mid-19th century by four male dancers (all brothers) from Thanjavur who are credited with restoring the art's purity by turning back to its ancient roots.

To become proficient at Bharata Natyam one must be not only talented but extremely dedicated. It requires at least seven years training to master Bharata Natyam's gestures and poses; head, eyes, neck, hands, body – each and every movement is charged with meaning. In addition the dancer must fully understand the symbolism contained within the stories behind the dance in order to infuse the performance with its own unique flavour or *rasa* – something conveyed through particular emotions, or *bhavas*. The skill of the artist in conveying the rasa is of more importance to the audience than the story's plot – which is usually well known anyway.

EDDIE GERALD

A single gesture, seven years in the making: Baratha Natyam, Mamallapuram (Mahabalipuram), Tamil Nadu.

Bharata Natyam is sometimes performed by men but more common-ly by women, in a solo performance. There are strict guidelines laid down regarding every single aspect of the art, right down to the attributes required in order to be an accomplished dancer. Some of these guide-lines are listed in Mrinalini Sarabhai's *Understanding Bharata Natyam*:

...the danseuse should possess a good figure, should be young, with round breasts, experienced, charming, well-versed in rhythm, skilled in the movements of the body and the intricacies of the steps... with large, well-shaped eyes, tastefully apparelled and bejewelled, endowed with a sparkling face, not too stout or too thin, not too tall or too short...

The dance will normally be accompanied by a singer *'...who should not shake his head while singing, nor show any unbecoming facial gri-maces...',* who chants the lines of the story, often using small cymbals for heightened emphasis in certain parts.

The song/performance of Bharata Natyam is invariably an intimate expression of a devotional love: the major theme of the art form is of worship of God through pure devotion and love, so the words of the song may include such as these:

Oh Lord! you alone I desire, you are my protector always,
With abundant love for you, who adorn the city of Tanjore,
Oh Lord of the Great Temple.
Quickly come to me! I am endowed with virtues, and immersed in the
    happiness of this love.
With deep desire in my heart I await you.
Oh, compassionate one, do not slight me now, but come!
Lips sweet with rapture and abundant love are thine,
In the ocean of love am I, unable to find the shore
Come quickly to me, why this indifference?
Am I not desirable and of incomparable qualities?

In Bharata Natyam, the dancer is a devotee who has been separated from the object of her devotion (God). In her yearning for him, she expresses all the emotions of a tragic heroine yearning for her lover.

Not too stout or too thin, not too tall or too short... women Baratha Natyam dancers, Mamallapuram (Mahabalipuram), Tamil Nadu.

EDDIE GERALD

A drummer and one or two musicians on stringed instruments may also accompany the dancers. A typical Bharatya Natyam performance lasts about two hours.

The Natyanjali School of Dance One of the most remarkable organisations operating in Bangalore today is the Natyanjali School of Dance. Unexciting as the name sounds, the school itself is remembered by all who see its Bharata Natyam and Kuchipudi performances, for the simple fact that most of the dancers are either totally blind or otherwise visually impaired.

The school was set up by Mr A Ashok Kumar, who trained as a classical Indian dancer. When he was approached to ask if he would help to teach visually impaired (he prefers to call them differently abled) people to dance, he doubted whether it was possible. After a preliminary lesson, however, his pupils were so enthusiastic that he decided to persevere. In retrospect he claims that the pupils themselves became the teachers, showing him how best to communicate the dance steps to them.

By a gradual process, he would demonstrate a position, the dancer would feel it with his hands and then imitate it. The group started with folk dances – which are less technically difficult and in which rhythm is of great importance. With the success of these initial experiments, and the confidence that this brought, they moved on to classical Indian dance. This intensely complex and technical discipline places huge emphasis on the exact use of the hands, feet and facial expressions to convey the meaning of the dance.

An intimate expression of devotional love: Baratha Natyam, Mamallapuram (Mahabalipuram), Tamil Nadu.

Initially the dancers were taught the positions of the feet (a process which took two years) and then of the hands. The facial expressions were the most difficult to convey. The dancers learnt all of the expressions by painstaking imitation of what they could feel with their hands. 'For example', says Mr Kumar, 'When you smile, various things happen. Your cheeks lift, the edges of your eyes crinkle, the sides of your mouth pull back'. By feeling all of this and imitating it exactly the visually impaired dancers learned the intensely complicated dance routines.

The company's shows last for around two hours, and the disabled dancers move around the stage as freely as their sighted counterparts. Some of the differently abled performers have trained for 12 years to reach this level of skill, and what might take an hour to teach to a sighted pupil can take four hours of painstaking practice for a handicapped dancer to learn. Their patience, dedication and sheer ability to memorise whole dances are awesome.

The company receives no state funding whatsoever, and exists solely on its earnings as a professional dance company. What motivates them? For the dancer-turned-choreographer Mr Kumar (who incidentally also writes the music and choreographs the dances himself) it is simple: 'We want to show the world that nothing is impossible'.

Although the Natyanjali School of Dance often tours during the summer months, it usually manages four or five performances in Bangalore between October and January. Information about performances can be gathered from the newspapers or by ringing Mr Kumar (☎ 641507).

EDDIE GERALD

EDDIE GERALD

Kathakali

Kerala's colourful and theatrical dance form is of more recent origin than Bharata Natyam. Although some of its traditions hark back a very long way indeed (to pre-Hindu times), its present form owes a major debt to the Raja of Kottarakkara who in the 17th century created his own dance troupe when a neighbouring prince refused to lend his. Rejecting the more conventional Sanskrit, the raja used the vernacular, Malayalam, as the language through which the stories (including the *Ramayana* and the *Mahabharata*) were to be conveyed. And so it remains today.

Usually only men become Kathakali dancers, but occasionally women also train in the art.

Kathakali isn't simply another form of dance/drama, it incorporates elements of yoga and ayurvedic medicine. Training for professional Kathakali performers begins from an early age, and is extremely rigorous and demanding: gymnastics and physical exercises are performed daily from 3 am to 7 am, and the routine includes some of the most extreme yogic postures that you are likely to see.

Kathakali in Kochin, before and after: applying make-up (this page) to become one of the 'katti', or evil, class of character (facing page).

EDDIE GERALD

Make-Up & Costume The make-up and costumes employed in Katha-kali are not only spectacular, they are symbols that are deeply inscribed with specific meanings, which can be broken down into five major groups or classes:

Paccha ('green')

This is the green-faced group of characters. They are the noble, kingly, divine or heroic types, and include among their ranks such characters as Arjuna, Vishnu, Indra and Krishna. With their crimson lips, ridged white 'beards' (*chutti*), billowing skirts, towering headpieces and the sacred mark of Vishnu on their foreheads, they are one of the most instantly recognisable icons of Keralan culture.

Katti ('knife')

These evil, arrogant characters wear the same white chuttis and golden head-dress as the noble paccha characters, and will usually have the same green-coloured face, to indicate that they are high-born too. But they don't have the sacred mark of Vishnu on their foreheads: there, instead, is a white knob. These characters also wear a white knob on the tips of their noses, and have a red mark that stretches from their noses to their cheeks, ending in an upturned point, like a moustache. Characters in this class include Jarasandha (a wicked king) and Vajraketu (an *asura,* or demon, who abducts young women during the course of one of the plays).

Kathakali dancer sleeps during make-up application, which can take as long as two hours.

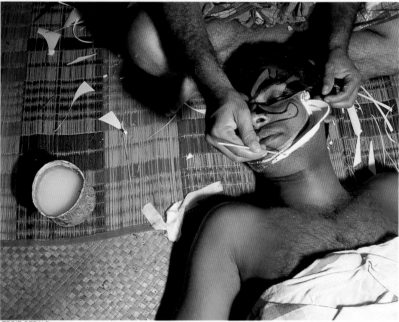

EDDIE GERALD

Tadi ('beard')

    This class is distinguished by the beards that the characters wear. There are three different types of beard signifying distinct differences in character – red (*chuvanna tadi*), black (*karutta tadi*) and white (*vella tadi*). The red-bearded characters are brutal, wicked and base; the black-bearded ones are wild and primitive, and the white-bearded characters are virtuous and spiritually higher beings.

Kari ('black')

    These are female characters, with false breasts, and jet-black faces dotted with red and white marks. They are also the most foul and despised characters of Kathakali.

EDDIE GERALD

EDDIE GERALD

A show in its own right: the make-up before the performance.

Minukku ('radiant')

These characters are distinguished by their minimal costume and make-up, which makes a startling contrast to the sheer extravagance of that of all of the other characters of Kathakali. The pared-down look signifies purity, humility and spirituality. The face make-up is a warm yellow tint, and usually the only head-dress is a cloth (no Kathakali actor performs bare-headed). Characters in this class include Parvati, Sita and Draupadi (all women), as well as Brahmins and sages.

There are several other characters which don't fit into any of the general make-up categories. These characters include the man-lion Narasimha, and the bird-vehicle Garuda.

All the materials used in the elaborate, ritualised make-up process are made from natural ingredients – powdered minerals and the sap of certain trees for the bright green make-up; the beaten bark of certain trees, dyed with fruits and spices, for wigs; coconut oil for mixing up the colours; and lamp-black mixed with coconut oil for the thick, lustrous black face paint.

The make-up process before the dance is quite a show in its own right. A professional make-up artist will usually start off the application of the hero's 'face', including the skilfully applied white paper 'beard' (chutti) which frames the lower part of the face, but the job is completed by the actor himself. The finishing touch is the small seed tucked under the eyelids, making the whites of the eyes turn red – an essential feature in Kathakali, which places great emphasis on the movement and expressions of the eyes.

The majority of Kathakali dancers are men...

The application of the make-up can take a couple of hours or more (during which time the actor will lay on his back and often fall asleep)

EDDIE GERALD

and is a process which visitors allowed in to watch find almost as fascinating as the performance itself.

Kathakali Performances There are more than 100 different arrangements of plays, all of them based on stories from the *Ramayana* and *Mahabharata*.

Performances traditionally begin just after sunset (at around 8 pm), and continue all through the night until dawn, but since most tourists don't have the inclination to stay up all night, the centres in the list following which put on the dance offer shortened versions, lasting about 1½ hours.

The dancers are usually accompanied by two drummers and two singers, who stand at opposite ends of the back of the stage. One of the drummers plays a cylindrical drum called the *chenda* which is held vertically and played with drum-sticks; the other drummer provides rhythm with his *maddalam*, which he holds in a horizontal position, playing one of the ends with his palm and the other end with his fingers. Of the two singers, one will have a gong and the other a pair of cymbals. They sing the story of the play, verse by verse, adding extra emphasis and emotion with their instruments.

...which can lend a distinctly pantomine quality to the female roles.

EDDIE GERALD

To catch a performance, try any of the following:

Art Kerala (☎ 366238), within a stone's throw of the See India Foundation, stages rooftop performances at a competitive Rs 80. Make-up begins at 6 pm and the show runs from 7 to 8 pm.

Cochin Cultural Centre (☎ 367866), Souhardham, Manikath Rd, is south of Ernakulam Junction train station. The dance is held in a specially constructed air-conditioned theatre designed to resemble a temple courtyard. Some visitors find the introductions disappointing and extra may be charged for photography. Make-up begins at 5.30 pm and the performance runs from 6.30 to 8 pm.

Kerala Kathakali Centre stages performances at the Cochin Aquatic Club on River (Calvathy) Rd, Fort Cochin, near the bus stand. Enthusiastic performances from young Kathakali artists nicely balance the more formal introduction to the art at the See India Foundation. Make-up begins at 5 pm, and the performance runs from 6.30 to 7.30 pm. The last ferry from Fort Cochin to Ernakulam departs after the performance at 9.30 pm. Admission is Rs 75.

See India Foundation (☎ 369471), Devan Gurukalum, Kalathiparambil Rd, is near the Ernakulam Junction train station. The show features an extraordinary presentation by PK Devan, who explains the dance's history and makes a plucky attempt to simplify the main elements of Hinduism for visitors. Make-up begins at 6 pm, and the performance runs from 6.45 to 8 pm, with time for questions afterwards. It costs Rs 100, though you may be offered a discounted ticket from hotel staff in Ernakulam.

The Great Elephant March – drummers and folk dancers.

PAUL BEINSSEN

If, after viewing one of these performances, you wish to experience more of this fascinating art, you can attend a traditional all-night performance. Once a month the Ernakulam Kathakali Club hosts all-night performances by major artists at the TDM Hall on Durbar Hall Rd, Ernakulam. Programs covering the story in English are distributed from tourist offices a week in advance. The cost is Rs 100 (as donation).

Traditional Kathakali is also performed almost every night at Sree Vallabha Temple, Tiruvilla, Kerala, as an offering by the devotees. Tiruvilla is near Kottayam and almost all the trains from Ernakulam to Thiruvananthapuram stop there. See the Around Kottayam section in the Kerala chapter.

Courses A government-run school, near Palakkad in north-east Kerala, teaches Kathakali dancing. Courses in Kathakali can also be taken at the Vijnana Kala Vedi Centre at the village of Aranmula. See Around Kottayam in the Kerala chapter.

Kuchipudi

Andhra Pradesh's own dance-drama, Kuchipudi, originated in a small village from which the dance takes its name. Like Kathakali, its present-day form harks back to the 17th century when it became the prerogative of Brahmin boys from this village. It often centres on the story of Satyambhama, wife of Lord Krishna. Once a men-only dance, women are the main performers today.

Folk dancers, Thanjavur, Tamil Nadu.

EDDIE GERALD

Mohiniattam

A semi-classical form is *Mohiniattam*, which is based on the story of Mohini, the mythological seductress. Containing elements of Bharata Natyam and Kathakali, it combines songs in Malayalam with Carnatic (South Indian) music and is performed mainly in Kerala.

Yakshagana

Unique to south-west Karnataka, Yakshagana has long served as a vehicle for the popular dissemination of moral tales and legends, usually centred on the cosmic struggle between good and evil. The focus in Yakshagana is less on the dance or movement aspect of performance, since (and unlike in the tradition of Kathakali) the actors have vocal roles to play, singing and speaking. As in Kathakali, the costumes and make-up are not only striking, they are deeply symbolic of a particular character's essential traits. Mangalore hosts frequent performances of this particular performing art; for further information inquire at the tourist office in that city (see the Mangalore section in the Karnataka chapter).

Serious students of Karnataka's folk culture may be interested to know that there is an organisation dedicated to studying this particular genre. It is funded by the Ford Foundation. Contact: the Regional Resources Centre, MGM College, Udipi 576102, Karnataka.

Folk dancer in a street festival, Mamallapuram (Mahabalipuram), Tamil Nadu.

PAUL BEINSSEN

Folk Dances

South India has many kinds of folk dance. These include the *Puravi-attams*, or dummy horse dances (Karnataka, Tamil Nadu); the *Koklikatai* dance from Tamil Nadu in which dancers move about on stilts that have bells attached and the *Kolyacha* fishers' dance from the Konkan Coast. Goa's stylised *Mando* song/dance is a waltz-like blend of Indian rhythms and Portuguese melody accompanied by Konkani words, and is performed by men and women dancing together.

Various forms of trance-dancing (including the relatively recent Western import, *Goa Trance*, which accompanies the generic electronic music that also goes by the name of *Goa Trance*) and dances of exorcism occur throughout the South; and almost all of the tribal peoples, including the Todas of Tamil Nadu and the Banjaras of Andhra Pradesh, retain their own unique dance traditions.

As in Kathakali, Teyyam dancers of Kerala apply elaborate, symbolic make-up (this page) and extraordinary head-dresses (following page, photograph by Paul Beinssen).

Teyyam

Kannur, in Kerala, is a good base to witness the fascinating ritual of *Teyyam,* an ancient dance form practised for centuries by tribal people and villagers in the north Malabar region. The bizarre head-dresses, costumes and body painting and trance-like performances are extraordinary. The Sri Muthappan Temple in Parassinikkadavu, 18km from Kannur, stages Teyyam performances twice daily, in the early morning and the evening. To see the morning performance, organise a taxi the night before to pick you up from your hotel at 4 am. During the day there are buses to Parassinikka-davu and there is basic accommodation available near the temple. During the January to April period, there are Teyyam performances in villages throughout the region. Ask at the tourist office or the very helpful staff at the Yatri Niwas Hotel about these rituals.

PAUL BEINSSEN

Nrityagram

This dance village, 30km north-west of Bangalore (in Karnataka), was established in the early 1990s to revive Indian classical dance. Under the auspices of well-known Odissi dancer, Protima Gauri, it offers the long-term study of classical dance and its allied subjects, such as choreography, philosophy, music, mythology and painting. The village, designed by award-winning Goan architect, Gerard Da Cunha, welcomes visitors and accommodates guests. Contact Nrityagram's Bangalore office (☎ 846 6314).

Facts for the Visitor

PLANNING

When to Go

October to March is the best time to visit South India, although there are variations; see the regional chapters for details. At this time it is relatively dry and cool, although in November and the beginning of December parts of Tamil Nadu and Kerala come in for a drenching as the monsoon retreats across them. In the popular beach resorts of Goa many facilities (such as beach shacks) don't open until November and, in the weeks immediately after the monsoon (ie October), there can be strong rips which make swimming hazardous. The Western Ghats can get misty in winter (late December, January) and the nights are often cold regardless of the time of year.

Temperatures start to rise rapidly in most places in March and by April South India sizzles. The mountains, where it's not nearly as hot and the atmosphere isn't as dusty, can be pleasant in April and May, just before the monsoons. The cooling monsoon rains arrive in June and last until the end of September or early October. For more information about when to go where, see the Climate section in the previous chapter.

Maps

Lonely Planet's *India Travel Atlas* breaks down the country into over 100 pages of maps, and so gives unequalled coverage. It is fully indexed and the book format means it is easy to refer to, especially on buses and trains.

Nelles Verlag publishes a good series that covers the whole of India. Part 4 of the series, *Southern India* (1:1,500,000), includes city maps of Chennai and Bangalore.

Trekkers may want to pick up the relevant maps from the *TPC* or *ONC* series published by the US Defense Mapping Agency Aerospace Center (available from most specialist map shops). The topographical detail is excellent, but heights are in feet and detail on roads and villages is very poor.

The *Discover India* series of road maps published by TTK Pharma and available widely throughout South India is reasonably good for showing roads, villages and tourist attractions.

The Survey of India has maps covering all of India. In order to obtain a map for anywhere within about 150km of the land and sea borders (which in the case of the latter means most of South India) you will need special permission from the District Commissioner, something that is difficult if not impossible to obtain. However, in 1998 there were plans to release these maps to the public, so it's worth checking. The Survey of India's office in Delhi is opposite the tourist office on Janpath.

What to Bring

If you are only travelling to a single destination, eg Goa or Kerala, you can pretty much bring what you like. Heavy luggage presents few problems if all you've got to do is get it into the taxi and to a hotel.

If you are undertaking a longer trip, the usual budget travellers' rule applies – bring as little as possible. In South India that's easy to do as you will seldom need more than light clothing.

If you are spending time in the hills, especially during the cool season, you will need a reasonably warm top or jacket for chilly nights.

Modesty rates highly in South India, as in the rest of the country. Although men wearing shorts are accepted as a western eccentricity, they should at least be of a decent length. Wearing shorts or a T-shirt in a more formal situation is definitely impolite.

If you are visiting temples or other sacred places, please be sensitive to dress requirements. Sleeveless tops and short skirts/shorts are unacceptable in such situations. A reasonable clothes list would include:

- underwear and swimming gear
- one pair of cotton trousers
- one pair of shorts (men only)
- one long (ankle-length) cotton skirt (women)
- a few T-shirts or lightweight shirts
- sweater for cool nights in the hills
- one pair of sneakers or shoes
- socks – useful for visiting temples, especially for traipsing over areas exposed to the sun
- sandals
- flip-flops (thongs) – handy to wear when showering
- lightweight jacket or raincoat
- a set of 'dress up' clothes
- a hat – South Indians commonly use umbrellas instead of hats, which can be sweaty and uncomfortable. Umbrellas can be bought cheaply everywhere.

If you are going camping or trekking you will need to take:

- walking boots – these must give good ankle support and have a sole flexible enough to meet the anticipated walking conditions. Ensure your boots are well broken in beforehand.
- warm jacket
- wool shirt or pullover
- breeches or shorts – shorts are ideal but should not be worn in places where they may cause offence to locals.
- shirts – t-shirts are OK, but shirts with collars and sleeves will give added protection against the sun.
- socks – a sufficient supply of thick and thin pairs should be taken.
- a sunhat

Bedding A sleeping bag, although a hassle to carry, can come in handy. You can use it to spread over unsavoury looking hotel bedding, as a cushion on hard train seats, and as a seat for long waits on railway platforms. If you are planning on camping or spending time in the hills (especially during the cool season) a sleeping bag is essential. If you are planning to travel in Andhra Pradesh be aware that in budget and mid-range accommodation you are seldom provided with any sheets or pillowcases and a sleeping bag is a good idea – in the cool season especially. For those intending to stick to the coast, a sheet sleeping bag is a good alternative.

Generally (in Tamil Nadu, Goa, Kerala and Karnataka) guesthouses and hotels provide a sheet to cover the bed, an extra sheet and a pillowcase. Not all places provide a sheet to put over you – this is when you'll be pleased you brought that sheet sleeping bag. This is sufficient for most places because of the heat. In the hill country blankets are usually provided as well.

For visitors on a package tour or those staying in mid-range hotels (more than Rs 350 a night) in places where there is a good tourist infrastructure, bedding will definitely be available in your hotel room.

Toilet Paper Indian sewerage systems are generally overloaded enough without having to cope with toilet paper as well. However, if you can't adapt to the Indian method of a jug of water and your left hand, toilet paper is widely available. A basket is sometimes provided in toilets for used toilet paper. Use it. Do not put sanitary napkins or tampons in toilets.

Toiletries Soap, toothpaste, shampoo and other toiletries are readily available. Conditioner can be hard to find; some brands combine shampoo and conditioner in one. If this doesn't appeal, bring your own supplies. A sink plug is worth having since few cheaper hotels have plugs. A nail brush or even something sturdier can be very useful for scrubbing the dirt and grit off your feet at the end of the day. For women, tampons are available in most major cities; sanitary pads are more widely available, however. Bring condoms with you, as the quality of locally made condoms may be suspect.

Men can safely leave their shaving gear at home. One of the pleasures of Indian travel is a shave in a barber shop every few days. With AIDS becoming more widespread in India, however, choose a barber's shop that looks clean, avoid roadside barbers, and make sure that a fresh blade is used. For just a few rupees you'll get the full treatment – lathering, followed by a shave, then the process is repeated, and finally there's the hot, damp towel and sometimes talcum powder, or even a scalp massage.

Miscellaneous Items Some handy items to stow away in your pack could include the following. See the Health section later in this chapter for details about medical supplies.

- a padlock, especially for budget travellers. Most cheap hotels and quite a number of mid-range places have doors locked by a flimsy latch and padlock. You'll find having your own sturdy lock on the door does wonders for your peace of mind
- a knife (preferably Swiss Army); it has a whole range of uses, such as peeling fruit, etc
- a miniature electric element to boil water in a cup
- a sarong – it can be used as a bed sheet, an item of clothing, an emergency towel, and a pillow on trains
- insect repellent, a box of mosquito coils or an electric mosquito zapper – you can buy them in most places; try any medical store (remember, however, that many parts of South India are subject to power cuts). A mosquito net can be very useful, although setting it up might be a problem if it hasn't got its own supports (if it doesn't come with a portable frame, bring tape with you)
- a torch (flashlight) and/or candles – power cuts are not uncommon ('load shedding' as it is euphemistically known) and there's little street lighting at night
- a voltage stabiliser – for those travellers who may be bringing sensitive electronic equipment
- moisture-impregnated disposable tissues – to use on your hands and face
- a spare set of glasses and your spectacle prescription
- earplugs (to shut out the din in some hotels) and a sleeping mask
- a sun hat and sunglasses; if you hate sweaty hats, buy an umbrella in India. It provides shade plus air circulation
- a water bottle; it should always be by your side. If you're not drinking bottled water, use water purification tablets (and choose not to add to India's growing problem with plastic trash)
- high-factor sunscreen; it's becoming more widely available in India, but it's *expensive*! Lip balm might come in handy if you are planning to spend a lot of time at the beach

- a bit of string; very useful as a makeshift clothes line – double-strand nylon is good to secure your clothes if you have no pegs. You can buy small, inexpensive sachets of washing powder everywhere
- a pair of binoculars if you plan to be bird-watching and wildlife spotting
- a high-pitched whistle; some women carry them as a possible deterrent to would-be assailants

How to Carry It For visitors travelling only to one destination, eg Goa or Kerala, and who really only intend travelling by taxi from the airport to their hotel, a suitcase is a good option. It's lockable, keeps your clothes flat and is less likely to get damaged by careless luggage handlers at the airport.

For others, a backpack is still the best carrying container. Many packs these days are lockable, otherwise you can make it a bit more thief-proof by sewing on tabs so you can padlock it shut. It's worth paying the money for a strong, good quality pack as it's much more likely to withstand the rigours of Indian travel.

An alternative is a large, soft, zip bag with a wide shoulder strap. This is obviously not an option if you plan to do any trekking.

SUGGESTED ITINERARIES
Andaman & Nicobar Islands

Port Blair – Ross Island – Havelock – Cinque Island – Jolly Buoy or Redskin Islands – Diglipur. (10 to 20 days)

Pristine water, empty beaches, coral reefs, dense (but diminishing) forest and a rather tragic history is what the Andamans are all about. Actually getting to the islands (either by plane or boat) leaves the traveller with a real sense of achievement. Once there, island hopping is a favourite activity. So is snorkelling, diving or simply beachcombing. Unless you have bags of money to charter a boat, your choice of islands will depend on the vagaries of scheduled ferry services. Regular buses travel the main trunk road, broken by ferry crossings, and if you want to travel to North Andaman you can catch the bus to Diglipur, the second largest settlement on the Andamans.

Andhra Pradesh

Hyderabad – Nagarjuna Sagar – Nagarjunakonda – Nagarjuna Sagar-Srisailam Tiger Reserve (also known as the Rajiv Gandhi Tiger Reserve) – Vijayawada – Warungal – Hyderabad.
(10 to 15 days)

The lack of tourist infrastructure in Andhra Pradesh adds to the challenge of traversing dusty desert-like landscapes and exploring ruins of fallen empires. Time loses meaning as you meander through the labyrinthine bazaars of Hyderabad. Train is the best way to cover the vast distances of what is still one of India's poorest states, but you'll have to take the bus from Hyderabad for the long one-day trip to Nagarjuna Sagar. Here you can catch the boat to see the recovered treasures from the ancient Buddhist settlement of Nagarjunakonda.

The bus will take you through part of the Nagarjuna Sagar-Srisailam Tiger Reserve and on to Vijayawada where the waters of the Krishna River form a huge delta. After visiting ancient Hindu cave temples and the Buddhist ruins at Amaravathi take the train to Warangal where the 600-year-old fort stands as a testament to the skills and determination of the early Kakatiyas. At Palampet the 1000-pillared, 1000-year-old temple has been carefully restored, each sculptured column revealing a rich synthesis of myth and history. It's just a short 150km journey by train back to Hyderabad.

Kerala

(1) Kochi – Kottayam – Kumily/Thekkady – Munnar – Thrissur – Guruvayor (Punathur Kota).
(Seven to 10 days)

This route highlights the spice trade and spice-growing with an opportunity to view wildlife, spectacular mountain scenery, picturesque tea estates and a stable of temple elephants. After arriving in Kochi and exploring the bazaars of Fort Cochin and Mattancherry catch a bus to the Cardamom Hills via the rubber-producing centre of Kottayam. A relaxing day could be spent around Kottayam at the Kumarakom Bird Sanctuary on the shore of Vembanad Lake. From Kottayam head to the spice-growing centre of Kumily and the Periyar Wildlife Sanctuary. While you probably won't see a tiger, an early morning jungle walk will give you a taste of wild India, and chances are you will see elephants, monkeys, squirrels and birds.

A scenic road connects Kumily with the tea-growing centre of Munnar. You may wish to spend several days in Munnar exploring the groomed hills and Eravikulam National Park or just enjoying the cool mountain climate. The bus ride from Munnar down the Western Ghats escarpment to the cultural centre of Thrissur is spectacular. Near Thrissur is the important temple town of Guruvayoor and the temple elephant stable at Punnathur Kota. In the grounds of an old palace more than 40 elephants are cleaned, preened and fed by their *mahouts* (elephant caretakers).

(2) Thiruvananthapuram – Kovalam – Varkala – Kollam – Alappuzha – Kottayam – Kochi.
(Seven to 10 days)

Tropical beaches and idyllic backwaters fringed with swaying coconut palms are the attractions of southern Kerala. Head directly for Kovalam, avoiding Thiruvananthapuram, the busy and dusty capital. As well as the sun, salt and sand you can visit ancient wooden palaces, quiet hill stations and backwater villages in day trips from Kovalam. Varkala is a little more relaxed than Kovalam. The sacred beach here is *the* place to unwind. A short train ride from Varkala is Kollam; from this ancient port you can embark on a voyage of discovery as you experience life on the waters' edge. You can mingle with other tourists on the scheduled cruises or hire your own *kettuvalaam* (traditional Keralan rice barge) for the memorable trip to Alappuzha. From Alappuzha there are further backwater experiences on the way to Kochi, either directly along Vembanad Lake or via the rubber-producing centre of Kottayam.

Tamil Nadu

Chennai – Mamallapuram – Pondicherry – Gingee – Madurai – Kodaikanal – Ooty – Mudumalai Wildlife Sanctuary – Kanchipuram – Chennai.
(20 to 30 days)

This itinerary will provide a fair slice of the uniqueness and diversity of Tamil Nadu. The coastal regions see relatively few tourists, the cuisine demands extensive exploration and the numerous temples portray the complexity and dynamism of Dravidian culture. However, should you become 'templed out', the Western Ghats offer respite from the heat and chaos of the plains. The walking possibilities in these mountains should satisfy the serious trekker as well as the casual stroller, although detailed trekking information is as rare as the Bengal tiger.

At Mudumalai you can exchange glances with such animals as deer, elephants and (if luck is on your side) tigers. Buses are frequent and distances manageable in Tamil Nadu. Catch the bus down the coast to Mamallapuram and Pondicherry. From Pondicherry take the train for the remainder of the journey, using buses for short trips out to Kodaikanal and the Mudumalai Wildlife Sanctuary.

Karnataka

Bangalore – Mysore – Belur & Halebid – Sravanabelagola – Chitradurga – Hampi – Lakkundi – Badami – Bijapur. (Two to three weeks)

Bangalore, with its excellent travel connections, is a good place to start any tour of Karnataka. With its cosmopolitan feel, it's a far cry from the rest of India but it's a good place to ease yourself into India slowly, or to unwind when you've had enough.

A three hour bus journey gets you to Mysore, once the seat of the Maharajahs of Mysore – the Wodeyars. The palace, in the hybrid Indo-Saracenic style, was built in 1912, and is one of the most memorable buildings in South India.

The nearby fortress of Srirangapatnam, where Tipu Sultan held out against the British, is fun to explore. Mysore has plenty of good accommodation and places to eat, and is also a good base from which to explore the surrounding area.

Nearby are Belur and Halebid, which boast the best-preserved temples built during the reign of the Hoysala dynasty (11th to 13th centuries) in South India; they're gems

of early Indian architecture. Also within striking distance is Sravanabelagola, home of the unique 17m-high statue of the Jain deity Gomateshvara, which is carved from a single piece of rock.

Return to Bangalore and continue northwards by bus to the ancient fortress of Chitradurga – perfect for a day's lazy exploration. From here it's only a short bus journey to Hampi, and the breathtaking ruins of the ancient city of Vijayanagara. Allow three days here if possible, longer still if you can. The ruins extend over a vast area, and the best way to discover them is to wander around, exploring under your own steam.

From Hampi it's only a short hop to Badami (via the temples at Lakkundi if you have time). Badami and the surrounding sites at Aihole and Pattadakal were all former capitals of the ruling Chalukyas, and became experimenting grounds for South Indian architecture from the 4th to the 8th centuries.

From Badami you could continue north to Bijapur to see the awesome Golgumbaz – the mausoleum of Mohammed Adil Shah. Alternatively, if you need a break from architecture, take the bus or train down to the coast – Goa is only a matter of hours away, and Gokarna on the Karnatakan coast is on one of the most peaceful and beautiful stretches of Indian coastline that you're likely to find. From either of these you can get the Konkan Railway northwards to Mumbai, or take connections south to Bangalore.

Goa

Decide which beach appeals to you the most, base yourself there, and make excursions if you feel like it. This is practical not only because the beaches are generally by far the most pleasant places to stay, but because the best-value hotels and all the facilities that the visitor will want are naturally based around the beaches, too. There is little need for an itinerary, because everything in Goa is close enough to be within a day's travel (there and back) from wherever it is you're staying.

HIGHLIGHTS
Temples
Temples are prolific in South India. The ornate *gopurams* (Dravidian gateway towers) rise majestically above rice paddies, dusty towns and crowded cities. Some temples perch precariously on mountain tops. Others are carved into rocks or constructed on beaches. Reflected in the splendid architecture of these temples is the history of South India. At almost any time of the year, pilgrims will be on the road, journeying from one temple to another, paying homage to their favoured deities and seeking balance and peace in their lives.

Visiting temples demands a lot of energy. Some are vast and can easily absorb an entire day. Many become impossibly crowded and noisy. It is therefore easy to overdose on the temple experience. For this reason you should plan your visits carefully and try not to see more than one temple in a day. Read about the temple before your visit; this will enhance your enjoyment. Temple guides are often on hand but be prepared to negotiate for a good price for their services, and be prepared to be confronted by all kinds of shysters and touts.

If your visit coincides with a temple festival (a highly likely occurrence since festivals happen almost every month) you'll witness some spectacular, bizarre and often quite moving devotional practices.

For its sheer size and uniqueness, the Sri Meenakshi Temple at Madurai is a must. At Mamallapuram the famous shore temple as well as the ancient structures known as the five *rathas* are highly recommended. Around Kanchipuram there are many temples, so you'll have to pace yourself carefully. The temple at Tiruvannamalai is in an imposing setting. If you need to work off all that curry and rice, it's worth climbing up to the Rock Fort Temple at Trichy or the hill temple at Palani where the views are breathtaking. At Tirupati in Andhra Pradesh millions of devotees sacrifice their hair to their god. This place draws a phenomenal 100,000 people every day and easily rivals the Vatican and Mecca as a venue for pilgrims. It is extremely well organised and well worth a visit.

Karnataka has some of the most famous temples in South India. Once home to the great dynasties of the Chalukyas and Hoysalas, and later of the Vijayanagara kings, its historic and artistic legacy is rich and varied: from the intricate detail of the stone carving on the temples at Belur, Halebid and Somnathpur to the larger, but equally impressive, decoration that crowds the walls of the Chalukya temples in Badami, Pattadakal and Aihole. Also impressive are the massive stone slab temples of Hampi, built on such a monumental scale that it's hard to believe their extent.

Although these sites have the best known of Karnataka's temples, there are ancient places of worship scattered throughout the state. Of great interest too are the numerous pilgrimage centres in Karnataka, of which Dharmastala, Sringeri, Udipi and Gokarna are the best known. Each of these has a unique history and has inherited centuries of tradition, and they all draw tens of thousands of pilgrims annually.

Temple	Place	State	Page
Arunachaleswar	Tiruvannamalai	TN	529-30
Brihadishwara	Thanjavur	TN	561-2
Gangakon-dacholapuram	near Kumbakonam	TN	554
Cave Temples	Badami	Kar	329-31
Channekeshava	Belur	Kar	259
Durga	Aihole	Kar	333
Hoysaleswara	Halebid	Kar	257-8
Kamakshi Amman	Kanchipuram	TN	523
Kumari Amman	Kanyakumari	TN	595
Malaikovil	Palani	TN	610
Nataraja	Chidambaram	TN	546-8
Ramanathaswamy	Rameswaram	TN	590-1
Shore Temple	Mamallapuram	TN	512
Sri Meenakshi	Madurai	TN	580
Veerabhadra	Lepakshi	AP	384-6
Venkateshwara	Tirupati	AP	379
Vinayaka, Thayu-manaswamy	Trichy	TN	566-8
Virupaksha	Hampi	Kar	311
Virupaksha	Pattadakal	Kar	333
Vittala	Hampi	Kar	312-13

Bazaars

Almost every town has a bazaar. Big cities such as Hyderabad and Chennai have many bazaars which seem to merge into each other. For the traveller, bazaars are more about looking than shopping. It is here that you'll see acres of unbelievable plastic kitsch alongside some of the finest silks and cottons as well as mountains of cooking implements.

In many towns Tibetans have travelled south to set up their temporary bazaars of woollen clothing. These are especially popular around the hill stations. The food stalls present an olfactory as well as a visual delight. Some bazaars such as the Charminar Bazaar in Hyderabad specialise in jewellery. Tailoring is a speciality of the bazaars around the Meenakshi Temple in Madurai. Others seem to have everything including chickens, goats, flowers, human hair and dental equipment. The antique shops around Jew Street (Jew Town) in Fort Cochin (Kerala) offer endless hours of hunting and bartering.

Although Bangalore and Mysore appear very modern, both have colourful, noisy and busy bazaars that are a striking contrast to their surroundings.

Bazaar	Place	State	Page
Charminar	Hyderabad	AP	351
City Market	Bangalore	Kar	226
Devaraja Market	Mysore	Kar	243
Jew Town	Fort Cochin	Ker	433-4
Laad	Hyderabad	AP	352
Meenakshi Temple	Madurai	TN	580
Theagaraya Nagar	Chennai	TN	496

Backwaters

The myriad canals, rivers and lakes that make up Kerala's famed backwaters are more than just aquatic thoroughfares. Much of the area which makes up the backwaters was reclaimed from swamps and lakes hundreds of years ago. Fishing, prawn farming, sand mining, lime burning, boat building, coir making, commerce and rice farming are just some of the traditional activities you will witness as you slowly cruise through the palm-lined waterways.

Route	State	Page
Alappuzha-Kottayam	Ker	416-17
Kollam-Alappuzha	Ker	416-17
Village Tours	Ker	416-17

Beaches

Only a few beaches have resort developments where travellers can laze and gaze, many beaches escape package deal mediocrity. The Tamil Nadu coastline is dotted with small fishing industries. Watching the boats come and go is a great way to spend time. At some places like Rameswaram it is possible to negotiate a ride on a fishing boat. At other beaches the waters are considered to be particularly auspicious, and are believed to contain a myriad healing properties.

At Kanyakumari, on the southern tip of India, crowds gather at the bathing ghats and partake of the special waters. The beaches in the Andaman & Nicobar Islands are still pristine and deserted. Here you can be left alone to string a hammock between trees, star gaze at night and snorkel or dive during the day. The beach is always a respite from the oppressive heat of the interior and in cities such as Chennai, an evening or morning stroll along the beach can recharge your depleted batteries.

In southern Kerala the water is warm, blue and inviting. You can choose between luxurious resorts or a basic budget hotel, between the lively crowds of Kovalam or the more laid-back scene at Varkala. A world away from the touristed beaches are the quiet fishing villages and beaches of northern Kerala. Although not an attractive swimming proposition, their postcard-like beauty and pastoral tranquillity are sure to lift the spirits.

Goa is a mecca for beach lovers but recently other places have been added to the traveller's map. Gokarna has four small but beautiful and peaceful beaches, and there are other beaches along the Karnatakan coast which foreigners rarely (if ever) visit. The problem with many of these is that there are few facilities. For those with a lot more cash to spare, it would be hard to beat the white sand perfection of the Lakshadweep Islands, but unfortunately due to travel restrictions they are out of reach to travellers on a modest budget.

Place	State	Page
Anjuna	Goa	202-5
Bekal Fort	Ker	455-6
Benaulim	Goa	211-14
Chapora & Vagator	Goa	205-7
Cinque Island	A&N	664-5
Colva	Goa	211-14
Elliot Beach (Chennai)	TN	480
Gokarna	Kar	299-302
Havelock Island	A&N	662-3
Kanyakumari	TN	594
Kovalam	Ker	398-406
Mamallapuram	TN	514
Marina (Chennai)	TN	478
Rameswaram	TN	591
Varkala	Ker	407-10

Forts

Although forts can be exhausting places to explore, they invariably offer a palpable sense of history. They are visual reminders of fallen empires as well as human folly, courage and tenacity. Some forts are relatively intact but it's the ones that have fallen back towards a state of nature that hold a magical allure. Often you'll share these places only with eagles, the occasional goat, a few snakes and the inevitable bats. Within the fort complex you'll often find an exquisite lake, a well and an ancient temple.

Gingee Fort, not far from Tiruvannamalai, is a vast sprawling complex where tourists generally don't go. Golconda Fort in Hyderabad is popular with tourists but is well worth a visit. Devakonda Fort, like Gingee, is eerie, isolated and captivating. Much of Warangal Fort is in ruins but these are massive edifices isolated within an extensive landscape. Be prepared to spend the better part of a day exploring some forts. In Kerala you can stay in the small guesthouse within the ramparts of Bekal Fort, and nod off to a serenade of foxes.

The battered and ramshackle fort at Gulbarga gets few visitors, and Bidar Fort gets

even fewer, which is a pity as they're both impressive, the latter in particular. Much easier to get to is the excellent fort at Chitradurga. The most famous remains of a fortified city are at Hampi, although there's little left to see of the fortifications themselves. Hampi draws huge numbers of visitors.

Place	State	Page
Bekal Fort	Ker	455-6
Bidar	Kar	343
Chitradurga	Kar	320-1
Devakonda	AP	364-5
Gingee	TN	530-1
Golconda	AP	354, 356-7
Gulbarga	Kar	340
Warangal	AP	371

Hill Stations

If you've had too many bus rides, if your temper is becoming dangerously frayed, your patience has expired and your sense of humour is conspicuously absent, maybe it's time to head for the hills. In spite of intense and often unchecked development, hill stations can still offer a welcome break. They are relatively cool in summer and almost cold (especially at night) in winter. If you can visit during an off season, you'll be able to bargain for lower priced accommodation.

Walking and horse riding are popular pastimes in hill stations. Sitting in front of a log fire and sharing travel experiences is also a great way to while away time. Residents of the plains look upon residents of hill stations as being a little crazy. Perhaps they are, but there's nothing like a dash of altitude to save you from complete insanity.

Place	State	Page
Kodaikanal	TN	601-9
Munnar	Ker	425-9
Ooty	TN	622-9

The Great Outdoors

If hill stations sound a bit too sedate, dust off your hiking boots and head for the Western Ghats in Karnataka and the Nilgiris in Tamil Nadu. Kodagu is a great place to go trekking and hill climbing, and you can rest up on a coffee plantation afterwards. At Jog Falls, not far away, the scenery and hiking are fantastic. Or, if you want a quick escape, head for the rock-climbing places near Bangalore.

One of the delights of rock climbing in India is that when you get to the top of the cliff you will very likely find a little temple perched peacefully there. If you are not a rock climber, try Nandi Hill, also near Bangalore; great for hiking and views, with several peaceful places to stay and eat.

Because Nagarhole National Park in Karnataka is more remote than many national parks and sanctuaries, it's pleasantly uncrowded and peaceful. The resthouses inside and the resorts outside the park are excellent and you have a good chance of seeing wild elephants.

Place	State	Page
Jog Falls	Kar	294
Kodagu (Coorg)	Kar	264-79
Nandi Hill	Kar	236
Nargarhole National Park	Kar	273-5
Nilgiris	TN	615-39

Festivals

Richly caparisoned elephants, fireworks, dancing, ritual – South India's festivals are certainly lively. In Kerala, for example, you can see frantic, colourful snakeboat races or take in a measured, meandering elephant procession. One of the South's most colourful and lively events is the Pooram Festival in Kerala. Kerala also plays host to one of the South's most popular festivals: Aranmula Valamkali, or Snakeboat Festival, which is held in connection with Onam (the August/September lunar period). For more information on festivals, see the Holidays & Festivals section later in this chapter.

Event	State	Page
Dussehra Festival	Kar	244
Great Elephant March	Ker	415
Feast of St Francis Xavier	Goa	192-3
Mamallapuram Dance Fest	TN	514
Pooram Festival	Ker	449
Snakeboat Races	Ker	414-15

TOURIST OFFICES
Local Tourist Offices

The national (Government of India) tourist office has offices in all major centres in South India's states and territories. Individual states also run their own tourist offices, eg the Tamil Nadu Tourism Development Corporation (TTDC), the Karnataka State Tourism Development Corporation (KSTDC) and the Kerala Tourism Development Corporation (KTDC). In addition districts within states sometimes have their own offices (eg the District Tourism Development Corporation at Kollam, Kerala). Sometimes the various national and state offices are linked; other times they are not. State and national offices may in fact compete with one another. And the relationship these offices have with private operators also varies from place to place. See the chapters on specific states for more details.

Offices vary widely in their usefulness, although they are generally good places for picking up brochures and maps. Some seem to do little more than sell tours, which are run by private operators. For trekking information you are advised to contact the adventure clubs and agencies listed in the Karnataka and Tamil Nadu chapters.

Some tourist offices run their own accommodation networks. For example, the KSTDC operates a chain of hotels under the name of Hotel Mayura and these are situated at some of the best spots in the state, are usually clean and can be pre-booked through the tourist office. For more information including contact details see the relevant sections in the state chapters.

Government of India tourist offices in the four major international gateways to India include:

Calcutta
    (☎ 033-242 1402, 242 3521)
    4 Shakespeare Sarani
Chennai (Madras)
    (☎ 044-852 4295) 154 Anna Salai
Delhi
    (☎ 011-332 0005) 88 Janpath, New Delhi
Mumbai (Bombay)
    (☎ 022-203 2932)
    123 Maharishi Karve Rd, Churchgate

Tourist Offices Abroad

The Government of India Department of Tourism maintains a string of tourist offices in other countries where you can get brochures, leaflets and some information about India. The tourist office leaflets and brochures are often very informative and worth getting hold of. On the other hand, some of the foreign offices are not always as useful for obtaining information as those within the country. There are also smaller 'promotion offices' in Osaka (Japan) and in Dallas, Miami, San Francisco and Washington DC (USA).

Australia
(☎ 02-9232 1600; fax 9223 3003)
Level 1, 17 Castlereagh St, Sydney,
NSW 2000
Canada
(☎ 416-962 3787; fax 962 6279)
60 Bloor St West, Suite No 1003, Toronto,
Ontario M4W 3B8
France
(☎ 01 42 65 83 86; fax 01 42 65 01 16)
8 Blvd de la Madeleine, 75009 Paris
Germany
(☎ 69-23 54 23; fax 23 47 24)
Kaiserstrasse 77-III, D-6000
Frankfurt-am-Main-1
Italy
(☎ 02-80 49 52) Via Albricci 9, 20122 Milan
Malaysia
(☎ 3-242 5285; fax 242 5301)
Wisma HLA, Lot 203 Jalan Raja Chulan,
50200 Kuala Lumpur
Netherlands
(☎ 20-620 8991; fax 638 3059)
Rokin 9-15, 1012 KK Amsterdam
Singapore
(☎ 235 3800; fax 235 8677)
United House, 20 Kramat Lane, Singapore 0922
Sweden
(☎ 8-21 50 81; fax 21 01 86)
Sveavagen 9-11, S-III 57, Stockholm 11157
Switzerland
(☎ 22-732 18 13; fax 731 56 60)
1-3 Rue de Chantepoulet, 1201 Geneva
Thailand
(☎ 2-235 2585) KFC Bldg,
3rd floor, 62/5 Thaniya Rd, Bangkok 10500
UK
(☎ 0171-437 3677; 24 hour brochure line
☎ 01233-211999; fax 0171-494 1048)
7 Cork St, London W1X 2LN

USA
(☎ 212-586 4901; fax 582 3274)
30 Rockefeller Plaza, 15 North Mezzanine,
New York NY 10112
(☎ 213-380 8855; fax 380 6111)
3550 Wilshire Blvd, Suite 204, Los Angeles
CA 90010

VISAS & DOCUMENTS

Passport

You must have a passport with you all the time; it's the most basic travel document. Ensure that your passport will be valid for the entire period you intend to remain overseas. If your passport is lost or stolen, immediately contact your country's embassy or consulate in Delhi.

Visas

Virtually everybody needs a visa to visit India. The application is (in theory) straightforward and the visas are usually issued with a minimum of fuss.

Tourist visas are issued for six months, are multiple entry, and are valid from the date of issue of the visa, not the date you enter India. This means that if you first enter India five months after the visa was issued, it will be valid only for one month. One year visas are only available to businesspeople or students. Tourist visas are not extendable. If you want to stay longer than six months you will have to go to a neighbouring country, eg Sri Lanka (but not Nepal, see below), and get a new six month visa.

Six month multiple entry tourist visas cost A$55 for Australians, UK£19 for Britons, US$50 for Americans, and FF 200 for French passport holders.

Nepal According to a recent report from travellers, it is no longer possible to get a new Indian visa in Kathmandu if you already have a six month visa in your passport. Some travellers have managed to get a short visa extension, however, by having their current visas changed to three/six months from date of entry instead of from date of issue.

Pakistan The high commission in Islamabad is quite efficient, although if there is an Indian embassy in your home country they may have to fax there to check that you are not a thief, wanted by the police or in some other way undesirable. The process takes a few days, and of course you have to pay for the fax.

Sri Lanka In addition to the Indian Embassy in Colombo, it is possible to obtain an Indian visa in Kandy. The issuing process take approximately seven working days. The office is at 47 Rajapilla Mawatha, not far from the Castle Hill Guesthouse.

Thailand It takes four working days for non-Thai nationals to obtain an Indian visa.

Visas for Neighbouring Countries

Bhutan Although Bhutan is an independent country, it handles its external relations primarily through its embassy in Delhi. All tourist visas must be channelled through the Tourist Authority of Bhutan (TAB) (☎ 975-2-23251, 23252; fax 23695), PO Box 126, Thimphu, Bhutan. You may also try the Bhutan Foreign Mission (☎ 011-688 9809; fax 688 6710), Chandragupta Marg, Chanakyapuri, New Delhi 110021.

Bhutan has a rigid set of rules for foreign tourists, designed to limit the number of visitors each year and subsequently protect the kingdom's traditional culture. Tourists pay an all-inclusive US$200 per night in Bhutan, and must travel on a scheduled itinerary.

Myanmar (Burma) The embassy in Delhi is fast and efficient and issues four-week visas. There is *no* Burmese consulate in Calcutta, although there is one in Kathmandu in Nepal and Dhaka in Bangladesh.

Nepal The Nepalese Embassy in Delhi is on Barakhamba Rd, New Delhi, quite close to Connaught Place, not out at Chanakyapuri like most other embassies. It is open Monday to Friday from 10 am to 1 pm and 2 to 5 pm. Single entry, 30-day visas take 24 hours and cost US$25 (payable in rupees). A 30 day visa is available on arrival in Nepal for

US$25, and can be extended, but doing so involves rather a lot of form filling and queuing – it's better to have a visa in advance, if possible.

There is a consulate in Calcutta, and it issues visas on the spot. You'll need one passport photo and the rupee equivalent of US$25.

Sri Lanka Most western nationalities do not need a visa to visit Sri Lanka, but there are diplomatic offices in Delhi, Mumbai, and Chennai.

Thailand There are Thai embassies in Delhi and Calcutta. One month visas cost about US$10 and are issued in 24 hours. They can be extended in Thailand. If you are flying into and out of Thailand and don't intend to stay more than 15 days, a visa is not required, but you cannot extend your period of stay.

Tax Clearance Certificates

If you stay in India for more than 120 days you need a tax clearance certificate to leave the country. This supposedly proves that your time in India was financed with your own money, not by working in India or by selling things or playing the black market.

Basically all you have to do is find the Foreign Section of the Income Tax Department in Delhi, Calcutta, Chennai or Mumbai and turn up with your passport, visa extension form, any other similar paperwork and a handful of bank exchange receipts (to show you really have been changing foreign currency into rupees officially). You fill in a form and wait anything from 10 minutes to a couple of hours. You're then given your tax clearance certificate and away you go. We've never yet heard from anyone who has actually been asked for this document on departure.

Photocopies

It's a good idea to carry photocopies of your important travel documents, which obviously should be kept separate from the originals in the event that these are lost or stolen.

Take a photocopy of the first page of your passport (with your personal details and photograph), as well as a copy of the page with your Indian visa. A photocopy of your travel insurance policy could be handy. Keep a record of the travellers cheques you have exchanged, where they were encashed, the amount and serial number. Encashment receipts should also be kept separate from your travellers cheques. Photocopy your airline ticket and your credit card. It's not a bad idea to leave photocopies of your important travel documents with a friend or relative at home.

Restricted Area Permits

Even with a visa you are not allowed everywhere in South India. Certain places require special additional permits. These are covered in the appropriate sections in the relevant chapters, but briefly they are:

Andaman & Nicobar Islands For those flying in, permits for a stay of up to 30 days are issued on arrival at the airport in Port Blair. If you're arriving by ship, you need a permit in advance; the shipping company won't let you buy a ticket without one. Permits are obtainable from an embassy or consulate abroad, from the Ministry of Home Affairs in Delhi, or from the Foreigners' Registration offices in Chennai (☎ 044-827 8210; Shastri Bhavan Annex, Haddows Rd) or Calcutta (☎ 033-247 3301; 237 Acharya JC Bose Rd).

Getting the permit in Delhi could take several days; in Calcutta or Chennai it's generally a few hours. If you think there's a chance you might visit the Andamans on your Indian trip, get a permit when you get your Indian visa; it costs nothing and could save time later.

Lakshadweep Lakshadweep permits are not a problem as long as you are booked with a recognised trip/resort. For foreigners this means that you must either have booked with the exclusive and extremely

expensive Bangaram Island Resort, or with Laccadives (a diving company based on Kadmat Island). Foreigners may only visit Kadmat and Bangaram and only as part of these packages. Domestic tourists require permits too, and may visit other islands but only as part of an organised cruise on the Lakshadweep supply ship MV *Tippu Sultan*. See the Lakshadweep section for more details.

Trekking Permits

Foreigners must have permits for trekking in certain areas of the Nilgiri Hills (Tamil Nadu), Kodagu (Karnataka) and in most areas in or around national parks. The permits are obtainable from forest departments. In theory these permits aren't difficult to get, but as the wheels of bureaucracy tend to grind slowly and sometimes halt altogether, it is wise to allow two days per permit. Alternatively you can join an organised trek where the company arranges your permit and any other paperwork for you. For more details see the relevant sections on outdoor activities in the Karnataka and Tamil Nadu chapters.

Onward Tickets

Many Indian embassies and consulates will not issue a visa to enter India unless you are holding an onward ticket, which is taken as sufficient evidence that you intend to leave the country.

Travel Insurance

A travel insurance policy to cover theft, loss and medical problems is a wise idea. There is a wide variety of policies and your travel agent will be able to recommend the best one for you. The international student travel policies handled by STA Travel, Council Travel and other student travel organisations are usually good value. Some policies offer a range of medical expense options, including options which cover scuba diving, trekking and other adventurous activities. The more expensive options are chiefly for countries like the US which have extremely high medical costs. Check the small print:

- Some policies specifically exclude 'dangerous activities', which can include motorcycling and even trekking. If such activities are on your agenda you don't want that sort of policy. A locally acquired motorcycle licence may not be valid under your policy.
- You may prefer a policy which pays the doctors or hospitals directly rather than you having to pay on the spot and then claim later. If you have to claim later make sure you keep all documentation. Some policies ask you to call back (reverse charges) to a centre in your home country where an immediate assessment of your problem is made. Keep a photocopy of your policy, with this number, separate from the original, for reference in the event that the latter is stolen.
- Check if the policy covers ambulances, an emergency helicopter airlift out of a remote region, or an emergency flight home with a medical escort. If you have to stretch out you will need two seats and somebody has to pay for them!

Driving Licence & Permits

If you are planning to drive in India, get an International Driving Permit from your local national motoring organisation. In many places in South India it is possible to hire a motorbike; see the Motorcycles section in the Getting Around chapter for more information. An International Permit can also be used for other identification purposes, such as plain old bicycle hire.

Other Documents

A health certificate, while not necessary in India, may be required for onward travel. These days student cards are virtually useless – many student concessions have either been eliminated or replaced by 'youth fares' or similar age concessions. Similarly, a Youth Hostel (Hostelling International – HI) card is not generally required for India's many youth hostels, but you do pay slightly less at official youth hostels if you have one.

It's worth having a batch of passport photos for visa applications and for obtaining permits to remote regions. If you run out, Indian photo studios will do excellent portraits at pleasantly low prices.

EMBASSIES
Indian Embassies & Consulates

India's embassies, consulates and high commissions abroad include:

Australia
   (☎ 02-6273 3999; fax 6273 3328)
   3-5 Moonah Place, Yarralumla, ACT 2600
   (☎ 02-9223 9500; fax 9223 9246)
   Level 27, 25 Bligh St, Sydney, NSW 2000
   (☎ 03-9386 7399; fax 9384 1609)
   15 Munro St, Coburg, Melbourne, Vic 3058
   (☎ 09-221 1485; fax 221 1206)
   The India Centre, 49 Bennett St, Perth, WA 6004
Bangladesh
   (☎ 02-503606; fax 863662)
   120 Road 2, Dhamondi, Dhaka
   (☎ 031-211007; fax 225178)
   1253/1256 or Nizam Rd, Mehdi Bagh, Chittagong
Belgium
   (☎ 2-640 98 02; fax 648 96 38)
   217 Chaussee de Vleurgat, 1050 Brussels
Bhutan
   (☎ 0975-22162; fax 23195)
   India House Estate, Thimpu, Bhutan
Canada
   (☎ 613-744-3751; fax 744-0913)
   10 Springfield Rd, Ottawa K1M 1C9
China
   (☎ 8621-6275 8881; fax 6275 8885)
   1008, Shanghai International Trade Centre, 2200 Yan An Xi Lu, Shanghai
Denmark
   (☎ 31 18 28 88; fax 39 27 02 18)
   Vangehusvej 15, 2100 Copenhagen
France
   (☎ 01 40 50 70 70; fax 01 40 50 09 96)
   15 rue Alfred Dehodencq, 75016 Paris
Germany
   (☎ 228-5 40 51 32; fax 23 32 92)
   Baunscheidtstrasse 7, 53113 Bonn
Israel
   (☎ 3-5101431; fax 510 1434)
   4 Kaufman St, Sharbat House, Tel Aviv 68012
Italy
   (☎ 6-488 46 42; fax 481 95 39)
   Via XX Settembre 5, 00187 Rome
Japan
   (☎ 3-3262 2391; fax 3234 4866)
   2-2-11 Kudan Minami, Chiyoda-ku, Tokyo 102
Myanmar (Burma)
   (☎ 1-82550; fax 89562)
   545-547 Merchant St, Yangon (Rangoon)
Nepal
   (☎ 71-410900; fax 413132)
   Lainchaur, PO Box 92, Kathmandu

The Netherlands
   (☎ 70-346 9771; fax 361 7072)
   Buitenrustweg 2, 252 KD, The Hague
New Zealand
   (☎ 4-473 6390; fax 499 0665)
   180 Molesworth St, Wellington
Pakistan
   (☎ 51-814371; fax 820742)
   G5 Diplomatic Enclave, Islamabad India
   House, 3 Fatima Jinnah Rd, Karachi
   (☎ 21-522275; fax 568 0929)
South Africa
   (☎ 11-333 1525; fax 333 0690)
   Sanlam Centre, Johannesburg
Sri Lanka
   (☎ 1-421 605; fax 446 403)
   36-38 Galle Rd, Colombo 3
Thailand
   (☎ 2-258-0300; fax 258-4627)
   46 Soi 23 (Prasarnmitr), Sukhumvit Rd,
   Bangkok
   (☎ 53-24 3066; fax 24 7879)
   113 Bumruangrat Rd, Chiang Mai 50000
UK
   (☎ 0171-836 8484; fax 836 4331)
   India House, Aldwych, London WC2B 4NA
   (☎ 0121-212 2782; fax 212 2786)
   8219 Augusta St, Birmingham B18 6DS
USA
   (☎ 202-939 7000; fax 939 7027)
   2107 Massachusetts Ave NW, Washington
   DC 20008
   (☎ 212-879 7800; fax 988 6423)
   3 East 64th St, Manhattan, New York, NY
   10021-7097
   (☎ 415-668 0662; fax 668 2073)
   540 Arguello Blvd, San Francisco,
   CA 94118

Embassies & High Commissions in India

Most foreign diplomatic missions are in the nation's capital, Delhi, but there are also quite a few consulates in the other major cities of Mumbai, Calcutta and Chennai. Consulates in Chennai include the following (the telephone area code is 044):

France
   (☎ 827 0469) 16 Haddows Rd
Germany
   (☎ 827 1747) 22C-in-C Rd
Japan
   (☎ 826 5594) 60 Spur Tank Rd,
   Chetput

Sri Lanka
   (☎ 827 2270)
   9-D Nawab Habibullah Rd, off Anderson Rd
UK
   (☎ 827 3136) 24 Anderson Rd
USA
   (☎ 827 3040) Gemini Circle, 220 Anna Salai

Embassies and consulates in Delhi include the following (the telephone area code for Delhi is 011):

Australia
   (☎ 688 8223; fax 688 5199)
   1/50-G Shantipath, Chanakyapuri
Bangladesh
   (☎ 683 4065; fax 683 9237)
   56 Ring Rd, Lajpat Nagar-III
Bhutan
   (☎ 688 9809; fax 687 6710)
   Chandragupta Marg, Chanakyapuri
Canada
   (☎ 687 6500; fax 687 6579)
   7/8 Shantipath, Chanakyapuri
China
   (☎ 687 1585; fax 688 5486)
   50-D Shantipath, Chanakyapuri
France
   (☎ 611 8790; fax 687 2305)
   2/50-E Shantipath, Chanakyapuri
Germany
   (☎ 687 1831; fax 687 3117)
   6/50-G Shantipath, Chanakyapuri
Ireland
   (☎ 462 6733; fax 469 7053)
   13 Jor Bagh Rd
Israel
   (☎ 301 3238; fax 301 4298)
   3 Aurangzeb Rd
Italy
   (☎ 611 4355; fax 687 3889)
   50-E Chandragupta Marg, Chanakyapuri
Japan
   (☎ 687 6581)
   4-5/50-G Shantipath, Chanakyapuri
Myanmar (Burma)
   (☎ 600251; fax 687 7942)
   3/50-F Nyaya Marg, Chanakyapuri
Nepal
   (☎ 332 8191; fax 332 6857) Barakhamba Rd
The Netherlands
   (☎ 688 4951; fax 688 4856)
   6/50-F Shantipath, Chanakyapuri
New Zealand
   (☎ 688 3170; fax 687 2339)
   50-N Nyaya Marg, Chanakyapuri

Pakistan
   (☎ 467 6004; fax 637 2339)
   2/50-G Shantipath, Chanakyapuri
South Africa
   (☎ 614 9411; fax 614 3605)
   B-18 Vasant Marg, Vasant Vihar
Sri Lanka
   (☎ 301 0201; fax 301 5295)
   27 Kautilya Marg, Chanakyapuri
UK
   (☎ 687 2161; fax 687 2882)
   50 Shantipath, Chanakyapuri
USA
   (☎ 688 9033; fax 687 2028)
   Shantipath, Chanakyapuri

CUSTOMS

The usual duty-free regulations apply for India; that is, one bottle of whisky and 200 cigarettes. You're allowed to bring in all sorts of western technological wonders, but big items, such as video cameras, are likely to be entered on a 'Tourist Baggage Re-Export' form to ensure you take them out with you when you go. This also used to be the case with laptop computers, but it seems this restriction has been waived. It's not necessary to declare still cameras, even if you have more than one.

Note that if you are entering India from Nepal you are not entitled to import anything free of duty.

MONEY
Costs

From top to bottom: if you stay in luxury hotels, use car-and-driver combinations for sightseeing and fly from city to city you can spend a lot of money. South India has plenty of hotels at US$50 or more a day and some where a room can cost US$200 plus. Lakshadweep (the island group off the coast of Kerala) is an especially pricey destination. The high taxes levied against luxury accommodation (up 30% in Tamil Nadu) also need to be taken into account. At the other extreme, if you scrimp and save, stay in the cheapest hotels (or hostels and dormitories), always travel 2nd class on trains, and learn to exist on *dal* (lentils, pulses) and rice, you can see South India on less than US$7 a day.

Most travellers will probably be looking for something between these extremes. Prices can be dramatically lower in off-the-beaten-track places, but for those visiting the usual travellers' haunts and prepared to splash out on occasional tours (eg Kerala's backwaters) expect to average about US$20 to US$25 a day. If you are planning to go diving you will be up for rather more. See the sections on the Andaman & Nicobar Islands (Tamil Nadu) and Lakshadweep (Kerala) for more details on diving costs.

Carrying Money

A moneybelt worn around your waist beneath your clothes is probably one of the safest ways of carrying important documents such as your passport and travellers cheques on your person. Some travellers prefer a pouch attached to a string which is worn around the neck, with the pouch against the chest concealed beneath a shirt or jumper. Leather pouches worn over the clothing are inadvisable; they are too conspicuous (as are 'bum bags'). Many temples insist that all leather be removed anyway.

Cash

Cash – US dollars or pounds sterling – is useful to carry, especially if you intend travelling in areas, eg parts of Andhra Pradesh,

---

Banknotes

Indian banknotes circulate far longer than in the west and the smaller notes in particular get very tatty. A note can have holes right through it (most do in fact, as they are bundled together with staples when new) and be quite acceptable, but if slightly torn at the top or bottom on the crease line then it's no good and you'll have trouble spending it. Even a missing corner makes a bill unacceptable. If you do receive a torn note, the answer is to simply accept it philosophically. Some banks have special counters where torn notes will be exchanged for good ones.

that have limited money changing facilities and where you think you might have trouble changing travellers cheques or using credit cards.

Travellers Cheques

Although it's usually not a problem to change travellers cheques, it's best to stick to the well known brands – American Express, Visa, Thomas Cook, Citibank and Barclays – as more obscure ones may cause problems. Occasionally a bank won't accept a certain type of cheque – Visa and Citibank in particular – and for this reason it's worth carrying more than one flavour.

Travellers cheques are easily changed in the main cities, but beyond these, facilities can be limited. For example, outside of Hyderabad in Andhra Pradesh travellers cheques can be cashed at the State Bank of Hyderabad. Few branches however, offer this service and it is limited to weekdays. For more details see the relevant section in the state chapters.

Most star-rated hotels and government emporiums accept travellers cheques, but the exchange rates are generally slightly less favourable than those from a bank.

A few simple measures should be taken to facilitate the replacement of travellers cheques, should they be stolen (see Stolen Travellers Cheques in the Dangers & Annoyances section later in this chapter).

Credit Cards

Credit cards are widely accepted at midrange and upmarket hotels, for buying rail and air tickets, and in many shops. Be warned, however, that you won't be able to use your credit card in the Andaman & Nicobar Islands. Here it's cash or travellers cheques only.

On a MasterCard, Visa card, or Japanese Credit Bureau card you can now get cash advances (in rupees) on the spot in main cities.

International Transfers

Don't run out of money in India unless you have a credit card against which you can draw travellers cheques or cash. Having money

---

Credit Card Warning

A trap that many foreigners fall into in North India's touristy places (Agra, Jaipur, Varanasi, Delhi, Calcutta) but one to bear in mind generally, centres on buying with a credit card. You may be told that if you buy the goods the merchant won't forward the credit slip for payment until you have received the goods, even if it is in three months time. This is total bullshit. No trader will be sending you as much as a postcard until he or she has received the money in full for the goods you are buying. What you will find is that within 48 hours of you signing the credit slip the merchant has telexed the bank and the money will have been credited to his or her account.

Also be aware of any shop that takes your credit card out the back and comes back with the slip for you to sign. It has occurred that, while out of sight, the vendor will imprint a few more forms, forge your signature, and you'll be billed for items you haven't purchased. Get them to fill out the slip right in front of you.

---

transferred through the banking system can be time consuming. It's usually straightforward if you use a foreign bank, Thomas Cook or American Express in Delhi; elsewhere it may take a fortnight and will be a hassle.

Currency

The rupee (Rs) is divided into 100 paise (p). There are coins of five, 10, 20, 25 and 50 paise, Rs one, two and five, and notes of Rs one, two, five, 10, 20, 50, 100 and 500.

You are not allowed to bring Indian currency into the country or take it out of the country. You are allowed to bring in unlimited foreign currency or travellers cheques, but you are supposed to declare anything over US$10,000 on arrival.

Currency Exchange

In Delhi and other gateway cities you can change most foreign currencies or travellers cheques – Australian dollars, Deutschmarks, yen or whatever – but for the rest of the country it's best to stick to US dollars or pounds sterling. Thomas Cook and American Express are both popular travellers cheques, and can be exchanged readily in most major tourist centres. Thomas Cook has offices in Chennai (three city offices and a counter at the international airport), Bangalore, Hyderabad, Kochi, Thiruvananthapuram and Goa (Panaji) and changes all major currencies and travellers cheques. Because banks can be slow, it can be easier to deal with agencies such as these – and they are open longer hours.

Thomas Cook issues a little booklet of discount coupons that includes one offering commission-free exchange of foreign currency notes and travellers cheques. At the time this book was in production, the exchange rates were as follows:

A$1	=	Rs 25.50
C$1	=	Rs 28.10
NLG 1	=	Rs 21.20
DM 1	=	Rs 23.95
FF 10	=	Rs 71.50
ILS 1	=	Rs 11.50
JPY 100	=	Rs 29.10
NPR 100	=	Rs 69.90
NZ$1	=	Rs 21.60
UK£1	=	Rs 69.50
US$1	=	Rs 42.70

Outside the main cities, the State Bank of India is usually the place to change money, although occasionally you'll be directed to another bank, such as the local state bank.

In the more remote regions, few banks offer exchange facilities, so utilise the banks in the main tourist centres. Even some larger towns and some of the more touristed areas have no money changing facilities (eg Gulbarga and Badami in Karnataka).

For more details refer to the Money sections in the regional chapters. Some banks charge an encashment fee, which may be levied for the entire transaction, or on each cheque. Find out how much the bank is going to charge to exchange your cheques before you sign them.

Black Market

The rupee is a fully convertible currency; that is, the rate is set by the market not the government. For this reason there's not much of a black market, although you can get a couple of rupees more for your dollars or pounds cash. In the major tourist centres and major cities, especially around train and bus stations, you will have constant offers to change money. There's little risk involved although it is officially illegal.

Encashment Certificates

All money is supposed to be changed at official banks or moneychangers, and you are

---

Change

A perennial problem when you are travelling around South India is the lack of small change. The Reserve Bank of India has ceased printing Rs 1, Rs 2 and Rs 5 notes, and coins are to be used in their stead. However there never seem to be enough small denomination notes or coins, which leads to all sorts of hassles when it comes to settling bills. If you are taking an auto-rickshaw it's wise to have some idea of how much the ride will cost. Always have several Rs 10 notes with you for these occasions and better still, a selection of Rs 2 and Rs 5 notes or coins. Handing over a Rs 50 note will invariably elicit the response: 'No change'. Everybody seems to want to get their hands on Rs 5 notes, but they are in short supply and if you acquire some, hang on to them for occasions when you are making a small purchase. Some places (supermarkets especially) will issue sweets as a substitute for small change.

Banks will invariably give you bundles of Rs 100 or Rs 50 notes when you change money. Rs 500 do exist but banks will often say they have run out. This means if you are changing a lot of money you should expect to emerge from the bank with a wad of rupees that you can barely squeeze into your moneybelt.

supposed to be given an encashment certificate for each transaction.

Banks will usually give you an encashment certificate, but occasionally they don't bother. Ask for one. It is worth getting them, especially if you want to re-exchange excess rupees for hard currency when you depart India.

The other reason for saving encashment certificates is that if you stay in India longer than four months, you have to get an income tax clearance. See Tax Clearance Certificates earlier in this chapter for details.

Tipping & Bargaining

In tourist restaurants or hotels, where service is usually tacked on in any case, the normal 10% figure usually applies. In smaller places, where tipping is optional, you need only tip a few rupees, not a percentage of the bill. Hotel porters expect Rs 5 to Rs 10; other possible tipping levels are Rs 2 for bike-watching, Rs 10 or Rs 15 for train conductors or station porters perform-

---

Baksheesh

In most Asian countries tipping is virtually unknown, but India is an exception to that rule – although tipping has a rather different role in India than in the west. The term *baksheesh* encompasses tipping and a lot more besides. You 'tip' not so much for good service, but to get things done.

Judicious baksheesh will open closed doors, find missing letters and perform other small miracles. Tipping is not necessary for taxis nor for cheaper restaurants, but if you're going to be using something repeatedly, an initial tip will ensure the standards are kept up.

While everyone in Tamil Nadu will know what you mean by 'baksheesh' the Tamil word for it is actually *inam*. (Similarly the Tamil for the Hindu term *wallah* (eg taxi-wallah, chai-wallah) is *karan*.)

---

ing miracles for you, and Rs 5 to Rs 15 for extra services from hotel staff.

How much you pay for a wide range of goods and services from souvenirs to accommodation is very often subject to negotiation. Government emporiums and larger shops invariably have fixed prices (often rather higher than similar goods would fetch in the bazaars) as do small, general purpose shops. But in other places, eg bazaars, you will generally have to bargain. If you have no idea how much something should cost a rough guide is to slash the initially proposed price in half. This will invariably elicit an incredulous response. But at least the shopkeeper knows that you are not about to be taken for a ride and you can proceed to negotiate. Some shopkeepers will lower their 'final price' if you move towards the door saying that you'll 'think about it'. Another way around this is to peruse the prices at fixed price stores for items you might like to bargain for in bazaars, and ask fellow travellers as well as reliable locals what they might pay themselves.

POST & COMMUNICATIONS
Post

The Indian postal and poste restante services are generally excellent. Expected letters are almost always there and letters you send almost invariably reach their destination, although they may take up to three weeks. American Express, in its major city locations, offers an alternative to the poste restante system.

Postal Rates It costs Rs 6 to airmail a postcard and Rs 6.50 to send an aerogramme anywhere in the world from India. A standard airmail letter (up to 20g) costs Rs 11. Post office-issued envelopes cost Rs 1 within India. The larger post offices have a speed post service. International rates are Rs 200 for the first 200g and Rs 60 for every additional 200g. Internal rates are Rs 20 for places within 500km and Rs 30 for places beyond 500km. You can buy stamps at larger hotels, saving a lot of queuing in crowded post offices.

Posting Parcels Most people discover how to do this the hard way, in which case it will take half a day. Go about it as described below, which can still take up to an hour:

• Take the parcel to a tailor, or to a parcel-stiching-wallah (occasionally found just outside post offices) and ask for your parcel to be stitched up in cheap linen. Negotiate the price first.
• At the post office, ask for the necessary customs declaration forms. Fill them in and glue one to the parcel. The other will be stitched onto it. To avoid excise duty at the delivery end it's best to specify that the contents are a 'gift'.
• Be careful how much you declare the contents to be worth. If you specify over Rs 1000, your parcel will not be accepted without a bank clearance certificate, which is a hassle to get. State the value as less than Rs 1000.
• Have the parcel weighed and franked at the parcel counter.

Books or printed matter, can go by bookpost, which is considerably cheaper than parcel post, but the package must be wrapped a certain way: make sure that the package can either be opened for inspection along the way, or that it is wrapped in brown paper or cardboard and tied with string, with the two ends exposed so that the contents are visible. To protect the books, it might be worthwhile first wrapping them in clear plastic. No customs declaration form is necessary.

The maximum weight for a bookpost parcel is 5kg, which costs about Rs 1000 airmail and Rs 175 seamail. Parcels must be sent by 'open packet' mode, meaning they must be able to be easily opened and inspected. The packaging technique is best left to the professionals either at the post office or through major bookshops. Rates for airmail bookpost are:

200g	Rs 45
250g	Rs 54
500g	Rs 102
760g	Rs 159
1000g	Rs 195
1260g	Rs 252
1500g	Rs 288
2000g	Rs 363

Be cautious with places which offer to mail things to your home address after you have bought them. Government emporiums are usually OK.

Receiving Mail Have letters addressed to you with your surname in capitals and underlined, followed by the poste restante, GPO, and the city or town in question. Many 'lost' letters are simply misfiled under given (first) names, so always check under both your names. Letters sent via poste restante are held for one month only, after which, if unclaimed, they are returned to the sender.

Having parcels sent to you in India is an extremely hit-and-miss affair. Don't count on anything bigger than a letter getting to you. And don't count on a letter getting to you if there's anything of market value inside it.

Telephone
All over South India, even in the smallest places, you'll find private STD/ISD call booths with direct local, interstate and international dialling. These phones are usually found in shops or other businesses, but are well signposted with large STD/ISD signs advertising the service. A digital meter lets you keep an eye on what the call is costing, and gives you a printout at the end. You then just pay the shop owner – quick, painless and a far cry from the not so distant past when a night spent at a telegraph office waiting for a line was not unusual. Direct international calls from these phones cost around Rs 70 per minute, depending on the country you are calling. To make an international call, you will need to dial the following:

00 (international access code from India) + country code (of the country you are calling) + area code + local number

In some centres, STD/ISD booths may offer a 'call back' service – you ring your folks or friends, give them the phone number of the booth and wait for them to call you back. The booth operator will charge about

Rs 2 to Rs 3 per minute for this service, in addition to the cost of the preliminary call. Advise your caller how long you intend to wait at the booth in the event that they have trouble getting back to you. The number your caller dials will be as follows:

(caller's country international access code) + 91 (international country code for India) + area code + local number (booth number)

The Central Telegraph offices/Telecom offices in major towns are usually reasonably efficient. Some are open 24 hours.

Also available is the Home Country Direct service, which gives you access to the international operator in your home country. You can then make reverse charge (collect) or credit card calls, although this is not always easy. If you are calling from a hotel beware of exorbitant connection charges on these sorts of calls. You may also have trouble convincing the owner of the telephone you are using that they are not going to get charged for the call. The countries and numbers to dial are listed in the Home Country Direct Phone Numbers table.

Fax

Fax rates at telegraph offices (usually found at or near the central post office) are Rs 60 per page for neighbouring countries, Rs 95 per page to other Asian destinations, Africa, Europe, Australia and New Zealand, and Rs 110 to the USA and Canada. Main telegraph offices are open 24 hours. Rates within India are Rs 30 per page for A4 size transmissions.

Many of the STD/ISD booths also have a fax machine for public use but they cost between 5% and 30% more than government telegraph offices. If your fax doesn't go through you may still be liable for a fee. Private places will also usually accept incoming faxes, but charge a small amount. However, many hotels turn off their machines and store them in cupboards when they're not sending faxes. This makes it somewhat difficult for incoming messages.

Email

There are bureaux where you can send and receive email in major cities (eg Chennai, Bangalore). While this is the cheapest way to send text, offices may charge more for receiving email than for receiving a fax. Some of the star-rated hotels have business centres with email facilities which, for a fee, are available to residents and non-residents. Outside of the big cities email rarely exists. See the Information sections in the relevant chapters for reliable email bureaux.

Telegram

It's still possible to send telegrams. From telegraph offices the cost is around Rs 2.50 per word.

BOOKS

India is one of the world's largest publishers of books in English. You'll find a great number of interesting, affordable books on India by Indian publishers, which are generally not available in the west. South India's major cities, especially Chennai and Bangalore, have excellent bookshops. Even smaller places such as Fort Cochin and Ernakulam in Kerala have well-stocked stores offering plenty of choice in English and in some cases, French.

Recently published British and American books also reach Indian bookshops remark-

Home Country Direct Phone Numbers

Country	Number
Australia	0006117
Canada	000167
Germany	0004917
Italy	0003917
Japan	0008117
The Netherlands	0003117
New Zealand	0006417
Singapore	0006517
Spain	0003417
Taiwan	00088617
Thailand	0006617
UK	0004417
USA	000117

ably fast and with very low mark-ups. If a bestseller in Europe or America has major appeal for India they'll often rush out a paperback in India to forestall possible pirates.

Several Indian publishers including Penguin publish many South Indian authors who either write in English who or have been translated into English; catalogues are available for those interested. Macmillan India recently launched a project specifically aimed at publishing 55 English translations from 11 Indian languages, including South Indian languages.

Lonely Planet

It's pleasing to be able to say that for more information on India and its neighbours, and for travel beyond India, most of the best guides come from Lonely Planet!

Lonely Planet's *India* has comprehensive information on the whole of the country. The Himalaya is well covered, with a trekking guide and a regular travel guide (*Indian Himalaya*). *Trekking in the Indian Himalaya* is by Garry Weare, who has spent years discovering the best trekking routes in the Himalaya; his guide is full of practical descriptions and excellent maps. There are also Lonely Planet guides to *Delhi*, *Rajasthan* and *Goa*, for travellers spending more time in these places.

Lonely Planet guides to other places in the South Asian region include: *Nepal*, *Trekking in the Nepal Himalaya*, *Bhutan*, *Tibet*, *Karakoram Highway*, *Pakistan*, *Bangladesh*, *Myanmar*, *Sri Lanka*, *Maldives*, and *South-East Asia*.

Guidebooks

Blue Guide's *Southern India* by George Michell provides excellent information on the region's architecture, art, archaeology and history. The author has written numerous other books on the history and art of South India. See the relevant sections below. Railway buffs should enjoy *India by Rail* (Bradt Publications, 1997) by Royston Ellis.

Travel Writing

Dervla Murphy's classic on South India *On a Shoestring to Coorg* is still one of the most comprehensive accounts of travelling in this region although much has changed in the ensuing decades. *Om – An Indian Pilgrimage* by Geoffrey Moorhouse provides a fascinating insight into the lives of a wide range of people in South India, from humble coir makers to royalty to holy men.

Chasing the Monsoon by Alexander Frater is an Englishman's account of, as the title suggests, a journey north from Kovalam in Kerala all the way to one of the wettest places on earth (Cherrapunji in Meghalaya), all the while following the onset of the monsoon as it moves north across the country. It's a fascinating insight into the significance of the monsoon, and its effect on people.

The Smile of Murugan by Michael Wood is an account of the author's time in Tamil Nadu in the mid-1990s and includes an interesting depiction of a video bus pilgrimage.

In *Where the Streets Lead* Sarayu Ahuja, an architect and town planner, takes the reader on a tour of several of South India's major settlements and cities, offering interesting insights into not just the structures, but the lives of the people who inhabit them.

In *Tranquebar* author Georgina Harding travels to this former Danish port on the Tamil Nadu coast with her young son. There is plenty of interesting background that reveals a part of Indian history often overlooked.

Third Class Ticket by Heather Wood is a funny and at times poignant account of a 15,000km journey by a group of poor Bengali villagers across India.

Novels

Keralan-born Arundhati Roy grabbed the headlines in 1997 by becoming the first Indian to win the Booker Prize for her novel *The God of Small Things*. The story, centring on the fate of seven-year-old twins, is set in Kerala which is evoked in beautiful, sensuous language.

One of India's best-known writers, RK Narayan, hails from Mysore and many of his stories centre on the fictitious South Indian town of Malgudi. His most well known works include: *Swami & His Friends, The Financial Expert, The Guide, Waiting for the Mahatma* and *Malgudi Days*.

A Matter of Time by Shashi Deshpande centres on the problems a middle-class family faces when the husband walks out. Deshpande, who hails from Bangalore, takes the reader back through several generations to demonstrate how family tradition affects contemporary behaviour.

Sharanpanjara, or Cage of Arrows, by a Karnatakan author who simply calls herself Triveni, is hailed as one of the great novels in the Kannada language (it's now available in English translation). The story centres on an upper-class Mysore woman facing the stigma of mental illness.

The Revised Kama Sutra by Richard Crasta takes an irreverant look at growing up in Mangalore in the 1960s and 1970s. It's a book that leaves you with a lasting insight into the local life of Mangalore and similar South Indian cities. More importantly it gives a first hand account of the tensions of growing up as an intelligent and well educated youngster with frustratingly few opportunities to shine.

Nectar in a Sieve by Kamala Markandaya is a harrowing, although at times uplifting, account of a woman's life in rural South India and the effect of industrialisation on traditional values and lifestyles.

The first part of Salman Rushdie's *The Moor's Last Sigh* is set in Kochi in Kerala.

History & Culture

The most established work on the history of this region is *A History of South India From Prehistoric Times to the Fall of Vijayanagar* by Nilakanta Sastri. Heavy going at times, it nevertheless provides comprehensive and detailed coverage. If you want a thorough introduction to Indian history general then look for the Pelican two volume *A History of India*. In the first volume Romila Thapar follows Indian history from 1000 BC to the coming of the Mughals in the 16th century. Volume two by Percival Spear follows the rise and fall of the Mughals through to India since Independence.

The Wonder That Was India by AL Basham gives good descriptions of the Indian civilisations, origins of the caste system and social customs, and detailed information on Hinduism, Buddhism and other religions in India. It is also very informative about art and architecture.

The Career and Legend of Vasco da Gama by Sanjay Subrahmanyam is one of the best recent investigations of the person who is credited with 'discovering' the sea route to India. For more background on the Indian Ocean trade Kenneth McPherson's *The Indian Ocean – A History of People and the Sea* provides a comprehensive overview.

Robert Sewell's *A Forgotten Empire* is a classic on the Vijayanagar Empire.

The Archaeological Survey of India publishes a series of booklets on major sites and works (eg *Chola Temples*) which are inexpensive and widely available in India.

India – A Celebration of Independence 1947 to 1997 is a photographic record of the first 50 years of Indian Independence. It begins with an image of Mahatma Gandhi and ends more than 200 images later with a picture of chaos at Bombay port. Some of the world's leading photographers including Henry Cartier-Bresson, Mary Ellen Mark and Sebastiao Salgado are represented in this evocative photographic study.

South Indian Customs by PV Jagadisa Ayyar seeks to explain a range of practices from the smearing of cow dung outside the home to the formation of snake images beneath the banyan tree.

The Anger of Aubergines by Bubul Sharma is subtitled Stories of Women and Food. It's an amusing and unique culinary analysis of social relationships, interspersed with mouth watering recipes.

The Remembered Village by MN Srinivas is an entertaining & revealing account of the author's field research during the late 1940s and early 1950s in a Karnataka village. Srinivas, one of India's most distinguished sociologists, has also written *Religion and Society Among the Coorgs of*

South India and *Social Change in Modern India*.

Architecture, Art, Music & Literature

The History of Architecture in India: From the Dawn of Civilisation to the End of the Raj by Christopher Tadgell provides a good overview including important sites in South India and has plenty of illustrations.

Architecture and Art of Southern India by George Michell provides details on the Vijayanagar Empire and its successors, encompassing a period of some 400 years. Michell's *The Hindu Temple* is an excellent introduction to the symbolism and evolution of temple architecture.

Indian Art by Roy Craven gives a succinct and well illustrated introduction to Indian art from earliest times to the Mughals. Basil Gray's *The Arts of India* is a more extensive survey of art forms with plenty of illustrations.

Appreciating Carnatic Music (Ganesh & Co) by Chitravina Ravi Kiran is available in India for Rs 125 and is aimed at helping those more familiar with western music get to grips with this South Indian art form. It's a compact little book with masses of useful information including a question-and-answer section.

Thirukkural Couplets is an English translation of a series of 1330 aphorisms by the famous Tamil scribe Thiruvalluvar. The poems are believed to be some 2000 years old.

Arts & Crafts

Arts and Crafts of India by Ilay Cooper & John Gillow covers the entire country, including information on folk arts in South India.

The Arts and Crafts of Tamilnadu by Nanitha Krishna with photography by VK Rajamani is a beautifully crafted volume that is much more than a coffee-table book. There is detailed information on a wide range of crafts including textiles, bronzes, terracotta, woodcraft, stone carving, basketry and painting. The text is supported by highly professional photography.

Religion

A Handbook of Living Religions edited by John R Hinnewls provides a succinct and readable summary of all the various religions you will find in India, including Christianity and Judaism.

The English series of Penguin paperbacks are among the best and are generally available in India. In particular, *Hinduism* by KM Sen is brief and to the point. If you want to read the Hindu holy books these are available in translations: *The Upanishads* and *The Bhagavad Gita*. *Hindu Mythology*, edited by Wendy O'Flaherty, is an interesting annotated collection of extracts from the Hindu holy books.

A Classical Dictionary of Hindu Mythology & Religion by John Dowson (Rupa, Delhi, 1987) is an Indian paperback reprint of an old English hardback. As the name suggests, it is in dictionary form and is one of the best sources for unravelling who's who in Hinduism.

Travels Through Sacred India by Roger Housden is a very readable account of popular and classical traditions and contains a gazetteer of sacred places plus a roundup of ashrams and retreats.

Am I a Hindu? is a Hinduism primer edited by Viswanathan which attempts to explore and explain the fundamental tenets of Hinduism through a discourse of questions and answers.

Why I am not a Hindu by Kancha Ilaiah is an insightful and provocative analysis of the caste system in modern India. Ilaiah is a reader in political science at Osmania University in Hyderabad. He is also a political activist with a long involvement in the movement for civil liberties and the rights of the Dalits.

The Riddle of Ganesha by Rankorath Karunakaran is a beautifully illustrated and informative book that explains some of the nuances and complexities of the many sides of the famous elephant headed god.

Hinduism, an Introduction by Shakunthala Jagannathan is a popular, well illustrated book that seeks to explain what Hinduism is all about. If you have no prior knowledge of the subject matter, this book is a good starting point.

The Marriage of East and West by Bede Griffiths is the famous book by the equally famous monk who lived for many decades in Tamil Nadu. The author examines the essence of eastern and western thought in an attempt to forge a fresh approach to spirituality.

Indian Mythology by Veronica Ions is a comprehensive and well illustrated book that covers all of the major religions in India.

Women

For an assessment of the position of women in Indian society, it is well worth getting hold of *May You Be the Mother of One Hundred Sons* by Elisabeth Bumiller. The author spent 3½ years in India in the late 1980s and interviewed Indian women from all walks of life. Her book offers some excellent insights into the plight of women in general and rural women in particular, especially with regard to arranged marriages, dowry deaths, *sati* and female infanticide.

Author Anees Jung was born in Hyderabad and brought up as a child in *purdah*. Her book *Unveiling India* touches on her own experiences and those of other women from both rural and urban backgrounds and explores various issues that affect women all over India today.

Caste As Woman by Vrinda Nabar looks at what feminism really means in India in a variety of contexts.

Tribal People (Adivasis)

The Todas of South India: A New Look by Anthony R Walker is a comprehensive study of the Toda people of South India. Illustrated with drawings and some photography, it's an accessible read on one of the most documented Indian tribal groups.

The scholarly *Tribes of India – The Struggle for Survival* by Christoph von Fürer-Haimendorf documents the sometimes shocking treatment of India's tribal peoples.

Blue Mountains Revisited: Cultural Studies

on the Nilgiri Hills edited by Paul Hockings is a fascinating collection of essays on culture, language and anthropology. It will appeal to the serious scholar with a particular interest in tribal customs and beliefs.

Environment & Wildlife

The Book of Indian Animals by SH Prater was first written in 1948 but remains one of the best overviews of India wildlife and includes colour illustrations. Unfortunately it's hard to get outside of India. The Insight Guide *Indian Wildlife* provides interesting background and plenty of colour illustrations. It's widely available.

The National Book Trust of India publishes a series of books on such topics as *Endangered Animals of India* by SM Nair, *Flowering Trees* by MS Randhawa, and *Our Environment* by Laeeq Futehally. Though mainly aimed at children the books are informative, illustrated, cheap (Rs 35) and easy to find in India.

The National Council for Science and Technology and the Bombay Natural History Society have jointly published a series of small books, all with black covers and priced at Rs 125. For a brief, readable overview of such topics as *Indian Elephants*, *Moths of India* and *Extinction is Forever* they are worth picking up.

Cheetal Walk: Living in the Wilderness by ERC Davidar describes the author's life among the elephants of the Nilgiri Hills and looks at how they can be saved from extinction.

This Fissured land: An Ecological History of India by Madhav Gadgil & Ramachandra Guha provides an excellent overview of ecological issues.

For a comprehensive list of titles on regional birdlife, see the illustrated Birds of South India section in the Facts about South India chapter.

WWF in Delhi has a bookshop which is a great source for works and information on wildlife and the environment; for their contact details see the boxed text 'Conservation Contacts' in the Facts about South India chapter.

General

An Indian Summer by James Cameron is an autobiographical account of Independence and South India.

Everybody Loves a Good Drought by Mumbai-based journalist Palagummi Sainath is a collection of reports on the living conditions of the rural poor. This excellent book, researched in the mid-1990s, provides an unsentimental insight into how the poorest of India's people survive and how well intentioned programs aimed at assisting them can lead to all sorts of absurdities. Many of the stories are from North/Central India, but some centre on Tamil Nadu.

For an interesting and perceptive examination of contemporary India get hold of *The Idea of India* by Sunil Khilnani.

The Vintage Book of Indian Writing 1947-1997 is a collection of essays and short stories edited by Salman Rushdie & Elizabeth West. It's one of the many books published in celebration of India's 50 years of independence and it contains some excellent writing by such acclaimed authors as Jawaharlal Nehru, Nayantara Sahgal, Anita Desai, Vikram Seth and Arundhati Roy.

The Garden of Life: An Introduction to the Healing Plants of India by Naveen Patnaik is a magnificently illustrated book on an intriguing subject. If you want to know the healing properties of such plants as basil, asparagus, hemp, coconut, lotus, mango, garlic, liquorice and many more, this book will help. The text is interspersed with fine drawings and some evocative poetry. The author is a founding member of the India Trust for Art and Cultural Heritage.

French anthropologist Chantal Boulanger has written a book about traditional sari styles in India, including South India, called *The Art of Indian Drape* (Shakti Press International). For details on this book and others written by this author visit the Web site at: www.devi.net for details.

Phrasebooks

Lonely Planet publishes phrasebooks for Hindi/Urdu, Bengali and Sinhalese. These will be useful if you plan to travel widely.

CD ROM

The following CD Roms are all available in India but only at major bookstores. *India: A Multimedia Journey* includes videos, slides, maps and travelling tips. *Karnataka* (very expensive at Rs 2500) includes a luscious coffee table book about the state. *India Mystique* highlights Indian philosophy, history and religion. *Tarla Dalal's Desi Khana: The Best of Indian Vegetarian Cooking* provides a step-by-step guide to more than 140 recipes from all over India. *Indian Wildlife* has more than 650 pictures and slides as well as information about more than 30 national parks, including some in South India. *Kerala: The Green Symphony* (Indus Media) has plenty of cultural, geographical and historical information, and lots of graphics.

ONLINE SERVICES

There are numerous online services relevant to India, but services come and go with some frequency. The Lonely Planet Web site (www.lonelyplanet.com) has up-to-date advice, photographs, travel tales and general information on travelling throughout the region, with many links to other relevant sites.

For news it's worth checking out the Web sites run by India's best-known newspapers and magazines. They include:

- www.asian.age.com (the Asian Age)
- www.hinduonline.com or www.the-hindu.com (the Hindu)
- www.india-today.com (India Today)

NEWSPAPERS & MAGAZINES

Of the English-language dailies the *Asian Age* is arguably the best in South India. Its foreign coverage is excellent. National newspapers include the *Times of India*, the *Hindu*, and the *Indian Express*. They are printed in Bangalore and carry a section dedicated to the particular states in which they are distributed.

The *Hindu* is one of the more comprehensive papers and has an excellent literary supplement on Sunday that examines books published both in and outside India. The

Deccan Herald available throughout South India appears to have little critical comment and virtually no world news. The *Economic Times* is a serious publication for those interested in business and economic analysis. The *Indian Review of Books* is published monthly in Chennai.

There's a very wide range of general interest magazines published in English in India. *India Today* is an excellent national magazine available from most news stands. After 21 years of publishing fortnightly, the magazine became weekly from June 1997. It costs Rs 15. *Frontline* is a fortnightly magazine published by the *Hindu* newspaper group. It has comprehensive coverage of national, political and social events as well as a reasonable foreign news section. It also costs Rs 15.

Gentleman is a glossy magazine for male yuppies. *Sportstar*, published by the *Hindu* group, is a weekly national magazine, containing reams of information on cricket. *Better Photography* is a high quality, monthly national magazine published in Mumbai. *Biznet* is a self-described 'cyber mag' dedicated to Web surfers and is published in Mumbai. In addition to feature articles and cyber news it contains reviews and addresses of Indian and foreign Web sites. It costs Rs 30 and is a 'sister' publication to *Gentleman*.

Time and *Newsweek* are only available in the main cities, and anyway, once you've become used to Indian prices they seem very expensive.

You can also find newspapers like the *Herald Tribune* and *Guardian* and magazines like *Der Spiegel* and its English, French and Italian clones in the major cities and at expensive hotels but, again, they're not cheap.

RADIO & TV

Radio programs can be heard on All India Radio (AIR) which provides the usual interviews, music and news features. There is also an FM band. Some programs are in English. Details on programs and are found in the major English-language dailies.

Satellite TV runs 24 hours and includes up to 30 channels including BBC, CNN, Discovery and Asianet. Various local channels broadcast in the vernacular. The national broadcaster is Doordarshan.

PHOTOGRAPHY & VIDEO
Film & Equipment

Colour print film processing facilities are readily available in larger cities. Film is relatively cheap and the quality is usually (but not always) good. Kodak 100 ASA colour print film costs around Rs 140 for a roll of 36 exposures. Always check the use-by date on local film stock. Heat and humidity can play havoc with film, even if the use-by date hasn't been exceeded. Developing costs are around Rs 25, plus Rs 5 per photo for printing.

If you're taking slides bring the film with you. Colour slide film is only available in the major cities. Colour slides can be developed only in Delhi, and quality is not guaranteed – take your film home with you. Kodachrome and other 'includes developing' film will have to be sent overseas.

Remember, if you buy film from street hawkers you do so at your own risk. Some travellers report that old, useless film is loaded into new-looking canisters. The hapless tourist only discovers the trick when the film is developed back home.

Equipment

A UV filter permanently fitted to your lens will not only cut down ultraviolet light, but will protect your lens. Spare batteries should be carried at all times. Serious photographers will consider bringing a tripod and fast film (400 ASA) for temple and fort interior shots. It might be a good idea not to carry your gear round in a flash new bag. Either get an old battered-looking one or put your expensive bag inside a less salubrious carrier.

Photography

In general, photography is best done in the early morning and late afternoon. The stark midday sun eliminates shadows, rendering less depth to your photographs.

Film manufacturers warn that, once exposed, film should be developed as quickly as possible; in practice the film seems to last, even in South India's summer heat, without deterioration for months. Try to keep your film cool, and protect it in water and air-proof containers if you're travelling during the monsoon. Silica gel sachets distributed around your gear will help to absorb moisture. As places such as coastal Kerala can be very humid year-round, silica is useful any season.

It's worthwhile investing in a lead-lined (X-ray proof) bag, as repeated exposure to X-ray (even so-called 'film proof' X-ray) can damage film. *Never* put your film in baggage which will be placed in the cargo holds of aeroplanes. It will probably be subjected to large doses of X-ray which will spoil or completely ruin it.

Restrictions

Be careful what you photograph. India is touchy about places of military importance – this can include train stations, bridges, airports and military installations. Some temples prohibit photography in the *mandapa* (forechamber of a temple) and inner sanctum.

At Mysore (Karnataka) you are not allowed to take a camera inside the palace itself at all; you must check it in at a special counter just inside the front gate. If in doubt, ask. Some temples, and numerous forts and palaces, levy a fee to bring a still camera or video camera onto the premises. See the relevant state chapters for more information.

Photographing People

Some people are more than happy to be photographed, but care should be taken when pointing cameras at women. Again, if in doubt, ask.

A zoom is a less intrusive means of taking portraits – even when you've obtained permission to take a portrait, shoving a lens in your subject's face can be disconcerting. A reasonable distance between you and your subject will help to reduce your subject's

discomfort, and will result in more natural shots.

Video

Properly used, a video camera can give a fascinating record of your holiday. As well as videoing the obvious things – sunsets, spectacular views – remember to record some of the everyday details of life in South India. Often the most interesting things occur when you're actually intent on filming something else. Remember too that, unlike still photography, video 'flows' – so, for example, you can shoot scenes of countryside rolling past the train window, to give an overall impression that isn't possible with ordinary photos.

Video cameras these days have amazingly sensitive microphones, and you might be surprised how much sound will be picked up. This can also be a problem if there is a lot of ambient noise – filming by the side of a busy road might seem OK when you do it, but viewing it back home might simply give you a deafening cacophony of traffic noise.

One good rule to follow for beginners is to try to film in long takes, and don't move the camera around too much. Otherwise, your video could well make your viewers seasick! If your camera has a stabiliser, you can use it to obtain good footage while travelling on various means of transport, even on bumpy roads. And remember, you're on holiday – don't let the video take over your life and turn your trip into a Cecil B de Mille production.

It is possible to obtain video cartridges easily in South India's large towns and cities, but make sure you buy the correct format. It is usually worth buying at least a few cartridges duty-free to start off your trip.

Finally, remember to follow the same rules regarding people's sensitivities as for still photography – having a video camera shoved in their face is probably even more annoying and offensive for locals than a still camera. Always ask permission first.

TIME

India is 5½ hours ahead of GMT/UTC, 4½ hours behind Australian EST and 10½ hours ahead of American EST. It is officially known as IST – Indian Standard Time.

ELECTRICITY

The electric current is 230-240V AC, 50 cycles. Electricity is widely available in the main towns and cities and tourist destinations. Sockets are of a three round-pin variety, similar (but not identical) to European sockets. European round-pin plugs will go into the sockets, but as the pins on Indian plugs are somewhat thicker, the fit is loose and connection is not always guaranteed.

Power cuts ('load shedding') and 'brown outs' (partial power cuts, ie when the power drops below normal levels, dimming lights and slowing fans, etc) are common in Karnataka, Kerala, Kodaikanal (Tamil Nadu) and the Andaman & Nicobar Islands in particular, but can occur anywhere in South India. If you are bringing sensitive electronic equipment, eg a notebook computer, a voltage stabiliser is essential.

You can buy small immersion elements, perfect for boiling water for tea or coffee, for Rs 50. For about Rs 70 you can buy electric mosquito zappers. These are the type that take chemical tablets which melt and give off deadly vapours (deadly for the mosquito, that is). There are many different brands and they are widely available.

WEIGHTS & MEASURES

Although India is officially metricated, imperial weights and measures are still used in some areas of commerce. Some of the measures you will frequently come across in the media are: one lakh (100 thousand); and one crore (10 million). A conversion chart is included on the inside back cover of this book.

LAUNDRY

All of the top-end hotels, most of the mid-range hotels and some of the budget hotels and guest houses offer a laundry service, and costs are minimal.

HEALTH

Travel health depends on your predeparture preparations, your daily health care while

---

Medical Kit Checklist

Consider taking a basic medical kit including:

❏ **Aspirin or Paracetamol** (acetaminophen in the US) – for pain or fever

❏ **Antihistamine** (such as Benadryl) – useful as a decongestant for colds and allergies, to ease the itch from insect bites or stings, and to help prevent motion sickness. Antihistamines may cause sedation and interact with alcohol so care should be taken when using them; take one you know and have used before, if possible

❏ **Antibiotics** – useful if you're travelling well off the beaten track, but they must be prescribed; carry the prescription with you

❏ **Loperamide** – (eg Imodium) or Lomotil for diarrhoea; prochlorperazine (eg Stemetil) or metaclopramide (eg Maxalon) for nausea and vomiting

❏ **Rehydration mixture** – for treatment of severe diarrhoea; particularly important when travelling with children

❏ **Antiseptic** such as povidone-iodine (eg Betadine) – for cuts and grazes

❏ **Multivitamins** – especially for long trips when dietary vitamin intake may be inadequate

❏ **Calamine lotion** or aluminium sulphate spray (eg Stingose) – to ease irritation from bites or stings

❏ **Bandages** and Band-aids

❏ **Scissors**, tweezers and a thermometer (note that mercury thermometers are prohibited by airlines)

❏ **Cold and flu tablets** and throat lozenges. Pseudoephedrine hydrochloride (Sudafed) may be useful if flying with a cold, to avoid ear damage

❏ **Insect repellent**, sunscreen, chap stick and water purification tablets

❏ A couple of **syringes**, in case you need injections in a country with medical hygiene problems. Ask your doctor for a note explaining why they have been prescribed travelling and how you handle any medical problem that does develop. While the potential dangers can seem quite frightening, in reality few travellers experience anything more than upset stomachs.

Predeparture Planning

Immunisations For some countries no immunisations are necessary, but the further off the beaten track you go the more necessary it is to take precautions. Be aware that there is often a greater risk of disease with children and in pregnancy.

Plan ahead for getting your vaccinations: some of them require more than one injection, while some vaccinations should not be given together. It is recommended you seek medical advice at least six weeks before travel.

Record all vaccinations on an International Health Certificate, available from your doctor or government health department.

Discuss your requirements with your doctor, but vaccinations you should consider for this trip include:

Hepatitis A The most common travel-acquired illness after diarrhoea, Hepatitis A can put you out of action for weeks. Havrix 1440 and VAQTA are vaccinations which provide long term immunity (possibly more than 10 years) after an initial injection and a booster at six to 12 months. Gamma globulin is a ready-made antibody collected from blood donations. It should be given close to departure because, depending on the dose, it only protects for two to six months.

A combined hepatitis A and hepatitis B vaccination, Twinrix, is also available. This combined vaccination is recommended for people wanting protection against both types of viral hepatitis. Three injections over a six-month period are required.

Typhoid This is an important vaccination to have for travel to South India. It's available either as an injection or oral capsules.

Diphtheria & Tetanus Diphtheria can be a fatal throat infection and tetanus can be a fatal wound infection. Everyone should have these vaccinations. After an initial course of three injections, boosters are necessary every 10 years.

Hepatitis B This disease is spread by blood or by sexual activity. Travellers who should consider a hepatitis B vaccination include those visiting countries where there are known to be many carriers, where blood transfusions may not be adequately screened or where sexual contact is a possibility. It involves three injections, the quickest course being over three weeks with a booster at 12 months.

Polio Polio is a serious, easily transmitted disease, still prevalent in India. Everyone should keep up to date with this vaccination. A booster every 10 years maintains immunity.

Yellow Fever There is no risk of becoming infected with yellow fever in South India, but if you are arriving from a yellow-fever infected area (certain countries in Africa and South America) you will need to prove that you have had the jab.

Rabies Vaccination should be considered by those who will spend a month or longer in South India, especially if they are cycling, handling animals, caving, travelling to remote areas, or for children (who may not report a bite). Pretravel rabies vaccination involves having three injections over 21 to 28 days. If someone who has been vaccinated is bitten or scratched by an animal they will require two booster injections of vaccine, those not vaccinated require more.

Japanese B Encephalitis This mosquito-borne disease is not common in travellers, but occurs in South India. Consider the vaccination if spending a month or longer in a rural area, making repeated trips to rural areas or visiting during an epidemic. It involves three injections over 30 days. The vaccine is expensive and has been associated with serious allergic reactions so the decision to have it should be balanced against the risk of contracting the illness.

Tuberculosis TB risk to travellers is usually very low. For those who will be living with or closely associated with local people in rural South India, there may be some risk. As most healthy adults do not develop symptoms, a skin test before and after travel to determine whether exposure has occurred may be considered. A vaccination is recommended for children living in these areas for three months or more.

Malaria Medication Antimalarial drugs do not prevent you from being infected but kill the malaria parasites during a stage in their development and significantly reduce the risk of becoming very ill or dying. Expert advice on medication should be sought, as there are many factors to consider including the area to be visited, the risk of exposure to malaria-carrying mosquitoes, the side effects of medication, your medical history and whether you are a child or adult or pregnant. Travellers to isolated area in high-risk countries may like to carry a treatment dose of medication for use if symptoms occur.

Health Insurance Make sure that you have adequate health insurance. See Travel Insurance under Visas & Documents earlier in this chapter for details.

Travel Health Guides If you are planning to be away or travelling in remote areas for a long period of time, you may like to consider taking a more detailed health guide.

Staying Healthy in Asia, Africa & Latin America, Dirk Schroeder, Moon Publications, 1994. Probably the best all-round guide to carry; it's detailed and well organised.
Travellers' Health, Dr Richard Dawood, Oxford University Press, 1995. Comprehensive, easy to read, authoritative and highly recommended, although it's rather large to lug around.
Where There is No Doctor, David Werner, Macmillan, 1994. A very detailed guide intended for someone, such as a Peace Corps worker, going to work in an underdeveloped country.

Travel with Children, Maureen Wheeler, Lonely Planet Publications, 1995. Includes advice on travel health for younger children.

There are also a number of excellent travel health sites on the Internet. From Lonely Planet's home page there are links at www.lonelyplanet.com/weblinks/wlprep.htm to the World Health Organisation and the US Center for Diseases Control & Prevention.

Other Preparations Make sure you're healthy before you start travelling. If you are going on a long trip make sure your teeth are OK. If you wear glasses take a spare pair and your prescription.

Nutrition

If your food is poor or limited in availability, if you're travelling hard and fast and therefore missing meals, or if you simply lose your appetite, you can soon start to lose weight and place your health at risk.

Make sure your diet is well balanced. Cooked eggs, pulses and lentils (dal) and nuts are all safe ways to get protein. Fruit you can peel (bananas, oranges or mandarins for example) is usually safe (melons can harbour bacteria in their flesh and are best avoided) and a good source of vitamins. Try to eat plenty of grains (including rice) and bread. Remember that although food is generally safer if it is cooked well, overcooked food loses much of its nutritional value. If your diet isn't well balanced or if your food intake is insufficient, it's a good idea to take vitamin and iron pills.

In hot climates make sure you drink enough – don't rely on feeling thirsty to indicate when you should drink. Not needing to urinate or small amounts of very dark yellow urine is a danger sign. Always carry a water bottle with you on long trips. Excessive sweating can lead to loss of salt and therefore muscle cramping. Salt tablets are not a good idea as a preventative, but adding salt to food can help.

If you require a particular medication take an adequate supply, as it may not be available locally. Take part of the packaging showing the generic name, rather than the brand, which will make getting replacements easier. It's a good idea to have a legible prescription or letter from your doctor to show that you legally use the medication to avoid any problems.

Basic Rules

Food There is an old colonial adage which says: 'If you can cook it, boil it or peel it you can eat it … otherwise forget it'. Vegetables and fruit should be washed with purified water or peeled where possible. Beware of ice cream which is sold in the street or anywhere it might have been melted and refrozen; if there's any doubt (eg a power cut in the last day or two) steer well clear. Shellfish such as mussels, oysters and clams should be avoided as well as undercooked meat (in fact it's generally safer to avoid meat altogether, and very easy to do so in vegetarian South India). Steaming does not make shellfish safe for eating.

If a place looks clean and well run and the vendor also looks clean and healthy, then the food is probably safe. In general, places that are well patronised will be fine, while empty restaurants are questionable. The food in busy restaurants is cooked and eaten quite quickly with little standing around and is probably not reheated.

Water The No 1 rule is *be careful of the water* and especially ice. If you don't know for certain that the water is safe assume the worst. Reputable brands of bottled water or soft drinks are generally fine, although in some places bottles may be refilled with tap water. Only use water from containers with a serrated seal – not tops or corks. Take care with fruit juice, particularly if water may have been added. Milk should be treated with suspicion as it is often unpasteurised, though boiled milk is fine if it is kept hygienically. Tea or coffee should also be OK, since the water should have been boiled.

Water Purification The simplest way of purifying water is to boil it thoroughly.

Consider purchasing a water filter for a long trip. There are two main kinds of filter. Total filters take out all parasites, bacteria and viruses, and make water safe to drink. They are often expensive, but they can be more cost effective than buying bottled water. Simple filters (which can even be a nylon mesh bag) take out dirt and larger foreign bodies from the water so that chemical solutions work much more effectively; if water is dirty, chemical solutions may not work at all.

It's very important when buying a filter to read the specifications, so that you know exactly what it removes from the water and what it doesn't. Simple filtering will not remove all dangerous organisms, so if you cannot boil water it should be treated chemically. Chlorine tablets (Puritabs, Steritabs or other brand names) will kill many pathogens, but not such parasites as giardia and amoebic cysts. Iodine is more effective in purifying water and is available in tablet form (such as Potable Aqua). Follow the directions carefully and remember that too much iodine can be harmful.

Medical Problems & Treatment

Self-diagnosis and treatment can be risky, so you should always seek medical help. Although we do give drug dosages in this section, they are for emergency use only. Correct diagnosis is vital.

An embassy, consulate or five-star hotel can usually recommend a good place to go for advice. In some places standards of medical attention are so low that for some ailments the best advice is to get on a plane and go somewhere else. Antibiotics should ideally be administered only under medical supervision. Take only the recommended dose at the prescribed intervals and use the whole course, even if the illness seems to be cured earlier. Stop immediately if there are any serious reactions and don't use the antibiotic at all if you are unsure that you have the correct one. Some people are allergic to commonly prescribed antibiotics such as penicillin or sulpha drugs; carry this information when travelling, eg on a bracelet.

Hospitals Although India does have a few excellent hospitals such as the Christian Medical College Hospital in Vellore, Tamil Nadu, the Breach Candy Hospital in Mumbai and the All India Institute of Medical Sciences in Delhi, most Indian cities do not have the quality of medical care available in the west. Usually hospitals run by western missionaries have better facilities than government hospitals where long queues are common. Unless you have something very unusual, these Christian-run hospitals are the best places to head for in an emergency.

India also has many qualified doctors with their own private clinics which can be quite good and, in some cases, as good as anything available anywhere in the world. The usual fee for a clinic visit is about Rs 100; Rs 250 for a specialist. Home calls usually cost about Rs 150.

Environmental Hazards
Fungal Infections In hot, humid South India, fungal infections can be a problem. They are usually found on the scalp, between the toes or fingers, in the groin and on the body (ringworm). You get ringworm (which is a fungal infection, not a worm) from infected animals or other people. Moisture encourages these infections.

To prevent fungal infections wear loose, comfortable clothes, avoid artificial fibres, wash frequently and dry carefully. If you do get an infection, wash the infected area at least daily with a disinfectant or medicated soap and water, and rinse and dry well. Apply an antifungal cream or powder like tolnaftate (Tinaderm). Try to expose the infected area to air or sunlight as much as possible and wash all towels and underwear in hot water, change them often and let them dry in the sun.

Heat Exhaustion Dehydration and salt deficiency can cause heat exhaustion. Take time to acclimatise to high temperatures, drink sufficient liquids and do not do anything too physically demanding.

Salt deficiency is characterised by fatigue, lethargy, headaches, giddiness and muscle cramps; salt tablets may help, but adding extra salt to your food is better.

Heatstroke This serious, occasionally fatal, condition can occur if the body's heat-regulating mechanism breaks down and the body temperature rises to dangerous levels. Long, continuous periods of exposure to high temperatures and insufficient fluids can leave you vulnerable to heatstroke.

The symptoms are feeling unwell, not sweating very much (or at all) and a high body temperature ($39°C$ to $41°C$ or $102°F$ to $106°F$). Where sweating has ceased the skin becomes flushed and red. Severe, throbbing headaches and lack of coordination will also occur, and the sufferer may be confused or aggressive. Eventually the victim will become delirious or convulse. Hospitalisation is essential, but in the interim get victims out of the sun, remove their clothing, cover them with a wet sheet or towel and then fan continually. Give fluids if they are conscious.

Jet Lag Jet lag is experienced when a person travels by air across more than three time

---

Everyday Health
Normal body temperature is up to $37°C$ or $98.6°F$; more than $2°C$ ($4°F$) higher indicates a high fever. The normal adult pulse rate is 60 to 100 per minute (children 80 to 100, babies 100 to 140). As a general rule the pulse increases about 20 beats per minute for each $°C$ ($2°F$) rise in fever.

Respiration (breathing) rate is also an indicator of illness. Count the number of breaths per minute: between 12 and 20 is normal for adults and older children (up to 30 for younger children, 40 for babies). People with a high fever or serious respiratory illness breathe more quickly than normal. More than 40 shallow breaths a minute may indicate pneumonia.

zones (each time zone usually represents a one-hour time difference). It occurs because many of the functions of the human body (such as temperature, pulse rate and emptying of the bladder and bowels) are regulated by internal 24-hour cycles. When we travel long distances rapidly, our bodies take time to adjust to the 'new time' of our destination, and we may experience fatigue, disorientation, insomnia, anxiety, impaired concentration and loss of appetite. These effects will usually be gone within three days of arrival, but to minimise the impact of jet lag:

- Rest for a couple of days prior to departure
- Try to select flight schedules that minimise sleep deprivation; arriving late in the day means you can go to sleep soon after you arrive. For very long flights, try to organise a stopover
- Avoid excessive eating (which bloats the stomach) and alcohol (which causes dehydration) during the flight. Instead, drink plenty of non-carbonated, non-alcoholic drinks such as fruit juice or water – consider taking your own supply on board
- Avoid smoking
- Make yourself comfortable by wearing loose-fitting clothes and perhaps bringing an eye mask and ear plugs to help you sleep
- Try to sleep at the appropriate time for the time zone you are travelling to

Motion Sickness Eating lightly before and during a trip will reduce the chances of motion sickness. If you are prone to motion sickness try to find a place that minimises movement – near the wing on aircraft, close to midships on boats, near the centre on buses. Fresh air usually helps; reading and cigarette smoke don't. Motion-sickness preparations, which can cause drowsiness, have to be taken before the trip commences. Ginger (available in capsule form) and peppermint (including mint-flavoured sweets) are natural preventatives.

Prickly Heat Prickly heat is an itchy rash caused by excessive perspiration trapped under the skin. It usually strikes people who have just arrived in a hot climate. Keeping cool, bathing often, drying the skin and

using a mild talcum or prickly heat powder or resorting to air-conditioning may help.

Sunburn In South India's hot climate you can get sunburnt surprisingly quickly, even through cloud. Use a sunscreen with a high SPF, wear a hat, and avoid exposure between the hours of 11 am and 3 pm. Calamine lotion or stingose are good for mild sunburn. Protect your eyes with good quality sunglasses, particularly when you're at the beach, where the glare is particularly harsh.

Infectious Diseases
Diarrhoea Simple things like a change of water, food or climate can all cause a mild bout of diarrhoea, but a few rushed toilet trips with no other symptoms is not indicative of a major problem.

Dehydration is the main danger with any diarrhoea, particularly in children or the elderly as dehydration can occur quite quickly. Under all circumstances *fluid replacement* (at least equal to the volume being lost) is the most important thing to remember. Weak black tea with a little sugar; soda water, or soft drinks allowed to go flat and diluted 50% with clean water are all good. With severe diarrhoea a rehydrating solution is preferable to replace minerals and salts lost. Commercially available oral rehydration salts (ORS) are very useful; add them to boiled or bottled water. In an emergency you can make up a solution of six teaspoons of sugar and a half teaspoon of salt to a litre of boiled or bottled water. Urine is the best guide to the adequacy of replacement – if you have small amounts of concentrated urine, you need to drink more. Keep drinking small amounts often. Stick to a bland diet as you recover.

Lomotil or Imodium can be used to bring relief from the symptoms, although they do not actually cure the problem. Only use these drugs if you do not have access to toilets, eg if you *must* travel. For children under 12 years Lomotil and Imodium are not recommended. Do not use these drugs if the person has a high fever or is severely dehydrated.

In certain situations antibiotics may be required: diarrhoea with blood or mucus (dysentery), any diarrhoea with fever, persistent diarrhoea not improving after 48 hours and severe diarrhoea. In these situations gut-paralysing drugs like Imodium or Lomotil should be avoided.

A stool test is necessary to diagnose which kind of dysentery you have, so you should seek medical help urgently. Where this is not possible the recommended drugs for dysentery are norfloxacin 400mg twice daily for three days or ciprofloxacin 500mg twice daily for five days. These are not recommended for children or pregnant women. The drug of choice for children would be co-trimoxazole (Bactrim, Septrin, Resprim) with dosage dependent on weight. A five-day course is given. Ampicillin or amoxycillin may be given in pregnancy, but medical care is necessary.

Amoebic dysentery is more gradual in onset than other types of dysentry, with cramping abdominal pain and vomiting less likely; fever may not be present. It will persist until treated and can recur and cause other health problems.

Giardiasis is another type of diarrhoea. The parasite causing this intestinal disorder is present in contaminated water. The symptoms are stomach cramps, nausea, a bloated stomach, watery, foul-smelling diarrhoea and frequent gas. Giardiasis can appear several weeks after you have been exposed to the parasite. The symptoms may disappear for a few days and then return; this can go on for several weeks. Tinidazole, known as Fasigyn, or metronidazole (Flagyl) are the recommended drugs. Treatment is a 2gm single dose of Fasigyn or 250mg of Flagyl three times daily for five to 10 days.

Hepatitis Hepatitis is a general term for inflammation of the liver. It is a common disease worldwide. The symptoms are fever, chills, headache, fatigue, feelings of weakness and aches and pains, followed by loss of appetite, nausea, vomiting, abdominal pain, dark urine, light-coloured faeces, jaundiced (yellow) skin and the whites of the eyes may turn yellow. **Hepatitis A** is transmitted by contaminated food and drinking water. The disease poses a real threat to the western traveller. You should seek medical advice, but there is not much you can do apart from resting, drinking lots of fluids, eating lightly and avoiding fatty foods. People who have had hepatitis should avoid alcohol for some time after the illness, as the liver needs time to recover.

Hepatitis E is transmitted in the same way, and can be very serious in pregnant women.

There are almost 300 million chronic carriers of **Hepatitis B** in the world. It is spread through contact with infected blood, blood products or body fluids, for example through sexual contact, unsterilised needles and blood transfusions, or contact with blood via small breaks in the skin. Other risk situations include having a shave, tattoo, or having your body pierced with contaminated equipment. The symptoms of type B may be severe and may lead to long term problems. **Hepatitis D** is spread in the same way, but the risk is mainly in shared needles.

Hepatitis C can lead to chronic liver disease. The virus is spread by contact with blood usually via contaminated transfusions or shared needles. Avoiding these is the only means of prevention.

HIV & AIDS HIV, the Human Immunodeficiency Virus, develops into AIDS, Acquired Immune Deficiency Syndrome, which is a fatal disease. HIV is a major problem in many places including India which has more AIDS sufferers than any other country. Goa has up to three times the national average of HIV cases, an estimated 20,000. Thirty-five per cent of Goa's prostitutes are HIV positive.

By the year 2001 there could be as many as 50 million Indians infected with the virus. Any exposure to blood, blood products or body fluids may put the individual at risk.

The disease is often transmitted through sexual contact or dirty needles – vaccinations, acupuncture, tattooing and body piercing can be potentially as dangerous as intravenous drug use. HIV/AIDS can also be spread through infected blood transfusions; some developing countries cannot afford to screen blood used for transfusions.

If you do need an injection, ask to see the syringe unwrapped in front of you, or take a syringe pack with you.

Fear of HIV infection should never preclude treatment for serious medical conditions.

Intestinal Worms These parasites are most common in rural, wet areas of South India. The different worms have different ways of infecting people. Some may be ingested by eating such food as undercooked meat; some enter through your skin (particularly bare feet). Infestations may not show up for some time, although they are generally not serious, if left untreated some can cause severe health problems later. Consider having a stool test when you return home to check for these and determine the appropriate treatment.

Typhoid Typhoid fever is a dangerous gut infection caused by contaminated water and food. Medical help must be sought.

In its early stages sufferers may feel they have a bad cold or flu on the way, as early symptoms are a headache, body aches and a fever which rises a little each day until it is around 40°C (104°F) or more. The victim's pulse is often slow relative to the degree of fever present – unlike a normal fever where the pulse increases. There may also be vomiting, abdominal pain, diarrhoea or constipation.

In the second week the high fever and slow pulse continue and a few pink spots may appear on the body; trembling, delirium, weakness, weight loss and dehydration may occur. Complications such as pneumonia, perforated bowel or meningitis may occur.

The fever should be treated by keeping the victim cool and giving them fluids to prevent dehydration. Ciprofloxacin 750mg twice a day for 10 days is good for adults.

Chloramphenicol is recommended in many countries. The adult dosage is two 250mg capsules, four times a day. Children aged between eight and 12 years should have half the adult dose; and younger children one-third the adult dose.

Insect-Borne Diseases
Filariasis, lyme disease, leishmaniasis and typhus are all insect-borne diseases, but they do not pose a great risk to travellers. For more information on them see Less Common Diseases at the end of the health section.

Malaria This serious and potentially fatal disease is spread by mosquito bites. It is extremely important to avoid mosquito bites and to take tablets to prevent this disease. Symptoms range from fever, chills and sweating, headache, diarrhoea and abdominal pains to a vague feeling of ill-health. Seek medical help immediately if malaria is suspected. Without treatment malaria can rapidly become more serious and can be fatal.

If medical care is not available, malaria tablets can be used for treatment. You need to use a malaria tablet which is different to the one you were taking when you contracted malaria. The treatment dosages are mefloquine (three 250mg tablets and a further two six hours later), or fansidar (single dose of three tablets). If you were previously taking mefloquine and cannot obtain fansidar then other alternatives are halofantrine (three doses of two 250mg tablets every six hours) or quinine sulphate (600mg every six hours). There is a greater risk of side effects with these dosages than in normal use if used with mefloquine, so medical advice is preferable.

Travellers are advised to prevent mosquito bites at all times. The main strategies are:

- wear light-coloured clothing
- wear long trousers and long-sleeved shirts
- use mosquito repellents containing the compound DEET on exposed areas (prolonged overuse of DEET may be harmful, especially to children, but its use is considered preferable to being bitten by disease-transmitting mosquitoes)
- avoid wearing perfumes or aftershave
- use a mosquito net impregnated with mosquito repellent (permethrin) – it may be worth taking your own
- impregnating clothes with permethrin effectively deters mosquitoes and other insects

Dengue Fever This viral disease is transmitted by mosquitoes and occurs mainly in tropical and subtropical areas of the world. Generally, there is a small risk to travellers except during epidemics, which are usually seasonal (during and just after the rainy season).

The *Aedes aegypti* mosquito which transmits the dengue virus is most active during the day, unlike the malaria mosquito, and is found mainly in urban areas, in and around human dwellings.

Signs and symptoms of dengue fever include a sudden onset of high fever, headache, joint and muscle pains (hence its old name, 'breakbone fever') and nausea and vomiting. A rash of small red spots appears three to four days after the onset of fever. Dengue is commonly mistaken for other infectious diseases, including influenza. Infection can be diagnosed by a blood test.

You should seek medical attention if you think you may be infected. There is no specific treatment for dengue. Aspirin should be avoided, as it increases the risk of haemorrhaging. Recovery may be prolonged, with tirednesss lasting for several weeks. Severe complications are rare in travellers, but include dengue haemorrhagic fever (DHF), which can be fatal without prompt medical treatment. DHF is thought to be a result of second infection due to a different strain (there are four major strains), and usually affects residents of the country rather than travellers.

There is no vaccine against dengue fever. The best prevention is to avoid mosquito bites at all times – see the malaria section for more details.

Japanese B Encephalitis This viral infection of the brain is transmitted by mosquitoes. Most cases occur in rural areas as the virus exists in pigs and wading birds. Symptoms include fever, headache and alteration in consciousness. Hospitalisation is needed for correct diagnosis and treatment. There is a high mortality rate among those who have symptoms; of those that survive many are intellectually disabled.

Cuts, Bites & Stings
Rabies is passed through animal bites. See Less Common Diseases for details of this disease.

Bedbugs & Lice Bedbugs live in various places, but particularly in dirty mattresses and bedding, evidenced by spots of blood on bedclothes or on the wall. Bedbugs leave itchy bites in neat rows. Calamine lotion or Stingose spray may help.

All lice cause itching and discomfort. They make themselves at home in your hair (head lice), your clothing (body lice) or in your pubic hair (crabs). You catch lice through direct contact with infected people or by sharing combs, clothing and the like. Powder or shampoo treatment will kill the lice and infected clothing should then be washed in very hot, soapy water and left in the sun to dry.

Insect Bites & Stings Bee and wasp stings are usually painful rather than dangerous. However in people who are allergic to them severe breathing difficulties may occur and require urgent medical care. Calamine lotion or Stingose spray will give relief and ice packs will reduce the pain and swelling.

There are some spiders with dangerous bites but antivenenes are usually available. Scorpion stings are notoriously painful and can actually be fatal. Scorpions often shelter in shoes or clothing.

There are various fish and other sea creatures which can sting or bite dangerously or which are dangerous to eat. Again, follow local advice and warnings.

Cuts & Scratches Wash well and treat any cut with an antiseptic such as povidone-iodine. Where possible avoid bandages and sticking plasters, which can keep wounds wet. Coral cuts are notoriously slow to heal and if they are not adequately cleaned, small pieces of coral can become embedded in the wound.

Jellyfish Local advice is the best way of avoiding contact with these sea creatures which have stinging tentacles. Dousing in vinegar will de-activate any stingers which have not 'fired'. Calamine lotion, antihistamines and analgesics may reduce the reaction and relieve the pain.

Leeches & Ticks Leeches are present throughout South India's mountain ranges and forested areas; they attach themselves to your skin to suck your blood. Trekkers often get them on their legs or in their boots. Salt or a lighted cigarette end will make them fall off. Do not pull them off, as the bite is then more likely to become infected. Clean and apply pressure if the point of attachment is bleeding. An insect repellent may keep them away.

You should always check all over your body if you have been walking through a potentially tick-infested area as ticks can cause skin infections and other more serious diseases. If a tick is found attached, press down around the tick's head with tweezers, grab the head and gently pull upwards. Avoid pulling the rear of the body as this may squeeze the tick's gut contents through the attached mouth parts into the skin, increasing the risk of infection and disease. Smearing chemicals on the tick will not make it let go and is not recommended.

Snakes There are a few species of poisonous snakes in South India, including the deadly king cobra. To minimise your chances of being bitten always wear boots, socks and long trousers when walking through undergrowth where snakes may be present. Don't put your hands into holes and crevices, and be careful when collecting firewood.

Snake bites do not cause instantaneous death and antivenenes are usually available. Immediately wrap the bitten limb tightly, as you would for a sprained ankle, and then attach a splint to immobilise it. Keep the victim still and seek medical help, if possible with the dead snake for identification. Don't attempt to catch the snake if there is a possibility of being bitten again. Tourniquets and sucking out the poison are now comprehensively discredited.

Less Common Diseases
The following diseases pose a small risk to travellers in South India, and so are only mentioned in passing. Seek medical advice if you think you may have any of these diseases.

Cholera This is the worst of the diarrhoeas and medical help should be sought. Outbreaks of cholera are generally widely reported, so you can avoid such problem areas. *Fluid replacement is the most vital treatment* – the risk of dehydration is severe as you may lose up to 20 litres a day. If there is a delay in getting to hospital then begin taking tetracycline; the adult dose is 250mg four times daily. It is not recommended for children under nine years or for pregnant women. Tetracycline may help shorten the illness, but adequate fluids are required to save lives.

Leishmaniasis This is a group of parasitic diseases transmitted by sandfly bites, found in many parts of the Middle East, Africa, India, Central and South America and the Mediterranean. Cutaneous leishmaniasis affects the skin tissue, causing ulceration and disfigurement. Visceral leishmaniasis affects the internal organs. Seek medical advice as laboratory testing is required for diagnosis and correct treatment. Avoiding sandfly bites is the best precaution. Bites are usually painless, itchy and are yet another reason to cover up and apply repellent.

Rabies Rabies is a fatal viral infection. Many animals can be infected (such as dogs, cats, bats and monkeys) and it is their saliva which is infectious. Any bite, scratch or even lick from a warm-blooded, furry animal should be cleaned immediately and thoroughly. Scrub with soap and running water, and then apply alcohol or iodine solution. Medical help should be sought promptly to receive a course of injections to prevent the onset of symptoms and death. Note that even if the victim has had a rabies vaccination, injections are still required if bitten by an infected animal.

Tetanus Tetanus occurs when a wound becomes infected by a germ which lives in soil and in the faeces of horses and other animals. It enters the body via breaks in the skin. All wounds should be cleaned promptly and adequately and an antiseptic cream or solution applied. Use antibiotics if the wound becomes hot, throbs or if pus is seen. The first symptom may be discomfort in swallowing, or stiffening of the jaw and neck; this is followed by painful convulsions of the jaw and whole body. The disease can be fatal.

Tuberculosis (TB) TB is a bacterial infection usually transmitted from person to person by coughing but may be transmitted through consumption of unpasteurised milk. Milk that has been boiled is safe to drink, and the souring of milk to make yoghurt or cheese also kills the bacilli. Travellers are usually not at great risk as close household contact with the infected person is usually required before the disease is passed on.

Typhus Typhus is spread by ticks, mites or lice. It begins with fever, chills, headache and muscle pains followed a few days later by a body rash. There is often a large painful sore at the site of the bite and nearby lymph nodes are swollen and painful.

Typhus can be treated under medical supervision. Seek local advice on areas where ticks pose a danger and always check your skin (including hair) carefully for ticks after walking in a danger area such as a tropical forest. A strong insect repellent can help, and serious walkers in tick areas should consider having their boots and trousers impregnated with benzyl benzoate and dibutylphthalate.

Women's Health
Gynaecological Problems Sexually transmitted diseases are a major cause of vaginal problems. Symptoms include a smelly discharge, painful intercourse and sometimes a burning sensation when urinating. Male sexual partners must also be treated. Medical attention should be sought and remember in addition to these diseases HIV or hepatitis B may also be acquired during exposure. Besides abstinence, the best thing is to practise safe sex using condoms.

Antibiotic use, synthetic underwear, sweating and contraceptive pills can lead to fungal vaginal infections when travelling in hot climates. Maintaining good personal hygiene, and loose-fitting clothes and cotton underwear will help to prevent these infections.

Fungal infections, characterised by a rash, itch and discharge, can be treated with a vinegar or lemon-juice douche, or with yoghurt. Nystatin, miconazole or clotrimazole pessaries or vaginal cream are the usual treatment.

Pregnancy It is not advisable to travel to South India while pregnant as some vaccinations normally used to prevent serious diseases are not advisable in pregnancy. In addition, some diseases are much more serious for the mother (and may increase the risk of a stillborn child) in pregnancy, eg malaria.

Most miscarriages occur during the first three months of pregnancy. Miscarriage is not uncommon, and can occasionally lead to severe bleeding. The last three months should also be spent within reasonable distance of good medical care. A baby born as early as 24 weeks stands a chance of survival, but only in a good modern hospital. Pregnant women should avoid all unnecessary medication; vaccinations and malarial prophylactics should still be taken where needed. Extra care should be taken to prevent illness and particular attention should be paid to diet and nutrition. Alcohol and nicotine, for example, should be avoided.

WOMEN TRAVELLERS
South India is generally perfectly safe for women travellers, even for those travelling alone. An exception is the heavily touristed beach areas of Goa. Here you are advised not to walk in isolated spots (down lonely alleys, along the beach) on your own – after dark especially. Two Swedish women were packraped at Anjuna in 1997. If you are in doubt about whether it's safe or not, ask.

Cities are generally quite OK although if you are on your own, take reasonable care if you are out after dark. Staying safe is really a matter of common sense, although a few tips from those who have gone before always help. See the boxed text for more information.

Although you are unlikely to be at any physical risk, one of the wearying aspects of

---

Advice for Women Travellers

Western women in India are frequently a source of curiosity, especially when travelling alone, and particularly so in remote areas. By dressing and behaving in a culturally appropriate manner you will avoid offending local sensibilities and attracting unwanted attention. Below are some tips from a seasoned traveller.

- Dress modestly. Long skirts are better than short skirts, slacks (loose fitting) are better than jeans. Shorts and sleeveless blouses or tight-fitting clothing are frowned on.

- Walk confidently in the street, as though you were going somewhere, and answer men's glances with a haughty look.

- Treat service people (who are almost always men) impersonally. Don't invite their confidences. Ignore any personal remarks and report bad behaviour to the proper authorities, eg hotel and restaurant managers, the police, train conductors etc.

- Don't go home with people you meet on the street – you'll be asked frequently to visit family homes. Most of the time it will be safe, but why take chances?

- Lock your hotel room when you are in it. If you don't know who is knocking at your door, phone down to the desk first before opening it.

- Try to arrive in towns before nightfall. If you do arrive late, refuse to get in a rickshaw or taxi with the driver's brother, cousin or friend.

- Take a book with you to restaurants. It keeps your eyes from roaming around too much and attracting attention from men who will be looking at you anyway. If anyone approaches you, tell him to get lost or you will call the manager.

- If you are being followed, go to the nearest tourist hotel and wait for a few minutes. Most Indians (excluding businessmen) are discouraged from entering, and your follower will get tired of waiting and leave. Museums and other public sights are also good.

- Remember, Indians are basically modest and passersby will be more than willing to help a woman being bothered. Ask anyone on the street who looks respectable – uniformed or suit-coated men are good.

- If you want to go out to a movie or entertainment in the evening, try to arrange a rickshaw during the day to pick you up in the evening. Inform your hotel – even if it is only a hostel – where you are going and when you expect to return. If anything does happen they will know both who the driver is and where you went. Make sure that your driver understands he is to come and pick you up again.

Mary Anne Morel (Canada)

travelling in some parts of South India, especially if you are alone, is the (unwanted) attention you will attract from young local men from time to time. If you don't want to be the constant object of what is euphemistically called 'Eve teasing' (harassment in various forms) then pay attention to the local norms of dress and behaviour. Dressing modestly helps. This means not wearing sleeveless tops, shorts or even jeans. Loose clothing that covers your legs and shoulders is best.

The *salwar kameez* or traditional Punjabi shirt and pyjama combination is becoming increasingly popular among western women travellers because it's practical and cheap and, most of all, it's considered respectable attire. A cotton salwar kameez is also surprisingly cool in South India's steamy heat and keeps the burning sun off your skin. A scarf (or the *dupatta* that is worn with the salwar kameez) is handy if you intend travelling in the stricter Muslim areas of South India, eg parts of Andhra Pradesh, where women invariably cover their heads.

Many places to eat in South India have separate areas for women and families. This is usually called the 'family room'. If you are on your own and the main eating area is full of men, and you feel uncomfortable with this, head for the family room. The food is the same as 'outside' but sometimes you may be charged a little more. The service is generally very good.

On buses, the front seats are usually deemed the area unofficially reserved for unaccompanied women, and families. If you are travelling alone you may feel more comfortable sitting in this part of the bus. Long distance trains often have special carriages reserved for women and children. Having said that, they can be so noisy with small children you may rather have wished you had opted for the ordinary carriage.

On the whole, a woman travelling alone is still very unusual in South India and much of the time you will find that there is great concern for your safety and welfare, and that people will go out of their way to assist you.

GAY & LESBIAN TRAVELLERS

While overt displays of affection between members of the opposite sex, such as cuddling and hand-holding, are frowned upon in India, it is not unusual to see Indian men holding hands with each other or engaged in other close affectionate behaviour. This does not necessarily suggest that they are gay. The gay movement in India is confined almost exclusively to larger cities and Mumbai is really the only place where there's a gay 'scene'. Since marriage is seen as very important, to be gay is a particular stigma – most gays stay in the closet or risk being disowned by their families.

As with relations between heterosexual western couples travelling in India – both married and unmarried – gay and lesbian travellers should exercise discretion and refrain from displaying overt affection towards each other in public.

Legal Status

Homosexual relations for men are illegal in India. Section 377 of the national legislation forbids 'carnal intercourse against the order of nature' (that is, anal intercourse). The penalties for transgression can be up to life imprisonment. Because of this gay travellers could be the subject of blackmail – take care. There is no law against lesbian relations.

Publications & Groups

Bombay Dost is a gay and lesbian publication available from 105 Veena Beena Shopping Centre, Bandra (W) Mumbai; The People Tree, 8 Parliament St, New Delhi; and Classic Books, 10 Middleton St, Calcutta. Support groups include Bombay Dost (address above); Pravartak, Post Bag 10237, Calcutta, West Bengal 700019; Sakhi (Lesbian Group), PO Box 3526, Lajpat Nagar, New Delhi 110024; and Sneha Sangama, PO Box 3250, RT Nagar, Bangalore 560032.

DISABLED TRAVELLERS

Travelling in South India can entail some fairly rigorous challenges, even for the able-bodied traveller – long bus trips in crowded vehicles between remote villages and endless queues in the scorching heat at bus and train stations can test even the hardiest traveller. If you can't walk, these challenges are increased many-fold. Few buildings have wheelchair access; toilets have certainly not been designed to accommodate wheelchairs; footpaths, where they exist (only in larger towns), are generally riddled with holes, littered with obstacles and packed with throngs of people, severely restricting mobility.

If your mobility is restricted you will require a strong, able-bodied companion to accompany you, and it would be well worth considering hiring a private vehicle and driver.

Publications & Groups

Disability Express Travel & Disability Resource Directory
(☎ 417-836 4773; fax 836 5371)
South-west Missouri State University, USA.

Royal Association for Disability & Rehabilitation
(☎ 171-250 3222; fax 250 0212)
12 City Forum, 250 City Rd, London,
England EC1V 8AF

SENIOR TRAVELLERS

Unless your mobility or vision is impaired or you're in any other way incapacitated, and if you're in reasonable health, there is no reason why the senior traveller should not consider India as a potential holiday destination. It may be helpful to discuss your proposed trip with your local GP.

TRAVEL WITH CHILDREN

Children can often enhance your encounters with local people, as they often possess little of the self-consciousness and sense of the cultural differences which can inhibit interaction between adults. South India has a very family orientated society.

Children are welcome in places to eat and stay; most hotels provide family rooms or will happily provide extra beds. You would certainly not be discouraged from bringing children on temple visits. However, there are few facilities dedicated solely to children's entertainment so it would be wise to bring books, favourite toys, games and so forth with you.

Travel in most South Indian states presents no problems from a logistical point of view but Andhra Pradesh may be inadvisable for children given the distances and difficulties involved in getting from A to B.

Travelling with children can be hard work, and ideally the burden needs to be shared between two adults. For more information, see the Health section earlier in this chapter, and get hold of a copy of Lonely Planet's *Travel with Children* by Maureen Wheeler.

DANGERS & ANNOYANCES
Theft

Common sense is your best safeguard when it comes to protecting your valuables. there's no need to be paranoid about the risk of theft; just make sure you don't set yourself up as an easy target. The less you look like a tourist, the less of a target you will be.

Never leave those most important valuables (passport, tickets, health certificates, money, travellers cheques) in your room; they should be with you or secured in a hotel safe. Either have a passport pouch under your shirt, a moneybelt or simply extra internal pockets in your clothing.

When travelling on trains at night keep your gear near you; padlocking a bag to a luggage rack can be useful, and some of the newer trains have loops under the seats which you can chain things to. Never walk around with valuables casually slung over your shoulder. Take extra care on crowded public transport.

Thieves are particularly active in places most frequented by tourists. These include beach resorts such as those in Goa and Kerala as well as popular temple town destinations such as Madurai.

Don't accept drinks or food from strangers no matter how friendly they seem, particularly if you're on your own. Be aware that in India there are occasional instances where travellers are drugged and their belongings stolen.

Beware also of your fellow travellers. Unhappily there are more than a few backpackers who make their money go further by helping themselves to other people's.

Remember that backpacks are very easy to rifle through. Don't leave valuables in them, especially during flights. Remember also that something may be of little or no value to a thief, but to lose it would be a real heartbreak to you – like film. Finally, a good travel insurance policy helps.

If you do have something stolen, you're going to have to report it to the police. You'll also need a statement proving you have done so if you want to claim on insurance.

Insurance companies, despite their rosy promises of full protection and speedy settlement of claims, are just as disbelieving as the Indian police and will often attempt every devious trick in the book to avoid paying out on a baggage claim.

Note that some policies specify that you must report an item stolen to the police within a limited amount of time of your observing that it is missing.

Stolen Travellers Cheques If you're unlucky enough to have things stolen, some precautions can ease the pain. All travellers cheques are replaceable, although this does you little immediate good if you have to go home and apply to your bank. What you want is instant replacement. Furthermore, what do you do if you lose your cheques and money and have a day or more to travel to the replacement office? The answer is to keep an emergency cash-stash in a totally separate place. In that same place you should keep a record of the cheque serial numbers, proof of purchase slips, encashment vouchers and your passport number.

American Express makes considerable noise about 'instant replacement' of their cheques but a lot of people find out, to their cost, that without a number of precautions 'instantly' can take longer than they think. If you don't have the receipt you were given when you bought the cheques, rapid replacement will be difficult. Obviously the receipt

should be kept separate from the cheques, and a photocopy in yet another location doesn't hurt either. Chances are you'll be able to get a limited amount of funds on the spot, and the rest will be available when the bank has verified your initial purchase of the cheques. American Express has a 24 hour number in Delhi (☎ (011) 687 5050) which you must ring within 24 hours of the theft.

LEGAL MATTERS

If you find yourself in a sticky legal predicament, contact your embassy. You should carry your passport with you at all times.

In the Indian justice system it seems the burden of proof is on the accused, and proving one's innocence is virtually impossible. The police forces are often corrupt and will pay 'witnesses' to give evidence.

Drugs

For a long time India was a place where you could indulge in all sorts of illegal drugs with relative ease – they were cheap, readily available and the risks were minimal. Things have changed. Penalties for possession, use and trafficking in illegal drugs are strictly enforced. If convicted on a drugs-related charge, sentences are long (*minimum* of 10 years) and accompanied by a hefty fine, even for minor offences, and there is no remission or parole. In some cases it has taken three years just to get a court hearing.

In Goa the police have recently taken a tough new anti-drugs line. A special court, the Narcotic Drugs and Psychotropic Substances Court, with its own judge, has been established expressly to try drug offences. It seems as though the prevailing attitude is 'if in doubt, convict' on the basis that the accused can always appeal to a higher court if they wish to do so.

Child Prostitution

Since 'Anglo-Indian' Freddy Peat was convicted in 1996 of a number of horrific sex crimes against children in Goa, there has been increasing acceptance in that state that child prostitution is a problem that needs to be tackled. There is now greater vigilance by police and locals and the legal procedure is now in place to deal with paedophiles. Offenders face life imprisonment in an Indian jail if convicted.

The international watchdog organisation ECPAT (End Child Prostitution, Pornography and Trafficking) included Goa in a series of research papers produced for the 1996 World Congress Against the Commercial Sexual Exploitation of Children.

The Indian Penal Code and India's Immoral Traffic Act impose penalties for kidnapping and prostitution. In addition, the international community has responded to what is essentially a global problem with laws that allow their nationals (including those from Australia, New Zealand, Germany, Sweden, Norway, France, USA) to be prosecuted for child sex offences upon their return home.

If you know of anyone engaged in these activities you should report it to police in the country you're in and again to the police when you get home.

BUSINESS HOURS

Officially, business hours are 9.30 am to 5.30 pm (8.30 am to 5.30 pm in the Andaman Islands) Monday to Friday. Unofficially they tend to be more around 10 am to 5 pm. Government offices seem to have lengthy lunch hours which are sacrosanct and can last from noon to 3 pm. Many public institutions such as museums, galleries and so on close at least one day during the week. Banks are open from 10 am to 2 pm Monday to Friday, and 10 am to noon on every second Saturday.

Travellers cheque transactions usually cease 30 minutes before the official bank closing time. In some tourist centres there may be foreign exchange offices that stay open for longer hours. Thomas Cook is open from 9.30 am to 6 pm Monday to Saturday. Post offices are open Monday to Saturday from 9.30 am to 5.30 pm. In the capital cities the GPO and head post offices are open to 8 pm every day.

HOLIDAYS & FESTIVALS

It would be virtually impossible to spend any amount of time in South India and not happen upon a festival of some description. The south shares major festivals – eg Holi, Independence Day and Dussehra – with the rest of the nation, and the various southern states all have plenty of their own, unique celebrations. Kerala, for example, is justly famous for its frantic snake boat races; Karnataka's Mahamastakabhisheka Festival, held once every 12 years, draws thousands of devotees and curious onlookers to witness the monks pouring hundreds of pots of ghee and coconut water over the head of the giant Jain statue of Bahubali.

Most festivals follow the Indian lunar calendar and therefore change from year to year according to the Gregorian calendar. Some nationwide festivals are listed below. For information on festivals pertaining to specific states, see the relevant chapters. Muslim holidays and festivals, which follow the Islamic calendar, are listed at the end of this section.

January

Republic Day Republic Day on 26 January celebrates the anniversary of India's establishment as a republic in 1950; there are activities in all the state capitals but most spectacularly in Delhi, where there is an enormously colourful military parade. As part of the Republic Day celebrations, three days later a *Beating of the Retreat* ceremony takes place outside Rashtrapati Bhavan, the residence of the Indian president, in Delhi.

February-March

Holi This is one of the most exuberant Hindu festivals, with people marking the end of winter by throwing coloured water and powder *(gulal)* at one another. In much of South India, which doesn't really have a winter as such, it isn't as widely celebrated as it is in the north. In tourist places it might be seen as an opportunity to take liberties with foreigners; don't wear good clothes on this day, and be ready to duck. On the night before Holi, bonfires are built to symbolise the destruction of the evil demon Holika.

Sivaratri This day of fasting is dedicated to Shiva, who danced the *tandava* on this day. Temple processions are followed by the chanting of mantras and anointing of lingams.

March-April

Mahavir Jayanti This Jain festival marks the birth of Mahavira, the founder of Jainism.

Ramanavami In temples all over India the birth of Rama is celebrated on this day. In the week leading up to Ramanavami, the *Ramayana* is widely read and performed.

Good Friday This Christian holiday is celebrated in Goa and Kerala.

May-June

Buddha Jayanti This 'triple blessed festival' celebrates Buddha's birth, enlightenment and attainment of nirvana.

June-July

Rath Yatra (Car Festival) Lord Jagannath's great temple chariot makes its stately journey from his temple in Puri, Orissa, during this festival. Similar festivals take place in South India.

July-August

Naag Panchami This festival is dedicated to Ananta, the serpent upon whose coils Vishnu rested between universes.

Raksha Bandhan (Narial Purnima) On the full moon day of the Hindu month of Sravana, girls fix amulets known as *rakhis* to their brothers' wrists to protect them in the coming year. The brothers reciprocate with gifts.

August

Independence Day This holiday on 15 August celebrates the anniversary of India's independence from the UK in 1947.

Drukpa Teshi This festival celebrates the first teaching given by the Buddha.

August-September

Ganesh Chaturthi This festival, held on the fourth day of the Hindu month Bhadra, is dedicated to Ganesh.

Shravan Purnima After a day-long fast, high-caste Hindus replace the sacred thread which they always wear looped over their left shoulder.

September-October

Dussehra This is the most popular of all the Indian festivals and takes place over 10 days, beginning on the first day of the Hindu month of Asvina. It celebrates Durga's victory over the buffalo-headed demon Mahishasura. In Mysore there are great processions.

October-November

Diwali (or *Deepavali*) This is the happiest festival of the Hindu calendar. At night, countless oil lamps are lit to show Rama the way home from his period of exile.

November-December

Nanak Jayanti On this day the birthday of Guru Nanak, the founder of the Sikh religion, is celebrated.

Christmas Day This is also a holiday in India, and especially important in India.

Muslim Holidays

The dates of the Muslim festivals are not fixed, as they fall about 11 days earlier each year.

Id-ul-Fitr This festival celebrates the end of Ramadan, the Muslim month of fasting. Falls on about 18 January 1999.

Id-ul-Zuhara This festival commemorates Abraham's attempt to sacrifice his son. Falls on 20 March 1999.

Muharram This 10-day festival commemorates the martyrdom of Mohammed's grandson, Imam Hussain. Falls on 18 April 1999.

Milad-un-Nabi This festival celebrates the birth of Mohammed. Falls on 27 June 1999.

ACTIVITIES
Cycling & Motorcycling

There are some organised tours but it's not difficult or expensive to organise things for yourself. See the Bicycle and Motorcycle sections in the Getting Around chapter.

Walking, Hiking & Trekking

Within easy reach of two of South India's largest cities – Chennai and Bangalore – are peaceful, rural spots that provide a good antidote to big-city life – a chance to stretch your legs and breathe some fresh air. See the Outdoor Activities sections in the Tamil Nadu, Chennai and Karnataka chapters.

The Western Ghats are full of potential for hikers, trekkers and other outdoor enthusiasts. Kodagu in Karnataka is particularly lovely, but there are also plenty of places to explore in Tamil Nadu. In some cases you will need to get a special permit (usually easily obtained from the local forestry department). For more details see the relevant sections in the chapters on Karnataka and Tamil Nadu. In Kerala there is hiking and

Considerations for Responsible Trekking

South India's remaining forests and wilderness areas are already under enough pressure. Please consider the following tips when trekking and help preserve their beauty and fragile ecology.

Rubbish

* Carry out all your rubbish and make an effort to carry out that left by others. Don't overlook easily forgotten items, such as silver paper, orange peel, cigarette butts and plastic wrappers. Empty packaging weighs very little and can be stored in a dedicated rubbish bag.
* Never bury your rubbish: digging disturbs soil and groundcover and encourages erosion. Buried rubbish will more than likely be dug up by animals, who may be injured or poisoned by it.
* Minimise the waste you must carry out by taking minimal packaging and essential items only. Combine small-portion packages into one reusable container before your trek.
* Don't rely on bought water in plastic bottles. Disposal of these bottles is creating a major problem. Use iodine drops or purification tablets instead.
* Sanitary napkins, tampons and condoms should also be carried out: they burn and decompose poorly.

Human Waste Disposal

* Contamination of water sources by human faeces can lead to the transmission of hepatitis, typhoid and intestinal parasites, such as giardiasis, amoebas, and roundworm.
* Where there is a toilet, use it; where there is none; dig a small hole 15cm deep and at least 100m from any watercourse. Use toilet paper sparingly and cover it and the waste with soil and a rock.

Washing

* Don't use detergents or toothpaste in or near watercourses. For personal washing, use biodegradable soap and a water container (or even a lightweight, portable basin) at least 50m away from the watercourse. Widely disperse the waste-water to allow the soil to filter it fully before it finally makes it back to the watercourse.
* Wash cooking utensils 50m from watercourses using a scourer such as sand instead of detergent.

Erosion

* Hillsides and mountain slopes are prone to erosion. It is important to stick to existing tracks and avoid short cuts that bypass a switchback. If you blaze a new trail straight down a slope it will turn into a watercourse with the next heavy rainfall and eventually cause soil loss and deep scarring.
* Walk through mud patches across tracks: walking around them will increase their size.
* Avoid removing the plant life that keeps topsoil in place.

Fires & Low Impact Cooking

* Don't depend on open fires for cooking. Cook on a light-weight kerosene, alcohol or Shellite (white gas) stove and avoid those powered by disposable butane gas canisters.
* Avoid accommodation that uses wood fires to heat water or cook food.
* Fires may be acceptable in remote areas. Use only a minimal amount of dead, fallen wood which should be lit within an existing fireplace. Remember the adage 'the bigger the fool, the bigger the fire'. Use minimal wood, just what you need for cooking.
* Ensure that you fully extinguish a fire after use. Spread the embers and douse them with water. A fire is only truly safe to leave when you can comfortably place your hand in it.

Wildlife Conservation

* Do not engage in or encourage hunting. It is illegal in all parks and reserves.
* Don't buy items made from endangered species.
* Do not feed the wildlife.

wildlife viewing in places around Munnar (for more details see the Kerala chapter).

Windsurfing
Four and five-star hotels at Goa's beach resorts rent windsurfers and there are independent windsurfing operators at Bogmalo Beach (Splash Water Sports) and Candolim Beach (Venture Sports). Windsurfers can also hired in Muthukadu (Tamil Nadu) and Port Blair (Andaman Islands).

Boating & River Rafting
There is some rafting along the Cauvery River (Karnataka). Boating is available near Chennai (refer to Outdoor Activities under Around Chennai for details). There are boating facilities at Hussain Sagar Lake in Hyderabad. In Kerala you can go drifting around the Backwaters. (See the Kerala chapter for more details.)

Diving & Snorkelling
You can dive and snorkel in Goa, Lakshadweep and the Andaman Islands. *Goa Diving* at Bogmalo Beach offers courses and is PADI affiliated. See the chapters on the Andaman & Nicobar Islands and Lakshadweep for more details on courses and diving conditions there.

Swimming
Goa and Kerala have many beaches; see those chapters for details. In other places the four and five-star hotels may allow nonguests to use their pools for a fee, but ring first.

Horse Riding & Polo
The Andhra Pradesh riding club in Hyderabad offers regular polo and cross-country riding (☎ (040) 393328).

Golf
India's golf clubs were once affiliated with the Royal Calcutta Golf Club (established in 1829) which followed rules laid down by St Andrews in Scotland. Golf today is under the aegis of the Indian Golf Union which is affiliated with the World Amateur Golf Council. In Tamil Nadu there are links in Chennai (at

the Gymkhana Club and the Cosmopolitan Club), Kodaikanal and Ooty. Temporary membership is available at all these places. In Karnataka there are golf links at Bangalore and at Mysore. In Mysore the Jayachamaraja Wadiyar Golf Club is next to the racecourse and allows nonmembers to play on the 18 hole course.

COURSES
Arts & Crafts
The Madras Craft Foundation (☎ (044) 491 8943; fax 434 0149) at 6 Urur Olcott Rd, Besant Nagar, Chennai organises one day workshops in pottery, *kalamkari* (applying vegetable dyes to a drawing on cotton), enamel jewellery, embroidery and story telling. Prices, around Rs 225, include lunch. Special children's workshops are conducted in clay sculpting, tie dyeing, making cards and stuffed elephants.

The Cholmandal Artists Village (☎ (044) 492 6092) on the outskirts of Chennai will accept serious students. See the Chennai chapter for details.

Dance & Music
Professional teachers are naturally interested in serious students and if you really want to learn, say, Indian classical dance, be prepared to commit yourself for at least three years' hard work. If you aren't that keen but still want to learn something of South India's classical art and music you could hire a tutor for private sessions through a cultural organisation such as the Music Academy (☎ (044) 827 5619), corner of TTK Rd and Dr Radhakrishnan Salai, Chennai, or the Kalakshetra Foundation (☎ (044) 491 1169), Tiruvanmiyur, Chennai.

The Nrityagram dance village near Bangalore in Karnataka has courses in dance and music. For details see the Karnataka chapter.

Martial Arts
You can study the ancient martial art of Kalarippayatt at the CVN Kalari in Thiruvananthapuram, Kerala. See that chapter for details.

Finding An Indian Voice

It was more than music. Learning classical singing in South India (Carnatic Sangeetam) meant becoming a disciple of a master musician, and being accepted into a Brahmin family as a daughter. Classes were three times a week, but every few months there were festivals, such as Ganesh Chaturthi and Deepavali. These festivals entailed giving ritual offerings to my teacher, as well as to anyone who worked for me. At my Brahmin family's house I would participate in cooking for the family. In South India society, this was a very great honour.

I first started singing *bhajans* in the ashram of a world famous guru. It was the best thing there – everything else was gender-segregated eating halls and bookshops and a dour and rigid discipline. But the devotional music had a great spirit of joy and invocation of the deity. Later on I went to visit the sacred mountain Arunachala in Tiruvannamalai (Tamil Nadu), and there I was introduced to my music guru. I had to be formally inducted on an auspicious day at an auspicious hour; the almanac was consulted. Here I learned some of the intricacies of a music tradition that is at least 1000 years old and is passed on orally in an old fashioned guru-disciple relationship. It has no indigenous notation.

From the basic rhythm patterns I progressed to memorising 14 *varanams* over three years, and many other songs and smaller works. The vocal music is taught with incredible precision, and every slide and quaver has to be reproduced and memorised. Once enough complex musical works are mastered, then the ultimate achievement is in improvisation. Here you take the note forms that are particular to the *raga* (conventional patterns of melody and rhythm) and create new music.

To become accomplished in the tradition takes about six years – I gave it only three. Still, that was long enough to be able to find my Indian voice, which I can call on at will, anywhere in the world.

Di Cousens (Sunyata)

Yoga & Ayurveda

At Varkala Beach in Kerala there are places where you can learn yoga and ayurvedic massage. See that chapter for details. The astanga school of yoga in Mysore offers courses costing around US$400 per month. You should book well in advance. Contact: Mr K Pattabhi Joise (☎ (0821) 25558), Astanga Yoga Nilaya, 876/1 Laxmipuram, 1st Cross, Mysore, Karnataka.

Languages

The following institutes offer language courses for visitors:

Hindi Prachar Sabhar,
  (☎ 044-434 1824),
  Chennai, Tamil Nadu (Hindi language)
International Institute of Tamil Studies
  (☎ 044-827 2650),
  Central Polytechnic, Adyar, Chennai,
  Tamil Nadu (Tamil language)

VOLUNTARY WORK

Numerous charities and international aid agencies have branches in South India and, although they're mostly staffed by locals, there are some opportunities for foreigners. Though it may be possible to find temporary volunteer work after you arrive, you'll probably be of more use to the charity concerned if you write in advance and, if they need you, stay for long enough to be of help.

Overseas Aid Agencies

For long-term posts, the following organisations may be able to help or offer advice and further contacts:

Australian Volunteers Abroad: Overseas Service
  Bureau Programme
  (☎ 03-9279 1788; fax 9416 1619)
  PO Box 350, Fitzroy Vic 3065, Australia
Co-ordinating Committee for International
  Voluntary Service
  (☎ 01-45 68 27 31)
  c/o UNESCO, 1 rue Miollis, F-75015 Paris,
  France

continued on page 131

South Indian Food

CHRISTINE NIVEN

South India's states have their own very distinctive cuisine, which for travellers accustomed to 'Indian' basics of tandoori meats and restaurant-issue curries, will be nothing less than a revelation. South India shines in exciting vegetarian and rice-based cooking and skilful handling of spices – spices, after all, were the primary attraction for the early seafaring Europeans to visit India's shores.

Bigger cities and tourist centres throughout the region provide internationally recognised cooking too: tandoori chicken, pilaus, biryanis, Kashmiri lamb, and *saag panir* (spinach and fresh cheese braised in spices), for example, are widely available, as well as traditionally northern breads, such as *chappatis* (wholemeal unleavened bread cooked on a *tawa* or griddle), *paratha* (flaky, pan-fried bread), *puri* (deep-fried wholemeal bread) and *naan* (Punjabi leavened bread). The tastes of the truly homesick or nervous traveller are also well catered for (sometimes rather too well): you can order fish and chips in Goa, porridge for breakfast in Kerala, a hamburger in Bangalore, and banana pancakes almost everywhere.

On the whole, food in South India is tasty and cheap, and lentils and pulses (*dal*) are king. This particularly applies to the *thali* – often referred to as a 'meal' on the menu and almost always served during lunchtime (between about noon and 3pm), usually the main meal of the day. Thalis come in two basic varieties: veg and nonveg (nonveg being more expensive); normally both of these are 'all you can eat' deals – your waiter will keep topping up your thali until you've had enough.

Sometimes thalis will be served on a flat, stainless steel dish after which they are named (the accompaniments are arranged on the plate in small metal bowls called *katoris*); often they will be served on a banana leaf. In this case, after your leaf is spread before you, a waiter will bring some water to sluice it down. You will then be dished out a large serving of rice and another waiter will arrive with a cluster of katoris in which reside a selection of *sambars* (tart, thick vegetable curries based on tamarind, dal or buttermilk), chutneys, pickles, curd (*thayir*) or curd rice (*thayir sadam*), *rasams* (piquant, soupy curries based on tomato, tamarind, lime and dal) and if you are eating meat, a meat-based dish. Some thalis will also include a sweet to round off the meal, such as *barfi*, which is made from ghee (clarified butter), sugar, and reduced milk. You will also usually receive a crispy pappadam (lentil wafer), and sometimes a ghee chappati as well.

South Indian food is eaten with the fingers – foreigners will usually be offered a spoon and fork, but eating with your fingers feels

GREG ELMS

South India is one of the world's centres of spice production; packaged spices make good little souvenirs.

EDDIE GERALD

SARA-JANE CLELAND

EDDIE GERALD

Corn, sugar cane, tomatoes, snake gourds and squash thrive in the perpetually hot South: char-grilling corn on the streets of Chennai (top); crushing sugar cane for an instant drink (bottom right); at Mysore's Deveraja Market (bottom left).

Introduced to India by Portuguese traders, the ubiquitous chilli (top) is an essential ingredient in most South Indian *rasams* and *sambar* (centre right). Other regulars at table include *idli*, *vadai* and *puri* (bottom right), *naan* (bottom left) and *chappatis* (centre left).

GREG ELMS

The ideal all-you-can-eat, eco-friendly lunch, South Indian thalis are often served on banana leaves.

and tastes much better. You take a small portion of sambar or rasam, mix it with a bit of rice and transport neat little balls of the mixture to your mouth. If you have a chappatti you can use that as a scoop to save drips and spillage if you're not adept with your fingers. Remember to use your right hand only, but pick up your glass of water with your left.

Many places serve thali meals for around Rs 20; for Rs 45 in a city like Chennai you can get all the trimmings and certainly as much as – or more than – you could possibly eat. Invariably, if the first round doesn't fill you up, your leaf (or plate) will be topped up a second or third time – or at least until you've had your fill.

Breakfast foods in South India also appear at other times during the day as snack foods. Everywhere in the south you will come across *idlis* (steamed rice and semolina cakes) which are accompanied by chutney (often coconut) or sambar and frequently both. Usually idlis are served in portions of two at a time. Also popular, and often eaten with idlis, are *vadai*, which are deep-fried dal and vegetable cakes (sometimes called *ulundu vadai* in South India). These come with a sambar and chutney. Less common is *uppuma*, which is a savoury dish made from semolina, pounded rice, vegetables and spices. *Puttu* is a sweet breakfast dish made of pounded rice and coconut (and called *pittu* in Sri Lanka).

Equally popular as snacks or breakfast are the wafer-like rice-flour pancakes called *dosa*. Dosa come in a number of different forms: *masala dosa* (stuffed with a potato masala); *uttapam* (a thicker dosa topped with chopped spiced vegetables); and paper, or semolina, dosa (lacy, thinner than other dosa and with no filling). Dosa usually come with coconut chutney and a sambar, and are generally about the size of a dinner plate, but sometimes they are rather larger. Udipi in Karnataka is considered the home of the masala dosa.

In Kerala especially you will come across *appams*, which are pancakes made from fermented rice flour and coconut milk. The final

EDDIE GERALD

Pulses and lentils, collectively called dal, are South Indian staples. Dal also refers to the finished dish made from dal, spices and vegetables.

product is crispy at the edges and rather like a pikelet in the middle. Appams are often accompanied by a hard boiled egg in a curry sauce and this is a snack you'll find in *chai* (tea) shops everywhere. Travellers familiar with Sri Lankan cuisine will recognise appams as they are the same as hoppers in that country – as are the *idiyappams* that come in vermicelli strands and which are often served with milk and sugar. In Sri Lanka these are known as string hoppers.

Other snacks that you'll find in chai shops everywhere are *samosas* (triangular pastries stuffed with curried vegetables), *namkin* (spiced nibbles), *bajji* (bite-sized pieces of vegetable dipped in chickpea flour), *bonda* (spiced potato or vegetable balls dipped in batter and deep fried), *pakora* (deep-fried vegetable cakes), *sundal* (spiced whole chick peas), *puri* (usually served with spiced potatoes) and *paratha* (usually served with spiced vegetables including onion).

When it comes to meat and fish, there are many regional specialities in South India. In Kerala, famous for its fish (notably prawns and the freshwater fish known as *karimeen* as well as the flounder-like *pomfret*) there are numerous variations to try. Many fish dishes here use coconut milk and on occasion roasted coconut to give a thick, dark sauce. Jaggery or palm sugar is sometimes added as well.

Goa is similarly famous for fish and indeed fish curry and rice is the staple diet. Kingfish probably features most frequently on the menu but there are many others. Among the most famous Goan dishes is *ambot tik*, a slightly sour curry dish which can be prepared with fish (most commonly) or meat. *Caldeirada* is a mildly flavoured dish of Portuguese origin in which fish or prawns are cooked into a kind of stew with vegetables and often flavoured with wine. Also of Portuguese origin is the famous and very fiery vindaloo: Goans, being mainly a Christian people, will make it with pork. Pomfret is sometimes sliced open, stuffed with a chilli sauce and then baked; the result is delicious. *Chicken sukka* is made with grated coconut and coconut milk.

Chick peas are ubiquitous in all Indian cooking – besan, a flour made from chick peas, is the essential pastry-making ingredient for samosas and pakoras. Here chick peas form the basis of a big, spicy stew.

EDDIE GERALD

continued from page 127

Council of International Programs (CIP)
  (☎ 703-527 1160)
  1101 Wilson Blvd Ste 1708, Arlington VA
  22209, USA
International Voluntary Service (IVS)
  (☎ 0131-226 6722)
  St John's Church Centre, Edinburgh EH2
  4BJ, UK
Peace Corps of the USA
  (☎ 202-606 3970; fax 606 3110)
  1990 K St NW, Washington DC 20526, USA
Voluntary Service Overseas (VSO)
  (☎ 0181-780 2266; fax 780 1326)
  317 Putney Bridge Rd, London
  SW15 2PN, UK

Other Voluntary Work Opportunities

Archaeology Students of archaeology may like to contact the Archaeological Survey in Hyderabad with a view to securing an attachment. See the section on Hyderabad in the Andhra Pradesh chapter for more information.

Conservation & the Environment The Palani Hills Conservation Council in Kodaikanal (Tamil Nadu; ☎ 044-40711) offers a range of opportunities for volunteers with specific skills and interests in conservation issues. Interested travellers should write to the President, PHCC, Amarville House, Lower Shola Rd, Kodaikanal 62410.

The Annamali Reforestation Society (ARS) (☎ 044-23645; fax 23645) at Tiruvannamalai, Tamil Nadu, is dedicated to regenerating the forest cover of the sacred mountain Arunachala.

The ARS runs workshops for villagers and local schools to raise environmental awareness. It also operates a large temple garden and has established a productive permaculture demonstration farm. If you are interested in volunteering please write to the society: 60-B/1, ROA Colony, Tiruvannamalai, 606 603, Tamil Nadu.

ACCOMMODATION

South India has a huge range and variety of accommodation, from the most basic hostels and cheap hotels to upmarket jungle lodges and former royal palaces. Apart from the truly luxurious places to stay, the best value for money is in the middle price range – Rs 250 to Rs 500 per night for a double. For this in a city like Chennai you can easily get a clean room, a private bathroom (with hot water most of the time), colour satellite TV, room service (a 10% surcharge usually applies), a telephone and a fan (sometimes air-con). However, in places where there is little tourist infrastructure, such as Andhra Pradesh, don't expect anywhere near the same standard. Accommodation outside Hyderabad, for example, is hard to get and low-budget accommodation generally is very basic and often filthy. Even medium-range accommodation can be unclean or worse. Price isn't necessarily proportional to cleanliness. A higher rate may simply buy you a piece of carpet (dirty) or a TV (which may not work).

At the budget end of the market it's important to distinguish between services for pilgrims and cheap accommodation. While it may appear there is an abundance of accommodation, it may be primarily for pilgrims and provided by temples at no, or very low, cost. This is particularly so in Andhra Pradesh. In such situations it is unfair for foreign visitors to expect tourist facilities.

Many hotels claim to provide hot water, but in reality don't. If the hotel claims '24 hour running water' it may mean that a room boy will run up to your room with a bucket of hot water. This is usually a much better option than waiting for hot water to appear via the shower. Don't be afraid to inspect the room first and try the plumbing. Very often hot water only comes on for a few hours in the evening or morning, so ask.

All over South India you will come across the word 'hotel'. This doesn't automatically signal a place to stay. A hotel may simply be a place to eat. It might be worth checking, if you can, in advance.

Having arrived at the hotel of your choice, you may be told that it's full. It's sometimes worth persevering in these cases, especially if you're travelling off the beaten track. If you're a foreign visitor it may be assumed that you want air-conditioning and a western sit-down toilet. If you're happy with a ceiling fan and a squat toilet, say so.

It's amazing how often a room, exactly to your requirements, suddenly and magically appears.

Hotels very often want at least two nights' payment in advance. If you only stay one night the balance is happily refunded. You will usually be offered a receipt, but if you aren't, ask for one. Many places operate on a 24 hour basis, ie your 24 hours starts when you check in. Generally you can't pay by the hour if you go over the limit; you will be asked for another 24 hours payment even though you may only want the room for three or so hours extra. Four and five-star hotels generally have a noon checkout rule.

Youth Hostels

Indian youth hostels (HI – Hostelling International) are generally very cheap. You are not usually required to be a YHA (HI) member (as in other countries) to use the hostels, although your YHA/HI card may get you a lower rate. The charge is typically Rs 15 for members, Rs 30 for nonmembers.

Private Jungle Lodges

To cater for upmarket Indian and foreign tourists visiting the major national parks, increasing numbers of private resorts and lodges are being constructed close to, but never inside, the parks. The settings, standards, prices and facilities vary amazingly. Prices can range from about Rs 500 a double (singles are rarely available) to an impressive US$250. At the cheaper places, rates are room only; everything else is extra: meals start at Rs 100 for a decent buffet and you will be charged for every second that you hire a guide or jeep. As you would hope, at the expensive places, everything is included: meals, guides, jeep and boat tours, park entrance fees and so on.

These places are often hard to reach by public transport so you will probably have to charter a vehicle some of the way or organise something with the lodge (but you will pay heavily for any transfers). You must always pre-book, often months ahead for peak times. Never just turn up expecting an empty room and a meal.

Some lodges have the best possible settings, and the best equipment, vehicles and facilities for viewing wildlife – usually far better than that possessed by the forest departments (and better than you could hope to organise yourself). So if you *really* want to see some wildlife, especially tigers and elephants, you may have to dig deep into your wallet. In any case, splurging on a lodge or two during your trip is not a bad idea for sheer decadence, decent wildlife trips and genuine relaxation.

Forest Department Bungalows

Several government departments – notably the State Electricity Board (EB) and the Public Works Department (PWD), as well as the various forest departments and the Department of Irrigation – have inspection or holiday bungalows. They are ostensibly for staff, but if rooms are available, tourists can sometimes use them. You are far more likely to be successful with the bungalows or dormitories run by the forest departments.

These bungalows are often excellent value. Prices range from Rs 40 to Rs 150 a double (singles are never available), and while facilities are rustic, the rooms are usually clean. Importantly, they are often located in the most idyllic positions, eg in the middle of an isolated national park or overlooking a waterfall. Food is always available, but it may be little more than dal and rice, so bring your own supplies if you wish to liven up your meals. Alcohol and smoking are often not allowed in the bungalows, but this is also often, sadly, ignored by guests.

These bungalows *must* be pre-booked with as much advance notice as you can provide. The difficulty in finding out how and where to book these bungalows is often a disincentive, but the information provided in the following chapters (Karnataka, Tamil Nadu) should steer you in the right direction.

Tourist Bungalows

Usually run by the state government, tourist bungalows often serve as replacements for the older government-run accommodation units. Tourist bungalows are generally excellent value, although they vary enormously in facilities and level of service offered.

They usually have dorm beds as well as rooms – typical prices are around Rs 40 for a dorm bed, and Rs 120 to Rs 350 for a double room. The rooms have a fan, two beds and bathroom; air-con rooms are often also available at around Rs 500. Generally there's a restaurant or 'dining hall' and often a bar.

Train Retiring Rooms

These are just like regular hotels or dormitories except they are at railway stations. To stay here you are generally supposed to have a railway ticket or Indrail Pass. The rooms are, of course, extremely convenient if you have an early train departure, although they can be noisy if it is a busy station. They are often very cheap and in some places they are also excellent value. In Andhra Pradesh, retiring room staff may be the only ones able to assist English-speaking travellers. Railway retiring rooms are let on a 24 hour basis. The main problem is getting a bed, as they are very popular and often full.

Tea Plantations & Coffee Estates

An interesting accommodation option is to stay at a coffee estate in the Kodagu district of Karnataka or at a tea plantation in the Nilgiri district of Tamil Nadu. These can be beautiful and quiet places to relax, go hiking and watch the tea or coffee being picked and processed (in season). Prices and facilities vary considerably (there are upmarket resorts, plain rooms in the back of the family home and just about everything in between). They are nevertheless a worthy option. See the relevant sections in the Karnataka and Tamil Nadu chapters for details. Tourist offices and travel agents in South India may be able to assist with lists of new places offering this sort of accommodation.

Railway Waiting Rooms

For emergency accommodation when all else fails or when you just need a few hours rest before your train departs at 2 am,

railway station waiting rooms are a free place to rest your weary head. The trick is to rest in the (usually empty) 1st-class waiting room and not the crowded 2nd-class one.

Officially you need a 1st-class ticket to be allowed to use the 1st-class room and its superior facilities. In practice, luck, a 2nd-class Indrail Pass or simply a foreign appearance may work. In some places your ticket will be checked.

Cheap Hotels

There are cheap hotels all over South India, ranging from filthy, uninhabitable dives (but with prices at rock bottom) to quite reasonable places in both standards and prices. Ceiling fans, mosquito nets on the beds, private toilets and bathrooms are all possibilities, even in rooms which cost Rs 120 or less per night for a double.

Although prices are generally quoted in this book for singles and doubles, most hotels will put an extra bed in a room to make a triple for about an extra 25%. In some smaller hotels it's often possible to bargain a little. On the other hand these places will usually put their prices up if there's a shortage of accommodation in the area.

Many hotels in South India, and not only the cheap ones, operate on a 24 hour system. If you want to spend a couple of extra hours in the room (say you are due to check out at 1 pm but want to stay until 3 pm) you may be allowed to (it's up to the discretion of the manager). But generally if you want to stay a few hours over the limit you will be required to fork out for an additional 24 hours accommodation.

Expensive Hotels

South India's big, air-con, swimming-pool places are for the most part confined to the major tourist centres and the large cities. There are a number of big hotel chains in India. The Taj Group has some of India's flashiest hotels, including the Taj Coromandel in Chennai, the Fort Aguada Beach Resort in Goa and the Malabar Hotel in

Kochi (Cochin). The Oberoi chain is as well known outside India as within it.

Most expensive hotels operate on a noon checkout basis, prices are quoted in US dollars for foreigners and taxes can be very high (eg 30% in Tamil Nadu).

Home Stays

Staying with an Indian family can be a real education. It's a change from dealing strictly with tourist-oriented people, and it can give an intimate insight into everyday Indian life. In Chennai it's often referred to as paying guest accommodation. Contact the Government of India Tourist Office in Anna Salai Rd, Chennai, for details. Word of mouth, however, is one of the best ways to find out about home stay accommodation; places come and go all the time.

Other Possibilities

There are YMCAs and YWCAs in big cities – some of these are modern, well equipped and cost about the same as a mid-range hotel (but are still good value). There are also a few Salvation Army Hostels, eg in Chennai. Travellers with their own transport can almost always find hotels with gardens where they can park and camp.

Taxes & Service Charges

There are various levels of taxation in South India and these can add substantially to your costs, especially if you are using top-end accommodation. Always check at hotels and restaurants which taxes apply.

In Andhra Pradesh a 10% luxury tax is applied to all accommodation, even though there may be little luxury involved. In the more upmarket hotels there is a 10% 'hotel expenditure tax' on top of the 10% luxury tax.

In Tamil Nadu 10% to 30% tax is common on accommodation; 30% applies to four and five-star hotels. Some places that charge only 10% or 20% luxury tax add a further 10% as a 'service tax'.

In the Andaman Islands star-rated hotels may levy a 10% luxury tax during peak season.

In Karnataka luxury tax is 5% on accom-

modation in the Rs 150 to Rs 200 bracket, 7% on Rs 201 to Rs 400 and 15% on anything above Rs 400. Service tax seems to be left up to individual establishments and varies from place to place; most of the mid and upper range places to stay and eat add a service charge.

In Kerala luxury tax on accommodation is up to 7.5% on a standard room in a budget hotel (10% on an air-con room); 7.5% to 10% on a standard room in a mid-range hotel (10% to 15% for air-con); and 25% on a top-end hotel (usually made up of 15% luxury tax plus 10% luxury expenditure tax). Luxury tax is applied in mid-range and top-end restaurants and is usually about 6%.

Seasonal Variations

In popular tourist places, eg Kerala, Hampi in Karnataka and Goa, hoteliers crank up their prices in the high season by a factor of two to three times the low-season price. The high season tends to coincide with the cooler, non-monsoon, months of November to February. Prices in this book are high-season rates.

Touts

Touristed areas attract hordes of touts all vying for your time and money. Accommodation touts, touts who work for arts & crafts places and touts pitching for tour operators are generally employed on a commission basis and can be most persuasive, very skillful and extremely annoying. Very often they are the rickshaw-wallahs who meet you at the bus or railway station. They earn a commission for taking you to a particular hotel, which may not be the hotel of your choice. Some very good cheap hotels simply refuse to pay the touts and you'll then hear lots of stories about the hotel you want being full or closed or whatever.

Take particular care in Mamallapuram and Madurai (Tamil Nadu). The practices of touts in these places are of particular concern to the local authorities. Despite warnings at bus stands and other places frequented by foreigners, travellers keep getting taken in. You have been warned.

Touts do have a use though – if you arrive in a town when a big festival is on or during peak season finding a place to stay can be very difficult. Hop in a rickshaw, tell the driver how much you're prepared to pay for a room, and off you go. The driver will know which places have rooms available and unless the search is a long one you shouldn't have to pay the driver too much. Remember that he will be getting a commission from the hotel too.

FOOD
Western Food
For some foreign travellers Indian food can occasionally get to be simply too much. For these people the Indian-food blues are most likely to hit at breakfast time – idlis aren't corn flakes, after all. This is when eggs really come into their own – fried, boiled, scrambled, poached or omelette are all widely available. Toast and jam may also be tempting at such times, but the toast will often be disappointingly soggy. Generally only white bread is available and it tends to be loaded with sugar.

That peculiar Raj-era term for a midmorning snack still lives – tiffin. Today tiffin means any sort of light meal or snack. One western dish which Indians have adopted is chips (French fries, or finger chips as they are known in the south). Unfortunately ordering chips is very much a hit and miss affair – sometimes they're excellent, and at other times truly dreadful.

There are fast-food outlets in major cities. Bangalore in Karnataka, for example, has KFC and Pizza Hut plus a few mediocre burger places. For more details, including where to get good western breakfasts, see the Karnataka chapter.

Other Cuisines
Chinese food is widely available, particularly in Kerala and Goa. While in general the food is quite good, and often makes a very tasty alternative to local dishes, it has to be said that you are extremely unlikely to find much genuinely Chinese cuisine in South India.

Fruit
Bananas, pineapples, mangoes, jackfruit, custard apples, watermelons and papaya are all locally grown. Watermelons are often sold by the slice on roadside stalls. Green and gold-coloured coconuts (gold ones are less oily) are available everywhere; when you have drunk the coconut water the vendor will hack off the top so you can scoop up the jelly-like flesh.

Sweets
South Indians love sweets, which are generally made from reduced milk, ghee and honey or jaggery. Favourites include: *kulfi*, similar to ice cream and sometime flavoured with pistachio; *gulab jamuns*, made from deep fried milk powder dough and steeped in rose-flavoured syrup; *jalebis*, deep-fried orange-coloured squiggles with syrup inside; *laddoos*, cardamom flavoured balls of chickpea flour; *payasam*, a milk pudding made from rice and usually reserved for festive occasions; *kul kuls*, pastry rolls in sweet syrup; and *barfi*, a fudge-like sweet made from reduced milk.

Paan
An Indian meal should properly be finished with *paan* – the name given to the collection of spices and condiments chewed with betel nut. Found throughout eastern Asia, betel is a mildly intoxicating and addictive nut, but by itself it is quite inedible. After a meal you chew paan as a mild digestive.

Paan sellers have a whole collection of little trays, boxes and containers in which they mix either *saadha* 'plain' or *mithaa* 'sweet' paans. The ingredients may include, apart from the betel nut itself, lime paste (the ash not the fruit), the powder known as *catachu*, various spices and even a dash of opium in a pricey paan. The whole concoction is folded up in a piece of edible leaf which you pop in your mouth and chew. When finished you spit the leftovers out and add another red blotch to the pavement. Over a long period of time, indulgence in paan will turn your teeth red-black, addict you to the betel nut, and perhaps even lead to mouth cancer. Trying one occasionally shouldn't do you any harm. See also the separate South Indian Food section in this chapter.

DRINKS
Nonalcoholic Drinks
Tea & Coffee South India grows both tea and coffee, but the preferred drink in most places is coffee. Tea and coffee are always served with milk and sugar; westerners may find the coffee a bit weak and milky and far too sweet. A few places serve filter coffee (usually upmarket hotels and restaurants catering to tourists) and this is about the closest you'll get to coffee as you might expect it in the cafes of Australia or Europe.

Often the coffee you order at hotels will be of the instant variety. Tea of course is served as *chai* in the little shops that cater to dedicated tea drinkers, but it also comes in pots or more usually thermos containers in hotels with the milk and sugar served separately. However, don't expect leaf tea; usually what you'll get are teabags.

Water You should not drink water unless it comes out of a sealed bottle, or you know that it has been boiled or sterilised. Although top-class hotels would never serve anything other than safe water, in some mid-range places the water is only filtered and not boiled. The local water filters remove solids but don't remove bacteria. Water is generally safer in the dry season than in the monsoon.

Bottled Water Most visitors to South India stick to bottled water, available just about everywhere. (Stock up before you hit the road or embark on a long train trip in Andhra Pradesh and in parts of rural Tamil Nadu. In the Andaman Islands the only place you'll be able to buy it readily is Port Blair.) The price for a one litre bottle ranges from about Rs 12 to Rs 20. Expect to pay a little more in restaurants. Virtually all so-called mineral water is actually treated tap water.

Generally, if you stick to bottled water, any gut problems you might have will be from other sources – food, dirty utensils,

dirty hands and so on. (See under Basic Rules in the Health section earlier.)

Soft Drinks Soft drinks are a safe but not healthy alternative for water. Coca-Cola and Pepsi are widely available, especially in cities. There are also many indigenous brands with names like Campa Cola, Thums Up, Limca, Gold Spot or Double Seven. They are reasonably priced at around Rs 10 for a 250ml bottle (more in restaurants). Coca-Cola also comes in cans for about Rs 13.

Juices & Other Drinks Coconut water is a popular drink in South India. Just about everywhere you'll see vendors standing by mounds of coconuts, machete at the ready. One drinking coconut costs about Rs 8 – more in some places. Another alternative to soft drinks is soda water, a bottle of which costs around Rs 8. Add the juice of a lemon and you have a delicious, safe lemon soda.

In the cities particularly you'll come across sugarcane and fruit juice vendors. Be cautious if you decide to try fruit juice; it may have been mixed with ordinary (dodgy) water. Finally there's lassi, a refreshing and delicious iced curd (yoghurt) drink. But again, be careful of the water (and ice) used in its making.

Alcoholic Drinks
A cool beer can be something you really look forward to in South India, even if you're not usually a beer drinker. Leading brands include Kingfisher, Kingfisher Diet, Royal Challenge, United Breweries (UB), Eagle, King's, Arlem, London Pilsener, Kalyani Black Label, and Sandpiper. Strong beers include Cannon 1000, Haywards 5000, Knockout and Charger. A 750ml bottle in Tamil Nadu costs Rs 40 to Rs 45 in a mid-range hotel and about Rs 100 to Rs 140 in a more upmarket one. The price drops considerably in Pondicherry, where beer is *sans* tax; here you'll pay Rs 25 a bottle. Goa is one of the cheapest states in India for alcohol and consequently is a popular destination for Indians from neighbouring states.

Be aware that icy cold beer is rather rare;

usually it's just coolish. And liquor is not always easy to get (except in Goa). Strictly speaking alcohol is not to be consumed in public places – or at least in places not specifically designated for such consumption (eg permit rooms). Having a beer with your meal can therefore be an interesting experience. Often, in an effort to please, restaurant staff will send out a boy to buy the requested liquor. On his return the bottle will be discreetly presented, wrapped awkwardly in newspaper, and frequently placed under the table with the mosquito coils. Sometimes even glasses are wrapped up, which is more likely to attract attention than avert it. At Kovalam Beach in Kerala alcohol is easily purchased, but at Varkala Beach you may be served beer in a teapot. However, a restaurant owner who does this is risking a heavy fine. (See the Bangalore section of the Karnataka chapter for details on Bangalore's pubs.)

Indian interpretations of western alcoholic drinks are known as IMFL (Indian Made Foreign Liquor). They include imitations of Scotch and brandy under a plethora of different brand names. The taste varies from hospital disinfectant to passable imitation Scotch.

Indian white wines range from sweet to sherry-like. The best of the bunch is Riviera, a dry white wine which is OK, but far from cheap. Indian red wines tend to be more like port.

Local brews made from the sap of the coconut tree are called *feni* in Goa and toddy in Kerala and Tamil Nadu. Feni is also made from cashews in Goa. After a second distillation the alcoholic strength of these concoctions can be as much as 35% proof. Although usually drunk straight, they can be quite good mixed. Feni tastes great with Coke or Pepsi.

ENTERTAINMENT

South India is not exactly the night-time entertainment capital of the world. A late night in Chennai, Hyderabad and other cities is usually around 10.30 to 11 pm. Discos, dance parties and nightclubs do exist in the southern cities but they are pretty mild, even by Delhi and Mumbai standards. Much entertainment is self-made and opportunities are limited only by your imagination.

Temple Festivals It would be just about impossible to travel through South India and not happen upon at least one festival. Although the origins and rituals of each festival may be different, they are generally a spectacle of passion and colour. They can involve massive temple cars (raths, or chariots) as well as music, dance, and colourfully garbed and garlanded deities. For entertainment value they are hard to beat. See the following chapters for details.

Wedding Watching January/February is the wedding season in Tamil Nadu and Andhra Pradesh. The colourful ceremonies take place in hotels, wedding halls, temples, city streets and village homes. Some of the more elaborate weddings involve elephants, horses and bands of roaming musicians. As an outsider you may be invited to partake in the ritual blessing of the couple.

Helping the Boats Come In Throughout the day along the Tamil Nadu coast, fishers bring in their catch. Watching them land their crude but amazingly sturdy catamarans is a great way to spend time. Helping them bring the boats in will generate much laughter and camaraderie. You may even score some fish or an offer of a ride on the next boat out.

Stargazing – at the Movies The huge MGR studios in Chennai are often buzzing with movie stars. This is where many Tamil and Telugu films are shot. The studios are open to the public and it's perfectly acceptable to wander about and gaze at the stars. If you're lucky you may be 'discovered' and invited to prove your mettle in front of the cameras (see the boxed text 'the Southern Cinema Invasion' in the Chennai chapter).

Stargazing – at the Planetarium Planetariums are especially popular in Andhra Pradesh; even relatively small towns have one. Most planetariums offer shows in Telugu or Hindi; some have English.

Cinemas This is a must. To experience the movie culture is to experience India. It doesn't matter if you don't speak the language. In Tamil or Telugu cinema, the plot can usually be figured out less than a minute into the film. Besides, it's the visual rather than the verbal narrative that counts. Tamil cinema in particular lends a whole new meaning to that often quoted phrase from Federico Fellini that 'Going to the movies is like dreaming with your eyes open'. The audience reaction is usually as entertaining as the film itself.

Water Theme Park If Umberto Eco ever updates his book *Travels in Hyperreality*, the Black Thunder water park in Tamil Nadu deserves special mention. Located on the road from Coimbatore to Ooty, this expensive (and environmentally devastating) playground for the middle and upper classes represents a new face of India. See the Tamil Nadu chapter for details.

Sound-and-Light Shows Sound-and-light shows are popular at tourist spots such as the Tirumalai Nayak Palace in Madurai, the Cellular Jail in Port Blair and the Golconda Fort near Hyderabad. The shows usually consist of a few coloured lights and an audio recording played to maximum distortion. Most shows take place in the early evening and patrons must usually compete with the mosquitoes for space. See the following chapters for details.

Performing Arts Performances of classical dance and music are held at numerous venues including star hotels, the Music Academy in Chennai, the arts village of Dakshinachitra just south of Chennai and Osmania University in Hyderabad, and on the harbour front at Fort Cochin, Kerala. Some of the finest performances take place in small villages during festivals such as Pongal (harvest festival) in Tamil Nadu. Consult tourist offices for details of specific festivals. See the colour section on performing arts in the Facts about South India chapter, and following chapters for details.

In major cities, cultural bodies such as Alliance Française, the British Council, the Goethe Institute and various diplomatic missions will sometimes sponsor performing arts including stage plays, concerts and films. Consult the newspapers for details.

SPECTATOR SPORT
Cricket
India's No 1 spectator sport enjoys a healthy following in South India. If you are from a cricketing country yourself, you will meet people all over South India able to rattle off the names of your top players and knowledgably discuss the successes or otherwise of your country's international performances to date.

First-class matches attract huge crowds (Chennai's Chidambaram stadium seats 40,000) and leading cricketers like Bombay-born Sachin Tendulkar are idolised.

Chennai has played host to some fascinating international contests, including the first World Cup match to be staged in the Indian subcontinent, between India and Australia in October 1987. International Test matches generally take place in India between February and April or between October and December, and Chennai usually stages the first Test.

In March 1998 Chennai was the scene of the opening Test between India and Australia. India won the series 2-1, including the Chennai game, despite Australian spin bowler Shane Warne having emergency rations of baked beans flown in because he didn't like the local food!

Cricket has been played in Chennai since the 18th century.

If you are interested in attending a game, check the local English-language dailies for details. The tourist office or your hotel may be able to assist with information. South India's main cricketing venues are:

- MA Chidambaram Stadium (usually called Chepauk after the Chennai suburb in which it's located) is near the University of Madras Most test matches are held around the time of the Pongal harvest festival (January) during the three day public holiday
- Chinnaswammy Stadium, Bangalore
- Lal Bahadur Stadium, Hyderabad

Football (Soccer)

Football has a passionate following in Goa and Kerala. The local newspapers carry details of important matches and tourist offices should be able to assist with more information.

Horse Racing

There is horse racing every Sunday and on public holidays at Hyderabad's Malakpet Race Course, in Andhra Pradesh. Horse racing is popular in Bangalore and Mysore in Karnataka. The seasons usually run from May to July and from November to February. You can find out when and where races are to be held by checking the local newspapers. See the relevant sections of the Karnataka chapter for more details.

Traditional Sports

Kambla or buffalo racing is a local pastime in rural southern Karnataka during January and February. A pair of buffaloes and their handlers can cover about 120m in around 14 seconds. See the boxed text 'Buffalo Surfing' in the Karnataka chapter..

Other traditional sports include *kho-kho* and *kabaddi*, (see the boxed text on kabaddi in the Chennai chapter) which are both essentially a variation of tag. The Kho-kho Federation of India (KKFI) has branches in all states. Kabaddi is known in South India as *chedugudu* or *hu-tu-tu*.

SHOPPING

South India produces fabulous textiles including the famous Kanchipuram silk. It's also known for woodcarving, especially sandalwood, and various forms of metalwork. Fort Cochin in Kerala has one of India's foremost antique markets. Some of the best devotional kitsch in the world is available from temple bazaars.

Popular purchases such as Kashmiri papier mâché and carpets, Tibetan rugs, Rajasthani and Tibetan jewellery, Rajasthani miniature painting and other products from the north are also available, mainly in the larger cities and tourist centres.

Government emporiums can be found in major cities and usually stock a large range of local crafts. Prices are fixed and are a little higher than one would pay in the bazaar, but for novices who don't know the going rates for crafts or who are unversed in judging quality, the emporiums are a reasonably safe bet. Shipping can be arranged at these places.

Some small handicraft shops exist as outlets for particular cultural groups and are sometimes operated by NGOs. The Victoria Technical Institute in Chennai is such a place. Just south of Chennai on the coast road the purpose built arts village of Dakshinachitra showcases a wide range of crafts from around South India. Visitors can watch artisans working with wood, clay, glass, metals and fibre. Many of the products are for sale. The Cholamandal Artists' Village, also on the coast road south of Chennai, was set up by a group of practising artists to foster the development of contemporary art. The place is dotted with studios and the artists work with stone, paint, metals and other materials. Much of the work created here is sent to galleries of contemporary art around the country and even abroad. For more details see the relevant sections of the chapter on Tamil Nadu.

Metalwork

Bidri is a craft of north-eastern Karnataka (Bidri is named for Bidar, its place of origin in Karnataka) and Andhra Pradesh, where silver is inlaid into gunmetal. Hookah pipes, lamp bases and jewellery boxes are made in this manner. Bidri employs the technique of sand-casting – artisans make a mould from sand, resin and oil.

Small bronze figures of various deities are available in Tamil Nadu, especially in and around major temple towns. The bronze makers (called *shilpis*) still employ the centuries' old lost-wax method of casting, a legacy of the Chola period when bronze sculpture reached its apogee in skill and artistry. A wax figure is made, a mould is formed around it and the wax is melted and poured out. The molten metal is poured in and when it's solidified the mould is broken open. Figures of Shiva as Lord of the Dance, Nataraja, are among the most popular. Small copper bowls, cigarette boxes and paan containers are still handmade in Hyderabad, Andhra Pradesh. Bell metal lamps are a good buy in Thrissur, Kerala.

Jewellery

South India's most important jewellery making centres are Hyderabad, Bangalore, Mysore, Ooty and Thanjavur. Hyderabad is a major centre for cultured pearls. Tirunelveli in southern Tamil Nadu is a centre for many types of jewellery, particularly the large chunky pieces that are made by hammering gold or silver over wax. South Indian jewellery is generally distinguished from that made in the north by its use of motifs patterned on nature – lotus buds, flowers, grass stalks and in Kerala, birds.

Leatherwork

Indian leatherwork is not made from cowhide but from buffalo-hide, camel, goat or some other substitute. *Chappals*, those basic sandals found all over India, are a popular purchase. There isn't a lot of variety in leatherwork, but prices are relatively low.

Textiles

South India produces one of India's most famous types of silk at Kanchipuram, not far from Chennai in Tamil Nadu. Gold and silver is woven into the more expensive Kanchipuram saris, which are all handloomed. The saris are available in major cities, but Chennai has a particularly good selection. For more information on Kanchipuram silk see the colour section 'Silks and Saris'. Dhamavaram in Andhra Pradesh is known as the silk centre of this state; it's not far from Puttaparthi. Kozhikode in Kerala and Mysore in Karnataka are also good places to go shopping for silk saris.

Khadi emporiums (known as Khadi Gramodyog) can be found in every city in South India, and these are good places to buy handmade items of homespun cloth, such as the popular 'Nehru jackets' and the *kurta pyjama*. Bedspreads, tablecloths, cushion covers or material for clothes are other popular khadi purchases.

Ikat production is a very export-oriented activity in Pochampalli (Andhra Pradesh), much of it going to Europe to be used in clothing and furnishings. Ikat is a fabric-making technique in which distinctive patterns are created by individually dyeing the yarn prior to weaving.

The ancient art of drawing on cloth with pen and using vegetable dye is known as *kalamkari* and is very much alive, especially in the town of Sri Kalahasti in Andhra Pradesh. A pattern is traced on the cloth with a pen or pencil then dye is painted on the fabric to create a picture. The images usually depict scenes from the great epics of the *Ramayana* and the *Mahabharata*. although in days gone by artists often chose to paint scenes from courtly life.

Woodwork

Mysore is South India's main centre of sandalwood carving (sandalwood was once reserved solely for carving deities); all manner of things are made, from solid pieces of furniture to keyrings and delicate fans. Rosewood is used for making furniture and carving animals; elephants are a speciality of Kerala. Kerala, along with coastal Karnataka, are centres for marquetry, which uses woods of various hues (including rosewood) and, in Mysore, ivory substitutes. Carved wooden furniture and other household items, either in natural finish or lacquered, are also made in various locations. Wood carvers' skills are very much in evidence in the major temples towns of Tamil Nadu.

Wooden boxes and chests, once major dowry items, are available in the antique shops of Fort Cochin in Kerala. Although they are still made by local artisans, metal cupboards and trunks are replacing the wooden versions and they are becoming rarer. Dowry boxes are usually made from the wood of the jackfruit tree (sometimes rosewood) and are reinforced with brass hinges and brackets.

Wooden toys are also made in many parts

of South India. Brightly painted buses and trucks are made in Thiruvananthapuram.

The small village of Kondapalle in Andhra Pradesh has acquired a reputation for its brightly painted wooden dolls. In a tradition stretching back more than 200 years, the handmade dolls are carved by men and painted by women and children. The artisans operate from their homes and they welcome visitors. The dolls are packaged and distributed throughout India as well as abroad (see the colour section in the Andhra Pradesh chapter).

Paintings & Drawings

In Kerala, and, to a lesser extent, Tamil Nadu, you'll come across vibrant miniature paintings on leaf skeletons enclosed on a printed card depicting domestic and rural scenes as well as gods and goddesses. Just outside Chennai an artists' village called Cholmandal specialises in contemporary art and the gallery here has some fine work.

Kalamkari are drawings on cloth that depict various stories from the *Ramayana* and the *Mahabharata*. Vegetable dyes are used to add colour. This artwork is available in Andhra Pradesh as well as Tamil Nadu, usually in the emporiums.

Basket Weaving

Materials from palm leaves to bamboo and grasses are used to construct attractive baskets, mats and boxes which are available throughout South India.

Stone Sculpture

Mamallapuram is the stone sculpture capital of India. There are literally hundreds of sculptors creating images of all shapes and sizes. Most outlets liaise with Chennai shipping companies in case you want to take home that three-tonne Ganesh statue.

Books

Major cities such as Hyderabad, Chennai, Madurai and Bangalore have excellent bookshops. Even with the cost of packaging and postage, purchases can still be cheaper than in foreign countries.

Musical Instruments

A good place to see skilled artisans is at the Development Centre for Musical Instruments in Chennai where the techniques used in making as well as playing the instruments are displayed. Although you can't buy musical instruments here staff will advise you on good places to do so.

Antiques

The antique market that winds its way through Jew Town in Fort Cochin (Kerala) is one of India's best. Especially popular purchases are quaint spice chests and boxes, dowry boxes and bronze statues. But also on show are discarded figurines from Keralan churches, clocks, Dutch and Chinese crockery, glassware of various vintages and faded prints. Dealers regularly come from London and New York to buy container-loads of collectibles. Ferreting through the cobwebbed, dusty warehouses for something special to take home is one of the pleasures of a visit to Fort Cochin. Shops here are well used to shipping purchases all over the world; sometimes they dispatch huge articles such as carved wooden columns and old, sewn boats.

Articles more than 100 years old are not allowed to be exported from India without an export clearance certificate. If you have doubts about any item and think it could be defined as an antique, you can check with branches of the Archaeological Survey of India. Contact a Goverment of India Tourist Office (see the Tourist Offices section earlier in this chapter) for details.

More Things to Buy

Other great buys in South India include:

- handmade paper from Pondicherry (see the boxed text 'From Rags to Riches' in the Tamil Nadu chapter)
- painted tiles from Pondicherry
- tea, coffee and spices (Munnar, Kerala, for tea; Kumily in Kerala for spices)
- tribal shawls from Toda villages in Tamil Nadu.
- handmade toys (see the colour section in the Andhra Pradesh chapter), Lambadi mirrorwork in Goa (blouses & skirts embroidered with mirrors and sequins)

Getting There & Away

Most visitors to South India will enter via Chennai. Those visiting Goa can only fly direct if they are on a charter; otherwise the trip involves a flight to Mumbai followed by another flight, or rail or bus trip, for the 600km south to Goa. If you're travelling to South India from South-East Asia, Australia or New Zealand it would be worth checking fares to Chennai, as it's cheaper to fly there than to Mumbai.

The first section of this chapter deals with travel from international destinations to India, as well as information on Delhi's international airport, international airline offices, and accommodation in the capital. See the Mumbai and Chennai chapters for details on their respective airports and accommodation. The second part of this chapter has information on domestic airlines in India, and travel from within India

to destinations in South India. Additional information on travelling from Mumbai to South India can be found in the Mumbai chapter.

India

AIR
Buying Tickets
The plane ticket will probably be the single most expensive item in your budget, and buying it can be an intimidating business. There is likely to be a multitude of airlines and travel agents hoping to separate you from your money and it is always worth putting aside a few hours to research the current state of the market. Start early: some of the cheapest tickets have to be bought months in advance and some popular flights sell out early. Talk to other recent travellers – they may be able to stop you making some of the same old mistakes. Look at the ads in newspapers and magazines, consult reference books and watch for special offers. Then phone around travel agents for bargains. (Airlines can supply information on routes and timetables; however, except at times of inter-airline war, they do not supply the cheapest tickets.) Find out the fare, the route, the duration of the journey and any restrictions on the ticket. Then sit back and decide which is best for you.

You may discover that those impossibly cheap flights are 'fully booked', but we have another one that costs a bit more...' Or the flight is on an airline notorious for its poor safety standards and leaves you in the world's least favourite airport in mid-journey for 14 hours. Or they claim only to have the last two seats available for the whole month you want to travel, which they will hold for you for a maximum of two hours. Don't panic – keep ringing around.

Use the fares quoted in this book as a

guide only. They are approximate and based on the rates advertised by travel agents at the time of going to press. Quoted airfares do not necessarily constitute a recommendation for the carrier.

If you are travelling from the UK or the USA, you will probably find that the cheapest flights are being advertised by obscure bucket shops whose names haven't yet reached the telephone directory. Many such firms are honest and solvent, but there are a few rogues who will take your money and disappear, to reopen elsewhere a month or two later under a new name. If you feel suspicious about a firm, don't give them all the money at once – leave a deposit of 20% or so and pay the balance when you get the ticket. If they insist on cash in advance, go somewhere else. And once you have the ticket, ring the airline to confirm that you are actually booked on the flight.

You may decide to pay more than the rock-bottom fare by opting for the safety of a better-known travel agent. Firms such as STA Travel, who have offices worldwide, and Council Travel in the USA are not going to disappear overnight, leaving you clutching a receipt for a nonexistent ticket, but they do offer good prices to most destinations.

Once you have your ticket, write down its number, together with the flight number and other details and keep the information somewhere separate. If the ticket is lost or stolen, this will help you get a replacement. It's sensible to buy travel insurance as early as possible. If you buy it the week before you fly, you may find, for example, that

you're not covered for delays to your flight caused by industrial action.

Round-the-World Tickets & Circle Pacific Fares

Round-the-World (RTW) tickets have become very popular in the past few years. The airline RTW tickets are often real bargains, and can work out to be no more expensive, and sometimes even cheaper, than an ordinary return ticket.

The official airline RTW tickets are usually put together by a combination of two airlines and permit you to fly anywhere on their route systems so long as you do not backtrack. Other restrictions are that you (usually) must book the first sector in advance and cancellation penalties then apply. There may be restrictions on how many stops you are permitted and usually the tickets are valid for 90 days up to a year. An alternative type of RTW ticket is one put together by a travel agent using a combination of discounted tickets.

Circle Pacific tickets use a combination of airlines to circle the Pacific – Australia, New Zealand, North America and Asia. As with RTW tickets there are advance purchase restrictions and limits to how many stopovers you can take. These fares are likely to be around 15% cheaper than RTW tickets.

Travellers with Special Needs

If you have special needs of any sort – you've broken a leg, you're vegetarian, travelling in a wheelchair, taking the baby, terrified of flying – you should let the airline know as soon as possible so that they can make arrangements accordingly. You should remind them when you reconfirm your booking (at least 72 hours before departure) and again when you check in at the airport. It may also be worth ringing around the airlines before you make your booking to find out how each one of them can handle your particular needs.

Airports and airlines can be surprisingly helpful, but they do need advance warning. Most international airports will provide escorts from check-in desk to plane where needed, and there should be ramps, lifts, and accessible toilets and telephones for wheelchair-bound travellers. Aircraft toilets, on the other hand, are likely to present a problem; travellers should discuss this with the airline at an early stage and, if necessary, with their doctor.

Guide dogs for the blind will often have to travel in a specially pressurised baggage compartment with other animals away from their owner; smaller guide dogs will be subject to the same quarantine laws (six months in isolation, etc) as any other animal when entering or returning to countries currently free of rabies, such as Australia.

Deaf travellers can ask for airport and inflight announcements to be written down for them.

Children under two travel for 10% of the standard fare (or free on some airlines), as long as they don't occupy a seat. They don't get a baggage allowance either. 'Skycots' should be provided by the airline if requested in advance; these will take a child weighing up to about 10kg. Children between two and 12 can usually occupy a seat for half to two-thirds of the full fare and do get a baggage allowance. Push chairs can often be taken as hand luggage.

International Arrivals & Departures – Delhi

Information for Delhi is included below. For information on Mumbai and Chennai, please refer to those chapters.

The names of the airports in Delhi are a little confusing. Terminal IA is for arrivals on domestic flights within India; and next door, Terminal IB (ignore the large name on the top 'Indira Gandhi International Airport') is for domestic departures. Both are 15km from Connaught Place, and sometimes collectively known Palam airport. The *real* Indira Gandhi International Airport, also called Terminal II, is 20km from Connaught Place, and used for all international arrivals and departures.

If you have just arrived and have an onward connection to another city in India it may be with Air India. If that is the case, you must check in at the international ter-

minal (Terminal II) rather than the domestic terminal.

If you need to change money there are 24 hour State Bank of India and Thomas Cook foreign exchange counters in the international arrivals hall. There are also exchange offices in the new arrivals and departures lounges, opposite the terminals, though they may not always be staffed.

Many international flights arrive and depart in the early hours of the morning, usually before dawn. Take special care if this is your first foray into India and you arrive exhausted and jet-lagged. We continue to hear stories of travellers arriving in India for the first time on their own and being taken to a hotel they don't want (and charged Rs 1500 or more for a room) by unscrupulous taxi drivers.

If you are unsure, sit out the rest of the night in the 24 hour arrivals lounge or stay at the Airport Dormitory (see Places to Stay below). At the very least use the pre-paid taxi service, pre-book your hotel room (there is a 24 hour hotel booking counter in the international arrivals hall – but it only deals with star-rated hotels), and never allow a stranger to accompany you as a passenger in your taxi.

Several (but not all) airlines now require you to have the baggage you're checking in X-rayed and sealed, so do this at the machines just inside the departure hall before you queue to check in.

The international departure tax (Rs 500) can be paid at the State Bank of India counter in the departures hall, also before check-in, or, if you are flying with Air India, you can pay it at the Air India office when you confirm or book your flight.

Facilities within the international airport are poor: there are the requisite overpriced cafes, but the large, recently constructed arrivals and departure lounges (which cost Rs 10 to enter each and are opposite the terminals) are quiet and comfortable and make the endless waiting a little more bearable.

Places to Stay There are literally hundreds of places to stay in the capital, including some budget options in the bazaar known as Paharganj (which is only a stone's throw from the New Delhi train station) or any of the many hotels convenient to the airports.

City Paharganj has dozens of cheap hotels. Some of the best along Main Bazaar, the major thoroughfare, also boast excellent restaurants. All of the following are on Main Bazaar:

Hotel Vivek (☎ 777 7062) is popular and central. Singles/doubles are from Rs 150/200, though you pay a lot more for air-con.

Hotel Vishal (☎ 753 2079) has rooms for Rs 160/200, or Rs 250 for a room with a bathroom.

Hare Krishna Guest House (☎ 753 3017) has clean rooms from Rs 130/170; more with a private bathroom.

In the mid-range, *Gold Regency (☎ 354 0101)* has new, clean and quiet rooms for a negotiable Rs 900.

Outside Paharganj, the Ys are often a good mid-range option (and available to either gender).

YMCA Tourist Hotel (☎ 336 1887), on Jai Singh Rd, has singles/doubles for Rs 815/1365.

YWCA International Guest House (☎ 336 0133), 10 Sansad Marg (Parliament St), is better value from Rs 385/655.

Retiring Rooms at the Old Delhi and New Delhi train stations cost Rs 150/250 for a fan-cooled double for 12/24 hours; or Rs 250/450 with air-conditioning.

Airports & Environs The *Airport Dormitory* (no telephone) is OK if you have one of those terrible late night or early morning arrivals or departures (though it's not ideal for unaccompanied women, as the dorms are mixed and not that safe). It is at the bus stand, 300m down the road from the international terminal. A dorm bed costs Rs 65 per person for 24 hours.

The *Centaur Hotel (☎ 565 2223)*, with rooms for US$150/170, is the most convenient top-range place. It's on Gurgaon Rd, 2km south of the international terminal and 5km from the domestic terminals.

To/From the Airport Three companies ply the airport-city route. They can drop you off at the domestic and international airports, as well as at Ajmer Gate (on the other side of New Delhi train station to Paharganj), Old Delhi train station and their offices around Connaught Place. The time it takes to get from the airport to Connaught Place varies depending on traffic, but averages around 40 minutes. You can only catch these buses at the airports or at their ticket offices.

One company, EATS (☎ 331 6530), has an office opposite the Palika Bazaar on Radial Road, Connaught Place. The other two, Delhi Transport Corporation (DTC) (☎ 331 6745) and Blue/White Line, share an office at Super Bazaar, Connaught Place. A coach (from one of the companies) leaves the international airport every 30 minutes, but departures to the airport (every 30 to 60 minutes) are shared, so you will have to inquire at one of the offices beforehand about exact schedules. You are probably better off using EATS *to* the airport, as the DTC-Blue/White Line office is not easy to find. The coaches stop immediately outside the domestic arrivals terminal, and to the left as you exit the international (arrivals) terminal. Tickets, which can be pre-booked, cost Rs 30, plus Rs 5 for baggage.

Public bus No 780 travels about every 30 minutes between Super Bazaar at Connaught Place and the bus stand (300m from the international terminal), but this bus gets very crowded, and should be avoided at night, when it's not very safe. It takes anything from 30 to 90 minutes to make the journey.

Taking the coach into the city from the airport is fine if you are doing it during daylight hours, otherwise take a pre-paid taxi from the stand immediately to your right as you exit the international (arrivals) terminal (or outside the domestic arrivals terminal. The fares are displayed at the counter. It costs Rs 150 to Paharganj or Connaught Place plus Rs 2 for baggage. There's a 25% surcharge between 11 pm and 5 am. Ignore *any* offers from drivers who are not part of the pre-paid taxi service.

Auto-rickshaws (about Rs 150 from

Connaught Place) can take you to the international terminal, (not a great idea unless you want to fly home smelling like exhaust fumes) but are not allowed to collect arriving passengers. For the domestic terminals (about Rs 120), auto-rickshaws are easier.

There is also a free coach service run by Air India and Indian Airlines between the international and domestic airports for bona fide passengers needing to change flights. This coach leaves from a special, easy-to-find, bay at the international airport every hour, on the hour. Alternatively, you can take a pre-paid taxi or airport coach between the airports.

International Airlines Offices of the major international airlines in Delhi (telephone area code: 011) are as follows:

Aeroflot
  (☎ 331 2873; airport ☎ 329 6331)
  BMC House, 1st Floor, N1,
  Middle Circle, Connaught Place
Air Canada
  (☎ 372 0043; airport ☎ 565 2850)
  Room 1421, New Delhi Hilton,
  Barakhamba
Air France
  (☎ 373 8004; airport ☎ 565 2099)
  Scindia House, Janpath
Air India
  (☎ 331 1225; airport ☎ 565 2050)
  Jeevan Bharati Bldg, Sansad Marg 1,
  Connaught Place
Air Lanka
  (☎ 336 8843; airport ☎ 565 2957)
  Student Travel Information Centre,
  Room 1, Janpath Hotel
Air Mauritius
  (☎ 373 1225; airport ☎ 565 2050)
  c/o Air India (street address above)
  Connaught Place
Alitalia
  (☎ 332 1006; airport ☎ 565 2349)
  2nd floor, DCM Bldg, Barakhamba
American Airlines
  (☎ 332 5876)
  105 Indra Prakash Bldg,
  Barakhamba
ANA
  (☎ 331 0012)
  42 Connaught Circus, Connaught Place
Austrian Airlines
  (☎ 331 6284)
  C28, Prem House, Connaught Circus

Biman Bangladesh
  (☎ 545 2943)
  Indira Gandhi international airport
British Airways
  (☎ 332 7428; airport ☎ 565 2077)
  DLF Bldg, Sansad Marg
Cathay Pacific Airways
  (☎ 332 3919) Tolstoy House, Tolstoy Marg
Delta Air Lines
  (☎ 332 5222; airport ☎ 565 2093)
  Chandralok Bldg, 36 Janpath
DrukAir(Bhutan)
  (☎ 331 0990; airport ☎ 565 3207)
  Chandralok Bldg, 36 Janpath
El Al Israel Airlines
  (☎ 332 3960; airport ☎ 565 3038)
  G-57, Connaught Place
Emirates
  (☎ 332 4665; airport ☎ 329 6861)
  Kanchenjunga Bldg, 18 Barakhamba Rd
Gulf Air
  (☎ 332 7814; airport ☎ 565 2065)
  G12, Connaught Circus
Japan Airlines
  (☎ 332 4922; airport ☎ 565 2060)
  Chandralok Bldg, 36 Janpath
KLM Royal Dutch Airlines
  (☎ 372 1139; airport ☎ 565 2420)
  Prakash Deep, 7 Tolstoy Marg
Korean Air
  (☎ 331 5454; airport ☎ 565 3304)
  303/4 Prakash Deep, 7 Tolstoy Marg
Lufthansa Airlines
  (☎ 332 3310; airport ☎ 565 2063) 56 Janpath
Malaysian Airlines
  (☎ 332 4308; airport ☎ 565 2395)
  G55, Connaught Place
Pakistan International Airlines (PIA)
  (☎ 373 7791; airport ☎ 565 2841)
  Kailash Bldg 26, KG Marg
Qantas Airways
  (☎ 332 9027) Mohan Dev Bldg, Tolstoy Marg
Royal Nepal Airlines Corporation (RNAC)
  (☎ 332 1164; airport ☎ 329 6876), 44 Janpath
Scandinavian Airlines (SAS)
  (☎ 335 2299; airport ☎ 565 3708)
  1st floor, Amba Deep Bldg, KG Marg
Singapore Airlines (SIA)
  (☎ 335 0131; airport ☎ 565 3072)
  International Business Centre, M-38/1,
  Middle Circle, Connaught Place
South African Airways (SAA)
  (☎ 332 5262) B1, Connaught Place
Swissair
  (☎ 332 5511; airport ☎ 565 2531)
  DLF Bldg, Sansad Marg

Thai Airways International
   (☎ 623 9133; airport ☎ 329 6526)
   Park Royal Hotel, America Plaza,
   Nehru Place, Chanakyapuri
United Airlines
   (☎ 371 5550; airport ☎ 565 3910)
   Amba Deep Bldg, 14 KG Marg

Africa

Due to the large Indian population living in Nairobi there are plenty of flights between East Africa and Mumbai. Typical fares from Mumbai to Nairobi are about US$550 return with Ethiopian Airlines, Kenya Airways, Air India or PIA (via Karachi). Flights between Nairobi and Chennai are via Mumbai and typically cost around US$967 return, with Kenya Airways, Air India or PIA. Aeroflot operates a service between Delhi and Cairo (via Moscow).

Australia & New Zealand

Advance purchase return fares from the east coast of Australia to Chennai range from A$1349 to A$1699 depending on the season. Fares are slightly more expensive to Mumbai. From Australia fares are cheaper from Darwin or Perth than from the east coast. The low travel period is from March to October; peak is from November to February.

Tickets from Australia to London or other European capitals, with an Indian stopover, range from A$900 to A$1500 one-way and A$1775 to A$2300 return, again depending on the season.

Return advance purchase fares from New Zealand to India range from NZ$1950 to NZ$2350 depending on the season.

Bangladesh

Bangladesh Biman and Indian Airlines fly from Calcutta to Dhaka (US$66) and Chittagong (US$55), both one-way fares.

Continental Europe

Fares from continental Europe are mostly far more expensive than from London. Amsterdam, however, can be a good place for a cheap ticket, but make sure the travel agent you use has an 'SGR' certificate or you may never see your money again. A return ticket

to Mumbai from London is around £329 in the low season; high season fares range from £259 one way to £419 return. Excursion fares can be much more: DFL 1596/UK£465 to Mumbai and DFL 1830/UK£530 to Chennai. In Amsterdam, NBBS is a popular travel agent.

Hong Kong

Hong Kong is the discount ticket capital of the region. Its bucket shops are at least as unreliable as those of other cities. Ask other travellers for advice before buying a ticket.

Malaysia

Not many travellers fly between Malaysia and India because it is cheaper from Thailand, but there are flights between Penang or Kuala Lumpur and Chennai. You can generally pick up one-way tickets for the Malaysia Airlines flight from Kuala Lumpur to Chennai for RM$776 one way and between Penang and Chennai for RM$894. Kuala Lumpur-Mumbai is RM$1199 one way and RM$2109 return.

The Maldives

From Thiruvananthapuram (Trivandrum) in southern India to Male' in the Maldives, costs US$60 one way. This is cheaper than flying there from Colombo in Sri Lanka.

Myanmar (Burma)

There are no land crossing points between Myanmar and India (or any other country), so if you want to visit Myanmar your only choice is to fly there. Myanmar International Airways flies Calcutta-Yangon (Rangoon); Bangladesh Biman flies Dhaka-Yangon.

From Bangkok via Myanmar, the one-way Bangkok-Yangon-Calcutta fare is around US$403 with Thai or Myanmar Airways.

Calcutta-Yangon costs US$356 one way on Indian Airlines.

Nepal

Royal Nepal Airlines Corporation (RNAC) and Indian Airlines share routes between India and Kathmandu. Both airlines give a 25% discount to those under 30 years of age on flights between Kathmandu and India; no student card is needed. There are flights between Kathmandu and Mumbai (US$257 one-way) and many more between Kathmandu and Delhi (US$142).

Pakistan

PIA and Air India operate flights from Karachi to Delhi for US$100 one way and Lahore to Delhi for US$67 one way.

Singapore

Singapore is a great cheap ticket centre and you can pick up Singapore-Chennai tickets for about S$415.

Sri Lanka

There are flights to and from Colombo and Mumbai, Chennai, Tiruchirappalli or Thiruvananthapuram. Flights are most frequent on the Chennai-Colombo route (US$90).

Thailand

Bangkok is the most popular departure point from South-East Asia into Asia proper because of the cheap flights from there to Calcutta, Yangon in Myanmar, Dhaka in Bangladesh or Kathmandu in Nepal. It will cost about US$250 to fly from Bangkok to Chennai.

The UK

Charter flights are probably the least expensive way to get from the UK to Goa or Kerala. The most common scheduled route is Air India via Mumbai or Air Lanka via Colombo. As a guide, at the time of writing The Charter Flight Centre (☎ 0171-565 6788/6777) was advertising return flights to Kerala or Goa for UK£299. The best source for information on charter flights is the *Evening Standard* newspaper.

Various excursion fares are available from London to India, but you can get better prices through London's many cheap-ticket specialists. Check the travel page ads in the *Times*, *Business Traveller* and the weekly 'what's on' magazine *Time Out*; or check give-away papers like *TNT*. Some travel agents to try include:

Bridge the World
(☎ 0171-911 0900)
1-3 Ferdinand St, Camden Town, London NW1
Quest Worldwide
(☎ 0181-547 3322)
29 Castle St, Kingston, Surrey KT1 1ST
SD Enterprises
(☎ 0181-903 3411; fax 903 0392)
103 Wembley Park Dr, Wembley, Middlesex
STA Travel
(☎ 0171-937 9962)
74 Old Brompton Rd, London SW7
(☎ 0171-465 0484)
117 Euston Rd, London NW1
Trailfinders
(☎ 0171-938 3939)
194 High St, Kensington, London W8 7RG
(☎ 0171-938 3366)
46 Earls Court Rd, London W8

From London to Mumbai, fares range from around UK£189/329 one way/return in the low season or UK£259/459 one way/return in the high season – cheaper short-term fares are also available. The cheapest fares are usually with KLM or Alitalia. You'll also find very competitive airfares to the subcontinent with Bangladesh Biman or Air Lanka. Lufthansa Airlines has some of the best deals but on these special offers once you've bought the ticket no changes to dates of travel are allowed.

If you want to stop in India en route to Australia expect to pay between UK£349 and UK£589 for a one-way fare through to Australia.

Most British travel agents are registered with ABTA (Association of British Travel Agents). If you have paid for your flight with an ABTA-registered agent which then goes out of business, ABTA will guarantee a refund or an alternative. Unregistered bucket shops are riskier but also sometimes cheaper.

The USA & Canada

The cheapest return airfares from the US west coast to India are around US$1300. Another way of getting there is to fly to Hong Kong and get a ticket from there. Tickets to Hong Kong cost about US$675 one way and around US$700 return from San Francisco or Los Angeles. In Hong

Kong you can find one-way tickets to Mumbai for US$595 or Chennai for US$825. Alternatively, you can fly to Singapore for around US$780/900 one way or return, or to Bangkok for US$765/850 one way or return, and pick up a cheap onward ticket from there.

From the east coast you can get return flights to Mumbai for US$1059/2004 in the low/high season, and to Chennai for US$1177/2565 (low/high). Another way of getting to India from New York is to fly to London and buy a cheap fare from there.

The *New York Times*, the *San Francisco Examiner*, the *Chicago Tribune* and the *LA Times* all produce weekly travel sections in which you'll find any number of travel agents' ads. Council Travel and STA Travel have offices in major cities nationwide. The magazine *Travel Unlimited* (PO Box 1058, Allston, Mass 02134) publishes details of the cheapest air fares and courier possibilities for destinations all over the world from the USA.

Fares from Canada are similar to the USA fares. From Vancouver the route is like that from the US west coast, with the option of going via Hong Kong. From Toronto it is easier to travel via London.

Travel CUTS has offices in all major Canadian cities. The *Toronto Globe & Mail* and the *Vancouver Sun* carry travel agents' ads. The magazine *Great Expeditions* (PO Box 8000-411, Abbotsford BC V2S 6H1) is useful.

Cheap Tickets in India

Although you can get cheap tickets in Chennai, Mumbai and Calcutta, it is in Delhi that the real wheeling and dealing goes on. There are a number of bucket shops around Connaught Place, but inquire with other travellers about their current trustworthiness. And if you use a bucket shop, double-check with the airline itself that the booking has been made. A one-way fare from Chennai to London is US$482 on British Airways.

Although Delhi is the best place for cheap tickets, many flights between Europe and South-East Asia or Australia pass through Mumbai. If you're heading east from India to Bangladesh, Myanmar or

Thailand you'll probably find much better prices in Calcutta than in Delhi, even though there are fewer agents.

LAND

Drivers of cars and riders of motorbikes will need the vehicle's registration papers, liability insurance and an international driver's permit in addition to their domestic licence. Beware: there are two kinds of international permit, one of which is needed mostly for former British colonies. You will also need a *carnet de passage en douane*, which is effectively a passport for the vehicle, and acts as a temporary waiver of import duty. The carnet may also need to have listed any expensive spares that you're planning to carry with you, such as a gearbox. This is necessary when travelling in many countries in Asia, and is designed to prevent car import rackets. Contact your local automobile association for details about all documentation.

Liability insurance is not available in advance for many out-of-the-way countries, but has to be bought when crossing the border. The cost and quality of such local insurance varies wildly, and you will find in some countries that you are travelling uninsured. In India insurance only covers about 40% of the value of the vehicle.

Anyone who is planning to take their own vehicle with them needs to check in advance what spares and petrol are likely to be available. In India, unleaded fuel is available only in Delhi, Mumbai, Calcutta and Chennai and a few other large cities.

Cycling is a cheap, convenient, healthy, environmentally sound and above all fun way of travelling. But come prepared; you won't necessarily be able to buy that crucial gizmo for your machine when it breaks down.

For more details on driving your own vehicle in India, cycling or motor biking in South India, see the Getting Around chapter.

Bangladesh

The main crossings are at Benapol and Haridaspur on the Calcutta route and Chilahati and Haldibari on the Darjeeling route. The

Tamabil/Dauki border crossing, in the north-east corner on the Meghalaya route, and the Akaura/Agartala crossing into Tripura in the east are also open. Crossing via lesser routes such as Bhurungamari is sometimes also possible.

No exit permit is required when leaving Bangladesh. If border officials mention anything about a permit, remain steadfast. However, if you enter Bangladesh by air and exit via land, you do need a road permit, which can be obtained from the Passport & Immigration office, 2nd floor, 17/1 Segunbagicha Rd in Dhaka, and if you are driving from Bangladesh in your own vehicle, two permits are required: one from the Indian High Commission (☎ 504897), House 120, Road 2, Dhanmondi in Dhaka, and one from the Bangladesh Ministry of Foreign Affairs (☎ 883260), Pioneer Rd (facing the Supreme Court), Segun Bagicha in the centre of Dhaka.

Europe

Many travellers combine travel to the sub-continent with the Middle East by flying from India or Pakistan to Amman in Jordan or one of the Gulf states.

A number of London-based overland companies operate bus or truck trips across Asia on a regular basis. See Tours under UK in the Organised Tours section later in this chapter for details.

For more detail on the Asian overland route see the Lonely Planet guides to Pakistan, Iran and Turkey.

Nepal

There are direct buses from Delhi to Kathmandu, but these generally get bad reports from travellers. It's cheaper and more satisfactory to organise this trip yourself. The most popular routes are from Raxaul (near Muzaffarpur), Sunnauli (near Gorakhpur), and Kakarbhitta (near Siliguri). If you are heading straight to Nepal from Delhi or elsewhere in western India then the Gorakhpur to Sunauli route is the most convenient. From Calcutta, Patna or most of eastern India, Raxaul to Birganj is the best entry point. From Darjeeling it's easiest to go to Kakarbhitta.

To give an idea of costs, a 2nd-class rail ticket from Delhi to Gorakhpur costs US$6 and buses from Gorakhpur to the border and then on to Kathmandu cost another US$6.

Pakistan

Due to the continuing unstable political situation between India and Pakistan, there's only one border crossing open. This may change.

For the Lahore (Pakistan) to Amritsar (India) train you have to take one ticket from Lahore to Attari, the Indian border town, and another from Attari to Amritsar. The train departs Lahore daily at 11.30 am and arrives in Amritsar at 3 pm after a couple of hours at the border passing through immigration and customs. Going the other way, you leave Amritsar at 9.30 am and arrive in Lahore at 1.35 pm. Pakistan immigration and customs are handled at Lahore station. Sometimes, however, border delays can make the trip much longer. From Amritsar you cannot buy a ticket until the morning of departure and there are no seat reservations – arrive early and push.

Few travellers use the road link between India and Pakistan. It's mainly of interest to people with vehicles or those on overland buses. By public transport the trip from Lahore entails taking a bus to the border at Wagah between Lahore and Amritsar, walking across the border and then taking another bus or taxi into Amritsar.

From Lahore, buses and minibuses depart from near the general bus terminal on Badami Bagh. The border opens at 9.15 am and closes at 3.30 pm. If you're stuck on the Pakistan side you can stay at the *PTDC Motel*, where there are dorm beds and double rooms.

South-East Asia

The South-East Asian overland trip is still wide open and as popular as ever. From Australia the first step is to Indonesia – Timor, Bali or Jakarta. Although most people fly from an east-coast city or from Perth to Bali, there are also flights from Darwin and from Port Hedland in the north of Western Australia. The shortest route is the flight between Darwin and Kupang on the Indonesian island of Timor.

From Bali you head north through Java to Jakarta, from where you either travel by ship or fly to Singapore or continue north through Sumatra and then cross to Penang in Malaysia. After travelling around Malaysia you can fly from Penang to Chennai in India or, more popularly, continue north to Thailand and eventually fly out from Bangkok to India, perhaps with a stopover in Myanmar. Unfortunately, crossing by land from Myanmar to India (or indeed to any other country) is forbidden by the Myanmar government.

There are all sorts of travel variations possible in South-East Asia; the region is a delight to travel through, it's good value for money, the food is generally excellent and healthy, and all in all it's an area of the world not to be missed. For full details see Lonely Planet's guide *South-East Asia*.

SEA

The ferry service from Rameswaram in South India to Talaimannar in Sri Lanka has been suspended for some years due to the unrest in Sri Lanka. This was a favourite route for shipping arms and equipment to the Tamil guerrilla forces in the north of the country. The service between Penang and Chennai also ceased some time ago.

The shipping services between Africa and India only carry freight (including vehicles), not passengers.

DEPARTURE TAX

For flights to neighbouring countries (Pakistan, Sri Lanka, Bangladesh, Nepal) the departure tax is Rs 150, but to other countries it's Rs 500. The airport tax applies to everybody, even to babies who do not occupy a seat. The method of collecting the tax varies but generally you have to pay it before you check in, so look out for an airport tax counter as you enter the check-in area.

ORGANISED TOURS

There are numerous foreign ecotravel and adventure travel companies which can pro-

vide unusual and interesting trips in addition to companies that provide more standard tours. There are too many to include them all here; check newspapers and travel magazines for advertisements, and journals such as *Earth Journal* (USA) for listings. Companies that organise tours to various parts of India include the following:

Australasia
Ferris Wheels Classic Enfield Motorcycle Safaris
(☎ 02-9904 7419)
61 Elizabeth St, Atarmon 2064, Australia
Peregrine Adventures
(☎ 03-9663 8611)
258 Lonsdale St, Melbourne 3000, Australia.
Also offices in Sydney, Brisbane, Adelaide,
Perth and Hobart.
Venturetreks
(☎ 09-379 9855; fax 09-377 0320)
164 Parnell Rd (PO Box 37610),
Parnell, Auckland, New Zealand
Window on the World
(☎/fax 03-9874 7029)
79 Rooks Rd, Nunawading 3131,
Melbourne, Australia
(☎/fax 0431-430832)
27 Chandra Nagar, Srirangam, Tiruchirappalli
(Trichy), India 62006
World Expeditions
(☎ 02-9264 3366; fax 02-9261 1974)
3rd Floor, 441 Kent St, Sydney 2000, Australia
(☎ 03-9670 8400; fax 03-9670 7474)
1st Floor, 393 Little Bourke St, Melbourne
3000, Australia

UK
Encounter Overland
(☎ 0171-370 6845)
267 Old Brompton Rd, London SW5 9JA
Exodus Expeditions
(☎ 0181-673 0859)
9 Weir Rd, London SW12 0LT
Imaginative Traveller
(international reservation office)
(☎ 081-742 3113; fax 081-742 3046)
14 Barley Mow Passage, Chiswick,
London W4 4PH

USA
Adventure Center
(☎ 800-227 8747)
1311 63rd St, Suite 200, Emeryville, CA 94608
All Adventure Travel, Inc
(☎ 303-440 7924)
PO Box 4307, Boulder, CO 80306 Asian
Pacific Adventures (☎ 800-825 1680) 826 S
Sierra Bonita Ave, Los Angeles, CA 90036

Inner Asia Expeditions
(☎ 415-922 0448; fax 415-346 5535)
2627 Lombard St, San Francisco, CA 94123

South India

AIR

All South India's states are serviced by air as are the Union Territories Lakshadweep and the Andaman & Nicobar Islands. Major international and domestic airports in South India are in Andhra Pradesh (Hyderabad); Tamil Nadu (Chennai); Andaman & Nicobar Islands (Port Blair); Kerala (Thiruvananthapuram, Kochi: Willingdon Island domestic airport & Kochi international airport); Lakshadweep (Agatti); Karnataka (Bangalore, Mangalore, Belgaum); and Goa (Dabolim). See the relevant chapters for more information.

Charter Flights

For charter flights between the UK and Goa and Kerala, see the UK paragraph of the Air section earlier in this chapter.

Domestic Airlines

With deregulation, Indian Airlines no longer has a monopoly on domestic air services. At least four local operators fly to South India. For the Mumbai and Chennai addresses of domestic operators servicing South India, see those chapters.

Delhi The addresses in Delhi (telephone area code: 011) for airlines serving South India are:

Indian Airlines
(☎ 331 0517)
Malhotra Bldg, F Block, Connaught Place
Jet Airways
(☎ 685 3700)
3-E Hansalaya Bldg, 15 Barakhamba Rd
NEPC
(☎ 332 2525) G39,
4th Floor, Pawan House, Connaught Circus
Sahara India
(☎ 332 6851)
GF, Ambadeep Bldg, Kasturba Gandhi Marg

Domestic Air Services

South India has a busy network of air services. There are regular services between major cities. Some Indian Airlines flights are operated by its subsidiary Alliance Air (flight code CD). Indian Airlines has a 14/21 day 'Discover India' pass which costs US$500/750. This allows unlimited travel on its domestic routes, but you aren't allowed to backtrack. There's also a 25% youth discount if you're under 30. This also applies to Jet Airways.

Buying Tickets

Computerised booking is the norm, so getting flight information and reservations is relatively simple – it's just getting to the head of the queue that takes time. In some Indian Airlines offices you are required to enter your name in a book at the counter and then wait your turn. All flights are heavily booked and you need to plan as far in advance as possible.

Air tickets must be paid for with foreign currency or by credit card, or rupees backed up by encashment certificates. Change, where appropriate, is given in rupees. Infants up to two years old travel at 10% of the adult fare, children aged from two to 12 the reduction is 50%. There is no student reduction for overseas visitors but there is a youth fare for people 12 to 29 years old. This allows a 25% reduction.

Refunds on adult tickets attract a charge (usually Rs 125) and can be made at any office. There are no refund charges on infant tickets. If a flight is delayed or cancelled, you cannot refund the ticket. If you fail to show up 30 minutes before the fight, this is regarded as a 'no-show' and you forfeit the full value of the ticket.

Indian Airlines accepts no responsibility if you lose your ticket. They absolutely will not refund lost tickets, but at their discretion may issue replacements.

Check-In

Check in one hour before departure. On some internal routes, as a security measure, you are required to identify your checked-in baggage on the tarmac immediately prior to boarding.

BUS

Because of the long distances involved between major northern cities and southern ones, Mumbai to Goa is the only long-haul bus trip that travellers would consider tolerable and practical. However, it is likely that the now-completed Konkan Railway will make this trip less popular. In Mumbai, Goan government Kadamba buses depart from the State Road Transport Terminal close to Mumbai Central train station. There's only one government bus to Goa each day. It departs at 5 pm and arrives in Panaji at 9 am the following day; tickets cost Rs 220.

Private long-distance buses are much more comfortable and can be booked at booths along J Boman Behram Marg, near the entrance to the State Road Transport Terminal. Tickets to Goa cost between Rs 200 and Rs 300 for deluxe buses, and between Rs 400 and Rs 500 for sleeper or air-con buses. Buses depart between 2 and 5 pm and many start from just south of the Metro Cinema on MG Rd. The journey takes 17 hours.

TRAIN

There are regular services between North and South Indian cities. See the following chapters for details on services within South India. See the Mumbai chapter for details on trains from that city. In Delhi, trains to Chennai Central train station and other South Indian destinations leave from New Delhi train station. The fastest express train to Chennai Central takes around 36 hours to make the 2195km trip. Express fares are: Rs 1495 (1st class); Rs 806 (air-con chair); Rs 341 (sleeper class); and Rs 246 (2nd class).

Express services from New Delhi include the *Tamil Nadu Express* (46½ hours; departs Delhi at 10.30 pm); the *Andhra Pradesh Express* (43 hours; leaves New Delhi at 5.50 pm, arrives at Hyderabad at 8.15 pm and then Chennai Central at 1 pm); and the *GT Express* (36 hours; leaves New Delhi at 6.40 pm and arrives at Chennai Central at 7 am).

The *Kerala Express* leaves New Delhi train station at 11.30 am and arrives at Ernakulam in Kerala at 11.35 am (48 hours later), continuing on to Kollam (Quilon) at 2.45 pm and Thiruvananthapuram at 4.55 pm. The fare to Thiruvananthapuram is: Rs 1923 (1st class); Rs 1017 (air-con chair); Rs 407 (sleeper class); and Rs 294 (2nd class). The *Navyug Express* continues through to Kanyakumari (57½ hours; leaves New Delhi at 2 pm and arrives at Kanyakumari at 11.30 pm).

There is a special foreign tourist booking office upstairs in the New Delhi train station. It is open Monday to Saturday from 7.30 am to 5 pm. This is the place to go if you want a tourist-quota allocation, are the holder of an Indrail Pass or want to buy an Indrail Pass (for information on these passes, see the Getting Around chapter). The main ticket office is on Chelmsford Road, between New Delhi train station and Connaught Place. It is well organised but incredibly busy.

CAR & MOTORCYCLE

Few people bring their own vehicles to India. If you decide to bring a car or motorcycle to India it must be brought in under a carnet (a customs document guaranteeing its removal at the end of your stay). Failing to do so will be very expensive. For more information on driving in India, see the Car section of the Getting Around chapter.

Rental

Renting a self-drive car in any of the main cities in India and driving to South India is possible but not recommended. India holds the unenviable record of having the most dangerous roads in the world. Hertz maintains offices in Delhi (☎ 011-697 7188), Mumbai (☎ 022-492 1429) and Chennai (☎ 044-433 0684) as well as in Panaji (☎ 0832-223998) in Goa. Costs are around Rs 1000 a day, drivers must be 25 years old or over and a deposit of Rs 5000 is required.

It would be possible to travel to South India by hiring a car and driver. Car hire companies offer chauffeur-driven services, or alternatively you can make your own arrangements. The best way to do this is to check prices with various car-hire companies and the tourist office, then negotiate a rate with the driver of your choice – your driver may have been recommended by word of mouth (other travellers) or by your hotel.

The 600km trip from Mumbai to Goa, for example, takes about 14 hours. Many drivers will happily do this in one stretch, although it would probably be safer to have an overnight rest. You'll have to pay for the taxi's return

trip, so the cost will be between Rs 6000 and Rs 8000.

BOAT

The Mumbai-Goa ferry runs five days a week and the trip takes around eight hours. There have been a few breakdowns, but the authorities maintain that the problem has been sorted out. See the Mumbai chapter for more details.

Getting Around

AIR

All states in South India are serviced by air. This is handy if you want to get from say, Kochi (Kochin) on the west coast to Chennai (Madras) on the east, quickly and with no hassle. There are flights between Calcutta and Chennai via the Andaman Islands, but these are heavily booked (at least three months advance reservation is required). At the time of writing there were three return flights a week from Kochi in (Kerala) to Agatti (Lakshadweep) and three return flights from Goa to Agatti. The plane from Kochi is an Islander and due to lack of space/power, passengers may only take 10kg of luggage each. However, the situation changes periodically, so it's worth double-checking. Air travel within some of the larger states is feasible. Goa is too small to make air travel within it worthwhile.

Domestic Air Services

India's major domestic airline, the government-run Indian Airlines, flies extensively throughout South India. Some services are operated by its subsidiary, Alliance Air. The country's international carrier, Air India, has a domestic run between Mumbai (Bombay) and Chennai.

There are four independent operators. The best of them (indeed the best airline in India) is Jet Airways. It has an extensive network throughout India. The other operators are NEPC, Sahara India and Spanair. Sahara India flies between major cities including daily flights between Delhi and Chennai. Spanair flies between Mumbai and Goa. NEPC runs charter flights in addition to its usual services. Contact details for domestic airlines are in the Getting There & Away chapter.

BUS

Generally you will find there are two main types of bus: private and state. Both ply the same routes, although private buses tend to offer more choice in terms of frequency. Private buses also tend to be a bit more expensive and rather more comfortable.

In South India, signs at bus stands and on the buses themselves tend to be in the local script. This means you will have to keep checking to ensure you are in the right spot and that you are getting on the right bus.

One of the hair-raising aspects of bus travel in India, including the South, is the speed at which the buses travel (combined with the knowledge that the level of maintenance among profit-driven companies is probably not as good as it should be). In some instances you may prefer taking the train – in Andhra Pradesh especially. The roads there are generally in poor condition and the buses seem even more battle scarred than in other parts of India.

Beware of touts selling tickets for private buses. At many bus stands they will sell tickets to any destination of your choice (and even not of your choice). While some tickets may be valid, many travellers have been caught forking out rupees for services which simply did not exist. Every bus stand has an office where people are generally quite helpful – better to locate it than to trust the touts.

Classes

Buses vary widely from state to state, although generally bus travel is crowded, cramped, slow and uncomfortable. In some states there is a choice of buses on the main (or long-haul) routes: ordinary, superfast (this Kerala category simply means the bus stops more often than does the express or super express), express, super express, semi-luxe, deluxe and deluxe air-con. The main distinctions are as follows:

Ordinary These generally have five seats across, although if there are only five people sitting in them consider yourself lucky. They tend to be frustratingly slow, are usually in an advanced state of decrepitude and stop frequently – often for seemingly no reason – and for long periods. They're certainly colourful and can be an interesting way to travel on short journeys; on longer trips you'll probably wish you'd stayed at home.

Express These are a big improvement in that they stop far less often. They're still crowded, but at least you feel like you're getting somewhere. The fare is usually a few rupees more than on an ordinary bus – well worth the extra.

Semi-Luxe & Deluxe These are also five seats across, but they have more padding and 'luxuries' such as tinted windows, and the buses stop infrequently. The fare is about 20% more than the ordinary fare, which discourages many of the locals who can only afford the cheapest mode of travel. The big difference between deluxe and semi-luxe is that deluxe buses have only four seats across and these will usually recline.

Reservations

State buses and some private operators have computer booking. This means you can book well ahead and, as you will be allocated a seat number, you won't have to join a scrum to get a place to sit. It also means that you can usually get a partial refund if you cancel your ticket. See the following chapters for detail on the various states.

Baggage

Baggage is generally carried for free on the roof, so it's an idea to take a few precautions. Make sure it's tied on properly and that nobody dumps anything heavy or smelly on your gear. One traveller reported having cases of fish placed on his backpack; the fish leaked into his belongings (they weren't in plastic bags), which stank for a long time afterwards. At times a tarpaulin will be tied across the baggage – make sure it covers your gear adequately.

Theft is unlikely to be a problem, but keep an eye on your bags if you stop for any length of time. Having a large, heavy-duty bag into which your pack will fit can be a good idea, not only for bus travel but also for air travel. If someone carries your bag onto the roof, expect to pay a few rupees for the service.

TRAIN

The first step in coming to grips with South India's rail network is to get a timetable. *Trains at a Glance* (Rs 15) is a handy, 100-page guide covering all the main routes and trains. It is usually available at major train stations, and sometimes on news stands in the larger cities. Alternatively, for information on South Indian trains alone, get hold of a copy of *Southern Central Railway*, also available from the same place.

Life on board trains in South India is quite communal. You not only share a compartment, but food, water, conversation (even if

Fares at a Glance

Distance (km)	1st class (air-con)	1st class	Air-con chair	2nd class express, sleepers	2nd class express, seat	2nd class passenger
50	Rs 226	Rs 102	Rs 80	Rs 66	Rs 17	Rs 9
100	Rs 362	Rs 153	Rs 94	Rs 66	Rs 27	Rs 14
200	Rs 545	Rs 246	Rs 190	Rs 66	Rs 49	Rs 26
300	Rs 763	Rs 341	Rs 211	Rs 95	Rs 68	Rs 36
400	Rs 976	Rs 435	Rs 257	Rs 119	Rs 85	Rs 43
500	Rs 1153	Rs 511	Rs 303	Rs 142	Rs 102	Rs 50
1000	Rs 1885	Rs 832	Rs 462	Rs 230	Rs 166	Rs 72
1500	Rs 2548	Rs 1116	Rs 618	Rs 288	Rs 207	Rs 89
2000	Rs 3166	Rs 1385	Rs 750	Rs 325	Rs 235	Rs 106

you don't have a lot of language in common), newspapers and so on. The meals served on board trains are generally pretty good.

Some travellers report problems with theft. *Trains at a Glance* contains information on the Railway Vigilance Organisation, which can be located at all major train stations and which is there to deal with reports of bribery and corruption. The booklet also details the procedure for reporting theft.

During and shortly after the monsoon, rail services can be drastically affected by floods and high rivers, particularly where major rivers reach the sea, such as the coastal regions of Andhra Pradesh and Tamil Nadu.

South India is slated to have a new luxury train in 1999, the result of a joint effort by Indian Railways and Sterling Holiday Resorts. It will travel south from Bangalore to Mysore, then on to Chennai, Kodaikanal, Kanyakumari, Thiruvananthapuram (Trivandrum), Udhagamandalam (Ooty) and Kochi (Cochin). Tourist offices in Chennai and other major cities should have details if this service goes ahead.

Classes

There are generally two classes – 1st and 2nd – but there are a number of subtle variations on this basic distinction. For a start there is 1st class and 1st class air-con. The air-con carriages only operate on the major trains and routes. The fare for 1st class air-con is more than double normal 1st class. A slightly cheaper air-con alternative is the air-con two-tier sleeper, which costs about 25% more than 1st class. These carriages are a lot more common than 1st class air-con, but are still only found on the major routes.

Between 1st and 2nd class there are two more air-con options: the air-con three-tier sleeper and air-con chair car. The former has three levels of berths rather than two, while the latter, as the name suggests, consists of carriages with aircraft-type reclining seats. Once again, these carriages are only found on the major routes, and the latter only on day trains. The cost of air-con three tier is about 70% of the 1st class fare; air-con chair is about 55% of the 1st class fare.

Sleepers

There are 2nd class and 1st class sleepers, although by western standards even 1st class is not luxurious. Bedding is available but only on certain 1st class and air-con two-tier services, and then only if arranged when booking your ticket. First class sleepers are generally private compartments with two or four berths in them, sometimes a toilet as well. Usually the sleeping berths fold up to make a sitting compartment during the day. First class air-con sleepers are more luxurious, and much more expensive, than regular 1st class sleepers.

Second class sleepers are known as three tier. They are arranged in doorless sections of six berths each. During the day, the middle berth is lowered to make seats for six or eight. At night they are folded into position, everybody has to bed down at the same time and a Travelling Ticket Examiner (TTE) ensures that nobody without a reservation gets into the carriage. However, this doesn't always happen.

One couple reported having to sleep with 17 people in a three-tier (six-place) compartment. In such cases you may need to assert your rights. What will probably happen is that, after some discussion, ticket checking and looks of dismay, the intruder will vacate the seat/sleeper and move to their allocated one.

Broad-gauge, three-tier sleeping carriages also have a row of narrow two-tier (upper and lower) berths along one side. These are not only narrower than the 'inside' berths, but are about 20cm shorter. When reserving 2nd class berths, always write 'inside' on the Accommodation Preference section of the booking form. Sleeping berths are only available between 9 pm and 6 am.

Types

What you do not want is a passenger train. No Indian train travels very fast, but at least the mail and express trains keep moving more of the time. Air-con 'superfast' express services operate on certain main routes, and because of tighter scheduling and fewer stops they are much faster.

Costs

Fares operate on a distance basis. The timetables indicate the distance in kilometres between the stations and from this it is simple to calculate the cost between any two stations.

Reservations

The cost of reservations is nominal and most of the time computerisation will make the process relatively fast. Major cities such as Chennai have a place set aside to deal exclusively with foreigners, which allows you to avoid the crowds. Reservations can be made up to two months in advance.

Reservation costs are: Rs 30 (air-con 1st class); Rs 20 (1st class and air-con chair class); Rs 15 (2nd class three-tier sleeper); Rs 10 (2nd class sitting). There are rarely any 2nd class sitting compartments with reservations. There are also some superfast express trains that require a supplementary charge.

For any sleeper reservation you should try to book at least several days ahead. If the train is fully booked, it's often possible to get a Reservation Against Cancellation (RAC) ticket. This entitles you to board the train and get a seat. Once the trip is under way, the TTE will find a berth for you, but it may take an hour or more. This is different from a wait-listed ticket, as the latter does not give you the right to actually board the train.

At most major city stations there is usually a separate section or counter(s) in the booking hall (often called Tourist Cell) which deals with the tourist quota. Only foreigners and nonresident Indians are allowed to use this facility. You must pay in foreign currency (cash or travellers cheques in US dollars or pounds sterling) or be prepared to show your encashment certificate if you only have rupees. Change will be given in rupees.

Refunds

Booked tickets are refundable, but cancellation fees apply. If you present the ticket more than one day in advance, a fee of Rs 10 to Rs 50 applies, depending on the class. Up to four hours before departure, you lose 25% of the ticket value; less than four hours before departure and up to three to 12 hours after

departure (depending on the distance of the ticketed journey), you lose 50%. Any later than that and you can keep the ticket as a souvenir.

Tickets for unreserved travel can be refunded up to three hours after the departure of the train, and the only penalty is Rs 10 per passenger.

Indrail Passes

Indrail passes permit unlimited travel on Indian trains for the period of their validity, but they are expensive and generally not worth the expense. Costs range from US$80/150 (2nd class/1st class) for a seven day pass, to US$235/530 for a 90 day pass. In purely dollar terms, to get the full value out of any of the passes you need to travel around 300km per day; with the speed of Indian trains that's at least six hours travel, day in and day out.

Also, although the pass covers the cost of reservations, it doesn't get you to the front of the queue. Nor does the pass give you any advantage when it comes to trying to get a berth or seat on a fully booked train; you join the waiting list like anybody else. The only occasion when it's going to save you time is if you want to travel unreserved on a train, when you can simply hop on without queuing for a ticket. As these journeys are likely to be far fewer and shorter than those when you want to have a reserved berth, it's not much of a gain.

If you are still interested, children from the age of five to 12 years of age pay half-fare. Indrail passes can be bought overseas through some travel agents or in India at certain major booking offices. Payment in India can be made only in either US dollars or pounds sterling, cash or travellers cheques, or in rupees backed up with encashment certificates. Second-class passes are not available outside India. Indrail passes cover all reservation and berth costs at night, and they can be extended if you wish to keep on travelling.

CAR

Few people bring their own vehicle to India. If you do decide to bring a car or motorcycle to India, it must be brought in under a carnet, a customs document guaranteeing the vehicle's removal at the end of your stay. Failure to do so will be very expensive.

Road Rules & Conditions

Driving in India is legally (but often only theoretically) on the left side of the road, in right-hand drive vehicles, as in the United Kingdom.

Because of the extreme congestion in the cities and the narrow bumpy roads in the country, driving is often a slow, stop-start process – hard on you, the car and fuel economy. Service is so-so in India and parts and tyres not always easy to obtain, although there are plenty of puncture-repair places. In all, driving is no great pleasure except in rural areas where there's little traffic.

Rental

Budget and Hertz maintain offices in the major cities. But given India's crazy driving conditions, it's far better and much more

straightforward to hire a car and driver. As a guide, for a Maruti 800cc four seater, expect to pay Rs 2000 per day (one to six days) and Rs 1900 per day (seven to 13 days). For a Maruti Esteem 1300cc five seater, expect to pay Rs 4300 (one to six days) and Rs 4200 (seven to 13 days). These prices include unlimited mileage but exclude fuel and road taxes.

Purchase

Buying a car is expensive and not worth the effort unless you intend to stay long-term.

Fuel

Petrol is around Rs 27 per litre (Rs 29 with oil). Diesel is much cheaper at Rs 9 per litre. Petrol is readily available in all larger towns and along main roads.

MOTORCYCLE

Biking gives you the freedom to go where you like when you like, and it is becoming increasingly popular. In Goa it is almost *de*

Some Indian Rules of the Road

Drive on the Left Theoretically vehicles keep to the left in India – as in Japan, Britain or Australia. In practice most vehicles keep to the middle of the road on the basis that there are fewer potholes in the middle than on the sides. When any other vehicle is encountered the lesser vehicle should cower to the side. Misunderstandings as to status can have unfortunate consequences.

Overtaking In India it is not necessary to ascertain that there is space to complete the overtaking manoeuvre before pulling out. Overtaking can be attempted on blind corners, on the way up steep hills or in the face of oncoming traffic. Smaller vehicles unexpectedly encountered in mid-manoeuvre can be expected to swerve apologetically out of the way. If a larger vehicle is encountered it is to be hoped that the overtakee will slow, pull off or otherwise make room for the overtaker.

Use of Horn Although vehicles can be driven with bald tyres or nonexistent brakes, it is imperative that the horn be in superb working order. Surveys during the research for Lonely Planet's *India* revealed that the average driver uses the horn 10 to 20 times per kilometre, so a 100km trip can involve 2000 blasts of the horn. In any case the horn should be checked for its continued loud operation at least every 100m. Signs prohibiting use of horns are not to be taken seriously.

Driving at Night It is a matter of courtesy to turn your headlights off as you approach blind corners – so as not to bedazzle anyone coming the other way. How that oncoming driver is supposed to be aware of your presence around the blind corner is another matter altogether.

rigueur. To get a taste of what long-distance motorcycling is like in India on an Enfield get hold of a copy of *Bullet up the Grand Trunk Road* by Jonathan Gregson.

This section is based largely on information originally contributed by intrepid Britons, Ken Twyford and Gerald Smewing, with updates from Mike Ferris, Jim & Lucy Amos and Bill Keightley.

What to Bring

An International Driving Permit is technically not mandatory, but you'd be foolish not to bring one. The first thing a policeman will want to see if he stops you is your licence, and an international permit is incontrovertible.

If you know you will be biking, bring quality riding gear with you. Helmets, boots, gloves and jackets are available in India but the quality can be suspect. If you are planning to be in South India during the monsoon, bring a good set of wet-weather gear. A few small bags will be a lot easier to carry than one large rucksack.

Rental

Renting is a viable option if you are only spending a few weeks in South India. Finding a dealer who will rent is usually a matter of asking around (see the section below for more detail). You should be able to negotiate a late-model bike in good condition for about US$100 a week, perhaps less if you are renting it for a month or longer. You may have to lodge a substantial deposit. Be sure tools and a few spares are included in the deal; you'll probably need them.

Purchase

Second-Hand India has few used-vehicle dealers, motorbike magazines or weekend newspapers with pages of motorcycle classifed advertisements. To purchase a second-hand machine you simply need to inquire. Whether buying or selling, it's best to go to a reputable dealer who has a good track record. In Delhi, Lalli Singh's Inder Motors (☎ (011) 572 5879), at 1744/55 Hari Singh Nalwa St in Karol Bagh, enjoys a good reputation among travellers.

New When buying second-hand, all you need to give is an address, but if you're buying a new bike, you'll need to have a local address and be a resident foreign national. However, unless the dealer you are buying from is totally devoid of imagination and contacts, this presents few problems. New bikes are generally purchased through a showroom. There is an Enfield showroom in Panaji (Goa) at MS Auto Guides (☎ 0832-225865) on Dr Dada Vaidya Rd, and at Marikar Motors (☎ 0484-341083), Lissie Junction, Ernakulam, Kerala (Marikar Motors also sells second-hand Enfields). Enfield motorcycles are manufactured at Eicher Motors (☎ 044-543066), 17km outside Chennai.

Documents A needless hint perhaps, but do not part with your money until you have the ownership papers, receipt and affidavit signed by a magistrate authorising the owner (as recorded in the ownership papers) to sell the machine. Not to mention the keys to the bike and the bike itself!

Each state has a different set of ownership transfer formalities. Get assistance from the agent you're buying the machine through, or from one of the many 'attorneys' hanging around under tin roofs near Motor Vehicles Department offices. They will charge you a fee of up to Rs 300, which will consist largely of a bribe to expedite matters.

Alternatively, you could go to one of the many typing clerk services and request them to type out the necessary forms, handling the matter cheaply yourself – but with no guarantee of a quick result.

Check that your name has been recorded in the ownership book and stamped and signed by the department head. If you intend to sell your motorcycle in another state then you will need a 'No Objections Certificate'. This confirms your ownership and is issued by the Motor Vehicles Department in the state of purchase, so get it immediately when transferring ownership papers to your name. The standard form can be typed up for a few rupees, or more speedily and expensively through one of the many attorneys.

Silk & Saris

The sari is synonymous with Indian style and a brocade bridal sari from Kanchipuram is among the most coveted of garments. Kanchipuram silk saris, named after the temple town near Chennai where they are still woven by hand, come in a gorgeous array of colours. The more expensive are shot through with gold and silver as well.

The silk from which Kanchipuram saris are made is bought in its raw state from silkworm farms on the Tamil Nadu/Karnataka border. Transported to Kanchipuram, the yarn is bleached and colour added, sometimes using a vegetable dye but increasingly these days a chemical one.

Next comes the weaving. Handlooming silk is an ancient skill which has been passed from one generation to the next since the days of the Pallava kings, who made Kanchipuram their capital in the 6th century. To this day it remains a cottage industry that engages the entire family.

About 80% of Kanchipuram's population depends on handlooming for a living. Powerlooms, favoured elsewhere, haven't eclipsed this industry so far. This is partly because a machine-made garment could never really replace a real Kanchipuram product; part of its appeal lies in the knowledge that the designs are not mass produced. In addition, since the mid-1950s, weavers have formed cooperatives that have become powerful forces in ensuring workers are not exploited. It's estimated that one powerloom would replace around 1000 handloom workers.

Generally a weaver will turn out three or four saris of a single design. Taking into account the setting up involved, the first 5.5m-long sari takes about 35 eight-hour working days to complete and 10 days to finish each subsequent sari.

The fabric itself lasts about 15 years, but the more expensive saris

Kanchipuram silk saris are still woven by hand (above) and make a splash of colour as they are spread out to dry on the Nandi Hills (left).

PETER DAVIS

SARA-JANE CLELAND

PETER DAVIS

Who's sari now? Clockwise from top: at the beach, Poompuhar; stitching it up, Chennai; bathing at the ghats, Nandi Hills.

may live on in a slightly different form. This is because they include gold and silver brocade borders which can be melted down and recycled into a new garment. This brocade, called *zari*, can also be cut out of an unwanted silk sari and reattached to another. Zari is usually sourced from Surat and Gujarat.

Kanchipuram saris are also known for their distinctive patina which is said to come from special qualities of the local river water, which is used for bleaching and colouring.

How much a Kanchipuram sari costs depends to a large extent on the amount of zari used. A simple sari with no zari (it would probably weigh about 250g) costs around Rs 2500, but you should expect to pay at least Rs 25,000 for a wedding garment with lots of brocade and weighing around 1.5kg.

Insurance & Tax As in most countries, it is compulsory to have third party insurance. The New India Assurance Company or the National Insurance Company are just two of a number of companies who can provide it. The cost for fully comprehensive insurance is around Rs 1000 for 12 months, and this also covers you in Nepal.

Road tax is paid when the bike is bought new. This is valid for the life of the machine and is transferred to the new owner when the bike changes hands.

Which Bike?

The big decision to make is whether to buy new or second-hand. Obviously cost is the main factor, but remember that with a new bike you are less likely to get ripped off as the price is fixed, the cost will include free servicing and you know it will be reliable. Old bikes are obviously cheaper, and you don't have to be a registered resident foreign national, but you are far more open to getting ripped off, either by paying too much or by getting a dud bike.

Everyone is likely to have their own preferences and there is no one bike which suits everybody. Here is a rundown of what's readily available:

Mopeds These come with or without gears. As they are only 50cc capacity, they are really only useful around towns or for short distances.

Scooters There are the older design Bajaj and Vespa scooters, or the more modern Japanese designs by Honda-Kinetic and others. The older ones are 150cc while the Honda is 100cc and has no gears.

Scooters are economical to buy and run, are easy to ride, have a good resale value, and most have built-in lockable storage. The 150cc Bajaj Cheetak costs Rs 28,400 and has plenty of power and acceleration for Indian road conditions. It's reliable as long as the plug is kept clean; newer models have electronic ignition so there's no need to adjust the points. Many riders rate these bikes well; here's what one wrote:

A big plus for the scooter is the spare tire. I've experienced a puncture nearly every 150km and believe me, pushing a dead motorcycle through the hot Indian sun is a pain. Wheel removal on a scooter is a breeze – five nuts and that's it. No dirty chains to screw around with, no broken spokes to replace. Another inherent plus of this machine is the front end, which protects the rider from numerous surprise projections as well as mud and other flying excretions. Let someone else ride deafening Enfields with their greasy temperamental chains, no spare tire and gas tank between their legs. I'll take a 'bulletproof' scooter any day!

Bill Keightley (USA)

100cc Motorcycles This is the area with the greatest choice. The four main Japanese companies – Honda, Suzuki, Kawasaki and Yamaha – all have 100cc, two-stroke machines, while Honda and Kawasaki also have four-stroke models.

There's little to differentiate between these bikes; all are lightweight, easy to ride, very economical and reliable, with good resale value. They are suitable for intercity travel on reasonable roads, but they should not be laden down with too much gear. Spares and servicing are readily available. The cost of a new bike of this type is about Rs 35,000 to Rs 40,000.

If you're buying second-hand avoid the Rajdoot 175 XLT, based on a very old Polish model, and the Enfield Fury, which has a poor gearbox, spares that are hard to come by and a low resale value.

Bigger Bikes The Enfield Bullet is the classic machine and is the one most favoured among foreigners. Attractions are the traditional design, thumping engine sound, and the price, which is not much more than the new 100cc Japanese bikes. It's a wonderfully durable bike, easy to maintain and economical to run, but mechanically they're a bit hit and miss, largely because of poorly engineered parts and inferior materials – valves and tappets are the main problem areas. Another drawback is the lack of an effective front brake – the small drum brake is a joke, totally inadequate for what is quite a heavy machine.

In addition to the 350, the Bullet is available in a 500cc single cylinder version. It has a functional front brake and 12V electrics which are superior to the 350's 6V. If you opt for a 350cc, consider paying the Rs 5000 extra to have the 500cc front wheel fitted.

If you are buying a new Enfield with the intention of shipping it back home, it's definitely worth opting for the 500cc as it has features – such as folding rear footrest and longer exhaust pipe – which most other countries require. The emission control regulations in some places, such as California, are so strict that there is no way these bikes would be legal. You may be able to get around this by buying an older bike, as the regulations often only apply to new machines. Make sure you check all this out before you go lashing out on a new Enfield, only to find it unregisterable at home. The price is around Rs 58,000, or Rs 65,000 for the 500cc model. There's a hopelessly underpowered diesel version for Rs 66,000.

The Yezdi 250 Classic (or Monarch, or Deluxe) is a cheap, basic, rugged machine, and one which you often see in rural areas.

The Rajdoot 350 is an imported Yamaha 350cc. It's well engineered, fast and has good brakes. Disadvantages are that it's relatively uneconomical to run, and spares are hard to come by. These bikes are also showing their age badly as they haven't been made for some years now. They cost around Rs 12,000.

If you've Rs 530,000 to spare, the BMW F650 is now available in India.

On the Road

It must be said that, given the general road conditions, motorcycling is a reasonably hazardous endeavour, and one best undertaken by experienced riders only.

In the event of an accident, call the police straight away (if you're able), and don't move anything until the police have seen exactly where and how everything ended up. One foreigner reported spending three days in jail on suspicion of being involved in an accident, when all he'd done was take a child to hospital from the scene of an accident.

Don't try to cover too much territory in one day. A high level of concentration is needed to survive and long days are tiring and dangerous. On the busy national highways expect to average 50km/h without stops; on smaller roads, where driving conditions are worse, 10km/h is not an unrealistic average. On the whole you can expect to cover between 100km and 150km in a day on good roads. Night driving should be avoided at all costs.

Putting the bike on a train for really long hauls can be a convenient option. You'll pay about as much as a 2nd-class passenger fare for the bike. It can be wrapped in straw for protection if you like, and this is done at the parcels office at the station, which is also where you pay for the bike. The petrol tank must be empty, and there should be a tag in an obvious place detailing name, destination, passport number and train details.

Repairs & Maintenance

In India anyone who can handle a screwdriver and spanner can be called a mechanic, so be careful. If you have any mechanical knowledge, it may be better to buy your own tools and learn how to do your own repairs. This will save a lot of arguments over prices. If you are getting repairs done by someone, don't leave the premises while the work is being done or you may find that good parts have been ripped off your bike and replaced with old ones.

Original spare parts bought from an 'authorised dealer' can be rather expensive compared to the copies available from your spare-parts-wallah.

If you buy an older machine you would do well to check and tighten all nuts and bolts every few days. Indian roads and engine vibration tend to work things loose, and constant checking could save you rupees and trouble. Check the engine and gearbox oil level regularly. As the quality of oil available is poor, it is advisable to change it and clean the oil filter every 2000km.

Punctures Chances are you'll be requiring the services of a puncture-wallah at least once a week. They are found everywhere, often in the most surprising places, but it's advisable to at least have tools sufficient to remove your own wheel and take it to the puncture-wallah. Given the annoyance of frequent punctures, it's worth lashing out on new tyres if you buy a second-hand bike with worn tyres. A new rear tyre for an Enfield costs around Rs 600.

Fuel Should you run out, try flagging down a passing car (not a truck or bus since they use diesel) and beg for some. Most Indians are willing to let you have fuel if you have a hose or siphon and a container.

Organised Motorcycle Tours

Classic Bike Adventure (☎ 0832-273351; fax 277624, 277343), Casa Tres Amigo, Socol Vado No 425, Assagao, Bardez, Goa, is a German-based company that organises tours on well-maintained Enfields, with full insurance. Costs are from DM2450 to DM 3680. Ferris Wheels (☎/fax (02) 9904 7419; email: ferriswheels@australia.net.au), 61 Elizabeth St, Artarmon, NSW 2064, Australia, also organises tours in South India on Enfields.

BICYCLE

South India offers plenty of variety for the cyclist. There are (relatively) smooth-surfaced highways, rocky dirt tracks, coastal routes through coconut palms, winding country roads through spice plantations and more demanding routes in the Western Ghats. The following information comes from Ann Sorrel, with updates from various travellers.

Information

Before you set out, read some books on bicycle touring such as the Sierra Club's *The Bike Touring Manual* by Rob van de Plas (Bicycle Books, 1993). Cycling magazines provide useful information, including listings for bicycle tour operators and the addresses of spare-parts suppliers. They're also good places to look for a riding companion.

For a real feel of the adventure of bike touring in strange places, read Dervla Murphy's classic *Full Tilt*, Lloyd Sumner's *The Long Ride* or Bettina Selby's *Riding the Mountains Down* (subtitled 'A Journey by Bicycle to Kathmandu').

Your local cycling club may be able to help with information and advice. In the UK, the Cyclists Touring Club (☎ 01483-417217) 69 Meadrow, Godalming, Surrey GU7 3HS, has country touring sheets that are free to members. The International Bicycle Fund (IBF; ☎ 206-628 9314), 4887 Columbia Drive South, Seattle, Washington 98108-1919, USA, publishes two handy guides: *Selecting and Preparing a Bike for Travel in Remote Areas* and *Flying With Your Bike*.

If you're a serious cyclist or amateur racer and want to contact counterparts while in India, there's the Cycle Federation of India; contact the Secretary, Yamun Velodrome, New Delhi.

Using Your Own Bike

If you are going to keep to sealed roads and already have a touring bike, by all means consider bringing it. Mountain bikes, however, are especially suited to countries such as India. Their smaller, sturdier construction makes them more manoeuvrable and less prone to damage, and allows you to tackle rocky, muddy roads unsuitable for lighter machines. An imported multi-geared machine is generally considered essential for the serious cyclist in India.

There is a disadvantage: your machine is likely to be a real curiosity and subject to much pushing, pulling and probing. If you can't tolerate people touching your bicycle, don't bring it to India.

Spare Parts If you bring a bicycle to India, prepare for the contingencies of part replacement or repair. Bring spare tyres, tubes, patch kits, chassis, cables, freewheels and spokes. Ensure you have a working knowledge of your machine. Bring all necessary tools with you as well as a compact bike manual with diagrams in case the worst happens and you need to fix a rear derailleur or some other strategic part. Indian mechanics can work wonders and illustrations help overcome the language barrier. Roads don't have paved shoulders and are very dusty, so keep your chain lubricated. Most of all, be ready to make do and improvise.

Although India is officially metricated, tools and bike parts follow 'standard' or 'imperial' measurements. Don't expect to find tyres for 700cc rims, although 27 x 1¼ tyres are produced in India by Dunlop and Sawney. Some mountain-bike tyres are available but the quality is dubious. Indian bicycle pumps cater to a tube valve different from the Presta and Schraeder valves commonly used in the west. If you're travelling with Presta valves (most high-pressure 27 x 1¼ tubes), bring a Schraeder (car-type) adaptor. In India you can buy a local pump adaptor, which means you'll have an adaptor on your adaptor. Bring your own pump as well; most Indian pumps require two or three people to get air down the leaky cable.

In major cities Japanese tyres and parts are available but pricey – although so is postage, and transit time can be considerable. If you receive bike parts from abroad, beware of exorbitant customs charges. Say you want the goods as 'in transit' to avoid these charges. They may list the parts in your passport!

For foreign parts try Metre Cycle, Kalba Devi Rd, Mumbai, or its branch in Thiruvananthapuram, Kerala; the cycle bazaar in the old city around Esplanade Rd, Delhi; Popular Cycle Importing Company on Popham's Broadway, Chennai; and Nundy & Company, Bentinck St, Calcutta. Alternatively, take your bicycle to a cycle market and ask around – someone will know which shop is likely to have things for your 'special' cycle. Beware of Taiwanese imitations and do watch out for tyres which may have been sitting collecting dust for years.

Luggage Your cycle luggage should be as strong, durable and waterproof as possible. Don't get a set with lots of zippers, as this makes pilfering easier. As you'll be frequently detaching luggage when taking your bike to your room, a set designed for easy

removal from the racks is a must; the fewer items, the better. (*Never* leave your bike in the lobby or outside your hotel – take it to bed with you!)

Bike luggage that can easily be reassembled into a backpack is also available and is just the thing when you want to park your bike and go by train or foot.

Theft If you're using an imported bike, try to avoid losing your pump (and the water bottle from your frame) – their novelty makes them particularly attractive to thieves. Don't leave anything on your bike that can easily be removed when it's unattended.

Don't be paranoid about theft – outside the major cities it would be well-nigh impossible for a thief to resell your bike as it would stand out too much. And aren't widely recognised quick-release levers on wheel. Your bike is probably safer in India than in western cities.

Purchase
Finding an Indian bike is no problem: every town will have at least a couple of cycle shops. Shop around for prices and remember to bargain. Try to get a few extras – bell, stand, spare tube – thrown in. There are many brands of Indian clunkers – Hero, Atlas, BSA, Raleigh, Bajaj, Avon – but they all follow the same basic, sturdy design. A few mountain-bike lookalikes have recently come on the market, but most have no gears. Raleigh is considered to produce bikes of the finest quality, followed by BSA, which has a big line of models, including some sporty jobs. Hero and Atlas both claim to be the biggest seller. Look for the cheapest or the one with the snazziest plate label.

Once you've decided on a bike, you have a choice of luggage carriers – mostly the rattrap type varying only in size, price and strength. There's a wide range of saddles available but all are equally bum-breaking. A stand is certainly a useful addition and a bell or airhorn is a necessity. An advantage of buying a new bike is that the brakes actually work. Centre-pull and side-pull brakes are also available but at extra cost and may actually make the bike more difficult to sell. The average Indian will prefer the standard model.

Sportier 'mountain bike' styles with straight handlebars are popular in urban areas. In big cities and touristy areas it's also possible to find used touring bikes left by travellers. Also check with diplomatic community members for bikes.

Reselling is no problem. Count on getting about 70% of what you originally paid if it was a new bike. A local cycle-hire shop will probably be interested or you could ask the proprietor of your hotel if they know any prospective purchasers.

Spare Parts As there are so many repair 'shops' (some consist of a pump, a box of tools, a tube of rubber solution and a water pan under a tree), there is no need to carry spare parts, especially as you'll only own the bike for a few weeks or months. Just take a roll of tube-patch rubber, a tube of Dunlop patch glue, two tyre irons and the wonderful 'universal' Indian bike spanner, which fits all the nuts. There are plenty of puncture-wallahs in all towns and villages who will patch tubes for a couple of rupees, so chances are you won't have to fix a puncture yourself anyway. Besides, Indian tyres are pretty heavy duty, so with luck you won't get too many flats.

On the Road
The 'people factor' makes cycling in South India both rewarding and frustrating. Those with Indian bikes are less likely to be mobbed by curious onlookers.

At times the crowd may be unruly – schoolboys especially. If the mob is too big, call over a lathi-wielding policeman. The boys will scatter pronto! Sometimes the hostile boys throw rocks. The best advice is to keep pedalling; don't turn around or stop, and don't leave your bike and chase them as this will only incite them further. Appeal to adults to discipline them. Children, especially boys seven to 13 years old, are unruly and dangerous in crowds. Avoid riding past a boys' school at recess.

Routes
You can go anywhere on a bike that you would on trains and buses, with the added pleasure of seeing all the places in between. If mountain bicycling is your goal, give serious consideration to the hill stations of South India.

The downside of leaving the congested highways is the deterioration in the quality of the road surfaces. Some stretches, especially away from the coast, have become so potholed that village tracks become a much more attractive option. The Eastern and Western Ghats of South India provide excellent cycling with wonderful scenery. Again the roads here are paved but the paving varies considerably in quality and the roads themselves in terms of traffic density. Travelling on major highways for any length of time is frustrating. Highway 17 between Goa and Kochi is a case in point. The melee continues all the way down this highway and on through Highway 47 all the way to Kanyakumari. One solution is to plan your trip so that you get regular breaks at national parks and reserves; the verdant lushness of these areas is a welcome respite from the hot, dusty roads outside them.

Steven Ireland (Australia)

Distances
If you've never cycled long distances, start with 20km to 40km a day and increase this as you gain stamina and confidence. Cycling long distances is 80% determination and 20% perspiration. Don't be ashamed to get off and push the bike up steep hills. For an eight hour pedal, a serious cyclist and interested tourist will average 90km to 130km a day on undulating plains, or 70km to 100km in mountainous areas.

Accommodation
There's no need to bring a tent. Inexpensive places to stay are widely available, and a tent pitched by the road would merely draw crowds. Bring a sleeping bag, especially if you intend exploring the Ghats. Consider buying a mosquito net if you're heading off the beaten track; they are inexpensive in India and available widely. There's no need to bring a stove and cooking kit (unless you cannot tolerate Indian food), as there are plenty of tea stalls and restaurants (called

hotels). When you want to eat, ask for a hotel. On major highways you can stop at *dhabas*, the Indian version of a truck stop.

Transporting Your Bike

Sometimes you may want to quit pedalling. For sports bikes, air travel is easy. With luck, airline staff may not be familiar with procedures, so use this to your advantage. Tell them the bike doesn't need to be dismantled and that you've never had to pay for it. Remove all luggage and accessories and let the tyres down a bit.

Bus travel with a bike varies from state to state. Generally it goes for free on the roof. If it's a sports bike stress that it's lightweight. Secure it well to the roof rack, check it's in a place where it won't get damaged and take all your luggage inside.

Train travel is more complex – pedal up to the train station, buy a ticket and explain you want to book a cycle in for the journey. You'll be directed to the luggage offices (or officer) where a triplicate form is prepared. Note down your bike's serial number and provide a good description of it. Again leave only the bike, not luggage or accessories. Your bike gets decorated with one copy of the form, usually pasted on the seat, you get another, and God only knows what happens to the third. Produce your copy of the form to claim the bicycle from the luggage van at your destination. If you change trains en route, *personally* ensure the cycle changes too!

As part of a small group chartering a boat to ply the backwaters from Alapphuzha (Alleppey; Kerala) to Kollam (Quilon) my bike proved little problem lashed to the stern of the cabin. This was the case on other river crossings where in some situations the only means of crossing was a simple outboard-motor canoe. Aboard buses the bike is loaded on the roof and luggage is stowed inside the bus. Check for yourself that your bike is properly secured. Toe clip straps are an ideal method of restraint. A small charge will apply for the bike. If you are transporting your bike on a domestic flight, international rules apply (handlebars straightened, tyres deflated). There is no requirement that your bike be packed in a box.

Steven Ireland (Australia)

HITCHING

Hitching is never entirely safe in any country in the world, and we don't recommend it. Travellers who decide to hitch should understand that they are taking a small but potentially serious risk. If you do choose to hitch travel in pairs and let someone know where you are planning to go.

That said, hitching is not a realistic option in South India anyway. There are not that many private cars so you are likely to be on board trucks. You are then stuck with the old quandaries of: 'Do they understand what I am doing?', 'Should I be paying for this?', 'Will the driver expect to be paid?', 'Will they be unhappy if I don't offer to pay?', 'Will they be unhappy if I offer or will they simply want too much?'.

It is a very bad idea for a woman on her own to hitch. India is a country far less sympathetic to rape victims than the west, and that's saying something. A woman in the cabin with a truck driver on a lonely road has, needless to say, only her own strengths and resources to call upon if things turn nasty.

BOAT

Apart from ferries across rivers (of which there are many), the only real boating possibilities are the trips through the backwaters of Kerala – not to be missed (see the Kerala chapter for more details) – and the jetfoil between Mumbai and Goa (see the Mumbai chapter).

The only other ferries connecting coastal ports are those from Calcutta and Chennai to the Andaman Islands (see Getting There & Away in the Port Blair section of the Andaman & Nicobar Islands chapter).

LOCAL TRANSPORT

Taxi

Taxis are generally Ambassador cars. Rates differ depending on whether you are simply travelling within a city or whether your journey is further afield. And there are usually two ways to pay: per hour or per kilometre. Generally the rate per kilometre is Rs 4.40 (non air-con) and Rs 8.10 (air-con) plus the driver's expenses (known as *batta* and usually amounting to around Rs 125 per day). If you are travelling interstate then you will also be liable for road toll fees, which are minimal. You will always have to pay the return fare (eg Mysore-Kochi-Mysore) whether or not you are making the return trip. Very often your hotel will be able to arrange a car and driver (as taxis are often known) for you.

Within a city a non air-con Ambassador car, including driver and fuel, costs either Rs 385 (five hours; 50 km) or Rs 750 (10 hours; 100 km). For air-con expect to pay Rs 560 and Rs 1120 respectively. Out-station trips (as they are known in South India and calculated for 24 hours from midnight) cost Rs 1300 for non air-con (200km; Rs 4.40 for every extra kilometre) and Rs 1800 for air-con (200km; Rs 7 for every extra kilometre). Air-con is a good idea in South India if you expect to be in the car for half a day or more; the heat can be really oppressive otherwise.

As an example, if you are going on a trip from Chennai to Mamallapuram and Kanchipuram expect to pay Rs 825 (non air-con) or Rs 1375 (air-con).

Auto-Rickshaw

An auto-rickshaw (or 'auto' or 'three wheeler') is a noisy three-wheel device powered by a two-stroke engine with a driver up front and seats for two (or sometimes more) passengers behind. Because of their size auto-rickshaws can manoeuvre through heavy traffic more adeptly than taxis, but they don't offer nearly as much protection in the event of a collision.

Auto-rickshaws invariably have meters which invariably don't work (or so the driver will claim). However, there are enough working meters in major cities such as Bangalore, Chennai (Chennai has about 18,000 auto-rickshaws) and Mysore for you to insist on getting one. Flag fall is Rs 7 and it's generally about Rs 3 per kilometre after that. Sometimes meters are tampered with and tick over at an alarming speed. Keep an eye on the meter just in case. If you can't find a metered vehicle, or your requests to have the meter turned on are laughed at, be sure to settle on a price before you get in. Expect to pay more at night and during holidays. Avoid

taking a rickshaw from the rank outside your hotel, especially if it is an upmarket hotel. Prices will be higher. Walk a few hundred metres and hail a rickshaw in the street.

Drivers will very often wait if you are making a return journey (as opposed to a 'drop only'). Generally the 'waiting' fee will be about Rs 50 for one hour; Rs 10 to Rs 15 for a quick stop. Drivers vary widely in their knowledge of their cities. It helps, however, if you are going to a fairly obscure destination, to have it written down in the vernacular to show the driver.

Cycle-Rickshaw

This is effectively a three-wheeler bicycle with a seat for two passengers behind the rider. Cycle-rickshaws are rare in South India, but generally prices are a lot lower than auto-rickshaws and the service is friendly and efficient.

Bicycle

India is a country of bicycles. They're a great way to get around the sights in a city or make longer trips (see the section on touring India by bicycle earlier in this chapter). In Andhra Pradesh and Tamil Nadu hourly rates for bicycle hire begin at Rs 2, and daily rates range from Rs 12 to Rs 20. These prices vary slightly in other states, and in touristed areas (such as Goa and parts of Kerala) expect to pay considerably more – Rs 40 per day in Goa and Rs 30 per day in Hampi (Karnataka).

ORGANISED TOURS

State tourist offices all run tours and very often they are good value for money if you have little time and want to see as much as possible. In Kerala the backwater village tours can be quite good. There are a great many private operators as well. Rather than join a state-run bus tour, many travellers prefer to use private agencies which can put together a package and arrange a car and driver – or in some cases team you up with others in order to fill a minibus. For more detail, see the relevant sections in the following chapters.

Mumbai (Bombay)

Mumbai is the capital of Maharashtra and the economic powerhouse of India. It's an exhilarating city, fuelled by entrepreneurial energy, determination and dreams. Compared with the torpor of the rest of India, it can seem like a foreign country.

An island connected by bridges to the mainland, Mumbai is also the finance capital of the nation, the industrial hub of everything from textiles to petrochemicals, and responsible for half of India's foreign trade. But while it aspires to be another Singapore, it's also a magnet for the rural poor. It's these new migrants who are continually reshaping the city, making sure Mumbai keeps one foot in its hinterland and the other in the global market place.

Most travellers tend to stick around long enough only to reconfirm their plane tickets or organise transport to Goa, scared off by the city's reputation for squalor and the relatively high cost of accommodation. But Mumbai is a safe and charismatic city that fully rewards exploration; if you have a day or two to spare on your way into or out of India there's plenty to see and do in Mumbai.

INFORMATION

The efficient Government of India Tourist Office (☎ 203 3144; fax 201 4496) is at 123 Maharshi Karve Rd, opposite Churchgate station. It's open weekdays from 8.30 am to 6 pm, and Saturday from 8.30 am to 2 pm.

American Express (☎ 204 8291), on the corner of SBS Marg and Shivaji Marg in Colaba (next to the Regal Cinema), handles foreign exchange transactions and provides cash advances on American Express credit cards between Monday and Saturday from 9.30 am to 6.30 pm. Thomas Cook (☎ 204 8556), at 324 Dr D Naoroji Rd in the Fort, also provides speedy foreign exchange and is open Monday to Saturday from 9.30 am to 6 pm.

The GPO is on W Hirachand Marg near Victoria Terminus. Poste restante is open

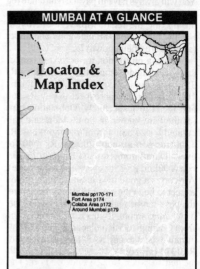

MUMBAI AT A GLANCE

Locator & Map Index

Mumbai pp170-171
Fort Area p174
Colaba Area p172
Around Mumbai p179

Population: 15 million
Main Languages: Hindi & Marathi
Telephone Area Code: 022
Best Time to Go: September to April

Highlights

- Taking in the carnival atmosphere of Chowpatty Beach at night
- Catching a ferry to Elephanta Island to see the triple-headed carving of Shiva
- Getting lost in the cacophonous bazaars of Kalbadevi

Monday to Saturday from 9 am to 6 pm. There's a post office in Colaba on Henry Rd.

Interzone (☎ 287 2641; fax 287 2640; email mktg@dbsindia.com), on the 1st floor of Raheja Chambers, is a good, though expensive, place to send and receive email. They charge Rs 200 per hour (Rs 150 for students).

For personal service and discounted tickets you won't get much better than the tiny little travel agency, Transway International (☎ 262 6066; fax 266 4465, email tran-skam.etm@smt.sprintrpg.ems.vsnl.net.in), on the 2nd floor of Pantaky House, 8 Maruti Cross Lane, off Maruti Lane, Fort. It can be a challenge to find but the service is worth the hunt – ask locals for the old Handloom House (now burnt down) on Dr D Naoroji Rd; Maruti Lane is behind it.

THINGS TO SEE & DO

The city's greatest attraction is the superb Victorian townscape of the **Fort** Victoria Terminus, Bombay University and Horniman Circle are just some of the main landmarks, but there are several dozen other architectural gems.

Nearly everyone who comes to Mumbai visits the **Gateway of India**, an exaggerated arch of triumph on the Colaba waterfront which has become the de facto emblem of the city. More rewarding are the exhibits in the **Prince of Wales Museum** and the **National Gallery of Modern Art**, both located between Colaba and the Fort. The one excursion not to miss is the one-hour boat trip to **Elephanta Island** (see Around Mumbai, later in this chapter).

If you have a little more time, pay a visit to the **Jain Temple** and **Hanging Gardens** on Malabar Hill at the north end of Marine Drive, or visit **Haji Ali's Mosque**, a fairytale-like construction at the end of its own causeway.

Mumbai's markets are great places to explore. The colourful, indoor **Crawford Market** is a definite legacy of British Bombay, while the tumultuous, densely packed **Kalbadevi Bazaars**, to the north, are far more Indian.

Most of the best Mumbai experiences, however, don't involve going to 'see' anything in particular. Take an evening stroll along Marine Drive to **Chowpatty Beach**, where you can munch on *bhelpuri* (a spiced chicken snack) and soak up the area's carnival atmosphere. Loiter at sunset at a rooftop table in Cafe Naaz on the edge of Malabar Hill's **Kamala Nehru Park** and watch the lights of Marine Drive come on; or spend an hour or two watching the cricket on the maidans.

The Maharashtra Tourism Development Corporation (MTDC) offers rushed tours of Mumbai for Rs 75. Bookings can be made at the MTDC Tours Division and Reservation Office (☎ 202 6713; fax 285 2182), CDO Hutments, Madame Cama Rd, Nariman Point. Tours last four hours and depart daily from the MTDC office at 2 pm; passengers are also picked up near the Gateway of India in Colaba.

PLACES TO STAY

Mumbai is India's most expensive city to stay in, and pressure for accommodation – even at the bottom end of the market – is intense. If you haven't made a booking, there's no guarantee that you'll be able to find a room in your preferred price range on your first night, especially if you arrive late in the day. Most travellers gravitate towards Colaba, which has plenty of budget and mid-range hotels, though the Fort is a great place to pick up on the buzz of Mumbai, and Marine Drive has the advantage of a seafront location.

Airport

The *Hotel Aircraft International* (☎ 612 1419, 179 Dayaldas Rd), is one of the cheapest hotels near the airports, with air-con singles/doubles from Rs 850/950.

Avion Hotel (☎ 611 3220, Nehru Rd), has some single rooms for Rs 1175, but the majority of the rooms are in the Rs 1525 to Rs 1825 bracket.

Centaur Hotel (☎ 611 6660; fax 611 3535), right outside the domestic terminal, has all the usual five-star amenities. Rooms cost US$185.

Leela Kempinski (☎ 836 3636; fax 836 0606), 1km from the international terminal, is an award-winning five-star establishment charging US$315/335 for singles/doubles.

Colaba

The *Salvation Army Red Shield Hostel* (☎ 284 1824, 30 Mereweather Rd), is the cheapest place to stay in Colaba. A bed in a separate-sex dorm costs Rs 100 (including breakfast) or Rs 140 (full board).

MUMBAI

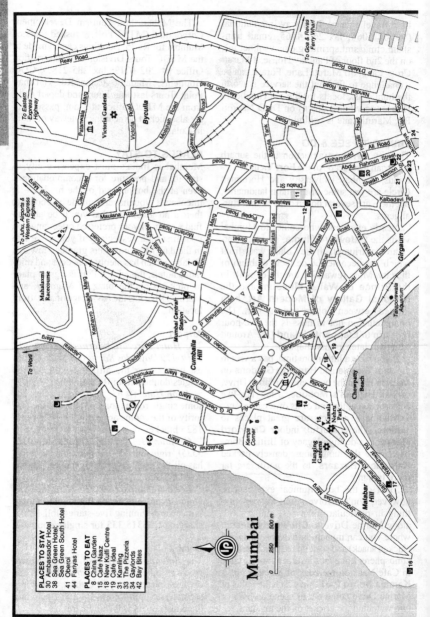

PLACES TO STAY
30 Ambassador Hotel
38 Sea Green Hotel;
   Sea Green South Hotel
41 Oberoi
44 Fariyas Hotel

PLACES TO EAT
8 China Garden
15 Cafe Naaz
18 New Kulfi Centre
19 Cafe Ideal
31 Kamling
33 The Pizzeria
34 Gaylords
42 Bay Bites

Mumbai

0   250   500 m

To Goa & Revas Ferry Wharf
P D'Mello Road
Nandlal Jani Road
Mazgaon Road
Tilak Road

To Eastern Express Highway
Reay Road
Patarwala Marg
Victoria Gardens
Victoria Road
Mohatah Road
Baiwant Singh Road
Jail Road
Babula Tank Road
Mohammed Ali Road
Abdul Rahman Street
Sheikh Memon
Kalbadevi Rd

To Juhu, Airport & Western Highway
Clerk Road
Bapurao Jagtap Marg
Maulana Azad Road
Clare Road
Jillphoy Road
Maulana Azad Road
Dhabu St
Puplaji Road
Morland Road
Sudal Street

Sane Guruji Marg
Arthur Road
Dr Anadrao Nair Road
Sitaram Road
J Boman Behram Marg
Kamathipura
Maulana Shaukatali Road
Sardar Patel Road
Vithalbhai Patel Road
N Desai Road
Girgaum

Mahalaxmi Racecourse
Keshavro Khade Marg
Mumbai Central Station

Lala Lajpatrai Marg
J Dadajee Road
Cumbella Hill
P Bapurao Road
Tardeo Road
Dr B hadakm Road
Artemi Marg
B Khadaevi Road
Sardar Road
Jagannath Shankar Shet
Girgaum Road
Tatapurewala Aquarium

To Worli
B Dahanukar Marg
SK Barodawala Marg
Dr G Deshmukh Marg
A Krani Marg
Fly-over
Pandita
Chowpatty Beach

Bhulabhai Desai Marg
Kemps Corner
Hanging Gardens
Kamala Nehru Park
Walkeshwar Rd
Bal Gangadhar Kher Marg
Bhuleshwar Khar Marg
Jagmohandas Marg
Malabar Hill

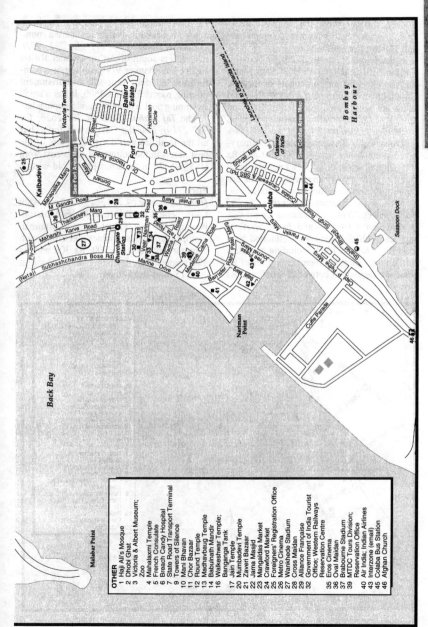

OTHER
1 Haji Ali's Mosque
2 Dhobi Ghat
3 Victoria & Albert Museum;
  Zoo
4 Mahalaxmi Temple
5 French Consulate
6 Breach Candy Hospital
7 State Road Transport Terminal
9 Towers of Silence
10 Mani Bhavan
11 Chor Bazaar
12 Round Temple
13 Madhavbaug Temple
14 Babulnath Mandir
16 Walkeshwar Temple;
  Banganga Tank
17 Jain Temple
20 Mumbadevi Temple
21 Zaveri Bazaar
22 Jama Masjid
23 Mangaldas Market
24 Crawford Market
25 Foreigners' Registration Office
26 Metro Cinema
27 Wankhede Stadium
28 Cross Maidan
29 Alliance Française
32 Government of India Tourist
  Office; Western Railways
  Reservation Centre
35 Eros Cinema
36 Oval Maidan
37 Brabourne Stadium
39 MTDC Tours Division;
  Reservation Office
40 Air India; Indian Airlines
43 Interzone (email)
45 Colaba Bus Station
46 Afghan Church

Carlton Hotel (☎ 202 0642, 12 Mereweather Rd), is basic but rooms with common bath and TV cost just Rs 275/400.

Hotel Volga II (☎ 202 6320), on Nawroji Fardunji Rd near the corner of SBS Marg, has the cheapest air-con rooms in Colaba. Small, clean doubles start from Rs 450, and there are also some rooms without air-con from Rs 275. Reservations are not accepted.

Bentley's Hotel (☎ 284 1474; fax 287 1846, 17 Oliver Rd), offers enormous and ordinary-sized doubles for between Rs 700 and Rs 935, including breakfast. It's a popular hotel but the prices have risen steeply over the last year and reservations are recommended.

YWCA International Centre (☎ 202 5053; fax 202 0445, 18 Madame Cama Rd), accepts both women and men. Spotless singles/doubles/triples with attached bath cost Rs 551/1085/1603, including breakfast and dinner. There's a membership fee of Rs 60 and a deposit of between Rs 650 and Rs 1800 is required. It's very popular so phone at least a week in advance to secure a room.

Fariyas Hotel (☎ 204 2911; fax 283 4992), two streets south of Arthur Bunder Rd on Justice Devshanker V Vijas Marg, is a comfortable, modern four-star establishment offering rooms from Rs 4500. It has a small swimming pool, a restaurant and a popular bar.

The *Taj Mahal Hotel* (☎ 202 2626; fax 287 2719), near the Gateway of India, has all the facilities you'd expect in one of the best hotels in the country. Rooms cost from US$290/320 in the atmospheric old wing.

Fort

Hotel Lawrence (☎ 284 3618), at Rope Walk Lane, behind the Prince of Wales Museum, is one of the best budget hotels in Mumbai. Plain, clean singles, doubles and triples with common bath cost Rs 200, Rs 300 and Rs 400 respectively, including taxes. Book at least 15 days in advance.

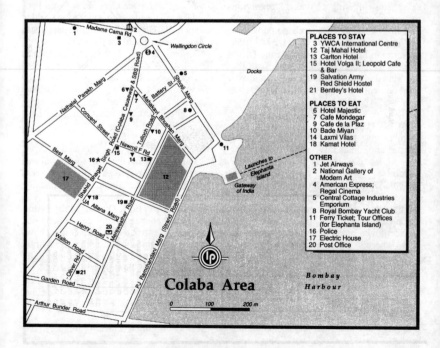

PLACES TO STAY
3 YWCA International Centre
12 Taj Mahal Hotel
13 Carlton Hotel
15 Hotel Volga II; Leopold Cafe & Bar
19 Salvation Army Red Shield Hostel
21 Bentley's Hotel

PLACES TO EAT
6 Hotel Majestic
7 Cafe Mondegar
9 Cafe de la Plaz
10 Bade Miyan
14 Laxmi Vilas
18 Kamat Hotel

OTHER
1 Jet Airways
2 National Gallery of Modern Art
4 American Express; Regal Cinema
5 Central Cottage Industries Emporium
8 Royal Bombay Yacht Club
11 Ferry Ticket; Tour Offices (for Elephanta Island)
16 Police
17 Electric House
20 Post Office

Colaba Area

Benazeer Hotel (☎ *261 1725, 16 Rustom Sidhwa Marg)*, in the heart of the Fort, has simple air-con rooms with attached bath and TV for Rs 600. It's clean, friendly and well run.

Hotel Residency (☎ *262 5525; fax 261 9164)*, on the corner of Dr D Naoroji Rd and Rustom Sidhwa Marg, is a quiet, comfortable air-con hotel with immaculate singles/doubles with attached bath and TV from Rs 1150/1230.

Marine Drive

The *Sea Green Hotel* (☎ *282 2294, 45 Marine Drive)*, and its adjacent twin *Sea Green South Hotel* (☎ 282 1613) are good-value hotels charging Rs 1085/1400 for decent-sized air-con singles/doubles with TV, fridge and attached bath.

Ambassador Hotel (☎ *204 1131; fax 204 0004)*, near the corner of Veer Nariman Rd and Marine Drive, is a modern four-star establishment with a freakish revolving restaurant sprouting from its roof. Rooms cost from US$135 but there's no pool.

The Oberoi (☎ *202 5757; fax 204 1505)*, at Nariman Point, overlooks Marine Drive and the Arabian Sea. It competes with the Taj Mahal Hotel in a bid to be Mumbai's most opulent hostelry. Singles/doubles cost from US$305/330.

PLACES TO EAT

Mumbai has the best selection of restaurants of any Indian city.

Colaba

Leopold Cafe & Bar on Colaba Causeway is a Mumbai institution and a meeting point for travellers. Unfortunately its popularity has pushed prices up and the quality of service down, but it remains as popular as ever. There's an extensive continental, Chinese and veg/non veg menu, and the food isn't bad.

Cafe Mondegar may be cramped but it's highly popular among budget travellers, mainly due to its convivial atmosphere and the CD jukebox. Food ranges from western breakfasts to continental and Indian mains.

Beer is consumed in large quantities in the evening, which seems to make the surly waiters even more temperamental.

Bade Miyan, a permanent evening stall on Tulloch Rd, is a fun place to eat. It serves excellent grilled kebabs to customers milling on the street or seated at a motley assortment of benches on the side of the road.

Kamat Hotel is one of the better Indian restaurants on Colaba Causeway. It serves delicious, sensibly priced vegetarian food such as masala dosas (curried vegetables wrapped inside a pancake) for Rs 18 and thalis for Rs 25.

Cafe de la Plaz, on the 2nd floor of the Metro Plaza on Colaba Causeway, is a tiny outdoor terrace cafe serving juices, burgers and sandwiches. It's a nice place to perch yourself to escape from the hubbub of the street and to watch traffic accidents happening below, but it closes at around 9 pm.

Hotel Majestic, on the north side of Colaba Causeway, or *Laxmi Vilas*, on Nawroji Fardunji Rd, are the places to go for a big healthy cheap feed. They're both thali specialists, charging under Rs 20 for the works.

Tanjore, at the Taj Mahal Hotel, is a sumptuous restaurant with a select menu of tandoori dishes and thalis for between Rs 225 and Rs 545. It has Indian music and dance on Tuesday, Thursday and Saturday night. Formal dress is expected.

Fort

In the Jehangir Art Gallery, located midway between Colaba and the Fort, *Cafe Samovar* serves moderately priced light meals on a pleasant jungly verandah. It's open daily between 11 am and 7 pm.

Wayside Inn, on K Dubash Marg, is one of the most comfortable places to hang out in central Mumbai. Dr Ambedkar must have felt that way, since he wrote the initial draft of the Indian Constitution at a table here. It looks like an Italian trattoria but serves Raj-style fare, such as leek soup, roast chicken and orange soufflé. Light meals cost around Rs 35; substantial dishes are around Rs 65. It's open daily until 7 pm.

Mocambo Cafe & Bar is a fine spot in the

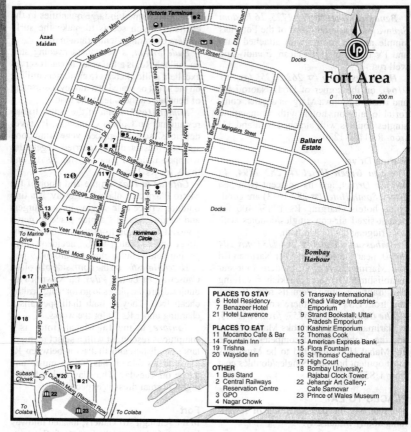

PLACES TO STAY
6 Hotel Residency
7 Benazeer Hotel
21 Hotel Lawrence

PLACES TO EAT
11 Mocambo Cafe & Bar
14 Fountain Inn
19 Trishna
20 Wayside Inn

OTHER
1 Bus Stand
2 Central Railways
   Reservation Centre
3 GPO
4 Nagar Chowk

5 Transway International
8 Khadi Village Industries
   Emporium
9 Strand Bookstall; Uttar
   Pradesh Emporium
10 Kashmir Emporium
12 Thomas Cook
13 American Express Bank
15 Flora Fountain
16 St Thomas' Cathedral
17 High Court
18 Bombay University;
   Rajabai Clock Tower
22 Jehangir Art Gallery;
   Cafe Samovar
23 Prince of Wales Museum

heart of the Fort serving a mixture of Indian and continental fare. The beer is cold, the sandwiches are good and the open street frontage lets you absorb the Fort's atmosphere.

Fountain Inn, in Nanabhai Lane, has a vast menu ranging from tandoori crab to simple potato chaat. The ground floor restaurant is generally packed to capacity and serves main courses for Rs 50 to Rs 70. Upstairs, in the air-con section, you pay Rs 70 to Rs 100 for the same dishes, but your beer is served in a silver tankard and your meal is accompanied by Western pop music.

Trishna, at 7 Rope Walk Lane, is currently the rage among the city's foodies. The emphasis is on succulent seafood dishes, with most in the Rs 50 to Rs 250 price range. Other dishes are between Rs 50 and Rs 80. The king crab and surmai tikka are superb. Bookings are advisable.

Churchgate & Nariman Point
There are hundreds of food vendors in the streets of Nariman Point catering to the area's office workers. They dish up tasty cheap fare and standards of hygiene are relatively high.

Bay Bites, at the end of J Bajaj Marg, is a snack shack set in a private garden looking over the water to Cuffe Parade. It's a good place for a cheap lunch and is a comfortable vantage point from which to watch Koli fishing boats heading out to sea.

The Pizzeria, on the corner of Marine Drive and Veer Nariman Rd, has the best pizzas in the city and beautiful views of the lights of Back Bay and Malabar Hill at night. Pizzas with the usual Western toppings, plus local variations like 'Bombay Masala', start from Rs 80.

Kamling, on Veer Nariman Rd, is a modest, well established Cantonese restaurant serving inexpensive fare.

Gaylords, also on Veer Nariman Rd, is an expensive restaurant with a popular sidewalk cafe (often optimistically described as 'Parisian'). It's a pleasant spot for a snack, and the adjoining pastry shop serves delicious sweets and eclairs.

Chowpatty Beach & Malabar Hill

The stalls lining Chowpatty Beach in the evening are atmospheric spots to snack on bhelpuri, drink fresh juices and indulge in your favourite kulfi.

Cafe Ideal is an amiable Iranian-style cafe on Chowpatty Seaface with a CD jukebox and the usual continental-Chinese-Indian hybrid menu. Most dishes cost around Rs 30; beer is Rs 48.

New Kulfi Centre, has some of the most delicious kulfi in Mumbai. It's weighed in 100g slabs, cut into cubes, and served to customers clustered on the pavement outside. Prices range from Rs 12 to Rs 25.

Cafe Naaz, on the edge of Malabar Hill's Kamala Nehru Park, is a multi-tiered terrace cafe with superb views of Back Bay and Chowpatty Beach. It's a great place to loiter around sunset as the lights of Marine Drive come on.

China Garden (☎ 363 0841, Om Chambers, Kemps Corner), is an elegant Chinese restaurant and cocktail bar. Locals unanimously agree that it has the best Chinese food in the city. Most main dishes are between Rs 120 and Rs 200; bookings are essential.

GETTING THERE & AWAY
Air

Mumbai is the main international gateway to India and a convenient entry point to South India, especially if you intend to explore Goa and the Malabar Coast. The international terminal (Sahar) is 30km north of central Mumbai. Its nearby domestic airport (Santa Cruz) is approximately 26km north of the city centre. There are regular shuttle buses between the two terminals. Facilities at Sahar include Government of India and MTDC tourist counters, 24 hour money-changing facilities and a prepaid taxi booth.

Most international flights land at Mumbai in the middle of the night. So if you arrive without a hotel reservation and are wary of tramping around an unfamiliar city in the early hours of the morning, you may want to wait until dawn before heading into the city.

If you're leaving India from Mumbai, your ticket several days before your departure. It's wise to check in three hours before your flight departs, since you'll need this time to handle the queues and bureaucracy. You can exchange any leftover rupees for a number of hard currencies at Sahar's State Bank of India, opposite the check-in desks. There's a Rs 500 departure tax on all international flights.

Domestic Airlines

The addresses in Mumbai (telephone area code: 022) of airlines serving South India are:

Indian Airlines
   (☎ 287 6161)
   Air India Bldg, Nariman Point
Jet Airways
   (☎ 285 5789)
   Amarchand Mansion, Madame Cama Rd
NEPC
   (☎ 610 2546)
   Santa Cruz airport, Vile Parle East
Sahara Indian Airlines
   (☎ 283 2369)
   ground floor, Maker Chambers V,
   J Bajaj Marg, Nariman Point
Spanair
   (☎ 610 8135)
   Santa Cruz airport, Vile Parle East
   NB: Spanair serves Goa

MUMBAI

Domestic Flights from Mumbai

There are regular flights between Mumbai and more than 35 Indian cities, including daily flights between Mumbai and Bangalore (US$110), Calcutta (US$185), Delhi (US$140), Goa (US$65), Jaipur (US$125), Kochi (US$135), Chennai (US$130) and Varanasi (US$190).

International Airlines

Most international airline offices in Mumbai are in or close to Nariman Point. Addresses of international carriers include:

Air Canada
   (☎ 202 1111)
   Amarchand Mansion, Madame Cama Rd
Air France
   (☎ 202 4818)
   1st floor, Maker Chambers VI,
   J Bajaj Marg, Nariman Point
Air India
   (☎ 202 4142)
   Air India Building, Nariman Point
Air Lanka
   (☎ 284 4156)
   12D Raheja Centre, ground floor,
   Nariman Point
Alitalia
   (☎ 204 5023)
   Industrial Assurance Building,
   Veer Nariman Rd, Churchgate
Biman Bangladesh Airlines
   (☎ 282 4659)
   199 J Tata Rd, Churchgate
British Airways
   (☎ 282 0888)
   Valcan Insurance Building,
   202B Veer Nariman Rd, Churchgate
Cathay Pacific Airways
   (☎ 202 9561)
   Taj Mahal Hotel, Apollo Bunder, Colaba
Delta Air Lines
   (☎ 288 5652)
   Taj Mahal Hotel, Apollo Bunder, Colaba
Emirates
   (☎ 287 1649)
   ground floor, Mittal Chambers,
   228 Nariman Point
Gulf Air
   (☎ 202 1626)
   ground floor, Maker Chambers V,
   J Bajaj Marg, Nariman Point

Japan Airlines
   (☎ 287 4939)
   ground floor, Raheja Centre,
   Free Press Journal Marg, Nariman Point
Kenya Airways
   (☎ 282 0064)
   199 J Tata Rd, Churchgate
KLM – Royal Dutch Airlines
   (☎ 283 3338)
   Khaitan Bhavan, 198 J Tata Rd, Churchgate
Kuwait Airways
   (☎ 204 5351)
   Chateau Windsor, 86 Veer Nariman Rd,
   Churchgate
Lufthansa Airlines
   (☎ 202 3430)
   ground floor, Express Towers, Nariman Point
Malaysian Airlines
   (☎ 218 1431)
   GSA Stic Travels & Tours,
   6 Maker Arcade, Cuffe Parade
Pakistan International Airlines
   (☎ 202 1598)
   4th floor, B Wing, Mittal Towers,
   Free Press Journal Marg, Nariman Point
Qantas Airways
   (☎ 202 9297)
   4th floor, Sakhar Bhavan, Nariman Point
SAS
   (☎ 202 7083)
   Podar House, 10 Marine Drive
Singapore Airlines
   (☎ 202 2747)
   Taj Mahal Hotel, Apollo Bunder
Swissair
   (☎ 287 2210)
   ground floor, Maker Chambers VI,
   J Bajaj Marg, Nariman Point
Thai Airways International (THAI)
   (☎ 215 5301)
   15 World Trade Centre Arcade, Cuffe Parade
TWA
   (☎ 282 3080)
   Amarchand Mansion, Madame Cama Rd

Bus

Long-distance government buses to Goa, Karnataka and other southern states depart from the State Road Transport Terminal close to Mumbai Central station. The terminal is fairly chaotic and no information is available in English. Bookings can be made between 8 am and 8 pm. There's one daily government bus to Goa (depart Mumbai 5 pm, arrive Panaji at 9 am the following day; Rs 220); one daily bus to Bangalore (depart 10.30 am; Rs 345); and four buses a day to Hyderabad (depart 10 am, 1.30 pm, 5 pm and 9 pm; Rs 265).

Much more comfortable are the private long-distance buses which can be booked at booths along J Boman Behram Marg, near the entrance to the State Road Transport Terminal. Tickets to Goa cost between Rs 200 and Rs 300 for deluxe buses, and between Rs 400 and Rs 500 for sleeper or air-con buses. Buses depart daily around 2 pm and 5.30 pm, many starting from just south of the Metro Cinema on MG Rd. If you turn up here at around 1.30 pm you can pick your coach, and try bargaining. The journey to Goa takes at least 17 hours. Private buses to both Bangalore and Hyderabad cost around Rs 300.

Train

Two systems operate out of Mumbai. The one you need for South India is Central Rail-

ways, which operates from Victoria Terminus (VT), also known as Chhatrapati Shivaji Terminus (CST). The reservation centre behind VT is open Monday to Saturday between 9 am and 1 pm, and 1.30 and 4 pm. Tourist-quota tickets and Indrail passes can be bought at counter No 8.

Note that a few useful expresses heading southwards depart from Kurla, which is inconveniently located 16km to the north of VT. Some Central Railways trains also depart from Dadar, several stops north of VT on the suburban line. They include the *Dadar Express*, one of the fastest trains to Chennai (Madras). You can still book tickets for these trains at VT.

Trains operating on the new Konkan Railway also operate from VT. At the time of writing there was only one train a day, departing at 10.30 pm, to Margao in Goa. This is bound to change, however, as more

Major Trains from Mumbai

Destination	Train Number & Name	Departure Time	Distance (km)	Duration (hours)	Fare (Rs) (2nd/1st)
Agra	2137 *Punjab Mail*	7.10 pm VT*	1344	21.30	264/1009
Ahmedabad	2009 *Shatabdi***	6.25 am MC	492	7.00	475/955
	9011 *Gujarat Express*	5.45 am MC		9.30	141/511
Aurangabad	1003 *Devagiri Exp*	9.20 pm VT	375	7.15	115/405
	7617 *Tapovan Exp*	6.10 am VT		7.15	
Bangalore	6529 *Udyan Exp*	7.55 am VT	1210	24.30	255/952
Calcutta	2859 *Gitanjali Exp*	6.00 am VT	1960	33.30	320/1335
	8001 *Howrah Mail*	8.15 pm VT		36.00	
Chennai	1063 *Chennai Exp*	7.45 pm D	1279	24.00	264/1009
Delhi	2951 *Rajdhani Exp***	4.55 pm MC	1384	17.00	1100/3120
	2925 *Paschim Exp*	11.35 am MC		23.00	277/1062
Kochi	1081 *Mumbai-Kanyakumari Exp*	3.35 pm VT	1840	39.00	308/1281
Pune	2123 *Deccan Queen*	5.10 pm VT	191	3.30	66/238
	1007 *Deccan Exp*	6.40 am VT		4.30	
Varanasi	1065 *Kurla-Varanasi Exp*	5.20 am K	1509	22.30	286/1116

* Abbreviations for train station: VT = Victoria Terminus; MC = Mumbai Central; D = Dadar; K = Kurla
** Air-con only; fare includes meals and drinks

Shatabdi 2009 runs daily except Friday
Rajdhani 2951 runs daily except Monday
Kurla-Varanasi Express 1065 runs Monday, Wednesday, Thursday only

services are introduced, and by the time this appears there should also be direct services to Mangalore. Currently the trip to Margao takes 12 hours.

Mumbai's other major railway stations, Churchgate and Mumbai Central, are the domain of Western Railways, which only handles services heading north.

Boat

The Mumbai to Goa ferry service is operated by Frank Shipping. The modern, 400-seat, air-con jetfoil leaves Mumbai Friday to Sunday at 10.30 pm, and on Tuesday and Thursday at 9 am. The journey takes about eight hours. On the return leg it leaves Panaji daily, except Tuesday and Thursday, at 9 am. The fare is Rs 1400/1600 in economy/business class, and includes meals. For bookings in Mumbai contact the ferry terminal (☎ 373 5562; fax 373 3740), which is in the old dockyard, about 2km north-east of Victoria Terminus. In Panaji, contact (☎ 0832-228711). The ferry does not run during the monsoon (mid-May to October).

GETTING AROUND
To/From the Airports

An airport bus service operates between Sahar (international) and Santa Cruz (domestic) airports and the Air India Building at Nariman Point in central Mumbai. The journey from Sahar takes about 1¼ hours and costs Rs 50; from Santa Cruz it takes about an hour and costs Rs 40. In peak hour the trip can take well over two hours, so don't cut things too fine if you're catching a flight. Baggage costs Rs 5 per piece.

From Sahar, departures are at 2.30, 6.30, 8.30, 9.30 and 11.30 am, and at 2, 3.30, 5, 7.30, 9.30 and 10.30 pm; the buses leave from Santa Cruz half an hour later. From Nariman Point, departures are at 12.30, 4.15, 8.15, 10.15 and 11.30 am, and 1.15, 2.15, 3.45, 5.30, 7.15, 9.15 and 11.15 pm. Tickets can be bought on the bus or at the booth outside the Air India building in Nariman Point.

There's a pre-paid taxi booth at the international airport, with set fares to various city destinations. It costs Rs 245 to Colaba

during the day and Rs 285 at night; you pay Rs 5 per item of luggage. A pre-paid fare is higher than the meter rate but it saves haggling. Don't try to catch an auto-rickshaw from the airport to the city: they're prohibited from entering central Mumbai.

Bus

Despite popular mythology, Mumbai's red double-decker buses are one of the best ways to travel short distances in the city, as long as it's not during rush hours. Fares generally cost only a couple of rupees and are paid to the conductor once you're aboard. Route numbers and destination signs are very confusing so it's best to make as many friends as possible at the bus queue; somebody will always let you know when the right bus is coming.

Train

Mumbai has efficient but overcrowded suburban electric trains, and it's virtually the only place in India where it's worth taking trains for city travel. The main suburban route of interest to travellers is Churchgate to Mumbai Central (Rs 2/22 in 2nd/1st class), and onward to Dadar. There's a train every few minutes in either direction between 4.30 am and 1.30 am. Avoid rush hours.

Taxi & Auto-Rickshaw

Mumbai has a huge fleet of metered black-and-yellow taxis, but auto-rickshaws are confined to the outer northern suburbs. Taxis are the most convenient way to zip around the city but they're not cheap. You may have to approach a few vehicles before you find one willing to go where you want. Taxi meters are out of date, so the fare is calculated using a conversion chart which all drivers carry – ask to see it at the end of the journey. The rough conversion rate is around 10 times the meter reading.

Car

The tourist office's recommended rates for hiring a car with a driver are from Rs 750 per day or Rs 575 for half a day with limited kilometres.

AROUND MUMBAI
Elephanta Island

The rock-cut temples on Elephanta Island, 9km north-east of Apollo Bunder, are Mumbai's major tourist attraction. They are thought to have been created between 450 and 750 AD, when the island was known as Gharapuri, the Fortress City. The Portuguese renamed it Elephanta because of a large stone elephant near the shore. This statue collapsed in 1814, and the British removed the remaining pieces to the Victoria Gardens where it was reassembled and still stands today.

The caves are reached by a steep stairway that begins near the ferry landing. Palanquins are available for those who need to be carried up. It costs Rs 5 to enter the cave area at the top of the hill. There is one main cave with a number of large sculpted panels, all relating to Shiva. The most famous of these is the Trimurti, or triple-headed Shiva, in which the god is also depicted as Brahma the creator and Vishnu the preserver. The central bust of Shiva, its eyes closed in eternal contemplation, may be the most serene sight you witness in India.

The best time to visit Elephanta is during the week, since on weekends it has a carnival atmosphere which is not conducive to quiet enjoyment of the temples. When you've had your fill of the temples, the tree-top terrace of the MTDC's *Chalukya Restaurant & Beer Bar* at the head of the stairway is a fine spot to sit back and take in the expansive views of Mumbai Harbour.

Getting There & Away Launches depart from 8.30 am daily from the Gateway of India. Three different types of service are available: ordinary, luxury and deluxe. The ordinary service departs every 30 minutes, has wooden benches for seating and costs Rs 50 return. Rs 70 will get you a plastic bucket seat for the return trip on the luxury service, departing every 15 minutes, while Rs 125 is the price of a return ticket on the deluxe service. Deluxe has individual cushioned seats and makes just one return trip a day (between 9.30 and 10.30 am from the Gateway; from Elephanta at 1.30 pm).

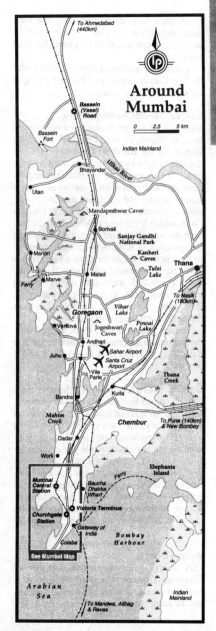

Around Mumbai

0   2.5   5 km

All three services take an hour one way. Boats depart from the Gateway between 8.30 am and 3.40 pm, and from Elephanta between 1 and 5 pm.

Ignore the hawkers at Apollo Bunder who try to persuade tourists that there's nothing to eat or drink on the island.

Sanjay Gandhi National Park

This 104 sq km protected area of forested hills on Mumbai's northern outskirts is best known for the **Kanheri Caves**, which line the side of a rocky ravine in the centre of the park. They were used by Buddhist monks between the 2nd and 9th centuries as *viharas* (monasteries) and *chaityas* (temples). The most impressive is cave 3, the Great Chaitya Cave, which has a long colonnade and a 5m-high *dagoba* (Buddhist religious monument composed of a solid hemisphere topped by a spire) at the back of the cave. Several other caves have interesting sculptures, though the majority are little more than shelters carved into the rock. Entry to the national park costs Rs 2; entry to the caves, a further 5km from the park entrance, is another Rs 2.

There's a **Lion Safari Park** 500m inside the national park entrance. 'Safari trips' run daily except Monday between 9 am and 5 pm; entry is Rs 10.

Getting There & Away Take the train from Churchgate to Borivali station (40 minutes) and then an auto-rickshaw for the 6km to Kanheri Caves. Be wary of rickshaw-wallahs who try to persuade you to allow them to keep the meter running while you explore the caves; if you fall for this trick, you'll return to the rickshaw to find the meter has been tampered with. On Sunday and public holidays there is a bus service from Borivali station to the caves. Kanheri can also be visited (quickly) on the MTDC's suburban tour.

Manori Beach

This sleepy beach near the Portuguese-flavoured fishing village of Manori is a weekend retreat for wealthy Mumbai families and the scene of occasional beach parties. It's in a surprisingly rural environment, about 40km from the city centre.

Places to Stay The *Manoribel Hotel (☎ 269 1301)* has a selection of cottages set in a shady beachside grove strung with hammocks. They cost between Rs 600 and Rs 1300 on weekdays, and between Rs 750 and Rs 1750 on weekends. Double rooms are Rs 400 to Rs 500 weekdays; Rs 100 more on weekends. Full board is available for an extra Rs 310. Be sure to book in advance.

DoMonica Beach Resort (☎ 444 9735), 100m further north, charges Rs 150 per head. Full board is available for an extra Rs 220. Advance bookings are essential on weekends.

To get to Manori, take the suburban electric train from Churchgate to Malad, then bus No 272 to Marve. A ferry (Rs 2.50) shuttles across Manori Creek, and it's a pleasant 2km walk or tonga (a two-wheeled horse carriage) ride from the Manori slipway to the beach and the hotels.

Bassein

The remains of the Portuguese fortified city of Bassein are on the northern side of the river which separates Greater Mumbai from the Indian mainland. After securing the area in 1534, the Portuguese built a city of such pomp and splendour – with a cathedral, five convents and 13 churches – that it came to be known as the Court of the North. In 1739 the Marathas besieged the city and the Portuguese surrendered after appalling losses. The weathered city walls are still standing and you can see the eerie ruins of some of the churches and the Cathedral of St Joseph. Bassein is 11km from the Bassein Road (Vasai Road in Marathi) train station.

Ajanta Caves

The Buddhist caves of Ajanta, 325km east of Mumbai, date from around 200 BC to 650 AD. As Buddhism gradually declined, the caves were abandoned and became forgotten until they were rediscovered when a British hunting party stumbled upon them in 1819. Their isolation had contributed to the fine state of preservation of many of the remarkable paintings, and today Ajanta is listed as a World Heritage Site by UNESCO.

The 29 caves are cut into the steep face of a horseshoe-shaped rock gorge on the Waghore River. Five of the caves are chaityas while the other 24 are viharas. The famous Ajanta 'frescoes' were created by coating the rough-hewn rock walls with a 1cm-thick layer of clay and cow dung mixed with rice husks. A final coat of lime was applied to produce the finished surface on which the artist painted. This was then polished to produce a high gloss. Although the Ajanta paintings are particularly notable, there are many interesting sculptures here as well.

If possible, avoid coming here at weekends or on public holidays when Ajanta seems to attract half the population of India. The hawkers at Ajanta are some of the most persistent in South India – if you don't want to buy, don't accept 'gifts' or make promises to 'just look'.

Places to Stay & Eat It's a long trip (at least two hours) by bus from Aurangabad, and many visitors prefer to stay close to the caves.

MTDC Travellers' Lodge (☎ 02-438 4226) is right by the entrance to the caves. The rooms cost Rs 125/200 with shared bathroom. Checkout time is 9 am. The food in the *restaurant* is reasonably good. You can make bookings at the MTDC in Aurangabad.

MTDC Holiday Resort (☎ 02-438 4230) at Fardapur, 5km from the caves, is more popular. Large, clean rooms along a pleasant verandah cost from Rs 150/200 to Rs 250/300 with hot shower. Each room has two beds, clean sheets and a fan. Dorm beds are Rs 50. The attached *Vihara Restaurant* serves uninspiring thalis, non veg food and cold beer. There are a number of chai and snack shacks along the main road in Fardapur, but none offer anything you could call a meal.

Getting There & Away You can catch a direct train from Mumbai to either Aurangabad (106km south of Ajanta) or the railway town of Jalgaon (60km north of Ajanta), which is a stop on the Mumbai-Delhi line. Alternatively, the MTDC office at CDO Hutments, Madame Cama Rd, Nariman Point, handles bookings for Ghadge Patil Transport's daily bus to Aurangabad (Rs 240), which departs from the MTDC office at 8 pm and takes 12 hours.

There are four daily buses from Aurangabad to the caves, and frequent buses from Jalgaon to Fardapur. The caves are 4km off the main Aurangabad to Jalgaon road, and Fardapur is 1km further down the main road towards Jalgaon. There are regular buses between Fardapur and Ajanta which cost Rs 4. Not all buses travelling along the main road call at Ajanta, so ensure you get on the right one to avoid a walk to the caves.

Shared taxis operate between the caves, Fardapur and Jalgaon. Prices are negotiable, but expect to pay around Rs 15 from Ajanta to Fardapur and Rs 50 to Jalgaon.

There's a 'cloakroom' at the Ajanta Caves where you can leave gear (Rs 2), so it is possible to arrive on a morning bus from Jalgaon, look around the caves, and continue to Aurangabad in the evening, or vice versa.

Goa

The former Portuguese enclave of Goa has for years been one of India's most popular destinations, known for its magnificent beaches, the relaxed friendliness of its people, and its renowned 'travellers' scene. White-washed churches, colourful Hindu temples, dense palm groves and crumbling forts all contribute to the unique scenery of India's tiniest state. For more information about Goa see Lonely Planet's *Goa*.

HISTORY

Goa had been a major trading centre for centuries when its destiny took an important turn in 1510 with the arrival of the Portuguese. The conquistadors captured the capital and made it the centre of their eastern empire. A brief but glorious age followed, during which the lucrative spice trade made the capital of Goa one of the richest cities in the world. By the 17th century, however, decline had set in, and although the territory gradually expanded in size, Goa's wealth evaporated and it became a colonial backwater. It was not until 1961 that the Portuguese were forced from Goa and the tiny area became a Union Territory of India. In 1987 it opted to become the 25th state of India.

BEACHES

Goa is justifiably famous for its beaches. Colva, Calangute and Baga tend to be dominated by package tourism and offer a complete range of accommodation, while beaches like Anjuna, Vagator and Chapora, where the backpackers tend to congregate, have much more basic places to stay.

Benaulim, with its beach shacks and low-key resorts, strikes a happy balance between the two. For the quietest beaches you have to look further afield. Arambol is still pretty much undeveloped, and there are empty stretches of sand both to the north and south of it. Palolem, further south, is also relatively quiet.

On the Beaches

Just because Goa is so welcoming and friendly, don't make the mistake of thinking that you can disregard local sensibilities. Nudism (that includes topless sunbathing) is actually

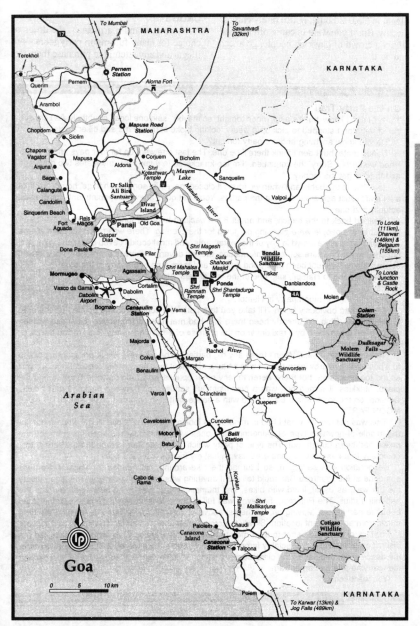

To Mumbai
MAHARASHTRA
To Savantvadi (32km)
17
KARNATAKA
Terekhol
Querim
Pernem
Pernem Station
Aldona Fort
Arambol
Chopdem
Siolim
Mapusa Road Station
Chapora
Vagator
Mapusa
Corjuem
Bicholim
Anjuna
Aldona
Shri Koteshwar Temple
Mayem Lake
Sanquelim
Baga
Calangute
Dr Salim Ali Bird Sanctuary
Divar Island
Mandovi River
Valpoi
Candolim
Sinquerim Beach
Reis Magos
Fort Aguada
Panaji
Old Goa
To Londa (111km), Dharwar (146km) & Belgaum (155km)
Gaspar Dias
Pilar
Shri Magesh Temple
Bondla Wildlife Sanctuary
Dona Paula
Agassaim
Shri Mahalsa Temple
Safa Shahouri Masjid
Tiskar
To Londa Junction & Castle Rock
Mormugao
Cortalim
Shri Ramnath Temple
Ponda
Shri Shantadurga Temple
Danblandora
4A
Vasco da Gama
Dabolim
Dabolim Airport
Molen
Bogmalo
Cansaulim Station
Verna
Colem Station
Majorda
Zuvari River
Rachol
Dudhsagar Falls
Molem Wildlife Sanctuary
Colva
Margao
Sanvordem
Benaulim
Arabian Sea
Varca
Chinchinim
Sanguem
Quepem
Cavelossim
Mobor
Cuncolim
Balli Station
Betul
Cabo da Rama
Konkan Railway
Agonda
17
Shri Mallikarjuna Temple
Paloiem
Chaudi
Cotigao Wildlife Sanctuary
Canacona Island
Canacona Station
Talpona
Goa
0 5 10 km
Polem
KARNATAKA
To Karwar (13km) & Jog Falls (489km)

GOA

illegal in Goa, although police rarely enforce the law. But if you want to cause offence and attract a crowd of gawking people, go ahead and do it.

DRUGS

Acid, ecstasy and marijuana – the drugs of choice for many full-moon partygoers – are illegal and any attempt to purchase them (let

On the Party Trail

'Party? I don't know, but it's a full moon tonight, so maybe', said one local, doubtfully. As I cruised out of Vagator, I stopped to pick up a weary looking bloke in torn jeans and biker boots.

'Do you know anything about a party tonight?'

'Dunno mate, but I don't think there'll be one. The last one went on for four days and only finished yesterday. Sorry', he continued, 'I'm too knackered to think. I lost my mates two days ago and they've got the money.'

I took him to the bank, and when we found it closed, gave him some cash to get home. 'Thanks a lot mate. Just ask around about the parties. You'll get quite a few disappointments before you actually find one.'

I headed back to the beach, and about 8 pm decided to do a round of the bars in Anjuna to find out where people were planning on going for the evening. There was no one around. Three was quite definitely a crowd in any of the restaurants, and most couldn't even boast one. Worried, I headed to the one sure source of information, the taxi drivers. 'Where is everyone?' They looked at me blankly. 'I've just been all around Anjuna, and there's no one in any of the bars.'

'They've gone to Hampi', said one of the taxi drivers, helpfully.

'Hampi?'

'Hampi – big full moon party in Hampi'.

My face had obviously fallen. 'I'll take you to a party', he continued, and pointed up the road to the Paraiso Club. I'd already been there and had met three disconsolate Japanese women who'd been taken there by a taxi driver on the promise of a 'full moon party', only to find the place all but deserted.

'Not that party', I said. 'Aren't there any big parties?' The driver's eyes lit up, and he pointed to a poster on a nearby lamp-post. It was an advertisement for a party at Makkies in Baga. It didn't sound too promising, but there weren't many other options, so I rode down to Baga to find the place. Makkies, it turned out, was a new nightclub sandwiched between package tour hotels. Outside, on the road, was a blackboard with a notice written in coloured chalk – TONITE! FULL MOON PARTY.

This was not exactly what I had in mind. I was looking for one of those illegal, impromptu, in-the-middle-of-nowhere type of gatherings; the ones where the DJs had been flown in and the police had been bought out. The type of party which my passenger had been at; where I, too, could say that I vaguely remembered having lost my friends two days ago.

Desperation was setting in, so I turned the bike around and headed for Vagator. Perhaps someone at the Primrose Bar could tell me if anything was happening tonight. The lane outside the bar was, as usual, lined with bikes, and thumping music was to be heard as I entered the half-mile radius. The Primrose, however, was full of bored-looking would-be ravers, rather than bonafide partygoers. Moving on, up the hill above Vagator, the Nine Bar was blasting the right music from an excellent location. Slowly the crowd grew until … silence. The police had arrived.

For lack of anything better to do, I motored back to the Paraiso Club, which at least had the distinction of having a respectably large number of people. I wandered a short way away from the dance area, and sat on the cliffs, contemplating the full moon. A shadowy figure approached me, carrying a large carrier bag.

'You want some?'

alone consume them) fraught with danger. Fort Aguada prison houses some foreigners serving lengthy sentences for drug offences, because for some time now authorities have been taking a hard line on the parties and the drugs.

Possession of even a small amount of *charas* (hashish) can mean 10 years. There

---

'What is it?'

'Chocolate: Kit Kat, Dairy Milk …'

It was obviously time to go home. On the way back, I passed lines of motorbikes heading in the opposite direction. No one, it seemed (apart from those in Hampi, presumably), knew where the party was, although on that particular night there were large numbers who wanted to find out.

Two nights later, having put my disappointment behind me, I left a bar in Calangute at around 1 am, and decided to take a motorbike taxi back to my hotel. 'Oh,' the driver said conversationally, as he walked towards the bike, 'you're not going to the party then?'

'Where is the party?' Incredible vagueness. 'How do you know there's a party?' Someone had heard from someone else. I asked for a second opinion from an Israeli backpacker loitering nearby: 'Do you know about a party?'

'No, but he says there's a party, so there must be one.'

Ten minutes later we were climbing into an ageing car, with flashing lights around the windscreen and a Dukes of Hazzard horn, and, deafened by reggae music, were heading up the coast to Arambol.

At a quarter to two we arrived at Siolim. In the darkness we could see the lights of the ferry approaching. Normally the ferry stops at 8 or 9 pm, but tonight it was running straight through. We crossed the estuary in darkness, with a ferry load of other travellers on an assortment of motorbikes and scooters. On the far side of the river we headed north until, after quarter of an hour, we reached a crossroads where the driver stopped. 'Normally,' he hesitated, 'the parties are up there, but we'll wait and see where the others are going.'

After two other taxis had headed past us into the night, he started again, but a few minutes later he stopped to question a fisherman who was on his way home.

'Party?'

'Straight… *string of Konkani*… party… *string of Konkani*… Arambol'

'Thank you.'

Eventually we arrived on the fringe of an area where the palm trees were lit up by the glow of a hundred Primus lamps, and the peace of the night was exploded by psychedelic dance music. The atmosphere was subdued (perhaps because people were still recovering from Hampi?). Groups of foreigners sat around on palm mats talking, smoking or just gazing at nothing in particular. A few tie-dyed sheets strung between the trees marked the extent of the dance area.

The Primus lamps are the property of the Indian women who always turn up at these events to provide refreshments. With their ready cups of tea and patient faces, I half expected them to start handing out sympathy as well: 'Never mind… it's just a difficult stage you're going through.' By four o'clock I was faltering, and decided that the excitement of the moment had passed. We went for a swim and then decided to head back home, leaving a couple of hundred hardier souls to continue to daylight.

This was as close as I got to a party, but on the way I picked up some useful tips on finding a *real* affair:

- There doesn't have to be a full moon out for there to be a full moon party on
- If you want to know what's going on, check in any of the following: the Anjuna taxi rank, the Primrose Bar, the Shore Bar
- Befriend an Israeli

GOA

have been cases of policemen approaching hapless tourists and threatening to 'plant' drugs on them unless they pay a relatively large amount of money on the spot. Most travellers comply – the prospect of several months awaiting trial, and then possibly a jail sentence, makes it only wise to do so.

Probably the best way to deal with the problem should it happen to you is to try persuasion, but if that fails to work, pay the baksheesh. While doing this, make a mental note of every distinguishing feature of the policeman you are paying. Immediately after the incident, write a letter describing exactly what happened, with as much detail as possible.

Copies of the letter should go to the Government of India Tourist Office in Panaji (not the Goan Tourist Department), any one (or all) of the three daily English language newspapers in Goa, and the Government of India Tourist Office in your own country.

MEDICAL SERVICES

If you're unlucky enough to be injured in a motorcycle accident, the best bone specialist in Goa is Dr Bhale (☎ 0832-217053), who runs a 24 hour x-ray clinic at Porvorim, 4km north of Panaji on the NH17 road to Mapusa.

ACCOMMODATION

Accommodation prices in Goa are based on high, middle and low seasons. The high season covers the period from mid-December to late January, the middle season from October to mid-December and February to June, and the low season from July to September. Prices quoted in this chapter are high season rates. If you're in Goa during the rest of the year, then count on discounts of about 25% in the middle season and up to 60% in the low season.

At all times of year there's a 5% luxury tax on rooms over Rs 100, 10% on rooms over Rs 500, and 15% for those over Rs 800. For most of the low-budget places, the prices quoted here include this tax, but in mid- and high-budget hotels you can expect tax to be added to the bill.

GETTING THERE & AWAY

Air

Goa's international airport, Dabolim, is 29km from Panaji, on the coast near Vasco da Gama. Most of India's domestic airlines operate services here, as well as several charter companies which fly into Goa direct from the UK and Germany.

There are numerous flights between Goa and Mumbai. Indian Airlines also has daily direct flights to and from Delhi (US$190), Chennai (Madras) (US$110), Kochi (Cochin) (US$95) and Bangalore (US$80). At the time of writing there were also flights from Goa direct to Agatti in the Lakshadweep Islands.

Bus

See the Getting There & Away sections under Panaji, Margao and Mapusa for details of long-distance bus travel.

Train

Goa's rail links have been disrupted over the last few years by two major engineering projects. The first, the conversion of the existing South Central Railways (SRC) line from metre to broad gauge, should have been completed in 1997, but is still dragging on. Some estimates are that the line may not open for another 18 months or so. When it finally opens, trains to Bangalore will take about 15 hours, and cost around Rs 185/610 in sleeper/1st class, or Rs 805 for an air-con two-tier sleeper. Getting to Delhi from Goa will take about 44 hours and cost around Rs 348/1410 in sleeper/1st class, and Rs 1675 for air-con.

The second project, the new 760km Konkan Railway from Mangalore, along the coast through Goa to Mumbai, is now finished. At the time of writing there were no through trains from Mumbai to Mangalore; trains from north and south terminated at Margao, where passengers had to change. The direct service from Mumbai to Mangalore is expected to start soon.

The trip from Margao to Mumbai takes 12 hours, and from Margao to Mangalore around six hours. There are several convenient stations including Mapusa Road for trains to Mapusa and Old Goa for trains to Panaji, but it's still undecided which stations will sell tickets, and where the express trains will stop. At the time of writing tickets could only be purchased at Margao.

The main station for both SCR and Konkan railway lines is at Margao, where there's a computerised booking office. Seats and sleepers can also be booked at the station in Vasco da Gama, and at the railway outagency on the 1st floor of the Panaji bus stand.

Taxi

It takes 14 hours to drive the 600km from Mumbai to Goa, but this can be done over two days. You'll have to pay for the taxi's return trip, so the cost will be around Rs 6000.

Boat

A catamaran service run by Frank Shipping plies the route between Mumbai and Panaji five times a week from October to May. In the past year it has been prone to occasional breakdowns, but the staff say that the problem has now been fixed.

From Goa to Mumbai it sails every Monday, Wednesday, Friday, Saturday and Sunday, departing at 9 am and arriving in Mumbai at 4.30 pm. Going the other way, on Tuesday and Thursday it departs Mumbai at 9 am, arriving in Panaji at 4.30 pm; on Friday, Saturday and Sunday it leaves Mumbai at 10.30 pm, arriving at 6.30 am. Bookings can be made through travel agents or at the company's offices in Mumbai (☎ (022) 374 3737) and Panaji (☎ (0832) 228711). Tickets aren't cheap: Rs 1400/1600 for economy/business class. Apart from the half-hour cruise up the Mandovi River, the trip is pretty unexciting as the catamaran is obliged to stay at least 15km away from the coast to avoid fishing fleets.

GETTING AROUND
Bus

The state-run Kadamba bus company is the main operator, although there are also many private companies. Buses are cheap and run

to just about everywhere. Services are frequent and destinations at the bus stands are signposted in English.

Car Rental

Self-drive car rental is available in the major centres of Goa, and several companies have counters at the airport. Hertz (☎ 0832-223998) charges from Rs 5950 for a small Maruti-Suzuki for a week. Wheels (☎ 0832-224304) offer a three-day rental with limited mileage for Rs 2750.

Motorcycle Rental

Hiring a motorcycle in Goa is easy, and popular with visitors. The machines available are old Enfields, more modern Yamaha 100s and gearless Kinetic Honda scooters. Per day in high season, you can expect to pay up to Rs 200 for a scooter, Rs 300 for the smaller bikes and Rs 400 for an Enfield; outside high season and if the demand is low the prices can drop by half.

While most bikes will have some sort of insurance, if you're involved in an accident you'll probably be required to pay for the damage to the rental bike, at the very least. You should be aware that India has the worst record for road accidents in the world, and inexperienced, helmetless foreigners on motorcycles are extremely vulnerable. Carry the necessary paperwork (licence, registration and insurance) at all times. Licence checks on foreigners are a lucrative source of baksheesh for the police. See the Getting Around chapter for more information on motorbike hire and travel.

Motorcycle Taxi

Goa is the one place in India where motorcycles are a licensed form of taxi. They are much cheaper than other forms of transport if you are travelling alone, and backpacks are no problem. Licensed motorcycles can be identified by their yellow front mudguard.

Bicycle

There are plenty of places to hire bicycles in all the major towns and beaches in Goa. Charges are around Rs 40 for a full day.

Boat
One of the joys of travelling around Goa are the flat-bottomed passenger/vehicle ferries which cross the many rivers in this small state. The main ferries are from Siolim to Chopdem (for Arambol and places to the north), Querim to Terekhol, Old Goa to Diwar, and Cavelossim to Assolna.

North Goa

Goa neatly splits itself into two districts: North and South Goa. North Goa has the state capital, Panaji; the former capital of Old Goa, with its world-heritage churches and cathedrals; and a string of beaches that runs right up the coast to Maharashtra.

PANAJI (Panjim)
Pop: 93,000 Tel Area Code: 0832
Built on the south bank of the wide Mandovi River, Panaji officially became the capital of Goa in 1843, when Old Goa was finally abandoned.

Information
Tourist Offices The Panaji tourist office (☎ 225715) is in the government-run Patto Tourist Home between the bus stand and the Ourem River. Excellent maps of Goa and Panaji are available for Rs 12. There's also a useful tourist booth on the ground floor of the bus terminal, and a third counter at the airport.

There's a Government of India Tourist Office (☎ 223412) in the Communidade Building, Church Square. Also on this square is the Karnataka Tourist Office (☎ 224110).

Money The State Bank of India is open from 10 am to 2 pm (until noon on Saturday). Thomas Cook opens from 9.30 am to 6 pm Monday to Saturday, and on Sunday (October to March only) from 10 am to 5 pm. The Bank of Baroda, on the Azad Maidan, can give cash advances on Visa and MasterCard.

Post & Communications The poste restante at the GPO is open from 9 am to 5 pm, Monday to Saturday. International telephone calls can be made from any number of STD/ISD booths around town. Cyber Inn (☎ 222988) is a good place to receive and send email. The Inn is in Model Complex, opposite St Inez Church, to the south-west of the city centre.

Visa Extensions Visa extensions are not granted as a matter of course in Panaji. If you're unsuccessful here, Mumbai and Bangalore are the nearest alternatives. The Foreigners' Registration Office is inside Police Headquarters in the centre of Panaji and is open from 9.30 am to 1 pm, Monday to Friday.

Travel Agencies Reasonably efficient travel agencies include Aero Mundial (☎ 224831), at the Hotel Mandovi; Georgeson & Georgeson (☎ 223742), opposite the GPO (1st floor); and MGM International Travels (☎ 225150), Mamai Camotin Building, near the Secretariat (they also have branches at Calangute and Anjuna).

Bookshops & Libraries The Mandovi and Fidalgo hotels have good bookshops which stock international magazines.

Three local English-language newspapers are published in Panaji. The 'establishment' paper is the *Navhind Times*, and the 'independent' papers are the *Herald* and the *Gomantak Times*.

The Alliance Française de Goa (☎ 223274) has a library at 37 Lake View Colony, Miramar, not far from the Youth Hostel.

Things to See
The narrow streets and tiled buildings of the old district of **Fontainhas** are fun to explore. The **Chapel of St Sebastian**, in the centre of the area, dates from the 1880s and contains a striking crucifix which originally stood in the Palace of the Inquisition in Old Goa.

The **Church of the Immaculate Conception** stands above the square in the main part of town. The original construction was consecrated in 1541. Panaji was the first port of call for voyages from Lisbon, so Portuguese sailors would visit this church to give thanks for a safe crossing before continuing to Old Goa.

The **Secretariat** is the other building of interest in Panaji. Dating from the 16th century, it was originally the palace of a 15th century Muslim ruler. Nearby is a statue of Abbé Faria, a famous hypnotist, who was born in Candolim but later emigrated to France.

Organised Tours

Tours of Goa are offered by Goa Tourism (book at the tourist office) and by private agencies. The one day tours of North Goa and South Goa (Rs 75 each) take in a lot of places but are pretty rushed. Other options include a two day tour to Dudhsagar Falls and the Bondla Wildlife Sanctuary (Rs 400).

There are also daily hour-long river cruises (Rs 60) along the Mandovi River at 6 pm and 7.15 pm. On full-moon nights, there are two-hour cruises from 8.30 pm for Rs 100. Boats leave from the jetty next to the huge Mandovi Bridge. There's also an all-day trip upriver to Old Goa for Rs 500.

Places to Stay – Budget

Patto Tourist Home (☎ 227972), in a complex which includes the tourist office, is near the bus stand. Beds in the single dormitory cost Rs 50, but as the management won't let Indians and foreigners share the same room, you'll be lucky to get a dorm bed. Triple rooms cost Rs 320.

The *Youth Hostel (☎ 225433)* is at Miramar, 3km west of Panaji. It's a fair way from the centre of town, and the atmosphere is distinctly institutional, but it's cheap. Dorm beds cost Rs 20 (Rs 40 for non-members) and there's a solitary double room with bathroom for Rs 70.

Udipi Boarding & Lodging in the old part of town, has basic double rooms for Rs 100, while the nearby *Elite Boarding & Lodging* has doubles for Rs 150, and a triple for Rs 200, all with private bathroom.

There are also two double rooms (with common bath) at the *Hotel Venite* restaurant for Rs 150.

Park Lane Lodge (☎ 220238) is one of the best places in Fontainhas. Family-run, it's an old Portuguese house that has good clean rooms and a relaxed atmosphere. A double with attached bathroom costs Rs 300. There are also two slightly cheaper rooms with common bathroom. Also recommended is the *Afonso Guest House (☎ 222359)*, in the same street as the Chapel of St Sebastian. Spotlessly clean doubles with attached bath cost up to Rs 500 in high season, but rapidly come down to more like half this by the end of February.

Orav's Guest House (☎ 226128, 31 January Rd), lacks the character of these last two places, but is also good. It's clean and well run, but checkout is 9 am. Doubles with attached bathroom are Rs 250.

Republica Hotel (☎ 224630), on José Falcão Rd, at the back of the Secretariat, is an old place with fine views of the Mandovi River. Double rooms with attached bath cost Rs 250.

Mandovi Pearl Guest House (☎ 223928), nearby, is popular but as it has only four rooms it's often full. Large triples with attached bathroom go for Rs 350 (Rs 250 outside high season).

Places to Stay – Mid Range

The unremarkable *Tourist Hotel (☎ 227103)* charges Rs 320/550 for doubles/triples, and Rs 550 for an air-con room. There's a terrace restaurant, bar, bookshop and a handicraft shop on the ground floor.

Hotel Aroma (☎ 43519, Cunha-Rivara Rd) is a modern place which fronts onto the Municipal Gardens. Clean, airy double rooms with attached bath are good value at Rs 350. The tandoori restaurant on the 1st floor is one of the best in Panaji.

Hotel Bareton (☎ 226405) is a clean and friendly place with spotless rooms for Rs 300/450. The only drawback is the checkout time: 8.30 am.

Mayfair Hotel (☎ 223317, Dr Dada Vaidya Rd) is very pleasant. A double with attached

GOA

bathroom is Rs 460. In the shoulder season, these rooms are good value at Rs 300; they also let them as singles for Rs 230.

Hotel Arcadia (☎ 220140, MG Rd) is in the same league as the Mayfair. Clean, pleasant rooms are Rs 200/300 (more for a room with balcony or air-con).

Hotel Summit (☎ 226736, Menezes Braganza Rd), has rooms for Rs 775/1100 during high season, but these come down soon after New Year to Rs 550/750. Also worth considering is the similarly priced *Hotel Sunrise* (☎ 220221, 18th June Rd),

although it's often booked out by Indian business-wallahs.

Keni's Hotel (☎ 224581, 18th June Rd) is also fairly good value. Singles/doubles cost Rs 400/550; air-con doubles cost Rs 650 with bathroom, hot water and colour TV. The hotel includes a bar, restaurant and shopping arcade.

Panjim Inn (☎ 226523) is by far the nicest, albeit the most expensive, place to stay in this price range. It's a beautiful 300-year-old mansion with a large 1st floor verandah. Singles/doubles cost Rs 585/675

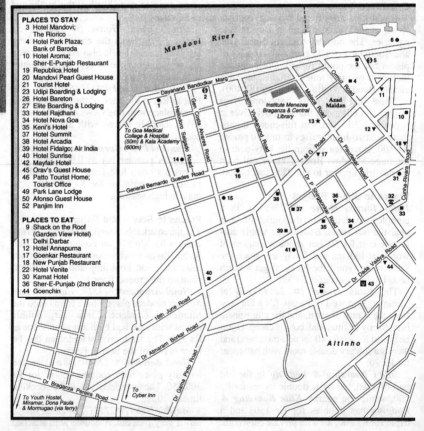

PLACES TO STAY
3 Hotel Mandovi;
   The Riorico
4 Hotel Park Plaza;
   Bank of Baroda
10 Hotel Aroma;
    Sher-E-Punjab Restaurant
19 Republica Hotel
20 Mandovi Pearl Guest House
21 Tourist Hotel
23 Udipi Boarding & Lodging
26 Hotel Bareton
27 Elite Boarding & Lodging
33 Hotel Rajdhani
34 Hotel Nova Goa
35 Keni's Hotel
37 Hotel Summit
38 Hotel Arcadia
39 Hotel Fidalgo; Air India
40 Hotel Sunrise
42 Mayfair Hotel
45 Orav's Guest House
46 Patto Tourist Home;
    Tourist Office
49 Park Lane Lodge
50 Afonso Guest House
52 Panjim Inn

PLACES TO EAT
9 Shack on the Roof
   (Garden View Hotel)
11 Delhi Darbar
12 Hotel Annapurna
17 Goenkar Restaurant
18 New Punjab Restaurant
22 Hotel Venite
30 Kamat Hotel
36 Sher-E-Punjab (2nd Branch)
44 Goenchin

Mandovi River

Dayanand Bandodkar Marg

Ormuz Road

Malaca Road

Azad Maidan

Institute Menezes Braganza & Central Library

Heliodoro Salgado Road

Gen Costa Alvares Road

To Goa Medical College & Hospital (50m) & Kala Academy (600m)

M.G. Road

Dr Pissurlekar Road

General Bernardo Guedes Road

Dr P Shirgaonkar Road

Cunha-Rivara Road

Dr Dada Vaidya Road

18th June Road

Dr Atmaram Borkar Road

Altinho

Dr Braganza Pereira Road

Dr Gama Pinto Road

To Cyber Inn

To Youth Hostel, Miramar, Dona Paula & Mormugao (via ferry)

with bathroom, plus 15% tax and an additional 12% between 21 December and 10 January.

Hotel Rajdhani (☎ 225362) is a good clean place, right in the centre on Dr Atmaram Borkar Rd. It charges Rs 695 for a double, Rs 795 with air-con. Checkout time is 10 am.

Hotel Park Plaza (☎ 222601) is centrally located on Azad Maidan. The cheapest rooms in high season are Rs 795/1000, but it's a reasonable place if you have this kind of money to spare.

Places to Stay – Top End
Hotel Mandovi (☎ 224405, Dayamond Bandokar) is the best of the top-end places. Rooms in this colonial-era hotel start at Rs 1375/1800. There's a good restaurant on the 1st floor and a pleasant bar on the balcony.

Hotel Nova Goa (☎ 226231, Dr Atmaram Borkar Rd) is the best of the modern hotels. Rooms normally cost Rs 1100/1600, but over Christmas/New Year you won't get in for less than Rs 2400. There's a shaded pool.

Hotel Fidalgo (☎ 226291, 18th June Rd)

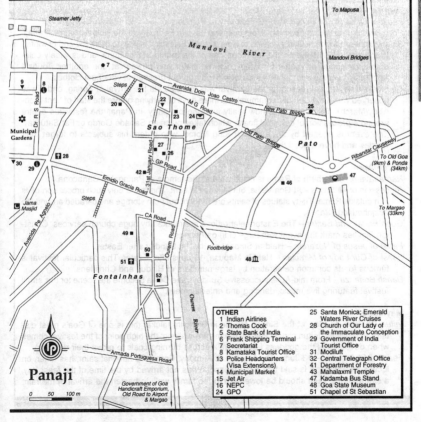

OTHER
1 Indian Airlines
2 Thomas Cook
5 State Bank of India
6 Frank Shipping Terminal
7 Secretariat
8 Karnataka Tourist Office
13 Police Headquarters (Visa Extensions)
14 Municipal Market
15 Jet Air
16 NEPC
24 GPO
25 Santa Monica; Emerald Waters River Cruises
28 Church of Our Lady of the Immaculate Conception
29 Government of India Tourist Office
31 Modiluft
32 Central Telegraph Office
41 Department of Forestry
43 Mahalaxmi Temple
47 Kadamba Bus Stand
48 Goa State Museum
51 Chapel of St Sebastian

Panaji

Government of Goa Handicraft Emporium, Old Road to Airport & Margao

0   50   100 m

GOA

HOLIDAYS & FESTIVALS

Goa has a huge number of holidays and festivals. Whereas most Christian festivals occur on set dates, Hindu religious festivals follow the lunar calendar and thus change from year to year.

In the following lists, national, state, and some of the more notable local holidays are given:

January

Feast of the Three Kings – 6 January. Reis Magos, Cansaulim and Chandor villagers celebrate this festival with re-enactments by local boys of the three kings arriving with gifts for Christ.

The Shri Bodgeshwar Zatra, or temple festival – takes place just south of Mapusa.

Festival of the goddess Shantadurga Prasann – at the small village of Fatorpa, south of Margao in Quepem province. There is a night-time procession of chariots bearing the goddess. As many as 100,000 people flock to the festival.

Republic Day – 26 January. The anniversary of India's establishment as a republic in 1950; Goa was not involved but it is celebrated here too.

February/March

Feast of Our Lady of Candelaria – 2 February at Pomburpa.

Pop, Beat & Jazz Music Festival – Held over two days in February at the Kala Academy, Panaji.

Shigmotsav or Shigmo – Goa's version of Holi, this Hindu festival is held to mark the end of winter. It normally takes place on the full moon day of the month of Phalguna, and is widely celebrated by gangs of youths throwing coloured water and powder at one another. Tourists frequently become a target – this is not a day to go out dressed in your best clothes.

Carnival – The original reason for the carnival was to celebrate the arrival of Spring, and it was observed within the Catholic community as three days of partying before the start of Lent (February/March). The Carnival is now really just one big party. In Panaji the festivities centre around a procession of colourful floats, which takes place on Sabado Gordo or Fat Saturday. The event is opened by the arrival of King Momo, who orders his subjects to forget their worries and have a good time.

March/April

Ramanavami – The birth of Rama is celebrated at the temple at Partagal in Canacona.

Procession of All Saints – At Goa Velha, 5th Monday in Lent. This is the only such procession of its sort outside Rome. Thirty statues of saints are brought out from storage and paraded around the neighbouring villages.

Good Friday and Easter – The Easter celebrations are marked by huge church services. Christian families mark the event with large clan gatherings.

Feast of Jesus of Nazareth – Held at Sindao, on the 1st Sunday after Easter.

Feast of Our Lady of Miracles – Held in Mapusa, 16 days after Easter. This particular festival is famous for its common celebration by large numbers of Hindus and Christians.

Beach Bonanza – From mid-April, successive Sundays see Colva become the scene for this small festival featuring live music, dancing and entertainment.

May/June

Igitun Chalne – In May, at the Sirigao temple in Bicholim taluka, this is one of Goa's most distinctive festivals. Igitun chalne literally means fire-walking; the high point of the festival comes when devotees of the goddess Lairaya walk across burning coals to prove their devotion.

Feast of St Anthony – 13 June. The feast of St Anthony, Portugal's national saint, has taken on local significance. It is said that if the monsoon has not arrived by the time of the feast day, a statue of the saint should be lowered into the family well, to hasten the arrival of the rain.

Feast of St John the Baptist (Sao Joao) – 24 June. Whereas St Anthony's feast day marks the onset of the rains, the Feast of St John is a thanksgiving for the arrival of the monsoon. Wells start to fill up again, and to mark the event young men jump into the water. Since each well owner by tradition has to supply feni to the swimmers, the feast day is marked by increasingly high spirits.

Feast of Saint Peter & Saint Paul – 29 June. Another celebration of the monsoon, this time by the fishing community, particularly in Bardez taluka. Fishermen tie their boats together to form rafts which serve as stages. After a church service and a large feast, tiatrs, folk dances and music are performed.

August

Independence Day – 15 August. A holiday to celebrate the anniversary of India's independence from the UK in 1947. The prime minister delivers an address from the ramparts of Delhi's Red Fort.

Feast of St Lawrence – This feast day is to celebrate the end of the monsoon.

Gokul Ashtami – Celebration of Krishna's birthday. In some temples the deity is symbolically placed in a cradle.

Bonderam – 4th Saturday of August on the island of Divar. Processions and mock battles commemorate disputes which took place over property on the island.

Navidades – 24 August. The offering of the first sheaves of rice to the head of state.

August/September

Ganesh Chaturthi – This Hindu festival is celebrated throughout the state, and commemorates the birth of Ganesh. Clay models of Ganesh are taken in procession around the areas of the temples, before being immersed in water. A period of fasting is observed.

September/October

Fama de Menino Jesus – A feast held at the Church of Our Lady of Mercy in Colva on the 2nd Monday of October. Celebrates the 'miraculous' favours granted by the 'Menino Jesus'.

October/November

Diwali (or Deepavali) – This Hindu festival, also known as the Festival of Lights, is second in importance only to Ganesh Chaturthi and marks the victory of Good over Evil.

Govardhana Puja – Hindu festival dedicated to Hinduism's holiest of animals, the cow.

November/December

Marathi Drama Festival – Takes place at Kala Academy from November to December.

Food & Cultural Festival – A five day festival held on Miramar beach in November or December to highlight Goan cuisine and entertainment.

Konkani Drama Festival – Held at Kala Academy, November to December.

Feast of Our Lady of the Rosary – Held on the 3rd Wednesday of November at Navelim.

Tiatr Festival – At Kala Academy, November.

State Art Exhibition – Held in December.

Feast of St Francis Xavier – The feast is celebrated in Old Goa on 3 December with processions and services.

Feast of Our Lady of Immaculate Conception – Held on or around 8 December in Panaji and Margao, and accompanied by a large fair.

Christmas Day – Christmas is celebrated as a holiday throughout Goa and India. Goa's Catholics flock to midnight mass services, traditionally called Missa de Galo or Cock crow because they used to go on well into the early hours of the morning. Christmas day itself is marked with large family gatherings and feasting.

GOA

also has a swimming pool, but is rather run down. Doubles start at Rs 1100.

Places to Eat
The *Hotel Venite (31 January Rd)* serves excellent Goan food and has long been popular with travellers. Goan sausages are Rs 75, as is another local dish, chicken cafrial. The Venite is open for breakfast, lunch and dinner daily, except Sunday.

Hotel Annapurna is a clean vegetarian restaurant around the back of the Hotel Aroma. Barefoot waiters serve excellent thalis for Rs 17, and dosas from Rs 10.

Kamat Hotel, on the south side of the Municipal Gardens, is part of an excellent chain of vegetarian restaurants.

New Punjab Restaurant, diagonally opposite the Kamat Hotel, offers good, cheap Punjabi food and more expensive tandoori specials. It's closed on Thursday.

Sher-E-Punjab, at the Hotel Aroma, has the best tandoori food in town. It serves excellent North Indian food for around Rs 75 (per main dish). There's a second branch on 18th June Rd, with an extensive menu and slightly lower prices.

Delhi Darbar, on MG Rd, is another recommended tandoori place, though it's a little more expensive than the Sher-E-Punjab. It's one of the most popular restaurants in town and often fully booked in the later part of the evening.

The *Goenchin (☎ 227614)*, just off Dr Dada Vaidya Rd, is an excellent Chinese restaurant but definitely a splurge. Main dishes are around Rs 75, and specials range from Rs 100 to Rs 150.

The Riorico, at the Hotel Mandovi, is supposedly the best restaurant for Goan cuisine, although some people find the food and service rather disappointing considering the high prices.

For cheap, authentic Goan food, the *Goenkar Restaurant*, with its bright, upstairs cafe and smart basement restaurant, is excellent. If you just want to chill out and enjoy a beer, the *Shack on the Roof* on top of the Garden View Hotel, at the north end of the Municipal Gardens, is a good spot.

Getting There & Away
Air Indian Airlines (☎ 223831) is at Dempo Building, D Bandodkar Marg, on the riverfront. Air India (☎ 231101) is next to the Hotel Fidalgo on 18th June Rd. Other airlines with offices in Panaji include Jet Airways (☎ 221472), and NEPC Ltd (☎ 220192).

Bus Goa, Maharashtra and Karnataka state road transport corporations (STRCs) all operate services out of Panaji's Kadamba bus stand. Typical fares and timings are: Mumbai (Rs 205, 17 hours), Bangalore (Rs 223, 14 hours), Belgaum (Rs 44, five hours), Hospet (Rs 102, 10 hours). If you miss the Hospet bus you can easily take a bus to Hubli (Rs 53, seven hours) and get onward transport from there. From Hubli to Hospet is another 4½ hours. The Karnataka State Road Transport Corporation (KSRTC) also has direct services to Bijapur, Badami and Shimoga.

Many private companies offer luxury, air-con and sleeper buses to Mumbai. There are also daily private buses to Bangalore, Pune and Mangalore. A couple of companies offer buses to Hampi, although these are only laid on when there's sufficient demand. There are several private operators' offices just outside the gates of the bus stand.

For journeys within Goa, there are frequent buses to Vasco da Gama, Margao, Old Goa, Calangute and Mapusa.

Getting Around
To/From the Airport There is one bus a day leaving at 11.45 am from the Indian Airlines office in Panaji to Dabolim airport (Rs 30). A taxi costs about Rs 300 for the 40 minute trip. A cheaper option is to catch a bus to Vasco, and take an auto-rickshaw from there.

Taxi & Auto-Rickshaw Taxis and auto-rickshaws are metered, but getting the drivers to use the meters is extremely difficult. Negotiate the fare before heading off. Typical taxi fares from Panaji include Rs 150 to Calangute and Rs 300 to Colva.

OLD GOA

Nine kilometres east of Panaji, half a dozen imposing churches and cathedrals (among the largest in Asia) are all that remain of a city that was once said to rival Lisbon in magnificence. Old Goa flourished under the conquistadors but, as trade waned, its fortunes changed. The decline was accelerated by the activities of the Inquisition and by a devastating epidemic which struck in 1635. In 1843 the city was finally abandoned and the capital was shifted to Panaji.

The Archaeological Survey of India publishes the excellent booklet *Old Goa*, by S Rajagopalan. It's available from the archaeological museum in Old Goa. Lonely Planet's *Goa* also gives a detailed historical perspective of the city.

The Main Buildings

The largest of the churches in Old Goa is the **Se Cathedral**, which was begun in 1562.

One of the bell towers collapsed in 1776, but the other still houses the Golden Bell, so called for its rich sound. To the west of the cathedral is the **Convent & Church of St Francis of Assisi**, which dates from 1661. The convent at the back of this church is now the **archaeological museum** (open Saturday to Thursday, 10 am to 5 pm; free entry).

The **Basilica of Bom Jesus** is famous throughout the Roman Catholic world as the resting place of the mortal remains of St Francis Xavier. The saint's body is kept in a silver casket, which rests in a side chapel of the basilica. The **Professed House**, next door to the basilica, was completed in 1585 and houses a small modern **art gallery**.

Other Buildings

The **Church of St Cajetan** is said to be modelled on St Peter's Basilica in Rome; construction began in 1655. The ruins of the **Church of St Augustine** provide the most

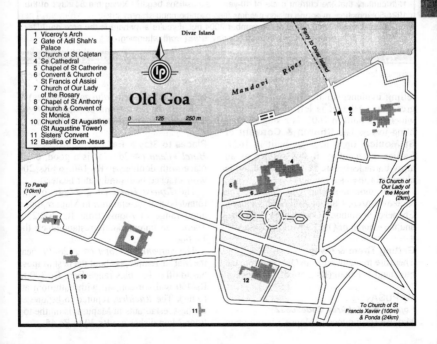

1 Viceroy's Arch
2 Gate of Adil Shah's Palace
3 Church of St Cajetan
4 Se Cathedral
5 Chapel of St Catherine
6 Convent & Church of St Francis of Assisi
7 Church of Our Lady of the Rosary
8 Chapel of St Anthony
9 Church & Convent of St Monica
10 Church of St Augustine (St Augustine Tower)
11 Sisters' Convent
12 Basilica of Bom Jesus

Divar Island

Old Goa

0   125   250 m

Mandovi River

Ferry to Divar Island

To Panaji (10km)

To Church of Our Lady of the Mount (2km)

Rua Direita

To Church of St Francis Xavier (100m) & Ponda (24km)

The Miraculous Body of St Francis Xavier

Goa's patron saint, Francis Xavier, had spent 10 years as a tireless missionary in South-East Asia when he died on 2 December 1552, but it was through his death that his greatest power in the region was released.

He died on the island of Sancian, off the coast of China. His servant is said to have emptied four sacks of quicklime into his coffin to consume his flesh in case the order came to return the remains to Goa. Two months later, the body was transferred to Malacca, where it was observed to be still in perfect condition, refusing to rot despite the quicklime. The following year, it was returned to Goa, where the people were declaring the preservation a miracle.

The Church was slower to acknowledge it, requiring a medical examination to establish that the body had not been embalmed. This was performed in 1556 by the viceroy's physician, who declared that all internal organs were still intact and that no preservative agents had been used. He noticed a small wound in the chest and asked two Jesuits to put their fingers into it. He noted, 'When they withdrew them, they were covered with blood which I smelt and found to be absolutely untainted.'

In comparison to 16th and 17th century church bureaucracy, modern Indian bureaucracy seems positively streamlined, for it was not until 1622 that canonisation took place. By then, holy relic hunters had started work on the 'incorrupt body'. In 1614, the right arm was removed and divided between Jesuits in Japan and Rome, and by 1636, parts of one shoulder blade and all the internal organs had been scattered through South-East Asia. By the end of the 17th century, the body was in an advanced state of desiccation, and the miracle appeared to be over. The Jesuits decided to enclose the corpse in a glass coffin out of view, and it was not until the mid-19th century that the current cycle of 10-yearly expositions began. During the 54 days of the 1994-5 exposition, over one million pilgrims filed past the ghoulish remains.

The next exposition is not until November 2004 but, if you're anywhere in the area on 3 December, the annual celebration of the saint's day is well worth attending.

telling evidence of the fate of this once great city. All that is left of this church, which was built in 1602, is a single crumbling tower. The **Church & Convent of St Monica**, opposite, was built in 1627. Earlier this century it saw service as an army barracks before being returned to the church for use as a nunnery.

Other monuments in Old Goa are the Viceroy's Arch, Gate of Adil Shah's Palace, Chapel of St Anthony, Chapel of St Catherine, and the Church of Our Lady of the Rosary.

Getting There & Away

There are frequent buses to Old Goa from the bus stand at Panaji (Rs 2.50, 25 minutes).

MAPUSA

Pop: 34,800 Tel Area Code: 0832

Mapusa (pronounced 'Mapsa') is the main centre of the northern *talukas* (provinces) of Goa, and the main town for supplies if you are staying at either Anjuna or Chapora.

Places to Stay & Eat

Hotel Vilena (☎ 263115) is a good, clean place with doubles at Rs 140, or Rs 200 with attached bath (and water heater).

The *Tourist Hotel (☎ 262794)*, on the roundabout at the entrance to Mapusa, has a good range of rooms from Rs 200/250. There's an unremarkable restaurant on the 1st floor.

The *Satyaheera Hotel (☎ 262849)*, near the Maruti Temple, is about the best Mapusa has to offer. Doubles range from Rs 300 to Rs 450 with air-con, all with bathroom attached. The *Ruchira*, reputed to be one of the best restaurants in Mapusa, is on the top floor. Main dishes are Rs 30 to Rs 45.

Mapusa

To Le Pavillon
Restaurant (1km)

To Anjuna (7km)
& Chapora (9km)

0   100   200 m

Municipal
Gardens

To Church
of Our Lady
of Miracles
(300m)

To Aguada (12km)
& Calangute (17km)

To Panaji
(13km)

6	Hotel Vilena;
	Tequila Restaurant
1	Police Station	7	Taxi & Motorcycle
2	GPO		Stand
3	Maruti Temple	8	Tourist Hotel
4	Satyaheera Hotel;	9	Kadamba Bus Stand
	Ruchira	10	State Bank of
5	Other India		India
	Bookstore	11	Market

GOA

Getting There & Away

On the Konkan Railway, Mapusa Road (6km north-east of town) is the nearest station, although it is not yet clear whether express trains will stop there in the future.

From the bus stand, there are public buses to Mumbai (Rs 205, 17 hours), Pune (Rs 138, 14 hours), Hubli (Rs 57, seven hours) and Belgaum (Rs 47, five hours). Private operators have kiosks by the taxi and motorcycle stand, and offer coaches to Mumbai, Bangalore, Hampi and Mangalore.

There are frequent bus departures for Panaji (Rs 4, 25 minutes), and buses at least hourly to Calangute and Anjuna (Rs 4). Other buses go to Margao, Chapora and Candolim. A motorcycle to Anjuna or Calangute costs Rs 40 and takes about 15 minutes. Rickshaws charge around Rs 60 and taxis about Rs 100 for the same trip.

FORT AGUADA & CANDOLIM
Tel Area Code: 0832

Built by the Portuguese in 1612, **Fort Aguada** overlooks the mouth of the Mandovi River and provides excellent views along the line of sandy beaches stretching

north towards Maharashtra. Sinquerim, the beach below the fort, and Candolim are popular with package tourists. Independent travellers can find accommodation here, although there's nowhere for those on a very tight budget.

Places to Stay

Moving south from Calangute, there's a clutch of places in an excellent position very close to the beach. *Dona Florina Beach Resort*, *D'Mello's* and *Shanu Holiday Home* all charge around Rs 400 to Rs 700 for a double room with attached bathroom.

Next is a group of guesthouses used by the cheaper end of the package market. The only one of note is the *Sea Side Rendezvous* (☎ 276323), which has a good restaurant and is also the base for Venture Sports, an outfit specialising in watersports.

Three places which are partially turned over to the package trade, but which are worth trying for pleasant rooms, are *Pretty Petal Guest House*, *Ave Maria* (☎ 277336) and *Tropicano Beach Resort* (☎ 277732).

Cheaper places in this area, with doubles from around Rs 250 to Rs 350, include *Monte Villa*, *Manuel Guest House* (☎ 277729) and the friendly *Lobo's Guest House*.

Moving south, but remaining in the Rs 500 to Rs 700 price range, there's the *Sea Shell Inn* (☎ 276131), the *Casa Sea Shell* (☎ 277879), the homely *Per Avel* (☎ 277074) and the spotlessly clean *Summer Ville Beach Resort* (☎ 277075).

Hotels (with pools) in the Rs 1000 to Rs 1500 range include the Portuguese-style villas of the *Aldea Santa Rita* (☎ 276868) and the *Aguada Holiday Resort* (☎ 276071). *Dona Alcina Resorts* (☎ 277453) is more expensive still at Rs 2000 during high season.

Marbella Guest House (fax 276308) is one of the nicest places in the whole area. It's a beautifully restored Portuguese villa hidden away down a quiet lane behind the Fort Aguada Beach Resort. The six airy rooms are superbly decorated, each in a different style. Rooms range from Rs 900 to Rs 1600 (Rs 650 to Rs 1300 in the middle season). It's highly recommended, but in the high season you'll need to book in advance.

The Taj Group (☎ 276201; fax 276044) operates a complex of three five-star deluxe hotels beside Sinquerim Beach, to the south of Candolim. The *Taj Holiday Village* charges US$210, *Fort Aguada Beach Resort* has rooms for US$225, and the luxurious villas of the *Aguada Hermitage* are priced from US$465 to US$575.

Places to Eat

Most hotels have restaurants attached, and

down on the beach there are dozens more places to try, all of which serve excellent seafood, snacks and cold drinks.

Coconut Inn is one of the more established places in the area and is a pleasant, open-air, upmarket place to eat.

The *Stone House* is a mellower place, with tables laid out in a raised garden, nonstop Marley and Dylan on the sound system, and suitably relaxed service.

The *Banyan Tree*, in the grounds of the Taj Holiday Village, is one of the best restaurants in the area. It's an open-sided

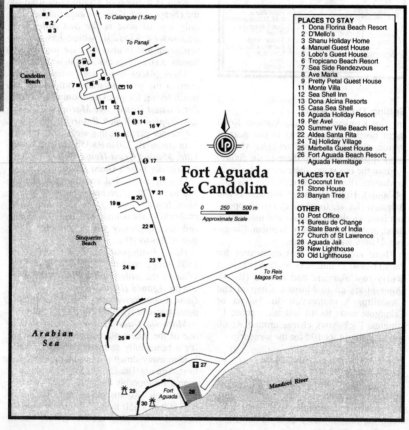

PLACES TO STAY
1 Dona Florina Beach Resort
2 D'Mello's
3 Shanu Holiday Home
4 Manuel Guest House
5 Lobo's Guest House
6 Tropicano Beach Resort
7 Sea Side Rendezvous
8 Ave Maria
9 Pretty Petal Guest House
11 Monte Villa
12 Sea Shell Inn
13 Dona Alcina Resorts
15 Casa Sea Shell
18 Aguada Holiday Resort
19 Per Avel
20 Summer Ville Beach Resort
22 Aldea Santa Rita
24 Taj Holiday Village
25 Marbella Guest House
26 Fort Aguada Beach Resort;
   Aguada Hermitage

PLACES TO EAT
16 Coconut Inn
21 Stone House
23 Banyan Tree

OTHER
10 Post Office
14 Bureau de Change
17 State Bank of India
27 Church of St Lawrence
28 Aguada Jail
29 New Lighthouse
30 Old Lighthouse

Fort Aguada
& Candolim

0   250   500 m
Approximate Scale

To Calangute (1.5km)
To Panaji
Candolim Beach
To Reis Magos Fort
Sinquerim Beach
Arabian Sea
Fort Aguada
Mandovi River

GOA

affair serving excellent Thai and Chinese cuisine. Main dishes are from Rs 150.

Getting There & Away

Buses run from Panaji to Sinquerim (14km) and continue north to Calangute. A pre-paid taxi from the airport is Rs 439.

CALANGUTE & BAGA
Tel Area Code: 0832

Calangute's days as a hippy haven have most definitely passed, and the area is now at the centre of Goa's rapidly expanding package tourist market. The beach isn't one of the best, and many people will find the place too crowded, but there is plenty going on and lots of good places to stay and to eat.

Information

Rama Bookshop offers a great range of books in many languages. You can buy, sell or exchange here.

Faxes can be sent and received at Telelink (fax 276124), near the petrol station. MGM Travels is nearby and there are several exchange offices that will change cash or travellers cheques. The Bank of Baroda, near the market, will advance cash on a MasterCard or Visa card.

Kerkar Art Complex

This complex in South Calangute has a gallery with paintings on sale by local artists, and concerts of Indian classical music and dance on Tuesday and Saturday at 6.45 pm. Tickets are Rs 250.

Places to Stay

Central Calangute In the centre of Calangute are a number of popular budget options.

Angela Guest House (☎ 277269) offers doubles for Rs 300 to Rs 400 over Christmas. It's a popular place to stay and the staff are friendly. If it's full, there are several other places nearby.

Conria Beach Resort and *Calangute Paradise* have rooms during high season at Rs 300 and Rs 250 respectively.

Hotel Souza Lobo has a great location right

on the beach and has four clean, basic rooms for Rs 300. Hot water is available between 3 and 6 pm when the restaurant is closed.

Hotel A Canôa (☎ 276082) has some nice rooms with sea views, and charges between Rs 150 to Rs 250; unfortunately it's often full.

Alfa Guest House (☎ 277358) is set back from the beach, with rooms from Rs 200 and Rs 250.

Victor Guest House (☎ 276966), also away from the beach, is very pleasant and has doubles with attached bath and hot water for Rs 300.

Coco Banana (☎ 279068), near Angela Guest House, is very popular. Rooms in this mid-range establishment surround a quiet courtyard and are very clean, and the owners are helpful. Prices jump to Rs 800 in mid-December, but are more reasonable once the rush is over.

The ugly *Calangute Tourist Resort* (☎ 276024) dominates the beach. Rooms cost between Rs 240 and Rs 300 for a double, and Rs 410 a triple, all with attached bath. There are dorm beds for Rs 50.

Falcon Resort (☎ 277033), near the tourist resort, offers clean, pleasant double rooms for Rs 400 to Rs 600.

Hotel O'Camarao is just north of the Tourist Resort and very close to the beach. Rooms are pleasant and good value at Rs 250. Nearby *La Bamba* is similarly priced.

Varma's Beach Resort (☎ 276077), in the same area, is peaceful, friendly and rather exclusive, with the rooms set around a leafy courtyard. At Christmas, doubles cost Rs 1400 (Rs 1600 with air-con).

Albenjoh (☎ 276422) is a very good choice, with rooms from Rs 200 to Rs 400, all with attached bathroom. The more expensive rooms have adjoining balconies and the place is spotlessly clean. It's at the start of the Calangute to Baga road.

Rodrigues Cottages, nearby, has a few rooms at Rs 100 with attached bathroom.

South Calangute There are a few cheap places left in this area, but they're in the minority.

GOA

NV Guest House, in an excellent location, is the best of the lot. It's run by a friendly family, and they charge Rs 250 for a double. The restaurant, only a few metres from the beach, serves fresh seafood.

Kismat Mahal (☎ 276067), near St Anthony's Chapel, is a friendly family-run place with doubles for Rs 300 (downstairs) and Rs 400 (upstairs).

Calangute to Baga Many of the hotels in this area have been tarted up to pull in the package tourists, so it should come as no surprise that prices are relatively high.

Johnny's Hotel (☎ 277458) is a modern brick building close to the beach. Rooms here go for Rs 500 during high season.

Stay Longer Guest House (☎ 277460) is the best of the smaller places to be found back on the main road heading north. It's run by a very friendly family; rooms are around Rs 400. The nearby *Saahil Hotel* has much the same prices. At Rs 600 the *Hotel Shelsta (☎ 276069)* is a bit more upmarket, with a pleasant garden.

Vila Goesa (☎ 277535), at the end of a lane opposite the Shelsta, is an upmarket hotel in an attractive garden setting, near to the beach. Rooms are from Rs 1375.

Estrela do Mar Beach Resort (☎ 276014), near the Vila Goesa, is slightly cheaper and rather less well looked after.

Graceland has a few small apartments for self-caterers, with attached kitchens, for around Rs 500.

Casa Esmeralda, next door to Graceland, is a good bet and also charges around Rs 500.

Joanita Guest House (☎ 277166), near Casa Esmeralda, has good rooms with attached bathroom for Rs 250 to Rs 400. The rooms face a pleasant, shady garden.

Hotel Linda Goa (☎ 276066) is one of a number of package tour hotels on the main road. Though it's looking a bit battered, it's probably the best value of the group, with rooms from Rs 500 to Rs 800. In the same area, with pools and rooms for around Rs 1050, there's the *Sunshine Beach Resort (☎ 276003)*, *Paraiso de Praia (☎ 276768)*, *Villa Bomfim (☎ 276105)*, *Ronil Beach Resort (☎ 276183)* and the *Beiramar (☎ 276246)*. This last place doubles its prices over Christmas.

Ancora Beach Resort (☎ 276096), down the next side lane (lined with persistent Kashmiri traders), is a reasonable bet with attached restaurant and bar. Rooms are around Rs 400.

Hotel Hacienda (☎ 277348) has some good rooms with bath and hot water for Rs 600; it's back on the main road.

Hotel Bonanza (☎ 276010), across the road, is more expensive at Rs 660, or Rs 860 with air-con.

Miranda Beach Resort, in the same area, has doubles for Rs 250 to Rs 300.

Baga If you're looking for a room or a house to rent, ask at any of the restaurants near the road in Baga. There are a number of houses available across the river, but they're often occupied by long-term visitors.

Villa Fatima Beach Resort (☎ 277418), set back from the road amid the coconut palm groves, is a popular place to stay, run by a lovely family. Double rooms with attached bathroom cost from Rs 200. There's a restaurant and TV area, and you can rent a safety deposit box for Rs 50.

Alidia Beach Cottages (☎ 276835) is slightly more upmarket. Over the Christmas fortnight the very pleasant rooms here go for around Rs 800.

Hotel Riverside (☎ 276062) has good rooms for Rs 800 to Rs 1000 in a quiet area.

Hotel Baia Do Sol (☎ 722470), charges around Rs 1000, but is closer to the beach.

Cavala Seaside Resort (☎ 276090) is cool and airy, and also has doubles with verandah and bathroom for around Rs 1000.

North of the river, away from the hubbub of Calangute and Baga, there are several pleasant and relatively inexpensive places to stay, although they're often booked up.

Nani's Bar & Rani's Restaurant (☎ 276313) has a few basic doubles with common bathroom for Rs 100, or Rs 350 with attached bathroom. *Divine Guest House* is similarly good value.

Jimi's Tepee Village (fax 276124) is by

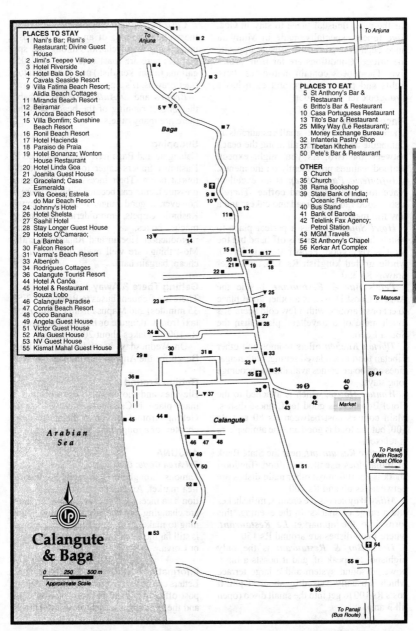

PLACES TO STAY
1 Nani's Bar; Rani's
   Restaurant; Divine Guest
   House
2 Jimi's Teepee Village
3 Hotel Riverside
4 Hotel Baia Do Sol
7 Cavala Seaside Resort
9 Villa Fatima Beach Resort;
   Alidia Beach Cottages
11 Miranda Beach Resort
12 Beiramar
14 Ancora Beach Resort
15 Villa Bomfim; Sunshine
   Beach Resort
16 Ronil Beach Resort
17 Hotel Hacienda
18 Paraiso de Praia
19 Hotel Bonanza; Wonton
   House Restaurant
20 Hotel Linda Goa
21 Joanita Guest House
22 Graceland; Casa
   Esmeralda
23 Vila Goesa; Estrela
   do Mar Beach Resort
24 Johnny's Hotel
26 Hotel Shelsta
27 Saahil Hotel
28 Stay Longer Guest House
29 Hotels O'Camarao;
   La Bamba
30 Falcon Resort
31 Varma's Beach Resort
33 Albenjoh
34 Rodrigues Cottages
36 Calangute Tourist Resort
44 Hotel A Cañoa
45 Hotel & Restaurant
   Souza Lobo
46 Calangute Paradise
47 Conria Beach Resort
48 Coco Banana
49 Angela Guest House
51 Victor Guest House
52 Alfa Guest House
53 NV Guest House
55 Kismat Mahal Guest House

PLACES TO EAT
5 St Anthony's Bar &
   Restaurant
6 Britto's Bar & Restaurant
10 Casa Portuguesa Restaurant
13 Tito's Bar & Restaurant
25 Milky Way (Le Restaurant);
   Money Exchange Bureau
32 Infanteria Pastry Shop
37 Tibetan Kitchen
50 Pete's Bar & Restaurant

OTHER
8 Church
35 Church
38 Rama Bookshop
39 State Bank of India;
   Oceanic Restaurant
40 Bus Stand
41 Bank of Baroda
42 Telelink Fax Agency;
   Petrol Station
43 MGM Travels
54 St Anthony's Chapel
56 Kerkar Art Complex

To Anjuna

To Anjuna

Baga

To Mapusa

To Panaji
(Main Road)
& Post Office

To Panaji
(Bus Route)

Arabian
Sea

Market

Calangute

**Calangute
& Baga**

0   250   500 m
Approximate Scale

GOA

far the most unusual place to stay in Goa. Five tepees, specially made in Mumbai, have been erected on the hillside opposite the bridge. Conditions are far from primitive. The tepees contain mattresses, fans, lights and power points, and each has a strongbox set in the floor.

Places to Eat

There are hundreds of small restaurants in Calangute and Baga and all along the beach between the two. As you might expect, seafood features prominently on the menus.

Infanteria Pastry Shop is an excellent place for a croissant and coffee. There's also a good range of bread and cakes, and a few full meals.

Hotel Souza Lobo is a perfect place to watch the sunset. Service is off-hand but the food is very good. Pepper steak is Rs 50, whole grilled kingfish Rs 125, and tiger prawns Rs 350.

Pete's Bar & Restaurant, beside the Angela Guest House, is another good place to eat or sit around with a few cold beers. It's much more of a travellers' place than the Souza Lobo.

Tibetan Kitchen offers momos and other Tibetan food in a relaxed setting, with magazines and board games available to encourage long stays.

Wonton House, which is attached to the Hotel Bonanza, is good for Chinese dishes. Main courses cost between Rs 80 and Rs 100, but the food is good and the atmosphere is relaxed.

Oceanic Restaurant, near the State Bank of India, does excellent seafood. Tandoori shark is Rs 100, most other main dishes are between Rs 60 and Rs 100.

Milky Way serves ice creams, milkshakes and a range of snacks. In the evenings this turns into the upmarket *Le Restaurant*, where main dishes are around Rs 150.

Tito's Bar & Restaurant is the only nightspot to speak of, and it boasts a high-powered sound system and a large terrace which is usually packed by about 11 pm. It costs Rs 100 to get into the small disco (open till 3 am).

Casa Portuguesa Restaurant, set within the walled grounds of an old villa, has a unique old-world charm. Among the specialities here are roast wild boar (Rs 105), galinha (a chicken dish) and the mandatory tiger prawns. It's a good place for a splurge.

Britto's and *St Anthony's* are probably the longest running of the beach bars, but there are many others.

Shopping

Calangute and Baga have been swamped by Kashmiri traders eager to cash in on the tourist boom. Their incessant hassling and pressure tactics can become tedious. There is, however, a good range of things to buy – Kashmiri carpets, embroideries, and papiermâché boxes, as well as genuine and reproduction Tibetan and Rajasthani crafts. Most things are well made, but nothing is cheap; bargain hard.

Getting There & Away

There are frequent buses to Panaji (Rs 2.50, 35 minutes) and Mapusa from Calangute. A taxi from Calangute or Baga to Panaji costs Rs 100 and takes about 20 minutes.

On Wednesday, boats leave from Baga Beach for the Anjuna flea market.

Getting Around

Bicycles and motorcycles can be hired at many places in Calangute and Baga. See the Getting Around section at the start of this chapter for a rough idea of types and prices.

ANJUNA
Tel Area Code: 0832

Famous throughout Goa for its Wednesday flea market, Anjuna has long had a reputation as a meeting point for travellers. Times are changing and package tourism is beginning to make its presence felt, but the place is still far more relaxed than Calangute, Baga or Colva.

Information

Letters can be sent to poste restante at Anjuna post office. Halfway between Nelson's Bar and the beach is a branch of MGM Travels, where you can make bookings and get flights confirmed.

The retail desires of the expatriate community are served by the Oxford Stores and the Orchard Stores, which stand opposite each other. You can change money here and at several other places around the village.

Take great care of your possessions in Anjuna, particularly on party nights, as theft is a big problem. The bank has safety deposit boxes which you can use. You should take care not to waste water because there's an acute shortage, especially late in the season.

Places to Stay

There are guesthouses around the village, and even a couple of hotels, but finding a place to stay during the high season can still be a problem.

Poonam Guest House (☎ 273247) is an attractive place built around a garden. The rooms here, all of which have attached bath-

rooms, are much in demand in high season, and priced accordingly: Rs 600 for a double with a sea view, Rs 500 for a room without the view, and Rs 800/1000 for the two new suites.

Mary's Holiday Home is slightly cheaper than the nearby Poonam; doubles with attached bath go for Rs 300 to Rs 400.

Sonic Guest House (☎ 273285) charges Rs 300 for double rooms with a common bath.

Palmasol Cliff Resort (☎ 273236) has double rooms with attached bath and hot water for Rs 500.

White Negro (☎ 273326) is located near Palmasol. Older rooms with common bathroom are Rs 250. Ten newly built doubles with bathroom and hot water go for Rs 500.

Red Cab Inn (☎ 274427) is a bit flash for any self-respecting backpacker, but great if you can afford your creature comforts. Doubles are Rs 450 (or Rs 350 with common bathroom).

Cabin Disco (☎ 273254), back on the

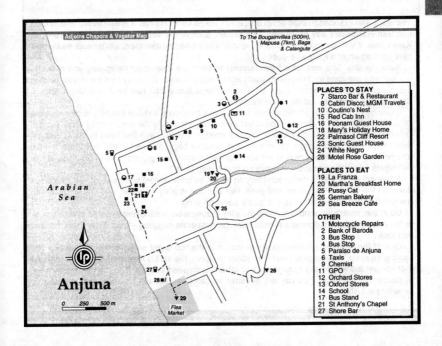

PLACES TO STAY
7 Starco Bar & Restaurant
8 Cabin Disco; MGM Travels
10 Coutino's Nest
15 Red Cab Inn
16 Poonam Guest House
18 Mary's Holiday Home
22 Palmasol Cliff Resort
23 Sonic Guest House
24 White Negro
28 Motel Rose Garden

PLACES TO EAT
19 La Franza
20 Martha's Breakfast Home
25 Pussy Cat
26 German Bakery
29 Sea Breeze Cafe

OTHER
1 Motorcycle Repairs
2 Bank of Baroda
3 Bus Stop
4 Bus Stop
5 Paraiso de Anjuna
6 Taxis
9 Chemist
11 GPO
12 Orchard Stores
13 Oxford Stores
14 School
17 Bus Stand
21 St Anthony's Chapel
27 Shore Bar

Adjoins Chapora & Vagator Map

To The Bougainvillea (500m),
Mapusa (7km), Baga
& Calangute

Arabian Sea

Anjuna

0   250   500 m

Flea Market

Mapusa road, charges Rs 150/200 for a single/double with common bathroom.

Starco Bar & Restaurant, nearby, is better value; the five double rooms, all with attached bathroom, go for Rs 250.

Coutino's Nest (☎ *274386*) is recommended. It's a clean place with rooms for Rs 150 with common bath (hot shower). It's run by a friendly family and there's a pleasant terrace.

Motel Rose Garden (☎ *273362*) has eight reasonable rooms at the back, all with attached bathrooms, which range from Rs 450 to Rs 750 in high season. You couldn't get much closer to the beach, although the proximity to the Shore Bar means that it's not for party poopers.

The Bougainvillea (☎ *273271; fax 262031*) is an upmarket place on the outskirts of Anjuna, with a swimming pool, garden and

---

Anjuna Flea Market

The Wednesday flea market at Anjuna is a major attraction for people from all the Goan beaches. It hosts a wonderful blend of Tibetan and Kashmiri traders, colourful Gujarati tribal women and blissed-out 1960s-style hippies. It's quite a scene. Whatever you need, from a used paperback to a new swimsuit, you'll find it here – though you have to bargain hard to get a reasonable deal. There's also lots of good Indian and western food. Traditional-style fishing boats are available for transport to the market from Baga Beach; you'll see notices advertising these in Baga's restaurants.

Anjuna is the Goa experience in concentrated form; a syrup of hippies, ravers, handicrafts, hard-sell and sunshine, undiluted by the harsh realities of rural India. One traveller described it like this:

There's a San Franciscan man down on the hot baked sand. He has a brown beard and talks in that San Franciscan way about how he was here back in 71. 'We were just saying, weren't we Karen, how it still has that feel about it... there was an earthquake then, while I was away, now here I am again and there she goes.'

Karen laughs. She was talking boisterously to someone else about delegating and networking, but now she joins in. 'His friends won't let him out anymore. They say he's the thread holding the plates together.' A whole circle of 40-somethings throw their hair back and laugh while a Brahmin bull noses around the circle's outside.

Close by on the sand, an Indian boy with Down's syndrome shadow boxes a dozen invisible Bruce Lees, lifting them above his head before pitching them onto the sand metres away. A small crowd of kids has gathered to watch. They're workers resting, swaddled head to toe in embroidered hats, waistcoats, lungis, tablecloths and shoulder bags, and rapt in the impromptu martial arts performance. The boy next to me sparkles with mirrors and giggles, and when I look at him he forgets to say, 'yes madam you looking now cheap price'.

A little girl struggles up the beach carrying an old suitcase almost twice size of her. She plops down on the sand in front of us and sings. Her suitcase is a squeezebox, and she works it with her small brown hand and sings out loud a beautiful song.

Up at the market the wind is blowing the silks around a bit, but the embroidered blankets suck in the heat and there's nowhere to hide from the desperate haggling - 'look sister, look madam, you *look*'.

One of the hippy stallholders starts to lose it in the too bright sunlight. 'He hit me with the fucking bamboo!' he screams. 'Argh!' he screams again. His stall is right next to the one that has T-shirts painted with freaky mushroom and other trip-inspired designs. The man selling these is at peace with the world. You can tell, because he can sit in that sun for hours, without moving, or selling a T-shirt.

bar. In high season, well-appointed rooms start at Rs 1500.

Places to Eat

Anjuna has the usual beachside cafes, but there's some refreshingly different food available, too.

The *German Bakery* serves herbal tea, espresso coffee and all manner of other goodies. It's the perfect place to while away a hot afternoon.

Motel Rose Garden is by the beach and has excellent seafood and cold beer.

Sea Breeze Cafe has reasonable food with main dishes in the Rs 30 to Rs 40 range.

La Franza is also popular and serves huge portions.

White Negro has a good bar and restaurant. Main dishes are around Rs 50 to Rs 60.

Martha's Breakfast Home is, as the name suggests, a good place to start the day, with coffee and pancakes.

The *Pussy Cat*, nearby, is another good place for lassi, ice cream, fruit juice and milk shakes.

Entertainment

For most people, the evening begins with several beers on the steps of the *Shore Bar*, watching the sunset. The *Primrose Cafe* in Vagator stays open late and is a popular place to move on to. *Paraiso de Anjuna* is the only other guaranteed alternative to an early night.

Getting There & Away

There are buses every hour or so to Anjuna and Chapora from Mapusa. A motorcycle taxi to Anjuna costs about Rs 50 and takes 15 minutes.

CHAPORA & VAGATOR
Tel Area Code: 0832

This is one of the most beautiful and interesting parts of Goa's coastline. Much of the inhabited area nestles under a canopy of dense coconut palms, and Chapora village is dominated by a rocky hill on top of which sits an old Portuguese fort. Along with neighbouring Anjuna, the area is a meeting point for travellers.

Places to Stay

Most people who come here stay for a long time. Initially, you'll have to take whatever is available and ask around, or stay at Calangute or Baga and 'commute' until you've found something.

Chapora The popular *Shertor Villa* has about 20 rooms and charges Rs 150 for a double with common bathroom (reductions for long stays).

Baba Restaurant has eight doubles for Rs 150.

Sea View Guest House has some extremely basic rooms (little more than a mattress on the floor) from Rs 70 to Rs 100.

Helinda Restaurant (☎ 274345) has probably the best rooms in Chapora. The place is clean and has a friendly, easy-going atmosphere, but is often booked solid; doubles with attached bathroom are Rs 250.

Vagator Run by a very friendly family, *Dolrina Guest House (☎ 273382)* has a good range of rooms. Doubles with common bathroom are Rs 230, or Rs 260 with bath attached.

The *Anita Lodge*, nearby, is cheaper, but basic.

Jolly Jolly Lester has good doubles with attached bathroom at Rs 350.

Reshma Guest House has rooms with common bath for Rs 150/200, or Rs 300 with attached bath.

Bethany Inn Guest House is newly built. Only three rooms have been completed so far; there are two spacious doubles (Rs 450) and a larger family room, all with attached bathroom, hot water and fridge.

Sterling Vagator Beach Resort (☎ 273-276), Vagator Beach, is the most upmarket place in this area. It's friendly and, as beach resorts go in Goa, quite good. Over high season, rooms cost Rs 1150/2350.

Hill Top Motel is set back a fair distance from Little Vagator Beach and has singles/doubles for Rs 90/160.

Nearer the beach, several of the houses around the *New Daynite* restaurant have *rooms* to let.

GOA

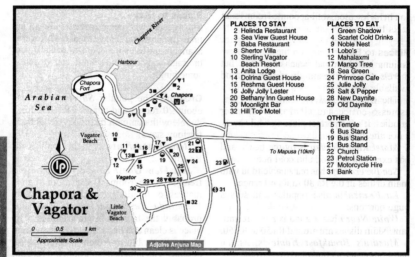

PLACES TO STAY
2 Helinda Restaurant
3 Sea View Guest House
7 Baba Restaurant
8 Shertor Villa
10 Sterling Vagator
    Beach Resort
13 Anita Lodge
14 Dolrina Guest House
15 Reshma Guest House
16 Jolly Jolly Lester
20 Bethany Inn Guest House
30 Moonlight Bar
32 Hill Top Motel

PLACES TO EAT
1 Green Shadow
4 Scarlet Cold Drinks
9 Noble Nest
11 Lobo's
12 Mahalaxmi
17 Mango Tree
18 Sea Green
24 Primrose Cafe
25 Julie Jolly
26 Salt & Pepper
28 New Daynite
29 Old Daynite

OTHER
5 Temple
6 Bus Stand
19 Bus Stand
21 Bus Stand
22 Church
23 Petrol Station
27 Motorcycle Hire
31 Bank

Chapora & Vagator

Arabian Sea

Chapora Fort

Harbour

Vagator Beach

Little Vagator Beach

To Mapusa (10km)

Adjoins Anjuna Map

0   0.5   1 km
Approximate Scale

The **Moonlight Bar** has five double rooms available for Rs 150 (common bath).

Places to Eat

There are numerous restaurants along the main street of Chapora village. *Scarlet Cold Drinks*, *Green Shadow* and *Helinda Restaurant* are all popular, as are *Baba Restaurant* and *Noble Nest*.

Lobo's and *Mahalaxmi* are among several busy restaurants just above Vagator Beach. Further back from the waterfront, *Sea Green* serves up tasty Chinese food on a shady patio area, and *Mango Tree* also has a fair selection.

To the south, *Julie Jolly* is a friendly place which often shows a video in the evenings. On the lane leading west towards the beach there are a selection of places to while away a lazy afternoon or evening, including *Salt & Pepper*, and the *Old Daynite* and *New Daynite*.

Primrose Cafe is the place to go at night. It stays open late and is invariably packed.

Getting There & Away

There are fairly frequent buses to Chapora from Mapusa throughout the day. A bus to Vagator is almost as convenient. It's often easier and quicker to take a motorbike taxi from Mapusa or to get a group together and hire a taxi.

ARAMBOL (Harmal)

One of the more remote beaches in Goa, Arambol still draws plenty of people but has managed to avoid much development. Accommodation is basic, but the seashore is beautiful and the village is quiet and friendly.

Buses from Mapusa stop at the modern part of Arambol, on the main road. From here, a side road leads 1km down to the village, and the beach is about 500m further on. There are a couple of small stores in the village, and two or three places that will change money. The main beach is a good place to swim, but to the north are several much more attractive bays – follow the path over the headland.

Places to Stay & Eat

Long-term residents rent rooms from the villagers. The most basic places are often no more than four walls and a roof. You can rent mattresses, cookers and all the rest from the shops at the village.

The most pleasant accommodation is in the little *chalets* on the next bay north. They're basic, but the sea views are superb. At the height of the season these places are much in demand, and rooms are Rs 250.

Villa Oceanic, in the village, is a private house with immaculate rooms, and a friendly atmosphere. All rooms are doubles with common bathroom, and cost Rs 150. The house is set just back from the south end of the beach, and is accessible from the road by a path that's difficult to follow – ask directions.

Laxmi Niwas, 500m back from the beach and above Ganesh Stores, has several double rooms at Rs 250 with attached bathroom.

Mrs Naik Home is pleasant, and as a consequence usually fully booked. It's on the road to the beach, and has doubles with attached bathroom for Rs 250 to Rs 300.

There are several bars lining the main beach, in which all the usual fare is available. Set back from the beach, the *Garden of Meals* is open every evening and usually has a set special, which is different each night.

Getting There & Away
There are buses from Mapusa to Arambol every couple of hours. On Wednesdays there are boats to the Anjuna flea market: Rs 75 one way, or Rs 150 return.

TEREKHOL FORT
On the north bank of the Terekhol River stands a small Portuguese fort, which has been converted into a hotel.

The *Hotel Tirakhol Fort Heritage* (☎ 0834-782240; fax 782326) is an interesting, if isolated, place to stay. There's little else here – even the beach is reached via the ferry – but the setting is spectacular, and the rooms in the old fort are unique. Doubles are Rs 850, deluxe suites cost Rs 1750.

South Goa

Although the beaches of the southern district of Goa include tourist centres like Colva and

Benaulim, and a sprinkling of upmarket resort complexes, there's generally less tourism development here than in the north. Margao is both the capital of the region and the transport hub.

VASCO DA GAMA
Tele Area Code: 0834
Close to Mormugao Harbour and 3km from Dabolim airport, Vasco da Gama is of little interest, unless you need to catch an early flight from Dabolim.

Places to Stay
Hotel Westend (☎ 511575) has clean doubles for Rs 200.

Tourist Hotel (☎ 513119) has doubles for Rs 250, dropping to Rs 200 in the low season.

Hotel Maharajah (☎ 514075) is the best of the mid-range bunch. Doubles range from Rs 275 to Rs 800.

Hotel La Paz Gardens (☎ 512121; fax 513302) is the top hotel, with singles/doubles for Rs 900/1100.

Places to Eat
Nanking Chinese Restaurant, near Hotel La Paz Gardens, is a friendly place with good food. Szechuan chicken is Rs 40.

Goodyland is a fast-food joint near the Nanking, serving excellent pizzas (Rs 40), sausage rolls and ice cream.

Sweet N Sour, in the Hotel La Paz Gardens, is a more expensive Chinese place with an excellent reputation.

The *vegetarian restaurant* at the Hotel Annapurna is a good, cheap option, with thalis for Rs 18.

Getting There & Away
There are frequent buses to Margao and Panaji (Rs 7, one hour). Long-distance private buses can be booked at the kiosks outside the train station. A taxi to the airport costs Rs 50.

BOGMALO
Eight kilometres from Vasco, and only 4km from the airport, is Bogmalo, a small, sandy cove dominated by the five-star Park Plaza

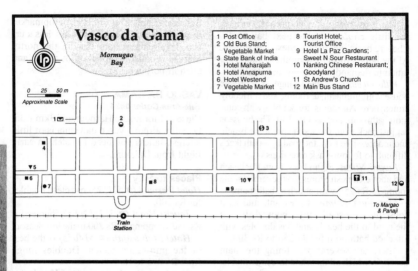

Vasco da Gama

Mormugao Bay

0   25   50 m
Approximate Scale

1. Post Office
2. Old Bus Stand; Vegetable Market
3. State Bank of India
4. Hotel Maharajah
5. Hotel Annapurna
6. Hotel Westend
7. Vegetable Market
8. Tourist Hotel; Tourist Office
9. Hotel La Paz Gardens; Sweet N Sour Restaurant
10. Nanking Chinese Restaurant; Goodyland
11. St Andrew's Church
12. Main Bus Stand

To Margao & Panaji

Train Station

Resort. There's little here apart from the mediocre beach, a few expensive cafes and the small village of Bogmalo.

Rooms at the *Park Plaza Resort* (☎ 513291; fax 512510) cost from US$170 plus taxes.

In the village, the *Petite Guest House* (☎ 555035) has doubles for around Rs 1100.

Cheaper, but generally booked up by package tour companies, is *Joets Guest House* (☎ 555036), which has doubles with attached bathroom from Rs 500. The guesthouse is also the base for a diving school.

MARGAO (Madgaon)
Pop: 79,800 Tel Area Code: 0834
Margao is the capital of Salcete taluka and the main centre of South Goa. It is a pleasant provincial town which still displays reminders of its Portuguese past. The **Church of the Holy Spirit** is worth a visit, as is the colourful **covered market**.

Margao is the service and transport centre for people staying at Colva and Benaulim.

Orientation & Information
The tourist office (☎ 722513) is in the Tourist Hostel, in the centre of town. The main

(Kadamba) bus stand is about 1.5km from the centre of town, on the road to Panaji.

The State Bank of India is opposite the Municipal Gardens. You can get advances on a Visa or MasterCard at the Bank of Baroda near the covered market.

Paramount Travels (☎ 731150) can arrange tickets for the Frank Shipping catamaran to Mumbai. Menezes (☎ 720401), behind the Secretariat, is an Indian Airlines agent.

The GPO is on the north side of the Municipal Gardens, but the poste restante has its own office (open only from 8.30 to 10.30 am and 3 to 4.30 pm), 300m south-west of the GPO. Fax and email services are available from the Business Inn (☎ 733232, email cyberinn@bom2.vsnl.net.in), Kalika Chambers (on the same street as the Banjara restaurant).

Places to Stay
Rukrish Hotel (☎ 721709) is probably the best of the cheapies. It has good, clean singles with small balconies for Rs 85, or doubles with bathroom for Rs 180. The rooms are rented on a 24 hour basis.

Tourist Hostel (☎ 721966), near the

market in the middle of town, is run by Goa Tourism. It's a reasonable place with singles/doubles for Rs 200/250.

Hotel La Flor (☎ 731402), Erasmo Carvalho St, is well run by friendly staff. The rooms, all with TV and attached bath, are clean and cost from Rs 180/250.

Woodlands Hotel (☎ 721121), Miguel Loyola Furtado Rd, is probably the best hotel in Margao. It has a bar, a restaurant and a wide range of rooms, from basic singles/doubles with TV and attached bath for Rs 170/200 to air-con suites at Rs 600.

Places to Eat

Tato, east of the Municipal Gardens, is the best vegetarian restaurant in Margao. A thali costs Rs 20, and the place is spotlessly clean.

Banjara is a subterranean restaurant near Tato that has excellent north Indian food in very civilised air-con surroundings. Main dishes are Rs 70 to Rs 80.

Longuinhos, opposite the tourist office, is recommended for its Goan cuisine. Goan sausages are Rs 30. They also do pastries, sweets and good tandoori dishes, and there's a busy bar; draught beer is Rs 15.

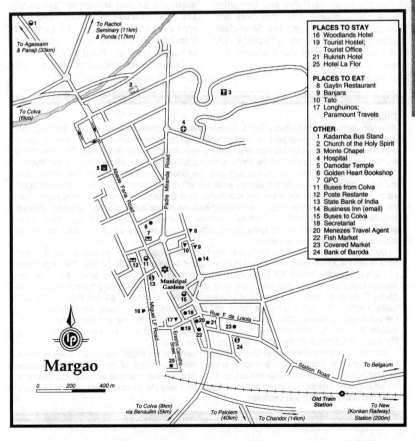

PLACES TO STAY
16 Woodlands Hotel
19 Tourist Hostel;
     Tourist Office
21 Rukrish Hotel
25 Hotel La Flor

PLACES TO EAT
8 Gaylin Restaurant
9 Banjara
10 Tato
17 Longuinhos;
     Paramount Travels

OTHER
1 Kadamba Bus Stand
2 Church of the Holy Spirit
3 Monte Chapel
4 Hospital
5 Damodar Temple
6 Golden Heart Bookshop
7 GPO
11 Buses from Colva
12 Poste Restante
13 State Bank of India
14 Business Inn (email)
15 Buses to Colva
18 Secretariat
20 Menezes Travel Agent
22 Fish Market
23 Covered Market
24 Bank of Baroda

To Rachol
Seminary (11km)
& Ponda (17km)

To Agassaim
& Panaji (33km)

To Colva
(6km)

Abade Faria Road

Padre Miranda Road

Municipal
Gardens

Miguel LF Road

Rue F de Loiola

Erasmo Carvalho
Street

Margao

0   200   400 m

To Colva (8km)
via Benaulim (5km)

To Palolem
(40km)

To Chandor (14km)

Station Road

To Belgaum

Old Train
Station

To New
(Konkan Railway)
Station (200m)

GOA

Woodlands Hotel has a good-value restaurant. Fish curry rice is Rs 21, fried
chicken is Rs 31 (plus 10% service charge).

Gaylin is an excellent and very popular
Chinese restaurant. Main dishes are around
Rs 70.

Getting There & Away

Bus From the Kadamba bus stand, there are
daily buses to Mumbai (Rs 287, 17 hours),
Bangalore (Rs 225, 14 hours), Hubli (Rs 52,
six hours) and Belgaum (Rs 42, five hours).
There are numerous buses to Karwar, all of
which stop at Chaudi, near Palolem.

Regular buses to Colva and Benaulim
(Rs 4, 20 minutes) run from both the
Kadamba bus stand and the Municipal
Gardens (east side). Buses to Panaji (Rs 10,
one hour) depart from the Kadamba bus
stand every 15 minutes.

Train The new station now handles all
trains for the Konkan Railway and also for
the South Central Railway (when it reopens). See the Getting There & Away
section at the start of this chapter for train
information.

To get to Colva, you can take a motorcycle for about Rs 35 (no objection to
backpacks), auto-rickshaw (around Rs 45)
or taxi (about Rs 65).

AROUND MARGAO

Six kilometres from Margao, **Rachol Seminary & Church** date from 1610, and are
interesting for their architecture and murals.
The attached **Museum of Christian Art** is
open daily except Monday. There are buses
from Margao, but make sure you get on one
to Rachol Seminary, not Illa de Rachol.

Twenty kilometres east of Margao, in the

Dhirio

Although football is indisputably Goa's number one sport, *dhirio*, or traditional bullfighting, has
until recently come a close second. Until recently, that is, because amid much protest the sport
was banned in 1996 under laws governing the prevention of cruelty to animals. The movement
advocating the reinstatement of the dhirio is strong, however, and political lobbying continues.

Unlike in Spanish and Portuguese bullfights, the Goan version of the sport does not involve
matadors. In dhirio two bulls are pitched against each other. The animals, which are primed for
each fight, charge their opponent and lock horns, thus starting an immense shoving match that
can go on for as long as an hour. The fight only ends when one bull is pushed from the makeshift
ring, or when one turns and runs from its opponent. The struggle rarely ends in injury beyond su-
perficial wounds caused by scraping horns, although occasionally an animal does get fatally
injured by the horns of its opponent.

Up until the time of the ban, dhirio was big business for a few families who owned the best
bulls. Fees for a champion to take part in a fight could be as high as Rs 50,000. The large sums
of money, however, reflect the investment which is made in the animals, which are raised on
special feed from calves, and which are used only as fighting bulls, being trained daily for the
dhirio. Quite apart from the expense of keeping and feeding such an animal, the risk of a bull
losing a fight is very real. Losing one fight is just about acceptable, but losing two effectively ends
the bull's fighting career. If this happens the bull, in which so much time and money has been invested, is suddenly worth almost nothing. The animals are often sold, or sent back to ploughing
the fields on a fraction of the rations that they once enjoyed.

No one seems to know whether dhirio will be reinstated in the future, but in the meantime there
are rumours that occasional impromptu contests still occur. Most of the activity was formerly
centred around Salcete taluka (province), so if you find yourself in a rural area and stumble on a
crowd around a makeshift ring, go and investigate. You may still be able to witness one of Goa's
most distinctive and popular pastimes.

village of Chandor, is the **Menezes Braganza House**, one of the grandest colonial-era mansions in Goa. The family has lived here since the 17th century, and the rooms are furnished with antiques and hung with chandeliers. Check with the tourist office to ensure that the house will be open when you visit.

COLVA & BENAULIM
Tel Area Code: 0834

Colva is the main tourism centre for south Goa. Despite this, the area is still less de-

veloped than Calangute and Baga, and it's not hard to escape the crowds. Just walk a kilometre or two in either direction from the busy part of the beach and you'll find plenty of space.

Information

Colva village has a tiny post office where letters can be sent to poste restante. There's a small Bank of Baroda next to the church in Colva, and there's another branch at the crossroads in Benaulim. The Silver Sands Hotel and Colva Beach Resort will change

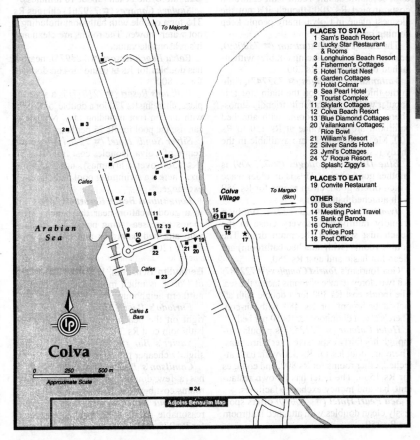

Colva

To Majorda

Arabian Sea

Colva Village

To Margao (6km)

Cafes

Cafes

Cafes & Bars

0   250   500 m
Approximate Scale

Adjoins Benaulim Map

PLACES TO STAY
1 Sam's Beach Resort
2 Lucky Star Restaurant & Rooms
3 Longhuinos Beach Resort
4 Fishermen's Cottages
5 Hotel Tourist Nest
6 Garden Cottages
7 Hotel Colmar
8 Sea Pearl Hotel
9 Tourist Complex
11 Skylark Cottages
12 Colva Beach Resort
13 Blue Diamond Cottages
20 Vailankanni Cottages; Rice Bowl
21 William's Resort
22 Silver Sands Hotel
23 Jymi's Cottages
24 'C' Roque Resort; Splash; Ziggy's

PLACES TO EAT
19 Convite Restaurant

OTHER
10 Bus Stand
14 Meeting Point Travel
15 Bank of Baroda
16 Church
17 Police Post
18 Post Office

GOA

travellers cheques. Meeting Point Travel (☎ 710413) has a shop in Colva and a booth in Benaulim.

Places to Stay

Colva *Hotel Tourist Nest (☎ 723944)*, in a rambling old Portuguese house, is good value. Doubles are Rs 100 with common bathroom, or Rs 150 with attached bathroom. The *Garden Cottages*, close by, is similarly priced.

Fishermen's Cottages (☎ 734323) is one of the closest places to the beach. During high season a double room with bathroom costs around Rs 200; though it's not the cleanest place in Colva, many people keep coming back.

The *Lucky Star Restaurant (☎ 730069)*, nearby, also has sea-facing doubles with attached bathroom for Rs 200.

Vailankanni Cottages (☎ 737747), right in the thick of things on the main street, is popular with travellers for its friendly atmosphere. Clean double rooms with attached bathroom are good value at Rs 150 to Rs 200. Meals and snacks are available in the shady restaurant.

Blue Diamond Cottages (☎ 737909) is another good choice. This is an older place which offers good, clean rooms for Rs 250 with attached bathroom.

Jymi's Cottages (☎ 737752) is run by a friendly family and is very close to the beach just south of the main drag. The double rooms (with attached bathroom) are clean but basic and cost Rs 250.

Goa Tourism's *Tourist Complex (☎ 722287)* is a two storey terrace of rooms facing the sea. The rooms cost Rs 300 for a double with attached bathroom, or Rs 480 with air-con. There's also a dormitory for Rs 50 per bed.

Hotel Colmar (☎ 721253) is popular, although it's fairly expensive over Christmas. There are doubles for Rs 450 with bath attached, other rooms for Rs 800, and cottages for Rs 1500. The hotel has its own restaurant, bar and money exchange facilities.

Sea Pearl Hotel (☎ 730070) offers spotlessly clean doubles with attached bathroom for Rs 350.

Sam's Beach Resort (☎ 735304), about 500m further along the same road, is a new place with spacious double rooms laid out around a central garden. It's peaceful and, at Rs 200, the rooms are good value.

'C' Roque Resort (☎ 738199), midway between Colva and Benaulim, is a good choice if you want to stay right on the beach. The clean, simple double rooms, all with attached bathroom, are good value at Rs 300. The place doesn't have access from the road, so you'll have to get a lift to the seafront at either Colva or Benaulim, and walk along the beach (about 10 minutes).

Skylark Cottages (☎ 739261) charges Rs 315 for a double with bathroom including a hot water shower. The rooms are clean and it's reasonable value.

Colva Beach Resort (☎ 721975), nearby, has doubles for Rs 600 and air-con doubles for Rs 800.

William's Resort (☎ 721077) is a superior place, charging Rs 770 for a double, or Rs 990 with air-con (not including tax). Nonguests can use the pool for Rs 25 per hour.

Silver Sands Hotel (☎ 721645) is in the centre of Colva. Doubles cost from Rs 950 (Rs 1500 over Christmas), not including tax. There's a swimming pool and currency exchange.

Longhuinos Beach Resort (☎ 731645) is in a good location near the beach. Most rooms have sea-facing balconies; doubles with attached bathroom and hot water go for Rs 1200.

Benaulim Benaulim, less than 2km south of Colva, is much more peaceful than its northern neighbour.

Furtado's Beach House (☎ 720776) is right on the beach; rooms with attached bathroom cost Rs 300.

Xavier's Bar (☎ 730780), nearby, has slightly cheaper rooms at Rs 200.

Camilson's Beach Resort (☎ 722917) has a few doubles at Rs 250, but most rooms cost between Rs 600 and Rs 900.

L'Amour Beach Resort (☎ 733720) has reasonable rooms with attached bathroom for Rs 275 to Rs 550.

O Palmar Beach Cottages (☎ *722901)*, opposite, is similar and has doubles with attached bath for Rs 360. Neither of these places has much in the way of shade, but they're both very close to the beach and are often full in the high season.

Most of the other places are scattered around the village of Benaulim, about 1km back from the beach, where accommodation is cheaper.

Rosario's Inn (☎ *734167)* is very popular and has rooms with verandah and attached bathroom for Rs 170. There are also cheaper rooms with common bathroom.

Savio Rest House (☎ *735954)* charges just Rs 60 for a single room with common bathroom, or Rs 70 for a double.

Jacinta Moraes Tourist House (☎ *722706)*, nearby, has good doubles at Rs 100 with bath.

Kenkre Tourist Cottages is excellent value at Rs 80 for a double with attached bath.

Liteo Cottages offers reasonable doubles

with attached bath for Rs 250, as does the nearby *Tansy Cottages* (☎ *734594)*.

D'Souza Guest House (☎ *734364)*, a short distance north along the road to Colva, is a small, upmarket guesthouse in a Goan bungalow with an extensive garden. Spotlessly clean rooms cost up to Rs 375 in high season, but prices drop to half this at other times.

Palm Grove Cottages (☎ *722533)*, further south, is an excellent place to stay. Set in a peaceful garden, it has a range of rooms (all with attached bath) from Rs 175 to Rs 750.

O Mangueiro Guest House (☎ *734164)* has five doubles and a single that people often rent long term; the doubles go for Rs 100. There's a kitchen and common bath.

Oshin Cottages (☎ *722707)* is in a very peaceful area, set back from the road. There are 17 doubles, all with attached bath, for Rs 275.

Carina Beach Resort (☎ *734166)* is currently the top hotel in Benaulim. It's a

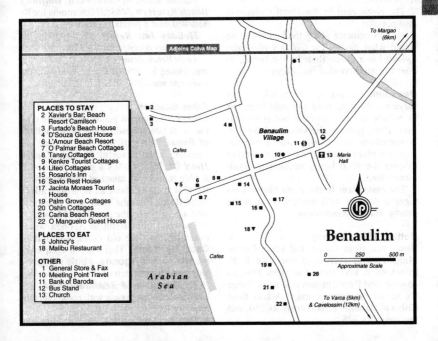

PLACES TO STAY
2 Xavier's Bar; Beach Resort Camilson
3 Furtado's Beach House
4 D'Souza Guest House
6 L'Amour Beach Resort
7 O Palmar Beach Cottages
8 Tansy Cottages
9 Kenkre Tourist Cottages
14 Liteo Cottages
15 Rosario's Inn
16 Savio Rest House
17 Jacinta Moraes Tourist House
19 Palm Grove Cottages
20 Oshin Cottages
21 Carina Beach Resort
22 O Mangueiro Guest House

PLACES TO EAT
5 Johncy's
18 Malibu Restaurant

OTHER
1 General Store & Fax
10 Meeting Point Travel
11 Bank of Baroda
12 Bus Stand
13 Church

To Margao (6km)

Adjoins Colva Map

Benaulim Village

Maria Hall

Cafes

Cafes

Arabian Sea

Benaulim

0   250   500 m
Approximate Scale

To Varca (5km) & Cavelossim (12km)

low-key affair with a garden and a pool. Rooms are Rs 990 to Rs 1200, but they have a few cheaper rooms without attached bathroom.

Places to Eat

Colva The most popular places to eat (and drink) are the string of open-air, wooden restaurants which line the seafront. Sadly these have been under threat for some time, and may be forced to close altogether in the near future, due to government plans to clear the beaches.

Back from the beach there are a number of popular places.

Convite restaurant in the A Concha Resort has excellent Chinese food, although the prices are rather higher than many of the other places; main dishes cost Rs 60 to Rs 80.

The *Rice Bowl* also serves good Chinese food, but for more reasonable prices.

The *Sea Pearl Hotel* is an excellent place for seafood.

The *restaurant* in the Hotel Colmar is also popular.

A short distance along the beach can be found what passes for Colva's nightlife. *Splash* has a dance floor by the beach, as does the neighbouring bar, *Ziggy's*.

Benaulim Almost all the beach shacks serve excellent seafood and cold beer, but as in Colva their future existence is in question. The largest of the shacks, *Johncy's*, is something of an institution, a popular meeting place, and seems set to survive despite the food being nothing to write home about.

The *restaurant* in the Palm Grove Cottages is popular with foreigners, as is the nearby *Malibu Restaurant*.

Getting There & Away

Buses run from Colva and Benaulim to Margao about every half hour (Rs 4, 20 minutes). A taxi from Colva to Margao costs around Rs 65; motorcycle taxis charge Rs 35 for the same journey. A taxi from Colva to Dabolim airport costs Rs 250, and to Panaji, Rs 325.

Getting Around

If you're not staying at any of the northern beaches, it's worth making the day trip to the Wednesday flea market at Anjuna. Trips are advertised at the beach bars and cost about Rs 95. The D'Souza Guest House in Benaulim also sells tickets.

VARCA & CAVELOSSIM
Tel Area Code: 0834

The 10km strip of pristine beach south of Benaulim has become Goa's upmarket resort beach, with at least half a dozen hotels of varying degrees of luxury.

Places to Stay

In Varca, the *Resorte de Goa* (☎ 745066; fax 745310) has rooms and villas set around a swimming pool for Rs 1850 and upwards.

The nearby *Goa Renaissance Resort* (☎ 745208; fax 745225) is a true five-star establishment. Rooms cost from US$207.

Further south, in Cavelossim, *Gaffino's Beach Resort* (☎ 746385) has rooms for Rs 350/400, and a popular restaurant.

Holiday Inn Resort (☎ 746303; fax 746333) has doubles for Rs 4500.

Leela Beach Resort (☎ 746363; fax 746352) was closed in 1997/8 for 'upgrading'; the room rate was US$330 before the upgrade.

Other Beaches

Opposite the narrow peninsula occupied by the Leela Beach Resort is the fishing village of **Betul**. North of the village, near the harbour, is the peaceful *Oceanic Tourist Hotel* (☎ 768101). It's a small place with double rooms with attached bathroom from Rs 175. It takes about an hour to walk to Betul Beach from the hotel, so it's better to take a boat across the estuary to Mobor.

The road from Betul to Agonda winds over hills, past the old Portuguese fort of **Cabo de Rama**. There are a couple of places to stay in **Agonda**, a little village by an empty 2km stretch of sand.

The *Dunhill Bar & Restaurant* (☎ 647328) has simple double rooms with common bathroom for Rs 150.

Two hundred metres further down the

track, **Carferns** (☎ 647235) charges Rs 200 for simple double rooms.

In the far south of Goa is **Palolem**, a beautiful palm-fringed cove of white sand. There's accommodation at the **Palolem Beach Resort** (☎ 643054), a low-key affair with basic doubles at Rs 250 to Rs 300, and tents (better, since they catch the breeze) for Rs 175.

About 50m down the road from the beach is **Tonricks Royal Cottages** (☎ 643239), where doubles with attached bathroom go for Rs 350. Similarly priced is **Cocohuts**, which has some thatched beach huts built on stilts among the palm trees. There are also plenty of rooms available in villagers' houses.

There are only two buses a day from Margao to Palolem, but frequent services from Margao to Chaudi (Rs 10); get off at the Palolem junction, 1.5km before Chaudi. It's then a 2km ride in an auto-rickshaw (Rs 25) or by motorbike (Rs 15).

PONDA

The central, inland town of Ponda boasts an old mosque and, in the surrounding area,

numerous unique Hindu temples. There are regular buses from Panaji and Margao, but to get to the temples it's best to have your own transport.

Among the most important temples in the area are those of **Shri Manguesh**, **Shri Mahalsa**, **Shri Ramnath**, **Shri Naguesh** and **Shri Shantadurga**.

BONDLA WILDLIFE SANCTUARY

Up in the lush foothills of the Western Ghats, Bondla is the smallest of the Goan wildlife sanctuaries (8 sq km), but the easiest one to reach. Unless you're prepared to spend a few days here, and put in the time on an observation platform, you're unlikely to see much. There is accommodation in chalets, which can be booked through the Department of Forestry in Panaji.

To get to Bondla, take any bus heading east out of Goa along the NH4A, and ask to be let down at Usgao Tisk. From there, catch a motorcycle taxi to the park (Rs 50).

DUDHSAGAR FALLS

On the eastern border with Karnataka are Goa's most impressive waterfalls. Once the

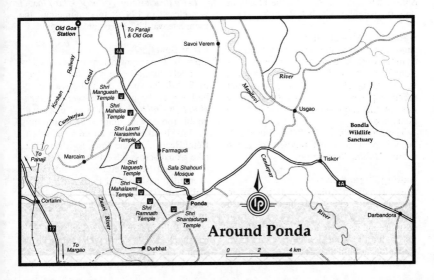

Around Ponda

SCR trains are running again, the best way to get here will be as a day trip by train from Margao. Until then the falls can only be reached by jeep (expensive) and only during the dry season.

MOLEM & COTIGAO WILDLIFE SANCTUARIES

These wildlife sanctuaries are larger than Bondla, but you will need your own transport to get to them. There's a treetop watchtower in Cotigao, but the animals manage to remain well hidden, so you won't see a lot.

Accommodation is available at Molem in the **Tourist Resort** (☎ 834-600238). There's no accommodation at Cotigao, although you can stay in the **Forest Resthouse**, nearby, if you get permission from the Department of Forestry in Panaji, half a block south of the Hotel Fidalgo.

Karnataka

The eighth-largest state in India (both in area and in population), Karnataka marks the dividing line between the Dravidian south and the Indo-Aryan north. It is an area above all of variety. On the Kanaran Coast, the waterlogged paddy fields allow for the local sport of buffalo racing, while on the parched northern plains, cotton and groundnuts (peanuts) are the main products. In between these two lie the dense forests of the Western Ghats, where crops of teak, sandalwood and coffee are grown.

Ruled by a succession of dynasties over its turbulent history, Karnataka has a range of architectural gems to entice the visitor. To the north one can find impressive relics of the Muslim past: the huge dome of the Golgumbaz in Bijapur, and the massive fortress at Bidar. Further to the south are the awesome ruins of the ancient city of Vijayanagar with their huge temples and monolithic sculptures. The state is also notable for its unique and well-preserved collection of early religious architecture. Superbly crafted Hoysala and Chalukya temples date from the 6th century onwards, while the 10th century Jain sculpture at Sravanabelagola is one of the most famous monuments in India.

But there is much more to Karnataka than monumental architecture. The state is home to a number of nature reserves where trekking, fishing and birdwatching are all possibilities. The cultural legacy of the state is such that it is still possible to watch the famous Yakshagana dance drama or see the *kambla* (buffalo races) that are so popular in the areas along the southern Karnatakan coast. Some of the most famous pilgrimage sites in India are to be found in Karnataka and you can soak up the atmosphere of these peaceful places in Sringeri, Kollur and Gokarna among other places. Lastly, with more than 300km of coastline, Karnataka offers beaches that are not as well known as those to the north in Goa, and are correspondingly quieter and more relaxed.

KARNATAKA AT A GLANCE

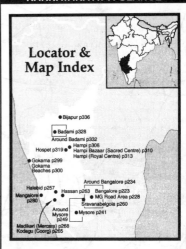

Locator & Map Index

Population: 51 million
Area: 191,791 sq km
Capital: Bangalore
Main Language: Kannada
Best Time to Go: October to February

Highlights
- Exploring the extensive ruins of Vijayanagar, then taking a corracle across the river to watch the sunset from the peaceful northern banks of the Tungabhadra
- Clambering around the ancient fort at Chitradurga
- Visiting the famous temple ruins at Badami, Pattadakal and Aihole
- Relaxing on the beaches of northern Karnataka

Festivals
March/April – Vairamudi, Melkote
October – Dussehra, Mysore
October – Tula Sankramana, Telecauvery
Dates Vary – Muharram, Hospet

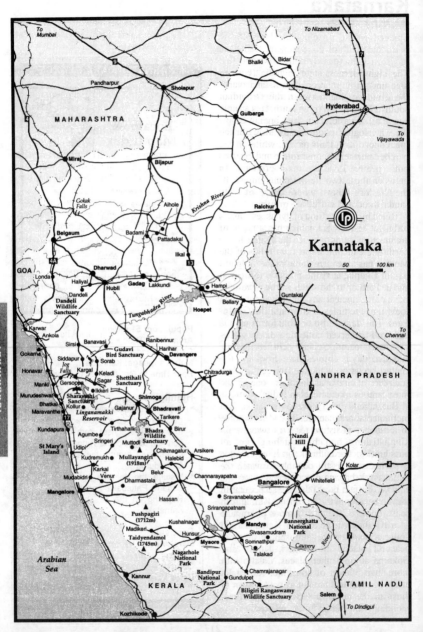

Karnataka

HISTORY

Situated on the dividing line between the north and south of the continent, Karnataka has seen numerous dynasties rise and fall. Some have been among the greatest empires that India has ever seen, while others have infringed on only part of the area from north or south. The genealogy of Karnataka's early ruling houses is complex, but a brief overview gives a valuable insight into the state's development and its cultural affiliations.

The earliest important rulers in the region were the Shatavahanas, who ruled large areas of north Karnataka from about 30 BC to 230 AD. From this point the area fell under the control of the powerful Pallavas of Kanchi (modern-day Kanchipuram), a long-lived southern kingdom which appears to have ruled much of Karnataka via a feudatory state known as the Chutus of Banavasi. The arrangement lasted for around a century until the Pallava overlordship was challenged on two fronts. In the south-east of the area (near Kolar) an important house known as the Gangas grew up. The Gangas held considerable power from around 350 onwards and, as feudatories to larger states, continued to control the area for several hundred years. In western Karnataka, Banavasi became the capital of the Kadamba kingdom which was founded in 345 and soon grew to control almost the whole of the area that is today Karnataka.

Kadamba rule came to an end around 540 when the dynasty was overthrown by the Chalukyas of Badami, (c.540-c.753). The first great monarch, Pulikesin I, built the fort at Badami and his grandson Pulikesin II (609-42) extended the empire over a vast area.

There was a brief hiccup in the dynastic aspirations when the Pallavas captured Badami in 642 but the Chalukyas soon regained the initiative and occupied the Pallava capital of Kanchi only a few years later. At its height this empire spanned all of modern-day Karnataka and Maharashtra, along with large parts of almost all the neighbouring states, and was truly one of the great Indian empires. The major legacy of the Badami Chalukyas is the enormous wealth of temple architecture which they left behind, particularly at Badami, Pattadakal and Aihole.

Chalukyan fortunes changed in 753 when Dantidurga, the chief of a feudatory state known as the Rashtrakutas (c.753-c.973), overthrew the last Chalukyan monarch and seized power. The ensuing empire lasted for around 200 years, and was said by an Arab traveller of the time to be the largest in India. Despite all this power, in 973 the Rashtrakutas disappeared from the stage, usurped by the Chalukyas of Kalyan (c.973-c.1189), who claimed descent from the earlier Chalukyas of Badami.

The Chalukyas of Kalyan established their capital at Kalyana (modern-day Basava Kalyana in Bidar district) and ruled for nearly two centuries. Like their counterparts of Badami, they left behind them a superb legacy of architectural monuments, the best of which can be seen at Ittagi, Gadag and Lakkundi. Towards the end of their reign, however, the region was slowly being divided between two main emerging kingdoms – the Yadavas from the north and the Hoysalas in the south. The Hoysalas (c.1180-c.1340) are by far the better remembered of the two kingdoms, due to the impressive monuments that they left behind

Taxes in Karnataka

Karnataka, like other states, levies luxury tax on food and accommodation. There are occasional variations but generally the rates are: 5% tax on prices from Rs 150 to Rs 200, 7.5% tax on prices from Rs 200 to Rs 400, and 15% tax on anything above Rs 400.

Bear in mind that hotels rarely quote prices with tax included – that will be extra when you come to pay the bill. Some of the more expensive hotels will also charge their own extras (which they won't declare either, unless you read the small print). Usually this is a 10% to 15% 'service charge', but in a couple of places it can be even more.

them – particularly the temples at Belur, Halebid and Somnathpur. Hoysala power was effectively ended by the arrival of the Muslim armies of the Sultan of Delhi at the end of the 13th century.

In the midst of the confusion that surrounded the brutal invasions from the north, the Vijayanagar Empire (c.1336-c.1565) came to power, and minor South Indian states flocked to join the alliance against the Muslims. A standoff persisted through the next two centuries, with the rough dividing line between the Muslim and Hindu forces being the line of the Tungabhadra River.

To the north, the Bahmani sultans (c.1347-c.1480) initially had their capital in Gulbarga, but later moved it to Bidar when the kingdom was extended to the east. The kingdom finally split up in the 1480s and five independent sultanates were formed – the most important of which was the kingdom of Bijapur (c.1480-c.1686).

Under Bahmani leadership the Muslim forces had been able to achieve great things and had effectively controlled the Deccan Plateau. As separate kingdoms, often at odds with each other, they failed to provide a cohesive force to overcome the Vijayanagar armies.

For half a century there was no real challenge to Vijayanagar power until, piqued by the arrogant behaviour of the Vijayanagar kings, the Muslim states finally joined in a coalition, and in 1565 inflicted a decisive rout at the Battle of Talikota.

In the wake of the Battle of Talikota, the Vijayanagar Empire still theoretically held power, but most of the smaller kingdoms that had been allied to it soon declared independence.

The two most important kingdoms to rise from the ashes were the Keladis of Ikkeri (c.1565-c.1763), who subsequently came to control most of the Karnatakan Coast, and the Wodeyars of Mysore (c.1565-c.1761), whose influence spread south. Further interference from the north was temporarily ceased by the arrival of the Mughals and

Karnataka Holidays & Festivals

In addition to the numerous Hindu, Muslim, Jain and other festivals that are celebrated throughout South India, there are many that are specific to Karnataka. For the most part these are localised and are festivals or *jatras* in honour of a local deity. Some of the most important ones are listed below.

Date	Place	Deity Honoured/Event	Duration (days)
January*	Udipi	Krishna	7
January	Banashankari	Banashankari Fair	7
January	Srirangapatnam	Ranganatha Swamy	1
January-February	Bijapur	Siddheshwara	8
February	Hampi	Virupaksha Swamy	4
March	Gulbarga	Sharana Basaveshvara	15
March	Gokarna	Mahabaleshwara (Shivaratri)	7
March-April	Melkote	Vairamudi	6
April	Gadag	Thontada Siddhalingeshwara	1
April	Bangalore	Dharmaya	1
October	Mysore	Dussehra	10
November	Bangalore	Basavanna	1
November	Dharmastala	Manjunatheshwara	3
November	Kollur	Mookambika	10
**	Sravanabelagola	Gomateshwara	13

* every second year
** once every 12 years – next to take place in 2005

then the Marathas who put pressure on the kingdom of Bijapur.

After two centuries of expansion by the Mysore rajas, however, the throne of the kingdom was usurped by a commander in the Mysore army, Hyder Ali, in 1761.

Hyder Ali soon brought the Keladis into his kingdom and enlarged Mysore's territory to cover a huge area. Hyder and his son Tipu Sultan pursued an anti-British policy which eventually met with disaster when the fortress at Srirangapatnam was stormed by British troops in 1799 and Tipu was killed.

In the aftermath of the death of Tipu the British restored the Wodeyars of Mysore to the throne, while also giving sections of the kingdom to the ruler of Hyderabad.

A disagreement followed in 1830 and the British took the region back under their own direct administration for the next 50 years, only returning it to the Mysore Rajas in 1880.

The Mysore Rajas pursued an enlightened course on education and social affairs, and were so popular that, after Independence, the former Maharaja was the first to be elected as the region's governor.

Unification Movement

As early as 1924 calls were being made for the unification of the Kannada-speaking districts into one large state.

Under British rule the area that today constitutes Karnataka was split up into a myriad pieces, each administered by a different authority: the coastline was under two separate administrations, some areas came under the Bombay Presidency, others under the Madras Presidency and so on.

The demands for statehood became louder after Independence and the calls became a political issue which in 1953 led to a series of peaceful protests.

Finally a commission was set up to examine the case and in November 1956 the districts that make up the modern state were brought together as one large region known as Mysore State. The name was changed to Karnataka in 1973.

Southern Karnataka

BANGALORE
Pop: 5.2 million Tel Area Code: 080

The fifth largest city in India, Bangalore rivals Chennai (Madras) as the most influential metropolis in the south. Unlike Chennai, however, Karnataka's capital city has a distinctively hi-tech feel to it. With its many computer industries, international corporations and huge Indian conglomerates, Bangalore is at the very heart of modern India. Future projects include a new international airport, a self-contained business park and the 560m Golden Tower which, if it ever gets built, will be the highest tower in the world.

As one might expect in a bastion of modern industrialism, peace, a slow pace of life and clean air are not the main ingredients of life in Bangalore. The city is as busy, crowded and hectic as any other place in India and, with a population that has almost doubled over the last 15 years, overcrowding and other environmental problems are pressing. Many people find that the permanent traffic jams, fumes and noise are too much, and move on quickly.

Nonetheless, after a few weeks roughing it around the South, Bangalore can be a surprisingly civilised place in which to arrive. Thanks to the long, wide avenues that are the legacy of its garrison town past, the city has retained a feeling of space that Mumbai and Chennai have not.

Two large parks still provide the opportunity to escape the streets, and the city's relatively high altitude (914m) gives it a pleasant climate.

Excellent shops and cinemas, good places to eat and drink, and convenient transport links all make Bangalore a city worthy of a day or two of your time. It's also a useful place to arrange trips to Karnataka's national parks and wildlife sanctuaries.

History
Like almost all of South India, the area where

Bangalore now stands was once part of a feudatory kingdom of the Vijayanagar Empire. The city itself was founded in 1537 by a local chief named Kempegowda who is credited with having built a mud fort and four watchtowers that marked out an area which he hoped the city would one day cover. The kingdom grew faster than he could have anticipated for, with the fall of the Vijayanagar Empire in 1565, the smaller kingdoms of the south were free to proclaim their independence. Within the next century the Gowdas came to control a wide area, but their good fortune didn't go unchallenged. In 1637 the sultans of Bijapur took Bangalore and it was subsequently passed on to the Marathas who held it until 1687, when it came into possession of the Rajas of Mysore.

When Hyder Ali usurped the throne of Mysore in 1761 he began a rapid expansion and fortification of the city, and it became a centre for the manufacture of armaments. Bangalore was captured by the British in 1791, but was returned to Tipu Sultan under the terms of a treaty. Eight years later, with Tipu's death at the storming of Srirangapatnam, the city was handed back to the Rajas of Mysore. A further change of hands occurred in 1830, when the British took over direct administration, and the city became an important garrison for the army. In 1881 Bangalore was returned to the Rajas of Mysore, but the military cantonment remained in British hands until Independence in 1949 when the two parts of the city were joined under the same administration.

Bangalore became the state capital in 1956. The foundations for its rapid growth were laid in the 1960s when the government set up key defence and telecommunications research centres here. The city's pool of expertise began to attract foreign investors in the 1980s and investment in Bangalore reached a peak in the early 1990s.

With the massive expansion of the city's business interests have come inevitable problems, almost all of which are due to the city's inadequate infrastructure. Clogged roads, water shortages, and regular power cuts are just some of the problems that need to be addressed if Bangalore is to maintain its position as India's most go-ahead city.

Orientation

Bangalore is a sprawling, disorienting city, composed of endless traffic-clogged arterial roads that appear to have no purpose other than to connect one large ugly roundabout with the next. Thankfully travellers usually only need to concentrate on fathoming two areas of the city: Gandhi Nagar in the west and the Mahatma Gandhi (MG) Rd area 4km to the east.

The Central bus stand and the City train

India's Silicon Valley

Bangalore's meteoric recent growth is founded on an aspect of modern India that is seen in few other places in the country – world-class technological excellence. During the last 20 years the city has become home to a number of businesses including, in particular, India's booming computer software industry. By the mid-1990s India was the world's largest software exporter after the USA. Multinationals have piled in to the country to take advantage of the large pool of expertly trained talent which is being turned out of South India's technical training colleges.

Sadly it's not only a case of a high calibre workforce – graduates are cheaper to employ, too. A programmer of several years experience and seniority in India is still paid less than his counterpart in the west. Signs are that this is changing, though, as more and more Indians set up their own companies and develop their own products. Recently a Bangalore entrepreneur was bought out by Microsoft, and every day Indian companies are proving that they are at the cutting edge of the industry.

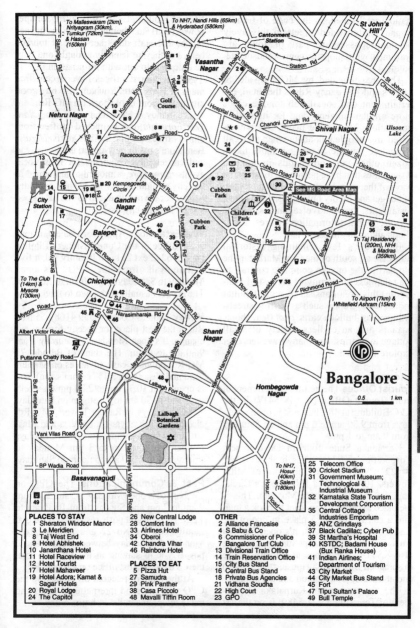

KARNATAKA

Bangalore

0   0.5   1 km

PLACES TO STAY
1 Sheraton Windsor Manor
2 Le Meridien
8 Taj West End
9 Hotel Abhishek
10 Janardhana Hotel
11 Hotel Raceview
12 Hotel Tourist
17 Hotel Mahaveer
19 Hotel Adora; Kamat & Sagar Hotels
20 Royal Lodge
24 The Capitol

26 New Central Lodge
28 Comfort Inn
33 Airlines Hotel
34 Oberoi
42 Chandra Vihar
46 Rainbow Hotel

PLACES TO EAT
5 Pizza Hut
27 Samudra
29 Pink Panther
38 Casa Piccolo
48 Mavalli Tiffin Room

OTHER
2 Alliance Francaise
4 S Babu & Co
6 Commissioner of Police
7 Bangalore Turf Club
13 Divisional Train Office
14 Train Reservation Office
15 City Bus Stand
16 Central Bus Stand
18 Private Bus Agencies
21 Vidhana Soudha
22 High Court
23 GPO

25 Telecom Office
30 Cricket Stadium
31 Government Museum; Technological & Industrial Museum
32 Karnataka State Tourism Development Corporation
35 Central Cottage Industries Emporium
36 ANZ Grindlays
37 Black Cadillac; Cyber Pub
39 St Martha's Hospital
40 KSTDC; Badami House (Bux Ranka House)
41 Indian Airlines; Department of Tourism
43 City Market
44 City Market Bus Stand
45 Fort
47 Tipu Sultan's Palace
49 Bull Temple

station are located on the edge of Gandhi Nagar. The crowded streets in this lively but unprepossessing part of town are crammed with shops, cinemas and budget hotels.

The area bounded by MG, Brigade, St Mark's and Residency Rds is the retail, entertainment and social hub for the city's more affluent citizenry and for its student population. This is the bland, internationalised area people talk about when they call Bangalore 'yuppie heaven': it looks like a dozen other neighbourhoods in modern Asian cities that have been keen to adopt the ways of the west. Here you'll find a mixture of budget and luxury hotels, fast-food joints, restaurants, bars, travel agencies, airline offices, tourist information centres, bookshops and craft shops.

Bangalore's few remaining historical relics are all south of the City Market in the old part of the city. In complete contrast to the relentless modernity of the rest of Bangalore, this area consists of more-familiar Indian iconography such as narrow streets, old temples, bullock carts, *chai* (tea) shops, bazaars and an endless variety of small cottage industries. Not many travellers ever explore this area.

Information

Tourist Offices The helpful Government of India Tourist Office (☎ 558 5417) in the KFC Building at 48 Church St is open weekdays from 9.30 am to 6 pm and on Saturday from 9 am to 1 pm.

Karnataka State Tourism Development Corporation (KSTDC) has its head office (☎ 221 2901) on the 2nd floor of Mitra Towers, 10/4 Kasturba Rd, Queen's Circle, opposite the Government Museum. This is the place to come if you want to book a tour, hire a car, or reserve a place in one of the KSTDC's Mayura hotels; it's open from 10 am to 5.30 pm daily except Sunday. There are also KSTDC operations at Badami House (also called Bux Ranka House; ☎ 227 5869) and at the City train station and the airport.

The Government of Karnataka Department of Tourism (☎ 221 5489) is on the 1st floor of F block, Cauvery Bhavan, Kempegowda (KG) Rd – behind the Indian Airlines office. The staff don't see a lot of tourists here, but they're friendly enough, and may be able to help out with information.

All the tourist offices have decent free maps of Bangalore. You can also buy good city maps from bookshops on MG Rd.

The handy what's-on guide, *Bangalore This Fortnight*, can be picked up free from tourist offices and hotels. The *Deccan Herald*, Bangalore's major newspaper, is a lively read and carries advertisements for most local events. *Bangalore*, a monthly mag aimed at the city's middle-class readership, provides listings for the month ahead as well as a good insight into the city itself.

Visa Extensions Apply for visa extensions at the office of the Commissioner of Police (☎ 225 6242 ext 251) on Infantry Rd, a five minute walk from the GPO. It's open Monday to Saturday from 10 am to 5.30 pm. The process usually takes two to three days.

Money Thomas Cook (☎ 559 4168), 55 MG Rd, is the best place for speedy foreign exchange. It's open Monday to Saturday from 9.30 am to 6 pm. The Bank of Baroda, 72 MG Rd, provides cash advances on MasterCard and Visa (with a 1% commission), and is open from 10.30 am to 2.30 pm on weekdays and 10.30 am to 12.30 pm on Saturday. ANZ Grindlays in Raheja Towers, MG Rd, also gives cash advances on Visa and MasterCard, with no commission. ANZ Grindlays is open from 10 am to 3 pm Monday to Friday and from 10 am to noon on Saturday.

Post & Communications The GPO on Cubbon Rd is open Monday to Saturday from 9 am to 7 pm and Sunday from 10.30 am to 1 pm. The efficient poste restante service is at inquiry counter No 22 and is open from Monday to Saturday between 10 am and 6 pm. If you're staying in the MG Rd area, there's a handy post office on Brigade Rd.

At the modern telecom office next to the GPO you can send international faxes and make telephone calls 24 hours a day.

The swanky Coffee Day Cyber Cafe at 13-15 Brigade Rd offers email and Internet access for Rs 60 for half an hour, and also has the best coffee in Bangalore. The helpful staff can set up a local email address for you. There have been mixed reports about Cyber Net (☎ 558 5678 ext 1003) on Church St. At Rs 100 per hour, the rates are cheaper than at the Cyber Cafe, and you're unlikely to have to queue as is often the case down the road. One woman traveller, however, reported having received a lot of hassle from the manager.

Travel Agencies Jungle Lodges & Resorts (☎ 559 7025, fax 558 6163) runs a number of upmarket resorts around Karnataka including a camp site at the Cauvery Fishing Camp (see Outdoor Activities in the Around Bangalore section) and lodges near the Dandeli, Nagarhole and Biligiri Rangaswamy national parks; refer to the relevant sections for details. Its office is on the top floor of the Shrungar Shopping Centre on MG Rd. Advanced bookings are highly recommended, and also possible at Seagull Travels in Mysore (see the Travel Agencies section under Mysore for details).

Bookshops There are several excellent bookshops in town. One of the best is the Premier Bookshop, 46/1 Church St, around the corner from Berrys Hotel. Books on every conceivable subject are piled from floor to ceiling. The owner somehow seems to know where everything is. Gangarams Book Bureau, 72 MG Rd, is also good. There's a branch of Higginbothams a couple of doors away at No 68.

Libraries & Cultural Centres The British Library (☎ 221 3485) on St Mark's Rd has a good range of newspapers, magazines and books, and is a pleasant place to relax and catch up on the news. It's open Tuesday to Saturday from 10.30 am to 6.30 pm.

Alliance Française (☎ 225 8762) is on Thimmaiah Rd near Cantonment train station. It has a library with French newspapers and magazines, and is open Monday, Tuesday,

Thursday and Friday between 9 am and 1 pm and from 4 to 7 pm; open mornings only on Wednesday and Saturday. It also holds exhibitions, music evenings and video nights.

Medical Services In an emergency, phone (☎ 102). For anything less urgent, try St Martha's Hospital (☎ 227 5081), Nrupathunga Rd. The Mallya Hospital (☎ 227 7991) has also been recommended.

National Parks Most national parks in Karnataka are a fair way from Bangalore, so permits and bookings for resthouses are usually handled by the forest departments in the district capitals. For permits to trek in the Bangalore district, or to book accommodation at the resthouses at Namada Chilume, Bandipur (though Mysore is a better place to handle bookings) and Nagarhole (though Hunsur is better for bookings) go to the Wildlife Office (☎ 334 1993) on the 2nd floor of the Karnataka Forest Department, in the tall, white building called Aranya Bhavan, at 18th Cross, Malleswaram (about 2.5km north of City train station). The office is not particularly helpful but the library on the ground floor is interesting.

Vidhana Soudha
Located at the north-western end of Cubbon Park, this massive, granite, neo-Dravidian style building is one of Bangalore's most imposing. Built in 1954, it houses both the Secretariat and the State Legislature. It's floodlit on weekend evenings and on public holidays, but is not open to the public.

Cubbon Park & Museums
This 120 hectare park, laid out in 1864, is one of the main 'lungs' of the city. It's not the most beautiful of gardens but is nonetheless a pleasant escape from the surrounding urban chaos. On its fringes are the superbly restored neoclassical High Court, the grand Public Library, two municipal museums and a dull aquarium. Also in the gardens is a huge **children's park**, which adults are wisely not allowed into unless accompanied by a minor.

The **Government Museum**, one of the

oldest in India, was established in 1886 and houses a poorly presented collection of stone carvings, pottery, weapons, paintings, and some good pieces from Halebid. The museum is open daily except Monday from 10 am to 5 pm; entry is Rs 1.

The **Visvesvaraya Technological & Industrial Museum** usually has schoolchildren pressing buttons on exhibits which reflect India's technological progress. It's open daily except Monday between 10 am and 6 pm; entry is Rs 7.

Lalbagh Botanical Gardens
This pleasant 96 hectare park in the southern suburbs of Bangalore was laid out in the 18th century by Hyder Ali and his son Tipu Sultan. It contains many centuries-old trees which are labelled for identification, one of India's largest collections of rare tropical and sub-tropical plants, a glasshouse modelled on London's Crystal Palace, one of Kempegowda's watchtowers and a surreal lawn clock surrounded by Snow White and the seven dwarfs. There are major flower displays here in the week preceding Republic Day and the week before Independence Day. The gardens are open daily from sunrise to sunset.

City Market
If you've spent all your time on MG Rd then this bustling market south-west of Cubbon Park is all you need to remind you that you're still in India. It contains a tarpaulin-covered fruit and vegetable bazaar, a spice market, plenty of garland sellers, cloth shops and an entire colourful street lined with hole-in-the-wall tailor shops. It's not exactly a mainstream tourist attraction, but the vendors here see few travellers and are extremely friendly.

Fort & Tipu Sultan's Palace
Kempegowda built a mud-brick defence structure on this site in 1537, and in the 18th century it was solidly rebuilt in stone by Hyder Ali and Tipu Sultan. It's a sturdy little fort, though much of it was destroyed during the wars with the British. It's worth a quick visit if you're exploring the City Market.

Tipu Sultan's modest palace is notable for its elegant teak pillars. It was begun by Hyder Ali, and completed by Tipu in 1791. The palace is a five minute walk south-west of the City Market.

Bull Temple
Situated on Bugle Hill at the southern end of Bull Temple Rd, this is one of Bangalore's oldest temples. Built by Kempegowda in the Dravidian style in the 16th century, it contains a huge granite monolith of Nandi (Shiva's bull vehicle) similar to the one on Mysore's Chamundi Hill. Non-Hindus are allowed to enter the temple and the priests are friendly. It's especially interesting on weekends, when there are often musicians, wedding processions and even *pujas* (prayers) to bless new motor cars.

Ulsoor Lake
This pretty picnic spot is on the north-eastern fringe of the city centre. You can hire rowboats for Rs 60 per hour or have a 10 minute spin around the lake in a motorised dinghy for the same price. There's a decent pool (Rs 5) here, with carefully regulated separate-sex swimming hours. One of Kempegowda's watchtowers stands nearby.

Activities
Swimming Nonguests can use the pools at the following hotels for a fee: Le Meridien (Rs 350), Taj West End (Rs 400) and the Sheraton Windsor Manor (Rs 390). There's also a public swimming pool at Ulsoor Lake.

Horse Racing Bangalore's winter race season runs from November to February and its summer season from May to July. Races are generally held either on Friday or weekends and can be a lot of fun. Contact the Bangalore Turf Club (☎ 226 2391) for details.

Outdoor Activities For information about outdoor activities around Bangalore, see the Around Bangalore section later in this chapter.

Organised Tours
The KSTDC offers a huge range of tours, which can be booked in any of its offices. They all start at Badami House (also known as Bux Ranka House). They include a city sightseeing tour, run twice daily at 7.30 am and 2 pm, which costs Rs 80. It quickly covers the city's best attractions and spends a lot of time at a government-owned silk and handicraft emporium. There's also a tour to Srirangapatnam, Mysore and Brindavan Gardens departing daily at 7.15 am and returning at 11 pm. It costs Rs 200, excluding all entrance fees. There are also tours to Nandi Hill, Belur, Halebid and Sravanabelagola, and a weekend tour to Hampi.

Maharaja Tours (☎ 333 4442) offers cultural tours tailored to foreign visitors which include introductions to Indian arts, a visit to a temple, a yoga demonstration, a concert and dance, and a visit to an Indian home. Tours last about six hours, and may start either in the morning or afternoon according to demand. They cost Rs 800, including a vegetarian meal.

Places to Stay – Budget
Bus Stand Area A dozen or more budget hotels line Subedar Chatram Rd in the heart of Gandhi Nagar, just east of the bus stands.

Royal Lodge (☎ 226 6575), at No 251, is one of the cheapest, largest and oldest. It has clean singles/doubles with common bathroom for Rs 100/140 and doubles with attached bathroom and hot water in the morning for Rs 253.

Hotel Adora (☎ 220 0324), almost opposite at No 47, has decent rooms with attached bath for Rs 145/231.

Hotel Mahaveer (☎ 287 3670), immediately south of the City train station and Central bus stand, is a spotless, modern, upmarket budget hotel with small rooms with TV, attached bath and hot water in the morning. Rooms cost Rs 180/250; air-con doubles cost Rs 500.

Hotel Tourist (☎ 226 2381) is a little further afield at 5 Racecourse Rd. It's good value at Rs 75/120 for rooms with attached bath and hot water in the morning.

Janardhana Hotel (☎ 225 4444, Kumara Krupa Rd) has spacious singles/doubles/triples with balconies, attached bath and hot water for Rs 311/385/465. The rooms are good, but the hotel isn't in a great location. Checkout time is 24 hours.

Retiring rooms at the City train station can also be good value, although they're often full by the afternoon.

MG Rd Area Finding decent budget accommodation around the MG Rd area can be tricky, particularly in December and January, so it's worth making a reservation by telephone a couple of days in advance.

New Central Lodge (☎ 559 2395, 56 Infantry Rd) is a pretty uninspiring place. The rooms are overpriced, but are clean and will do for a night if you get stuck. Singles/doubles with common bath are Rs 120/250 and with attached bath they're Rs 300/320. There's hot water from 6 to 9 am.

Imperial Lodge (☎ 558 5473, 93-4 Residency Rd) has singles/doubles/ triples with attached bath for Rs 170/300/380. It's in a handy location but on a noisy main road.

Airlines Hotel (☎ 227 3783, 4 Madras Bank Rd) is off the road in its own leafy grounds and has a range of facilities including a garden restaurant – with drive-in service – a supermarket and a bakery. Singles/doubles/triples with attached bath and hot water in the morning cost Rs 250/370/450. Unfortunately it's so popular that you need to make a reservation 10 to 15 days in advance.

Brindavan Hotel (☎ 558 4000, 108 MG Rd) has decent rooms with attached bath for Rs 160/280 and air-con rooms for Rs 425/850. The hotel is fairly quiet since it's set back from the road, but it's also often full.

City Market Area This is the place to stay if you enjoy being in the thick of the noise, bustle and atmosphere of the bazaar. It's a 25 minute walk from the City train station.

Chandra Vihar (☎ 222 4146, Avenue Rd) charges Rs 145/275 for clean, decent-sized rooms with attached bath, bucket shower and hot water in the morning. There are great views of the market from some rooms.

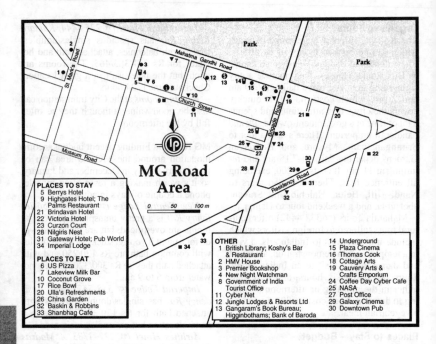

MG Road Area

0   50   100 m

PLACES TO STAY
5 Berrys Hotel
9 Highgates Hotel; The Palms Restaurant
21 Brindavan Hotel
22 Victoria Hotel
23 Curzon Court
28 Nilgiris Nest
31 Gateway Hotel; Pub World
34 Imperial Lodge

PLACES TO EAT
6 US Pizza
7 Lakeview Milk Bar
10 Coconut Grove
17 Rice Bowl
20 Ulla's Refreshments
26 China Garden
32 Baskin & Robbins
33 Shanbhag Cafe

OTHER
1 British Library; Koshy's Bar & Restaurant
2 HMV House
3 Premier Bookshop
4 New Night Watchman
8 Government of India Tourist Office
11 Cyber Net
12 Jungle Lodges & Resorts Ltd
13 Gangaram's Book Bureau; Higginbothams; Bank of Baroda
14 Underground
15 Plaza Cinema
16 Thomas Cook
18 Cottage Arts
19 Cauvery Arts & Crafts Emporium
24 Coffee Day Cyber Cafe
25 NASA
27 Post Office
29 Galaxy Cinema
30 Downtown Pub

Rainbow Hotel (☎ 670 2235, Sri Nara-simharaja Rd), opposite the City Market bus stand and a big white mosque, is OK value at Rs 125/205/308 for singles/doubles/triples with attached bath, though it's not keen on un-accompanied women travellers.

Places to Stay – Mid-Range
Most of the hotels in this price range are in the MG Rd area but there are a few near the racecourse, a rather dull area which is a short auto-rickshaw ride from the City train station and Central bus stand.

MG Rd Area The *Victoria Hotel (☎ 558 4076, fax 558 4945, 47-8 Residency Rd)* is a throwback to the days of the Raj, and is set in grounds filled with huge shady trees. It's a popular place, and a haven from the busy cityscape outside the gates, but by the time they've added luxury tax and their own 10% service charge it's not great value.

Singles/doubles with attached bath cost Rs 420/1050, deluxe double rooms are Rs 1170 and a suite costs Rs 1300. There's a bar and restaurant with indoor and garden dining. There are not many rooms so you need to make an advance reservation.

Curzon Court (☎ 558 2997, fax 558 2278, 10 Brigade Rd) offers comfortable air-con rooms with TV and attached bath from Rs 800/1000.

Nilgiris Nest (☎ 558 8401, fax 558 5348, 171 Brigade Rd) is on the 3rd floor above a supermarket of the same name. It has clean, spacious, airy rooms with TV and attached bath for Rs 600/800. Checkout time is 24 hours.

Berrys Hotel (☎ 558 7211, 46/1 Church St) is a large, standard, mid-range establish-ment that's rarely full. Huge musty and rather depressing rooms with attached bath cost Rs 400/450. The deluxe rooms cost Rs 500/550, and are in much better condition.

Highgates Hotel (☎ 559 7172, fax 559 7799, 33 Church St) is a tasteful, modern, three-star hotel at the top of this price range. Comfortable air-con rooms with TV, fridge and attached bath cost Rs 1195/1600. It has a restaurant, a lobby coffee shop and a patio. Reservations are recommended.

Comfort Inn (☎ 559 1800, fax 559 2276, 66 Infantry Rd) is a good option is you like your creature comforts but don't want to pay Taj prices. The air-con rooms are modern and extremely comfortable; singles/doubles go for Rs 1330/1695.

Racecourse Area The *Hotel Raceview (☎ 220 3401, 25 Racecourse Rd)* has doubles (no singles) for Rs 500, or Rs 900 with air-con. Keen punters may be interested to know that some of the more expensive rooms have a good view of the racetrack.

Hotel Abhishek (☎ 226 2713, 19/2 Kumara Krupa Rd) has singles/doubles with TV and attached bath for Rs 720/780, or Rs 810/900 with air-con.

Places to Stay – Top End
Bangalore's importance as an industrial and business centre has resulted in a plethora of swanky hotels, most of them around MG Rd or in the more peaceful northern part of town, close to the golf and race courses. The Oberoi and the Taj West End vie for the title of best hotel in town. To all of the prices quoted below you can add 25% for luxury tax and service charge.

Gateway Hotel (☎ 558 4545, fax 558 4030, 66 Residency Rd) is a four-star member of the Taj Group. It has excellent rooms from US$80/95, including breakfast. Facilities include a swimming pool and a restaurant specialising in Malabar Coast cuisine.

The Capitol (☎ 228 1234, fax 225 9922, Raj Bhavan Rd), opposite the GPO, charges US$75/85 for a single/double room.

Le Meridien (☎ 226 2233, fax 226 7676, 28 Sankey Rd) has rooms from US$145/165.

Taj Residency (☎ 558 4444, fax 558 4748, 41/3 MG Rd) charges US$130/145.

Sheraton Windsor Manor (☎ 226 9898, fax 226 4941, 25 Sankey Rd) occupies a beautiful old manor house where rooms cost from US$145/160.

Oberoi (☎ 558 5858, fax 558 5960, 37-9 MG Rd) has luxurious rooms which open onto an immense tranquil garden for US$245/275. There's a swimming pool and all the usual five-star amenities.

Taj West End (☎ 225 5055, fax 220 0010, Racecourse Rd) is a classy five-star hotel occupying a carefully restored 19th century mansion and several villas set in a beautiful eight hectare garden. Rooms start from US$195/215.

Places to Eat
MG Rd Area There are a huge number of places to eat around MG Rd, though most are expensive and mediocre imitations of western fast-food or pizza joints. Their attractiveness will probably be determined by how long you've been in India. Despite the burger-pizza overload, you'll find western-style breakfasts in very short supply.

Ulla's Refreshments (1st floor, General Hall, MG Rd) is a local favourite and a great spot for snacks (Rs 15) and South Indian vegetarian dishes (Rs 30 to Rs 40). It has an indoor area and a big, convivial terrace.

US Pizza (Church St) makes pretty good pizza, with prices starting at around Rs 80, but there's little atmosphere, and they don't serve beer.

Coconut Grove, also on Church St, is a friendly, semi-open-air restaurant with a mouthwatering array of South Indian regional dishes. Main courses cost between Rs 90 and Rs 110. In the same area, a good place for a splash-out meal is *The Palms*, the rooftop restaurant belonging to the Highgates Hotel. It's a peaceful and relaxing place, specialising in South Indian cuisine. Crab in chilli gravy, pork cooked Coorg style, and Kerala stew are all Rs 85.

Rice Bowl (Brigade Rd) is a cosy Chinese joint run by Tibetans. The food is average but it certainly comes in hearty proportions; main dishes cost around Rs 60. Less cramped and with a pleasant atmosphere is the *China Garden* which is down a side street off Brigade Rd. The dining area is outdoors and main courses cost between Rs 70 and Rs 100.

Shanbhag Cafe (Residency Rd) dishes up decent South Indian thalis for Rs 23, and a more luxurious North Indian variety for Rs 61.

Victoria Hotel (47-8 Residency Rd) has a nice shady garden restaurant and an old-fashioned dining hall that are both interesting eating places if you have the patience to handle the lacklustre service. The food is multicuisine, and there's a lunchtime buffet for Rs 75.

Casa Piccolo (131 Residency Rd) has western food, a relaxed atmosphere and sensible prices – pizzas and burgers start from Rs 36 and steaks from Rs 58. It's not a bad spot, but don't expect culinary wonders.

Lakeview Milk Bar (38 MG Rd), and *Baskin & Robbins (Residency Rd)* are the places to go for ice cream. Lakeview is one of the few places on MG Rd to open early and serve western breakfasts.

Koshy's Bar & Restaurant is a good place for western snacks (including breakfasts), or if you just fancy a quiet relaxed drink. The menu proudly boasts that Koshy's has been 'Caterers to our late prime minister Jawaharlal Nehru and the Queen of England'. No one was on hand to specify when they actually catered to the queen, so this one remains a mystery.

Mac Fast Food (MG Rd) has been recommended for its burgers and pizzas.

Elsewhere The *Kamat Hotel* and *Sagar Hotel* are the two best options in Subedar Chatram Rd in Gandhi Nagar. The former dishes up South Indian veg fare, and the latter Andhra-style cuisine.

Samudra (25 Lady Curzon Rd) has delicious North Indian fare and more impressive fish tanks than Bangalore's aquarium. Main dishes cost Rs 50. It's a 10 minute walk north of MG Rd.

The Pink Panther (Ramanathree Chambers), just south of Samudra, is another western clone restaurant and cafe, but worth a visit. It serves some fascinating dishes including paneer spinach chips (Rs 65) and chicken tikka pizza (Rs 80). Most memo-

rable is the surprisingly tasty mashed potato, baby corn and cheese toasted sandwich (Rs 40).

Mavalli Tiffin Room, near Lalbagh Botanical Gardens, may not look much, but it's a legendary dosa and snack joint with excellent lassis.

Paradise Island at the Taj West End is the most interesting of the five-star hotel restaurants. Set in a beautiful garden pavilion, it serves excellent Thai and Chinese cuisine.

Pizza Hut (Cunningham Rd), is new and has better pizza than US Pizza in the MG Road area. Cold Kingfishers can be had here too.

Entertainment

Bars Bangalore's affluence has bred a pub culture that wouldn't be out of place in any western country but which comes as a complete culture shock in India. Flashy bars, well-lit discos and draught beers are all the rage with well-heeled young people and office workers. Needless to say, you won't feel like a social reprobate for drinking a beer here as you might do in the 'black holes' of Tamil Nadu.

Most of the pubs are fairly similar male-dominated theme bars, with deafeningly loud music and TV screens showing Sky sports. They tend to have carefully structured seating arrangements that prevent too much social interaction between strangers; women are often quarantined in 'family only' areas.

Bars are open during lunchtime and from 5 to 11 pm. Draught beer usually costs around Rs 25 for a mug or Rs 60 for a bottle. Nearly all bars serve snacks.

Pub World, next to the Gateway Hotel, is symptomatic of Bangalore's restless mimicry of the west. It's a confused mix of a British pub, Wild West saloon and Manhattan cocktail bar, all in one room. The music is shatteringly loud and the place is generally packed. Other theme bars include *NASA (Church St)*, which is decked out like a spaceship and has laser shows, and *Underground (MG Rd)*, which is (supposedly) modelled on a London tube station.

New Night Watchman, near Berrys Hotel,

has a nifty cubist park bench arrangement, a few bar stools and, thankfully, no theme décor.

Black Cadillac *(50 Residency Rd)* has quieter music and a cover charge on Friday and Saturday night (which includes the price of four drinks). Unlike most of the other places the clientele is not entirely male, and the atmosphere is much more relaxed.

Cyber Pub next to *Black Cadillac* wins the prize for being the oddest place in town. The tiny modern bar has absolutely no atmosphere; users have their beer and snacks brought to them as they sit in front of the computer screens.

If you just fancy a quiet beer, two good places are the veranda of the *Victoria Hotel* and the old fashioned tea-room style *Koshy's Bar & Restaurant (St Mark's Rd)*. For a more lively scene, the *Downtown Pub*, opposite Gateway Hotel, has good music, a relaxed atmosphere and a couple of pool tables.

Nightclubs Like the pub and bar scene, Bangalore's collection of nightclubs is constantly changing. A good new place is *The Club* which is about 14km west of the city centre, on the Mysore road. With a bit of haggling, a rickshaw should cost around Rs 125 one way. Entry to the nightclub costs Rs 150, for which you get a free beer.

Cinema The *Plaza (MG Rd)* and the *Galaxy (Residency Rd)* both show first-run English-language films. Regional films are best watched at one of the many cinemas along KG (Kempegowda) Rd in Gandhi Nagar.

Shopping

Bangalore is a good place to purchase silk, sandalwood and rosewood items, and Lambadi tribal jewellery.

The most pleasant shopping experience is to be found on Commercial St, north of MG Rd. This street is home to a number of silk, handicraft and clothes shops. Stunning, hand-embroidered saris are reasonably priced and fabric is cheaper here than in the silk emporiums lining MG Rd.

There are plenty of handicraft shops on MG Rd. Cauvery Arts & Crafts Emporium at

No 23 stocks the same range of statues, jewellery, ceramics, carpets and *agarbathis* (incense) that you've seen in a thousand other tourist towns across the country. Cottage Arts at No 52 and Central Cottage Industries Emporium at No 144 also stock the usual range of artefacts.

HMV House on St Mark's Rd has a selection of Hindi cassettes and CDs and a small range of western music. There are several places around the city that sell genuine (ie not pirated) cassettes of western music for around Rs 100 – a real bargain. CDs are for sale too, but are not nearly such good value.

Don't assume shops are closed because they look dark and gloomy; it's probably just one of Bangalore's frequent power cuts.

Getting There & Away

Air The Indian Airlines office (☎ 221 1914) is in the Housing Board Buildings, KG Rd. Other operators include Jet Airways (☎ 227 6617), Sahara (☎ 558 6976) and NEPC Skyline (☎ 526 2842).

There are daily connections (prices in US$) to Calcutta ($215), Kozhikode ($55), Delhi ($210), Hyderabad ($80), Chennai ($55) and Mumbai ($110), plus numerous flights to Ahmedabad ($180), Goa ($80), Kochi ($60), Mangalore ($56), Pune ($115) and Thiruvananthapuram ($90).

The only direct international flights from Bangalore are to Muscat, Sharjah and Singapore. However, there are a number of international connecting flights via Mumbai. These include services to the Gulf and to Paris, London, New York and Singapore. The advantage of these services is that you can go through customs and immigration procedures in relative peace at Bangalore airport. Facilities at Bangalore airport include foreign exchange counters and a pre-paid taxi booth.

International airlines with offices in Bangalore include:

Air France
(☎ 558 7258)
Sunrise Chambers, 22 Ulsoor Rd
Air India
(☎ 227 7747)
Unity Bldg, Jayachamaraja Rd

British Airways
(☎ 227 4034)
7 St Mark's Rd
KLM
(☎ 226 8703)
West End Hotel, Racecourse Rd
Lufthansa
(☎ 558 8791)
44/2 Dickenson Rd
Qantas Airways
(☎ 220 2067)
Westminster Bldg, Cunningham Rd
Singapore Airlines
(☎ 221 2822)
51 Richmond Rd

Bus Bangalore's huge and well-organised Central bus stand is directly in front of the City train station. All the regular buses within the state are operated by the Karnataka State Road Transport Corporation (KSRTC; ☎ 287 3377). Interstate buses are operated by KSRTC as well as the state transport corporation of Andhra Pradesh (APSRTC; ☎ 287 3915; platform 11), Tamil Nadu's JJTC (☎ 287 6974; platform 12) and Goa's Kadamba (near the computerised reservation booths). Computerised advance booking is available for all KSRTC super-deluxe and express buses, which makes planning travel and getting a place refreshingly easy. It's advisable to book in advance for long-distance journeys.

KSRTC operates horrifyingly fast buses to Mysore every 15 minutes from 5 am to midnight (Rs 36/53 ordinary/deluxe, three hours). It also has four daily departures to Ernakulam (16 hours), 11 to Hospet (eight hours), four to Jog Falls (eight hours), 12 to Chennai (eight hours), two to Mumbai (24 hours), four to Udhagamandalam (Ooty; eight hours) and two to Panaji (15 hours).

Kadamba buses depart for Panaji at 5.30 and 6 pm (Rs 223, 13 hours). The APSRTC has plenty of buses to Hyderabad (12 hours); one departs at 7.45 am and the remainder leave in the evening. JJTC has frequent departures to Madurai (10 hours) and Coimbatore (11 hours), plus seven daily buses to Chennai (eight hours).

In addition to the various state buses, numerous private companies offer more comfortable and more expensive buses between Bangalore and the other major cities in central and southern India. The private bus fare to Goa, for example, is around Rs 225. You'll find private operators lining the street facing onto the Central bus stand. Most private buses depart in the evening.

Train There are two train stations in Bangalore. The main one, the City train station, is the place to make reservations. Cantonment train station is a useful spot to disembark if you're arriving in Bangalore and heading for the MG Rd area.

Rail reservations in Bangalore are computerised but there are no tourist quotas on any trains and bookings are heavy on most routes. On the other hand, it's usually possible for travellers to get into the emergency quota – to do so, however, you have to buy a ticket first and throw yourself on the mercy of the assistant commercial manager in the Divisional Office building immediately north of the City train station. The reservation and inquiry office is on the left as you're facing the station and is open Monday to Saturday from 8 am to 8 pm; Sunday 8 am to 2 pm. Counter number 14 is reserved for 'foreign tourists, freedom fighters, and senior citizens'. Luggage can be left at the City train station.

Bangalore is connected by direct daily express trains with all the main cities in southern and central India. The only lines disrupted by conversion from metre to broad gauge at the time of writing were the stretches between Mysore and Hassan, Hassan and Mangalore, and Londa and Goa. While work on the Goa line continues (which could be another year or more) the quickest and most comfortable way to get there is by train to Londa with onward transport by bus.

See the table over the page for a selection of major trains from Bangalore.

Getting Around
To/From the Airport The airport is 13km east of the City train station and about 9km east of the MG Rd area. There are pre-paid taxis from the airport to the city (Rs 170). If

Major Trains from Bangalore

Destination	Train Number & Name	Departure Time	Distance (km)	Duration (hours)	Fare (RS) (2nd/1st)
Calcutta	5625 Guwahati Exp	11.30 pm Thur & Fri	2025	38.00	325/1385
Ernakulam	6526 Kanyakumari Exp	9.10 pm	638	13.00	172/620
Hospet	6592 Hampi Exp	9.55 pm	491	9.30	141/511
Hyderabad	7686 Kachiguda Exp	5.05 pm	790	16.30	199/722
Chennai	2608 Lalbagh Exp	6.30 am	361	5.20	110/395
	2640 Brindavan Exp	2.30 pm			
	2008 Shatabdi Exp*	4.20 pm		4.55	410/815
Mumbai	1014 Kurla Exp	12.10 am	1211	24.00	255/952
	6530 Udyan Exp	8.30 pm			
Mysore	6222 Kaveri Exp	7.15 am	139	2.30	36/187
	6206 Tippu Exp	2.25 pm			
	6216 Chamundi Exp	6.15 pm			
	2007 Shatabdi Exp*	10.55 am		2.00	205/405
Delhi	2627 Karnataka Exp	6.25 pm	2444	41.45	364/1637
	2429 Rajdhani Exp**	6.45 am Wed & Fri		33.43	1600/4635
Thiruvananthapuram	6526 Kanyakumari Exp	9.00 pm	851	18.15	208/737

* Air-con only; fare includes meals and drinks; daily except Tuesday
** Air-con only

you plan to take an auto-rickshaw, avoid the touts who hang around outside the building, demanding two or three times the correct fare (many of them have a faked card showing 'special airport rates'). Walk a couple of hundred metres away from the building towards the main road and you'll soon find a driver willing to use the meter. Going to the airport from the centre of town, you may have to haggle for a price since drivers will be reluctant to use their meters – count on around Rs 100 for a taxi or Rs 40 for an auto-rickshaw. Bus Nos 13 and 333 go from the city to the airport for around Rs 15.

Bus Bangalore has a comprehensive local bus network. Most local buses run from the City bus stand next to the Central bus stand; a few operate from the City Market bus stand to the south.

To get from the City train station to the MG Rd area, catch any bus from platform 17 at the City bus stand.

Auto-Rickshaw Bangalore residents are proud to tell you that auto-rickshaw drivers are required by law to use their meters (which are properly calibrated, incidentally), and locals will *insist* on them being used. Although many drivers are reluctant to use the meter, if you persevere you'll soon find one who'll oblige. Outside the train and bus stations there are rickshaw ranks supervised by a policeman who ensures that the meter is used. Flagfall for autos is Rs 7 and then Rs 3.60 for each extra kilometre. Expect to pay about Rs 17 from the train station to MG Rd. After 9 or 10 pm, you'll almost certainly have to haggle and agree on a fare.

Car Europecar (☎ 221 9502), 85 Richmond Rd, provides the best-value car hire. It has self-drive Maruti 800s for Rs 825 per day (up to 150km) and charges Rs 5.50 per kilometre thereafter. A chauffeur-driven Maruti costs Rs 625 for eight hours or 80km, whichever comes first. After this point it's Rs 150 extra

KARNATAKA

per hour and Rs 6.25 extra per kilometre. If you're planning to go further afield consider getting a driver and car from KSTDC (at its office on Kasturba Rd). The rate is Rs 3.25 per kilometre, for a minimum of 250km, in addition to which you must pay Rs 100 as an allowance for the driver. Car hire is the ideal way to visit some of the attractions listed below

Taxi By the time this book appears a new type of taxi (small Maruti cars) will have started to appear on the streets of Bangalore. They should, like the rickshaws, all have functioning meters.

Walking Negotiating Bangalore on foot is an unrewarding slog since the city is diffuse and the pavements wayward. Crossing the street in some parts of town is more dangerous than travelling on the Bangalore-Mysore bus.

AROUND BANGALORE
Whitefield Ashram
About 20km east of Bangalore is Sai Baba's summer ashram, where he usually in residence between March and May. His main ashram, Puttaparthi, is in neighbouring Andhra Pradesh (see that chapter for further detail).

Transport to both the Whitefield Ashram and Puttaparthi can be arranged in Bangalore at S Babu & Co (☎ 226 1351), a travel agency in the Cauvery Continental Hotel, 11 Cunningham Rd. Between March and May, half-day tours to Whitefield for either morning or evening *darshan* (audience with the guru) cost Rs 250. You can also get to Whitefield on bus No 333-E or 319-C from platform 17 at the City bus stand.

Bannerghatta National Park
This modest national park, 21km south of Bangalore, is home to a small population of leopards. There's also a staged 'safari' where you can see lions, tigers and elephants in a fenced-in area, plus a crocodile and snake farm. It's open daily except Tuesday; catch bus No 365 from platform 15 at the City bus stand.

Nrityagram
This village, 30km north-west of Bangalore, was established in the early 1990s to revive Indian classical dance. Under the auspices of well-known Odissi dancer, Protima Gauri, it offers the long-term study of classical dance and its allied subjects, such as choreography, philosophy, music, mythology and painting. The village, designed by award-winning Goan architect Gerard Da Cunha, welcomes visitors and accommodates guests. Contact Nrityagram's Bangalore office (☎ 846 6314).

Antharganga Hill
One of the best places for hiking and scenery has to be Antharganga Hill, at Kolar, 70km from Bangalore. There are steps all the way to the top (40 minutes) which pass a temple where Hindus can wash away their sins, and the climb finishes at a delightful plateau, where you can explore the village

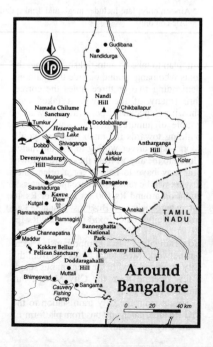

and enjoy the undisturbed birdlife. There are plenty of easy trails leading all over the place: take your pick.

It is easy enough to take a day trip from Bangalore, or you could stay in Kolar at the *Sri Anjanadri Lodge* (☎ 08152-22460), immediately opposite the bus stand. Rooms are pleasant, if a little noisy, but are a bargain at Rs 50/100/175. Buses travel between Bangalore and Kolar (Rs 17) about every 40 minutes. From the bus stand walk about 3km along the road to the hills (they are easy to spot), or charter an auto-rickshaw to the entrance. There is no entrance fee.

Devarayanadurga Hill

This hill (1188m) is another fantastic place for scenery. A 10 minute walk up the steps from the car park brings you to two temples dedicated to Yoganarasimha and Bhoganarasimha. Another two minutes along the trail starting behind the water tower takes you to the remains of another small temple, and those staggering views.

The hill is 70km north-west of Bangalore, just off the road to Tumkur, and 20km from Dossabet. It can easily be combined with a trip to Shivaganga and Nandi Hill (see over the page). You must hire your own vehicle (from Bangalore, Tumkur or Dossabet) because the road to the top is very steep and long, and there is no public transport.

Kokkre Bellur

One of the more successful conservation programs in South India is Project Pelican, at the tiny village of Kokkre Bellur (see the boxed text on this page). However, this is mainly of interest to bird enthusiasts (and only during the correct season, from the end of February to April); villagers and conservationists do not want hordes of tourists wandering around disturbing the birds.

Kokkre Bellur is easy to reach from Mysore or Bangalore. Take one of the very regular buses between the two cities (but not the nonstop express), and get off at Maddur. From there, wait for the irregular and crowded bus or, better, charter an auto-rickshaw to Kokkre Bellur, a bumpy but scenic one hour ride away.

A very pleasant, but often heavily booked, hotel at Maddur is the *Hotel Priyadarshini* (☎ 08232-32725), which costs Rs 250 a

KARNATAKA

Project Pelican

One of 10 known nesting spots in India for the endangered spot-billed pelican (*Pelicanus philippensis*) is at Kokkre Bellur. These large and graceful creatures are very fussy, and Kokkre Bellur is home to the best types of trees for nesting. However, branches and leaves are often cut off or shaken to obtain animal fodder, and the chicks, which often fall to the ground, cannot be rescued because the adult pelicans don't have enough room to land and fly off. The pelicans almost disappeared in Kokkre Bellur until the establishment of Project Pelican in 1994.

Members of the project hand-rear fallen chicks, and villagers are encouraged not to damage trees, but there are continual problems: 1kg of fish is needed per bird per day (fish farms are being built to cope with this); alternative sources of firewood and fodder must be found for the villagers; resources to fund the project are limited; and, ironically, detrimental effects from well-meaning tourists are becoming apparent.

One heartening aspect of the project is that the villagers are involved at a grassroots level, and are keen to avoid government interference. The best time to visit is from the end of February to April, when the branches are often drooping from the weight of 360 birds and their nests. For more information, and donations, contact the Mysore Amateur Naturalists (☎ 0821-541 744), 571 9th Cross, Anikethana Rd, Kuvempu Nagar, Mysore 570 023; or visit the Web site (www.eco-canada.com) run by one of the foreign supporters.

double. The *Hotel Mayura*, on the main road in Maddur, is a great place for a meal and a beer. The hotel boasts what one visitor boldly proclaimed to be 'the cleanest toilets in India'.

Namada Chilume Sanctuary

This gorgeous pocket of forest is worth visiting, especially if you have a vehicle and you're going to Devarayanadurga. There is a small deer park, some birds and a few hiking trails, but the serenity and access to granite ridges for climbing are the main attractions. Part of a state forest, it is open from 6 am to 6 pm every day. Entrance costs Rs 1. You can even rent one of the handful of quaint and clean *Forest Inspection Bungalows* from the Karnataka Forest Department Wildlife Office in Bangalore (see the National Parks section under Bangalore).

The forest is 10km from Devarayanadurga, and easy to reach with your own vehicle. If you are relying on public transport, take a rickshaw or taxi from Tumkur (10km away).

Nandi Hill

Nandi Hill is one of the most majestic places in the region, and should be included on your itinerary. There is nothing much to do but admire the views across the plains and do some hiking, but the place is very serene and relaxing. It is an ideal day trip or better, a place to stay for a few days.

Often mistakenly referred to as a hill station, there is a small, enclosed area on top of Nandi Hill (1615m). It was a popular summer retreat during the reign of Tipu Sultan, and was predictably enjoyed by British colonialists, though no hint of the colonial era remains. The trails within the area are a little confusing, but it shouldn't take more than hour to see everything (plus time for getting a little lost, and admiring the views).

Entrance only costs Rs 2, and it is open every day during daylight hours. Avoid Sunday when this place is bumper-to-bumper with day-trippers.

Hiking & Rock Climbing There are no properly established hiking trails, so just walk wherever you fancy. There are some sheer rock faces for the experts, but those without a masochistic streak or good equipment should climb from the eastern side. Start your climb from the closest point to the hill from the road between Chikballapur and Doddaballapur. For information on rock-climbing agencies see the Outdoor Activities Around Bangalore section.

Places to Stay & Eat If you are hankering for somewhere to relax for a few days, this is probably as good as it gets. But as accommodation is limited, booking ahead is strongly advisable.

Hotel Mayura Pine Top only has two rooms (Rs 125 per double), so bookings are essential (at the KSTDC office in Bangalore). The restaurant boasts what must be the best views of any restaurant in South India, and offers a good selection of cheap meals and drinks including western breakfasts and beer.

Nehru Nilaya Guest House (☎ 08156-78621) has pleasant and clean double rooms for Rs 150, or separate, quaint cottages dotted along the trail for Rs 200. For bookings between 15 March and 15 July contact the Horticultural Department at the Lalbagh Botanical Gardens in Bangalore; for other times, ring the Nehru Nilaya Guest House.

You can eat at the Nehru Nilaya, Hotel Mayura, or at the unsavoury *Vegetarian Hotel*, next to the Mayura.

Getting There & Away From Bangalore, there are about six direct buses per day (Rs 17, two hours) via Chikballapur or Doddaballapur. On the way back, you can also jump on whatever is going down the hill, and look for onward transport from wherever it stops. If you have the energy, the scenic trail down the hill (8km) ends at the road between Chikballapur and Doddaballapur, from where you can hail down a passing bus to Bangalore.

Shivaganga

For temples, views across the plains and a chance to stretch your legs, head to Shivaganga Hill (1367m). The steep steps which lead to the top (allow at least an hour) pass several incredible underground cave temples, a natural spring called Pathalaganga and finish at two temples, Gangadareswara and Honna Devi. Other temples and hiking opportunities are in the vicinity and easy to find.

The hill is 56km north-west of Bangalore. Get off the Bangalore-Tumkur bus at the town of Dobbo, 8km away from Shivaganga and charter an auto-rickshaw or taxi. Alternatively, take one of the direct buses which travel about every two hours between Bangalore and Shivaganga. There are plenty of places to eat in the village.

Outdoor Activities Around Bangalore

Bangalore gets our vote as one of the worst places in India for air pollution, so if you are hankering after some fresh air, head for the hills. The region surrounding Bangalore is full of great places to go trekking and rock climbing, and to enjoy a multitude of other outdoor activities. The definite advantages are that everything is close to Bangalore and easy to reach, and equipment can be hired from several reliable agencies.

Refer to the general Around Bangalore section for information about other great places to go for some outdoor fun, namely Antharganga Hill, Namada Chilume, Nandi Hill, Devarayanadurga and Shivaganga. It is worth considering hiring a vehicle so you can visit a few places in one day.

Rock Climbing The region around Bangalore is the best place in South India for rock climbing. There are sheer cliffs for the expert (and crazy), but you can also just hike up or (often) use steps to the top. In most cases equipment or a guide is not needed if you look for an easier side of the hill to climb. Many rocks have temples on the peak. The best time for rock climbing is early November to early March; at other times the rain and heat can make a climb difficult, unpleasant and dangerous.

Briefly, the best places to head for are:

Kutgal
About 10km from Ramnagaram (see following entry), just off the road to Magadi, this rock is less accessible and more challenging than others, and even if you use the steps and chain to the

250-year-old temple at the top, it is a tough climb. Take a rickshaw or taxi from Ramnagaram.

Ramnagaram
Within a 2km radius of this town are several stunning, sheer granite cliffs, but anyone with some determination can climb up an easier side. The best place to head for are the three separate peaks, huddled together, at the village of Ramnagiri – these hills also have a few small caves to explore. Take any bus heading towards Mysore (not the nonstop express, though) or Mandya from Bangalore, and get off at Ramnagaram. From there, rent an auto-rickshaw to Ramnagiri, about 5km away. There are a couple of hotels near the bus stand in Ramnagaram.

Savanadurga
This 500m sheer rock face is the largest near Bangalore, and great for purists and masochists. (Savanadurga means Fort of Death in Kannada.) Others will enjoy climbing the two peaks, Karigudda or Karibetta (Black Hill), and Biligudda or Bilibetta (White Hill), 1207m high. Temples dedicated to Narasimha and Veerabadra are on top of the hills, and there are ruins of a 16th century fort built by Kempegowda. About 3km away (ask directions), a reservoir is ideal for kayaking and windsurfing. (This can be arranged by Ozone or Woody Adventures.) You have to pay a Rs 1 entrance fee at the gate to the Savanadurga State Forest, a few hundred metres from the village. The steps to the top of Bilibetta (which takes about two hours to hike up) start from behind the temple in the village. The region is famous for medicinal plants and pristine vegetation, and is great for hiking on flat land. Savanadurga village is about 60km from Bangalore, and about 10km from Magadi. Four buses a day travel directly to the village from Bangalore central bus stand, or go to Madagi and get onward transport there.

Trekking Rock climbing is a major outdoor activity around Bangalore, but trekking is certainly possible in several regions:

Channarayanadurga
These hills, the highest of which is 1139m, boast the ruins of 17th century forts, several cave temples, and stunning views. They're about 95km from Bangalore, and about 35km from Tumkur.

Nandidurga
This is another great area for rummaging around old forts and abandoned temples. The highest hill (about a 45 minute climb) has a shrine dedicated to Narasimha. The principal town, and

starting point for hiking, is Gudibana, exactly 100km from Bangalore.

Muttali to Sangama

This is one of the best overnight hikes in the region. Start in Muttali village and hike 20km to the convergence of the Cauvery and Arkavathi rivers, camping along the way. You can combine it with a visit to the Cauvery Fishing Camp (see the entry for Fishing, later in this section) at Bhimeswari. Though you follow a river, the region is hot and dry. You need permission from the Wildlife Office in Bangalore (see under National Parks in the Bangalore section), but a guide is not needed. You can extend this to a four or five day trek (80km), by starting at Shimsha and hiking via Bhimeswari, Sangama, Sunnadgedde (famous for limestone caves), Ungya and Hogenakal, which has several picturesque waterfalls. You will need a guide for this trek – the Ozone agency can arrange this.

Rangaswamy Hills

Among these hills, you can climb Doddaragahalli Hill (about 1100m), which has deep caves and awesome views from the fort on top. As it is near the Bannerghatta National Park, you will need permission from the Wildlife Office in Bangalore. The best place to start and to find a guide is Kanakapura, about 60km from Bangalore.

Outdoor Adventure Agencies

With the exception of the Adventure Academy, all of the following agencies can arrange any trekking or rock climbing trips mentioned above, as well as other activities such as paragliding in the Nilgiris district of Tamil Nadu, and visits to national parks and wildlife sanctuaries in Karnataka and Tamil Nadu. They also have camping, cooking and rock climbing equipment,for hire and can arrange guides, trainers and private transport.

Adventure Academy

(☎ 221 0454, 3rd floor, State Youth Centre, Nrupathunga Rd, Bangalore). If you ask the tourist office in Bangalore anything about outdoor activities, they will send you to the Academy. While it only organises trips for local youth, staff are happy to answer any general questions.

Clipper Holidays

(☎ 559 9032, fax 559 9833, email cliphol@clipper.wiprobt.ems.vsnl.net.in, Suite 406, Regency Enclave, 4 Margath Rd (off Brigade Rd), Bangalore 560 025). Clipper is a very professional outfit which organises special-interest holidays, from wildlife tours to ayurvedic retreats.

Ozone

(☎/fax 331 0441, email nomads@giasbga.vsnl.net.in or outdoorzone@hotmail.com, 5 5th Main, 12th Block, Kumara Park West, Bangalore 560 020). This impressive outfit, run by capable young men, can organise a vast range of treks all around Karnataka, as well as in Tamil Nadu and Kerala. It is the only place in Bangalore which can arrange mountain bike trips (along established hiking trails).

Spark

(☎ 664 0880, fax 664 0293, email sparkina@giasbga.vsnl.net.in, Corporation Stadium Complex, Jayanagar III Block, Bangalore 560 011). Part of the nationwide National Adventure Foundation, Spark has access to about 15 camp sites near Bangalore, and can get permits with ease. As a nonprofit organisation run by enthusiasts, its prices are very reasonable. Ring (in the evening) before you visit the office.

Woody Adventures

(☎ 226 4218 or 225 9159, Sri Sailam 4, 2nd Cross Rd, Gandhi Nagar, Bangalore 560 009). This is another excellent agency which can organise rock climbing and trekking trips to anywhere mentioned above, and to more remote places in Karnataka, and as far as Kodagu (Coorg) district. It has a wide range of equipment for hire.

Costs

Costs vary, of course, depending on where you're going, what sort of activity you want to do and how many there are in your group. As a general rule of thumb, the prices per person per day for equipment are: rock climbing gear (Rs 50); sleeping bag (Rs 20); camping stove (Rs 30); backpack (Rs 15); and two/four-person tents (Rs 45/60). A guide will cost about Rs 200 per day, or about Rs 250 if you take a more knowledgeable and professional guide recommended by one of the agencies listed above.

As a general guide, a rock climbing trip may come to Rs 400 to Rs 500 per person per day, for a group of two, including private transport, food, guide and equipment. Expect to pay up to Rs 1000 per person per day for a professional, all-inclusive trek over several days.

Other Activities

Karnataka offers the outdoor enthusiast a range of other adventure and leisure activities:

Air Sports

For something different (and expensive), try paragliding and parachuting. Contact Agni Aero Sports Adventure Academy (☎ 553 3203, fax 553 5696, 99/A Abhishek, 17th B Main Rd, 5th Block, Koramangala, Bangalore), but you are more likely to find them at Jakkur Airfield, on the road to Doddaballapur. The Ozone agency (see the Outdoor Adventure Agencies section) can arrange all-inclusive parasailing and paragliding trips around Nandi Hill, among other places, for Rs 1250 per person.

Fishing

One of the best places to fish in South India, is at the Cauvery Fishing Camp, set up by Jungle Lodges & Resorts (see Travel Agencies in the Bangalore section). The best season is December to March. Prices are not low: US$80 per person per day including food, plus another US$45 per person per day if you want to go fishing. The camp is located about 100km south of Bangalore, on the road to Kanakapura and near the village of Bhimeswari.

Helicopter Tours

Deccan Aviation (email decanair@blr.vsnl.net.in) is a Bangalore-based helicopter charter company. They offer a range of fully catered packages, from a US$50 per person helicopter tour over Bangalore and surrounds, to a US$600 per couple luxury getaway to the Biligiri Rangaswamy Wildlife Sanctuary.

Horse Riding

The only horse riding club that we know of in South India is the very keen Embassy Ranch (at the time of research prices were not available). The club is located at Torhunse, Jala Hobli, 24km from Bangalore, on the road to Doddaballapur. Contact it in Bangalore (☎ 227 0018, fax 227 0828, email mktg@embassyindia.com) at 101 Embassy Chambers, 5 Vittal Mallya Rd, Bangalore 560 001.

Motorcycling

Any motorbike enthusiast with a valid licence should contact the Karnataka Motorsports Club (☎ 546 0050) and find out what activities it has on offer.

Running

The worldwide Hash House Harriers has a club in Bangalore (☎ 530 0915). They go for a run every Sunday – no doubt followed by a cleansing ale (or two).

Water Sports

If you are looking for something a little more adventurous than a paddle on Ulsoor Lake in Bangalore, try windsurfing at Hesaraghatta Lake, about 30km from Bangalore, on the road to Tumkur; or at Kanva Dam, 13km north of Ramnagaram. Contact the Bangalore Sailing Club (details were not available at the time of research). Kayak hire from Ozone or Woody Adventures costs Rs 175/350 per day for single/double seat; a life jacket costs Rs 20.

MYSORE

Pop: 735,000 Tel Area Code: 0821

This charming, easy-going city has long been a favourite with travellers – it's a manageable size, enjoys a good climate and has chosen to retain and promote its heritage rather than replace it. The city is famous for its silk and is also a thriving sandalwood and incense centre, though don't expect the air to be any more fragrant than that of the next town.

History

Mysore is named after the mythical Mahisuru, where the goddess Chamundi, the favoured deity of the Wodeyar Rajas, slew the demon Mahishasura. Up until the middle of the 16th century the Wodeyars were in the service of the Vijayanagar emperor, but with the fall of the empire in 1565 the Mysore rulers were among the first to declare their independence. Although they maintained many of the old traditions of the parent kingdom (notably the Dussehra festival, which is a direct descendant of the Mahanavami celebrations that were so important in Vijayanagar), the new state wasn't slow to assert its independence. Srirangapatnam was soon added to the kingdom, and over the next two centuries Mysore's territories were expanded slowly but surely.

In 1761 the Wodeyars suffered a setback when one of their officers, named Hyder Ali, usurped the throne. He and his son Tipu Sultan developed the kingdom at an astounding rate via a course of aggressive military action. During this period, Tipu's plans to lay out a new capital included razing most of the existing city so that he could start again.

With Tipu's defeat by the British in 1799 the kingdom was returned to the Wodeyars, although Mysore was sadly lacking in its old buildings. Colonel Arthur Wellesley (later to become the Duke of Wellington) recorded that the new raja (aged only five years old)

KARNATAKA

had to be crowned in a tent, because there were no suitable buildings in which to perform the ceremony.

Within the next few years a replacement was built for the old wooden palace, and the rajas were involved in large-scale rebuilding of the city. When the wooden palace was partially destroyed by fire in 1897, however, plans were made to build a new palace that would properly reflect the position of the rajas. The palace which still dominates the city is the result, and today is a major attraction for tourists. The Rajas of Mysore continued to rule until Independence in 1947, and were widely recognised as running a model state, with large amounts invested in building and education. In 1956, when the new state was formed, the former Maharaja was the first to be elected as the governor.

Orientation

The train station is on the north-western fringe of the city centre, about a kilometre from the main shopping street, Sayaji Rao Rd. The Central bus stand is on the Bangalore-Mysore Rd, on the north-eastern fringe of the city centre. Mysore Palace occupies the entire south-eastern sector of the city centre. Chamundi Hill is an ever visible landmark to the south.

Information

Tourist Offices The KSTDC tourist office (☎ 22096) is in the Old Exhibition Building on Irwin Rd and is open Monday to Saturday from 10 am to 5.30 pm. There are also counters at the train station (☎ 30719), the Central bus stand (☎ 54497) and a transport office (☎ 423652) next to the Hotel Mayura Hoysala.

For information about what's on in Mysore, pick up a copy of any of the three local news-sheets. *Andolana* and *Samachar* (both 50 paise) have information on films, some events and even horse racing. The weighty *Star of Mysore* (Rs 1) runs to eight pages and has the best news and listings.

Money The State Bank of Mysore, on the corner of Irwin and Ashoka Rds, has efficient foreign exchange facilities, as does its branch office on Sayaji Rao Rd. The Bank of Baroda on Gandhi Square provides cash advances on MasterCard and Visa.

Post & Communications The GPO is on the corner of Irwin and Ashoka Rds. It's open between 10 am and 6 pm, though the poste restante facility is only open until 4 pm. There's a handy local post office on the 1st floor of a building fronting KR Circle.

The central telegraph office is on the western side of the palace and is open 24 hours.

Travel Agencies Seagull Travels (☎ 529732, fax 34653) under the Hotel Ramanshree, has helpful staff and is the place in Mysore to book upmarket accommodation near the national parks, including anything run by Jungle Lodges & Resorts.

Bookshops Geetha Book House, on KR Circle, is the best bookstore in Mysore, with a good selection of general interest books, as well as a substantial number of books about local history and culture. The Ashok Book Centre on Dhanvantri Rd, near the junction with Sayaji Rao Rd, is also worth checking out.

Medical Services The Basappa Memorial Hospital (☎ 512401), a couple of kilometres west of the city centre, is considered the best hospital in Mysore.

National Parks To book accommodation for bungalows within Bandipur National Park (though you can also book in Bangalore), go to the Aranya Bhavan Building, one block up from the main road through Ashokapuram. The office (☎ 480901), helpfully marked 'Reservation for Bandipur Cottages', is upstairs, in room 105. The office for Project Tiger is next door. Bus No 61 will take you to Ashokapuram from the city centre, but an auto-rickshaw is easier.

Mysore Palace

The beautiful profile of this walled Indo-Saracenic palace, the seat of the maharajas of

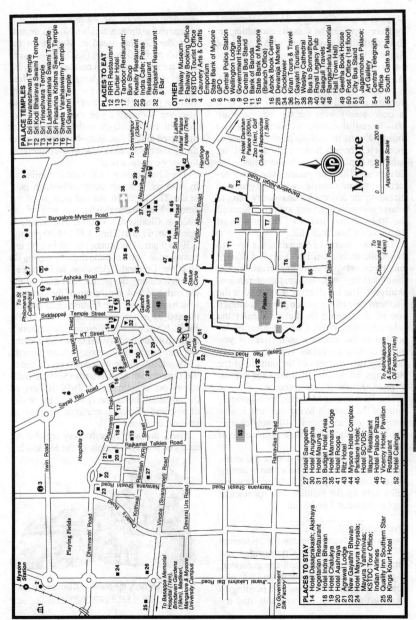

PALACE TEMPLES
T1 Sri Bhuvaneshwari Temple
T2 Sri Kodi Bhairava Swami Temple
T3 Sri Trineshwara Temple
T4 Sri Lakshmiramana Swami Temple
T5 Sri Prasanna Krishna Swami Temple
T6 Shweta Varahaswamy Temple
T7 Sri Gayathri Temple

PLACES TO EAT
12 RRR Restaurant
13 Durbar Hotel
17 Tandoor Restaurant;
    Shilpashri
22 Kwality Restaurant
29 Indra Cafe; Paras
    Restaurant
32 Shilpashri Restaurant
    & Bar

OTHER
1   Railway Museum
2   Railway Booking Office
3   KSTDC Tourist Office
4   Cauvery Arts & Crafts
    Emporium
5   State Bank of Mysore
6   GPO
7   Central Police Station
8   Wellington Lodge
9   Government House
10 Central Bus Stand
11 Bank of Baroda
15 State Bank of Mysore
    (Branch Office)
16 Ashok Book Centre
28 Devaraja Market
34 Clocktower
36 Gayatri Tourism
38 Wesley Cathedral
39 Bus to Somnathpur
40 Royal Legacy Pub
42 Seagull Travels
48 Rangacharlu Memorial
    Hall (Town Hall)
49 Geetha Book House
50 Post Office (1st floor)
51 City Bus Stand
53 Jaganmohan Palace;
    Art Gallery
54 Central Telegraph
    Office
55 South Gate to Palace

Mysore

0   100   200 m

Approximate Scale

PLACES TO STAY
14 Hotel Dasaprakash; Akshaya
18 Hotel Indra Bhavan
19 Hotel Chalukya
20 Hotel Aashraya
21 Agrawal Lodge
23 New Gayathri Bhavan
24 Hotel Mayura Hoysala;
    Mayura Yathnivivas;
    KSTDC Tour Office;
    Indian Airlines
25 Quality Inn Southern Star
26 Kings Kourt Hotel
27 Hotel Sangeeth
30 Hotel Maurgana
33 Hotalesan Restaurant
35 Hotel Mannars Lodge
41 Hotel Roopa
43 Ritz Hotel
44 Mysore Hotel Complex
45 Parklane Hotel;
    Hotel SCVDS
46 Hotel Palace Plaza
47 Viceroy Hotel; Pavillon
    Restaurant
52 Hotel Calinga

Mysore, graces the city's skyline. Designed by Henry Irwin, who was the consulting architect of the Government of Madras, the Amba Vilas Palace was completed in 1912 at a cost of Rs 4.2 million. The former Maharaja is still in residence at the back of the palace.

Inside it's a kaleidoscope of stained glass, mirrors, gilt and gaudy colours. Some of it is undoubtedly over the top but there are also beautiful carved wooden doors and mosaic floors, as well as a whole series of mediocre, though historically interesting, paintings depicting life in Mysore during the Edwardian Raj. The palace even has a selection of Hindu temples within its grounds, including the Shweta Varahaswamy Temple whose *gopuram* (gateway tower) influenced the style of the later Sri Chamundeswari Temple on Chamundi Hill.

The main rooms of the palace are open to the public daily from 10.30 am to 5.30 pm, and the crowds can sometimes rival those in the departure lounge of a major international airport. The Rs 10 entry fee is paid at the southern gate of the palace grounds, though you need to retain the ticket to enter the palace building itself. Cameras must be deposited at the entrance gate (free) if you intend to enter the palace buildings; visitors can only take pictures of the outside of the buildings. Shoes are left at the shoe deposit counter near the palace entrance.

The Residential Museum, incorporating some of the palace's living quarters, is also open. It costs an extra Rs 10 entry charge, and is rather dull after the magnificence of the palace itself.

On Sunday nights and during the entire Dussehra Festival, there's a carnival atmosphere around the palace as 97,000 electric bulbs light up the building in a spectacular display between 7 and 8 pm.

Chamundi Hill
Overlooking Mysore from the 1062m summit of Chamundi Hill, the **Sri Chamundeswari Temple** makes a pleasant half-day excursion. Pilgrims are supposed to climb the 1000-plus steps to the top, but those not needing to improve their karma will probably find descending easier on the leg muscles. There is also a road to the top, and bus No 201 departs from the City bus stand in Mysore for the summit every 30 minutes (Rs 2.75). A taxi to the top from Mysore will cost around Rs 150.

Before exploring the temple visit the free **Godly Museum** near the car park. Here you can ponder the price of various sins and discover some sins you may never have thought existed. Gym enthusiasts may be distressed to find that 'body-building' is a bad thing, since it's a clear case of over-attention to 'body consciousness'.

The Chamundeswari Temple is dominated by a towering seven storey, 40m-high gopuram. The statue in the car park is of the demon Mahishasura, who was one of the goddess Chamundi's victims. The temple is open from 6 am to 2 pm, 3.30 to 6.30 pm and 7.30 to 9 pm. If the queues to get in look unmanageable, you can jump them by paying Rs 10 at the 'Demand Tickets Special Entrance'.

After visiting the temple start back to the car park and look for the top of the stairway, which is behind the Mahishasura Statue, marked by a sign proclaiming 'Way to Big Bull'. It's a pleasant descent since there's some shade on the way and the views over the city and surrounding countryside are superb.

Two-thirds of the way down you come to the famous 5m-high **Nandi** (Shiva's bull) carved out of solid rock in 1659. It's one of the largest in India and is visited by bevies of pilgrims offering *prasaad* to the priest in attendance there.

You'll probably have rubbery legs by the time you reach the bottom of the hill and it's

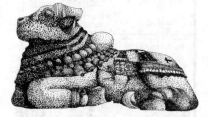

Standing 5m high, the Nandi of Chamundi Hill is one of the biggest in India.

still a couple of kilometres back into the centre of Mysore. Fortunately there are usually auto-rickshaws waiting to ferry pedestrians back to town for around Rs 30. Local tourist literature reports that the summit is 13km from the city, but this is by the winding, switchback road; via the steps it's only about 4km.

Devaraja Fruit & Vegetable Market
The Devaraja Market, stretching along the western side of Sayaji Rao Rd, south of Dhanvantri Rd, is one of the most colourful in India and provides excellent subject material for photographers.

Jaganmohan Palace & Art Gallery
The Jayachamarajendra Art Gallery in the Jaganmohan Palace, just west of Mysore Palace, has a collection of kitsch objects and Wodeyar memorabilia, including weird and wonderful musical machines, rare instruments and paintings by Raja Ravi Varma. The palace was built in 1861 and served as a royal auditorium. It's open daily; entry is Rs 5.

Mysore Zoo
Mysore has one of India's better kept zoos, set in pretty gardens on the eastern edge of the city centre. It's open daily (8.30 am to 5.30 pm) except Tuesday; entry is Rs 8.

Rail Museum
Mysore's paltry rail museum boasts a maharani's saloon carriage, complete with royal toilet, dating from around 1899. It's east of the train station, just across the railway track, and is open daily, though closed for lunch between 1 and 2 pm; entry is Rs 2.

Folklore Museum
The Folklore Museum, which has been recommended, is to be found on the Mysore University campus, in the north-west corner of the city. The museum is open from 10 am to 5 pm Monday to Saturday, although it's closed on every second Saturday; entry is free. You'll need to take a rickshaw out to the university, and allow a little time to locate the building, which is tucked away in the middle of the campus, just off Kavempu Ave.

Other Buildings
Mysore has several fine buildings and monuments in a variety of architectural styles. Dating from 1805, **Government House**, formerly the British Residency, is a 'Tuscan Doric' building set in 20 hectares of gardens. West of Government House is **Wellington Lodge**, where Arthur Wellesley lived after the defeat of Tipu Sultan.

In front of the north gate of Mysore Palace, a 1920 statue of Maharaja Chamarajendar Wodeyar stands in the New Statue Circle, facing the 1927 **Silver Jubilee Clock Tower**. If he glanced sideways he'd see the imposing town hall, the **Rangacharlu Memorial Hall** of 1884. The next traffic circle west is the 1950s Krishnaraja Circle (KR Circle), graced by a statue of Maharaja Krishnaraja Wodeyar.

St Philomena's Cathedral, north of the GPO, was built between 1933 and 1941 in neo-Gothic style, and is one of the largest churches in India. It looks rather gloomy from the outside but the whitewashed interior is airy and full of birdsong from the resident pigeons and sparrows.

Converting maharajas' palaces into hotels is a popular activity, and the grand **Lalitha Mahal Palace** of 1921, 7km east of town, is a prime example. It's worth driving here from the city centre (Rs 40 return by auto-rickshaw) since the road passes several exquisite colonial residences and the bougainvillea-clad **Commissioner of Police** building. The former **Hotel Metropole** (now sadly closed) also started life as a guesthouse of the maharajas, and the 1910 **Chaluvamba Vilas** on Madikeri Rd was a maharaja's mansion.

The Royal City by TP Issar (INTACH, Mysore, 1991) is a comprehensive survey of the city's architecture.

Activities
Swimming The swimming pool at the Lalitha Mahal Palace Hotel is open to nonguests for Rs 180 per day; Quality Inn Southern Star also charges Rs 180.

Golf The Jayachamaraja Wadiyar Golf Club (☎ 35108), next to the Racecourse on Race

KARNATAKA

Course Rd, has a rather parched 18 hole course. Nonmembers are charged Rs 100 for a round; you can hire clubs for Rs 50, and the going rate for caddies is Rs 20. Dress regulations don't allow T-shirts, jeans or tennis (ie short) shorts.

Horse Racing The well-maintained race course has regular meets between the end of May and the end of February – check the local press for details.

Adventure Sports Garuda Aerosport (☎ 37018), 631/A Hyder Ali Rd, is a yet-to-get-off-the-ground concept by Mr Somender Singh, who runs the business from his motorcycle garage (sorry, tune-up centre). He's got a couple of microlights from which you could enjoy a birds-eye view of the area, although the flights aren't cheap and as for insurance, you'd better have your own. Rs 500 buys you a quick circuit of the town, and Rs 3000 gets you an hour in the air.

Yoga Mr K Pattabhi Jois runs the Ashtang Yoga School (☎ 25558). The shortest of the courses last for three months and cost US$400 per month.

Organised Tours
The KSTDC's Mysore city tour covers the city sights plus Chamundi Hill, Somnathpur Temple, Srirangapatnam and Brindavan Gardens. The tour starts daily at 7.30 am, ends at 8.30 pm and costs Rs 90. It's a pretty good tour, though some of the sights are a bit rushed.

The KSTDC also runs a Belur, Halebid and Sravanabelagola tour every Tuesday, Wednesday, Friday and Sunday (daily in the high season), starting at 7.30 am and ending at 9 pm. The cost is Rs 160. This is an excellent tour if your time is short or you don't want to go to the trouble of making your own way to these places. The time you get at each destination is sufficient for most people.

KSTDC tours can be booked through any of the city's KSTDC offices or through Dasaprakash Travel (☎ 24949), in the courtyard of the Hotel Dasaprakash.

Dussehra Festival
This 10 day festival in the first and second weeks of October is a wonderful time to visit Mysore. The palace is illuminated every night and on the last day the former Maharaja leads one of India's most colourful processions. Richly caparisoned elephants, liveried retainers, cavalry, and the gaudy and garlanded images of deities make their way through the streets to the sound of jazz and brass bands, and through the inevitable clouds of incense.

Places to Stay
Accommodation can be hard to find during the Dussehra Festival (October), and in December and January too, so it pays to book in advance.

Places to Stay – Budget
Mysore has plenty of budget hotels. The main areas are around Gandhi Square and in the area between Dhanvantri and Vinoba Rds.

Hotel Maurya (☎ 426677, Hanumantha Rao St II), off Sardar Patel Rd is well run and excellent value. Clean singles/doubles/triples with attached bathroom and bucket shower cost Rs 105/175/250.

Hotel Dasaprakash (☎ 24444), near Gandhi Square, is part of a South Indian hotel chain. It's a huge, airy place built around a central courtyard with basic but acceptable rooms with attached bath from Rs 110/225 to Rs 190/300. Checkout is 24 hours. You get a newspaper under your door in the morning, there's an excellent vegetarian restaurant, an ice cream parlour, a travel agent and, for emergencies, an astro-palmist on call.

Hotel Mannars Lodge (☎ 35060), off Gandhi Square towards the Central bus stand, has modern, good-value singles/doubles/triples with attached bath for Rs 145/180/250.

Parklane Hotel (☎ 430400, fax 428424, 2720 Sri Harsha Rd) is the most popular budget hotel in the city. It's a travellers' hangout with decent rooms with attached bath for Rs 99/124 on the ground floor and Rs 124/149 on the upper floor. There's a courtyard bar and restaurant downstairs. You'll need to reserve a room days in advance.

Hotel Anugraha (☎ 430768), in the centre

of town near the junction of Sayaji Rao and Sardar Patel Rds, is a standard Indian hotel offering adequate rooms with attached bath from Rs 90/150. Checkout is 24 hours.

Hotel Calinga (☎ 431019), opposite the City bus stand, is an old hotel with rudimentary rooms with attached bath for Rs 140/180.

New Gayathri Bhavan (☎ 421224, Dhanvantri Rd) is a cheap, friendly, large place with a wide variety of rooms starting from Rs 50/100 with common bath and Rs 145 with attached bath.

Hotel Sangeeth (☎ 424693, 1966 Narayana Shastri Rd) has clean rooms with attached bath for Rs 125/175.

Agrawal Lodge (☎ 422730), just off Dhanvantri Rd and down a side street, has rooms with attached bathroom for Rs 100/150.

Hotel Aashraya (☎ 427088), on another nearby side street, has overpriced doubles with attached bath from Rs 250 and minuscule singles for Rs 80.

Hotel Chalukya (☎ 427374) has rooms with attached bath for Rs 95/175, and deluxe doubles for Rs 300.

Hotel Indra Bhavan (☎ 423933) is a relatively clean hotel but it has seen better days. Singles/doubles with attached bath cost Rs 125/130 and there are also better doubles for Rs 170 or Rs 240. There's a 'meals' hall downstairs.

Other options include the cluster of budget hotels east of the Jaganmohan Palace, though they see few foreign tourists, and the good *Retiring Rooms* at the train station.

Places to Stay – Mid-Range
Ritz Hotel (☎ 422668), a few hundred metres from the Central bus stand, is a friendly place with plenty of old-world charm. There are only four rooms: spacious doubles with mosquito nets, attached bath and 24 hour hot water are Rs 180, and a four-bed room costs Rs 280. You'll need to book a month in advance to secure a room. There's a restaurant and bar downstairs.

Hotel Mayura Hoysala (☎ 425349, 2 Jhansi Lakshmi Bai Rd) is a good KSTDC hotel on the opposite side of the city centre. It has a relaxing ambience and offers decent

rooms with enormous attached bath for Rs 250/300. The hotel has its own quiet gardens, as well as a bar and restaurant.

Mayura Yathrinivas (☎ 423652), a KSTDC annexe next door, has characterless doubles with attached bath for Rs 240 and dorm beds for Rs 50.

Hotel Palace Plaza (☎ 430034, 2716 Sri Harsha Rd) is a recommended modern hotel offering a variety of rooms ranging from Rs 275 with TV and attached bath to Rs 700 with air-con and (brace yourself) circular beds, fantasy curtains and mirrored ceilings.

Hotel SCVDS (☎ 421379), next door to the Parklane Hotel, has modern rooms with mosquito nets, TV and attached bath from Rs 199/350. It's keen to attract foreign travellers, so offers discounts on these rates.

There are two very ordinary modern hotels, both popular with domestic tourists, south of the Central bus stand.

Mysore Hotel Complex (☎ 426217, 2729 Bangalore-Nilgiri Rd) has characterless doubles with attached bath from Rs 275 or with air-con for a pricey Rs 800.

Hotel Roopa (☎ 33770), on the opposite side of the road, is better value but still nothing special. Average doubles cost from Rs 240, or Rs 500 with air-con.

Hotel Darshan Palace (☎ 520794, Lokaranjan Mahal Rd) is further out, to the south-east of the Hardinge Circle. The rooms are not quite as good as the outside suggests, but the hotel is in a quiet part of town, and at Rs 225 for a double with TV and hot water, it's good value.

Viceroy Hotel (☎ 424001, fax 433391, Sri Harsha Rd) is a new place that seems to cater largely to a well-heeled business clientele. Extremely comfortable non air-con rooms cost Rs 475/525, or Rs 650/750 with air-con.

Places to Stay – Top End
Kings Kourt Hotel (☎ 421142, fax 438384) is a large, modern establishment a couple of hundred metres south of the Hotel Mayura Hoysala. It charges from Rs 1190/1390 for air-con rooms, though at slack periods you may get a good reduction on this tariff.

Quality Inn Southern Star (☎ 438141,

fax 421689, 13-14 Vinoba Rd) is a plush, modern hotel. It boasts a swimming pool, health club, poolside barbecue, restaurant and coffee shop. The hotel is centrally air-conditioned and rooms cost Rs 1695/2495 including breakfast.

Lalitha Mahal Palace Hotel (☎ 571265, fax 571770), 7km from the city centre, is Mysore's most luxurious hotel. This huge, gleaming white structure was once one of the Maharaja's palaces. Standard rooms cost US$140/160, though there are some cramped 'turret' rooms for US$60/70. The rooms in the older part of the building have the most character, but they can be gloomy and lack balconies. Facilities include a rather ordinary swimming pool, a tennis court, and a large bar with reputedly the best billiard table in India.

Places to Eat

Shilpashri Restaurant & Bar (Gandhi Square) is very popular with travellers and for good reason: the food is excellent, the prices are reasonable and the rooftop is a lovely place to dine at night. It serves western breakfasts and Indian, Chinese and continental mains costing between Rs 30 and Rs 50. If Shilpashri is full (and it often is), the *Durbar Hotel* opposite also has a roof bar; it's rather scruffy and the food is average, but at least you won't have to queue. The restaurant on the ground floor also does a very cheap western 'Brake Fast'.

Akshaya Vegetarian Restaurant in the Dasaprakash Hotel has excellent 'limited' meals for Rs 20 and superb 'special meals' for Rs 30. There's also a good ice cream parlour in the courtyard.

RRR Restaurant (Gandhi Square) is a typical vegetarian place with 'meals' for between Rs 24 and Rs 40; travellers rave about the all-you-can eat thalis.

Parklane Hotel (Sri Harsha Rd) has a convivial courtyard restaurant that's long been a travellers' favourite. It serves everything from tandoori chicken and chop suey to sandwiches and beer. The red lights above your table are for signalling the waiters, not for ambience.

Ilapur is a clean, air-con place adjacent to the Parklane Hotel. It serves North Indian and spicy Andhra food for between Rs 35 and Rs 50.

Ritz Hotel, close to the Central bus stand, has a large restaurant-bar which is popular with locals. Indian, Chinese and continental fare is on offer, the food is good and the staff are friendly. The hotel's line in self promotion is nothing if not unusual: the tariff card boldly states: 'Rooms: bad, Food: bad, Service: bad. Try us for a change, you will like us!'. It's a good spot.

Paras Restaurant (Sayaji Rao Rd) is a popular local eatery serving South Indian (Rs 25) and North Indian (Rs 50) thalis at lunchtime. *Indra Cafe*, downstairs, has snacks, juices and sweets; expect to queue for a seat at lunchtime.

Tandoor Restaurant (Dhanvantri Rd) is a hole-in-the-wall eatery serving Punjabi fare and cheap western breakfasts. The nearby *Bun Shop* sells tasty potato buns which make a fine light lunch for just Rs 3.

Kwality Restaurant (Dhanvantri Rd) serves veg and nonveg fare as well as Chinese and tandoori specialities. Most meals are between Rs 35 and Rs 50.

The Pavilion Restaurant in the Viceroy Hotel is smart, air-conditioned, and serves reasonably priced food (main courses around Rs 55).

Lalitha Mahal Palace Hotel offers Mysore's most sumptuous dining experience, though some find the over-refined atmosphere and the baby-blue Wedgwood-style décor in the grand dining hall unsettling to the digestion. Dinner for two here will set you back around Rs 600, not including drinks. The food is superb and there's live Indian classical music. The à la carte menu is replaced by a buffet outside the busy tourist season. The hotel travel counter can arrange a taxi back into town for around Rs 125.

Entertainment

The *Royal Legacy (Nazarbad Main Rd)*, not far from the Central bus stand, is a compact Bangalore-style pub selling beer by the mug

(Rs 23), pint (Rs 46) or bottle (Rs 60). It's a popular joint with music and dancing upstairs. More relaxed places for a beer include the *Parklane Hotel* (Rs 39), *Shilpashri Restaurant & Bar* (15 varieties of beer from Rs 37 to Rs 47), or the gentleman's club-style bar at the *Lalitha Mahal Palace Hotel* (Rs 125).

There are plenty of cinemas in the area between the Central bus stand and Gandhi Square.

Shopping

Mysore is famous for its carved sandalwood, inlay work, silk saris, incense and wooden toys. The best place to see the whole range is at the Cauvery Arts & Crafts Emporium on Sayaji Rao Rd. It's open daily except Sunday from 10 am to 1.30 pm and 3 to 7.30 pm. It accepts credit cards, foreign currency or travellers cheques and will arrange packing and export, though it's not cheap by Indian standards.

There are a number of other souvenir and handicraft shops in the precincts of the Jaganmohan Palace and along Dhanvantri Rd. Silk shops can be found along Devaraj Urs Rd.

You can buy silk and see weavers at work at the Government Silk Factory on Jhansi Lakshmi Bai Rd. The factory is open to visitors from 10.30 am to noon, and 2.30 to 4 pm, although you need to allow a little extra time to get your permit from the office just

---

Sandalwood City

Mysore is one of the major centres of incense production in India, and scores of small, family-owned *agarbathi* (incense) factories around town export their products all over the world.

The incense sticks are handmade, usually by women and children, and a good worker can turn out at least 10,000 a day. They are made with thin slivers of bamboo, dyed red or green at one end, onto which is rolled a sandalwood putty base. The sticks are then dipped into small piles of powdered perfume and laid out to harden in the shade.

---

inside the front gate. Hand looms are no longer in use inside the factory. You can also visit a nearby sandalwood oil extracting plant in the suburb of Ashokapuram and purchase oil and scented incense sticks.

Getting There & Away

Air There are no flights to Mysore but Indian Airlines (☎ 421846) has an office next door to the Hotel Mayura Hoysala. It's open Monday to Saturday from 10 am to 1.30 pm and 2.15 to 5 pm.

Bus The Central bus stand handles all of the KSRTC long-distance buses. There is a timetable in English, although its accuracy is doubtful, and you should double-check details at the inquiry desk. Reservations can be made six days in advance. The City bus stand, on KR Circle, is for city, Srirangapatnam and Chamundi Hill buses. Private long-distance bus agents are clustered around the road junction near the Wesley Cathedral.

Nonstop KSRTC buses hurtle off to Bangalore (Rs 36/53 ordinary/deluxe, three hours) every 15 minutes. There are also numerous ordinary services to Bangalore, which stop at Srirangapatnam. If you're heading for Belur, Halebid or Sravanabelagola, the usual gateway is Hassan (Rs 31, three hours). Buses depart every 30 minutes.

There's one direct bus to Sravanabelagola, which leaves at 7 am (Rs 26, three hours), but buses depart every 30 minutes to Channarayapatana, only 10km from Sravanabelagola; you can pick up a local bus from there.

Those heading to Hampi have a choice of three buses to its nearest service centre, Hospet (Rs 90/130, 12 hours). Ten buses a day head to Ooty (Rs 45, five hours) via Bandipur National Park. Private minibuses also ply the route to Ooty taking more like three hours (Rs 100); agencies around Gandhi Square sell tickets.

There are plenty of buses to Mangalore (Rs 60/80, seven hours) and Kannur (Rs 75, six hours) and three buses to Ernakulam (Rs 171, 12 hours). One bus heads to Gokarna (Rs 155, 14 hours) at 6 am and one bus heads to Chennai (Rs 132, 10 hours) at 7 pm.

KARNATAKA

In addition to the KSRTC buses, there are a number of private bus companies which run to such places as Bangalore, Mumbai, Goa, Hyderabad, Chennai, Mangalore, Ooty and Pune. Fares on these buses are more than the KSRTC buses but they are definitely more comfortable. To book tickets, try Gayatri Tourism, opposite the Ritz Hotel, and nearby Kiran Tours & Travel.

Train The booking office at the pretty pink Mysore train station is computerised and rarely has long queues, but there's no tourist quota. The office is open Monday to Saturday from 8 am to 2 pm and 2.15 to 8 pm; Sunday, 8 am to 2 pm. There are three daily express trains to Bangalore (Rs 36 in 2nd class, three hours), plus the air-con high-speed *Shatabdi Express* (Rs 205, two hours) which runs daily except Tuesday. The *Shatabdi* continues on to Chennai (Rs 475, seven hours).

At the time of writing, conversion from metre to broad gauge had closed all other services from Mysore, including those to Hassan, Arsikere and Mangalore. Services to Hassan, Arsikere, Shimoga and Hubli were expected to recommence at the time of this book's publication; several expresses a day should undertake the journey. The line to Mangalore may not reopen for another couple of years. Until these lines are back in operation, to catch an express to any major Indian city requires a change in Bangalore.

Passenger services between Mysore and Bangalore stop in Srirangapatnam, an alternative to catching the bus.

Getting Around
Bus From the City bus stand, bus No 201 goes to Chamundi Hill (Rs 2.75) every 40 minutes. Buses No 303 and 304 go to Brindavan Gardens (Rs 4.25), departing every 30 minutes. Buses No 313 and 316 leave every 40 minutes for Srirangapatnam (Rs 3.75). A direct private bus to Somnathpur (1½ hours) runs along Nazarabad Main Rd at around 11.45 am, but there are plenty of similar buses on this stretch heading to T Narsipur or Bannur, where you can change to another bus for Somnathpur.

Car If you intend to explore the many sights around Mysore in a car, KSTDC recommended rates for car and driver hire are Rs 3.30 per kilometre for a minimum of 250km per day. Expect to pay Rs 70 per day for the driver's expenses. Some private travel firms offer variations on these rates, but they usually end up with the same sort of price by the time they've added 'extras'.

Taxi & Auto-Rickshaw There are plenty of auto-rickshaws. The Central bus stand and the train station both have supervised rickshaw 'ranks' where a policeman ensures that the drivers use the meter, but away from these areas you'll have to insist that the meter is used. Flagfall is Rs 7 for the first kilometre and then around Rs 3 for each subsequent kilometre. Taxis are considerably more expensive and do not have meters so fares must be negotiated.

AROUND MYSORE
Somnathpur
Tel Area Code: 08227
Situated some 33km east of Mysore and 32km south-east of Srirangapatnam, Somnathpur is a tiny village notable for the remarkable **Keshava Temple** which stands near the side of a dusty lane. Although the Hoysalas (who ruled in this area from the 11th to the 14th centuries) left behind them numerous examples of their exquisite temple architecture, the Keshava Temple is famous both for its fantastic detail and for the fact that, unlike the temples in Halebid and Belur, this one was actually completed.

According to the inscription on the stone slab that stands just inside the main entrance, the community of Somnathpur was founded by a Hoysala minister named Somanatha, during the reign of king Narasimha III (1254-91). Somanatha granted the area to a group of Brahmins in order to form an *agrahara* (scholastic community). A separate Hoysala inscription in Harihara (where Somanatha also sponsored some temple building) claims that this community was so learned that even the parrots were able to hold discussions! Perhaps impressed by this phenomenon, Somanatha – 'great minister, champion with a sword and bravest at riding wild horses' – petitioned the king for funds to found a new temple. The Keshava Temple, built in 1268, was the result.

The temple is enclosed within a walled courtyard which is entered at the east end via a gate and porch. Around the north, west and south sides of the courtyard run colonnaded cloisters with the doorways to 64 separate cells, all of which originally held sculptures of various deities. The temple itself sits on an irregularly shaped, multifaceted platform, which rises almost a metre from the ground level of the courtyard.

At each of the sharp angles on the basement is the image of an elephant, so that the beasts appear to be bearing the burden of the temple. The layout of the temple is known as *trikutachala* – ie having three shrines, above each of which rises a separate tower.

The outside of the temple is adorned with

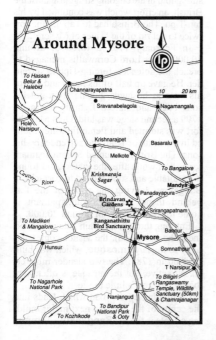

Around Mysore

To Hassan Belur & Halebid
Channarayapatna
0   10   20 km
Sravanabelagola
Nagamangala
Hole Narsipur
Krishnarajpet
Basaralu
Melkote
To Bangalore
Country River
Krishnaraja Sagar
Mandya
Panadayapura
Brindavan Gardens
To Madikeri & Mangalore
Srirangapatnam
Ranganathittu Bird Sanctuary
Bannur
Mysore
Hunsur
Somnathpur
T Narsipur
To Nagarhole National Park
To Biligiri Rangaswamy Temple, Wildlife Sanctuary (50km) & Chamrajanagar
Nanjangud
To Bandipur National Park & Ooty
To Kozhikode

KARNATAKA

so much detail that it's hard to know where to look first. At the eastern end of the temple (ie near the entrance) the upper walls are set with pierced screens to allow light into the outer hall. Below these screens, bands of decoration stretch all the way to the ground. Working upwards, they show elephants, horsemen, scrollwork and scenes from the epic poems. Above this fourth layer is a row of images, mostly of Vishnu, interspersed with carved pillars, and above these are another two rows of figures.

As you move around to either the south or north sides of the building, the layout changes. For the remainder of the exterior, there are six bands of decoration, comprising elephants, horsemen, scrollwork, scenes from the epics, a row of *makaras* (mythical creatures) and a row of swans. Above these, a series of large images, each one flawlessly sculpted, surround the temple walls. The 194 images that surround the temple in this 'layer' are all of gods and goddesses – and the majority are of Vishnu in his various forms.

Many of the images are signed by the sculptors who carried out the work, and from the signatures we learn that the principle craftsman was a man named Mallithama who is personally responsible for 40 of these large sculptures.

Inside the temple, the triple shrines all face into the middle hall. The north sanctum holds an image of Janardhana and the south sanctum, opposite, holds an image of Krishna playing his flute. The image of Keshava that originally adorned the main (central) shrine is sadly no longer in place. The middle hall is notable for its huge and perfectly turned pillars. The deep-carved ceiling panels that adorn both the middle and outer halls are particularly worthy of note.

The temple is open daily from 9 am to 5.30 pm; entry is Rs 2.

Places to Stay The only place to stay or eat in Somnathpur is the run-down KSTDC *Hotel Mayura Keshava*, which is just outside the temple compound. It has a fantastic, peaceful location, but sadly is in poor condition. There are only a couple of functional

The Incredible Flying Temple

In a temple which is so meticulously laid out, it is surprising to find that one of the largest individual features, the towering stone pillar that stands at the eastern end of the building, is not in fact aligned with the rest of the structure. The cause is explained by a local story. Legend has it that when it was finished, the temple was so perfect that the gods wished to take it away for their private enjoyment. Only at the last minute, as the building began to lift from its foundations, did the craftsmen realise that something was amiss. Acting swiftly, they took a chisel to the sculptures on the outer walls, and defaced the nearest of them. With its perfection now flawed, the temple slowly rested on the ground once more – albeit in a slightly different position to the one it had originally occupied.

rooms with attached bathroom which go for Rs 60/110. The restaurant is very basic, but fine for a snack or cold drink.

Getting There & Away Somnathpur is just a few kilometres south of Bannur and 10km north of T Narsipur. See the earlier Mysore Getting Around section for details on public transport.

Talakad & Sivasamudram

The remains of the capital of the 4th to 5th century Ganga dynasty, built on a bank of the Cauvery River at Talakad, are now largely buried by sand. A few buildings, including a 12th century Hoysala temple, still poke through the surface. Once every 12 years this surreal temple is dug out for the performance of Panchalinga Darshan, though it doesn't take long for it to be smothered once again by the sand. Talakad is 50km south-east of Mysore.

A further 25km downstream, the Cauvery suddenly drops more than 50m at the twin waterfalls at Sivasamudram, best seen immediately after the monsoon.

Srirangapatnam

Sixteen kilometres north-east of Mysore, on an island in the Cauvery River, stand the ruins of the capital from which Hyder Ali and Tipu Sultan ruled much of southern India during the 18th century. In 1799, the British finally conquered them with the help of disgruntled local leaders. Tipu's defeat marked the real beginning of British territorial expansion in southern India.

The first important settlement on this site was in the 9th century when the forerunner of the present Ranganatha Temple was founded. The temple was expanded in the 12th century by the Hoysala prince Vinayaditya. In 1454 the rulers of the area were granted permission by the Vijayanagar king to build a fort, and after the fall of the Vijayanagar Empire, the Rajas of Mysore made it their new capital.

When Hyder Ali usurped the throne in 1761, Srirangapatnam became his main stronghold in the ongoing struggle against the British, an effort which was continued by his son Tipu. The British had to capture the fort twice to get rid of the 'Tiger of Mysore'.

In February 1792 a force of around 40,000 under Lord Cornwallis managed to breach the defences, forcing Tipu to surrender. He gave up half of his lands and two of his sons as hostages, but he soon got his sons back and started fighting again. In 1799 a second siege was laid. On 4 May the fort was stormed and fierce fighting resulted in the death of Tipu, and surrender by his sons. The British occupied Srirangapatnam for a short while after the victory, but found it unsuitable and soon moved to barracks in Bangalore, leaving the ruins of the fort behind them. Today Srirangapatnam is home to a community of around 20,000.

Entering through the main gate of the fort (near the bus stand), the visitor comes initially to the large **mosque**, which was built by Tipu in 1787. The two slender minarets are attractive, but the mosque is often kept locked, so there's little to see.

Continuing up the road which leads into the centre of the fort, the next major building of note is the **Sri Ranganatha Temple**.

This wonderful old temple is dedicated to a form of Vishnu, and the town is named after the deity. A temple was first built on this spot in the 9th century, and it was renovated and added to by successive dynasties over the years. As you penetrate deeper into it from the impressive front entrance, you walk through three progressively older areas. The pillared front hall, thought to have been built by Hyder Ali, gives way to a middle area with impressive sculptures both to the left and right of the entrance. The inner hall, however, is the most impressive, with huge pillars and a clear view of the sanctum which contains the reclining form of the deity. A passageway leads around the outside of the sanctum.

North of the temple, by the wall of the fort, is the **dungeon** where Colonel Baillie, who was defeated by Tipu at the Battle of Pollilore in 1780, was held along with hundreds of other British prisoners. Conditions are reputed to have been appalling and many, including Baillie, died in captivity.

Just to the east of the dungeon, along the dusty road leading back towards the entrance to the fort, you come to the **Water Gate**. The small reinforced gate gives access to the riverside, an area now in use as the *dhobi ghats* (area where clothes are washed). It was near here that Tipu met his death, and in addition to the small plaque on the gateway, there's also a simple stone slightly further to the east that marks the spot where he fell.

Accounts of the sultan's death vary slightly, but most agree that he was wounded while trying to retreat to the palace. As Tipu was being carried to safety, an enemy soldier tried to snatch his jewelled sword belt; when Tipu fought back he was shot through the head.

One kilometre east of the fort, set in ornamental gardens, is Tipu's **summer palace**, also known as the **Daria Daulat Bagh**. The palace was built in 1784 when Tipu's power was at its height, and every square centimetre of the inner walls is covered with murals depicting his armies and the splendour of his kingdom. The west wall has an enormous mural of Tipu's victory in the Battle of Pollilore, and other scenes show him review-

ing his troops and taking part in various court rituals.

After Tipu Sultan's defeat, the palace was temporarily the home of Colonel Arthur Wellesley (later the Duke of Wellington). The museum inside has an interesting collection of paintings, portraits, coins and other bits and pieces. The museum is open daily except Friday; entry is Rs 2. Two kilometres further east is the impressive onion-domed **Gumbaz**, or mausoleum, of Tipu and his father, Hyder Ali. Tipu was buried with full military honours on the day after his death.

Places to Stay The best place to stay is the KSTDC's *Hotel Mayura River View* (☎ 52114), peacefully located beside the Cauvery River, a couple of kilometres west of the bus stand and train station. It has well-kept double cottages for Rs 350 (no singles) plus an indoor/outdoor restaurant-bar. Corracle rides can be arranged with locals, but don't go for a dip unless you want to be crocodile bait.

Getting There & Away Srirangapatnam is on the main road between Mysore and Bangalore, and is thus served by scores of buses. It's also possible to get to Srirangapatnam on Mysore to Bangalore passenger trains. See the earlier Mysore Getting Around section for details.

Getting Around Walking around the sights is not really an option as the points of interest are very spread out. The best plan is to hire a bicycle on the main street in the fort, about 500m from the bus stand. All the sites are signposted so it's not difficult to find your way around. There are also *tongas* (horse and open carriages) and auto-rickshaws for hire.

Brindavan Gardens
Tel Area Code: 08236
These tranquil ornamental gardens, laid out below the immense Krishnaraja Sagar dam, look like they belong in a tidy European spa resort rather than the south of India. The gardens are a popular picnic spot and crowds come each night to see the illuminated fountains.

The gardens are illuminated Monday to Friday between 6.30 and 7.25 pm (7 to 7.55 pm in summer) and on weekends until 8.25 pm (to 8.55 pm in summer). Entry is Rs 5, plus Rs 15 for a camera permit. Due to fears the dam will be sabotaged, 'movie cameras, explosives and suspectable items' are prohibited. If you arrive by car after 4.30 pm or without a booking, you'll have to walk the pleasant 1.5km stretch from the main gate across the top of the dam to the gardens.

Places to Stay Since the closure of the *Hotel Krishnaraja Sagar*, the *Hotel Mayura Cauvery* (☎ 57252) is the only place to stay. Clean, basic rooms with attached bathroom and partial views of the garden cost Rs 168/215. There's a restaurant with a limited menu.

Getting There & Away The gardens are 19km north-west of Mysore, and one of the KSTDC tours stops here briefly. See the earlier Mysore Getting Around section for details on public transport.

Tibetan Settlements
There are many Tibetan refugee settlements in the low, rolling hills west of Mysore, in the area between Hunsur and Madikeri. These date back to the 1960s when the Indian government made an offer of land to homeless Tibetan families who were fleeing from occupied Tibet. Since that time, much has changed. The communities have grown enormously and have established themselves with employment, schools and temples. There's still a strong feeling of tradition, though, and entering the area from the main Madikeri road, it's striking to see gaggles of red-cloaked Buddhist monks wandering down the lanes, and prayer flags fluttering in the wind.

Bylakuppe is one of the main areas of settlements, with nearly 20 villages, and the largest population of Tibetans in the whole of India. The villages are well spread out, so it's a good idea to have your own transport or to spend a couple of days and wander at your leisure. One of the villages, Sera Je, is

the site of the Sera Je Monastic University, one of the three largest Tibetan Monasteries in exile. Approximately 8km from the main road, the settlement has a guesthouse and an enormous, newly completed monastery. There are several handicrafts operations in the area, including carpet factories (where you can get Tibetan carpets made to your own design), an incense factory and various social organisations.

The *Siddhartha Guest House* (☎ 08276-74981) has clean doubles with attached bathroom for Rs 125, and there's a good restaurant downstairs. The guesthouse is run as a profit-making enterprise for the monastic school next door. Few travellers make it here, but the atmosphere is very friendly and welcoming.

Mandya District
There are several beautiful Hoysala temples in the Mandya district, which stretches north and east of Mysore.

Approximately 50km north of Mysore, via the town of Pandayapura, the dusty little village of **Melkote** is home to the Cheluvarayaswami Temple. The temple was built in the 12th century and later came under the patronage of the Mysore maharajas and even of Tipu Sultan. Today it is a recognised centre of traditional Sanskrit learning, as well as being an important place of pilgrimage. During the Vairamudi Festival, which is held in March/April each year, the temple image is adorned with jewels belonging to the former maharajas of Mysore. Around 200,000 people crowd into the tiny village for the main day of the festivities.

The temple is fronted by a large, rose-coloured gopuram which is topped with images of four lions' heads – facing the four points of the compass. Passing through the large doorway you enter the dim hall, where the large metallic statues used in the festival are stored. The interior of the temple is plain, but it's worth wandering around the cloister area which surrounds the main temple as some of the pillars have extremely ornate carving.

Although the Cheluvarayaswami Temple

is the most important place of worship in the village, it's not the most imposing. The village and surrounding area are dominated by a large rocky scarp which rises abruptly from the surrounding countryside. On the top of this perches the Narasimha Temple, worth the climb to visit.

Nagamangala, to the north of Melkote, was an important town even in the days of the Hoysalas. Its principal attraction is the Saumyakeshava Temple, which was built in the 12th century and later added to by the Vijayanagar kings. The temple is fronted by a large and intricately structured gopuram, but the interior is almost without ornamentation compared to other temples in the area. The sanctum is kept locked except at prayer times.

Hosaholalu village near Krishnarajpet, about 20km west of Melkote, is home to the Lakshminarayana Temple, a superb example of 13th century Hoysala architecture which rivals in artistry the temples at Belur and Halebid. The temple is small and the entrance is not particularly inspiring to look at, but the western end of the shrine has the same rich detail that one sees on other temples of the time. Particularly noticeable is the use of almost the same design (although on a smaller scale) as that used on the Keshava Temple at Somnathpur.

The temple is raised above ground level, with carvings of elephants guarding each of the corners of the stone dais. On the lower parts of the walls are six bands of carving; from the bottom upwards these show elephants, horsemen, floral designs, scenes from the epics, *makaras* (mythical creatures), and swans. On the south side of the sanctuary the epic scenes are taken from the *Ramayana*, while on the north side they are from the *Mahabharata*. Above the bands are carvings of the deities, including Vishnu, Sarasvati, Brahma and Laxmi Narayana among others. The interior of the temple is very plain.

Basaralu village, some 25km north of Mandya, is home to the tiny but exquisite 12th century Mallikarjuna Temple, executed in early Hoysala style. It's adorned with beautiful sculptures, including a 16-armed

Shiva dancing on Andhakasura's head, and Ravana lifting Kailasa, the Himalayan mountain home of Shiva.

Getting There & Away Getting to any of these towns involves the use of numerous local buses; you'll have to ask around to find the right ones as the timetables are all in Kannada. Mysore is your best base for all of them except Basaralu, for which Mandya might be better. There's a range of modest accommodation in Mandya.

Biligiri Rangaswamy Temple Wildlife Sanctuary

Set among the dramatic Biligiri Rangana (BR) Hills (about 1350m), this sanctuary is cooler and more scenic, but harder to reach, than others in Karnataka. Stretching over 540 sq km, you may see wild elephants and sloth bear, with luck, but you are more likely to see gaur (in fact, local conservationists believe there are too many gaur), barking deer, sambar and wild dog. Though there aren't many birds – about 60 species – they go about their business undisturbed and are easy to spot.

The best time to see wildlife is between June to October, when the animals come out for water at the end of the dry season, but the more comfortable time to visit is winter to early summer (ie November to May). Every

The Soliga Tribal People

The Soligas (who numbered 16,390 in 1981, the most recent record available) live in or near the Biligiri Rangaswamy Hills. They consider themselves to be an integral part of the hills, and rely on the forest for food (eg tubers), and bark and wood for basket-weaving, among other things. They speak the unique Soliga language, but use the Kannada script. Though officially Hindu, Soligas often incorporate traditional beliefs into their religion, eg when performing naming rites and worshipping ancestors.

April, you can witness the wonderful Ratha Festival at the Biligiri Rangaswamy Temple (see the following entry). Permits to enter the sanctuary are required (and easy to get) from the Forest Department in Chamrajanagar if you are not staying at the resort.

Trekking Within the sanctuary, and along the nearby BR Hills, trekking is possible with permission and a guide; both are available from the resort or Forest Department, Chamrajanagar. On the highest peak of the range, Biligiri Rangana Betta, is the revered **Biligiri Rangaswamy Temple**, focus of the annual Ratha Festival mentioned above. You may also stumble across the ruins of some pre-colonial forts in the area.

Places to Stay & Eat The Deputy Conservator of Forests at Chamrajanagar (☎ 08224 -2059) was particularly uninterested in providing information about resthouses in the sanctuary. You may have more luck; it is worth ringing them anyway.

The only alternative is the camp site/resort set up by the Jungle Lodges & Resorts company (see under Travel Agencies in the Bangalore section for details). Though not as luxurious as other places set up by Jungle Lodges, the setting is superb and relaxed, and the tents have private bathrooms and hot water. Prices, which are around US$110 per person per night, include game drives by jeep or elephant and good food.

Getting There & Away BRT Sanctuary is about 90km from Mysore, along a rough road via Chamrajanagar. There are a couple of direct buses from Mysore every day; alternatively catch a bus or train to Chamrajanagar, and then arrange a jeep – a great idea if you have a small group to share the costs.

Ranganathittu Bird Sanctuary

If you have a few hours up your sleeve, and you're interested in birdlife, you should visit the Ranganathittu Bird Sanctuary. The sanctuary is set around a handful of tiny islands in the Cauvery River, and is home to dozens of species of waterbirds, including cormorant, heron, ibis and spoonbill. You can also see a few crocodiles lazing on rocks in the sun. There are walkways around the sanctuary, but for a closer look, charter a rowboat to take you along the river. Boat trips cost Rs 2 per person or Rs 20 if you take the whole boat to yourself.

The sanctuary is open from 8.30 am to 6 pm daily, but in order to see the most birdlife you should go either in the early morning or late afternoon. The best time of year to visit is June to November. The Rs 100 entrance fee for 'foreigners' is annoying, but worth paying. A visit to the sanctuary can be easily combined with a visit to Srirangapatnam, 3km away. Refer to the earlier section on Srirangapatnam for ideas of where to stay; otherwise it's easy to reach from Mysore. Take the regular bus to Srirangapatnam from Mysore, and charter an auto-rickshaw (Rs 80 return with a one hour wait at the sanctuary) or a very slow, but most enjoyable, tonga (Rs 50 to Rs 100).

BANDIPUR NATIONAL PARK

Once part of a private hunting ground owned by the Maharaja, Bandipur was established in 1931, and subsequently enlarged to 874 sq km. It joins the more popular Mudumalai National Park in Tamil Nadu, and forms part of the Nilgiri Biosphere Reserve. Bandipur was the first park (in 1973) created under the banner of Project Tiger. At the time of research, the park was closed temporarily due to the nefarious activities of a smuggler (see the boxed text 'The Brigand of Bandipur', opposite).

Flora & Fauna

Located in the midst of the mighty Western Ghats, Bandipur is mainly pristine moist deciduous forest, with over 50 species of trees such banyan, teak and sandalwood, and nearly 200 species of flowers, plants and shrubs. Given its proximity to major towns, and the good system of roads within the park, poaching and smuggling is a major problem.

There are very few tigers (about 75) and panthers (about 90), but there are jackals, foxes, sambar, barking deer, mouse deer,

---

The Brigand of Bandipur

One of the continuing sagas in the struggle against poaching and smuggling in the hills where the borders of Tamil Nadu, Kerala and Karnataka meet involves a brigand known as Veerappan. Almost regarded as a local version of Robin Hood, he has, however, reportedly killed over 100 forest officers and government officials and 2000 elephants, and smuggled 40,000kg of sandalwood and ivory – though these figures may be somewhat exaggerated.

At the time of research, a special taskforce, established in 1990, with hundreds of heavily armed specialists, had still not captured Veerappan and his motley bunch of six compatriots. He has almost certainly survived this long because of protection from corrupt government and forest officials, and ineptitude by, and lack of cooperation between, the three state governments.

In late 1997 he kidnapped, but returned safely, 22 forest officers and researchers. This lead to the closure of Bandipur National Park and possible trekking routes in the Nilgiris. Given that Veerappan has been in hiding for 20 years, he is likely to be there for a while longer. Before trekking around the hills in this region, seek advice from the forest departments.

---

wild dogs, flying squirrels, Malabar squirrels and a plethora of common langur. Bandipur is one of the best places to see chital and wild elephants (about 3500); gaur are more prevalent after a debilitating epidemic 30 years ago. In the forests there are over 180 species of birds including great Indian horned owls, kingfishers, jungle babblers, peacocks, tawny eagles, coucals, woodpeckers and shrikes.

Trekking

No hiking is allowed inside the park, but it's easy enough to organise scenic day hikes in the region through the resorts listed below (and see under Hiking in the Mudumalai National Park section). The popular hike to the Mysore Ditch – an impressive 260m gorge on the Moyar River – takes you along the border between Bandipur and Mudumalai. This is reason enough to take a guide: the parks have no fences and wild animals can't read border signs

Visiting the Park

The best time to see wildlife is during late summer (ie March to April), but some elephants tend to migrate to Wynad (Kerala) and Mudumalai (Tamil Nadu) national parks at this time. The most comfortable time to visit is between November (which is when many elephants migrate *from* Kerala) and February. Try to avoid coming on a Sunday, when hordes of tourists from Mysore and Ooty shatter the serenity.

Foreigners have to fork out Rs 150 at the reception-cum-interpretation centre (☎ 0822 9-30) in Bandipura village. Cameras cost an extra Rs 10; video cameras, Rs 100. To bring your own vehicle into the park costs another Rs 100, but you can't use it to tour the park.

The only way to get around is on the unsatisfactory minibus tour (Rs 15, one hour) run by the Forest Department (book at the reception centre). These leave anytime between 6 and 9 am, and 4 and 6 pm, depending on demand. More ecologically sound, but *very* bumpy, are elephant rides (Rs 20 per person; minimum of four people required), which run at the same time as the bus tours. Some artificial salt licks have been created to help attract the wildlife, which you can observe from one of the *machans* (watchtowers), however you may find your visit unsatisfying, because the wildlife is elusive, the network of roads in the park is limited, and visitors can only tour on the uncomfortable bus.

Places to Stay & Eat

You can come for the day from Mysore or Ooty (in the Nilgiris), but Bandipur is a relaxing area to stay awhile.

Bungalows In the village of Bandipura, in the middle of the park, the forest department manages some *bungalows* (from Rs 75 to Rs 150 per double) and *dormitories* (Rs 20 per bed). Though basic, it is very cheap, central and pleasant. Make sure you tell the staff that you want meals; otherwise, bring your own food and rent out the kitchen (Rs 50 per day), or head into Gundlupet for meals. A maximum of two nights is allowed, but extensions are possible if there are no more bookings. Book at the reservations office at Mysore or the Wildlife Office in Bangalore – see under National Parks in those sections for contact details.

Hotels Another cheap option is to stay in nearby Gundlupet, a reasonable mid-sized town on the main road from Mysore. The best hotels are the *Hotel Shrinagar* in the centre of town (look for the sign), where noisy doubles cost Rs 180; and the *Ganga Lodge* (☎ 08229-2235), which costs Rs 250 a double.

Hotel Mayura Prakruthi (☎ 08229-7301) is another good KSTDC-run place. Pleasant double rooms, or quieter cottages away from the main road, with TV and an airy bathroom, cost Rs 414 per double. You can ring them direct, or book at the KSTDC offices in Mysore or Bangalore. Nonguests can enjoy a meal (Rs 40 to Rs 50) there, or relax with a beer after visiting the park. The hotel is about 5km north of Bandipura, on the main road from Mysore.

Resorts There are a number of luxurious resorts near Bandipur. All prices include meals, wildlife tours and all taxes and charges; and rooms must be pre-booked direct or at Seagull Travels in Mysore – preferably with several weeks' notice.

Bush Betta is about 4km from Bandipur's main entrance, just off the road to Mysore. Singles/doubles cost US$85/155. Book at its office in Bangalore (☎ 080-551 2631, fax 559 3451), Gainnet, Raheja Plaza, ground floor, Richmond Rd. Guests are picked up at the reception centre in Bandipur.

Tusker Trails, run by the daughter of the last Maharaja of Mysore, has comfortable twin-bed cottages, with a pool, for US$88/

144. It is in Mangala village, near Bandipur. Book at the Tusker Trails office (☎ 080-334 2862, fax 226 4674) at Hospital College, Bangalore Palace, Bangalore.

Tiger Ranch is another 'eco-tourist' resort with bamboo cottages in the middle of the 'jungle' (well, forest). One advantage here is that you will not be forced to pay an exorbitant 'foreigners' price': all visitors are charged Rs 940 per person. Book at Ranch Colorado Resorts (☎ 080-337 4558, fax 337 3508), 1135 Ramshiv Complex, 1st Main Rd, Yeshwanthpur, Bangalore.

Getting There & Away

Bandipur is very easy to reach. Any of the regular buses (which leave every 30 to 60 minutes) between Ooty, in the Nilgiris, and Mysore will drop you off at the reception centre, Bandipura village, Gundlupet or Hotel Mayura Prakruthi. To other resorts you will have to arrange private transport.

BELUR & HALEBID
Tel Area Code: 08177

The Hoysala temples at Halebid (Halebeed, Halebidu) and Belur, along with the one at Somnathpur, east of Mysore, are widely acknowledged as being among the best examples of Hindu architecture in India. Their sculptural decoration rivals that of Khajuraho (Madhya Pradesh) and Konark (Orissa), or the best of European Gothic art.

Halebid

Halebid is thought to have been inhabited since the 9th century, but it remained relatively unknown until the beginning of the 12th century, when it became capital of the Hoysala Empire. Known as Dorasamudra, a name that referred to the huge artificial lake to the east of the city, the capital was surrounded by walls and a moat, and was famed for its wealth and culture. The prize drew the attention of neighbouring monarchs and in the early part of the 14th century Dorasamudra was attacked and pillaged twice by the armies of the Sultans of Delhi.

The capital, and the Hoysala Empire, finally came to an end when the last king,

Ballala III, was killed in battle against the Sultan of Madura in 1342. The city was never properly reoccupied, and became known as 'Halebidu' or 'Old City' to distinguish it from the newer developments nearby.

Hoysaleswara Temple The main structure in Halebid is the Hoysaleswara Temple, construction of which began around 1121. Despite more than 80 years of labour it was never completed and, in a couple of places, you can still see gaps which the sculptors had yet to fill. But along with the Channekeshava Temple in Belur, this ranks as one of the most outstanding examples of Hoysala art. Every inch of the outside walls and much of the interior is covered with an endless variety of Hindu deities, sages, stylised animals and birds, and friezes depicting the life of the Hoysala rulers.

Entrance to the garden surrounding the temple is from the north, but the temple itself faces east towards the huge tank from which the ancient city got its name. On the eastern side, two large pavilions house huge monolithic statues of Nandi, facing inwards to the twin halls, and twin sanctums, of the temple.

```
1  Museum
2  Hoysaleswara Temple
3  Mayura Shantala
4  Kedareswara Temple
5  Jain Bastis
```

To Banavar

Bidarakere Tank

To Belur

Tippamahalli Tank

3 ■ ■ 2

4

5

Halebid

Dorasamudra Lake

0   0.5   1 km

As with the temple at Somnathpur, the Hoysaleswara Temple sits on a stone platform. The lower walls are decorated with 'layers' of friezes (from the bottom upwards: elephants, lions, scroll work, charging horsemen, scroll work, scenes from the epics, mythical beasts known as *makaras*, and swans). Above these lines of decoration, which run continuously around the walls, are larger figures of the gods and goddesses of Hindu mythology.

Although all of the detail is breathtaking, you should take a look at the carving around the doors for some of the best work on the structure. The south door (ie furthest from the entrance to the garden) has an inscription on the lintel recording that it was carved by a sculptor named Kalidasi. The central figure is Shiva, trampling the demon Andhakasura beneath his feet. The figures on either end of the lintel (warriors fighting with lions) are symbols of the Hoysala royal household.

The interior of the temple is just as impressive as the exterior, with huge latheturned pillars, and delicate ornamentation. The lingam in the south shrine is dedicated to the Hoysala king, Vishnuvardhana, in whose reign work on the temple was started. The one in the north shrine is dedicated to his queen, Santalesvara.

There's a small museum adjacent to the temple, housing a collection of sculptures. The first sculpture directly inside the gate is another depiction of the Hoysala crest – the founder of the house, battling with a tiger. The temple is open daily from sunrise to sunset; entry is free. The museum is open daily from 10 am to 5 pm except Friday.

Kedareswara Temple A short distance to the south-east of the Hoysaleswara Temple is the smaller Kedareswara Temple. Although the sculptures around the outside walls show that this once matched its neighbour for artistic flair, it has suffered with time, and patches of the exterior have been poorly repaired. It's still a lovely structure though, and is set in its own quiet garden.

Jain Bastis Between the two Hindu temples is a small enclosure containing

KARNATAKA

The Hoysala Crest

The crest of the Hoysala household is seen on temples throughout the south. Often the figures on either sides of the doors incorporate the theme, or there are carvings on the lintels.

The motif shows the founder of the dynasty, Sala, engaged in fierce struggle with a tiger. According to legend this image represents a real encounter which took place when a monk with whom Sala was travelling was attacked by a tiger. In his panic, he cried out to the future king 'Hoy Sala' (Kill it, Sala). The fearless warrior did just that, overcoming the tiger in straight combat, and earning for himself the title by which his dynasty became known.

The Hoysalas, who ruled this part of the Deccan between the 11th and 13th centuries, had their origins in the hill tribes of the Western Ghats and were, for a long time, feudatories of the Chalukyas. They did not become fully independent until about 1190 AD, though they first rose to prominence under their leader Tinayaditya (1047-78 AD), who took advantage of the waning power of the Gangas and Rashtrakutas. Under Bittiga (1110-52 AD), better known by his later name of Vishnuvardhana, they began to take off on a course of their own and it was during his reign that the distinctive temples at Belur and Halebid were built.

Typically, these temples are squat, star-shaped structures set on a platform to give them some height. They are more human in scale than the soaring temples found elsewhere in India, but what they lack in size they make up for in the sheer intricacy of their sculptures.

It's quickly apparent from a study of these sculptures that the arts of music and dancing were highly regarded during the Hoysala period. As with Kathakali dancing in Kerala, the arts were used to express religious fervour, the joy of a victory in battle, or simply to give domestic pleasure. It's also obvious that these were times of a relatively high degree of sexual freedom and prominent female participation in public affairs.

The Hoysalas converted to Jainism in the 10th century, but then took up Hinduism in the 11th century. This is why images of Shaivite, Vaishnavite and Jain sects coexist in Hoysala temple.

three Jain temples (*bastis*). The exterior of these three structures is strikingly plain, especially in comparison to the intense ornamentation of their neighbours. None the less, the artistry inside the temples is stunning, and the huge Jain deities which are carved from black stone lend a special atmosphere. As with the Kedareswara Temple, just down the lane, few of the many visitors to the Hoysaleswara Temple come to see these other structures, which are consequently much more peaceful.

Places to Stay & Eat The only place to stay in Halebid is the KSTDC's *Mayura Shantala* (☎ 3224), set in a pleasant garden across the road from the Hoysaleswara Temple. There are four cottages with attached bathrooms which go for Rs 157 (Rs 100 for single occupancy). The tiny *canteen* has drinks, toast and omelettes and can

rustle up basic meals. There's a small tourist office inside the grounds of the hotel.

Close to the temple there's a cluster of snack stands and a basic restaurant catering to Indian tourists.

Belur

Belur came to prominence as a major town of the Hoysalas at the beginning of the 12th century. In order to commemorate an important victory against the Cholas in 1116, the king, Vishnuvardhana, built a series of temples. One of these, the Channekeshava Temple, is recognised today as a pinnacle of the Hoysala sculptors' and architects' achievements.

Channekeshava Temple The temple was begun in 1116 and was worked on for over a century. As with other temples of the time, the names of the sculptors have, in many cases, been recorded under the work they executed. It is interesting to note that two of the most prominent artists who worked on this temple came from North Karnataka, and the area controlled by the Kalyana Chalukyas. Nagoja of Gadag, and Masana of Lakkundi can only have brought experience of the northern temple design south with them.

The exterior of the temple is not, in the lower friezes, as extensively sculpted as the other Hoysala temples, but the work higher up on the walls is unsurpassed in detail and artisanship. Particularly arresting are the freestanding bracket figures, which are angled between the upper walls and the over-hanging eaves. There are 38 such sculptures around the outside of the temple, most of them depicting female figures dancing or in ritual poses. The guides will be only too happy (for a small fee) to explain the signif-icance of each one.

Also notable is the line of sculptures which stands out from the ledge approxi-mately 2m above the ground. There are literally hundreds of figures here, all de-picted in minute detail. Also interesting is the repetition of the Hoysala motif (a man fighting a tiger) on each side of the three doors into the temple.

The interior of the temple is perhaps the most impressive part of it. The hall is con-structed in a cruciform, above the centre of which is a stunning dome some 4m square and 2m deep. The immense pillars are of varied design, but are all perfectly execut-ed. The work over the door to the sanctum is equally beautiful.

The temple stands in the centre of a paved compound, which includes a well, a bathing tank and several other, smaller temples. The most important of the minor temples in the compound is the **Kappe-Chennigaraya Temple**, which stands directly to the south of the Channekeshava Temple. Built on the orders of Queen Santaladevi, it was conse-crated at the same time as the major temple, and mimics its layout.

Entrance to the compound is via a gate-way surmounted by a seven storey gopuram. The original gateway was destroyed in the 14th century during a Muslim raid, but was rebuilt during the time of the Vijayanagar Empire.

Places to Stay & Eat The *Hotel Mayura Ve-lapuri* (☎ 22209), a spotlessly clean KSTDC operation, is the best place to stay in Belur. It's only 300m from the temple and a five minute walk from the bus stand. Excellent singles/doubles with attached bath cost Rs 168/200 in the new wing; rooms in the old wing are cheaper at Rs 135/163. Its bland canteen-bar has a limited menu, but is a good place for a snack. There's a small tour-ist office next door to the canteen.

Swagath Tourist Home (☎ 22159) has basic rooms with attached bath for Rs 60. It's 50m before the temple on the left side of the road.

Shri Raghavendra Tourist Home (☎ 22372), to the right of the temple entrance, near the massive temple chariot, has basic rooms with common bath and mattresses on the floor for Rs 50, or rooms with attached bath for Rs 75.

Sri Vishnu Krupa (☎ 22263) is on the town's main road, a few minutes walk from the bus stand. It has fine deluxe doubles with attached bath for Rs 125 and scummy cheaper rooms with attached bath for Rs 40/100. It also has a veg restaurant.

Hotel Shankar is the most popular of the town's handful of basic restaurants. It's 200m before the temple on the left side of the road.

Getting There & Away
Halebid and Belur are only 16km apart. Crammed buses shuttle between the two towns every 30 minutes from around 6 am to 9 pm; the fare is Rs 4. If you're visiting the temples from Hassan, the last bus from the Halebid bus stand back to Hassan leaves at around 5.30 pm; from Belur, there are plenty of buses to Hassan, even late into the evening. There are a few buses a day from Halebid to Mysore and many buses from Belur to Mysore. If you're heading to Hampi, you'll need to catch a bus from Halebid to Shimoga (three hours) and pick up a bus to Hospet (five hours) from there.

While rail services to Hassan are disrupted,

KARNATAKA

Arsikere (40km north-east of Halebid) is the closest operational railhead. There are seven buses a day from Arsikere to Halebid and Belur (Rs 15, two hours). Arsikere has three passenger trains a day to Bangalore and a couple of inconveniently scheduled expresses. It also has an express connection to Miraj (for trains to Goa) and an express four times a week to Mumbai.

KSTDC offices in Bangalore and Mysore run tours which visit both Halebid and Belur. See the Organised Tours sections in those cities for details.

SRAVANABELAGOLA
Pop: 4000 Tel Area Code: 08176
This is one of the oldest and most important Jain pilgrimage centres in India, and the site of the huge 17m-high naked statue of Bahubali (Gomateshvara), said to be the world's tallest monolithic statue. It overlooks the sedate country town of Sravanabelagola from the top of the rocky hill known as Indragiri. Its simplicity and serenity is in complete contrast to the complexity and energy of the sculptural work at the temples of Belur and Halebid. The word Sravanabelagola means the Monk of the White Pond.

Although you can visit Sravanabelagola throughout the day, it's worth noting that to see any of the monuments you must climb the rocky steps up either of the two main hillsides. Since the steps lead to holy sites, visitors are required to leave their shoes at the bottom of the hill which can be a problem, as by midday the stone has become blisteringly hot. Either try to get here in the morning or evening, or bring a pair of socks to protect your feet.

History
Sravanabelagola has a long historical pedigree going back to the 3rd century BC when Chandragupta Maurya came here with his guru, Bhagwan Bhadrabahu Swami, after renouncing his kingdom. In the course of time Bhadrabahu's disciples spread his teachings all over the region, firmly establishing Jainism in the south. The religion

found powerful patrons in the Gangas who ruled the southern part of what is now Karnataka between the 4th and 10th centuries, and it was during this time that Jainism reached the zenith of its influence.

Information
The helpful tourist office is at the foot of the stairway climbing Indragiri Hill and is open daily except Sunday from 10 am to 5.30 pm. There's no entry fee to the site, but you are encouraged to make a donation.

Indragiri Hill
Starting from the bottom of the hill, where visitors are required to leave their shoes, pilgrims follow a series of some 500 steps, hewn into the rock face, which bring them to the main temple and the statue at the top of the hill. It's a short but steep climb; porters are available to help disabled visitors for around Rs 75 (return).

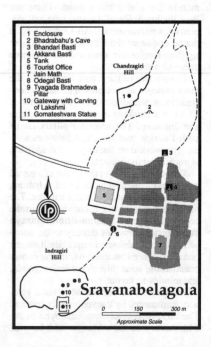

1 Enclosure
2 Bhadrabahu's Cave
3 Bhandari Basti
4 Akkana Basti
5 Tank
6 Tourist Office
7 Jain Math
8 Odegal Basti
9 Tyagada Brahmadeva Pillar
10 Gateway with Carving of Lakshmi
11 Gomateshvara Statue

Chandragiri Hill

Indragiri Hill

Sravanabelagola

0   150   300 m
Approximate Scale

After the first part of the climb (which covers about three-quarters of the distance to the top) an encircling wall is reached, and you pass through a gateway. Straight ahead as you come through the gate is the **Odegal Basti,** easily recognisable from the stone props which shore up the walls of the platform on which it stands. The building dates from the Hoysala period and has three shrines inside, each containing a beautifully carved image. The main shrine contains a statue of Sri Adinath, the first Jain *tirthankar* (master). To the left is Sri Shanthinatha, the 16th tirthankar, and to the right is Sri Neminatha, the 22nd tirthankar.

Continuing to the bottom of the next set of steps, you pass a small pavilion which houses the **Tyagada Brahmadeva Pillar.** The carving is very fine; a number of intricately depicted creepers are coiled around the pillar, and all four sides are covered with inscriptions. According to the inscription on the north face, the pillar was erected by Chamunda Raya, the same officer who was responsible for the huge Gomateshwara statue that crowns the hilltop.

The steps above the pavilion lead to a gateway with a fine carving on the lintel of Lakshmi flanked by two elephants. On either side of this gateway are small shrines with images of the two brothers Bahubali (Sri Gomateshvara) and Bharatha (Sri Bharatheshvara). Beyond this, the stairs pass through two more gates to enter the outer courtyard of the temple on the hilltop.

In front of the entrance to the inner enclosure is a two storey pavilion with, on the lower level, the statue of a woman facing towards the doorway of the enclosure. The story goes that when Chamunda Raya came to pay his respects by anointing the statue, he poured his generous offering onto the monolith, but it failed to cover the huge figure. A little old woman named Gullakayajji was present and gave him her humble pot of ghee, which promptly covered the statue from head to foot. The old woman was actually Padmavati in disguise, who came to teach Chamunda Raya to control his pride. The statue is of Gullakayajji.

The huge and famous **Gomateshvara Statue** stands in the middle of a high walled courtyard, the sides of which are inset with cells containing images of Jain saints. According to inscriptions, the immense carving was commissioned by an officer named Chamunda Raya, during the reign of the Ganga king, Rachamalla.

The statue is a depiction of Bahubali, the son of the Emperor Vrishabhadeva, who became the first Jain tirthankar, Adinath. When Vrishabhadeva died, Bahubali and his elder brother Bharatha competed fiercely for the right to succeed their father. Having beaten his brother in three successive contests and thereby won the title, Bahubali suddenly realised the futility of the struggle and renounced his kingdom. He withdrew from the material world and entered the forest, where he meditated in complete stillness until he attained enlightenment.

Bahubali's brother Bharatha erected an image in his honour, but the area around it soon became overgrown, and the statue was lost to sight. Chamunda Raya tried in vain to find the statue and, being unable to do so, decided to erect another image. He shot an arrow which landed on the boulder on the top of Indragiri Hill and he directed sculptors to carve the image from the boulder that stood there.

Although opinions vary slightly on the exact date on which the work was done, the best guess is that it was completed in around 981, and indeed celebrations to mark the millennium of the statue's existence were held in 1981.

The stance and facial expression of the image show the Gomateshvara completely at peace, with a serene smile on his face. The sense of the saint meditating in complete stillness is enhanced by the way in which the vines have grown around his legs and arms. There are anthills on either side of him, and he is equally unaware of the snakes that move around him. The statue's nudity marks the ultimate renunciation of worldly things.

Once every 12 years the statue of Bahubali is anointed with thousands of pots of coconut milk, yoghurt, ghee, bananas, jaggery, dates, almonds, poppy seeds, milk, saffron and sandalwood during the Mahamastakabhisheka Ceremony. This will next take place in the year 2005.

Chandragiri Hill

To the north of the village Chandragiri Hill rises 52.5m above the plain and is climbed via a set of steps cut into the rock. Almost all of the monuments stand within a walled enclosure.

As you enter the enclosure, immediately ahead is the impressive **Kuge-Brahmadeva Pillar**, believed to have been erected in about 974. To the west of this a simple shrine known as the **Santinatha Basti** houses a 3.3m-high standing figure of Santinatha, the 16th tirthankar. The statue is thought to date from the Hoysala period. Just north of this shrine is an odd, rough carving of Sri Bharatheshvara, the brother of Bahubali. The statue is incomplete and has no lower legs.

To the north of the Kuge-Brahmadeva Pillar is the **Parsvanatha Basti,** which is fronted by an enormous lamp tower. The basti houses the largest statue on Chandragiri – an elegant 4.5m-high image of Parsvanatha, the 23rd tirthankar. Unfortunately, like several other buildings in the enclosure, it is also home to colonies of both rats and bats, so it's not a place to linger.

North of the Parsvanatha Basti, on the edge of the enclosure, is the **Chamunda Raya Basti,** which many claim is the finest of the temples on the hill. According to inscriptions within the temple, the main part of the building was erected around 982. The upper storey, from which you get a good view across to the main hill, was added by Chamunda Raya's son in about 995. There are many other shrines within the enclosure.

Just to the east of the enclosure is a small cave which has had a porch built on to it. The cave interior is bare and cramped, with only a pair of carved footprints on the floor. This, according to tradition, is where the sage Bhagwan Bhadrabahu Swami came to pass his last moments. His disciple, the Emperor Chandragupta, remained here worshipping the footprints until he too died, by the Jain ritual of starvation.

Other Temples

In addition to the temples on the two hills, there are several interesting structures in the village itself. The largest of these is the **Bhandari Basti**, which was erected in 1159 under the orders of the *bhandari* or treasurer of the Hoysala king Narasimha I. The shrine contains images of all 24 of the Jain tirthankars. The **Akkana Basti** was erected in 1181 and is another good example of the Hoysala style. The central feature of the village, however, is the enormous **tank** which is surrounded by a wall. The tank is said to have been completed during the reign of Krishnaraja Wodeyar (1713-31).

Places to Stay & Eat

Nearly all of Sravanabelagola's accommodation is run by the local Jain organisation SDJMI, which has a central accommodation office (☎ 57258) that handles bookings for 21 guesthouses in town. Most of these guesthouses are efficiently run and indistinguishable. They generally cost Rs 50 for a double, though the pick of the bunch, *Yatri Nivas*, costs Rs 100. The accommodation office is just before the bus stand, on the way into town. It's on the right-hand side, set back 50m from the road.

The friendly *Hotel Raghu* (☎ 57238), 50m from the bottom of the stairway climbing Indragiri Hill, is the only privately owned establishment. Basic but decent singles/doubles/triples with attached bath cost Rs 50/75/100. It also has a popular veg restaurant.

There is a very basic *refreshment canteen* in the bus stand, and *chai shops* and *vegetarian restaurants* in the street leading to the foot of Indragiri Hill.

Getting There & Away

There are four buses a day to Hassan (Rs 11, one hour); three buses to Belur (Rs 18, 2½ hours); three buses to Bangalore (Rs 28, three hours); and one to Mysore (Rs 17, 2½ hours) at 7.30 am. Nearly all long-distance buses leave in the morning or at lunchtime; there's very little transport after 2 pm. If you're having trouble making transport connections, catch a local bus 10km north-west to Channarayapatna, which is on the main Bangalore-Mangalore road.

The KSTDC operates tours from Mysore and Bangalore to Sravanabelagola; see the Organised Tours sections in those cities for details.

HASSAN
Pop: 121,000 Tel Area Code: 08172
Traditionally Hassan has been the most convenient base from which to explore Belur, Halebid and Sravanabelagola, since it's the nearest railhead to all three sights. However, at the time of writing, virtually all rail services to Hassan had ceased while the Mysore and Mangalore lines were converted from metre to broad gauge. The line to Hubli via Shimoga is expected to reopen in late 1998, and the line from Hassan to Mangalore looks as though it will take considerably longer to convert.

There are ample bus connections to compensate, so you'll still almost certainly pass through here. Whether you decide to stay is another matter, since there's now a fine KSTDC hotel at Belur and ample accommodation at Sravanabelagola. Hassan does have several good budget hotels, though, and the region's only upmarket establishment.

Information
The tourist office (☎ 68862) is open from 10 am to 5.30 pm. For foreign exchange, go to the State Bank of Mysore.

Places to Stay
Vaishnavi Lodging (☎ 67413), a one minute walk from the bus stand, is excellent value at Rs 100/140 for clean singles/doubles with attached bath.

Hotel Lakshmi Prasanna (☎ 68391), in the centre of town, has good rooms with attached bath and bucket shower for Rs 80/210.

Hotel Palika (☎ 66307, Racecourse Rd) has been undergoing renovation and should have reopened by the time this book appears. Comfortable economy rooms with attached bath formerly cost from Rs 205/275, but the management strangely claim that after the refurbishment is finished they'll be charging less than this!

Hotel Hassan Ashok (☎ 68731, fax 68324) on the Bangalore-Mangalore road is the best hotel in town and is popular with tour groups. Including tax, rooms with attached bath and TV cost Rs 1005/1250, or Rs 1195/1300 with air-con. It has a restaurant and a comfortable bar.

The one *Retiring Room* at the train station costs Rs 25; a bed in the six-bed dorm costs Rs 15.

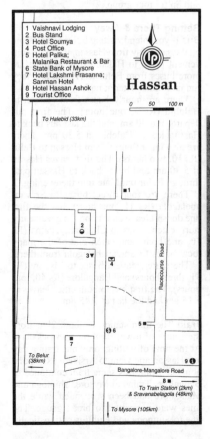

1 Vaishnavi Lodging
2 Bus Stand
3 Hotel Soumya
4 Post Office
5 Hotel Palika;
   Malanika Restaurant & Bar
6 State Bank of Mysore
7 Hotel Lakshmi Prasanna;
   Sanman Hotel
8 Hotel Hassan Ashok
9 Tourist Office

Hassan

0   50   100 m

To Halebid (33km)

Racecourse Road

To Belur (38km)

To Mysore (105km)

Bangalore-Mangalore Road

To Train Station (2km) & Sravanabelagola (48km)

KARNATAKA

Places to Eat
Sanman Hotel and *Lakshmi Prasanna* have popular veg restaurants with thalis for Rs 12.

Hotel Soumya has two separate sections. The North Indian part is a bit dingy, but is reasonably priced and the food is good.

Malanika Restaurant & Bar, in the Hotel Palika, should be a good bet once the hotel reopens after renovations. Formerly it served decent veg/nonveg fare for around Rs 40.

Hotel Hassan Ashok offers Indian and continental cuisine, though its à la carte menu (Rs 100 to Rs 125 for main courses) tends to be replaced by buffets (from Rs 175) laid on for tour groups.

Getting There & Away
Bus If you intend visiting Belur and Halebid on the same day from Hassan, it's more convenient to go to Halebid first, as there are more buses from Belur to Hassan and they run until much later at night.

There are hourly buses from Hassan to Halebid (Rs 7, one hour). The first bus departs at 6.30 am, and the last bus back to Hassan leaves Halebid at 5.30 pm. There are also lots of buses from Hassan to Belur (Rs 10, two hours). The first leaves Hassan at 5.30 am and buses back to Hassan pass through Belur until late into the evening.

There are four direct buses to Sravanabelagola (Rs 11, one hour), but the first one doesn't leave until noon. To get an early start, catch a bus to Channarayapatna (Rs 10, one hour) and catch one of the many local buses to Sravanabelagola from there.

There are frequent buses to Mysore (Rs 31, three hours) and Bangalore (Rs 40, four hours). The first bus to both cities leaves at 5.15 am and the last at 7.45 pm.

Train The train station is about 2km from the centre of town; Rs 8 by auto-rickshaw. At the time of writing, only one train a day left Hassan and went to Arsikere (Rs 9, one hour) at 3 pm; this same train continued to Bangalore. Trains to Mysore, Shimoga and Mangalore had been suspended while the lines were converted to broad gauge. The line to Shimoga and Hubli is optimistically

scheduled to reopen in mid-1998, and the Mysore line is supposed to be completed soon, too. It is thought that the Mangalore line will take much longer – at least a couple of years. Note that the route to Mangalore is prone to landslides during the monsoon months from June to September.

Kodagu (Coorg)

Kodagu (which means something like Dense Hilly Country) is more commonly known by its former name, Coorg. Kodagu is the smallest district (4104 sq km) in Karnataka, and one of the smallest in India. It is a delightful area in the middle of the Western Ghats, with rolling hills, forests, coffee plantations and hiking opportunities. The people, known as Kodavas, have a unique culture (see the boxed text 'The People of Kodagu' in this section).

According to brochures, Kodagu is famous for three things: excellent coffee, beautiful women and high-ranking military personnel. But if these things don't appeal, the fresh air, national parks, temples, mountains and friendly people probably will. Kodagu is the nicest and coolest place to break up a journey between Mysore or Bangalore and the coast – but don't be put off by the lacklustre capital, Madikeri.

The best time to come is winter: ie October to February. Summer (March to May) is bearable because the elevation and forests makes it cool, but try to avoid the period of very heavy rainfall between June and September.

HISTORY
The region of Kodagu, which was once bigger than it is now, featured in ancient literature as the home of the revered Cauvery (Kaveri) River. Its fiercely independent Kodava people were never completely subjugated by any empire, but the area was occupied in parts by the Gangas, Cholas, Hoysalas and Nayakas. The region was then ruled by the Haleri dynasty of Kodagu from 1592, and by Tipu Sultan during the late

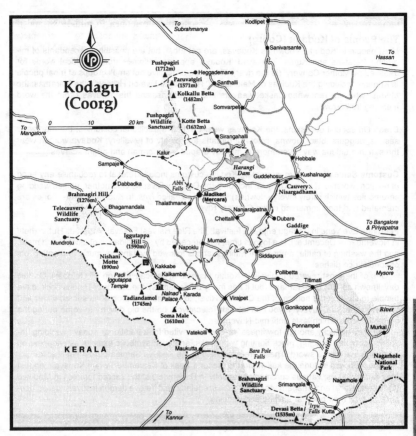

18th century. The British annexed the region in 1834. Even then, the colonialists never enjoyed absolute control, but they did leave one important legacy: coffee.

In 1947, when India gained independence from Britain, Coorg was a separate state. But in 1956 Kodagu, as it became known, was integrated into Karnataka, much to the anger of many Kodavas.

FLORA & FAUNA

Thirty per cent of Kodagu is covered with evergreen and semi-evergreen forests. It is home to over 50 species of trees, and dozens of ferns and orchids, but the plants you are most likely to see and smell are coffee, pepper, cardamom and ginger. The aroma of coffee during the time of blossoms (April) and picking (December-January) will make most coffee lovers swoon. One unappealing tree, known colloquially as the poison nut tree *Strychnos nux vomica*, produces strychnine.

The herds of wild elephants which used to roam around Kodagu are mostly confined to the Nagarhole National Park, but suffer because natural corridors between protected

The People of Kodagu (Coorg)

Most people in Kodagu, known as Kodavas, are not tribal, but are possibly descendants of migrating Persians and Kurds. The word 'Kodava' apparently comes from the local words for 'Blessed by Mother Cauvery' (ie the river). There are distinctive but small groups of tribal people in Kodagu, including the Kudiyas or Malaikudis ('Those Who Live on Hilltops'); the Marathas; the Medas, who are renowned basket-weavers and musicians; and the Yeravas (from the word meaning 'to borrow').

Dress On special occasions, the Kodavas wear distinctive traditional costumes: the men wear sashes, daggers, black gowns, colourful turbans and plenty of jewellery; Kodava women wear the sari in a unique way (even more complexly draped than normal) and bright scarves.

Customs Some of the more interesting Kodava customs include refusal to recognise any head of religion; worship of unique deities, including the Cauvery River as Godmother; unique wedding ceremonies (which rarely involve dowries); and homes called *lyns*. In Kudiya funerals, bones are cremated and then immersed in the Cauvery River.

Festivals Everyone in Kodagu enjoys a festival. The Rice Harvest Festival, known as Huthri (held in November or December), is a joyous time. It is preceded by an avoidance of alcohol and meat, and the washing of cattle, among other things; and is followed by dancing, music and eating lots of special rice dishes.

One of the most revered festivals in Kodagu is held at Telecauvery (on 17 October). On this day, known as Tula Sankramana (but it has many other names), thousands of Hindus flock to the temple to swim at the source of the Cauvery River, to take home a drop of its sacred water and to pray to the Sri Cauvery. If you cannot visit Telecauvery on the big day, try to come during the month of Jatra, which lasts until mid-November.

You may be lucky enough to witness, or even be invited to, a traditional Kodava wedding, involving complex dancing, mock fighting with sticks, and such symbolic exploits as chopping off a banana leaf with a sword. These are often held at the Kodava Samaja building in Madikeri.

Other festivals include the *kail muhurtha* (second week of September) when Kodava men test their archery skills; various ceremonies (usually in December) at the sacred temples in Madikeri (Omkareshwara) and Bhagamandala; and the irregularly held Yerava demon festivals, called *pandalatas*, with their peculiar singing and dancing.

areas are threatened (see the boxed text 'Elephant Conservation in the Facts about South India chapter). Kodagu is home to plenty of squirrels, langur and macaques, as well as the rare slender loris. It also has over 100 species of birds including golden eagles, kites, green bee-eaters, and purple honeysuckers which enjoy the products from a multitude of hives; and the silent, grey and ominously named goat sucker.

The enormous mahseer fish (which can weigh up to 40kg), Karnataka carp and murral apparently jump out of the Cauvery in front of your eyes – or at least used to, before the advent of dynamite fishing and industrialisation along the river.

Anyone with an interest in the local environment should contact the Coorg Wildlife Society (no telephone) in Madikeri. The helpful staff can provide information about local wildlife, but nothing much about trekking and other outdoor activities. It is only open from 10 am to 1 pm on weekdays.

BOOKS & NEWSPAPERS

The four page, English-language dailies, the

The Kodagu State Freedom Movement

Many inhabitants are still angry that Kodagu was incorporated into Karnataka in 1956 without a referendum. They believe that because Kodagu is the richest (and highest tax-paying) district in the state, but has not been developed to the extent it deserves, and that the people have a unique language, culture and heritage, the district should become a separate state, like Goa. The Kodagu Rajya Mukthi Morcha (KRMM), or Kodagu State Freedom Movement, has recently gained momentum: it is a well-organised, popular and seemingly well-funded movement, but its slogan – 'Struggle Until Victory' – is being blatantly ignored by an unsympathetic Karnataka government.

At the time of research, protest activities organised by the KRMM included the typically Indian *bundh* (a district-wide 12 hour strike by all workers, whether sympathetic or not to the cause), and public rallies. A short time later, there was some small-scale rioting in Virajpet, death threats against newspaper editors, and a refusal by sympathisers to pay state taxes. Original KRMM members are seriously concerned that the movement, and the independence cause generally, has been overrun by rogue elements, bent on a more violent approach. We can only fervently hope that the situation does not deteriorate as it has in the north-eastern states of Assam and Nagaland.

Kodagu Front ('The Newspaper with a Difference') and the *Coffeeland News* ('The First English Daily of Kodagu'), compete for limited readership, but these are your main source about what is going on. Both are surprisingly hard to find; try the newsagents at the public and private bus stands.

If you are interested in local history and culture, pick up the *Gazetteer of Coorg* (Rs 150) by G Richter, a colonial account first published in 1870 and available from the Coorg Wildlife Society in Madikeri, or *A Study of the Origins of Coorgs* (Rs 300), by KC Ponnappa, available at Komal Stores, opposite the fort.

ACTIVITIES

Fishing The stretch of the Cauvery River between Siddapura and Guddehosur is a protected area, and managed by the Coorg Wildlife Society. With a licence and equipment from the Society, you can fish for (but you must return to the river) mural, mully or gigantic mahseer. The best season for fishing is March to April.

Walks Refer to Walking in Kodagu later in this section for details.

Water Sports Harangi Dam will be developed in the future for water sports, such as kayaking. If you're game, you can raft down stretches of the Cauvery (best during the monsoon season). For more information, check the adventure agencies listed in the Walking in Kodagu section, especially the Coorg Adventure Club.

MADIKERI (MERCARA)
Pop: about 35,000 Tel Area Code: 08272

The elevated market town of Madikeri, also known by its former name of Mercara, is the capital of Kodagu. It is not a particularly pretty town, but it's a lot nicer than other so-called 'hill stations', such as Ooty in the Nilgiris. Madikeri is the perfect place to base yourself while you enjoy the rest of Kodagu.

Orientation

Madikeri is spread out along a series of ridges, but the two bus stands and most of the hotels and restaurants are within walking distance of each other, and not far from the main road through town, General Thimmaiah Rd. The best map of Kodagu is available from the Coorg Wildlife Society for the 'foreigners' price of Rs 100.

Information

Tourist Offices The small tourist office (☎ 2850) is full of empty desks and staff

KARNATAKA

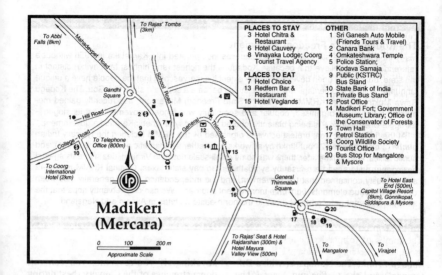

Madikeri (Mercara)

PLACES TO STAY	OTHER
3 Hotel Chitra & Restaurant	1 Sri Ganesh Auto Mobile (Friends Tours & Travel)
6 Hotel Cauvery	2 Canara Bank
8 Vinayaka Lodge; Coorg Tourist Travel Agency	4 Omkateshwara Temple
	5 Police Station; Kodava Samaja
PLACES TO EAT	9 Public (KSTRC) Bus Stand
7 Hotel Choice	10 State Bank of India
13 Redfern Bar & Restaurant	11 Private Bus Stand
15 Hotel Veglands	12 Post Office
	14 Madikeri Fort; Government Museum; Library; Office of the Conservator of Forests
	16 Town Hall
	17 Petrol Station
	18 Coorg Wildlife Society
	19 Tourist Office
	20 Bus Stop for Mangalore & Mysore

who wish they were somewhere else. It can provide nothing more than a basic brochure or two. Open from 10 am to 1.30 pm and 2.15 to 5.30 pm, every day but Sunday, it is located on the ground floor of the badly signed, three storey PWD Building. The Walking in Kodagu section lists better travel and trekking agencies.

Forest Departments There is a confusing array of departments which are somehow linked with the word 'forest'. Ignore the Deputy Conservator of Forests (☎ 28019), next to the Hotel Mayura Valley View, unless you want to book certain bungalows (which are mentioned later). The Office of the Conservator of Forests (☎ 25708), upstairs in the Deputy Commissioner's Building in the Madikeri Fort, is helpful, knowledgeable and allows foreigners to stay in some of its bungalows.

Money The Canara Bank will change cash and travellers cheques – but take a good book, as service is a little slow. It was unclear at the time of research if the State Bank of India will change money.

Post & Communications The post office is on a bend along General Thimmaiah Rd. The new telephone office south of the State Bank of India is inconvenient so use one of the many private telephone stalls around town.

Rajas' Seat

Built for the enjoyment of former kings, the views from the small garden known as Rajas' Seat are magnificent, especially at daybreak or dusk – but only when the clouds disappear. It's an inspiring place to walk to from the town centre, before enjoying breakfast or dinner at the nearby Hotel Mayura Valley View (see Places to Stay).

Next door you can take a ride on the *Baba Saheb Express* **miniature train**, which chugs around two small loops for about five minutes. It costs Rs 3 per person (minimum of 10), or if you want to feel like a real sahib you can charter the whole train for Rs 30.

Abbi Falls

Abbi Falls (Abbi actually means 'falls') is a pretty place, about 8km from the town centre. You can combine it with a visit to the Rajas' Tombs, and hike most or all of the way from the tombs – look for the signs to 'Abbi Fals' or 'Tourisum Place' – or from the centre of Madikeri (see the Walking in Kodagu section).

Auto-rickshaw drivers are getting savvy and overcharging tourists: try not to pay more than Rs 100 return, including 30 minutes waiting time at the falls, and 15 minutes at the tombs.

The best time is during or just after the monsoons (June to September), and certainly before it dries up in summer. The falls are located in a private coffee estate, and entrance is (surprisingly) free. Try to get there early or late, otherwise busloads of tourists will shatter the serenity, and avoid Sunday, when it is bumper-to-bumper with picnickers.

Rajas' Tombs

The tombs of former Kodava kings, Veeraraja, Lingarejendra, Biddanda Bopu and his son, Biddanda Somaiah, are located in the northern suburbs. The tombs are permanently locked, so find the caretaker, who lives in a house at the back; he will naturally want a small tip for opening them. Though the inside of the tombs are empty and uninteresting, the views from the top are wonderful. Entrance is free, and the site is unfenced and permanently open. It is a gentle 3km stroll from Gandhi Square, or take an auto-rickshaw.

Madikeri Fort

Certainly a disappointment compared with the fort in Mysore, this small stone building was the former palace of the Kodava kings. Built in 1812, it now houses local government offices, such as the Office of the Conservator of Forests; a musty **library**; and St Mark's Church, which is now the **Government Museum**, with a very modest and unusual collection which includes British weapons, a boomerang and a stuffed leopard. The museum is open from 9 am to 5 pm, every day except Monday and alternate Saturdays, and entrance is free. The views from the top of the fort are worth the walk.

Omkateshwara Temple

This small Hindu temple, built in 1820 by the former king, Lingarejendra, is an interesting blend of Keralan, Gothic and, strangely enough, Islamic architectural styles: it has a dome in the middle of a square lake and a minaret at each corner. It is easy to reach on foot from the town centre, and is open daily (daytime only).

Places to Stay

Refer to the rest of the Kodagu and Walking in Kodagu sections below for other worthy accommodation options in hotels, coffee plantations and national parks. Ask the Coorg Tourist Travel Agency (see the Walking in Kodagu section) about coffee plantations which have recently opened rooms to tourists.

Vinayaka Lodge (☎ 29830) is the best value in the budget range, though it's a little noisy because of its proximity to the bus stands. Simple, clean singles/doubles cost Rs 100/215.

Hotel Cauvery (☎ 25492) is good value for single travellers, though the single rooms (Rs 150) have no fan. Doubles, with a fan, cost Rs 250, but there is no TV. This place is clean, friendly and not too noisy, despite its central location.

Hotel East End (☎ 26496) is about the same price and standard as the Cauvery, but it's inconveniently located, and on a noisy road.

Hotel Chitra (☎ 25191) is the best place in town. Large, airy twin/triple rooms (with hot water only available in the morning) cost Rs 220/275 – plus another Rs 50 for a TV. The generator offsets regular power cuts in the town.

Hotel Mayura Valley View (☎ 27301) has the best views, but this state-run (KSTDC) place has been sadly neglected for years. The tariff of Rs 322/430 for a single/double, plus Rs 50 for a TV, is negotiable when they're not busy. However, before handing over any money, make sure the fan, TV and hot water work – all three may not function at all. The restaurant is excellent, however.

Hotel Rajdarshan (☎ 29142), opposite the Rajas' Seat, and the three-star *Coorg International Hotel* (☎ 28071), are the top places. The former is overpriced at Rs 400/500 for singles/doubles but is modern and clean; the latter, 2km from town, costs from Rs 1412/1477, including horrendous taxes and charges.

Capitol Village Resort (☎ 26929) is a charming place, beautifully located among paddy fields and coffee, cardamom and pepper plantations. Modern semidetached cottages cost Rs 500/650 for a double/triple; meals are an extra Rs 50. Hiking can be arranged to nearby hills, plantations and waterfalls. It is owned by the manager of the Hotel Cauvery, so you can also book there. It is about 8km from Madikeri, on the road between Chettali and Siddapura, and accessible by hourly buses from Madikeri, or by auto-rickshaw.

Places to Eat

There isn't a great choice, but you won't go hungry. The cheapest vegetarian restaurants can be found along the start of College Rd, not far from Gandhi Square.

Hotel Veglands is the best, and most popular, vegetarian restaurant in town. In fact, if you go at normal lunch or dinner times, you may have trouble finding a seat. Tasty meals cost from Rs 15.

Hotel Choice is one of our favourites. The menu is extensive, the service is friendly and the meals are cheap – from Rs 15 to Rs 30. It is one of the few places open early for a western breakfast.

Hotel Mayura Valley View has a bar and restaurant on the ground floor. It has great service and views; it's the perfect place to finish off a stiff walk from the town centre, via the Rajas' Seat down the road. Meals are a little pricey, from Rs 40 to Rs 60, but worth a splurge. It is also open early for a western breakfast.

Hotel Chitra has a bar and restaurant on the ground floor too. It is also a little pricey, but the servings of Indian (about Rs 40) and Chinese (about Rs 50) meals are big and tasty. Large, cold Kingfisher beers are Rs 45.

Redfern Bar & Restaurant is one of the few independent restaurants in town. It serves Indian and Chinese food and cold beers in a pleasant setting but prices are a little high.

Market Days in Kodagu

One way to meet the real Kodavas, and other tribal people, is on market days. Before making a long trip to the countryside, however, it is worth double-checking the market days with some locals.

Day	Location
Monday	Napoklu
Wednesday	Virajpet
Thursday	Murnad
Friday	Madikeri
Saturday	Sanivarsante
	(Sanivarsante means
	'Saturday Market')
Sunday	Gonikoppal

Getting There & Away

Madikeri is well connected to most places in this part of India, though there is no train service. The hopelessly chaotic private bus stand has services to just about everywhere within Kodagu, except Kushalnagar (for which you catch the Bangalore bus). The individual sections below list details of costs and times.

The public bus stand handles state-run (KSRTC) buses to anywhere outside Kodagu, and advanced bookings are possible for overnight services. To Bangalore, buses leave every 30 minutes in the morning and afternoon, and every hour in the evening, for Rs 83/99 for semideluxe/superdeluxe; to Mysore (Rs 38/46), every 20 to 30 minutes; to Mangalore (Rs 44/53), every 30 minutes; to Hassan (Rs 30 for express service only), every 90 minutes; to Chikmagalur (Rs 48), one bus leaves at 7 am or get a connection at Hassan; and to Shimoga (Rs 68), three express buses leave every day (currently: 6.30 am, 2 and 7.30 pm). For Mangalore and Mysore you can also jump on buses passing by General Thimmaiah Square.

Getting Around

Madikeri is easy enough to walk around, though some roads are steep. There are plenty of unmetered rickshaws, which cost about Rs 15 for a short trip.

BHAGAMANDALA & TELECAUVERY

Bhagamandala is located at the convergence of three revered rivers, the Cauvery, Sujyothi (which is underground) and Kanike. The Hindu **Sri Bhagandeshwara Temple** at Bhagamandala, like the Omkareshwara Temple in Madikeri, has a Keralan influence. It is a serene place, with a copper-plated roof, and intricate carvings. A dip in the bath at Trevni Sangama nearby is meant to revive the spirits of all jaded travellers – but ask at the temple first.

Telecauvery (meaning Head of Cauvery) is also very significant to Hindus. It is the start of the mighty Cauvery River (one of the seven sacred rivers in India) which flows through Karnataka and Tamil Nadu. Telecauvery is the site of a majestic festival (see the 'People of Kodagu' boxed text earlier in this section), held at the two **temples** dedicated to Shiva and Ganesh.

Steps (300 in total) lead to the top of Brahmagiri Hill (1276m), for breathtaking views of just about everywhere in Kodagu. Telecauvery is located inside the Telecauvery Wildlife Sanctuary. Though the sanctuary is not open to the public you are allowed access to the temples at Brahmagiri Hill.

Places to Stay

Hotel Threvani, on the main street in Bhagamandala, is very basic; the *Lucky Star Hotel* in 'upper' Bhagamandala is better. The Deputy Conservator of Forests, next to the Hotel Mayura Valley View in Madikeri, has a tiny *bungalow* at Telecauvery, about 200m down from the temples; and the PWD in Madikeri (☎ 26301) has a *bungalow* at Bhagamandala. Both are reluctant to cater for foreigners – but you may have some luck.

Getting There & Away

Buses leave Madikeri about every hour (Rs 15, 90 minutes) for the very scenic ride to Bhagamandala. These buses may or may not continue on to Telecauvery, but between Bhagamandala and Telecauvery (Rs 6, 40 minutes), buses leave every 30 to 40 minutes.

Telecauvery is 8km up a steep road from Bhagamandala, but it's an easy walk down. Refer to Walking in Kodagu later in this section about this and other hikes in the area.

KUSHALNAGAR

A few kilometres beyond Bylakuppe, on the main road, is Kushalnagar, a small market town which lies about 90km west of Mysore. Since the opening up of guesthouses at Bylakuppe itself, there's no particular reason to visit Kushalnagar, except that getting a bus onward from the area is easier from the bus stand here. There are plenty of buses from Kushalnagar to Mysore, Bangalore and Mangalore via Puttur. If you arrive in Kushalnagar you can easily get a rickshaw the short distance to Bylakuppe.

Should you decide to stay in Kushalnagar rather than the settlements themselves, there are several places available.

Safalya Lodge (☎ 08276-74615), on the main road 1km east of the bus stand, has plain rooms with attached bath for Rs 120/150. *Kodagu Plaza* (☎ 08276-73052), on the same road 250m west of the bus stand, has huge modern doubles with attached bath for Rs 275. Across the road from the bus stand is the *Kannika International* (☎ 08276-74728), the plushest place in town with doubles from Rs 225 upwards.

CAUVERY NISARGADHAMA

One glorious place for fresh air, tranquillity and short walks is this park, on an island (2.5 sq km) in the middle of the Cauvery River. It's sometimes overrun by screaming school-kids, and less boisterous monks from the nearby Bylakuppe Tibetan settlement camp on the weekends, but the island is serene most of the time. You can easily combine it with a visit to Harangi Dam and/or Dubare.

Visiting the Park

The park is open every day from 9.30 am to 5 pm, but you can stay there overnight (see Places to Stay & Eat). Tickets, which cost Rs 2, are available from the reception centre (☎ 08276-74454) at the two bridges. The 3.8km path around the island (indicated on a map inside the park) passes an uninteresting deer park and a motley orchidarium, and there is no wildlife to admire, but the views of the forests and river are the highlight. Elephant and boat rides are possible from mid-December to mid-June.

Places to Stay & Eat
The Office of the Conservator of Forests in Madikeri has *cottages*, with four single beds, or charming *wooden houses*, with double beds, on stilts above (and almost leaning into) the river. They cost Rs 400, and Rs 200 respectively. Arrange meals (Rs 40) at the canteen by the bridges.

If you can't get a room on the island, you can stay at the nearby town of Kushalnagar, about 2km away. *Mahalaxmi Lodge*, at the back of the bus stand, has quiet doubles for a reasonable Rs 120. *Sri Radhakrishna Lodge (☎ 74822)* is the tall, pink and green place near the entrance to the bus stand. Singles/doubles are a bargain Rs 65/90.

Getting There & Away
Catch any of the hourly Madikeri-Bangalore buses to Kushalnagar (Rs 12, 50 minutes) from the public bus stand, and then take an auto-rickshaw to the park. Alternatively, get off at the park entrance, about 3km before you reach Kushalnagar – look for the wooden arch on the right as you come from Madikeri. From the main road a short path leads to the ticket office and the two hanging bridges leading to the island.

HARANGI DAM
This surprisingly large and impressive dam, not far from Kushalnagar, is worth a look around. It is an ideal place for a picnic, and there are some short walks along designated paths – but get permission from the PWD office near the entrance to the dam before venturing any further. Sadly, the magnificently located *bungalow* run by the PWD is not currently open to the public. Harangi Dam will be developed for water sports in the future (see the Kodagu Activities section).

There are irregular buses to the dam from Kushalnagar, but the easiest way is to take an auto-rickshaw from Kushalnagar (about

9km) or from Guddehosur (6.5km). Both roads are great for a short hike (refer to the Walking in Kodagu section).

DUBARE
The village of Dubare, about 15km south of Kushalnagar along the Cauvery, is home to an elephant camp. While you can get a close look at the elephants and learn about their domestication, most will find their captivity and treatment distressing. The best time to see the mighty beasts being washed, and going to/coming from the forests, is between 6 and 7 am, and 4 to 6 pm. While Dubare is not set up as a tourist attraction as such, visitors are welcome.

The Forest Department (next to the Hotel Mayura Valley View in Madikeri) has a musty *bungalow*, built about 100 years ago, on the banks of the river. An auto-rickshaw from Kushalnagar will cost about Rs 100 return, including one hour or so waiting time at Dubare. Alternatively, catch a bus from Kushalnagar or Siddapura to Nanjarajpatna, walk 1.5km to the river, and then take a short boat ride (Rs 5) to Dubare.

KAKKABE
Under the mighty Tadiandamol peak (refer to the Walking in Kodagu section for details), and near Kakkabe, are two places worth visiting. The **Nalnad Palace**, built in 1791 as a hunting lodge, is now used for horticultural purposes and as a children's camp site, but tourists are welcome to look around.

The **Padi Iggutappa Temple** is probably the most important temple in Kodagu. If you visit with a local guide or friend, you will feel more comfortable, and be able to enjoy a lunch (free, but a donation is requested) with devotees. It is about 2km north of Kakkabe, just off the main road; or a 6km hike from the Palace Estate (see Places to Stay). If you ask around you may be able to visit a **honey farm**: Kakkabe has some of the largest farms in Asia.

Places to Stay
Palace Estate (☎ 08272-38346) is the only place to stay, and one of the nicest in Kodagu.

It is a home on a coffee plantation, in the majestic foothills, and only 200m up from the Nalnad Palace. Charming rooms, with buckets of hot water on request, cost Rs 150/250 for singles/doubles. Excellent traditional meals cost Rs 30 to Rs 80 each; guides cost Rs 125 per day. This place is bound to become popular, so bookings are essential, either directly, or at the Coorg Tourist Travel Agency in Madikeri (see the Walking in Kodagu section).

Getting There & Away
From Madikeri, there is at least one direct bus every day to Kakkabe (Rs 15, 90 minutes) – it currently leaves at 6 am, thereby allowing a day trip. It is far easier to get a connection at Napoklu. From Kakkabe, save your legs and charter a jeep (Rs 75 one way) up to the Palace Estate or Nalnad Palace. The three to 4km walk down from the palace to the junction at Kaikamba is very pleasant, and a lot easier than the uphill climb.

IRPU FALLS
In the remote stretches of southern Kodagu, the 60m Irpu Falls is in another marvellous area for hiking (see the Walking in Kodagu section). According to a legend, the **Shri Rameshwarna Temple** on the Lakshman-thirtha River, and accessible by a vehicular road, was dedicated to Lord Shiva by Sri Rama. Before entering the temple you must take off your shoes.

A trail (800m) to Irpu Falls starts from behind the temple. You can swim in a pond halfway up the falls, though the water is *very* refreshing. If you have the energy, and don't mind the odd leech or two, you can hike further up the trail to the very top of the falls.

Places to Stay
Chilligeri Estate (☎ 08274-44265) is the only place to stay in the area, and is one of the handful of coffee plantations likely to open up for tourists in the future. The setting is very pleasant, but the price of Rs 250 a double is a little high. The friendly family owners speak little English, so before you hire any guides or vehicles make sure you fully understand what you're getting for the price. The estate is 5km from Irpu Falls and 10km from Nagarhole National Park. Book directly, or at Coorg Tourist Travel Agency (see the Walking in Kodagu section).

Getting There & Away
A direct bus travels every two to three hours between Madikeri and Kutta, but it's better and quicker to get a connection in Gonikoppal. From Kutta, you can hire a jeep to the falls or estate. Otherwise, look for the sign 'Irpu Shri Rameshwarna Temple' on the Gonikoppal-Kutta road; it is then a pleasant 3km walk to the temple.

NAGARHOLE NATIONAL PARK
Also known as the Rajiv Gandhi National Park, the serene Nagarhole National Park (643 sq km) was created in 1955. Once part of the maharajas' private hunting grounds, Nagarhole is pleasantly cool most of the year. It is not easy to reach, however, and not, thankfully, developed (so far), so it's

The Tribal People of Nagarhole vs Taj Hotels
Nagarhole is home to 33,000 Jenu Kurumbas as well as other tribal people or *adivasis*. The Taj Group of Hotels hoped to build the Gateway Tusker Lodge at Murkal, but with some assistance from local and foreign NGOs, the adivasis mounted a legal battle against the hotel chain and the Karnataka government. This was one of the very, very few environmental cases to go to court and, even more incredibly, to win.

Problems began with a lack of sympathy, and occasional violence, on the part of the forest department towards the adivasis. Building large resorts in a national park has significant detrimental effects on delicate park ecology, and the Gateway Tusker Lodge would have displaced adivasis, exiling them from their source of income, food and medicines, as well as their grave sites and temples.

KARNATAKA

far quieter than other parks. Nagarhole is a great place to relax for a few days, especially if you don't mind if you don't see a lot of wildlife.

Some of the forest was destroyed by fire in 1992 when tensions between officials involved in anti-poaching activities and local graziers and farmers erupted in a frenzy of arson. The damage is now hard to see, and won't affect your visit in any way. However, many tribal people, such as the Jena Kurumbas who still live in *hadis* (villages) inside the park, aren't happy about potential development

Flora & Fauna
Nagarhole's lushness is greatly appreciated by the wildlife: there is plenty of mixed deciduous forest, including teak and rosewood; and rivers, (such as the Kabini), creeks, dams and swamps. About 15% of the park is covered with coffee plantations.

The park hosts 55 to 60 tigers, leopards and wild elephants (1000 to 1200), but you are far more likely to see gaur, four-horned deer and barking deer, wild dogs, bonnet macaques and common langur. You may also spot the rare slender loris. Of the 250 varieties of birds, you may see and hear common babblers, crested hawks and great Indian warblers. Though Nagarhole means Snake River in the Kannada language, there aren't too many slitherers among the undergrowth.

Hiking
Hiking inside the park is strictly forbidden. You can walk to (or from) the western entrance from Kutta, but not within the park.

Visiting the Park
The reception centre (☎ 08274-44221), in the village of Nagarhole, is open 24 hours. The Rs 150 entrance fee for foreigners includes a bus tour – cameras cost another Rs 10. Visitors can only travel around the park on the unsatisfactory official bus tour (minimum of two people), between 6 and 8 am, and 3 and 5.30 pm; a little later in summer. If staying at the resorts (see Places to Stay & Eat), you will have better options. There are no elephant rides; and private ve-

hicles are not allowed into the park between 6 pm and 6 am.

The best time to see wildlife is during late summer (April-May), when the animals struggle to find adequate water and venture to accessible rivers and salt licks – but the park will close if there any bushfires at this time. The most comfortable time to visit is in winter (November-February). Avoid the heavy monsoon period (July-August), when the park may also close for a few days.

Places to Stay & Eat
Bungalows There are rustic but charming *bungalows* (for Rs 75 to Rs 150 per double) and *dormitories* (Rs 20 per bed) in Nagarhole village. Surrounded by herds of spotted deer, it is a great place to relax. You may want to bring some extra goodies to supplement the basic, (but filling), vegetarian meals. Bookings are possible at the Wildlife Office in Bangalore, but you will probably have more luck at the Office of the Deputy Conservator of Forests in Hunsur (☎ 08222-52041), 2km west of the bus stand. You must get a receipt before staying at the bungalows, but you pay at the park reception centre. There is a two night maximum stay but this can be extended if there are no other guests.

Resorts *Wild Lands Resorts*, run by the Karnataka Forest Development Corporation (☎ 080-345192), next to the Wildlife Office in Bangalore, has lodges at Murkal. The cost of a cottage for foreigners is too high – Rs 450/600 for doubles/triples – but the dormitory is better value at Rs 100 per bed. However, it's a hassle to reach the park without transport.

Orange County Resort (☎ 08274-58481, fax 58485, email orangecounty@rhrl. wipro.bt.vsnl.net) is only useful if you have transport and heaps of money. Luxurious cottages in the 'ye-olde-English' style are set in the midst of a gorgeous coffee plantation and cost Rs 1250 for a double, plus meals. It is located near Siddapura; you will have to arrange transport to the park through the management of the resort.

Kabini River Lodge is the best of the lot

simply because for some reason it has access to far more of the park than the Forest Department, so you're more likely to see tigers and elephants. It has a magnificent setting on the Kabini River, which the owners insist is full of elephants in late summer (April-May).

The lodge offers a range of rooms, cottages and tents from US$110 per person including meals and tours by jeep and boat. Bookings are essential: contact Jungle Lodges & Resorts in Bangalore, or Seagull Travels in Mysore – see the relevant sections for details. The lodge is near Karapur village, on the road between Mysore and Manantavadi (in neighbouring Mysore district).

Getting There & Away
From Mysore the direct daily bus (Rs 33, three hours) to Nagarhole village leaves at 9 am, and returns from Nagarhole at 4 pm. From Madikeri (Rs 25, 2½ hours), one direct daily bus leaves at 7.15 am, and returns from Nagarhole at 3.30 pm. These bus timings (which you should double-check) allow you a quick day trip, but try to stay overnight.

It is easier to catch regular buses to Gonikoppal from Madikeri or Mysore, and then another (Rs 12, one hour) to Kutta, from where you can hire a jeep. You could also hire a jeep to travel to – but not around – the park from Gonikoppal or Titimati.

HUNSUR
There is only one reason to visit or stay in Hunsur: to book the forest bungalow in Nagarhole National Park or, maybe, the one on top of the magnificent Brahmagiri Hill, in southern Kodagu. The Office of the Deputy Conservator of Forests (☎ 08222-52041) is 2km west of the bus stand.

The best place to stay is the *Hotel New Dreamland*, where singles/doubles cost Rs 120/180. It is about 3km east of the bus stand. Buses travel between Mysore and Madikeri every 20 to 30 minutes, and stop off at Hunsur. From Hunsur to Nagarhole, get a connection at Gonikoppal.

WALKING IN KODAGU
Though so much of Kodagu is begging to be explored on foot, several important factors will limit your trekking:

- There are few designated long-distance walking routes. The lists below give some idea of what is available, but seek further advice if planning to walk long distances independently. Otherwise, get one of the agencies (mentioned below) to arrange everything, or ask the YHA what walks you may be able to join.
- You cannot simply trek anywhere. Kodagu is surrounded by hills – difficult to climb and easy to get lost in; the south-western stretch is close to Kerala (and border patrols); much of the interior is made up of vast, private coffee plantations, with trails meandering all over the place; and there are many protected areas.
- You are not permitted to walk independently in Nagarhole National Park.

Don't be put off though: the advantages are that the hills are fairly gentle and you can avoid the higher peaks if you want to, birdlife is prolific, and you certainly won't be bumping into other foreigners along the way. However, this part of India is prone to fog so try not to scream too much if you have struggled for five hours to the top of a peak only to find you can't see anything. And when the rains come, so do the leeches.

Information
Getting decent advice and information is not easy. Don't waste your time with the tourist office in Madikeri: even if you're walking independently, contact one of the agencies listed below, or the Office of the Conservator of Forests in Madikeri Fort.

Maps Take one of the ONC or TPC maps published by the US Defense Mapping Agency Aerospace Center (not available in India). The best local map is sold by the Coorg Wildlife Society (see under Flora & Fauna earlier in the Kodagu section). The survey departments will not issue you detailed maps of Kodagu for security reasons, because of its proximity to the coast.

Permits & Guides For day hikes and walks along main roads and not in protected areas

KARNATAKA

you do not need permits or guides. For two or three day treks, especially anywhere in a protected area, you may need a permit, and a guide is recommended, though not compulsory. Refer to the individual sections below for details.

For longer treks across great distances of Kodagu, particularly near the border with Kerala, you need permission from the Principal Chief Conservator of Forests (☎ 080-334 1993), Karnataka Forest Department, Bangalore. If you are walking independently, the PCCF will give you permission (allow a week), but the Office of the Conservator of Forests in Madikeri will still allocate you a compulsory guide. If you arrange a long trek with an agency, they will do all the paperwork for you.

If you want a reliable guide who speaks English and knows the trails, the agencies listed below will find one for about Rs 300 per day. Organising one yourself for Rs 200 to Rs 250 per day is cheaper, but the guide may not be as reliable. A porter will cost about Rs 100 per day. The hotels, resorts and coffee plantations around Kodagu can also arrange local guides and porters. See also the boxed text 'Looking for a Good Guide' in the Tamil Nadu chapter.

Climate
It is vital to time your walk properly. Do not come during the monsoon period (June to September) when between four and 5m of rain will fall: leeches and boggy roads will also make your life a misery. The rest of the year is OK: summer (April-June) in Kodagu is cooler than the rest of the region, but November-March is certainly the best time. It may rain a little between early October and mid-November, but not too much.

Food & Accommodation
You can usually stay in temples, homes, forest bungalows or schools along the way, but guides (especially those working for the YHA and Friends Tours & Travels) will be able to organise this better than you can. This means you do not have to carry a tent: there are a lot of hills in this part of India,

so you will soon realise the importance of carrying as little as possible.

Someone near where you stay should be able to cook a very basic, but cheap, meal, also obviating the need to carry cooking equipment. Whether you buy food along the way, or take your own, you will be expected to feed any guide or porter.

Equipment
Not every agency listed below rents equipment, but the Coorg Tourist Travel Agency and Friends Tours & Travel do rent two person tents for about Rs 250 per night. The YHA has a camp site near Madikeri (see Agencies, following). Alternatively, contact the Coorg Adventure Club to see what equipment they have available.

Agencies
With the exception of the Coorg Adventure Club, all agencies are based in Madikeri (Telephone area code: 08272):

Coorg Adventure Club (☎ 08273-47722)
Based in Gonikoppal, this club organises outdoor activities for local youth, but is happy to provide advice about trekking, mountain climbing and rafting.

Coorg Tourist Travel Agency (☎ 25817)
This friendly place is not a dedicated trekking agency, but it is one of the best travel agencies in Madikeri. It can organise walks, and accommodation in coffee plantations around Kodagu. It is beneath the Vinayaka Lodge.

Friends Tours & Travel (☎ 29102)
This agency is run by the most knowledgeable and enthusiastic trekker in town; he also runs the local branch of the YHA. He can arrange treks (and accommodation along the way), guides and equipment. The office is currently upstairs along Hill Rd; if you can't find it, ask at Sri Ganesh Auto Mobile shop. But the manager plans to move to an office along College Rd, which he promises will be well-signed and easy to find.

Hotel Cauvery
Mr Ganesh Aiyanna, the manager of the Hotel Cauvery (see Places to Stay in Madikeri), is a font of local knowledge and can arrange treks for foreigners, but has no particular trekking agency as such.

Ozone, Clipper, & Woody Adventures
Though based in Bangalore, these three agencies arrange trekking and climbing in Kodagu, and have a wide range of equipment for hire. Refer to the Outdoor Activities Around Bangalore section for contact details.

Palace Estate
This is the best place to organise a climb up Tadiandamol near Kakkabe, and for hiking in the general area. For details see Places to Stay in the Kakkabe section.

Youth Hostels Association (YHA) of India (☎ 29974)
The YHA boasts over 600km of walking routes in Kodagu. The YHA has a camp site at Thalathmane, about 5km from Madikeri, which can be used by foreigners between November and June. On-site tents cost Rs 150 per tent (and hold up to a dozen people). Though the YHA is basically set up for Indians, foreigners with a genuine interest in trekking are able to join a group already organised (which may be full of kids). The YHA doesn't bother arranging treks for small groups – for this, contact Friends Tours & Travel.

Day Hikes

Most of the hills can also be climbed in one day – refer to the Hills section below.

Harangi Dam With permission from the PWD office near the entrance to Harangi Dam, you could hike around the dam, and to points such as Madapur. You do not need permission to hike along the main road (9km) between the dam and Kushalnagar, though you will need to ask directions. The road (6.5km) to/from the obvious turn-off at Guddehosur is shaded, and easier to follow.

Irpu Falls From the Chilligeri Estate (see the main Irpu Falls section above), it is a tough 8km hike uphill to the Irpu Falls. It is far easier to hire a jeep up to the falls, and walk back. A guide is needed, and available at the Chilligeri Estate or in Kutta.

Kushalnagar to Dubare One hike which is easy to follow is along the western side of the Cauvery River, between Kushalnagar (15km) or Cauvery Nisargadhama (12km) and Dubare. If the banks become muddy or impassable, simply walk between 100m and

1km to the road which parallels the western bank. You must seek permission and advice (but no guide is necessary) from the Coorg Wildlife Society (see under Flora & Fauna earlier in the Kodagu section), because this stretch of the Cauvery is protected. Refer to the individual sections above about how to reach the starting points. With permission, you could continue this trek by camping overnight along the river, or staying at the forest bungalow at Dubare, and finishing (or starting) in Siddapura.

Day hikes into the forest at Dubare are possible with permission from the forest department (next to the Hotel Mayura Valley View in Madikeri), but you must take a local guide because there are some angry elephants in the forest still trying to avoid capture.

Abbi Falls to Madikeri Between Abbi Falls and Madikeri (or vice versa), the path is a little steep in parts. The best idea is to take an auto-rickshaw to the falls, from where it is a 6km hike to the Rajas' Tombs (see under Madikeri), and then another 2km down the main road to the centre of Madikeri.

Madikeri to Suntikoppa This easy hike (13km) takes you past endless coffee plantations. The advantages are that it's easy to organise, no permission or guide is needed and you can get on or off a bus along the way: it is a main road, albeit not that busy. Surprisingly there is nowhere to eat on this stretch of the road. From Madikeri the walk is mostly downhill: start walking east from the Rajas' Tombs.

From the Rajas' Seat Several trails just begging to be explored head down into the valley from the Rajas' Seat. If you have the time and confidence, follow a trail until it eventually hits a main road and then wait to flag down onward transport back to Madikeri. If you ask directions, the trail to Capitol Village Resort (see Places to Stay in the Madikeri section) is very pleasant.

Telecauvery to Bhagamandala Downhill from Telecauvery to Bhagamandala, you can

(a) walk down the main road (8km); (b) trudge along the old mud trail (about 6km); or (c) follow the winding Cauvery River (about 12km). The police at the Telecauvery Temple will give you directions to the start of the hikes along the river and mud trail. Refer to the relevant sections earlier for more information about these two sacred places.

Longer Walks
All these treks take at least one night, so you will need to take a tent or rely on accommodation in villages, or forest bungalows. For these treks, you will need permission and guides. Refer to Permits & Guides earlier in this section.

Telecauvery to Nagarhole This epic seven day trek starts at Brahmagiri, the hill at Telecauvery. Walking between 10km and 15km each day you visit and stay at or near: Nishani Motte Temple on Nishani Motte peak (890m); Nalnad Palace; Vatekolli or Maukutta; Bara Pole Falls; Irpu Falls; and the entrance to Nagarhole National Park. The trek takes you along mountain ridges and is about 95km long. You can add another day and climb Tadiandamol or Iggutappa hills; and another two days if you head south-west to the village of Mundrotu. It is a great idea to break up the journey and stay at the Palace Estate at Nalnad Palace (see Places to Stay in the Kakkabe section).

Telecauvery to Pushpagiri This five or six-day trek (about 75km) also starts at Brahmagiri Hill at Telecauvery. The trail heads north, via Dabbadka village; Sampaje, where you can stay in a forest bungalow if you ask in the village; Kotte Betta (it's better to take two days for this stretch, and stay at Kalur); and then a final assault to – and up – Pushpagiri.

Kakkabe to Telecauvery This six day trek is about 75km long and involves a lot of climbing. After conquering Tadiandamol (1745m), trek via Iggutappa (1590m); Nishani Motte peak (890m); Mundrotu village; and finish at Brahmagiri, the hill at Telecauvery.

This trek can be organised with the Ozone trekking agency in Bangalore.

Thalathmane to Abbi Falls & Return This is a popular five day circular trek organised for local youth by the YHA (though foreigners can join). It starts at its base camp, at Thalathmane, and meanders in one of several directions through tiny villages such as Kalur, via Abbi Falls. Distances per day range from 13 to 17km, and the trails are fairly gentle. The YHA charges a very reasonable all-inclusive Rs 490 per person.

Hills
Most of these hikes can be completed in one day. They do not normally require guides, though a guide will help you find the easiest paths to the peak; and no permission is required unless the hill is in a protected area.

Devasi Betta Devasi Betta (1535m), also known as Brahmagiri Hill (not to be confused with the one near Telecauvery) is the start of the important Lakshmanatirtha River. Admire the majesty of Devasi Betta from the Shri Rameshwarna Temple at Irpu Falls (see the main Irpu Falls section earlier).

As Devasi Betta is part of the Brahmagiri Wildlife Sanctuary (181 sq km), you must get permission and a guide from the forest ranger at Srimangala (☎ 08274-46331). If this fails, try the Office of the Deputy Conservator of Forests in Hunsur (see that section, earlier, for details). It is about 8km to the top of the hill from Irpu Falls. The forest department has a bungalow in a spectacular position on the hill; book through the forest ranger in Srimangala.

Gaddige This meandering, easy 15km hike goes up and down Gaddige Hill, which has two small temples on the peak. To start, catch a bus between Siddapura and Piriyapatna and get off at the gate at the border between Kodagu and Mysore districts. Ask the officers at the gate for directions to the trail up the hill. A popular 22km trek from Gaddige to Dubare is currently off limits because of wild elephants.

Iggutappa This 1590m hill, near Tadiandamol Hill, has two ancient temples near its peak. You will need a guide to show you which of the several peaks is Iggutappa, and to find it in the mist. Allow about five hours return from Padi Iggutappa Temple – see the Kakkabe section earlier for details about guides, accommodation and transport.

Kotte Betta The third-highest peak in Kodagu, Kotte Betta (1632m) has two ponds and a small temple at the peak. This trek to the top and back (about 13km; allow five to six hours) starts and finishes at Sirangahalli. The top is quite rocky, and if the clouds have parted it can be damn hot.

To climb it in one day from Madikeri, catch the 9 am bus (but double-check the departure time) towards Surlabi, but get off at Sirangahalli. If you can't get a bus back to Madikeri later in the day and you still have any energy left, hike 6km down the road from Sirangahalli to Madapur, where buses regularly pass by. The indigenous people around Kotte Betta aren't fond of tourists, so for this reason alone a guide is recommended.

Pushpagiri The second-highest peak in Kodagu, Pushpagiri (1712m) is a popular walk. However, it's not easy because a fair bit of walking is required before you even start the climb – therefore, take a tent or stay at Girigadde. It is part of the Pushpagiri Wildlife Sanctuary (103 sq km), so you should seek permission and advice from the Coorg Wildlife Society (see Flora & Fauna, earlier in the Hadikeri section) first. A guide is not compulsory, but is recommended. One disadvantage is that views are regularly obscured by mist, regardless of the time of the year.

From Madikeri, take the bus to Somvarpet. Then catch another bus, which stops about 4km before Heggademane, from where it is about 8km to the peak of Pushpagiri. This peak is significantly higher than the other two nearby peaks – Paruvatgiri (1571m) and Kolkallu Betta (1482m) – but it's easy to be confused if it's misty.

About 7km to the west of the peak, your guide (or ask directions if you don't have one) can take you to a home at Girigadde which rents *rooms* to trekkers. It is then another 7km to the village of Subrahmanya, from where you can catch onward public transport.

Soma Male The hike to the top of Soma Male (1610m), which has an old temple, starts and finishes at Karada (about 11km return). The last stretch is very hard and susceptible to blizzards, with some rock-climbing and narrow trails along the way. Hire a guide for this one. This trek can be arranged with Friends Tours & Travels (see under Agencies, earlier). Karada is linked by bus with Napoklu and Virajpet.

Tadiandamol The highest peak in Kodagu (1745m) is a popular climb, because it is easy to reach and organise. The trek is about 14km return from Nalnad Palace; allow about five hours. A guide (available at the Palace Estate) is not compulsory, but he will show you the most direct way, and make sure that you really climb Tadiandamol rather than some other smaller peak nearby. The start of the trail is gentle, but it gets tough and demoralising at the end.

You shouldn't start before 9.30 am, as this allows enough time for the wild elephants to slip back into the forest and for the early-morning fog to lift – even though you may come across fog at any time along the way. Refer to the Kakkabe section earlier for details about how to reach, and where to stay at, Tadiandamol.

Coast & the Western Ghats

MANGALORE
Pop: 480,000 Tel Area Code: 0824
Mangalore has been a trading centre for many centuries; some historians even point to a text by Pliny as evidence that the city was well known to travellers in the 1st century. Little

KARNATAKA

is known of its early history, but it appears to have been ruled for a considerable time by a tribe known as the Alupas.

From the 14th century the local rulers became feudatories of the Vijayanagar kings and in 1443 Abdur Razzak, a Persian emissary to the court at Vijayanagar, described Mangalore as a city 'which forms the frontier of the kingdom of Bidjanagar'.

With the arrival of the Portuguese in the late 15th century the power balance along the Malabar Coast changed forever, and over the following two centuries the con-

quistadors held a large measure of control over the area. A legacy of this presence is the city's distinctively European character, in evidence today in landmarks such as St Aloysius College and Rosario Cathedral.

In the latter half of the 18th century, control of Mangalore was disputed by Hyder Ali and the British. In 1784 the city fell to Tipu Sultan (Hyder's son) and thousands of Kanarese Christians (some estimates have put the number as high as 50,000) were marched off to captivity in Srirangapatnam. Stories abound about the inhumane treat-

PLACES TO STAY
4   Panchami Boarding & Lodging
10 Hotel Shaan Plaza
11 Hotel Navaratna Palace; Pai Cafe; Kerra Panna Restaurant
12 Hotel Manorama
13 Hotel Indraprastha; Tourist Office
15 Poonja International Hotel; Yuvraj Restaurant
18 Hotel Roopa; Kamadhenu Vegetarian Restaurant
21 Hotel Moti Mahal; Mangala Restaurant
25 Taj Manjarun Hotel; Galley Restaurant

PLACES TO EAT
16 Dhanyavad Restaurant
19 Palkhi Restaurant

OTHER
1   Sultan's Battery
2   Indian Airlines
3   KSRTC Bus Stand
5   Shreemanthi Bai Memorial Government Museum
6   Kadri Temple
7   Air India Office
8   Shree Asheervad Typing Centre
9   St Aloysius College Chapel
14 Higginbothams & Trade Wings
17 Canara Bank
20 Athree Book Centre
22 Milagres Church
23 Town Hall
24 State Bank of India; City Bus Stand
26 GPO
27 Rosario Cathedral
28 Mangladevi Temple

Mangalore

0   0.5   1 km
Approximate Scale

Map labels: To Vdipi • To Airport • Boloor • NH 17 • Bejan • Ferry Road • Bookapatna Road • Lalbagh Circle • Bejai Main Road • Kadri • North Sand Pit • Car Street • K S Rao Rd • Balmatta Rd • Falnir Road • Arabian Sea • Maidan Road • Falnir • Train Station • Rosario Church Road • Shetty Circle • To Kerala & Ullal • NH 17

KARNATAKA

ment that they received as prisoners, and it took many years for the community to recover. With Tipu's defeat in 1799 the city was finally incorporated into British India and became capital of South Kanara district.

Today Mangalore remains the administrative capital for the area (though it's now known as Dakshina Kannada) and the city is a centre for the export of cashew nuts and coffee. The completion of a deep water port in 1976 along with a recent influx of large businesses (including petrochemical factories and power plants) has made it one of the up and-coming cities in the south-west. This is cause for as many headaches as celebrations as the city's infrastructure is proving insufficient to deal with the demands made on it.

Mangalore has a languid tropical atmosphere, crowded streets and no worthwhile attractions, but it's a convenient transport hub and can make a good stopover for a night.

Orientation

Mangalore is hilly and has windy, disorienting streets. Fortunately, all the hotels and restaurants, the city bus stand and the train station are in or around the hectic city centre. The KSRTC long-distance bus stand is 3km to the north; you'll need to take an auto-rickshaw (about Rs 10).

Information

The tourist office (no phone) is in the Hotel Indraprastha, along with the KSTDC transport office (☎ 421692). It has a few brochures, but apart from this its information is next to useless. For up-to-date train and bus details you're better off going directly to the station or the bus stands. The tourist office is open daily except Sunday from 10.30 am to 5.30 pm, with an infinitely extendable lunch hour in the middle.

The best place to change money is the State Bank of India, next to the Taj Manjarun Hotel. Nearer to the centre of town, Trade Wings travel agency will change Thomas Cook and American Express travellers cheques. The Canara Bank on Balmatta Rd will give a cash advance on a Visa card; go to the MIPD section on the 2nd floor. The

service is friendly but the system is archaic, so allow plenty of time.

The GPO is about 15 minutes walk downhill (south) of the city centre, just past Shetty Circle. Email hasn't really caught on in Mangalore yet, but if you're desperate you could try the Shree Asheervad Typing Centre (☎ 443949, email: narain@mngcom.dcc. dartnet.com), Basement, Hotel Vandana Building, Near Bunt's Hostel, Karangalpady.

There's a Higginbothams bookshop on Lighthouse Hill Rd, but better is the Athree Book Centre (☎ 425161) at 4 Sharavathi Building, Balmata. There's an excellent selection of books on all subjects and the friendly owner, Mr Ashoka Vardhana, is an expert on trekking in the Western Ghats.

For information about events and news, try the local daily, the *Canara Times*. Mangalore also has its own monthly magazine, *Mangalore Today,* which covers events in the whole district of Dakshina Kannada.

Things to See

For some strange reason Mangalore has few, if any, sights worthy of note. **Sultan's Battery**, 4km from the centre on the headland of the old port, is a remnant of Hyder Ali's days, but the last remaining bastion, made out of rough blocks of laterite, really doesn't merit a special visit. A No 16 bus from the city centre will get you there; an auto-rickshaw round trip costs Rs 30.

The **Shreemanthi Bai Memorial Government Museum**, about 1km east of the KSRTC bus stand, is open daily from 9 am to 5 pm, but closed on Monday and every second Saturday. Bus No 19 passes the entrance. Further out in the same direction is the Kerala-style **Kadri Temple**. The temple is modern in design and layout, with little ornamentation. Nonetheless the silver doorways are beautifully executed, and the temple also houses a bronze statue of Lokeshwara believed to have been cast in 968 and reputed to be one of the best bronzes in India (bus Nos 3, 4 & 6).

St Aloysius College Chapel is known for its mural-covered walls and ceilings, which were painted by Reverend Antonio Moscheni at the beginning of the 20th century.

If nothing else, the scale of the thing is impressive, and the college is pleasantly peaceful after the mad crush of people and vehicles in the centre of town. The chapel is open from 8.30 to 10 am, 12.30 to 1 pm and 3.30 to 6 pm.

If you've still got time and energy to spare, try the **Rosario Cathedral**, a large, plain whitewashed edifice built in 1910; the dome was supposedly modelled on St Peter's Basilica in Rome. The **Mangladevi Temple,** which gave the town its name, is a short distance south of the cathedral. It's a tiny, modern temple, whose redeeming features are the three silver doorways which frame the image in the sanctum.

Places to Stay – Budget
Hotel Manorama (☎ 440306, KS Rao Rd) is good value, with large, clean singles/doubles with attached bathroom from Rs 145/231. Air-con doubles go for Rs 450.

Hotel Indraprastha (☎ 425750, Lighthouse Hill Rd) charges Rs 125/175 for big, old rooms with attached bath. The corridors are semi-derelict, but the rooms are OK.

Hotel Roopa (☎ 421271, Balmatta Rd) has reasonable rooms with attached bath for Rs 125/184 and air-con doubles for Rs 450.

Panchami Boarding & Lodging (☎ 211986), opposite the KSRTC bus stand, has singles/doubles/triples with attached bath for Rs 100/145/200.

There are also *Retiring Rooms* and *dormitories* at the train station.

Places to Stay – Mid-Range & Top End
Hotel Navaratna Palace (☎ 441104, KS Rao Rd) has well-furnished singles/doubles with attached bath for Rs 175/285, and air-con doubles for Rs 525.

Hotel Shaan Plaza (☎ 440312, KS Rao Rd) has rooms for Rs 270/330 or air-con doubles for Rs 530.

Poonja International Hotel (☎ 440171, fax 441081) is an upmarket place catering mainly to Indian businessmen. Large, comfortable rooms with TV and attached bathroom go for Rs 400/500, or Rs 700/800 with air-con.

Hotel Moti Mahal (☎ 441411, fax 441011,

Falnir Rd) is in a higher class, and boasts a bar, restaurant, coffee shop and swimming pool. Rooms cost Rs 550, or Rs 700 with air-con. Nonresidents can use the pool for Rs 30.

Taj Manjarun Hotel (☎ 420420, fax 420585, Old Port Rd) is the best hotel in town. Air-con rooms cost Rs 1850/1975. It has a good restaurant and a swimming pool (which nonguests can use for Rs 100).

Places to Eat
Despite its fishing port and the popularity of Mangalore-style seafood in places such as Mumbai, you'll be hard pressed to find a decent piece of seafood in the city. The two places which do serve some seafood are both expensive.

The *Galley Restaurant* at the Taj Manjarun Hotel has a few Mangalorean specialities such as ladyfish (Rs 120) and lobster (Rs 350).

The *Palkhi Restaurant (Balmatta Rd)* is a popular place with businesspeople, and serves a few local dishes such as 'prawns cooked in whole pounded spices' (Rs 150), and the Karnatakan equivalent of pomfret recheiado – pomfret stuffed with a spicy sauce. The rest of the items on the menu are rather cheaper, with main courses averaging around Rs 70 to Rs 100.

Roopa Hotel has several eateries, including the acceptable *Shin Min Chinese Restaurant*, the *Kamadhenu Vegetarian Restaurant* and the *Roopa Ice-Cream Parlour*.

Dhanyavad Restaurant (corner KS Rao and Lighthouse Hill Rds) is a popular veg restaurant serving snacks during the day and cheap 'meals' in the evening.

Pai Cafe, next to the Hotel Navaratna Palace, serves excellent thalis for around Rs 15.

Keera Panna Restaurant in the basement of the same building is popular with locals. Veg dishes are in the Rs 30 to Rs 50 bracket, nonveg dishes cost around Rs 50 to Rs 70, and beers are Rs 50.

Mangala Restaurant, at the Hotel Moti Mahal, is a pseudo-plush affair kitted out in the best décor the 1970s had to offer. Indian, Chinese and continental mains cost around Rs 70.

Yuvraj Restaurant, on the 1st floor of the

Poonja International, serves good Indian and continental food in ice cold air-con surroundings. Main courses cost around Rs 60 to Rs 80, and a western breakfast costs Rs 60.

Getting There & Away

Air Indian Airlines (☎ 455259) is based about 4km out of town on Hathill Rd in the Lalbagh area. The office is open from 9.25 am to 4 pm daily (including Sunday) with a lunchbreak from one to 1.45 pm.

Air India (☎ 493875) has a small office on the ground floor of the Pancha Mahal hotel in Kodialbail, not far from KS Rao Rd. You can make bookings here or reconfirm a ticket, but to collect a new ticket you have to go to the Indian Airlines office.

Indian Airlines flies daily to Mumbai (US$100) and four times a week to Chennai (US$80) via Bangalore (US$60). Jet Airways (☎ 441181) also has two flights daily (except Sunday) to Mumbai (Rs 3415 economy).

Bus The long-distance (KSRTC) bus stand is about 3km north of the city centre. It's fairly quiet and well organised. There are daily departures to Bangalore (Rs 113, nine hours), Goa (Rs 140, 10 hours), Hassan (Rs 56, four hours), Hospet (Rs 149, 11 hours), Karwar via Udipi (Rs 76, seven hours), Madikeri (Rs 34, four hours) and Mysore (Rs 100, seven hours). In addition, there are two daily buses to Chikmagalur (Rs 40) and many services to both Shimoga (Rs 68) and Dharmastala (Rs 20).

Private buses running to other destinations (including Sringeri, Venur, Karkal and Mudabidri) depart from the dusty patch of ground across the road from the city bus stand. This area is known variously as the 'private bus stand' or the 'temporary bus stand', because for some time it has been slated for development. The plan has been in stalemate for two years now, leading some Mangaloreans to refer to the area cynically as the 'permanent-temporary bus stand'.

Several private coach companies, serving all the main destinations, have offices on Falnir Rd, and there are other operators near the long-distance (KSRTC) bus stand.

Train The train station is on the southern fringe of the city centre. The new west-coast Konkan Railway connecting Mangalore and Mumbai is now open but at the time of writing there were no through trains along the length of the line. Instead there were two daily trains north, a passenger service departing at 7.10 am and an express train departing at 2.45 pm. These arrived in Margao (Goa) at 1.30 pm and 8.45 pm respectively, from where a service to Mumbai departed at 6.25 pm, arriving in Mumbai at 5.30 am. Approximate times from Mangalore to other main stations in Karnataka are: Udipi 1½ hours, Honnavar 3½ hours, Gokarna 4½ hours, Karwar five hours. Note that the express service does not stop at all stations – it passes straight through Gokarna Road, for example.

In 1998 all rail services heading east (ie to Hassan, Mysore and Bangalore) had been suspended while the Mangalore-Hassan line was converted to broad gauge. Nobody's going to say when this line will reopen – it could take at least a couple of years. Note when it does reopen that the section through the Western Ghats is prone to landslides during the monsoon season.

Plenty of expresses head to Kozhikode, and a couple of daily expresses run to Thiruvananthapuram (Rs 186/620 sleeper/1st class, 16 hours) via Ernakulam and Kollam. At the time of writing, two daily expresses to Chennai (Rs 220/775 sleeper/1st class, 18 hours) looped south to Kozhikode to avoid conversion work, and remained almost as fast as catching a bus.

Getting Around

To/From the Airport The airport is 20km from the city centre. Bus Nos 47B and 47C from the city bus stand will get you there. Alternatively, there's an airport bus which departs from the Indian Airlines office in Lalbagh at 8.45 am on Monday, Wednesday and Friday, and at 6.45 am other days. Share taxis (Rs 50 per person) can sometimes be picked up in front of the Poonja International and the Moti Mahal hotels. A normal taxi ride will cost around Rs 200.

KARNATAKA

Bus & Auto-Rickshaw The city bus stand is opposite the State Bank of India, close to the Taj Manjuran Hotel. There are plenty of auto-rickshaws and, following a showdown with the police in 1997, they all have correctly calibrated meters which they're generally willing to use. Flagfall is Rs 7.

AROUND MANGALORE
Ullal
Ullal, 13km south of Mangalore, boasts the *Summer Sands Beach Resort* (☎ 467690, *fax 467693*). The beach is OK and the resort makes a pleasantly quiet escape from the city. Its bungalows each have two double rooms with attached bath, large living room, kitchen and porch. The cottages cost Rs 1349 including taxes, or Rs 2340 with air-con. There's an OK restaurant and a swimming pool. Bus Nos 44A, 44C and 44D run from the city bus stand to Ullal.

Dharmastala
Dharmastala lies 75km east of Mangalore on the lower slopes of the Western Ghats. It's a well-known pilgrimage centre, and hundreds of Indians come to daily worship at its famous **Manjunatha Temple**.

The temple itself is fairly modern and not very exciting to look at but the constant bustle of pilgrims gives the place a special atmosphere. Particularly interesting is the mixture of faiths: the temple is a prominent Shaivite centre which is tended by Madhwa Vaishnava priests and looked after by a Jain family. The Jain influence is most noticeable in the huge (14m) statue of Bahubali which was erected in 1973 on the low hill above the temple. The posture, facial expression and designs of creepers around the arms of the figure are obviously taken from the similar statues at Sravanabelagola, and at nearby Karkal and Venur.

Opposite the temple is the **Manjusha Museum** (entry Rs 1) which houses a large and eclectic collection. Items range from ancient scripts on palm leaves, silver jewellery and religious statuary, to rows of cabinets showing the 'evolution' of spectacles, cameras, typewriters and sewing machines. Buses

to Dharmastala run regularly from the KSRTC bus stand in Mangalore.

Venur
This town, approximately 50km north-east of Mangalore, has eight bastis and the ruins of a Mahadeva temple. An 11m-high **Bahubali statue**, dating back to 1604, stands on the southern bank of the Gurupur River.

Mudabidri
There are 18 bastis in Mudabidri, 35km north-east of Mangalore. The oldest of them is the 15th century **Chandranatha Basti**, known colloquially as the 1000 pillar hall. The temple, which is to the north of the town centre, is impressive rather than beautiful. It sits within a walled enclosure, which is entered via an imposing gateway on the eastern side. Immediately inside the gate is a huge stone lamp tower. The steps up to the large open-sided *mandapam* (a pavilion at the front of a temple) are flanked by a pair of stone elephants, and from the hall you can see down the length of the temple to the glittering deity in the sanctuary.

The pillars of the hall are mostly plainly styled, but are massive and support a roof made of huge stone slabs. Overall the temple has a slightly strange appearance because the stone roof is surmounted by a gabled and tiled wooden roof. Visitors are not allowed any further than the second hall, but nonetheless the temple, which is still very much in use, is a pleasant and peaceful place to visit.

Karkal
A further 20km north of Mudabidri, at Karkal, are several important temples and a 13m-high **Bahubali statue**, which was completed in 1432. The statue is on a small, serene hillock on the outskirts of the town. There are good views of the Western Ghats from here, and to the north you can see the **Chaturmukha Basti**. The basti, which was built in the 16th century, is plain in design, and the ornamentation is limited to some low relief carvings. Like its counterpart in Mudabidri, the temple is built of massive

slabs of rock. From the front porch you can see the three deities in the sanctum.

SRINGERI
Tel Area Code: 08265

The southern seat of the orthodox Hindu hierarchy is in Sringeri, a small, unspoilt village nestled among the lush coffee plantations of Chikmagalur, approximately 100km north-east of Mangalore. The other three centres also founded by Shankaracharya, the 9th century Hindu theologian and saint, are Joshimath in the Himalaya (north), Puri (east) and Dwarka (west).

The main point of interest is the **Vidyashankar Temple,** which dates from the 14th century. The temple, built of golden-coloured stone, sits on a low platform in the middle of a large paved area. The mandapam is remarkable for its 12 zodiac pillars, known as *rasikambhas*, which are placed so that the early morning sun falls on a different one during each solar month. Each pillar bears a design of a rearing animal, with a rider on its back. The exteri-or of the temple is richly ornamented with sculptures.

A few metres to the north of the Vidyashankar Temple is the modern temple which is the focal point for pilgrims, and which is consequently a scene of almost constant activity. The image in the temple is that of Sri Sarada, an incarnation of Sarasvati, the figure of absolute knowledge and bliss. The temple is open from 6.15 am to 2 pm, and from 5 to 9.30 pm. To the south, steps lead down to the ghats on the riverbank, where pilgrims (and in particular their children) line the water's edge to throw food to a seething mass of sacred fish.

A concrete bridge across the river leads to the residence of the Acharya (swami). The present Acharya gives darshan here. Next to the residence itself are the *adhishtanams* (memorial halls) to three of the former Acharyas.

Places to Stay & Eat
There is a range of pilgrims' accommodation available; report to the reception centre

In the Shade of a Cobra

According to tradition the sacred *pitha* (religious centre), which stands on the banks of the Tunga River at Sringeri, has its origins in a particular event. The Hindu saint Sri Shankaracharya was passing the area when he saw an odd sight – a cobra spreading its hood to give shade to a frog. The sage was so taken with this image of peace between animals that he decided to found his pitha on the spot. He installed in a temple an image of Sri Sharada (the deity representing absolute knowledge and bliss) and spent the next 12 years there, teaching his disciples. After this he departed to found three other centres at Puri, Dwarka and Josimath.

Before Shankaracharya departed, his main disciple was installed as his successor, and since that time the succession of acharyas (swamis or gurus) has continued unbroken for over 1000 years. The sages of Sringeri have been recognised by monarchs and people alike, and have many times been called on to give assistance or wisdom. Among the most famous gurus have been Sri Vidyaranya, who is credited with having played a part in the founding of Vijayanagar. The present guru, the 36th in the line of succession, is His Holiness Jagadguru Sri Bharati Tirtha Mahaswamigal.

The most important annual festival in Sringeri is Navaratri, which is celebrated for nine days during the bright half of Aswayuja (September to October). The festival commemorates the victory of the goddess over the demons after a nine day struggle, and thus is a celebration of the triumph of good over evil. Sharada, the presiding deity at Sringeri, is worshipped in all her various forms during the festival, and the image of the deity is adorned with numerous precious ornaments. The town is crowded with pilgrims throughout the festivities.

(☎ 50123) next to the temple entrance to be allocated a room. In the new accommodation block, excellent double rooms with attached bath cost Rs 75. If you're really on a tight budget there are also rooms for Rs 60, and Rs 25.

There are a couple of alternative places in the village, the main one being *Padmashree Lodge (☎ 50363)*, near the bus stand. Single rooms cost Rs 150 and doubles are Rs 250; the rooms are clean and the place is friendly, but it can't compare for price with the temple's own accommodation.

If you're visiting Sringeri en route elsewhere, you can leave your bags in the reception centre while you look around.

There are numerous nondescript veg 'meals' restaurants along the main street.

Getting There & Away
The bus stand is 200m to the right of the temple entrance. There are plenty of buses from Sringeri to main points in Karnataka, including KSRTC buses to Bangalore (10 hours), Mysore (eight hours), Hassan (4½ hours) and Chikmagalur. Private buses run to the places that the KSRTC doesn't cover; there are regular services to Mangalore (four hours), Agumbe (one hour), Kudremukh (two hours) and Shimoga. The picturesque road to Mangalore follows the Tunga River for 10km and passes through the Kudremukh National Park.

AROUND SRINGERI
Agumbe
Seventy kilometres south-west of Shimoga and roughly 80km east of Udipi, Agumbe sits at the top of the Ghats, in the extreme south-western corner of Shimoga district. The spot is famous (according to tourist literature) for its wonderful sunsets and there's a small platform (next to the road) from which visitors can take in the view. Of more interest to travellers, however, is the tiny, peaceful village itself, and the small *PWD guesthouse* which would be a useful base from which to explore the area.

The guesthouse is just off the main road, and is easy to find as it is directly above the only eatery in the village, the *Hotel Classic*. A caretaker, who lives in the cottage next door, looks after the building. There are three rooms – a bathroom, an enormous bedroom (with two beds in the middle of the otherwise unfurnished room) and a large dining room (again with practically no furniture). Although there are only two beds, there is ample floor space for 10 or more people. There is running water, meals are available at the Hotel Classic and there's a tiny shop in the village. Bring candles.

The guesthouse must be booked in advance through the Assistant Executive Engineer (☎ 28532) at Tirthahalli. You'll need to be persistent to get results, as no one is particularly interested in taking responsibility. Once you get to the booking stage, it costs Rs 30 per person per day. There are buses to Agumbe from Mangalore, Shimoga and Sringeri.

Kudremukh
Ninety-five kilometres west-south-west of Chikmagalur, and roughly 40km due south of Sringeri, is the tiny hill town of Kudremukh, another possible base if you want to explore the area. Sadly the hills just to the north of the town have been badly defaced by open cast iron ore mining, but the village itself is shielded from this by a low ridge, so that the eyesore is at least hidden from view for some of the time.

The only place to stay is the surprisingly smart *Syadri Bhavan (☎ 08269-54148)*. Single rooms go for Rs 100 and doubles for Rs 150; you need to book in advance. There are buses to Kudremukh from both Sringeri and Chikmagalur.

A mellower, though more spartan, option is the *Kudremukh Nature Camp* in Bhagavati, about 15km north of Kudremukh town. The entrance is signposted off the main road, from which a rough track leads about 1.5km across the hillside to the camp. There are six tents, all set on concrete bases, and furnished with two bare steel beds apiece. There are toilets and basic washrooms (ie a tap in a cubicle).

You can swim in the waterhole nearby, but there are no facilities and no food, so you'll have to be self-sufficient. Security, too, might be a worry if you want to go trekking, though you could probably leave your gear with the warden who lives up by the main road. Unless you get a group of day-tripping locals coming for a swim, this is about as peaceful and secluded a spot as you're likely to find.

Reservations for the camp are handled through the Wildlife Office (☎ 080-334 1993) at Aranya Bhavan, 18th Cross, Mallesharam, Bangalore. If you haven't reserved in advance, you could try a visit to the local Forestry Officer in Kudremukh town, though they may just refer you to Bangalore. There is a possibility, if arranged in advance, of getting a guide to take you into the Kudremukh National Park (best season: December to February), although the closely wooded countryside and hilly terrain make the chances of spotting anything fairly remote.

CHIKMAGALUR
Tel Area Code: 08262
Chikmagalur (which literally means Younger Daughter's Village) is not a bad little town but there is little reason to stop unless you want to break up a journey or need to book accommodation for the Bhadra Wildlife Sanctuary. For this, go to the Bhadra Wildlife Division (☎ 20904), at the back of the Assistant Conservator of Forests, about 300m down from the bus stand. The State Bank of Mysore, not far from the ACF, will change money.

There are about a dozen hotels and lodges within 300m north of the bus stand, along IG Rd. The best of the cheapies is *Giri Hotel*. The best of the rest is the charming *Malnad Paradise Hotel* (☎ 32218) which charges a negotiable Rs 165/250 per single/double. It also boasts the best *restaurant* in town.

Direct buses to Shimoga and Hassan leave every 30 minutes, and every 90 minutes to Mangalore or Bangalore, but you can jump on one of the many other buses passing by.

AROUND CHIKMAGALUR
Hiremagalur
Hiremagalur, 4km outside Chikmagalur, is joined to its larger neighbour by history: its name literally means elder sister, and records how the places were gifted to two daughters of a local landowner. If you find yourself in the area and have an hour or two to spare, a visit to the tiny **Rama Temple** at Hiremagalur is extremely educational. Mr Kannan, the friendly chief priest at the temple, speaks excellent English and is only too happy to explain the history and traditions of the place. It's a welcome change to hovering on the threshold of yet another temple and wondering what it's all about.

Bhadra Wildlife Sanctuary
Based around the huge Bhadra Reservoir, this 492 sq km park was established in 1974. Though conveniently located between Shimoga and Chikmagalur towns, the sanctuary is not easy to reach or explore, so it attracts few visitors. Before making any plans, check to see if the sanctuary is open: tourists can currently only visit between November and March.

Flora & Fauna Most of the park is a mixture of dense moist and dry deciduous forest and there is plenty of bamboo and teak. The endemic *Strobilanthus cunthialum*, with its bright blue flowers, is not found in many places outside of Bhadra.

There is a chance to spot flying foxes, mongooses, sloth bears, wild elephants (there are about 160 in the sanctuary) and panthers, but you are more likely to see wild pigs, gaur, striped hyenas, flying squirrels and deer. Birdlife includes kingfishers, drongos, cranes, bluejays, falcons and hornbills.

Hiking You are allowed to hike within the sanctuary, but you must have permission and take a guide. An 8km circular 'nature trail' starts at the cottages at Muttodi, but the midges and ticks in summer, and the leeches in the wet season, will make it unpleasant unless you are fully armed with repellents. No hiking is allowed around the forest bungalows at the reservoir.

Bangalore-based trekking agencies, Woody Adventures, Ozone and Clipper, organise treks in the sanctuary, while Ozone also runs

KARNATAKA

trips up Mullayangiri Hill (at 1918m, the highest peak in Karnataka), near Chikmagalur. Refer to the Outdoor Activities Around Bangalore section for contact details.

Visiting the Park The park is run by the Assistant Conservator of Forests (ACF) in Chikmagalur (see the previous entry). At Muttodi, you can arrange jeep tours. The area is very scenic, but you are unlikely to see much wildlife. The best time to visit is between October and May, though by March the park will become very dry and there is a chance of bushfires in April-May. The rains last from June to September.

Places to Stay & Eat The ACF (at Chikmagalur) has two sets of *bungalows*. One overlooks the northern parts of the impressive Bhadra Reservoir, but the caretaker probably won't know about your arrival, so there may not be any food or electricity. The bungalow is about 1km up from the turn-off in the town of Bhadra River (aka BR) Project, on the road from Tarikere. The bungalow is unsigned, on the right before you cross the main bridge.

To better explore the park, you are better off staying at the *cottages* (Rs 150 per cottage) or *dormitory* (Rs 20 per person) at Muttodi, which occupies an attractive position on the Somavahini River. Adjacent on-site tents are sometimes also available – check with the Muttodi (aka Kesave) Wildlife Office in Muttodi village.

Getting There & Away Muttodi is 24km from Chikmagalur; private buses travel between both places every two hours. To BR Project, take one of the private buses which travel between Shimoga and Tarikere every 15 minutes, and ask to be dropped at the turn-off to the reservoir.

Kemmanagundi
Just 45km north of Chikmagalur, Kemmanagundi is a tiny collection of houses and botanical gardens also known as KR Hill Station. The surrounding scenery is spectacular and the highest point is the guesthouse

at an elevation of 1450m. Formerly a summer retreat, Kemmanagundi is now the base for the Royal Horticultural Society of Karnataka, and visitors come here not only to enjoy the views, but also to visit the rose gardens and the orchid house. If you have your own transport, other sites of interest in the area include Hebbe Falls (9km) and Kallahatti Falls (10km).

The *Raj Bhavan* guesthouse, which is on the top of the hill, has pleasant double rooms with attached bathroom for Rs 150. There are also rooms available lower down the hillside, near the forestry department offices, for Rs 70/130. Rooms must be booked in advance. From March 15 to July 15 bookings go through the office of the Chief Conservator of Forests (Wildlife) (☎ 080-334 1993) at Aranya Bhavan, 18th Cross, Malleswaram, Bangalore, but outside these dates you should contact the Special Officer at Kemmanagundi (☎ 08262-37126). There are veg and nonveg canteens near the forestry offices.

To get to Kemmanagundi by bus from Shimoga go to Tarikere and change, and from Chikmagalur go to Lingadahalli. Both of these towns are to the north of Kemmanagundi and the bus up the hill consequently approaches from the north. Although the scenery on this approach is excellent, if you have your own transport try the road which approaches Kemmanagundi from the south. It's far too windy and precipitous for the buses, and it passes near to the highest point in the Karnatakan Ghats – the scenery is fantastic.

SHIMOGA
Tel Area Code: 08182
Though Shimoga is a grotty town it's well positioned to break up a journey between Bangalore and Goa; to use as a base to visit nearby attractions (see the Around Shimoga section) and Bhadra Wildlife Sanctuary – though accommodation must be booked in Chikmagalur; or to book a forest resthouse at Jog Falls to the north.

Orientation & Information
The stretch of the main road, BH Rd, between the town centre and the bus stand, is the best

place to base yourself. There is nowhere in town to change money – the nearest places for this are Chikmagalur and Hubli-Dharwad. The Wildlife Division (☎ 22983) of the Deputy Conservator of Forests (DCF) is behind the Nehru Stadium. The new tourist office (no telephone service at the time of research), along Balaraj Urs Rd and 100m east of the DCF, is friendly, but fairly hopeless unless all you want is a few glossy brochures.

Keladi Shivappa Nayaka Palace

Also known as the Archaeological Museum, this 17th century building on the banks of the Tungabhadra River houses some mildly interesting carvings and statues. The pretty gardens are home to hundred of bats. It is open every day but Monday, from 9 am to 5 pm, and entrance is free. Take an auto-rickshaw. About 200m from here is the **Catholic Church of the Sacred Heart of Jesus**.

Places to Stay & Eat

Ashoka Lodge (☎ 23787), right opposite the bus stand, is good value at Rs 120 for a basic single, or Rs 184/253 for singles/doubles with TV. It is convenient, but the incessant blaring of horns is enough to wake the dead. There are plenty of places to eat in this area.

Sree Durga Lodge (☎ 23081, BH Rd) is good value (and a useful landmark). Cheerful rooms with TV are strangely priced at Rs 70/200, and the rooms away from the main road are hard to get so it's worth booking ahead. It has a veg *restaurant* on the ground floor.

Hotel Malanad (☎ 79736) is the best place in town. It is clean and friendly, though the immediate area, one block from the Sree Durga, is a bit grubby. Small, clean rooms with a fan, cost Rs 100/140; an extra Rs 25 for a TV – but avoid the overpriced air-con rooms. The *restaurant* is excellent, even if the service can be annoyingly over-attentive.

Blue Star Bar & Restaurant is just off BH Rd, about 100m down from the Sree Durga. It offers western music and satellite TV, but a lot of the reasonably priced dishes (from Rs 25) on the extensive menu are not available.

Getting There & Away

Bus For long-distance services, public buses leave from the sedate public bus stand at the top of BH Rd; for shorter distances catch a private bus from the adjacent, chaotic station. If you have no idea what to do, go to the private bus stand, and ask someone – you will be pointed in the right direction very quickly. Private buses go to Sagar (Rs 20) and Jog Falls (Rs 25) every 30 minutes; public buses go to Chikmagalur (Rs 28) every 30 minutes. To Mangalore and Bangalore, daily private coaches also leave from outside the bus stands.

Train Given the accessibility of the bus stands and the frequency of departures, few people bother with the train. Every day, two trains go to Bangalore (Rs 35/64/291 for ordinary/2nd class/1st class); to Talguppa (for Jog Falls), Rs 13 for ordinary class only; and to Hubli-Dharwad (Rs 41/77/354). The train station is 10 minutes by auto-rickshaw from the town centre.

AROUND SHIMOGA
Tunga Anicut Dam & Sacrebyle

This dam on the rocky Tungabhadra River is ideal for short hikes or a picnic. It is open from 10 am to 5 pm every day, and there is no entrance fee. Photos are not allowed for security reasons. Sadly, foreigners are not permitted to stay at the picturesque bungalows run by Department of Irrigation overlooking the dam, but you may be able to charter a boat (with a boatman) for a trip around the lake.

Take a regular, private bus towards Tirthahalli, and get off at the sign 'Tunga Anicut', about 3km south of Gajanur village. Alternatively, take an auto-rickshaw from Shimoga for about Rs 120 return, including about one hour waiting time at the dam, and a stop at Sacrebyle.

The forest department has an elephant camp in the unsigned village of Sacrebyle, a pleasant 3km walk further south along the main road from the Tunga Anicut Dam. Nothing is particularly set up for tourists. The elephants may be out 'working' when you arrive, so it's best to get there between 9

KARNATAKA

and 11 am, when you may see the elephants being washed in the lake.

Shettihalli Sanctuary

This sanctuary (395 sq km) of tropical evergreen and semi-evergreen forests is home to spotted deer, sambar, gaur, Malabar squirrels, jackals, wild dogs and sloth bears. The Tunga Anicut Dam inside the sanctuary is also home to plenty of happy otters and waterbirds. However, a large part of the sanctuary is inhabited by villagers, and it has suffered from the effects of grazing, as well as manganese mining and logging. The very few wild elephants in the park are often reduced to raiding crops to find food in the dry season. Smuggling of teak and poaching of wild boar is also common.

According to the DCF in Shimoga you can trek inside the park, but there are no trails, maps or guides, so there seems little point, and it may be dangerous anyway. Try to avoid the monsoons between May and October, when 2m of rain causes massive erosion, exacerbated by open-cut mines. Most visitors only visit the lacklustre tiger and lion reserve, because the sanctuary (but not the reserve) is usually closed from January to May. You can stay at the *forest bungalows* inside the sanctuary for Rs 75. Contact the DCF in Shimoga (see Orientation & Information in the Shimoga section) for bookings and further information.

The tiny **Thyvare Koppa Lion & Tiger Reserve** is part of the Shettihalli Sanctuary. Though lacklustre, the fact is that it's the closest you are likely to get to seeing a tiger 'in the wild'. The reserve is open every day but Tuesday, from 9 am to 5 pm. There is a playground, some caged birds and a canteen serving simple meals and drinks, but most visitors come for the whirlwind bus trip past some bored tigers and lions. Tours operate between 9.30 am and 1 pm, and 2.15 and 4.30 pm.

You can take an auto-rickshaw from Shimoga, but try not to pay more than Rs 60 one way. It is easy enough to catch any private or public bus (Rs 4, 20 minutes) between Shimoga and Sagar. Get off at the sign saying

'Shettihali Sanctuary' on the main road, and walk about 200m to the entrance.

UDIPI

Tel Area Code: 08252

The important Vaishnavite town of Udipi (Udupi) is 58km north of Mangalore on the coastal road. It was here that the 13th century religious leader, Madhvacharya, lived and preached, and the town's **Krishna Temple** continues to draw many pilgrims. Udipi has another claim to fame since, according to local legend, the ubiquitous masala dosa was first created here.

Orientation

Udipi is a small place and it is easy to find your way around. At the centre of the town is Car St – the area of the Krishna Temple and the eight monasteries *(mutts)*. Five kilometres to the west is the port of Malpe, and 4km to the east is the suburb of Manipal.

Information

The GPO is near the private bus stand, on Kanakadasa Rd. The only bank which will change foreign currency is the Syndicate Bank in Manipal. It's open from 10 am to 2 pm on weekdays, and from 10 am to noon on Saturday. As a matter of course, they will only change hard currency (US$, UK£) and American Express travellers cheques. However, they claim that if you turn up with another well-known brand of travellers cheques (Thomas Cook etc) and can produce the purchase record for the cheques then they can change these too.

Things to See

Sri Krishna Temple & the Mutts The Krishna Temple is not impressive to look at. A long corridor leads from the front entrance, with the sanctum through a doorway to the left of the corridor, and the water tank, where worshippers perform their ablutions, to the right.

There are 14 daily acts of worship by the swami in charge of the temple, and it's worth waiting to see the commotion that occurs whenever the next round of ceremonies

Heavy Krishna

Udipi's religious significance started with the arrival of the Hindu saint Madhvacharya in 1238. Krishna was so pleased with Madhvacharya's piety that he decided to come to the town, and contrived a scheme whereby an image of himself was transported across the sea, hidden in the ballast of a ship. The ship was wrecked in a storm just off the coast near Malpe, but Madhvacharya recovered the statue from the wreck and carried it to the monastery. After the statue had been cleaned the saint's disciples tried to move it to the temple, but it was too heavy for them. Madhvacharya, however, lifted the deity effortlessly and carried it to its present resting place, where it has sat ever since.

Some years later a saint named Kanaka came to the temple to worship the image and camped outside the west wall of the sanctuary. Krishna was so impressed that he caused a small earth tremor which opened a crack in the exterior wall, so that Kanaka could view the image as he prayed. The abbot of the monastery, rather than patching up the hole, had it made into a proper window, so that the sanctuary would be visible from the street. The window is still in use by pilgrims today.

A unique system has developed in Udipi for the supervision of the temple. Madvacharya's eight disciples all founded monasteries in the area, and the abbots of these monasteries take it in turns to tend to the Krishna Temple. The Paryaya system is notable mainly for the handover ceremony which occurs in mid-January in alternate years, and which is accompanied by elaborate festivities.

begin. Pilgrims are herded out of the way, the temple elephants trumpet and a row of chanting monks pass through in procession to carry out the next ritual.

St Mary's Island A couple of kilometres off the coast is St Mary's Island, supposed to have been the site of the first landfall that Vasco da Gama made when he arrived in India (though why he should have stopped here, when the coast was so tantalisingly close, seems uncertain). The island is barely 300m long and about 100m wide, and the only cover is provided by a few palm trees.

In particular the island is notable for the strange rock forms (columnar lava) which cause hexagonal crazy paving on the rocky outcrops around the shore. The island is a popular spot for day-trippers, especially at weekends, and it's possible to swim in the sandy inlets at the south end of the island.

Boats go to the island from Malpe Harbour. Sunday is the best day to go, as you shouldn't have to wait too long for a group of tourists to turn up, and the boat will be filled – costing each person Rs 35 for the return journey. On other days of the week, the boat

should still do the journey but it rather depends on how many other people there are who want to go. You can hire the boat all for yourself if you don't want to wait – the going rate is around Rs 800. Before doing this, however, hang around the harbour area for a little while, as the boat owners will happily take your money without letting you know that a coachload of other tourists is due to turn up in a few minutes. The journey to the island takes around half an hour.

Malpe Beach Walk due west from the bus stop at Malpe, leaving the harbour to your left, and you soon come to the beach. It's a peaceful place, and looks initially extremely picturesque, but its potential is ruined by the fact that it is used as a communal latrine by the villagers living nearby. Swimming excepted, it's a good spot. Walk north for about 1km, past the abandoned hulk of a half-built hotel, and rejoin the road to find the **Beach Guest House (☎ 26061)**, a newly built place with three double rooms, which go for Rs 250 to Rs 300. The area is wonderfully peaceful, and the rooms are good – it's a great place to get away from it all.

KARNATAKA

Places to Stay – Budget

Hotel Shaan (☎ 23901), near the private bus stand, is good value. It's a friendly place with large, clean double rooms with attached bathroom for Rs 170.

Hotel Mallika (☎ 21121, KM Marg) is slightly cheaper and the rooms are small and dark, but basically fine. Doubles with attached bath cost from Rs 135.

Hotel Sindhu Palace (☎ 20791, Court Rd) has small, basic, clean rooms with attached bath; singles go for Rs 100 and doubles for Rs 140.

Hotel Vyavahar Lodge (☎ 22568, Kanakadas Rd), near the Krishna Temple, is excellent value. Large clean doubles with attached bath cost Rs 140, and singles are Rs 80.

Hotel Brindavan (☎ 20037), near the city bus stand, is just the place if you're counting your pennies. Double rooms with attached bathroom go for Rs 75, and singles with common bath cost Rs 45. Bring a mosquito coil.

If you're really looking for a bargain, several of the monasteries around the central square have their own guesthouses, but they're often booked out with pilgrims.

Indraprastha Guesthouse on the south side of the square has double rooms for just Rs 45.

Places to stay – Mid-Range

Hotel Janardhan (☎ 23880), near the KSRTC bus stand, has pleasant rooms with attached bath; singles are Rs 165, doubles are Rs 200, or Rs 450 with air-con.

Kediyoor Hotel (☎ 22381), also near the bus stand, is an upmarket place with excellent service. Large double rooms with TV and attached bath go for Rs 300 (Rs 260 for single occupancy), and air-con rooms starts at Rs 600.

Places to Eat

Woodlands Restaurant (Dr UR Rao Complex), in the backstreets just to the south-west of Car St, is a popular place with a good range of vegetarian food. Dishes are mostly in the Rs 20 to Rs 40 bracket.

Mexican Garden, at the Hotel Kediyoor, has a pleasant garden setting, and has good veg dishes for around Rs 35, and nonveg dishes for Rs 50 to Rs 70. It also serves a limited selection of seafood. The *vegetarian restaurant* in the Kediyoor is also good value, with excellent thalis and dosas for Rs 10 to Rs 20.

Classic Dining Bar, near the KSRTC bus stand, is a modern place whose early evening clientele consists mostly of businessmen enjoying a beer. It serves the usual range of Indian and Chinese dishes, plus a few local specialities which are worth trying, such as Crab Sukka (Rs 50), which is crab cooked in spices and coconut.

Getting There & Away

There are three bus stands in Udipi, all within a stone's throw of each other, near the Hotel Kediyoor. Buses to Malpe (Rs 2.75) leave from the lower bus stand, while buses to Manipal (Rs 4) leave from the upper bus stand. The KSRTC bus stand is tucked away behind the building which houses the State Bank of India. Services run to (among other places) Gokarna, Panaji, Mangalore and Bangalore. There are numerous private operators who run coaches to destinations including Bangalore, Goa, Hospet, and Kochi.

Since the inauguration of the Konkan Railway, the most convenient way to get to Gokarna, Goa or Mumbai is by rail. At the time of writing there were two trains running north to Margao, a passenger service departing at 8.29 am, and an express departing at 4.02 pm. Heading south, the passenger service departed at 7.30 pm and the express at 12.58 pm.

THE COAST NORTH FROM UDIPI

With the opening of the Konkan Railway the Karnatakan Coast has suddenly become one of the best connected areas in the country. Not only does India's newest (and potentially fastest) rail link run the length of the coastal plain, but the main highway, the NH17, is one of the best maintained roads in India. The coastline is well worth exploring, and if nothing else there is access to some wonderful areas of the Western Ghats.

Kollur

Eighty kilometres north-east of Udipi, and nestled in the thickly forested slopes of the Western Ghats, is the tiny village of Kollur. The Mookambika Temple here is one of the most important pilgrimage destinations in Karnataka, and there has been a shrine on this site for over 1000 years.

Although the temple is interesting to visit in itself (especially if you make it here during the main annual festival in March), the area around the village is particularly worth exploring. The surrounding hillsides contain one of the largest forestry areas in Karnataka, and part of this region is designated as the Mookambika Nature Reserve.

Kollur village would make a good base from which to explore for a day or two. There are several lodges, including the *Sri Rathna Guesthouse*, where double rooms are Rs 130, and the *Devi Kripa Guesthouse* (☎ *08254-58274*), which has doubles for Rs 150 and air-con doubles for Rs 450.

If you really want to get away from it all, the *Mookambika Nature Camp* might be the ideal spot. The park is 4km south of Kollur, on the road down towards the coast. From the tarmac road (where it's clearly signposted) a rough vehicle track leads approximately 1.5km into the woods. At the end of the track you come to a small clearing in which there are concrete bases for six tents (which are set up only when required). There are also a couple of buildings that serve as storerooms/accommodation and a tiny visitors' bungalow, which was un ler renovation at the time of writing and should be ready for use by the time this book appears.

It's a lovely, tranquil place with the scope for excellent rambles in the forest (arborists will be delighted to find that the trees are all labelled). You can swim in the waterhole next to the clearing, and the woman who lives on site can provide simple meals.

Hardly anyone visits here, so you'd be best off bringing your own provisions just in case. Unless you have your own transport, you'll have to get a bus to Kollur village and then either walk or hitch a lift

from there. For reservations try contacting the Deputy Conservator of Forests (Wildlife Division) at Karkala (☎ 21183) or the Range Forest Officer based at Kundapura (☎ 58277). If you have your own transport you could do worse than to just turn up and see if there's accommodation available.

Maravanthe

There's a decent beach at Maravanthe, approximately 10km north of Kundapura (Coondapoor), where a sand spit has formed at the Sauparnika River delta. There's another beach, known as Gudajji, close by.

Buffalo Surfing

Kambla, the Canaran sport of buffalo racing, first became popular in the early part of the 20th century, when farmers would race their buffalo home after a day in the fields. The event really took off in the 50s and 60s, and today the best of the races are big business. At top events up to 50,000 spectators may attend, and one organiser in 1998 went to the trouble of procuring spotlighting and a photo finish. The racing buffaloes are extremely valuable, too, and are pampered and prepared like thoroughbreds for every race. A good animal can cost over Rs 300,000.

The events are held annually in the Dakshina Kannada region, between about October and March every year, when the paddy fields have enough water in them for racing. Although the racing 'season' is still observed, the exact timings are becoming less important as nowadays specially prepared tracks are often laid out. The 120m-long tracks are laid parallel to each other and the fastest pairs of buffalo can cover the distance through water and mud in around 14 seconds. There are two versions: in one the man runs alongside the buffalo, and in the other he rides on a board fixed to a ploughshare, literally surfing his way down the track behind the beasts. It's a truly awesome sight. For those who don't believe that these slow lumbering beasts can really move, look out!

KARNATAKA

Turtle Bay Beach Resort (☎ 08252-61313) is the only place to stay in the area. Prices are high for what you get, but it's pleasantly restful, right on the water's edge, and apart from fellow guests you're unlikely to see any other tourists at all. The resort has one proper double with attached bath (Rs 500); there are also two small but well laid-out wooden cabins (Rs 400) and three tents with frame beds and mattresses (Rs 200). The cabins and tents share the common bathrooms. There's a small restaurant.

There are buses to Kundapura from Udipi and Mangalore; you'll need to get a taxi or a local bus to Maravanthe from there. Alternatively catch a bus going to, say, Gokarna and ask to be dropped on the main road near Maravanthe. Next to the main road is a sign for the Turtle Bay Beach Resort which is 500m up a side lane.

Murudeshwar

Thirty-nine kilometres south of Honnavar, Murudeshwar is a famous pilgrimage destination. The temple itself is modern and architecturally uninspiring, and the beaches immediately next to the temple are often thronged with paddling pilgrims. The guesthouse next to the temple, however, opens up an opportunity to explore the beach which stretches away to the north. The *RN Shetty Trust Guesthouse* (☎ 08385-68860) has large double rooms with attached bathroom and balcony for Rs 275, and doubles with common bath for Rs 100.

JOG FALLS
Tel Area Code: 08186

Jog Falls may be the highest in India, but they're not the most spectacular: the Linganamakki Dam further up the Sharavati River significantly limits the water flow. The falls are more voluminous during the monsoons, but the most comfortable time to visit is winter (December-February), when the falls may be obscured some of the time by mist. There are actually four falls; the longest drop of 253m is known as 'The Raja'.

Though the amount of water cascading

over the falls may not be that impressive, the setting is superb, the nearby scenery is picturesque and the countryside is perfect for gentle hiking (see the boxed text 'Walks Around Jog Falls' over the page).

Places to Stay

Bungalows The Deputy Conservator of Forests in Shimoga manages and takes bookings for two self-contained *forest resthouses*. One is on the left (and signed in Hindi), about 1km down the road to the coast from the falls; the other is 300m further down on the right and unsigned behind a blue and green fence. They cost Rs 75 per person, but you must walk back to the falls for meals.

Unless you book months ahead, you are unlikely to get a room at the magnificent *bungalows* at the car park run by the Karnataka Electricity Board (in Bangalore). It is worth trying for a room at the *PWD Bungalow*, perched precariously on the northern part of the falls, about 3km from the car park. This is actually located in Uttar Kannad district, so bookings (preferably several weeks in advance) must be made at Siddapur.

Hotels *Tunga Tourist Home* (☎ 4732), at the car park, is pretty ordinary. Small doubles cost Rs 100 but prices are likely to rise after some (necessary) renovations. The nearby towns of Kargal and Sagar (see the Around Jog Falls section following) have cheap options, but you'll miss out on the ambience of the falls.

A *Youth Hostel* is a few hundred metres up from the car park, but several travellers have complained about unfriendly staff. Dorm beds cost Rs 100 per person, so it's not good value. If you are really counting your rupees, ask someone at the chai stalls about renting a *room* in a local home, or some space in a stall itself – but don't expect any sleep.

Hotel Mayura (☎ 4732), the state-run (KSTDC) hotel, is wonderfully situated overlooking the falls, about 150m from the car park. It offers spacious and quiet rooms (though some are a little musty) for Rs 250 to Rs 300 a double. It is friendlier than the barbed wire around the hotel suggests.

Places to Eat

One side of the car park at the falls is lined with about a dozen *chai stalls*. Most serve cheap and tasty omelettes, thalis, fried noodles and fried rice, as well as hot and cold drinks.

Hotel Mayura has a room which looks more like a dining room for guests, but the public are welcome. It is great for western-style breakfasts, eg omelette, toast and tea, and other basic but delicious meals cost about Rs 40. The *Tunga Tourist Home* has a small dining room, mainly for guests.

Getting There & Away

Bus For a small place, the falls are surprisingly well connected by bus. The roads to/from the coast are fairly tortuous – the road from Manki is more spectacular, but also more likely to make you car sick than the road from Bhatkal. For these trips, it's worth chartering a vehicle, so you can stop to admire the views and waterfalls along the way.

To Shimoga (Rs 26, 2½ hours), there are buses about every 45 minutes, so you could take a day trip. To Siddapur, there are three buses a day; to Karwar via Honavar, two a day (5 am and noon); to Gokarna via Kumta, one a day (4.30 pm); and to Bhatkal, another at 4.30 pm. Double-check these times with anyone working at a hotel or chai stall at the falls. If you are in a hurry to head east, take a regular bus to Sagar, and get an onward connection.

Train The nearest train station is at Talguppa, between Sagar and Jog Falls. There are two trains a day to Shimoga.

AROUND JOG FALLS
Kargal
Tel Area Code: 08186

This small, laid-back town is where you may have to get onward transport to/from Jog Falls, or make inquiries about the Gudavi or Sharavathi sanctuaries (see later in this section). For this, contact the friendly guys at the Assistant Conservator of Forests (ACF) (☎ 4134), on the left at the fork at the end of the main road.

As an alternative to Jog Falls, the cheapest

Walks Around Jog Falls

The best way to explore the countryside around Jog Falls is on foot. Try some of the following gentle hikes:

Jog Falls
  A steep path starting at the end of the line of chai stalls at the car park leads to the bottom of the falls. If there is any rain around be prepared for leeches.
Kargal to Jog Falls
  Follow the well-signed main road. You can hike one way (5km) and take a bus back.
Jog Falls to the PWD Bungalow
  Head down the road to the coast from the car park, cross the bridge and turn left at every fork in the road. It is about 6km return.
Jog Falls to Linganamakki Reservoir
  Head down the road to the coast from the car park, turn right before the bridge and follow the river upstream. It is about 10km one way.
Kargal to Linganamakki Reservoir
  From the southern (lower) end of Kargal, follow the well-signed Kargal-Bhatkal road and look for the turn-off to the dam. It is about 6km one way. You may be able to get public transport back to Kargal or Jog Falls.

---

place to stay is *Sri Vijaya Prasad* (☎ 4341), about 50m up from the ACF office. It is very basic, but it's hard to complain about the price: Rs 40/60 for singles/doubles. Otherwise, the *Rainbow Hotel & Lodge* (☎ 4346), on the main road, has decent rooms for Rs 120 a double.

Gersoppa

Gersoppa is a modest village situated on a lovely stretch of the Sharavati River. From a point about 250m from the end of the main street, motorboats and canoes cross the river. If you can charter a boat here, a trip up or down the river (between dams, that is) is magical.

If you can find a guide in the village or at the point where the boats leave, a wonderful walk (about 5km return), through the forest from the river, leads to an abandoned, ancient (but undated) **Jain Temple**, known locally as Chaturmukka Basthi (Four Faces Temple).

To reach Gersoppa, charter a jeep from Kargal or Jog Falls (about Rs 275 for a half-day), or catch a direct bus, which leaves Jog Falls and Kargal three or four times a day.

Gudavi Bird Sanctuary

This small (740 sq m) sanctuary is rarely mentioned in brochures handed out by the tourist authorities, but is worth a trip, especially in the right season. The sanctuary is based around a large reservoir, over 200 years old, on the Varada River.

Wildlife Nearly 200 species of birds are found in Gudavi; one-third are migratory waterbirds such as white egrets, cormorants, white and black ibises, snake birds, spoonbills and herons. The best time to visit is during the nesting season (which unfortunately coincides with the monsoons): June to October. Between the months of August and September, between 10,000 and 15,000 birds create a great canopy over the reservoir. From November to February, the more sedentary ducks, pheasants, coots and moorhens rule the roost. Early morning or late afternoon is the best time to visit.

Visiting the Park You can watch the birds from anywhere along the short path around some of the reservoir, or from one of the watchtowers. There are no binoculars to hire or buy in these parts, so bring them with you if possible. Entrance is free and the sanctuary is open daily during daylight hours. With permission from the ACF in Kargal (☎ 4134) you can camp at the sanctuary, but you must bring your own food. Or you can stay in Sagar.

Getting There & Away The best idea is to take a day trip from Jog Falls (but allow about three hours one way). Catch any bus to Sagar, and get a regular connection to Sorab,

from where you will have to charter an auto-rickshaw (about Rs 120 return, including one hour waiting time). There are two or three local buses to the park entrance from Sagar – inquire locally for exact departure times.

Sagar

This small, pleasant town is on the road between Jog Falls and Shimoga. It is a road and train junction, and somewhere to stay if you plan to spend a lot of time at the Gudavi Bird Sanctuary or if you want to visit the limited ruins of the **temples** at Keladi, 5km to the north, and Ikkeri, 3km to the south.

You can stay at the *Lakshimi Lodge*, along the main road, for Rs 30/60 for singles/doubles. You are more likely to get some sleep and not be eaten by bedbugs at the *Vaibhav Lodge* or *Sri Gajanana Lodge*, both about 150m west of the bus stand.

Keladi

Keladi, in Shimoga district, was once the capital of the Keladi Nayakas, a royal household which started as a feudatory to the Vijayanagar Empire. The first Keladi ruler, Chavdappa Nayaka (1499-1513), came to power when he was granted the land as a reward for valuable service in the Vijayanagar army. The grant was subsequently increased to include several coastal territories and ports, and Keladi wealth grew with trade.

After the fall of the Vijayanagar Empire, the Keladis effectively became independent, and successive rulers held considerable power on the west coast. One notable figure was Shivappa Nayaka, who ruled from 1645 to 1660, and fought the Portuguese for control of the coastline. The kingdom finally fell in 1763, captured by Hyder Ali; it subsequently became part of Mysore state.

Today Keladi's monuments are limited to three temples which sit within a single courtyard. The earliest of the structures is the rather plain **Ramesvara Temple**, which is the centre of the three. The **Virabhadra Temple**, which is to the south, is of similar design, but with an ornately carved ceiling. To the north is the whitewashed **Devi Temple**, the hall of which has an intricately carved wooden ceiling and pillars. There's a small museum on the opposite side of the road. To get to Keladi by bus take any service to Sagar, and change for a local bus there for the final 5km ride north.

Ikkeri

Sometime after about 1512, as their kingdom began to grow in wealth and power, the Keladi Nayakas moved their capital to Ikkeri. The capital was occupied until the mid-17th century when the Nayakas opted to move again – this time to a site further to the south. Nothing remains of the old town at Ikkeri, and the **Aghoreshwara Temple**, which dates from the 16th century, is the only relic of the period. The temple, set on a high platform, is relatively plain in design but its size is impressive. The mandapam is surprisingly large, with 16 huge pillars, and a carved panel in the centre of the ceiling. To get to Ikkeri take a bus to Sagar (3km to the north) and get onward transport from there.

Sharavathi Sanctuary

Half of this sanctuary (436 sq km), established in 1974, contains the enormous Linganamakki Reservoir. The ACF in Kargal intends to develop the sanctuary for tourists, but currently facilities and transport are limited.

The sanctuary is mostly wet tropical evergreen and semi-evergreen forest which shelters wild boar, barking deer, spotted deer, wild dogs, gaur, common langur, Indian porcupines, and bonnet and lion-tailed macaques. Many species of birdlife, including cormorants, large egrets and common and whistling teals, are attracted to the reservoir. There are over 120 villages in the sanctuary, so it's under constant threat from grazing, logging and development.

Halfway down the road between Kargal and Bhatkal, the Hindu **Bheemeswara Temple** hosts an annual pilgrimage. While this can be reached by road, other attractions must be approached on foot (and trekking will be allowed in the future): the **Kanoor Kote Fort**, built in the 16th century, the impressive Dabbe Falls and Hedi Gudda Hill (677m).

Before you visit, contact the ACF in Kargal (☎ 08186-4134). Avoid the heavy rains between June and late September, and lighter rains in April and May. The best time to visit is from October to February.

Places to Stay & Eat The Deputy Conservator of Forests in Shimoga has *bungalows* in the sanctuary, close to Jog Falls (see the earlier Jog Falls section). Inside the sanctuary and on the reservoir the ACF in Kargal plans to develop the existing *Nature Camp* for low-key tourism and water sports. Other camps may be set up in the sanctuary at Muppani, 15km from Kargal.

Getting There & Away There is no public transport option so you will have to hire a jeep from Jog Falls or Kargal. Contact the ACF in Kargal before you do this.

Banavasi

The unassuming town of Banavasi, 100km from Gokarna, has a placid appearance which belies its historical significance. The first record of the town dates from the 3rd century BC, when the Emperor Ashoka is said to have sent his Buddhist missionaries to 'Vanavasa'. Four centuries later the area was ruled by a tribe called the Chutus, who were feudatory chiefs of the Shatavahana dynasty.

Banavasi really came into its own in the 4th century AD, however, when it became capital of the Kadamba dynasty. This kingdom which came to include most, if not all, of modern Karnataka was one of the great empires of the south and lasted for around 200 years before being overthrown by the Chalukyas of Badami in c.540.

Fascinatingly for historians, the town of Banavasi holds clues to almost all of these periods. Several years ago, on the banks of the Varada River which flows through Banavasi, archaeologists discovered the remains of brick-built Buddhist monuments.

The **Madhukeshvara Temple** which today is the only remaining relic of the town's glorious past, holds clues to most of Banavasi's subsequent history. The oldest parts of the temple are said to date from around

The Kadambas of Banavasi

The Kadambas were one of the great early South Indian dynasties whose empire, at its height, stretched into Goa and beyond. History relates that the founder of the empire was a Brahmin scholar named Mayurasharma who, suffering an insult during an incident in the Pallava capital of Kanchi (modern-day Kanchipuram), resolved to rule for himself. He abandoned his studies and took to the sword, soon carving out a kingdom of his own, which in the end even the Pallavas had to acknowledge.

Mayurasharma is believed to have founded his empire in c.345 AD, and soon extended his grip over a considerable area. His successors enlarged the empire even further and an inscription dating from 450 AD proclaims Mayurasharma's great-great grandson, Shantivarma, as 'the lord of the entire Kannada land'. Although the Kadambas were overcome by the Chalukyas of Badami in c.540 AD, descendants of the dynasty continued to rule small areas, including Goa, for many years to come.

200, while the main shrine, with its distinctive square-shaped and layered *sikhara* (temple tower built above the sanctum) is attributed to the Kadambas themselves. The Parvati shrine, which is the other main building in the walled courtyard, and which stands to the right of the main temple, was built by the Chalukyas of Badami. To the left and behind the main temple, containing a fine sculpture in black stone, is a shrine to Narasimha which was erected during Vijayanagar times.

The dim, densely pillared mandapam of the main temple houses a huge Nandi bull, which indicates that the temple is dedicated to an incarnation of Shiva. The mandapam is modest in design and decoration, but the scale is impressive. The antaralya houses several lovely sculptures. In a small area to the left of the temple is a famous ornamental bed, carved entirely from stone. It comes into use only once a year when the statue of the deity is placed on it for worship. The temple precinct also houses a tiny museum.

Getting There & Away It's a long haul out to Banavasi by public transport – but perfectly possible. The best option is to take a bus to Sirsi (there are a couple from Gokarna, and several more from Kumta) and then get a connection to Banavasi itself.

GOKARNA
Tel Area Code: 08386

The unspoilt town of Gokarna, 50km south of Karwar, attracts an unlikely mixture of Hindu pilgrims, Sanskrit scholars, beach-loving travellers and a hardcore hippy element who shifted here when things got way uncool in Goa. For Hindus, Gokarna is one of the most sacred sites in the country. It's also a lovely mellow little town which has so far escaped the scourge of intensive tourism, although rumours abound about the plans for development in the future.

Orientation

It takes a matter of minutes to find your way around Gokarna. There are really only two streets, the narrow Main St which is lined with picturesque Kerala-style wooden houses, and Car St which leads to the Mahabaleshwara Temple. Beyond the temple a lane leads down to the beach, and directly to the south of the junction of the two main streets is the impressive temple tank. Cafes, shops, lodges and the bus stop are all within a five minute walk.

Information

The manager at the Om Hotel can change travellers cheques and currency, although the rates he gives are poor. The next nearest place is the Bank of India in Karwar, which will change travellers cheques only (and only Thomas Cook and American Express). There's a small sub post office at the junction of Car St and Main St. International phone calls can be made at a number of places, but Shivaram Services (☎ 56506) on Main St also has a fax and a friendly owner. Bicycles can be rented from stalls along Main St.

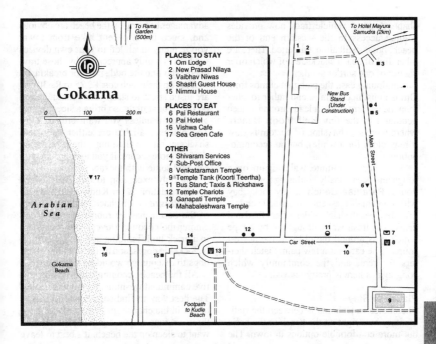

Gokarna

0   100   200 m

Arabian Sea

Gokarna Beach

To Rama Garden (500m)

To Hotel Mayura Samudra (2km)

New Bus Stand (Under Construction)

Main Street

Car Street

Footpath to Kudle Beach

PLACES TO STAY
1 Om Lodge
2 New Prasad Nilaya
3 Vaibhav Niwas
5 Shastri Guest House
15 Nimmu House

PLACES TO EAT
6 Pai Restaurant
10 Pai Hotel
16 Vishwa Cafe
17 Sea Green Cafe

OTHER
4 Shivaram Services
7 Sub-Post Office
8 Venkataraman Temple
9 Temple Tank (Koorti Teertha)
11 Bus Stand; Taxis & Rickshaws
12 Temple Chariots
13 Ganapati Temple
14 Mahabaleshwara Temple

KARNATAKA

Temples

The **Mahabaleshwara Temple**, where the sacred lingam resides, is at the western end of Main St, not far from the **Ganapati Temple**, which honours the role that Ganesh played in rescuing the lingam. At the eastern end of Main St is the **Venkataraman Temple**, and 100m south of this is the large temple **tank**, or *koorti teertha*, where locals, pilgrims, and immaculately dressed Brahmins perform their ablutions next to *dhobi-wallahs* (clothes washers) on the ghats. Near the Ganapati Temple, on Main St itself, are the two enormous **chariots** which are dragged along Main St amid much brouhaha on Shiva's birthday festival in February.

Beaches

Travellers have been drifting into Gokarna for some time now, lured by the stories of its deserted beaches which rival anything Goa

has to offer. Although some will be happy to settle for the beach near the town itself, with a bit of walking you can get to the real gems: a series of four perfect beaches, hemmed in by headlands and backed by the foothills of the Western Ghats.

Kudle Beach (pronounced 'kood-lee') is a 20 minute walk to the south of the town. To reach it, follow the footpath which begins on the southern side of the Ganapati Temple and heads south (ie not the path with an arrow to the koorti teertha). The track soon climbs to the top of a barren headland with expansive sea views, and then descends to the gently curving bay. There are four or five chai shops on Kudle, all of which serve limited food and have basic rental accommodation.

At the south end of Kudle, a track climbs over the next headland, swinging east as it does so. After 20 minutes you descend to **Om Beach**, so named because of its distinctive shape. A dusty vehicle track now provides limited access to the western end of the beach, but it's still almost deserted. There are a handful of beach shacks, all of which offer shelter of one sort or another.

Continuing east, the path that climbs from Om is indistinct at times, and rather rougher than the earlier tracks. It leads around a steep headland to the tiny **Half Moon Beach**, where there's a chai shop (if custom is slow it may close for a while), but no accommodation.

A further 20 minute walk, again on a rough and occasionally confusing path, leads you to **Paradise Beach**, a tiny rocky bay with two small crescents of sand. There's a primitive beach shack which offers food and drink, and fresh water brought in by a pipe which runs around the cliffs to the nearest source. The cafe has a few palm thatch shelters for rent, and the community which congregates here is pretty relaxed.

Places to Stay

The choice in Gokarna is between the rudimentary huts right on the beach or the basic but more comfortable options in town. The advantages of being on the beach are obvious and, since it's a decent hike from town, you're pretty much left to your own devices – which is highly appreciated by those travellers who like the odd spliff for breakfast.

Huts on the beach cost Rs 25 to Rs 30 and are just a space to stash your gear and sleep on the floor at night, so bring a sleeping bag or a bedroll unless you want bruised hips. The places available are either palm leaf shacks or mud-walled huts, the latter being slightly more secure; if you look around you can find some with lockable doors.

The only exception to this basic beach accommodation is on Kudle Beach where *Shiva Prasad* beach shack, at the south end of the beach, has 10 rooms set well back among the coconut groves. The rooms are in a brick-built building and have electricity, lockable doors, and a couple of big guard dogs to discourage would-be thieves.

All the beach accommodation has primitive communal washing and toilet facilities. The best way to find somewhere to stay is to ask in the chai shops – most places have three or four rooms out the back. If you want to sleep on the beach, it's best to leave

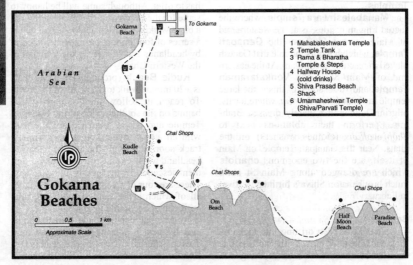

Gokarna Beaches

To Gokarna
Gokarna Beach
Arabian Sea

1 Mahabaleshwara Temple
2 Temple Tank
3 Rama & Bharatha Temple & Steps
4 Halfway House (cold drinks)
5 Shiva Prasad Beach Shack
6 Umamaheshwar Temple (Shiva/Parvati Temple)

Kudle Beach
Chai Shops
Chai Shops
Chai Shops
Om Beach
Half Moon Beach
Paradise Beach

0   0.5   1 km
Approximate Scale

KARNATAKA

The Tricking of Ravana

According to Hindu belief, Gokarna owes its prominence as a pilgrimage centre to an event which occurred shortly after the world was made. Rudra, wishing to see the new creation, arrived on this spot by squeezing through the ear of the earth. He was so pleased with this method of delivery that he named the place Gokarn, meaning 'ear of the cow'.

Rudra then retreated to meditate, and formed his essence into a lingam which had tremendous powers. The lingam's potential caught the eye of Ravana, the demon king of Lanka, who wished to possess it in order to strengthen his fight against the gods. He took the *lingam* from its resting place and started south, under the understanding that if he ever rested it on the ground he would be unable to pick it up again.

The gods schemed to find a way to make Ravana put down his burden, and in the end they sent Ganesh (Ganapati) to Gokarna to carry out their plan. Ganesh intercepted Ravana just before the time of prayer, and offered to hold the lingam for him while he prayed. As soon as Ravana was deep in prayer, Ganesh placed the lingam on the ground, and the gods anchored it firmly with the weight of three worlds. Try as he might Ravana couldn't budge the lingam and left in a fury.

Rudra now revisited Gokarna and declared that he would thenceforth live in the lingam. He further proclaimed that those who came to worship would receive abundant favours in response to their prayers. Thus Gokarna is one of the three most propitious Hindu places of worship, and the main annual festival, Mahashivaratri, which takes place in February, attracts tens of thousands of pilgrims.

your belongings at Vaibhav Niwas in town for a small fee. It's not a good idea to sleep alone on any of the beaches.

In the town, there are a handful of reasonable places. *Vaibhav Niwas* (☎ 56714) is a cosy guesthouse set back from the town's main street. Tiny but acceptable singles/doubles with common bath cost Rs 40/75 and rooms with attached bath cost between Rs 100 and Rs 125. There are also a few dormitory beds.

New Prasad Nilaya (☎ 56250), a starkly modern hotel whose design does not bode well for Gokarna's architectural integrity, probably has the town's best appointed rooms – though this is not saying much. They're plain, clean enough and cost Rs 175 with attached bath. The hotel is on a small side lane between Vaibhav Niwas and Om Lodge.

Om Lodge (☎ 56445), nearby, has basic doubles with attached bath for Rs 150, four-bed rooms for Rs 250, and five-bed rooms for Rs 300. Air-con doubles cost Rs 300.

Hotel Mayura Samudra (☎ 56236) is a neglected KSTDC hotel on a hilltop overlooking the sea, inconveniently located some 2km from town. Its three large double rooms,

all with attached bath, go for Rs 105. They could do with a coat of paint, but they're clean and spacious. A new bar and restaurant are planned and should be open by the time that this book appears.

Shastri Guest House (☎ 56220) is a slightly dingy but reasonable option near Vaibhav Niwas. Singles with private shower but common toilet facilities are good value at Rs 40, and doubles with attached bath and toilet cost Rs 120.

Nimmu House (☎ 56730) is a very pleasant and relaxed family-run place just back from the town beach. Rooms with common bath cost Rs 70/120.

Rama Garden, about 800m up a dusty track from the temple area, must be one of the mellowest places in Gokarna. The accommodation is basic, but the atmosphere more than makes up for it. At the cheapest end of the scale, a bed costs Rs 25, or it's Rs 50/60 for a hut, depending on whether or not it has a fan.

The place is often full of long-term residents, so you may have to wait for something to become available.

KARNATAKA

Places to Eat
The *chai shops* on all of the beaches can rustle up basic snacks and meals.

Pai Restaurant, halfway along the town's main street, has cheap vegetarian snacks and excellent thalis. *Pai Hotel*, nearby, has good masala dosas.

Om Lodge has a very seedy restaurant attached to it, but the terrace area on the 2nd floor is better; the food is reasonable and the beer is cold.

Vaibhav Niwas has an extensive menu of the usual traveller fare, and is a good place for breakfast: porridge, pancakes and toast are all on offer.

Near the beach, *Vishwa Cafe* has a large shady sitting out area which draws a crowd of travellers in the evenings. *Sea Green Cafe* is slightly further from the main thoroughfare, and consequently rather quieter.

Getting There & Away
The new Konkan Railway passes close to Gokarna. Express trains stop at Ankola and Kumta (both about 25km away), but the slower passenger train stops at Gokarna Road, 9km from the town. A bus from the town runs out to the station at 11 am in time to catch the train to Margao (which departs at 11.30 am); it waits to bring back passengers who've arrived on the same train. The slow train south departs Gokarna Road at 4.25 pm.

Direct buses head to Karwar (Rs 15, 1½ hours) at 6.45 and 8 am and at 4 pm. Otherwise you'll have to jump on one of the more frequent private buses to Ankola and change to a local Karwar-bound bus from there. There's a direct bus to Goa at 8 am (4½ hours), otherwise head for Karwar to pick up more Goa-bound buses. There are four buses to Hubli (Rs 45, four hours) in the morning and one just after lunch. There's a direct 6.45 am bus to Mangalore (Rs 60, eight hours). If you miss this, catch a local bus to Kumta and catch one of the more frequent Mangalore buses from there. There are also two daily buses to Bangalore (Rs 159, 12 hours), one bus to Hampi (Rs 90, 10 hours) at 7 am, and one direct bus to Mysore (Rs 150, 12 hours).

KARWAR
Tel Area Code: 08382
Karwar is a dull, sleepy port town near the mouth of the Kali Nadi River, only a short distance south of Goa. While the town holds little of interest, the area immediately to the south is very picturesque since the foothills of the Western Ghats come right to the coast, forming headlands that are separated by sweeping sandy bays. The tranquillity and beauty of the area is set to change radically when work eventually starts on a new naval base. The prospective date for this project to get underway was 1999, but as yet there's little sign of any activity.

You can take a boat across the Kali Nadi to the Jungle Lodges & Resorts enclave at the Devbag Forest Beach Resort, but this is about as exciting as the local entertainment opportunities get. The boat pier, which is next to the bridge over the Kali Nadi, is a Rs 20 private auto-rickshaw ride or Rs 3 share from the town centre.

Karwar's Indian Bank is the closest bank to Gokarna that handles foreign exchange transactions. It's open weekdays from 10 am to 2 pm and on Saturday from 10 am to noon. They will change only well-known brands of travellers cheques, and will not change any hard currency.

Places to Stay & Eat
Hotel Ashok (☎ 26418), close to the bus stand, is a reasonable place which offers singles/doubles with attached bath for Rs 60/105, or Rs 50/75 with common bath.

Anand Lodge (☎ 21256), a two minute walk from the bus stand, has acceptable doubles (only) with attached bath and balconies for Rs 100.

Hotel Navtara (☎ 20831, Kaikini Rd), about 500m from the bus stand, has clean bright rooms for Rs 90/130.

Hotel Bhadra (☎ 25212), near the Kali Nadi Bridge, has modern doubles with attached bath for Rs 200 and air-con doubles for Rs 450. It has a mediocre veg/nonveg restaurant and a bar.

Devbag Forest Beach Resort is administered by Jungle Lodges & Resorts (☎ 26596) from its office opposite the Hotel Bhadra. The resort is reached by a 10 minute boat ride from the dock next to the Kali Nadi Bridge. It's extremely peaceful, and the accommodation in huts set on stilts is very comfortable, but the price is over the top: foreigners pay Rs 1400 per person per night (Indians pay only Rs 700). There's a bar and restaurant (food is included in the price), and a secluded private beach. For the price of a Rs 50 return boat fare, you can visit the resort for the day.

Udipi Hotel and its sister restaurant *Hotel Savita*, both on Main Rd, are clean, veg snack and 'meals' specialists. *Hotel Sitara*, next to the Udipi Hotel, has a range of reasonably priced Indian, continental and Chinese dishes, and a pleasant roof garden.

Getting There & Away
Karwar is a main station on the Konkan Railway, meaning that both express and passenger trains stop here. The express train to Mangalore leaves at 9.30 am, and the passenger train leaves at 3.30 pm. The passenger train to Margao leaves at noon, and the express departs at 7.30 pm. The train station is 8km from the town centre.

The Karwar bus stand is on the southern edge of the town centre. There are four daily buses to Panaji (Rs 32, four hours), and many more to Margao. There are frequent services to Hubli (Rs 46, four hours), and five buses a day to Belgaum (five hours). There's a service at 3 pm to Londa, three buses to Shimoga, two to Jog Falls, one to Hassan, and one direct bus at 9.30 am to Hospet (eight hours).

There are five KSRTC buses a day to Gokarna, but private buses also shuttle between Karwar, Ankola and Gokarna. They depart from just outside the bus stand entrance.

AROUND KARWAR
The nearest beaches to Karwar are **Binaga** and **Arga**, three and 5km south of the town respectively. They're both scimitar-shaped swathes of sand and are generally deserted.

Krishna Resthouse (☎ 21613), set back from the beach at Binaga, is a great place to stay if you want some peace and quiet. It's

a basic family-run guesthouse with a two double rooms with common bath, and a small cottage, all of which go for Rs 150. You can either self cater or arrange food in advance with the owner. It's Rs 25 by autorickshaw or Rs 2 by bus from Karwar.

At the town of **Ankola**, 37km south of Karwar, are the 15th century ruins of King Sarpamalika's Fort and the equally old Sri Venkatraman Temple. In an unmarked mudbrick garage near the temple are two giant wooden chariots large enough to be pulled by elephants. They are carved with scenes from the *Ramayana*. There's a long deserted beach at **Belekeri**, 4km north of Ankola.

DANDELI
Tel Area Code: 08284
Dandeli is a reasonably nice town, perched in a magical location along the Kali River. It is the headquarters for a large timber industry, gateway to the Dandeli Wildlife Sanctuary (see following entry), and location of the Wildlife Division of the Deputy Conservator of Forests (DCF; ☎ 31585) – one of about a dozen 'forest departments' in Dandeli. The DCF is about 100m up, and on the right, from the Riverview Forest Bungalows.

Places to Stay & Eat
To take a day trip to the Dandeli Wildlife Sanctuary, you can stay in Dandeli town.

Riverview Forest Bungalows, right on the river, has a wonderful setting, but is often full of forest rangers living the good life. Try booking at the DCF in Dandeli, or the Forest Department (☎ 08383-27128) in nearby Haliyal. Rooms cost Rs 50 per person.

State Guesthouse (☎ 31299), opposite the bus stand, is the best place, but is popular so get there early or book ahead. Immaculately clean and comfortable rooms cost Rs 200; the deluxe rooms (Rs 250) have TV with remote control.

Tourist Lodge (☎ 31007), next door, is a dingy, cheaper alternative. Airless cubicles cost Rs 120/150 for a single/double. The *Prakash Lodge*, about 200m down from the bus stand, is the same price, but a little nicer and friendlier.

KARNATAKA

The best place for a meal or cold beer is the *Shetty Lunch Home*, close to the State Guesthouse.

Getting There & Away

Buses regularly go to Dharwad and/or Hubli (Rs 20, one hour) via Haliyal – this is a very pretty trip. There are also three buses a day to Karwar; to any other place, change at Hubli or Dharwad. Unfortunately, the connections to Goa, and Panaji in particular, are not good – you will have to get onward transport in Haliyal. The train service was not functioning at the time of research.

DANDELI WILDLIFE SANCTUARY

This 834 sq km park, the second largest sanctuary (after Bandipur) in Karnataka, was established in 1975. It is surprisingly neglected by visitors, but is well set up and a good detour on the way to or from Goa. Sadly, some of what the region has to offer, including hiking opportunities, is off limits to everyone – courtesy of the Karnataka Power Corporation which seems to build a dam on every available stretch of river.

Flora & Fauna

The sanctuary is mainly moist mixed deciduous and semi-evergreen forest, and you will find plenty of teak, bamboo, ferns and shrubs. Most of the wildlife consists of gaur, wild dogs, barking deer, mouse deer, common langur, flying squirrels and macaques, but you may see wolves, wild boar and one of the 40 wild elephants. Partridges, owls, eagles, peacocks and great pied hornbills are among the birdlife. Encroaching by domesticated animals, mining and logging are real problems, which result in crop-raiding by elephants, and subsequent reprisals by angry villagers.

Visiting the Park

The park is only open from 6 to 8 am, and 4 to 6 pm, and no amount of begging will get you in at any other time. The only way into the sanctuary is by private vehicle, which allows you to see a fair bit even if the wildlife is fairly scarce. Inquire at your

hotel or at the DCF in Dandeli about hiring a vehicle. Don't pay more than about Rs 100 per hour and a little less for a taxi. The entrance fee (which includes a guide from the sanctuary) costs Rs 100 per vehicle. Inside the park, ask the guide to show you the **Kavla Caves** and **Ulvi Temple**.

The park is closed during the rainy season, ie from June to October. The best time to visit is from December to May. There are four entrances, but the most convenient place is Kulgi, where the **Nature, Education & Interpretation Centre** (no telephone) is worth visiting. Visit the DCF in Dandeli before you arrange anything.

Places to Stay

You could take a day trip from Dharwad or Hubli, but Dandeli town (see the Dandeli entry) is the best place to base yourself.

Nature Camp, next to the Interpretation Centre in the park, is the most authentic option. Permanent tents, with a concrete floor and shared facilities, cost Rs 100, and hold four to five people. Bring your own sleeping bag and mattress; meals are available. Book at the DCF in Dandeli town.

Kali River Camp (☎ 08284-30266) is the only resort. Located on the other side of the river from Dandeli town, it offers luxurious tents, though some dearer rooms were being built at the time of research. This set up is not as impressive as other places run by Jungle Lodges & Resorts (see under Travel Agencies in the Bangalore section for booking details) but the prices, which include meals, wildlife viewing and boat trips, are lower: US$60 per person.

Central Karnataka

HAMPI

Pop: 930 Tel Area Code: 08394

Vijayanagar, near the village of Hampi, is one of the most fascinating historical sites in South India. Set in a strange and beautiful boulder-strewn landscape, the remnants of the great city have an almost magical quality, and the sheer size of the site is awesome.

Hampi has become a thriving travellers' centre and most people stay at least a couple of days to soak up the atmosphere and explore the area. If you're in a hurry, it is possible to see the main sites in one day, either by bicycle or, if you start early, on foot. Signposting in some parts of the site is inadequate, but you can't really get lost. It's not safe to wander around the ruins alone at dawn or dusk.

Orientation

There are two main points of entry to the ruins: Hampi Bazaar in the north and Kamalapuram, about 4km to the south. Kamalapuram is a sleepy little village with one hotel, a couple of restaurants and the site museum. The main travellers' scene is in Hampi Bazaar where there are numerous lodges and restaurants.

There are a few buses between Hampi Bazaar and Kamalapuram, and rickshaws are also available. To walk between the two villages takes around 40 minutes.

Information

The tourist office (☎ 41339) is on the main street of Hampi Bazaar and is open from 8 am to 5.30 pm daily during the high season (December to January) and 10 am to 5.30 pm at other times. It can arrange guides for Rs 350 per day or Rs 250 for half a day, and they also sell maps of the site. If it's out of stock, Aspiration Stores, near the entrance to the Virupaksha Temple, has a choice of three good maps for Rs 10 to Rs 15, as well as a selection of books on Hampi. Although it's not really about the monuments themselves, Robert Sewell's *A Forgotten Empire*, which was originally published at the end of the 19th century, is still a fascinating read.

Warning: Theft in Hampi

The problem of thefts and muggings in Hampi has now become serious enough for the police to require travellers arriving in Hampi Bazaar to register with them at the beginning of their stay. There is no compulsion to do so, but guesthouses such as the Shanthi Guesthouse prominently advertise the request, and draw travellers' attention to it on arrival. The police office is just inside the front entrance of the Virupaksha Temple, and travellers are asked to register their arrival in a log book, complete with visa details. You may be asked to show your passport.

The main purpose of this officialdom seems to be to get newcomers into the office for a quick briefing about the hazards of Hampi. There have been several incidents of tourists being robbed at knifepoint while touring the ruins. Recently the police have been searching for a thief known as 'Nagendra', whose mugshot you may see prominently displayed on the office wall (assuming that he hasn't been caught).

The advice is very simple:

- Don't carry your valuables with you when you travel around the ruins – leave them in a locker in your room.
- Don't wander around the ruins at dawn or dusk, and certainly not after sunset.
- Try to avoid visiting the ruins alone at any time of day.
- Don't accept food, drinks or cigarettes from strangers.

Particular trouble spots in the past have been near Matunga Hill, behind the Vittal Temple, and down by the riverside.

To put all of this into perspective there has so far been no violence (although it has obviously been threatened) in any of the attacks, and most visitors will have no problems whatsoever. And with Hampi's star in the ascendant as Karnataka's major tourist drawcard the authorities are doing as much as possible to ensure that all visitors are warned of the danger.

KARNATAKA

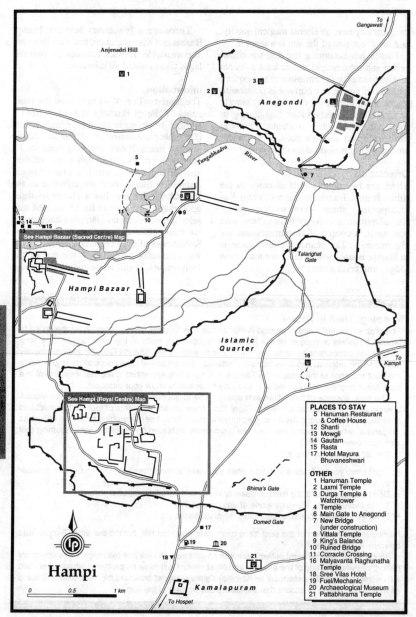

To Gangavati

Anjenadri Hill

Anegondi

Tungabhadra River

Talarighat Gate

See Hampi Bazaar (Sacred Centre) Map

Hampi Bazaar

Islamic Quarter

To Kampli

See Hampi (Royal Centre) Map

Bhima's Gate

Domed Gate

Hampi

0   0.5   1 km

To Hospet

Kamalapuram

PLACES TO STAY
5   Hanuman Restaurant
    & Coffee House
12 Shanti
13 Mowgli
14 Gautam
15 Rasta
17 Hotel Mayura
    Bhuvaneshwari

OTHER
1   Hanuman Temple
2   Laxmi Temple
3   Durga Temple &
    Watchtower
4   Temple
6   Main Gate to Anegondi
7   New Bridge
    (under construction)
8   Vittala Temple
9   King's Balance
10 Ruined Bridge
11 Corracle Crossing
16 Malyavanta Raghunatha
    Temple
18 Sree Vilas Hotel
19 Fuel/Mechanic
20 Archaeological Museum
21 Pattabhirama Temple

The **museum** at Kamalapuram is open between 10 am and 5 pm daily except Friday. On display are a number of fine sculptures and some of the artefacts that have been recovered from the excavations, as well as a large floor model of the layout of Vijayanagar. This in itself is worth making a visit for, as it gives an overall view of the scale of the site that is difficult to obtain if you're moving around the ruins themselves.

At the eastern end of Hampi Bazaar, near the monolithic Nandi, there's a small photo gallery. The display contrasts pictures taken in 1896 with shots taken from exactly the same positions in 1983. The amount of restoration that has taken place over the intervening century is clearly visible. Strangely the photos taken just over a century ago are much more striking than recently taken ones.

The best place to change money is the Canara Bank in Hampi Bazaar, open between 11 am and 2 pm on weekdays (except Wednesday) and from 11 am to 12.30 pm on Saturday. It will change travellers cheques but not cash, and can give advances on Visa and MasterCard. There are authorised moneychangers offering lower rates on the main street.

There's a small post office up the lane just to the left of the entrance to the Virupaksha Temple. Letters can be sent here for poste restante – have them addressed to you at Poste Restante, Hampi, 583239, Karnataka.

Several travel agents in Hampi will book train, bus and plane tickets.

History

The Empire Vijayanagar, 'City of Victory', was once the capital of one of the largest Hindu empires in Indian history. Founded in 1336, at a time when the Muslim armies of the north were conquering and pillaging almost at will, the new empire was an amalgam of the ancient Hindu kingdoms of the south. The alliance provided a solution that managed to hold the invaders at bay for over two centuries.

The site of the city is known to have been occupied long before the foundation of the new kingdom; local inscriptions suggest that the area was settled in the 1st century and that there was a Buddhist centre nearby. The history of the Vijayanagar Empire, however, starts in the small fortified enclave of Anegondi, on the northern bank of the Tungabhadra River. Anegondi was devastated in 1334 by the armies of Muhammed Tughluq, the Sultan of Delhi. A Muslim ruler was appointed, but as soon as the army retired from the region, he found the area ungovernable, and subsequently a local Hindu ruler was placed in authority. Stories vary about who this ruler was, but over the following years it seems that power fell into the hands of a minister named Harihara, and his brother Bukka. Within a short time Harihara managed to consolidate his position and declared independence. The Hindu kingdoms of the south, facing almost certain annihilation at the hands of the Muslim armies, rallied willingly to the call of a competent commander. Thus began the kingdom of Vijayanagar.

Just as there are several versions of the story, so there are different accounts of the founding of the city of Vijayanagar itself. In one, the first ruler of the dynasty, while out hunting, met the Hindu saint Madhavacharya, who advised him to build a new city on the site. In another the saint founded the city himself, and in yet another the holy man gave his blessing to a poor shepherd who subsequently came to rule the area and built the city as his capital.

Even if there is an element of truth in these tales, it seems most likely that the motives for moving the city from Anegondi would have been twofold. Lack of space to the north of the river may have been important, as may have been the attraction of placing the Tungabhadra River between their enemies and themselves. Whatever the exact reasons, the city on the present site was founded in c.1336 and almost immediately began to grow rapidly. Inscriptions suggest that even by 1340 the new rulers had acquired extensive territories, and under the rule of Bukka I (c.1343-79) the majority of South India was brought under the control of the new empire.

KARNATAKA

Despite a rapid growth in wealth and military power, the fledgling state was not immune from its northern neighbours, and for the next two centuries the history of the region was one of constant invasion and massacre. The Hindu armies occasionally got the upper hand, but generally the Deccan sultans inflicted the worst defeats, and had to be bought off several times with huge payments. The atrocities that were committed almost defy belief.

In 1366 Bukka I responded to a perceived slight by capturing the Muslim stronghold of Mudkal and slaughtering every inhabitant bar one, who escaped to carry the news to Muhammad Shah, the Sultan of the Deccan. Muhammad swore that he would not rest until he had killed 100,000 Hindus, but he far exceeded even his own predictions. The Muslim historian Firishtah estimates that half a million 'infidels' were killed in the ensuing campaign.

The Hindu armies took their rare opportunities to repay the blood debts whenever they could. In a campaign of 1419 they gained the upper hand by bribing one of the sultan's attendants to attack him during the battle. As the mortally wounded sultan left the field, the slaughter commenced. Firishtah observed:

The Hindoos made a general massacre of the mussulmauns, and erected a platform with their heads on the field of battle. They followed the sultan into his own country, which they wasted with fire and sword, took many places, broke down many mosques and holy places, slaughtered the people without mercy...

Revenge was not long in coming. In 1422 the sultan's successor, Ahmad Shah I, led an army across the Tungabhadra and surprised the Hindu forces, who fled in disarray:

Ahmad Shaw, not stopping to besiege the city, overran the open country, and wherever he came, put to death men, women, and children, without mercy ... Laying aside all humanity, whenever the number of slain amounted to twenty thousand, he halted three days and made a festival in celebration of the bloody work.

Vijayanagar's fortunes improved considerably

after 1482 when the Bahmani kingdom, which had controlled the whole of the northern Deccan, disintegrated leaving five fledgling, warring sultanates.

With little realistic opposition from the north, the Hindu empire reached its peak over the following years. A strong new dynasty was founded under Krishnadevaraya, and Vijayanagar controlled almost all trade to and from the southern peninsula. Among the most important exports were spices and cotton, while the most valued imports were high-quality horses for the Vijayanagar cavalry. The trade in horses was, by agreement with the Portuguese in Goa, tied up so that the Vijayanagar Empire bought all of the best horses in order to avoid the Muslims getting them. Taxes on trade and agriculture accrued a massive wealth, and almost the whole of the southern peninsula came under undisputed Vijayanagar control.

Within the structure of this success, however, lay the seeds of the empire's downfall. Krishnadevaraya strengthened his grip over the empire by assigning huge tracts of land to high-ranking military commanders on the proviso that they would supply him with troops and taxes. The system worked as long as there was a strong and undisputed monarch on the throne, but with the accession of weaker rulers, the policy of concentrating power in the hands of a few militarily powerful leaders was fatal. A series of uprisings followed, the largest of which, led by a noble named Rama Raya divided the kingdom fatally, just at a time when the Muslim sultanates were beginning to form themselves into a new alliance.

In 1565 a Muslim coalition engaged the Hindu armies at the Battle of Talikota. The result was a complete rout of the Vijayanagar forces, and the devastation of the City of Victory. The last of the Vijayanagar line escaped, and the dynasty, now without a capital, limped on for several years. In reality however, power in the region passed either to Muslim rulers, or to the local chiefs who had come to power as loyal followers of the Vijayanagar kings.

Krishnadevaraya

The Vijayanagar Empire reached its height during the reign of Krishnadevaraya, who came to the throne in 1509. A monarch renowned for his grace, he was also a commanding figure, who ruled his empire personally and led by example. The 16th century European traveller Domingo Paez described him as 'gallant and perfect in all things', and also gives us an insight into his physical presence: before dawn every day, according to Paez, the king would 'take in his arms great weights made of earthenware, and then, taking the sword, he exercises himself with it and then he wrestles with one of his wrestlers. After this labour he mounts a horse and gallops about the plain ...'.

Soon after coming to the throne, Krishnadevaraya asserted his command over the empire by engaging in a series of campaigns in which he enjoyed great success. He settled down to a fruitful reign in which he personally supervised several projects within the capital. He built the Krishna and Hazara Ramasvami temples, started work on the Vittala Temple, and commissioned the immense image of Narasimha. He constructed a new irrigation system which even today waters the area of the city, and he founded the 'new city' Nagalpura (now known as Hospet).

There was one thing that he longed to do, however, and that was to capture Raichur. The Muslim stronghold had for nearly two centuries been coveted by the Vijayanagar kings, although none had had the power to take it from their enemy. In May 1520, with an army estimated at nearly three-quarters of a million fighting men, Krishnadevaraya laid siege to Raichur and captured it, inflicting a decisive defeat on the Sultan of Bijapur's army. At last the Vijayanagar Empire was the undisputed power of the Deccan.

Some say that Krishnadevaraya's actions following his victory sowed the seeds of the empire's downfall. During the after-battle celebrations, a Muslim envoy arrived to make peace and Krishnadevaraya declared that if the sultan would kiss his foot, he would give him back the fortress. Since the sultan naturally did not reply to this slight, Krishnadevaraya set off in search of him, occupying Bijapur itself for a short time. The insult offered to one of their number, and the sight of a Muslim capital occupied by the Hindu enemy, was enough to galvanise the Muslim rulers of the Deccan and, 40 years later, they took their opportunity to finish off Vijayanagar once and for all.

Krishnadevaraya saw none of this, however. After a rule of some 20 years he fell sick and died in 1529, aged about 42.

The City To have founded a city so close to the northern boundary of the Hindu lands and also to have given it the title 'City of Victory', betrays a huge amount of self-confidence. The scale of the planning, too, was ambitious. At its height, the city covered an area of 43 sq km, was surrounded by seven lines of fortification, and was reputed to have had a population of about half a million.

Vijayanagar's wealth was nowhere better seen than in its busy bazaars, which were centres of international commerce. European travellers such as the Portuguese Fernão Nuniz and Domingo Paez described the scene:

In this city you will find men belonging to every nation and people, because of the great trade which it has, and the many precious stones there, principally diamonds.

The religion of the society of Vijayanagar was a hybrid of current Hinduism, with the gods Vishnu and Shiva being lavishly worshipped in the orthodox manner. At the same time, Jainism was also prominent, and there were even a number of mosques built for the use of the Muslim mercenaries. Brahmins were privileged; *sati* (the Hindu practice of self-immolation of the widow on the funeral pyre of her husband) was widely practised and sacred prostitutes frequently worked from the city's temples.

Excavation at Vijayanagar was undertaken in 1976 by the Archaeological Survey of

India in collaboration with the Karnataka state government.

General Layout

The ruins that are visible today cover only a part of the entire area of the city – Nagalpura (Hospet), for example, was a satellite town built to extend the main city in the reign of Krishnadevaraya. In outline, however, archaeologists tend to split the city into two main areas – the so-called Sacred Centre, which is to the north, and the Royal Centre, to the south. These two areas contain the major collections of ruins, but by no means all of them. To the north-east lies the Vittala Temple, and beyond that, on the northern side of the river, the ancient enclave of Anegondi. There are also important buildings to the south-east and east of the Royal Centre.

Sacred Centre

The Sacred Centre lies on the northern edge of the city, on the banks of the holy Tungabhadra River. It was here, according to various legends, that the Hindu sage Madhavacharya lived, in a shrine on the slopes of Hemakuta Hill. His role in advising the foundation of a new city has already been mentioned, and the same legends also have it that the first building erected was the temple of Pampapati, which is the modern Virupaksha Temple. The Portuguese traveller Nuniz repeats this story, claiming that Harihara I, the first ruler of the new empire, founded the temple in honour of his mentor. It seems likely that the name of the village which today exists around the ruins (Hampi) would have come from the name of the goddess enshrined in the temple – Pampapati.

Virupaksha Temple Wherever the truth lies, it is generally agreed that the Virupaksha Temple was indeed one of the earliest structures to be built in the new city, and that

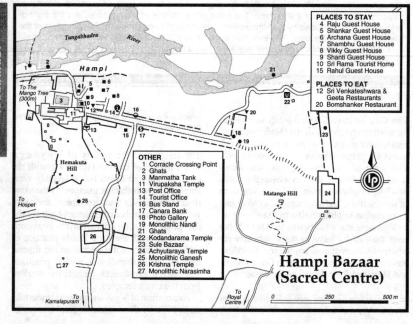

PLACES TO STAY
4 Raju Guest House
5 Shankar Guest House
6 Archana Guest House
7 Shambhu Guest House
8 Vikky Guest House
9 Shanti Guest House
10 Sri Rama Tourist Home
15 Rahul Guest House

PLACES TO EAT
12 Sri Venkateshwara & Geeta Restaurants
20 Bomshanker Restaurant

OTHER
1 Corracle Crossing Point
2 Ghats
3 Manmatha Tank
11 Virupaksha Temple
13 Post Office
14 Tourist Office
16 Bus Stand
17 Canara Bank
18 Photo Gallery
19 Monolithic Nandi
21 Ghats
22 Kodandarama Temple
23 Sule Bazaar
24 Achyutaraya Temple
25 Monolithic Ganesh
26 Krishna Temple
27 Monolithic Narasimha

Tungabhadra River

Hampi

To The Mango Tree (300m)

Hemakuta Hill

To Hospet

To Kamalapuram

Matanga Hill

To Royal Centre

Hampi Bazaar (Sacred Centre)

0   250   500 m

it was probably constructed on the foundations of an earlier temple.

The main gopuram, almost 50m high, is thought to have been built in 1442 (the girders that now support the entranceway are remnants of restoration work that took place during British rule). The second, smaller, gopuram was added in 1510 by Krishnadevaraya on the occasion of a festival in honour of his coronation. It was shortly after this that the intrepid Domingo Paez visited, and reported that this temple was 'the one which they hold in most veneration, and to which they make great pilgrimages …'. The sanctum, he noted:

… is like a chapel, where stands the idol which they adore … at the first gate are doorkeepers who never allow any one to enter except the Brahmans that have charge of it, and I, because I gave something to them, was allowed to enter…

The main shrine, at the west end of the inner courtyard, is dedicated to Virupaksha, a form of Shiva. The temple sits atop a raised platform, and with a large, pillared mandapam forms the entranceway. The solid stone pillars are carved with the figures of rearing creatures, and the ceiling of the central area is painted, although it has become blackened with soot over the years. On the north side of the shrine is a smaller sanctuary to the protector of the city, the goddess Pampadevi, an incarnation of Parvati. Up a small flight of steps, in the north-west corner of the inner courtyard, is an interesting spot where the temple builders experimented with the pinhole camera concept. Light is admitted through a narrow slit in the wall, and an inverted image of the front gopuram is cast onto the rear wall of the chamber.

Entry to the temple is free from 6.30 to 8 am and 6.30 to 8 pm, otherwise you pay Rs 1 for entry, Rs 50 to use a camera, and Rs 500 to use a video.

Hemakuta Hill Overlooking the Virupaksha Temple to the south, Hemakuta Hill contains some of the earliest structures in the whole ruins, some of them built before Vijayanagar

times. Most of the temples are Jain, demonstrating the diverse religious freedoms of early Vijayanagar. The view from the hill over Hampi Bazaar is well worth making the short climb for.

On the south side of the hill, next to the road leading to the bazaar, is a small temple housing a 4.5m-high statue of **Ganesh**, carved from a single block of stone. The size and artistry of this statue are only surpassed by the monolithic sculpture, some 300 to 400m to the south, of the man-lion god **Narasimha**. This immense (7m high) work of art was carved during the reign of Krishnadevaraya. As a result of the vandalism that took place when the city was sacked, the figure is missing its hands and toes, but otherwise it looks as fresh as the day it was carved. To the right of the Narasimha figure is a small square shrine which houses a huge Shiva lingam.

Lying between the Ganesh Temple and the statue of Narasimha are the remains of a **Krishna Temple**, also built during the reign of Krishnadevaraya. This enormous complex equalled the city's other major temples in size and design, but is now in a state of decay. The long avenue leading up to the entrance is now a ruined line of stones projecting into the fields, but it's still possible to imagine how the major temples of the city, each with its own bazaar, formed very definite centres of activity. Entrance to the temple is via a massive gateway, above which once stood a proud pagoda – though only the base of it now remains.

Hampi Bazaar Walking up Hampi Bazaar from the Virupaksha Temple, you pass the corrugated iron shed where the huge temple chariot is stored between religious festivals. The bazaar road stretches eastwards for 750m, and it's not difficult to imagine how the street must have been in its heyday. Domingo Paez, visiting in around 1520, described it as a street …

… of very beautiful houses with balconies and arcades, in which are sheltered the pilgrims that come to visit the temple, and there are also houses

for the lodging of the upper classes; the king has a palace in the same street...

At the far eastern end of the road is a pavilion containing a huge monolithic image of **Nandi**, Shiva's bull. In most Shiva temples the image of Nandi is a couple of yards in front of the sanctum, or perhaps just outside the temple itself looking in towards the deity. The size of this carving and the fact that it faces down the entire length of the bazaar to the Virupaksha Temple, give an idea of the scale of the architects' conceptions for this northern part of the city.

East of Hampi Bazaar Near the eastern end of Hampi Bazaar an obvious track, navigable only on foot, leads left towards the Vittala Temple, about 2km away. The track runs parallel to the river, past stepped ghats, to the tiny **Kodandarama Temple**, next to which there's a small drinks stall – perfect for a halfway stop. Just beyond this to the right are the impressive ruined lines of **Sule Bazaar**. At the southern end of this area is the **Achyutaraya Temple**, which has an isolated location at the foot of Matunga Hill, making it even more atmospheric than the Vittala Temple. The scale of the front gateway to the Achyutaraya Temple is a reminder of its former glory – even though the temple itself is in a poor state of repair.

Continuing north-east towards the Vittala Temple you climb a rocky path and pass a number of small piles of stones. By tradition, couples who want children visit this spot and place the stones as an offering. When the child is born, they are supposed to return to remove them. To the left, perched on Anjenadri Hill on the far side of the river, one can see the tiny whitewashed Hanuman Temple (see the Anegondi entry later in this section).

Vittala Temple Highlight of the ruins, this 16th century temple is one of India's three World Heritage Monuments. It's in a good state of preservation, though purists may well have doubts about the cement block columns which have been erected to keep the main structure from falling down. Work is thought to have started on the temple in the reign of Krishnadevaraya (1509-29), and although it was never finished or consecrated, the temple's incredible sculptural work is the pinnacle of Vijayanagar art.

The complex has three entrances, although today only the southern entrance is kept open. The temple itself is in the centre of the courtyard on a raised platform, and three similar, but smaller, halls are also in the temple precinct. The intricately carved pillars depict the figures of rearing animals. Most intriguing are the multitude of tiny columns which are so slender that they reverberate when tapped, producing a musical note. Unfortunately this means that almost every visitor to the temple for a number of years has hit the pillars to make them 'sing'. The practice is being actively discouraged as many of the pillars are becoming rather the worse for wear.

The temple is dedicated to Vishnu. To the east of the main sanctum is a chariot carved entirely from stone including stone wheels which were once capable of turning. The chariot houses an image of Garuda, Vishnu's bird vehicle.

Entry to the temple costs Rs 5, except on Friday, when it's free.

Near Vittala Just to the south-west of the temple stands the **King's Balance** – a simple stone archway and lintel where the king's weight in gold and jewels was measured annually, the glittering counterbalance to be given to the priests. A dusty path leads a short way south-west, down to the riverbank, where you can see the remains of a large **bridge**. There's a better view of it from the north bank looking south, but even from here you can appreciate the scale of the structure which was built on hundreds of pillars of granite.

Royal Centre
The name traditionally given to this part of the ruins is misleading, for the area contains numerous temples and civic buildings as well as the palaces, pavilions and stables which archaeologists believe were the property of the

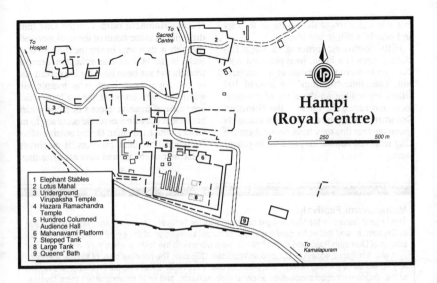

Hampi (Royal Centre)

0   250   500 m

1 Elephant Stables
2 Lotus Mahal
3 Underground Virupaksha Temple
4 Hazara Ramachandra Temple
5 Hundred Columned Audience Hall
6 Mahanavami Platform
7 Stepped Tank
8 Large Tank
9 Queens' Bath

To Hospet
To Sacred Centre
To Kamalapuram

Vijayanagar royals. It seems in fact as though this southern area of the city – separated from the Sacred Centre by the large irrigation canal which supplied water to the capital – might well have contained the bulk of the living area in the city.

Queens' Bath Approaching the area of the Royal Centre from Kamalapuram in the south-east, the first important building you come to is the Queens' Bath. This small square structure seems to have been designed for royal recreation. Inside the doorway, a colonnaded passage runs around a large central bathing tank. Doors and windows on all sides catch any available breeze, and with the shade of the passageways, and perhaps of an awning, it must have been an ideal spot to while away a hot afternoon.

You can still see the channel from the aqueduct by which the bath was filled, as well as the drainage outlet for when the water was changed. The ceiling of the passageway around the tank is divided into domes which have delicate plasterwork designs.

Royal Enclosure Area To the north-west of

the Queens' Bath is a large walled area containing a number of structures that appear to have been important in the civic life of the city. The **Mahanavami Platform** in the north-east corner of the enclosure is easily recognisable by the stairway running up the western side, and is thought to have been used in the celebration of religious festivals. The sides of the multilevel platform are covered with relief carvings showing elephants, horses, camels, warriors and dancers. According to accounts by foreigners who witnessed the festivities, it seems that the top of the platform was covered with a wooden structure and a cloth awning, and that the king sat here to survey the proceedings.

To the south of the platform is a deep **stepped tank** with regular and perfectly symmetrical steps on all sides. The mathematical precision of the design is further testimony to the skill of the Vijayanagar stonemasons, as are the nearby **aqueducts** and the **large tank** just to the south.

The scale of engineering that was undertaken to provide Vijayanagar with adequate water supplies is quite remarkable. The real triumph of the whole system was the canal that was cut through the centre of the city and which is still in use today.

In the north-west corner of the Royal Enclosure Area is a large, bare platform with steps up to a crumbling dais at its southern end. The stone 'footings' for around 100 pillars are visible on the floor of the platform and hence the name – the **Hundred Columned Audience Hall**. Archaeologists speculate that this may have been where the king received deputations and sat in judgement.

Hazara Ramachandra Temple One hundred metres to the north of the audience hall, through a gateway in the next section of wall, is the Hazara Ramachandra Temple, thought to have been built for the private use of the royal household. The temple sits within its own courtyard, the walls of which are made of massive blocks of stone which have been cut with incredible accuracy to interlock with each other. On the outside of the walls are low relief carvings of elephants, horsemen, warriors and dancers. The most

---

Mahanavami Festival

The largest festival in the Vijayanagar calendar was the festival of Mahanavami, which took place in September and lasted for nine days. Our principal knowledge of the event comes from the accounts of Domingo Paez and Fernão Nuniz, who witnessed the festival when they visited the city.

It was a religious occasion, but also an important civic one. The principal deity of the city was publicly honoured by the king himself, and presided over the events. It was also the time when the nobles of the kingdom pledged themselves anew to their monarch, and he in return granted them favours. Nuniz noted that the king would honour them by giving them '... scarves of honour for their personal use ... and this he does each year to the captains at the time when they pay him their land-rents'.

The festival started each day, according to Paes, with the king's visit to the statue of the deity, followed by the sacrifice of '... twenty four buffaloes and a hundred and fifty sheep'. After further elaborate rituals the morning ended with a royal audience in which '... all the captains and chief people come and make their salaam to him, and some, if they so desire, present some gifts to him'.

In the afternoon there was a further royal audience, which was carefully stage managed by, in Krishnadevaraya's time, the chief minister Salvatinica. 'This Salvatinica stands inside the arena where the festivals go on, near one of the doors, and from there gives the word for the admission of all things necessary for the festival.' The afternoon's events were dominated by displays of dancing women and by wrestling: '... their wrestling does not seem like ours, but there are blows (given), so severe as to break teeth, and put out eyes, and disfigure faces, so much so that here and there men are carried off speechless by their friends ...'.

Festivities continued after sunset with drama, fireworks, dancing and displays of wealth. Paez recalls in particular 'women clothed in the following manner ... collars on the neck with jewels of gold very richly set with many emeralds and diamonds and rubies and pearls ... on the waist many girdles of gold and of precious stones'. Nuniz, visiting some years later, was similarly impressed: 'These women are so richly bedecked with gold and precious stones that they are hardly able to move'. Each day was ended with further prayer and sacrifice.

The culmination of the festival came on the ninth and final day. 'On the last day there are slaughtered two hundred and fifty buffaloes and four thousand five hundred sheep.' The final event was a military review when the massive army was lined up '... in such a way that you could see neither plain nor hill that was not entirely covered with troops'. Foreign policy for the year ahead was decided by a very direct method. 'The Rao ... takes a bow in his hand and shoots three arrows, namely one for the Ydallcão [Sultan of Bijapur], and another for the king of Cotamuloco [Shah of Golkonda], and yet another for the Portuguese; it was his custom to make war on the kingdom lying in the direction where the arrow reached furthest.'

striking feature in the temple itself are the four huge, black stone pillars which support the ceiling of the second hall.

Zenana Enclosure Approximately 400m north of the Hazara Ramachandra Temple is a walled area commonly known as the Zenana Enclosure. This, it is speculated, may have contained a number of buildings that belonged to the royal households. The main building of interest in the first courtyard is the **Lotus Mahal**, an open-sided pavilion which may have been used as a reception area. Through a small gateway to the east is a second courtyard, which is dominated by the impressive **Elephant Stables**.

Underground Virupaksha Temple Returning to the Ramachandra Temple, take the road running west, and after 500m you come to the remains of the underground Virupaksha Temple. Much of the interior is now flooded, but you can still explore a certain amount of the building.

East of Kamalapuram

Approximately 1km east of the museum in Kamalapuram, the **Pattabhirama Temple** is one of the largest temples in the ruins, its size further exaggerated by the appearance of the huge bare courtyard that surrounds the central platform on which the temple stands. The temple faces east and has an impressively large pillared mandapam. To the south-east of this is another pillared platform similar to those in the Vittala Temple. The eastern entrance to the enclosure is surmounted by a towering brickwork gopuram, although much of the detail has crumbled.

Approximately 4km to the north-east of Kamalapuram, the fine **Malyavanta Raghunatha Temple** is largely overlooked by tourists because of its isolated position. The entrance from the road is via a concrete track which winds up a short incline. Inside the walled enclosure is the main temple, the sanctuary of which is built around a massive rock which protrudes from the ceiling. The eastern end of the temple is an impressive colonnaded hall. To the south of this is an even more remarkable hall with slender pillars similar to those at the Vittala Temple, and a large central area, perhaps for dancing. There are gopurams over the east and south entrances.

Passing through a gate in the western side of the enclosure wall you come to a tiny whitewashed shrine built against the side of a boulder, on the top of which is perched an even smaller shrine. From beside the boulder there's a good view across the whole area and you can even make out some of the buildings in the Royal Enclosure.

Anegondi

Access to Anegondi will soon be easier, with the completion of the new bridge which is being built across the river, just to the east of the Vittala Temple. At the time of writing the only other way to Anegondi was to take a corracle across the river. If you have a motorbike you can cross the river via the bridge at Kampli, approximately 10km to the north-east.

Anegondi is an old fortified stronghold, which can realistically lay claim to having been the first major settlement in the area, from which Vijayanagar was born. There's not too much to see here today, although much of the old defensive wall is intact.

Crossing the river at the site of the new bridge you come first to the massive **main gate**, which gave access to the river. Follow the dusty road north from the gate into the centre of the village where there's a small temple, outside which is parked a large wooden chariot for use in religious festivals. Beyond these, you come to the northern gate of the village.

To the west of Anegondi, in the rocky ridge which runs from north-west to south-east, are to be found the tiny **Durga Temple** and further up the ridge, a stretch of wall with a watchtower and some remaining buildings. Return to the road to pass to the north of the ridge. If you turn south just beyond it, a winding lane leads up to the **Laxmi Temple** where there's a large tank and an ashram.

Back on the road again, and slightly further

KARNATAKA

to the west, you can climb the steep steps to the tiny whitewashed **Hanuman Temple** which is perched on top of the prominent rocky hill, and which is clearly visible from Hampi Bazaar. The climb is hard work, but the views from the top are great.

The Corracles of Hampi

Corracles have been ferrying folk across the Tungabhadra River for centuries. To the visitor today it seems amazing that a mode of transport as old as the ruins themselves is still in use. The design has changed little, and the circular craft, constructed of interwoven strips of wood, look much as they must have done in the days of the Vijayanagar Empire itself. The only concession to the modern age is that they are no longer covered in animal hide, but now make use of plastic sacking covered with tar for waterproofing.

It's a memorable experience, squatting in the side of a basket boat and being paddled across the water in the early morning or at sunset. Relax and imagine that somehow the ruins have come to life. The descriptions of Domingo Paez, the Portuguese adventurer who visited Vijayanagar in 1520, seem totally contemporary: 'People cross to this place by boats which are round like baskets ... Men row them with a sort of paddle, and the boats are always turning round, as they cannot go straight like others ...'.

EDDIE GERALD

Places to Stay

Hampi Bazaar This is the best place to soak up Hampi's special atmosphere if you don't mind basic but adequate accommodation. The lane just to the right of the tourist office leads into an area where every second building is either a guesthouse or a restaurant, so there are plenty of places to choose from. A few of the better ones are mentioned here, but there are many others if they're full.

Shanti Guest House (☎ 41568) is one of the best places to stay and is a popular travellers' haunt. In high season (December to January) it charges Rs 150 for bare double rooms, with fans and common bathroom, set around a garden courtyard. To get here, walk up to the entrance of the Virupaksha Temple, turn right and follow the signposts.

Raju Guesthouse, across the street, has clean simple rooms with common bath for Rs 70/100. It has a rooftop eating area where you can relax when your room gets claustrophobic.

Shankar Guesthouse is a better option about 20m further down the lane. The Shankar only has three rooms, but is spotless, and run by a very friendly family.

Vikky Guesthouse, in the area behind the tourist office, has doubles with common bath for Rs 150 on the 1st floor, or Rs 200 on the ground floor. It's of a similar standard to Shanti but with less atmosphere.

Among the other lodges worth looking out for in this area are *Shambhu Guesthouse*, where rooms go for Rs 150 on the ground floor or Rs 200 on the 1st floor, and the *Archana Guesthouse*, where the double rooms also go for Rs 150.

Rahul Guesthouse is a friendly place with a congenial restaurant area. Clean spartan rooms cost Rs 100/125. There are common toilet and bathing facilities and some rooms have fans. The guesthouse is just south of the bus stand, on the street running parallel to the bazaar.

Sri Rama Tourist Home (☎ 51219), to the right of Virupaksha Temple, is popular with visiting Indians. It has reasonably well-appointed rooms, but lacks atmosphere. Doubles with attached bath cost Rs 100.

Across the River Although there's plenty of good, cheap accommodation in Hampi Bazaar, the real 'scene' is on the north side of the river. To get across, take a corracle (Rs 3) from the ghats, just to the north of the Virupaksha Temple. Four or five places offer accommodation (most can also provide meals), but as they have only a few rooms each, finding somewhere to stay is not necessarily easy. None of them have telephones so you'll just have to do the rounds, and see what you can find. Accommodation is rather more basic than in Hampi Bazaar, but the place has a wonderful easy-going atmosphere.

Rasta, the first guesthouse you come to as you walk up from the riverbank, has basic double rooms for Rs 70. Alternatively, you can sleep on the roof of the building for Rs 10, and leave your luggage in the owner's house for safekeeping. The tiny restaurant has excellent views across the river to the Virupaksha Temple.

Gautam has tiny thatched huts, bare except for a bed, for Rs 30 per day. The house next door has very basic cells for Rs 50. Further down the lane, *Mowgli* has thatched huts for Rs 40, and a couple of rooms for Rs 70/100. Next door, *Shanti* has three or four well appointed rooms for Rs 70.

One and a half kilometres to the northeast, the *Hanuman Restaurant & Coffee House* is most easily accessible by getting a corracle from near the ruined bridge. Basic thatched huts here cost Rs 50, and there are also a couple of rooms for Rs 100. The shady restaurant is a great place to stop for a thali and cold drink if you're exploring the area around Anegondi.

Kamalapuram The *Hotel Mayura Bhuvaneshwari* (☎ 08394-41574), just to the north of Kamalapuram, is a modern, well-kept KSTDC hotel. OK singles/doubles with attached bath and mosquito nets cost Rs 200/240, or Rs 330/385 with air-con. The hotel has a vegetarian/nonvegetarian restaurant and a bar. It's a good choice for those who want to be close to the ruins but consider a comfortable bed more important than ambience.

Places to Eat
Hampi Bazaar The simple restaurants and soft-drink stalls on the main street of Hampi Bazaar have largely been superseded by newer, smarter eateries in the streets just to the north. They're still congenial spots from which to observe the streetlife, however. *Sri Venkateshwara*, on the right as you near the Virupaksha Temple, is the most established restaurant. It serves tiffin and western snacks at lunch and thalis (Rs 15) in the evening. *Geeta* is a popular alternative.

In the streets north of the bazaar there are dozens of restaurants which cater exclusively to the travelling community, and in reality there's little to separate them. Most people find a favourite and stick with it, but the rooftop restaurants are inevitably popular in the evenings.

Slightly away from the crowd, the *Bomshanker Restaurant*, on the way to the Vittala Temple, serves great food and is run by a friendly family. The *Mango Tree* has to have the most secluded location – about 400m west of the ghats down a path through a banana plantation. The tiny house nestles under the shade of a clump of huge mango trees. There are no tables, just mats on the earthen terrace from which to enjoy the view of the river. The thalis are excellent.

Alcohol is not permitted in Hampi, because of the village's religious significance. There are still places where you can get a cold Kingfisher, but it's expensive and you'll have to keep the bottle hidden under the table. For a legal beer, there's a bar in the Hotel Mayura Bhuvaneshwari in Kamalapuram.

Kamalapuram This sleepy village has a few humble eateries, the most notable of which is the *Sree Vilas Hotel* opposite the bus stand. It's a rustic place serving idlis for breakfast, puris for lunch and dosas in the evening. It closes at 7.30 pm. The restaurant at the *Hotel Mayura Bhuvaneshwari* serves standard KSTDC fare.

Getting There & Around
Buses run roughly hourly along the 13km stretch between Hampi Bazaar and Hospet.

KARNATAKA

The first bus from Hospet is at 6.30 am, and the last one back leaves Hampi at 8.30 pm. There are also regular buses between Hospet and Kamalapuram. The first bus from Hospet leaves at 6.30 am; the last one back leaves Kamalapuram at 10 pm.

Only a few buses link Hampi Bazaar and Kamalapuram, but you can negotiate this short stretch easily in an auto-rickshaw for Rs 5 share or Rs 30 private.

You can also catch auto-rickshaws to Hampi from Hospet for Rs 50. A taxi for this trip costs around Rs 100.

It makes a lot of sense to hire a bicycle to explore the ruins once you've seen the Vittala and Achyutaraya temples and Sule Bazaar. The entire Royal Enclosure area is navigable by bicycle since a dirt road runs through it. Once you've got up the steep hill from the bazaar, the road between Hampi Bazaar and Kamalapuram can also be used to get to the ruins; key monuments are haphazardly signposted along its length. Bicycles cost around Rs 30 per day in Hampi Bazaar.

Walking is the only way to explore all the nooks and crannies of the site, but expect to cover at least 7km just to see the major ruins. If you're not fit to walk or cycle, auto-rickshaws and taxis are available for sightseeing, and will drop you as close to each of the major ruins as they can possibly get. A five hour tour costs Rs 250 by auto-rickshaw and Rs 350 by taxi.

Organised tours depart from Hospet; see that section for details.

HOSPET
Pop: 151,900   Tel Area Code: 08394

Many people who come to see the Vijayanagar ruins at Hampi use Hospet as a base. It's a fairly typical Karnataka country town with dusty roads clogged with bullock carts, bicycles, scooters and dilapidated buses.

Information

The tourist office (☎ 28357) is open daily between 7.30 am and 7.30 pm. It has free maps and information on Hampi and sights in northern Karnataka. Malligi Tourist Home changes travellers cheques at competitive

---

> ### Firewalking in Hospet
> For much of the year Hospet is not a particularly interesting place, but it comes alive during the festival of Muharram, which commemorates the martyrdom of Mohammed's grandson, Imam Hussain. If you're here at this time (the date varies from year to year) don't miss the firewalkers, who walk barefoot across the red-hot embers of a fire that's been going all day and night. Virtually the whole town turns out to watch or take part and the excitement reaches fever pitch around midnight. The preliminaries, which go on all day, appear to be a bewildering hybrid of Muslim and Hindu ritual. Those who are scheduled to do the firewalking must be physically restrained from going completely berserk just before the event.

rates, as does the branch of Neha Travels in the courtyard of the Hotel Priyardarshini.

Organised Tours

The daily KSTDC tour to the three main sites at Hampi (Hampi Bazaar, Vittala Temple and the Royal Enclosure) and to Tungabhadra Dam departs at 9 am and returns at 5.30 pm; it costs Rs 60. Bookings can be made at the Hospet tourist office, Malligi Tourist Home or the Hotel Priyadarshini. If possible, book a day in advance as this tour is often full. Lunch (not included in the price) is at the KSTDC's hotel in Kamalapuram.

Places to Stay

Hotel Vishwa (☎ 27171), opposite the bus stand, has large, clean rooms with attached bath which are good value at Rs 80/150, and four-bed rooms for Rs 289 including tax. The hotel is set back from the street so the rooms are quiet. There's hot water in the morning and some rooms have small balconies.

Hotel Priyadarshini (☎ 28838, Station Rd) is the smartest place in town, and also has a range of excellent rooms for those on a lower budget. Simple but clean and pleasant rooms with attached bath go for Rs 140/195, deluxe doubles for Rs 270 and air-con doubles for Rs 440. All rooms have balconies and hot water in the morning. There's a veg/nonveg garden restaurant and bar.

Malligi Tourist Home (☎ 28101, 6/143 Jambunatha Rd) has long been a favourite among travellers, but has lost its appeal recently. Dingy, mosquito-infested doubles with attached bath and hot water start from Rs 140. Semideluxe doubles, also with mosquitoes, go for Rs 250. If you're prepared to pay a little more, however, the air-con rooms from Rs 350 to Rs 700 are OK. On the positive side, the hotel has a foreign exchange facility, a small garden and a bookshop which has English and French books on Hampi.

Hotel Sandarshana (☎ 28574, Station Rd) has acceptable double rooms with common bath for Rs 100, and doubles with attached bath from Rs 130. The rooms are pretty bare, but are clean and airy.

Hotel Shalini (☎ 28910, Station Rd) is the town's budget option. It has basic singles/doubles/triples with bath for Rs 50/80/100. The rooms are bare and gloomy, but quite sufficient for a night.

Hotel Mayura Vijayanagar (☎ 39270) is a KSTDC operation 6km outside Hospet at Tungabhadra Dam. There's absolutely no reason for anyone to stay this far out of town, and consequently the place has a rather abandoned and unloved feel to it. Rooms with attached bath cost Rs 125/160. Buses between Hospet and the dam leave every 15 minutes. It's easier to pick up a bus to Hospet from the junction at the bottom of the dam road rather than at the dam itself.

Places to Eat

Madhu Paradise, at the Malligi Tourist Home, serves reasonably priced South Indian and North Indian veg fare and western breakfasts. *Waves* 'multicuisine restaurant' is part of a new complex being built by the hotel to attract business customers. The setting is upmarket and the food is good, but there's little atmosphere.

Eagle Garden Bar & Restaurant, behind the Malligi, has Indian and Chinese fare and 'American' breakfasts. It's a popular spot, with a thatched barn-like restaurant and tables outdoors. The food is good and main courses cost around Rs 50; Kingfishers are Rs 45.

Manasa Bar & Restaurant in the Hotel Priyardarshini serves nonveg Andhra-style dishes in a garden. The hotel also has an indoor veg restaurant.

Shanthi Restaurant in the Hotel Vishwa does excellent vegetarian thalis at lunchtime for Rs 15, and snacks the rest of the day.

Getting There & Away

Bus The busy bus stand in Hospet is fairly well organised, with bays marked in both English and Kannada, though buses in this part of the state are generally crowded and you'll need to fight to get on. A large backpack can make this an uncomfortable experience.

Buses to Hampi depart from Bay No 10. See the Hampi Getting There & Around section for details.

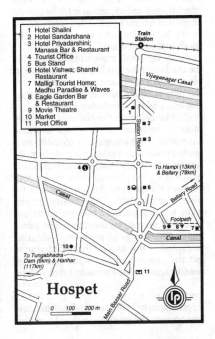

1 Hotel Shalini
2 Hotel Sandarshana
3 Hotel Priyardarshini;
   Manasa Bar & Restaurant
4 Tourist Office
5 Bus Stand
6 Hotel Vishwa; Shanthi
   Restaurant
7 Malligi Tourist Home;
   Madhu Paradise & Waves
8 Eagle Garden Bar
   & Restaurant
9 Movie Theatre
10 Market
11 Post Office

Train Station

Vijayanagar Canal

Station Road

To Hampi (13km)
& Bellary (78km)

Canal

Bellary Road

Footpath

Canal

To Tungabhadra
Dam (6km) & Harihar
(117km)

Main Bazaar Road

Hospet

0   100   200 m

More than 10 express buses run daily to Bangalore (Rs 91/132 ordinary/deluxe, nine hours). They are nearly all morning or night departures: no Bangalore buses depart between 1 and 9.30 pm. KSTDC (the tourist organisation) also runs its own deluxe bus to Bangalore departing daily at 10 pm from the tourist office (Rs 145).

There are only three buses a day to Badami, but if you miss them you can always get a bus to Gadag or Ilkal and transfer to another bus there. The journey takes five hours via Gadag and close to six hours via Ilkal.

There are many daily services to Hubli (Rs 41, four hours), all of which run via Gadag. There are four buses to Bijapur (Rs 60, six hours); five buses to Hyderabad (Rs 100, nine hours); and also daily departures to Hassan, Raichur, Mangalore and Shimoga. One bus heads to Gokarna (Rs 70, eight hours) each morning at 9 am.

Train Hospet train station is a 20 minute walk or Rs 10 auto-rickshaw ride from the centre of town. There is one direct train daily to Bangalore at 8.30 pm (Rs 157/531 in sleeper/1st class, 10½ hours). There are two expresses to Guntakal at 3.35 and 8.30 pm (2½ hours), where you can pick up many other expresses to Bangalore, and two expresses to Hubli at 7.40 and 11.10 am (four hours). To get to Badami and Bijapur, you'll need to catch a Hubli train, get off at Gadag, and pick up a connection from there.

AROUND HOSPET

If you find yourself with time to spare before catching onwards transport, you could always pay a visit to the **Tungabhadra Dam**, approximately 5km west of Hospet. The dam itself is over 2km long, and work started on it in February 1945. Ninety villages were affected, and over 54,000 people displaced, but today the project provides guaranteed irrigation for countless farms and towns. Do not try to take any photos near the dam itself, as it's a restricted zone due to a perceived threat of sabotage. Below the dam are some unspectacular gardens (entry Rs 2) where every evening there's a display of the 'musical fountain'.

CHITRADURGA
Tel Area Code: 08194

Almost exactly midway between Hospet and Bangalore, in the middle of the dusty central Karnatakan plateau, a series of granite hills rises unexpectedly out of the plain. The rounded hills, which are liberally scattered with huge boulders, are reminiscent of the rocky landscape of Hampi, and also house a fortress of impressive strength. Archaeological finds show that the area has been important since early times, but the region really came into its own under a feudatory dynasty of Vijayanagar called the Chitradurga Nayakas. When the City of Victory was sacked in 1565, these local chieftains became independent and the fortress became their main stronghold.

In 1779 the fort fell into the hands of Hyder Ali who, along with his son Tipu, strengthened and expanded it to the present shape that we see today. After Tipu's defeat by the British, the fort's usefulness as a defensive structure ended.

Today the small town which grew up in the shadow of the fort has spread outside its old walled confines and a more modern area contains facilities such as the bus and train stations, and the town's few hotels.

Despite being on the National Highway midway between northern and southern Karnataka, Chitradurga is a pleasant little market town with a relaxed atmosphere. Its position between Hospet and Bangalore makes it a good place to break the journey between the two, and the fort is perfect for a day's exploration. The massive granite walls blend seamlessly into the landscape around them, and this deceptive appearance makes Chitradurga all the more fascinating to explore – just as you think that you've got the measure of the place you notice another section that you hadn't seen before.

Fort

Approximately 500m south of the bus stand you come to the gateway to the old, walled

EDDIE GERALD

EDDIE GERALD

GREG ELMS

Karnataka
Awesome remnants of the great cities and empires at Vijayanagar near Hampi (top), Badami (bottom left), and Mysore (bottom right).

GREG ELMS

EDDIE GERALD

GREG ELMS

Karnataka
Even the cows are colourful (top right); flowers and *tika* dye powders at Mysore's photogenic Devaraja Market (top left & bottom).

town, where there's a tiny tourist office. Beyond the gate the bustle of the modern town is left behind and the lane climbs gently for a further 500m to the east gate of the fort. Entry is Rs 2.

From the ticket booth, the entrance to the fort lies over the old moat and through the first gate, a massive construction of precisely cut granite blocks. With the exception of a couple of simple motifs on the walls, there is little ornament; the emphasis here is on sheer strength of defences. The indestructible walls are complemented by a winding entranceway which made the main gate more difficult for attackers to penetrate.

Just inside the first gate a sign points left (south) to the **Banashankari Temple** and the **Grinding Stones**. The temple is in a tiny cave which has been enlarged to house the statues of two deities. The images have been defaced but the temple is still in use and is tended by a friendly priest who may well give you a quick rundown on the history of the place.

Twenty metres beyond the temple is a large stone-walled pit with four massive grinding stones arranged on the four sides. The stones, which were used in the manufacture of gunpowder, were turned by buffalo power. The central area around which the buffalo would have trudged is clear, but the elaborate cog system which must have turned the stones is now gone.

Returning to the main path inside the front gate, follow the paved way up through four more gates – each as strong as the first – until you arrive at the inner area of the fort, on a saddle between the rocky hilltops. Continue climbing to pass through a further gate into the old palace area, which contains a number of buildings that are still in good shape. Notable among these is an impressive temple built on the rocky promontory overlooking the gates through which you have just passed.

The highest of the buildings in the fort are reached slightly further up the hill, and the main one is constructed against the rock face. Behind the building, a series of shallow footholds have been cut in the steeply sloping rock. These can be followed up to the central bastion, which is perched on the pinnacle above. From here there are excellent views of the whole fort. Circular parapets crown each of the surrounding hilltops.

To the south is a series of fascinating semi-ruined, cone-shaped buildings, while to the west is a large water tank. Having sussed the layout from this vantage point, the best thing to do is simply to wander at leisure. The fort has plenty of pleasant shady spots to rest (you could picnic up here), and there's endless scrambling and exploring to be done.

Places to Stay & Eat
There isn't a huge choice of places to stay in Chitradurga.

Vashista Deluxe Lodge (☎ 24010), about 2km south of the bus stand on the Bangalore road, is a good place. Pleasant singles/doubles/triples with attached bath go for Rs 90/165/260. The place can easily get booked out, so phone in advance. There's a reasonable veg restaurant attached to the hotel.

Prakash Lodge (☎ 22958), directly opposite Vashista, is altogether more basic, but adequate for a night. Rooms with attached bath go for Rs 50/100.

Maruthi Inn, north of the town centre, just off the National Highway, is also worth a try. It boasts rooms with air-con, and an attached restaurant and bar.

Getting There & Away
Bus Being on the main highway between northern and southern Karnataka (the NH4 Belgaum to Bangalore road), and near to the junction with the NH13 which runs north to Hospet and Bijapur, Chitradurga is well served by buses. There are regular services to and from Bangalore (Rs 53, four hours), Hospet (Rs 40, three hours) and Hubli (Rs 55, five hours).

Train Although Chitradurga has a train station, it's actually on a branch line with very limited services, so transport by bus is a far better option.

RANIBENNUR BLACKBUCK SANCTUARY

This small (119 sq km), dry, scrubby sanctuary was established in 1974 for the sole purpose of preserving about 6000 threatened blackbuck antelopes, as well as great Indian bustards (of which only 14 are left in the sanctuary). The sanctuary also hosts wild foxes, hyenas, and langur. The best time to see blackbucks is between September and February; if you are lucky, bustards can be spotted between May and January. There are no wildlife tours, but you can go on small hikes near the resthouse. The downside is the annoying midges throughout the park.

Very pleasant *forest resthouses* (Rs 150 per person) are at the entrance to the sanctuary – book at the Assistant Conservator of Forests in Dharwad (☎ 0836-40302). Otherwise, stay in Ranibennur town at the *Hotel Renuka Lodge*, right opposite the bus stand, for Rs 200/250 per double without/with TV; or at the *Hotel Pushpak*, in the eastern part of town, for Rs 150 a double.

Ranibennur is easy to reach on one of the very regular buses from Bangalore, Shimoga (Rs 28, three hours) or Hubli-Dharwad. The sanctuary is 5km north of Ranibennur town; take an auto-rickshaw.

GADAG
Tel Area Code: 08372

Gadag is a medium-sized market town with a deceptive appearance, its low skyline and country town atmosphere belying the fact that the urban area actually spreads quite a long way. There's a marked Muslim presence, the remnants of some attractive old houses, and a feeling of being off the beaten track, as few travellers ever visit here. The only reason to stop here in fact, unless you are changing train or bus, is to visit the temple ruins at Lakkundi, 12km to the east.

Things to See

There are a couple of interesting temples in Gadag which don't really merit a special visit, but are definitely worth a look if you

Blackbucks

Also known as Indian antelopes, blackbucks *(Antelope cervicapra)* survive well in the dry, open scrubland of the Deccan Plateau and are believed by many tribal people to be sacred. When frightened, they can run up to 80km per hour for several kilometres (faster than a motor vehicle over the same rough terrain), and can jump over obstacles 4m high (which a motor vehicle can't do). They live for seven or eight years, and are about 80cm high.

The female blackbuck has no horns; males have distinctive hollow spiral horns (up to 50cm long) and an attractive coat (which is dark brown in South India), making them a prime target for poachers. Blackbucks are extinct in Bangladesh and Pakistan, and very rare in Nepal, so they are almost exclusively found only in India. The best place to see blackbucks in the south is the Ranibennur Blackbuck Sanctuary in Karnataka.

have time. Some way from the town centre, to the south, the **Trikuteshwara** and **Sarasvati** temples stand side by side in the same enclosure.

The temples date from the Kalyana Chalukya period. The Trikuteshwara Temple has a triple lingam in the sanctuary, and in the hall beyond (which is kept locked although the priest may open it for you) is a large sculpture of Nandi. The Sarasvati Temple is also locked but the porch area is worth seeing for its massive and intricately carved pillars, and a sloping roof made of huge stone slabs.

Nearer the centre of the town, two other ancient monuments stand on either side of a busy back road. The **Someshwara** and **Rameswara** temples are both still in partial use. The intricate stonework and amazingly fresh ancient designs make a startling contrast with the modern scenes which occur all around them.

Places to Stay

The choice of hotels in Gadag is pretty slim.

Hotel Welcome, next to the bus stand, is extremely basic, with bare little double rooms with attached bathroom for Rs 80. You are required to leave an additional Rs 80 as a deposit, although it's difficult to know what damage you could possibly do to these cell-like chambers.

Shanbhag Lodge (☎ 28856), on Nehru Rd between the bus stand and the train station, is better, with airy, spartan doubles for Rs 100 to Rs 125.

Hotel Durga Vihar (☎ 28878), on the road out of Gadag towards Hospet, undoubtedly wins the prize for best value. This relatively new hotel caters mostly to businessmen and their families. The cheapest double rooms (Rs 149) are spotlessly clean, large and modern. There are also 'deluxe air-cooled' rooms for Rs 250. There's a good veg restaurant downstairs. The hotel is about 2km from the bus stand and directions are complicated, so it's probably easiest to take a rickshaw. From the bus stand this should cost Rs 12; from the train station expect to pay more.

Places to Eat

There are restaurants in both Shanbhag Lodge and the Hotel Durga Vihar. If you're staying in the former place, a short walk towards the train station will take you past *My Food*, a very smart-looking vegetarian restaurant.

If you're staying in the Hotel Durga Vihar and want nonveg food or a beer with your meal, try *Vikram Hotel*, a couple of hundred metres back towards the centre of town. There's a good selection of South Indian and other Indian fare here, and the beer is ice cold.

Getting There & Away

On the main highway between Hospet and Hubli, and at the junction of both road and rail links north towards Badami and Bijapur, Gadag is well served by transport.

Bus There are regular buses daily to Badami (Rs 22, two hours), Hospet (Rs 25, 2½ hours) and Hubli (Rs 15, 1½ hours). There are four daily buses to Bijapur via Badami, which leave at 6 and 7.30 am, 1.30 and 2 pm; the journey takes around five hours and costs about Rs 60. There are seven buses a day to Gulbarga (Rs 75, nine hours) and six buses a day to Shimoga (Rs 61, six hours).

Train Gadag is on a junction between the main line running west to east, and the branch line running north through Badami and Bijapur to the junction at Sholapur. At the time of writing the train services north were disrupted by the ongoing conversion to broad gauge, and thus although there were regular trains via Badami to Bijapur, there were no through services as far as Sholapur. Check to see how work is progressing before you buy your ticket.

From Gadag to Bijapur is Rs 239 in 1st class or Rs 48 in 2nd class. Two express trains a day head eastwards and two go west. The eastbound trains depart at 1.15 and 6.17 pm and stop at Hospet (2½ hours) and Guntakal (five hours); the later of the two trains is the 6591 *Hampi Express* which continues to Bangalore, arriving at 7 am the next morning. From Gadag to Bangalore costs Rs 576 in 1st class, Rs 114 in 2nd class. The westbound

KARNATAKA

trains depart at 9.50 am and 1.05 pm, and reach Hubli about 1½ hours later. The later of the two trains is the 7225 *Amaravati Express*, which will eventually (once work is complete) continue straight through to Goa.

AROUND GADAG
Lakkundi
Twelve kilometres east of Gadag along the Hospet road is the tiny village of Lakkundi. Somehow this place seems to have escaped most tourist itineraries, which is odd as scattered among the tiny houses and dusty lanes are a number of stunning temples which date from the Kalyana Chalukya period (c.973–c.1189).

From the bus stand, the first spot to visit is only about 150m north of the road, behind the bus stand itself. The impressive **stepped tank** has an arched structure approximately two thirds of the way along it, which is said to have separated the bathing areas to be used by the men and women. The tank fills up to the level of the small shrines by the end of the monsoon, but by January or February the water is right down in the rocky bottom of the pit, revealing the striking design of the whole bathing area.

Directly across the road, a dusty lane leads past the tiny Vijaya Virupaksha Temple. Follow this track as it winds through the village to the southern side of the houses, to come to the **Kashi Vishveshwara Temple**, one of the finest structures in the group. Two shrines, raised on the same plinth, face each other. The roof between them has long since collapsed, but the quality of the carving is breathtaking. The south side of the temple, in particular, has amazingly detailed tracery and the four massive pillars that support the covered hall also carry intricate relief designs.

The sanctuary contains an image of the incarnation of Shiva to whom the temple is dedicated. On the other side of the lane stands the **Nanneshwara Temple**. As you climb the steps of the modern enclosure that surrounds the temple, three or four old stone steps are seen directly ahead. On the right side of these is the image of a man fighting

a tiger. This image was the symbol of the Hoysala dynasty, and originated from an ancient story about the founder of the dynasty fighting and slaying a tiger.

Head back towards the road in a northwesterly direction, and a couple of minutes' walk brings you to the pride of the collection, a large temple that stands in its own enclosure. The mandapam of the main temple has exquisitely turned stone pillars that were constructed in five parts – if you look very closely you can just see the joins. To the right of the entrance to the second hall is an inscription giving the original name of the town – Lokkikundi. The doorway to the sanctum is flanked by images of a four headed Brahma (right), and Padmavati (left). Next to the temple stands a small **museum**, which is open daily (except Friday) from 9 am to 5 pm, although you may have to ask around to find the curator.

Dealing with the children in the village can be hard work, and you can bank on spending a large part of your visit surrounded by a crowd demanding 'one pen, chocolate, what-is-your-name?'. Don't give them pens, money or sweets unless you want to foster a culture of dependency and exploitation; anyway it's actually cruel to dispense sweets to children who have no access to dentists. If you want to make a difference make a donation to an organised welfare group, or start your own.

There are also at least a couple of old men who turn up from nowhere and start straight in on a guided tour. The information isn't bad, but fix a price before you start, because their asking price when you get to the end is astronomical.

Getting There & Away Buses between Hubli and Hospet pass through Lakkundi, so there's no shortage of transport, and you could even visit Lakkundi en route between Hospet and Badami.

HUBLI
Pop: 728,000 Tel Area Code: 0836
Hubli is important to the traveller principally as a major railway junction on the routes

from Mumbai to Bangalore, Goa and northern Karnataka. At the time of writing, services to Goa were disrupted while the line was being converted from metre to broad gauge.

All the main services (hotels, restaurants etc) are conveniently close to the train station. The bus stand is on Lamington Rd, a 15 minute walk from the train station.

Places to Stay

Ashok Hotel (☎ 362271, Lamington Rd) is about 500m from the train station. It has acceptable rooms with attached bath for Rs 130/175 and air-con doubles for Rs 350. The management may initially try to palm you off with one of the dingier rooms, so ask to see a couple before you make a choice.

Hotel Vipra (☎ 362336), in the same building, is better value all round, with standard rooms from Rs 100/140 and deluxe doubles with balcony from Rs 250.

Hotel Kailash (☎ 52234), opposite the Ashok, is more upmarket. Comfortable rooms with attached bath, hot water and TV cost Rs 303/435 including tax. Air-con rooms go for Rs 435/575. There's a good veg restaurant on the ground floor.

Hotel Ajanta (☎ 362216) is a short distance off the main street and visible from the train station. It's a huge place so you'll always be able to find accommodation here. Average rooms cost Rs 55/90 with common bathroom or Rs 90/135 with attached bath. Checkout is 24 hours. There's a 'meals' restaurant on the ground floor.

Retiring Rooms at the train station cost Rs 100, or Rs 30 for a dorm bed.

Places to Eat

Parag Bar & Restaurant is next to the Modern Lodge, which is on the street facing the train station. It has a British pub-style restaurant and an open-air rooftop section. Passable veg and nonveg Indian and Chinese dishes cost around Rs 40.

Royal Palace, on a side street near the Ashok Hotel, is the best restaurant in this part of the city. North Indian mains cost around Rs 60.

Ravi's, below Hotel Kailash, serves excellent snacks, and South Indian thalis for Rs 15.

There's a cluster of eateries at the foot of the train station sliproad offering cheap thalis, biryanis and vegetarian snacks.

Getting There & Away

Air Hubli's airport was closed indefinitely at the time of writing.

Bus Hubli has a large and busy bus stand. The KSRTC has lots of buses to Bangalore (Rs 110, nine hours) and Hospet (Rs 41, four hours). There are also four buses daily to Mumbai (Rs 185, 15 hours); three to Mysore (Rs 176, 10 hours); two to Mangalore (Rs 125, 10 hours); and at least one daily departure to Bijapur, Gokarna and Jog Falls. There are four KSRTC buses to Panaji (Rs 52, five hours), and Goa's Kadamba Transport Corporation also runs a number of services.

Opposite the bus stand are plenty of private companies operating deluxe buses to Bangalore, Bijapur, Goa, Mangalore, Mumbai and Pune.

Train The train reservation office is open from 8 am to 8 pm daily. If you're heading for Hospet (four hours), there are expresses at noon and 5 pm. To reach Bijapur, you'll have to catch one of these trains and change at Gadag (1½ hours). There are also two to three expresses a day to Bangalore (10 hours) and usually two expresses to Mumbai (17 hours) via Londa (two hours). Londa is the closest junction with rail connections to Goa.

Northern Karnataka

BELGAUM
Pop: 453,000   Tel Area Code: 0831

On a rather bald plateau in the north-western corner of the state, Belgaum was a regional capital in the 12th and 13th centuries. In the 14th century it came under the influence of the Yadavas, before being taken by the great Bahmani statesman Mahmud Gawan in

1474. The fort was rebuilt at this stage, and the town became a major stronghold. In 1511 it was granted to a military officer named Asad Khan, in recognition of his bravery and assistance to the sultan. Over the coming years, Asad established himself as one of the major players in the Deccan, managing to outwit the Sultans of Bijapur, the Vijayanagar kings and the Portuguese to increase his own personal fortune.

After Asad's death Belgaum came back under the control of Bijapur, before passing to the Mughals, and then the Marathas. The British captured the town in 1818, and it became a military garrison – a function which is evident even today in the presence of a barracks within the old fortress. Today Belgaum is a busy modern town, notable to tourists mainly for its bus and train links, and for the fact that it has the only airport in northern Karnataka.

The old oval-shaped stone **fort** near the bus stand is of no great interest, although it makes a placid retreat from the bustle of the town. Mahatma Gandhi was locked up here once. The nearby mosque, **Masjid-Sata**, is reputed to have been built by Asad Khan and dates from 1519. There are also two interesting **Jain Temples**, one with an extremely intricate roof, and another with fine carvings of musicians. Belgaum's **watchtower**, on Ganapath Galli in the town centre, provides a panorama of the flat countryside and distant hills. **Sunset Point**, on the old racetrack road, also offers fine views

Places to Stay & Eat

Hotel Sheetal (☎ 429222), in Khade Bazaar, is about three minutes walk from the bus stand. Clean, bright rooms with attached bath cost Rs 90/150. It also has a veg restaurant.

Hotel Mayura Malaprabha (☎ 470781), on the NH4 bypass, just behind the lake, is a modern but rather neglected KSTDC operation. Cottages with attached bath cost Rs 160/190, and there's a tourist office in one of the buildings.

Hotel Keerthi (☎ 423332), a tall, white establishment 500m to the right as you leave the bus stand, offers clean, comfortable rooms

The Great Schemer

Asad Khan was one of the great figures in the Deccan during the early 16th century. A Turk who started life as a simple military officer named Khusru, his fortunes changed dramatically in 1511 when he distinguished himself in front of the sultan during the defence of Bijapur. He was immediately awarded the title of Asad Khan, and was granted the district of Belgaum, an area of which he remained chief for the rest of his life. He was undoubtedly talented, for he quickly rose to become chief minister, commander in chief of the army and confidant to the sultan. Witnesses at the time, however, were very much at odds as to where his real strengths lay.

The Muslim historian Firishtah was something of a fan, and declared him a great man, whereas the Portuguese regarded him as an arch manipulator, playing regional politics for all it was worth, in order to feather his own nest. On several occasions he is said to have played off the Adil Shah of Bijapur; Krishnadevaraya, the emperor of Vijayanagar; and the Portuguese governor general in Goa. According to the Portuguese historian Barros, Asad was capable of making all three rulers believe that he was secretly working for them, while quietly making approaches to the others, and bolstering his personal wealth along the way.

Detractors even claim that such episodes as Asad helping the sultan to escape from the battlefield after the defeat at Raichur in 1520 may have been staged to curry favour with the monarch. Wherever the truth lies, he is to be credited for a long and successful innings; unlike so many other powerful men in the region, Asad managed not only to play the game successfully but to survive it, too; he died a natural death in 1549.

with attached bath from Rs 130/200. The hotel is well run but tends to be quite noisy. It has a good veg/nonveg restaurant and a bar.

Hotel Sanman Deluxe (☎ 430777, College Rd) is a slightly more upmarket place with rooms from Rs 255/415. The rooms are comfortable and there's a currency exchange service at the reception.

Getting There & Away

Indian Airlines no longer has an office in Belgaum, but Span Air has flights between Belgaum and Mumbai daily (except Sunday) for Rs 3050. Mayur World Travels (☎ 424707) on College Road can assist with booking flights.

The bus stand is close to the old town area and there are buses to Mumbai, Bangalore, Panaji, Gadag and Hubli, among other places. You'll need to catch an auto-rickshaw to the train station, where several express trains plying between Bangalore (15 hours) and Mumbai (14 hours) stop. These trains pass through Londa (the closest rail junction with connections to Goa) and Hubli. There's also a daily express to Delhi (37 hours).

BADAMI

Pop: 18,200 Tel Area Code: 08357

Set in beautiful countryside at the foot of a red sandstone ridge, the small rural town of Badami was once the capital of the Chalukya Empire, which covered much of the central Deccan between the 4th and 8th centuries. At its height the empire was enormous, stretching from Kanchipuram in Tamil Nadu to the Narmada River in Gujarat. The earliest Chalukya capital was in nearby Aihole, after which the site was moved to Badami, with a secondary capital in nearby Pattadakal. The result of this relocation is that the whole area around Badami is strewn with temples, and there are over 150 in the three main centres alone.

The sculptural legacy left by the Chalukya artisans includes some of the earliest and finest examples of Dravidian temples and rock-cut caves, as well as the earliest structural temple in the whole of India. The forms and sculptural work at these sites provided

inspiration for the later Hindu empires which rose and fell in the southern part of the peninsula before the arrival of the Muslims.

History

The Chalukyas began their rise to power as feudatories of the powerful Kadambas, and during this time their capital was in Aihole. By the middle of the 6th century, however, the power balance had shifted. The first great ruler in the dynasty, Pulikesin I, moved the capital to Badami (known in inscriptions by its Sanskrit name of Vatapi) in c.543. In this naturally protected site he built a fort, and a huge tank (which is still in use) to collect the water running down off the surrounding hills. The southern end of the town was protected by walls and a moat, and the development of the new capital began, although much temple building continued at Aihole.

Over the next half-century the empire expanded gradually, but Chalukya fortunes really took off in 610, with the accession of Pulikesin II. He was undoubtedly one of the greatest rulers India has ever seen, and over

---

Eating Vatapi

According to legend, the area where Badami now stands was once inhabited by two demons who were brothers. Vatapi and Ilvala had a particularly nasty sense of humour, and liked nothing better than to invite guests to dinner and kill them in a very unusual way. Before the guests arrived, Ilvala would kill his brother Vatapi, and would cook his flesh. Having served the guests and watched them eating, Ilvala would cry 'Vatapi, come out', and his sibling would burst out of the guests' stomachs, thus killing them. The pair finally met their match in the sage Agastya, who they invited to dine with them. Having finished his meal, he quickly cried 'Vatapi, be digested', and thus the demon was unable to come back to life. According to this legend, the hills of Badami and Aihole are the remains of these two brothers.

the 42 years of his reign he pushed the boundaries of his empire far to the north and south.

The Chalukya army was regarded as invincible, and it is said that the mere sight of its banners, emblazoned with the dynasty's emblem (the boar Varaha), was enough to make enemies submit. Diplomatic missions were received from as far afield as Persia, and legendary Chinese traveller Xuan Zang also visited the court. Chalukya fortunes were set back when the Pallavas took Badami in 642, but in 655 Pulikesin's son, Vikramaditya, defeated them, and reclaimed the area.

By the early 8th century, the Chalukya Empire was at its height, and Vikramaditya II captured the Pallava capital of Kanchi (Kanchipuram). In memory of his achievement, his queens Lokamahadevi and Trailokanahadevi built the Virupaksha and Mallikarjuna temples at Pattadakal. Soon after this, however, weakened by constant warring, the empire began to decline, and the Chalukya army was finally defeated by the Rashtrakuta chief, Dantidurga in 753.

Badami came under the rule of the Rashtrakutas and then under the Chalukyans of Kalyan (a separate branch of the Western Chalukyans), the Kalachuryas, the Yadavas of Devagiri, the Vijayanagar Empire and the Adil Shahi kings of Bijapur.

Hyder Ali took Badami in the mid-18th century and rebuilt the fort, and Tipu Sultan was responsible for building the mosque here. The Marathas also briefly occupied the town, before it fell into the hands of the British in 1818.

Information

The tourist office (☎ 65414), based in a building by the entrance to the KSTDC's Hotel Mayura Chalukya, is open from 10 am to 5 pm daily. It has no leaflets to give out, and there are no organised tours, but the staff are helpful and can answer questions about local transport, and sightseeing.

Be sure to bring enough money with you to get to the next large town, since there is nowhere to change money in Badami, Pattadakal or Aihole.

Not even the plush Hotel Badami Court can change money, or accept credit cards or travellers cheques in payment. Staff say that they may, however, be prepared to allow payment in US$ cash in an emergency!

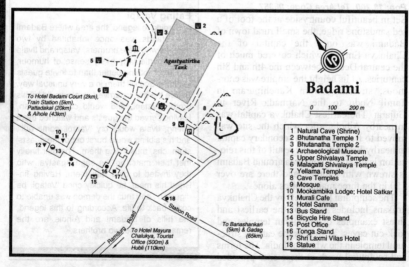

To Hotel Badami Court (2km),
Train Station (5km),
Pattadakal (20km)
& Aihole (43km)

Agastyatirtha Tank

Badami

0   100   200 m

To Hotel Mayura
Chalukya, Tourist
Office (500m) &
Hubli (110km)

Ramdurg Road

Station Road

To Banashankari
(5km) & Gadag
(65km)

1 Natural Cave (Shrine)
2 Bhutanatha Temple 1
3 Bhutanatha Temple 2
4 Archaeological Museum
5 Upper Shivalaya Temple
6 Malagatti Shivalaya Temple
7 Yellama Temple
8 Cave Temples
9 Mosque
10 Mookambika Lodge; Hotel Satkar
11 Murali Cafe
12 Hotel Sanman
13 Bus Stand
14 Bicycle Hire Stand
15 Post Office
16 Tonga Stand
17 Shri Laxmi Vilas Hotel
18 Statue

Caves

Although Badami was also an experimenting ground for designs of freestanding temples, the town is best known for its beautiful cave temples. The Chalukyan kings were Vaishnavites, but they were tolerant of those with other beliefs, and the caves cut into the face of the southern cliff above Badami reflect this. Two of them are dedicated to Vishnu, one to Shiva and the fourth is a Jain temple. There's also one natural cave which is a Buddhist temple. Entry to the caves costs Rs 2.

Cave One This cave, just above the entrance to the complex, is dedicated to Shiva. It is thought to have been carved during the 6th century and is the oldest of the four caves. As you approach the entrance, on the cliff wall to the right of the porch is one of the most impressive carvings in the whole complex. The beautiful image of Nataraja has 18 arms which hold, among other things, a snake, a musical instrument and a *trishula* (trident).

As you enter the porch area of the cave, on the right is a huge figure of Ardhanarishvara. The right half of the figure shows features of Shiva, such as matted hair and a third eye, while the left half of the image has aspects of Parvati, including braided hair and ornaments. On the opposite wall of the porch is a large image of Harihara the right half of which represents Shiva, and the left half Vishnu. Next to the image stands Nandi, with a human body and an ox's head. Near Nandi is Parvati holding a lotus, and to the left of Harihara is Garuda. The ceiling panels are also ornamented, and one image of particular note, on the central panel of the porch ceiling, is that of Naga, the snake, with five hoods. A headless Nandi sits in the middle of the cave, facing a tiny sanctuary, which is carved into the back wall.

Cave Two This cave is simpler in its design, and is dedicated to Vishnu. As with caves one and three, the front edge of the platform is decorated with images of dwarfs in various poses. Four pillars support the veranda, the top of each of which is carved with a bracket in the shape of a *yali*, or mythical beast. On

the left wall of the porch is the pig-headed figure of Varaha, an incarnation of Vishnu and the emblem of the Chalukya Empire. To his left is an image of Naga, the snake. On the right wall of the porch is a large sculpture of Trivikrama, another incarnation of Vishnu. His left leg is in the air and in his eight hands he holds a variety of weapons including a discus, a bow and a sword. The ceiling panels contain images of Vishnu riding Garuda, *gandharva* couples, swastikas and fish arranged in a wheel.

Between the second and third cave are two sets of steps to the right. The first gives access to a **natural cave**, the eastern wall of which contains a small Buddhist image of Padmapani, who stands on a lotus and holds another lotus in his hands. The second set of steps leads up a narrow defile to the hilltop **South Fort**; sadly these steps are barred by a metal gate.

Cave Three This cave was carved under the orders of Mangalesha, the brother of king Kirtivarma, in 578. It is dedicated to Vishnu and contains some of the best sculptures in the complex. Dr Burgess, the great 18th century historian of Indian archaeology, proclaimed it to be 'in some respects one of the most interesting Brahmanical works in India'. To the right as you enter the cave is a large image of Trivikrama and a huge, 3m-high sculpture of Narasimha. In his four hands Narasimha holds a discus, a fruit, a whisk and a mace. Varaha stands nearby, holding the goddess Prithvi in his left hand.

On the left-hand walls of the cave is a large carving of Vishnu, sitting on the coils of the snake; nearby is an image of Varaha with four hands. In addition to the main sculptures, the cave is particularly notable for the wealth of other detail. The pillars have carved brackets in the shape of yalis, and the sides of the pillars are also carved. The ceiling panels contain images including Vishnu, Indra riding an elephant, Shiva on a bull, and Brahma on a swan.

Cave Four Dedicated to Jainism, Cave Four is the smallest of the set and was the latest to

KARNATAKA

be created having been carved in the 7th to 8th centuries. The pillars, with their roaring yalis, are of a similar design to the other caves. The right wall of the cave has an image of Suparshvanatha, surrounded by more than 20 sculptures of Jain tirthankars. The sanctum contains an image of Adinath, the first Jain tirthankar.

Temples & Tank

The caves overlook the picturesque 6th century **Agastyatirtha Tank**. At the west end of the tank is a tiny temple, and a functioning mosque, the latter having been built by Tipu Sultan. The eastern end of the tank is dominated by the peaceful waterside **Bhutanatha temples**. The largest of these seems to have started off as a single compartment which was then enlarged. An 8th century inscription on the wall dates the structure. Just to the south of these is a large rock with some carvings. Beyond it, almost hidden under an overhanging rock, is a tiny **natural cave** which you must stoop to enter. The image contained in the cave is said by local legend to be that of a man whose leprosy was cured when he bathed in the large tank, and who thereafter became an ascetic. The figure looks very like a Jain image, however, so the story may well be fanciful.

At the north-west corner of the tank is the **Archaeological Museum**, which houses superb examples of local sculpture, including remarkable Lajja-Gauri images of a fertility cult which flourished in the area. It's open from 10 am to 5 pm daily except Friday.

The stairway behind the museum climbs through a sandstone chasm and fortified gateways to reach the **North Fort**, and the two Shivalaya temples that stand on the rocky outcrops within it. The **Upper Shivalaya Temple**, right on the top of the ridge, commands an excellent view of the surrounding countryside. This is one of the earliest temples in the area, and the massive blocks are adorned with large scale ornamentation, including four huge elephant heads carved around the steps up on to the temple platform, and rotund figures around the edge of the platform.

The **Lower Shivalaya Temple**, lower down the hillside, is reduced to only one tower. From beside the temple you get an excellent view down into the narrow streets below. This part of the town is well worth exploring for its old houses, tiny squares and the occasional Chalukyan ruin.

If you walk down into the town and head north a short way you come to the **Malagatti Shivalaya Temple**, which stands isolated on a rocky outcrop above the village. The temple was built during the 8th century and is regarded by many to be one of the best examples of temple architecture in Badami.

Places to Stay

Most visitors tend to use Badami as a base while they explore not only the temples and caves around the village itself, but also the important sites at Pattadakal and Aihole, as well as at Mahakuta and Banashankari. There's a limited but adequate range of accommodation here (the only other option is to stay in the very basic hotel in Aihole), and the atmosphere is relaxed and enjoyable.

Mookambika Lodge (☎ 65067), opposite the bus stand, has clean doubles with attached bath and hot water in the morning for Rs 200, and deluxe doubles for Rs 350. Checkout is 24 hours.

Hotel Satkar (☎ 65417) has clean, basic double rooms with attached bath and hot water in the morning from Rs 150. Checkout is 24 hours.

Shri Laxmi Vilas Hotel (☎ 65077), near the tonga stand, has acceptable doubles (only) with attached bath and bucket shower for Rs 100, but it can be noisy.

Hotel Mayura Chalukya (☎ 65046) is a KSTDC hotel on Ramdurg Rd, about 750m east off Station Rd. The neglected old section has tranquil gardens and overpriced doubles/triples with mosquito nets and attached baths with dodgy plumbing for Rs 200/300. A brand new wing which, it is promised, will contain six deluxe air-con rooms is still waiting to be completed. Don't leave your room open and unattended: the resident monkeys are fond of pinching things.

Hotel Badami Court (☎ 65230) is easily

the town's best hotel. It's 2km from the town centre, on the road to the train station. Impeccable doubles with bathtubs and TV cost Rs 750, or Rs 950 with air-con, including tax.

The sole *Retiring Room* at Badami's train station is a double costing Rs 50.

Places to Eat

Badami is the only one of the three sites with a selection of acceptable restaurants.

Hotel Sanman, close to the Badami bus stand, is popular with travellers and locals. It has cheap veg/nonveg food, a roof terrace, and cold beers.

Murali Cafe, nearby, is a basic veg restaurant serving thalis at lunchtime. The dosas are also good.

Hotel Mayura Chalukya has the usual KSTDC veg restaurant and beer bar; the food available is limited.

Pulikeshi Dining Room in Hotel Badami Court is an upmarket, multicuisine, silver service restaurant where dinner costs just under Rs 100 per head. It's also the place to come if you've got a hankering for home: fish and chips is Rs 55, and a continental breakfast costs Rs 90.

Getting There & Away

Bus The timetable at the bus stand in Badami is in English and Kannada but it's not particularly accurate. You'll also have to cope with the usual rugby scrum to get on a bus when it arrives. There are several direct buses daily to Bijapur (four hours), but if in doubt it might be easier to take one of the many buses to Bagalkot (the next large town to the north), and change there for Bijapur. There are four daily buses to Hubli (three hours), and three buses to Bangalore (12 hours). Only three buses run daily direct to Hospet (five hours), but you can catch any of the buses to Gadag (two hours) or Ilkal (two hours) to pick up a connection to Hospet.

Train Conversion work is still disrupting services to Bangalore, and the only trains running through Badami at the time of writing were those shuttling between Gadag and Bijapur-nearly all of them 2nd class passenger trains. Tickets for passenger trains go on sale about 30 minutes before the train arrives. Five trains head to Bijapur (Rs 20, four hours), the most convenient (ie departing at reasonable hours of the day) being at 11.36 am and 4.50 pm. The other three depart at 5.20 am, 8.09 pm and 12.37 am.

The most convenient of the five heading to Gadag are at 7.49 and 10.19 am, and 3.49 pm. The others depart at 2.32 am and 9.49 pm. There are connections from Gadag to Hospet and Hubli. From Bijapur you can also continue north to Sholapur in Maharashtra, which is a major railway junction where you can pick up services to cities such as Mumbai, Hyderabad and Bangalore.

It's worth noting that, once the rail conversion work is complete, the times and fares listed above will probably change, and direct services to Sholapur will resume.

Getting Around

Badami train station is 5km from town. Tongas congregate outside the station to meet the trains. A private tonga from the station into town costs Rs 25, or the fare is split between however many clamber aboard if it's shared. You have the choice of a tonga, auto-rickshaw (Rs 30) or taxi (Rs 50) when heading from town out to the train station. You can hire bikes in Badami for Rs 3 per hour, which is useful if you just want to nip out to the station to check the train timetable.

The best way to explore the surrounding area is by local bus, since there are plenty of them and they run pretty much to schedule. You can easily visit both Aihole and Pattadakal in one day from Badami, but it's best to start with Aihole since the last bus from Aihole to Badami is around lunchtime; the last bus from Pattadakal to Badami is around 5 pm. There are several early morning buses from Badami to Aihole (Rs 12, two hours). From Aihole, there's a bus at around 11.30 am to Pattadakal (30 minutes). The 1 pm service was temporarily ceased at the time of research but should have restarted now. From Pattadakal there are hourly buses and minibuses back to Badami. It's a good idea to take food with you.

KARNATAKA

Taxi drivers in Badami quote around Rs 450 for a day trip taking in Pattadakal and Aihole. Mookambika Lodge can arrange a car and driver to these two places and to other local sights on the way for Rs 150 per person (minimum of two people).

AROUND BADAMI
Pattadakal

This village, 20km from Badami, was the second capital of the Badami Chalukyas and was used in particular for the royal coronations. While most of the temples here were built during the 7th and 8th centuries, the earliest remains date from the 3rd and 4th centuries, and the latest structure is a Jain temple of the Rashtrakuta period (9th century). In Chalukya times, Pattadakal was known as Kisuvolal, or Red Town, due to the reddish colour of the local sandstone, from which the temples are constructed.

Pattadakal, like Aihole, was a developing ground for South Indian temple architecture. In particular, two main types of temple towers were tried out here. On the one hand there are the curvilinear sikharas of the Kasivisvesvara, Jambulinga and Galaganatha

temples, while on the other, the Mallikarjuna, Sangamesvara and Virupaksha temples have a square roof and receding tiers.

The most important monuments are the Virupaksha and Mallikarjuna temples, built to commemorate the victory of Vikramaditya II over the Pallavas of Kanchi. The temples are dated 740-745 AD on the basis of the pillar inscription put up to record a grant to the Vijayesvara Temple.

The **Virupaksha Temple** is a huge structure. The massive columns are covered with intricate carvings depicting episodes from the *Ramayana* and *Mahabharata*, and showing battle scenes, lovers and decorative motifs. Around the roof of the inner hall are sculptures of elephants' and lions' heads. To the east, and facing the temple, is a pavilion containing a massive Nandi. The exterior of the temple is covered with sculpture and ornament, some of it fairly eroded, but much of it still in good shape. The **Mallikarjuna Temple**, next to the Virupaksha Temple, is slightly more worn but almost identical in design.

A classical dance festival is held at Pattadakal, normally at the end of January.

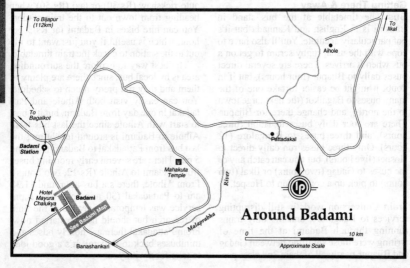

To Bijapur (112km)

To Ilkal

Aihole

To Bagalkot

Badami Station

Badami

Mahakuta Temple

Pattadakal

River

Hotel Mayura Chalukya

See Badami Map

Malaprabha

Banashankari

Around Badami

0   5   10 km

Approximate Scale

Aihole

Forty-three kilometres from Badami, Aihole was the Chalukyan regional capital between the 4th and 6th centuries. Here you can see Hindu temple architecture in its embryonic stage, from the earliest simple shrines, such as those in the Kontigudi Group and the Lad Khan Temple, to the later and more complex buildings such as the Meguti Temple.

Most of the temples at Aihole date from the first half of the Chalukya period, which started with the reign of Pulikesin I in 553 and ended during the time of Pulikesin II, when the Pallavas captured Badami in 642. After 13 years of Pallava occupation, the kingdom was restored by Vikramaditya I, and the main temple building activity moved to Pattadakal.

In the centre of the village is a fenced enclosure (entry Rs 2) with the most impressive building in Aihole – the **Durga Temple**, which dates from the 7th century. The temple is notable for its semicircular apse, which was copied from Buddhist architecture, and for the remains of the curvilinear sikhara. Even more striking than the formal layout are the outstanding carvings that crowd the colonnaded passageway around the sanctuary. The walls, pillars and brackets are covered with sculptures of breathtaking execution. Among the main figures who appear on the walls are Shiva, Vishnu, Narasimha and Durga.

The small **museum** behind the Durga Temple contains further examples of the Chalukyan sculptors' work, and is open from 10 am to 5 pm (closed Friday).

To the south from the Durga Temple are several other collections of buildings including some of the earliest structures in Aihole – the Gandar, Ladkhan, Kontigudi and Huccha-paya groups, which are of pavilion type with slightly sloping roofs. Six hundred metres to the south-east, on a low hilltop, is the **Meguti Temple**, which is almost certainly the latest building in Aihole. This Jain temple can be accurately dated by an inscription which puts its year of construction as 634-35.

Two hundred metres to the north-east of the village, another notable monument is the

Ravula Phadi cave temple, which was constructed in the latter half of the 7th century. The cave was never finished and much of the stone is still rough, bearing the clear marks of the sculptors' chisels. The temple has a central porch, off which there are three other chambers. To the left as you enter the cave is a large carving of a dancing Shiva, with his consort Parvati. Other figures include Ganesh and Harihara. The sanctuary holds a large lingam, and there are carved lotus motifs in the centre of the floor and ceiling. The area in front of the cave is fenced off and just inside the gate is a stone pillar, possibly once a lamp tower.

About 200m west of Ravula Phadi, the **Hucchimalli Gudi** is a simple stone shrine. The inner sanctum contains a massive plain lingam, and the outer wall surrounding the sanctum is pierced by square holes, a couple of which still retain their latticework screens. The carving on the ceiling of the porch is notable for its fine detail. Karttikeya is portrayed seated on a peacock, and surrounded by attendants. A simple square tank sits before the temple entrance.

Places to Stay Accommodation is available at the Department of Tourism *Tourist Home* (☎ 74641), 1km from the village centre on the Amingad road. The place is all but deserted; a large triple room with attached bath costs Rs 60 and food is available.

Mahakuta Temple

Approximately 10km east of Badami is another remnant of the Chalukyan rule. Mahakuta was made sacred by the presence of the sage Agastya, who lived here, and the temple is still active as a pilgrimage site. Within the walled courtyard are two main temples on either side of an old tank. The first of these, nearest the entrance, is still in use but the other one is now deserted. A number of smaller shrines in various states of dilapidation are arranged around the outside of the courtyard.

Banashankari

This small village, about 5km south-east of

The Banashankari Festival

The annual festival at the village temple in Banashankari is more than simply a religious event. The rites are as important as ever, but the festival is also an excellent excuse for a fair.

In the evenings villagers from all around the area pour in, and the lanes become crowded with overexcited children and only marginally less excited adults. Temporary cinemas, set up in ramshackle barns knocked together with corrugated iron, show the latest Bollywood movies. Fairyfloss, coconuts, *belpuri* (a chickpea snack), sweetmeats and other snacks are on sale.

Packing them in at the northern end of the road is a motorcycle wall-of-death act. It's not too surprising when the rider circles the cage, his body horizontal to the ground. Even when he takes his hands off the handlebars, or casually starts to take off his shirt, the crowd are unimpressed. Interest increases when a second motorcyclist joins the act, circling the cage at the same time. The highlight has everyone craning their necks in disbelief: two motorbikes, a bicycle and a small hatchback car, all overtaking each other on a vertical wall – what a great act! Across the road there's a circus, complete with big top, acrobats, clowns and raucous music.

The fair is more than just an excuse for fun, it's also a good place to do business. If you want to buy clothes, presents for the kids, a wooden trunk, or even a new door for your house, this is definitely the place to look. Just down the road towards Badami is the annual bull market which always coincides with the Banashankari festival. Farmers come here to buy and sell; only bulls are traded, and almost all of them are white. To make the bulls more attractive, their owners do a certain amount of cosmetic work. The horns are freshly painted – or decorated with ribbons – and the animals are tethered in long lines for easy inspection. A good bull can fetch around Rs 7500.

Badami, is home to an attractive temple, with a huge tank surrounded by a pillared cloister. Banashankari is particularly worth visiting during the annual temple festival, which usually falls in January. For days on end the streets around the temple are taken over by a huge fair, which is best visited in the evenings. Although the stalls peddling *prasaad* (sacred food offerings) outside the temple entrance are busy, the real activity takes place in the streets slightly further away, which become lined with stalls selling everything from sweets to jewellery to woodcarving. Temporary cinemas are set up in lean-to shacks, a circus is established in the nearby fields, and the streets are full of fairground entertainers. It's a wonderful place to wander, and the excitement of all the other visitors, intent on having a good evening out, becomes infectious.

BIJAPUR

Pop: 217,500 Tel Area Code: 08352

Modern Bijapur is a dull, undistinguished town blessed by the scattered ruins and still-intact gems of 15th to 17th century Muslim architecture. It is dotted with mosques, mausoleums, palaces and fortifications, including the famous Golgumbaz, whose vast dome is said to be the world's second largest. The austere grace of Bijapur's discoloured monuments is in complete contrast to the sculptural extravaganza of the Chalukyan and Hoysala temples further south. The Ibrahim Roza Mausoleum, in particular, is considered to be one of the most finely proportioned Islamic monuments in India.

History

The history of Bijapur goes back to the 6th century, when it was part of the kingdom of the Chalukyas of Badami. After their fall from power, the town passed through the hands of the Rashtrakutas, Kalyana Chalukyas, Kalachuris, Yadavas and Khiljis, before falling into the hands of the Bahmani sultans who ruled the north Deccan from their capital in Gulbarga. As the power of the Bahmanis waned, the semi-autonomous cities became increasingly powerful, and in

1489 the governor of Bijapur, Yusuf Adil Khan (later Adil Shah), declared independence and founded his own dynasty, the Adil Shahis.

In all, nine sultans of the dynasty ruled the kingdom of Bijapur, of whom Ali I, Ibrahim II and Muhammad were the most notable. The city enjoyed great prominence, the rulers at times controlling Goa, and particularly gaining in wealth following the fall of the Vijayanagar Empire in 1565. In 1686, however, the Mughal emperor Aurangzeb overthrew Sikander Adil Shah and put an end to the rule. Thereafter Bijapur saw the rule of the Nizams, Marathas and British.

Bijapur is still strongly Muslim in character, and some solo women travellers have reported being harassed here.

Orientation

The two main attractions, the Golgumbaz and the Ibrahim Roza, are at opposite ends of the town. Between them runs Station Rd (MG Rd) along which are most of the major hotels and restaurants. The bus stand is a five minute walk from Station Rd; the train station is 2km east of the centre.

Information

The tourist office has moved and is now in the building behind Hotel Mayura Adil Shahi Annexe on Station Rd. Apart from providing a map of the state, the staff here have nothing to do, and have little intention of increasing their workload. There are no organised tours of the city.

The post office, in the town centre, is also on Station Rd and is open Monday to Saturday from 8.30 am to 6 pm.

To change travellers cheques, head to the Canara Bank (open between 10.30 am and 2.30 pm on weekdays, 10.30 am and 12.30 pm on Saturday) north of the market. You'll need to provide the bank with photocopies of the pages in your passport which have your name and photograph in them and also of the page with your visa. Service is slow, and the rates tend to be poor. There is nowhere in Bijapur to get cash on a credit card.

Power cuts are frequent in Bijapur and often last for hours, so have candles handy.

Golgumbaz

Bijapur's largest and most famous monument is the Golgumbaz. Not long after Muhammad Adil Shah came to the throne in 1626 he started work on the monument which was to be his own sepulchre. Work was still in progress when he died in 1656, and it is believed that there would have been further ornamentation to the building had he lived a little longer. The mausoleum may not be particularly beautiful or graceful to look at, but it's certainly impressive. The enormous, square structure, which contains a single immense hall, is buttressed by octagonal seven storey towers at each of its corners. The enormous dome which covers the building has an internal diameter of 38m, and is said to be the world's second largest after St Peter's in Vatican City.

Around the base of the dome, high above the hall, is a gallery known as the 'whispering gallery', since the acoustics here are such that any sound made is said to be repeated 10 times over. 'Bedlam gallery' would be a more appropriate name, since it is permanently full of yelling tourists and children running amok. Access to the gallery is via a narrow staircase in the south-eastern tower and there are views of Bijapur from the outside of the dome before you enter the

Bijapur's biggest claim to fame: the Golgumbaz.

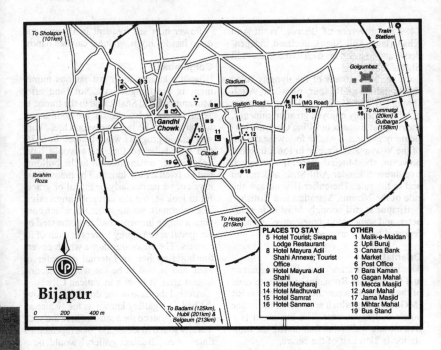

PLACES TO STAY
5 Hotel Tourist; Swapna Lodge Restaurant
8 Hotel Mayura Adil Shahi Annexe; Tourist Office
9 Hotel Mayura Adil Shahi
13 Hotel Megharaj
14 Hotel Madhuvan
15 Hotel Samrat
16 Hotel Sanman

OTHER
1 Malik-e-Maidan
2 Upli Buruj
3 Canara Bank
4 Market
6 Post Office
7 Bara Kaman
10 Gagan Mahal
11 Mecca Masjid
12 Asar Mahal
17 Jama Masjid
18 Mihtar Mahal
19 Bus Stand

gallery. In particular you can clearly see the extent of the old city walls. The views are clearest in the early morning, which is also the best time to test the acoustics, before the school groups arrive.

The caskets of Mohammed Adil Shah (1626-56), his two wives, his mistress (Rambha), one of his daughters and a grandson stand on a raised platform in the centre of the hall. The actual graves are in the crypt, accessible by a flight of steps under the western doorway.

The mausoleum is open from 6 am to 6 pm; entry costs Rs 2, except on Friday, when it's free. Shoes should be left outside near the entrance to the hall.

An **archaeological museum**, in the building in front of the mausoleum, is open between 10 am and 5 pm daily except Friday. The collection includes sculptures and carvings from Chalukyan temples, as well as more recent pieces dating from the Adil Shahi period. Particularly interesting is the painted plan of the old city, which shows the layout of the city defences, even down to the details of individual gun emplacements. To the west of the mausoleum is a large mosque.

Ibrahim Roza
The beautiful Ibrahim Roza was constructed at the height of Bijapur's prosperity by Ibrahim Adil Shah II (1580-1626) for his queen. As things turned out he died before she did, and thus the mausoleum became his and was named after him. His queen, Taj Sultana, his daughter, two sons, and his mother Haji Badi Sahiba, are all buried here with him.

Unlike the Golgumbaz, which is impressive only for its immensity, the emphasis here is on elegance and delicacy. The 24m-high minarets are said to have inspired those of the Taj Mahal. The structure, which is raised on a high stone platform, is approached via a path through formal gardens. On the plinth itself two buildings seem to mirror each other; to the east is the mausoleum itself with the six tombs, while to the west is a mosque. It's also one of the few monuments in Bijapur with substantial stone filigree and other decorative work. The entry fee is Rs 2; shoes should be left on the steps up to the platform on which the mausoleum stands. The building is closed at 6 pm.

Citadel

Surrounded by its own fortified walls and wide moat in the city centre, the citadel once contained the palaces, pleasure gardens and Durbar Hall of the Adil Shahi kings. Unfortunately, most of them are now in ruins, although some impressive fragments remain. The best is the **Gagan Mahal**, built by Ali Adil Shah I around 1561 to serve the dual purpose of a royal residence and a Durbar Hall. It looks like an opera stage set, and is completely open on one side so that an audience outside the hall had an unobstructed view of the proceedings on the raised platform inside.

Mohammed Adil Shah's seven storey palace, the **Sat Manzil**, is nearby, but substantially in ruins. Just across the road stands the delicate **Jala Manzil**, once a water pavilion surrounded by secluded courts and gardens. On the other side of Station Rd are the graceful arches of **Bara Kaman**, the ruined mausoleum of Ali II who ruled from 1656 to 1686.

Jama Masjid

The finely proportioned Jama Masjid has graceful arches, a fine dome and a large inner courtyard with room for 2250 worshippers. Spaces for them are marked out in black on the polished floor of the mosque. The flat roof is accessible by several flights of stairs. The masjid was built by Ali I (1557-80), who was also responsible for erecting the fortified city walls and the Gagan Mahal, and for installing a public water system. It is the largest mosque of its class in the Deccan, and is simple and plain in design with little ornamentation except in

the central archway. The mosque is impressive for its scale and symmetry rather than for anything else. There are 'cloisters' on the north and south sides of the courtyard, and the only ornate touches are the painted and carved mihrab in the west wall.

Mihtar Mahal

Moving west from the Jama Masjid towards the centre of the city you soon come to the Mihtar Mahal. The entrance to the courtyard was once via a gate underneath the extraordinary tower at the north-east corner of the complex. Today, however, you must enter by a gate on the north side of the compound. The façade of the small mosque is heavily carved, but the dark grey stone and squat form make it far from graceful.

Mecca Masjid

On the eastern side of the citadel is the tiny, walled, Mecca mosque, thought to have been built in the early 17th century. The name is supposed to have come from the fact that the mosque's layout resembles that of the Prophet's mosque at Mecca. Another interesting speculation, which has been arrived at due to the high surrounding walls and cloistered feel of the place, is that this mosque may have been for the use of ladies. The prayer hall itself has ornamental brackets and parapets, and a simple central dome.

Other Monuments

The **Asar Mahal**, to the east of the citadel, was built by Mohammed Adil Shah in about 1646 to serve as a Hall of Justice. The building was also used to house two hairs from the Prophet's beard. The rooms on the upper storey are decorated with frescoes and the front is graced with a square tank usually full of swimming kids. Women are not allowed inside.

Upli Buruj is a 16th century, 24m-high watchtower built on high ground near the western walls of the city. An external flight of stairs leads to the top, where there are a couple of hefty cannons and good views of the city and plains.

The **Malik-e-Maidan** (Monarch of the

Plains) is a huge cannon measuring over four metres long, almost 1.5m in diameter, and estimated to weigh 55 tonnes. It was cast in 1549 and brought to Bijapur as a war trophy thanks to the effort of 10 elephants, 400 oxen and hundreds of men.

Places to Stay

Accommodation can be hard to find in Bijapur, so to avoid trekking around hotels when you arrive, it's worth telephoning in advance to reserve a room.

Hotel Tourist (☎ 20655), in the centre of town, has reasonable rooms with attached bath for Rs 60/100 or Rs 70/125 for the 'special' rooms, which have nothing special about them.

Hotel Samrat (☎ 21620) is probably the best of the budget places to stay. It has good rooms with attached bath and mosquito nets for Rs 95/120. It's east of the town centre on Station Rd.

Hotel Megharaj (☎ 21458) is another reasonable option. Bare but clean doubles go for Rs 120, deluxe doubles are Rs 190, and aircon rooms cost Rs 350. Travellers staying there report that the rooms are clean but that there's a lot of noise from the traffic on Station Rd.

Hotel Sanman (☎ 21866), opposite the Golgumbaz, has rather dingy but acceptable doubles/triples with attached bath for Rs 115/145. Checkout time is 24 hours.

Hotel Mayura Adil Shahi (☎ 20934) is a KSTDC operation where many travellers end up staying. Rooms here are set around a quiet, leafy garden courtyard which doubles as an open-air restaurant. Acceptable singles/doubles with mosquito nets, soggy attached bathrooms and hot water in the morning cost Rs 130/183 including tax.

Hotel Mayura Adil Shahi Annexe (☎ 20401) nearby is also shrouded in greenery. It consists of four well-appointed air-con rooms with TV, attached bath and 24 hour hot water which cost Rs 506 including tax.

Hotel Madhuvan (☎ 25572) is a modern hotel off Station Rd with comfortable but overpriced doubles (only) with TV and attached bath for Rs 550, or Rs 650 with air-con.

Places to Eat

Swapna Lodge Restaurant, on the 2nd floor of the same building as the Hotel Tourist, is popular with travellers. It has good veg/nonveg food (including 63 different chicken dishes), cold beer, and a rooftop terrace which is perfect for evening dining. Don't be put off by the forlorn entry to this place as both the service and food are good.

Hotel Mayura Adil Shahi has a reasonable restaurant in the middle of its garden courtyard. It serves western breakfasts and modestly good Indian food, although the service is poor. If you can put up with the surliness of the staff, the garden makes a pleasant setting for an evening beer.

Hotel Madhuvan, *Hotel Sanman* and *Hotel Samrat* all have restaurants. The last of these boasts what may be the world's darkest bar; it's best to light a match if you want a waiter to see you.

Getting There & Away

Bus The timetable painted on the wall at the bus stand is pretty confused and seems to have changed long ago. There are five daily services to Badami, and buses almost hourly to Belgaum (five hours), Hubli (Rs 55, 4½ hours) and Gulbarga (Rs 43, four hours). Buses run every half hour to Sholapur. There are six evening services to Bangalore, two of which are 'superdeluxe' (Rs 203, 12 hours); Bangalore buses run via Hospet. Six buses go to Hyderabad (Rs 151, 10 hours) daily, and eight buses go to Mumbai via Pune (one bus departs early morning, the rest leave in the evening). There are three buses daily to Bidar (seven hours).

Train Because of the current disruption while the gauge is widened, only a handful of trains operate from Bijapur. Once normal services are resumed, however, Bijapur will once again be connected to the major rail junction at Sholapur and the less important junction at Gadag. Sholapur has connections to Mumbai, Hyderabad and Bangalore; Gadag has connections to Hospet, Hubli and Bangalore. Bijapur station has a healthy quota of sleeping berths allotted to it on all major expresses passing through Sholapur and Gadag, so you should have no problem getting a berth if you're making a long-distance connection.

Getting Around
Bus The uncrowded local bus system has only one route: from the train station, along Station Rd to the gate at the western end of town. Buses run every 15 minutes.

Auto-Rickshaw & Tonga Auto-rickshaw drivers charge what they think you will pay – intense haggling and Rs 15 should get you between the train station and the town centre. To zip between the Golgumbaz and Ibrahim Roza costs the same. Tonga drivers are eager for business and will offer to take you from the train station to the town centre for around Rs 10.

Around Bijapur
Some 20km east of Bijapur, along the Gulbarga road at **Kummatgi**, are the remains of a water pavilion built during Adil Shahi times. The desirability of a cool and well-watered place in which to escape the parched conditions of the north Karnatakan summer is understandable, and it appears that this small complex served that purpose.

The two main buildings are surrounded by a small moat. The building nearest to the gate is open sided and shady, catching the breezes and remaining wonderfully cool. The remains of murals can still be seen on the domed ceilings, and the arches are embellished with simple designs. Behind this first building is a two storey tower set within its own surrounding moat. Again the structure is open sided, and may well have had a sprinkler system to cool it further. A gate-like building 50m to the west stands on the edge of a reservoir, now dry during summer, which must have provided the water for the moats and sprinklers.

Although the buildings are not visually spectacular, the countryside is peaceful, and the shade and quiet make a pleasant change from crowded, noisy Bijapur. All Gulbarga buses pass Kummatgi, but many of them are

'express' services and therefore don't stop. It's easiest to catch a 'maxi cab' or 'tempo' – ie a privately owned small bus. These depart from the small lane leading north-eastwards away from the bus stand. The trip takes around 25 minutes and costs Rs 5.

GULBARGA
Pop: 349,500 Tel Area Code: 08472
Gulbarga was the first capital of the Bahmanis, who successfully established their independence from Delhi in 1347. The first sultan, Alla-ud-din, was responsible for much of the great architecture that still graces the city today, including the fort and the Jami Mosque.

Alla-ud-din's successors continued to rule from Gulbarga patronising the arts and sciences in particular until 1428 when the fourth sultan, Ahmed, moved the capital to Bidar. Within the century the kingdom was weakened, and split up into five independent sultanates – Bijapur, Bidar, Berar, Ahmednagar and Golconda. The five fought against each other for much of the time, only managing to form an alliance briefly to defeat the Vijayanagar forces at the fateful Battle of Talikota in 1565. When the great northern ruler Aurangzeb ranged southwards through the Deccan in the mid-17th century, he had little problem picking off the individual states, the last of which, Golconda, finally fell to his armies in 1687.

Today, dusty, scruffy Gulbarga is far from being a tourist spot, and few travellers ever make a stopover here. The atmosphere can be oppressive, and the children are as likely to throw stones as to come and talk. While many locals are friendly enough, women travelling alone may wish to give this place a miss. Having said all this, there are a couple of sights that are unique, and if you feel like escaping from the tourist trail, this is one place where you can certainly do just that.

Things to See
Fort Gulbarga's neglected fort is in poor condition, despite attempts to promote it as a tourist attraction. Although the fort was already in place when the Bahmanis came

to power, it was substantially rebuilt by the first sultan, Alla-ud-din, with 15 strong bastions in the outer wall.

The only building still completely intact inside the walls is the **Jama Masjid**, which also dates from Alla-ud-din's time. Built in 1367 by a Moorish architect, it is reputed to be modelled on the great mosque in Cordoba (Spain). The huge edifice is plain to look at, and the interior is almost devoid of ornament, but the masjid is said to be the largest completely covered mosque in South India.

North of the mosque, and just inside the fort's east gate (the main entrance from the city), is a dilapidated watchtower. Three massive cannon are still in place on the top of the tower and, standing near them, you get an excellent view over Gulbarga. To the east you can see the domes of the Haft Gumbad and mausoleum or *dargah* of Hazrat Gesu Daraz. To the west, on the skyline about 1.5km away, you can see the Chor Gumbad, a huge white mausoleum.

The most interesting part of the fort is around the north-west gate, which you can get to by following the street leading northwestwards from the watchtower. Near the gate, the narrow street is lined with old houses, painted in pastel colours, and still showing traces of the ancient stonework. The north-west gate gives a startling insight into the strength of the fortress. The huge metal-studded gates are adorned with massive spikes, which were designed to stop them being charged by elephants. In the unlikely event that anything ever made it past these outer defences, the fort's occupants again had the advantage. The road beyond the gate leads through a series of sharp turns, flanked on both sides by massive walls, from which defenders could fire down onto a trapped enemy.

Some locals claim that it's not safe to wander around the fort alone, so it pays to be careful, and if possible go in company.

Haft Gumbad To the east of the town centre are the Haft Gumbad, the tombs of the Bahmani kings. These massive, plain, box-like structures are surmounted by huge domes, and are so regular in appearance that they seem almost unreal. All of the tombs are kept locked, but you can still glimpse something of the interiors through the grilled doorways, and there are traces of the original ornament on the outside.

Dargah of Bande Nawaz A 10 minute walk east of the Haft Gumbad will bring you to a collection of buildings contained within a perimeter wall. The main building here is the tomb of Bande Nawaz, a great Sufi Muslim saint who came to Gulbarga in 1413. The tomb is a major centre for pilgrimage and, despite the hustle of the street outside the complex, once through the gates the setting is shady and tranquil. Locals come here not only to pray, but also to chat and even to doze in a shady spot.

The main tomb may only be entered by men; women have to stay outside and peer through the door. The inside of the building is truly memorable, as the huge dome and interior of the ancient structure have been covered with a mosaic of mirrors. The detail even includes Koranic verses picked out in black mirrors. The result is somewhere between breathtaking and incredibly tacky. For the more traditionally minded the mausoleum opposite has delicately decorated walls, and a magnificent cloth suspended above the tomb itself. Visitors must leave their shoes outside the complex; shorts are not considered acceptable dress.

Places to Stay & Eat

The *Hotel Mayura Bahmani (☎ 20644)* is a neglected KSTDC establishment set back off Station Rd in what is considered to be a municipal garden. It's been under renovation for some months, but staff promise that it will open again soon. Meanwhile the bar and restaurant remain open although neither have much of a clientele. The hotel is about 2km from the train station (Rs 10 by auto-rickshaw) and 3km from the bus stand (Rs 10).

Hotel Aditya (☎ 24040), on the opposite side of Station Rd, has well-appointed rooms with attached bath and hot water in the morning for Rs 200/250, deluxe doubles for Rs 350 and air-con doubles for Rs 550. The hotel is popular with businessmen and tends to be booked solid. Checkout is 24 hours. There's a clean veg restaurant in the hotel, with good thalis for Rs 20. Checkout is 24 hours.

Hotel Pariwar (☎ 21522), also on Station Rd, is another popular place, but with more reasonable prices. Rooms go for Rs 145/220, and air-con rooms start at Rs 600.

Hotel Sanman (☎ 22801), just off Station Rd and north of the Aditya, is the best-value place in town. Very clean singles/doubles with attached bath go for Rs 120/149, and the management is friendly.

Hotel Santosh (☎ 22661), at Bilgundi Gardens, University Rd, is well to the east of town and requires a Rs 15 rickshaw ride to get to it. Comfortable, standard double rooms go for Rs 250 and air-con doubles for around Rs 375. The hotel has a good garden restaurant which serves ice cold beers and veg/nonveg food. (Many of the restaurants in Gulbarga are strictly vegetarian and do not serve alcohol.)

Retiring Rooms at the train station are great value at Rs 30 per bed or Rs 50 per bed in an air-con room.

If you're stuck without a room, there are a number of undistinguished budget hotels catering to Indian tourists on the road into town from the bus stand.

Getting There & Away
There are plenty of government buses to Bijapur and Bidar (Rs 30, three hours), plus overnight buses to Bangalore. Four buses depart for Hyderabad, all of them in the evening.

An inordinate number of express trains pass through Gulbarga, giving it surprisingly good connections to Mumbai, Bangalore, Hyderabad and Cochin.

BIDAR
Tel Area Code: 08482
This little visited, walled town in the extreme north-eastern corner of the state has a long history stretching back at least to the time of the Kalyan Chalukyas (977-1190),

when it may have been known as Vidarbha. Later, the town came under the Yadavas of Devagiri followed by the Kakatiyas of Warangal (1322) and the Tughluqs of Delhi (1341), before finally falling to the Bahmanis. In 1428 Bidar became capital of the Bahmani kingdom, and was renamed Muhammadabad.

Favoured for its excellent defences and climate, the city became an important trading centre for horses, cloth, silk and pepper. Athanasius Nikitin, a Russian who travelled in the Deccan (under the assumed name of Khwaja Yusuf Khurasani) from 1469 to 1474, spent many months at Bidar, and described it as 'the chief town of the whole of Mohamedan Hindusthan'.

After the disintegration of the Bahmani kingdom, Bidar became capital of the Barid Shahi dynasty. In 1619 it fell to the forces of Bijapur, and in 1656 Aurangzeb captured the town and renamed it Zafarabad. Finally in 1724 Nizam-ul-Mulk Asaf Jah of Hyderabad established his authority over the area, and it remained part of the Nizam's territories until the British took over the area in the 19th century.

Today Bidar is a pleasant little town which sees few visitors, but which has a refreshingly relaxed atmosphere. Bidar is also something of a garrison town for the large airforce base which stands only a few kilometres away on the Gulbarga road.

Things to See
Fort The splendid 15th century fort dominates the north end of the town, and is really the main attraction. In its day, this was considered one of the most formidable strongholds in the country, with tunnels, deep wells and defences from which boiling oil could be poured on attackers. The fort was built by Ahmad Shah Bahmani when he moved his capital to Bidar, and is thought to have been constructed on the site of an older fortress, and built with the aid of foreign engineers. More than anything else, the sheer immensity of the structure is impressive. The huge inner area is surrounded by massive outer walls 5.5km long. There are

37 bastions and seven gates, and the whole lot is encircled by a triple moat hewn out of solid rock. The main parts of the fort are in excellent condition, and with its semi-ruined halls, it's an excellent place to explore.

The main entry from the town is from the south, via a series of three gates through which the roadway twists in an elaborate chicane. Just inside the gate to the left, the first building you come to is the **Rangin Mahal** or Coloured Palace. The palace was built by Ali Barid (1542-80), the second ruler of the Barid Shahi dynasty. If the outer door is locked, ask at the building opposite for access. The entrance gives onto a courtyard which contains the remains of a dried-up pool. The open-sided hall beyond has finely carved wooden pillars and beams. At the back of the hall is a doorway with mosaic designs around the edges. The rooms beyond have mosaic designs on the walls and mother-of-pearl inlay.

Mahmud Gawan, Statesman & Scholar

Mahmud Gawan travelled to India as a young merchant from Gilani in Iran and arrived at Bidar in 1453. By virtue of his outstanding abilities he was soon noticed and rose to become one of the greatest figures of his age, a renowned statesman, military commander and scholar. Despite the immense power which he came to wield, he was a lover of culture and learning, led a life of austerity, and used to spend most of his leisure time in the company of scholars in the *madrasa* (Islamic centre of learning) and by reading books.

Under Sultan Humayun, Gawan held office as the Governor of Bijapur. When Humayun was murdered in his sleep, in 1461, it fell to Gawan to take over the administration of the kingdom. The rightful heir to the throne was only eight years old, and so Gawan and the child's mother jointly managed the kingdom, while the statesman groomed the young heir to take over as soon as he became old enough. It was a time of considerable turbulence, when the very existence of the Bahmani kingdom was under threat, but Gawan handled affairs skilfully, and in 1466 he was formally appointed prime minister.

In the ensuing years he restored the kingdom to its former glory. Either by making peace treaties, or by conquering the state's enemies, he brought order and security. In 1469 he attacked Goa and wrested the region from the Vijayanagar Empire, at a time when the Hindu state was almost at the height of its powers. Having settled the kingdom he enacted reforms which included curbing corruption and improving the justice system. In recognition of his devotion to learning, he founded the madrasa in Bidar, where food and dress were provided free to students and there was a great library.

Such outstanding success was not without a price. Many of the nobles did not like the reforms and were jealous of the prestige enjoyed by Gawan, and they took it upon themselves to plan his downfall. In 1481, a group led by a nobleman named Malik Hassan hatched a plot by which they intended to destroy Gawan's reputation in the eyes of the sultan. They forged a letter, supposedly from Gawan to the King of Orissa, inviting him to invade the Bahmani kingdom. They got Gawan's seal affixed to the letter by bribing his secretary. Finally, they chose their moment carefully, and presented the letter to the Sultan of Bijapur one evening when he was drunk. The sultan immediately called for Gawan, and without listening to any argument, sentenced him to death. Gawan, seeing that argument was useless, immediately knelt in front of the monarch and was beheaded on the spot.

When the sultan sobered up and learnt the truth about the old man who had advised him faithfully throughout his reign, he was overcome with grief, and ordered that Gawan should be buried with full honours. From this time onwards, however, the Bahmani Empire began a rapid and inexorable decline.

Continuing westwards from the Rangin Mahal, you come to the **Solah Khamb Mosque**, which was built in 1423-24 by Qubli Sultani, and which is still in excellent condition. Plain in design, and surmounted in the centre by a large dome, it faces onto an open garden area, which has a pond and watercourse running through it. At the north end of this garden is a small **archaeological museum** with some bits and pieces of stone carving and a few other knick-knacks. Of note are the monumental old padlocks and the array of huge firearms. To the south of the garden is the **Tarkash Mahal**, an imposing multistorey edifice, supposedly built as the palace for a Turkish wife of the sultan, and subsequently used to house the royal harem.

To the west of the mosque and garden area are a number of ruined buildings which were undoubtedly extremely impressive in their day and which are thought to have been used as audience halls. The other buildings in the fort are in varying states of decay, and are scattered throughout the walled area. The best way to see them is simply to wander, and you could easily spend a morning or afternoon exploring at leisure.

Mahmud Gawan Madrasa Five hundred metres south of the main gate to the fort, near the middle of town, is the madrasa, or religious college, built by Mahmud Gawan, the chief minister of Mahmud Shah Bahmani III. Mahmud was an educated man who loved learning and built this college in 1472 to further education. At its height it contained a huge library of manuscripts, and was staffed by numerous scholars. The building was badly damaged by lightning in 1696 and has since suffered from neglect. A local story also accounts for the advanced state of ruin. The madrasa was at one time used as a cavalry barracks, and chambers in the left minaret were commandeered as the powder magazine. Unfortunately an accident resulted in a large part of the historic structure being blown up. Consequently the magnificence of the madrasa in its heyday is left somewhat to the imagination of the visitor, although the right-hand side of the building

is still intact, and houses a small mosque. There are a few remains of colourful mosaics on the outer walls.

Bahmani Tombs At Ashtur, 2km east of Bidar, is a series of impressive mausoleums, built to house the mortal remains of the sultans. Arranged in a long line along the edge of the road, the tombs are all regular in shape and feature, although there are slight differences between them if you look closely. One of the tombs has half fallen down, giving an interesting view of the dome construction in cross section. The best-preserved building still has some of the facing tile mosaics, and the finely carved black stone edging that has been used for the corners and decoration.

Places to Stay & Eat

Hotel standards in Bidar are mediocre and the choice is slim.

Hotel Ashoka (☎ 26249), near Deepak Theatre, is by far the best place in town. Pleasant double rooms start from Rs 130, or

---

KARNATAKA

The Bidriware of Bidar

During its Islamic heyday, Persian craftsmen of Bidar came up with a form of damascening now known as bidriware. It involves moulding imaginative blends of blackened zinc, copper, lead and tin, which are then embossed, and overlaid or inlaid with pure silver. In both design and decoration, the artefacts are heavily influenced by the typically Islamic decorative motifs and features of the time. Finely crafted pieces such as hookahs, goblets, paan boxes and bangles are exquisitely embellished with interwoven creepers and flowing floral patterns, and occasionally framed by strict geometric lines. The effect of the delicate silver filigree against the ebony-toned background is striking. These days artists still tap away at their craft in the backstreets of Bidar, as well as in the neighbouring city of Hyderabad.

Rs 230 for a deluxe double. There are air-con rooms for Rs 410.

Hotel Ratna (☎ 27218), *Sri New Venka-teshwara Lodge (☎ 26443)* and *Hotel Prince (☎ 25747)* all have acceptable singles/doubles with attached bath for between Rs 55/75 and Rs 95/115. The first two are on the main street in the town centre, the last is on Udgir Rd, on the way into town from the bus stand.

Hotel Mayura Barid Shahi (☎ 26571) is a KSTDC hotel on Udgir Rd which has run-down singles/doubles with attached bath for Rs 100/150. The restaurant on the ground floor is reasonably good value and serves good dosas.

Hotel Mayura Restaurant, opposite the bus stand, is a clean establishment where you can get reasonable Indian food and forget your accommodation woes over a beer.

Getting There & Away

Bus Bidar has plenty of bus connections, including two daily services to Raichur, several daily services to Gulbarga, six buses to Hyderabad, and two buses every day to Bangalore.

Train Bidar is on a branch line, and the services through here tend to be slow passenger trains, so bus connections are easier and quicker.

Andhra Pradesh

The biggest state in South India, Andhra Pradesh gets its name from an ancient people called the Andhras. By the 2nd century BC they had developed a flourishing civilisation which extended from the west to the east coasts of South India.

From the extensive coastline of over 400km, the coastal plain gives way to the Eastern Ghats. These in turn rise to one of the oldest geological formations in India, the Deccan Plateau, on which most of Andhra Pradesh is situated at approximately 500m above sea level. The Godavari and Krishna rivers cut their way through the plateau before fanning into large deltas and entering the sea on the east coast. Except for the Ganges, these are the largest river systems in India. Their surrounding fertile soils produce such crops as rice, beans and lentils.

The monsoons can wreak havoc in the low-lying areas, flooding the deltas and destroying lives and crops. On the dryer plateau, droughts may result in crop failure and exacerbate the impoverished conditions. Irrigation schemes are beginning to overcome these difficulties.

Over the centuries the Deccan ('south') provided a natural barrier from much foreign invasion. Now its dry landscape and eroded soils frequently deter the traveller. But this natural barrier has enabled unique and fascinating cultures to evolve and develop.

Another deterrent to travellers has been the monsoonal conditions which may obstruct or even destroy public transport systems and communications. Such events are rare and usually cause only temporary or minor inconvenience. Monsoons occur in May, October and November. Travellers can therefore avoid these times or make inquiries to assess the situation.

With careful planning the deterrents can be overcome. Indeed, for the adventurous traveller, there is much to experience in Andhra Pradesh. Here a diversity of cultures

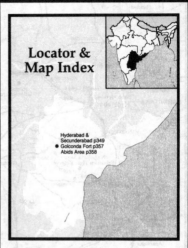

ANDHRA PRADESH AT A GLANCE

Locator & Map Index

Hyderabad & Secunderabad p349
● Golconda Fort p357
Abids Area p358

Population: 76 million
Area: 276,754 sq km
Capital: Hyderabad
Main Language: Telugu
Best Time to Go: October to February

Highlights

* Wandering the great bazaars of Hyderabad
* A picnic atop the ruins of Golconda Fort
* Shaving your head for darshan at Tirumala's Venkateshwara Temple
* Sampling the fiery Andhra cuisine

results in a fascinating blend of languages, religions, architectural styles and customs.

The capital, the twin cities of Hyderabad-Secunderabad has a rich Muslim heritage evidenced by its huge and lavish mosques. The nearby Golconda Fort marks the former capital of Persian kings, and the nearby Qutb Shahi Tombs was their burial place.

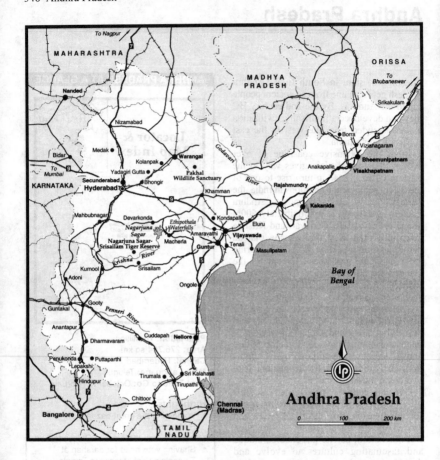

Andhra Pradesh

Warangal contains the ruins of Chalukyan-style architecture, while near Vijayawada there are ancient Hindu cave temples and Jain sites which can be visited. Incredible crowds at Tirumala make it one of the most frequented pilgrimage sites in the world, and pilgrims also flock to the well known ashram of Sri Sathya Sai Baba in Puttaparthi.

The reconstructed buildings and museums of Nagarjunakonda provide fascinating evidence of early civilisations as well as ancient Hindu-Buddhist societies. Although the coastal area is not developed for tourism, there are beach resorts in the north. The hills provide a cooler environment and are home to many of Andhra Pradesh's tribal people. Wildlife sanctuaries give refuge to animals including elephants, leopards and antelopes. The Nagarjuna Sagar-Srisailam Tiger Reserve is reputedly the largest in India.

Andhra Pradesh has a diverse cuisine of aromatic rices, charcoal breads, spiced meats and vegetables. Some foods suggest a delicate subtlety while others excite the palate with their fiery chillies.

Bookshops and bazaars, parks and gardens,

museums and warm hospitality all add to the experience of Andhra Pradesh.

HISTORY

By the 1st century AD the flourishing Satavahana dynasty reigned throughout the Deccan Plateau. It evolved from the Andhra people whose presence in southern India may date back as far as 1000 BC.

In the 3rd century BC the Emperor Ashoka, a recent convert to Buddhism, sent missionaries to the Andhras to bring to them this new philosophy. A people of many religions, the Andhras took Buddhism on board and built huge edifices in its honour. Their capital city, Amaravathi, contains the remains of their ingenious architecture and sculpture. They also hosted the huge Buddhist University where the architect of the Madhyamika school of thought, Nagarjuna, taught for over 60 years.

From the 7th to the 10th centuries the area was ruled by the Chalukyas, whose Dravidian style of architecture was prominent particularly along the coast and was to influence successive administrations. The Chalukya and Chola dynasties merged in the 11th century to be overthrown by the Kakatiyas who introduced pillared temples and pavilions into South Indian religious architecture.

Following the Kakatiya rule Vijayanagar sovereignty rose to become reputedly one of finest empires not only of the region, but of India. From the mid-14th to 16th centuries this empire fought to successfully resist the expansionist attempts of the northern Muslim rulers.

By the 16th century the Qutb Shahi dynasty, with all its Islamic splendour, was established in Hyderabad. This sovereignty was to fall in 1687 to the Mughal emperor Aurangzeb. In the 1600s and 1700s as the British and French vied for trade, the Hyderabad rulers, known as the nizams, managed to retain relative control by negotiating with the various colonial administrations. In 1947 the region became part of the new independent India.

Some 40 years earlier however, a movement to create a state for the Andhra people had begun. It was argued that the culture and Telugu language of the Andhras were unique and that a state encompassing the

Andhra Pradesh Holidays & Festivals

There are many important events celebrated in Andhra Pradesh. Those listed here are either unique or have a particular significance for Hyderabad or the state. Many of the festivals have variable dates being linked to planetary positions and influences. For more details inquire at your hotel, tourist office or obtain a copy of the Tourist Guides *Channel 6* or *Prime Time Prism*.

Date	Event	Place
January	Samkranti Harvest Festival	Statewide
Jan/Feb	Hyderabad Industrial Exhibition	Exhibition Centre, Mozamjahi Rd
February	Sivaratri honours the deity Shiva	Statewide at Shiva temples
March	Ugadi – Telugu New Year	Statewide
	Id-ul-Zuhara – celebrates Abraham's faith	Muslim communities
June/July	Mrigasira – marks beginning of rainy season	Hyderabad
	Mahankali Jatra – celebrates the goddess Kali	Statewide at Kali temples; focused on Secunderabad Mahankali Temple
1 November	Andhra Pradesh Formation Day	Statewide
Last week in November	Pandit Motiram-Maniram Sangeet Samaroh – four day festival of Hindustani music	Hyderabad

ANDHRA PRADESH

Telugu-speaking people should be instituted. Opposition to states divided along linguistic lines was strong but conversely served to intensify desire for the new state.

In 1952, supporters of a Telugu state held a hunger strike in which a cherished activist, Sri Potti Sri Ramulu, fasted to his death.

The Andhra state was instituted in 1953 from the Telugu areas of former Madras. In 1956 this process was furthered and the current Andhra Pradesh was created by combining Andhra state with parts of the Telugu-speaking areas of the former nizam's territory. Thus Andhra Pradesh became the fifth largest of the Indian states.

In 1991 Andhra Pradesh's former chief minister, Narasimha Rao became the first prime minister from the southern Indian states.

Security

Hyderabad is a city of many cultures. Most of the time the cultures live together in harmony and goodwill. Occasionally, however there are moments of tension and sometimes violence.

North of Hyderabad, and in the districts of Anantapur, Kurnool and Cuddapah, family feuds over land have resulted in violence and death. Such incidents are usually targeted and contained within the disputing parties. If you intend to travel in these areas inquire locally about the current situation. Keeping informed of prevailing circumstances can assist and safeguard your security.

HYDERABAD & SECUNDERABAD
Pop: 4.3 million   Tel Area Code: 040

Situated far into the central west of Andhra Pradesh, the capital, Hyderabad, is the sixth-largest city in India. With Secunderabad to the north, it forms a twin city, combining Hindu and Islamic cultures.

Hyderabad is a city of alluring contradictions. It is a busy, noisy place, where narrow, ancient lanes meet large vehicle-choked roads. Centuries-old Islamic monuments stand alongside modern office blocks and shopping centres. In the bustling markets skilled jewellers string pearls and fashion diamonds.

Hyderabad has played host to the world's reputedly richest royals – the Nizams of Hyderabad, yet many of its inhabitants are very poor. As the main city in a state proud of its Telugu-speaking heritage, Hyderabad is unique among southern cities in that Urdu is the major spoken language. As capital to a 95% Hindu state, its population is almost 50% Muslim. And as capital of a state still advocating prohibition, it has its own small wine industry.

History

Towards the end of the 16th century the royal residence of the Qutb Shahi dynasty at Golconda was facing a water shortage. As a result the shah, Muhammad Quli, moved his headquarters 11km away to the banks of the Musi River, where he established the new city of Hyderabad in 1590. He named the city after his wife and queen, Hyder Mahal. Although well positioned to withstand military attack, Hyderabad was overrun in 1687 by the Mughal Emperor Aurangzeb. Subsequently the rulers of Hyderabad were viceroys, installed by the Mughal administration in Delhi.

After Aurangzeb's death, Mughal power waned. In 1724 the Hyderabad viceroy, Asaf Jah, took advantage of the situation declaring Hyderabad an independent state with himself as its head. He was also known as Nizam-ul-Mulk or 'regulator of the land'. So began the dynasty of the nizams of Hyderabad, under which the traditions and customs of Islam flourished. Given the disintegration of the Mughal supremacy, the Hyderabad sovereignty attained particular significance. It became the centre of Muslim India. People from all over the world, but particularly from the Muslim world, came to observe and participate. Hyderabad developed into a locus for arts, culture and learning. Its abundance of rare gems and minerals furnished the nizams with enormous wealth, and stories abound of their extravagances and eccentricities.

The Nizam dynasty survived numerous internal and external threats to its existence, but a struggle for the throne in the 1750s led to the murders of several heirs. Stability was restored in 1763, but was jeopardised again by wars with the Marathas. Further difficulties occurred as the French and British competed to win the support of successive nizams. Whilst most of the nizams cultivated diplomatic policies to ensure their own continued sovereignty as well as good rela-

tionships with the later colonists, their power still weakened considerably.

In the early 1800s the British established a military barracks just north of Hyderabad at Secunderabad, named after the Nizam, Sikander Jah.

In 1908 severe flooding destroyed several parts of Hyderabad. This resulted in a rebuilding program which included a library, hospital, town hall and university. With Independence in 1947, most of the states opted to be part of the Indian Union. The then Nizam of Hyderabad, Osman Ali Khan, resisted. As

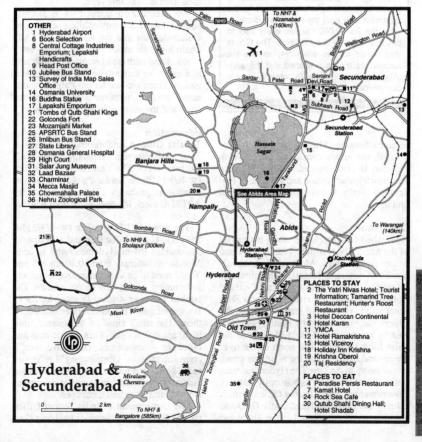

OTHER
1 Hyderabad Airport
6 Book Selection
8 Central Cottage Industries Emporium; Lepakshi Handicrafts
9 Head Post Office
10 Jubilee Bus Stand
13 Survey of India Map Sales Office
14 Osmania University
16 Buddha Statue
17 Lepakshi Emporium
21 Tombs of Qutb Shahi Kings
22 Golconda Fort
23 Mozamjahi Market
25 APSRTC Bus Stand
26 Imlibun Bus Stand
27 State Library
28 Osmania General Hospital
29 High Court
31 Salar Jung Museum
32 Laad Bazaar
33 Charminar
34 Mecca Masjid
35 Chowmahalla Palace
36 Nehru Zoological Park

PLACES TO STAY
2 The Yatri Nivas Hotel; Tourist Information; Tamarind Tree Restaurant; Hunter's Roost Restaurant
3 Hotel Deccan Continental
5 Hotel Karan
11 YMCA
12 Hotel Ramakrishna
15 Hotel Viceroy
18 Holiday Inn Krishna
19 Krishna Oberoi
20 Taj Residency

PLACES TO EAT
4 Paradise Persis Restaurant
7 Kamat Hotel
24 Rock Sea Cafe
30 Qutub Shahi Dining Hall; Hotel Shadab

Hyderabad & Secunderabad

0   1   2 km

To NH7 & Bangalore (585km)

ANDHRA PRADESH

Life Wasn't Meant to be Wheezy

Each June, at the festival of Mrigasira, on a date chosen by astrologers, asthma sufferers from all over India converge on a house in Hyderabad. They come to receive free and unconventional treatment.

The cure, taken by some 500,000 people in 1997, is a 5cm-long fish, known locally as murrel, which is stuffed with a secret herbal mixture developed by the Goud family – then swallowed live.

The family says that a Himalayan saint gave their ancestor the secret formula 152 years ago in gratitude for the hospitality shown to him. They refuse payment for the treatment and pool their own resources to raise the Rs 40,000 needed every year to buy the herbs for the medicine. The Gouds also refuse to give absolutely anyone the formula, as the saint warned that the wriggling remedy would lose its potency if it were commercialised.

---

tensions between Muslims and Hindus increased, the nizam considered joining with Pakistan. But riots ensued, resulting in police and military intervention and the state of Hyderabad finally became part of the Indian union.

Orientation

Hyderabad has developed along both sides of the Musi River, which is easily traversed by its four bridges. Most of Hyderabad's places of interest, historical monuments, museums, hotels and restaurants extend from both sides of the river for two to 3km. South of the river is the main landmark, the Charminar, surrounded by bustling bazaars. Nearby are the huge Mecca Masjid and the Salar Jung Museum. Just north of the river are several bazaars, and the main bus stand, one of many in the city. The Hyderabad train station (known locally as Nampally station), Government of India Tourist Office, British Library, the Lepakshi Handicrafts, GPO and public gardens are located in the Abids and

Nampally areas. There is also ample budget accommodation here.

Further north again and beyond Hussain Sagar, the city's main water supply, lies Secunderabad. The head post office and Andhra Pradesh Travel & Tourist Development Corporation (APTTDC) tourist office are located here. Many trains terminate at Secunderabad train station, though quite a few continue on to Hyderabad train station. Eight kilometres north of the city is the Hyderabad airport.

Four kilometres to the north-west of the main city, the scenic Banjara Hills provide sanctuary for the wealthy. Luxury accommodation is available here.

The Nehru Zoological Park is slightly south-west of the city while the ruins of Golconda Fort and the tombs of the Qutb Shahi kings lie about 11km directly west.

Road and address systems are intriguing and make for some quite challenging navigation. There are two Sardar Patel Rds; one runs from the Charminar to the south of the river and the other is in Secunderabad.

Information

Tourist Offices Andhra Pradesh Travel & Tourist Development Corporation (APTTDC) has two offices. The Yatri Nivas Hotel office (☎ 460 1519) on Sardar Patel Rd in Secunderabad is primarily a booking office for APTTDC tours. It's open daily from 6.30 am to 7 pm.

The other APTTDC office (☎ 473 2554/555) is at Gagan Vihar (5th and 11th floors), Mozamjahi Rd in Hyderabad and is open Monday to Saturday from 10.30 am to 5 pm. You'll need to be very persuasive to get any information, and it may be out of date. The booklet *Discover Andhra Pradesh* for Rs 15 is a useful guide if you can prize one out of them. The small kiosk on the ground floor (6.30 am to 7 pm daily) has a basic map and brochure – sometimes. Otherwise they'll refer you upstairs. Upstairs they'll refer you to the kiosk! The tourist information kiosks at Secunderabad train station and at the airport are similar, if you find them open.

The Government of India Tourist Office (☎ 763 0037) in the Sandozi Building (2nd

Wet & Dry in Andhra Pradesh

In December 1994, just minutes after a new state government was sworn in, Andhra Pradesh became a 'dry' state. The decision to ban the sale of alcohol follows a remarkable campaign by village women who were fed up with husbands drinking away the housekeeping money. Such was the strength of their movement that the local Telugu Desam party won a resounding victory in the state election by promising to introduce prohibition.

But prohibition didn't prove the panacea its proponents might have hoped. The distilling of bootleg liquor became a major cottage industry in the villages of Andhra Pradesh, and fortunes were made in the smuggling of alcohol from neighbouring 'wet' states, leading to widespread corruption of police and officials.

In May 1997 the state government relented and legalised the sale of Indian-made foreign liquor (IMFL) throughout Andhra Pradesh (incidentally generating crores of rupees for the state coffers from licensing fees).

Despite this relaxation of prohibition, the situation in Andhra Pradesh remains 'fluid'. Alcohol is banned on Tuesday, public holidays and the first day of the month. Few places serve booze and you should check with a tourist office before you carry it into the state.

floor) on Himayatnagar Rd has the usual range of brochures. It's open weekdays from 6 am to 7 pm.

The useful monthly 'what's on' guides, *Channel 6* and *Prime Time Prism* for Rs 10 each, can usually be tracked down at bookstores or the major hotels. The *Hyderabad Guide*, published by Disha Books for Rs 65 is available at most bookshops. Long-term visitors may find the *Guide to Hyderabad and Secunderabad* (Rs 100) from ICRISAT (International Crops Research Institute for the Semi-Arid Tropics) a useful reference.

Guide maps are available from the Survey of India (☎ 701 8943) at Vigyan Chowk Nagarik, Vinaya Kendra, Tarnaka. For information on archaeological sites, visit the Archaeological Survey of India (☎ 465 1012) 1-9-1113/30/1/C, Dayanandnagar, Vidyanagar.

Money The most efficient foreign exchange office is Thomas Cook (☎ 231988) in the Nasir Arcade on the first floor, AG's Office Rd. They charge an encashment fee of Rs 20 on travellers cheques other than Thomas Cook, and are open Monday to Saturday from 9.30 am to 6 pm.

There are a number of banks in the Abids

Circle area including the State Bank of India. It is down a very narrow passageway off Bank St. Just follow the 'do not spit' signs. Like most banks it's open weekdays from 10.30 am to 2.30 pm and until 12.30 pm on Saturday.

Post & Communications Post offices are open from 9.30 am to 5.30 pm Monday to Saturday. The GPO is on Abids Circle, Hyderabad, and is open for general business from 9.30 am to 8 pm every day and for poste restante collection on weekdays from 10 am to 3 pm (Saturday until 1 pm). In Secunderabad the post office (HPO) is in Rashtrapati Rd near the corner of Sardar Patel Rd. It has the same hours as the GPO.

There are plenty of direct-dial, fax and email kiosks around town, particularly in the Nampally and Abids districts. Many hotels also have direct dial STD/ISD and fax.

Travel Agencies Travel agents proliferate. It's a good idea to shop around before making any commitments. You'll find prices and service vary markedly. Sita World Travel (☎ 233638; fax 234223) is at 3-5-874 Hyderguda. Deccan Travels (☎ 770 3200; mob 9848 045170) is at the Hotel

ANDHRA PRADESH

Basera, 9-1-167/188 Sarojini Devi Rd, Secunderabad. Hussain Travels, (☎ 849045) 103 Parklane near the Nanking Restaurant in Secunderabad, offers a similar service.

Bookshops & Cultural Centres A good bookshop in Abids is AA Hussain & Co on MG Rd (also known as Abids Rd). Book Point is at 3-6 272 Himayatnagar Rd and Book Selection is in Sarojini Devi Rd in Secunderabad, about 150m east of MG Rd.

Alliance Française (☎ 236646; fax 231684) is right next to the Birla Planetarium. It screens weekly movies in French and organises cultural events. A German equivalent, the Max Mueller Bhavan (☎ 591410), is at Eden Bagh, Ramkote.

The British Library, Secretariat Rd (☎ 23-0774) is open from 10 am to 6 pm (closed Sunday and Monday); members and British citizens admitted. The State Library at Afzalganj (☎ 500107) has a collection of more than three million books and is open daily from 8 am to 8 pm, except Friday and public holidays.

Charminar

The principal landmark in Hyderabad, the Charminar (four towers) was built by Muhammad Quli Qutb Shah in 1591, reputedly to commemorate the end of a devastating epidemic in Hyderabad. This four-columned structure stands 56m high and 30m wide and creates four arches facing each of the cardinal points. Each column has a minaret on top. The intricately decorated sides clutch elegant balconies, and Arabic inscriptions surrounded by sculpted roses proclaim the name of God.

The small mosque with 45 prayer spaces on the 2nd floor is the oldest in Hyderabad. Spiral staircases lead up the columns to views of the city at the top, but they're currently closed for 'chemical renovations' to repair damage done by pollution. Nestled at the south-east corner of the Charminar is a small Hindu shrine honouring the goddess Lakshmi.

It's fitting that the Charminar, built to commemorate the end of widespread illness,

now stands sentry to the Nizam's General Hospital, a former palace of the nizams.

On roads leading to the Charminar four large archways constructed in 1594 acted as royal gateways to the palaces and to the city centre. You'll see them as you walk north away from the Charminar.

The lower area of the Charminar is open daily from 9 am to 4.30 pm. Each evening it is illuminated from 7 to 9 pm. Resist the services of the 'archaeological guide'. He'll charge a fortune to tell you less than any guidebook.

Bazaars

The narrow streets surrounding the Charminar make up some of India's most exotic bazaars. Just north of the Charminar in Sardar Patel Rd is the centre of India's pearl trade, and you'll also find perfumeries, silk merchants, exquisite saris and maybe even antique books.

Leading west from the Charminar, **Laad Bazaar** is renowned for its *bidriware*, an ancient artform in which fine strands of zinc and copper alloy are set into etched surfaces of plates, vases and other objects. Some 600 years ago the Persians brought the art to the town of Bidar in Karnataka – hence its name. You'll also see Hyderabad's famous *lac* bangles, but you can buy almost anything here. It's a busy, bustling market, yet it has a relaxed air about it. (See the 'Laad Bazaar' colour section).

Chowmahalla Palace

The Laad Bazaar lane leads towards the Chowmahalla Palace. Although visitors are not permitted entry, you can still get a good idea of the architecture from the outside. This palace was begun in 1751 by the then nizam and underwent several subsequent additions. The nizams used the palace's main hall to hold court.

Mecca Masjid

Adjacent to the Charminar is the Mecca Masjid, one of the largest mosques in the world – accommodating up to 10,000 worshippers. Construction began in 1614, during

Laad Bazaar

The entry sign to Laad Bazaar (in Hyderabad's old town, west of the Charminar) instructs patrons 'No entry to autos from 10 am to 9 pm'. No one takes any notice. They jostle in regardless. Carts of colourful *lac* bangles line the street. Bright brocades hang outside shops, silver and gold sequins glitter in the sun. In small boutiques, druggists sit and face their huge old scales, large bottles of medications arranged carefully behind them. In glass cases, incense sticks are stacked up beside ointments for piles. For Rs 1000, a man can hire a Maruti for his wedding and for a further Rs 250 he can purchase a *shamla* (decorative hat with veil at back). Bookstalls sell exam papers for the higher degree.

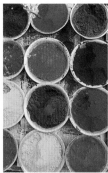

At intervals along the tiny street, men wash and carefully arrange betel leaf, the lime-green colour contrasting markedly with the dust and dung of the street. Dye merchants create mountains with their coloured powders while nearby tiny boys stand proudly by their trolleyloads of plastic kitsch. Noodles, nuts and beans are piled up alongside brass foundries and locksmiths.

Traders are interspersed with craftspeople. The lacquer workers from the town of Nirmal add bright colours with gold trimming to their handcrafted pieces of furniture. The rhythms of the silversmiths can be heard as they beat leather pouches containing silver destined to become silver leaf, a decorative (and edible) addition to sweets and meals. Next door, drum makers carefully trim the leather that will accept the beat and create the percussive resonance. As they test their creations, they synchronise their rhythm to those of the silversmiths. Together they set a calm, continual vibration to which the entire market pulsates.

High above the street large poster ads for soap portray blonde women, their hair flowing freeing around them. They smile down on the women in the street who peer back through the slits in their black veils.

Camels drift slowly across the scene, appearing as if they had always been there; disappearing as if they had never been.

Laad Bazaar has existed for centuries. Except for a few concessions to modern times, it continues as it always has.

Bazaar scenes: little mountains of coloured tika *powders (above) and crowded thoroughfares (left), where ancient traditions collide with contemporary vitality.*

Village of the Dolls

Kandapalle dolls demand dexterity and an eye for detail.

Brightly coloured wooden elephants complete with their *mahouts* and elaborate *howda*, birds of every conceivable shape and size, dancers in classical repose and elaborate images of folk heroes and gods – these are the wooden dolls of Kondapalle.

The road through the village is dotted with hawkers and their colourful dolls. If you follow the gentle but persistent tapping of the carpenter's chisel you'll venture off the road along the earthern walkways, around a few boulders and past the inevitable chickens, bullocks and goats to the swept forecourts of the village houses. This is where the dolls are born. No one seems quite sure of when the practice started but everyone agrees that it goes back more than 100 years.

Outside each home are dozens of dolls in various stages of production. The men carve the local timber known as *ponki* while the women and children design and paint. Each stage demands great dexterity and an eye for detail. The doll makers welcome visitors and proudly demonstrate their craft.

Today 50 Kondapalle households are engaged in the craft. As well as dolls and toys they make bowls, kitchenware and educational toys to be assembled by kindergarten children. The products are exported all over the world. With government support for training and marketing, the doll makers of Kondapalle have achieved a significant level of self sufficiency.

PETER DAVIS

EDDIE GERALD

the reign of Muhammad Quli Qutb Shah, but wasn't finished until 1687, by which time the Mughal Emperor Aurangzeb had annexed the Golconda kingdom. The minarets were originally intended to be much higher but, as he did with the Bibi-qa-Maqbara in Aurangabad, Aurangzeb sacrificed aesthetics to economics. The high wall on the western side provides the mihrab, the indicator for the direction of Mecca. The other sides comprise 15 arches supported by large columns. Several bricks embedded above the gate are said to be made with soil from Mecca – hence the name. The colonnades and door arches, with their inscriptions from the Qu'ran are made from single slabs of granite. These massive stone blocks were quarried 11km away and dragged to the site by a team of 1400 bullocks.

Unfortunately, the mosque has been disfigured by huge wire mesh awnings, erected in a vain attempt to stop birds nesting in the ceiling and liming the floor. The steel supports that have been carelessly cemented into the tiled and patterned floor to hold this netting are nothing short of vandalism.

To the left of the mosque is an enclosure containing the tombs of Nizam Ali Khan, who died in 1803, and his successors.

Salar Jung Museum

Nearer the river from the Mecca Masjid is the Salar Jung Museum. Its huge collection, dating back to the 1st century, was put together by Mir Yusaf Ali Khan (Salar Jung III), the prime minister, or grand-vizier, of the seventh nizam, Osman Ali Khan. It contains 35,000 exhibits from all corners of the world and includes sculptures, woodcarvings, religious objects, Persian miniature paintings, illuminated manuscripts, armour and weaponry, and over 50,000 books. In the Jade Room you'll see the swords, daggers and clothing of the Mughal emperors and of Tipu Sultan. A children's section contains toys, puppets and model trains. All this is housed in 36 rooms of one of the ugliest buildings imaginable.

The museum is open daily except Friday from 10 am to 5 pm but avoid Sunday when

it's bedlam. Entry is Rs 5. From Abids, bus No 7 will drop you at the Musi River Bridge; just cross the river and take the first turn left.

Not far west of the Musi River Bridge, facing each other across the river, are the spectacular **High Court** and **Osmania General Hospital** buildings, built in the florid Indo-Saracenic style.

Birla Mandir Temple

This stunning Hindu temple was built of white Rajasthani marble in 1976 and graces one of the twin rocky hills, Kalabahad, (black mountain) overlooking the south end of Hussain Sagar. Dedicated to Lord Venkateshwara, the temple is a popular Hindu pilgrimage centre. Finely carved sculptures depict scenes from the *Mahabharata* and *Ramayana*. Statues of Hindu gods and goddesses line the path to the temple. There are excellent views over the city from the temple, especially at sunset. It's open to Hindus and non-Hindus alike, from 7 am to noon and 3 to 9 pm.

Planetarium & Science Museum

On Naubat Pahar (drum rock), the hill adjacent to the Birla Mandir Temple, are the Birla Planetarium & the Science Museum (☎ 235081). The planetarium has presentations in English (at 11 am, 4 pm and 6 pm daily; 3.45 pm on public holidays), Telugu (at 12.15, 3, 5 and 6.45 pm; 4.30 pm on public holidays) and Hindi (7.30 pm. and 2.15 pm on public holidays). It's closed on the last Thursday of each month; admission is Rs 10. The museum is open from 10.30 am to 8.15 pm daily (closed on the last Tuesday of each month); admission is Rs 6.

Buddha Statue & Hussain Sagar

Andhra Pradesh played an important role in the history of Buddhism and Hyderabad boasts one of the largest stone Buddhas in the world. The brainchild of Telugu Desam's president, NT Rama Rao, work on the project began in 1985 at Raigir, some 50km from Hyderabad, and was completed in early 1990. The 17.5m high, 350 tonne monolith was transported to Hyderabad and

ANDHRA PRADESH

loaded onto a barge for ferrying across Hussain Sagar to be erected on the dam wall.

Unfortunately, disaster struck and the statue sank into the lake taking with it eight people. There it languished for two years while ways of raising it were discussed. Finally, in mid-1992, a Goan salvage company raised it once more (undamaged!) and it was erected on a plinth in the middle of the lake.

Frequent boats make a 30 minute round trip to the statue from **Lumbini Park**, just north of Secretariat Rd, between 9 am and 6 pm for Rs 10 per head. You'll also need to pay the Rs 2 entrance fee for the park, which is a pleasant spot to enjoy Hyderabad's blood-red sunsets (open from Tuesday to Sunday from 9 am to 9 pm).

The **Tankbund** skirts the eastern shore of Hussain Sagar. It has great views of the Buddha statue and is a popular promenade and jogging track. An evening stroll along Tankbund is a most pleasant way to while away time and to encounter Hyderabadis in their more relaxed state. Flanking the entire 1.5km stretch are 35 statues of people who have played a significant role in the history of Andhra Pradesh. Most statues are of freedom fighters or political leaders. In the early evenings, the walkway is crowded with ice cream vendors, fortune tellers, and lovers seeking respite from the heat of the day.

Archaeological Museum
The Archaeological Museum is in the public gardens to the north of Hyderabad train station. The museum contains a small collection of archaeological finds from the area, together with copies of paintings from the Ajanta Caves in Maharashtra.

The museum's opening hours are 10.30 am to 5 pm daily, except Friday, and entry is Rs 0.50.

Also worth a quick visit is the nearby **Health Museum**, which is open from 10.30 am to 1.30 pm and 2 to 5 pm; admission is free.

The gardens feature an **aquarium** in the Jawahar Bal Bhavan. It's open daily from 10.30 am to 5 pm except Sunday.

Osmania University
This university, an important centre for Persian, Urdu and Arabic studies, is situated to the east of the city in University Rd within well-landscaped botanical gardens. It is noted for its architecture, a combination of Indian and European design. The domed ceiling of the Arts College is particularly impressive.

Nehru Zoological Park
One of the largest zoos in India, the Nehru Zoological Park is spread over 1.2 sq km of landscaped gardens with animals living in large, open enclosures. The 3000 animals and birds here don't look any less bored than animals in zoos anywhere else in the world, but at least an effort has been made, which is more than can be said for most Indian zoos. There's a prehistoric animal section, a toy train around the zoo (every 15 minutes, Rs 1) a lion safari trip (every 15 minutes, Rs 5) and a nocturnal section.

The park is across the Musi River, south of the city, and is open daily except Monday from 9 am to 5 pm; entry costs Rs 1, or Rs 20 if you're in a private car. Once again, it's chaos on Sundays.

Tombs of Qutb Shahi Kings
These graceful domed tombs are about 1.5km north-west of Golconda Fort's Balahisar Gate. They are surrounded by landscaped gardens, and a number of them have beautifully carved stonework. The tombs are open daily except Friday from 9.30 am to 4.30 pm and entrance costs Rs 2, plus Rs 5 if you have a camera (Rs 25 for a video camera). Most people walk from Golconda to the tombs, but there are usually a few auto-rickshaws willing to take you for a handsome price.

Golconda Fort
This 16th-century fortress is regarded as a must-see. Like many of the great forts in India, Golconda exudes a palpable sense of history. Once you have spent some time exploring the massive structure, it's easier to appreciate the history of Hyderabad and its environs (see the boxed text, pages 356-7).

Knowledgeable guides congregate at the entrance to the fort. They're geared towards groups and they'll ask Rs 250 for a 90 minute tour and rapidly lose interest in any offer below Rs 150. If you don't want a guide, dismiss them firmly before you enter the main gate. Alternatively, the *Guide to Golconda Fort & Qutb Shahi Tombs* may be on sale. For Rs 10 it's a good investment.

The fort is open from 8 am to 6.30 pm daily, and entrance costs Rs 2 (free on Friday). To get to the fort's main entrance, Balahisar Gate, take city bus No 119 or 142 from Nampally High Rd (Public Gardens Rd), outside the public gardens. The 11km trip takes an hour and costs about Rs 2. An auto-rickshaw from Abids costs around Rs 120 to Rs 150 return, including waiting charges. Early morning is a better time if you want relative peace and quiet. Tour groups begin arriving around 11am.

See the following Organised Tours section for details of the hour-long sound & light show.

Organised Tours

The APTTDC (☎ 473 2554/555, bookings 460 1519/20) conducts daily tours of the city which pick up at 7.45 am from Yatri Nivas Hotel, 7.55 am from Secunderabad train station and 8.30 am from Gagan Vihar on Mozamjahi Rd, and finish at 5.15 pm at the Birla Mandir. The cost is Rs 85 (children over four, Rs 60) plus entry charges and includes a vegetarian lunch. The tours visit Buddha Purnima, Qutb Shahi Tombs, Golconda Fort, Salar Jung Museum, Mecca Masjid, Charminar, Nehru Zoo, the inevitable handicrafts emporium, Birla Mandir Temple and the Planetarium. Brief stops are all you'll get, but if you only have a day in town the tour is good value. Check when you book. Some tours do not include all sites.

A tour to Nagarjuna Sagar leaves daily at 6.30 am and returns at 9.30 pm (adult/child Rs 190/140). The round trip is 360km and stops at the dam, museum (except Friday when it's closed) Ethipothala Falls, and includes lunch. Since public transport to these sites is limited, this tour is a good option.

If you wish to arrange your own tour with a guide, the APTTDC office (☎ 473 2554/555) at Gagan Vihar, as well as the numerous Travel Agents, can organise this for you. At the various sites you will often meet helpful guides who for a negotiated fee will escort and inform you.

APTTDC also conduct weekend tours to Tirupathi (adult/child Rs 600/500), Srisailam (adult/child Rs 310/260). Fare includes travel and accommodation.

An interesting alternative is the *Deccan by Dusk* tour, also operated by the APTTDC, which visits Lumbini Park and the Qutb Shahi tombs before going on to Golconda Fort for a quick tour and the sound & light show. This tour departs Yatri Nivas Hotel at 2 pm, returns at 8.45 pm and costs Rs 60 (including ticket for sound & light show). If you make your own way to the fort you can see the sound & light show for Rs 20. It starts at 6.30 pm (November to February) and 7 pm (March to October). Sessions are in Telugu on Thursday, Hindi on Tuesday and Friday, and English on Wednesday, Saturday and Sunday. It doesn't operate on Monday.

Places to Stay – Budget

The best of the cheap hotels are all in the Nampally/Abids area between Abids Circle and Hyderabad (Nampally) train station.

Royal Lodge, *Royal Home*, *Royal Hotel*, *Neo Royal Hotel* and *Gee Royal Lodge* are built around a courtyard opposite the station on Nampally High Rd (Public Gardens Rd). They're all very similar – count on Rs 90/170 for singles/doubles with attached not very clean bathroom. All rooms have fans. Hot water is usually only available in the mornings. The Royal Lodge claims to take only Indian residents.

New Asian Hotel (☎ 201275), across the road, is a typical, no-frills Indian boarding house, but it's adequate at Rs 40/150 for older rooms and Rs 75/250 for newer rooms which look just as old. All rooms have attached bathrooms (though many have semi-detached plumbing) and fan. Bucket hot water is generally available in the mornings.

Apsara Hotel (☎ 502663) is 10 minutes

ANDHRA PRADESH

Golconda Fort

There's an echo at Golconda that shatters the silence of the granite hill. It ricochets off the massive walls which sheltered some armies and helped to destroy others. It traverses the space that concealed dazzling jewels and spawned fabulous wealth. This is the place that inspired tales from the Arabian Nights. Golconda was much more than just a fortress. It was, for a short time, the epicentre of an empire.

Today much of the fort is in ruins, the bulk of which dates from the time of the Qutb Shahi kings (16th to 17th centuries). However, the origins of the fort have been traced to the earlier Hindu periods when the Yadavas and, later, the Kakatiyas ruled this part of India.

In 1512, Sultan Quli Qutb Shah, a Turkoman adventurer from Persia and governor of Telangana under the Bahmani rulers, declared independence. Golconda became his capital. It remained that way for 78 years until 1590, when the court was moved to the new city of Hyderabad.

The fort didn't remain empty for long. In the 17th century, Mughal armies from Delhi were sent against the Golconda kingdom to enforce payment of tribute. Abul Hasan, the last of the Qutb Shahi kings, held out at Golconda for eight months against the massive army commanded by the Emperor Aurangzeb. Even under the constant barrage of Mughal artillery, the walls of the fort proved impenetrable. Aurangzeb finally succeeded via the treacherous actions of an insider named Abdullah Khan Pani. On a September night in 1687, he opened the gates to the seriously exhausted and somewhat depleted Mughals. Abul Hasan was badly wounded in the ensuing battle. His death in prison 12 years later marked the beginning of Mughal rule.

Following Aurangzeb's death early in the next century, his viceroys (later the nizams) made Hyderabad their capital and once again, Golconda was abandoned.

When standing atop the fort, it's easy to see how the Mughal army came close to total defeat. The citadel is built on a granite hill 120m high and is surrounded by crenellated ramparts constructed of large masonry blocks. The massive gates are studded with large pointed iron spikes, intended to prevent elephants from battering them down. They are further protected by a cordon wall to check direct attack. Outside the citadel stands another crenellated rampart, surrounding the base of the hill, with a perimeter of 11km. Outside this wall is a third wall, made up of boulders and incorporating natural defences in the landscape. All these walls are in an excellent state of preservation. The fort once had eight gates, but of these only four are still used – the Fateh, Mecca,

---

walk south-east of the station on Nampally Station Rd (also known as Station Rd) and has rooms for Rs 100/150 with attached bathroom (bucket shower), fan and hot water in the mornings.

Nithya Lodge (☎ 595317), upstairs in a shopping arcade on Nampally Station Rd nearer Abids Circle, is friendly and is also better value. Clean, straight rooms with bucket shower are Rs 200 inclusive of taxes; Star TV will cost you Rs 25 extra. There's no restaurant, but there are plenty of places to eat quite close to the hotel.

Hotel Sri Brindavan (☎ 320 3970) on Nampally Station Rd near the junction with Abids Circle is also good value. It offers

singles/doubles with attached bathroom for Rs 200/250. Hot water is available from 4 to 7.30 am. Rooms are arranged around a quiet courtyard. This is a popular place for the few backpackers who pass through Hyderabad. In the forecourt of the hotel is an excellent restaurant offering veg and nonveg meals.

Hotel Suhail (☎ 510142) is clean and quiet with standard rooms for Rs 110/135, deluxe rooms for Rs 135/150 and air-con doubles for Rs 250. All the rooms have TV and attached bathroom with hot water, and most have a balcony.

The *YMCA* (☎ 756 4670) accepts male and female residents and has six branches. The Secunderabad branch at the northern end

Banjara and Balahisar gates. Halfway up the fort is a small mosque; its structures softening the somewhat awesome shapes of the fort.

Many of the buildings inside the citadel – the palaces and harem of the Qutb Shahi kings, assembly halls, arsenal, stables and barracks – have suffered a great deal from past sieges and the ravages of time, but enough remains to give a good impression of what the place must once have looked like. Restoration of the buildings around the Balahisar Gate (the main entrance) has been underway for years – even the wrought iron has been replaced. At the top, near the entrance to the royal palaces, is a Hindu cave temple dedicated to the deity Mahakali.

Survival within the fort was attributable not only to the walls, but also to the highly sophisticated water supply. A complex series of concealed glazed earthen pipes would carry water to where it was needed. Some of these pipes can still be seen. Survival was also aided by the acoustics: sounds from the Grand Portico would echo across the fort complex, making anonymity was impossible. Even today, silence only comes with stillness, and it is worth standing still to consider the great tides that have moved through the fort.

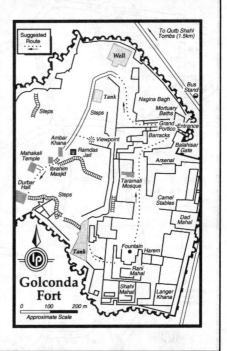

Golconda Fort

of Nampally Station Rd has singles/doubles for Rs 65/90. The branch of greater Hyderabad on Narayunguda Rd has rooms for Rs 75/100. The rooms at both these branches are without attached bathroom. They are basic but relatively clean.

Only Secunderabad train station has *Retiring Rooms*. Air-con single/double are Rs 150/220 non air-con single/double Rs 50/80. Dormitory rates are Rs 30 for 24 hours. It tends to be well patronised so it may be difficult to get a place.

Places to Stay – Mid Range
The *Yatri Nivas Hotel* (☎ 840005; fax 867448) on Sardar Patel Rd in Secunderabad

is no longer completely government run. It is now in joint management between the APTTDC and Amogh Hotels Ltd. It has recently been completely refurbished and issued a three-star rating. The rooms are large, clean and well positioned for peace and quiet. Air-con rooms are Rs 500/550, without air-con Rs 400/425. It has two restaurants, the Tamarind Tree and the Hunter's Roost. If there's a wedding in the forecourt you'll witness a spectacle rich in sound and colour. At the tourist office here they give useful verbal information.

Hotel Rajmata (☎ 320 1000) faces the 'royal' courtyard opposite the Hyderabad train station and has 'deluxe' rooms (no air-con)

ANDHRA PRADESH

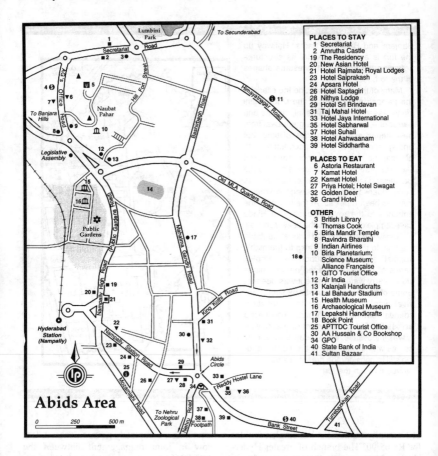

Abids Area

0   250   500 m

PLACES TO STAY
1 Secretariat
2 Amrutha Castle
19 The Residency
20 New Asian Hotel
21 Hotel Rajmata; Royal Lodges
23 Hotel Saiprakash
24 Apsara Hotel
26 Hotel Saptagiri
28 Nithya Lodge
29 Hotel Sri Brindavan
31 Taj Mahal Hotel
33 Hotel Jaya International
35 Hotel Sabharwal
37 Hotel Suhail
38 Hotel Aahwaanam
39 Hotel Siddhartha

PLACES TO EAT
6 Astoria Restaurant
7 Kamat Hotel
22 Kamat Hotel
27 Priya Hotel; Hotel Swagat
32 Golden Deer
36 Grand Hotel

OTHER
3 British Library
4 Thomas Cook
5 Birla Mandir Temple
8 Ravindra Bharathi
9 Indian Airlines
10 Birla Planetarium;
    Science Museum;
    Alliance Française
11 GITO Tourist Office
12 Air India
13 Kalanjali Handicrafts
14 Lal Bahadur Stadium
15 Health Museum
16 Archaeological Museum
17 Lepakshi Handicrafts
18 Book Point
25 APTTDC Tourist Office
30 AA Hussain & Co Bookshop
34 GPO
40 State Bank of India
41 Sultan Bazaar

with colour TV, hot water, towel and soap for Rs 290/360. There's an attached restaurant with veg and nonveg food.

Hotel Saptagiri (☎ 460 3601) on Nampally Station Rd is a relatively new place and spotlessly clean. The rooms are small but still good value at Rs 135/180, and Rs 350 for a double with air-con. All the rooms have a balcony and an attached bathroom with hot water.

Hotel Aahwaanam (☎ 590301), off Nehru Rd and right opposite the noisy Ramakrishna Cinema (through the gates with the Nandi

on top), is huge and has decent rooms for Rs 190/225 or Rs 275/320 with air-con, including tax. All the rooms have attached bathroom (bucket showers) with hot water and TV. There's an air-con refreshments kiosk opposite.

Hotel Jaya International (☎ 475 2929; fax 475 3919), in Reddy Hostel Lane off Bank St, has clean comfortable rooms for Rs 200/300 or Rs 450/550 with air-con and TV. There's no restaurant.

Hotel Sabharwal (☎ 461 0100), opposite the Hotel Jaya International, is along a short laneway. The rooms are basic and some are relatively clean. Prices are Rs 300/400 with air-con.

Hotel Siddhartha (☎ 590222; fax 461 1400), nearby on Bank St, is a quiet place with a grand foyer that totally belies the quality of the rooms. Singles/doubles cost Rs 250/300 or Rs 425/500 with air-con. There are also more expensive suites. The hotel has its own restaurant and air-con coffee shop, plus secure parking.

Taj Mahal Hotel (☎ 237988), at the junction of MG and King Kothi Rds, is a huge, rambling place set in its own grounds and is deservedly popular. Spacious rooms with attached bathroom, hot water and TV cost Rs 275/475, or Rs 400/550 with air-con. Facilities include two vegetarian restaurants, coffee shop and car parking.

Hotel Saiprakash (☎ 461 1726; fax 461 3355), on Nampally Station Rd, five minutes walk south-east of Hyderabad station, is quite comfortable but somewhat impersonal. Singles/doubles cost Rs 450/550 or Rs 550/650 with central air-con. The popular Woodland restaurant is on the ground floor.

Hotel Ramakrishna (☎ 834567, 831133; fax 846609) is five minutes walk from Secunderabad train station and directly opposite the Railway Reservation Complex. This new establishment, with 70 rooms, is already showing signs of age. Nevertheless, the rooms are clean, the water is piping hot and it's good value. Choose a room at the back, away from the noisy traffic. Non air-con single/double rooms are Rs 275/350, and air-con single/doubles are Rs 350/425. The hotel has a good veg and nonveg restaurant. Alcohol is prohibited.

Places to Stay – Top End
Hotel Viceroy (☎ 753 8383; fax 753 8797), on the Tankbund towards Secunderabad, overlooks Hussain Sagar and has comfortable and well appointed singles/doubles for Rs 1400/1700 or Rs 1600/1900 with a lake view. Suites are available from Rs 2800 to Rs 3500. All rates include a buffet breakfast. This centrally air-con hotel has the usual facilities, including a pool, Hertz car rental and

a business centre with email facility that is available to non hotel guests.

Hotel Deccan Continental (☎ 840981; fax 840980), on Sir Ronald Ross Rd in Secunderabad, is only 1km from the airport. A spotless hotel with 84 large rooms (some with splendid views) and numerous facilities including swimming pool and an hourly courtesy airport bus, this hotel is good value. Air-con rooms are Rs 750/850, non air-con Rs 400/600. Executive rooms are also available. As well as two multicuisine restaurants, the hotel has a beer garden.

Hotel Karan in SD Rd, Secunderabad has air-con single/doubles with attached bathrooms from Rs 550/700 and suites at Rs 900 to Rs 1350. They have 24 hour hot and cold water, a multicuisine restaurant (closed from 3 to 7 pm) and they accept credit cards.

Amrutha Castle (☎ 598664; fax 241850), on Secretariat Rd, must be the most bizarre hotel in India. Modelled on Mad King Ludwig's Austrian folly, Neuschwanstein (by way of Disneyland and Camelot), this theme park, complete with suits of armour, bad oil paintings and suites with names such as 'Suleiman the Magnificent' is a tribute to hyperreality. Thoroughly modern, well appointed rooms start at Rs 1000/2000, and suites range from Rs 1600 to Rs 3500. Facilities include fax in every room, restaurant, coffee shop, gym and a rooftop pool. As the glossy brochure exclaims, 'now it's a lot more than what the European Royal blue blood had exuberated!'

The Residency (☎ 204060; fax 204040), in Public Gardens Rd, is a newly built hotel deserving its claim of providing five-star comfort for three-star prices. Standard rooms are Rs 895/1150. Executive and deluxe rooms are also available. Its numerous assets include its plush (quiet) lobby and a 24 hour coffee shop.

Most of the five-star hotels are on Road No 1 at Banjara Hills, west of Hussain Sagar. They're all centrally air-conditioned and have excellent restaurants and the full complement of facilities. All attract 20% tax.

Taj Residency (☎ 399999; fax 392218) is pleasantly situated on an artificial lake. Rates from Rs 2000 to Rs 3000 in the executive rooms include breakfast.

Holiday Inn Krishna (☎ *393939; fax 392682)*, just off Road No 1, has modern, luxurious rooms from Rs 2200 to Rs 4200.

Krishna Oberoi (☎ *392323; fax 393079)* is a palatial hotel with rooms costing from Rs 2200 to Rs 8500.

Ritz Hotel (☎ *233571)*, the former palace of the nizams of Hyderabad, is now closed for renovations. It may reopen as a government guesthouse.

Places to Eat

Hyderabad is justifiably proud of its delicious Andhran cuisine but be warned, some of the vegetarian chilli dishes can be real tear-jerkers. A few savoury specialities to look out for include kulcha (charcoal-baked bread), biryani (fragrant steamed rice with meat or vegetables), haleen (pounded wheat with a lightly spiced mutton sauce) and nihari (spiced tongue and trotters). Don't miss the delicious marinated fruits, which are served cold at the end of meals to refresh the palate.

Fresh fruit is available on the many stalls that edge the streets, but try the Mozamjahi Market at the junction of Mukarramjahi and Jawaharlal Nehru Rds. Not only is it a great place for fruits and vegetables but the architecture is alluring. Nizam Shahi Rd is the spot for ginger and garlic – stacks of these line the street and pervade it with exciting, pungent smells.

Woodland restaurant, on the ground floor of Hotel Saiprakash on Nampally Station Rd, does excellent South Indian veg breakfasts, snacks and meals. There's also a more expensive (but nowhere near as good) multicuisine restaurant called *Rich and Famous*. All major credit cards are accepted.

Grand Hotel, just around from the Hyderabad GPO, is far from grand but it has cheap nonveg local food such as biryani and mutton cutlets and is immensely popular at lunchtime.

Any *Kamat Hotel* dishes up good cheap meals. The menu includes South Indian vegetarian and North Indian as well as Chinese

and 'finger chips'. Soups are Rs 17 to Rs 30, rice dishes Rs 9 to Rs 25. There's one in Secunderabad on Sarojini Devi Rd, another in Abids on AG's Office Rd opposite Indian Airlines, and a third on Nampally Station Rd.

Priya Hotel on Station Rd has basic veg meals for Rs 25 and nonveg meals from Rs 20 to Rs 45. It's a good place to eat here, in air-con comfort.

Hotel Swagat, also on Station Rd and almost next door to the Priya, has similar fare without air-con, but cheaper.

Astoria Restaurant opposite the Kamat Hotel on AG's Office Rd is a popular open-air dinner spot.

Qutub Shahi Dining Hall (downstairs) and *Hotel Shadab* (upstairs) are at High Court Rd, Madina Circle. Upstairs is slightly more expensive but good value and a pleasant environment. Meals from around Rs 36.

Rock Sea Cafe is just near Mozamjahi Market. It's good for drinks, quick snacks and sweets. Puris from Rs 5.

Golden Deer on MG Rd, not far from Abids Circle, is more expensive, but a good choice for dinner. It specialises in Chinese and Indian meals starting around Rs 40, and is blissfully air-conditioned.

Hotel Ramakrishna opposite the Railway Reservation Complex in Secunderabad is also air-conditioned and has dosas from Rs 11, curries from Rs 22 to 38 and biryanis from Rs 25.

Paradise Persis Restaurant near the corner of Sardar Patel Rd and MG Rd in Secunderabad is famous for its authentic Hyderabadi cuisine. Established in 1953, this is *the* place to eat in Secunderabad, and prices are reasonable. It's a multilayered labyrinth of eating venues (including open-air patios) adorned with flashing fairy lights. Vegetarian and nonveg fare is available. Tandooris and biryanis start at Rs 35. The food's good, especially the vegetables laced with hot chilli. At the sidewalk takeaway area you can get juicy kebabs for Rs 95, freshly baked rotis, oven-fresh biscuits and hot coffee. Don't bother with the coffee. It's not a patch on the good stuff you get almost everywhere else.

The Hunter's Roost and the *Tamarind*

Tree are relaxing and attractive outdoor venues attached to Yatri Nivas. The Hunter's Roost is multicuisine with a bar and has indoor air-con as well as outdoor dining. Both venues are friendly, well priced and quiet.

Vazik in Laad Bazaar serves drinks, chappati and other snacks – welcome fare if you're hot, dusty and desperate.

Top-end hotels all have excellent restaurants and coffee shops, in particular the *Dakhni* at the Taj Residency and the *Firdau* at the Krishna Oberoi. Expect to pay at least Rs 250 to Rs 500 per person. The Taj Residency's *Kabab-e-Bahar* is a less formal barbecue/kebab restaurant set outdoors in a small lake, with excellent veg and nonveg dishes for around Rs 100.

Entertainment

For cultural shows go to the **Ravindra Bharati Theatre** where you can enjoy nightly performances of music, drama and dance. Details are available from tourist offices and local papers.

Discos are held in the larger hotels. Try the Gateway Hotel at Banjara Hills (☎ 222222). Clubs may also have discos but usually admit members only. One exception is the Country Club, which permits admission of nonmembers to its disco, Pyramid. With the recent relaxation of liquor laws, many hotels are now providing music and dance venues.

There is a plethora of cinemas in Hyderabad. You'll have no trouble locating them. They show Tamil and Telugu films. Usually women and men are segregated. The **Hyderabad Film Club** (☎ 290265/841) runs screenings of foreign films, sometimes in conjunction with the Alliance Française.

Hyderabad is a popular venue for cultural festivals, art exhibitions, forums, workshops, book fairs and car rallies. And if you're into rocks, you may like to contact the **Save the Rocks Society** (☎ 238253). It organises regular rock walks through the surreal landscape of Andhra Pradesh. These walks aim to raise awareness of how rocks are being destroyed through intensive quarrying. The 'What's On' section of the city guide *Chan-nel 6* or the daily paper will have all the details.

Shopping

Laad Bazaar (see the 'Laad Bazaar' colour section) near Charminar is the heart of old Hyderabad, and where you'll find Hyderabadi specialities such as pearls, glass and lac bangles, *bidri* ware and enamel jewellery. An interesting market closer to Abids is Sultan Bazaar on Turrebazkhan Rd.

The best place to buy arts and crafts from all over India is Kalanjali on Nampally High Rd. This shop is well laid out, has fixed prices, accepts credit cards, and will reliably send purchases anywhere round the world. It's open daily from 10 am to 8 pm. Also good is the Central Cottage Industries Emporium at 94 Minerva Complex on Sarojini Devi Rd, Secunderabad. Lepakshi Handicrafts, with a wide variety of crafts, is also in this complex. Lepakshi Emporium is on Tankbund.

Silk and sari shops dominate a section of Nampally Station Rd. One of the biggest is Gianey's Silks and Saris, opposite Pulla Reddy Sweets. Even if you're not buying, it's worth watching the Hyderabadi women seriously engrossed in selecting some of the finest silks in the country. Another place for silk is near Charminar – Fancy Silks, 21-2-28, Pathergatti.

Getting There & Away

Hyderabad is connected by air, road and rail to most major Indian cities. It also has connections to some international cities.

Air The Air India office (☎ 237224) is opposite the Legislative Assembly. International flights leave for Kuwait (twice weekly) Muscat (three weekly) and Sharjah (three weekly). Air India also has flights to Mumbai and Chennai.

Indian Airlines (☎ 236902) is nearby and open daily from 10 am to 1 pm and 2 to 5.25 pm. There are Indian Airlines flights in either direction between Hyderabad and Bangalore (daily, US$80), Mumbai (three daily, US$90), Calcutta (daily except Sunday, US$170), Delhi (twice daily, US$165),

Chennai (three daily, US$80), Nagpur (three weekly, US$80), Vizag (three weekly, US$85) and Tirupathi (three weekly, US$65).

Jet Airways (☎ 33222) flies daily to Bangalore, Mumbai, Calcutta and Chennai.

Bus There are several bus stands in Hyderabad. The main one is the Andhra Pradesh State Road Transport Corporation (APSRTC) Hyderabad/Imlibun complex at Gowliguda. Buses leave Imlibun bus stand (☎ 513955) for all parts of the state. The buses are well organised into separate bays, and there's an inquiry counter, a timetable in Telugu and English and a computerised advance booking office which is open daily from 8 am to 9 pm. North of the city in Secunderabad, the Jubilee bus stand (☎ 780 2203) operates a similar service with buses to destinations in the north and west.

There are also a number of private bus companies offering superdeluxe video services to Bangalore, Mumbai, Chennai, Nagpur and Tirupathi. Most of their offices are on Nampally High Rd close to the Hyderabad train station entrance road. Most have one departure daily, usually in the late afternoon. To Bangalore or Nagpur it's Rs 220 and 12 hours; to Mumbai or Chennai it's Rs 250 and 14 hours.

Train Secunderabad is the main train station and this is where you catch through trains (that is, all trains not originating in Hyderabad). However, trains starting at Hyderabad can be boarded here too. Bookings for any train can be made either at Hyderabad station or Secunderabad station Monday to Saturday from 8 am to 2 pm and 2.15 to 8 pm, and on Sunday from 8 am to 4 pm. Both stations have a tourist quota. For general inquiries phone 131; for reservations, cancellations and availability phone 135.

Trains leave for every part of the country. To Calcutta, you must first take a train to Vijayawada and then change to one of the east coast express trains such as the *Coromandel Express*. The fare to Calcutta is Rs 292/1169 in 2nd/1st class and the 1600km trip takes 32 hours. A good buy is the *South Central Railway Time Table* (Rs 15 from station inquiry counters). Apart from all the regular train times and fares, the book recommends no less than 35 circular tours (departing from and returning to Hyderabad or Secunderabad). These tours attract a range of discounted prices and cover distances from 2000km to nearly 9000km. It is possible to break each tour for a number of days but be sure to check the nature of your ticket first.

Getting Around

Hyderabad can be a confusing city to negotiate. Streets are often not marked. Large signs are often misleading, being simply advertisements rather than indicators for streets and/or buildings. The system of multi-numbered addresses adds to the confusion and often places are not on major streets but set back from them in small alleyways or hidden within 'complexes'. Languages other than Telugu, Hindi and Urdu are rarely spoken or understood. And all maps have their inaccuracies. However all this is more than compensated by the cooperation of local people. State clearly where you want to go. You may not be immediately understood but someone will quickly find help. People on the street and auto-rickshaw drivers will persist until they understand what you want. As always, take your time, enjoy the local humour and all will be well.

To/From the Airport The airport is at

Bus Services from Hyderabad

Destination	Frequency (Daily Departures)	Fare (Rs)
Aurangabad	2	135
Bangalore	9 (mainly evening)	195
Bidar	19	35
Mumbai	10	285
Gulbarga	7	95
Hospet	2	105
Kurnool	20	85
Chennai	1 (4.30 pm)	225
Nagpur	2	165
Nizamabad	32	50
Tirupathi	11	175
Vijayawada	30	95

Train Services from Hyderabad

Destination	Train Number & Name	Departure Time	Distance (km)	Duration (hours)	Fare (Rs) (2nd/1st)
Aurangabad	7664 *S-A Exp*	7.30 pm S	517	13.30	146/526
Bangalore	5092 *G/S-Bangalore Exp*	6.20 pm S	790	15.50	199/736
Mumbai	7032 *Hyderabad-Mumbai Exp*	8.20 pm H	800	17.15	199/736
Calcutta	8046 *East Coast Exp*	7.30 am S	1591	30.00	292/1169
Chennai	7054 *Hyderabad-Madras Exp*	3.45 pm H	794	14.25	199/736
Delhi	2723 *Andhra Pradesh Exp*	7.10 am H	1397	26.20	277/1062
	7021 *H Nizamuddin Exp*	8.00 pm H		33.30	
Tirupathi	7603 *Venkatadri Link Exp*	3.50 pm S	741	17.40	191/696

Abbreviations for train stations: S – Secunderabad, H – Hyderabad
Abbreviations for trains: S-A Exp: *Secunderabad-Aurangabad Express*; G/S-Bangalore Exp: *Gorakhpur/Secunderabad-Bangalore Express*
Fares are for sleeper class

Begampet, about 8km north of Abids. There is no airport bus. An auto-rickshaw from Abids should cost about Rs 35 by the meter, though drivers usually refuse to use it for this ride so you'll have to haggle. Taxi drivers ask about Rs 100.

Bus Getting on any city bus in Hyderabad, other than at the terminus, is (as one traveller put it) 'like staging a banzai charge on Guadalcanal'. He wasn't exaggerating. Buses you might find useful include:

No 2 – Secunderabad station to Charminar
No 7 – Secunderabad station to Afzalganj and return (this is the one to catch if you're heading for Abids, as it goes down Tankbund and Nehru Rd via the GPO)
No 8 and 8A – connect Secunderabad and Hyderabad train stations
No 119 and 142 – Nampally High Rd to Golconda Fort

There are several city bus stands with the main one, the Hyderabad station, being located adjacent to the Imlibun (state service) in Gowliguda. On most routes, the first 10 seats are reserved for women and some services are for women only.

You can also buy a 'Travel As You Like' ticket at any of the major bus stands or Secunderabad train station. This permits unlimited bus travel anywhere within the city area for the day of purchase.

Auto-Rickshaw & Taxi By the meter, auto-rickshaws cost Rs 6 for the first 2km plus Rs 3 for each additional kilometre. There is a minimum fee of Rs 5.6. Most drivers need prompting to use the meter, and some may refuse, preferring a higher negotiated price. Try to go by meter. You'll usually find it's cheaper, but not always – old meters require extra payment. Between 10 pm and 5 am you may have to pay a 50% surcharge. A return trip to Golconda Fort by auto is around Rs 120 to Rs 150, including waiting time.

Taxis cost about twice as much as autos.

Car You can rent a car and driver from the APTTDC for Rs 450 for an eight-hour day within the city area. Outside the city, rates vary from Rs 3.5 to Rs 4 per kilometre, depending on the company. You can arrange car travel at many hotels. Hertz cars can be rented from Hotel Viceroy (☎ 618383) and Alpha Motors (☎ 201306), 17 Abids Shopping Centre. For long-distance travel in particular, shop around. Services and rates vary.

AROUND HYDERABAD
There are many places around Hyderabad which may be visited in a day trip or on the way to other sites.

Medak
Medak, 100km north of Hyderabad, was

ANDHRA PRADESH

originally an important Buddhist site. Later dynasties included the Kakatiyas and the Qutb Shahis. Now however it is a **Christian Church** that has assumed prominence. The church was built by the Reverend Charles Posnett in gratitude for the end of a famine. Commenced in 1914, it was consecrated in 1924. Its huge dimensions accommodate a congregation of 5000. In Neo-gothic style, the church is famed for its stained glass windows depicting various biblical scenes. The church is particularly popular for Christmas festivities.

The **fort** at Medak was built by the Kakatiyas and developed later by the Qutb Shahis. It's renowned for the huge Mubarek Mahal, one of its several gateways and also its brass gun which is almost 3m long.

You can get to Medak by bus from Hyderabad or Warangal. Buses also run there from most major towns in the area.

Devakonda

Ninety kilometres south-east of Hyderabad on the main road to Nagarjuna Sagar is the small town of Mallapally. Seven kilometres directly south of here and off the main road, you'll see evidence of an old fort as you approach the village of Devakonda. The walls of the fort are high on a hill to the right. On the left you'll see the *dargah* (burial place and monument) of the popular Muslim saint, Abdul Khader, who lived 400 years ago. Each year, the people of the village hold commemorative rituals to celebrate his life and work. His dargah, a combination of huge rocks and white mosque-like shapes, is prominent on the landscape.

A wide staircase of 300 steps leads from the base of the fort to a small enclosed area known as the Tortoise Den. From here a path continues past a small encatchment which once provided water to the fort. About 300m further up the hill, and off the path, a checkpoint enabled observations up to 7km away. Continuing along the path and up the steps you'll arrive at an archway. The frieze on the right column is a Telugu, Hindu symbol for learning. This symbol now graces the front of school texts in Andhra Pradesh. Further

along the path, the gun point area is shaded by a large tamarind tree. The small window overlooking the valley enabled the watcher to remain unseen while observing the surrounding country and directing the troops to take action. A second gun point is a little further on just before a stone structure with several smaller sections which were used as 'guest rooms'.

Thirty metres further on, to the left of the path, is Sita's well. Here another tamarind tree provides shade. A staircase descends from ground level to the waters. A few metres further along the path a small temple honours Shiva. The elephant god Ganesh stands guard outside whilst within, the familiar Nandi faces the lingam. Believed to have been constructed by Krishnadevaraya, the temple no longer functions except on the festival honouring Shiva, *Sivaratri,* in February/March.

Next to the temple is the old storehouse and further along the path is a small and picturesque lake known locally as Kornehru. Opposite on the huge rock is an inscription of a lotus within which is the OM symbol. Local people believe that a statue of Lakshmi together with images of other deities lie at the bottom of the lake. The towering solitary rock nearby was once a place of punishment: criminals were left on its narrow top, and with no chance of escape they either fell or waited for the slow inevitable death.

From the lake you can return to the Shiva temple, walk along the side of it through the scrub and up the stony hill behind it to the summit. Here you will see a tiny temple to Rama. The 360° view is stunning. From here you can retrace your steps.

The path at the fort is overgrown, there are no signs and many of the steps have crumbled away, all of which can make navigation somewhat difficult. However the isolation of this landscape and its ancient ruins make it a worthwhile site to explore even if you don't make it to the summit.

At the fort you may encounter Banjaras, tribal people who came to the area some 400 years ago from Rajasthan (see the boxed text).

The Banjaras of Andhra Pradesh

The older women are the most readily identifiable. They sustain their cultural identity through their traditional dress. The vibrant colours are elaborately adorned with hundreds of sequins and tiny pieces of reflective glass. Around their wrists, necks and ankles they wear brass, silver and sometimes bone. Silver rings cascade from their ears almost to their shoulders. In public they cover their heads with a long cloth known as an odhi.

These are the Banjara people of Andhra Pradesh, also known as the Lambadis. They migrated to the Deccan from Rajasthan around 600 years ago. Nobody seems certain as to when or how the Banjara people first arrived in Rajasthan. One theory is that they are descendants of gypsies who, more than 2000 years ago, drifted across the rugged mountains of Afghanistan and landed in Rajasthan.

It was war and deprivation that forced the Banjaras to undertake a mass migration from the north to the south of India. They were fleeing the advancing armies of Aurangzeb, the last of the great Mughal emperors. Although they were used to a semi-nomadic existence, the journey south was plagued by persecuting armies, near starvation and a landscape that was as alien as the new language they had to learn. They survived by doing what they had known for many hundreds of years. They herded cattle (their herds were vast, sometimes exceeding 10,000) and they employed their skills in transportation. Many of them worked for the Mughals as carriers of goods.

Today there are an estimated 30,000 Banjara people in Andhra Pradesh although the true number could be much higher since many have become fully integrated into the culture and the customs of the state. They speak Telugu and Urdu as well as their own dialect known as Kutni. Some of their unique ancient customs and beliefs remain but mostly they share a number of Hindu beliefs. They pay homage to family deities, the main one of which is Lord Venkateshwara which, like many from the north, they call Balaji. It's not unusual to see Banjara families making the long pilgrimage from their settlements around Hyderabad to Tirupathi, the abode of their deity. At the temple they'll partake in the rituals including the shaving of their heads and the donation of their hair to the god.

Movement is still part of life for many Banjara people. They tend not to own land, living instead in settlements called *tandas* (hamlets) on the edge of towns. Each year they may spend a few weeks or even months roaming from job to job. Some buy salt from the mines and hawk it in bags from one marketplace to another. Others graze cattle or work in road construction gangs, breaking rocks or perhaps sealing a new road. Their transport is most often a small cart drawn by oxen.

Festivals are an important part of Banjara life. Their settlements explode with song and dance on the occasions of weddings, the new year and a new child. A traditional Banjara wedding ceremony used to last up to one month. Nowadays the music and dance extend for just three days.

Today older Banjara people are concerned that the young Banjara women are turning away from their traditional garb in favour of conventional Indian dress. As one elderly woman said 'My daughters want to be modern. They wear saris. This makes me sad, we will become invisible'.

To get to Devakonda take the bus, which leaves every hour from Imlibun bus stand in Hyderabad and takes about 1½ hours to make the journey. From the Devakonda bus stand you'll see the fort in the distance, about 1.5km away. You can either walk to the base of the fort or catch an auto-rickshaw.

Keesara Gutta

Just 27km north-east of Hyderabad the Shiva Temple of Ramalingeswara Swamy sits atop the steep hill (*gutta*). It is named after Rama because according to legend he brought the lingam here and directed Hanuman, the monkey god, to bring another 111 lingam.

This temple is particularly significant for

ANDHRA PRADESH

the celebration of Sivaratri (the night of Shiva) which takes place around February/March. Pilgrims come this temple to observe the rituals. They fast throughout the day and night and in the evening they chant continually while every three hours the lingam is bathed in milk, curd, ghee and honey. Legends relate that these are Shiva's favourite rituals and that he looks kindly on those who perform them. Devotees are therefore enthusiastic in their observance. The following morning, after the priests have eaten, the devotees may break their fast.

The main temple area has recently been restored and is surrounded by brightly coloured walls of decorative ironwork. The top presents views of the surrounding landscape. Buses leave Hyderabad every half hour for Keesara Gutta. From the bus stand, follow the signs. It's an easy 500m walk up the hill to the temple.

Bhongir

Bhongir has an impressive fort which can be seen from the main Hyderabad-Warangal Rd 47km north-east of Hyderabad. The fort was begun by the Chalukyas in the 10th and 11th centuries, developed further by the Kakatiyas and finally taken by the later Muslim rulers. Much of the outer walls and gun point sections remain. Both buses and trains frequent the town. The road to the fort is just behind the bus stand. From there it's an easy 500m walk past the area where people make drinking pots to the bottom of the fort. Once you negotiate the initial flat rock slabs it's a fairly easy ascent to the top, up a wide staircase. Along the way there are magnificent views of the surrounding landscape.

Yadagiri Gutta

This hill, some 60km north-east of Hyderabad, resembles a ski resort without the snow. It was a favourite haunt of monkeys, but now all but a few of them remain. They have been displaced by multitudes of pilgrims who swarm to the area, the site of one of the few Vaishnavite temples. It is believed that Vishnu appeared here to one of his devotees.

The principal shrine is his and there is also one for Lakshmi.

Pilgrims come in the belief that they will be cured of all disease if they bathe in the waters here. They come particularly for the Brahmotsavam, in March-April, when chanting and scriptures are recited. Images of the deities are taken within chariots in procession around the temple.

The fees for entry start at Rs 2, increasing depending on the type of darshan required. At the top of the 375 steps, a complex maze of unsightly wired structures (common in many temples now) ensures that devotees file through the temple using the queue system.

Frequent buses from Hyderabad will take you directly to the temple. Dormitory accommodation for pilgrims starts at Rs 25 per person. For a little extra you can stay in a lodge. The APTTDC organises two tours daily to the temple, leaving Hyderabad at 8 am and 2 pm and taking five hours.

Kolanpak

Kolanpak is situated 7km west of Aleru, which is 71km north-east of Hyderabad. This was an important capital for the Chalukyas in the 11th century and also a significant centre for both Jainism and Saivism. The 2000 year old Jain Mahavira Temple is here. The inner wall of the temple is lined with shrines honouring the Jain saints (or tirthankaras).

The image of Mahavira, considered the most significant tirthankara, is set in a 1.5m high jade statue. Craftsmen are employed in restoring the structure, and recreating the intricate sculptural designs. It's worth spending time just to watch the painstaking work of the dozens of artisans who, like the stones they work with, have travelled from Rajasthan. The work is scheduled for completion by the end of 2003.

Opposite the temple is a large dining area where daily meals are prepared for the hundreds of devotees. There's a small museum which opens only once a year for a few days in October around the birthday of Mahavira.

Regular trains and buses come here from Hyderabad.

NAGARJUNAKONDA
Tel Area Code: 08680

Nagarjunakonda, on the Krishna River in the central hill country of Andhra Pradesh, is 150km south-east of Hyderabad. Evidence suggests that human activity began here as early as 200,000 years ago. Remnants from prehistoric times, including tools such as stone axes, have been located and identified. About 3000 BC agrarian communities of a more permanent nature settled along the banks of the Krishna. From the 2nd century BC until the early 3rd century AD Nagarjunakonda and nearby Amaravathi became the site of powerful Hindu and Buddhist empires.

Nagarjunakonda was originally known as Sripavata and encompassed the city of Vijayapuri (the victorious city). Its current name may have derived from Nagarjuna, one of the most revered Buddhist monks, who governed the *sangha* for nearly 60 years around the turn of the 2nd century AD. He founded the Madhyamika school, which studied and developed the teachings of Mahayana Buddhism. The school attracted students from as far afield as Sri Lanka and China, and its philosophical concepts still form the basis of debate among Buddhist scholars.

By the 3rd century AD the Hindu Ikshvakus had settled in the region. They constructed a large amphitheatre and trading centre, which may have been influenced by contact with Romans. They also honoured their gods, Vishnu and Shiva, with huge monuments.

The area was subsequently taken over firstly by the Pallavas and later by the Chalukyas. These dynasties influenced the culture and architecture. A 14th century hill fort was possibly the work of the Vijayanagar Empire. From the 16th century the region was deserted.

In 1926 the archaeologist AR Saraswathi discovered the remains of the earlier civilisations. In 1950 the area was chosen as the site for a huge reservoir, the **Nagarjuna Sagar** to supply water for irrigation and the generation of electricity. At almost 1000km

from the source of the Krishna River, the reservoir when full has a level of 180m and is 175km wide. Before the flooding in 1960, excavations were undertaken which unearthed the remains of stupas, viharas, chaityas and mandapams, as well as some outstanding examples of white marble carvings and sculptures depicting the life of the Buddha. Some 100 significant sites were detected. Many of the ancient monuments and structures were removed and rebuilt within the walls of the nearby hilltop fort, now an island in the middle of the dam.

The **Nagarjunakonda Museum** is also on the island. It's well laid out with information in Telugu, Hindi and English. Stone age picks, hoes, axes, hammers and spears are on display. Coin moulds, as well as the coins themselves, are also there, some of which belonged to the local rulers, the Satavahanas and later Ikshvakus. Others are Roman from the years 37 to 141 AD.

Impressive sculptures of large, voluptuous women stand side by side with exquisite Buddhas. The Jataka stories are beautifully sculpted on long, slim slabs. A large model of the Nagarjunakonda Valley indicates the original positioning of the stupas, tanks, monastery and university. The exhibits give a fascinating insight into the ancient Buddhist and Hindu civilisations.

The museum is open daily (except Friday) from 9 am to 4 pm. Launches depart for the island from the small village of Vijayapuri, on the banks of Nagarjuna Sagar, at 9.30 am and 1.30 pm each day (not Friday). The trip takes one hour and costs Rs 20 (adults) and Rs 10 (children). Tickets are sold from 30 minutes prior to the departure of the launch. There are no advance bookings. The trip is one hilarious affair with much laughter, singing and directions to stay put lest the boat overbalance and sink. There's little chance of that.

The launch stays at the island for 30 minutes. Even with the extra 20 minute leeway, which locals refer to as 'Indian time', this is hardly enough to see everything. Certainly you won't get to see all the outside exhibits. To do the place justice take

ANDHRA PRADESH

the morning launch out to the island and the afternoon launch back. You may be told that you require a permit to do this – you don't. When things get very busy additional express launches may run for Rs 30/20. It's best to avoid weekend visits when the place can become quite crowded.

Light refreshments are available on the island but you may like to take some additional food. There used to be an informative booklet in the museum, but they are now very tired. If you're desperate, you can pick one up in Vellore, in Tamil Nadu!

Places to Stay

Nagarjunakonda is popular with domestic tourists and accommodation can be very tight during May school holidays. It's also rather basic; you'll probably appreciate your sleeping sheet!

Vijay Vihar Complex (☎ 2125) is operated by the APTTDC. This spacious, breezy and crumbling hotel is directly opposite the jetty and many rooms have balconies overlooking the water. The rooms may be large but the beds and mattresses are in urgent need of replacements. As for the sheets – bring your own. Singles/doubles are Rs 300/450. The downstairs restaurant offers a good range of veg and nonveg meals.

Project House (☎ 2040) is also APTTDC operated. Situated 3km from the jetty in a landscaped garden at Colony Hill, it offers basic singles/doubles for Rs 200/300. You'll need plenty of insect repellent here and plenty of patience with the plumbing. The hot water is still 'coming'. The vegetarian restaurant is OK. There's a friendly tourist office but they have no maps, no brochures and no information.

There is also an OK *Youth Hostel* in Hill Colony.

A number of basic, clean, and inexpensive *private rooms* are available directly opposite Project House. They cost around Rs 100 per room per day. Ask at the Suranthi Wine Shop for Mr Mastan Rao. He's the man with the key and he'll show you a whole range of rooms. Rooms with a window are the best.

Getting There & Away

The easiest way to visit Nagarjunakonda from Hyderabad is to take the tour organised by the APTTDC (☎ 816375). It departs Hyderabad daily (if demand warrants it) at 6.30 am from Yatri Nivas Hotel, returns at 9.30 pm and costs Rs 120 (child), lunch included. The tour includes visits to the Nagarjunakonda Museum (closed Friday), Nagarjuna Sagar and Ethipothala Waterfalls.

If you'd prefer to make your own way there, regular buses link Hyderabad, Vijayawada and Guntur with Nagarjuna Sagar. The nearest train station is 22km away at Macherla (a branch line running west from Guntur) from where buses leave regularly for Nagarjuna Sagar.

AROUND NAGARJUNAKONDA
Ethipothala Waterfalls

These falls, 60m high and some 21km east of Nagarjunakonda are named after a priest *(ethi)* who meditated in the caves above *(opathalla* – upper place). The falls consist of several cascades emanating from the Chandravanka River. There are quite a few small cave temples in the area. Some are places of worship for the local tribal people, the Lambadi.

It's best to avoid the early morning for your visit since fog often hangs over the dam and river. There is no public transport to the site so you may prefer to take the tour outlined above. Alternately, you can hitch a ride.

Nagarjuna Sargar-Srisailam Tiger Reserve

Just 130km south of Hyderabad, this reserve (formerly the Rajiv Gandhi Wildlife Sanctuary) boasts a range of wildlife including tigers, panthers, wolves, langurs and many more.

Extending over 3568 sq km, the sanctuary was declared a tiger reserve in 1983. Although since Rajiv Gandhi's death it has been renamed, it is still generally referred to by its former title. Averaging 500m above sea level, the reserve's highest peak is Durgamkonda, at 917m. The forests within the park include tropical, and dry and deciduous. Tribal people, Chenchu, are said to inhabit the area. They are reputed to be food gatherers who favour a barter system for trade among themselves. A 'social upliftment' program for the tribal people has been instigated for them by the park authorities!

Like most national parks and wildlife sanctuaries, this one is highly promoted by tourist and forest authorities, but admittance to the sanctuary is via a test in diplomacy, labyrinthine bureaucratic processes, tolerance, humour and sly negotiations. Passing the test does not ensure entry, and conditions for entry vary constantly. It seems however, that despite all advice to the contrary, the best procedures to follow if you wish to enter the park, are the following:

- Apply to the, Chief Considerator of Forests, AP Forest Department, Aranya Bhavan, Hyderabad (☎ 230561). Ignore all advice which suggests you don't require this permission. Wait through the numerous lunch breaks, meetings, holidays and outstation trips. The first thing you'll be asked for when you turn up at the forest checkpoint is the permission from Hyderabad, but the difficulties back in Hyderabad will probably mean you won't have the required permission.
- There are two entry points via checkpoints. If approaching from Hyderabad the entry point is at Achampet. The other checkpoint is south at Sundipenta near Srisailam.
- Visitors will require their own transport – preferably 4WD. It's probably best to hire this from Hyderabad. Ignore anyone who tries to tell you that there are jeeps for visitors at the park; it's simply not true. If you arrive at the reserve without transport you may be able to arrange it at Achampet, the northernmost entry. Otherwise you'll need to go on to Srisailam some 100km away on the eastern side of the park, where you can organise transport with Mr T Narayan, Canteen 1 (☎ 87154/87330) for Rs 1000 per day plus diesel. Organising transport at the park leaves you in a very weak position for bargaining. Also transport at Srisailam is conditional on permission to enter the park!
- With your own vehicle and permission you approach one of the two checkpoints. You cannot enter the park without a ranger. There are 10 attached to the reserve, but it can often be difficult to locate even one.

- There are no entry fees apart from the usual 'small consideration'.
- Entry to the park is only between the hours of 6 am and 6 pm. No traffic is permitted between 9 pm and 6 am.
- There is a basic style Forest Resthouse (Rs 25) at Mannanur near the northern Achampet entrance and another at Srisailam.
- There is an Environment Office at Mannanur which is open every day from 8.30 am to 6.30 pm (closed from 12.30 to 2.30 pm). The 5.30 pm daily film screenings provide extensive and interesting information – on 'African lions'.
- To the right of the Environment Office there's a small shrine to the 'god of the forest'. Divine intervention may be required.

Having survived all these processes you may find the only wildlife you experience is a wild goose! The checkpoints are officially staffed 24 hours a day, but are often completely deserted.

Srisailam

Srisailam is almost 230km south of Hyderabad and set within the heavily forested Nallamalai Hills. The intricately carved temple here is an impressive sight. It's dedicated to Shiva and Parvati, known here as Mallikarjuna and Bhramaramba.

Numerous legends surround the temple. Most focus on the beauty of a young woman (sometimes Sita, sometimes Parvati) who worshipped Shiva with jasmine flowers and built the temple in his honour. Others relate a quarrel between Shiva and Parvati's sons, Ganesh and Subrahmanya. The parents arrived to appease the latter's wrath, and remained permanently. As such they acquired the reputation for settling disputes and creating harmony and thousands of pilgrims flock for their blessings.

The temple is also popular because of its non-discriminatory policy – it welcomes people of all castes.

A further attraction is the temple's significance in housing one of only twelve of India's 'jyothirlingams'. These naturally occurring stone formations are believed by devotees to be self-created, or created by

ANDHRA PRADESH

divine force, and are therefore particularly revered.

Although the temple's history may date from the 2nd century AD, most of the present day structures are of the 14th century. The temple is surrounded by a finely sculptured 8.5m-high wall. Elephants in various poses form the base. Hunting scenes, and Shiva in his many guises, are positioned in the rows above. Within the large compound are numerous shrines, mandapams and the sanctum containing the lingam. As with many other temples, Srisailam has wire structures which force crowds into single-file queues. The more you pay at the entrance, the more your access to the temple is facilitated. The temple is open from 5.30 to 11 am and 4.30 to 8 pm.

Srisailam is a tiny town consisting only of the temple and accommodation for pilgrims. You will easily find your way around.

Being a pilgrim town, Srisailam is almost totally administered by the temple custodians. Except for a few private services, all accommodation and facilities are arranged through them.

On arrival at the town toll gate (Rs 10 for four-wheel vehicles; Rs 2 for motorcycles) visitors must register at the Reception Centre, Srisaila Devasthanam. To get there, from the toll gate turn right and proceed 400m. At the Reception Centre, accommodation will be allocated ranging from *choultries* (accommodation for pilgrims) at no cost to rooms from Rs 25 to Rs 400. Cottages with two double rooms and attached bathrooms start at Rs 150. The whole process is well organised. Payment for at least two nights accommodation will be taken, and the balance refunded if you stay for one night only.

There is also some private accommodation at *Jagatguru Matam Guest House* which has two-bedroom cottages for Rs 600, or Rs 800 with air-con. Although the temple may welcome all castes, accommodation is apparently organised according to caste.

There are two places to eat – Canteen 1 and Canteen 2. Both provide good food at low costs – a few rupees will get you a thali.

Visitors who prefer non-spicy food are advised to eat at Canteen 1.

Since rituals begin at 4.30 am each day, it's generally fairly quiet after about 9 pm. Also because of forest regulations no one may leave the town between 9 pm and 6 am.

To get to Srisailam take the train from Hyderabad to Mahbubnagar then take the bus. Buses also leave from Kurnool. However you may find it easier to take a day or overnight tour directly from Hyderabad. Overnight tours cost Rs 310 which includes fares and accommodation.

WARANGAL
Pop: 537,000 Tel Area Code: 08712

About 157km north-east of Hyderabad, Warangal (one stone) is named after one of the many huge rocks nearby. It was the capital of the Kakatiya kingdom which spanned the greater part of present-day Andhra Pradesh from the latter half of the 12th century until it was conquered by the Tughlaqs of Delhi early in the 14th century. The Hindu Kakatiyas were great builders and patrons of the arts, and it was during their reign that the Chalukyan style of temple architecture and decoration reached the pinnacle of its development.

If you have an interest in the various branches of Hindu temple development and have either visited or intend to visit the early Chalukyan sites at Badami, Aihole and Pattadakal in neighbouring Karnataka state, then an outing to Warangal is worthwhile. Facilities are adequate for an overnight stop, or it can be visited in a long day trip from Hyderabad.

Warangal is a cotton market town. You may see the bullock trains laden with bales on their way from auction to factory. In the mid-1990s the cotton industry experienced crisis in this district. Many crops failed, irrigation was inadequate and the farmers fell victim to the unscrupulous practices of moneylenders. Faced with these difficulties many farmers committed suicide.

There's also a colourful **wool market** here in the cooler months around the bus stand area. As in many other southern towns,

Tibetans from the north come and set up shop.

Orientation & Information

The main locations of interest and information are Warangal, Hanamkonda (3km north-west of Warangal) and Kazipet (some 10km south-west of Warangal). This arrangement is somewhat disjointed and can be confusing.

The Warangal train station and bus stand are directly opposite each other. Station Rd, running left as you leave the train station, is the main area for facilities in Warangal. The Warangal post office is on the right towards the end of Station Rd. The Police station is almost at the end on the left. Main Rd connects Warangal and Hanamkonda. There is a post office on this road 2km west of Hanamkonda.

Kazipet is the train junction for northbound trains. There is a Regional Tourist Information Bureau 3km north of here at the Tourist Resthouse, and a smaller one in the Kazipet train station. Both have very limited resources so a visit to them is hardly worthwhile. The Forest Department is close by the tourist office and is an excellent place to witness entropy in its finest form.

Bank times are Monday to Friday, 10.30 am to 2.30 pm and until 12.30 pm on Saturday. Almost every bank is represented here but few handle foreign exchange. It's best to go to the State Bank of Hyderabad, opposite the Kazipet Tourist Information Bureau and next to the Engineering College. But they won't change travellers cheques on Saturdays. Few places accept credit cards.

There are numerous local/STD/ISD booths, many open 24 hours.

Fort

Warangal's fort, reputedly the largest of its kind in India, was a huge construction with three distinct circular strongholds surrounded by a moat. The two outer circuits were earthen walls originally some 5m high, but now very much eroded. The inner fortress of granite was slightly higher. Four paths with decorative gateways, set according to the cardinal points, led to the centre where a huge Shiva temple once existed. Now the gateways are still obvious, but much of the fort is in ruins. Even the remaining statues have large pieces missing. Even so, the fallen pillars and raised mandapam still permit an insight into the ingenuity of the past. There are other Shiva shrines here where prayer and rituals still occur. From the hill you can view the activities around the tank below. Washing creates a colourful patchwork on the wide grey stones.

The fort area is a popular picnic ground, no doubt due to its tranquil atmosphere. It's 5km from Warangal and easily reached by bus or auto-rickshaw.

Hanamkonda

Built in 1163, the **1000-Pillared Temple** on the slopes of Hanamkonda Hill 400m from the Hanamkonda crossroads, is a fine example of Chalukyan architecture. It is dedicated to three deities-Shiva, Vishnu and Surya. Now, carefully restored, it stands on a 1m-high platform and measures 31m by 25m. It is in two main sections with a central, very impressive Nandi. Its numerous pillars are intricately carved. Small lingam shrines dot the surrounding gardens. This is another serene area where you can wander at leisure to the sounds of the puja bells, the gentle squeals of the eagles and the tapping of the stonemasons. It's open from 6 am to 6 pm.

Down the hill and 3km to the right is the **Siddheshwara Temple**, a small temple, which contains the customary shrine to the lingam.

The **Bhadrakali Temple** featuring a stone statue of the goddess Kali, seated and with a weapon in each of the eight hands, is high on a hill almost half way between Hanamkonda and Warangal.

Planetarium

The planetarium on Main Rd, just 500m south of the Siddheshwara Temple runs daily sessions (except Monday), at 2.30, 4, 6 and 7.45 pm. Entry is Rs 5 and all sessions are in Telugu. The depiction of the northern

ANDHRA PRADESH

sky is serenaded by a mixture of pumped-up techno beats and new-age sci-fi music.

Places to Stay

Accommodation facilities are modest. In addition to room charges, several hotels have a once only guest charge of Rs 20 to Rs 30. Most of the hotels are on Station Rd, which runs parallel to the train line; turn left as you leave the station.

Vijaya Lodge (☎ 61781/2) on Station Rd, three minutes from the train station, is OK value at Rs 58/95 for rooms with attached bathroom, or Rs 110 for a double room with phone.

Hotel Shanthi Krishna (☎ 26607) also on Station Rd, behind the post office, is similar with prices at Rs 65/100 for non aircon and air-con doubles are Rs 200. It's friendly but take some incense.

Anand Lodge Station Rd, has dormitories for men only at Rs 25 for 24 hours. This includes the use of a locker.

Kathic Lodge has singles/doubles for Rs 70/100 for shared bathrooms and toilets.

Vikas Lodge (☎ 24194), up behind the bus stand and near the huge market, has basic rooms with bathroom for Rs 50/70.

Ashok (☎ 85491), which is on Main Rd at Hanamkonda, is 7km from Warangal train station and has non air-con single/doubles for Rs 175/250; with air-con is Rs 330/410. It's spacious, noisy and the 'hot water is coming' – one day perhaps. It has two very good restaurants, one of which serves liquor.

Hotel Ratna (☎ 60645; fax 60096), newer than Ashok, has singles/doubles Rs 180/250 and for air-con doubles Rs 400 and Rs 500. It accepts Master Card and Visa.

Chariot, the AP tourist resthouse, is on the main road (about 3km before Kazipet bus stand) directly opposite the Regional Engineering College. The basic but spacious double rooms are Rs 125. Singles are not available but a dormitory of six beds will set you back Rs 300. The resthouse has a good vegetarian restaurant. The Regional Tourist Information Bureau is also located here

Retiring Rooms at the Warangal train station are Rs 30/60 (non air-con) and Rs 50/100 (air-con). There are also *Retiring Rooms* at Kazipet train station.

Places to Eat

There are several small snack houses but few eating places in Warangal. Hotels Ashok and Ratna have attached restaurants with good food.

Ruchi Restaurant in central Station Rd serves nonveg dishes.

Kapila Restaurant at the Hanamkonda crossroads has veg meals from Rs 20 and nonveg from Rs 95. Its internal, darkened and air-con section serves the same meals at slightly higher prices.

Getting There & Away

Regular buses run between Warangal and Hyderabad, Nizamabad and other major centres. Local buses connect Warangal with Kazipet and Hanamkonda.

Warangal is a major railway junction and there are regular trains to and from main cities such as Delhi and Chennai, as well as Hyderabad or Secunderabad (152km, three hours, Rs 66/200 in 2nd/1st class) and to Vijayawada (209km, four hours, Rs 75/252 in 2nd/1st class). The three-hour journey from Hyderabad makes a one-day trip to Warangal and surrounds possible.

Getting Around

The bus stand is directly opposite the entrance to the train station. Bus No 28 will take you the 5km to the fort at Mantukonda. Regular buses go to all the other sites. You can also rent bikes in Station St for Rs 2 an hour or Rs 12 a day. Only bikes with crossbars and no gears are available. Autorickshaws and cycle-rickshaws are other alternatives.

AROUND WARANGAL
Palampet

Sixty kilometres north-east of Warangal the **Ramappa Temple**, (dating from 1234), provides another very beautiful example of Kakatiya architecture. Built by Recherla, a general of Ganapatadevi, its many pillars are ornately carved and its overhanging eaves envelop fine statues of female forms. The temple is open from 6 am to 6.30 pm daily.

Just over 1km south of the temple the **Ramappa Cheruvu**, a huge lake, also constructed by Recherla, now assumes a natural presence within the landscape. There are no facilities at the temple so take water, and food if you wish.

The *Vanavihar Guesthouse,* situated on the banks of the lake, has three double rooms with attached bathrooms and ceiling fans for Rs 10 per person. If you want to stay, you must book with the Tourist Information Bureau in Kazipet prior to leaving Warangal. You'll need to bring all your own provisions including food.

Pakhal Wildlife Sanctuary

This sanctuary, covering some 900 sq km, surrounds the shores of another lake created by the Kakatiyas in 1213. The tourist literature promotes the sanctuary as a home of wild leopards, deers, hyenas, bears and even tigers. To enter the park you must report to the District Forest Officer in Main Rd 3km north of Kazipet. Here you will receive a map of the park and the paths you may follow. You must provide your own four-wheel vehicle with driver. There is no accommodation in the park.

VISAKHAPATNAM
Pop: 1.15 million Tel Area Code: 0891

This coastal city is the commercial and industrial heart of Andhra Pradesh's isolated north-east corner, and is home to India's largest shipbuilding yard. Originally it was two separate towns – the northern and more urbane Waltair and the southern port town of Visakhapatnam (known as Vizag). However, as Vizag grew (and continues to rapidly do so), the pair gradually merged.

These days the twin towns have little to offer tourists and the pall of industrial smoke that hangs in the air makes them unenticing. Vizag's best known sight is the rocky promontory known as the **Dolphin's Nose** jutting into the harbour. The hilly seaside area of Waltair is edged by long beaches affording views across the Bay of

Bengal and the busy Calcutta-Chennai shipping lane.

At Simhachalam Hill, 10km north of town, there's a fine 11th century **Vishnu Temple** in Orissan style. The best beach is **Rishikonda**, also about 10km north.

The APSRTC (☎ 546400) operates full-day tours of Vizag and Waltair for Rs 75 per person.

Orientation & Information
The train station and bus stand are about 1.5km apart. Both are about 2km from the city centre, based loosely around the Poorna Market area. The beach hotels are all located in Waltair, which is the most pleasant place to stay.

The tourist office in the train station has precious little information.

Places to Stay & Eat
There's no shortage of places to stay to suit all budgets. The *Retiring Rooms* at the train station include men-only dorm beds for Rs 10 and comfortable doubles at Rs 125.

City Centre A good area for cheap hotels is Main Rd near the Poorna Market.

Hotel Poorna (☎ 62344) is down an alley off Main Rd, and has clean singles/doubles with attached bathroom from Rs 80/120.

Hotel Prasanth (☎ 65282), opposite, is similar with rooms for Rs 90/135.

Swagath Restaurant nearby on Main Rd has a small rooftop garden and cheap vegetarian meals and snacks.

Hotel Daspalla (☎ 564825) has rooms for Rs 350/400, or Rs 800/1000 with air-con. The three-star hotel has several restaurants serving Chinese, Continental, tandoori and spicy local cuisine.

Dolphin Hotels Limited (☎ 567000) is a centrally located four-star place with a swimming pool and restaurant. Rooms range from Rs 520/750 to Rs 1300/1500, and breakfast is included in rooms priced above Rs 750/1000.

Beach Area Located at the northern end of Beach Rd, *Palm Beach Hotel (☎ 554026)*

ANDHRA PRADESH

is old and run-down, but it's OK if you just want to be close to the beach. Rooms are Rs 250/300 or Rs 350/500 with air-con.

Park Hotel (☎ 554488; fax 554181), next door, looks old and ugly from the outside but the rooms are modern and comfortable. Air-conditioned rooms, all with a sea view, cost Rs 1200/2050. There's a swimming pool, bookshop and three restaurants, and the staff are friendly.

Taj Residency (☎ 567756; fax 564370), Vizag's best, is a luxurious, tiered hotel that climbs the hill from Beach Rd. It has a swimming pool and a restaurant, and room prices range from Rs 1650 to Rs 4500 plus 20% tax.

Getting There & Away

Vizag's airport is 13km west of town; Rs 85 by auto-rickshaw. Indian Airlines (☎ 546501) flies to Calcutta (US$115) and Chennai (US$90) daily except Wednesday and Sunday, and to Hyderabad (US$85) on Monday and Saturday. NEPC Airlines (☎ 574151) flies Thursday and Saturday to Chennai (US$105) and Wednesday and Friday to Calcutta (US$125) via Bhubaneswar (US$82). NEPC (☎ 574151) flies to Mumbai (US$182) via Hyderabad (US$78) on Wednesday, Friday and Sunday.

Visakhapatnam Junction station is on the main Calcutta to Chennai line. To Calcutta the best train is the overnight *Coromandel Express* (879km, 15 hours, Rs 213/758 in 2nd/1st class). Heading south, the same train goes to Vijayawada (352km, 5½ hours, Rs 108/390) and Chennai Central (784km, 17 hours, Rs 198/772).

From the well-organised bus stand, the APSRTC (☎ 546400) has services to destinations within Andhra Pradesh, as well as Puri in Orissa.

AROUND VISAKHAPATNAM

About 25km north-east of Vizag is **Bheemunipatnam**, one of the safest beaches on this part of the coast. It's also the site of the ruins of the east coast's oldest Dutch settlement. A little way inland from here is **Hollanders Green**, the Dutch cemetery.

Some 90km north of Vizag are the million-year old limestone **Borra Caves** which are filled with fascinating stalagmite and stalactite formations. A further 30km north is the **Araku Valley**, home to a number of isolated tribal communities.

VIJAYAWADA
Pop: 853,300 Tel Area Code: 0866

Vijayawada was originally known as Bejjawada (from *bejjam*, Telugu for tunnel) after the numerous channels the river makes to the sea. Its current name is believed to have come from the legendary Arjuna, of the Mahabharata, who was victorious (vijaya) in winning Shiva's blessings. Originally an important Buddhist site, in the 7th century it became the main centre for the Eastern Chalukyas who created large cave temples within the rocky hills. For many, it is the heart of Andhra culture and language. The main attractions here are Hindu temples, including the ancient rock cave temples, two 1000 year old **Jain temples** and the Buddhist site at Amaravathi.

Orientation & Information

Vijayawada sits at the head of the delta of the mighty Krishna River. Its position has established it as a major port and an important junction on the east coast train line from Calcutta to Chennai. About 265km east of Hyderabad and 70km inland from the sea, it's an important industrial centre and a fairly hectic town.

There is a tourist information kiosk at the train station, open from 7 to 11 am and 2 to 6 pm, but not public holidays. You can also get tourist information from Krishnaveni Motel (☎ 426382) just over the Prakasam Barrage in Seethanagaram, Tadepalli.

Lepakshi Handicrafts Emporium (☎ 573 129) is in Ghandinagar.

Kanaka Durga Temple

This temple on Indrakila Hill is dedicated to the goddess and protector of the city. Legend has it that the area was once the domain of powerful demons whom no man could destroy. It was the goddess who defeated them and now receives continual gratitude and honour from her followers. She is considered to embody prosperity, power and compassion and many devotees credit her with the prosperous development of Vijayawada.

Mogalarajapuram Caves

Located 3km east of Vijayawada, these cave temples, dedicated to such deities as Nataraja and Vinyaka, date from the 5th century.

Undavalli Caves

About 8km from Vijayawada, across the river, are the ancient Hindu cave temples of Undavalli. The rocks into which they are set were formed in an Antarctic-Indian collision some 16 million years ago. These caves, carved in the 7th century, house temples dedicated to Anantasayana (another name for Vishnu) and the Trimurti (the triad – Brahma, Vishnu and Shiva) which is the incomplete top section. Small, finely crafted statues of deities line the first floor. An inscription dated 1343 registers donations to the temple by an official of the area, Machamareddi. Deep within the right side of the caves a huge statue of Vishnu lies peacefully. You'll need to find the man with the key to get in. Once in, he'll light a candle to display the sculpture.

There is a regular bus service to the caves which by general standards seems fine, yet even the tolerant locals complain about it. Few travellers see the caves, but they are well worth a visit.

Gandhi Stupa

Built in memory of Mahatma Gandhi, this tall monument stands over 15m high and creates an impressive landmark in the city. You can get a good idea of the city from the wide ranging views at the top of Gandhi Hill, on which the stupa is located.

Prakasam Barrage

This structure which creates a road bridge over the Krishna River is also part of a major irrigation project which has resulted in the Vijayawada area becoming one of the richest grain producing areas in the state.

People bathe in the ghats below. Since legends accord the creation of the Krishna River to Shiva, it is believed that the waters hold beneficial qualities.

Places to Stay & Eat

Most of the hotels have attached restaurants. Vijayawada is noted for its cuisine and its fruits, particularly mangoes. It has delicious curd too.

Hotel Swapna Lodge (☎ 575386) on Durgaiah St near the Navrang Theatre, about 2km from the train station, offers the best value among the cheapies. It's on a quiet backstreet and is friendly and clean. Rooms cost Rs 90/120.

Sree Lakshmi Vilas Modern Cafe (☎ 57-2525) on Besant Rd at Governorpet, a bustling shopping district about 1.5km from the train station, has rooms with common bathroom for Rs 80/90, or Rs 90/165 with attached bathroom and bucket shower. The hotel has a good vegetarian restaurant, a generator facility and a 'conveyance service' to the bus or train station: cycle-rickshaw Rs 6, and auto-rickshaw Rs 12.

Sree Nivas Hotel (☎ 573338), behind the UTI Office off Bandar, Governorpet, is good value with singles/doubles at Rs 200/275 or with air-con Rs 400/475.

Brundavan Lodge (☎ 574665) on Besant Rd is OK with singles/doubles Rs 80/150 and air-con doubles at Rs 330. 'Room guest' charges for air-con are an additional Rs 30.

Krishnaveni Motel (☎ 426382) is very good value with doubles (only) Rs 250 and air-con Rs 350. Set in pleasant gardens by the river, it's away from the noise and chaos of the city. The staff are helpful. Boating facilities are available.

Hotel Raj Towers (☎ 571311), on Congress Office Rd, Governorpet, 1.5km from the train station, has rooms with attached bathroom for Rs 265/355 and Rs 460/535 with air-con. The double deluxe at Rs 600 are very good value. It also has a veg restaurant and bar.

Hotel Manorama (☎ 571301/ 577221), on MG Rd about 500m from the new bus stand, is similar, with rooms with attached

ANDHRA PRADESH

bath for Rs 390/490, or Rs 590/690 with air-con. All major credit cards accepted. It has a veg restaurant and a nonveg serving Chinese and continental dishes.

Hotel Ilapuram (☎ 571282; fax 575251) on Besant Rd, Gandhinagar, is one of the best value places in town. Singles/doubles are Rs 450/550, or Rs 550/650 with air-con and there are more expensive suites. The hotel has both nonveg and veg restaurants and a bar. Tours can also be organised here.

Hanuman Dormitory (for men only) at the bus stand is Rs 20 for 24 hours. A hot shower is Rs 2 extra. Due to 'funny business' there are no dormitories for women.

The *Deluxe Lounge* next door to the dormitory provides a banana lounge environment with TV for men and women for Rs 3 per hour.

The *Retiring Rooms* at the train station are well maintained. Singles/doubles cost Rs 75/125 and for an air-con double Rs 220. The air-con suite at Rs 330 is particularly appealing with its iridescent blue lounge, lavender toilet and bright pink basin. Dormitories (for men only) cost from Rs 30 non air-con and Rs 115 for air-con.

Hotel Nandini, upstairs at the bus stand, serves standard South Indian veg meals from 10 am to 3 pm and from 7 to 10 pm. Downstairs it's open round the clock.

Modern Bakery & Ice-Cream Parlour on Besant Rd is OK for snacks.

Getting There & Away

Air The airport is 20km from the city. NEPC Airlines (☎ 476493) flies to Chennai and Visakhapatnam on Tuesday, Thursday and Saturday.

Bus The enormous bus stand on Bandar Rd near the river is about 1.5km from the train station. It's well organised and has dormitories, waiting rooms, a cloakroom and a restaurant. All signs here are in Telugu, but for non-Telugu speakers there is a helpful inquiry desk. From here, buses travel to all parts of Andhra Pradesh; every 30 minutes to Hyderabad (six hours), eight times daily to Warangal (six hours) and Visakhapatnam

seven times daily (10 hours). Buses also leave for Chennai twice daily (10 hours).

Train Vijayawada is on the main Chennai to Calcutta and Chennai to Delhi lines and all the express trains stop here. The quickest train from Vijayawada to Chennai is the *Coromandel Express* (seven hours, Rs 126/464 in 2nd/1st class). The same train to Calcutta (20 hours) costs Rs 255/952.

There are plenty of trains via Warangal to Hyderabad (6½ hours, Rs 87/312); one of the quickest is the *Godavari Express*. The *Tamil Nadu Express* to New Delhi (27 hours) costs Rs 308/1228 in 2nd/1st class.

To Tirupathi (nine hours), the daily *Howrah-Tirupathi Express* costs Rs 92/308 in 2nd/1st class. Heading north to Puri (Orissa), take the *Howrah-Tirupathi Express* to the junction, Khurda Rd, then a passenger train or bus for the last 44km to Puri.

There are also direct weekly trains to Kanyakumari and Bangalore, trains four times weekly to Varanasi and daily to Thiruvananthapuram (Trivandrum).

AROUND VIJAYAWADA
Amaravathi

Some 30km due west of Vijayawada, near the bank of the Krishna River, stands Amaravathi, one of the most significant ancient Buddhist centres and the former capital of the Andhras. Here, in the museum, you can see a small replica of the 2000 year old **stupa** with its intricately carved pillars and marble-surfaced dome. The carvings depict the life of the Buddha as well as scenes from everyday life. The remains of the original stupa, a grass covered mound, are a few metres past the museum.

Other exhibits in the museum include Buddha statues, sculptures of the lotus and the swastika – an early symbolic representation of the Buddha. Entry to the museum is free. Hours every day except Fridays and public holidays are 10 am to 5 pm.

If you have a particular interest in Buddhist history and monuments, you will no doubt wish to visit Amaravathi. There's no direct route from Vijayawada to Amaravathi so it's necessary to travel the 30km to Guntur and then a further 30km to Amaravathi. Buses run from Vijayawada to Amaravathi (via Guntur) every hour from 6 am to 9 pm. The APTTDC also organises bus tours for Rs 60 as well as boat trips for Rs 75 return. Ask at the tourist information kiosk at Vijayawada train station or at the APTTDC's counter at the Krishnaveni Motel (☎ 426382) in Seethanagaram, Vijayawada. There is no accommodation at Amaravathi and few places to get drinks and snacks.

Kondapalle

Once famous for its 14th century fort, the village of Kondapalle is now also noted for the production of brightly painted wooden figures, including deities, animals, small bowls and kitchenware. The items, made out of light wood known as *poniki* create a colourful picture as you enter the town. (See *between* pages 352 & 353.)

Kondapalle is situated some 20km northwest of Vijayawada, via the major trucking stop at Ibrahimpotam. To get there catch the train to Ibrahimpotam and then a bus (or walk) for the last 4km. Alternately, catch the city bus directly there.

Khamman Fort

Compared to other fort sites in Andhra Pradesh, Khamman Fort has little of its original structure remaining. However it's an interesting and attractive place to visit and a popular meeting place and picnic spot. In the central fort area within the rock cavity there is a small water catchment. Within the fort wall, narrow tunnels create escape passages. Local children delight in giving demonstrations. To get there catch the bus to the Khamman bus stand and walk along the road adjacent to the fort wall for about 500m until you reach a small mosque. From here you will see the ascent to the fort.

TIRUMALA & TIRUPATHI
Pop: 191,000 Tel Area Code: 08574

The 'holy hill' of Tirumala in the extreme south of Andhra Pradesh is one of the most important pilgrimage centres in India, and is claimed to be the busiest in the world – eclipsing Jerusalem, Rome and Mecca in the sheer number of pilgrims.

Because it hosts an army of pilgrims from all over India and the world, everything at Tirumala and at its service town of Tirupathi, 20km away, is organised to keep visitors fed, sheltered and moving. Most are housed in special pilgrims' choultries in both Tirupathi and Tirumala. Organisation is administered by the very efficient Tirumala Tirupathi Devasthanams (TTD). The private hotels and lodges are in Tirupathi, so a fleet of buses constantly ferries pilgrims up and down the hill between Tirupathi and Tirumala from before dawn until well after dusk.

Tirumala is an engrossing place where you can easily spend a whole day just wandering around. It's one of the few places in India which allows non-Hindus into the temple sanctum sanctorum but, despite this, the place sees few non-Hindu visitors. Maybe they are deterred by the crowds. Yet Tirumala has a sense of generosity and surprising ease about it. It's well organised with ample facilities, including shopping complexes, banks, a post office, rail reservation office, and even a Lepakshi Handicraft Emporium. It's well worth a visit, even if you're not a pilgrim.

Venkateshwara Temple

Pilgrims flock to Tirumala to visit the ancient temple of Venkateshwara, an avatar of Vishnu. This is the god whose picture graces the reception areas of most lodges and restaurants in South India, with his eyes covered (since his gaze would scorch the world) and garlanded in so many flowers that only his feet are visible.

The history of the temple may date back almost 2000 years – it is mentioned in the Sangam poetry of the first few centuries AD. Numerous temple inscriptions from the 9th century record details of the temple and contributions made by both Pallava and Chola kings. Under the Vijayanagars the temple prospered and expanded. In 1517, Krishnadevaraya, on one of his many visits to the temple, donated gold and jewels enabling the vimana (inner shrine) roofing to be gilded.

For devotees, the deity Venkateshwara symbolises goodness. With his conch he creates the cosmic sounds that destroy ignorance. He is said to embody the Hindu trinity, that is the three deities – Brahma, Vishnu and Shiva. As such he is considered to be very powerful. Among the powers attributed to Venkateshwara is the granting of any wish that is made in front of the idol at Tirumala. The image is said to be self-created and immortal. Sandalwood paste is placed on it and develops an impression. This is highly prized by devotees, who believe it has assumed the powers of the deity.

There are never less than 5000 pilgrims here at any one time and, in a single day, the

total is often as high as 100,000. The temple staff alone number 18,000!

Such popularity makes the temple one of the richest in India, with an annual income of a staggering one billion rupees. This is administered by a temple trust which ploughs the bulk of the money back into hundreds of choultries and charities such as homes for the poor, orphanages, craft training centres, schools, colleges and art academies.

It's considered auspicious to have your head shaved when visiting the temple. People donate their hair to the deity, an act symbolic of renouncing the ego. Hundreds of barbers sit patiently, as devotees offer their heads to be shaved. If you see bald headed people in South India, you can be pretty sure they've recently been to Tirupathi – this applies to men, women and children.

The Brahmotsavam festival is celebrated here in September/October. The sacred texts are recited and each day, morning and evening, images of the deities are taken in a colourful procession around the temple. The chariot for Brahma, believed to be the instigator of the festival, leads the procession.

As you face the entrance to the temple, there is a small **museum** at the top of the steps to the left. Among other things, it has a good collection of musical instruments, including a tabla-type drum called a *ubangam*! The museum is open from 8 am to 8 pm and entry is Rs 1.

Sri Padmavathi Amma Vari Temple
Down the hill from the main temple is one to the deity's consort, Lakshmi. The entrance leads to a white pillared hall with the familiar images of Hanuman the monkey god, Krishna and others. This is the temple of the goddess of abundance and prosperity and the priests here have certainly adopted such notions. On leaving, visitors may be harassed for money (even large sums), and the demand is for US dollars.

Organised Tours
The APTTDC runs weekend tours to Tirupathi from Hyderabad. The tours leave at 3.30 pm on Friday and return at 7 am on

---

Special Darshan at Tirumala
After paying Rs 30 for 'special darshan', you'll be allowed to enter Tirumala's Venkateshwara Temple. Special darshan means you can go in ahead of all those who have paid nothing for their ordinary *darshan* (viewing of a god) and who have to queue – often for 12 hours or more – in the claustrophobic wire cages which ring the outer wall of the temple.

Although special darshan is supposed to get you to the front of this immense queue in two hours, on weekends when the place is much busier it can take as long as five hours, and you still have to go through the cages. A signboard at the entrance keeps you briefed on the waiting time. To find the start of the queue, follow the signs to 'Sarvadarshanam', around to the left of the temple entrance.

No matter which darshan you experience, once inside the temple, you'll have to keep shuffling along with everyone else and, before you know it, you'll have viewed Venkateshwara and will be back outside again.

You can however pay considerably more than Rs 30 and secure a position for other special darshans, some of which involve minimal waiting.

Monday and include accommodation and 'special darshan'. The cost is Rs 600. It's also possible to take the bus only; this costs Rs 150 one way.

It's probably best to approach Tirupathi from Chennai. (For details of organised Tours see the section in the Chennai chapter.)

Tirupathi in included in some of the circular rail tours conducted by South Central Railway. See their booklet or contact Secunderabad station for details.

Places to Stay

Hotel prices can vary, especially at festival times when there may be dramatic increases.

Tirupathi Tirupathi is the town at the bottom of the hill and the transport hub. It has plenty of hotels and lodges, so there's no problem finding somewhere to stay. A number of hotels are clustered around the main bus stand, 500m from the centre of town, and there are *Retiring Rooms* at the train station.

Vasantha Vihar Lodge (☎ 20460), 141 G Car St, is a friendly place about a minute's walk from the train station. It has small, basic single/double rooms for Rs 55/80 with fan and attached shower.

Hotel Bhimas Paradise (☎ 25747; fax 25568) at Renigunta Rd, has double rooms only from Rs 400, and Rs 650 to Rs 850 for air-con. As well as the 10% tax, there's a guest charge of Rs 100.

Hotel Bhimas (☎ 25744), a block away at 42 G Car St, has rooms for Rs 75/250 and doubles with air-con for Rs 500.

Bhimas Deluxe Hotel (☎ 25521), opposite at 34-38 G Car St, and apparently not associated with its namesakes, is a two-star hotel with air-con single/double rooms for Rs 525/625. All the rooms have attached bathroom and TV. There are good views to the hills.

Hotel Mayura (☎ 25925; fax 25911) at 209 TP Area is a three-star hotel close to the main bus stand. Rooms with attached bathroom cost Rs 450, or Rs 675/720 with air-con. There's a restaurant serving Indian and Mughlai cuisine, and some good views.

India Quality Inn Bliss (☎ 21650; fax 29514) is a new hotel with singles/doubles for Rs 375/450 for non air-con and Rs 700/850 with air-con. All have TV. There are two restaurants – a veg and nonveg, a cake shop and a bar. It's a friendly place with great views.

Hotel Guestline (☎ 28800; fax 27774), at 14-37 Karakambadi Rd, is 3.5km out of town away from the bustle. Rates are Rs 850 single to Rs 1895 for a deluxe suite. There are several restaurants offering a wide range of cuisine and a bar. As well as a swimming pool, shops and a health clinic, they offer 'special darshan assistance' (queue-jumping help) for around Rs 1000.

Tirumala There is a huge variety of accommodation, from free dormitories to upmarket apartments and cottages, on the Tirumala Hill close to the temple. It's well organised, pleasant and has all facilities, including a post office, several shopping complexes and hospital.

Most pilgrims stay in the vast *dormitories* which ring the temple – beds here are free and open to anyone. If you want to stay, check in at the Central Reception Office and you'll be allocated a bed or a room. It's best to avoid weekends when the place becomes outrageously crowded.

Guesthouses and *cottages* range from Rs 250 for a suite to Rs 6500 for an entire guesthouse. Accommodation in these may be organised through the Central Reception Office.

You can also make advance (up to 30 days) bookings for accommodation if you wish. To do this, you must write (not phone) giving all details of your requirements and including a bank draft for Rs 100 to the Asst Executive Officer (Reception-I), TTD, Tirumala 517 504. However in the busy seasons there are no reservations. It's first come, first served.

Places to Eat

Tirupathi A good vegetarian restaurant called *Lakshmi Narayana Bhavan* is opposite the main bus stand. The *Bhimas Hotel* also has a good vegetarian restaurant, including

ANDHRA PRADESH

an air-con dining hall. The ***Bhimas Deluxe Hotel's*** popular basement restaurant serves both northern Indian and southern Indian cuisine until late at night – the Kashmiri naan here is an extravagance to behold.

Tirumala Huge ***dining halls*** serve thousands of free meals daily to keep the pilgrims happy. Other than that, there are numerous very good restaurants serving vegetarian meals. The service is amazingly quick given the numbers to be fed. It's all very easy and very pleasant.

Getting There & Away

It's possible to visit Tirupathi on a long day trip from Chennai, but staying overnight makes it far less rushed. If travelling by bus or train, it's possible to purchase 'link tickets' which cover the transport to Tirupathi and then up the mountain to Tirumala. These can save considerable time and confusion once you arrive.

Air The Indian Airlines office (☎ 22349) is in the Hotel Vishnupriya complex, opposite the main bus stand in Tirupathi. Flights come from Chennai (Tuesday, Thursday, Saturday for Rs 1015) and Hyderabad (Tuesday, Thursday, Sunday for Rs 2180).

Bus Tamil Nadu's state bus company has express buses (route Nos 802, 848, 883 and 899) from the state express terminus in Chennai from 5.15 am. There are eight services daily. Ordinary buses are more frequent but much slower. The express buses take about four hours to do the 150km trip, cost Rs 35 and can be booked in advance in Chennai.

To Chennai, there are express buses from Tirupathi's main bus stand every 20 minutes from 2.30 am.

Buses to Hyderabad (12 hours, Rs 175) leave in the late afternoon and evening. There are hourly buses to Vijayawada (Rs 130) as well as plenty of services to Vellore (2½ hours, Rs 175) in neighbouring Tamil Nadu and most other major towns in Andhra Pradesh and Tamil Nadu.

Train Tirupathi is well served by express trains. There are three trains daily to Chennai (147km, three hours) which cost Rs 66/200 in 2nd/1st class.

The daily *Venkatadri Express* runs to Secunderabad (741km, 17½ hours, Rs 191/696 in 2nd/1st class) and there are three daily express trains to Vijayawada (389km, nine hours, Rs 117/427). There's also an express train to Madurai (663km, 18 hours, Rs 175/632) via Vellore, Chidambaram and Tiruchirappalli, as well as a twice weekly service to Mumbai (1132km, 31 hours, Rs 242/1183).

Getting Around

Bus Tirumala Link buses operate from two bus stands in Tirupathi: the main bus stand which is about 500m from the centre of town and the Tirumala bus stand near the train station. The 20km trip takes 45 minutes and costs Rs 10/20 one way/return on an ordinary bus, or Rs 15/30 on an 'express' bus.

To get on a bus in either Tirupathi or Tirumala, you usually have to go through a system of crowd-control wire cages which are definitely not for the claustrophobic. At busy times (weekends and festivals), it can take up to two hours to file through the cages and get onto a bus. If you're staying in Tirupathi, it's worth buying a return ticket which saves you some queuing time in the cages at the top of the hill. You can avoid going through the cages at Tirupathi by catching a bus from the main bus stand (where there are no cages), but if you decide to leave from the Tirumala bus stand near Tirupathi train station, you will have to go through them.

Finding the queue for the buses at the Tirumala bus stand in Tirupathi can also be a task. You must walk through a choultry to reach the cages and ticket office – the choultry is about 200m from the entry to Tirupathi train station (turn to the right as you exit the station) opposite the bottom of the footbridge over the train line.

The one-way road to Tirumala winds precariously upwards and the bus drivers have perfected the art of maniacal driving. The road they drive down is the old one and is very narrow and winding, but this will change because it's undergoing renovations. It has 57 hairpin bends, which means 57 adrenaline rushes for you as the bus hurtles down – the whole experience is total lunacy.

Taxi If you're in a hurry, or don't like the cages, there are share taxis available all the time. Seats cost around Rs 40, depending on demand. A taxi all to yourself costs about Rs 250 one way.

Walking You can walk with the pilgrims up a very pleasant 15km path. It takes between four to six hours depending on your pace. You can deposit your luggage at the toll gate at Alipiri near the huge Hanuman statue. It will be transported free of charge to the Reception Centre. It's best to walk in the evening when it's cooler, but there are several rest points protected from the sun along the way, and even a canteen.

AROUND TIRUMALA & TIRUPATHI
Around Tirumala there are several other temples as well as naturally occurring sites. All are linked with mythologies of deities, entities and their myriad manifestations.

Sila Thoranam
This rock formation, just a couple of kilometres up the hill from the temple, is one of only three similar structures in the world and the only one of its kind in Asia. Geologists date the arch structure (8m wide by 3m high) at 1.5 million years. For devotees it is the place where the deity came to earth. Behind the arch are rock impressions of a foot and wheel. The foot, they believe, belongs to Vishnu. The wheel is one of his identifying features.

There is no transport up to the arch, but it's easy to walk, or you can take a taxi and include Narayanagiri and Dharmagiri. Depending on waiting time it will cost from Rs 200 to Rs 300 for all three sites.

Narayanagiri
The road from Sila Thoranam leads up hill

to the highest point on Tirumala. From here you can see stunning views over the surrounding areas. A side road takes you to **Dharmagiri**, where the School for the Study of Vedic Sciences is located.

Chandragiri
Some 12km west of Tirupathi, Chandragiri was an important Vijayanagar capital from the late 15th to 17th centuries. There is a fort complex here which consists of the fort itself with palaces and temples. The palaces, in particular, are impressive with their towers, arcades and verandahs. They provide another good example of Vijayanagar architecture. Buses for Chandragiri depart from the Tirupathi bus stand every 10 minutes. Then there's a 20 minute walk to the ruins or you can take a rickshaw (cycle or auto). There's a small museum; entry costs Rs 2, and Rs 25 for video cameras (closed Friday).

SRI KALAHASTI
Sri Kalahasteeswara Temple
Some 36km east of Tirupathi the Sri Kalahasti Temple derives its name from the legend which relates how three animals, a snake (sri), a spider (kala) and an elephant (hasti) all worshipped the deity, Shiva. Here Shiva is known as Sri Kalahasteeswara and the female deity is Sri Gnana Prasoonambika. The temple is linked to four others which together honour Shiva as one of the elements. Here the element is air or wind. Symbolising this, within the inner shrine, just beside the lingam, one flame flickers continually.

Some 10m below the temple there is a small shrine to the elephant god, Ganesh. The narrow staircase and hazardous entrance are suggestive of one of this deity's aspects – god of obstacles. Devotees believe that Ganesh dispenses particularly auspicious blessings from this shrine because of the difficulties endured to get there.

Sri Kalahasti may be visited as a day trip from Tirupathi or Chennai. If you wish to stay, accommodation from Rs 75 to Rs 250 is available through the temple administration. Regular buses run here from Tirupathi.

ANDHRA PRADESH

From Chennai catch bus No 200 to Tirupathi which goes via Sri Kalahasti.

Kalamkari Drawing

Sri Kalahasti is also noted for the art form known as kalamkari. Artists create designs by drawing figures onto cotton and applying vegetable dyes of various colours. Only white, washable material may be used. To enhance the images, the material is soaked in a mixture of *myrabalam* (resin) and cow's milk for one hour. A sharpened bamboo stick is used like a pen and dipped into a mixture of fermented *jaggery* (palm sugar) and water to apply the figures to the cloth. Alum is then brushed onto those sections of the cloth where colour is to be allotted. The cloth is placed in a solution which reacts to the alum resulting in colour on the material.

Various processes are employed to obtain the different effects. These include the use of cow dung, ground seeds, plants and flowers. The cloth is regularly washed in the river to remove dust and surplus colour. River water is preferred due to its flow and its mineral content.

Kalamkari is an ancient art, practised in South India over the centuries to produce aesthetic works for temples and royalty. The works, depicting flowers and plants, birds and animals, were bordered with rich patterns. The artists of Sri Kalahasti however, usually represent stories from the *Mahabharata* and the *Ramayana*. It was also important in trade to foreign countries including Indonesia and Britain.

In Sri Kalahasti, under the auspices of the All India Handicrafts Board, the art was revived in the late 1950s when a training centre was established. Whilst some places have adopted chemical dyes, the Sri Kalahasti artists retain the ancient methods and ingredients and continue to use vegetable dyes.

Visitors may meet the artists and see them at work at Sri Vijayalakshmi Fine Kalamkari Arts, 15/622 BP Agraharam, Sri Kalahasti (☎ 08578-62228). The work from the artists of this small workshop is highly regarded and has received awards from the Victoria Technical Institute in Chennai.

AROUND SRI KALAHASTI

On the way to Sri Kalahasti from Chennai there's the chance for interesting outdoor activities at the **Pulicat Bird Sanctuary** and in the hills near **Varadayyapaliyam**. See details in the Around Chennai section in the Chennai Chapter.

PUTTAPARTHI
Tel Area Code: 08555

Prasanthi Nilayam, the main ashram of Sri Sathya Sai Baba, is in the south-western corner of Andhra Pradesh at Puttaparthi. Sai Baba's followers were once predominantly Indian and include former Prime Minister Narasimha Rao. Now Sai Baba also has thousands of western devotees, among them the founder of the Hard Rock Cafe franchise.

Sai Baba was born Sathyanarayana in the village of Puttaparthi on 23 November 1926. From a young age, he is reputed to have shown concern for his fellow human beings and to have performed numerous miracles. Over time his message of service to others has become very popular, swelling his followers to perhaps millions. Some 40 years ago he established the ashram, known as the **Abode of Highest Peace**, at Puttaparthi. Sai Baba spends most of the year here but sometimes moves to Whitefields Ashram near Bangalore in neighbouring Karnataka or Kodaikanal in Tamil Nadu during the hot, dry season.

There is no doubting the many significant benefits from the guru's teachings of administering to others. The ashram now sponsors numerous services. Medical staff work voluntarily at a huge, state-of-the-art hospital which treats thousands of people all for free. Schools, a university, a planetarium and sports grounds all comprise the charitable services.

Inspired by the Baba message, devotees around the world have changed their lives dramatically, undertaking all manner of charitable work for the benefit of others. And people of different ethnicities, at war in their home countries, come together at the ashram in peace and understanding.

For devotees, ashram life and its codes

will no doubt be familiar. For aspiring devotees and newcomers, the ashram may seem like a military camp, where the 'commandants' continually issue orders to bring recruits into line. Devotees excuse such behaviour as a challenge to the ego and therefore a useful strategy. Many settle into routine, acceding to 'Baba's will'. Some people however never learn (or refuse to succumb) and therefore constantly attract the wrath of the commandants.

For newcomers, the following information may facilitate an ashram stay:

- On arrival at the ashram all visitors must register. During popular times such as Christmas, this process can take many hours.
- Passports must be surrendered by first-time visitors and will be returned after attendance at the orientation lecture.
- Forms, detailing name, age, education, employment are completed with absolute precision, in quadruplicate.
- Passport photos must be presented. You can get these from several booths in the village opposite the ashram and it's best to have them before you register. It saves time and confusion.
- When registration is completed you join the queue at the Public Relations Office where accommodation is allocated.
- Unless married, men and women stay in separate accommodation.
- All men and women are separated for meals, lectures and darshan.
- Separate sex queues exist for purchasing meal tickets.
- Language is simple – the words Sai Ram are used as greetings, apologies, acknowledgement, but most of the time silence is preferred.
- Lights must be out by 9 pm and you will be commanded to comply if you are late.
- Women are expected to wear a shawl to darshan.
- There is electronic security surveillance at darshan.

Places to Stay

Most people prefer to stay at the ashram. It's like a small village with all amenities. Ashram accommodation, although basic, is well maintained, comfortable and very reasonable. Inquiries as to availability can be made (☎ 08555/87583) but advance bookings are not taken. However there is usually ample accommodation. Meal costs are negligible, starting from Rs 2 for breakfast of tiffin.

With the numbers visiting the ashram ever growing, more accommodation is becoming available outside, mainly in the form of small pilgrim lodges and larger apartment developments. Most of these places are run by Sai Baba devotees and rules, similar to those in the ashram, apply.

The chief area for accommodation outside the ashram is Main Rd. Almost every building is 'deluxe accommodation' and almost all are called 'Sai Baba'. As with the name and description, the type does not vary.

Hotel Sai Sree Nivas (Main Rd), is typical of outside accommodation. It's basic with singles/doubles with attached bathroom for Rs 150/300. Prices fluctuate depending on demand. It's very similar to the ashram, at double the price.

Sri Sathya Sai Village (☎ *044 459951; fax 489-6069)*, 2km from the ashram on the road to the airport, is a newly constructed village with all facilities and a multicuisine restaurant. Various accommodation plans are available ranging from Rs 650 (double room only) to Rs 1000 (double room including breakfast and two major meals). Triple and quadruple rooms are also available. All rooms have air-con.

Places to Eat

Big Pizza – Long Noodles Restaurant, in the Sai Jyothi Complex, just off Chitravanthi Rd has reasonable meals starting at omelettes for Rs 24 and noodles for Rs 26.

Sai Bestways has every preparation of paneer imaginable for about Rs 35. Breads range from Rs 5 to Rs 30, and dal Rs 15.

Shopping

Whilst the ashram provides for the spiritual needs of the devotees, just outside a thriving community caters for material needs. Photos (required by the ashram), Indian dress (which seems to be an immediate requirement for all westerners), mattresses, gifts, crafts, medicinal supplies and fruits, are all available. And there's also a willing army of porters to transport the consumerables back to the ashram. Books about Sai Baba are available in the ashram. There's a wider variety outside at Prasanthi Sai Book Sellers (☎ 87525), Main Rd. They also sell music tapes.

Getting There & Away
Puttaparthi is most easily reached from Bangalore (see that section in the Karnataka chapter for details). From Hyderabad, catch the train to Dharmavaram from where buses depart regularly for Puttaparthi. If you're coming from Chennai the overnight 'high-tech' bus handles the bumpy ride. It leaves Parry's Corner at 7 pm each day and takes 11 hours for Rs 175. Indian Airlines flies to Puttaparthi from both Chennai (Wednesday and Sunday, US$55) and Mumbai (Monday and Thursday, US$110).

Getting Around
At the time of writing several changes were occurring in Puttaparthi. The ashram entrance and main bus station were being relocated. However, Puttaparthi is a well organised town and you should have no trouble finding you way. It's small and you can walk around easily. It's pleasant to amble; you may even get to meet Sai Gita (Sai Baba's elephant) on her daily stroll. However if you want to travel further afield the large bus station has regular buses to surrounding areas such as Dharmavaram and Hindupur. The timetable is listed in Telugu, Hindi and English. There are numerous auto-rickshaws and cars can be hired from travel agencies, such as Sri Sai Ravitheja (☎ 87429) opposite the ashram on Main Rd

AROUND PUTTAPARTHI
There are some interesting sites near Puttaparthi which may be visited in day trips, or on the way to or from Bangalore or Hyderabad.

Penukonda
This small dusty town 27km south-east from Puttaparthi has played an important role in the history of the region and contains many significant sites. For a short period in the 16th

century this town became the headquarters of the Aravidu rulers, following the demise of the Vijayanagars. In the 17th century the city was captured by the Qutb Shahis, then the Mughals and then the Marathas.

As you approach the town from the north, you can see vestiges of the ancient fort along the hills. Within the ancient city walls are a number of temples as well as the extensive remains of the **Sher Shah Mosque**. The mosque was built during the Qutb Shahi occupation and, despite the scattered ruins, it continues to function as a place of prayer. Gravestones are positioned throughout the complex. For many people (and goats) the precinct functions as a home, with the residents recumbent on top of the graves in somewhat similar poses as those beneath them. Visitors are welcomed but women are not permitted in the prayer areas. A headcovering is mandatory.

Make your departure a quick one. The above-ground bodies, so immobile on your arrival, suddenly become amazingly invigorated. You may be besieged by numerous and persistent beggars.

At the northern entrance of the city wall a 5m-high sculpted image of Hanuman stands proudly dressed in deep orange silk. Appropriately, monkeys (the real variety) amble about near their deity.

To see the temples in the town arrive early. They are closed from 10 am to 5 pm.

Penukonda has little in the way of tourist facilities. There is no tourist office or information. There are several small places for drinks and snacks but no accommodation. Buses leave from Puttaparthi. From Bangalore you can take a train. A popular stopping place for buses and trucks is the *Al Baba Restaurant* at Thimmapuram 500m from the 'Puttaparthi cross' (turnoff).

Lepakshi
If you're travelling between Puttaparthi and Bangalore, it's well worth detouring to the **Veerbhadra Temple** (also known as Virbhadra) at Lepakshi. The road takes you through a remarkable landscape in which hills of boulders rise out of the ground and

Temple of the Dancing Gods

According to legend, Lepakshi got its name when Ravana passed by this place and injured a bird after stealing Sita from her husband Rama. Rama, in pursuit of his wife, arrived at this spot and seeing the injured bird, called to it 'lepakshi', meaning 'bird get up', hence the name of the town.

The temple at Lepakshi is dedicated to Veerbhadra – Shiva in his ferocious form. Such divine ferocity, said to cast out ignorance, must have exerted its power at Lepakshi. Certainly there's no sign of ignorance here, just intricately carved beauty.

Constructed on two uneven concentric circles and on three different levels, the temple is entered through a small gopuram. To the left of the entrance inscriptions note the donors and the amounts of their donations from the time of construction in 1538. Pilgrim choultries line the wall, flanked by *yalis*, the mythical lions.

At the small structure honouring the goddess, huge meal plates – food containers for offerings – are sculpted into the ground. Beneath her shrine stands a more recent statue of the monkey god, Hanuman, now vying with the goddess for her acclaim. A huge right footprint of the celebrated Sita of the *Ramayana* is imprinted into the stone. The left foot is on the Penukonda Hill some 60km away. Water trickles into the foot; locals believe its source is a natural spring.

On a level beyond the foot is the Kalyana Mandapam, the marriage hall which depicts the union of Parvati and Shiva. At the entrance is a statue of Brahma, with his five heads and 10 hands, welcoming the wedding guests. Among them are numerous gods and saints including Menaka Devi and Parvat Raja (Parvati's parents), Indra the god of air, and Agni the god of fire. All stand exquisitely sculptured, exemplifying proud and happy guests. Beyond them the pandit blesses the couple, who stand together, Shiva holding Parvati's hand.

To the side of the marriage hall a gigantic Ganesh is carved into the rock. As is the custom, worshippers always pay homage to him, the remover of obstacles, before they proceed with further worship. Small sculptures are associated with the Kalahasti Temple, Shiva's temple on the eastern side of Andhra Pradesh. Beyond these a huge cobra impressively rears each of its seven heads around the lingam, as it returns the look of the Nandi (Shiva's vehicle – a bull) 500m away.

In the Natya Mandapam, the dance hall of 70 stone pillars, the deities and other heavenly beings play music and dance, a common activity in temples, but one that is particularly emphasised here.

Shiva dances whilst Parvati watches. Brahma beats the drum, Chandra the moon god plucks the veena and Suriya the sun god plays the flute. Cymbals, harmonium, drums and veena play as the dancers move under a 100-petalled flower canopy. Ceiling paintings depict the main sculptors, Jakana and Ampana. Next to them, seven women represent the seven days of preparation Parvati underwent prior to her wedding. A third shows Arjuna and Shiva fighting for a pig.

In the main temple, that of Veerbhadra, the perfect man and woman are depicted: he must have a long nose, broad chest, long hands, small diaphragm and flat feet, she must have a long nose equal in size to the width of her forehead, and the distance from her nose to chin. Her diaphragm must be small, her fingers and wrists round and her feet must be arched when walking.

In the area of the main shrine to Shiva, there are eight others including those dedicated to Parvati (as Badra Kali), Hanuman and Rama. Although the temple was never completed, its exquisite work gives a sense of overall balance and completion.

ANDHRA PRADESH

stand like ancient ruins, creating a curious horizon of awesome shapes. Leave yourself plenty of time for the bus or car to negotiate the herds of goats, buffaloes and donkeys. In Lepakshi it's greener and cooler.

At the entrance to the town sits the huge,

monolithic Nandi (the bull that is Shiva's vehicle). At 4½m high and 8½m long it is India's largest. You won't miss it. It faces the seven headed cobra, an equally huge sculpture at the temple.

Just 500m on you will come to the temple. (See the 'Temple of the Dancing Gods' boxed text for details.) Each year in February/March pilgrims flock to this temple for Sivaratri, the festival which particularly honours Shiva. Leave yourself plenty of time to enjoy the splendour of this temple. Information booklets in Hindi and Telugu are available at the entrance. There is also a very knowledgeable English speaking guide.

The temple is open every day. Buses leave from Puttaparthi. You can also get regular buses from Hindupur train station and Anantapur. Lepakshi is fast developing as a tourist destination and, as a consequence, places to stay are becoming more readily available. Check first for the latest information. Local people recommend the Hindupur Tourism Complex, or you can stay in Lepakshi itself at the *Abhya Griha Resthouse* run by the tourist office, but you have to be lucky to find it open. There are numerous places for snacks and drinks.

Dharmavaram

Some 40km north of Puttaparthi Dharmavaram is referred to as the **silk town** of Andhra Pradesh. On arrival there is little evidence of its industry and its importance to the state. However down its narrow lanes and within its small buildings, villagers transform thousands of small cocoons into colourful silk thread, which they then weave into lavish saris.

Sacks of cocoons are heaved into town on bullock carts. Almost every day between 11 am to 2 pm you can see the delivery and auction at the government supervised Silk Exchange Depot. From here the cocoons are taken and boiled, each forced to surrender its 800m of delicate thread. The thread is then spun and dyed. Hundreds of large reels capture the yarn as it spins to a thread. It is then placed on one of the 20,000 handlooms which position the threads so carefully woven by the villagers.

It takes one person one week to weave a sari. At this rate each person creates around five saris a month. Of the 400,000 population one quarter is employed in the silk industry. The silks of Dharmavaram are popular throughout India, but the industry has recently received a welcome boost with large orders for sarongs and shawls for the Sai Baba community.

Dharmavaram also has two temples, the **Lakshmi Chennakesavaswamy Shrine** in the Vijayanagar style and the **Ramalingeswara Temple** noted for its architecture and musical pillars.

To get to Dharmavaram, take the bus from the Puttaparthi bus stand. The bus stand at Dharmavaram is a few metres past the Silk Exchange Depot. After you've seen the activities at the depot ask for instructions to see the spinning and weaving. It all happens a few kilometres away – probably too far to walk, but an auto-rickshaw will take you there. Some travellers find that sharing a car from Puttaparthi is economical and enables them to see the sites quite easily. There's nowhere to stay in Dharmavaram, but there are places for drinks and snacks.

Kerala

Kerala, the land of green magic, is a narrow, fertile strip on the south-west coast of India, sandwiched between the Lakshadweep Sea and the Western Ghats. The landscape is dominated by rice fields, mango and cashew-nut trees and, above all, coconut palms. The Western Ghats, with their dense tropical forests, misty peaks, extensive ridges and ravines, have sheltered Kerala from mainland invaders and encouraged maritime contact with the outside world.

HISTORY

The early history of Kerala is documented in ancient Tamil scripts and Hindu mythology. According to legend Parasu Rama, an incarnation of Vishnu, threw his weapon from Kanyakumari across the sea. The sea subsequently receded to the point where the weapon landed, and the land of Kerala was born.

The kingdom of the Cheras ruled much of present-day Kerala up until the early Middle Ages. Its fortunes waxed and waned as it competed with empires, kingdoms and small fiefdoms for territory and trade.

People have been sailing to Kerala in search of spices, sandalwood and ivory for at least 2000 years. Long before Vasco da Gama led the Portuguese to India, the coast had been known to the Phoenicians, then the Romans, and later the Arabs and Chinese. The Arabs initially controlled the shipment of spices to Europe, which motivated the Portuguese to find a sea route to India to break the Arab monopoly. In those days (late 15th century to the 16th century) Kerala was not only a spice centre in its own right, but a transhipment point for spices from the Moluccas. And it was through Kerala that Chinese products and ideas found their way to the west. Even today, Chinese-style fishing nets are widely used.

Such contact with people from around the world has resulted in an intriguing blend of cultures and has given Malayalis (natives of

KERALA AT A GLANCE

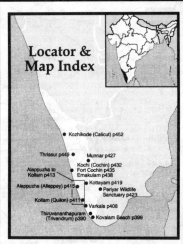

Locator & Map Index

Kozhikode (Calicut) p452

Thrissur p449 • • Munnar p427
Alappuzha to • Kochi (Cochin) p432
Kollam p413 • Fort Cochin p435
Ernakulam p438
Alappuzha (Alleppey) p415 • • Kottayam p419
• Periyar Wildlife
Sanctuary p423
Kollam (Quilon) p411 •
• Varkala p408
Thiruvananthapuram • • Kovalam Beach p399
(Trivandrum) p390

Population: 33 million
Area: 38,864 sq km
Capital: Thiruvananthapuram
Main Language: Malayalam
Best Time to Go: October to March

Highlights
- Exploring the backwaters aboard a *kettuvallam* (rice-barge houseboat)
- An evening of Kathakali dance theatre
- Sun, surf and seafood on the beach at Kovalam or Varkala
- An early morning jungle walk at Periyar Wildlife Sanctuary

Festivals
January – Great Elephant March, Thrissur, Alappuzha, Thiruvananthapuram
April/May – Pooram Festival,Thrissur
August/September – Onam, Statewide

Kerala) a cosmopolitan outlook, coupled with a tradition of seeking their fortunes

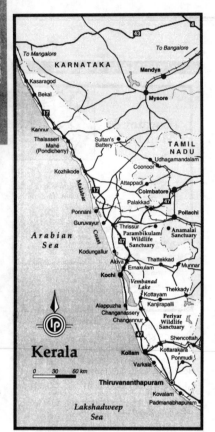

Name Changes

A number of towns and districts have been stripped of their anglicised names and given Malayalam names, but these are far from universally used. The major places affected include:

Old Name	New Name
Alleppey	Alappuzha
Calicut	Kozhikode
Cannanore	Kannur
Changanacherry	Changanassery
Cochin	Kochi
Palghat	Palakkad
Quilon	Kollam
Sultan's Battery	Suthanbatheri
Tellicherry	Thalasseri
Trichur	Thrissur
Trivandrum	Thiruvananthapuram

created in 1956 from Travancore, Cochin and Malabar. Malabar was formerly part of Madras state, while Travancore and Cochin were princely states ruled by maharajas. The maharajas of Travancore and Cochin paid considerable attention to the provision of basic services and education, and it was this early concern for public welfare which resulted in the post-Independence state being one of the most progressive, literate and highly educated in India.

Another of Kerala's distinctions was that it had one of the first freely elected communist governments in the world (elected in 1957). Communists have been in and out of office in Kerala ever since.

The relatively equitable distribution of land and income, found rarely to the same degree elsewhere in India, is the direct result of successive communist governments in the state. Kerala's progressive social policies have had other benefits: infant mortality in Kerala is the lowest in India, and the literacy rate of around 90% is the highest in the country.

Perhaps more than anywhere else in India, getting around Kerala can be half the fun, particularly on the backwater trips along the coastal lagoons. Even an agonisingly slow train trip can be a restful experience when

elsewhere in India or overseas. You can generally find a Malayali in any nook or cranny of the world.

When Vasco da Gama and his Portuguese fleet arrived on the Malabar Coast in 1498 the Zamorin of Calicut had established a wealthy kingdom based on the spice trade. Da Gama's arrival heralded an era of European contact with Kerala as Portuguese, Dutch and English interests fought the Arab traders and then each other for control of the spice trade.

The present-day state of Kerala was

Kerala's Religions

The population of Kerala is roughly 60% Hindu, 20% Muslim and 20% Christian. Hindus are mainly concentrated in southern Kerala, around Thiruvananthapuram, although Muslims are also a prominent and vocal component of the population in this area. The main Muslim area is in the northern part of the state, particularly around Kozhikode (Calicut).

Kerala's main Christian area is in the central part of the state, around Kochi and Kottayam. Christianity was established here earlier than almost anywhere else in the world. In 52 AD, St Thomas the Apostle, or 'Doubting Thomas', is said to have landed on the Malabar Coast near Cranganore (now Kodungallur), where a church with carved Hindu-style columns supposedly dates from the 4th century AD. There have been Syrian Christians in Kerala since at least 190 AD, and a visitor at that time reported seeing a Hebrew copy of the gospel of St Matthew. There are 16th century Syrian churches in Kottayam. When the Portuguese arrived here 500 years ago, they were more than a little surprised to find Christianity already established along the Malabar Coast, and more than a little annoyed that these Christians had never heard of the Pope.

---

you're in Kerala – watching the canals and palm trees cruising past the open windows of your carriage at 20km/h can bring on a state of near-spiritual inertia.

The state also has some of the best and most picturesque beaches in India: Kovalam, a little south of the capital Thiruvananthapuram (Trivandrum), is one of the most popular beaches with travellers. The smaller resort at Varkala Beach is less developed, but heading in the same direction as Kovalam – visit while it's still pleasantly understated.

Best of all, Kerala has an easy-going, relaxed atmosphere unlike the bustle you find elsewhere in India.

Southern Kerala

THIRUVANANTHAPURAM (Trivandrum)
Pop: 854,000 Tel Area Code: 0471

Built over seven hills, Thiruvananthapuram (City of the Sacred Serpent) is as noisy, polluted and bustling as any other Indian city – many travellers find it a hot, noisy shock after a few days of relative peace and quiet on the beaches of Kovalam or Varkala. Away from the busy centre, Thiruvananthapuram has managed to retain some of the

ambience characteristic of old Kerala: red-tiled roofs, narrow winding lanes, etc – but this link to a more easy-going past is disappearing fast. The overwhelming image is of frenetic activity.

Political and religious tensions are always simmering in this educated but poor populace. In the words of a cynical local, 'the only time we all get together is for clashes'. Political slogans, emblems and flags – especially those of the Communist and Muslim parties – are a notable feature of the urban landscape.

There are only a few 'sights' within the city, which can easily be seen in one or two days, so it makes sense to base yourself at Kovalam Beach, just 16km south, where you can enjoy a sea breeze and a cooling swim, and make short visits to the capital.

Phone Number Change
Phone numbers beginning with 6 in Thiruvananthapuram have changed. Replace the 6 with 32 for these numbers.

Orientation
Most of the services and places of interest are on or very close to MG Rd, which runs north-south, from the museums and zoo to the Sri Padmanabhaswamy Temple.

The Kerala State Road Transport Corporation (KSRTC) long-distance bus stand, train station, Tourist Reception Centre and many of the budget hotels are all close together, while the municipal bus stand is 10 minutes walk south, close to the temple. It's three to 4km from the southern cluster of hotels and transport facilities to Museum Rd, at the northern end of MG Rd. The large Secretariat building, halfway along MG Rd, is a handy landmark.

Information

Tourist Offices There's a handy though basic tourist information desk at the airport and an occasionally operating accommodation booking service for Thiruvananthapuram and Kovalam (don't count on it).

The Tourist Reception Centre (☎ 330031) in front of the KTDC Chaithram Hotel, near the train station and long-distance bus stand, is essentially there to promote KTDC guided tours (see Organised Tours later in this section). The Tourist Facilitation Centre (☎ 61132) on Museum Rd, opposite the museum and zoo, has a colourful map, but it can handle only the most basic of inquiries.

Money Travellers cheques can be cashed and credit card cash advances made at the Canara Bank near the South Park Hotel and at the Bank of India counter in the lobby of the Hotel Chaitram. Hours are 10 am to 2 pm Monday to Friday and 10 am to noon Saturday.

Post & Communications The main post office is tucked away down a small side street off MG Rd, about 10 minutes walk from the Central Station Rd area. Most of the counters, including poste restante, are open Monday to Saturday from 8 am to 8 pm.

The Central Telegraph Office, at the midpoint of MG Rd, is 20 minutes walk from either Museum Rd or Central Station Rd. The office is open 24 hours. There are numerous STD/ISD counters and kiosks around town.

Visa Extensions The office of the Commissioner of Police (☎ 60486) on Residency

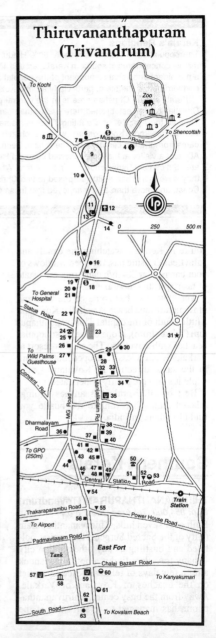

Thiruvananthapuram (Trivandrum)

Rd issues visa extensions, but the process takes four days to a week, and it's not guaranteed that an extension will be approved in all cases. You don't have to leave your passport, and it speeds things up if you give a Thiruvananthapuram hotel address rather than somewhere in Kovalam. The office is open every day from 10 am to 5 pm except Sunday.

Bookshops & Libraries The British Library (☎ 68716), in the YMCA grounds near the Secretariat building, is officially only open to members, but visitors are made to feel welcome. It has three day old British newspapers and a variety of magazines. The library is open Tuesday to Saturday from 11 am to 7 pm. Higginbothams bookshop is on MG Rd and the Continental Book Company is nearby. Though tiny, the handy bookshop

in the lobby of the Hotel Chaithram has a good range of books on Kerala and also sells a basic map.

Medical Services The General Hospital (☎ 443870) is west of MG Rd, about 1km along Statue Rd.

Sri Padmanabhaswamy Temple
Thiruvananthapuram's most interesting temple is open to Hindus only, and even they must wear a dhoti or sari. Still, it's worth visiting – even if you're just passing through town – to see the temple's seven storey carved *gopuram* (gateway tower) reflected in the nearby sacred tank. Constructed in the Dravidian style by the maharaja of Travancore in 1733, the temple is dedicated to Vishnu, who reclines on the sacred serpent, Ananda, which gives Thiruvananthapuram

its name. The temple's image of the reclining Vishnu is over 18 feet long and is viewed in three sections through three doors. A lotus grows from Vishnu's navel and Brahma resides in the lotus symbolising the new age.

In early November some of the temple's images, including that of Sri Padmanabha, are taken to Shanghumugham Beach for ritual bathing. the elaborate procession to the Arabian Sea is escorted by members of the Travancore royal family.

Puthe Maliga Palace Museum

The Puthe Maliga Palace Museum, adjacent to the temple, is housed in several wings of the 200 year old palace of the maharajas of Travancore. Notable mostly for its wonderful Keralan architecture, the museum also offers a rare glimpse into the formal and private lives of one of India's most celebrated royal families. It took 5000 workers four years to complete and the Maharaja only lived there for one year! Many of the exhibits are chattels reflecting the spice trade with China and Europe. There are two ornate thrones, one made entirely of Bohemian crystal.

It's open every day except Monday from 8.30 am to 12.30 pm and from 3 to 5.30 pm; entry is Rs 10, and use of a camera in the palace grounds is Rs 15, but note that photography is not permitted within the building. The palace hosts a classical music festival from 27 January to 3 February; tickets for the festival can be purchased at the museum. The musicians perform under the glow of oil lamps on the veranda – don't forget the mosquito repellent.

Other Museums, Gallery & Zoo

The zoo and a collection of museums are in a park in the north of the city. The museums are open Tuesday to Sunday from 10 am to 4.45 pm (from 1 pm on Wednesday). A single Rs 5 entry ticket covers all the museums and is obtainable from the Natural History Museum.

Housed in a whimsical, decaying, Keralan-style building dating from 1880, the **Napier Museum** has an eclectic display of bronzes, historical and contemporary ornaments, temple carts, ivory carvings and life-size figures of Kathakali dancers in full costume.

The **Natural History Museum** has a rudimentary ethnographic collection as well as an interesting replica of a *tharawad* – a traditional wooden residence of the Nair warrior family/caste.

The **Sri Chitra Art Gallery** has paintings of the Rajput, Mughal and Tanjore schools, together with works from China, Tibet, Japan and Bali. There are also many modern Indian paintings, including works by Ravi Varma, Svetoslav and Nicholas Roerich.

Hindus Only

Despite Kerala's high education standards and its religious diversity, almost every Hindu temple in the state hangs out the 'No Entry' sign for non-Hindus. Don't feel left out – there's at least one temple in the state which bans many Hindus as well. Hindu or not, women between the age of 10 and 50 are not allowed in the Sabarimala Temple in central Kerala. Why? Because women of menstrual age could 'defile' the temple.

In late 1994 the temple and the state government found themselves in a tricky situation when an investigation was launched into complaints by Sabarimala pilgrims about the standard of facilities at the temple. Controversy erupted when it was discovered that the Pathanamthitta District Collector who was instructed to visit the temple to investigate the complaints was a 42-year-old woman. The state's high court, which in 1990 had ruled that it was OK to ban women of menstrual age, hurriedly ruled that she could visit the temple, but only on her official duties – worshipping while in the temple was strictly forbidden! Although the case has focused attention on this clear example of discrimination in a supposedly even-handed state, the rule continues. Lower caste people were also banned from temples not so many years ago.

The **Zoological Gardens** are among the best designed in Asia – set among woodland, lakes and well maintained lawns – but some of the animal enclosures (and their inhabitants) are miserable. The zoo is open Tuesday to Saturday from 9 am to 5.15 pm. Entry is Rs 4 and there's an additional Rs 5 charge for a camera or Rs 250 for a video camera.

The **Science & Technology Museum** and **Planetarium**, about 100m west of the Mascot Hotel, cater mostly to high-school science students. The museum is open from 10 am to 5 pm daily and entry is Rs 2. The planetarium (☎ 446976) has 40 minute shows in English at noon daily (Rs 10) except Monday, when it's closed.

CVN Kalari Sangham

Located in East Fort, near the Sri Padmanabhaswamy Temple, is a small but remarkable building – part training centre, part temple and part hospital. The CVN Kalari Sangham was built in 1956. Its founders played a significant role in the revival of *kalarippayat*, the traditional martial art of Kerala, believed to be the forerunner of all eastern martial arts and integral to the technical development of all other performing arts in Kerala, including Kathakali (see the colour section 'Dancing for the Gods' on pages 64-80).

Individuals and small groups can view the training sessions and exercises for free between 6.30 am and 8.30 to 9 am every morning except Sunday, when it's closed. Ayurvedic diagnosis and treatment for ailments (especially soft tissue injuries) is available from 10 am to 1 pm and 5 to 7.30 pm Monday to Saturday, and 10 am to 1 pm on Sunday.

If you wish to join the combatants in the pit you must sign up for a course (three month minimum) at Rs 500 per month. You'll need to arrange your own accommodation, meals and transport.

Ganapathy Temple

Also in East Fort is the Ganapathy Temple, the largest of several temples dedicated to Ganesh in the city. It is worth a visit in the early morning before the traffic completely

dominates the senses. The sound of temple bells, the ritual smashing of coconuts and the smell of incense are magical, but all too fleeting as the chaos on MG Rd gets into full swing.

Organised Tours

The KTDC operates a variety of tours in the city and further afield. They all depart from the Tourist Reception Centre opposite the train station.

The daily Thiruvananthapuram city tour departs at 8 am, returns at 7 pm, and costs Rs 94 (child Rs 50). The tour visits the Sri Padmanabhaswamy Temple, the Napier Museum, art gallery, zoo, Veli Lagoon, an aquarium, and Kovalam Beach. This tour is of little interest to non-Hindu visitors since the temple is off limits and there is little fascination in gawping at fellow travellers sunbathing on Kovalam Beach. On Monday, when the museums and zoo are closed, the tour includes Neyyar Dam (see Around Thiruvananthapuram later in this chapter).

For those with less stamina there is a rather uninteresting half day tour (Rs 63) which leaves at 1 pm and includes Veli Lagoon and Kovalam Beach. On Wednesday this tour departs at 2 pm and includes the zoo, museum and art gallery, and Kovalam Beach.

The daily Kanyakumari (Cape Comorin) tour departs at 7.30 am, returns at 9 pm, and costs Rs 178 (child Rs 50). It includes Padmanabhapuram Palace (except on Monday) and Kanyakumari, and is good value if you want to avoid public buses or staying overnight in Kanyakumari. There's also a daily tour to the Ponmudi hill resort (see under Around Thiruvananthapuram) which departs at 7.45 am, returns at 7 pm, and costs Rs 157/50.

There are other long-distance tours including destinations such as Munnar, Thekkady and Madurai, but these are generally hopelessly rushed affairs or not operating due to insufficient numbers.

Places to Stay – Budget

There are many cheap places around Central Station Rd, near the train station and KSRTC long-distance bus stand, but most of them are very basic and the road is busy and noisy. The beach at Kovalam is a far more pleasant place to stay. If you have to stay overnight in Thiruvananthapuram, the best hunting ground is Manjalikulam Rd, which runs parallel to MG Rd. Despite its central location, it's quiet and has a collection of cheap to mid-range hotels.

Pravin Tourist Home (☎ *330753)* is a cheerful if not spotless place with large singles/doubles/triples for Rs 86/150/215; tea and coffee is available.

Sundar Tourist Home (☎ *330532)* has simpler rooms for Rs 30/65 with common bath for Rs 35/75 with attached bath.

Vijai Tourist Home (☎ *331727)* is friendly but the double rooms for Rs 125 have rather dingy attached bathrooms.

Sivada Tourist Home (☎ *330320)* has non air-con singles/doubles with attached bath for Rs 80/130 and air-con rooms for Rs 200/300.

Manacaud Tourist Paradise & Hotel (☎ *327578)*, at the Central Station Rd end of Manjalikulam Rd, has large, clean rooms with attached bathroom for Rs 100/200.

Hotel Sukhvas (☎ *331967)*, next door, is OK with standard rooms for Rs 100/200 or air-con rooms for Rs 460 but the some staff are happy to point out better deals elsewhere!

Hotel Ammu (☎ *331937)*, nearby, is small and popular and has singles/doubles with attached bath from Rs 150/210, more expensive rooms with TV (Rs 225/265) or TV and air-con (Rs 415). There is a small air-con restaurant.

Nalanda Tourist Home (☎ *471864)*, south of the train line, is on busy MG Rd, but the rooms at the back are not too noisy and it's cheap at Rs 65/95 (all with attached bath).

The *YWCA Guesthouse* (☎ *446518)* is four floors up, which is a bit of a drag, and it's on MG Rd, but clean singles/doubles/family rooms with attached bath cost only Rs 150/250/300. There are not many rooms and it is often full.

The *YMCA* (☎ *330059)* is open to members only and charges Rs 35/70 or Rs 80 for a double with attached bath.

There are *Retiring Rooms*, including a dormitory, at the train station.

Places to Stay – Mid-Range

The KTDC *Hotel Chaithram* (☎ *330977, fax 331446, Central Station Rd)*, next to the KSRTC long-distance bus stand, is an efficient, modern hotel that's rarely full. Rooms cost Rs 450/550, or Rs 700/850 with air-con. The tariff includes a buffet breakfast. Facilities include a bookshop, a Bank of India branch office, a bright and friendly bar, a good air-con veg restaurant and an average nonveg restaurant. Checkout is 24 hours.

Hotel Highland (☎ *333200, fax 332645, Manjalikulam Rd)* is welcoming and has a good choice of rooms from Rs 190/230 or from Rs 440/540 with air-con. You must pay extra for a TV. There's also an air-conditioned multicuisine restaurant.

Hotel Regency (☎ *330377, fax 331696, Manjalikulam Cross Rd)* has comfortable rooms for Rs 200/350, or Rs 450/550 with air-con, all with TV and phone. There are two restaurants, but at the time of writing the rooftop one was closed. Checkout is 24 hours.

Hotel Residency Tower (☎ *331661, fax 331311, Press Rd)*, just off Manjalikulam Rd, is clean and comfortable with friendly staff. Singles/doubles cost Rs 390/590, or Rs 790/990 with air-con. It has a bar, nonveg restaurant, direct dial phones and TV.

Hotel Navaratna (☎ *331784, YMCA Rd)*, just around the corner, is a favourite of Indian business travellers. It has rooms for Rs 190/220, or Rs 450 for an air-con suite. The modern rooms have satellite TV and direct dial STD, and there's a reasonable restaurant and coffee shop.

Wild Palms Guest House (☎/fax *478992, Puthen Rd)*, off Convent Rd, offers a break from the hotel environment. Situated in a quiet backstreet, this clean and cosy guesthouse has non air-con rooms for Rs 695 and air-con rooms from Rs 1145. Tariffs include breakfast, and dinner can be arranged.

Places to Stay – Top End

With the closure of Hotel Fort Manor, at the time of writing top-end accommodation in the city centre was exceedingly tight. So make sure you have a booking and perhaps check whether the Fort Manor has re-opened.

Hotel Luciya (☎ *463443, fax 463347)* is at East Fort, close to the Sri Padmanabhaswamy Temple. It's centrally air-conditioned and has rooms from Rs 1425/1775, as well as more expensive suites, all with satellite TV and direct dial STD/ISD. There's also a bar, restaurant, coffee shop, bookshop, business centre and pool.

South Park (☎ *333333, fax 331861),* a swank, centrally air-conditioned hotel further north on MG Rd, has rooms for US$50/60 to US$95/105. It has one of the city's best restaurants, a coffee shop, a terrific cake shop and a bar.

The KTDC *Mascot Hotel* (☎ *438990, fax 437745, Museum Rd),* north of the centre, is a pleasant hotel with a gloomy design. Rooms all have air-con and start from Rs 995/1195. There's an air-con restaurant, a coffee shop, and an open-air bar and ice cream parlour near the pool.

Hotel Pankaj (☎ *464645, fax 465020, MG Rd),* opposite the government Secretariat, has central air-con and rooms from Rs 950/1300 up to Rs 1990 for a suite. There's a bar and two restaurants, one offering fine views from the top floor and a daily buffet lunch. Rooms have direct dial STD and satellite TV, and there are foreign exchange and travel desks.

Places to Eat

Maveli Cafe is a bizarre, circular Indian Coffee House with a spiralling floor, next to the KSRTC long-distance bus stand. The food is good and cheap. Watch your knees on the tables.

Indian Coffee House, midway along MG Rd, is open even if the front of the building and the road are still under construction as they were at the time of writing.

Ambika Cafe, at the junction of Central Station and Manjalikulam Rds, is a good spot for a cheap breakfast.

Prime Square, adjacent to the Ambika Cafe, has good value veg and nonveg restaurants, as well as an ice cream parlour. It's a deservedly popular lunch spot.

Asok Veg Restaurant, further north along Manjalikulum Rd, is a typically inconspicuous but good value 'meals' restaurant.

Hotel City Tower (MG Rd), near the railway bridge, is another popular lunch spot; thalis are Rs 15.

Central Station Rd has a number of vegetarian restaurants serving the usual 'meals' thalis, and there are several good, cheap vegetarian places opposite the Secretariat on MG Rd, including *Sree Arul Jyothi, New Arul Jyothi, Sri Ram Sweets* and *Ananda Bhavan.*

Rangoli is south of the railway line, on MG Rd, and has a small entrance leading to a neat and tidy air-con 'family restaurant' upstairs.

Azad Restaurant, a few doors north, is also clean, air-conditioned and good value.

There are restaurants in many of the hotels. *City Queen Restaurant,* in the Hotel Highland on Manjalikulam Rd, does good Chinese dishes and also serves Indian and western food. *Gokulum* in the Hotel Chaithram is a good air-con veg restaurant.

Mascot Hotel, Hotel Pankaj and in particular the *South Park* all have popular lunchtime buffets.

Rooftop restaurants are all the go in Thiruvananthapuram, and for good reason: from an elevated position, away from the noise and dust at street level, the city appears green and parklike.

Sandhya Restaurant, on the 5th floor of the Pankaj Hotel, has particularly fine views. The *Hotel Regency* also has a top floor restaurant.

The *Mascot* and the *Chaithram*, both KTDC hotels, have outdoor ice cream parlours. Alternatively, try the engagingly named *Snoozzer (Press Rd)*; it has air-con and is a great escape from the midday heat.

Shopping

The SMSM Institute (☎ 330298, fax 331582), YMCA Rd, is a government sponsored handicrafts outlet with the usual sandalwood carvings, textiles and bronzes, etc. Visit here before paying big money in one of the private antique shops.

Getting There & Away

Air Indian Airlines (☎ 438288) is on Museum Rd, next to the Mascot Hotel; the office is open from 10 am to 5.35 pm daily, with a lunch break from 1 to 1.45 pm. Other airlines include Jet Airways (☎ 325267), Air India (☎ 328767), Air Lanka (☎ 328767), Air Maldives (☎ 461315), Gulf Air (☎ 322156) and Kuwait Airways (☎ 328651).

Indian Airlines has direct connections to Bangalore (four flights weekly, US$90); Mumbai (Bombay) (daily, US$155); Chennai (Madras) (daily, US$90) and Delhi (daily, US$290). Jet Airways also has daily flights to Mumbai and Chennai.

There are a number of connections to the Arabian Gulf with Air India, Gulf Air and Kuwait Airways. Air India also flies to Singapore on Monday and Saturday.

Thiruvananthapuram is a popular place from which to fly to Colombo (Sri Lanka) and Male' (Maldives). Air Lanka and Indian Airlines fly to Colombo daily for Rs 2190/4375 one way/return. Air Maldives and Indian Airlines have daily flights to Malé for Rs 2725/5450 one way/return.

Bus The KSRTC bus stand (☎ 323886), opposite the train station, is total chaos. The law of the jungle applies each time a battered old bus comes to a screeching halt in a cloud of dust.

Buses operate regularly to destinations north along the coast, including Kollam (Rs 15, 1½ hours), Alappuzha (Rs 47, 3¼ hours), Ernakulam (Rs 55, five hours) and Thrissur (Rs 70, 6¾ hours). Buses depart hourly for the two hour trip to Kanyakumari. There are three buses daily for the eight hour trip to Thekkady (Rs 80) for Periyar Wildlife Sanctuary.

Most of the bus services to destinations in Tamil Nadu are operated by Thiruvalluvar (the Tamil Nadu state bus service), which has its office at the eastern end of the long-distance bus stand. It has services to Chennai (four daily, 17 hours), Madurai (10 daily, seven hours), Pondicherry (one daily, 16 hours), Coimbatore (one daily), as well as Nagercoil and Erode. KSRTC also operates

several services daily to Coimbatore (Rs 66). Long-distance buses operate to Bangalore (Rs 195), but it's better to catch a train if you're going that far.

Train Although the buses are generally faster than the trains, KSRTC buses, like most others in South India, make no concessions to comfort and the drivers can be reckless. If you prefer to keep your adrenaline levels down, the train is a relaxing alternative.

The reservation office, on the 1st floor of the station building, is efficient and computerised but you should reserve as far in advance as possible because long-distance trains out of Thiruvananthapuram are heavily booked. The reservation office is open Monday to Saturday from 8 am to 2 pm and from 2.15 to 8 pm; Sunday from 8 am to 2 pm. If you're just making your way up the coast in short hops or to Kochi, there's no need to reserve a seat. The 'booking office' for buying tickets just prior to departure is open 24 hours.

Numerous trains run up the coast via Kollam and Ernakulam to Thrissur. Some trains branch off east and north-east at Kollam and head for Shencottah. Beyond Thrissur, many others branch off east via Palakkad to Tamil Nadu. It's 436km to Coimbatore (Rs 91/126/464 for 2nd/sleeper/1st class, nine hours). Coimbatore has connections to Mettupalayam and Ooty (Udhagamandalam).

Trains which go all the way up the coast as far as Mangalore in Karnataka include the daily *Parsuram Express* (departs 6 am; 15 hours) and *Malabar Express* (departs 5.40 pm). The daily *Cannanore Express* (departs 9 pm; 12¾ hours) goes as far north as Kannur. Each of these trains travels via Ernakulam, and there are several additional daily expresses to Kochi including the *Venada Express* (departs 5 am), the *Kerala Express* (departs 9.40 am) and the *Vanchinad Express* (departs 5.05 pm).

It's about 42km from Thiruvananthapuram to Varkala (Rs 16/92 in 2nd/1st class, 55 minutes), 65km to Kollam (Rs 22/109, 1½ hours); 224km to Ernakulam (Rs 56/274, five hours); and 414km to Kozhikode (Rs

99/125/451 for 2nd/sleeper/ 1st class, 10 hours).

South of Thiruvananthapuram, it's 87km to Kanyakumari (Rs 25/141, two hours).

For long-haulers, there's the Friday-only *Himsagar Express* to Jammu Tawi which goes via Delhi.

Getting Around

To/From the Airport The small and relaxed airport is 6km from the city centre or 15km from Kovalam Beach. A No 14 local bus from the Municipal bus stand will take you there for around Rs 2. Prepaid vouchers for taxis cost Rs 60 to Rs 80 to destinations in the city; Rs 180 to Rs 200 to Kovalam Beach.

Local Transport Auto-rickshaws are your best bet for transport around the city. The drivers aren't always willing to use their meters; flagfall is Rs 6, then around Rs 3 per kilometre. From the train station to the Napier Museum; it costs about Rs 15.

See the Kovalam section for transport information from Thiruvananthapuram to the beach.

AROUND THIRUVANANTHAPURAM
Ponmudi & The Cardamom Hills

Ponmudi, a small hill resort just 61km from Thiruvananthapuram, makes for a pleasant day trip or overnight excursion. That said, there is not a lot to do here other than walk in the lightly wooded hills and valleys, frequent the beer parlour or just enjoy the slight relief from the humid coastal climate. The sad-looking deer park is hardly an attraction. The journey to Ponmudi, through banana, rice, rubber, teak, and finally tea and pepper plantations, provides glimpses of the rugged village life in the hills and along the picturesque banks of the Kalar River.

There *are* good views here, though perhaps not as spectacular as those further north in the Ghats. Accommodation in the *Government Guesthouse* is arranged by ringing the manager (☎ 0471-890230), who will provide the various room rates. The KTDC runs the restaurant/beer parlour and

a small snack bar close to the guesthouse rooms.

The mix of lightly populated hills, carloads of young men from the city, and a bar suggests that women travellers should exercise due care, especially on weekends.

On the road to Ponmudi you will pass the turn-off to **Neyyar Dam** and the surrounding **Neyyar Wildlife Sanctuary**. These are popular picnic and day trip locations on weekends. Boats can be hired to explore the shores of the sanctuary. **Peppara Wildlife Sanctuary** is a small (53 sq km) reserve, which is best accessed from Ponmudi and for which you will need your own transport. The sanctuary offers good birdwatching and the possibility of seeing bigger fauna.

Getting There & Away Three or four KSRTC buses leave each day for Ponmudi from the long-distance bus stand. At Nedumangad you will change to a smaller bus capable of negotiating the hairpin corners. A taxi booked through a tour agent will cost about Rs 900 for a half-day trip. The KTDC organises tours which include Ponmudi and Neyyar Dam; see Organised Tours under Thiruvananthapuram for details.

Padmanabhapuram Palace

Padmanabhapuram Palace was once the seat of the rulers of Travancore, a princely state for more than 400 years, which included a large part of present-day Kerala and the western coast of Tamil Nadu.

The palace is superbly constructed of local teak and granite, and stands within massive stone town walls. The oldest parts of the palace date from 1550. The architecture is exquisite, with rosewood ceilings carved in floral patterns, windows laid with jewel-coloured mica, and floors finished to a high polish with a special compound of crushed shells, coconuts, egg white and the juices of local plants.

The 18th century murals in the *puja* (prayer) room on the upper floors have been beautifully preserved, and surpass even those at Mattancherry in Kochi. Ask your guide or at the curator's office for special access. You will have to wait around until any tour groups have left the vicinity and you will probably have to help the guide open the heavy trapdoor entrance.

The palace was occupied from 1550 to 1790 at which time the raja moved to Thiruvananthapuram. Of the 14 rajas that occupied this palace the 13th, Marthanda Varma, was the most powerful (1729-58). He dedicated the palace to Vishnu and changed its former name, Kalkulam, to the present mouthful.

Chinese traders sold tea and bought spices here for centuries and their legacy is evident throughout the palace. There are intricately carved rosewood chairs, screens and ceilings as well as large Chinese pickle jars. With its banqueting halls, audience chamber, women's quarters, recruiting courtyard and galleries, the palace shouldn't be missed if you are visiting this part of the country.

Getting There & Away Padmanabhapuram is just inside Tamil Nadu, 65km south-east of Thiruvananthapuram. To get there, catch a local bus from Thiruvananthapuram (or Kovalam Beach) to Kanyakumari and get off at Thuckalay, from where it is a short rickshaw ride or 15 minute walk to the palace. Alternatively, take one of the tours organised by the KTDC; see Organised Tours in the Thiruvananthapuram section for details. Another option is to organise your own taxi (about Rs 800 return) or arrange one through a private travel agent. The palace is open Tuesday to Saturday from 9 am to 4.30 pm. Entry costs Rs 4, a camera permit is Rs 5.

KOVALAM
Tel Area Code: 0471
Thirty years ago Kovalam was a hippy idyll: a picture-perfect tropical beach; a traditional Keralan fishing village providing fresh fish, fruit and toddy (coconut beer); and about as far from decadent western civilisation as you could get and still hear Jim, Janis and Jimi. It is no longer the mellow backpackers' hang-out catering to budget travellers that it once was. Today this tiny beach is the focus of a multi-million dollar business, ferrying

thousands of tourists from Britain and Europe on chartered jumbos for a two week dose of ozone, UV and a sanitised Indian 'experience'.

The result has been an influx of some get-rich-quick merchants, chaotic beachfront development, an uncontrollable avalanche of garbage, exorbitant prices, desperate souvenir sellers and hordes of ogling sightseers. All of which threatens to destroy the ambience that made Kovalam so attractive in the first place.

But while it's far from paradise, Kovalam retains a certain charm and is still popular with backpacking travellers craving some rest and recreation on the long haul across the subcontinent. The beaches are generally safe and clean (though much of the rubbish is buried just under the surface), and the powerful Arabian Sea swells are inviting and invigorating. There's little local colour left in the village behind the beach, though local fishermen still sail their boats out to sea each night.

Kovalam has an abundance of places to stay, ranging from cheap concrete boxes to five-star resorts, and there's an equally wide range of restaurants, many tuned in to the standard Asia travellers' menu.

Keep in mind that bold displays of naked flesh are offensive to local sensibilities, even on the beach.

Orientation
Kovalam consists of two palm-fringed coves (Lighthouse Beach and Hawah Beach) separated from less-populated beaches north and south by rocky headlands. The southern headland is marked by a prominent lighthouse which is red-and-white striped; the northern headland is topped by the Ashok Beach Resort. It's a 15 minute walk from one headland to the other. A maze of poorly lit paths runs through the coconut palms behind the beach, leading to a multitude of guesthouses and restaurants.

Information
There's a helpful tourist office just inside the entrance to the Ashok Beach Resort.

KERALA

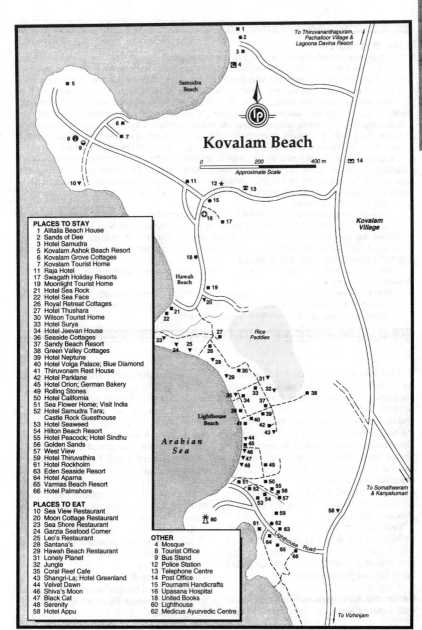

Kovalam Beach

0   200   400 m

Approximate Scale

Samudra Beach

To Thiruvananthapuram, Pachalloor Village & Lagoona Davina Resort

Kovalam Village

Hawah Beach

Rice Paddies

Lighthouse Beach

Arabian Sea

To Somatheeram & Kanyakumari

To Vizhinjam

Lighthouse Road

PLACES TO STAY
1 Alitalia Beach House
2 Sands of Dee
3 Hotel Samudra
5 Kovalam Ashok Beach Resort
6 Kovalam Grove Cottages
7 Kovalam Tourist Home
11 Raja Hotel
17 Swagath Holiday Resorts
19 Moonlight Tourist Home
21 Hotel Sea Rock
22 Hotel Sea Face
26 Royal Retreat Cottages
27 Hotel Thushara
30 Wilson Tourist Home
33 Hotel Surya
34 Hotel Jeevan House
36 Seaside Cottages
37 Sandy Beach Resort
38 Green Valley Cottages
39 Hotel Neptune
40 Hotel Volga Palace; Blue Diamond
41 Thiruvonam Rest House
42 Hotel Parklane
45 Hotel Orion; German Bakery
49 Rolling Stones
50 Hotel California
51 Sea Flower Home; Visit India
52 Hotel Samudra Tara;
   Castle Rock Guesthouse
53 Hotel Seaweed
54 Hilton Beach Resort
55 Hotel Peacock; Hotel Sindhu
56 Golden Sands
57 West View
59 Hotel Thiruvathira
61 Hotel Rockholm
63 Eden Seaside Resort
64 Hotel Aparna
65 Varmas Beach Resort
66 Hotel Palmshore

PLACES TO EAT
10 Sea View Restaurant
20 Moon Cottage Restaurant
23 Sea Shore Restaurant
24 Garzia Seafood Corner
25 Leo's Restaurant
28 Santana's
29 Hawah Beach Restaurant
31 Lonely Planet
32 Jungle
35 Coral Reef Cafe
43 Shangri-La; Hotel Greenland
44 Velvet Dawn
46 Shiva's Moon
47 Black Cat
48 Serenity
58 Hotel Appu

OTHER
4 Mosque
8 Tourist Office
9 Bus Stand
12 Police Station
13 Telephone Centre
14 Post Office
15 Pournami Handicrafts
16 Upasana Hospital
18 United Books
60 Lighthouse
62 Medicus Ayurvedic Centre

The Other Kovalam

With their heavy wooden boats, massive nets and rhythmic chants as their lithe muscles work in unison to haul in the catch, you can't miss Kovalam's fishermen. At dawn, when the powered vessels are returning to Vizhinjam after a night's fishing, the traditional vallams, with a huge coil of coir net and rope on board, are rowed out through the breakers on Kovalam's beaches.

The nets, weighted with stones and floated with large chunks of wood, are set in a wide arc with the aid of boys and young men on katamarans, simple boats made of three or four planks lashed together. Two ropes, which are attached to either end of the net, are brought to shore separately. Boys take up positions along these ropes, several hundred metres from shore, beating their hands on the water to drive the fish into the net as it is hauled towards the beach.

It can take over three hours and 30 men to set and haul the net. The result may be only a handful of *koyiyali* (pilchards). There are usually two or three hauls happening simultaneously (somehow the ropes don't get tangled) and while one net may be virtually empty, the second haul may bring in a truckload. The fishermen see the bad side either way – no fish no money, too many fish and it's a buyers' market.

The fish buying takes place right on the beach where the cod end of the net is inverted to reveal the catch. The buyers can be easily distinguished by their starched business shirts, flashy gold watches and brilliant white *lungis*, looking almost as conspicuous as the tourists. As the catch is unloaded into baskets the haggling starts: first, over what constitutes a full basket, and second, over the price being demanded or offered.

The main catches are *choora* (tuna), *chala* (sardine), *nemeen* (seerfish), *aargoli* (pomfret), *malav* (mullet) and koyiyali.

What the fishermen make of the ragtag jumble of cafes and sunburnt tourists littering the beach at Kovalam is anybody's guess. But if a line of chanting, straining fishermen is on the end of a rope is heading your way, you will be politely gestured to move.

The Central Bank of India has a counter at the Ashok Resort which changes travellers cheques quickly and without fuss. It's open Monday to Friday from 10.30 am to 2 pm and on Saturday from 10.30 am to noon. Up the road towards Kovalam village, Pournami Handicrafts is an authorised moneychanger, and is open from 9 am to 6.30 pm daily. Wilson Tourist Home also has an official moneychanging counter.

There's a post office and a telephone centre (open 9 am to 5 pm weekdays) in Kovalam Village.

Visit India (☎ /fax 481069), at the foot of Lighthouse Rd, is a friendly travel agency which can arrange ticketing, tours, and car hire. It is also an official moneychanger and has a fax and phone service.

Dangers & Annoyances Don't drink local well water at Kovalam. There are so many pit toilets adjacent to wells that you're guaranteed to get very sick if you do. Stick to bottled water or bring a purifying kit.

Theft from hotel rooms, particularly cheap hotels, does occur. Ensure your room has a decent bolt and windows which lock, and stash your gear out of sight in a cupboard or under the bed. Keep an eye on any possessions you take to the beach.

It's safest to swim between the flags, in the area patrolled by lifeguards. Strong rips at both ends of Lighthouse Beach carry away several swimmers every year.

Kovalam is subject to electrical supply 'load-shedding' for 30 minutes every evening. Carry a torch (flashlight) after dark.

Things to See & Do

Surfboards and boogie boards can be rented from young men on the beach for around Rs 50 per hour.

There are a number of ayurvedic centres in Kovalam. Some just offer an oily massage; others offer up to 21-day treatments including a special diet and daily massage. Recommended are Medicus Ayurvedic Centre (☎ /fax 480596), on Lighthouse Rd, which offers a one hour body massage for Rs 300, plus several intensive treatments from two to 21 days. The 10-day treatment (minimum recommended duration to achieve a noticeable effect) costs US$300 including ayurvedic food and massage or US$600 including food, massage and room. At the Ayurveda & Naturopathy Massage Centre at the Hotel Samudra Tara, a one hour body massage costs Rs 250. If you are serious about pursuing ayurvedic treatment for an existing ailment, Arsha Ayurvedic Hospital is the genuine article. Contact Visit India for details (see Information, opposite page).

Organised Tours

Several travel and tour agents in Kovalam organise tours which range from three-hour jaunts in the backwaters to eight-day tours of South India or trips to the Maldives. If you like boating, trekking or just seeing the sights and want minimal hassle then negotiate a deal with one of these agencies. The short backwater cruises on a traditional rice barge are a good counterbalance to the beach scene and the poisonous air of Thiruvananthapuram. As with all backwater tours in Kerala, you get to go ashore and witness toddy tapping, coir making and boat building/repairing. A three-hour boat trip costs about Rs 250 per person. If given the choice, elect to have a boat with proper sunshade – it's hot out there.

Places to Stay

There are dozens of places to stay at the budget end of the market – the coconut groves behind the beach are littered with small lodges, houses for rent and blocks of recently constructed rooms. Shop around, but you basically get what you pay for. Ask for a reduced rate if you are staying longer than a few days.

Prices climb the closer you get to the beach, and a few minutes walk can often mean lower prices or much better rooms for the same price. Prices climb even more dramatically when the package tourists begin to arrive – November to February is the high season but most places have a peak high season over the Christmas/New Year period when prices go even higher and rooms become scarce. From about 15 December to 7 January it is best to book ahead. Outside the high season it's a buyer's market; find the best place on the beach and bargain hard. The prices quoted here are typical high-season prices, unless otherwise stated.

Places to Stay – Budget

Most, though not all, of the cheapest places are along or just back from the beach. There are others along the road from Thiruvananthapuram and along Lighthouse Rd.

Eden Seaside Resort (☎ 481749, Lighthouse Rd), opposite the Varmas Beach Resort, is basic but all rooms have attached bathroom; doubles cost Rs 500, dropping to half that price in the low season.

Hotel Thiruvathira (☎ 480787), almost next door, has downstairs doubles for Rs 350 and upstairs doubles with balcony and bay views for Rs 450. In the low season, prices drop to Rs 200 and Rs 250.

Hotel Samudra Tara (☎ 481608), further down Lighthouse Rd towards the beach, has clean and comfortable non air-con rooms for Rs 300 (Rs 400 with a balcony) and air-con rooms for Rs 700. There's an ayurvedic massage and naturopathy clinic here as well (see Things to See & Do earlier).

Castle Rock Guesthouse (☎ /fax 481995), next door and sharing the same entrance off Lighthouse Rd, has clean, non air-con singles/doubles for Rs 500/800 (Rs 200/300 in the low season). Air-con doubles are Rs 1000 (including breakfast) in the high season, dropping to Rs 600 in the low season.

Green Valley Cottages (☎ 480636), in a wonderfully peaceful location next to the paddy fields, has clean, neat and colourful rooms with attached bathroom for Rs 450 in the high season and Rs 150 to Rs 250 in the low season.

Hotel Greenland, also well back from the beach, is attached to the well known Shangri-La restaurant. Simple but clean rooms cost Rs 300 for single or double occupancy.

Kovalam Tourist Home (☎ 480441), a long walk back from the beach, has simple rooms with attached bathroom for just Rs 150/300 in the low/high season, or Rs 350/400 with air-con. Little English is spoken.

Sandy Beach Resort (☎ 480012) has refurbished rooms for Rs 350/550 in the low/high season and an attached restaurant.

Hotel Jeevan House (☎ 480662), right behind the Coral Reef Cafe, has a range of accommodation from Rs 200 to Rs 1200 in the high season or Rs 100 to Rs 400 in the low season.

Other places worth considering include the no-frills **Hotel Surya** (☎ 481012), just back from the beach, with rooms from Rs100/200 in the low/high season and the beachfront **Sea Flower Home** (☎ 480554), a touch close to the drain but friendly and clean with rooms for Rs 200 downstairs and

Ayurveda

Most visitors head for Kerala's beaches and backwaters to recharge and relax. But some, on a more serious quest for better health, come expressly to sample Kerala's renowned ayurvedic treatments.

Ayurveda, the science of long life, is an ancient system that uses herbs and oils to treat a range of ailments. Fundamental to ayurvedic philosophy is the belief that we all possess three *doshas* or humours: *vataam* (wind or air); *pitam* (bile); and *kapham* (phlegm). Together these are known as the *tridoshas* and disease is viewed as the result of imbalance among them. Ayurveda aims to restore that balance, and hence good health, principally through two methods: *panchakarama* (internal purification) and *snehana* (massage). The herbs used for both grow in abundance in Kerala's moist climate, many of them in the hilly, forested areas of the hinterland where they are harvested by tribal people. Every town and village in Kerala has its ayurvedic pharmacy where the medicinal plants, fresh and dried, are sold.

Ayurvedic practise in Kerala places special emphasis on massage and is claimed to be particularly beneficial for those suffering such chronic ailments as arthritis and rheumatism. The type of oil used in massage differs according to the ailment being treated, but ranges from castor and neem to mustard and camphor. To these are added various powdered herbs, nuts and bark. The ayurvedic practitioner may conduct the massage using the palm of the hand, a cloth or a poultice of herbs wrapped up in a cloth – it all depends on the type of condition being treated.

Ayurvedic massage is also used on trainee Kathakali dancers and students of Kalarippayatt, Kerala's traditional form of martial art. The guru massages the student's head and shoulders with his hands, but uses his feet to stretch and flex the student's legs and back – flexibility being essential to classical dance and martial art.

Having an occasional ayurvedic massage, something offered at tourist resorts all over Kerala, is relaxing, but to reap any long term benefits necessitates rather more dedication – usually a 15-day or even a 41-day commitment which may involve certain dietary abstentions and exercises as well as regular massages from a qualified practitioner.

Ayurvedic practitioners traditionally hailed from families where the knowledge was passed from father to son over successive generations. These days there are ayurvedic colleges throughout South India where students train for several years. Properly qualified practitioners receive accreditation from the state government.

Ayurvedic hospitals and clinics in Kerala include: Aryavaidyashala (Kottakal, near Calicut); Aryavaidya Pharmacy (Coimbatore); Ayurvedic Medical College (Thiruvananthapuram); District Ayurvedic Hospital (Palghat); and Kerala Ayurvedic Pharmacy (Ernakulam).

Christine Niven

Rs 400 for a balcony. *Hotel Paradise Rock* (☎ 480658), nearby, obviously had trouble deciding on a name but offers clean, small rooms for Rs 100/150. *Seaside Cottages* (☎ 481937) has basic rooms for Rs 250 (single & double), and *Thiruvonam Rest House* (☎ 480661) is perhaps a tad overpriced at Rs 400, up to Rs 500 (with a balcony), but will rent an interesting looking air cooler for Rs 100. *Rolling Stones* has basic rooms for Rs 200 (single & double). Also worth a try is *West View* which is a few minutes stroll from the beach and has standard rooms from Rs 150 to Rs 250.

Places to Stay – Mid-Range
The best hunting ground for mid-range hotels is Lighthouse Rd. Many of the newer hotels in this category may be booked out by charter tourism groups from December to April, but there are usually rooms available in November. The charter companies have demanded higher standards than backpackers and certain luxuries such as fridges, telephones and hot water are often found in each room.

Hotel Seaweed (☎ 480391) is an excellent, friendly and secure place with sea breezes and bay views. There's a wide variety of rooms from Rs 500 to Rs 1200 and Rs 1000 to Rs 1300 with air-con. Prices drop 25% to 30% in the low season.

Hilton Beach Resort (☎ 481476), nearby, has air-con singles/doubles costing Rs 900/1200.

Hotel Peacock (☎ 481395) has non air-con rooms for Rs 500 and air-con rooms with fridge for Rs 750. Prices are inclusive of tax and there is a restaurant, the Sea Bee, attached.

Hotel Rockholm (☎ 480306), further up Lighthouse Rd (ie away from the beach), is also an excellent choice. It has great views over the small cove beyond the lighthouse. In the high season rooms cost Rs 900/1000 in the low season there's a 25% discount.

Hotel Aparna (☎ 480950) has doubles for Rs 1075 (inclusive of tax) in the high season. Credit cards and travellers cheques are not accepted.

Varmas Beach Resort (☎ 480478) has balconies overlooking a small cove. In the high season, doubles with air-con are Rs 1650, and without air-con, Rs 1290.

Hotel Palmshore (☎ 481481, fax 480495) fronts onto the private sandy cove south of the lighthouse headland, which is a pleasant escape from the frenetic activity on Lighthouse Beach. The rooms are pleasantly designed, all with attached bathroom and a balcony facing the sea. Doubles cost US$56 (US$62 with air-con) during the December/January peak, reducing to US$45/50 for the rest of the high season, and falling to US$20/25 during the low season.

Golden Sands (☎ 481476) is a new hotel built for the charter crowd with large, comfortable doubles for Rs 350/650 in the low/high season.

Hotel Neptune (☎ 480222) is set back from Lighthouse Beach and has standard rooms for Rs 500, balcony rooms for Rs 550 and air-con rooms for Rs 750 over the Christmas/New Year peak. Prices in the low season fall to less than Rs 300.

Hotel Volga Palace (☎ 481663) is similar with rooms ranging from Rs 400 for the ground floor to Rs 800 for the gloomy palace suite on the top floor.

Blue Diamond (☎ 481224), adjacent to Volga Palace, is of a similar standard and price but is usually booked out by a charter group.

Wilson Tourist Home (☎ 480051) is a few steps closer to the beach and slightly cheaper. It is large and friendly, with a range of non air-con rooms from Rs 300 to Rs 350 during the high season, and air-con courtyard rooms for Rs 850.

Hotel Sea Rock (☎ 480422, fax 480722) on Hawah Beach has been popular for years. The rooms are all doubles and have attached bathroom. Singles/doubles cost Rs 900/1000 dropping to Rs 550 in the low season.

Hotel Thushara (☎ /fax 481693), back in the coconut palms, has superbly built and beautifully furnished self-contained cottages and rooms for Rs 750 (Rs 250 in the low season).

Royal Retreat, next door, is a cluster of

brand new air-conditioned cottages from Rs 800 to Rs 900 a double. There are also non air-con singles from Rs 300 to Rs 750. Prices are halved in the low season.

Moonlight Tourist Home (☎ 480375, fax 481078), further up this road, is popular and squeaky clean. The spacious rooms have poster beds and mosquito nets; doubles, some with small balconies, cost Rs 600/900 in low/high season or Rs 1000/1400 with air-con.

Hotel Orion (☎ 480999) is a friendly place overlooking Lighthouse Beach just 20m from the high-tide mark, and its prime position is reflected in its tariff. Doubles are Rs 600/1250 in the low/high season and suites (with air-con and fridge) are Rs 900/2000.

Hotel Parklane (☎ 480058), a minute's walk back from the beach, is a good choice at the bottom of this range. Clean, comfortable doubles, some with a small balcony, cost Rs 700 including breakfast and taxes; rates are halved in the low season. The manager is friendly and there's a pleasant rooftop restaurant.

Raja Hotel (☎ 480355), well back from the beach, has sea-facing rooms with attached bathroom for Rs 750, falling to Rs 400 in the low season. It also has a bar and a veg/nonveg restaurant.

Places to Stay – Top End

The *Kovalam Ashok Beach Resort (☎ 480101, fax 481522)* is superbly located on the headland at the northern end of the second cove. The hotel is centrally air-conditioned and has a bar, restaurants, swimming pool, sports and massage facilities, bank and bookshop. Room prices are Rs 4000/4500 from mid-December to mid-February, dropping to Rs 3700/4200 during the rest of the year; uninspiring cottages are Rs 500 cheaper, while the Castle suite costs Rs 12,500/15,000 during the low/high season!

Hotel Sea Face (☎ 481835, fax 481320) is right on Hawah Beach. Standard rooms are Rs 2000 (Rs 2400 with air-con), deluxe rooms are Rs 3000, and suites are Rs 4500 (plus 20% tax). Rates fall in stages from June to October; at their lowest they are less than half the high season price. All rooms have TV and direct dial facilities, and the pool overlooks the beach.

Swagath Holiday Resorts (☎ 481148, fax 330990) is set in well tended gardens high above the beach looking over the coconut palms to the lighthouse. Comfortable rooms with TV and phone cost Rs 1300 to Rs 1750 (Rs 1500 to Rs 2500 with air-con) or Rs 3500 for an air-con suite; there are no low season price reductions. There's an excellent multicuisine restaurant (lawn-service available), but no pool. Be warned: rooms with a view of the lighthouse are strafed with brilliant light all night long.

Places to Eat

Open-air restaurants line Lighthouse Beach and are scattered among the coconut palms behind it. Almost all the restaurants offer the standard Asian travellers' menu: porridge, muesli, eggs, toast, jam and pancakes for breakfast, and curries or seafood with chips and salad for dinner.

At night, you stroll along the beachfront and select which fish you would like cooked from one of the many restaurants' seafood displays. The range of fresh seafood includes seer fish (delicious baked in a tandoor), barracuda, sea bass, catfish, king and tiger prawns, and crabs. Always check the prices when you order. Fish and chips with salad typically costs between Rs 70 and Rs 100, depending on variety and portion size; tiger prawns will push the price beyond Rs 200.

There's plenty of competition so don't be afraid to negotiate if the asking price is too high. The quality can vary widely from place to place and from month to month; ask other travellers or diners for their recommendations. Beer is available in most restaurants, but is expensive, even by Keralan standards – expect to pay at least Rs 70.

Santana's (which has the best sound system), *Hawah Beach*, *Coral Reef Cafe*, *Velvet Dawn*, *Garzia Seafood Corner*, *Leo's Restaurant* and the *Orion Cafe* at the Hotel Orion all have a reputation for quality and value. But almost without exception you must be prepared for a long wait; the length of time it takes to grill a fish is quite amazing.

Serenity, at the south end of the beach, turns out good travellers' breakfasts and recognisable 'spegatty'; nearby **Black Cat** and **Shiva's Moon** are similar. The **Sea View Restaurant** is popular all day long, and just beyond the headland the **Sea Shore Restaurant** is a wonderful spot to sip a beer while the sun sets. For cappuccino and apple strudel, try the rooftop cafe at the **German Bakery**.

There are quite a few places back from the beach, although seafood is not the number one concern.

Lonely Planet vegetarian restaurant is nicely situated by the paddy fields, and turns out some surprisingly good South Indian food. No, we have absolutely nothing to do with it and we are not planning to open a franchised chain!

Jungle is run by a couple of Italian guys; yes there's pasta as well as other western dishes and Indian and Chinese. The **Shangri-La**, **Hotel Sindhu**, and **Moon Cottage Restaurant** are also worth a look.

If you get tired of the interminable wait for meals at the beachside places, consider the mid-range hotels back from the beach. These places have better equipped kitchens than the beach shacks and can turn out more consistent food with much greater speed.

Lucky Coral rooftop restaurant at the Hotel Seaweed is ever-popular.

The **Rockholm's** celebrated restaurant includes a terrace overlooking the sea.

At the **Palmshore,** you can eat indoors or on the open balcony.

The **Sea Rock** has a balcony overlooking the beach.

For a splurge, head off to the **Ashok Beach Resort** or the **Swagath Holiday Resorts**, but don't expect a warm welcome if you haven't scrubbed up first.

Hotel Appu, well away from the beach, has the best cheap Indian food in Kovalam, and is packed with lunching locals from 1 to 1.30 pm.

On the beach, a number of local women sell fruit to sun worshippers. The ring of

'Hello. Mango? Papaya? Banana? Coconut? Pineapple?' will soon become a familiar part of your day. You'll soon establish what the going rate is and, after that, they'll remember your face and you don't have to repeat the performance. The women rarely have any change, but they're reliable about bringing it to you later. Toddy (coconut beer) is available from shops in Kovalam Village.

Entertainment

During the holiday season, a shortened version of traditional Kathakali dance drama is performed every night except Sunday in Kovalam. Every Monday, Wednesday and Saturday at the Hotel Neptune, and Tuesday and Friday at the Ashok Beach Resort, you can watch make-up and dressing from 5 to 6.45 pm and the dance program with commentary from 6.45 to 8.15 pm. Cost is Rs 90.

For a less cultural pursuit, western videos are shown twice a night in a number of restaurants.

Shopping

Kovalam Beach has numerous craft and carpet shops (usually of Tibetan, Kashmiri and Rajasthani origin), clothing stores (ready to wear and made to order), book exchanges, general stores selling everything from toilet paper to sunscreen, travel agents, and even yoga schools. Beach vendors sell batik *lungis* (sarongs), beach mats, sunglasses and leaf paintings, while others offer cheap (and illegal) Kerala grass.

Getting There & Away

Bus The local No 111 bus between Thiruvananthapuram and Kovalam Beach runs every 15 minutes between about 6 am and 10 pm and costs Rs 3.50. The bus leaves Thiruvananthapuram from stand 19 on MG Rd, 100m south of the municipal bus stand, opposite the Hotel Luciya Continental. Although the bus starts out ridiculously overcrowded, it rapidly empties. At Kovalam, the buses start and finish at the entrance to the Ashok Beach Resort.

There are also direct services to Ernakulam (Rs 60, 5½ hours) and Kanyakumari

(Rs 20, 1½ hours) which are good ways of avoiding the crush at Thiruvananthapuram. Kanyakumari (Cape Comorin, Tamil Nadu), is two hours away and there are four departures daily. One bus leaves each morning for Thekkady in the Periyar Wildlife Sanctuary (Rs 90, 8½ hours). Direct buses go to Kollam (Rs 20, 2 hours) if you want to do the backwater trip.

Taxi & Auto-Rickshaw A taxi between Thiruvananthapuram and Kovalam Beach will cost Rs 150 to Rs 200, depending on pick-up and set-down point. Auto-rickshaws make the trip for Rs 60 to Rs 80. It's best to arrive at the lighthouse (Vizhinjam) end of the beach because this is much closer to the hotels and there usually aren't as many touts around. Prepaid taxis from Thiruvananthapuram airport to the beach cost around Rs 200. Don't assume a rickshaw will be cheaper than a taxi – shop around.

AROUND KOVALAM
Vizhinjam
The small fishing village of Vizhinjam (pronounced *Virinyam*), just 1km south of Kovalam Beach, is a sobering reminder of your geographic and cultural situation after the resort atmosphere of Kovalam. Its big artificial harbour is dominated by a pink and green mosque on the northern end and a huge Catholic church to the south; from Kovalam you can sometimes hear them trading amplified calls to prayer and mass in the early hours. Christian/Muslim relations have been tense during resettlement programs following the harbour project, erupting in periodic violence in recent years in which several villagers have died. The peace is now maintained by a permanent police presence and a 'no mans land' between the two harbourside settlements.

It would be easy to offend locals and court danger by wandering into Vizhinjam in the same manner as going down to Kovalam Beach from your hotel. Dress appropriately, be sensitive to the economic divide and take care in 'no mans land' – its edges are well used public toilets.

The beach is packed with boats which set out to fish at sunset. From the beach at night, you can see their lights strung like a necklace along the horizon.

Vizhinjam (then Vilinjam) was a capital of the 7th to 11th century Ay kingdom, and a number of rock-cut temples have been found around the village – reminders of the period when the kingdom was under Tamil influence.

Pulinkudi & Somatheeram
At Pulinkudi, 8km south of Kovalam, are two interesting alternatives to Kovalam's crowded beaches.

Surya Samudra Beach Garden (☎ 480413, fax 481124) is a small and very select hotel with individual cottages, many of them constructed from transplanted traditional Keralan houses. There are private beaches, a fantastic natural rock swimming pool and music, and martial arts or dance performances at night. The food is superb, though expensive by local standards. From December to February, room rates range from Rs 3500/4000 to Rs 4000/4500, and gradually reduce throughout the low season.

Somatheeram Ayurvedic Beach Resort (☎ 481600, fax 480600), a little further south on Somatheeram Beach, combines beach life with ayurvedic medical treatment. In the high season, room prices start at US$45 and stop at US$170. Various treatment packages are available which cost extra, as do meals. There is a sister resort, *Manaltheeram*, nearby.

Samudra Beach & Pozhikkara Beach
At Samudra Beach, about 4km by road north of Kovalam, are a number of resorts competing for space with the local fishing villages. Some of the ostentatious newer resorts are closed to all but charter tourists, and the steep and rough beach, often crowded with fishermen, is not as amenable for swimming as the beaches further south. The pace is more relaxed than Kovalam, but this may change with the influx of charter tourists. Also, local resentment to tourism is discernible.

The KTDC *Hotel Samudra* (☎ 480089, fax 480242), a pleasant retreat from hectic Kovalam, has its own bar and restaurant. Air-con doubles cost Rs 3495, dropping to Rs 2800 in the low season.

Sands of Dee (☎ 480887) would appear to be vulnerable to a king tide and certainly offers beach frontage. Pleasant rooms go for Rs 400/750 in the low/high season and there is a restaurant attached.

Alitalia Beach House (☎ 480042), run by the amiable Shah Jahan, has singles for Rs 250/500 and doubles for Rs 500/1000 in the low/high season. There is also a rooftop restaurant.

As well as the restaurants associated with the hotels, there are several seafood/tandoori restaurants set up on the beach, such as the *Fat Fish*, producing the usual offerings found at Kovalam's beachfront restaurants.

Lagoona Davina (☎ 480049, fax 450041), at Pachalloor village, behind Pozhikkara Beach, 5km north of Kovalam, is a small, exclusive resort with several tiny cabins which cost from Rs 1675/3350 for room and breakfast in the low/high season. Lunch and dinner (and you are a long hike from other restaurants) costs Rs 650/900 per person. It's quiet, peaceful and isolated. There is a boat which shuttles across the narrow lagoon to the beach, and backwater trips are available.

VARKALA
Pop: 41,400 Tel Area Code: 0472
Varkala is a developing beach resort 41km north of Thiruvananthapuram. One look and it's apparent that authorities have not learned from the mistakes which have allowed Kovalam Beach to become a shambles. Several inappropriate developments (mostly designed to house package tourists from Britain and Europe) already mar the beach, and the garbage is piling up fast. Nevertheless, an Arabian Sea sunset viewed from the clifftop is unlikely to be forgotten in a hurry.

Orientation & Information
The town and the train station are 2km from the beach, which lies beneath towering cliffs and boasts a mineral water spring.

Most places to stay are at the beach, either at temple junction, on Beach Rd, or 500m north along the clifftops. As at Kovalam, prices vary seasonally, and it pays to shop around. Varkala's beach can disappear almost entirely during the monsoon, gradually reappearing in time for the tourist onslaught from November to February.

The very friendly Bureau de Change (☎ 602749) at temple junction encashes travellers cheques, has an STD/ISD phone service, cold drinks and film, and can arrange taxis at fair rates. It also has bus and train timetables pinned up on the wall. It is open daily from 9 am to 10 pm.

The Tourist Helping Centre, at the beach end of Beach Rd, is a friendly travel agent which organises elephant rides (full day, Rs 800 including Keralan lunch) and backwater trips (full day, Rs 600 including lunch). It also arranges longer, overnight trips to the tea plantations, rubber factories and forests near the Tamil Nadu border (Rs 1000 including food and accommodation). There are a number of other travel agents, such as Cliff Tours & Travels, along the clifftop, that can organise sightseeing trips, taxis, air tickets and hotel reservations.

The small Kerala Store on the clifftop has a limited range of food items plus a few handy essentials such as soap, toilet paper, batteries and razors.

Things to See & Do
Despite initial perceptions, Varkala is first and foremost a temple town with a sacred beach. The **Janardhana Temple** is at temple junction at the beginning of Beach Rd. Non-Hindus are not permitted to enter the sanctum sanctorum but you may well be invited to wander around the temple grounds in which there is a huge banyan tree and shrines devoted to deities such as Ayappa (an incarnation of Shiva, and lord of forests and wild animals), Hanuman and others.

Sivagiri Mutt, a hill in Varkala village, is the headquarters of Sree Narayana Dharma Sanghom Trust (☎ 602221, fax 0471-550651). The ashram is devoted to Sree Narayana Guru (1855-1928) who preached 'one caste, one religion, one god for man' and attracted a large following among the lower castes. Inquiries are welcome.

There are two centres for **yoga** and **massage** on the clifftop. At the Progressive Yoga Centre a one-week yoga course is Rs 450, lessons in ayurvedic massage cost Rs 1750 for one week, and a massage costs Rs 180 for just over an hour of treatment. Meditation is taught by Swami Sukshmaanda from Sivagiri Mutt. At the Scientific School of Yoga & Massage you can enjoy a 1½ hour massage combining ayurvedic and Swedish techniques (Rs 200), attend a meditation course (Rs 500), learn yoga over five days (Rs 500) or learn ayurvedic and Swedish massage techniques over 10 days (Rs 3000; Rs 5000 per couple).

Places to Stay – Budget

Anandan Tourist Home (☎ 602135), opposite the train station, is neat and orderly and

has rooms for Rs 60/150 or Rs 300 with aircon and TV.

Government Guest House (☎ 402227), north of the Janardhana Temple, near the Taj Garden Retreat, has cavernous rooms in a large annexe of the former summer palace of

PLACES TO STAY
1   Prasanthi Cliff Guest House
2   Hill Palace
6   Hill Top Beach Resort
8   White House
11   Red House
12   Preethi Resort
13   Green House
20   Udatha Cliff Hostel;
    Sea Spring Restaurant
22   Varkala Marine Palace
24   Eden Garden
25   Taj Garden Retreat
26   Government Guest House
27   Sea Pearl Chalets
29   Panchavadi Beach Resort
30   Akshay Beach Resort
31   Gratitude Inn
37   JA Tourist Home;
    Anna Two Wheeler Agencies

PLACES TO EAT
3   Sea Breeze Restaurant
4   Sea Queen
9   Sea Breeze Restaurant;
    Hill View Lodge
14   Shiva's Moon
15   Seaview Restaurant
16   Kadaloram No 1
17   Sunset Restaurant
18   Manos
19   Prasanthi Cliff Cafe Italiano
28   Mama Chompos Pizzeria
33   Sree Padman Restaurant

OTHER
5   Scientific School of Yoga & Massage
7   Kerala Store
10   Durga Temple
21   Nature Cure Hospital
23   Tourist Helping Centre;
    The Beach Restaurant
32   Devaswom Building
34   Bureaux de Change
35   Auto-Rickshaw Stand
36   Janardhana Temple

Varkala
0   50   100 m
Approximate Scale
Arabian Sea
Spring
Helipad
Cliffs
Rice Paddies
Beach Road
To Train Station (2km)
Tank
To Progressive Yoga Centre

the Raja of Travancore. There are two even larger but more run-down rooms in the spooky palace. At Rs 52 these rooms, with bath, are a bargain, but it is a long haul to the beach and cheap restaurants.

JA Tourist Home (☎ 602453), close to the Janardhana Temple, has basic accommodation ranging in price from Rs 75 to Rs 150.

Gratitude Inn (Beach Rd) has small, clean singles/doubles for Rs 100/150. You may also be asked to purchase handicrafts from the owner's Cottage Emporium.

Akshay Beach Resort (☎ 602668) has single rooms with shared facilities for Rs 100 and singles/doubles with bath for Rs 150/200.

Varkala Marine Palace (☎ 603204) has rooms from Rs 200 to Rs 500. There's a 50% discount in the low season. It also has an open-air tandoor restaurant overlooking the beach.

On the cliffs, 10 minutes walk north (follow the indistinct path beside the Varkala Marine Palace), accommodation is provided by small hotels and local families who offer rooms from Rs 75 to Rs 150 in the low season to Rs 300 in the high season. Some places to stay haven't yet acquired names, so just look for the *White House, Green House* or *Red House*, all with rooms at around Rs 200 to Rs 300 in the high season.

Prasanthi Cliff Guest House, further around the cliffs, is run by the folks at Cafe Italiano (make inquiries there) and has three small, charmingly decorated rooms with common bath for Rs 250.

Hill Palace has very basic though acceptable rooms for Rs 75 with shared facilities or Rs 125 with bath attached.

Hill Top Beach Resort has simple rooms with attached bathroom for Rs 200 downstairs and Rs 300 upstairs. There's a restaurant attached.

Places to Stay – Mid-Range & Top End

Eden Garden (☎ 603910, fax 481004), overlooking the paddy fields, is delightfully situated. The 10 rather small, low-ceilinged rooms are Rs 350 for doubles. There is an in-house masseur.

Akshay Beach Resort (☎ 602668, Beach Rd) has OK air-con doubles for Rs 500, but it is primarily a budget hotel.

Panchavadi Beach Resort (☎ 600200), almost opposite, has six small rooms for Rs 300 and two family rooms (each with two double beds) for Rs 600. Prices increase by Rs 100 during the Christmas peak. There's hot water but no air-con.

Preethi (☎ 600942) is a new, squeaky clean resort set back from the cliff. Standard rooms are Rs 500, deluxe rooms (with hot water and a balcony) are Rs 700, and cottages (two double beds) are Rs 1400.

Sea Pearl Chalets (☎ 605875) consists of 10 concrete wigwams on the headland south of Beach Rd. The four rooms overlooking the sea cost Rs 500 a double, the others are Rs 400. The wigwams are self-contained and the beds have mosquito nets.

Udatha Cliff Hostel is a spotless home on the clifftop with nine comfortable rooms, four with attached bath. Prices range from Rs 150 downstairs to Rs 500 to Rs 800 for the rooms on the top floor. Sea Spring restaurant is attached.

Taj Garden Retreat (☎ 603000, fax 602296), a resort set among terraced gardens and coconut palms overlooking the beach, eclipses every other building in this tiny hamlet and is certainly a harbinger of future developments. Standard air-con rooms are US$95/105 to US$110/120 from Christmas to the end of February and US$15 cheaper throughout the rest of the year. There's a restaurant, bar, pool, tennis courts and health club.

Places to Eat

Anandan Tourist Home, opposite the train station, has a restaurant downstairs.

Sree Padman Restaurant, perched right at the edge of the tank at temple junction, is popular with locals and travellers alike.

Mama Chompos Pizzeria (Beach Rd) has delicious pizza, foccacia, pasta, homemade cheeses and crusty Italian bread, as well as decent coffee.

Most of the other eating places are seasonal, opening up along the clifftop at the northern part of Varkala Beach from November to February.

Sea Breeze, Shiva's Moon, Seaview, Prasanthi Cliff Cafe Italiano, Manos, Sunset Restaurant, Kadaloram No 1 and others all offer similar standards (shaky tables and a diverse collection of rickety chairs), similar food (fresh fish on display out the front at night) and similar service (usually incredibly slow). A small tuna cooked in the tandoor served with rice or chips and salad costs about Rs 75.

Sea Queen tries to be different with some Spanish influence in the menu.

Entertainment

Kathakali dance drama can be experienced in the atmospheric, though stiflingly hot, surroundings of the old Devaswom building beside the tank at temple junction. Facial make-up and costume dressing is from 5 to 6.45 pm and the dance program with English commentary is from 6.45 to 8.15 pm. Performances are every Sunday, Wednesday and Friday during December and January and cost Rs 75.

Getting There & Away

Varkala is 41km north of Thiruvananthapuram (by train, Rs 16/92 in 2nd/1st class, 55 minutes) and just 24km south of Kollam (Rs 13/79, 45 minutes). There are regular buses to/from Thiruvananthapuram and Kollam which terminate at temple junction. Look for the timetables in the Bureau de Change. From Varkala, it's easy to get to Kollam in time for the morning backwater boat to Alappuzha. A taxi from Thiruvananthapuram direct to Varkala Beach costs about Rs 500 (Rs 600 from Kovalam).

Getting Around

Auto-rickshaws shuttle back and forth between the train station and the Varkala temple junction for Rs 15. A taxi to the beach costs about Rs 50. You can hire a 350cc Enfield Bullet (Rs 350 per day), a small Yamaha (Rs 300 per day), a Kinetic Honda (Rs 250 per day) or a Hero bicycle (Rs 40 per day) from Anna Two Wheeler Agencies, on the ground floor of JA Tourist Home on Beach Rd.

AROUND VARKALA

One of the earliest British East India Company factories was established at nearby **Anjengo** in 1684. While the ruins are not much to look at, the solid fortifications make it not too difficult to appreciate the courage and determination that was needed to do a little trading on the spice coast. The risks were high but so were the rewards.

Anjengo is about 15km from Varkala – about Rs 100 for the return trip by autorickshaw, and the trip alone is time well spent. You travel alongside the beach through thatched fishing villages, first Muslim then Christian/Hindu, always accompanied by the smell of fish drying in the sun.

KOLLAM (Quilon)
Pop: 374,400 Tel Area Code: 0474

Nestled among coconut palms and cashew tree plantations on the edge of Ashtamudi Lake, Kollam, still referred to as Quilon (pronounced 'koy-lon'), is a typical Keralan market town, with old wooden houses whose red-tiled roofs overhang winding streets. It's also the southern gateway to the backwaters of Kerala, and is most well known as the starting or finishing point for the Kollam-Alappuzha backwater cruise (see the boxed text 'The Backwaters' in the Alappuzha section, pp 416-7).

The Malayalam era is calculated from the founding of Kollam in the 9th century. The town's later history is interwoven with the Portuguese, Dutch and English rivalry for control of the Indian Ocean trade routes and the commodities grown in this part of the subcontinent.

Information

There's a very helpful DTPC Tourist Information Centre near the KSRTC bus stand (open Monday to Saturday from 9 am to 5.30 pm) and another at the train station. Chani Books is in the Bishop Jerome Nagar shopping centre.

You can encash travellers cheques at the

Bank of Baroda, opposite the Hotel Sudarsan, or avoid the long wait in the bank and go to the DTPC Tourist Information Centre, which changes money between 10 am and 2 pm at government rates.

Things to See & Do

If you have the time, wander along Main Rd, an old thoroughfare (almost peaceful compared with Alappuzha Rd) where **jewellery** and **sari** shops with polished marble and brass entrances incongruously abut dusty, dirty footpath/sewers and the potholed road is full of well-polished chauffer-driven cars.

The extraordinary-looking **Shrine of Our Lady of Velamkanni**, near the KSRTC bus stand, attracts a large and vocal crowd in the evening. There are also Chinese fishing nets on **Ashtamudi Lake** and the ruins of a Portuguese/Dutch **fort** and also some 18th century churches at **Thangasseri**, 3km from Kollam's centre.

Organised Tours

Guided tours on foot and in traditional country boats through the myriad paths and canals of **Monroe Island** in Ashtamudi Lake are organised by the DTPC (inquire at the Information Centre). The first part of the journey is by road through the outskirts of Kollam, passing cashew nut processing factories. The boat trip starts at a quiet backwater village, and the next few hours are spent observing village life – prawn and fish farming, coir making, copra drying, even matchstick making. Also, there are wonderful opportunities for birdwatching, with scores of kingfishers, bee-eaters, egrets, Brahminy kites and others. The tour lasts from 9 am to 1 pm and costs Rs 250 per person.

Places to Stay – Budget

The **Government Guest House** (☎ 70356), 3km north of the centre by the water's edge on Ashtamudi Lake, is a large, forgotten relic of the Raj. The immense rooms are sparsely furnished and decorated with old willow pattern plates, large Chinese pickle jars and old lithographs depicting British victories in the War of Independence/Mutiny. Rooms

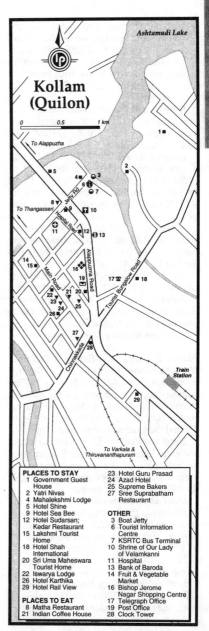

Kollam (Quilon)

Ashtamudi Lake

0   0.5   1 km

To Alappuzha

To Thangasseri

Jetty Rd

Hospital Road

Alappuzha Road

Main Road

Chinnakkada

Tourist Bungalow Road

Train Station

To Varkala & Thiruvananthapuram

PLACES TO STAY	
1	Government Guest House
2	Yatri Nivas
4	Mahalekshmi Lodge
5	Hotel Shine
9	Hotel Sea Bee
12	Hotel Sudarsan; Kedar Restaurant
15	Lakshmi Tourist Home
18	Hotel Shah International
20	Sri Uma Maheswara Tourist Home
22	Iswarya Lodge
26	Hotel Karthika
29	Hotel Rail View

PLACES TO EAT	
8	Matha Restaurant
21	Indian Coffee House
23	Hotel Guru Prasad
24	Azad Hotel
25	Supreme Bakers
27	Sree Suprabatham Restaurant

OTHER	
3	Boat Jetty
6	Tourist Information Centre
7	KSRTC Bus Terminal
10	Shrine of Our Lady of Velamkanni
11	Hospital
13	Bank of Baroda
14	Fruit & Vegetable Market
16	Bishop Jerome Nagar Shopping Centre
17	Telegraph Office
19	Post Office
28	Clock Tower

with attached bath are a bargain at Rs 52 per person but getting into town can be difficult because of the scarcity of auto-rickshaws.

Lakshmi Tourist Home (☎ 741067), down an alley off Main Rd, is a no-frills lodge with clean singles/doubles costing Rs 50/90 with attached bath.

Hotel Karthika (☎ 76241) is a large, popular place built around a central courtyard. Decent rooms are Rs 111/200 with attached bathroom or Rs 310 with air-con.

Iswarya Lodge (☎ 77801, Main Rd), nearby, is slightly cheaper at Rs 70/129.

Sri Uma Maheswara Tourist Home (☎ 743712) has basic doubles with bath for Rs 110. The staff are friendly and the premises clean.

Mahalakshmi Lodge (☎ 79440), opposite the KSRTC bus stand, is cheap but very basic with rooms with common bathroom for just Rs 44/64.

Hotel Shine is nearby and offers better rooms for Rs 100/115 with bath attached.

Hotel Rail View (☎ 76918), opposite the train station, has rooms for Rs 60/90 and an attached bar and restaurant.

There are *Retiring Rooms* at the station.

Places to Stay – Mid-Range & Top End

Hotel Sudarsan (☎ 744322, fax 740480) is good value at Rs 160/190 or from Rs 360/395 with air-con, although rooms at the front can be noisy because of the traffic. There is an executive suite for Rs 750/850. All rooms have TV and there are restaurants and a bar.

Hotel Sea Bee (☎ 75371, Jetty Rd) is conveniently located, but the plush foyer gives no indication of the unkempt and grotty rooms. Singles/doubles cost Rs 150/200, or Rs 500 for an air-con double.

Hotel Shah International (☎ 742362, fax 75368) is in a quieter location and has pleasant rooms for Rs 150/220, or Rs 330/380 for air-con. There's also an executive suite for Rs 650/950, and a restaurant.

The KTDC *Yatri Nivas* (☎ 745538), just across the inlet from the boat jetty, is large and rather lost looking. Rooms are from Rs 110/165 to Rs 165/220, or Rs 385 for an air-con double. The riverside location is terrific:

there's a pleasant waterfront lawn and the staff will run you across the river to the boat jetty in the hotel's speedboat if you ask nicely. Alternatively you can arrange for the DTPC to send an auto-rickshaw to you at the hotel for about Rs 10.

Palm Lagoon (☎ 451014, fax 523974) is an idyllic resort 18km from Kollam on the shores of Ashtamudi Lake. Self-contained thatched cottages cost Rs 1500 for bed & breakfast or Rs 2250 for full board. There are backwater tours and ayurvedic rejuvenation programs available. There's a 10% discount if you book through the DTPC. A taxi to Palm Lagoon will cost about Rs 100 or you can take the KTDC speedboat for Rs 250.

Places to Eat

Matha Restaurant, near the jetty, serves up a wickedly spicy fried chicken and is a firm favourite with the rickshaw-wallahs. The menu is in Malayalam but you will receive plenty of cheerful help in discerning where the various deep-fried bits used to belong on a chicken.

New Restaurant, opposite the bus stand and next to Mahalakshmi Lodge, is the place to head for coffee or chai while waiting for a KSRTC bus or a ferry.

Hotel Guru Prasad (Main Rd) is a fairly ordinary vegetarian place where a 'meal' (thali) costs just Rs 10.

The *Azad Hotel,* on the same side of the road, is a rather brighter restaurant with both

---

Not Just a Fish

For many Malayalis the best fish in the backwaters is the karimeen, or pearl spot *(Etroplus suratensis)*. But not just any karimeen will do. Those caught in waters where the bottom is composed of black mud are distinguished by their black skin with pearly silver spots and, it is said, have the sweetest of flavours. These fish bring the highest prices. Lesser karimeen are a dull white colour.

veg and nonveg meals. Main Rd also has a decent branch of the *Indian Coffee House*.

The *Sree Suprabatham Restaurant*, hidden away in a courtyard directly opposite the clock tower, is another typical South Indian 'meals' restaurant.

The restaurants in the *Iswarya Lodge* and the *Mahalakshmi Lodge* both have good vegetarian food.

Kedar Restaurant, in the Hotel Sudarsan, is an air-con haven with white tablecloths, etc, but relatively cheap meals. The food is good, with Indian mains for about Rs 40, though the service is way too relaxed and you may need to send back your meal to be properly heated. Western and Chinese cuisine is also available. It's a good spot for breakfast before a backwater cruise.

Hotel Shah International also has a reasonable restaurant.

Jala Subhiksa, a converted Keralan rice barge moored at the ferry pier, was Kollam's floating restaurant. It had been moved to the Palm Lagoon Resort at the time of writing but it, or a replacement, may be back in place by the time you arrive – ask at the Information Centre.

Supreme Bakers, opposite the post office, is great for a treat. Select a cake and enjoy the air-con with a coffee or Pepsi as the wealthy ladies and fat children buying sweets offer a glimpse of yet another side to Indian life.

Kollam is a cashew-growing centre and the nuts are on sale in shops and hotels and from street vendors. Small packets can be bought for Rs 10 to Rs 20.

Getting There & Away

Bus Many of the buses leaving the KSRTC bus stand are en route from elsewhere, so it's the usual pandemonium when a bus arrives. Thankfully, seats in express buses can be reserved in advance. Kollam is on the well serviced Thiruvananthapuram-Kollam-Alappuzha-Ernakulam bus route. Superexpress services take 1½ hours to Thiruvananthapuram (Rs 25); 1¾ hours to Alappuzha (Rs 26); and 3½ hours to Ernakulam (Rs 55).

Alappuzha to Kollam

Train Kollam is 159km south of Ernakulam and the three to four hour trip costs Rs 24/204 in 2nd/1st class. The *Trivandrum Mail* from Chennai goes through Kollam, as does the *Mumbai to Kanyakumari Express* and the Mangalore to Thiruvananthapuram coastal service.

The *Quilon Mail* between Kollam and Chennai (Egmore station) via Madurai covers the 760km in 20 hours for Rs 134/657. The trip across the Western Ghats is a delight.

Boat See the boxed text 'The Backwaters' in the Alappuzha section for information on the popular backwaters cruise to Alappuzha. Although the public ferry to Alappuzha is still not operating, there are public services across Ashtamudi Lake to the villages of Guhanandapuram (one hour), Muthiraparam (2½ hours) or Perumon (2½ hours); fares are around Rs 6 return. The daily ATDC and DTPC tourist boats to Alappuzha can be booked at various hotels around town. They either start by bus from the KSRTC bus stand or from one of the town jetties, depending on water levels and the state of the canal blockage.

Getting Around
The KSRTC bus stand and the boat jetty are side by side, but the train station is on the opposite side of town. Auto-rickshaw drivers are reasonably willing to use their meters; expect to pay around Rs 10 from the train station to the boat jetty. The *Yatri Nivas* speedboat can be hired to explore the waterways around Kollam for Rs 300 an hour.

ALAPPUZHA (Alleppey)
Pop: 274,000 Tel Area Code: 0477
Like Kollam, this is a pleasant, easy-going market town surrounded by coconut plantations and built on the canals which service the coir industry of the backwaters. With the possible exceptions of an incongruous 8m-high concrete mermaid or the Rajiv Gandhi Memorial Old Age Home for Coir Workers, there's precious little to see for most of the year; but the annual Nehru Cup snakeboat race is an event not to be missed. Any other day of the year, the backwater trip to or from Kollam is the only reason to pass through. There is a quiet though not terribly clean beach a short auto-rickshaw ride (Rs 30) from the town centre.

Orientation & Information
The bus stand and boat jetty are conveniently close to each other, and within easy walking distance of most of the cheap hotels. The train station is 4km south-west of the town centre. The DTPC Tourist Reception Centre at the boat jetty is very helpful. The Bank of India on Mullakal Rd will encash travellers cheques.

Alappuzha's water is notoriously unhealthy – take the brown colour as a warning. Even if you drink tap water in other places, it's advisable to give Alappuzha's water a miss.

Nehru Cup Snakeboat Race
This famous regatta takes place on the second Saturday of August each year. It's held on Vembanad Lake to the east of the town. Scores of long, low-slung *chundan vallams* (snakeboats) with highly decorated sterns compete for the cup. Each boat is crewed by up to 100 rowers shaded by gleaming silk umbrellas, all of whom are watched avidly from the banks by thousands of spectators. The annual event celebrates the seafaring and martial traditions of ancient Kerala.

Tickets for the race are available on the day from numerous ticket stands on the way to the lake where the race is held. This entitles you to a seat on the bamboo terraces which are erected for the occasion and which give an excellent view of the lake. Ticket prices range from Rs 10 for standing room to Rs 250 for the Tourist Pavilion, offering best view at the finishing point.

Take food and drink to the race because there's little available on the lakeshore. An umbrella is another necessity because the race takes place during the monsoon and the weather can alternate between driving rain and blistering sunshine.

The race is now repeated during the tourist season as the ingeniously named **Tourism**

Snakeboat Race, on the third day of the Great Elephant March in mid-January.

Places to Stay – Budget

Komala Hotel (☎ 243631), just north of the North Canal, is quite popular and has a good range of rooms. Singles/doubles/triples/quads are Rs 97/130/165/200 and air-con singles/doubles are Rs 385/495 (taxes included).

Sheeba Lodge (☎ 244871), behind the Komala, is cheap and habitable at Rs 70/80, with some more expensive doubles upstairs (Rs 120).

Hotel Karthika, nearby, is probably the poorest choice of the three hotels in this area. seriously neglected doubles cost Rs 100. There is, however, a useful ISD/STD kiosk downstairs.

Hotel Arcadia (☎ 251354), opposite the boat jetty, has a renovated lobby but the rooms are a bit shabby. Non air-con singles/doubles/triples with bath attached are Rs 60/100/150. There's a restaurant downstairs.

Krishna Bhavan Lodge (☎ 60453), nearby, has small, rock-bottom rooms built around a courtyard/rubbish pile. It's cheap at

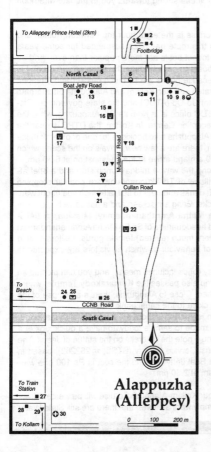

To Alleppey Prince Hotel (2km)

Footbridge

North Canal

Boat Jetty Road

Mullakal Road

Cullan Road

To Beach

CCNB Road

South Canal

To Train Station

To Kollam

Alappuzha (Alleppey)

0   100   200 m

PLACES TO STAY
1 Hotel Karthika; STD/ISD Office
2 Sheeba Lodge
4 Komala Hotel
9 Kuttanad Tourist Home
12 Krishna Bhavan Lodge
15 Kadambari Tourist Home
26 St George's Lodging
27 Hotel Brothers
28 Hotel Raiban

PLACES TO EAT
11 Hotel Annapoorna
18 Hotel Aryas
19 Indian Coffee House
20 Hotel Rajas
21 Sree Durga Bhavan Restaurant
29 Indian Coffee House

OTHER
3 Alappuzha Tourism Development
   Corporation (ATDC)
5 Mermaid Statue
6 Boat Jetty
7 DTPC Tourist Reception Centre &
   Restaurant
8 Bus Stand
10 Vembanad Tourist Services
13 Blue Lagoon
14 Penguin Tourist Boat Service
16 Temple
17 Temple
22 Bank of India
23 Temple
24 Telegraph Office
25 Post Office
30 Hospital

The Backwaters

Fringing the coast of Kerala and winding far inland is a vast network of lagoons, lakes, rivers and canals. These backwaters are both the basis of a distinct lifestyle and a fascinating thoroughfare. Travelling by boat along the backwaters is one of the highlights of a visit to Kerala. The boats cross shallow, palm-fringed lakes studded with cantilevered Chinese fishing nets, and travel along narrow, shady canals where coir (coconut fibre), copra (dried coconut meat) and cashews are loaded onto boats.

Along the way are small settlements where people live on narrow spits of reclaimed land only a few metres wide. Although practically surrounded by water, they still manage to keep cows, pigs, chickens and ducks and cultivate small vegetable gardens. Prawns and fish, including the prized *karimeen*, are also farmed, and shellfish are dredged by hand to be later burnt with coal dust to produce lime. On the more open stretches of canal, traditional boats with huge sails and prominent prows drift by. The sight of three or four of these sailing towards you in the late afternoon sun is unforgettable.

Tourist Cruises The most popular backwater cruise is the eight hour trip between Kollam and Alappuzha. The regular public ferry service on this route has been suspended for some years due to a canal blockage at the Kollam end, but tourist boats are more popular than ever. And although water levels currently allow the tourist boats to pass through the troublesome area, it is unlikely that the slow ferry service will return because buses are so much quicker and cheaper.

There are virtually identical daily cruises operated between Kollam and Alappuzha on alternate days by the private Alleppey Tourist Development Co-Op (ATDC) and the state government District Tourism Promotion Council (DTPC). The ATDC office is in Komala Rd, Alappuzha, while the Alappuzha DTPC can be found at the Tourist Reception Centre. In Kollam, the DTPC is near the KSRTC bus terminal. Many hotels in Kollam and Alappuzha take bookings for one or other of these services. The cost is Rs 150 one way. In addition, there are a few new arrivals on the scene which are competitively priced. Cruises depart at 10.30 am and arrive at their destination at 6.30 pm.

Generally only two major stops are made along the way: a midday lunch stop and a brief afternoon chai stop. Ayiramthengu or the coir village of Thrikkunnappuha are popular stopping places. The crew have an ice box full of fruit, soft drinks and beer to sell, although you might want to bring along additional refreshments and snacks. Bring sunscreen and a hat as well.

Boats also pause to drop visitors off at the **Matha Amrithanandamayi Mission** (☎ 0476-621279) at Amrithapuri. This is the residence and headquarters of Sri Sri Matha Amrithanandamayi Devi, one of India's very few (but in this case very much revered) female gurus. Visitors should dress conservatively and there is a strict code of behaviour to which all visitors are expected to adhere.

You can stay at the ashram for Rs 100 per day (price includes meals), and you can pick up an onward or return cruise a day or two later. The trip also passes the **Kumarakody Temple**, where the noted Malayalam poet Kumaran Asan drowned. Close to Alappuzha, there's a glimpse of the 11th-century **Karumadi Kuttan Buddha Image** close to the canal bank.

The cruise between Alappuzha and Kottayam is shorter – about 4½ hours (it follows a longer route than the ferry, see below) – and stops are made to sample toddy, to have a quick look at a snakeboat, and to visit an old church in Pulincunnu – note the umbrella on the statue of Jesus. The operator is a new cooperative, the Bharath Tourist Service Society (BTSS; ☎ 262262), based in Alappuzha at the Raiban Shopping Complex on Boat Jetty Rd, and the cost is Rs 100 one way. Boats depart Alappuzha at 9.30 am, and Kottayam at 2.30 pm.

Public Ferries Most passengers on the eight hour Kollam-Alappuzha cruise will be western travellers. If you want the local experience, or you simply want a shorter trip, there are still State Water

EDDIE GERALD

PAUL BEINSSEN

LINDSAY BROWN

LINDSAY BROWN

Backwaters
On Kerala's famed Backwaters, *kettuvallams* and other boats ferry loads of coir, copra and cashews across shallow, palm-fringed lakes and along narrow, shady canals.

Backwaters
The Backwaters are the basis of a unique lifestyle, too: freighting, fishing, bathing, and competing in the Snakeboat Races.

Transport boats from Alappuzha to Kottayam (six boats daily, Rs 6, 2½ hours) and Changanassery (two boats daily, Rs 9, three hours). The trip to Kottayam crosses Vembanad Lake and then runs along a fascinating canal. Changanassery is on the road and railway line, 18km south of Kottayam and 78km north of Kollam.

The DTPC also runs a popular four hour cruise which departs Alappuzha at 10 am and returns at 2 pm. This cruise is daily during December and January, and on weekends during the rest of the year. The cost is Rs 100, or Rs 60 concession (students and children). Many people prefer this shorter trip to a full day on a boat, and it also navigates some of the narrower waterways, offering a more intimate glimpse of backwater life.

Houseboats & Charters A very popular, but more expensive, option is to hire a houseboat, converted from a *kettuvallam*, or traditional rice barge. There are many companies in Alappuzha providing these houseboats, all following in the footsteps of the ATDC. Boats can also be chartered through the DTPC in Kollam and Alappuzha. Not surprisingly, there is quite a range in quality and service. Houseboats cater for groups (up to eight bunks) or couples (one or two double bedrooms). They can be hired either on a day-basis (Rs 3500 per boat) or overnight (Rs 5000), allowing you to make the Kollam-Alappuzha trip over two days, mooring in the backwaters overnight. Delicious Keralan food can be provided (including a cook) for an extra Rs 400 per person.

The DTPC also hires four-seat speed boats for Rs 300 per hour, and slower six-seaters for Rs 200 per hour. Between a group of people, this can be quite an economical proposition and allows you to make stops and plan your own itinerary – an option not available on the public ferries or tourist cruises. In Alappuzha, the baby blue tourist boats are moored across the North Canal from the boat jetty. Go directly to the boats if you don't want to deal through an intermediary tout. A one way trip to Kottayam costs about Rs 500. Alternatively, there are boat operators like the efficient Penguin Tourist Boat Service (☎ 261522) on Boat Jetty Rd. It has a long list of suggested backwater trips from Alappuzha. Vembanad Tourist Services (☎ 251395) and Blue Lagoon (☎ 260103), both in Alappuzha, also have boats for hire.

Backwater Village Tours An increasingly popular way to explore the backwaters is on a village tour. Usually this involves small groups of less than 10 people, a knowledgeable guide and an open work boat or covered kettuvallam. The tours last from 2½ to six hours. You are taken to villages to watch coir making, boat building, toddy tapping and fish farming, and on the longer trips a traditional Keralan lunch is provided. These tours are more rewarding to the tourist and the villagers, and they are very accessible – some of the best village tours operate out of Kochi, Kollam and Thiruvananthapuram (see Organised Tours in the relevant sections).

Backwater Ecology Although the backwaters have become an important tourist attraction, they are severely threatened by population growth and industrial and agricultural development. Kerala has 29 major lakes on the backwater system, seven of which drain to the sea. It's estimated that the area of these lakes has fallen from 440 sq km in 1968 to less than 350 sq km today due to legal and illegal land reclamation projects and urban development. The vast Vembanad Lake has dropped from 230 sq km to 179 sq km. The backwaters are only one-third of their mid-19th century levels.

Ecological damage includes pollution, the extinction of mangroves, crocodiles and migratory fish and the destruction of oyster beds. Many migratory birds no longer visit the backwaters and destructive fishing (using dynamite, poison and very fine nets) has caused great damage. To the casual eye, the most visible danger is the unhindered spread of water hyacinth (African moss or Nile cabbage), which clogs many stretches of canal and causes great difficulties for the boat operators.

Rs 30/50 with common bath and Rs 45/65 with bath attached, but barely habitable.

Kadambari Tourist Home (☎ *252210*), around the corner on Mullakal Rd, is marginally better and has rooms for Rs 60/100. There's a small Ganesh temple at its entrance.

St George's Lodging (☎ *61620, CCNB Rd*), opposite South Canal, is the best of the cheapies. Clean rooms cost Rs 33/58 with common bath or Rs 45/83 with bath.

Hotel Brothers (☎ *251653*), near the train station, has OK rooms for Rs 65/130/195 and musty air-con doubles for Rs 288. There is a veg/nonveg restaurant attached.

Places to Stay – Mid-Range & Top End
Hotel Raiban (☎ *251930*) is south of the South Canal, en route to the train station. Rooms are Rs 100/135, or Rs 300 for an air-con double. There's a restaurant and an ice cream parlour offering some intriguing flavours like 'Apricot Quark' and 'Bunny'.

Alleppey Prince Hotel (☎ *243752, AS Rd*), 3km north of the centre, is centrally air-conditioned and the best place in town. It has a bar, an excellent restaurant (opens at 7 pm) and an inviting swimming pool. Rooms are Rs 600/700. It's popular, so book ahead. An auto-rickshaw from the jetty or town centre should cost about Rs 20 (the rickshaw drivers get a sizeable commission so you should be able to drive a good bargain; a taxi is Rs 80.

Places to Eat
The *restaurant* attached to the DTPC Tourist Reception Centre on the North Canal is cheap, clean and airy and serves a wide variety of breakfasts, snacks and meals.

There's an *Indian Coffee House* branch on Mullakal Rd in the town centre and another south of the South Canal, opposite the hospital.

The *Hotel Aryas (Mullakal Rd)* serves good, cheap vegetarian meals. *Hotel Rajas* is a basic veg/nonveg restaurant.

Sree Durga Bhavan is a cheerful place where a good masala dosa will only set you back Rs 8.

Komala Hotel and *Hotel Raiban* have OK restaurants, and there are two *Annapoorna* veg restaurants; one next door to the Hotel Raiban and the other on Book Jetty Rd.

The *Vembanad Restaurant* at the Alleppey Prince Hotel is the best restaurant in town. It's comfortable and air-conditioned (or you can elect to eat by the pool) and serves excellent veg/nonveg food.

Getting There & Away
Bus On the Thiruvananthapuram-Kollam-Alappuzha-Ernakulam route, buses operate frequently. From Thiruvananthapuram, it's about 3¼ hours and Rs 40/55 to Alappuzha by superfast/express bus. It takes 1¾ hours and costs Rs 18/25 to reach Ernakulam from Alappuzha. To Kottayam a superfast is Rs 15 and to Changanassary it's Rs 8.50.

Train The train station is about 4km south-west of the town centre, close to the seafront. An auto-rickshaw from town costs about Rs 20. The 57km journey to Ernakulam takes one hour and costs Rs 20/109 in 2nd/1st class. There are also plenty of trains to Kayankulam (Rs 16/92).

Boat Alappuzha is the best starting point to explore the backwaters. See the boxed text 'The Backwaters' for general information on this fascinating means of travel.

KOTTAYAM
Pop: 172,000 Tel Area Code: 0481
Kottayam was a focus for the Syrian Christians of Kerala. Today, it's a centre for rubber production. There are direct buses from here to Periyar Wildlife Sanctuary, and ferries or tour boats to Alappuzha, so you may well find yourself passing through. The backwater trip from here to Alappuzha is a shorter alternative to the Alappuzha to Kollam trip.

Kottayam is the headquarters for India's second-largest daily newspaper in terms of circulation, the *Malayala Manorama*. It's published in Malayalam, and has a circulation of around 8.2 million – second only to the English-language daily the *Times of India*, with 11.1 million.

Orientation & Information

There's a private bus stand in the town centre where you can catch buses to Ernakulam. It is a secondary stop with no office or information provided – just hop on a bus with 'Ernakulam' on it and pay the conductor. The train station (2km from the city centre), boat jetty (3km) and KSRTC bus stand are all some distance from the centre.

The once useless Tourist Information Centre in the centre of town has been demolished. At the time of writing, inquiries were being 'handled' by the District Tourism Office at the Collectorate – don't waste your time trying to find them in the labyrinthine Collectorate. The telegraph office is open 24 hours daily for STD/ISD and local calls. The main benefit of making your calls from here rather than the many private booths is that there is little traffic noise. You can cash travellers cheques and get Visa cash advances at the Canara Bank on KK Rd.

Things to See

The **Thirunakkara Shiva Temple** in the centre of town is built in typical Keralan style and is only open to Hindus. About 3km north-west of the centre are two interesting Syrian Christian churches. **Cheriapally**, St Mary's Orthodox Church or the 'small' church, has an elegant façade spoilt by tacked-on entrance porches. The interior is notable for the 400-year-old vegetable dye paintings on the walls and ceiling.

Valiyapally, St Mary's Church or the 'big' church, is 100m away, and is actually smaller than its neighbour. The church was built in 1550. The altar is flanked by stone crosses, one with a Pahlavi Persian inscription. The cross on the left is probably original, but the one on the right is a copy. The guestbook goes back to 1899, and was signed by Haile Selassie of Ethiopia in 1956, among others. The extraordinary disembodied arms projecting from the wall relate to a story in the

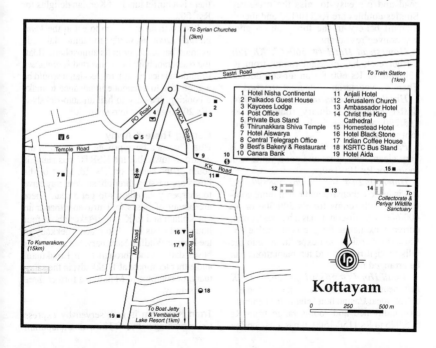

To Syrian Churches (3km)

Sastri Road

To Train Station (1km)

PO Road

YMCA Road

Temple Road

KK Road

MC Road

TB Road

1 Hotel Nisha Continental
2 Paikados Guest House
3 Kaycees Lodge
4 Post Office
5 Private Bus Stand
6 Thirunakkara Shiva Temple
7 Hotel Aiswarya
8 Central Telegraph Office
9 Best's Bakery & Restaurant
10 Canara Bank
11 Anjali Hotel
12 Jerusalem Church
13 Ambassador Hotel
14 Christ the King Cathedral
15 Homestead Hotel
16 Hotel Black Stone
17 Indian Coffee House
18 KSRTC Bus Stand
19 Hotel Aida

To Collectorate & Periyar Wildlife Sanctuary

To Kumarakom (15km)

To Boat Jetty & Vembanad Lake Resort (1km)

Kottayam

0   250   500 m

book of Daniel, which will be happily given to you to read. A donation towards restoration and upkeep will be expected.

Christ The King Cathedral is an immense, Johnny-come-lately landmark which is helpful for orientation.

Places to Stay

Kaycees Lodge (☎ 563440, YMCA Rd) is central, and has good rooms with attached bathroom for Rs 80/135.

The KTDC *Hotel Aiswarya (☎ 581254)* is also close to the centre, just off Temple Rd. Singles/doubles are Rs 150/200, Rs 400/500 (deluxe) or Rs 600/750 with air-con. It has a multicuisine restaurant and a beer parlour, and the lift goes all the way to the roof from where you can get a good view of the grounds of the Thirunakkara Shiva temple.

The *Ambassador Hotel (☎ 563293, KK Rd)* is less conveniently located. Keep a sharp lookout because it's set back from the road and it's easy to miss the driveway. Singles/doubles are Rs 110/137 and there's a small bakery in the lobby and a good veg/nonveg restaurant.

Homestead Hotel (☎ 560467, KK Rd), further east, has pleasant rooms from Rs 130/280, or Rs 600 for an air-con double. There's a vegetarian restaurant attached.

Hotel Nisha Continental (☎ 563984, Sastri Rd) has ordinary rooms for Rs 195/270, and has a fairly ordinary restaurant as well.

Paikados Guest House (☎ 584340) is very clean, very quiet and good value with rooms for Rs 100/160.

Hotel Aida (☎ 568391, fax 568399, MC Rd) is more expensive and much more comfortable with rooms for Rs 300/500 or Rs 400/600 with air-con. It has a bar, restaurant, currency exchange for guests and cable TV. Backwater cruises and expeditions into the hills to visit rubber and tea plantations can be arranged here.

Anjali Hotel (☎ 563661, fax 563669, KK Rd), near the town centre, is part of the excellent local Casino hotel chain. It's centrally air-conditioned and rooms range from Rs 675/975 to Rs 1150/1500. It has a bar, coffee shop and an air-con restaurant which serves snacks and cool drinks outside meal times.

Vembanad Lake Resort (☎ 564866), 2km south of the town centre, has cottages in a pleasant lakeside setting for Rs 450, or Rs 690 with air-con.

Places to Eat

Indian Coffee House (TB Rd) serves the usual snacks and breakfast.

The nearby *Hotel Black Stone* has basic vegetarian food.

Best's Bakery & Restaurant is another fairly typical South Indian restaurant fronted by a decent bakery where you can stock up on cakes, biscuits and chocolates for the long bus ride to Kumily or a backwater trip.

The excellent, partly air-con *Thali Restaurant (KK Rd)*, at the Homestead Hotel, does good thalis for Rs 20.

The restaurant at the *Anjali Hotel* has superb food, and at the *Ambassador Hotel* there is a buffet lunch of Keralan delights for Rs 100.

It's worth an excursion to eat at the *Vembanad Lake Resort*'s romantic lakeside evening barbecue, or in its atmospheric floating restaurant built in a converted *kettuvallam* (traditional rice barge). In Dec-Jan it would be a good idea to telephone in advance to make a booking. It's easy to hail an auto-rickshaw (Rs 20) to get back into town.

Getting There & Away

Bus There's a busy private bus stand in the centre of town, but the KSRTC bus stand is south of the centre, on TB Rd. Most of the buses are passing through, so you may have to sharpen your elbows to get a seat. There are plenty of buses to Thiruvananthapuram via Kollam and to Kochi. It takes about four hours and costs Rs 34 to reach Thekkady in the Periyar Wildlife Sanctuary. Seven express buses daily come through from Ernakulam and either terminate at Thekkady, in the sanctuary, or continue to Madurai, a further three hours away.

Train Kottayam is well served by express trains running between Thiruvananthapuram and Ernakulam. Destinations served include Kollam (100km, Rs 27/153 2nd/1st class), Thiruvananthapuram (165km, Rs 43/213, three hours) and Ernakulam (65km, Rs 20/109, two hours).

Boat The boat jetty, on a stretch of canal almost choked with weed, is about 3km from the town centre. Six ferries daily make the 2½ hour trip to Alappuzha for Rs 6 or you can take the BTSS 4½ hour cruise for Rs 100 (see the boxed text 'The Backwaters' in the Alappuzha section). This interesting trip is worthwhile if you don't have the time or the inclination for the day-long cruise between Kollam and Alappuzha. You can also charter your own boat for Rs 400 to Rs 500, although it's easier to do this from Alappuzha.

Getting Around
An auto-rickshaw from the train station to the ferry (ask for 'jetty') is Rs 30. From the train station or KSRTC bus stand to the town centre is about Rs 15.

AROUND KOTTAYAM
Kumarakom Bird Sanctuary
This bird sanctuary on Vembanad Lake is 16km west of Kottayam in a former rubber plantation. Local water fowl can be seen in abundance, as well as overwintering migratory species. Recently, several luxury resorts have opened at Kumarakom.

Places to Stay The KTDC *Kumarakom Tourist Village* (☎ 0481-524258) has houseboats with one double bedroom for Rs 1200 and with two double bedrooms for Rs 2000. To cruise the lake costs an extra Rs 600 per hour.

Coconut Lagoon Resort (☎ 0481-524491; *Kochi* ☎ 668221), part of the luxury Casino Group, has bungalow rooms for US$95/105 and mansion rooms for US$105/115. The setting is beautiful and there's a swimming pool.

Taj Garden Retreat (☎ 0481-524371; *Kochi* ☎ 668377) is small but luxurious and is similarly priced. All of these resorts have expensive house restaurants.

Getting There & Away Buses run regularly from Kottayam to Kumarakom. The Coconut Lagoon Resort can be reached by boat from near Kottayam, from Thanneermukkom (50km from Kochi) or all the way from Alappuzha.

Ettumanur
The Shiva temple at Ettumanur, 12km north of Kottayam, is noted for its superb woodcarvings and murals. The murals are similar in style to those at Mattancherry Palace in Kochi. To get there, hire an auto-rickshaw or catch a bus.

Vijnana Kala Vedi Centre
The Vijnana Kala Vedi Cultural Centre at Aranmula, a village 12km from Changanassery (Changanacherry), offers courses in Indian arts under expert supervision in a village setting. Subjects include Kathakali, Mohiniattam and Bharata Natyam dancing, Carnatic vocal music, percussion instruments, woodcarving, painting, Keralan cooking, languages (Hindi, Malayalam, Sanskrit), *kaulams* (auspicious decorations), Kalarippayat (Keralan martial art), ayurvedic (traditional Indian) medicine, mythology, astrology and religion.

You can put your own course together and stay as long as you like, though a minimum commitment of one month is preferred. Fees, which include full board and lodging and two subjects of study, start at around US$200 a week – less for longer stays. For further details, write to The Director, Vijnana Kala Vedi Cultural Centre, Tarayil Mukku Junction, Aranmula 689533, Kerala. Changanassery is just south of Kottayam and makes an interesting backwater trip from Alappuzha.

Sree Vallabha Temple
Traditional, all-night **Kathakali** performances are staged almost every night of the year at Sree Vallabha Temple, 2km from the town of Tiruvilla. The performances are an offering by the temple's devotees but non-Hindus are allowed to watch. Tiruvilla is about 35km south of Kottayam on the rail

route between Ernakulam and Thiruvananthapuram. Most trains stop at Tiruvilla. There is budget and mid-range accommodation available in Tiruvilla.

The Western Ghats

PERIYAR WILDLIFE SANCTUARY
Tel Area Code: 04869
Periyar is South India's most popular wildlife sanctuary, but if you go hoping to see tigers, you're almost certain to be disappointed. The great cats require an enormous amount of territory on which to lead their solitary lives and it's estimated the 777 sq km sanctuary has just 35 tigers and leopards. If, on the other hand, you treat Periyar as a pleasant escape from the rigours of Indian travel, a nice place to cruise on the lake, and an opportunity to see some wildlife and enjoy a jungle walk, then you will probably find a visit well worthwhile. The park encompasses a 26 sq km artificial lake, created by the British in 1895 to provide water to Madurai, and spreads into Tamil Nadu. It is home to bison, antelopes, sambar, wild boar, monkeys, langur, a wide variety of birds, and some 750 elephants.

Orientation & Information
Kumily is the junction town straddling the Kerala/Tamil Nadu border just north of the park boundary. It's a small place bustling with spice dealers, about 4km from Thekkady. Thekkady is the centre inside the park where the KTDC hotels and the boat jetty are located. When people refer to the sanctuary, they tend to use Kumily, Thekkady and Periyar interchangeably, which can be confusing. The name 'Periyar' is used to refer to the whole park.

There's a Wildlife Information Centre near the boat jetty in Thekkady. It's advisable to bring warm clothes and waterproof clothing to Periyar. Admission to the park costs Rs 50 (or US$2) for foreigners and only Rs 2 for Indians. An auto-rickshaw into the park from Kumily will cost Rs 25, plus Rs 5 entry fee for the rickshaw.

Visiting the Park
Boat trips on the lake are the usual way of touring the sanctuary, but spend one day at Periyar and take a midday boat trip and you're unlikely to see anything. 'As soon as a shy animal sticks its head up', reported one visitor, 'all aboard shout and scream until it goes again'.

The standard two-hour boat trips cost Rs 25 on the lower deck and Rs 50 on the upper deck in the larger KTDC craft, or Rs 15 in the sad-looking Forest Department craft. There are five KTDC cruises a day: at 7, 9.30 and 11.30 am and 2 and 4 pm and four Forest Department cruises (same times minus the early morning departure). The first and last departures offer the best wildlife-spotting prospects. It's better to get a small group together (the smaller the better) and charter your own boat. They're available in a variety of sizes from Rs 500 per cruise for a 12-person boat.

Jungle walks can also be interesting. A daily three hour walk departs at 7.30 am and costs Rs 10 per person. Guides can also be arranged from the Wildlife Information Centre for walks further into the park. This activity isn't promoted because it is not official park business, rather a sideline for some of the guides, so you must ask insistently about it. Visitors are not allowed to walk in the park without a guide. Some of the guides are very knowledgeable and they're certainly cautious in areas where animals may be present.

The third way to see wildlife is to spend a night in one of the *observation towers* or *resthouses*, although these are often booked out weeks in advance. Observation towers cost Rs 100 a night plus the boat drop-off charge and you must bring your own food supplies; resthouses cost Rs 300 per night plus Rs 60 for meals and the boat drop-off charge. Elephant rides (Rs 30 for two people for 30 minutes) are for fun, not for serious wildlife-viewing.

The best time to visit the sanctuary is between September and May. The hot season

(February to May) may be less comfortable but will offer more wildlife sightings because other water sources dry up and the wildlife is forced to come down to the lakeside. Weekends and public holidays are best avoided because of noisy day-trippers.

What you see is a matter of luck, but even those elusive tigers do show themselves occasionally. One guide reported that in the three years he had spent at the park, he had seen tigers only twice: on one occasion, he saw a tiger swimming in the lake close to the Lake Palace Hotel.

Organised Tours

A two day Periyar Wildlife Sanctuary tour leaves Thiruvananthapuram most Saturdays at 6.30 am and gets back on Sunday at 9 pm. It costs Rs 300, does not include food or accommodation, and must be one of the silliest tours in India, since there's no time to see any wildlife – even if it were possible in the company of a busload of garrulous honeymooners.

The grand-sounding Thekkady Tourism Development Council operates out of the Rolex Tourist Home. It has a brochure on Periyar, a rough map, and can organise tours to viewpoints, spice and tea plantations and temples in the district.

Many of the spice shops advertise tours to spice plantations, where you can see cinnamon, cardamom, pepper, cloves and many other spices in their pre-packed state.

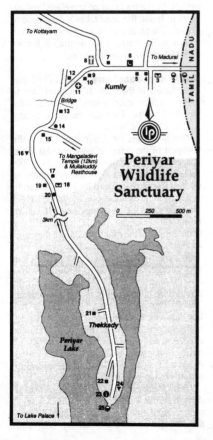

PLACES TO STAY
4   Hotel Regent Tower
5   Muckumkal Tourist Home
7   Lake Queen Tourist Home
9   Rolex Tourist Home
10 Woodlands Tourist Bhavan
12 Karthika Tourist Home
13 Spice Village
15 Hotel Ambadi
17 Leela Pankaj Resorts
19 Ambika Tourist Home
21 Periyar House
22 Aranya Nivas Hotel

PLACES TO EAT
16 Coffee Inn
24 Snack Bar

OTHER
1   Tamil Nadu Bus Station
2   Bus Stand & Tourist Taxis
3   Post Office
6   Mosque
8   Church
11 Hospital
14 Forest Checkpoint
18 Post Office
20 Park Entry Post
23 Wildlife Information Centre
25 Boat Jetty

KERALA

Places to Stay & Eat

Outside the Sanctuary Kumily is a one-street town, but it has accommodation ranging from dirt cheap to luxurious. Although it's 4km from the lake, you can catch the semi-regular bus, take an auto-rickshaw, hire a bicycle or set off on foot; it's a pleasant, shady walk into the park. If you're here in the low season, you should be able to negotiate a discount on these rates.

Muckumkal Tourist Home (☎ 22070) is close to the bus stand. Avoid the back rooms, which can be noisy if the hotel generator is switched on. Rooms with attached bathroom are Rs 75/150; air-con doubles are Rs 450. The hotel's *Little Chef Restaurant* is a reasonable place to eat.

Hotel Regent Tower, nearby, is run by the same folk. Rooms cost 107/215, which includes tax, and there is a restaurant, the *Maharani*.

Lake Queen Tourist Home (☎ 22084), next to the Kottayam Rd junction, has 54 rooms from Rs 107.50/161.25 (including tax). It is run by the Catholic Church and all profits go to charity. The *Lakeland Restaurant* is downstairs.

Rolex Tourist Home (☎ 22081), along the road to the park, has clean singles/doubles with bathroom for Rs 100/200.

Woodlands Tourist Bhavan (☎ 22077), close by, is cheap but very basic and gloomy. Rooms are Rs 80, or Rs 100/150 with attached bath. You might also find a cheap bed in one of the two large dorms.

Ambika Tourist Home (☎ 22004) has very small, very basic, singles with bucket shower for Rs 50. One double room has a shower and costs Rs 100.

Karthika Tourist Home (☎ 22146), opposite the hospital, has rather grotty rooms with bath for Rs 100/150 and a vegetarian restaurant.

Spice Village (☎ 22314) is a well designed Casino Group resort with attractive cottages in a pleasant garden with a swimming pool. The tariff is US$85/95 or US$115/125 for deluxe bungalows. Dinner in the restaurant starts at 7.30 pm and will blow your budget.

Hotel Ambadi (☎ 22193) has damp semi-detached cottages for Rs 380 to Rs 650 and rooms for Rs 900. It's in a beautiful setting and has quite a good restaurant serving Indian, Chinese and western dishes.

Leela Pankaj Resorts (☎ 22392) has cute, clean cottages for Rs 500 (Rs 250 from June to August) and mosquito netting is provided. There is a restaurant featuring Indian, Chinese and continental cuisines.

There are a few cheap *meals* places along Kumily's main drag.

Coffee Inn is a popular outdoor cafe with an eclectic selection of music and good travellers' fare (including home-made brown bread). In the tradition of travellers' restaurants in India, the food takes a *long* time to arrive. There are also a couple of small rooms with shared bath available for Rs 125/150 including mosquito net.

Inside the Sanctuary The KTDC has three hotels in the park. It's a good idea to make advance reservations, particularly for weekend visits. This can be done at any KTDC office or hotel.

Periyar House (☎ 22026, fax 22282), the cheapest of the three, is very popular. from August to May, rooms start at Rs 500/700, including breakfast and either lunch or dinner. The price drops to Rs 300/500 during June and July. You can hire bicycles, have a massage and change money here. If you're doing the 7.30 am jungle walk, tell the restaurant staff the night before and they will arrange an early, light breakfast.

Aranya Nivas (☎ 22023, fax 22282) has very pleasant rooms for Rs 1100/2000 and air-con suites for Rs 1150/2200. These prices drop considerably in the low season. There's a bar, garden area, TV lounge, postal and banking facilities and a small handicrafts shop. Food in the restaurant is excellent, and most nights there's a Rs 250 buffet (nonguests welcome). Guests at the Aranya Nivas are entitled to a free morning and afternoon boat trip.

Lake Palace (bookings & reception at Aranya Nivas ☎ 22023, fax 22282) is well away from the noise of day-trippers. Guests are transferred to the hotel by boat and should arrive at the Thekkady boat jetty by 4 pm for the final trip of the day back to the hotel. The six suites in the palace, at one time the maharaja's game lodge, cost Rs 4000/6000 a night, including meals and boating. If you can afford it, it's a delightful place to stay and you can actually see animals from your room. With a guide, it's possible to walk to the Lake Palace from the boat jetty in about an hour.

There are **resthouses** in the sanctuary at Manakavala (8km from Kumily), Mullakudy (39km) and Edappalayam (5km). Not all of them may be open for visitors but you can find out and book at the Wildlife Information Centre. The resthouses cost Rs 200/300 and have a keeper who will cook for you, although you must bring your own food.

There are also **observation towers** for Rs 100, which can be booked at the Wildlife Information Centre. Although they're primitive, and you must provide all your own food and bedding, you stand the best chance of seeing animals if you rent one. One of the watchtowers is a short stroll from the Lake Palace.

Near the boat jetty in Thekkady, there's a **snack bar** offering basic food, snacks and drinks.

Getting There & Away
Bus The bus stand in Kumily is just a bit of spare land at the eastern edge of town near the state border. All buses originating or terminating at Periyar start and finish at Aranya Nivas in Thekkady, but they also stop at the Kumily bus stand.

Buses operate on the Ernakulam Kottayam Kumily Madurai route. There are three express buses each way daily between Ernakulam and Kumily. Buses to Ernakulam take six hours and cost between Rs 46 and Rs 54.50, depending on the bus and the ticket seller.

The 110km trip from Kottayam takes about four hours and costs Rs 34. Regular buses go every half hour. The buses pass through rubber plantations and villages with pastel-coloured churches and rocket-like shrines. The road then climbs steadily through a mass of tea, coffee and cardamom plantations.

At least two direct buses daily make the eight hour trip to Thiruvananthapuram (Rs 80). Another goes to Kovalam (nine hours), and another to Kodaikanal (6½ hours). Only private buses make the spectacular trip to Munnar (Rs 30, 4½ hours). They all leave Kumily in the morning (6, 6.30, 8 and 9.30 am).

Getting Around
There is supposed to be a bus operating regularly between Kumily and Thekkady but few, if any, have seen it. An auto-rickshaw costs Rs 25. The KTDC Periyar House and Aranya Nivas both have bicycles for rent at Rs 25 a day.

AROUND PERIYAR
On the road to Munnar, about 20km from Kumily, is an isolated luxury resort called **Carmelia Haven** (☎ 04869-70252, fax 70268). Set in spice and tea plantations, a variety of rooms cost from Rs 1250/1500 in cottages to Rs 3250/3500 in a treehouse! There's even a cave! All rooms are equipped with modern amenities and satellite TV, and there are activities such as trekking and fishing.

The **Mangaladevi Temple**, 12km from Kumily, is just a jumble of ruins but the views are magnificent. At present, the road to the temple is closed. If it reopens, it's possible to get there by rented jeep or by bicycle, but the trip is uphill all the way from Kumily. By jeep from Kumily, count on a three to four hour round trip, including a lunch stop.

MUNNAR
Tel Area Code: 04865
Set amid South India's most dramatic mountain scenery in what was once known as the 'High Range of Travancore', the tiny hill town of Munnar (1524m) is the commercial centre of some of the world's highest tea-growing estates.

The combination of craggy peaks, manicured tea estates and crisp mountain air makes Munnar a delightful alternative to the better known hill stations of Tamil Nadu. But if you don't make the effort to get away from the scruffy immediacy of the main bazaar you may altogether miss the beauty and tranquillity of the countryside.

Information

The official Government Tourist Information Office is inconveniently located on Alwaye Munnar Rd (AM Rd), 2km from the bus stand and town centre, and is of little help apart from providing bus information, a STD/ISD phone service and organising a couple of sightseeing tours. The small Munnar Tourist Information Centre is similar. Instead, head for the Tourist Information Service (☎ 30349), a small shop in the bazaar, not far from the bus stand. Here you will receive information on things to do as well as assistance in arranging accommodation, auto-rickshaws and tours, etc.

A convenient and relatively quiet STD/ISD booth can be found at Happy Associates near the footbridge. It also stocks a small selection of ice cream. The Munnar Supply Association store stocks most grocery items.

For changing money, the State Bank of Travancore is efficient and friendly.

Things to See & Do

The stone **Christ's Church** (1910) is now administered by the Church of South India. Inside the well kept church are touching brass plaques in memory of the tea planters.

While the **walks** out of Munnar in any direction offer spectacular views, it's worth taking an auto-rickshaw (Rs 125 return) for the 16km to **Eravikulam National Park** (entrance Rs 50) where you can see the rare, but almost tame, Nilgiri tahr (a type of mountain goat), or clamber over the slopes of **Anamudi** (2695m), which is South India's highest peak.

A little further afield is **Top Station**, on Kerala's border with Tamil Nadu, which has spectacular views over the Ghats. There is precious little left of the ropeway which was used to transport tea – just some cement foundations. Be prepared to arrive and find the view obscured by cloud. Regular buses from Munnar make the steep 32km climb to Top Station in around an hour. Catch one of the private buses going to Koviluo, at the bus stand near Happy Associates. Koviluo is the next stop after Top Station. At Koviluo the bus turns around and heads back to Munnar – giving you

The High Range

According to local historians, the first European to enter the high ranges of Travancore was a young Duke of Wellington in pursuit of the slippery Tipu Sultan. While this romantic story may not stand up to academic scrutiny, it wasn't too long afterwards, in the early 19th century, that the Great Trigonometrical Survey brought British officers to these wild lands frequented by elephants, gaur, tigers and leopards. But by no means was the High Range uninhabited. The Mudhuvans had lived in the area around Munnar for centuries, and they had had constant contact with traders plying well trodden paths between the plains of Madurai and the towns of the spice coast.

It wasn't until the late 1870s that the region was confirmed as part of the independent Kingdom of Travancore and land concessions were distributed to the wealthy and influential. The area that came to be known as the Kanan Devan Hills boomed with plantings of coffee, cinchona (quinine is extracted from its bark) and tea. Labour had to brought in from Tamil Nadu, but elephants remained a problem, trampling crops and bungalows.

Disaster struck the small and still very isolated community in 1924. A heavy monsoon saw major landslides and flooding change the face of Munnar. There was a great loss of life and property, but the townsfolk recovered, rebuilt and replanted. Tea became the most economically viable crop and remains so to this day.

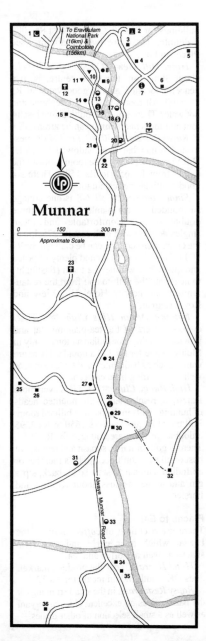

PLACES TO STAY
3 Hotel Brothers
4 Edassery Eastend
5 Government Guest House
6 Isaac's The Residency
9 Ambat & Krishna Lodges
15 PWD Guest House
25 Poopada Tourist Home
26 Kannan Devan Hills Club
30 Sree Narayana (SN) Tourist Home
32 High Range Club
34 Hotel Hill View
35 Royal Retreat
36 Sinai Cottages

PLACES TO EAT
10 Rapsy Restaurant
11 Suganthi Tea Stall

OTHER
1 Mosque
2 Temple
7 Munnar Tourist Information Centre
8 Produce Market; Hotel Hazrath
12 Church
13 Buses to Kumily & Ernakulam
14 Christian Shrine
16 Tourist Information Service
17 Buses to Top Station
18 State Bank of Travancore
19 Post & Telegaph Office
20 Petrol Station
21 Happy Associates
22 Tata Tea Regional Office
23 Christ's Church (Church of South India)
24 Raja Cycles
27 School
28 Government Tourist Information Office
29 Munnar Supply Association
31 CTC & RMTC Buses to Tamil Nadu
33 KSRTC Bus Stand

about an hour at Top Station. Or hire a jeep for the return trip for around Rs 600.

Organised Tours
Tata Tea conducts free tours of **tea processing factories**. Put your name down for a tour at the regional office in town. You will probably get to do the tour the next day if there are sufficient numbers of interested people. On the other hand, you may be asked to wait for the appropriate staff member to

arrive and find yourself wasting precious hours waiting for the tour to start.

Places to Stay

Munnar is crying out for a cheap, clean travellers' lodge in a quiet part of town. As it stands there are a few budget options, which are OK but are close to the noisy bazaar. Most accommodation in and around Munnar is in the middle to top range, catering mainly to honeymooners.

Places to Stay – Budget

The *PWD Guest House* is a ramshackle old bungalow with rock-bottom rooms for Rs 50.

Sree Narayana Tourist Home (☎ 30212, AM Rd), near the Tourist Information Office, is an average Indian lodge with doubles starting at Rs 300. Some rooms have a TV, shower and western toilet and cost Rs 400.

Ambat Lodge (☎ 30661) in the bazaar has tiny cell-like rooms for Rs 60/125. Doubles have bath (bucket) attached, singles share a bathroom. This place suffers from noise from the bazaar and rowdy staff who feel the need to make as much noise as possible at 6 am.

Krishna Lodge (☎ 30669), next door, has larger rooms for Rs 75/150 with bath attached.

Hotel Brothers (☎ 30436) is a small, friendly Indian lodging place with doubles/triples for Rs 200/300. Two rooms have attached bath, and there is a small restaurant (see Places to Eat).

Places to Stay – Mid-Range & Top End

The *Government Guest House* has spacious, clean doubles with shower and hot water for Rs 550.

Poopada Tourist Home (☎ 30223), about 400m west of the Government Tourist Office, has rooms with Indian bathroom (ie squat toilet) for Rs 495 a double. There's also a good, cheap restaurant.

Isaac's The Residency (☎ 30501, fax 30317) has large, comfortable rooms with cable TV and hot water for Rs 500/600. Credit cards are accepted, guests can change money, and there's a restaurant and bar.

Edassery Eastend (☎ 30451, fax 30227) has rooms in attractive plantation-house

buildings for Rs 650. Cottages cost Rs 1000 a double. There are two restaurants (see Places to Eat).

Hotel Hill View (☎ 30567, fax 30241), about 3km from the town centre, is in a peaceful location and is good value at Rs 250/400. All rooms have TV, telephone and hot water. There's an OK multicuisine restaurant and tours and fishing can be arranged.

Royal Retreat (☎ 30240, fax 30440), next to and somewhat overshadowed by Hotel Hill View, offers very nice rooms with all the extras from Rs 650 to Rs 1500. There's a good multicuisine restaurant.

Sinai Cottages (☎ 30560) is one cottage surrounded by tea plantations, with three double rooms. Comfortable and clean singles/doubles with bath cost Rs 275/350 or the entire stone cottage can be claimed for Rs 1000. There is hot water and plenty of peace and quiet. You will need a torch (flashlight) to negotiate the path to and from the restaurants at the nearby Hotel Hill View and Royal Retreat.

Kannan Devan Hills Club (☎ 30252) evokes the era of the tea-planting Raj and provides lodgings for Indian nationals only in Muir Cottage for Rs 350 a double. There are games such as badminton and table tennis, as well as a spiffing little canteen.

High Range Club (☎ 30253) is even more Rajesque, resplendent with mounted heads of hunting spoils in the bar and billiard room. Full board ranges from Rs 1650 to Rs 2295 a double, or there are cottages for Rs 1950. There is golf, billiards, squash and tennis, but best of all you don't need to be a member or an Indian national to stay, so sit back, sip a gin and argue the toss about Kipling and Forster.

Places to Eat

There are a couple of *coffee stalls* in the bazaar which open early and sell tiffin snacks as well as coffee and tea.

Hotel Hazrath, near the produce market, does OK South Indian meals for Rs 12.

Rapsy Restaurant, in the arcade running off the bazaar, does an excellent chicken biryani as well as a small selection of other dishes.

Suganthi Tea Stall, almost opposite Rapsy in the arcade, is a popular and busy place with savoury and sweet snacks but a shortage of seats.

Edassery Eastend has two restaurants: upstairs, through the main entrance, is the upmarket one, and downstairs (enter from the back of the building) is the simpler, much cheaper, one. Both are good quality (they use the same kitchen), but there is a smaller range and bigger serves downstairs.

Hotel Brothers has a basic but authentic restaurant. Usually there is only one meal available – 'Keralan Dish' – which consists of fish curry and tapioca (Rs 15).

The middle and top-end hotels all have good restaurants, usually with the three cuisines ubiquitous to hotels in Kerala: Indian, Chinese and continental. On average it is better to stick with the Indian menu.

Getting There & Away

Munnar is 130km east of Kochi via Aluva (Alwaye) and 70km north of Periyar. It's best reached by direct bus from Kochi (five daily, 4½ hours), Kottayam (five daily, five hours), Kumily (one daily, 4½ hours), Thiruvananthapuram (four daily, nine hours), Coimbatore (two daily, six hours) or Madurai (one daily, five hours).

There are five KSRTC buses each day to Thiruvananthapuram. Two go via Ernakulam (Rs 42, depart 8.40 and 11 am) and three via Kottayam (Rs 45, 12.25 and 3.30 pm). In addition, there are private buses which tend to stop more often and take longer.

To go to Kumily (Periyar) you will need to catch a private bus from the bus stand near the post office. There are only two direct buses a day (12.25 and 3 pm); other buses (1.20 and 2.45 pm) run to Poopara, from where you can catch a Kumily-bound bus.

Getting Around

Bicycle At Raja Cycles, south of the bazaar, an old Hero is only Rs 1.50 per hour. A little further south from Raja is a place with mountain bikes for Rs 5 per hour. Or you could pay Rs 10 per hour at the Government Tourist Information Office for similar bikes.

AROUND MUNNAR

Thattekkad Bird Sanctuary

This sanctuary is 20km from Kothamangalam, on the Ernakulam to Munnar road. It's home to Malabar grey hornbills, woodpeckers, parakeets, and rarer species such as the Sri Lankan frogmouth and rose-billed roller.

Boat cruises are available from Boothathankettu to Thattekkad. The best time to visit is from 5 to 6 am. There's an *Inspection Bungalow* at Boothathankettu, as well as a few mid-range *hotels* in Kothamangalam. From Munnar, Ernakulam bound buses stop at Kothamangalam.

PALAKKAD

Tel Area Code: 0491

Located in a natural depression in the Western Ghats and linking Kerala to the plains of Tamil Nadu, this small, dusty town is the centre of a large rice-growing region. Its former strategic importance is highlighted by the imposing **fort** built by Hyder Ali in 1766. All that remains of the neglected fort are the clumsily repaired bastions and a large wooden door, off its hinges, slowly disintegrating alongside worn stone carvings of fish and flowers. There is a functioning jail within the grounds, but that is about as interesting as it gets.

Situated as it is near the border with Tamil Nadu, travellers moving between these states can use Palakkad as a base to visit Parambikulam Wildlife Sanctuary and Silent Valley National Park (see Around Palakkad).

The Tourist Information Office is in West Fort Rd, beside the fort and near the Fort Palace Hotel. It has minimal information but helpful staff will provide train times and help organise accommodation at Thunakadavu (for Parambikulam) or Mukkali (for Silent Valley).

Palakkad's banks are small branches not authorised to encash travellers cheques or cards. Hotel Indraprastha will change money for guests only. There is a good bookshop within Hotel Indraprastha with travel guides, novels and a good selection of recipe books, primarily in English.

Places to Stay & Eat

Surya Tourist Home (☎ *538338)* is just 300m south of the private bus stand. It's a little hard to find: look for the sign to *Hotel Cauvery,* a popular veg/nonveg restaurant, on the ground floor. Reception for the Surya is on the 3rd floor. Clean singles/doubles are Rs 150/250, Rs 200/250 with cable TV or Rs 400 with air-con.

Hotel Ambadi (☎ *531244),* across the road from the private bus stand, has non air-con doubles for Rs 225, and air-con doubles for Rs 400. There is an attached multicuisine restaurant.

Hotel Kairali (☎ *534611)* is a good budget option near the KSRTC bus stand. Singles/doubles cost Rs 70/120, or Rs 330 with air-con.

Fort Palace Hotel (☎/fax *534621, West Fort Rd),* a Rs 5 rickshaw ride from the bus stands, is a good mid-range choice. Rooms are Rs 300/375, or Rs 400/500 with air-con. However, a ludicrous charge of Rs 75 for water and electricity will be added onto the bill along with the usual taxes.

Hotel Indraprastha (☎ *534641, fax 534645, English Church Rd)* is the top hotel in town. Non air-con rooms are Rs 600 a double, air-con rooms are Rs 800. There is an air-con restaurant (Indian and Chinese) and an excellent coffee/snack shop at the entrance which is clean, comfortable and reasonably priced.

Getting There & Away

Bus Buses to Coimbatore (51km, Rs 12.50, 1½ hours) depart the KSRTC bus stand every 15 minutes. To Thrissur (70km, Rs 19, two hours) buses depart every 20 minutes up to 9.45 pm. To Kozhikode (130km, Rs 30, four hours) buses leave about every 30 minutes.

For Parambikulam (Annamalai) catch one of the many regular buses to Pollachi in Tamil Nadu from the private bus stand. For Silent Valley catch one of the regular buses to Mannakkad, also from the private bus stand.

Train Palakkad Junction is 5km from town, with many trains heading east to Tamil Nadu and beyond, and west to Shoranur, the major junction with Kerala's north-south train, where connections can easily be made. There are several trains a day heading south to Ernakulam and Thiruvananthapuram, fewer heading north. The *Delhi-Mangalore Express* via Kozhikode departs Palakkad at 6.50 am; the *Palakkad-Kannur Express* departs at 1.30 pm. Fares to Chennai are Rs 167/564 in 2nd/1st class, to Ernakulam Rs 51/223, Kozhikode Rs 35/200 and Mangalore Rs 89/415.

AROUND PALAKKAD
Parambikulam Wildlife Sanctuary

The Parambikulam Wildlife Sanctuary, 135km from Palakkad (via Pollachi), stretches around the Parambikulam, Thunakadavu and Peruvaripallam dams, and covers an area of 285 sq km adjacent to the Annamalai Wildlife Sanctuary in Tamil Nadu. It's home to elephants, bison, gaur, sloth bears, wild boar, sambar, chital, crocodiles and a few tigers and panthers. The sanctuary is open all year, but is best avoided from June to August due to the monsoon.

The sanctuary headquarters are at Thunakadavu, where the Forestry Department has a *Forest Resthouse* and a treetop hut (book through the Forest Inspection Bungalow (☎ 04253-7233) at Thunakadavu. At Parambikulam, there's a *PWD Resthouse* and a Tamil Nadu government *Inspection Bungalow* (book through the Junior Engineer, Tamil Nadu PWD, Parambikulam). There are also two *watchtowers*: one at Anappadi (8km from Thunakadavu) and another at Zungam (5km from Thunakadavu).

The best access to the sanctuary is by bus from Pollachi (40km from Coimbatore and 49km from Palakkad). There are four buses in either direction between Pollachi and Parambikulam via Anamalai daily. The trip takes two hours. Boat cruises operate from Parambikulam and rowboats can be hired at Thunakadavu.

Silent Valley National Park

A rare remnant of primary evergreen forest, along with a population of the rare lion-tailed macaque and some tigers, are protected within this national park 80km from Palakkad in the Kundali Hills. The name derives from the eerie quietness resulting from the lack of cicadas. This is an important biosphere reserve and refuge of tribal peoples. Facilities are limited.

Accommodation is in the *Forest Department resthouse* (Mannakkad; ☎ 0492-453225) at Mukkali, 22km from the national park. It costs US$10 per person per day and there are local hotels in Mukkali for food. There are regular buses to Mannakkad from Palakkad (45km) from where it is easy to organise a lift to Mukkali.

WAYANAD WILDLIFE SANCTUARY

Also known as Muthanga Wildlife Sanctuary, Wayanad is a remote rainforest reserve connected to Bandipur National Park in Karnataka and Mudumalai Sanctuary in Tamil Nadu. At the time of writing, access to Wayanad Sanctuary was denied to all but those involved in the pursuit of a gang of bandits/poachers led by long-time fugitive Veerappan.

The nearest town is **Sultan's Battery**, 16km west, on the road routes from Mysore and Ooty to Kozhikode. The town is named after Tipu Sultan but **Tipu's Fort** is in fact a Jain temple. It is a little hard to find: the temple is set back about 50m from the road, 1km west of the private bus stand on the Mysore Rd. There is a large iron gate through which you can see a stone building. On first appearances apparently deserted, the caretaker will eventually appear to unlock the gates to the chambers. You will need your own torch (flashlight) to see the stone carving in the ceilings.

Twelve kilometres south of Sultan's Battery, near Ambalavayal, is the important archaeological site of **Edakkal Caves**, which feature prehistoric petroglyphs.

Places to Stay

Along the main drag in Sultan's Battery, and within walking distance of the private bus stand, are several lodges including the *Viyager Tourist Home* and the friendly *Hotel Jaya*, both with singles/doubles for Rs 40/60.

The Resort (☎ 0493-620510, fax 620583) is the best place in town. Rooms start at Rs 200/275, or Rs 500 for air-con. All rooms have attached bath and TV and there is a decent restaurant. It is close to the private bus stand and about 1km from the KSRTC bus stand.

Getting There & Away

There are regular KSRTC buses between Sultan's Battery and Kozihikode (Rs 28, 3½ hours) which are always crowded so it's worthwhile booking a seat. There are many buses running between Mysore or Ooty and Kozhikode which stop at Sultan's Battery.

Northern Kerala

KOCHI (Cochin)
Pop: 602,000 Tel Area Code: 0484

With its wealth of historical associations and its beautiful setting on a cluster of islands and narrow peninsulas, the fascinating city of Kochi perfectly reflects the eclecticism of Kerala. Here, you can see the oldest church in India, winding streets crammed with 500-year-old Portuguese houses, cantilevered Chinese fishing nets, a Jewish community whose roots go back to the Diaspora, a 16th-century synagogue, and a palace built by the Portuguese and given to the Raja of Cochin. The palace, which was later renovated by the Dutch, contains some of India's most beautiful murals. Another must-see is a performance of the world-famous Kathakali dance drama.

The older parts of Fort Cochin and Mattancherry are an unlikely blend of medieval Portugal, Holland and an English country village grafted onto the tropical Malabar Coast – a radical contrast to the bright lights, bustle and big hotels of mainland Ernakulam.

Kochi is one of India's largest ports and a major naval base. The misty silhouettes of huge merchant ships can be seen anchored off the point of Fort Cochin, waiting for a berth in the docks of Willingdon Island, an artificial island created with material dredged up when the harbour was deepened. All day, ferries scuttle back and forth between the various parts of Kochi. Dolphins can often be seen in the harbour.

History

Kochi is first and foremost a trading city. Arab and Jewish spice traders had settled here in the 1st century AD. Trade with the Middle East and eastern Mediterranean countries saw these communities prosper under the patronage of the local rajahs. Kochi's for-

tunes received a boost in the 14th century when the nearby ancient port of Cranganore (Kodungallor) silted up; the increase in business would eventually see Kochi become the most important port on the Malabar Coast.

For centuries the Rajas of Kochi were competing with the Zamorins of Calicut for territory and the spice trade. This rivalry saw the Portuguese welcomed in the early 1500s. The Portuguese lost their domination of the spice trade and Kochi to the Dutch in 1663 but just over a century later the British were in control.

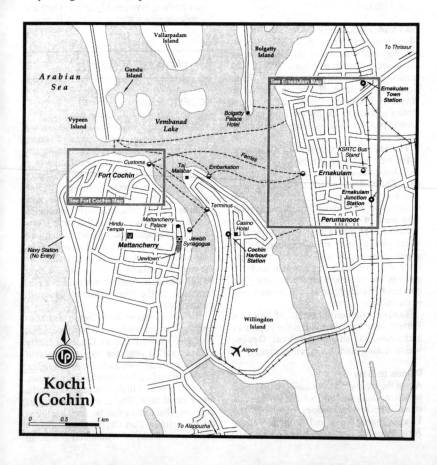

Kochi (Cochin)

Orientation

Kochi consists of mainland Ernakulam; the islands of Willingdon, Bolgatty and Gundu in the harbour; Fort Cochin and Mattancherry on the southern peninsula; and Vypeen Island, north of Fort Cochin. All these areas are linked by ferry; bridges also link Ernakulam to Willingdon Island and the Fort Cochin/Mattancherry peninsula. Most hotels and restaurants are in Ernakulam, where you'll also find the main train station and bus stand and the Tourist Reception Centre.

Almost all the historical sites are in Fort Cochin or Mattancherry, and although accommodation and restaurant facilities are limited here, it is a much more tranquil setting than Ernakulam. The domestic airport and two of the top hotels are on Willingdon Island. The new international airport is on Vypeen Island.

Information

Tourist Offices The KTDC's Tourist Reception Centre (☎ 353234) on Ernakulam's Shanmugham Rd has limited information but will organise accommodation at the Bolgatty Palace Hotel and arrange conducted harbour cruises. The office is open from 8 am to 7 pm daily. The tiny Tourist Desk (☎ 371761) at Ernakulam's main ferry jetty is privately run but much more helpful. It has a good map and tourist literature and will recommend and book accommodation and tours; it's open daily from 9 am to 5 pm. The *Jaico Time Table* or *Hello Cochin* are handy travel information booklets available from bus stands, news stands or bookshops.

The Government of India Tourist Office (ITDC; ☎ 668352) is next to the Taj Malabar Hotel on Willingdon Island, and offers a range of leaflets and maps. There's a Tourist Information counter at Kochi airport which is staffed for flight arrivals.

Money In Ernakulam, there is a State Bank of India opposite the Tourist Reception Centre and a very efficient Thomas Cook office in MG Rd. In Fort Cochin there is a State Bank of India near the Mattancherry Palace.

Post & Communications The main post office (including poste restante) is at Fort Cochin, but you can have mail sent to the main post office on Hospital Rd in Ernakulam, as long as it's specifically addressed to that office. STD/ISD booths are found all over town. You can send and receive email at Raiyaan Communication (☎ 351387, fax 380052, email raiyaan@giasmd01.vsnl.net.in) at Raiyaan Complex, Padma Junction, MG Rd. The cost is Rs 25 for transmission (per 2500 characters) and Rs 10 to receive email.

Visa Extensions Apply at the office of the Commissioner of Police (☎ 360700), at the northern end of Shanmugham Rd, Ernakulam. Visa extensions can take up to 10 days to issue and you have to leave your passport at the office during that time.

Bookshops Bhavi Books on Convent Rd, Ernakulam, is a good bookshop. There are a number of bookshops along Press Club Rd, although they chiefly stock books in Malayalam. Try Cosmo Books or Current Books for titles in English. Higginbothams is on Chittoor Rd, at the junction with Hospital Rd, and DC Books, with a huge collection of English-language classics, is out along Banerji Rd.

In Mattancherry, opposite the synagogue, there is an excellent bookshop called Idiom. It's open every day until about 6 pm. There are comprehensive sections on Indian art, culture, literature, religion, etc. Most books are in English but there is a decent collection of French-language titles. Opposite Idiom is another very good bookshop. It's called Incy Bella, and it stocks a good range of reference books on India.

Film & Photography A useful camera and film supplier is SP & Co on Convent Rd, Ernakulam.

Fort Cochin

St Francis Church India's oldest European-built church was constructed in 1503 by Portuguese Franciscan friars who accompanied the expedition led by Pedro Alvarez Cabral.

The original structure was made out of wood, but the church was rebuilt in stone around the mid-16th century; the earliest Portuguese inscription found in the church is dated 1562. The Protestant Dutch captured Kochi in 1663 and restored the church in 1779. After the occupation of Kochi by the British in 1795, it became an Anglican church and it is presently being used by the Church of South India.

Vasco da Gama, the first European to reach India by sailing around Africa, died in Cochin in 1524 and was buried here for 14 years before his remains were transferred to Lisbon in Portugal. His tombstone can be seen inside the church. Rope-operated *punkahs*, or fans, are one of the unusual features of this church.

Sunday services are held in English at 8 am and in Malayalam at 9.30 am.

Santa Cruz Basilica This large, impressive church dates from 1902, and has a fantastical pastel-coloured interior.

Chinese Fishing Nets Strung out along the tip of Fort Cochin, these fixed, cantilevered fishing nets were introduced by traders from the court of Kublai Khan. You can also see them along the backwaters between Kochi and Kottayam, and between Alappuzha and Kollam. They're mainly used at high tide, and require at least four men to operate their system of counterweights.

Mattancherry

Mattancherry Palace Built by the Portuguese in 1555, Mattancherry Palace was presented to the Raja of Cochin, Veera Kerala Varma (1537-61), as a gesture of goodwill (and probably as a means of securing trading privileges).

The palace's alternative name, the 'Dutch Palace', resulted from substantial renovations by the Dutch after 1663. The two storey quadrangular building surrounds a courtyard containing a Hindu temple.

The central hall on the 1st floor was the coronation hall of the rajas. Their dresses, turbans and palanquins are now on display. More important are the astonishing **murals**, depicting scenes from the *Ramayana, Mahabharata* and Puranic legends connected with Shiva, Vishnu, Krishna, Kumara and Durga. These beautiful murals rarely seem to be men-

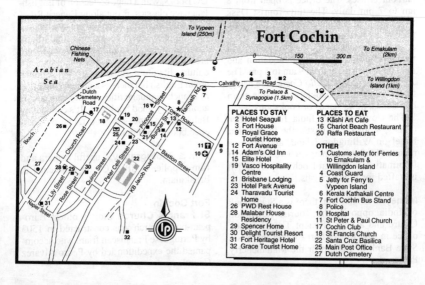

Fort Cochin

Arabian Sea

To Vypeen Island (250m)

To Emakulam (2km)

Chinese Fishing Nets

Dutch Cemetery Road

To Palace & Synagogue (1.5km)

To Willingdon Island (1km)

Calvathy Road

PLACES TO STAY	PLACES TO EAT
2 Hotel Seagull	13 Kāshi Art Cafe
3 Fort House	16 Chariot Beach Restaurant
9 Royal Grace Tourist Home	20 Raffa Restaurant
12 Fort Avenue	**OTHER**
14 Adam's Old Inn	1 Customs Jetty for Ferries to Emakulam & Willingdon Island
15 Elite Hotel	4 Coast Guard
19 Vasco Hospitality Centre	5 Jetty for Ferry to Vypeen Island
21 Brisbane Lodging	6 Kerala Kathakali Centre
23 Hotel Park Avenue	7 Fort Cochin Bus Stand
24 Tharavadu Tourist Home	8 Police
26 PWD Rest House	10 Hospital
28 Malabar House Residency	11 St Peter & Paul Church
29 Spencer Home	17 Cochin Club
30 Delight Tourist Resort	18 St Francis Church
31 Fort Heritage Hotel	22 Santa Cruz Basilica
32 Grace Tourist Home	25 Main Post Office
	27 Dutch Cemetery

tioned, although they are one of the wonders of India. The ladies' bedchamber, downstairs, is worth seeing. It features a cheerful Krishna using his six hands and two feet to engage in foreplay with eight happy milkmaids.

The palace is open Saturday to Thursday from 10 am to 5 pm; entry is free but you may be asked to make a 'donation'. Photography is not permitted but there is good booklet with colour reproductions of the murals on sale for Rs 35.

Cochin Synagogue Originally constructed in 1568, the synagogue was destroyed by cannon fire during a Portuguese raid in 1662 and was rebuilt two years later when the Dutch took over Kochi. It's an interesting little place, with handpainted, willow pattern floor tiles brought from Canton in China in the mid-18th century by Ezekial Rahabi, who was also responsible for the erection of the building's clock tower.

A synagogue built at Kochangadi in 1344 has since disappeared, although a stone slab from this building, inscribed in Hebrew, can be found on the inner surface of the wall which surrounds the Mattancherry synagogue.

The area around the synagogue is known as **Jewtown** and is one of the centres of the Kochi spice trade. Scores of small firms huddle together in old, dilapidated buildings and the air is filled with the pungent aromas of ginger, cardamom, cumin, turmeric and cloves. Many Jewish names are visible on business premises and houses, and there are several interesting curio shops on the street leading up to the synagogue.

The synagogue is open Sunday to Friday, from 10 am to noon and from 3 to 5 pm. Entry is Rs 1. The synagogue's guardians are friendly and keen to talk about the building and the Jewish community.

Ernakulam
Parishath Thampuram Museum This museum contains 19th century oil paintings,

The Jews of Kochi
Kochi (Cochin) is home to a tiny, isolated and unexpected Jewish community descended from Jewish settlers who fled Palestine 2000 years ago. The first Jewish settlement was at Kodungallur (Cranganore), north of Kochi. Like the Syrian Orthodox Christians, the Jews became involved in the trade and commerce of the Malabar Coast. Preserved in the Mattancherry synagogue are a number of copper plates bearing an ancient inscription granting the village of Anjuvannam (near Kodungallur) and its revenue to a Jewish merchant, Joseph Rabban, by King Bhaskara Ravi Varman I (962-1020). You can see these plates with the permission of the synagogue guardian.

Concessions given to Joseph Rabban by Ravi Varman I included permission to use a palanquin and parasol. Palanquins and parasols in those days were the prerogative of rulers, so in effect, Ravi Varman I had sanctioned the creation of a tiny Jewish kingdom. On Rabban's death, his sons fought each other for control of the 'kingdom' and this rivalry led to its break-up and the move to Mattancherry.

The community has been the subject of much research. An interesting study by an American professor of ethnomusicology found that the music of the Cochin Jews contained strong Babylonian influences, and that their version of the Ten Commandments was almost identical to a Kurdish version housed in the Berlin Museum Archives. Of course, there has also been much local influence, and many of the hymns are similar to ragas.

The community has diminished rapidly since Indian Independence; it now numbers only about 20, and lacks enough adult males to perform certain rituals without outside assistance. There has been no rabbi within living memory, so all the elders are qualified to perform religious ceremonies and marriages.

The Konkan Railway

When the British scratched a spiderweb of railway lines across the map of India they left one blank space: the Konkan Coast. The thin strip of land that stretches all the way down the western flank of India was once only accessible by train at points where tortuous rail routes were engineered through the Western Ghats. Proposals to construct a line along the coast itself were aired as long ago as 1894, but were never taken seriously because of the appalling terrain that would have to be crossed.

The problem was that to build a line running from north to south, the builders had to go against the grain of the country. Rocky spurs from the Ghats run westwards to the sea to create headlands that had to be either tunnelled through or removed. Scores of rivers drain from the Ghats into the Arabian Sea, each of which had to be bridged. Add to this the fact that in places the soil is soft and unstable, and the construction problems in the area are obvious.

On Republic Day 1998, however, after seven years of work, the opening of the new 760km Konkan Railway was confirmation of a great technological success. With nearly 2000 bridges (the largest of which is over 2km long) and 92 tunnels (the longest stretching 6.5km) the work is a major achievement. Constructed under a Build-Operate-Transfer scheme, the project has been jointly funded by the Ministry of Railways, the governments of the states involved, and the public. The cost has been enormous – estimates put it at around US$860 million, but it is hoped that the benefits to industry, tourism and social infrastructure will validate the heavy outlay.

Certainly communications with the coastal regions have instantly become easier. Although in early 1998 the initial services on the line were slow (to allow time for settling of the embankments), this route has been designed to be the fastest in India – with the capacity to take trains travelling at up to 160km/h. Once services are running at full speed, the journey from Mumbai to Goa will take 10 hours instead of the 20 hour haul that was formerly endured, and from Mumbai to Kochi will take 24 hours instead of 36 hours.

The project has not been without controversy, and work on the Goa section of the line was halted for several months in 1993 while environmental protesters took their case to the courts. Only time will tell who's right in many of the issues. Environmentalists claim that by building the line, with its high earthen embankments, across the low lying *khazans* (areas which rely on frequent drainage) the natural drainage of the area has been disrupted. If the water cannot flow away properly during the monsoon, environmentalists argue, fields will become waterlogged. If large areas of water are allowed to become stagnant, there could also be an increase in mosquito borne disease. The engineers claim that there is ample drainage.

There are other question marks too. How will the earthen embankments and the huge tunnels stand up to the testing monsoon conditions? Will the railway have the capacity to handle the weight of traffic that is likely to be forthcoming in the next few years? Although the Konkan Railway Company owns sufficient land for expanding the railway by double tracking, such a project would be phenomenally expensive.

In the meantime, however, the line is an undeniable achievement, and eases transport to the south considerably. The *Netravati Express* now connects Mumbai with Kochi via the Konkan Railway, it leaves Mumbai at 4.40 pm from Kurla train station and takes 28 hours to cover the 1300km journey. Fares are Rs 350/1000 in 2nd/1st class. In the other direction, the *Netravati Express* leaves Kochi at 4.45 am. The *Rajdhani Express* connects Kerala with New Delhi, also on the Konkan Railway.

old coins, sculptures and Mughal paintings, but apart from some interesting temple models, it's nothing special. It is housed in an enormous, traditional Keralan building (previously Durbar Hall) on Durbar Hall Rd, and is open Tuesday to Sunday from 10 am to 12.30 pm and from 2 to 4.30 pm; entry is free.

Vypeen & Gundu Islands
Ferries shuttle across the narrow strait from Fort Cochin to Vypeen Island. The island boasts a lighthouse at Ochanthuruth (open from 3 to 5 pm daily), good beaches, and the early 16th century Palliport Fort (open Thursday). Gundu, the smallest island in the harbour, is close to Vypeen and belongs to the Taj Group and will no doubt be developed.

Organised Tours
The KTDC offers daily boat cruises around Kochi Harbour which visit Willingdon Island, Mattancherry Palace, the Jewish synagogue, Fort Cochin (including St Francis Church), the Chinese fishing nets and Bolgatty Island. The 3½ hour tour departs from the Sealord Boat Jetty, just north of the Tourist Reception Centre, at 9 am and 2 pm, and costs Rs 50. The KTDC Sunset Cruise from 5.30 to 7 pm costs Rs 30, but is frequently cancelled, so check early in the day to avoid disappointment.

Village backwater cruises in open country boats or covered kettuvallams are all the rage in Kochi. They visit coir villages, coconut plantations and fish farms and give plenty of opportunity for birdwatching and to see how life is lived along the narrow canals. It is a very relaxing way to experience traditional Kerala, and hopefully the many operators will continue to manage this mini tourist boom sensitively. There are several trips offered, from two to six hours; the only downside is having to fight through Ernakulam's traffic at the start. Some recommended operators in Ernakulam include the following:

The Tourist Desk (☎ 371761) by the Main Jetty operates three-hour village backwater cruises in traditional open canoes, which include bus transport (45 minutes each way) from the jetty car park to the starting point. The trips depart at 9 am and 2 pm and cost Rs 275 (student card holders get a discount of Rs 50). There is free hotel pick-up if you are staying in Ernakulam. Similar cruises operated by the KTDC depart at 8.30 am and 2.30 pm and cost Rs 300.

Indo World (☎ 370127), Heera House, MG Rd, offers a full-day (six hour, Rs 800) cruise along canals and Vembanad Lake in a kettuvallam which includes a traditional Keralan lunch served on a banana leaf.

Salmon Tours (☎ 369669), Crystal Complex, Banerji Rd, has a four hour cruise (Rs 450) which also includes the opportunity to catch your lunch at a fish farm. This tour leaves at 9 am and returns at 2 pm.

Places to Stay
Ernakulam has accommodation in all price brackets. Fort Cochin has a handful of cheap places, a growing but still insufficient number of mid-range places and a handful of top-end places. Bolgatty Island has one unique top-end place and Willingdon Island has a mid-range and two top-end places.

Places to Stay – Budget
Fort Cochin During December and January budget hotel space is severely limited at Fort Cochin. If you crave a bit of peace and quiet, though, it is worth the effort to avoid Ernakulam. Outside the Dec-Jan high season you should be able to secure a discount on accommodation.

Royal Grace Tourist Home (☎ 223584) is a modern, concrete budget hotel opposite the St Peter & Paul Church. Large double rooms with attached bath are from Rs 150 to Rs 250, or Rs 300 with air-con; breakfast is extra. Under the same management is the smaller, but similarly priced, *Grace Tourist Home (KB Jacob Rd)*, south of the basilica.

Tharavadu Tourist Home (☎ 226897, *Quiros St)* is an airy and spacious traditional house with good views of the surrounding streets from the rooftop area. Doubles with bathroom are Rs 135, or there's two top floor rooms for Rs 155 and Rs 205 which share a bathroom.

Elite Hotel (☎ 225733, *Princess St)* is a long-term favourite and has doubles with attached bathroom for Rs 125 to Rs 250. There's a popular but not especially good restaurant downstairs.

Brisbane Lodging (☎ 225962), a couple of doors away, has seven presentable rooms from Rs 125 to Rs 150.

KERALA

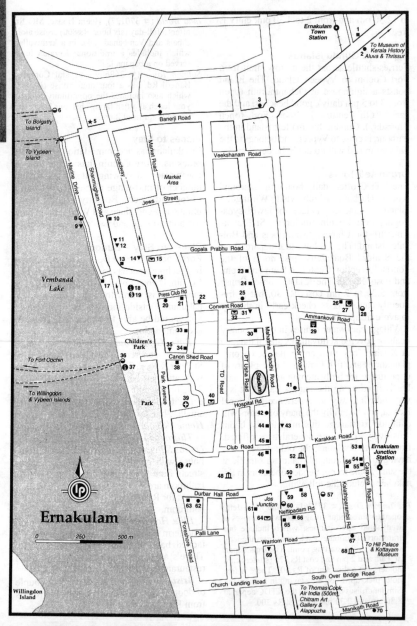

To Bolgatty Island

To Vypeen Island

Vembanad Lake

To Fort Cochin

To Willingdon & Vypeen Islands

Ernakulam Town Station

To Museum of Kerala History Aluva & Thrissur

Banerji Road

Veekshanam Road

Market Area

Jews Street

Gopala Prabhu Road

Press Club Rd

Convent Road

Ammankovil Road

Children's Park

Canon Shed Road

Park Avenue

Park

Hospital Rd

Karakkat Road

Club Road

Durbar Hall Road

Jos Junction

Nettipadam Rd

Palli Lane

Warriom Road

Church Landing Road

South Over Bridge Road

To Thomas Cook, Air India (500m), Chitram Art Gallery & Alappuzha

Manikath Road

Willingdon Island

Ernakulam

0   250   500 m

Broadway

Market Road

Shanmugham Road

Marine Drive

Mahatma Gandhi Road

Chittoor Road

PT Usha Road

TD Road

Stadium

Foreshore Road

Kalathiparambil Rd

Caravara Road

Ernakulam Junction Station

To Hill Palace & Kottayam Museum

PWD Resthouse is nicely situated near the waterfront, but has just two double rooms for Rs 100 each. The enterprising housekeeper will organise village day trips using public transport, and personally guide you around.

Vasco Hospitality Centre (☎ 229877), near St Francis Church, has basic doubles for Rs 100; two rooms have bath attached.

Adam's Old Inn (☎ 229495), in quiet Burgher St, has comfortable singles for Rs 100 and doubles from Rs 150 to Rs 250, or Rs 350 with air-con.

Delight Tourist Resort (☎ 228658, Rose St), opposite the old parade ground. More a friendly guesthouse than a resort, this large Dutch colonial home has seven double rooms from Rs 125 to Rs 400. All rooms have attached bath and mosquito netting on the windows.

Spencer Home (☎ 275409, Parade Rd), nearby, has clean and simple, bath-attached singles for Rs 90 and doubles from Rs 200 to Rs 300. Note checkout is noon.

Ernakulam There is no shortage of budget accommodation in Ernakulam. If you plan to stay in Fort Cochin during the busy Dec-Jan period it may pay to check in to a place in Ernakulam and book a room for subsequent nights in Fort Cochin. This avoids the stressful and often disappointing search for on-the-spot vacancies in Fort Cochin.

Basoto Lodge (☎ 352140, Press Club Rd) is small, simple, friendly and popular, so get there early. Singles with common bathroom cost Rs 50, and doubles with attached bathroom are Rs 100.

Hotel Seaking (☎ 355341, fax 372608) is set back from busy MG Rd and is excellent value with singles/doubles for Rs 180/280, or Rs 450 with air-con. There is an attached restaurant.

Hotel Hakoba (☎ 369839, Shanmugham Rd), conveniently located on the busy waterfront, is another good choice, although construction has spoilt the views. Doubles with attached bathroom start at Rs 172, or Rs 330 with air-con (prices include tax), and there's a sad-looking restaurant, a noisy bar and even a (not very reliable) lift.

Maple Tourist Home (☎ 371711, Canon Shed Rd), near the main jetty, is good value with doubles for Rs 230, or Rs 400 with air-con. The rooftop garden overlooks the jetty.

Bijus Tourist Home (☎ 381881), corner of Canon Shed and Market Rds, is a friendly place with rooms for Rs 140/230, and air-con doubles for Rs 400. It's good value and even has hot water. The management will help organise backwater/village tours as well as trips to martial arts displays and Kathakali dances.

Coastal Lodge (☎ 373083, Market Rd), a little further north, has basic rooms for Rs 70 with shared bath or Rs 90 and Rs 100 with bath attached. You will need a mosquito net here.

Queen's Residency (☎ 365775) is a quaint Indian-style hotel with rooms from Rs 140/200, or Rs 400 with air-con.

Hotel KK International (☎ 366010), opposite the Ernakulam Junction train station, is good value at Rs 162/270 including tax.

Geetha Lodge (☎ 352136, MG Rd), has simple rooms for Rs 150/250.

Anantha Bhavan (☎ 382071), nearby, has rooms from Rs 100/170 to Rs 160/260 and air-con doubles for Rs 550.

Hotel Luciya (☎ 381177), close to the KSRTC bus stand, is the best choice in this area. It has efficient and friendly staff and good value rooms at Rs 100/200, or Rs 225/350 with air-con. It has a restaurant, TV lounge, STD/ISD and laundry service.

Places to Stay – Mid-Range
Fort Cochin See some of the above Budget hotel listings which also have mid-priced rooms – they are the best choice in this price range.

Hotel Seagull (☎ 228128, Calvathy Rd) is right on the waterfront overlooking the harbour, and was created by converting a number of old houses and warehouses. Once one of the better places to stay in Fort Cochin, standards have slipped. All rooms are double and cost Rs 300, or Rs 400 with air-con. You can watch ships come and go from the bar and restaurant.

Hotel Park Avenue (☎ 222671, cnr Bastion and Peter Celli St) is a compromise between Fort Cochin's development restrictions and hoteliers' greed. The height of the original two-storey building was preserved but three storeys of hotel rooms were squeezed in, and then the whole lot was covered in marble! Most rooms are very tiny, some with no windows at all. Singles range from Rs 200 to Rs 550, doubles are from Rs 250 to Rs 750. The more expensive rooms have air-con.

The Fort House (☎ 226103, fax 222066, Calvathy Rd) is good value at Rs 650 a double, which includes breakfast and all taxes. It has a good location and rooms are clean and comfortable.

Fort Heritage (☎/fax 225333, Napier St) has very spacious rooms in an old Dutch building. It has been in the same Syrian Christian family for a very long time and is furnished with antique rosewood furniture. It has a good restaurant including a tandoori BBQ eating area with lawn service out in the back garden. Rooms are US$30/45 including breakfast. Air-con costs an extra US$10.

Ernakulam There are a number of mid-range places near Ernakulam Junction train station.

Paulson Park Hotel (☎ 382170, fax 370072) has good value rooms for Rs 240/450, or Rs 450/600 with air-con. There's a choice of multicuisine or tandoori restaurants.

Hotel Sangeetha (☎ 368487, Chittoor Rd) is a block west. Rooms are from Rs 220/330 to Rs 325/420, or Rs 400/450 with air-con; prices include breakfast.

Hotel Joyland (☎ 367764, fax 370645, Durbar Hall Rd), nearby, is well appointed and features a rooftop restaurant (Indian, Chinese and continental). Rooms are Rs 400/550, or Rs 475/675 with air-con.

Woodlands Hotel (☎ 368900, fax 382080,

MG Rd), a little north of Club Rd, is a long-time favourite. Rooms here are Rs 300/425, or Rs 475/650 with air-con. All rooms have TV and hot water, and the hotel has a vegetarian restaurant and a roof garden.

Hotel Aiswarya (☎ 364454), near Jos Junction, is a pleasant new hotel with clean rooms for Rs 250/350, or Rs 450 with air-con. All rooms have hot water and TV, plus there's complimentary tea or coffee in the morning.

Hotel Excellency (☎ 374001, fax 374009, Nettipadam Rd), south of Jos Junction, has a three-star rating and rooms from US$10/12, or US$22/24 with air-con. It has good facilities, a restaurant, and even throws in 'bed coffee'.

Bharat Hotel (☎ 353501, fax 370502, Durbar Hall Rd) is a huge place next to the Indian Airlines office. It has rooms from Rs 430/500, or Rs 600/750 with air-con. It has vegetarian and North Indian nonveg restaurants, a coffee shop, and a marriage hall on the roof!

Hotel Cochin Tower (☎ 340910, fax 370645) on busy Lissie Junction is close to Ernakulam Town train station. Comfortable rooms with satellite TV start at Rs 410/500, or Rs 570/730 with air-con. There are a couple of restaurants on the premises.

The Metropolitan (☎ 369931), near the Junction Railway station, is a glossy, centrally air-conditioned hotel with rooms for Rs 575/900. There's a decent restaurant and a bar.

The *Avenue Regent (☎ 372660, fax 370129, MG Rd)* is a centrally air-conditioned four-star hotel, not far from Jos Junction. Rooms start from US$38/58. There's a restaurant, and round-the-clock coffee shop.

Grand Hotel (☎ 382061, fax 382066, MG Rd) is a spacious olde-worlde establishment with two restaurants. The rooms all have air-con and cost Rs 450/500 in the old wing, Rs 550/600 in the new wing.

Sealord Hotel (☎ 382472, fax 370135, Shanmugham Rd) is centrally air-conditioned and good value, though the rooms are showing signs of age. Singles/doubles are Rs 600/700, or Rs 800/1100 for deluxe

rooms. There's two restaurants: one air-con with live music, the other on the rooftop with a bar.

Places to Stay – Top End

Fort Cochin Recent renovations have seen a few of the grand old buildings developed for top-end accommodation, and at the time of writing the Casino Group was building a large hotel which will service this price bracket.

The Malabar House Residency (☎/fax 221199, Parade Rd), across the playing field from St Francis Church, has beautifully furnished, centrally air-conditioned rooms for US$100 and suites for US$120. At least some of the rooms have short, Indian-style beds and for all that money you would expect leg room. The restaurant has a good reputation for Indian and Italian cuisine and prices to match, and also has theme evenings with set menus and dance performances.

Bolgatty Island In a magnificent setting on the southern tip of this island there is a unique place to stay.

Bolgatty Palace Hotel (☎ 355003, fax 354879) was built in 1744 as a Dutch palace, then later became a British Residency. At the time of writing, extensive renovations were underway. The palace will be restored as much as possible to its original splendour, providing four luxurious suites. There will be a further 16 rooms in an adjoining annexe. Plans include a swimming pool and extensive landscaping which can only enhance this magical location. Currently there are 10 semi-detached cottages at Rs 1200/1500 for singles/doubles. There is a restaurant and bar.

Telephone first or inquire at the Tourist Reception Centre, Shanmugham Rd, otherwise you'll waste a lot of time if the hotel is full. Ferries (Rs 0.40) leave the High Court Jetty in Ernakulam for Bolgatty Island every 20 minutes from 6 am to 10 pm; at other times, private launches are available.

Willingdon Island *Taj Malabar (☎ 666-811)* is a five-star hotel wonderfully situated at the tip of the island, overlooking the harbour. The hotel boasts the full range of facilities, including a swimming pool and ayurvedic massage. Rooms start at US$95/110, but this is a hotel where a room with a harbour or sea view (singles from US$115 to US$155, doubles from US$130 to US$170) is worth the extra cost; deluxe suites are US$250 to US$300.

Casino Hotel (☎ 668421) also has an excellent range of facilities, including a pool. It's much cheaper at US$65/70, but its location near the train station and warehouses is no match for the Taj Malabar's.

Ernakulam *Hotel Abad Plaza (☎ 381122, fax 370729, MG Rd)* is a modern, air-conditioned Indian business hotel. Rooms start at Rs 950/1200. It has restaurants, a coffee shop, a health club and a rooftop swimming pool with great views over the city.

Taj Residency (☎ 371471, fax 371481, Marine Dve), a more business-oriented sister to the Taj Malabar, is on the waterfront. It offers all mod cons (except a swimming pool), boasts the Harbour View Bar, and charges US$80/90, or US$100/115 for rooms with a sea view.

Places to Eat

Fort Cochin Eating options in the touristed area of Fort Cochin are limited, but by taking a walk along the streets behind and between Mattancherry and Fort Cochin you can find good cheap food cooked the way the locals like it – spicy.

Badhariya is a small nonveg restaurant where beef curry and paratha can be had for around Rs 10.

Ramathula Hotel, near the junction of Irimpichi Rd and New Rd, is better known by the chef's name, Kayika. It has excellent chicken or mutton biryanis for around Rs 25. Be there between noon and 3 pm so you don't miss out.

For snacks, the various samosa and wada (fried pastry balls) *stalls* near the Chinese fishing nets tend to do all their frying in the morning, the food becoming progressively tepid and stale throughout the day, so get there early.

Behind the Chinese fishing nets, just west of the Kerala Kathakali centre, are a couple of *fishmongers* and an even greater selection of *fish friers*. The idea is you buy a fish (or prawns, scampi, lobster, etc; Rs 50 to Rs 300 per kg) and have it cleaned by the fishmonger. Then you take your seafood to one of the kitchens where they will cook it and serve it to you at one of their tables (about Rs 30 for a large fish). The main drawbacks appear to be the attention all this brings from the mangy kittens, bold crows and sticky flies. It is obviously also in your interest to be able to determine the freshness of the catch and whether or not it has been properly stored on ice.

Kashi Art Cafe (Burgher St) is a bright new eating venue which also exhibits contemporary art. It opens at 8.30 am with a set breakfast (eg whole wheat porridge or bread pudding, muffin, fresh fruit, coffee or tea) for Rs 55 followed by lunch (soup, quiche or salad, coffee or tea) for Rs 45. Home-baked cakes are Rs 25 and filter coffee (likely to be the best coffee you will have in Kerala) is Rs 30 (two cups).

Elite Hotel (Princess St) is the old travellers' standby. It has a small range of fairly basic food including fish curries for around Rs 20.

Raffa, nearby, has budget Indian meals and ice cream but the limited choice of bland dishes is a sellout to tourists' bland tastes.

Chariot Beach Restaurant (Princess St) turns out uninspired Indian and western snacks and light meals, but it's a popular place to sit in the open, sip a cold drink and watch the world pass by.

Hotel Seagull (Calvathy Rd) has a reasonable restaurant and a bar with good views of the harbour.

The new top-end hotels have good quality restaurants. The cheapest is at the *Fort Heritage*. The biggest prices, smallest serves and longest waits are at *The Malabar House Residency*, which serves Indian and Italian dishes. The *Fort House* has already earned a good reputation for its preparation of seafood but it requires at least two hours notification of your order!

Willingdon Island In the Taj Malabar, the *Waterfront Cafe* offers a lunchtime buffet for Rs 275 (plus taxes). The Malabar's Chinese *Jade Pavilion* and the plush *Rice Boats* restaurants serve excellent seafood.

Casino Hotel has a buffet in its gloomy restaurant, or there's a brighter outdoor seafood restaurant by the pool which is only open for dinner.

Ernakulam The *Indian Coffee House*, corner of Canon Shed Rd and Park Ave, is opposite the Main Jetty. Its quaintly uniformed waiters in cummerbunds offer good snacks and breakfasts. It's popular with locals and is always busy.

Bimbi's (Shanmugham Rd) is a modern, self-serve restaurant near the Sealord Hotel. There is fast food (North and South Indian plus some western snacks) as well as sweets. An excellent masala dosa costs Rs 12. There's another branch near Jos Junction.

South Star (Shanmugham Rd) is an air-con restaurant above Bimbi's. It is good value with mains for around Rs 50.

Lotus Cascades/Jaya Cafe (MG Rd), in the Woodlands Hotel, turns out excellent vegetarian thalis for Rs 30.

Pandhal Restaurant (MG Rd) could easily be a modern western chain restaurant. It turns out excellent North Indian food and OK pizzas (Rs 90) but the burgers should be avoided.

Chinese Garden Restaurant (Warriom Rd), just off MG Rd, has good food and attentive service.

The *Ancient Mariner (Marine Drive)* is a mediocre floating restaurant.

Caravan Ice Cream, near the Tourist Reception Centre, is cool and dark and has good ice cream and milkshakes (Rs 20) – try the cardamom or fig.

Arul Jyoti (Shanmugham Rd) is a straightforward 'meals' place with basic vegetarian meals for Rs 15.

The *Bharath Coffee House (Broadway)* offers similar fare.

Chariot Restaurant (entrances on Convent and Narakathara Rds), has a similar menu as the Chariot Beach Restaurant in Fort Cochin.

Sealord Hotel (Shanmugham Rd) has two restaurants and two menus: Chinese and Indian/continental. The reasonably priced food is consistently good. The choice of venue is between air-con and live 'easy listening' rock or up on the roof where conversation is accompanied by traffic noise wafting up on photochemical thermals.

The classy but reasonably priced *Regency Restaurant (MG Rd),* in the Hotel Abad Plaza, offers good Indian, Chinese and western food.

The Paulson Park Hotel, near the Ernakulam Junction train station, has the *Moghul Hut* tandoori restaurant in its central atrium area.

Shopping

There are a number of handicraft and antique emporiums along MG Rd, Ernakulam, just south of Durbar Hall Rd. In Jew St, Mattancherry, There is a plethora of shops selling antiques and reproductions. Some of the larger warehouses are a joy to wander through, although one does begin to wonder how all these beautiful old carvings, obviously from churches, temples and grand houses, were came by. Along with the tourists there is a steady stream of interior decorators from California and London vying for the old teak columns and Chinese urns. Needless to say, bargains are few, but you should be able to squeeze a better price than you'd expect to pay in the west.

One of the more exciting developments in Kochi recently has been the encouragement of contemporary artists, including hometown talent. In Fort Cochin, Kashi Art Cafe, Burgher St, exhibits and sells works by up-and-coming artists. Draavidia Art & Performance Gallery, Jew St, Mattancherry, also exhibits new artists and has live performances of classical Indian music in the evenings. Also in Mattancherry, Galleria Synagogue exhibits and sells the works of several contemporary Indian artists.

In Ernakulam, Chitram Art Gallery, MG Rd (opposite Thomas Cook), and Galleria Mareecheka, Chittoor Rd, also exhibit works by well known and emerging artists.

If you fancy yourself with a sitar or set of tabla, head to Manuel Industries, Banerji Rd, Ernakulam. A sitar will set you back Rs 3500, while a set of tabla is Rs 1500.

A new Enfield Bullet 350cc is yours for Rs 50,000 at Marikar Motors, on Lissie Junction. Second-hand models from its workshop can be had for much less.

Getting There & Away

Jaico Time Table and *Hello Cochin* are handy booklets listing schedules, journey times and air, bus and train fares. They can be hard to track down, but the Jaico timetable is usually available at a stall at the KSRTC bus stand for Rs 5. Also try bookshops and news stands.

Air The Indian Airlines office (☎ 370242) is on Durbar Hall Rd, next to the Bharat Tourist Home. Air India (☎ 351295) is on MG Rd opposite Thomas Cook. Jet Airways (☎ 369423) and NEPC (☎ 369713) also have services to and from Kochi.

Indian Airlines has daily flights to Bangalore (Rs 2100), Mumbai (Rs 4552), Delhi (via Goa, Rs 9025), Goa (Rs 3315) and Chennai (Rs 3090). Jet Airways also flies to Mumbai, while NEPC flies to Bangalore, Chennai and Agatti (Lakshadweep).

Bus The KSRTC bus stand (☎ 372033) is by the railway line in Ernakulam, between the train stations. Because Kochi is in the middle of Kerala, many of the buses passing through Ernakulam originated in other cities. Although it's still often possible to get a seat on these buses, you cannot make advance reservations; you simply have to join the scrum when the bus turns up. You can make reservations up to five days in advance for many of the buses which originate in Ernakulam. The timetable is in English as well as Malayalam, and the bus stand staff are usually very helpful.

There are also private bus stands: the Kaloor stand is north-east of Ernakulam Town train station, and the Ernakulam South stand is right outside the entrance of Ernakulam Junction train station.

The fares and times that follow are for superexpress buses unless otherwise noted. Superfast services are usually a few rupees cheaper and stop more often.

Southbound There are two routes to Thiruvananthapuram (221km): one via Alappuzha and Kollam, and the other via Kottayam. Over 60 KSRTC buses a day take the Alappuzha to Kollam route. Superexpress buses take 4½ hours to Thiruvananthapuram and cost Rs 80. The intermediate distances, fares and times for superexpress buses are: Alappuzha (62km, Rs 25, 1½ hours), Kollam (150km, Rs 55, three hours), and Kottayam (76km, Rs 30, 1½ hours). There are also at least two direct buses a day to Kanyakumari (302km, Rs 103, 8¾ hours).

Eastbound At least four direct buses a day run to Madurai (324km, Rs 111, 9¼ hours). For those with phenomenal endurance, there are direct buses to Chennai (690km, Rs 210, 16½ hours).

The Madurai buses pass through Kumily, near the Periyar Wildlife Sanctuary on the Kerala/Tamil Nadu border. There are three buses direct to Kumily and Thekkady, the centre within the sanctuary (192km, Rs 46 by fast passenger bus, six hours). Departure times are 6.30 and 8.15 am, and 3.30 pm, and you can book a seat on the morning departures. You will need to book your journey through to Kumbam (the end of a section) but disembark at Kumily. The 8.15 am service is a Madurai-bound bus.

There are several KSRTC buses a day to Munnar (Rs 42). Or you can choose to take one of the many private buses to Kothamangalam from the bus stand outside Ernakulam Junction train station. From Kothamangalam there are many buses to Munnar.

Northbound There are buses every half hour to Thrissur (Trichur) (81km, Rs 30, two hours) and Kozhikode (219km, Rs 75, five hours). A couple of buses a day run right up the coast beyond Kozhikode to Kannur (Cannanore), Kasaragod and across the Karnataka state border to Mangalore.

KERALA

Half a dozen interstate express buses go to Bangalore (565km, Rs 192, 15 hours) daily via Kozhikode, Sultan's Battery and Mysore.

In addition to the KSRTC state buses, there are a number of private bus companies which have superdeluxe video buses daily to Bangalore, Mumbai and Coimbatore. Check out Princy Tours (☎ 354712) in the GCDA Complex on Shanmugham Rd, opposite the Sealord Hotel. Others include Conti Travels (☎ 353080) at the Jos Junction of MG Rd, and Silcon A/C Coach (☎ 394596), Banerji Rd.

Train Ernakulam has two stations, Ernakulam Junction and Ernakulam Town, but the one you're most likely to use is Ernakulam Junction. Note that none of the through trains on the main trunk routes go to the Cochin Harbour station on Willingdon Island.

Trains run regularly along the coast from Thiruvananthapuram via Kollam and Kottayam to Ernakulam; less frequently they continue on to Thrissur, Kozhikode, Thalasseri and Kasaragod. Two trains daily run right through to Mangalore in Karnataka. The daily *Vanchinad Express* runs between Thiruvananthapuram and Ernakulam in just over four hours, but other services are somewhat slower.

If you're heading to/from Ooty, there are quite a few expresses which stop at Coimbatore (198km, Rs 75/252, six hours). At the time of research there were no direct trains

to Goa, but check at any train station when you arrive to see if any services have been introduced. The fastest way to Goa is by train to Mangalore and bus or the Konkan Railway from there.

Getting Around
To/From the Airport A bus to the airport costs Rs 2 from Ernakulam or Fort Cochin. A taxi from either Ernakulam or Fort Cochin to the airport on Willingdon Island costs around Rs 80; and takes about 20 minutes. An auto-rickshaw ride is about half the price, and roughly the same duration.

Bus, Auto-Rickshaw & Taxi There are no convenient bus services between Fort Cochin and the Mattancherry Palace/Jewish synagogue, but it's a pleasant 30 minute walk through the busy warehouse area along Bazaar Rd. Auto-rickshaws are available, though the drivers will need persuasion to use the meters – this is tourist territory.

In Ernakulam, auto-rickshaws are the most convenient mode of transport. The trip from the bus or train stations to the Tourist Reception Centre on Shanmugham Rd should cost about Rs 15 – a bit less on the meter. Flagfall is Rs 6, then Rs 3 a kilometre.

Local buses are fairly good and cheap. If you have to get to Fort Cochin after the ferries stop running, catch a bus in Ernakulam on MG Rd, south of Durbar Hall Rd.

Major Trains from Ernakulam

Destination	Train Number & Name	Departure Time	Distance (km)	Duration (hours)	Fare (Rs) (2nd/1st)
Bangalore	6525 *Bangalore Express*	3.47 pm ET*	637	14	163/563
Chennai	6320 *Madras Mail*	5.35 pm ET	697	13	172/597
Delhi	2625 *Kerala Express*	2.35 pm EJ	2833	48	382/1702
	2431 *Rajdhani Express***	12.05 am Sat EJ		40.30	2390/4775
Kozhikode	6307 *Cannanore Express*	5.00 pm EJ	190	4.15	48/217
Mangalore	6329 *Malabar Express* ET	11.00 pm	414	10.45	119/410
	6349 *Parsuram Express*	11.00 am ET		10	
Mumbai CST*	6332 *Mumbai Express*	8.45 pm EJ	1840	36.45	304/1213
Thiruvananthapuram	6303 *Vanchinad Express*	5.50 am EJ	224	4.30	56/249

* Abbreviations for train stations: CST – Chhatrapati Shivaji Terminus (Victoria Terminus),
   ET – Ernakulam Town, EJ – Ernakulam Junction
** Air-con only; catering charge extra

The fare is Rs 3. Auto-rickshaws will demand at least Rs 50 once the ferries stop running after about 10 pm.

Taxis charge round-trip fares between the islands, even if you only want to go one way. Ernakulam to Willingdon Island could cost up to Rs 150 late at night.

Boat Ferries are the main form of transport between the various parts of Kochi. Nearly all the ferry stops are named, which helps to identify them on the timetable at Main Jetty in Ernakulam. The stop on the east side of Willingdon Island is called Embarkation; the one on the west side, opposite Mattancherry, is Terminus. The main stop at Fort Cochin is known as Customs.

Getting onto a ferry at Ernakulam can sometimes involve scrambling across several ferries to get to the boat you want. If you have to do this, make sure you get onto the right ferry or you may find yourself heading for the wrong island – ask the skipper or deck hand.

Ferry fares are all Rs 2 or less.

Ernakulam to Fort Cochin/Mattancherry
There are services to Fort Cochin every 45 minutes from around 6 am to 9.30 pm. It's a pleasant 20 minute walk from the Fort Cochin pier to Mattancherry. There are also seven ferries a day direct to/from Mattancherry. The ticket office in Ernakulam opens 10 minutes before each sailing.

Ernakulam to Willingdon/Vypeen Islands
Ferries run every 20 minutes from about 6 am to 10 pm. There are also ferries to Vypeen Island (sometimes via Bolgatty Island) from the High Court Jetty on Shanmugham Rd.

Ernakulam to Bolgatty Island Ferries for Bolgatty Island depart from the High Court Jetty every 20 minutes between 6 am and 10 pm. It's a five minute walk from the public jetty to Bolgatty Palace Hotel.

Fort Cochin to Willingdon Island Ferries operate between Customs Jetty and the Taj

Malabar/Tourist Office Jetty about 30 times daily, except on Sunday.

Fort Cochin to Vypeen Island Ferries cross this narrow gap virtually nonstop from 6 am until 10 pm. There is also a vehicular ferry every half hour or so.

Hire Boats Motorised boats of various sizes can be hired from the Sealord Jetty or from the small dock adjacent to the Main Jetty in Ernakulam. They're an excellent way of exploring Kochi harbour at your leisure and without the crowds; rates start at around Rs 300 an hour. Rowboats shuttle between Willingdon Island and Fort Cochin or Mattancherry on request for about Rs 40.

AROUND KOCHI
Tripunithura
The **Hill Palace Museum** at Tripunithura, 12km south-east of Ernakulam, en route to Kottayam, houses the collections of the Cochin and Travancore royal families. It's open Tuesday to Sunday from 9 am to 12.30 pm and from 2 to 4 pm; entry is Rs 1. Bus No 51 or 58 from MG Rd will take you there.

Edapally
The **Museum of Kerala History,** at Edapally, 10km north-east of Ernakulam en route to Aluva (Alwaye) and Thrissur, is open Tuesday to Sunday from 10 am to noon and from 2 to 4 pm; entry is Rs 2. Bus No 22 from MG Rd runs to Edapally.

Parur & Chennamangalam
About 35km north of Kochi is a busy little town a world away from touristed Kochi but with which it shares much history. Parur encapsulates the cultural and religious medley of this region, where international trade dominated for countless numbers of years. Just to the north of the central bus stop, beside the ochre-red former British Residency buildings, is the small though clearly signposted Jew St. There is one Jewish family remaining in Parur and they live on the premises of the disused synagogue. The dusty synagogue was built around the same

time as its famous counterpart in Mattancherry, but the original pulpit and arch were shipped to Israel and many of the Belgian glass lamps are now cracked.

At the end of Jew St is a canal where a market is held midweek. Nearby is an *agraharam*, (place of Brahmins) a small street of neat, close-packed houses which was settled by Tamil Brahmins who were brought here by the Rajas of Cochin. Behind the large Roman Catholic church are the remains of the third church erected on this site. It was built in 1308 and partly demolished in 1964. The first church was built, so some believe, by the Brahmins converted by St Thomas the Apostle (Doubting Thomas) in the first century AD. Parur also boasts a Syrian Orthodox church, a Krishna temple and a temple to the mute goddess Mookambic.

Four kilometres from Parur, on the banks of the Periyar River not far from the historic port of Kodungallor (Cranganore), is the village of Chennamangalam. Here stands the oldest **synagogue** in Kerala – virtually in ruins, abandoned and locked, and slowly disintegrating under the ineffectual guardianship of the Archaeological Survey of India.

There is a **Jesuit church** (now Roman Catholic) and the ruins of a Jesuit college, the Vaippikotta Seminary, which was wrecked by Tipu Sultan in 1790. The Jesuits first arrived in Chennamangalam in 1577 and, soon after their arrival, the first book in Tamil (the written language used in this part of Kerala at this time) was printed here by John Gonsalves.

You can walk to the **Hindu temple** on the top of the hill overlooking the Periyar River. On the way you'll pass a **16th century mosque** as well as Moslem and Jewish **burial grounds**.

Also in Chennamangalam is a 17th century **palace** built by the Dutch after they defeated the Portuguese at Cranganore, and presented to the Palayathachan – a dynasty of chief ministers to the royal family of Cochin. The palace is now in the hands of a trust which looks after the 60-odd Hindu temples in the immediate region.

Getting There & Away To get to Parur, catch a ferry to Vypeen Island and from there a bus runs north to Parur. From Parur you can catch a bus, rickshaw or taxi to Chennamangalam. Whereas Parur is compact and there are lots of locals to point you in the right direction, Chennamangalam is best visited with a guide. Indo World (☎ 370127) in Ernakulam can organise transport and a local retired history teacher to guide you.

THRISSUR (Trichur)
Pop: 77,700 Tel Area Code: 0487
Its name means the 'town with the name of Lord Shiva', Thrissur features one of the largest temples in Kerala, the Vadakkunathan Kshetram. An important religious and cultural centre for centuries, Thrissur was occupied by the kingdoms of Kochi from the 16th to the 18th century. It briefly fell into the hands of the Zamorin of Kozhikode and then Hyder Ali in the late 18th century. Today Thrissur is still distinguished by its cultural importance with several government arts colleges.

Orientation & Information
Thrissur radiates out from Vadakkunathan Kshetram. The encircling roads are named Round North, Round East, Round South and Round West. The Tourist Information Centre has minimal information.

The State Bank of India on Town Hall Rd encashes American Express and Thomas Cook travellers cheques but not cards. Canara Bank on Round South can handle cash advances on Visa cards.

Things to See
Famed for its murals and artwork, the Hindu-only **Vadakkunathan Kshetram** temple sits atop a hill in the centre of Thrissur. There are also two impressively large churches: **Our Lady of Lourdes Cathedral** and the **Puttanpalli Church**. Skip the sad **zoo**, and the amazingly dusty and decrepit **State Museum** in the zoo grounds. However, the **Archaeological Museum**, further along Museum Rd, has temple models, stone reliefs, Gandharan pieces and reproductions

KERALA

Caste in Kerala

Ritual purity was enforced in old Kerala with more vehemence than just about anywhere else in India. A low-caste person could pollute someone of higher caste not just by touch, but by mere proximity. There were rules that dictated how close a low-caste person could come to a high-caste person without polluting them. A low-caste person was expected to shout a warning if they saw they were approaching a higher-caste person and they were expected to cup their left hand over their mouth when speaking to their superiors. Those of the lowest caste were banned from temples and even from walking along main roads. If polluted, a high-caste person was expected to undergo ritual cleansing.

How this came to be is neatly explained in one of Kerala's best-known founding myths. The story goes that the god Parasurama, having slain all those of warrior caste in India, tried to make good by handing over the country to holy men. But having done this he found himself with nowhere to live and appealed to the holy men to grant him a piece of land. They agreed, saying that he could claim all the land within the area of a single throw of his axe. He threw his axe from Kanyakumari in the extreme south to an area that's now Goa, whereupon the sea receded and Kerala was created.

Parasurama brought in Brahmins, known as Nambudiris, to populate the new land – and gave them total control. The Nairs, a warrior caste, were created to serve the Brahmins and beneath them came a range of polluting castes.

In practice Nambudiri Brahmins were the major landholders in old Kerala and Nairs served them as supervisors – and as warriors in times of strife. Syrian Christians and Muslims, who also owned land and engaged in trade, were similar in status to Nairs. Below them were people who cultivated coconut trees and worked on the land – the Tiyya in northern Kerala and the Ezhava in southern Kerala. Artisans were roughly of the same status and below these were the slave castes, the Pulayas or Parayas who did all the heavy, unpleasant work.

But by the 1920s things were changing. The activity of European missionaries who campaigned against slavery, changing economic fortunes which benefited lowly castes, and the ability or otherwise of particular castes to adapt to changing times – including the cash economy – sealed the fate of an otherwise rigid system.

---

of some of the Mattancherry murals. There may be an entry fee, but when we called in there was no-one there to collect it. The museum is open from 10 am to 5pm. The zoo and museums are closed on Monday.

Special Events

The annual April/May **Pooram Festival** is one of the biggest in the south. It includes fireworks, colourful processions and brightly decorated elephants. This festival was first introduced by Sakthan Thampuram, the maharaja of the former state of Kochi.

Places to Stay

Ramanilayam Government Guest House (☎ 332016), at the junction of Palace and Museum Rds is excellent value at Rs 45/50 for singles/doubles, or Rs 175/275 with aircon., but ring first as it's often full.

The KTDC *Yatri Nivas* (☎ 332333, Stadium Rd), nearby, has rooms for Rs 100/150, or Rs 350/400 with air-con. There's a restaurant and bar.

Chandy's Tourist Home (☎ 421167, Railway Station Rd) is close to the bus and train stations. It has rooms for Rs 75 with shared bath or Rs 85/250 with attached bath. There are several lodges nearby with similar standards and prices.

Jaya Lodge (☎ 423258, Kuruppam Rd), around the corner, is unexciting but cheap with rooms for Rs 50/90; doubles with bathroom are Rs 100.

LINDSAY BROWN

EDDIE GERALD

EDDIE GERALD

PAUL BEINSSEN

Kerala
Images of Kochi (Cochin): an Escher-esque building coming together in Ernakulam (top left); sculpted images of Ganesh for sale in Fort Cochin (top right & bottom left) and a *rangoli* (flour-drawing) decorating a street.

PAUL BEINSSEN

LINDSAY BROWN

Kerala
Crowds of tourists throng Kerala's famous Kovalam Beach (top), while small groups of tea pickers pluck a living in the high ranges around Munnar (bottom).

Pathan's (☎ 425620, Chembottil Lane), just off Round South, has rooms for Rs 100/200, or Rs 225 with TV. The rooms are on the 4th floor so it's worth checking to see if the elevator is working.

Hotel Elite International (☎ 421033, fax 442057), across the road, is a more comfortable option; rooms are Rs 210/260, or Rs 340 with TV. Air-con rooms are Rs 410/480. It has a bar and an air-con restaurant.

Hotel Luciya Palace (☎ 424731, fax 427290, Marar Rd), just off Round South, has clean, comfortable rooms with TV for Rs 275/350, or Rs 450/500 with air-con. There's an air-con restaurant and bar.

Sidhartha Regency (☎ 424773, fax 425116, corner of TB and Veliyannur Rds) is close to buses and the train station. It is centrally air-conditioned and the pleasant rooms with TV and phone start at Rs 600/750. There is also a good restaurant and a bar.

Casino Hotel (☎ 24699, TB Rd), close to the bus and train stations, was being renovated and extended at the time of writing. Singles/doubles are Rs 350/400, or Rs 550/600 with air-con.

Places to Eat
A cluster of **snack stalls** sets up near the corner of Round South and Round East each evening.

There's an abundance of **Indian Coffee Houses**: you can find them on Round South; PO Rd, near Railway Station Rd; and upstairs in President Bazaar, on Kuruppam Rd.

Upstairs in **Pathan's** (junction of Chembottil Lane and Round South), there's a good, basic vegetarian restaurant with an air-con section. A floor above Pathan's is the **Ming Palace** Chinese restaurant.

Hotel Bharath, further down Chembottil Lane, is a very good, very busy vegetarian place.

The middle and top-end hotels have decent restaurants which usually have air-con. The **Luciya Palace** has a popular outdoor bar area.

Getting There & Away
Bus There are regular KSRTC buses to Guruvayur (Rs 10, one hour), Kozhikode (Rs 36,

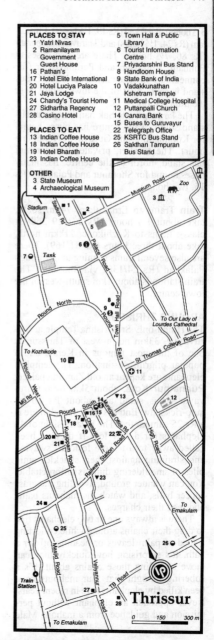

PLACES TO STAY	5 Town Hall & Public
1 Yatri Nivas	Library
2 Ramanilayam	6 Tourist Information
Government	Centre
Guest House	7 Priyadarshini Bus Stand
16 Pathan's	8 Handloom House
17 Hotel Elite International	9 State Bank of India
20 Hotel Luciya Palace	10 Vadakkunathan
21 Jaya Lodge	Kshetram Temple
24 Chandy's Tourist Home	11 Medical College Hospital
27 Sidhartha Regency	12 Puttanpalli Church
28 Casino Hotel	14 Canara Bank
	15 Buses to Guruvayur
PLACES TO EAT	22 Telegraph Office
13 Indian Coffee House	25 KSRTC Bus Stand
18 Indian Coffee House	26 Sakthan Tampuran
19 Hotel Bharath	Bus Stand
23 Indian Coffee House	
OTHER	
3 State Museum	
4 Archaeological Museum	

Thrissur

0   150   300 m

3½ hours), Palakkad (Rs 19, 1½ hours), Ernakulam (Rs 24, 1½ hours) and Thiruvananthapuram (Rs 80, 7½ hours). There are also buses to Ponnani, Kottayam and Perumpavoor (for connections to Munnar). The KSRTC bus stand is south-west of the town centre, near the train station.

The large, private Sakthan Tampuran bus stand south of the centre has buses bound for Kodungallor and Guruvayur (Rs 6, one hour). The smaller, private Priyadarshini bus stand, north of the centre, has many buses bound for Shoranur and Palakkad (Rs 15, two hours).

Train Trains to Ernakulam, 74km south, take about 1½ hours (Rs 23/129 2nd/1st class); trains to Kozhikode, 118km north, take about three hours (Rs 31/169). There are also several trains running to or through Palakkad (Rs 24/130) via Shoranur. The train station is about 1km south-west of the town centre.

AROUND THRISSUR
The Hindu-only Sri Krishna Temple at **Guruvayur**, 33km north-west of Thrissur, is one of the most famous in Kerala and a popular pilgrim destination. The temple's elephants are kept at an old Zamorin palace, **Punnathur Kota**, about 5km from Guruvayur's bus stand and about Rs 20 by auto-rickshaw. Entry is free, though there is a Rs 25 camera fee. The bizarre sight of 43 elephants (or a few less if they've been called away to a temple festival) swaying and straining against their shackles amid piles of smouldering dung is unforgettable. You can wander around, avoiding the grass soccer balls, and watch the mahouts bathe and feed their charges.

There is always one or two elephants free to drag their chains around while collecting a feed of palm leaves or heading off for a bath. It's surprising how quickly they can move and fling those chains about. It's a sobering thought that four mahouts have been killed by elephants here in recent years. Never approach an elephant without permission and guidance from a mahout. Male elephants in *musth*, mating season, are particularly dangerous and should be given a wide berth. You can tell when an elephant is in musht because there is a gland behind the eye which secretes a visible discharge, but the erections are even more obvious!

See under Thrissur for Getting There & Away information.

KOZHIKODE (Calicut)
Pop: 871,600 Tel Area Code: 0495
Vasco da Gama landed at Kappad Beach near Kozhikode in 1498, becoming the first European to reach India via the sea route around the southern cape of Africa.

His arrival heralded the period of Portuguese supremacy in India and the history of Kozhikode after 1498 was certainly dramatic. The Portuguese attempted to conquer the town, a centre of Malabar power under the Zamorins, or Lords of the Sea. The Portuguese attacks in 1509 and 1510 were both repulsed, although the town was virtually destroyed in the latter assault. Tipu Sultan laid the whole region to waste in 1789, and British rule was established in 1792.

Information
If the town's banks won't change your travellers cheques, try PL Worldways, 3rd floor, Lakhotia Computer Centre, at the junction of Mavoor and Bank Rds. Mavoor Rd is also known as Indira Gandhi Rd.

Things to See
Despite its colourful past, there is little of interest in the town. The central Ansari Park features musical fountains in the evening, and there's a mediocre beach with open drains running into it, 2km from the town centre. Five kilometres from town, at East Hill, the archaeological displays at the **Pazhassirajah Museum** include copies of ancient mural paintings, bronzes, old coins and models of temples and megalithic monuments. Next door, the dusty and musty **Krishna Menon Museum** has memorabilia of this former statesperson of India, while the **Art Gallery** has paintings of Raja Ravi Varma and Raja Raja Varma.

The three places are open Tuesday to Sunday from 10 am to 5 pm, except on Wednesday when the Krishna Menon Museum and the Art Gallery open at noon.

Places to Stay – Budget

All of the following have bathroom attached.

Metro Tourist Home (☎ 766029) at the junction of Mavoor and Bank Rds has singles/doubles for Rs 125/175, or air-con doubles with TV for Rs 425.

Hotel Sajina (☎ 722975, Mavoor Rd) has basic rooms for Rs 80/120.

Two basic lodges share a courtyard with the Indian Coffee House (see Places to Eat). *NCK Tourist Home* has rooms for Rs 125. Across the way the friendlier *Delma Tourist Home* charges Rs 120.

Lakshmi Bhavan Tourist Home (☎ 722027, GH Rd) is similar standard and costs Rs 75/150.

Hotel Maharani (☎ 722541, Taluk Rd) is slightly off the beaten track, and quiet. Rooms are Rs 140/175, or Rs 440 for an air-con double. There's a bar and a garden.

The KTDC *Hotel Malabar Mansion (☎ 722391, Mananchira Square)* is in the centre of town, near Ansari Park. Rooms are Rs 175/225, or Rs 360/400 with air-con. There's an air-con restaurant, beer parlour, snack bar and tourist information at the reception counter.

Kalpaka Tourist Home (☎ 720222, Town Hall Rd) is good value with singles/doubles for Rs 140/188, or air-con rooms for Rs 500. Prices include taxes. There is an OK restaurant.

Places to Stay – Mid-Range & Top End

Seaqueen Hotel (☎ 366604, fax 365854, Beach Rd) is by the waterfront, but Kozhikode's beach is nothing to get excited about. Rooms are Rs 375/500 or Rs 650/775 with air-con.

Paramount Tower (Town Hall Rd) was undergoing extensive renovations at the time of writing, so rooms should be bright and clean.

Hotel Malabar Palace (☎ 721511, fax 721794, GH Rd) is centrally air-conditioned and rooms cost Rs 1125/1375.

Taj Residency (☎ /fax 766448, PT Usha Rd) has rooms starting at US$65/75.

Places to Eat

There's an *Indian Coffee House* hidden away just off Mavoor Rd. The glossy *Woodlands* vegetarian restaurant is in the easily spotted White Lines building on GH Rd.

The restaurants in the *Metro*, *Kalpaka* and *Malabar Mansion* hotels are very reasonably priced, if not terribly exciting.

The air-con restaurant at the *Malabar Palace* is good and there's an ice cream

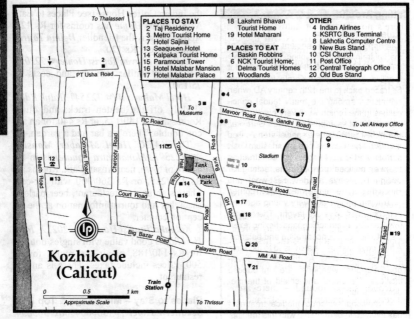

PLACES TO STAY
2 Taj Residency
3 Metro Tourist Home
7 Hotel Sajina
13 Seaqueen Hotel
14 Kalpaka Tourist Home
15 Paramount Tower
16 Hotel Malabar Mansion
17 Hotel Malabar Palace
18 Lakshmi Bhavan
   Tourist Home
19 Hotel Maharani

PLACES TO EAT
1 Baskin Robbins
6 NCK Tourist Home;
   Delma Tourist Homes
21 Woodlands

OTHER
4 Indian Airlines
5 KSRTC Bus Terminal
8 Lakhotia Computer Centre
9 New Bus Stand
10 CSI Church
11 Post Office
12 Central Telegraph Office
20 Old Bus Stand

Kozhikode (Calicut)

parlour, *Tom 'n Jerry*, in the garden outside the hotel.

The restaurant at the *Seaqueen Hotel* has good snacks and seafood and you can have a cold beer.

Getting There & Away

Air The Indian Airlines office (☎ 766243) is in the Eroth Centre on Bank Rd, close to the Mavoor Rd junction. Indian Airlines flies daily to Bangalore (Rs 2090), Mumbai (Rs 4130) and Chennai (five days a week via Coimbatore and five days a week via Madurai, Rs 2480), and three days a week to Goa (Rs 2695). Jet Airways (☎ 356052) on Mavoor Rd also connects daily with Mumbai.

Bus The KSRTC bus stand is on Mavoor Rd, close to the junction with Bank Rd. There's also the New bus stand, further east along Mavoor Rd, for long-distance private

buses, and the Old bus stand, at the intersection of GH and MM Ali Rds, for local buses. There are regular buses to Bangalore, Mangalore, Mysore, Ooty, Madurai, Coimbatore, Pondicherry, Thiruvananthapuram, Alappuzha, Kochi and Kottayam.

The bus to Ooty and Mysore (5½ hours) climbs over the Western Ghats and has spectacular views from the left-hand side.

Train The train station is south of Ansari Park, about 2km from the New bus stand. It's 242km north to Mangalore (Rs 56/274 in 2nd/1st class, 4½ to 5½ hours), 190km south to Ernakulam (Rs 48/239, five hours) and 414km to Thiruvananthapuram (Rs 90/451, 9½ to 11 hours).

Heading south-east, there are trains via Palakkad (Palghat; Rs 35/185) to Coimbatore (Rs 47/235). These trains then head north to the centres of Bangalore, Chennai and Delhi.

Getting Around
There's no shortage of auto-rickshaws in Kozhikode, and the drivers will use their meters. It's about Rs 10 from the train station to the KSRTC bus stand or most hotels.

MAHÉ
Tel Area Code: 0497
Mahé, 60km north of Kozhikode, was a small French dependency handed over to India at the same time as Pondicherry, at Independence. It is still part of the Union Territory of Pondicherry. Like Karaikal and Yanam on the east coast of India, there's little French influence left and Mahé's main function seems to be supplying passing truck drivers with cheap alcohol.

The English factory established here in 1683 by the Surat presidency to purchase pepper and cardamom was the first permanent English factory on the Malabar Coast. The East India Company also built a fort here in 1708.

Alcohol shops abound – there are 75 outlets selling Pondicherry whisky and Goan beer, as well as other Indian and some foreign spirits. In addition to the cheap booze (as little as one-third of the price for the same bottle in Kerala) there is some very cheap accommodation.

Places to Stay & Eat
It's far more pleasant to stay at Thalasseri, 8km north, though there are a few basic options in Mahé itself.

Government Tourist Home (☎ *332222*), near the river mouth, about 1km from the bridge, has singles/doubles for just Rs 12/20 with bath attached, but it's generally full. There is a very cheap 'meals' restaurant here as well.

Municipal Tourist Home (☎ *332233, Church Rd*), beside the courthouse, is in the same price range with singles/doubles/family rooms for Rs 12/22/30.

Hotel Arena (☎ *33242*), at the junction of Church and Cemetery Rds, has doubles with bath attached for Rs 100, or Rs 325 with air-con. Its restaurant was closed at the time of writing but breakfast was being provided.

Aswathi Guest House is across Church Rd, east down Old Syndicate Bank Rd. Basic doubles with bath attached cost Rs 120.

Zara Resorts (☎ *332503, Station Rd*), 1km east of Church Rd, has standard doubles with TV for Rs 150, or Rs 275 with air-con. There is a restaurant and a bar.

Getting There & Away
Mahé is too small to warrant a bus stand, so buses from Thalasseri stop on the northern side of the bridge and at various places along Church Rd south of the bridge. There are regular buses to Thalasseri, Mangalore and Kozhikode. There is also a service between Mahé and Pondicherry on the east coast of India – make inquiries at the Government Tourist Home or the nearby Government Guest House.

THALASSERI (Tellicherry)
Tel Area Code: 0497
Thalasseri is not worth a special detour but, if you are making your way along the coast, it's a pleasant, unhurried place to stop for the night. The town's fishing fleet returns in the late afternoon, and the beach becomes an animated fish market as people haggle over the catch. You may even be lucky enough to catch an impromptu circus act in the street: Thalasseri is home to a circus school.

Near the waterfront, right behind the fire station, the East India Company's 1708 **fort** is neglected but relatively intact, with a fine gateway flanked by two comical guards. There are at least two secret tunnels, one leading to the sea. The tunnels will be either 'closed', 'under repair' or 'inhabited by a cobra' but bring a torch (flashlight) and ask nicely at one of the government offices inside the fort and you may be offered a glimpse of a damp chamber. There's a disused lighthouse perched on one corner of the fort.

Between the fort and the sea are two churches and a school. The smaller Church of South India is disused and crumbling, its stained glass windows suffering from wayward cricket balls from St Joseph's schoolyard. Its congregation is in decline in this region of Kerala. Its fascinating cemetery is overgrown and neglected, save for one grave which belongs to Edward Brennan 'A Sterling, upright Englishman and founder of Brennan College' who died in 1859 aged 75. Brennan College is a highly respected institution in Kerala to this day.

Logan's Rd runs from Narangapuram, near the bus and train stations, to the town's main square near the fort.

Places to Stay

Most of the following places have rooms with bathroom attached.

Hotel Pranam (☎ 220634) (turn left at Logan's Rd from the train station, then immediately right) has comfortable rooms for Rs 86/165, or Rs 335 with air-con. There's an attached restaurant.

For all other accommodation listed below take a right turn into Logan's Rd from the bus and train stations.

Brothers Tourist Home (☎ 21558), at the Narangapuram end of Logan's Rd, shares a courtyard with Shemy Hospital. It is cheap, with rooms for Rs 50/85.

Impala Tourist Home (☎ 220484), nearby, is similar with rooms for Rs 45/65.

Minerva Tourist Home (☎ 221731) is a little further along Logan's Rd and has basic rooms for Rs 50/80.

The Residency (☎ 232357), a few doors uphill from the easily seen Paris Presidency, has good rooms from Rs 86/129, or Rs 248/275 for air-con. Prices include tax.

The *Chattanchal Tourist Home (☎ 222967, Convent Rd)* is beyond the square opposite the fire station. Rooms cost Rs 138 a double or Rs 345 with air-con.

Paris Presidency Hotel (☎ /fax 233666), close to the end of Logan's Rd, is welcoming and comfortable. It's good value at Rs 240/300, or Rs 390 for air-con doubles.

Paris Lodging House (☎ 231666), adjacent, is cheaper with rooms from Rs 70/115, up to Rs 288 for an air-con double.

Places to Eat

Parkview, near the railway crossing, is a simple nonveg eatery. Upstairs is the more comfortable though not much more expensive *Kings Park*, which has a much greater range and friendlier staff.

Hotel New Westend in the busy main square at the end of Logan's Rd has good nonveg food – the fish curry is excellent.

The *New Surya Restaurant*, a couple of doors away, has great chilli chicken.

Kwality Sweets is one of a number of ice cream parlours and 'cool' shops around the square: they only sport the sign 'cool' or 'cool bar' after 10 am.

The *Paris Presidency* has an air-con restaurant but odd rules. Don't ask for a cup of tea or coffee at lunchtime because that is 'rush time', and even if you are the only guest, the six or more staff couldn't possibly find the time to boil water.

Getting There & Around

Frequent trains and buses head north along the coast to Mangalore and south to Mahé, Kozhikode and Kochi. You can walk from the train station or bus stand to most of the hotels which are on Logan's Rd. An autorickshaw to any of the town's hotels should cost around Rs 10.

KANNUR (Cannanore)
Tel Area Code: 0497

Kannur's days of glory were under the Kolathiri Rajas, and its importance as a spice-trading port was mentioned by Marco Polo. From the 15th century various colonial powers exerted their influence over this rich region of the Malabar Coast. Kannur has been under Portuguese, Dutch and British rule.

Information

There is a Tourist Information Centre on South Bazaar that has a brochure (Rs 3) and map (Rs 7) of the district. Opposite is the State Bank of Travancore, which will encash American Express travellers cheques. For other brands and for cash advances on credit cards try the State Bank of India on Fort Rd.

Things to See

The Portuguese built **St Angelo Fort** in 1505 on the promontory north-west of town. Under the British it became a major military base and today the Indian Army occupy the cantonment area beside the fort. The fort is a Rs 7 rickshaw ride from town, but you will need to negotiate a waiting fee while you examine the grounds (entry is free). The solid laterite fortifications were modified by the British who also remodelled many of the buildings within the walls. There is some maintenance going on but this appears to be little more than patching with cement. A number of cannons have been set in cement and placed in very non-strategic positions but the constant sound of gunfire from the nearby army camp does lend a certain authenticity.

Places to Stay & Eat

Centaur Tourist Home (☎ 68270) is directly across from the train station entrance, about 200m down MA Rd. Basic singles/doubles are Rs 100/160. There are plenty of similar lodges in the vicinity.

The KTDC *Yatri Niwas (☎ 500717)* is a short walk behind the train station – take care and walk across the tracks. The hotel is clean and good value with rooms for Rs 100/150, or Rs 350/400 with air-con. The reception staff are very friendly and keen to help with inquiries or organising transport, especially if you show an interest in the cultural offerings of the region. The restaurant is unfortunately comically inadequate and dirty with only one or two dishes available from its menu.

Kamala International (☎ 66910, fax 50189, SM RD) is rather expensive with rooms with TV for Rs 500/540, or Rs 600/750 with air-con. There are two restaurants, including one on the roof, and a coffee shop.

Getting There & Away

There are direct buses to/from Mysore as well as regular buses to Mangalore and Kozhikode. Kannur is on the main train link between Mangalore and Kozhikode.

BEKAL FORT

Tel Area Code: 0499

Bekal, in the far north of the state, has long, palm-fringed **beaches** and a rocky headland topped by a huge fort built between 1645 and 1660. This fort, with views from the battlements north and south, is extensive but there is no interpretive information provided. Its early history is obscure but it has been under the control of the Kolathiri Rajas and the Vijayanagar Empire. The British East India Company occupied it for a period after the defeat of Tipu Sultan. There are slow-moving plans to build a large resort here, but meanwhile there's hardly a tourist in sight. Don't believe the hype about the beach – this is no embryonic Varkala or Kovalam. The beach is steep and coarse, the water murky brown because of all the river entrances, and there is no surf, just a nasty shore break and strong currents – don't come here for the swimming.

Places to Stay & Eat

You can stay inside the Bekal Fort walls at the excellent value *Tourist Bungalow*. There are just two rooms for Rs 40/60 with bath attached. To book, ring the District Collector, Kasaragod (☎ 430400/010). Cold mineral water and soft drinks are available from the caretaker but for food you will have to head to the villages north of the fort. You will need a torch (flashlight) if returning to the fort after dark, as there is a 1km walk from the gate to the bungalow – the howling is just foxes!

Eeyem Lodge (☎ 736343) is 3km north of the fort, at the village of Palakunnu, and has rooms with bath for Rs 45/55.

Hotel Sri Sistha, nearby, is a fairly basic restaurant but one of the few open during Ramadan. Meals and a good masala dosa can be had for under Rs 10.

Fortland Tourist Home (☎ 736600) is a few kilometres further north at the village of Udma. Comfortable singles/doubles cost Rs 75/125, or Rs 350 with air-con. There is a restaurant, the *Sealord*, attached.

Getting There & Around

The train station for Bekal Fort is Kotikulum but it is in the village of Palakunnu, and despite its size, trains regularly stop. Running north to Mangalore trains depart at

6.12, 7.53 and 9.10 am and 6.15, 6.58 and 10.23 pm. Trains going south depart at 6.54, 7.45 (express) and 9.14 am and 5.02, 7.30 and 9 pm. There are many buses to/from Kasaragod, the nearest town of any size, and it's not too hard to find an auto-rickshaw or a bus at Bekal Junction to take you to/from Palakunnu and Udma.

KASARAGOD
Tel Area Code: 0499

Kasaragod is about 20km north of Bekal and 47km south of Mangalore. There is a large fort nearby at **Chandragiri** built by Shivappa Nayaka, but this town is at most a rest-stop. There are a number of hotels in Kasaragod along MG Rd, near the junction with NH17.

Places to Stay

Enay Tourist Home (☎ 521164) has single or double rooms for Rs 100 with attached shower. Of a similar standard are the *Ceeyel*

Tourist Home (☎ 521177) and the *Aliya Lodge (☎ 522897);* the latter can be found behind the post office.

Hotel City Tower (☎ 521324) at the bus stand end of MG Rd is a green-and-cream landmark and the best place to stay in town. Rooms are Rs 172/299, or Rs 545 with air-con (prices include tax).

Getting There & Away

Bekal is a Rs 3 to Rs 5.50 bus ride from Kasaragod, depending on the bus and the route. Private buses leave for Bekal and Mangalore from the Municipal bus stand near the Hotel City Tower. More regular buses leave from the KSRTC bus stand 1½km south of the Municipal stand. Buses to Kahangad will drop you off at Udma, Palakunnu or Bekal. It's only one to 1½ hours between Kasaragod and Mangalore by express train (Rs 19). The train station is a couple of kilometres south of the town centre.

Lakshadweep

Between 300km and 400km off the coast of Kerala lie a group of islands that make up India's smallest Union Territory. Lakshadweep is an archipelago of coral atolls spread out along a roughly north-south axis, along a huge underwater ridge which is believed to be an extension of the Aravali mountain range in North India. To the west of the ridge the ocean floor drops some 4000m, while to the east, between the islands and the Indian mainland, the Lakshadweep Sea plummets to depths of over 2000m. Exposed to the might of the Arabian Sea, the 12 tiny atolls shelter 35 islands, 10 of which are inhabited. The total area enclosed within the reefs is around 300 sq km, but the total area of the islands themselves is only 32 sq km.

Up until they were renamed in 1973, the islands were often considered as three groups, known as the Aminidivi, Laccadive and Minicoy islands. The northernmost group (the Aminidivi Islands) consists of Chetlat, Bitra, Kiltan, Kadmat and Amini. Just to the south of these, and almost due west of Kochi on the Indian coast, the Laccadive Islands comprise Agatti, Andrott, Kavaratti and Kalpeni. Much further south, opposite Thiruvananthapuram on the mainland, is Minicoy, an island which has more in common with the Maldives to the south, than with the rest of the Lakshadweep archipelago.

The islands were for many years closed to visitors, and tourists still require a special permit. Foreigners can only visit the resort on Bangaram Island and the tourist facilities on Kadmat. Indian nationals are allowed to visit other islands, although only as part of an organised cruise.

The expense and restrictions of a visit to Lakshadweep will not appeal to everyone. For diving enthusiasts, however, the islands are a dream come true. A unique marine environment exists in the lagoons and the kilometres of coral reefs. Because of the limited number of visitors who make it to the islands, the dive sites are undisturbed

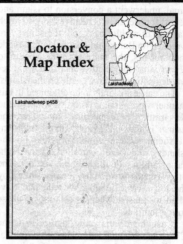

LAKSHADWEEP AT A GLANCE

Locator & Map Index

Lakshadweep p458

Population: 51,681
Area: 32 sq km on 35 islands, 10 of which are inhabited
Capital: The main administration is on Kavaratti.
Main Languages: The people of the northern islands speak Malayalam – albeit a different version from that spoken on the mainland. The islanders of Minicoy speak Mahl.
Best Time to Go: mid-November to early April

Highlights
* Deserted beaches
* Fantastic diving and snorkelling

and the coral undamaged. The Bangaram Island Resort, though expensive, has its own attractions. Away from telephones and TV, there's little to do except relax on an idyllic desert island, and stagger up the beach for a cold beer in the evening.

HISTORY

The early history of the islands is a matter of speculation. According to popular legend, the archipelago was discovered when the legendary ruler of Kerala, Cheraman Perumal, underwent a conversion to Islam and set off for Mecca. His relatives sent a search party to bring him back, but the ships were wrecked on Bangaram Island. Having made their repairs, the mariners sailed home to report what they had found, and were rewarded with the right to settle on the islands.

The earliest islands to be colonised in this manner were Amini, Andrott, Kalpeni and Kavaratti. These became known as the *tarwad* islands (in reference to the traditional social system which prevails on the islands), and were controlled by the high-caste families of the original settlers. The other islands were subsequently settled by the lower-caste inhabitants who had travelled to Lakshadweep as servants of these ruling families.

Most historians now agree that the Cheraman Perumal legend has little foundation in fact, but there's no concrete evidence to suggest who the first settlers really were.

Instead there are a number of tantalising clues.

The discovery of a Buddhist statue points to the islands having been settled as early as the 8th century, perhaps by mariners from Sri Lanka. On the other hand, the caste organisation, language and the matrilineal system of inheritance all suggest that the first inhabitants may have come from the Hindu mainland sometime around the 11th century. Finally, some have suggested that the islanders' Muslim faith could point to initial settlement by Arab traders.

A compromise between these theories seems most probable. The islands of Lakshadweep lie on trade routes that have been in use for at least 2000 years. With their supply of fresh water and coconuts, the islands would have been well known to early mariners, and they may have had temporary residents from early times. Which particular group settled here first will never be known.

Around the 12th century the islands came under the control of the mainland rulers, the Ali Rajas of Cannanore. This clan held complete power over trade until the 16th century, when the Portuguese, tempted by the com-

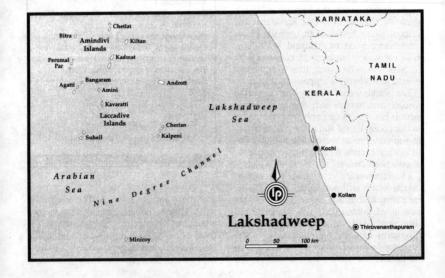

Coral Atolls

The most widely credited theory for the formation of coral atolls remains the one put forward by Charles Darwin in the 19th century. Observing that coral could grow only in shallow waters, Darwin suggested that rings of coral might have formed originally around islands that had gradually subsided into the sea. If the subsidence was very slow, he reasoned, the rate of growth of coral could keep pace with it. Thus while the island itself sank, the reef around the edge would grow upwards, forming a circular barrier around an inner lagoon.

Coral atolls are in a constant process of change. The living coral must remain healthy, not only to counteract the subsidence of the rocks below it, but also to counter the damage caused by the sea. By process of erosion, fragments of dead coral are deposited in the waters of the lagoon. These are slowly swept onto the lee side of the lagoon and piled up into sandbanks, which, over time, become small islands. The final stages of the development of the island begin with its colonisation by sea birds. The birds' droppings form a rich layer in which seeds (also carried by the birds) eventually take root. Once plants are growing on the island, human habitation is only a step away.

The development of each of the Lakshadweep atolls is at a different stage. Almost all of the islands are still growing, although in many cases exposed shores are also subject to erosion. The 'newest' islands are little more than sandbanks, while others are covered with a thatch of palm trees, but as yet do not have groundwater supplies sufficient to support habitation. One of the 'oldest' islands, Andrott, now fills the whole area within the reef, leaving no lagoon at all.

Coral parasite, the crown-of-thorns starfish.

mercial value of the coir produced in the islands, demanded a huge annual levy. The sum required was so large that the Ali Raja soon defaulted, and in 1525 Portuguese troops occupied the islands. Over the following years the conquistadors exploited the inhabitants ruthlessly. One attempt by the islanders to get their revenge occurred in 1545, when they poisoned the entire garrison on Amini. The Portuguese retaliated swiftly, slaughtering several hundred islanders.

As Portuguese power waned, the islands came back under the control of the Ali Rajas, who reasserted the old trade monopolies. The islanders were only permitted to sell their coir to the Ali Raja – at his prices

– and had to put up with the atrocities committed by his agents. In 1783 the inhabitants of the northern (Aminidivi) islands decided that they'd had enough and sent a deputation to Hyder Ali asking him to take the islands into his kingdom, which he subsequently did. The Laccadive Islands continued under the rule of the Ali Raja, along with Minicoy, which he had also acquired.

Within a few years all had changed again. The British defeated Tipu Sultan (Hyder Ali's son) and took the northern islands. They blockaded the Bibi of Cannanore and forced her to pay a levy on the southern islands. The amount and payment of this tax caused constant disagreement throughout the

Island Culture

The culture of the Lakshadweep islanders has been formed by a peculiar mixture of Indian and foreign influences, and Lakshadweep society displays, in particular, a cross between Hindu and Arab traditions.

Status of Women One of the most unusual features of the islands' society, particularly bearing in mind the islanders' Muslim faith, is the relative independence enjoyed by the women. This is largely due to a matrilineal system of inheritance, in which property is passed down the female side of the family. Even after marriage the wife continues living in her own house, which her husband visits for the night. Having her own property, the woman is not reliant on her husband, and therefore has more freedom than many Indian women enjoy. It seems possible that the tradition grew from the necessities of island life, where the men were often away at sea for long periods. Marco Polo called Lakshadweep the 'female islands', perhaps for this very reason.

Caste System All of the islands have a caste system which is thought to have been brought by early settlers from the mainland. In the northern islands there are three main castes: *koyas* or landlords, *malmis* or sailors, and *melacheris* or labourers. In Minicoy the sailors are divided into two sub-castes, and the groups are named differently, but the system still applies. Caste has been a source of considerable communal friction throughout the islands' history.

Language One of the pieces of evidence which is cited for the descent of the islanders from Keralan stock is the fact that they speak an ancient form of Malayalam. Although this undoubtedly shows an early connection, it's interesting to note that the islanders write their Malayalam in Arabic script.

Religion The Lakshadweep islanders are, to a person, Muslim. A popular story tells of the advent of the faith on the islands. It is said that an Arab holy man named Ubaid-Allah was shipwrecked on Amini, and started preaching to the people. The inhabitants threatened the saint, who fled to Andrott where he converted the entire population by performing a miracle. Over the next few months he visited other islands and performed a succession of miracles until all of the islanders had embraced the faith. Although this story is regarded as a myth by many today, the mosque on Andrott which houses the tomb of Ubaid-Allah is still revered as a particularly holy spot, and even today sailors passing the island offer prayers.

19th century until, in 1908, the islands were formally ceded to the British government.

Although British rule of the islands was even-handed, there was no attempt to develop them in any way. It is said that when India achieved independence in 1947 it was several months before the islanders knew anything about it. For the next 10 years this situation persisted, until, in 1956, the Indian government decided that the islands were so far behind the rest of the country in development that they should be centrally administered by the government in Delhi as

a Union Territory. In 1973, the three sets of islands were renamed Lakshadweep.

The Islands Today

Since 1956 huge progress has been made. Because of the classification of the indigenous population as Scheduled Tribes, the inhabitants of the islands have been given preferential treatment in education and in funding. There are now a number of schools in the islands, and many of the children progress to further education on the mainland. Perhaps the best indicator of the success in this area is in literacy rates. In 1951 only 15.3% of the population were literate, whereas by 1991 this was up to 79.23%. The literacy rate for women is particularly impressive – 70.88% compared with the Indian average of 39%.

All islands now have electricity, and almost all have medical facilities. Communications have been immeasurably improved with the building of all-weather docks on the leeward side of some of the islands, and with the establishment of regular flights from Kochi, and a helicopter service between the islands in the monsoon months.

There are, predictably, some problems – among them overcrowding. With good medical facilities and better food, the population of these tiny islands is burgeoning. At the beginning of the 20th century the total number of inhabitants of all islands was just 13,882. By 1981 the figure had leapt to 40,249, and in 1991 the islands were home to 51,681 people. Despite the appearance of peace and tranquillity in comparison with the mainland, the islands are one of the most densely crowded areas in India, with an average population density of 1615 people per sq km. Overcrowding in turn brings its own problems, high among which is that of the fresh water supply. The islands rely for their fresh water entirely on the monsoon rain, which filters through the sand to a thin layer of ground water only a metre or two below the surface, so it must be conserved carefully, and protected from contamination.

The main sources of livelihood for the islanders are the traditional trades of coir production (coconuts are the only crop of economic importance) and fishing. Apart from these there have been few other developments – a tuna canning factory in Minicoy and two small boatyards on other islands. Even the fishing industry which is judged to have potential for considerable expansion has not been developed much.

CLIMATE

Rainfall is marginally higher on Minicoy than on the other islands (average annual rainfall is 150cm), but temperature is pretty much constant across the whole archipelago. The months from November to March are settled, with average temperatures of between 24°C to 34°C. The temperature starts to rise during April and May, and the south-west monsoon arrives in June. The islands are affected by both the south-west and north-east monsoon, and consequently receive their annual rainfall from June through to October. The northern islands, however, lie in the rain shadow of the Kerala coastline, and hence do not receive as much of the later rain as Minicoy does.

FLORA & FAUNA

The vegetation on the islands is dominated by coconut palms, of which two main varieties occur. There are a number of other plants which grow naturally, or which have been introduced for cultivation, including banana, chilli, cucumber, drumstick (an Indian vegetable rather like a squash, but with a shape like a drumstick) and breadfruit. Attempts to grow rice have largely failed.

The fauna of the islands is, as might be expected, limited. Domestic animals such as cattle, goats and poultry are reasonably common. Cats are also to be found on the islands, and rats present a huge hazard to the coconut crop.

There are several types of sea birds, a few lizards and some coral snakes, but no land snakes. There are a variety of insects, including mosquitoes.

INFORMATION
Tourist Offices

The Society for the Promotion of Recreational Tourism & Sports in Lakshadweep (SPORTS) is the main Lakshadweep Tourism organisation. Its office (☎ 0484-668387; fax 668155) is on IG Rd, Willingdon Island, Kochi, 682003.

The Lakshadweep Tourist Office in Delhi is useless for Bangaram bookings, but may be able to provide other information. Contact Mr Pukoya (☎ 011-338 6807; fax 378 2246), Liaison Office, UTF Lakshadweep, F306, Kusum Road Hostel, Kasturba Gandhi Marg, New Delhi, 110001.

LAKSHADWEEP

LAKSHADWEEP

Diving

The Lakshadweep Islands are a paradise for sub-aqua enthusiasts. Not only are the islands surrounded by miles of perfect coral reefs but they have tremendous variety, too. Within the lagoons, the shallow waters are perfect for novice divers and also provide the possibility of diving even in rough weather. Outside the reefs, there are dives of varying depths with crystal clear waters giving excellent visibility. Near Bangaram Island there are a couple of wrecks that provide interesting excursions, (the 200-year-old wreck of the *Princess Royal* is a regular dive site) and around both Bangaram and Kadmat there are specific areas which are known to harbour particularly rich marine life. Sharks, rays, hawksbill and green turtles and barracudas are among the larger inhabitants of the reefs, but there are innumerable others, too, including butterfly fish, damsel fish, surgeon fish and parrot fish. Octopus are plentiful in the lagoons.

There are only two dive centres in the islands. Bangaram Island Resort has a well run dive school which is available for use by guests. Experienced divers have a range of options, but newcomers are also able to dive. A 'resort course' package for a beginner, consisting of a couple of lessons followed by a reef dive, costs US$120, and an open-water certificate course costs US$250. Experienced divers pay US$222 for a six-dive package, US$420 for 12 dives or US$600 for 18 dives. No dives are permitted below 35m. Information is available through the Casino Hotels office (see Places to Stay & Eat).

The oriental sweetlip, one of the most striking fish of Lakshadweep.

Permits & Restrictions

The reasons for the restrictions on travel to the islands seem to be twofold. Firstly the population of the islands are almost entirely classed by the government as Scheduled Tribes, and there is a concerted effort to protect not only their way of life, but also the unique environment of the islands. Just as important is India's deep concern about the security of its coastline. Although the islands cover an area of only 32 sq km, they are of considerable importance to the nation, as they add 15,000 sq km to India's territorial waters, and economic zone.

In practice, the only way to get to the islands is to book with one of the recognised travel organisations listed below. Allow plenty of time for the permit application to be processed (Laccadives recommend a month, minimum).

Foreigners are only permitted to visit Bangaram Island and Kadmat, whereas Indian nationals may also visit Kavaratti, Kalpeni and Minicoy. Both foreign and domestic tourists can travel on the cruise ship MV *Tipu Sultan*, which has accommodation on board.

Organised Tours

SPORTS (see Tourist Offices, earlier) offers a five day Coral Reef cruise (Indian tourists only) which leaves from Kochi and stops at Kavaratti, Kalpeni and Minicoy. A full day is spent getting to the islands (and back), and one day is allowed on each island, before passengers re-embark for an overnight

Lacadives, a new dive school which has been set up on Kadmat Island, offers slightly more reasonable prices than the costly Bangaram Resort. A week-long package with two dives a day, accommodation and food costs US$800. Transport to and from the island by plane or ship can be organised by Lacadives at an additional cost.

Bookings are via the company's office in Mumbai, at E20, Everest building, Tardeo, Mumbai, 400034 (☎ 022-494 2723; fax 495 1644; email: lacadives@hotmail.com). Lacadives will also arrange travel and permits. Visitors can opt to travel to or from the island by ship, on the MV *Tipu Sultan*. Lacadives' agent in the US is Natural Mystic Adventure Travels (☎ 212-683 3989; fax 212-683 2831; email: info@naturalmystic.com), Suite 320, 300 East 34th St, New York, NY 10016.

Because of weight restrictions on aircraft, most divers rely on equipment provided on the islands. Those who are going to Bangaram Island, however, can apply to the Casino Hotel office for an increased baggage allowance.

When to Go The best time to dive is between October and mid-May. Diving is still possible in the lagoons during the monsoon, and is also possible at times outside the reefs, but the weather can limit these opportunities severely.

Responsible Diving

* Avoid touching living marine organisms. Some can be damaged by even the gentlest contact. Never stand on coral, even if it looks solid and robust.
* Be conscious of your fins. Even without contact the surge of heavy fin strokes near the reef can cause damage.
* Practise and maintain proper buoyancy control. Major damage can be done by divers descending too fast and colliding with the reef.
* Resist the temptation to collect or buy corals or shells.
* Dispose of your rubbish sensibly, including litter you find.
* Minimise your disturbance of marine animals.

cruise to the next island. The cruise costs Rs 6000 in tourist class, Rs 8000 in 1st class and Rs 10,000 in deluxe class.

An alternative (which foreign tourists are allowed to take) is a five day cruise to Kadmat and back, with the middle three days being spent in tourist cottages on the island.

The cruise costs Rs 8000 in tourist class, Rs 9000 in 1st class, Rs 10,000 in executive class and Rs 10,500 in deluxe two-berth AC. Another version of this, with three days on Kavaratti, is open to Indians only, and costs Rs 9000 in 1st class and Rs 9500 in deluxe two berth.

THE ISLANDS

The following is a brief rundown of the main (inhabited) islands in the group. Note that not all of them are open to visitors (see under Permits & Restrictions). The northern group of islands was traditionally known as the Aminidivi Islands. **Amini**, which is thought to have derived its name from the Arabic word meaning 'faithful', was one of the earliest islands to be settled, and is still the centre of administration for the group.

About ten kilometres north of Amini is **Kadmat**, one of the five islands open to tourists (and one of only two islands open to foreigners); it is the base for the Laccadives dive centre. The discovery of some gold coins on Kadmat belonging to the Roman emperors of the 1st and 2nd centuries leads to the conclusion that the island was visited by traders well before it was finally settled.

Lakshadweep Islands:
Area & Population

Island	Area (sq km)	Population (1991)
Andrott	4.84	9119
Minicoy	4.37	8313
Kavaratti	3.63	8664
Kadmat	3.13	3983
Agatti	2.71	5667
Amini	2.59	6445
Kalpeni	2.28	4079
Kiltan	1.63	3075
Chetlat	1.04	2050
Bangaram*	0.58	61
Bitra	0.10	225

* Only 10 islands are properly inhabited. Bangaram is 'inhabited' only by the staff of the tourist resort.

Bitra is the smallest inhabited island in the territory, with an area of just 10.52 hectares. Sixty-five kilometres north of Amini is **Chetlat**, the northernmost inhabited island. To the south lies **Kiltan**, which is only about 3km long.

The southern group of islands was known traditionally as the Laccadive Islands. Over 400km from Kochi is **Agatti**, the westernmost island of the group. Roughly 6km long and only 1km wide at its broadest point, Agatti has the only airstrip in the islands. Although all visitors arriving by plane must stage through Agatti, the island is not open to tourists.

Bangaram, to the north of Agatti, is just visible on the horizon and is about two hours away by boat. **Andrott** is the nearest island to the mainland, and is also the largest of the group, being 5km long and 2km broad. According to tradition, the people of Andrott were the first islanders to embrace Islam, and the religious teachers of the island are still regarded with veneration.

Kalpeni, 87km south of Andrott, is another of the islands believed to have been colonised from early times. It was one of the islands worst affected by a great storm which struck in 1847: out of a population of 1642 islanders, 246 people were drowned and a further 112 died of disease or starvation in the weeks that followed. Of the island's 100,000 palm trees, under 1000 were left standing. **Kavaratti** is the headquarters of the whole Union Territory. The island is 6km long and about 1km wide. The people are renowned for their skill as woodcarvers and stonemasons.

Minicoy, 211km south of the southern group, is supposed to have been visited by Marco Polo, who referred to it as the 'female island'. The island is more than 10km in length and has a large, deep lagoon. A small island at the northern tip of the main island was once used by the inhabitants for isolating smallpox patients.

PLACES TO STAY & EAT
The *Bangaram Island Resort* is run by Casino Hotels, and is administered from its hotel in Kochi (☎ 0484-668221; fax 668001; email: casino@giasmd01.vsnl.net.in).

The resort on the uninhabited island of Bangaram has been well designed to minimise the impact on the island. There are only 30 rooms, allowing a maximum of 60 guests. Double rooms with full board are US$240 (plus 10% tax) between mid-December and May; single occupancy is US$230. Prices drop considerably during the low season. It's worth shopping around with travel agents in other countries, as some tour operators book through Casino and appear to be able to get a better deal as part of a larger package.

The resort has a good restaurant and a bar; and activities include diving, snorkelling, deep-sea fishing and sailing. Casino Hotels will organise travel and permits for the islands.

Apart from the low row of thatched buildings that make up the accommodation, bar and restaurant, there's almost nothing else on the tiny island. If you go exploring among the palm trees, you'll probably stumble on the staff accommodation, and if you wander around to the far side of Bangaram (you can stroll around the entire island in under an hour) you may find some fishermen from

Agatti, who occasionally stop off here. Apart from this the layout is remarkably simple. The low island is covered entirely with a dense mass of palm trees and ringed with a thin ribbon of white sand.

Laccadives runs a dive centre based on Kadmat Island. Packages include accommodation and all meals. See the boxed text 'Diving', earlier in this chapter.

GETTING THERE & AWAY
Air
At the time of writing Indian Airlines operated five flights a week from Kochi to Agatti (US$300 return), and two flights a week from Goa to Agatti (US$310 return). The plane used for the Kochi flights is a tiny Islander aircraft, and passengers are restricted to 10kg of luggage. If you're staying on Bangaram Island, extra luggage can be left in the Casino Hotel on Willingdon Island. The transfer from Agatti to Bangaram costs an extra US$30 by boat or, in the event of rough seas, US$80 by helicopter. The transfer takes around 1½ hours

Boat
Timings for the departure of the MV *Tipu Sultan* on its various cruises can be picked up from the SPORTS office on Willingdon Island. See under Organised Tours, above, for information on SPORT'S boat cruises.

LAKSHADWEEP

Chennai (Madras)

Now the fourth-largest city in India and the capital of Tamil Nadu, Chennai has grown from a number of small coastal villages including its former namesake Madraspatnam. Though many still call it Madras, it is now officially known by its Tamil name of Chennai. The city is large, bustling and often horribly polluted. It sprawls over more than 70 sq km and rather than claiming a centre, it retains its former regional hubs. Chennai is, however, an enthusiastic and friendly city that continues to cling to its many rich traditions. Although, like many Indian cities, it is experiencing unprecedented development, the locals are proud of the relaxed manner in which change is embraced. In the words of one long-time resident, 'On the outside Chennai is changing; but inside it will always be the same. It will not lose its soul'.

The billboards are perhaps the most striking outward expressions of the city. These gargantuan icons of popular culture dwarf city buildings in their eagerness to promote everything from soap, shoes, and herbal remedies to power tools and blockbuster movies. The movie billboards are an art in themselves. Many are three dimensional with gaudy larger-than-life characters in every clichéd repose. Each day an army of barefoot billboard erectors scurry over flimsy scaffolding to demolish the old and erect the new.

Chennai is not pedestrian friendly. As with most Indian cities, might is clearly right and there is a lot of might in the trucks and buses that plough relentlessly along the city streets. Traffic police exist but no one takes any notice of their feeble hand signals.

The pavements are another story. Often they don't exist. Where they do they resemble bomb sites, peppered with enormous pot-holes. Cow (and human) dung litters the pavements and hawkers, beggars and the inevitable fixers of everything cram between the dung and holes. These 50cm-high pavements demand all of your concentration.

CHENNAI AT A GLANCE

Locator & Map Index

Chennai (Madras) pp468-469
Anna Salai, Egmore
& Triplicane p486

Population: 5.9 million
Main Language: Tamil
Telephone Area Code: 044
Best Time to Go: December to February
& July to September

Highlights & Festivals
* **mid-Dec to mid-Jan** – Festival of Carnatic Music & Dance
* Kalakshetra Arts Village
* Excellent restaurants

Improvements are continual but just as one section is completed, another collapses.

In spite of the crowds, the traffic, the noise and the pollution, Chennai conveys a sense of spaciousness and ease lacking in many other big Indian cities. It's as if the serenity exuded by the cows that amble the streets has somehow infected the sprawling metropolis. Its streets are a little wider than average and its citizens a little less hurried. And in the aftermath of the monsoons, a gentle sea breeze takes the edge off the fumes.

In Chennai, the slums and beggars are less apparent and smaller in number than in other major cities, and public services are easily accessible and remarkably efficient. Here, it's possible to use public buses and urban commuter trains without undue discomfort (except during peak hour). However, the city suffers from water shortages in the summer months, especially if the last monsoon season has been a poor one. At such times water is trucked into the city, with hotels receiving priority. Thrifty use of water by visitors therefore may reduce the difficulties experienced by locals.

Many of the main Indian languages, especially those of South India, are spoken in Chennai. These include Telugu, Malayalam, Hindi, Urdu and of course English. The main language is Tamil and the people of Chennai are zealous guardians of their language and culture, which they regard as inherently superior to the hybridised cultures further north. They have, for instance, been among the most vociferous opponents to Hindi being established as the national language.

Chennai was not as significant to Tamil culture as some of the nearby towns such as Kanchipuram and Mamallapuram. It did,

Street Name Changes

It's not only the city that's been renamed; many streets have had official name changes, so there is a confusing melange of names used in the vernacular. Some of them include:

Old Name	New Name
Mount Rd	Anna Salai
Poonamallee High Rd	Periyar EVR High Rd
Popham's Broadway	Prakasam Rd
North Beach Rd	Rajaji Salai
South Beach Rd	Kamarajar Salai
Pycroft's Rd	Bharathi Salai
Adam's Rd	Swami Sivananda Salai
Mowbray's Rd	TTK Rd
Broadway	NSC Chandra Bose Rd

however, make a significant contribution to European colonial history of India. Strategically, Madras became the linchpin in the rapid expansion of the British Empire, although long before the presence of the colonial powers, commerce was the way of life for the villagers who dwelt along the thriving seaboard. The availability of spices, cotton and silk, not to mention easy port access, lured many traders from distant lands. In the 18th century, British and French colonial traders fought bitter battles to secure control of the highly prized port region.

In recent decades, Chennai has experienced a phenomenal expansion of both heavy and light manufacturing. Car assembly plants, railway coach and truck works, engineering plants, food processing and cigarette factories have injected much vigour into the local economy. The service sector has also expanded. Chennai boasts many esteemed educational institutes as well as a number of large sophisticated film studios. In fact Chennai is the centre for Tamil film-making. With a strong and sometimes volatile tradition of journalism and newspaper publishing, Chennai remains a focus for serious and diverse public discourse. There are enough newspapers, magazines and books in the city to satiate even the most voracious appetite.

One of the main attractions for travellers to Chennai is the ease and abundance of transport to other parts of the country. Train, air and bus connections are frequent, car hire is easy and banks and telecommunications readily accessible. For travellers with an interest in the rich and volatile colonial history of India, Chennai and its environs have much worth exploring.

HISTORY

Vigorous commerce, blatant opportunism, colonial conquests, entrepreneurial zeal and military might have combined to shape the history and destiny of Chennai. Situated on the east coast of India, the area has always been a popular place for seafarers, spice traders and cloth merchants. More than 2000 years ago the occupants of the villages that grew into the city of Chennai engaged with

CHENNAI

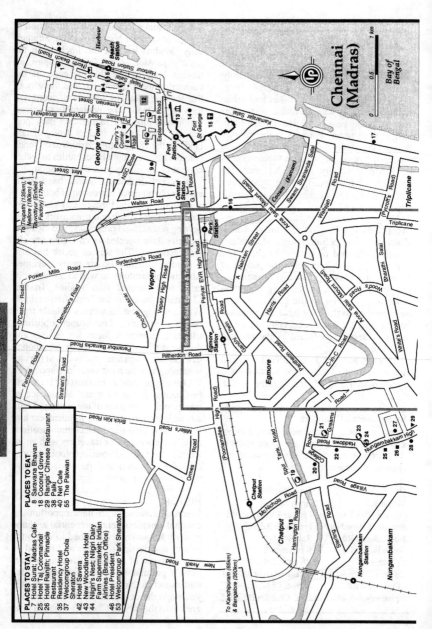

Chennai (Madras)

Bay of Bengal

0   0.5   1 km

PLACES TO STAY
7   Hotel Surat; Madras Cafe
25 Hotel Taj Coromandel
26 Hotel Ranjith; Pinnacle
    Restaurant
35 Residency Hotel
37 Welcomgroup Chola
    Sheraton
42 Hotel Savera
43 New Woodlands Hotel
44 Nilgiri's Nest; Nilgiri Dairy
    Farm; Supermarket; Indian
    Airlines (Branch Office)
46 Hotel President
53 Welcomgroup Park Sheraton

PLACES TO EAT
8   Saravana Bhavan
18 Coconut Grove
29 Rangis' Chinese Restaurant
38 Palki
40 Net Cafe
55 The Pakwan

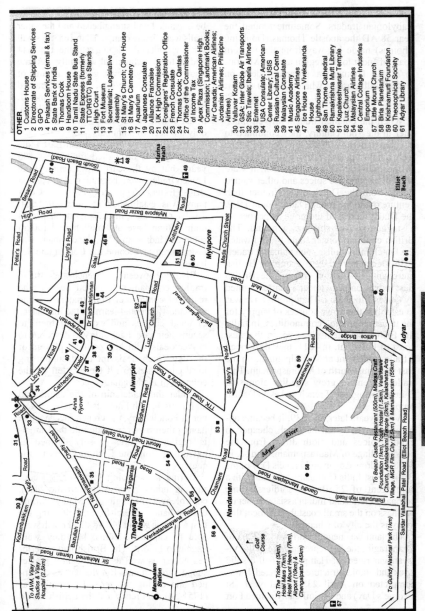

OTHER
1 Customs House
2 Directorate of Shipping Services
3 GPO
4 Prakash Services (email & fax)
5 State Bank of India
6 Thomas Cook
9 Handloom House
10 Tamil Nadu State Bus Stand
11 State Express (formerly TTC/RGTC) Bus Stands
12 High Court
13 Fort Museum
14 Secretariat; Legislative Assembly
15 St Mary's Church; Clive House
16 St Mary's Cemetery
17 Aquarium
19 Japanese Consulate
20 Alliance Francaise
21 UK High Commission
22 Foreigners' Registration Office
23 French Consulate
24 Thomas Cook; Qantas
27 Office of the Commissioner of Income Tax
28 Apex Plaza (Singapore High Commission; Landmark Books; Air Canada; American Airlines; Jordanian Airlines; Philippine Airlines)
30 Valluvar Kottam
31 GSA; Inter Globe Air Transports
32 Stic Travels; Iberia Airlines
33 Emternet
34 USA Consulate; American Center Library; USIS
36 Russian Cultural Centre
39 Malaysian Consulate
41 Music Academy
45 Singapore Airlines
47 Ice House – Vivekananda House
48 Lighthouse
49 San Thome Cathedral
50 Ramakrishna Mutt Library
51 Kapaleeshwarar Temple
52 Luz Church
54 Malaysian Airlines
56 Central Cottage Industries Emporium
57 Little Mount Church
58 Birla Planetarium
59 Krishnamurti Foundation
60 Theosophical Society
61 Adyar Library

Chinese, Greek, Phoenician, Roman and Babylonian traders. Sometime around the year 58 AD the apostle Thomas (Doubting Thomas) made his way from the western coast of India to the region around Madras. In 78 AD, Thomas was speared to death on a small hill close to where Chennai airport now lies. The hill is now known as St Thomas Mount.

When the colonial traders arrived much later in the 16th century, they continued to develop patterns of trade. First on the scene were the Portuguese, followed by the Dutch. In the mid-16th century, the British were content to purchase spices and other valued goods from the Dutch traders rather than venture out to the foreign land. But in 1599, the Dutch increased the price of pepper by a staggering five shillings a pound. The British could no longer stand by and watch the Dutch monopolise such valuable trade.

In December 1599 a group of British merchants in London formed the British East India Company under a charter granted by Queen Elizabeth I. Their prerogative was to establish their own sources of supply for the treasured trading commodities. Initially the British set themselves up on the west coast of India but, in 1611, they developed a trade settlement at Machilpatnam, on the east coast just north of Madraspatnam. This trade settlement grew steadily alongside Dutch, Portuguese, French and even Danish outposts.

A few years later, in 1639, it became apparent that it would be much cheaper to export spices and cloth direct from the coastal village of Madraspatnam. And so, in 1640, Andrew Cogan and Francis Day of the British East India Company, together with a contingent of 25 British soldiers, some company clerks and Indian assistants, set up business on the small coastal settlement that today is the city of Chennai.

The land was negotiated from the Raja of Chandragiri, the last representative of the Vijayanagar rulers of Hampi. In 1640 a solid brick and granite structure was erected. It was completed on April 23 of that year (St George's Day) and was officially named Fort St George in 1642. The structure continued to be expanded and strengthened and the outer walls were finally completed in 1653. A small fort was built at the fishing settlement in 1644 and a town, which subsequently became known as George Town, grew in the area of Fort St George. The settlement was granted its first municipal charter in 1688 by James II. This makes it the oldest municipality in India, a fact which Tamil Nadu state officials are only too keen to point out.

The supremacy of the British East India Company was unrivalled for almost 100 years, but by the early 18th century, the French traders were beginning to impact on British fortunes. The French East India Company was established at Surat in 1664. Twelve years later, in 1676, it established its main Indian base at Pondicherry, 100km south of Madras (in 1719, the company was restructured to become the Compagnie des Indes).

Rivalry between the French and British trading companies extended beyond the realm of commerce. Both traders became particularly adept at learning the intricacies of local politics and exploiting them to secure their base. Each side was desperate to broker deals with key political players of the day. Such deals included supporting local candidates to fill the gap left by the collapse of the Mughals.

Under the leadership of the astute and ambitious Joseph Francois Dupleix, Governor of Pondicherry, the French succeeded in having their own candidate rule the Carnatic region (the area loosely defined as extending from the Eastern Ghats to the coast).

During the ongoing Anglo-French conflicts in India (known as the Carnatic Wars), control over the region of Madras would change hands several times. Following the first Carnatic war (1740-48) the French were able to capture Madras, but they were unable to hold it. The British had superior sea power as well as significantly greater support from home. But the battles continued and during the second Carnatic war (1751-54) the French and the British would regularly pitch their armies against each other to gain the upper hand.

The third Carnatic war erupted in 1756 and coincided with Anglo-French conflicts in Europe. It was during this period that the French were forced to withdraw to Pondicherry leaving the British to develop Fort St George.

One key player in the British campaign against the French was Robert Clive (known widely as Clive of India). He began his career as a 'writer' for the British East India Company (a position about as low as you could get). Despite continual bouts of depression and a serious attempt on his own life, Clive worked his way through the ranks to become commander of the British army in India and Governor of Bengal. It was from Fort St George that Clive recruited an army of 2000 *sepoys* (locally engaged troops) and launched a series of strikingly successful military expeditions against the French.

Through his cunning military and financial exploits Clive secured a vast, somewhat formidable fortune for himself and the British East India Company. However, the swashbuckling entrepreneur was eventually disgraced by allegations of corruption. He was tried back in England and, though acquitted, he succumbed to severe depression and opium addiction. He took his life, by cutting his throat in 1774.

As the first major base for the British in India, Madras played a key role in the development of the British empire. It was also significant in the formation of the modern Indian army. Major Stringer Lawrence, a mentor to Robert Clive, was regarded as the founder of the Indian army. It was he who assembled the Madras Regiment in anticipation of further French sieges. The Madras Regiment later became known as the 102nd Royal Madras Infantry and then as the Dublin Fusiliers. To this day it remains the oldest regiment of the Indian army.

In the 19th century, the city became the seat of the Madras Presidency, one of the four divisions of British Imperial India. In the decades that followed, increased trade and immigration gave the city an intellectual as well as an industrial strength. A number of key players in India's struggle for independence from Britian came from Madras. Following Independence the city continued to boom, consolidating its current position as India's fourth-largest metropolis and a significant gateway to the South.

ORIENTATION

Chennai is basically a conglomerate of overgrown villages, and can thus be conveniently divided into a number of sections that facilitate orientation. The two main sections are either side of Periyar EVR High Rd (one of the main thoroughfares in the city). George Town is north-east of this road near the harbour area. In these narrow, overcrowded streets are the shipping agents, cheaper hotels and restaurants, bazaars and the GPO. The area's focal point is Parry's Corner – the intersection of Prakasam Rd (or Popham's Broadway as it's popularly known) and NSC Bose Rd. Many of the city buses terminate here; the Tamil Nadu state bus stands (the two long-distance bus stands) are close by on Esplanade Rd.

The other main section of the city is south of Periyar EVR High Rd. Through it runs Chennai's main road, Anna Salai (also known as Mount Rd), home to many of the city's airline offices, theatres, banks, bookshops, craft centres, consulates, tourist offices and top-end hotels and restaurants.

Egmore and Central, Chennai's two main train stations, are close to Periyar EVR High Rd. Many of the budget and mid-range hotels are clustered around Egmore train station. Egmore is also the departure point for most trains to destinations in Tamil Nadu. If you're going interstate, you'll probably leave from Chennai Central.

Nungambakkam, south-west of Egmore, houses the consulates and airline offices. Further south-west, the district of Theagaraya Nagar is crammed with markets and shops. South-east of Anna Salai, the Triplicane area includes the extensive Marina Beach and popular cheap hotels. In the Mylapore area, south of Triplicane, are the Kapaleeshwarar Temple and San Thome

CHENNAI

Cathedral. Further south is Adya district, home to MGR Film City, the Theosophical Society's World headquarters, and the arts village at Kalakshetra.

INFORMATION
Emergency Numbers

Chennai emergency numbers are: Police ☎ 100, Fire ☎ 101 and Ambulance ☎ 102.

Tourist Offices

The Government of India Tourist Office (☎ 852 4295; fax 852 2193) at 154 Anna Salai is open Monday to Friday from 9.15 am to 5.45 pm, and Saturday and public holidays from 9 am to 1 pm. It's closed Sunday. The staff here are knowledgeable, friendly, and give out heaps of free brochures, including the monthly *Hallo! Madras* guide which lists the city's services (it's also available for Rs 5 from bookstalls around town). Indian Tourism Development Corporation (ITDC) tour bookings can be made here as well. Bus No 11 or 18 from Parry's Corner or Central station will bring you here.

There are Government of India tourist information counters at the domestic and international airports.

The ITDC (☎ 827 8884) is at 29 Victoria Crescent, on the corner of C-in-C Rd. It's open from 5.30 am to 7 pm daily (mornings only on Sunday). This is not a tourist office as such, but all the ITDC tours can be booked, and start from, here.

The Tamil Nadu Tourism Development Corporation (TTDC) has stopped providing tourist information and now concentrates on selling tours and accommodation. Its office at 143 Anna Salai has been reduced to a desk (☎ 830 3390) under the stairs selling tours (10 am to 5 pm, Monday to Friday). You can book TTDC hotels and lodges from the office at the Hotel Tamil Nadu (☎ 582916). There are TTDC tourist booths at Central station and the State Express Division I (formerly TTC) bus stand.

There are no tourist police in Chennai. Problems can be reported to the Government of India Tourist Office at its city or airport offices.

The Railway Protection Force (RPF) at the We Care desk at Central station is very cooperative. It provides information on matters as diverse as rail services, drinking water and wheelchairs.

The Automobile Association of South India (☎ 852 4061), 187 Anna Salai, is in the American Express (administrative) building (4th floor). It sells a national road atlas.

Foreign Consulates

Foreign missions in Chennai are open from Monday to Friday and include:

France
(☎ 827 0469)
16 Haddows Rd
Germany
(☎ 827 1747)
22 C-in-C Rd; 9 am to noon
Japan
(☎ 826 5594)
60 Spur Tank Rd, Chetput; 9 am to 5 pm
Singapore
(☎ 827 3795/6393)
Apex Plaza, 3 Nungambakkam High Rd;
9 am to 5 pm
Sri Lanka
(☎ 827 0831/826 3515)
9D Nawab Habibullah Rd, off Anderson Rd;
9 am to 5 pm
UK
(☎ 827 3136/3137; fax 826 9004)
24 Anderson Rd; 8.30 am to 4 pm
USA
(☎ 827 3040)
Gemini Circle, 220 Anna Salai;
8.15 am to 5 pm

Visa Extensions & Permits

The Foreigners' Registration Office (FRO, ☎ 827 8210) is in the Shashtri Bhavan annexe (rear building, on the ground floor) at 26 Haddows Rd, Nungambakkam. Visa extensions (up to six months) are possible. They cost Rs 725 but can be very difficult to obtain. You'll need one passport photo and it helps to have assistance from someone resident in India who knows you. The office is open weekdays from 9.30 am to 1.30 pm and 2 to 6 pm. Bus Nos 27J and 27RR, from opposite the Connemara Hotel, pass by.

If you're planning to visit the Andaman & Nicobar Islands by boat, you'll need a permit before buying your boat ticket (air passengers can get the permit on arrival in Port Blair). Collect a form from the Directorate of Shipping Services (☎ 522 6873) at 6 Rajaji Salai in George Town. If you hand this form, together with two photos, into the FRO in the morning, you should be able to collect the permit on the same day between 4 and 5 pm.

Tax Clearance

Income tax clearance certificates are available from the Office of the Commissioner of Income Tax (☎ 827 2011 ext 4004), 121 Nungambakkam High Rd. You need to complete form 31 and have your passport. The procedure takes about 30 minutes.

Money

Both American Express and Thomas Cook give reasonable rates for cash and travellers cheques. The American Express exchange office (☎ 852 3638), G-17 Spencer Plaza, Anna Salai, is open Monday to Saturday from 9.30 am to 6.30 pm.

Thomas Cook charges Rs 20 to cash non-Thomas Cook travellers cheques. It has the following branches:

Egmore
  (☎ 855 1475)
  45 Ceebros Centre, Montieth Rd;
  Monday to Saturday from 9.30 am to 6 pm
George Town
  (☎ 534 2374)
  20 Rajaji Salai; similar opening hours
International airport
  (☎ 233 2882)
  open 24 hours
Nungambakkam
  (☎/fax 827 4941)
  Eldorado Bldg, 112 Nungambakkam High Rd; weekdays from 9.30 am to 1 pm and 2 to 6.30 pm, Saturday to noon

The State Bank of India's main branch is on Rajaji Salai in George Town. There are also branches on Anna Salai, and at the international (open 24 hours) and domestic (open from 5 am to 8 pm) airport terminals.

Several of the banks in Spencer Plaza, next door to the Hotel Connemara, give cash advances on MasterCard and Visa. Central Bank (Montieth Rd, Egmore) handles Visa cards.

Street cash transactions are best done in the Egmore area. Dealers are generally upfront and the exchange usually takes place in a shop or restaurant with the minimum of fuss.

Post & Communications

The GPO is on Rajaji Salai. There's also a post office in Kennet Lane, near the Egmore train station. If you're staying in Egmore or the Anna Salai area, for poste restante, it's more convenient to use the Anna Salai post office. The full address is Poste Restante, Anna Salai (Mount Rd) Post Office, Anna Salai, Chennai 600002. Poste restante is open from 10 am to 6 pm Monday to Saturday; the post office itself is open Monday to Saturday from 8 am to 8.30 pm, and Sunday from 10 am to 5 pm. The Anna Salai post office is also the best place to post parcels because it's much less congested than the GPO. A cheap and super-efficient packing service is available in the small office, just inside (from 10 am).

Both the GPO and the Anna Salai post office have 24 hour telegraph offices where you can make international phone calls. Otherwise, use one of the many STD/ISD/fax booths around town. Central station has an efficient fax service. In George Town, you can send faxes to anywhere outside India for Rs 60 per page (less than half the price charged in Egmore) at Prakash Services (☎ 534 0214; fax 534 1022), 146 Thambu Chetty St. It's open 24 hours for faxes and phone calls. It's also possible to send and receive email at this office between 10 am and 7 pm Monday to Saturday (Sunday opening is not guaranteed). Charges are Rs 30 per page plus Rs 10 if you don't type the message yourself. The email address is mdsaaa53@giasmd01.vsnl.net.in.

The recently established Net Cafe (☎ 826 3779) at 101/1 Kanakasri Nagar, Cathedral Rd (near the Music Academy), is excellent. It's possible to send and receive email as well as browse the net. (Be wary of them storing your supposedly dispatched email on a central server before finally transmitting it some days later.) Net Cafe charges Rs 80/150 for 30/60 minutes. It's open daily from 7 am to 10 pm.

Cheaper and more crowded (though equally efficient) is Enternet. There are two branches; the Kodambakkam branch (☎ 480 2956) is at 36/3 Taylors Estate, Station View Rd. Catch the train to Kodambakkam, then walk towards the Liberty Theatre for 200m. Turn left after the Muslim Mission and you'll see the office on the right hand side. The other, more central, branch is at 225, SI Plaza Centre (known also as SI Property Plaza; ☎ 822 2171), 2nd floor, 129 GN Chetty Rd (near Anna Flyover). Both branches open every day from 8 am to 10.30 pm. The cost of surfing the Net and reading/sending email is Rs 1 per minute and the staff are very helpful.

Travel Agencies
The American Express Travel Service (☎ 852 3628) in Spencer Plaza on Anna Salai and Thomas Cook (☎ 855 3276), 45 Ceebros Centre, Montieth Rd, Egmore, are both good.

Bookshops
Landmark Books, in the basement of Apex Plaza, at 3 Nungambakkam High Rd, has one of the best selections of books in South India. It's open from 9 am to 9 pm Monday to Friday, and noon to 9 pm Saturday and Sunday. It accepts credit cards. Higginbothams, at 814 Anna Salai, and (to a lesser extent) The Bookshop in Spencer Plaza, have reasonable assortments of novels and coffee-table books. Higginbothams also has kiosks at Central station and the domestic airport. Shanti Books, at 44 Anna Salai, has a small selection.

Giggles is now an institution. The proprietor, Nalini Chettur, started the shop in 1975, 'just for a giggle'. Since 1994, Giggles has been in temporary premises in the arcade near the Connemara Hotel car park. Here, in an extraordinary cubbyhole, books occupy every inch of space and are stacked

precariously to the ceiling. Browsers must demonstrate the dexterity of a yogi when negotiating their way. The collection is excellent; and so is Nalini's knowledge. Don't be afraid to ask for a deeply buried title. Nalini is more than willing to shift the mountains of books for your request. She will also mail your purchases home.

Libraries & Cultural Centres
The British Council Library (☎ 852 5412) is at 737 Anna Salai. Casual visitors are not actively encouraged but you can take out temporary membership for Rs 100 a month. It's open Tuesday to Saturday from 11 am to 7 pm.

The American Center Library (☎ 827 3040), attached to the US consulate, is open daily except Sunday from 9.30 am to 6 pm. The Alliance Française de Chennai (☎ 827 2650) at 3/4A College Rd, Nungambakkam, is open weekdays from 9 am to 1 pm and 3.30 to 6.30 pm, and on Saturday morning.

In Mylapore district, the Ramakrishna Mutt Library at 16 Ramakrishna Mutt Rd, not far from the Kapaleeshwarar Temple, specialises in philosophy, mythology and Indian classics. The Krishnamurti Foundation (☎ 493 7803) is further south, at 64 Greenway's Rd.

Across the river, in the grounds of the Theosophical Society, is the Adyar Library (☎ 413528), with a huge collection of books on religion, philosophy and mysticism. To use the library, however, you must apply to the Theosophical Society with a letter of introduction from a member. If accepted, there is a reading fee (deposit Rs 100 and subscription Rs 12 per annum) and a borrowing fee (deposit Rs 300, Rs 18 subscription per annum). There are many public holidays on which the library is closed so check before you visit. Even if you don't get library membership, you can visit the Headquarters Building, and enjoy peaceful gardens that contain the famous banyan tree (said to be one of the largest in the world), as well as shrines to all the major religions (see the boxed text, opposite).

The society grounds are open Tuesday to

Under the Spreading Banyan Tree

Set in sprawling and shady grounds not far from the Adyar Estuary is the world headquarters of the Theosophical Society. The characters and events that have shaped this society since its beginnings over 100 years ago have contributed significantly not just to the cultural development of India but to the development of thought and ideas around the world.

It all began with a talented Russian aristocrat named Helena Petrovna Blavatsky and a veteran of the American Civil War named Colonel Henry S Olcott. Madam Blavatsky was an accomplished musician and writer. The influential partnership of these strong-willed individuals began with their first meeting in the USA at the Vermont farmhouse of Mary Baker Eddy, founder of the Christian Science movement. After beginning the Theosophical Society in New York in November 1875 Madam Blavatsky and Colonel Olcott moved to India. In 1882 they acquired 11 hectares in Madras and, in 1886, they established the Theosophical Society Headquarters. The charter of the Theosophical Society has always been to create a 'universal brotherhood of humanity, without distinction of race, creed, sex, caste or colour'. The society encourages discourse while seeking truth in the wisdom of all great religions. Today it has 1200 branches in 60 different countries.

Expansion of the society headquarters occurred in 1907 under the presidency of the British suffragette, Annie Besant. A passionate speaker, thinker, journalist and educator, Annie Besant made India her home and she played a significant role in the Indian movement for home rule.

Today the 100 hectares surrounding the society buildings are divided into a series of beautifully developed gardens commemorating the founders. A key feature in the landscape is the great spreading banyan tree. Hundreds of visitors arrive every day to sit in its shade and read, reflect or meditate.

The vast collection of the Adyar library contains many rare manuscripts, some of which are well displayed downstairs. As well as ancient Sanskrit texts there is a 300-year-old book on embalming (written by a London surgeon), a 500-year-old Latin text on astronomy, Martin Luther's German translation of the Bible and 800-year-old scroll pictures depicting the life of Buddha. One of the oldest books in the library, *Sphehera Mundi,* was written by Joannis de Monteregio and printed in Florence in 1490. The book, in Latin, contains diagrams and charts that prove de Monteregio knew the earth was round.

Many significant figures and institutions in India have been spawned by the Theosophical Society. Annie Besant assumed the guardianship of two children who would become particularly influential players in the cultural and philosophical development of India. One was a boy named Jiddu Krishnamurti who became a guru on the world stage and attracted a wide following for his ideas on achieving salvation through self-realisation. The other was a girl named Rukmini Devi, who brought Maria Montessori to India and established the first Montessori school in the country. She also founded the Kalakshetra, or Temple of Art (see the boxed text in this chapter), and became a powerful advocate of free education, vegetarianism and animal welfare.

CHENNAI

Sunday from 8.30 to 11 am and 1.30 to 5 pm. To get to any of these three libraries, take bus No 5 or 19M from Anna Salai.

The Madras Craft Foundation (☎ 491 8943; fax 434 0149) at 6 Urur Olcott Rd, Besant Nagar, offers workshops in a range of crafts including pottery and print making. For travellers with a serious interest in traditional craft, the foundation has a small but well stocked library of journals and books with a focus on South India. The volunteer librarian works from 2 to 4.30 pm and visitors should telephone first.

The foundation also administers the craft village of Dakshinachitra on the East Coast Rd (see the boxed text 'Showcasing Traditional and Contemporary Arts' in the Tamil Nadu chapter).

Medical Services

For 24 hour emergency services, head to Apollo Hospital (☎ 827 6566) at 21 Greams Lane, or the Vijaya Hospital (☎ 483 9166) at NSK Salai, Valapalani.

Fortune Teller

If you're not able to get the information you require from the contacts listed above you could always try Nadi Joshim (☎ 236 6264), a popular palm leaf reader who charges Rs 250 for a session. Phone for an appointment (see the boxed text 'A Fortune Told, A Fortune Made', under Vaitheeswarankoil, in the Tamil Nadu chapter). The popular Chennai-based monthly magazine *Star Teller* has information and articles on astrology as well as listings of astrologers.

HIGH COURT BUILDING

This red Indo-Saracenic monstrosity at Parry's Corner is the main landmark in George Town. Built in 1892, it is said to be the largest judicial building in the world after the Courts of London. You can wander around and sit in on the sessions; court No 13 has the finest furniture and décor.

Also in the High Court Building compound, is the 1844 **lighthouse**, superseded in 1971 by the ugly modern one on the marina.

FORT ST GEORGE

Built around 1653 by the British East India Company, the fort has undergone much alteration since. It presently houses the Secretariat and the Legislative Assembly. The 46m-high flagstaff at the front is actually a mast salvaged from a 17th century shipwreck.

The **Fort Museum** has a fascinating collection of memorabilia from both the British and the French East India Companies, as well as the Raj and Muslim administrations. Entry is Rs 2 and it's open from 9 am to 5 pm; closed Friday. Upstairs the banqueting hall, built in 1802, has paintings of officials of the British regime. Included is a picture of Sir Arthur Havlock (governor of Madras in 1896) painted by Ravi Varma. This self-taught artist produced many paintings, often on mythological themes.

The Rat Catchers

Floods, drought, fluctuating prices and land taxes are the bane of most farmers' lives. So are rats. For the rice farmers around Chennai, rats are particularly devastating. These unwanted visitors contribute to the destruction of almost a quarter of the entire crop. Modern pesticides help but they are very expensive and potentially harmful to the delicate ecosystem.

Enter the Irula people, the indigenous inhabitants of Chengalpattu district, 50km south-west of Chennai. The Irulas used to live a nomadic life as hunters and gatherers. Until the 1970s they supported themselves by catching snakes for the leather industry but that trade was eventually outlawed. Now they have turned their skills to rats.

About 100 Irulas have formed a cooperative which they call the Rat and Termite Squad (RATS). Their methods are highly labour intensive. They identify the rat burrows, crouch down at the entrance and listen carefully. If they hear a rat they respond with extraordinary dexterity by thrusting an iron bar into the ground and blocking the escape route. Then they simply lift the protesting creature into a sack. If there is a large colony of rats, the Irulas might smoke them out using clay pots filled with straw.

In a scheme supported by the Department of Science and Technology, the Irulas are paid about Rs 2 for each rat. A typical year will yield around 100,000 rodents. In what has become a commercially viable enterprise, some of the rats end up as dinner for crocs at the Crocodile Bank near Mamallapuram. However, quite a few rats will be skinned, chopped, curried and consumed by the catchers. The Irulas claim that with rice as a staple diet, the rats are a particularly tasty and highly nutritious supplement.

St Mary's Church, built in 1678-80, was the first English church in Madras, and is the oldest surviving British church in India. There are reminders in the Church of Clive, who was married here in 1753, and of Elihu Yale, the early governor of Madras who went on to found the famous university bearing his name in the USA. About 1km west of the church is the cemetery in Pallavan Salai.

Opposite the church is the **pay accounts office**. It was formerly Robert Clive's house, and one downstairs room, known as Clive's Corner, is open to the public but there's little to see.

If you're coming to Fort St George by auto-rickshaw, ask for 'Secretariat'.

ST MARY'S CEMETERY

This overgrown burial ground is the final resting place of many of the key players and their families from the British administration. A number of the 19th-century inscriptions can still be read. In the south-western corner is the fenced-off and well maintained section containing war graves and a memorial. Both cemeteries may be visited on any day. However, the warden for the war cemetery is not available on Sunday. The St Mary's caretaker tells (unsubstantiated) stories of huge cobras lurking in the undergrowth.

ST ANDREW'S CHURCH

Near Egmore station, St Andrew's Church was completed in 1821 in the classical style. Inside, the impressive blue dome is decorated with gold stars. There are excellent views from the 55m steeple. Services are at 9 am and 6 pm on Sunday.

GOVERNMENT MUSEUM

Well worth a visit, the government museum is on Pantheon Rd, between Egmore and Anna Salai. The buildings originally belonged to a group of eminent British citizens, known as the Pantheon Committee, who were charged with improving the social life of the British in Madras.

The main building has an excellent **archaeological section** featuring pieces from all the major South Indian periods in-cluding Chola, Vijayanagar, Hoysala and Chalukya. It also houses a good ethnology collection.

The **bronze gallery**, in an adjacent build-ing, has a superb collection of Chola bronze art. One of the most impressive pieces is the bronze of Ardhanariswara, the androgynous incarnation of Shiva with one child-bearing hip and breast.

Next door is a poorly lit and unimpres-sive **art gallery**.

The museum complex is open from 9.30 am to 5 pm; closed Friday and public holi-days. Entrance is Rs 3 (Rs 20 for a camera), and the ticket includes entry to the bronze gallery, which the city bus tours omit.

MOSQUES

The **Wallajah Mosque** (also known as the Big Mosque) on Tripilcane High Rd just down from the Wallajah Rd, was built in 1795 by the Nawab of Arcot. Its huge, wide stairs form an imposing entrance. It may be viewed from its entrance or from the sur-rounding buildings. The original **Thousand Lights Mosque** on the corner of Peter's Rd and Anna Salai has been superseded by a more recent structure, but it is worth visiting for its impressive architecture. It is most easily viewed from the Anna Salai side. Both mosques are often listed in the tourist litera-ture, but while visitors are welcome, the mosques should not be considered as tourist sites; they are places of prayer and teaching.

DEVELOPMENT CENTRE FOR MUSICAL INSTRUMENTS

Numerous examples of Indian musical in-struments, both ancient and modern, are made and exhibited at this centre. The staff are happy to give demonstrations, and you are welcome to try the various instruments. You can blow the ancient *sankhu* (conch shell), to produce a haunting mellow tone. An Om bell makes a great sound when a stick is moved slowly around its rim, and a cobra-shaped instrument mimics the sound of the snake. The centre also has some in-teresting modern innovations. Fashioned on ancient instruments, these include stringed

CHENNAI

instruments with carved animal bases and gourds which act as extra resonators.

The centre has had several homes since its establishment 40 years ago. It is now in the Tamil Nadu Handicrafts building at 759 Anna Salai, and is well worth a visit. It's actually just off Anna Salai, down the lane and right next to Air Lanka. The centre is open from Monday to Friday, 9.30 am to 6 pm and Saturday 9.30 to 1 pm. You can't purchase musical instruments here but the staff can advise on the best places to go.

VALLUVAR KOTTAM

The Valluvar Kottam, on the corner of Kodambakkam High Rd and Village Rd (often referred to as Valluvar Kottam High Rd) honours one of the most acclaimed Tamil poets – Thiruvalluvar. His classic work, the Kural, deals with ethical issues and is reputed to be about 2000 years old. For many, it is the Tamil equivalent of the Bible.

The memorial is on three levels and is interesting from an architectural and literary point of view. The lower level comprises an auditorium 70m by 30m, which can seat up to 4000 people. Its grid ceiling obviates the necessity for supporting pillars. The next level consists of the Kural balcony, which overlooks the lower level. Here the 1330 couplet verses of the Kural are inscribed on granite tablets. Each tablet is positioned near a small window which casts light on the inscriptions. The third and highest level with its reflection ponds (though a bit too murky for reflection) has an octagonal sanctum at one end which houses an impressive sculpture of the poet. The sanctum sits on a huge stone car, or chariot, intricately carved and drawn by two stone elephants.

Valluvar Kottam was opened in 1976 and replicates ancient Tamil architecture. It is surrounded by pleasant gardens where another statue of the poet sits high on a column. It is open every day from 8 am to 6 pm. Entry is Rs 2.

SRI PARTHASARATHY TEMPLE

This temple off Triplicane High Rd (also known as Quaid-e-Milleth High Rd) is dedicated to Krishna. Built in the 8th century by the Pallavas, and renovated in the 16th century by the Vijayanagars, it is believed to be one of the oldest surviving temples in Chennai. It is noted for its various depictions of Vishnu. It's open from 6 am to noon and 4 to 8 pm.

Non-Hindus may visit the temple but are not usually permitted into the inner shrine.

MARINA & AQUARIUM

The sandy stretch of beach known as the Marina extends for 13km. The guides on the city tour insist that this is the longest beach in the world! The aquarium, on the seafront near the junction of Bharathi Salai and Kamarajar Salai, is worth missing just to encourage its closure. South of the aquarium is the **Ice House** (see the boxed text, opposite).

SAN THOME CATHEDRAL

Built in 1504, then rebuilt in neo-Gothic style in 1893, this Roman Catholic church is said to house the remains of St Thomas the Apostle (Doubting Thomas). There's a small crypt which is entered by a stairway just before the altar. Christ is portrayed rising from a lotus and flanked by two huge peacocks. The cathedral is near Kapaleeshwarar Temple, at the southern end of Kamarajar Salai (South Beach Rd), close to the seafront.

KAPALEESHWARAR TEMPLE

This ancient Shiva temple, off Kutchery Rd in Mylapore, was constructed in Dravidian style and displays the same architectural elements – *gopurams, mandapams,* tank – that are found in the famous temple cities of Tamil Nadu. Like most other temples in the state, non-Hindus are usually not allowed into the inner sanctum. The main festivals celebrated at this temple are Thai Pusam in January, when bronze images of the deities, Shiva and Parvati, are floated on the temple tank; and, during March/April, the Marriage of Shiva and Parvati, during which the temple's 63 bronze statues are taken in ceremonial procession and presented to the elaborately adorned images of the deities.

The Ice House

This relic of the Raj era was used to store enormous blocks of ice cut from the Great Lakes in North America and shipped to India as a crude but highly effective form of refrigeration.

Initially ice was a luxury in the colony, but it soon became an essential ingredient for an expanding economy. Although it took as long as four months for the ice-carrying clippers to sail from North America to the shores of India, the melting of the ice blocks was severely retarded by a wrapping of felt and pine sawdust. The ice blocks were still huge when the clippers moored off the coast of Madras. The ice was loaded onto small boats that were rowed to the shore. From there, groups of porters would lift each block onto their heads and carry them across the sand to the ice house.

The Madras ice house was one of several in India. Others were in Calcutta and Mumbai (Bombay). The first shipment of ice arrived in India in 1833 and over a period of 50 years considerable fortunes were made in the ice transportation business. The inevitable demise came with the invention of mechanical refrigeration.

After 1885, the Madras ice house experienced a number of transformations. It was a private residence for a wealthy lawyer and later, in 1897, it became the venue from which Swami Vivekananda would issue his daily address to the crowds. It was here that he implored them to take pride in their country, lead a simple life and devote themselves to the less fortunate. The teachings of Vivekananda had a great impact on Gandhi and many others. It was from the Madras ice house that a disciple of Swami Vivekananda, known as Swami Ramakrishnananda began the Ramakrishna movement in South India.

In the 1930s the ice house was a widow's home and today it functions as a hostel for the adjacent teachers college. The building is also known as Vivekananda House and every year, on 12 January (the Swami's birthday) many thousands of devotees gather to pay homage.

Surrounding the temple is a labyrinth of narrow streets with bustling markets and tiny shops selling everything from elegant saris to dental equipment.

Fees for photography in the temple are Rs 5 for hand held cameras and Rs 101 for video/movie cameras using temple electricity.

The temple is open for *puja* (prayers) from 4 am to noon and 4 to 8 pm. Bus No 21 runs here from Anna Salai or the High Court.

LUZ CHURCH

Dedicated to Our Lady of Light, this Portuguese church was built in the 16th century, and is the oldest church in Chennai.

Many Portuguese sailors owed their lives to a mysterious light that would guide them safely into the port. Despite much searching, they were never able to locate the source of the light, and the church was built as an expression of their gratitude.

BIRLA PLANETARIUM

Stargazing at the film studios is one thing. But to stargaze at the Planetarium offers a very different view of the world. Constructed in the name of a well known industrialist (BM Birla) the planetarium on Gandhi Mandapam Rd (also known as Kotturpuram High Rd) offers a welcome break from the chaos of street life in Chennai. The planetarium is open daily except Monday. Shows in Tamil are at noon and 2.30 pm. English-language shows are 10.45 am, 12.15 & 3.45 pm. Entry is Rs 7.

LITTLE MOUNT

This tiny cave is where St Thomas lived and preached when he came to India around 58 AD. Known to the locals as Chinnamalai, the cave is entered via the Portuguese church which was built in 1551. Inside the cave is an altar with a large image of St Thomas. The story goes that every day St Thomas would

CHENNAI

walk from his cave to the beach near Myla-pore. Near the old Portuguese church is a new church, erected to Our Lady of Health to commemorate St Thomas' martyrdom. Each year, a month after Easter, a two day festival is held at Little Mount.

GUINDY NATIONAL PARK, CHILDREN'S PARK & SNAKE PARK

These three establishments are adjacent to each other in the southern area of Chennai, just 1km from Guindy station. The Guindy National Park is the smallest national park in India, but at 270 hectares it's large for a city park. It contains mainly blackbuck, spotted deer, civet cats, jackals, mongoose, various species of monkey and many birds. You're unlikely to see much in this park and it's not really worth a visit. To enter you require a written permit from the ranger in the Chil-dren's Park, which has a few rides as well as sculptured animals.

As well as snakes, the Snake Park has lizards, crocodiles and turtles. It is well maintained with reasonably generous enclo-sures and plenty of shade. Large information boards in Tamil and English debunk many myths about reptiles and provide significant detail on habitat and behaviour. Here you can learn that of the 2750 species of snake throughout the world, India claims 244.

Each hour there's a demonstration, which is truly pythonesque! A bored keeper picks up snakes with a hook and goes through the motions to the accompaniment of an over-amplified pre-recorded spiel on snakes. It makes airline safety demonstrations posi-tively exciting.

Entry to each of these places is Rs 2 for adults and Rs 1 for children. It's Rs 10 for a still camera permit and Rs 75 for a video. The parks are open daily from 8.30 am to 5 pm, except Tuesday.

The easiest way to Guindy is by train from Egmore station to Guindy station. It's then a 1km walk east to the park or a short ride in an auto-rickshaw.

FILM STUDIOS

The film industry in Chennai is now bigger than Bollywood (Mumbai). Last year 289 films in Tamil and Telugu languages were produced (see the boxed text 'Tamil & Telugu talkies). Many of these would have been at least partially shot in studios in Chennai. One of the biggest studios is MGR Film City (☎ 235 2424). This is the only one routinely open to the public. It's also the only studio with outdoor sets, Mughal gardens, a Graeco-Roman amphitheatre and a giant concrete shark. Universal Studios it most certainly isn't, but it can be wonderfully entertaining if shooting is taking place out-doors.

If you've always fancied your chances as a film star, extras are occasionally needed. You can telephone the studios or simply try your luck and wander about waiting to be spotted. Entry to the studio is Rs 15 plus Rs 50 for a camera. Video cameras are prohib-ited. MGR Film City is open daily from 8 am to 8 pm. It's near Indira Nagar, about 10km south of Egmore. Bus 23C runs from Egmore, bus 5C from Parry's Corner.

Chennai's other big film studios, Vijaya (☎ 483 8787), Prasad (☎ 483 3715) and AVM (☎ 483 6700), are in the south-western suburb of Kodambakkam. You need the managers' permission to visit and it's not readily given. In 1997 shooting at these studios was seriously affected by industrial disputes.

ELLIOT BEACH

This stretch of beach near Adyar district is quieter and more relaxing than Marina Beach. You can stroll along the sand and watch the stray cows watching the horizon. At the southern end of the beach, just past the Castle Restaurant, is the **Velankanni Church**, built in honour of the Madonna of health. Devotees believe in the power of the Madonna to cure all ills, and they flock to the church in search of healing. Just near this church is the **Ashtalakshmi Temple**, which is dedicated to the goddess Lakshmi and celebrates each of her eight manifestations. A recent 1976 gopuram (gateway tower) displays a contemporary style of Dravidian architecture. Apart from the Mahalakshmi

PETER DAVIS

EDDIE GERALD

EDDIE GERALD

Chennai
A bustling, friendly city (clockwise from top left): an astrology robot tells fortunes; auto-rickshaws buzz around Egmore train station; tourists explore the belly of a film-set shark.

Chennai

Dust jackets and movie posters are a gaudy art in themselves, and some of the most striking outward expressions of Chennai culture.

Temple in Mumbai this is the only temple on the Indian coast dedicated to the goddess in all her manifestations.

ENFIELD FACTORY

The Enfield in India is manufactured by Eicher Motors in Tiruvottiyur, 17km north of Chennai. It's possible to visit the factory if you phone the product manager in advance (☎ 543300). You can also contact Enfield by email at: enfield@giasmd01.vsnl.net.in.

ORGANISED TOURS

Tours of Chennai and the nearby temple cities are run by the TTDC and the ITDC. For details on where to book, see Tourist Offices at the start of this chapter. TTDC tours can also be booked at the State Express Division I (formerly TTC) bus stand on Esplanade Rd (☎ 534 1982) between 6 am and 9 pm, or at Central station (☎ 563351).

A few examples of tours include:

City Sightseeing Tour
This tour includes visits to Fort St George, the government museum, Valluvar Kottam, the Snake Park, Kapaleeshwarar Temple and Marina Beach. The daily tours are fairly good value, although somewhat rushed. The morning tour is from 8 am to 1.30 pm, and the afternoon tour from 1.30 to 6.30 pm; the cost is Rs 75 per person. The TTDC tour commentary is not very enlightening, but the guides are helpful.

Kanchipuram & Mamallapuram (Mahabalipuram)
These full-day tours go from 6.20 am to 7 pm, and cost Rs 180 or Rs 260 (air-con bus) including breakfast and lunch and a visit to a crocodile farm on the return trip. It's good value if you're strapped for time, but otherwise it's a breathless dash.

Tirupathi
This full-day tour to the famous Venkateshwara Temple at Tirumala in southern Andhra Pradesh is good value if you don't have time to do it yourself. Be warned that at least 12 hours are spent on the bus. The price includes 'special *darshan*' (for details, see the boxed text 'Special Darshan at Tirumala' under Tirupathi in the Andhra Pradesh chapter). This usually takes two hours, but on weekends and holidays it can take five hours, which means the bus doesn't get back to Chennai until mid-

night. The daily tours officially last from 6 am to 10 pm. The fare is Rs 260 or Rs 500 (air-con), and includes breakfast, lunch and the Rs 30 special darshan fee.

Cultural & Spiritual Tours
A company called Window to the World specialises in tours of temples and other cultural sites around India, especially South India. Based in Tiruchirappalli (Trichy) and run by an Australian woman, this company caters for people whose interests lie beyond ordinary tourism. Participants in the tours are briefed on many aspects of Indian culture and the groups are usually no more than 14 people. Contact Faith Hawley (☎ 431-430832), 27 Chandra

---

The Biker's Bike

There's something comforting and reassuring about Enfield motorcycles; perhaps the lack of pretension. These motorcycles look like motorcycles. They're not sleek, futuristic-looking machines that cocoon the rider from the environment. Enfield enthusiasts claim that on their bikes they really feel the terrain – they know they are travelling. At the same time they also feel safe. Enfields are renowned for reliability and sturdiness. In short, they are ideally suited to Indian roads and that's why Enfield motorcycles are favoured by police and military in India. The Enfield Bullet, as it is known, has become something of a legend.

These machines have been chugging off the production line in India since the British company, Royal Enfield, set up a factory on the outskirts of Chennai in 1955. In the 1970s the triumph of the Japanese motorcycle market heralded the demise of the British market. In India, however, Enfield production continued unabated.

Touring India on an Enfield is becoming increasingly popular. Royal Enfield Motors (☎ 543300) organise 14-day tours of South India. A road captain assists with riding skills, and a back-up jeep, with mechanic on hand, carries spare parts. The tour groups have a maximum of 14 people.

The Southern Cinema Invasion

Chennai has long been the centre of the vibrant South Indian film industry. For decades writers, directors, technicians and of course the stars of the screen have been lured to the city. From 1931 to 1997, 4783 Tamil films and 4313 Telugu films were produced. The output of films from the Chennai studios is now so prolific that Chennai rather than Mumbai is considered the capital of the massive Indian film industry.

It all began back in 1917 with the production of a silent film titled *Keechaka Vadha* by RN Mudaliar, a Madras-based industrialist.

During the silent period, 147 films came out of Chennai. When the 'talkies' began the industry really flourished. As with cinema the world over, the battles within South Indian cinema continue to be about art and integrity versus commercial viability. Many of the past films have been cliché ridden and much of the current output is a high-octane romp of sex (Indian style), violence and unadulterated melodrama.

Tamil cinema has, on the other hand, been characterised by clever use of the medium for social awareness. A number of prolific writers and directors have made their mark in Tamil cinema with stories containing strong messages of justice and equality.

One of the pioneers of Tamil cinema was K Subrahmanayam, whose famous film *Balayogini* portrayed the ill treatment of a Brahmin widow and satirised both the caste system and aspects of western society. Subrahmanayam paved the way for a wide range of what became known in Tamil cinema as 'social films'. In 1949, the writer CN Annadurai wrote the screenplay for *Velaikkari*, a film that promoted anti-caste sentiments. He spawned many other writers and directors who struggled to balance the demand for a star-based industry with scripts of quality.

The power and influence of screen culture upon political culture in Tamil Nadu is evidenced by the fact that two ex-movie stars have risen to the position of State Chief Minister. One was Jayalalitha Jayaram. The other was MG Ramachandran, a screen actor who cultivated enormous popularity during the 1960s and 1970s as a champion of the downtrodden. The vast government film studios in Chennai bear his name.

Like Tamil cinema, Telugu cinema has its fair share of pioneers who demonstrate a passion for their craft and a loyalty to their culture. When Boag Rd in Chennai was recently renamed BN Reddi Rd, one such pioneer was given his due recognition. Bommireddi Narasimha Reddi was born in 1908 in Kothapalli, a village in Cuddapah district in Andhra Pradesh. He died in 1977 after a life dedicated to making quality films in his native Telugu tongue.

The influence of Tamil and Telugu directors is now being felt in the centre of the Hindi film industry in Mumbai, otherwise known as *Bollywood*. Dubbed in the local media as the 'southern invasion', these directors are impacting on the traditional high-decibel song sequence of Hindi films.

Nagar, Srirangam, Tiruchirappali. Window to the World also has an office in Melbourne, Australia: (☎/fax 61-3-9874 7029) 79 Rooks Rd, Nunawading, Victoria, 3131

Welcome Tourrs (sic) and Travels
This travel agency (☎ 852 0908; fax 858 6655) at 150 Anna Salai (Mount Rd) is approved by the Government of India Tourist Board and can organise everything from simple car hire to an extensive customised tour to suit your tastes.

The drivers are well trained, good humoured and safety conscious. Further information is available on their Web site at www.sysprom.com/welcome.

SPECIAL EVENTS

Between mid-December and mid-January, Chennai is host to the prestigious Festival of Carnatic Music & Dance. Performances are held at various music academies, featuring

The Day I Was Discovered

'You look like an actor, you should go to the studios and try your luck.' These words were spoken to me by Mr Film News Anandan (yes that really is his name). I was interviewing the septuagenarian award winning film historian about his collection of film stills from every Telugu and Tamil film ever made. I took his advice and ventured to MGR Film City. Within an hour I was 'discovered' by an urbane gentleman all dressed in white: 'My name is Arjun, I'm an associate director and I've been observing you. I'd like to invite you to be in my film'.

From that moment I was swept into the macho world of a swashbuckling Tamil blockbuster. Last month they were shooting in Switzerland. Next month they head for Malaysia but for now they're picking up shots in the Chennai studios. First they gave me lunch, then a car and a driver. I was rushed to 'wardrobe' (a concrete cell somewhere in the bowels of Film City). Only then did I (a Jewish man from Melbourne) learn that I was to play a Catholic priest.

The wardrobe department clearly wasn't geared up for western sizes. The search for white trousers that wouldn't render me a eunuch took many precious minutes. They put a white surplice (frock) over me, a crucifix around my neck, rosary beads in my right hand and a bible (in Tamil) in my left hand. Make-up consisted of a broken comb and an even more broken mirror. Then it was off to location – a paddock in the studio grounds where a mock grave had been dug and a black coffin was waiting to be lowered. My role was to preside over the burial of a young boy who had been shot by the villain.

Lighting technicians ran cables across wet grass (and issued warnings not to touch one light stand which had become 'live'). The camera crew prepared their lenses, and a large crowd of onlookers assembled. Three Indian tourists from Kerala requested my autograph and posed with me for their snaps. Into the mayhem came the cleanest car I had seen in Chennai and out stepped the denim clad, mobile phone toting hero. The crowds deserted me. They rushed their hero, who makes Arnold Schwarzenegger look like a wimp, for his autograph. He had come not to act, but to direct my scene (in Tamil Films the hero is often allowed to direct some scenes).

Only when they yelled 'action!' and then 'rain!' did I learn that the burial was to take place during the monsoonal downpour. Water from a fire hose gushed over me and my bible. As the coffin was slowly lowered, I muttered my mantra (what the hell am I doing here?), fondled my rosary and looked appropriately forlorn. Because it was a one camera shoot we had to do three takes from as many angles. Within two hours the shoot was over. Mr Arjun discreetly pressed my Rs 200 appearance fee into my hands and thanked me profusely. 'Call me when you're next in town' he said.

The film is called *Thayin Mani Kodi*, a patriotic title which loosely translates as *Mother Country*. And, surprisingly, it's about a hero who single-handedly defends his nation and wins the heart (and the body) of the heroine.

Peter Davis

some of the country's top classical dancers and musicians. Contact the Government of India Tourist Office for details.

PLACES TO STAY

Egmore, on and around Kennet Lane, is the main budget and mid-range accommodation hub, but competition for rooms can be fierce. Book in advance or arrive early. Two other areas for cheap hotels are George Town,

between Mint St, NSC Bose Rd and Rajaji Salai; and Triplicane, a suburb to the southeast of Anna Salai, which is less chaotic than Egmore and preferred by many budget travellers. The top hotels are mainly along Anna Salai and the roads leading off it. If you'd like to stay in a private home, contact the Government of India Tourist Office for a list of home-stays. Prices range from Rs 100 to Rs 600 per person per week.

CHENNAI

Hotel Tax

Hotel tax in Tamil Nadu is currently among the highest in the country – 15% on rooms costing between Rs 100 and Rs 199, and 20% for anything above. The top hotels will also add a 5% to 10% service charge. Prices given in this section are before tax.

PLACES TO STAY – BUDGET
Egmore

The **Salvation Army Red Shield Guest House** (☎ 532 1821, 15 Ritherdon Rd), is a 20 minute walk from Egmore station and welcomes both men and women. It's a clean, quiet place in leafy surroundings. A dorm bed costs Rs 40 and doubles/triples are Rs 175/200. Rooms have clean sheets and fans. Bathroom facilities are communal. Checkout is 9 am.

Alarmel Lodge (☎ 825 1248, 17-18 Gandhi Irwin Rd), is across the road from Egmore station. Singles/doubles with a very smelly common bathroom are just Rs 65/95 but rooms are usually filled with long-term lodgers.

The **Tourist Home** (☎ 825 0079, 21 Gandhi Irwin Rd), fills up quickly. Rooms, all with attached bath, start at Rs 120/150, or Rs 225 for a double with air-con.

Shri Lakshmi Lodge (☎ 825 4576, 16 Kennet Lane), is clean and quiet and has rooms with attached bathroom for Rs 150/300, or Rs 80/130 without. The rooms face a quiet central courtyard.

Hotel Sri Durga Prasad (☎ 825 3881, 10 Kennet Lane), nearby, is similarly priced and also often full.

Dayal-De Lodge (☎ 822 7328, 486 Pantheon Rd), at the southern end of Kennet Lane, is set back from the road and quieter than some of the other hotels, although the street noise still penetrates the front rooms. There are rooms from Rs 180/240; all have attached bathrooms with 24 hour hot water. Family rooms are available for Rs 330. The beds are particularly firm.

People's Lodge (☎ 853 5938, Whannels Rd), is a relic which has been popular for years. Rooms are Rs 110/150 but it no longer has attached bathrooms and the hot water is also 'finished'.

The **Retiring Rooms** at Central and Egmore stations have doubles from Rs 145 or Rs 260 with air-con. At Rs 80 for 12 hours, dorm beds (for men only) are quiet, clean and have air-con. There's a small sitting area. Washing and toilet facilities are right next door. Smoking, eating and alcohol are not permitted.

Hotel Masa (☎ 825 2966, 15 Kennet Lane), is a reasonable place with rooms with attached bath from Rs 215/275/325. There are also air-con doubles/triples for Rs 400/450. The long dark corridors of this hotel make an excellent echo chamber. Combine this with the street noise and you have a great place for those who can't tolerate silence.

Hotel Impala Continental (☎ 825 0484, 12 Gandhi Irwin Rd), opposite Egmore station, is at the top end of the lower price bracket. Encircling a quiet courtyard, this hotel offers a range of rooms (some of which are dark, dingy and in need of a serious clean) from singles/doubles at Rs 180/250 to deluxe doubles at Rs 280 and air-con doubles/triples at Rs 380/420. All rooms have attached bathrooms and there's 24 hour hot water. A TV can be hired for Rs 35 a day. Credit cards are not accepted.

Hotel Imperial (☎ 825 0376; fax 825 2030, 6 Gandhi Irwin Rd) is fair value, but look at a few rooms as some are far from spotless. Like the Impala, it's set around a courtyard containing shops, massage parlours, a news stand and travel agents. Some travellers find the setting less than salubrious. Singles/doubles are Rs 160/300 or Rs 450/475 with air-con. There are also air-con suites for Rs 550/600. The hotel has two restaurants (one open-air), a nightclub and a popular bar.

Triplicane

You can reach this area on bus No 30, 31 or 32 from Esplanade Rd, outside the State Express Division I (formerly TTC) bus stand, in George Town. From Egmore station, take bus No 29D, 22 or 27B.

Broadlands (☎ *854 5573, 16 Vallabha Agraharam St)*, is off Triplicane High Rd, opposite the Star Cinema. It's something of a travellers' institution, though it's now getting mixed reports, particularly because it has an unofficial policy of excluding Indians. It's a characterful old place set around courtyards. The simple rooms are reasonably clean and have wicker easy chairs, a table and fan. Singles cost from Rs 150 with common bath, Rs 160 with attached bath. The cheapest doubles are singles with an extra bed, which costs an extra Rs 50. Larger doubles are Rs 340 with common bath, Rs 350 with bath attached. There are also dorm beds for Rs 50. As a rule, the higher the room number, the better the room (Nos 43 and 44 are tops); the cheapest rooms are rather gloomy. There's a good notice board, and you can hire bicycles, but their entry policy means that if you're Indian and living abroad you'll have to show your passport to prove it.

Paradise Guest House is right next door to Broadlands. While it's a long way from any sense of paradise, it is clean with basic rooms at Rs 150/200. A deluxe double is Rs 250. It seems there is no hot water in Paradise but the staff promise to 'find some if you want it'.

Hotel Comfort (☎ *855 7661, 22 Vallabha Agraharam St)*, is near Broadlands. It's modern and characterless but the rooms are good and cost Rs 250/350 with attached bathroom. Larger rooms are available for Rs 350/485. All rooms have air-con.

Hotel Himalaya (☎ *854 7522, 54 Triplicane High Rd)* is not a bad option, with singles/doubles/triples from Rs 300/360/480 and also some air-con rooms. Exact room dimensions are prominently displayed above the door just in case you need to know them. There's a vegetarian restaurant and 24 hour hot water.

George Town
The **Hotel Surat** (☎ *589236, 138 Prakasam Rd)*, above the Madras Cafe, is not bad value – singles/doubles cost Rs 150/195 with attached bathroom, Rs 100/170 without. Avoid

the rooms at the front as they are incredibly noisy. Some of the rooms at the rear overlook a putrid rubbish tip.

Indira Nagar
The **Youth Hostel** (☎ *412882, 2nd Ave, Indira Nagar)*, is about 10km south of Egmore in a peaceful residential area. Dorm beds cost Rs 40 for nonmembers, Rs 20 for members, and it's possible to camp in the garden. Phone in advance for a reservation and directions, and bring a padlock for your locker. Meals are available on request (Rs 10 for a thali). If the Salvation Army Red Shield Guest House is full and you don't mind the long journey to get here, for real shoestringers this is a pleasant place to stay.

The easiest way to get to the Youth Hostel is by auto-rickshaw or by Bus No 18S from Parry's Corner to Indira Nagar and then an auto-rickshaw to the hostel.

PLACES TO STAY – MID-RANGE
Egmore
The **YWCA International Guest House** (☎ *532 4234; fax 532 4263, 1086 Periyar EVR High Rd – most often referred to by its former name, Poonamallee High Rd)*, is an excellent place but so popular you'll need to book well in advance. The rooms are bright and spacious. In the low season (April-July; September-October) singles/doubles/triples with clean bathrooms cost Rs 360/430/580, or Rs 520/580 with air-con. Add around Rs 50 per room for the high season (August, and November to March). The guesthouse accepts both men and women, but there's a transient membership fee of Rs 20 – valid for one month. The restaurant serves Indian and western food. Because this is a service organisation, taxes do not apply. However, certain rules do: checkout is usually by noon, visitors are forbidden in the rooms, lunch and dinner in the restaurant must be ordered in advance, alcohol is not served and meals usually finish by 9 pm.

Hotel Vaigai (☎ *853 4959, 3 Gandhi Irwin Rd)*, is a plain hotel which has doubles at Rs 275 to Rs 325, or Rs 500 with air-con. You'll need your own bedding here – the sheets

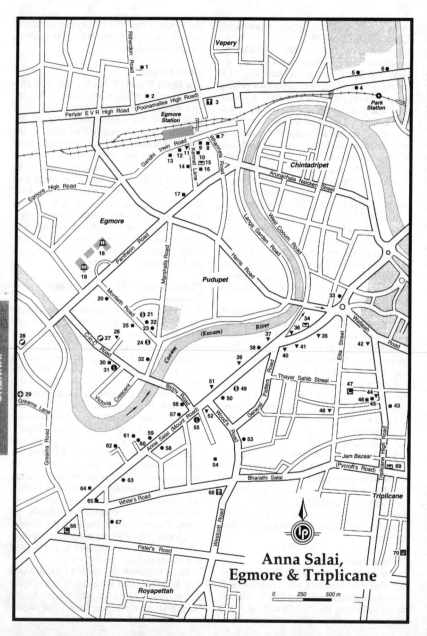

Vepery

Ritherdon Road

■ 1
■ 2
🚻 3
5 ●
6 ●
● 4

Park Station

Periyar E V R High Road (Poonamallee High Road)

Egmore Station

Gandhi Irwin Road

■ 7

Whannels Road

8
9
■ 12 11
● 10
□ 15
■ 13
■ 14 Kennet Lane
■ 16

Chintadripet

Arunachala Naicken Street

West Cooum Road

■ 17

Egmore High Road

Egmore

🏛 18

Pantheon Road

🏛 19

Langs Garden Road

Harris Road

Marshalls Road

Pudupet

● 20

Montieth Road

❸ 21
■ 22
● 23
● 24 ❸

River (Kuvam)

33

34
36
▼ 35

42 ▼

Wallajah Road

● 25
■ 26
▼ 27

Club Road

37
38 ▼
▼ 41
40

Ellis Street

28 ❸

● 32

39 ▼

Cooum

30 ●
31 ❶

Victoria Crescent

Binny Road

51 ▼

❹ 49
● 50

Thayar Sahib Street

47
□
44 ▲
■ 46 45
▼ 48
■ 43

29 ✚
Greams Lane

56 ●

57 ●
▼ 52
55 ●

Woor's Road

General Peters Road

Greams Road

61 ● 59
● 60
62 ●
● 58

Anna Salai (Mount Road)

● 53

● 54

Jam Bazaar
(Pycroft's Road)

🚉 69

Triplicane High Road

64 ■
65 ▲

White's Road

● 63

❸ 66

● 67

68 🚻

Bharathi Salai

Triplicane

Westcott Road

70 🏨

Peter's Road

Royapettah

Anna Salai, Egmore & Triplicane

0   250   500 m

CHENNAI

look like they've never been washed. Rooms with tiled floors are a safer option than those with the red carpet: nasty things lurk in the carpet mould. The hotel has a veg/nonveg restaurant and a bar.

Hotel New Victoria (☎ 825 3638; fax 825 0070, 3 Kennet Lane), charges Rs 850/1100 for air-con rooms with attached bath and phone conveniently located right beside the loo. Try to avoid the cell-like rooms without windows.

The hotel also has a bar stocked with 'Indian and foreign liquors' and a multicuisine restaurant.

Hotel Pandian (☎ 825 2901; fax 825 8459, 9 Kennet Lane), is a popular place. It's clean and comfortable but the cheaper rooms aren't great value as the plumbing is temperamental. Ordinary singles/doubles are Rs 450/550; air-con rooms start at Rs 700/800. The hotel has an excellent restaurant with a veg/nonveg menu, and a bar. The staff are particularly pleasant. Credit cards are accepted.

Hotel Chandra Towers (☎ 823 3344; fax 825 1703, 9 Gandhi Irwin Rd) has a lush lobby that belies the somewhat cramped singles/doubles for Rs 1095/1295. Some of the doubles have double beds. There's a good restaurant, 24 hour coffee shop, a bar and a Saturday and Sunday 'dance party' where Hindi and western pop is pumped at maximum decibels from the darkened bowels of the hotel.

Hotel Kanchi (☎ 827 1100; fax 827 2928, 28 C-in-C Rd) is south of Egmore. Spacious but seriously neglected singles/doubles, all with small balconies, are Rs 530/550 or Rs 700/725 with air-con. As with so many hotels, the ceiling fans do a better job than the air-con and you may be happy to trade the spaciousness for a cleaner environment. The hotel has an enclosed rooftop restaurant open from 11 am to 3 pm and 6 to 11 pm. There is a cheaper ground-floor dining hall and a bar.

Mylapore

The *New Woodlands Hotel (☎ 827 3111, 72/75 Dr Radhakrishnan Salai)*, has three categories of air-con rooms. The cottages are Rs 1100, deluxe rooms are Rs 650 and doubles are Rs 500. There are also some non-air-con singles for Rs 250. The hotel has a billiard room, two restaurants and a pool that nonresidents can use for Rs 60. An ayurvedic masseur is also on the premises. The hotel is frequently full and bookings at least one week in advance are advised

Nilgiri's Nest (☎ 827 5222; fax 826 0214, 58 Dr Radhakrishnan Salai) is a good choice. Bright, modern singles/doubles cost Rs 750/1050 including breakfast. Semi-deluxe rooms are Rs 925/1350 and deluxe rooms are Rs 1150/1700.

Nilgiri's Nest has a good restaurant, a supermarket next door and a branch of the Saravanaas/Saravana Bhavan chain of restaurants around the corner. This place is very popular: advanced bookings are advised and securing a room may be difficult.

Nungambakkam

Hotel Ranjith (☎ 827 0521; fax 8277688, 9 Nungambakkam High Rd), is convenient for the consulates and airline offices. There are singles/doubles for Rs 720/864, or Rs 1150/1280 with air-con. There are two restaurants, a bar and travel booking facilities.

Airport Environs

Hotel Mars (☎ 840 2586), at Pallavaram, is well priced. Singles start at Rs 300 and doubles are Rs 395. It's clean and tidy, and has hot water. Lone women travellers find the prevalence of female staff here comforting.

Hotel Mount Heera (☎ 234 9563; fax 233 1236) 287 MKN Rd, Alandur), has pleasant staff, and has similar services to Hotel Mars. Both are about 20 minutes by taxi from the airport.

PLACES TO STAY – TOP END

Many of the best hotels are situated in an arc stretching from Nungambakkam High Rd, south-west of Anna Salai, through to Dr Radhakrishnan Salai. There are also a few along or just off Anna Salai itself. Unless otherwise stated, all the following hotels have central air-con, a swimming pool, multicuisine restaurants, and a bar.

Hotel Connemara (☎ 852 0123; fax 852 3361, Binny Rd), just off Anna Salai, is an institution. Owned by the Taj Group, it was renovated recently and lost a little of its old-fashioned appeal in the process. Rooms cost from Rs 3850/4330 for standard singles/doubles, Rs 5000/5500 for 'superior' and Rs 6500/7000 for 'old world'. There's a pool, shopping arcade and astrologer.

Hotel Ambassador Pallava (☎ 855 4476; fax 855 4492, 53 Montieth Rd), is a modern four-star place which offers smart rooms from Rs 1975/2475.

The *Grand Orient (☎ 852 4111; fax 852 3412, 693 Anna Salai)*, used to be called Hotel Madras International. With its new name it has new prices. Rooms are from Rs 1195/1800. There's no pool.

Residency Hotel (☎ 825 3434; fax 825 0085, 49 GN Chetty Rd, Theagaraya Nagar), is popular with middle-class Indian families. Singles/doubles start at Rs 1195/ 1600. There's no pool here, but there is a multicuisine restaurant and bar.

Hotel Savera (☎ 827 4700; fax 827 3475, 69 Dr Radhakrishnan Salai), has well appointed singles/doubles for Rs 1800/2400.

Hotel President (☎ 853 2211; fax 853 2299, 16 Dr Radhakrishnan Salai) has rooms from Rs 975/1275. This is a big place with spacious rooms. It has a bar and a 24 hour coffee shop, as well as a swimming pool.

The *Indian Express Guest House* (☎ 858 6614, Club House Rd), behind the Government of India Tourist Office, is operated by the Indian Express newspaper mainly for its clients. However, it has four rooms available for travellers, which are large, clean and very quiet. The guesthouse overlooks a garden and gives the feeling of a rural retreat. All four rooms have air-con and cost Rs 1200/1500 including breakfast. There is no state tax on this place. Veg and nonveg meals are available on order.

Chennai has no shortage of five-star hotels where a room will cost from US$130/150. The choice includes:

Hotel Taj Coromandel
(☎ 827 2827; fax 825 7104, 17 Nungambakkam High Rd); as luxurious as all the Taj Group hotels.

The Trident
(☎ 234 4747; fax 234 6699, 1/24 G S T Rd); is the closest luxury hotel to the airport (5km) but it's a long haul from the city centre. Rooms cost Rs 5000 to Rs 7500.

Welcomgroup Chola Sheraton
(☎ 828 0101; fax 827 8779, 10 Cathedral Rd, the extension of Dr Radhakrishnan Salai); is closer to the centre than the Park Sheraton. Rooms range from Rs 3500/3800 to Rs 6500/6800.

Welcomgroup Park Sheraton
(☎ 499 4101, 132 TTK Rd, Alwarpet); epitomises executive-class opulence. Rooms from Rs 3500/3800 to Rs 6500/6800, suites from Rs 8500 to Rs 22,000.

PLACES TO EAT

There are thousands of vegetarian restaurants in Chennai, ranging from the simple 'meals' restaurants where a thali lunch (rarely available in the evening) is served on a banana leaf for under Rs 20 to sumptuous spreads for 20 times that amount in the major hotels. Breakfast at the simpler restaurants, which open shortly after dawn, consists of such staples as dosa, idli, curd and coffee.

You'll find nonvegetarian restaurants are much thinner on the ground, and western-style breakfasts are almost impossible to find outside mid-range and top-end hotels. If you're a strict carnivore or simply want a break from South Indian cuisine, it's probably best to go for lunch or dinner at one of the larger hotels.

For excellent vegetarian meals look out for branches of the *Saravanaas/Saravana Bhavan* chain. These are clean and cheap self-service restaurants open from 7 am to 11.30 pm. Thalis are from Rs 18 to Rs 50, masala dosas from Rs 11, lassis and curries from Rs 20, and there is a wide range of ice creams and fresh fruit juices. From 3 to 11.30 pm North Indian dishes are served, as well as Chinese food and pizzas. Other dishes are available at different times, but there's always a good selection of 'any timers'. Pay for your meal first, then take the receipt to the serving area. While you wait, enjoy the kitchen spectacle. Most branches also have a sit-down restaurant; the food's the same but there's a small service charge. If your meal comes to more than Rs 100 you can even pay by credit card.

George Town

In this old part of town there are many vegetarian restaurants, although few stand out. *Madras Cafe* on Prakasam Rd dishes out good, cheap thalis. *Saravana Bhavan* has a large branch on NSC Bose Rd.

Egmore

Most of the restaurants are along Gandhi Irwin Rd, in front of Egmore station. *Rajabhavan* is a vegetarian restaurant at the entrance to the Hotel Imperial. *Bhoopathy Cafe* is recommended, and is directly opposite the station.

Vasanta Bhavan, on the corner of Gandhi Irwin Rd and Kennet Lane, is bustling with waiters and features an upstairs dining hall, from which you can watch the street scene below. The stall at the front sells milk-based sweets.

Raj Restaurant at the Hotel Pandian is clean and quiet and serves good veg and nonveg dishes (Rs 55 to Rs 90). A beer costs

CHENNAI

Rs 50. At the *Omar Khayyam* restaurant in the Hotel Imperial nonvegetarian food is good.

The *Hotel Kanchi Rooftop Restaurant* offers an excellent range of North and South Indian dishes. Thalis are Rs 50. The waiter delights in offering guests lessons in Tamil cuisine and etiquette. The downstairs restaurant offers a range of dishes including dosas from Rs 11. The restaurant at the *Hotel New Victoria*, 3 Kennet lane, is also good.

Ponnusamy Hotel in Wellington Estate, 24 C-in-C Rd (opposite Hotel Kanchi), is a nonveg restaurant serving meat and fish curry and biryani dishes ranging from Rs 35. A few veg dishes are also on the menu. The *Milky Way Galaxy of Icecreams*, several doors down, is a favourite hang-out for the Chennai cool set.

Triplicane

The *Maharaja Restaurant*, just around the corner from Broadlands, is where most backpackers seem to end up at least once. The varied vegetarian menu includes toasted sandwiches, lassis, lunchtime thalis (Rs 23) and snacks until midnight. *Hotel Tirumulai*, further north, serves luscious banana-leaf thalis (Rs 25) and the biggest dosas you're ever likely to see – ask for the 'Tirumulai special dosa'.

The *Srinivasa Hotel*, on Ellis St, has also been recommended. There's a partitioned area for women and couples. If you're after fruit, vegetables or spices, head south along Ellis St to the junction of Bharathi Salai where you'll find the colourful *Jam Bazaar*.

Anna Salai Area

A branch of *Saravanaas* is in the forecourt of the Shanti Theatre on Anna Salai. It's a great place for a quick meal. *Mathura Restaurant*, on the 2nd floor of the Tarapore Tower on Anna Salai, is an upmarket vegetarian restaurant. Its Madras thali (Rs 55) comes with ice cream for dessert and is served from 11 am to 3 pm. *Buharis Restaurant*, on the opposite side of the road, looks rather less impressive but serves excellent tandoori (Rs 40 for a half tandoori chicken).

There's an air-con dining hall and an open-air terrace which is pleasant in the evening. *Chungking* is an excellent and very popular Chinese restaurant near Buharis.

Manasa, near Higginbothams bookshop on Anna Salai, has also been recommended. *Dasaprakash Restaurant* (also known as AVM Dasa) is an excellent upmarket cafe-style restaurant at 806 Anna Salai. It serves vegetarian fare, with some interesting choices such as broccoli crêpes (Rs 80). There are fresh salads (Rs 100) and the ice creams are good.

Aavin is a stand-up milk bar a few doors from the Government of India Tourist Office on Anna Salai. It serves lassis, ice cream and excellent cold milk, plain or flavoured.

The Other Room, at the Hotel Ambassador Pallava, serves pretty good western dishes. Beckti Lombardia (fish stuffed with spinach and cheese) is reasonably priced at Rs 115. It also has buffets, featuring various European cuisines, beside the pool for a set price at Rs 450.

Annalakshmi (☎ 855 0296, 804 Anna Salai), is run by the devotees of Swami Shantanand Saraswati who established Shivanjali, a trust which conducts education in the fine arts and provides medical care for impoverished women and children. The restaurant has swiftly gained the reputation of being the best vegetarian restaurant in the city.

The lunchtime buffet costs Rs 150 and the staff take the trouble to carefully explain what's in each dish. Set menus including various dishes start at Rs 200. There's also the seven-course meal for Rs 300, beginning with Ambrosia, an ayurvedic health drink which 'restores harmony to our modern stressed-out physical and emotional being'. Or if you're not so hungry, have a dosa for about Rs 55. There's a Rs 100 minimum charge.

If you toss in an extra Rs 40,000 you can purchase the exquisitely handcrafted table from which you have just dined (this includes the fine upholstered chairs). Even more rupees will secure a large rosewood relief of the goddess Lakshmi in voluptuous repose. The waiters at Annalakshmi advise that all the furniture and the adornments in the restaurant are for sale. Many of these fine objects are crafted by groups sponsored by the Shivanjali supporters. The proceeds support the operation of free clinics and schools. Annalakshmi is open from noon to 3 pm, and from 7.30 to 10 pm, daily except Monday.

Hotel Connemara has a wonderful pastry shop, but for a real treat there's the Rs 350 lunchtime buffet served in the coffee shop. Also in the Connemara is the *Raintree* restaurant, which is open in the evening. The outdoor setting is superb, with live classical dancing and music some nights. It's not difficult to spend Rs 400 to Rs 500 on an à la carte meal here. Booking is recommended as it tends to be popular.

Nungambakkam High & Cathedral Rds

The *Welcomgroup Chola Sheraton* has an excellent dinner buffet for Rs 260 including taxes. For serious coffee fiends, this hotel has a coffee shop offering no less than 20 varieties of caffeine from all over the world. The prices however are global (exorbitant) and the best coffee happens to be that of South India!

The *Palki*, 1 Cathedral Rd (150m down from the Chola Sheraton), offers good North Indian food in a pleasant environment. If you've become addicted to the local coffee, it's served here, even though it's not on the menu.

The restaurant at the *New Woodlands Hotel*, on Dr Radhakrishnan Salai, the extension of Cathedral Rd, is popular with locals. The dosas, tandoori fare and milk burfis all get rave reviews. Thalis are Rs 50. It seems few foreign visitors get here, yet the food is excellent, the service very good and the restaurant is cool, pleasant and well organised.

The *Pinnacle* at Hotel Ranjith, 9 Nungambakkam High Rd, is a rooftop restaurant where one tandoori platter is sufficient for two, the beer is cold and the view over the chaos of Chennai traffic adds to the ambience.

Rangis' (☎ 825 6041, 142 Uttamar Gandhi Salai), across the road from Landmark Books, is an intimate Chinese restaurant with tasty dishes at reasonable prices – Rs 30 to Rs 60 for a meal.

The *Net Cafe* (☎ 826 3779, 101/1 Kanakasri Nagar, Cathedral Rd), near the music academy, is where students surf the net while downing burgers and cappuccino. Western-style cakes sit in rows, more for display than consumption. Net Cafe is open every day from 7 am to 10 pm. (See Post and Communications earlier in this chapter.)

Elsewhere

Beach Castle Restaurant (☎ 491 4510, 34 Elliot Beach Rd) is in an idyllic setting with thatched pagodas (some on stilts) right on the beach. Vegetarian snacks are available during the day (the pizzas are excellent) and full veg and nonveg meals are on offer from 7.30 pm. The special fish soup is superb. Prices begin at around Rs 70 for a serious curry. If you want a splurge, try the tandoor platter for Rs 160. Cold beer is available for Rs 80. You can't hurry at this place; the waiters seem to be in a perpetual dream state. But with the ocean just over the fence why hurry?

Coconut Grove (☎ 826 8800, 95 Harrington Rd), is similar to Beach Castle with an outdoor setting beneath leafy trees. The menu focuses on dishes from Kerala, which are delicious, and the service is attentive. Prices are reasonable: from Rs 65 to Rs 80 for main dishes.

The Pakwan at The Dakshin Hotel, 35 Venkatanarayana Rd, is just around the corner from the Central Cottage Industries Emporium in Temple Towers. This is an excellent place to break for lunch while shopping for crafts. The menu is diverse and the dishes are superbly prepared. A two-course meal will be around Rs 200.

Hotel Runs gets the prize for South India's best-named restaurant. It's a cheap veg and nonveg place in Adyar, in the far south of the city, near ANZ Grindlays bank.

Self-Catering

The *Nilgiri Dairy Farm* supermarket, next to the Nilgiri's Nest Hotel on Dr Radhakrishnan Salai, is a good place for dairy products, boxed tea, coffee and other edibles (closed Tuesday).

CHENNAI

Kalakshetra – A Temple of Arts

Not far from the centre of Chennai, at a village called Tiruvanmiyur, near the temple of Marundeeswarar, is a 40-hectare estate where the traditional arts of music, dance and craft are passionately nurtured. Meander through the well-kept grounds and you may hear the seductive sounds of Carnatic instruments emanating from one of the classrooms. From another room you'll hear the rhythmic stomping of strong feet on wooden floors. To the tapping of music sticks and the clapping of hands, young women in exquisite dress are learning the intricate and powerful, yet delicate, steps of classical dance.

The Kalakshetra, which literally means Temple of the Arts, was founded in 1936. The story behind this institute is essentially the story of a remarkable woman by the name of Rukmini Devi, who sustained a passionate vision throughout her long life. Born in 1904, Rukmini was adopted at an early age by Annie Besant, president of the Theosophical Society. She was only 16 when she married 40 year old George Sydney Arundale, an Australian who was brought to India by Annie Besant as principal of the Theosophical School. In 1926 Rukmini journeyed with him to Australia and studied dance under the great Russian dancer, Anna Pavlova. A decade later she founded the Kalakshetra. She continued teaching, lecturing and writing up until her death in 1986 at the age of 82.

The atmosphere at Kalakshetra is decidedly creative. Described by the Indian media as a 'cultural empire', the centre has hosted many of India's finest musicians, dancers and artisans, who have come there to teach. Students are drawn from around the world. In 1993, the Kalakshetra was declared by the Indian parliament to be an institution of national importance.

ENTERTAINMENT

Cinema

There are 94 cinemas in Chennai (many seat around 1000) – a reflection on the vibrant film industry (see the boxed text 'The Southern Cinema Invasion' earlier in this chapter). Most cinemas screen Tamil films; some screen foreign-language movies. Devi Complex (☎ 855 5660) on Anna Salai, Sathyan (☎ 852 3813) and Woodlands Symphony (☎ 852 7355) often show English films. Melody Cinema (☎ 831371) has regular Hindi films. Check the local papers for details.

The British Council and Alliance Française have weekly film showings and there are film festivals held at the United States Information Service (USIS, ☎ 827 3040) 220 Anna Salai, and the Russian Cultural Centre (☎ 499 0050) 27 Kasturi Ranga Rd. Both the Chennai Film Society and Madras Film Club (☎ 854 0984) have regular screenings of Indian and foreign films.

Classical Music & Dance

The Music Academy (☎ 827 5619), on the corner of TTK Rd and Dr Radhakrishnan Salai, is Chennai's most popular public venue for Carnatic classical music and Bharat Natyam dance performance, a traditional and ancient dance form unique to South India. Contact the tourist office or check the English language daily newspaper *The Hindu* to find out what's on. Expect to pay about Rs 175 for a good seat.

Another concert venue is Kalakshetra, or the Temple of Art (☎ 491 1169; fax 491 4359) which was founded in 1936 and is committed to the revival of classical dance and music, and traditional textile design and weaving (see boxed text, above). Occupying a 40-hectare campus in the southern suburb of Tiruvanmiyur, this place attracts students from around the world. It offers complete courses under the tutorship of a guru in the Indian tradition of *gurukulam*, where education is inseparable from other life experiences. Visitors are encouraged to watch the classes which take place each weekday from 9 to 11.15 am and from 1.25 to 4.45 pm (mornings only on Saturday, closed Sunday). For small groups a lecture explaining the techniques and history can be arranged with prior contact.

The college puts on regular public performances including a special 10-day arts festival that takes place over December and January. Performances are in the evenings from 6.30 pm. Tickets are available during the day at the Bharta Kalakshetra Auditorium and range from Rs 20 to Rs 100. Entry is through the main gate on the northern side opposite the auditorium.

During the arts festival, many of the mid-range and top-end hotels run free buses to shuttle tourists between Kalakshetra and a number of city locations. Check with any tourist office. If you can't get onto one of these buses, bus No 19M from Parry's Corner will take you to Kalakshetra.

Bars & Nightclubs

Outside the top-end hotels, nightlife in Chennai is pretty tame. In most cases it's early to bed and up at sparrow's fart. The **Hotel Connemara** has a plush bar with plush prices and overamplified music. Beers (Rs 140) are served in gleaming tankards and are presented with a mouth-watering platter of snacks. **Sherry's**, at the Hotel Imperial, is a popular place and attracts a lively bunch of locals. **Maxim's** is a nightclub-cum-dance show at the Hotel Imperial which closes at 11 pm.

For dance, there's the choice of **Gatsby** (☎ 499 4101) at the Park Sheraton, or the **Cyclone** (☎ 853 2211) at the Hotel President but only at weekends and it's best to ring first. The weekend dance party in the bowels of the **Hotel Chandra Towers** is popular with the hip set of Chennai. The music begins to throb at 3 pm every Saturday and Sunday and continues until 10.30 pm. Men will be admitted if accompanied by a woman and there are no restrictions on entry for women. Tickets (per couple) cost Rs 150 but women are often admitted free. The entrance fee includes a bottle of beer.

SHOPPING

For conventional souvenirs, there's a whole range of craft shops and various government emporiums along Anna Salai. The emporiums have more-or-less fixed prices.

continued on page 496

CHENNAI

Permit Rooms

Until the early 1990s, the whole of Tamil Nadu was a 'dry' state. Anyone who wanted an alcoholic drink had to obtain a liquor permit from the tourist office before being allowed to buy a beer from a 'permit room' (bar). These permits were farcical, since they enabled patrons to purchase enough liquor to get cirrhosis of the liver.

Although prohibition has been abolished, the name 'permit room' survives and drinking alcohol in a bar in Tamil Nadu can still leave you with the feeling that you're doing something sinful. Enter a hotel (where most permit rooms, except those in the back of wine shops, are located) and ask for the bar, and unless you're in a five-star hotel, the receptionist will inevitably point down towards the basement where natural light never penetrates, and where the artificial lighting is so dim you could almost believe you're up to no good.

With Tamil Nadu now boasting the highest per-capita consumption of alcohol in the country, the prohibition lobby is stronger than ever. For this reason, you'll find health warnings on beer labels, dry days (such as Gandhi's birthday) and draconian government taxes on alcohol which ensure that the price of a beer in Tamil Nadu is one of the highest in India (over Rs 40).

If you're anywhere near Pondicherry while you're in the south it's worth knowing that part of the French legacy in this Union Territory is a relaxed attitude towards alcohol and beer costs around Rs 20 here.

Southern Music

A performance of Carnatic music involves a singer or a main melody instrument, a secondary melody instrument, one or more drones and one or more percussive instruments. Musical instruments used in a Carnatic performance include:

Veena This stringed instrument has 24 frets and seven strings, which are plucked with the right hand. It is a commonly used melody instrument.

The 24-fretted veena, commonly used to provide melody.

Chitravina (Gottuvadyam) A melody instrument with 21 strings, the chitravina has no frets. The right hand plucks the strings. A piece of wood or plastic is used in the left hand to slide up and down the neck of the instrument, rather like a slide guitar.

Violin, Viola These instruments, used as secondary melody instruments in ensembles, are also popular for solo performances. Like the mandolin and the guitar, they have been adopted from the west but are played in a uniquely Indian way.

Venu This is a side-blown bamboo flute with eight finger holes. Musicians these days also use the clarinet and the saxophone. The venu is commonly used in Carnatic music as a melody instrument.

Nagaswaram Used as a melody instrument, the nagaswaram looks rather like an oboe. It has a double reed and finger holes.

Mridangam This is a double-ended drum capable of producing tones of a definite pitch.

Tabla This double drum is really a North Indian instrument, but it is sometimes used in South Indian music.

Ghatam A clay pot beaten in such a way to produce a variety of hollow sounds.

Morsing A metallic jew's harp used as a drone.

Kanjira A tambourine.

Traditionally a North Indian instrument, the tabla (left) is occasionally played in Carnatic music. The tambora (below left) is used as a drone.

Tambora This is a four-stringed fretless instrument used as a drone. It is sometimes replaced with a *sruti* or hand-pumped harmonium.

Festival of Carnatic Music & Dance

Chennai's Festival of Carnatic Music & Dance, which takes place from mid-December to mid-January, is one of the largest of its kind in the world. It's a celebration of the classical music of South India, with songs in all the main languages – Tamil, Telugu and Kannada. Try to catch a performance if you're around.

At each venue there's usually a lecture and demonstration in the morning, followed by several concerts, each lasting around three hours, in the afternoon and evening. Most concerts start with a *varnam*, an up-tempo introduction. There are then several songs, *kirtis* or *kirtanas*, before the main number. The *raga* is the basis of Carnatic music: five, six or seven notes arranged in ascending or descending scales. There are 72 main ragas and several hundred variations of each, all organised into a complex classification.

Performers to look out for include vocalists KV Narayanaswami, MS Subbulakshmi, T Brinda, Balamurali Krishna, TN Seshagopalan, DK Pattammal and Semmangudi Srinivasier; violinists TN Krishnan, VV Subramanian, MS Gopalkrishnan, Lalgudi Jayaraman and GLR Krishnan; veena players Gayatri and Chittibabu; flautists N Ramani, T Viswanathan and Sikkil Sisters; gottuvadyam player N Ravi Kiran; nagaswaram players Shaik Chinna Moulana Sahib and Namagiripettai; and mridangam players TK Murthy, Palghat Raghu, Vellore Ramabhadran, Umayalpuram Sivaram and TV Gopalkrishnan.

Programs are advertised in the newspapers; it's also worth asking the tourist office for a list of venues.

Kabaddi

The game of kabaddi is rapidly claiming its place alongside cricket, soccer and hockey as a popular sport throughout India. In South India the game is also known as Hu-Tu-Tu and it is especially popular in Tamil Nadu.

Players need no special facilities or equipment, just a good pair of legs and lungs. Kabaddi is similar to a game of 'tag' and it requires two teams of 12 players each. Only seven players from each side can be on the field for any one game. Each team claims a defined space in a marked-out field. This space is known as a court. One player is then selected to cross into the court of the opposing team. The player must move with lightning speed to touch as many opponents as possible while resisting being touched by them. At the same time, the player must hold his or her breath while chanting the word 'kabaddi' at a volume audible to the spectators. Each 'touched' player is declared out. One match consists of 20-minute halves for men and 15-minute halves for women and juniors. Top kabaddi players are able to hold their breath for two to three minutes and the winning team is the one able to get most opponents out within the specified time.

Kabaddi is believed to have originated almost 4000 years ago, possibly in China. But it wasn't until 1951 that a code was established. The Kabaddi Association of India was formed in the same year. In the 1980s an amateur association was established and a series of slightly different codes were developed. Kabaddi has recently gained acceptance at the Asian Games and it has become so popular in Tamil Nadu that major organisations such as railways, banks, bus companies and even post offices are fielding their own workplace teams and staging lunchtime competitions.

continued from page 493

Also on Anna Salai is the Victoria Technical Institute, a rambling old three-storey place selling a range of traditional crafts from hand-made clothing, batik greeting cards and papier-mâché, to elaborately carved statues and furniture. Much of the work supports various development groups. It's closed Sunday, open Monday to Friday 9.30 am to 6 pm and Saturday morning. It accepts credit cards and will export goods.

Another place for quality arts and crafts is the Central Cottage Industries Emporium in Temple Towers, 476 Anna Salai, Nandanam. This store has some interesting displays and a fair range of works from all over India. It is refreshingly free from the pressure to buy often experienced at private stores – so free in fact that the service is seriously under-whelming and you virtually have to plead to be shown specific items. No 18 bus along Anna Salai will drop you here, but you may find it a long way to go for what it offers.

For top-grade silks and cottons, head to either the government-sponsored Hand-loom House, 7 Rattan Bazaar, George Town, or the more expensive India Silk House on Anna Salai.

The Theagaraya Nagar district (known locally as T Nagar) is a great place to shop. Sir Mohamed Usman Rd is particularly exciting. Here eggplants and banana leaves, anklets and underpants vie for position with crafts and cottons, pearls and silks, cows, tailors and pavement artists. Numerous buses frequent this popular shopping area. From Parry's Corner you can take 9, 9B, 10, 10C, 11, 11A, 11D or 11E.

For musical instruments, try AR Dawood & Sons, 286 Triplicane High Rd, not far from the Broadlands Hotel.

GETTING THERE & AWAY

Air

Chennai is an international arrival point and has an important domestic airport. The Anna international airport is well organised and not too busy, making Chennai a good entry or exit point. Next door is the relatively new domestic airport.

A departure tax of Rs 150 is payable for flights from Chennai to Sri Lanka and the Maldives, Rs 500 for other international destinations.

Domestic Airlines Addresses of domestic carriers that fly into Chennai include:

Indian Airlines
(☎ 855 3039; fax 855 5208)
19 Marshalls Rd, Egmore; open Monday to Saturday from 8 am to 8 pm
Jet Airways
(☎ 855 5353)
43 Montieth Rd, Egmore
NEPC Airlines
(☎ 434 4580)
43/44 Montieth Rd, Egmore

International Airlines Addresses of international airlines with offices in Chennai include:

Air Canada
(☎ 826 2409, ☎ 825 0882)
GSA: Jetair, G1/A Apex Plaza,
3 Nungambakkam High Rd
Air France
(☎ 855 4899)
Thapa House, 43/44 Montieth Rd, Egmore
Air India
(☎ 855 4477)
19 Marshalls Rd, Egmore;
open daily from 9.30 am to 1 pm
and 1.45 to 5.30 pm
Air Lanka
(☎ 852 4232)
Mount Chambers, 758 Anna Salai
Air New Zealand
(☎ 822 6149)
GSA: Inter Globe Air Transports,
Malavikas Centre, 144 Kodambakkam High Rd, Nungambakkam

Domestic Flights from Chennai

Destination	Time (hours)	IC	Fare (US$)	D5	Fare (US$)	9W	Fare (US$)
Agatti	3.55			2w	256		
Ahmedabad	3.35	3w	195				
Bangalore	0.45	4d	55	6w	57		
Bhubaneswar	4.20	3w	160				
Calcutta	2.10	10w	180				
Coimbatore	2.00	1d	70	6w	82	1d	73
Delhi	2.45	2d	210			2d	210
Goa	2.30	4w	110				
Hyderabad	1.00	2d	80			1d	80
Kochi (Cochin)	1.35	4w	90	6w	98		
Kozhikode (Calicut)	3.10	10w	70				
Madurai	1.15	4w	70	6w	82		
Mangalore	2.00	4w	80				
Mumbai (Bombay)	1.45	3d	130			3d	139
Port Blair	2.00	3w	175				
Pune	3.00	5w	140			1d	140
Puttaparthi	0.55	2w	55				
Tiruchirappalli (Trichy)	0.45	3w	60				
Tirupathi	0.25	3w	45				
Thiruvananthapuram	1.45	1d	90			1d	90
Visakhapatnam	2.40	3w	90				

* Abbreviations for airlines: IC – Indian Airlines; D5 – NEPC Airlines; 9W – Jet Airways
Note: Air India & Sahara India Airlines also have regular flights to Delhi.
Air India has daily flights to Mumbai.

CHENNAI

Alitalia
(☎ 434 9822)
GSA: Ajanta Travel, 548 Anna Salai
American Airlines
(☎ 826 2409)
GSA: Jetair, G 1/A Apex Plaza,
3 Nungambakkam High Rd
British Airways
(☎ 855 4680)
Alsamall, Khaleeli Centre, Montieth Rd,
Egmore
Cathay Pacific Airways
(☎ 852 2418)
Spencer Plaza, 769 Anna Salai
Gulf Air
(☎ 855 3091)
Indian Red Cross Bldg, 52 Montieth Rd
Iberia Airlines
(☎ 433 0659)
GSA: Stic Travels, Temple Tower,
476 Anna Salai
Japan Airlines
(☎ 852 4832)
GSA: Global Travels, 733 Anna Salai
Jordanian Airlines
(☎ 826 2409)
GSA: Jetair, G 1/A Apex Plaza,
3 Nungambakkam High Rd
KLM – Royal Dutch Airlines
(☎ 852 0123)
Hotel Connemara, Binney Rd
Kuwait Airways
(☎ 855 4111)
Thaper House, 43/44 Montieth Rd, Egmore
Lufthansa Airlines
(☎ 852 5095)
167 Anna Salai
Malaysian Airlines
(☎ 434 9291)
Karumuthu Centre, 498 Anna Salai
Nepal Airways
(☎ 433 0659)
GSA: Stic Travels, Temple Tower,
476 Anna Salai
Philippine Airlines
(☎ 826 2409)
GSA: Jetair, G 1/A Apex Plaza,
3 Nungambakkam High Rd
Qantas Airways
(☎ 827 8680)
G3, Eldorado Bldg, 112 Nungambakkam
High Rd
Saudia
(☎ 434 9666)
GSA: Arafaath Travels,
7 Century Plaza, 560 Anna Salai

Scandinavian Airlines (SAS)
(☎ 822 6149)
GSA: Inter Globe Air Transports, Malavikas
Centre, 144 Kodambakkam High Rd,
Nungambakkam
Singapore Airlines (SIA)
(☎ 852 1871)
West Minster, 108 Dr Radhakrishnan Salai
South Africa
(☎ 822 6149)
GSA: Inter Globe Air Transports, Malavikas
Centre, 144 Kodambakkam High Rd,
Nungambakkam
Swissair
(☎ 852 2541)
191 Anna Salai
Thai
(☎ 822 6149)
GSA: Inter Globe Air Transports, Malavikas
Centre, 144 Kodambakkam High Rd,
Nungambakkam
United Airlines
(☎ 822 6149)
GSA: Inter Globe Air Transports, Malavikas
Centre, 144 Kodambakkam High Rd,
Nungambakkam

International Flights There are flights to
and from Colombo (Air Lanka and Indian
Airlines), Dubai (Air India), Frankfurt (Air
India and Lufthansa), Jakarta (Air India),
Kuala Lumpur (Malaysian Airlines, Air
India and Indian Airlines), Male' (Indian
Airlines), London (British Airways), Penang
(Malaysian Airlines), Riyadh (Saudia), and
Singapore (Singapore Airlines, Malaysian
Airlines, Air India and Indian Airlines).

Bus

The Tamil Nadu state bus company was
called the Thiruvalluvar Transport Corporation (TTC). It was affiliated to the interstate
company Rajiv Gandhi Transport Corporation (RGTC). Now both companies have
been renamed the Tamil Nadu State Transport Corporation (STC) and the bus terminal
is known as the State Express bus terminus
(Division I and Division II). However, you
will find that previous names and local variants are used interchangeably in Chennai and
throughout the state. This can make life quite
challenging! The bus terminal is on Es-

Bus Services from Chennai

Destination	Route No	Frequency (d-daily)	Distance (km)	Travel Time (hours)	Fare (Rs)
Bangalore	831, 828	30d	351	8	85
Chidambaram	300	6d	233	7	45
Kanyakumari	282	9d	700	16	140
Kodaikanal	461	1d	511	12	90
Madurai	135, 137	37d	447	10	95
Mysore	863	2d	497	11	125
Ooty	468, 860	2d	565	15	115
Pondicherry	803, 803F	37d	162	5	30
Rameswaram	166	1d	570	13	95
Thanjavur	323	18d	321	18	60
Tiruchirappalli	123, 124	46d	319	8	60
Tirupathi	902/911	3d	150	4	48
	811/848/863	80d	150	4	48
Thiruvananthapuram	794	6d	752	17	150
Vellore	831, 863	26d	145	4	35

planade Rd in George Town, behind the High Court building. Both intrastate and interstate buses leave from here.

The bus reservation offices are upstairs: intrastate (formerly TTC, ☎ 534 1835) and interstate (formerly RGTC, ☎ 534 1836). They are computerised and open from 4 am to 11 pm daily. There's a Rs 2 reservation fee, and you have to pay Rs 0.25 for the form! See the table 'Bus Services from Chennai' for information on some of the STC bus services.

There is another state bus stand on the west side of Prakasam Rd, the road which flanks the State Express terminal. This terminal is total chaos but an army of boys attach themselves to every foreigner, and for a couple of rupees they'll find your bus.

The main reason to use this stand is for buses to Mamallapuram (Rs 15, two hours). There are a number of services, the most direct being No 188 and 188A/B/D/K (20 times daily). The other Mamallapuram services are Nos 19A, 19C, 119A (via Covelong, 21 times daily) and 108B (via Chennai airport and Chengalpattu, four times daily).

There are also private bus companies with offices opposite Egmore station which run superdeluxe video buses daily to cities such as Bangalore, Coimbatore, Madurai and Trichy. Prices are similar to the state buses, although the private buses tend to be more comfortable.

Train

The reservation office at Central station is on the 1st floor of the Reservation Complex. It's adjacent to the station, on the south side and set back a little from the road. You can also make reservations here for trains originating in most larger cities in the country. For Indian residents, the inquiry counter provides the details required to complete the application form. For visitors, the very helpful Foreign Assistance Tourist Cell deals with Indrail Pass and tourist-quota bookings.

The reservation office (☎ 131, 132, 133) is open Monday to Saturday from 8 am to 2 pm and 2.15 to 8 pm; Sunday from 8 am to 2 pm. At Egmore the booking office is in the station itself, and keeps the same hours as the office at Central station. See the Train Services table for a selection of trains from Chennai.

Boat

Services to the Andaman & Nicobar Islands

Train Services from Chennai

Destination	Train Number & Name	Departure Time	Distance (km)	Duration (hours)	Fare (Rs) (2nd/1st)
Bangalore	2007 *Shatabdi Exp***	6 .00 am MC	356	5.00	370/740
	6007 *Bangalore Mail*	10.00 pm MC		7.00	79/395
Calcutta	2842 *Coromandel Exp*	9.05 am MC	1669	28.00	302/1228
	6004 *Howrah Mail*	10.30 pm MC		32.20	
Coimbatore	2023 *Shatabdi Exp****	3.10 pm MC	494	6.50	565/-
Delhi	2621 *Tamil Nadu Exp*	9.00 pm MC	2194	34.00	341/1495
Hyderabad	7059 *Charminar Exp*	6.10 pm MC	794	14.20	199/736
Kochi (Cochin)	6041 *Alleppey Exp*	7.35 pm MC	700	14.30	181/657
Madurai	6717 *Pandian Exp*	6.45 pm ME	556	11.00	154/554
Mettuppalayam	6605 *Nilgiri Exp*	9.15 pm MC	630	10.00	172/620
Mumbai	1064 *Chennai Exp*	6.40 am MC	1279	24.00	264/1009
	7010 *Mumbai Mail*	10.20 pm MC		30.30	
Mysore	2007 *Shatabdi Exp***	6.00 am MC	500	7.15	142/511
Rameswaram	6713 *Sethu Exp*	5.55 pm ME	656	14.30	175/632
Thanjavur	6153 *Cholan Exp*	9.00 am ME	351	9.30	79/395
Tiruchirappalli	2635 *Vaigai Exp*	12.50 pm MC	337	5.50	76/378
Tirupathi	6057 *Saptagiri Exp*	6.25 am MC	147	2.45	38/200
Trivandrum	6319 *Trivandrum Mail*	6.55 pm MC	921	16.45	220/775
Varanasi	6039 *Ganga Kaveri Exp*	5.30 pm MC	2144	39.00	341/1495

Abbreviation for railway stations: MC – Madras Central; ME – Madras Egmore
** Air-con only; fare includes meals and drinks
*** Not Wednesday; air-con only; fare includes meals and drinks

are prone to change, so inquire about the latest schedules. There is currently one boat, the MV *Nancowry*, which sails from Chennai every 10 or so days to Port Blair (60 hours), administrative capital of the Andamans. Once a month, the boat sails via Car Nicobar. This voyage takes an extra two days; foreign nationals are not allowed to disembark at Car Nicobar. Foreigners are also not allowed to travel on the boat between May and August.

Cabin fares per person are Rs 3450 (deluxe cabin, two-berth), Rs 2852 (A-class cabin, usually two berth) and Rs 2243 (B-class cabin, four to six berth). There's also a 'bunk class' for Rs 955 per person. Meals are available on board for about Rs 100 per day. Some bedding is supplied but you should carry at least a sleeping sheet.

Tickets are issued at the Directorate of Shipping Services (☎ 522 6873), 6 Rajaji Salai (opposite the Customs House, in the little office by Gate No 5) in George Town. Foreigners must get a permit for the islands before they buy a boat ticket (see Visa Extensions & Permits under Information at the start of this chapter).

If you need a shipping agent, try Hapag Lloyd (☎ 522 9282), 37 Rajaji Salai, George Town.

GETTING AROUND
To/From the Airport
The domestic and international terminals are 16km south of the city centre. The cheapest way to reach them is by suburban train from Egmore to Tirusulam, which is only about 500m across the road from the terminals. The trains run from 4.15 am until 11.45 pm, the journey takes about 40 minutes, and the fare is Rs 6/80 in 2nd/1st class. These trains are not overly crowded, except during peak hours.

Public buses are not such a good bet, particularly if you've got a lot of luggage. Nos 18J, 52, 52A/B/C/D and 55A all start and finish at Parry's Corner and go along Anna Salai.

There is also an airport bus. It leaves from outside the Hotel Chandra Towers, near Egmore station, and stops at the domestic and international airports.

The airport bus is purple and easy to spot. It runs every 30 minutes (or about every 45 minutes when not busy, which is often); departure times are available at the booth, opposite Egmore station. Prior bookings are not possible.

There's also a minibus service for Rs 80 (Rs 50 during the day) between the airport and the major hotels (it also drops at Broadlands) but it's a slow way to get into town because of the number of stops it makes. The booking counter is next to the taxi counters at the international terminal.

If the booking counter is closed, the taxi drivers will try to tell you the service is no longer running; the bus should nevertheless be waiting outside and you can pay on board.

An auto-rickshaw to the airport costs Rs 70 by the meter but since all drivers refuse to use meters on this journey you'll need to haggle hard to pay anywhere near this. About Rs 100/150 for a day/night trip is what they'll normally charge.

A yellow-and-black taxi costs Rs 200. At the airport itself, you can buy a ticket for a taxi ride into the city for Rs 200 to Rs 250 (depending on the distance) at the pre-paid taxi kiosk inside the international terminal. There's also a pre-paid kiosk in the baggage collection area inside the domestic terminal – it's about 10% cheaper.

Bus

The bus system in Chennai is run by the newly named Metropolitan Transport Corporation (MTC). It's less overburdened than those in the other large Indian cities, although peak hour is still best avoided.

The seats on the left-hand side and the rear seat of buses are generally reserved for women. Some useful routes include:

Nos 16, 23C, 27, 27B, 27D, 29, & 29A
   Egmore (opposite People's Lodge) to Anna Salai
Nos 31, 32 & 32A
   Triplicane High Rd (Broadlands) to Central station and Parry's Corner. The No 31 continues on to Rajaji Salai (for the GPO and the Directorate of Shipping Services)
Nos 22, 27B & 29A
   Egmore to Wallajah Rd (for Broadlands)
Nos 9, 9A, 9B, 10, 17D, 17E, 17K
   Parry's Corner to Central and Egmore stations
Nos 11, 11A, 11B, 11D, 17A, 18 & 18J
   Parry's Corner to Anna Salai

Train

The suburban train is an excellent way to get between Egmore and Central station (Rs 2), Egmore and George Town (Rs 2), to Guindy (Rs 4) or the airport (Rs 4). There are relatively uncrowded ladies' compartments.

Motorcycle

If you're feeling brave you can hire a moped from U-Rent (☎ 567398) at the Picnic Hotel, 1132 Periyar EVR High Rd.

U-Rent charges Rs 150 per day but a year's membership of their rental scheme is also required (Rs 250). Helmets and insurance are mandatory and cost Rs 25 each per day. An international driving licence is generally needed but they may accept your home-country licence.

Taxi

Rates are Rs 25 for the first 1.5km and Rs 4 for each kilometre after that. Most drivers will try to quote you a fixed price rather than use the meter, so negotiate.

If you're really pushed for time you may like to hire a tourist taxi. For Rs 700 for a full day (Rs 350 for a half day) you'll get your own private guided tour. These tours may be booked from any travel agency.

Auto-Rickshaw

On the meter it's Rs 7 for the first kilometre, then Rs 2.50 per kilometre. Again, persuasion may be required before drivers will use the meter. There's a pre-paid booth outside Central station.

Car Hire

Almost without exception, car hire means you hire the car with a driver. Many of the mid-range and top-end hotels have travel desks which can arrange car hire. It's wise to use a travel agent approved by the Government of India Tourist Office. Rates can vary but a general guide for travelling within the city is Rs 800 per day (eight hours). For travelling outstation (beyond the city limits) costs are Rs 5 per kilometre (Rs 7 with aircon) with a minimum of 250km per day. Driver fees (for food and accommodation) are often additional, up to Rs 125 per day.

Around Chennai

PULICAT LAKE

Just over the border in Andhra Pradesh, huge Pulicat Lake is definitely worth exploring, and thankfully hasn't been developed. It has long, quiet beaches and a lake for fishing, boating and hiking, but you will have to arrange everything yourself. The best way to explore the lake is to rent a boat, and boatman, from Therunattam or Sullurpet for a few days. The Forest Department in Chennai has boats at several places around the lake. You can rent these, but you should take your own fuel. Camping around the lake region is possible if you can find somewhere secluded. If you have cooking equipment, you could buy fish for your meals.

The most accessible point is Therunattam, the village on the northern side of the inlet. It has a long beach, and you can climb the **lighthouse** if the keeper allows you in.

Getting There & Away

A direct bus leaves infrequently from the Broadway stand, a few hundred metres from Tamil Nadu state bus stand, but it's far easier to catch a local train to Ponneri (one hour) from Central station. Take any train heading towards Gummidipundi or Sullurpet; they leave at least every hour. Tickets costs Rs 7/70 in 2nd/1st class. From Ponneri, walk to the bus stand (ask directions) and catch the old bus which leaves about every 20 minutes to Pulicat village (Rs 4, 30 minutes). From the end of the main street in Pulicat, boats leave every few minutes to Therunattam.

OUTDOOR ACTIVITIES

There are good watersports and trekking opportunities not far from Chennai.

Watersports

The best places are: Muttukadu Beach, 30km south of Chennai and easily accessible by local bus; Kovalam, (also known as Covelong), 38km south of Chennai, off the main road to Mamallapuram (easy to reach by local bus); and Pulicat Lake.

Winter (December to February) is the best season for all watersports.

Rippling Grove (☎ 04114-45469) is a camp site beautifully set on Muttukadu Lagoon. Comfortable tents cost Rs 450 for a double and Rs 300 for a smaller tent with shared facilities. The price includes food. Canoes/windsurfers cost Rs 75/150 per hour, and you can hire equipment even if you aren't staying here. The entrance is in the village of Sholinganallur, along Mamallapuram Rd. For bookings, contact Sylvan Retreats (see Trekking Agencies).

Fisherman's Cove (☎ 04114-44304; fax 44303) is an upmarket resort on pleasant Kovalam Beach. Accommodation costs from US$110/125 a single/double, and hiring catamarans and windsurfers is also expensive.

Fishing

There is little set up for visitors, and nowhere to hire equipment in Chennnai, but if you have your own gear you can always go to a fishing village and rent a boat (and boatman) to run along some of the backwaters, such as Ennore (18km north of Chennai and easy to reach by local train), Kovalam and Pulicat Lake.

Swimming

If Marina Beach is too crowded, you could try Elliot Beach, 12km south, which has a few cafes nearby. Further south are excellent, quieter beaches at Muttukadu and Kovalam. For a completely unspoilt beach, head for Therunattam, on Pulicat Lake.

Ennore is promoted as a swimming beach in local brochures, but the area is now industrialised and polluted so give it a miss.

Trekking & Rock Climbing

Avoid mid-summer and the monsoons for these activities.

You can get information, guides and equipment from the trekking agencies listed below. Guides (but not equipment) should be available in major towns in the trekking areas. The most popular place in Tamil Nadu for outdoor activities is the Nilgiris (see the Nilgiris section in the Tamil Nadu chapter).

Where to Go Discreet camping is allowed in these places. No permits are required but guides are recommended.

Elagiri Hills (Javadi Hills)
A great three-day hike taking in the tribal villages of Samiyar Mulai and Athanavur, Muruyan Temple and Jalagamparai Falls. Start in Vaniyampadi, along a main road and train line from Chennai. These hills are great for rock climbing.
Gudiyam Caves
These caves were probably inhabited 30,000 years ago, but are now home to bees and bats. The small lake nearby is perfect for a picnic. The caves and lake are near Pondi, not far from Tiruvellore, and easily accessible by any train or bus heading towards Vellore. You don't need a guide, if you don't mind asking for directions.
Kambakkam
This is a popular place for birdlife, waterfalls, and rock climbing although industrialisation has spoiled the serenity a little. The rock faces are steep, so equipment and experience is required. It is close to Varadayyapalaiyam in the Nagari Hills, just over the border of Andhra Pradesh. Take the bus to Sullurpet, and get a connection to Varadayyapalaiyam.
Kolli Hills
The Kolli Hills are a fair way from Chennai, but another great three-day hike with inspiring views, tribal culture, temples and little rain. Starting from Namakkal (take the train to

Salem, and a local bus to Namakkal), hike to Sendamangalam village, then to Agasa Kangaii waterfall and up Mt Chethuragiri (1356m), finishing in Tammampatti.
Kovalam to Mamallapuram
This is a popular 20km hike along the beach. You can camp or stay at any resort overnight along the way.

Trekking Agencies To arrange trekking or other outdoor activities near Chennai (or anywhere else in Tamil Nadu) or to hire equipment, the following trekking agencies are worth contacting:

Sylvan Restreats & Trails
(☎ 491 2947; fax 491 8747) T29/B, VII Avenue, Besant Nagar, Chennai 600 090.
Wildertrails Adventure Club
(☎ 644 2729; fax 644 2499) 26 Thirunarayana, Kilpauk, Chennai 600 010. This outfit arranges rock climbing, trekking and camping trips for locals but travellers are welcome.
Youth Hostels Association
(Tamil Nadu Branch, ☎ 489 0976) E-1, 56th St, Ashok Nagar, Chennai 600 083 or contact the Youth Hostel, Indira Nagar, Chennai (see Chennai Places to Stay for details). Part of the India-wide National Adventure Foundation, this branch of the YHA is well organised, has an extensive range of outdoor equipment for hire and organises trips all over Tamil Nadu at reasonable rates.

Guides & Porters Be careful if you choose to hire a guide yourself as he may not be as knowledgeable about the trails and local attractions as you had hoped. Expect to pay about Rs 150 per day plus a little more if you expect him to carry any equipment or do any cooking. You must also pay for his travel costs and food. Porters will cost about Rs 100 per day, and can usually be found by your guide, but most trails are fairly gentle and short, so you will probably end up carrying your own stuff anyway.

Most guides will speak English, so get the details about agreed prices on paper, and have both parties sign the 'contract' before and after the trip. Guides and porters will expect a tip, and if you feel inclined, about 10% is fairly standard.

CHENNAI

Tamil Nadu

Tamil Nadu is the land of the Tamils. In the southernmost part of India, its location and land formations have spared it many of the brutal invasions that have shaped so much of the north. While its history is not without incursions and conflict, the people of Tamil Nadu have existed in comparative peace and isolation. As such the area has been largely free to develop and foster continuing traditions. It is often referred to as the cradle of Dravidian culture, a culture distinguished by its unique languages, belief systems and customs. It is one of the oldest continuous cultures in existence. The icons of this ancient culture are everywhere; they are the huge temples with their towering gateways (*gopurams*), the intricate rock carvings, the evocative music and, of course, the complex classical dance.

The landforms of Tamil Nadu have not only deterred intruders; they have inspired its people to designate particular places to celebrate events of significance. These places are the ancient pilgrimage sites that for centuries have witnessed a continual flow of devotees. They include Kanchipuram, Chidambaram, Kumbakonam, Tiruchirappalli, Thanjavur, Madurai, Kanyakumari and Rameswaram. These names are certainly on the tourist map of Tamil Nadu, but it is their significance as potent contours of the cultural map that guides pilgrims in their celebration of the land and its legends.

To the east, Tamil Nadu is surrounded by ocean – the Bay of Bengal. Its western border with Kerala is flanked by the Western Ghats with their rugged hills and unique biosphere. To the north is the extensive Deccan Plateau. The major river, the Cauvery, rises in the Western Ghats and dissects the state as it flows east, entering the sea at the ancient port of Poompuhar, some 340km south of Chennai. Tamil Nadu contains the most southerly point of the mainland – Kanyakumari; a point where the Arabian Sea, the Indian Ocean and the Bay of Bengal

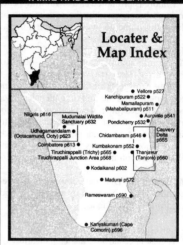

TAMIL NADU AT A GLANCE

Locater & Map Index

Vellore p527
Kanchipuram p522
Mamallapuram (Mahabalipuram) p511
Nilgiris p616
Mudumalai Wildlife Sanctuary p632
Auroville p541
Pondicherry p532
Udhagamandalam (Ootacamund, Ooty) p623
Chidambaram p546
Cauvery Delta p555
Coimbatore p613
Kumbakonam p552
Tiruchirappalli (Trichy) p565
Tiruchirappalli Junction Area p568
Thanjavur (Tanjore) p560
Kodaikanal p602
Madurai p572
Rameswaram p590
Kanyakumari (Cape Comorin) p596

Population: 61.5 million
Area: 130,069 sq km
Capital: Chennai (Madras)
Main Language: Tamil
Best Time to Go: November to February; the hills are generally good year-round.

Highlights

- Temple towns, Madurai in particular
- Mamallapuram's rock-cut temples and beach
- Kodaikanal – peaceful hill station
- The former French colony of Pondicherry

Festivals

Some of Tamil Nadu's biggest and brightest festivals include the *Mamallapuram Dance Festival* (Mamallapuram, January) and the 10-day *Temple Car Festivals* at Chidambaram (April/May, December/January)

For a complete list of festivals, see the table at the end of the chapter.

merge and from where one can symbolically regard all that is India.

Though highly industrialised, Tamil Nadu is not an urban state: most of its people are farmers and live in its 60,000 villages.

It is a land rich in history and legend; a land where poetry, dance and music have flourished and where temple rituals celebrate such art forms. Almost every inch of its land rings with the stories of its past. Its monuments and rituals give expression to these stories.

The coastline has beach resorts and delightful fishing villages. Mountain towns, such as Udhagamandalam (better known as Ooty) and Kodaikanal, provide a cool haven and welcome respite from the hot summer months. National parks offer much unique flora and the chance to glimpse a wild elephant or, more rarely, a tiger.

Budget accommodation is plentiful but mid-range and upmarket hotels in Tamil Nadu attract a hefty hotel tax, currently among the highest in the country. It's 15% on rooms costing between Rs 100 and Rs 199, and 20% for anything above. The top hotels will also add another 5% to 10% service charge.

Tamil cuisine is representative of one of the oldest continuously vegetarian cultures in the world. Breads, dosas (crispy-soft pancakes served with chutneys, sambars, rasams, spices and vegetables), and idlis (steamed rice dumplings) are some of the specialities. Sweets are a favourite, and here in the south coffee is just as popular as tea.

Meals are regularly served on banana leaves (the perfect picnic plate) and eaten with the hand (always the right hand). Foreign visitors will usually be offered cutlery, but the full sensual experience of a hands-on meal shouldn't be missed. A tolerant society, Tamil Nadu has accepted the opening of many nonvegetarian eating places and has even incorporated its own brand of yuppiedom – meat-eating! All Tamil Nadu food is great value and of consistently good quality.

Unfortunately, you'll rarely have the same pleasure drinking alcohol (to find out why, see the boxed text on Permit Rooms in the Chennai chapter) and, if you like a beer with your meal, it's good to remember that many nonvegetarian restaurants will serve alcohol while exclusively vegetarian restaurants will not.

To say that Tamil Nadu is a state rich in myth and legend would be a clear understatement. This is a state where myth and legend continue to shape its very consciousness. For tourists Tamil Nadu is not a state of beach resorts and theme parks, though these can be found if you look for them. It is a state where the ancient past continues to shape a dynamic present. As such, it is a state of temples and pilgrims, of music and dance and of stories told and retold.

Tamil Nadu has catered for pilgrims and visitors for many centuries. It's a relaxed state, where exciting cuisines, ample services and transport systems make travel easy and enjoyable.

HISTORY

Tamil Nadu is the home of the Tamils and their Dravidian culture. It is not known exactly from where or when the original Dravidians came. Human activity in the area now known as Tamil Nadu may have begun as early as 300,000 years ago. There is speculation that the first Dravidians were part of early Indus civilisations and came south after invasions in the north from 1500 BC. By 1200 BC, a civilisation distinguished by huge stone monuments and sculptures existed in South India. The people shared cultural characteristics with people from the ancient Middle East. It may be that these people were the descendants of emigrants from the Middle East to South India via the north or that they migrated directly by sea. It is from these people, with their unique languages and customs, that Dravidian culture emerged.

Over the centuries vital trade links were established with the Greeks and Romans, where commodities such as spices, cotton, sandalwood, ginger, rice and pearls were exported.

By the 4th century BC three major dynasties had taken power in the area. The Cholas and Pandyas governed in the east while the Cheras ruled in the area now known as Kerala and the south-western part of Tamil Nadu. Under these jurisdictions Hinduism burgeoned and artistic pursuits prospered. Art forms such as music, dance and poetry were part of religious practice. They celebrated life, productivity and abundance. Society was organised around the monarch and a set of ethical guidelines. This period, and for some three centuries after the birth of Christ, was the classical period of Tamil literature – the Sangam Age – which produced the influential Poet's Establishment at Madurai.

The domains of these three dynasties changed many times over the succeeding centuries. Their continual struggles for supremacy led to loss or extensions of their power base. An overthrown dynasty sometimes regained its authority at a later stage and sometimes in a different area. At times the conqueror was an external power. The Pallava dynasty, who were to base their capital at Kanchipuram, were influential particularly in the 7th and 8th centuries when they constructed many of the temples and monuments at Mamallapuram. Although all these dynasties engaged in continual skirmishes, their steady patronage of literature, architecture and the performing arts was to consolidate and expand the Dravidian civilisation, with its Hindu belief systems and customs.

In the 13th century, with threats of Muslim invasions from the north, the southern Hindu dynasties combined to thwart their northern assailant. The Muslims were defeated and the empire of Vijayanagar, which incorporated all of South India, was firmly established. The Vijayanagaras were keen patrons of the arts and under their authority existing monuments were restored and new ones were established. However, in the 16th century, the Vijayanagar Empire began to weaken. By the 17th century South India was ruled by various provincial leaders, most notably the Nayaks, who continued the development of monumental architectural works.

In 1640, however, the British, under the auspices of the British East India Company, negotiated the use of Madraspatnam (now Chennai) as a trading post. Subsequent interest on the part of the French, Dutch and Danes led to continual conflict and finally almost total domination by the British. Small pocketed areas – Pondicherry and Karaikal – remained under French control. Under British colonial rule most of South India, including the area now known as Tamil Nadu, was integrated into the region called the Madras Presidency.

Increased dissatisfaction with colonial rule and a strong desire for an independent India developed. Many Tamil people played a significant part in the struggle which finally achieved success in 1947. With the establishment of Andhra Pradesh in 1956, the Madras Presidency was disbanded and Tamil Nadu was established as an autonomous state.

Northern Tamil Nadu

The coast road from Chennai to Mamallapuram is dotted with several beach resorts, big theme parks, recreation areas and artists' communities.

ARTISTS' VILLAGES

A few kilometres south of Chennai are two very different artists' communities, one nurturing contemporary arts and the other traditional arts. Both encourage visitors. **Cholamandal Artists' Village** (☎ 492-6092) is 18km from Chennai along the coast road. Set on 3½ hectares of land, this is an independent community of about 30 artisans dedicated to the practice and development of contemporary art. Since its establishment in 1965, the community has battled numerous obstacles to enhance the acceptance of contemporary Indian art. Some of the original artists still live here and many younger ones enjoy short-term residencies before moving to other cities to establish similar communities. There is a gallery with fine paintings

Old Arts & New

Cholamandal In a culture steeped in ancient tradition and mythology, the acceptance of contemporary art has not been easy. While many Indian artists today seek to sustain the age-old traditions, others have sought new forms of expressions and new venues for their creative restlessness. This is how the artists' village of Cholamandal came into being in the mid-1960s.

The idea that a group of artists from the traditional Madras School of Arts and Crafts would purchase land from the sales of craft work in order to set up a place for artistic experimentation seemed outrageous. But this is exactly what happened. The artist Sri KCS Paniker was one of the instigators. Through sheer tenacity he was able to convince no less than 40 fellow painters and sculptors to join him in what he termed a search for 'a contemporary expression of the Indian spirit'.

In its early days the community faced seemingly insurmountable battles. A cyclone destroyed some of the first dwellings and a lack of infrastructure added to transport and communication difficulties. The greatest hurdle, however, was the entrenched attitudes of the establishment. The artists were regarded as renegades for turning their back on tradition and they were subsequently ostracised from much mainstream activity. For many of the artists, such controversy simply strengthened their resolve to generate a form of expression beyond the established comfort zone.

Today Cholamandal is firmly established as a community where artistic expression (which is clearly derivative of both Asian and European tradition) is pushed beyond the bounds of convention.

Dakshinachitra This four hectare site is referred to by local media as an architectural collage of South India. It's a sort of living museum that aims to preserve and promote the arts, crafts and folk traditions of Tamil Nadu, Andhra Pradesh, Karnataka and Kerala.

Many of the traditional buildings on the site have been translocated from villages around the southern states that were scheduled for demolition to make way for modern developments. At Dakshinachitra the structures have been painstakingly reassembled, complete with internal fittings, artefacts and practising artisans.

The Madras Craft Foundation is the driving force behind Dakshinachitra. Motivated by the rapid urbanisation of India and the consequential threat to traditional arts and crafts, members of the foundation wanted to establish a living showcase of village life. In particular, they have sought to reveal the interconnectedness of architecture, environment and artistic expression. Not only have they succeeded in generating a strong sense of authenticity that pays homage to the rich traditions of the region, they have also created a catalyst that is helping to rekindle certain artistic practices.

Dakshinachitra is much more than a museum. It is a living reminder not only of what has been, but also of what can be.

and sculptures (many of the paintings appear derivative of a synthesis of classical European and Indian art). Unframed as well as framed pictures are available (prices vary from Rs 2500 to Rs 25,000 and above). Credit cards are accepted.

Visitors can roam through the complex, enjoy the sculpture garden and engage with artists in their studios. Those with a serious interest in contemporary art can stay in the community at the *Cholamandal Guest House*. This rambling dwelling with a balcony facing the Bay of Bengal contains work studios as well as self-catering facilities. Only non air-con rooms are available and the cost is Rs 175. Preference is given to practising artists. Indian artists are eligible to apply for an 11 month residency to further their skills.

Entry to the village is free and it is open every day from 10 am to 7 pm. From Chennai catch city bus No 19, 19S, 19R, 19RR or 51RR.

About 12km further south from Cholamandal is the arts and crafts village called **Dakshinachitra** (☎ 091-04114). The name means 'Vision of the South' and that's exactly what this ambitious project of the Madras Craft Foundation offers (see the boxed text). The village is a showcase of traditional art, craft, architecture and lifestyle from the four states of South India. The carefully reconstructed 19th century dwellings authentically convey aspects of traditional village life. The artisans who live and work in the complex produce high quality ceramics, glass and sculpture. The Tamil Nadu section has an excellent display on the evolution of the Tamil language.

The complex also has an amphitheatre in which performances of classical dance are staged, and an archival library for research. So far, the Tamil Nadu and Keralan sections have been completed. Andhra Pradesh and Karnataka are expected to be finished within three years.

Although it has a certain museum feel to it, this place is definitely worth a visit. A one hour tour costs Rs 50 for locals and Rs 175 for foreigners. If you have a student card you can enter for Rs 25. Entry for children is Rs 10. The village is open every day except Tuesday. Many of the artisans' products are on sale in the shop, shipping can be arranged, and credit cards are accepted. Further information is available in Chennai from the Madras Craft Foundation (☎ 044-491 8943; fax 434 0149). Bus Nos 19 and 49 from Chennai call frequently at Dakshinachitra.

OTHER COASTAL ATTRACTIONS
Muthukadu
The **Boat House**, operated by the TNTDC, is an ideal spot for picnics, boating and other water sports including windsurfing and canoeing. It's just 500m north of Dakshinachitra.

Kovalam, also known as Covelong, is a fishing settlement with a fine beach, 38km south of Chennai. This is the site of a large historic fort, where goats meander through the ruins. The rest of the site has been converted into the Taj Group's luxurious *Fisherman's Cove Resort* (☎ 04114-44304).

Locals delight in saying that Queen Elizabeth II stayed here on her 1997 India tour. The rooms are priced from US$105/115, and sea-facing cottages from US$150 (all plus 30% tax).

The Little Folks (☎ 04114-46270), some 40km south of Chennai, is a children's theme park which contains a range of rides, a toy train, water slides, and picnic areas.

Further south and just 15km before Mamallapuram is the **Crocodile Bank**. This successful breeding farm was set up to augment the crocodile populations of India's wildlife sanctuaries. Visitors are welcome and you can see crocs and alligators of all sizes as well as turtles. The crocs eat many things including rats captured by the Irula people, indigenous inhabitants of Chengalpattu District (see the boxed text 'The Rat Catchers' in the Chennai chapter).

Numerous signs instruct that alligators can stay under water for six hours without coming up for air, and that crocs are more closely related to birds than to lizards or snakes! There's also a **Snake Farm** where antivenene is produced.

You can get to the Crocodile Bank by bicycle or on the 119A bus from Chennai. It's open daily except Tuesday from 8.30 am to 5.30 pm, but it's best to be there during the feeding frenzy (4.30 pm on weekends). Entrance fees are Rs 10 plus Rs 20 if you want to see the feeding. Entry to the Snake Farm is a further Rs 4. Photography is Rs 10 for still cameras and Rs 75 for videos. The Snake Farm opens an hour later and closes an hour earlier than the Crocodile Bank.

MAMALLAPURAM (Mahabalipuram)
Pop: 13,300 Tel Area Code: 04114
Mamallapuram is famous for its shore temple. It was the second capital and seaport of the Pallava kings of Kanchipuram, the first Tamil dynasty of any real consequence to emerge after the fall of the Gupta Empire.

Though the dynasty's origins are lost in the mists of legend, it was apparently at the height of its political power and artistic creativity between the 5th and 8th centuries AD,

TAMIL NADU

during which time the Pallava kings established themselves as the arbiters and patrons of early Tamil culture. Most of the temples and rock carvings here were completed during the reigns of Narasimha Varman I (630-68) and Narasimha Varman II (700-28). Narasimha Varman I was also known as Mahamalla, the great wrestler. It is from him that Mamallapuram derives its name.

The rock carvings at Mamallapuram are notable for the delightful freshness and simplicity of their folk-art origins, in contrast to the more grandiose monuments built by later larger empires such as the Cholas. The shore temple in particular strikes a very romantic theme and is one of the most photographed monuments in India. It, and all the other places of interest in Mamallapuram, are floodlit each night.

The wealth of the Pallava kingdom was based on agriculture (as opposed to pastoralism) and the increased taxation and produce which could be attained through this settled lifestyle. The early Pallava kings were followers of the Jain religion, but the conversion of Mahendra Varman I (600-30) to Shaivism, by the saint Appar, was to have disastrous effects on the future of Jainism in Tamil Nadu, and explains why most temples at Mamallapuram (and Kanchipuram) are dedicated to either Shiva or Vishnu.

The sculpture here is particularly interesting because it shows scenes of day-to-day life – women milking buffaloes, pompous city dignitaries, young girls primping and posing at street corners or swinging their hips in artful come-ons. In contrast, other carvings throughout the state depict mostly gods and goddesses, with images of ordinary folk conspicuous by their absence.

Stone carving is still very much a living craft in Mamallapuram, as a visit to any of the scores of sculpture workshops in and around town will testify. Many of the artisans (there are approximately 200 of them) line the streets as they chisel away from dawn to beyond dusk. Some make a good living with lucrative export contracts. In fact Mamallapuram is now famous for its sculptors.

Positioned at the foot of a low-lying, boulder-strewn hill where most of the temples and rock carvings are to be found, Mamallapuram is a pleasant little village and very much a travellers' haunt. This is one of the more westernised towns on the northern Tamil Nadu coast. It is especially popular with young backpackers and also with the middle classes of Chennai who use it as a weekend and holiday retreat. Prices in this town match its popularity.

Mamallapuram has an excellent combination of cheap accommodation, mellow restaurants catering to western tastes, a good beach, handicrafts shops *and* the fascinating remains of an ancient Indian kingdom. Accommodation is very tight in January during the Mamallapuram Dance Festival.

Orientation & Information

Some 50km south of Chennai, Mamallapuram covers an area of approximately eight sq km. It's easy to get around and visit the many places of interest.

The tourist office (☎ 42232) is in East Raja St (also known as Covelong Rd), on the way into Mamallapuram from Chennai. It has a range of leaflets as well as information on bus and train times. It's open daily from 9.45 am to 5.45 pm. You'll need to be persistent to obtain brochures, which are all stored beneath the counters.

You can change most travellers cheques at the Indian Overseas Bank on Tirukkalikundram Rd. It is open on weekdays from 10 am to 2 pm and Saturday until noon. You can also change travellers cheques (10 am to 6 pm, no commission) at the Foreign Exchange Bureau in East Raja St.

The post office is down a lane just east of the tourist office.

If you need a doctor, Dr Gladys Indhira has been recommended. Her surgery is behind Arafath Medicals, near the Indian Overseas Bank.

For information on the area's various sites visit the Archaeological Survey of India, next to the museum in East Raja St. Staff will not only provide information but also offer a free guided tour. Just down from

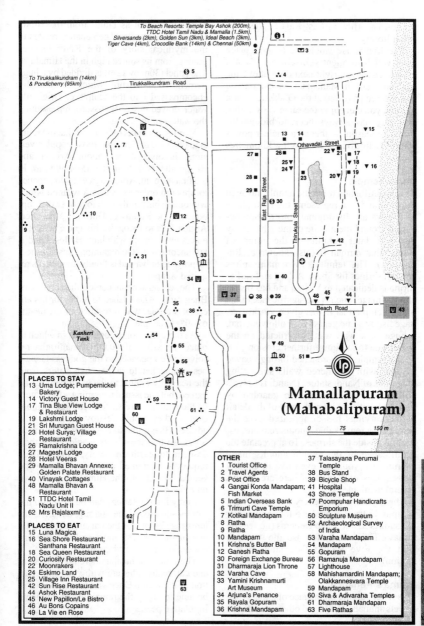

To Beach Resorts: Temple Bay Ashok (200m),
TTDC Hotel Tamil Nadu & Mamalla (1.5km),
Silversands (2km), Golden Sun (3km), Ideal Beach (3km),
Tiger Cave (4km), Crocodile Bank (14km) & Chennai (50km)

To Tirukkalikundram (14km)
& Pondicherry (95km)

Tirukkalikundram Road

Othavadai Street

East Raja Street

Thirukula Street

Beach Road

Kanheri Tank

Mamallapuram (Mahabalipuram)

0   75   150 m

PLACES TO STAY
13 Uma Lodge; Pumpernickel Bakery
14 Victory Guest House
17 Tina Blue View Lodge & Restaurant
19 Lakshmi Lodge
21 Sri Murugan Guest House
23 Hotel Surya; Village Restaurant
26 Ramakrishna Lodge
27 Magesh Lodge
28 Hotel Veeras
29 Mamalla Bhavan Annexe; Golden Palate Restaurant
40 Vinayak Cottages
48 Mamalla Bhavan & Restaurant
51 TTDC Hotel Tamil Nadu Unit II
62 Mrs Rajalaxmi's

PLACES TO EAT
15 Luna Magica
16 Sea Shore Restaurant; Santhana Restaurant
18 Sea Queen Restaurant
20 Curiosity Restaurant
22 Moonrakers
24 Eskimo Land
25 Village Inn Restaurant
42 Sun Rise Restaurant
44 Ashok Restaurant
45 New Papillon/Le Bistro
46 Au Bons Copains
49 La Vie en Rose

OTHER
1 Tourist Office
2 Travel Agents
3 Post Office
4 Gangai Konda Mandapam; Fish Market
5 Indian Overseas Bank
6 Trimurti Cave Temple
7 Kotikal Mandapam
8 Ratha
9 Ratha
10 Mandapam
11 Krishna's Butter Ball
12 Ganesh Ratha
30 Foreign Exchange Bureau
31 Dharmaraja Lion Throne
32 Varaha Cave
33 Yamini Krishnamurti Art Museum
34 Arjuna's Penance
35 Rayala Gopuram
36 Krishna Mandapam

37 Talasayana Perumai Temple
38 Bus Stand
39 Bicycle Shop
41 Hospital
43 Shore Temple
47 Poompuhar Handicrafts Emporium
50 Sculpture Museum
52 Archaeological Survey of India
53 Varaha Mandapam
54 Mandapam
55 Gopuram
56 Ramanuja Mandapam
57 Lighthouse
58 Mahishamardini Mandapam; Olakkannesvara Temple
59 Mandapam
60 Siva & Adivaraha Temples
61 Dharmaraja Mandapam
63 Five Rathas

TAMIL NADU

the tourist office in East Raja St there's a small library.

The lighthouse would be a good place from which to orient yourself, but it's still closed. However, right next door above the Mahishamardini Mandapam (a *mandapam* is a pillared pavilion) at the Olakkannesvara Temple you can enjoy the same views. Photography has always been forbidden for 'security reasons' – there's a nuclear power station visible on the coast, a few kilometres south.

Shore Temple

This beautiful and romantic temple, ravaged by wind and sea, represents the final phase of Pallava art. Its original construction occurred around the middle of the 7th centruy but was later rebuilt in the reign of Narasimha Varman II (also known as Rajasimha). The temple's two main spires contain shrines for Shiva. A third and earlier shrine is dedicated to Vishnu and has his reclining image. Such is the significance of the Shore Temple that it was given World Heritage listing some years ago. Following that, a huge rock wall was constructed on the ocean side to minimise further erosion.

The temple is approached through paved gardens with weathered walls supporting long lines of Nandi statues (Nandi is Shiva's bull vehicle). Entrances are guarded by mythical deities. Although most of the detail of the carvings has disappeared over the centuries, a remarkable amount remains, especially inside the shrines. To appreciate the significance of the temple and its many adornments, you may even like to employ the services of a guide. There are always several available.

The temple is open every day from 9 am to 5 pm. Entry fees are Rs 5 for people over 15, and Rs 25 for video cameras (no fees on Friday). The entrance fee also allows you to visit the Five Rathas (see later in this section).

Arjuna's Penance

This relief carving on the face of a huge rock depicts animals, deities and other semi-divine creatures as well as fables from the Hindu *Panchatantra* books. The penance relates to the mythical story of the River Ganges issuing from its source high in the Himalaya. The panel (30m by 12m) is divided by a huge perpendicular fissure which is skilfully encompassed into the sculpture. Originally water flowed down the fissure, representing the waters of the Ganges.

Varying accounts exist as to what the relief actually means. The two most popular versions involve stories about Arjuna and Bhagiratha, both from the *Mahabharata*. In the first account, Arjuna agrees to do penance to Shiva in order to receive a weapon which will obtain his family's victory over their opponents, the Kauravas. During his penance, Arjuna fails to recognise his god Shiva, and enters into combat with him. He loses and is left unconscious. On regaining consciousness he prays to Shiva and is finally granted his required weapon.

The second account depicts the penance of Bhagiratha, who wished to atone for his ancestor's crime, which resulted in the deaths of 60,000 people.

As there was not enough water in which to place the ashes of 60,000, Bhagiratha resolved to do penance to the goddess Ganga, beseeching her to deliver her waters from the heavenly realms to the earth below. She agreed, but she issued a warning – the waters of the Ganga were so forceful that without control, they would destroy the earth. She advised Bhagiratha to request the powers of Shiva, so that the waters would make their descent to earth in safety. Bhagiratha's request was granted and the waters of the Ganga flowed into the Himalaya and down onto the plains.

Many interpretations can be read into the stories and indeed the ongoing debate is interesting. Whatever the carving depicts, it's one of the freshest, most realistic and unpretentious rock carvings in India.

The touts and hustlers here are persistent and can really interfere with your appreciation of the panel. Once you move on, you'll be able to enjoy the remaining monuments in relative peace.

A gilded jumbo joins in the Great Elephant March, Kochi, Kerala.

PAUL BEINSSEN

EDDIE GERALD

EDDIE GERALD

Extraordinary festivals and street performances happen year-round: performers pay tribute to the tiger (top & centre), and drummers provide the beat for Kochi's Great Elephant March (bottom).

Ganesh Ratha

This *ratha* (a rock-cut Dravidian temple which is built to resemble a chariot) is directly west of Arjuna's Penance. Once a Shiva temple, it became a shrine to Ganesh (the elephant-headed god) after the original lingam was removed and locals reclaimed the sacred space for Ganesh. It's a beautifully carved small temple, with a tiny *yali*-pillared porch. (A yali is a mythical lion creature.) An inscription, repeated in other temples and mandapams, repeatedly curses those who do not follow Shiva!

Take care as you make your way to the Ganesh ratha: the nearby area is used as a public toilet.

Trimurti Cave Temple

North of the Ganesh Ratha, the Trimurti Cave Temple honours the Hindu trinity – Brahma, Vishnu and Shiva. A separate section is dedicated to each deity.

Mandapams

There are many mandapams scattered over the main hill. They are mainly of interest for their internal figure sculptures. The **Kotikal Mandapam**, a little south-west of the Trimurti Cave Temple, is dedicated to Durga.

One of the earliest rock-cut temples, predating the penance relief, is the **Krishna Mandapam**. It features carvings of a pastoral scene showing Krishna lifting up the Govardhana mountain to protect his kinsfolk from the wrath of Indra, the rain god. Beneath his protection, people continue their normal activities – milking cows, playing flutes and dancing.

Dharmaraja Mandapam is perhaps the oldest monument surviving in Mamallapuram. It was constructed as a Vishnu temple with shrines to Shiva and Brahma. Now very little, except the shell, remains.

Ramanuja Mandapam, just north of the lighthouse, has three sections which were probably dedicated to Brahma, Vishnu and Shiva. Most of the sculptures have now been dislodged. The same inscription as that in the Ganesh Ratha curses those who do not follow Shiva.

Mahishamardini Mandapam & Olakkannesvara Temple

is just a few metres south-west of the lighthouse. It depicts scenes from the *Puranas* (Sanskrit stories dating from the 5th century AD). The sculpture of the goddess Durga, in all her wrath, is considered to be one of the finest in Mamallapuram. She is shown, with the weapons of the gods in each of her eight hands, having just shot an arrow from her bow. Opposite, Vishnu reclines with contrasting composure.

Above this mandapam are the remains of the Olakkannesvara Temple, built in the 8th century. Once it may have approximated the Shore Temple but now only the lower level remains. Panels on the other walls show Shiva as teacher, as a dancing warrior and, with Parvati, overpowering Ravana. Before the construction of the lighthouse, this temple served the purpose. It affords spectacular views of Mamallapuram and the environs.

Five Rathas

The five rathas are sculptured temples in the style of chariots (rathas). Set close by the sea they are carved from solid rock. An impressive sight, they provide another fine example of Pallava architecture. Popular belief is that the chariots depict the story of the Pandava brothers, heroes of the *Mahabharata* (the great Vedic epic poem). However, there is no evidence to confirm this.

The first ratha, **Draupadi Ratha**, on the left after you enter the gate, is dedicated to the goddess Durga. Carefully sculptured guardians protect both sides of the entrance. The shrine within honours the goddess, who stands on a lotus, her devotees on their knees in worship. She looks ahead to her vehicle, the huge sculptured lion, which stands proud in front of her temple.

Right behind the goddess, to the south, sits a huge Nandi heralding the next chariot, the **Arjuna Ratha**, which is dedicated to Shiva. On the external walls numerous deities are depicted, including Indra the rain god with his vehicle, the elephant. The shrine within this temple once housed a Shiva lingam but only the cavity where it stood remains.

The next temple chariot, **Bhima Ratha,** honours Vishnu. Within its walls a large sculpture of this deity lies in repose.

The **Dharmaraja Ratha** is the tallest of the chariots and the farthest south. The outside walls portray many deities including both the sun god, Surya and the rain god, Indra, as well as the Shiva/Vishnu combination – the Harihara. The north-eastern corner is sculptured into a Shiva/Parvati combination. The symmetry this sculpture attains is said to symbolise the true equality of men and women.

The final ratha, the **Nakula-Sahadeva Ratha,** derives its name from the champions of the *Mahabharata* and is dedicated to the rain god, Indra. His mount is represented in the fine sculptured elephant which stands next to the temple. However, other accounts suggest that this ratha may have been meant for Subrahmanya who was also, in ancient times, associated with the elephant. The sculpture of the elephant faces the sea. Those who approach from the north, which all visitors do as they enter the gate, will see its back first, hence its name: gajaprishthakara (elephant's backside). The life-sized image is regarded as one of the most perfectly sculptured elephants in India and it provides a focal point for the five rathas.

Up until 200 years ago these structures were hidden in the sand. Excavations by the British revealed the treasures. Pictures in the museum document the excavation process.

Museums

South of the bus stand in East Raja St is the **Sculpture Museum,** containing more than 3000 sculptures by local artisans who work with wood, metal, brass and even cement. Some fine paintings are also on display. The museum is connected to the College of Traditional Art and Architecture located 2km along the highway towards Chennai. Many of the Mamallapuram sculptors are graduates of this college. The museum is open every day from 9 am to 6 pm. Entry is Rs 0.50; for a camera it's Rs 10.

Opposite Arjuna's Penance is the tiny **Yamini Krishnamurti Art Museum,** which displays a few small sculptures. Entrance is Rs 1.

Beach

The village itself is only a couple of hundred metres from the wide beach, north of the Shore Temple, where local fishers pull in their boats. The local toilet is also here, and a walk along the beach is an exercise in side-stepping the turds. South of the Shore Temple, or 500m or so north, it becomes cleaner.

Special Events

The four-day harvest festival, **Pongal,** is celebrated in mid-January.

From early January, and lasting for four weeks, is the very popular **Mamallapuram Dance Festival**. Dances from all over India are staged here including the Bharata Natyam (Tamil Nadu), Kathakali (Kerala), Kuchipudi (Andhra Pradesh) as well as tribal dances, puppet shows and classical music. Many events take place on an open-air stage against the imposing backdrop of Arjuna's Penance. Pick up a leaflet of events at the local tourist office or in Chennai. The local hotels will also advise on the program and how to get tickets.

Massage, Yoga & Ayurveda

The popularity of Mamallapuram with travellers has resulted in a mushrooming of places for massage, reiki, yoga and other forms of ayurvedic practices. One masseur who is highly recommended by many male and female travellers is Krishna, who operates his Ayurvedic Health Home from the Sri Murugan Guest House. He charges Rs 300 for a one hour massage (longer if necessary) and he even claims to have the remedy to make smokers kick their habit.

Places to Stay

If you don't mind roughing it a bit, it's possible to stay in *home accommodation* with families in the area around the Five Rathas, a 15 minute walk from the bus stand. Rooms are generally nothing more than thatched huts, with electricity and fan if you're lucky,

A Party on the Boil

The word *pongal* means 'boil'. It is the word that villagers yell out when the recently harvested rice begins to boil over in the new clay pots. The cry of 'pongal' is a cry of thanksgiving for the abundant harvest. Pongal is a secular festival enjoyed by Hindus, Christians, Buddhists and Muslims. It is a time to thank the sun for all that is harvested, to thank the animals for their contribution and to discard the old and usher in the new. Intellectuals and religious leaders regard Pongal as a celebration of integration and renewal.

January is the time of the four-day Pongal festival in India. The actual dates are set according to the lunar cycle. The festival varies across states, but in Tamil Nadu, the land of rich harvests, Pongal is particularly significant, especially in the villages.

Each of the four days is given a particular emphasis. The first day is Bogii Pongal. This is a time of almost frenetic preparation. Houses and streets are swept even more thoroughly than usual. Old appliances, particularly cooking utensils, are discarded and new ones brought into the home. Pongal pots line the street, as people make their new purchases. It is not unusual for villagers to have communal bonfires into which they cast all that is no longer needed, or at least something that symbolises the past. Large sticks of sugar cane are brought into the home as a special treat.

On the second day, Pongal Day, the new crop of rice is cooked until it boils over, signifying abundance. People flock to the temple, church or mosque to offer thanks for the harvest. In some villages (and tourist hotels) there is music and dancing. In a typical Pongal dance, women balance a decorated pongal pot on their heads as they move with great joy and rhythm to the music.

On Mattu Pongal, the third day, animals are honoured for their contribution to the harvest. Farmers paint the horns (and sometimes the hides) of their cattle in primary colours. Many cattle have fresh flowers placed ceremoniously around their necks. Village women rise earlier than usual to prepare sticky rice balls which they feed to the birds, especially the crows. In some villages, even the goats and sheep are adorned.

The final day, Kanum Pongal, is essentially a day of fun and physical activity. Soccer, cricket, basketball and tug-of-war are popular. Another activity is *jallikata*, the 'taming of the bulls'. This event is especially celebrated in the village of Alanganallur, near Madurai, where the tradition is at least 600 years old. Specially bred bulls are released into a makeshift arena. Young men (mostly village boys) seek to prove their macho mettle by pitting themselves against the tormented beasts. It is a practice that honours the great feats of Lord Krishna who is supposed to have tamed seven wild bulls in order to impress one of his many consorts. The bulls usually survive (at least physically) but each year many of the men (and some spectators) sustain serious injuries. Fatalities are not uncommon. Some 'bull tamers' are accused of subduing the beasts with alcohol and the practice of jallikata receives much media criticism. Tourists are usually kept in a 'safe' enclosure.

If you are travelling during Pongal time, try to get out of the city and into a small village where the true spirit of Pongal can be experienced.

and basic washing facilities. Reports from travellers on this type of accommodation are invariably positive. Touts who hang around the bus stand will find you accommodation in the village but, of course, you'll pay more if you use them. The usual cost is around Rs 250 per week (more if a tout takes you) and if you stay for less than a week the cost is about Rs 50 per day. Competition among the locals offering this sort of service is fierce.

If you intend to stay a month or more check with local home owners about the possibility of *long-term room rental* and self-catering. The proprietor of Hotel Surya offers such a facility at his home for around

Rs 1500 per month. Such arrangements can reduce the cost of your stay considerably. Reputable restaurateurs will put you in touch with others offering this service.

Hotel accommodation is abundant and new lodges as well as star resorts are under construction. Accommodation however can be tight during weekends, holidays and the peak seasons of November to March and July/August. Be careful of the scams operating at the bus stand where auto-rickshaw drivers convince you that the hotel you want is full and whisk you to one where they receive a substantial commission which eventually comes out of your pocket. The best strategy is to check out places yourself

---

Kolams

The rice-flour designs, or *kolam*, that adorn thresholds in Tamil Nadu, especially during the Pongal harvest festival and the Hindu month of Markali (mid-December to mid-January), are much more than mere decorations. The whole ritual of kolam-making draws directly on Tamil beliefs about the concept of sacred and non-sacred space.

The Tamil word kolam means play, form or beauty. A kolam is traditionally made of rice flour (although chalk and sometimes paint are used these days), which is intended to be eaten by ants and other small creatures, a mark of respect for all life. Kolams are traditionally made in the early morning, an auspicious time. Giving as one's first act of the day is similarly regarded as auspicious. A kolam is also an offering to Lakshmi, goddess of rice, wealth and happiness. By making a kolam, a woman (and kolam-makers are invariably women) is inviting Lakshmi (and hence prosperity) into her home. During Markali the divine is considered to be especially accessible and a beautiful kolam is seen as a way of attracting beneficial deities into the home.

Kolams can transmit all sorts of information to those who understand their nuances. A kolam can signal to sadhus and holy men that they can expect food at that particular house. It may be a sign of the family's prosperity generally, in addition to its hospitality. The absence of a kolam might signal ill fortune or a death in the household. Or it might simply mean that the household has no women, or that the women are too busy working in the fields to take the time to make a kolam. Some believe the kolam protects against the evil eye, acting as a sort of deflector of ill intentions, envy and greed.

White and red are favoured colours in kolam-making, although others such as blue may be used. Black is never used because of its association with dark and evil forces. Motifs used in kolam design vary. Some kolams feature complex geometric shapes; others lotus flowers and sundry bird and animal creations.

To save time these days it is possible to purchase bamboo or plastic tubes into which are punched holes. When the tube is filled with chalk dust it can be rolled over a patch of moistened, hard-packed ground to make an attractive, 'instant' kolam design.

Tamil Nadu doesn't have a monopoly on this art. Kolams, also called *rangoli*, flourish in other South Indian states. During the Onam festival in Kerala, for example, kolams are made using a variety of media including coloured dyes and flower petals.

EDDIE GERALD

and look as if you know what you're doing and where you're going.

Places to Stay – Budget

Mrs Rajalaxmi's place is still the best. Her rooms have fans and electricity, and there's a communal toilet and bucket shower. Meals are available on request. Like many villagers, she decorates her doorstep each morning with rice-flour designs known as *kolams*.

Lakshmi Lodge (☎ *42463*), near the beach and very popular with backpackers, was once a brothel. There are light, airy rooms with fans from Rs 100/130 to Rs 200/250. Indian and western food is served on 'private terraces' or you can dine on the roof under the stars and the sweeping beam of the lighthouse. A 'jealousy stone' is suspended above the entrance of this hotel; it will fall on the head of anyone envious of this hotel's success at attracting foreign travellers!

Tina Blue View Lodge & Restaurant (☎ *42319*), near Lakshmi Lodge, is run by the friendly Xavier and has more of a family-style atmosphere. Singles with bathroom cost Rs 80 and doubles are Rs 120 to Rs 250. There's also a four-bed cottage. The upstairs restaurant, which catches the sea breeze, is a great place to eat or to linger over a cold beer.

Uma Lodge (☎ *42322*), in the same area, has clean doubles at Rs 60/90 with common/attached bathroom, and larger rooms with toilets for between Rs 120 and Rs 250. There is no air-con and no hot water. The Pumpernickel Bakery is here.

Mamalla Bhavan (☎ *42250*), opposite the bus stand, has simple doubles (no singles) with bathroom and mosquitoes for Rs 75. Checkout time is noon.

Magesh Lodge (☎ *42997, 129 East Raja St*) is somewhat basic and a little dingy. However, it is clean. Standard/deluxe doubles are Rs 250/350.

Vinayak Cottages (☎ *42445*), entered from either East Raja St or Thirukula St, boasts four lovely cottages (all doubles) set in a garden. They're good value at Rs 150 for a square cottage, or Rs 200 for a larger round one. All have mosquito nets and private bath-

room. There are also clean double rooms in the main building for Rs 150.

Victory Guest House (☎ *42179, 5 Othavadai St*) offers clean basic non air-con double rooms (no singles) for Rs 200 with attached bathroom. This hotel boasts of its 'snazzy ambience'. There are also vegetarian and nonvegetarian restaurants and a resident reiki therapist.

Sri Murugan Guest House (☎ *42662, 42 Othavadai St*) is close to the beach with clean, well-priced rooms at Rs 150 downstairs and Rs 250 upstairs. Only double rooms are available. An Ayurvedic masseur operates from this guesthouse.

Ramakrishna Lodge (☎ *42431, 8 Othavadai St*) is clean, friendly and justifiably popular. Rooms begin at Rs 75/125 with attached bath but prices can be higher in the high season when advanced bookings are advised. Hot water is available from outside (they bring a bucket to your room). The roof terrace is a pleasant place to while away time.

Places to Stay – Mid-Range & Top End

Government hotel tax currently adds 20% to rooms priced at Rs 200 and above.

Mamalla Bhavan Annexe (☎ *42260, 104 East Raja St*) is very popular and is sometimes booked out with tour groups. All rooms are doubles with attached bathrooms. Here you can relax to the rhythmic tapping of the sculptors, which penetrates the rooms until well after sundown. Non air-con is Rs 300. Air-con is Rs 475, and Rs 600 for deluxe rooms.

There's an excellent veg restaurant. You may also take your meals on the balconies or within the courtyard area. Credit cards are accepted.

Hotel Veeras (☎ *42288*), quite near (and similar) to the Mamalla Bhavan Annexe, has comfortable doubles for Rs 250, or Rs 400 with air-con and fridge. The hotel has a restaurant and bar.

La Vie en Rose (☎ *42068*), better known as a restaurant, has a few pleasant, clean rooms for Rs 300/500 with all the facilities you'd expect for mid-range lodgings. Many rooms face a central courtyard. The lodge boasts a 'mini library' which, at last count, contained six books – among them, one of German translation, and Lonely Planet's *India*!

Hotel Surya (☎ *42292, Thirukula St*) is friendly and has a peaceful garden setting. The proprietor is a retired archaeologist with good knowledge of the local area. He is also a sculptor (he was commissioned to build an entire temple in Japan) and much of his work adorns the landscaped gardens of this hotel.

Surya's rooms are very clean and cost from Rs 150/250. Double rooms with a balcony overlooking either the sculpture garden or the lake are Rs 300/350, air-con rooms are Rs 450, deluxe are Rs 650.

TTDC Hotel Tamil Nadu Unit II (☎ *42287*), in pleasant shady grounds near the Shore Temple, has double cottages at Rs 250 to Rs 450 depending on their position and amenities. All have attached bathroom and fan and the hotel's facilities include a bar, a restaurant, a children's play area, and a large sign inviting guests to enjoy 'jolly walk in garden'.

The other mid-range and top-end hotels are scattered for several kilometres along the road north to Chennai. Each is positioned on its own narrow strip of land, about 300m from the road and as close as possible to the beach. All of these so-called beach resorts offer a range of facilities which usually include a swimming pool, bar, restaurant(s) and credit card facilities.

Temple Bay Ashok Beach Resort (☎ *42251, fax 42257*) is 200m from the edge of town. Superdeluxe singles/doubles with air-con cost Rs 1700/2400 in either the main block or the detached cottages. Nonguests can use the small pool for Rs 100 per day.

TTDC Hotel Tamil Nadu Beach Resort (☎ *42235*) is 1.5km north. This place has the best setting of all the resorts – a forested garden and a swimming pool – but it's very shabby. Doubles in sea-facing cottages, all of them with attached bathroom and balcony, cost from Rs 400; Rs 750 with air-con.

Mamalla Beach Resort (☎ *42375, fax 42160*) is further north, but not as close to the sea. It's a good place with clean doubles from Rs 360 downstairs and Rs 400 upstairs. A veg/nonveg restaurant has recently been established and staff are particularly friendly.

Silversands (☎ *42228*) has a plethora of inland rooms and cottages, but only the expensive suites and three-bed villas (Rs 2700) are on the beachfront. It's overpriced for what it offers, with seasonal rates ranging from Rs 300/400 to Rs 600/800 for normal singles/doubles.

Golden Sun Beach Resort (☎ *42245*) is 3km from Mamallapuram. Singles/doubles here start at Rs 550/650, or Rs 700/800 with air-con. There are sea-facing rooms from Rs 1200/1320. This place is often full on weekends even though the beachside disco no longer functions. There's also a health club and pool.

Ideal Beach Resort (☎ *42240, fax 42243*), 3km from town, is one of the best. This place is small enough to retain the owner's intended warm and intimate atmosphere and, as such, is popular with expats and foreigners. Rooms/cottages cost Rs 425/500. An air-con cottage costs Rs 780. All have mosquito nets and are well furnished. There's a nice pool which nonguests can use for Rs 100, and good food.

Places to Eat

Mamallapuram has, as you might expect, many places to eat catering to almost every traveller's need. Beachside restaurants serve attractively presented seafood in relaxed settings. Most will show you the fresh fish, prawns, crabs and squid before cooking them so you can make your choice. Be sure, however, to ask the price before giving the go-ahead, as some items – king prawns for example – can be very expensive. At many of the restaurants it is possible to 'customise' your meal according to budget and/or appetite. Beer usually costs Rs 50 at the beach bars and Rs 35 in the numerous wine shops.

Sea Shore Restaurant, on the beach, offers excellent fresh seafood. Tiger prawns are Rs 250 and there's also lobster and crab.

Grilled prawns and salad costs Rs 40, and the grilled baby shark is delicious.

Santhana Beach Restaurant is next door and offers similar fare. For two people, fresh lobster is Rs 450 and king prawns Rs 400 (you get about 30 on the plate). The staff are friendly and will invest time discussing the permutations and combinations of cooking prawns. They stay open late.

Luna Magica, also on the beach, has a tank full of live lobsters and prawns at prices similar to the Sea Shore. Coconut milk prawn curry is Rs 55; fried fish with chips and salad costs Rs 25.

Moonrakers (*Othavadai St*) is a late night 'hang-out' that attracts travellers like moths to a lamp. It's run by three friendly brothers. The food is good and it's one of the few places in town that offers muesli for breakfast. Prawns in garlic sauce costs Rs 60. It also has a good collection of western magazines and music tapes.

Village Inn Restaurant is run by the family who started the original Village Restaurant, one of the first in town. Their current restaurant is as popular as the original. It has an indoor section plus an intimate garden terrace where you can dine under coconut palms. Multicuisine food including fresh seafood is served by very attentive staff. Meals start from a few rupees to Rs 350 for seafood.

Village Restaurant, just down from the Village Inn and near Hotel Surya in Thirukula St, serves multicuisine fare.

Eskimo Land is proud of its warm atmosphere! It serves good Chinese cuisine as well as Indian, European and fresh seafood.

Tina Blue View is a good place to eat, especially in the heat of the day, as the shady upstairs area catches any breeze that might be around. The service is slow but the mellow atmosphere makes up for that. Cold beers are available.

Sea Queen Restaurant, next to Tina Blue, is reliable for good seafood.

Pumpernickel Bakery, at Uma Lodge, is part German run and does a wonderful range of bread and cakes. You can also get full meals, and there's beer and good music.

New Papillon/Le Bistro, on the road to the Shore Temple, is a tiny place run by an enthusiastic crew. Cold beers are available, as well as early morning breakfasts.

Au Bons Copains, also on the road to the Shore Temple, is a friendly little cafe. Prawn fried rice is Rs 30.

Sun Rise Restaurant, behind the New Papillon and across the playing field, has a wide range of fish dishes that are good value.

Curiosity Restaurant has moved opposite Lakshmi Lodge. The new food, especially the breakfast, is good and the prices are still on the high side.

La Vie en Rose, on the 1st floor of a building at the southern end of East Raja St, is partly French run. This lovely little place offers a different nonvegetarian menu each day and has main course meals for about Rs 70, and good coffee.

Mamalla Bhavan, opposite the bus stand, is an excellent place for South Indian vegetarian food. You can eat well at standard Indian 'meals' prices here. Around the back of the main restaurant, the special thali section serves different thalis every day for Rs 20. The main restaurant is also open for dinner.

Golden Palate Restaurant in the Mamalla Bhavan Annexe is the top vegetarian restaurant in town. The eggplant masala fry with special cashew gravy (Rs 25) is excellent.

Ashok Restaurant is set in pleasant gardens near the Shore Temple. It's not bad for breakfast with dosas from Rs 15.

Shopping

Mamallapuram has revived the ancient crafts of the Pallava stonemasons and sculptors, and the town wakes every day to the sound of chisels chipping away at pieces of granite. Some excellent work is turned out. The yards have contracts to supply images of deities and restoration pieces to many temples throughout India and Sri Lanka. Some even undertake contract work for the European market and a recent requisition has come from South Korea for funerary art. You can buy examples of this work from the Poompuhar Handicrafts Emporium (fixed

TAMIL NADU

prices – in theory) or from any of the dozens of craft shops which line the roads down to the Shore Temple and to the Five Rathas (prices negotiable).

Prices of the sculptures range from Rs 300 (for a small lightweight piece that will fit into your baggage) to Rs 400,000 for a massive Ganesh which requires a mobile crane for lifting. Should you have the inclination (and budget) for a large piece, most of the artisans have connections with Chennai shipping companies. Shipping to Europe or the USA can cost around Rs 6000 and take up to three months.

Exquisite soapstone images of Hindu gods, woodcarvings, jewellery and other similar products are also for sale. There are several Kashmiri shops, too.

If you want a hammock, this is quite a good place to buy one. For a book exchange service, try Himalaya Handicrafts on the main street (East Raja St).

Getting There & Away

The most direct route to/from Chennai (Rs 15, 50km, two hours) is on bus Nos 188 and 188A/B/D/K of which there are 20 daily. Bus Nos 19C and 119A go to Chennai via Kovalam and there are 21 buses daily. To Chennai via the airport you need to take No 108B of which there are nine daily.

To Pondicherry (Rs 18, 95km, 3½ hours) take bus No 188 or 188A of which there are eight daily. There are five daily buses (No 212A/H) to Kanchipuram (Rs 10, 65km, two hours) via Tirukkalikundram and Chengalpattu (Chingleput). Alternatively, take a bus to Chengalpattu and then another bus from there to Kanchipuram.

Taxis are also available from the bus stand but long-distance trips require hours of haggling before the price gets anywhere near reasonable. It's about Rs 400 to Chennai airport.

Getting Around

The easiest way to get around is on foot. You can hire bikes for Rs 15 per day from the bicycle shop opposite the bus stand. Mopeds can be rented from Lakshmi Lodge for Rs

125 per day (petrol extra) or from Poornima Travels (☎ 42463) at 33 Othavadai St for the same cost. Helmets are not available and you don't need a licence. At this same place you can also make air, train and bus bookings, rent a taxi and purchase stone carvings, silks and postcards.

Auto-rickshaws are also available but, since this is a tourist town, they won't use meters and negotiation is even more cryptic and challenging than usual. Many travellers find that sharing a taxi for the day is a good way to get around and see the places nearby.

AROUND MAMALLAPURAM
Tiger Cave

This shady and peaceful place is almost 5km north of Mamallapuram and signposted off to the right of the road. Dedicated to Durga, this rock-cut shrine possibly dates from the 7th century. It has a small mandapam featuring a crown of carved heads of the yali, the mythical lion creature from which the shrine japparently derived its name. It is therefore inappropriately named! It's a popular picnic spot on weekends.

Tirukkalikundram

Fourteen kilometres from Mamallapuram, this popular pilgrimage centre is also known as Tirukazhukundram, which means Hill of the Holy Eagles. Its hilltop Vedagirishvara Temple, dedicated to Shiva, is famous as the place where two eagles come each day, just before noon, to be fed by a priest. Legend has it that they come from Varanasi (Benares) and are en route to Rameswaram. The reality is that they often don't even turn up. If you really want to see them and you miss out, don't be too perturbed. Eagles glide around most temples.

Five hundred and fifty steep steps lead to the top of the hill, and you must ascend bare footed. Some less-fit visitors get themselves carried up in baskets. The temple contains two tiny and very beautiful shrines. Even if it's closed you may be able to find the custodian to let you in, for a small consideration. Views from the top encompass the larger Bhaktavatsaleshavra Temple and its gopurams, temple tanks, rocky hills and rice paddies.

You can get here from Mamallapuram by bus or by bicycle. The temple is open from 8.30 am to 1 pm and from 5 to 7 pm. *Puja* (prayer) time is 6 pm. Entry is Rs 1; Rs 5 for cameras. The tiny food stall, *Sri Ganesh*, at the temple entrance, serves drinks and snacks.

KANCHIPURAM
Pop: 184,000 Tel Area Code: 04112
The road to Kanchipuram, some 76km south-west of Chennai, travels through lush rice fields, scrubby bush and brightly coloured silk hanging in the sun to dry. Kanchipuram is a temple town and one of the seven sacred cities of India. While the other cities are dedicated to either Shiva or Vishnu, Kanchipuram is unique in that it is dedicated to both. It is also one of three cities in India (and the most important) where the goddess Shakti (known here as Kamakshi) is worshipped.

In South India, Kanchipuram is very significant for Shiva worshippers. It is linked to four other centres, each of which represent one of the five elements. Kanchipuram represents earth. Because of this, the most important Shiva temple in Kanchi, the Sri Ekambaranathar Temple, has a lingam made of sand (covered with metal). Of the original 1000 temples, there are still about 200 left spread out across the town.

Originally Kanchipuram was a major Buddhist centre established by the Mauryan emperor Ashoka in about the 3rd century BC. By the 3rd century AD it is reputed to have been a sophisticated city with diverse cultures and languages. Its numerous monasteries and temples indicated its focus as a significant place of Buddhist scholarship, although Hinduism and Jainism were also prevalent.

The Pallava dynasty established Kanchipuram as its capital and under its rule Kanchipuram was to witness a prospering of the arts, especially in the fields of literature, music and dance. The first South Indian stone temples were constructed. The inhabitants of Kanchipuram adopted Hinduism, worshipping the god Shiva, following the conversion from Jainism of their king, Mahendra Varman I.

Subsequent dynasties, among them the Cholas and Pandyas, continued their support of a prosperous Kanchipuram. When the Vijayanagar Empire took control Kanchipuram became part of the empire which extended throughout the whole of South India. New temples were built, old ones were renovated and extended, and Shaivism continued to be the major belief system.

With the arrival of the British, Kanchipuram was eventually merged into the British Empire.

As well as being a significant temple city and pilgrimage site, Kanchipuram is an important centre of commerce. It's also famous for its handwoven silk fabrics. This industry originated centuries ago, when weavers were employed to produce clothing and fabrics for royalty. The shops which sell silk fabrics, such as those along the road to the Devarajaswami Temple, are frequented by busloads of tourists in a hurry and prices are consistently higher than in Chennai. To get any sort of bargain you need to know your silk well and have done some legwork checking out prices in Chennai.

Kanchi attracts many pilgrims and tourists, especially during the temple car festivals (January, April and May). As such, there is usually an army of hangers-on. Have plenty of small change handy to meet various demands for 'small considerations, as you like' from 'temple watchmen', 'shoe minders', 'guides' and assorted priests. Be particularly wary of the 'priests' who pressure you for large sums of money, but you will also meet many who are generous with their time and information. All the temples are closed between noon and 4 pm.

Other than temples and silks, Kanchipuram is a dusty and fairly nondescript town.

Orientation & Information
Kanchipuram is on the main Chennai-Bangalore road, on the northern bank of the Palar River. It's divided into several districts, the

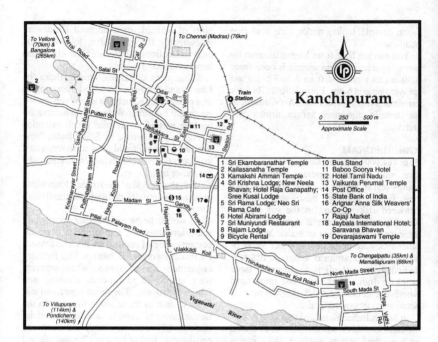

Kanchipuram

0   250   500 m
Approximate Scale

1 Sri Ekambaranathar Temple
2 Kailasanatha Temple
3 Kamakshi Amman Temple
4 Sri Krishna Lodge; New Neela
   Bhavan; Hotel Raja Ganapathy;
   Sree Kusal Lodge
5 Sri Rama Lodge; Neo Sri
   Rama Cafe
6 Hotel Abirami Lodge
7 Sri Muniyundi Restaurant
8 Rajam Lodge
9 Bicycle Rental
10 Bus Stand
11 Baboo Soorya Hotel
12 Hotel Tamil Nadu
13 Vaikunta Perumal Temple
14 Post Office
15 State Bank of India
16 Arignar Anna Silk Weavers'
   Co-Op
17 Rajaji Market
18 Jaybala International Hotel;
   Saravana Bhavan
19 Devarajaswami Temple

main ones being Shiva-Kanchi in the north, and Vishnu-Kanchi and Jaina-Kanchi in the south-east and west respectively.

The tourist information counter at the Hotel Tamil Nadu (☎ 22461), 78 Kamakshi Amman Sannathi St, just opposite the train station, will probably refer you to the small magazine stand in Gandhi Rd for information! Guides are available at most temples. The post office is on Station Rd, the Indian Overseas Bank and the State Bank of India are in Gandhi Rd but the State Bank (like most hotels) does not accept travellers cheques or Amex. Some hotels accept credit cards.

Kailasanatha Temple

Dedicated to Shiva, Kailasanatha is the oldest temple in Kanchi and for some, the most beautiful. It was built by the Pallava king, Rayasimha, in the late 7th century, though its front was added later by his son,

King Varman III. It is the only temple at Kanchi which isn't cluttered with the more recent additions of the Cholas and Vijayanagar rulers, and so reflects the freshness and simplicity of early Dravidian architecture.

Fragments of the 8th century murals which once graced the alcoves are a visible reminder of how magnificent the temple must have looked when it was first built. Small shrines, 58 in all, honour Shiva and Parvati and their sons, Ganesh and Murugan, in a variety of ways. Some are intricately painted.

The temple is run by the Archaeology Department and non-Hindus are allowed into the inner sanctum, where there is a prismatic lingam. This unique 16-sided black granite stone represents 16 aspects of the deity. It is said to be some 2000 years old and therefore much older than the temple itself. It is the largest lingam in Kanchi and the third-largest in Asia.

On the wall behind the lingam is a beautiful sandstone sculpture of the Somaskanda – an image which combines the three deities, Shiva, Parvati and Murugan (also known as Skanda). In a small shrine next to the sanctum the dance competition between Shiva and Parvati is beautifully depicted. Shiva is erect, his body lean and pliable. Parvati, on the side wall, watches. Brahma and Vishnu stand in carefully sculpted judgement on either side.

Both the guide and the priest here are knowledgeable and generous with information.

Sri Ekambaranathar Temple

The Sri Ekambaranathar Temple is dedicated to Shiva and is one of the largest temples in Kanchipuram, covering 12 hectares. Its 59m-high gopuram (pyramid-shaped gateway tower) and massive outer stone wall were constructed in 1509 by Krishnadevaraya of the Vijayanagar Empire, though construction was originally started by the Pallavas and the temple was later extended by the Cholas. Inside are five separate enclosures and a 1000-pillared hall (which actually contains 540 differently decorated pillars).

The temple's name is said to be a modified form of Eka Amra Nathar – the Lord of the Mango Tree – and in one of the enclosures is a very old mango tree, with four branches representing the four *Vedas* (sacred Hindu texts). The fruit of each of the four branches is said to have a different taste, and a plaque nearby claims that the tree is 3500 years old. The tree is revered as a manifestation of the god and women wanting a child pray beneath it. It is the only 'shrine' that non-Hindus are allowed to walk around. You can also partake of the sacred ash (modest contributions gratefully accepted). This is still a functioning Hindu temple and non-Hindus cannot enter the sanctum.

For Shiva devotees, this temple is particularly significant, because of its association with the elements. (See the introduction to Kanchipuram.) With the permission of the temple priest it's possible to climb to the top of one of the gopurams.

A 'camera fee' of Rs 5 goes towards the upkeep of the temple but the visit could cost you more, as this is undoubtedly one of the worst temples for hustlers.

Kamakshi Amman Temple

This imposing temple is dedicated to the goddess Parvati in her guise as Kamakshi, the goddess who accedes to all requests. Because of this, the temple is very popular with visitors, who leave precious gifts for the goddess in the hope of having their requests fulfilled.

Just within the entrance to the temple, Meenakshi, the temple elephant, stands brightly painted, accepting money offerings from visitors in return for a blessing – a gentle stroke on the head with her trunk.

To the right of the entrance is the marriage hall with its ornate pillars. Directly ahead the main shrine is topped with its more recent plating of gold.

As with many other temples, this temple has an annual Car Festival, held on the 9th lunar day in February/March. Ornate wooden carriages housing statues of deities are hauled through the streets in procession. In October/November the birthday of the goddess is celebrated. Special rituals conferring authority to her are conducted.

Devarajaswami Temple

Like the Sri Ekambaranathar Temple, this is an enormous monument. Dedicated to Vishnu, it was built by the Vijayanagar emperors. It has massive outer walls and a beautifully sculpted, 1000-pillared hall (in name only – just 96 pillars remain). Many of the pillars honour Vishnu in his various incarnations, including those of the fish, turtle and pig. The marriage hall on the raised platform in the centre commemorates the wedding of Vishnu and Lakshmi. One of the temple's most notable features is a huge chain carved from a single piece of stone.

There is a large tank beside the hall. Submerged within its waters is a 10m statue of the prostrate Vishnu. For 40 days once every 40 years the waters of the tanks are drained enabling a viewing of the statue. In 1979, the last time such an event occurred, it is claimed 10 million people came to make offerings to the temple.

Entrance is Rs 1 and there is a camera fee of Rs 5.

Vaikunta Perumal Temple

Dedicated to Vishnu, this temple was built between 674 and 800, shortly after the Kailasanatha Temple. The cloisters inside the outer wall consist of lion pillars and are representative of the first phase in the architectural evolution of the grand 1000-pillared halls of later temples. Wall sculptures depict historical events of the temple, with explanatory details given in 8th century script below the sculptures.

The main shrine is on three levels which contain images of Vishnu in standing, sitting and reclining positions.

The Weavers of Kanchipuram

Kanchipuram has prosperous silk and cotton weaving industries. Opposite the Kailasanatha Temple is the Thalapathi Cotton Weaving Centre, where you can see weavers almost buried within deep earthen holes – the pit looms from which they work. Above the holes are the looms which they dexterously manipulate to weave 2m of cloth each, per day.

Contrary to popular belief it is only in the last 50 years that the Kanchipuram weavers have been making pure silk saris. Prior to this the saris were cotton with a woven silk border. It's not known when the weavers first came to Kanchi. One theory is that they arrived in the 12th century, another suggests that the Vijayanagar emperor, Krishnadevaraya, in his desire to see the arts advance, issued them an invitation. Today chemical dyes are used, but originally, vegetable dyes were mixed with the waters of the nearby Palar River as the weavers believed that the river possessed particular powers of colour-enhancement. Many of the weavers working here today are direct descendants of the original artisans.

Kanchi's numerous silk merchants inhabit its narrow lanes. You can also witness the intricacies of the weaving process at these places, as well as purchase the finished product. The Arignar Anna Silk Weavers' Co-op is in Gandhi Rd. There are also many other places to buy silk in this road. Common belief has it that Kanchi silks are the highest quality in India and therefore the most expensive.

Places to Stay

Most of the cheap (and noisy) lodges are clustered in the centre of town, just a few minutes walk from the bus stand.

Rajam Lodge (☎ 22519, 9 Kamarajar St), next to the restaurant of the same name, is close to the bus stand. It's a friendly place which has basic singles/doubles/triples with attached bathroom for Rs 60/90/150.

Hotel Abirami Lodge (☎ 20797, 109 Kamarajar St) has spotless rooms from Rs 90/150, but most have a claustrophobic feel as there are no outside windows. Those at the back are quietest. The hotel has a good 'meals' restaurant.

Sri Rama Lodge (☎ 22435, 20 Nellukkara St) is reasonably clean and friendly with rooms from Rs 70/120, or Rs 260/350 with air-con. All the rooms have attached bathroom with hot and cold running water and the hotel has a good vegetarian restaurant, Neo Sri Rama Cafe.

Sree Kusal Lodge (☎ 23342), opposite Sri Rama Lodge, has clean, marble-lined rooms from Rs 95/150; air-con doubles are Rs 360. A TV is available for hire at Rs 30.

Sri Krishna Lodge (☎ 22831), next door, has extremely basic rooms for Rs 70/110 with bath.

Hotel Tamil Nadu (☎ 22553; fax 22552, Station Rd) is on a quiet, leafy backstreet near the train station. It's not one of the tourism department's best. Standard doubles are Rs 275, air-con doubles are Rs 450 and Rs 460. Deluxe air-con rooms (they're only marginally bigger) are Rs 600. There's a bar and simple restaurant.

Baboo Soorya Hotel (☎ 22555; fax 22556, 85 East Raja Veethy), near the Vaikunta Perumal Temple, is the swankiest hotel in town. The staff are friendly and helpful. Clean and well-appointed singles/doubles cost Rs 275/325, or Rs 425/475 with effective air-con. The hotel has a good vegetarian restaurant. You can get nonveg food in your room.

Hotel Jayabala International (☎ *24348, 504 Gandhi Rd*) is newly built and well positioned. Spotless rooms are available from Rs 120/325 to Rs 400/450 with air-con. All major credit cards are accepted and a branch of the Saravana Bhavan operates its excellent and fast veg restaurant from the hotel forecourt.

Places to Eat

The best and fastest meals are available from the Saravana Bhavan (part of the Chennai chain of vegetarian restaurants but with a slightly different spelling) at the Hotel Jayabala International. There are also many small vegetarian places in the vicinity of the bus stand where you can buy a typical plate meal for around Rs 12.

Hotel Abirami Lodge (*Kamarajar St*) has OK meals.

Sri Muniyundi Restaurant (*Kamarajar St*) does reasonable nonveg food.

Baboo Soorya Hotel has a good vegetarian restaurant. Thalis are Rs 23, veg spring rolls cost Rs 16.

New Neela Bhavan and *Hotel Raja Ganapathy* are adjacent to each other between the Sri Krishna Lodge and the Sree Kusal Lodge. Both offer cheap and good South Indian veg dishes.

Getting There & Away

Bus As elsewhere, the timetable at the bus stand is in Tamil, but if you don't understand, there is no problem finding a bus in the direction you want to go. Look for direct, or 'Point-to-Point' buses; they're the fastest – No 76B runs to Chennai (Rs 11.25, 1½ hours). There are five direct buses daily to Mamallapuram (No 212A, Rs 10, about two hours). Alternatively, take one of the more frequent buses to Chengalpattu and then catch another one from there to Mamallapuram.

There are direct STC buses to Tiruchirappalli (No 122), Chennai (No 828) and Bangalore (No 828).

There are also plenty of PATC buses to Chennai, Vellore and Tiruvannamalai, as well as private buses to Pondicherry.

Train From Chennai Egmore change at Chengalpattu (Chingleput) for Kanchipuram (Rs 14, three hours). There are services from Chengalpattu at 8.20 am and 5.45 and 8.20 pm and in the opposite direction at 6.05, 7 and 8.33 am and 6.13 pm, but these services do not run on national public holidays (see the Facts for the Visitor chapter for dates of public holidays). It's also possible to get to Kanchipuram from Chennai (or Tirupathi), and vice versa, via Arakkonam on the Bangalore-Chennai Central broad-gauge line, but there are only two connections per day in either direction: at 7.50 am and 5.30 pm from Arakkonam to Kanchipuram, and 9.23 am and 6.55 pm in the opposite direction.

Getting Around

Bicycles can be rented for Rs 2 per hour (Rs 15 for a day) from shops near the bus stand. Cycle-rickshaws should cost around Rs 60 for a temple tour but they'll try for Rs 150. Auto-rickshaws are also available.

VEDANTANGAL BIRD SANCTUARY

About 35km south of Chengalpattu and 52km from Mamallapuram, this is an important breeding ground for waterbirds. Cormorants, egrets, herons, storks, ibises, spoonbills, grebes and pelicans come here to breed and nest for about six months from October/November to March, depending on the monsoons. At the height of the breeding season (December and January), there can be up to 30,000 birds here.

After entering the sanctuary you can stroll along the 500m walkway. Rice paddies are on one side and there's a wide waterway on the other, which separates you from the island on which the birds nest. Signs in Tamil and English provide information on the birds, their habitat and breeding times. An observation tower with powerful binoculars (at no cost) enables you to get a much better

TAMIL NADU

view. Field naturalists frequent this park and are more than happy to offer advice and guidance. As well as the birds, you will no doubt see cattle, goats, dogs and even the odd cobra slithering along the branches of trees.

The best times to visit are early morning and late afternoon. The sanctuary is open from 6 am to 6 pm every day. Entry is Rs 1, camera Rs 5 and video camera Rs 50.

The only place to stay is in one of the basic two-room suites at the *Forest Department Resthouse*, just 500m before the sanctuary. Charges are Rs 25 per person. Officially reservations must be made in advance with the Wildlife Warden (☎ 044-413947), 4th Floor, DMS Office, Teynampet, Chennai. Unofficially if you arrive and they have a vacancy, you're in.

To get to Vedantangal take a bus from Chengalpattu to the Vedantangal bus stand. Then walk the 1km south. Often the buses take you right there. Another alternative is to get a bus from any of the major centres to Madurantakam, the closest town of any size, and then hire transport to take you the last 8km. There are small kiosks for drinks and snacks.

VELLORE
Pop: 330,200 Tel Area Code: 0416

Vellore, 145km from Chennai, is a dusty, semi-rural bazaar town. For tourists, it is noteworthy only for the Vijayanagar Fort and its temple, which are in an excellent state of preservation and worth visiting.

The town has a modern church built in an old British cemetery, which contains the tomb of a captain who died in 1799 'of excessive fatigue incurred during the glorious campaign which ended in the defeat of Tipoo Sultaun'. Here, too, is a memorial to the victims of the little known 'Vellore Mutiny' of 1806. The mutiny was instigated by the second son of Tipu Sultan, who was incarcerated in the fort at that time, and was put down by a task force sent from Arcot.

Vellore is famed for its hospital – a leader in research and health care. The people who come here from all over India for medical care give this unassuming town a cosmopolitan feel.

Vellore Fort

The fort is constructed of granite blocks and surrounded by a moat which is supplied by a subterranean drain fed from a tank. It was built in the 16th century by Sinna Bommi Nayak, a vassal chieftain under the Vijayanagar kings, Sada Shivaraja and Sriranga Maharaja. Later, it became the fortress of Mortaza Ali, the brother-in-law of Chanda Sahib who claimed the Arcot throne, and was taken by the Adil Shahi sultans of Bijapur.

In 1676 the fort passed briefly into the hands of the Marathas until they in turn were displaced by Nawab Daud Khan of Delhi in 1708. The British occupied the fort in 1760, following the fall of Srirangapatnam and the death of Tipu Sultan. It now houses various public departments and private offices, and is open daily.

The small **museum**, near the church inside the fort complex, contains sculptures and 'hero stones' dating back to Pallava and Chola times. Shoes must be taken off before entering. It's closed on Friday.

At the entrance to the fort the Archaeological Survey of India has a small information stall. It has some fascinating literature – on Nagarjunakonda in central Andhra Pradesh! Tamil readers may find additional information at the tiny Radhakrishna book depot in the market area.

Jalakanteshwara Temple

This temple was built about the same time as the fort (around 1550) and, although it doesn't compare with the ruins at Hampi, it is still a gem of late Vijayanagar architecture and has some stunning carvings in the main mandapam. During the invasions by the Adil Shahis of Bijapur, the Marathas and the Carnatic nawabs, the temple was occupied by a garrison and it ceased to be used. However, it has reopened and is now a popular place of worship.

The entrance faces a stature of Ganesh. To the left of the entrance is the pillared mandapam famed for its sculptures of yali and other mythical creatures and considered to be a masterpiece of its time. Nearby is another large Ganesh, this time on his vehicle, the rat. The familiar planets and icons of numerous saints line the next wall. There are shrines to Nataraja (Shiva in his incarnation as Lord of the Dance), the lingam and the goddess. The temple is open daily from 6 am to 1 pm and 3 to 8 pm, and it costs Rs 0.25 to leave your shoes.

After leaving the temple you may like to take anthropologist Madame Boulanger's suggestion and visit the tiny shrine nearby.

Turn right as you leave the temple and follow the path to the police hospital. Within the grounds is a tiny goddess shrine within the trunk of a huge banyan tree.

Christian Medical College & Hospital (CMC&H)

Vellore is now well known for the pioneering work of its hospital, one of the largest and best in the country. Established with one bed in 1900 by American, Dr Ida S Scudder, the hospital has increased to 1200 beds and treats up to 2000 patients a day. Its

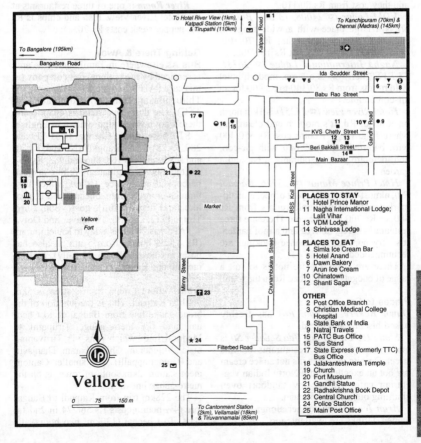

PLACES TO STAY
1 Hotel Prince Manor
11 Nagha International Lodge; Lalit Vihar
13 VDM Lodge
14 Srinivasa Lodge

PLACES TO EAT
4 Simla Ice Cream Bar
5 Hotel Anand
6 Dawn Bakery
7 Arun Ice Cream
10 Chinatown
12 Shanti Sagar

OTHER
2 Post Office Branch
3 Christian Medical College & Hospital
8 State Bank of India
9 Natraj Travels
15 PATC Bus Office
16 Bus Stand
17 State Express (formerly TTC) Bus Office
18 Jalakanteshwara Temple
19 Church
20 Fort Museum
21 Gandhi Statue
22 Radhakrishna Book Depot
23 Central Church
24 Police Station
25 Main Post Office

Vellore

0   75   150 m

TAMIL NADU

staff undertake research and training in all areas of medicine including transplants, cardiology and obstetrics. The hospital has been successful in obtaining support from church and secular organisations throughout the world.

Places to Stay

Vellore's cheap hotels are concentrated along the roads south of and parallel to the hospital.

Srinivasa Lodge (☎ 26389, 14 Beri Bakkali St) is a clean place run by friendly people. All rooms have bathroom attached and they cost from Rs 80/110.

VDM Lodge (☎ 24008, 13 Beri Bakkali St) is a large place with a wide range of rooms. Ordinary rooms are Rs 70/100, deluxe rooms with TV cost Rs 180/200.

Nagha International Lodge (☎ 26731, 13 KVS Chetty St) is a large, modern hotel with rooms from Rs 80/140 to Rs 400 for an air-con double.

Hotel River View (☎ 25251) is 1km north on Katpadi Rd. It's modern and clean, but where's the view? Rooms cost Rs 350/400 with bathroom, Rs 500/600 with air-con, and there are three restaurants, a bar and a garden.

Hotel Prince Manor (☎ 27726, Katpadi Rd), almost opposite the post office, is an up-market hotel with double rooms from Rs 500, or Rs 700 with air-con. There are three restaurants – veg, nonveg and a roof garden. It's very popular, so advance bookings are recommended.

There are several more hotels to suit a range of budgets on Filterbed Rd in the south.

Places to Eat

Dawn Bakery (Gandhi Rd) has freshly baked biscuits and bread.

Simla Ice Cream Bar (Ida Scudder St) is one of many 'meals' restaurants on this street. Despite the name it's not an ice cream bar but an excellent little North Indian vegetarian cafe with a tiny tandoori oven churning out piping-hot naan.

Arun Ice Cream, further along, is aptly named. Drinks are available too.

Shanti Sagar (Beri Bakkali St), next to VDM Lodge, is a buzzing vegetarian restaurant with more than 50 items on the menu and an attractive open air courtyard.

Hotel Anand (Ida Scudder St) is an up-market vegetarian restaurant with an air-con room.

Chinatown, opposite Natraj Travels on Gandhi Rd, does passable Asian meals. Tom yum soup is Rs 20, main dishes cost around Rs 40.

Lalit Vihar (KVS Chetty St) has Gujarati meals for Rs 20 including all-you-can-eat chappatis.

River Room is one of three restaurants at the Hotel River View. Fish and chips is Rs 60, pepper steak costs Rs 70.

Getting There & Away

Bus As elsewhere in Tamil Nadu, the area is serviced by the regional bus company (in this case PATC), and the STC (formerly the Thiruvalluvar Transport Corporation or TTC). The dusty bus stand is chaotic and there's not a single sign written in English.

STC buses run to Chennai (Nos 139 and 280, Rs 28), Tiruchirappalli (No 104, Rs 50) and Madurai (Nos 168, 866 and 983, Rs 66). All these buses originate in Vellore and can be booked in advance. Others, which pass through en route from Chennai and Bangalore (and may be full), go to Bangalore, Tirupathi (2½ hours), Thanjavur and Ooty.

PATC has 26 buses a day to Kanchipuram (Rs 8, 2½ hours) from 5 am. It also has buses to Chennai (Rs 28, 30 daily), Tiruchirappalli and Bangalore.

Train Vellore's main train station is 5km north at Katpadi. This is the junction of the broad-gauge line from Bangalore to Chennai, and the metre-gauge Tirupathi to Madurai line (which runs via Tiruvannamalai, Villupuram, Chidambaram, Thanjavur and Tiruchirappalli). The smaller Cantonment station, 2km south of town, is on the metre-gauge line only.

The 228km trip from Katpadi to Bangalore (4½ hours) costs Rs 56/274 in 2nd/1st class. To Chennai (130km, two hours) it's

Rs 34/176. The daily train to Madurai (15 hours) leaves at 7.10 pm; to Tirupathi (105km, three hours) it's at the unsociable hour of 1.05 am or there's a passenger train (5½ hours) leaving at 9.15 am.

Getting Around

Buses wait outside Katpadi station for trains to arrive and the journey into Vellore (Rs 2) takes anything from 15 to 30 minutes. Autorickshaws charge Rs 50.

AROUND VELLORE
Vellamalai (18km)

Vellamalai, 18km from Vellore, is named after Valli, the second wife of Murugan (Shiva's second son). Several legends give accounts of this hill being the place of her birth. Murugan's attempts to be with Valli were all unsuccessful until his brother, Ganesh, intervened. There's a temple at the bottom of the hill but the main temple, carved from a massive rock, is at the top. It is dedicated to Murugan, and has images of his two wives Devasena and Valli, considered to be different aspects of the goddess.

Shoes must be removed at the base of the hill. At the top there's a good view of the bleak countryside around Vellamalai – the ground is strewn with boulders. The cloth knots you will see tied to trees are requests that wishes be granted. The one hour trip from Vellore on bus No 20 (hourly) costs Rs 7.

TIRUVANNAMALAI
Pop: 50,000 Tel Area Code: 04175

The small town of Tiruvannamalai, 85km south of Vellore, sits at the base of Arunachala Hill. The name is given different interpretations, from Red Mount to 'immovable force', suggesting a combination of the two deities Shiva and Parvati. Nowadays it is most frequently referred to by its Tamil name Annamalai – 'attained mount' or 'mountain of bliss'. Along with four other temples, this site represents one of the five elements – in this case, fire.

This is an important Shaivite town. As with many sites, this one has several legends and these have become intertwined, creating

the beliefs and rituals observed today at the Tiruvannamalai Temple (also known as the Arunachaleswar Temple). In this temple Shiva is revered as Arunachaleswar, an aspect of fire – the light which destroys the darkness of ignorance.

Legend has it that as Brahma and Vishnu were arguing over who was the most superior of the two, Shiva appeared as a column of fire, creating the original symbol of the lingam, and challenged the arguing gods to locate the beginning and end of the column of fire. Neither succeeded, but Brahma lied and said that he had found the head. Shiva, however caught him out, and Vishnu and Brahma were both forced to bow to Shiva's superiority. Shiva agreed to appear each year and re-enact the vision in order to remind his devotees of the dangers of egotism.

Each November/December full moon, the Karthikai Deepam Festival celebrates this legend with a huge fire on top of Annamalai Hill. The fire, lit from a 30m wick immersed in 2000L of ghee, lasts for several days and can be seen for at least 10km.

Covering some 10 hectares, the Arunachaleswar Temple is one of the largest in India. It dates from the 11th century, with much of the structure being built from the 17th to 19th centuries. It has four large gopurams, one at each cardinal point. The eastern gopuram, known as the Rajagopuram, is the largest: its 13 storeys rise 66m high. Several smaller gopurams act as entrances to different sections.

Many of the stalls leading to the entrance were destroyed in an electrical fire in the mid-1990s, leaving a relatively open area for the approach. Just inside the entrance the familiar shrine to Ganesh is prominent. To the right is a large 1000-pillared hall, its steps flanked by sculptured elephants. At a large tank on the left, people feed idli to the fish. More shrines honour Ganesh and Murugan, who is believed to have split apart a stone statue in another attempt to settle an argument about superiority.

A statue of Nandi faces west to the inner shrine and another gopuram provides entrance to a smaller tank (some 24m square).

A small shrine to Bhairava (a ferocious manifestation of Shiva) is positioned on the side of the tank, and the ceiling paintings on the outer mandapam depict the story of the temple and Shiva's confrontation with the deceitful Brahma.

Further west are the main shrines to Shiva and Parvati – known here as Arunachaleswar and Unnamulaiyamman. The entrance to Parvati's shrine is guarded by her two sons, and pillars depict her and her different aspects. Similarly the shrine to Shiva is defended by guardian statues.

The temple is open from 6 am to 1 pm and from 5.30 to 10 pm.

Sri Ramanasramam Ashram

Located 2km south-west of Tiruvannamalai at the foot of Annamalai, this small ashram draws devotees of Sri Ramana Maharishi, a guru who died in 1950 after nearly 50 years in peaceful and often silent contemplation (including 20 years in caves on the slopes of Arunachala).

Unlike some ashrams, Sri Ramanasramam is not didactic. As its literature states 'there are no rigid rules or schedules of activities and the homely environment leaves visitors free to pursue their individual spiritual practice'. At this place even the monkeys seem contemplative, ambling with peacocks and devotees through the peaceful grounds.

While casual visitors are not discouraged, the administrators prefer people who are familiar with the life and teachings of Sri Ramana Maharshi. Accommodation is available for devotees but you must apply in writing at least three months in advance to the President, Sri Ramanasramam, PO Tiruvannamalai, 606 603 (☎ /fax 22491). The ashram also has a Web site: www.rtanet.com/ramana. Office hours are 8 to 11 am and 2 to 5 pm.

Places to Stay and Eat

There are several lodges offering basic accommodation near the temple.

Park Lodge has basic singles/doubles for Rs 60/80.

Udupi Brindhavan Lodge (☎ 22693, 57A Car St) has simple rooms for Rs 60/80

and two air-con rooms for Rs 270. Most have attached bathrooms and bucket hot water. There's a large veg restaurant next door.

Trishul Hotel (☎ 22219, 6 Kanakaraya Mudali St) has rooms for Rs 375/450 and Rs 580/650 with air-con. From December to February rates increase by at least Rs 100. It's clean, comfortable and has running hot water. A good veg restaurant is attached. It's a three minute walk to the temple. The staff have a reputation for getting the bill wrong – almost every time! This upsets some guests, but most enjoy the fiasco.

Aruna Lodge, just to the right of the temple entrance, serves veg food.

GINGEE (Senji)
Tel Area Code: 04145

Gingee (pronounced 'shingee') is 37km east of Tiruvannamalai and is the site of an extensive fort complex. Set in a silent and surreal landscape of precariously perched boulders, the meandering structure exudes a palpable sense of history. Constructed mainly in the 16th century during the Vijayanagar Empire (though some of the structures date back to the beginning of the 13th century), the fort has been occupied by various armies, including the forces of Adil Shah from Bijapur who, in 1648, renamed the complex Badshahbad. Thirty years later the Marathas attacked and took control of the fort from 1677.

In 1698 the Mughals took the fort and successfully retained it until defeated by malaria. Then came the French, who held the fort from the middle of the 18th century until the British defeated them at Pondicherry. After a short occupation by the British the site was finally deserted around the turn of the 19th century.

Today's invading army consists of the occasional film crew who use the dramatic location for yet another good guy/bad guy Tamil blockbuster. Otherwise the fort is delightfully free of human activity except for the occasional tourist, some labourers from the Archaeological Survey and a cool-drink vendor. The only permanent occupants seem to be crows, eagles, lizards and the occasional cobra.

A walk around the fort can easily take an entire day. It is constructed on three separate hills (Krishnagiri to the north, Chandrayandurg to the south and Rajagiri to the east) and joined by 5km of fortified walls (up to 15m thick in some places). The structure is in varying degrees of dilapidation which somehow adds to the lure of the place.

Buildings within the fort include a granary, a Shiva temple and a mosque. The most prominent building is the recently restored audience hall, Kalyana Mahal, which contains a pagoda-like structure that was used for wedding ceremonies. Horse and elephant stables are dotted throughout the complex.

Of the three hills, Rajagiri is the highest (165m). It's worth negotiating the 1200 uneven (and often invisible) steps to the citadel but take great care and plenty of water and allow around one hour for the climb. Krishnagiri Hill is much easier to climb.

The fort is open from 9 am to 5 pm. A siren is sounded at 4.45 pm to warn stragglers that the gates are about to be locked (if you do find yourself locked in a 'small consideration' to the watchman should reveal the key to your freedom). Entry is Rs 2. Cameras are free but video is Rs 25.

The only accommodation in Gingee is *Devi Lodge* (☎ *2210*). This basic but very clean lodge is on the main road, 1.5km from town on the Pondicherry side. It has 50 rooms (some with a rear view to the fort) and costs Rs 45/60. Bucket hot water is available and simple meals can be ordered for your room. There are a number of cheap veg and nonveg eating places in town.

There are buses almost every hour from Tiruvannamalai. The fort is 2km before the town, so ask the driver for 'the fort'. It is also possible to make a day visit from Pondicherry.

PONDICHERRY

Pop: 789,416   Tel Area Code: 0413

Pondicherry, the former French colony settled in the early 18th century, is a charming Indian town with a few enduring pockets of French culture, and an ashram set beside the sea. Together with the other former French enclaves of Karaikal (also in Tamil Nadu), Mahé (Kerala) and Yanam (Andhra Pradesh), it now forms the Union Territory of Pondicherry.

As in Goa, there are plenty of reminders of the colonial days, despite the fact that the French relinquished control of 'Pondy' over 40 years ago. The Tricolour flutters over the grand French Consulate, there's a *Hôtel de Ville* (town hall), red *kepis* (caps) and belts are worn by the local police, and you can occasionally hear French spoken on the streets.

Tamils from outside Pondicherry dismiss the place with an almost French expression 'phhhh' and a put-down: 'It's just dolphins and bicycles'.

Extensive restoration work of the buildings in the centre has been undertaken by the Aurobindo Ashram, the Alliance Française, and other bodies. Many houses and institutions in the streets between the waterfront and the old canal are now somewhat chic and gentrified, their gardens ablaze with flowering trees and their entrances adorned with shiny brass plates. Yet Pondicherry is still very much an Indian city. It's just that on the eastern side of the canal, it's a bit more relaxed and people don't sleep on the streets.

The French influence is also reflected, as one might expect, in the food. There are some very good restaurants serving everything from authentic bouillabaisse to crème caramel to die for. As in their other colonies the French soon sought out a good source of mineral water, and bottled Pondicherry water is by far the best in India. Hotels are excellent value since Tamil Nadu's punitive taxes do not apply here. And the beer's only Rs 35!

You may come here to see the Sri Aurobindo Ashram, or to check up on ancestry, but you'll probably stay longer than you'd intended.

History

Long before a word of French was spoken in Pondicherry, significant things were happening around the area. The jury is still out

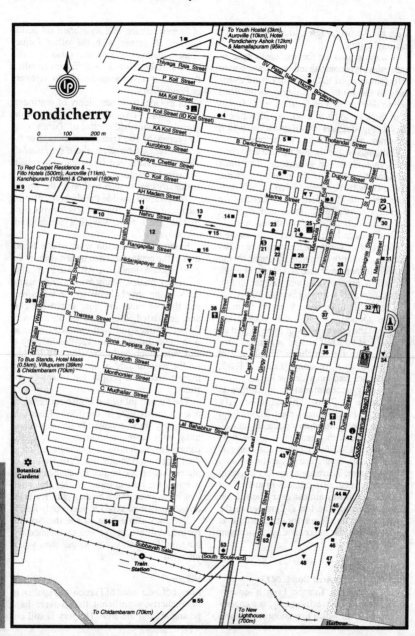

Pondicherry

0   100   200 m

To Youth Hostel (3km),
Auroville (10km), Hotel
Pondicherry Ashok (12km)
& Mamallapuram (95km)

To Red Carpet Residence &
Fillo Hotels (500m), Auroville (11km),
Kanchipuram (103km) & Chennai (160km)

To Bus Stands, Hotel Mass
(0.5km), Villupuram (39km)
& Chidambaram (70km)

Botanical
Gardens

Train
Station

To Chidambaram (70km)

To New
Lighthouse
(700m)

Harbour

Thiyaga Raja Street
P Koil Street
MA Koil Street
Iswaran Koil Street (ID Koil Street)
KA Koil Street
Aurobindo Street
Supraya Chettiar Street
C Koil Street
AH Madam Street
Nehru Street
Rangapillai Street
Nidarajapayer Street
SS Pillai Street
St Theresa Street
Sinna Pappara Street
Lapporth Street
Monthorsier Street
C Mudhaliar Street
Lal Bahabhur Street
Subbayah Salai
(South Boulevard)

SV Patel Salai (North Boulevard)
B Derichemont Street
Marine Street
L Thollandal Street
Dupuy Street
St Louis Street
Compagnie Street
St Martin Street
Manakula Vinayagar Koil Street
Francois Martin Street
Mahatma Gandhi Road
Mission Street
Canteen Street
Capt Xavier Street
Gingy Street
Victor Simonel Street
Romain Roland Street
Dumas Street
Coubert Avenue (Beach Road)
Suffren Street
Labourdonnais Street
Ellai Amman Koil Street
Covered Canal

Berath Street
Anna Salai (West Boulevard)

PLACES TO STAY		30	Le Cafe	24	Vak Bookshop
1	Ananda Inn; Hotel Surguru	34 43	Le Cafe (Seafront) Rendezvous & Satsanga	25	Sri Manakula Vinayagar Temple
5	Surya Swastika Guest House	45	Blue Dragon Chinese Restaurant	27	GPO; Telegraph Office
9	Hotel Aditya	47	Seagulls Restaurant	28	Library & Site of New
10	Victoria Lodge	48	La Terrasse		Museum
14	Aristo Guest House	49	Le Club	29	French Consulate
16	Amala Lodge	50	China Town Restaurant	32	Old Lighthouse
18	Hotel Kanchi			33	Gandhi Square
26	International Guest House	**OTHER**		35	Indian Overseas Bank; Hôtel de Ville
31	Sea Side Guest House	2	Sri Aurobindo Handmade Paper		(Town Hall)
36	Bar Qualithé Hotel		Factory	37	Government Square
39	Hotel Ram International	3	Drowpathiamman Temple	38	Church of the
44	Ajantha Guest House;	4	Clinic Nallam		Immaculate Conception
	Seaview Restaurant	6	Vijay Arya Moped	40	Kailash French
46	Park Guest House		Rental; Kitab Bookshop		Bookshop
55	Pondicherry Tourism Department Guest House	8 11	Sri Aurobindo Ashram Handloom (Tamil Nadu) Cooperative Shop	41	Notre Dame des Anges Church
		12	Market	42	Tourist Office
PLACES TO EAT		20	Cottage Industries	51	French Bookshop;
7	Bliss Restaurant	21	Canara Bank		Alliance Française
13	Hotel Aristo	22	Higginbothams		Library
15	India Coffee House	23	La Boutique d'Auroville;	52	Alliance Française
17	Hotel Dhanalakshmi		Police Station & Police	53	Bike Hire
19	Bamboo Hut		Museum	54	Sacred Heart Church

when it comes to issuing definitive statements on the early history but archaeologists claim to have evidence of two early settlements. One was called Podhigal and was identified as the abode of the Hindu saint called Agastya. The other settlement was called Vedapuri – here scholars would study the *Vedas*. Recent excavations in the district of Arikamedu, just near Pondicherry, have revealed significant trade connections with ancient Rome and Greece.

During the Chola period a prosperous settlement developed just west of Pondicherry known as Ozhukarai. This is an abbreviation of an earlier term meaning 'northern bank of the river'. The district has had many names over the centuries, including Ponduke and Pondukay.

The French had always sought to establish a colony in India and they finally arrived in Pondicherry in February 1673. Twenty years later the Dutch succeeded in wrestling the settlement from the French but the French were able to reclaim it in 1697 under the famous treaty of Ryswick. A strong French trading post was soon established and was regarded by many French as the beginning of a French empire in India. The British, however, keen to maintain the upper hand in the empire stakes, seized the settlement of Pondicherry three times during the 18th century in what became known as the Carnatic Wars. Much of the conflict during this period was an unofficial war between the British and the French East India companies. Britain finally returned Pondicherry to France in 1814. The French secured their presence for the next 140 years, establishing vestiges of French culture and strengthening links with mainland France. In 1954, six years after Indian Independence, France finally relinquished control of Pondicherry to the Union Territory of India.

TAMIL NADU

Orientation

Pondicherry is laid out on a grid plan surrounded by a congested boulevard. A north-south canal (now covered) divides the eastern side from the larger western part. In colonial days the canal separated Pondicherry's European and Indian sections.

It's fairly easy to navigate the town and locate landmarks and attractions, but there are some eccentricities with street names. Many streets start with one name then change to another. This is particularly so with east-west oriented streets. West Boulevard and North Boulevard are also known as Anna Salai and Sardar Vallabai Patel Salai (with numerous spelling variations) respectively.

The Aurobindo Ashram with its offices, schools and guesthouses, as well as the French institutions and many restaurants, are all on the eastern side, while most but not all of the hotels are west of the canal.

Phone Number Change

Phone numbers beginning with 3 or 4 in Pondicherry have changed. Add an additional 3 at the beginning of these numbers.

Information

The tourist office (☎ 39497), on Goubert Ave, is open daily from 8 am to 1 pm and 2 to 6 pm. It runs half-day sightseeing tours (Rs 40) covering the ashram, Auroville, the handmade paper factory and botanical gardens. Tours leave at 8 am and 2 pm.

The library in Rangapillai St (just around the corner from St Louis St) is open from 8.30 am to 8.30 pm, closed Monday.

The Indian Overseas Bank, in the courtyard of the Hôtel de Ville (town hall), accepts most travellers cheques. There's also a Canara Bank just off Nehru St. Both banks are open weekdays from 10 am to 2 pm and Saturday until noon.

The GPO, on Rangapillai St, is open from 10 am to 7.30 pm, Monday to Saturday. Next door is the 24 hour telegraph office.

The French consulate (☎ 34058), on Compagnie St, is open weekdays from 8 am to noon.

Clinic Nallam (☎ 35463), 74 Iswaran (also known as ID) Koil St, is a recommended place to go if you need a doctor.

Bookshops The Vak Bookshop, 15 Nehru St, specialises in books on religion and philosophy. Equally good, for French readers, is the Kailash French Bookshop (☎ 31872; fax 43663) at 169 Lal Bahabhur St. This shop (which has a branch in Paris) has a delightful garden in the forecourt and an excellent stock of books on India as well as novels and some academic texts. The French Bookshop on Suffren St, next to Alliance Française, is also good. There's a branch of Higginbothams on Gingy St. For second-hand books try Kitab on Dupuy St.

Sri Aurobindo Ashram

Founded by Sri Aurobindo in 1926, this ashram is one of the most popular in India with westerners, and also one of the most affluent. Its spiritual tenets represent a synthesis of yoga and modern science. After Aurobindo's death spiritual authority passed to one of his devotees, a Frenchwoman known as The Mother, who herself died in 1973, aged 97. These days, the ashram underwrites and promotes a lot of cultural and educational activities in Pondicherry, though there is a certain tension between it and the local people because it owns virtually everything worth owning in the Union Territory but is reluctant to allow local participation in the running of the society.

The main ashram building is on Marine St, and is surrounded by other buildings given over to the various educational and cultural activities of the Aurobindo Society. The ashram is open every day from 8 am to noon and 2 to 6 pm and you can be shown around on request. The flower-festooned *samadhi* (tomb) of Aurobindo and The Mother is under the frangipani tree in the central courtyard. Their old black Humber sits rusting in the garage just off the courtyard.

Opposite the main building is the educational centre where you can sometimes catch a film, slide show, play or lecture (forthcoming events are announced on the ashram's notice board). The centre is well stocked with books in almost every language. Entrance to Aurobindo's bedroom depends on your birthday: certain dates are selected by the ashram officials. If your birthdate corresponds with one of the selected dates, then you may be admitted to the bedroom! There is usually no entry charge (children under three are strictly prohibited) but a donation may be collected.

Sri Aurobindo Handmade Paper Factory

Quality handmade paper is a successful ashram enterprise (see the boxed text below). The paper is exported to many countries and visitors are welcome to wander through the factory and watch how it all happens. A wide range of products is available from the sales office. The factory is at

50 SV Patel Salai (☎/fax 34763). It's open daily except Sunday from 8.30 am to noon.

Museums

At the time of writing, the **Pondicherry Museum** was closed for renovation and relocation. Prior to its closure the museum contained everything from Pallava sculptures to a bed slept in by a peripatetic Dupleix, the colony's most famous governor. The museum is due to reopen in a new location at Rangapillai St, next to the library and just opposite Government Square. When it does, its hours will be from 10 am to 5 pm, Tuesday to Sunday.

Just next to the old lighthouse on Goubert Ave is the tiny **Jawahar Toy Museum**. It's actually a doll museum and although it's quite odd, it is rather charming. It houses 120 dolls, each of them carefully labelled and

---

From Rags to Riches

In the heart of Pondicherry among a garden of coconut trees, coloured handmade paper hangs in rows as the sun absorbs the moisture. Here, in small palm-roofed cottages, 240 workers convert waste cotton into high-quality paper. There is no tradition of papermaking in South India: the Aurobindo Ashram, which owns and manages this papermaking business, has undertaken extensive training for its workers, many of whom were previously part of the ranks of the long-term unemployed.

The paper factory is more an artists' workshop than an industrial plant. Despite the large mechanical presses there's a quiet, creative intensity about the place.

The papermaking process involves a synthesis of modern and ancient techniques. Huge bundles of waste cottons are boiled in vast vats of caustic soda and then soaked in a mild bleach. This prepares them for their 'beating': large machines cut, wash and separate the fibres of the rags until they disintegrate into a pulp, which can take up to eight hours. The pulp is then stored in large tanks and from there, it is scooped in small quantities onto specially designed frames. By sweeping their hands across the pulp the gum-booted workers give it the shape and size of a sheet of paper. Each sheet is placed between layers of felt for mechanical pressing to remove the water and then hung out to dry.

In the final processes, workers inspect and sort the sheets, discarding any defective ones which are returned to the beating machines. The paper is then ready for a final pressing and packing.

Such labour-intensive operations cannot hope to compete with commercial paper mills. For these reasons, those in charge of the papermaking decided way back in 1959 to produce only the highest quality papers, which can be used for art work, awards and exclusive stationery.

One sheet of paper takes almost three weeks to complete and 10,000 sheets are produced daily at various sizes and weights. Seventy-five per cent of the paper is now exported to almost every country in the world. This is literally a rags to riches process.

dressed in costumes from various Indian states. There's even a little 'fairyland' with a tiny Ganesh prominently ensconced. Entry is free and the museum is open from 10 am to 1 pm and from 2 to 5 pm. It's closed Monday.

At the police station you can see the **police museum**. This really is bizarre. To find it you have to walk through numerous rooms and numerous more gatherings of police officers, up some stairs and along a corridor. You'll be amply assisted. If you have an interest in 19th and 20th century police costumes and armaments this place will appeal: one display cabinet shows six types of hats worn by the police of Pondicherry.

Churches

There are several large churches and cathedrals around the town. The **Church of our Lady of the Immaculate Conception** in Mission St was completed in 1791. Its medieval architecture is in the style of many of the Jesuit constructions of that time. The church's rather imposing entrance gives way to a grand interior, softened by a peaceful ambience.

Consecrated at the turn of the century, the **Sacred Heart Church** on South Boulevard is an impressive sight with its Gothic architecture, stained glass and striking brown and white colours.

Parks & Gardens

Since their establishment by the French in 1826, the **Botanical Gardens** have received hundreds of different plant species from all over India and abroad. Successive curators and botanists conducted numerous experiments to investigate which particular species would survive here. Even a silkworm nursery was attempted! Now the gardens provide a peaceful environment where you can meander down the many pathways and enjoy the extensive variety of plants.

The **Government Park** in the centre of the eastern section, is the very antithesis of its earlier purpose. Once the location for the French military, destroyed by the British in 1761, its gardens now provide a pleasant space for relaxation.

Alliance Française

This worldwide French cultural organisation (☎ 38146), at 38 Suffren St, runs French, English and Tamil classes as well as a library and a computer centre. Its small monthly newsletter, *Le Petit Journal*, details forthcoming courses and events. The library (☎ 34351) is open daily from 9 am to noon and 4 to 7 pm. Temporary membership (valid for 15 days) is Rs 50.

Temples

Visitors rarely associate Pondicherry with temples and indeed the structures of Pondicherry have developed in such a way as to almost envelop the temples, squeezing them into tiny niches. Yet according to some sources there are over 150 temples in the Pondicherry area and 32 within the city itself. The Hindu people of Pondicherry are renowned for their devotion to Ganesh. His temple, the **Sri Manakula Vinayagar**, in Manakula Vinayagar Koil St is situated on the 'French' side of town – Ganesh is famous for his whimsical ways.

Compared to many better known temples, this one is small. The temple walls contain over 40 friezes of Ganesh in his various forms: sometimes he is honoured by his brother, Subrahmanya (also known by many other names, including Murugan), other times he is seated on a peacock, its feathers providing an intricate and colourful backdrop. The friezes are skilfully painted and with time and age their colours have turned to attractive muted shades. Hindus won't miss the opportunity to visit this temple. Non-Hindus will find the ambience and the artwork very appealing. At the 10-day annual festival in August/September the *Brahmotsavam* (reciting of sacred texts) takes place.

At the **Drowpathiamman Temple** (the address is at Iswaran Koil St, but the actual entrance is in MG Rd), the devotees are proud of their temple artist who has recently rejuvenated the temple's paintings and statues. Now they gleam ostentatiously in their new bright gloss. This temple is dedicated to the goddess of the area and is noted for its 24-day **festival of fire** held in July/August. During this time, an image of the deity is taken in a 2km procession in which saffron-clothed devotees cross burning coals as an expression of their faith. In preparation for the walk they fast for 40 days.

At the temple entrance is a brightly restored Gaja-Lakshmi, a depiction of the goddess with elephants. To the left is the 'security god' who, on the last days of the festival, is fed mutton, chicken, eggs and wine.

Places to Stay – Budget
Pondicherry Tourism Department Guest House (☎ 48276) (also called Tourist Home) on Dr Ambedkar Rd (near the train station) is by far the cheapest option in town, with basic but clean rooms. There are 17 single rooms for Rs 20 and 17 doubles for Rs 30. There is also a restaurant (called Le Cafe) which serves veg and nonveg meals.

Amala Lodge (☎ 38910, 92 Rangapillai St) is clean, popular with travellers and run by a friendly family. The rooms, on the other hand, are very basic. There are singles/doubles for Rs 50/90 with common bath, Rs 60/100 with attached bath.

Surya Swastika Guest House (☎ 43092) is an old-style little guesthouse with pleasant staff at 11 Eswaran (known also as Iswaran) Koil St. There are rooms for Rs 50/80 with common bath, Rs 55/85 with attached bath. Additional bodies are Rs 15 and a mat will be provided. The only drawback is that you have to be in by 9.30 pm.

Aristo Guest House (☎ 36728, 50A Mission St) is clean and friendly and has singles/doubles for Rs 70/100 as well as a few air-con doubles for Rs 550. All the rooms have attached bathrooms.

Victoria Lodge (☎ 36366, 79 Nehru St) is shabby but clean enough, and has rooms for Rs 75/150 with attached bathroom.

Hotel Kanchi (☎ 35540, Mission St) looks like a mid-range hotel until you see the rooms. It is, however, clean and quiet and some of the large, tiled rooms have a balcony. Singles/doubles with attached bathroom start at Rs 120/150.

Bar Qualithé Hotel (☎ 34325, Government Square) is predominantly a pub but it does have six rooms lining the 1st-floor veranda which overlooks the park. It has one single room for Rs 100. All the rest are four-bedded rooms with attached bath for Rs 350. The rooms lack the quality the name implies but this is compensated a little by the character of the place. Hopefully a current renovation program will improve the hotel.

Railway Retiring Rooms cost Rs 30/60 and are pretty quiet – the only action around is cows and goats grazing on the grass growing over the train tracks.

Places to Stay – Mid-Range & Top End
Ashram Guesthouses The best places to stay by far in Pondy are the guesthouses run by the Aurobindo Ashram. They're all immaculately maintained and in the most attractive part of town and, although classified here as mid-range, some offer rooms which are cheaper than those in the budget hotels mentioned above. However, given that such accommodation is set up to assist ashram devotees, certain conditions apply. There is a 10.30 pm curfew, though arrangements can usually be made with the doorkeeper to allow you to come back later. Smoking and alcoholic drinks are banned in all ashram guesthouses.

Park Guest House (☎ 34412, Goubert Ave) has the best facilities and position: all the rooms on the front side face the sea and have a balcony. However, unlike the other ashram guesthouses, the proprietors here prefer taking devotees rather than visiting tourists. Unless they're full, it's unlikely you'll be turned away; however, you may get a slightly cool reception. Singles/doubles range from Rs 200/250 to Rs 300/400 and all have private bathrooms. There's a vegetarian restaurant here.

International Guest House (☎ 36699) is on Gingy St. The cheapest rooms here are in the old wing where singles/doubles start at Rs 70/95. Doubles in the new wing cost Rs 100, and Rs 350 with air-con. All the rooms have attached bathrooms with hot water on request. The rules of the ashram apply here. The gates close at 10.30 pm and a sign says

'For peaceful stay avoid discussions'. Another sign says 'Drivers and servants of guests are not allowed'.

Sea Side Guest House (☎ 21825, 14 Goubert Ave), the third of the ashram guest-houses, has been tastefully renovated and has a far less institutional feel to it. This old house has eight very spacious rooms all with private bathroom. Rooms range from Rs 250 to Rs 400, some with air-con.

Other Hotels Attached to the restaurant/bar of the same name, *Ajantha Guest House (☎ 38898, 22 Goubert Ave)* is not a great place: all the rooms here are on the ground floor so there are no ocean views. There are no singles, and doubles cost Rs 250, or Rs 350 with air-con.

Hotel Surguru (☎ 39022, fax 34377, SV Patel Salai) is popular with business travellers. There are rooms from Rs 370/490, and Rs 490/710 with air-con, all with attached bathrooms and Star TV. The rooms are bright, clean and well furnished. The rear rooms are considerably less noisy. The hotel has a good vegetarian restaurant with very friendly service.

Ananda Inn (☎ 30711, fax 31241, SV Patel Salai) is a flashy neoclassical place, the top hotel in town. The comfortable air-con rooms are Rs 950/1200, there's a bar called Ecstasy, good nonveg and veg restaurants and an efficient travel desk.

Hotel Ram International (☎ 37230, 388 Anna Salai) is a sister to Hotel Surguru with similar facilities and clean and comfortable but slightly cheaper rooms. Singles/doubles are Rs 250/350, and Rs 500/575 with air-con.

Fillo Hotels (☎ 54690, Kumaraj Salai, Sathiya Nagar) is west of the centre and offers non air-con singles/doubles for Rs 150/200, and Rs 300/400 with air-con. The rooms are a little grubby except for one air-con double room which has recently been fitted out in bright pink! If you can lure the staff away from the TV you'll find they are actually quite helpful.

Hotel Mass (☎ 37221, fax 33654, Maraimalai Adigal Salai) is also west of the centre, and is comfortable, clean and a little

upmarket. The hotel has central air-con and standard rooms are Rs 550/700. Suites range from Rs 850 to Rs 1250. Each extra person is Rs 150. The hotel has a good patisserie, veg and nonveg restaurants and a 'late night bar' that closes at 10.30 pm. It also operates a weekend disco (6.30 to 10.30 pm Saturday and Sunday) for Rs 100 per couple.

Hotel Aditya (☎ 605011, 104 Kamaraj Salai) has comfortable rooms from Rs 200/250, and Rs 375/400 with air-con. There is a good vegetarian restaurant, and a helpful travel desk.

Hotel Pondicherry Ashok (☎ 65160; fax 65140) is a Portuguese villa-style hotel 12km north of town on the coastal road. Rooms here start at Rs 1195/2000. It's a great location but it's a little run down and the service doesn't quite match its claim as a three-star hotel.

Red Carpet Residence (☎ 53321, 3rd Cross, Ananda Ranga Pillai Nagar), near Ananda Rangar Mahal, is a series of seven comfortable apartments for long-term guests. Minimum stay is 24 hours, and it is possible to take out a 12 month lease. Each apartment has two bedrooms with balconies, two bathrooms, a lounge/dining area and a kitchen with a good stove, some utensils and crockery. Each has air-con and ceiling fans. Rates are Rs 650 per day. A 5% discount is available for a 30 day lease and 10% on a 90 day lease.

Places to Eat
Pondicherry has some excellent places to eat, some open-air, and most serve cheap beer. One of the cheapest places to eat is the ashram. If you purchase a meal ticket (Rs 15) in advance, you can eat lunch or dinner (in mandatory silence) in their dining room.

West Side The *Hotel Aristo* has a very popular rooftop restaurant. It has a 198 item Indian menu with everything made to order, so expect to wait at least 20 minutes for your food to arrive. Most main dishes are Rs 30 to Rs 50 and there are some interesting choices, such as walnut chicken with brown rice (Rs 50). Food is cheaper and served faster in the ground floor restaurant (closed Friday).

India Coffee House (Nehru St) is good value for breakfast and snacks.

Bamboo Hut (3 Rangapillai St) serves good and well-priced Chinese dishes from its rooftop garden.

Hotel Dhanalakshmi, opposite Amala Lodge in Rangapillai St, is somewhat downmarket. It serves multicuisine meals, has a bar and is very popular with locals as a drinking haunt.

East Side Near the ashram, *Bliss Restaurant* serves straightforward thalis for Rs 15 but is closed on Sunday.

Le Cafe, opposite the French consulate on Marine St, is a former garage turned snack bar offering good tea and samosas. It's not to be confused with the seafront *Le Cafe* on Goubert Ave, a crumbly old place that is frequented by the locals after their evening promenade. Basic South Indian food is available and you can dine with the waves crashing below.

Bar Qualithé Hotel, overlooking Government Square on Labourdonnais St, is an old refurbished place with comfy wicker chairs and bags of atmosphere. Have a plate of beef fry (Rs 25) with your beer (Rs 26). There's a range of more substantial dishes for around Rs 35.

Seagulls Restaurant (19 Dumas St) is right by the sea and serves quite good food. Alcohol is available.

Blue Dragon Chinese Restaurant (33 Dumas St) serves good Chinese food as does *China Town (Suffren St)*.

Seaview Restaurant and Bar (22 Goubert Ave), just above the Ajantha Guest House, has tremendous potential with its rooftop setting overlooking the ocean but the food is, at best, rather mediocre.

La Terrasse (5 Subbish Salai) is an excellent French-run pizza restaurant, open evenings only. Pizza costs from Rs 45 to Rs 65.

Rendezvous (30 Suffren St) is a lovely place with décor straight out of rural France – wicker chairs, gingham tablecloths and

shutters. It's open 8 to 11 am, noon to 3 pm and 6 to 10.30 pm. Bouillabaisse (Rs 60), lobster and mushroom quiche (Rs 90) and grilled prawns (Rs 150) are some of the excellent dishes on offer. They also do good tandoori food, and there's an attractive roof terrace.

Satsanga is just down the street from Rendezvous. French-run, the food's as good as it sounds – soupe de poisson (Rs 45), terrine de lapin (Rs 50), salade provençal (Rs 45), and poulet piment vert et frites (Rs 65). The coffee's superb, as is the crème caramel, and you can sit out in the garden. There's a range of jams, pickles and peanut butter for sale. There's a pricey art gallery, and they also have a couple of rooms for rent. It's closed on Thursday.

Le Club (33 Dumas St) is a rambling old mansion set in a pleasant garden. The cuisine is French, the décor peachy and the service immaculate. Tamil, Hindi, French, English and more are spoken and wine and beer are available. Breakfast is from 7.30 to 9.30 am but it's best to arrive after 8.30 am when the baguettes have arrived. (Sorry, no croissants.) Lunch is from noon to 2 pm and dinner from 7 to around 10.30 pm every day except Monday. Expect to pay Rs 150 for a glass of wine, around Rs 60 for an entree, and Rs 200 for a main course. You could follow this with a plate of profiteroles (Rs 65), but don't – they're stuffed with sweet ice cream. Try a cognac instead (Rs 175). Even if your budget only extends to a coffee (which they don't seem to mind) it's well worth a visit. There's a cheaper tandoori restaurant, *Le Bistro*, in the garden. Rumour has it that the owner of the building has recently returned to India and the restaurant may have to move. If it does, it will keep a similar menu and service.

Entertainment
People retire early in Pondy. Many take a walk along the seafront, eating ice creams, pursuing their amorous interests or simply watching others. But by nine or, at the latest, 10 pm, Pondy's a quiet, sleepy town. The residents do much of their entertaining at

TAMIL NADU

home. If they want to party they must seek permission from the police. Unless the traveller can secure an invite to one of these (hang around Le Club and you may get lucky!) there's not a great deal to do in Pondy in the evenings. The Bar Qualithé Hotel and the Ajantha Bar stay open until 10.30 pm and the Hotel Mass has a weekend disco that's also finished at 10.30 pm.

Shopping

Pondicherry specialises in a range of crafts which are available for sale throughout the area. Pottery, both clay and ceramic, is produced. While clay pottery is the oldest craft (over 2000 years) in the Pondicherry area, ceramics are a more recent introduction. Incense burners, vases, plant pots, ceramic bowls, platters, tea sets and jugs are just some of the items available. Fine handmade paper is sold from the sales office of the Sri Aurobindo factory (see the boxed text 'From Rags to Riches'). Pondicherry artisans also make jewellery, batiks, *kalamkari* (drawings of deities and other mythical beings), carpets and woodcarvings. Such products may be purchased from La Boutique d'Auroville (Nehru St) which stocks a range of high quality items.

Also on Nehru St is the Handloom (Tamil Nadu) Cooperative shop. Cottage Industries on Rangapillai St has a range of crafts. Another place for quality products, including stone carvings from Mamallapuram, Auroville products, top quality postcards and some chic handbags, is the seafront shop, Splendour, at 16 Goubert Ave.

Getting There & Away

Bus The STC (formerly TTC/RGTC) bus stand is by the roundabout on the road to Villupuram, to the west of the centre. It's quiet and well organised, with a computerised reservation service (Rs 2). There are buses to Chennai (Rs 30, 4½ hours) at least once an hour, and buses four times daily to Madurai (Rs 85, 7½ hours), Bangalore, Tirupathi and Coimbatore.

From the chaotic new bus stand, 500m to the west, there are regular buses to Banga-

lore (twice daily), Chidambaram (every half hour), Kanchipuram (four times daily), Karaikal (10 times daily), Kumbakonam (five times daily), Chennai (10 times daily), Mamallapuram (four times daily), Nagapattinam (three times daily), Tiruchirappalli (five times daily), Tiruvannamalai (nine times daily), Vellore (five times daily) and Villupuram.

Train Pondicherry's train station is not very busy as most people go by bus. It's more popular with goats than people! There are four daily passenger trains to Villupuram (Rs 7, 38km, one hour) on the Chennai to Madurai line. They depart Pondicherry at 5.10 and 8 am, and 4.15 and 9.30 pm. From Villupuram trains leave for Pondicherry at 3.55 am, and 1.25 and 9.10 pm. The computerised booking service at the station covers all trains on the southern railway.

Taxi Taxis to Chennai cost Rs 850, and Rs 750 to the airport.

Getting Around

One of the best ways to get around is by walking. Otherwise, large three-wheelers shuttle between the bus stands and Gingy St for Rs 3, but they're so overcrowded you might not want to use them. There are also plenty of cycle and auto-rickshaws. Autorickshaws are meterless and although official fares (starting at Rs 6 for up to 2km) are posted near the main stands, you'll have to haggle.

The most popular transport option is bicycle hire. This is also a good idea if you plan to visit Auroville. At many of the bike hire shops on MG Rd, Mission St and South Blvd you may be asked for Rs 500 or your passport as a deposit. The only way around this is to have proof of which hotel you are staying in (they may check this, too). The usual rental is Rs 2 per hour, or around Rs 20 per day.

Mopeds can be rented from Vijay Arya (☎ 36179), 9 Aurobindo St (no sign), for Rs 80 a day. You need to leave some ID (passport or driving licence).

AUROVILLE
Tel Area Code: 0413

Just over the border in Tamil Nadu, Auroville is the brainchild of The Mother and was designed by French architect Roger Anger. It was conceived as 'an experiment in international living where men and women could live in peace and progressive harmony with each other above all creeds, politics and nationalities'. Its opening ceremony on 28 February 1968 was attended by the President of India and representatives of 121 countries, who poured the soil of their lands into an urn to symbolise universal oneness.

The project has 80 settlements spread over 20km, and about 1200 residents (two-thirds of whom are foreigners), including children. The settlements include: Forecomers, involved in alternative technology and agriculture; Certitude, working in sports; Aurelec, devoted to computer research; Discipline, an agricultural project; Fertile, Nine Palms and Meadow, all engaged in tree planting and agriculture; Fraternity, a handicrafts community working in cooperation with local Tamil villagers; and Aspiration, an educational, health care and village industry project.

While most visitors attempt to 'see' Auroville in a day, you will not get the feel of the place unless you spend at least a few days here. Day-trippers and casual tourism are not actively encouraged, although visitors with a genuine interest in Auroville will not be made unwelcome. As the Aurovillians put it: 'Auroville is very much an experiment that is in its early stages, and it is not at all meant to be a tourist attraction'.

Information

In Pondicherry, La Boutique d'Auroville (☎ 27264) has information on the community. At Auroville itself, there is a visitor's centre (☎ 62239) near Bharat Nivas. This

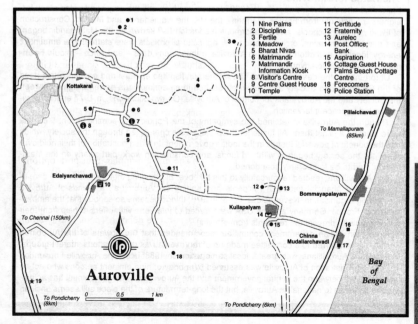

1 Nine Palms	11 Certitude
2 Discipline	12 Fraternity
3 Fertile	13 Aurelec
4 Meadow	14 Post Office;
5 Bharat Nivas	Bank
6 Matrimandir	15 Aspiration
7 Matrimandir	16 Cottage Guest House
Information Kiosk	17 Palms Beach Cottage
8 Visitor's Centre	Centre
9 Centre Guest House	18 Forecomers
10 Temple	19 Police Station

Kottakarai

Pillaichavadi

To Mamallapuram (85km)

Edaiyanchavadi

Bommayapalayam

Kullapalyam

To Chennai (150km)

Chinna Mudaliarchavadi

Bay of Bengal

Auroville

To Pondicherry (8km) 0 0.5 1 km

To Pondicherry (6km)

TAMIL NADU

centre has a permanent exhibition of the community's activities and the helpful staff will address any queries. It's open daily from 9.30 am to 5.30 pm. Next door is an Auroville handicrafts shop and a restaurant. If you're seeking detailed information on the range of activities at Auroville, read their monthly magazine *Auroville Today*. Many of the articles are refreshingly honest in their analysis and discourse. They certainly transcend the sort of public relations blurb common to so many ashrams. Copies of the magazine are sold at the visitor's centre. Extracts from particular issues are also available on the excellent Auroville Web site at www.auroville-india.org.

Matrimandir

The Matrimandir was designed to be the spiritual and physical centre of Auroville. Its construction has been very much a stop-start affair because the flow of funds has been less than steady. However, the meditation chamber and the main structure are now complete leaving only the finishing touches (metal discs) to be added to the external skin. Likewise, the extensive landscaping associated with the project is well under way with the assistance of a small army of local labourers.

The meditation chamber is lined with white marble and houses a solid crystal, 70cm in diameter and manufactured by the Zeiss company in Germany. It is said to be the largest crystal in the world. Rays from the sun are beamed into this crystal from a tracking mirror located in the roof. On cloudy days, solar lamps do the job.

The Battle for Auroville

For a time after Auroville's opening in 1968 idealism ran high and the project attracted many foreigners, particularly from France, Germany, the UK, the Netherlands and Mexico. Construction of living quarters, schools, and an enormous meditation hall known as the Matrimandir began, and dams, reforestation, orchards and other agricultural projects were started. The amount of energy, idealism and effort invested in Auroville in those early days – and since – should be immediately obvious to anyone.

Unfortunately the death in 1973 of The Mother, undisputed spiritual and administrative head of the Sri Aurobindo Society and Auroville, resulted in an acrimonious power struggle between the Society and the Aurovillians for control of Auroville. On two occasions, in 1977 and 1978, violence led to police intervention.

Though the Aurovillians retained the sympathy of the Pondicherry administration, the odds were stacked against them. All funds for the project were channelled through the society, which had the benefit of powerful friends in the Indian government. In a demonstration of their hold over Auroville, the society began to withhold funds; and construction work, particularly on the Matrimandir, had to be temporarily abandoned.

The Aurovillians reacted resourcefully to this takeover bid, pooling their assets to take care of the food and financial needs of residents and setting up 'Auromitra', a friends-of-Auroville fundraising organisation. Nevertheless, in early 1976, things became so serious that the ambassadors of France, Germany and the USA were forced to intervene with offers of help from their governments to prevent the residents from starving.

Finally, an Indian government committee recommended that the powers of the Aurobindo Society be transferred to a committee made up of representatives of the various interest groups, including the Aurovillians, with greater local participation. In 1988, under the Auroville Foundation Act, the administration of Auroville was assumed by a body of nine eminent persons who act as intermediaries between the central government and the Aurovillians. The government has actually gone so far as to nationalise Auroville, but the long-term future of the place still seems unclear.

While the Matrimandir is undoubtedly a remarkable edifice and certainly the focal point of the community, many of the more pragmatic Aurovillians would have preferred the money spent on community infrastructure and on projects of a more tangible nature. Others claim that without any such physical manifestation of Auroville's (and, therefore, The Mother's) spiritual ideal, the community may have splintered long ago, particularly in view of the financial and physical hardships endured by many of its less affluent members.

You can wander around the gardens between 9.30 am and 3.30 pm. Only between 3.30 and 4.30 pm are visitors allowed inside the Matrimandir, but you need to get a ticket (free) in advance from the visitor centre, before 4 pm.

Places to Stay & Eat

Palms Beach Cottage Centre is by the big Pepsi sign in the village of Chinna Mudaliarchavadi on the way to Auroville from Pondy. Not quite what the name suggests, it's a good 15 minutes from the beach. Clean toilets and showers are shared, and there's an open-air gazebo for eating and relaxing in. Meals are available, main dishes cost around Rs 45. Singles/doubles cost Rs 80/150.

Cottage Guest House is a little further on, down the lane on the right opposite the turnoff to Auroville. It offers basic singles/doubles with mosquito nets in a thatched-roof, semi-concrete block for Rs 60/120 with shared bathroom. Doubles with attached bathroom in the new block are Rs 180. There's a communal dining area and all meals are available.

You can also stay with virtually every one of the 40 community groups here; however, they prefer people to stay at least a week and, although work isn't obligatory, it's very much appreciated. You come here, after all, to get to know people involved in Auroville. You should note that none of these community groups will offer free accommodation in exchange for work. For most groups, money is tight. Conditions, facilities and costs vary a great deal. Some places are

quite primitive with minimal facilities; others have the lot. Prices range from Rs 80 to Rs 350, with some accommodation in the *Centre Guest House (☎ 62155)*, very close to the Matrimandir. A list of accommodation places, complete with map and details of facilities, is available at the visitor's centre.

The only place in Auroville where casual visitors will find a meal – and it's a good one – is the brightly decorated cafeteria next to the visitor's centre. It's open daily for lunch (Rs 25 for a healthy meal of the day) as well as for dinner on Friday and Saturday night. Savoury snacks, cakes, tea and coffee are sold as well.

Getting There & Away

The best way to enter Auroville is from the coast road, at the village of Chinna Mudaliarchavadi. Ask around as it's not well signposted. It's also possible to enter from the main Pondicherry to Chennai road at Promesse. The turn-off, 1km after the police station, is signposted.

Once at Auroville, you'll need something other than your feet to get around as everything is very spread out. If you rent a bike or scooter in Pondicherry, you can count on cycling at least 30km there and back. It's mostly tarmac roads or good gravel tracks. Most of the community centres (eg Matrimandir, Bharat Nivas, etc) are signposted but the individual settlements tend to be hidden and difficult to locate.

HOGENAKKAL
Tel Area Code: 043425

This quiet village, nestled in the forested Melagiri Hills, 170km south of Bangalore, is at the confluence of the Chinnar and Cauvery (Kaveri) rivers. From here the Cauvery enters the plains in a series of impressive waterfalls which have recently found fame as the backdrop for some of Indian cinema's more tragic love scenes. Sadly, in the last few years, the falls have also attracted dozens of disconsolate real-life lovers who have jumped to their deaths here.

Despite this, Hogenakkal is a popular day trip for families from Bangalore, and can make a peaceful respite for travellers wanting a break from temple hopping through Tamil Nadu. It's most impressive in July/August, when the water is at its peak.

No visit to Hogenakkal is complete without a ride in a corracle. These little round boats, known locally as *parisals*, are made from waterproof hides that are stretched over lightweight wicker frames. Another of Hogenakkal's treats is an oil massage – more than 100 masseurs ply their trade here so you shouldn't have to queue.

Places to Stay & Eat

Private homes, near the police station (to the right just as you enter the village), have rooms to let. The stalls at the bus stand all sell tasty fried fish.

Hotel Tamil Nadu (☎ 447) has doubles for Rs 350, or Rs 550 with air-con, including tax, plus about 30% at weekends. The large, airy rooms have monkey-proof balconies. Dorm beds (men only) in the attached *youth hostel* are Rs 70. The hotel has an uninspiring restaurant where you can get a thali for Rs 15. Nonvegetarian food should be ordered several hours in advance.

Tourist Resthouse and *Tourist Home* next to the bus stand both offer basic rooms for between Rs 80 and Rs 150.

Getting There & Away

Hogenakkal straddles the border of Tamil Nadu and Karnataka but can be accessed only from Tamil Nadu. The nearest main town is Dharampuri, 45km east on the Salem to Bangalore road. From here, there are several daily buses to Hogenakkal (Rs 90, 1¼ hours).

YERCAUD

Tel Area Code: 04281

This hill station (altitude 1500m) is 33km uphill from Salem. Surrounded by coffee plantations in the Servaroyan hills, it's a good place for relaxing, walking, or boating on the town's artificial lake.

Places to Stay

Unfortunately the peace you might expect at a hill station is sometimes shattered. Around

the lake area raucous music blasts out through loudspeakers. Choose a place away from the lake if you prefer solitude.

Hotel Tamil Nadu (☎ 22273, *Yercaud Ghat Rd*), near the lake, has double rooms from Rs 300 to Rs 450. Dorm beds cost Rs 75. Prices increase to Rs 400 and Rs 600 in the high season. In the scheme of things it's OK, with many rooms overlooking the lake. There's a restaurant and bar, but in spite of being surrounded by coffee plantations with the smell of roasting beans permeating the area, all you'll get is instant coffee! There's a small playground for children as well as boating facilities.

Hotel Shevaroys (☎ 22288; *fax 22387*, *Hospital Rd*) has double rooms from Rs 475/675 in the low season and Rs 625/825 in the high season. It's set in pleasant gardens with two restaurants serving Indian and Chinese cuisine as well as a 'Bears Cave Bar'. At the front door there's a chookyard containing the most bizarre birds and producing the usual chook whiffs each time you pass! They accept credit cards and change money.

Panchayat Union Guesthouse (☎ 22233) (also known as the Township Resthouse) is a good choice set among the trees overlooking dusty playing fields. For just Rs 75 you can have a two-room, two-bathroom lodge. A cook will bring food to your room. It's good value but you'd do well to take some incense to beat the stale smell! Before you stay, you must get permission from the Panchayat Union office just near the Hotel Tamil Nadu. It's open from 10.30 am to 5 pm every day. To get to the guesthouse follow the narrow road with the stone fence from the Canara Bank in Main Rd for 2km.

Central Tamil Nadu

CHIDAMBARAM

Tel Area Code: 04144

Sixty kilometres south of Pondicherry, Chidambaram's great temple complex of Nataraja, the dancing Shiva, is another of

Tamil Nadu's Dravidian architectural highlights.

The best time to be here is during one of the many festivals. The two largest are the 10-day car festivals, the dates for which usually fall in April/May and December/January. In February the Natyanjali Dance Festival attracts performers from all over the country.

Orientation & Information

The main focus at Chidambaram is its Nataraja Temple and the small town is developed around it with streets conveniently named after the four cardinal points. This is an easy town for walking, with most accommodation being close to the temple. There are two post offices; one in North Car St; the other in South Car St. They open from 10 am to 3 pm every day except Sunday. During Pongal, the North Car St post office organises special boxes for greeting cards – just follow the postmaster's handwritten instructions on the gate. There are several banks in town but none provides foreign exchange.

Both the train and bus stands are close to the town. The tourist office (☎ 22739) is at the TTDC Hotel Tamil Nadu, and is open from 9 am to 5 pm Monday to Friday.

Nataraja Temple

Chidambaram was a Chola capital from 907 to 1310 and the Nataraja Temple was erected during later time of their administration. Set within a walled rectangular frame, the complex covers 22 hectares and has four

---

Beware of Brahmins Bearing Books

Hawkers and beggars have been hassling visitors at the well-known temples in India for a long time. Now even priests have got into the act. This is especially true at the Nataraja Temple at Chidambaram. Claiming a long ancestry back to a fabled time, the Brahmins of Chidambaram belong to a particular group known as the Dikshitas. Unlike other temples, where the government provides funds for their upkeep, the Chidambaram priests have waged a protracted and successful struggle to ensure that control of the temple remains solely within their jurisdiction. An old temple with exquisite artwork requires substantial upkeep, as do the 300 priests, and their families who now undertake this work. And who would deny them this? Their role as guardians of the temple, both physically and ritualistically, is crucial if such a fine edifice and its customs are to be preserved for the thousands of pilgrims and others who visit.

Some of the Dikshitas, however, have become very arrogant. The moment foreigners enter the temple they are assailed by one (often more) of these priests who command the visitors to enter details in what seems like a visitors book. Not only is your name and address required. So too is the size of your donation as well as a vow to continue donating on a regular basis.

Visitors are often intimidated by aggressive priests into signing away hundreds (even thousands) of their rupees. Once you've made a donation, you still can't expect peace and quiet. Around the next corner or at the next table, there'll be another Brahmin, with another book demanding his 'rightful' access to your hard-earned savings.

If you come to this temple seeking serenity and silence, forget it. Anger and aggression is common, even in the inner sanctum!

The Dikshitas' claim to an ancient ancestry makes them unique. For these reasons they retain the respect of many of the local people as well as the pilgrims. And they are sought after to conduct important rituals pertaining to life's transitions. However, some people claim the Dikshitas have lost their purpose; that they have forsaken their spiritual role for a materialistic one. Some locals now warn visitors: 'You'll know the priests, they're the one's with the books'. 'Don't look at them; don't even talk to them' they advise. 'It's no more looking to the god' says one, 'now it's only shopping!'

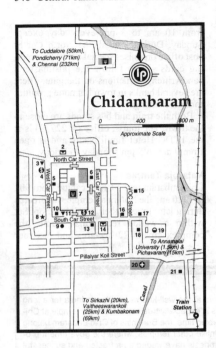

To Cuddalore (50km),
Pondicherry (71km)
& Chennai (232km)

Chidambaram

0   400   800 m

Approximate Scale

North Car Street

West Car Street

East Car Street

VOC Street

South Car Street

To Annamalai
University (1.5km) &
Pichavaram (15km)

Pillaiyar Koil Street

Canal

To Sirkazhi (20km),
Vaitheeswarankoil
(25km) & Kumbakonam
(69km)

Train
Station

PLACES TO STAY
5   Hotel Murugan
6   Hotel Akshaya; Aswini Restaurants
10 Ramyas Lodge
13 Star Lodge; Bakiya Lakshmi
    Restaurant
15 RK Towers
16 Shameer Lodge
17 Kalyanam Boarding & Lodging
18 Hotel Saradharam & Restaurant
21 TTDC Hotel Tamil Nadu; Tourist Office;
    Idli Shop

PLACES TO EAT
3   Kamala Vilas Hotel
11 Rams Ice Cream

OTHER
1   Tillai Kali Amman Temple
2   North Car Street Post Office
4   Indian Overseas Bank
7   Nataraja Temple
8   Police Station
9   Bike Hire
12 State Bank of India
14 South Car Street Post Office
19 Bus Stand
20 Hospital

large gopurams, the north and south ones towering 49m high. The temple is renowned for its prime examples of Chola artistry. It has been patronised by numerous dynasties since the original Chola construction, also see the illustrated 'Sacred Architecture' section on page 574.

As with most temples, but perhaps more so here, each of the entrances has long passageways where every imaginable (and unimaginable) item is on sale. The large gopurams, with finely sculptured icons depicting the various Hindu myths, face each of the directions.

To the left of the southern entrance the **Ganesh shrine**, set on a stepped pedestal, contains an impressive statue of the elephant god. Directly ahead of the entrance a Nandi looks towards the golden topped **Chit Sabha**, the hall of the inner sanctum, which houses the Nataraja icon and the lingam. The long, awesome corridors surrounding the sanctum contain sculptured pillared halls and numerous shrines.

The east and west gopurams have depictions of Shiva in the 108 poses of the classical dance (54 on each side of both), positions which form the basis for the Bharata Natyam.

At the north-eastern part of the complex, protected by sculptured elephants, is the 1000-pillared **Raja Sabha**, the king's hall, open on festival days. Guides will enthusiastically announce that there are 999 pillars – plus Siva's leg, constituting the final column. To the left of the king's hall and directly north in the complex is the **Sivaganga** (temple tank). Some 20m by 30m, the tank is the subject of many of the stories and the site where the legendary king bathed and was cured of his leprosy. The *Vedas* and the story of the competition dance are inscribed on the walls surrounding the tank. Eagles swoop down to collect small fish swimming in the tank.

TAMIL NADU

The portrait at the northern entrance is of the king Krishnadevaraya who visited the temple in 1516 and became one of its patrons. In the north-west corner Subrahmanya resides in all his glory, with several versions of his vehicle, the peacock, proudly standing sentinel, high on the walls by his shrine. Close by, to the south, his mother the goddess Parvati (here known as Sivakami) is honoured in her own temple. Illustrations

The Dancing Deity of Chidambaram

The legends of Chidambaram have lured millions of pilgrims over the centuries, and the temple remains popular today.

One of the most popular stories about the origins of the temple at Chidambaram involves a northern king who in the 5th century bathed in the waters of the Sivaganga (the temple tank) in the hope that he would be cured of his leprosy. In appreciation of his restoration to full health, he vowed to build a temple at the site of the Sivaganga. After his decision, some 3000 Brahmins are said to have followed him to Chidambaram. These Brahmins are said to be the ancestors of the Dikshita priests who currently operate the temple. The building dates from the 12th century but many alterations and additions have occurred in subsequent centuries.

It is at the Chidambaram Temple that Shiva is said to have won the dance competition with Parvati. Here he is honoured as Nataraja – the lord of the cosmic dance. Chidambaram is also significant because it is linked with four other sites which together represent the five elements. Here it is the element of ether or air – *akasha*. In representing this notion, the lingam here is transparent, and symbolises Shiva with no form. It also symbolises the deity as, like air, permeating everything.

The Symbolism of Nataraja

As Nataraja Shiva dances away evil and ignorance and is the human embodiment of apocalypse and creation. The circle of fire which usually surrounds the dancer symbolises the destruction and eternal flux of the universe: nothing is permanent.

Creation is given energy by the beat of the drum held in Shiva's upper right hand (top left from our point-of-view). His other right hand has the palm held out in a gesture of reassurance and protection.

Shiva's right foot tramples on a dwarf who symbolises ignorance, and his left hand pointing to his outstretched foot grants solace and balance.

The dance is a celebration of going beyond the limitations of rigid thought and action. It is an invitation to broaden ideas and experience. As master of the dance, Shiva creates the master plan for life.

leading to her shrine depict the temples at Madurai and Kanchipuram. In another depiction she holds audience with the gods.

The Nataraja Temple courtyard with its many shrines is open from 4 am to noon and 4.30 to 9 pm. Each day at about 5 pm a puja ceremony is held. The one on Friday evening is particularly striking. Although non-Hindus are not allowed into the inner sanctum, there are usually priests around who will take you in – for a fee, of course.

Places to Stay

As Chidambaram gains popularity new accommodation places are springing up every day. Most of the current (and it seems future) accommodation is in lodges, situated in 'complexes', down alleyways and up staircases.

Most of the new accommodation is generally well positioned, away from the noise, with balconies and fine village views.

Places to Stay – Budget

Railway Retiring Rooms at the station are good value at Rs 60/90 for a double/triple with attached bath. You must book through the station master on platform one. If the station master isn't working, then accommodation is not available and you'll be directed to Hotel Tamil Nadu, about 500m away.

Star Lodge (☎ 22743, South Car St) has clean and habitable rooms for Rs 50/70 with attached bathrooms. A triple room is Rs 100. The rooms have grills in the windows (no glass). It's a friendly place and there's a good restaurant downstairs.

Shameer Lodge (☎ 22983, Venugopal Pillai St) is good value at Rs 50/70/100 for rooms with attached bathroom and clean sheets.

Hotel Murugan (☎ 20419) is one of several similar places on West Car St. You receive a hearty welcome there and train and bus timings are conveniently listed. There are basic rooms with attached bath for Rs 50/100, and an air-con double for Rs 200. The dormitory with five beds costs Rs 180 and is good value for a family.

Kalyanam Boarding & Lodging (☎ 22707, 10 Venugopal Pillai St) is an old rambling place with basic rooms with shared bathroom for Rs 40/70. A double with air-con is Rs 300. The staff here will assist with information about the various attractions and events.

RK Towers (☎ 21077) is a new place near the bus stand at 20A VOC St. The rooms are airy and bright and the timber window frames add a stylish touch. There are no single rooms but at Rs 100 for a standard double this place is good value. Deluxe doubles are Rs 150 and a room with air-con is Rs 300.

Ramyas Lodge (☎ 23011, 36 South Car St) has basic but quiet rooms at Rs 60/100 with bathroom. A double deluxe is Rs 125, with air-con it's Rs 250.

TTDC Hotel Tamil Nadu (☎ 20056; fax 20061, Railway Feeder Rd) has recently spruced up its place. It offers a range of rooms from Rs 120/180 for a basic room, to Rs 300 for a double with air-con, plus Rs 50 for Star TV. It has a multicuisine restaurant.

Hotel Akshaya (☎ 20192; fax 22265, 17-18 East Car St) has very helpful and friendly staff. However, the prices are not good value for the standard offered. No singles are available. A double is Rs 195, deluxe Rs 300 and air-con is Rs 480. These prices include tax. The attached Aswini veg and nonveg restaurants offer good food at very reasonable prices. There is also a multicuisine rooftop restaurant. The hotel supplies a map and information about local points of interest.

Places to Stay – Mid-Range & Top End

Hotel Saradharam (☎ 22966; fax 22265, 19 VGP St), near the bus stand, is the best place in town with ordinary rooms with fan and TV for Rs 275/390 and air-con rooms from Rs 475/525. There's a bar and excellent veg and nonveg restaurants with thoughtful service.

Places to Eat

The choice of restaurants here is rather limited.

Bakiya Lakshmi Restaurant (formerly Babu Restaurant), on the ground floor of the Star Lodge, offers good vegetarian meals in full South Indian style – banana leaves and rock-bottom prices.

TTDC Hotel Tamil Nadu has veg and nonveg restaurants plus a very pleasant rooftop bar (beer is Rs 45).

Hotel Saradharam is an excellent place to eat; it's inexpensive, there's a bar and the beer's really cold! You need to get there early for lunch or dinner as it's very popular.

Rams Ice Creams, opposite the bike hire, serves cold drinks and good ice cream.

Kamala Vilas Hotel, near the Indian Overseas Bank, serves well-priced nonveg meals.

The Idli Shop, right next to the Hotel Tamil Nadu, is the place to go if you're hanging out for an idli. They're served from early morning to well into the evening.

Getting There & Away
The train station is a 20 minute walk south-east of the Nataraja Temple, or Rs 15 by cycle-rickshaw. Express and passenger trains leave for Chennai (six times daily), Kumbakonam, Thanjavur (twice daily), Tiruchirappalli and Madurai.

The bus stand, used by both STC and local buses, is more central. Point-to-Point bus No 157 (seven per day) is quickest to Chennai. Services for Pondicherry continue to Chennai every half hour (Nos 300, 324 and 326, Rs 35, seven hours) and go to Madurai (No 521, Rs 53, eight hours).

Getting Around
There's a bike hire shop on South Car St (Rs 1.50 per hour). No deposit is required. Only 'mens' bikes (with bars) are available.

AROUND CHIDAMBARAM
Pichavaram
The seaside resort of Pichavaram, with its backwaters and mangrove forest, is 15km east of Chidambaram. The small (and somewhat bizarre) entrance to the resort is more akin to a theme park than a peaceful paradise, but don't let that put you off. You can explore the beauty and seclusion of this place at your leisure. At the tourist office you can book a rowboat for Rs 10 per person

per hour (minimum one hour; maximum four hours). This includes a boatman which is essential unless you want to get lost among the 4000 canals and 1700 islands.

A Marine Research Institute is at nearby Parangipettai (Porto Novo), a former Portuguese and Dutch port.

The TTDC's *Aringar Anna Tourist Complex* (☎ 041445-89232) charges Rs 45 for a dorm bed and Rs 125 for a two-bedroom cottage. The complex is on a small island about 200m from the resort so you'll need to hire a boat to get there. There are no cooking facilities at the cottage but you can dine at the resort restaurant (which also has a bar) or have your meals delivered by boat. Regular buses go to Pichavaram from Chidambaram. There's a checkpoint just before you arrive: Rs 10 if you're in a car; free if you're in a bus.

Sirkazhi (Seerkazhi, Sirkali)
This small town, 20km south of Chidambaram, consists primarily of a temple. A few houses line its outside walls.

Legend has it that a small boy, Sambandar, came to the temple with his parents who were destitute. The boy had therefore not been fed for some time. In his anguish he emitted a long deep howl of pain. The goddess Parvati responded by providing him with sacred milk. Nourished by the milk, Sambandar began to compose the most beautiful poetry and songs.

Now three shrines embody idols of the deities Shiva (known here as Sri Brahmapureeswarar), Parvati (here referred to as the goddess Tirunilai Nayaki) and the child deity Gnanasambandar. The main festival in March-April celebrates the legend.

The temple is closed from noon to 4 pm. Regular buses come here but there's nowhere to stay.

Vaitheeswarankoil
About 25km south of Chidambaram, this tiny town is well known for its **Viadanatheeswarar Temple**, dedicated to Shiva and Parvati (known here as Viadanatheeswarar and Thaiyalnayaki). It is believed that the

A Fortune Told, A Fortune Made

Astrology is integral to Indian society. For many millions, significant decisions about employment, home-buying or new relationships will not be made without astrological advice. Farmers sometimes consult astrologers over which crops to plant or which animals to purchase. Even everyday decisions, such as the most appropriate times to start work or leave home, can be astrologically determined. The few souls who claim to be non-believers may still avail themselves of the service. Astrological consultancy, they claim, gives them a broader perspective by which to consider and resolve problems. And it provides an intermediate phase for important transitions such as marriage.

There are several types of astrology and numerous variations in astrological practice. In South India, the astrologers of Vaitheeswarankoil, south of Chidambaram, engage in a practice called Nadi. These astrologers claim to be the custodians of ancient palm leaf manuscripts that were originally scribed by sages known as Rishis. The Rishis, 18 saints in all, professed to have divine powers that enabled them to record future events. Their language was Sanskrit and their material was palm leaf.

Centuries later, Tamil kings arranged for these rare manuscripts to be stored and translated into the Tamil language. During the British administration, the manuscripts were auctioned and bought by families living in the Vaitheeswarankoil area. Their descendants now study the manuscripts and pass the knowledge on to whoever seeks information. Their method is to obtain a thumbprint (right for a male, left for a female) of the person seeking information. The ancient palm leaves are then searched for a match with the thumbprint. Sometimes no match is found, and thus no prediction can be made. In such circumstances, the client is advised and the process ceases. However, if there is a match, and sometimes this is achieved only with intense questioning of the client, then the appropriate leaves will be located and read. The leaves are stored in bundles of 50 to 100. In some cases many bundles may be relevant to the client so the process may be ongoing for years, even a lifetime. All manner of advice and predictions are made, including matters relevant to education, family, marriage, residence, occupation, illness and longevity.

Knowledge of the palm leaves is passed on from father to son or from guru to disciple. Training can begin from the age of nine and can take many years. For Nadi practitioners, astrology is strictly a male domain. They claim women are prohibited from reading the leaves and assuming the profession because 'it is a sacred profession and women have natural aspects which prevent association with the sacred'.

To believe or not to believe is a question faced by many who have considered seeking the services of the Nadi astrologers. They have a loyal and ever-growing number of satisfied clients. Others claim that these people invest more energy in making fortunes than in telling them. The fact remains that this is India, the astrologers are there, and your questions will be answered – in a manner of speaking.

aspect of Shiva revered here has healing powers, hence the name which means 'medicine Shiva'. People come to bathe in the waters of the tank in the belief that their illnesses will be cured. Other legends speak of Murugan, Shiva's son, receiving the *vel* (spear) from his father at this site. This event is symbolic of Murugan's power to banish ignorance and darkness – the vel being the weapon through which he achieves his purpose.

At the entrance, like many temples, there is a live elephant. This one is chained – by all four legs. Ironically, the elephant headed god Ganesh, dressed in red cloth, watches nearby with his familiar bemused look.

The town has another claim to fame – its **Nadi astrologers** make predictions according to the texts on ancient palm leaf manuscripts (see the boxed text opposite). Almost every building in the main street is an astrologer's agency. Only the canes of sugar, standing upright along the street, create an occasional break. Touts and brokers for the astrologers compete for custom. Sometimes their threatening behaviour can become aggressive and unpleasant. Stories abound of foreigners who have fallen prey to their harassment and subsequently parted with huge sums of money. It has been said that certain astrologers, who once were respected for their wise advice, have forsaken their skills at fortune telling for those of fortune making! However, many locals and foreigners use the services and find them very satisfactory.

If you want to secure the services of an astrologer, avoid the touts and find your own. Genuine astrologers apparently charge no advance and only accept payment afterwards. They charge between Rs 300 and Rs 1100 depending on the service and length of consultation. To provide comprehensive readings for foreigners, whose stay is usually brief, longer consultations (and their consequent fees) are advised. A cassette tape will be made on request for Rs 100. A postal service is available, but only after the initial reading has been given in person.

There are two accommodation lodges here, both operated by astrologers: *Sri Abirami Lodge (☎ 04364-79311, Mayiladuthurai Rd)* and *Sri Bhakkiam Lodge (☎ 04364-79460)*, just near the temple in South Car St (a continuation of the main street, Milladi St). They offer the usual basic singles and doubles as well as some deluxe rooms. You can get to Vaitheeswarankoil by train from Chidambaram (Rs 2) or Thanjavur (Rs 13). Buses travel here from Bangalore, Tirupathi, Chennai and Tiruchirappalli and all points along the way.

KUMBAKONAM
Tel Area Code: 0435
This busy, dusty commercial centre, nestled along the Cauvery River some 37km north-east of Thanjavur, is noted for its many temples with their colourful semi-erotic sculpture. According to legend, a *kumbh* (pitcher containing the 'seeds of creation') came to rest here after a huge flood (hence the town's name). Shiva broke the pot with his arrow, and its contents spilled and sprouted into Shiva lingams all over the countryside, which accounts for the large number of temples and shrines in the area.

Kumbakonam makes a good base from which to visit the very interesting nearby temple towns of Dharasuram and Gangakondacholapuram.

Temples
The **Sarangapani Temple** dates from the 13th century and is the largest temple in Kumbakonam dedicated to Vishnu: its gopuram stands at 45m with 12 storeys. The main sanctum is constructed in the style of a chariot or ratha. This is an expression of the legend which describes Vishnu's arrival here. In response to the requests of the sage Hemarishi, he descended from the heavens in a chariot.

At the entrance a painted elephant swinging its bells greets devotees and blesses them, in return for their offerings of rupees and bananas. The long hall, built in the Nayak period, leads to the inner shrine, its many pillars in a state of neglect.

North-west, the **Kumbeshwara Temple** is the largest of Kumbakonam's Shiva temples. During festival time, the image of Shiva is taken to the tank. This peaceful temple has a huge white gopuram which is some 39m high.

Nageshwara Temple is also in chariot style, and is dedicated to Nagaraja, the serpent king. The sculptures are exceptional examples from the Chola period. While structures around may impede light, on the three days during the Chithrai Festival (April/May) the sun's rays are said to cast light on the temple's lingam.

Just 600m south-east of the Nageshwara Temple is the palindromic **Mahamaham Tank**. The legend of the deluge (see earlier) relates that much of the contents of the

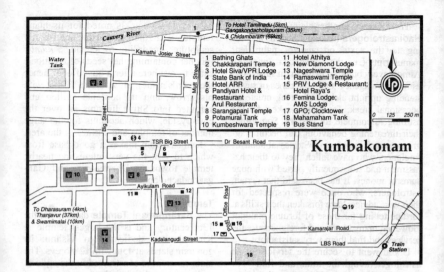

Kumbakonam

1	Bathing Ghats	11	Hotel Athitya
2	Chakkarapani Temple	12	New Diamond Lodge
3	Hotel Siva/VPR Lodge	13	Nageshwara Temple
4	State Bank of India	14	Ramaswami Temple
5	Hotel ARR	15	PRV Lodge & Restaurant;
6	Pandiyan Hotel &		Hotel Raya's
	Restaurant	16	Femina Lodge;
7	Arul Restaurant		AMS Lodge
8	Sarangapani Temple	17	GPO; Clocktower
9	Potamurai Tank	18	Mahamaham Tank
10	Kumbeshwara Temple	19	Bus Stand

pitcher flowed into this tank. Current belief is that once every 12 years, the waters of the Ganges flow into the tank, and at this time thousands of devotees flock here to a festival. The next festival will be held in early 2004.

All the temples are closed between noon and 4.30 pm.

Places to Stay

New Diamond Lodge (☎ 30870, 93 Ayikulam Rd) has basic singles/doubles for Rs 50/75 with common bath, Rs 65/85 with bath attached. It's fine but you should use your own padlock on the door. Rooms at the back have a great view over Nageshwara Temple.

Hotel Siva/VPR Lodge (☎ 21949) share the same reception at 104-5 TSR Big St in the main bazaar area. VPR Lodge offers excellent budget accommodation – Rs 75/100 for very clean rooms. The Shiva has huge, spotless doubles with attached bathroom, constant hot water, and a choice of Indian squat and western sit-down toilets (sometimes both in the same bathroom!) for Rs 195, Rs 350 with air-con.

Pandiyan Hotel (☎ 30397, 52 Sarangapani East St) is popular and often full. All of the rooms have bath attached and cost Rs 65/110.

Femina Lodge (☎ 20369, 8 Post Office Rd) is a small place with excellent-value rooms: spotless doubles with attached bath are Rs 150, a room with four beds is Rs 250.

AMS Lodge (☎ 22381) is adjacent to Hotel Femina. Rooms are basic but in the scheme of things they're pretty clean. Singles/doubles are Rs 70/100.

Hotel ARR (☎ 21234) is a large place at 21 TSR Big St. There are doubles for Rs 200 (Rs 450 with air-con). The hotel has a bar, but the restaurant attached to this hotel no longer functions (they've yet to remove the sign). If you require room service the friendly staff will take your order and your money, purchase a meal across the road and deliver it to your room.

Hotel Athitya (☎ 23262, Ayikulam Rd) has a range of good rooms from Rs 300/325 (ordinary) to Rs 450/475 (air-con). There's a veg and nonveg restaurant.

PRV Lodge (☎ 21820) is very basic and very busy. Rooms start at Rs 70/110 without air-con. A four-bed room is Rs 288 and a double with air-con is Rs 480.

Hotel Tamilnadu (☎ 30422, Poompuhar Rd), near the Men's Arts College, is 6km north of town. It's a spacious place with pleasant gardens. Double rooms only are available, and cost Rs 130, or Rs 300 with air-con. There's a restaurant and bar and for Rs 50 per night they'll bring a TV into your room.

Hotel Raya's (☎ 22545, 28-9 Head Post Office Rd) is the swishest place in town. It offers well-furnished doubles/triples (no singles) from Rs 350/475, or Rs 450/600 with air-con. Room 101 (Rs 600) is the 'lovers' room' – there are mirrors on every surface, including the ceiling above the bed.

Places to Eat

Arul Restaurant, opposite Hotel Pandiyan, is an excellent vegetarian place with a range of lunchtime thalis from Rs 10 to Rs 45 and an air-con dining hall upstairs.

PRV Lodge, next to Hotel Raya's and not to be confused with VPR Lodge, has a good vegetarian restaurant with meals from Rs 15, Rs 20 for specials. The naan are very good.

Hotel Raya's has a nonveg restaurant; main dishes are Rs 35 to Rs 45.

Getting There & Away

The bus stand and nearby train station are about 2km east of the town centre (Rs 20 by cycle-rickshaw).

STC has four buses a day to Chennai (No 303, Rs 55, seven hours) and there are frequent departures to Thanjavur via Dharasuram and to Gangakondacholapuram. Other buses pass through here on their way to Madurai, Coimbatore, Bangalore, Tiruvannamalai, Pondicherry and Chidambaram. Bus No 459 connects Kumbakonam with Karaikal.

There are at least four daily express trains via Chidambaram to Chennai, and three services to Thanjavur and Tiruchirappalli.

AROUND KUMBAKONAM

Not far from Kumbakonam are two Chola temples, Dharasuram and Gangakondacholapuram, both of which have been restored by the Archaeological Survey of India. They have knowledgeable guides. Few visitors go to these temples, which means that you have the opportunity to appreciate their beauty in peace. A copy of the booklet *Chola Temples* (for details see the later Brihadishwara Temple section in Thanjavur) may be useful when visiting these temples.

Dharasuram

The small town of Dharasuram is 4km west of Kumbakonam. Set behind the village, the **Airatesvara Temple** is a superb example of 12th century Chola architecture. It was built by Raja Raja II (1146-63) and is in a fine state of preservation.

The temple is fronted by columns with unique miniature sculptures. In the 14th century, the row of large statues around the temple was replaced with brick and concrete statues similar to those found at the Thanjavur Temple. Many were taken to the art gallery in the raja's palace at Thanjavur, but have since been returned to Dharasuram. The remaining empty niches are awaiting their replacements. The remarkable sculptures depict Shiva as Kankala-murti (the mendicant) and show a number of sages' wives standing by, dazzled by his beauty. Lower panels represent stories from the epics. And like many other temples, some have matching representations. On the one side Chandra, the moon god, clasps a closed lotus, while on the other, Surya, the sun god, has an open lotus. Buddha in teaching position is matched by Shiva, also in the same position. Many of Shiva's 25 aspects are skilfully depicted.

In one large sculpture a lion ferociously attacks an elephant, said to be symbolic of the triumph of Hinduism over Buddhism!

At the main shrine, a huge decorated lingam stands at the end of a long hall, the natural light illuminating it from sunrise to sunset. To the right is the saint, Kannappa, having sacrificed his eye to Shiva. And further right, Sarasvati, the goddess of wisdom and education, stands resolute.

A wide section around the temple is believed to have contained a water area surrounded by oil lamps. The Archaeological Survey of India has done quite a bit of restoration here. Although the temple is used very little at present, there is a helpful and knowledgeable priest who is an excellent English-speaking guide as well. He is available (for a small consideration) from 8 am to 8 pm daily. You can get to Dharasuram by bus or train. It's on the Chennai-Thanjavur line.

Gangakondacholapuram

Thirty-five kilometres north of Kumbakonam, this temple, dedicated to Shiva, was built by the Chola emperor Rajendra I (1012-44) in the style of (and with the same name as) the Brihadishwara Temple at Thanjavur, which was built by his father. Later additions were made in the 15th century by the Nayaks.

The original temple was in three main sections, with each of its four gates protected by the goddess Kali. Now only the main section remains. The ornate tower is almost 55m high and is said to weigh some 80 tonnes. Opposite, in the east, a huge Nandi sits looking back towards the tower. Within the recesses in the walls of the temple stand many beautiful statues, including those of Ganesh, Nataraja and Harihara, as well as Shiva granting blessings to gods and goddesses.

Outside in the garden is the Simhakinar, or Lion Well. This is approached by a staircase which descends through the sculptured body of a lion. It is thought that the Chola kings poured water from the Ganges into the well so that there would be a permanent supply for bathing the images of the gods – a customary temple practice. The same belief was associated with tanks which surrounded the temple, some one to 3km away. But now, only the ruins remain.

The temple is no longer used for Hindu worship. Much of it has already been restored and restoration continues. Like the temple at Dharasuram, this one is visited by few tourists, yet it is well worth the trip. A knowledgeable guide from the Archaeological Survey will show you around.

The temple is open from 6 am to noon and from 4 to 8 pm every day unless there is a funeral procession (very rare).

The palace, which was built in brick and located some 1.5km away, has long since fallen into ruin. As the locals say, 'the house of the gods must last forever; but the house for humans can wither away'. Even so, you can view some of the excavated remains of the palace in the small museum (closed Friday) next to the temple.

Buses will take you from Kumbakonam bus stand to the temple.

The nearby village is small and there's no accommodation.

Swamimalai

This site, 10km south-east of Kumbakonam, is another of Murugan's six abodes, marked by his temple on a small hill. For his devotees, Murugan is always a deity of considerable power, yet here his power takes on distinct qualities.

According to legend it was here that Shiva, powerless because of a curse, was required to surrender to Murugan's authority and wisdom.

Murugan, the child of Shiva, became for a short time his mentor and guru. The legend relates how Shiva forgot the momentous mantra, the Pranava, the mantra of the auspicious sound, Om. This loss left him bereft of the energy and potency of the sound. Desperate to regain this capacity, he turned to his son for help. Murugan therefore became his father's teacher and guide – hence the name of the site, Swamimalai (hill of the knower or guru).

Sixty steps lead up the hill to the shrine. The first deity, as always, is Vinayaka (Ganesh), the elephant-headed god and Murugan's brother. Here he is known as Netra Vinayaka (eyesight-giving Vinayaka) because of a blind man who reputedly regained his sight after worship.

The main festivals here are: Masi Magham in February/March, in which the meanings of the legend are celebrated; and Karthikai Deepam, in November/December, in which the focus is on Shiva and enlightenment.

Swamimalai is on the Chennai-Tiruchirappalli railway line. Both trains and buses come here frequently.

Tirubuvanam

About 10km east of Kumbakonam, this small town has a tiny 13th century Chola temple dedicated to Shiva (here known as Kampahareswarer), but Tirubuvanam is better known for its fine silk saris. Every second shop boasts even more silk, more colour and more luxuriance.

The town has a cooperative, the Tirubuvanam Silk Cooperative Society, which may be a useful place to start your pricing and perusals.

KARAIKAL (Karikal)
Tel Area Code: 04368

The former French enclave of Karaikal is part of the Union Territory of Pondicherry but there is little lingering French influence.

Karaikal is an important Hindu pilgrimage town with its Shiva **Darbaranyeswar Temple** and another, the **Ammaiyar Temple**, dedicated to Punithavathi, a female Shaivite saint subsequently elevated to the status of a goddess.

Unless you're a pilgrim, there's little to Karaikal apart from the cheap liquor. You'll see signs of it as soon as you cross the border. Even within sight of Tamil Nadu land, liquor shops flaunt their signs and *arrack* makers are hard at work.

There is a deserted, though windy, **beach** about 1.5km from town, and boating is possible on the nearby estuary.

The town's main drag is Bharathiar Rd. Along here you'll find accommodation, restaurants, the tourist office (☎ 2596) and, 1.25km further, the bus stand. Also on this road is a number of crowded bars, with signs blatantly displayed. Because Karaikal is part of the Pondicherry Union Territory, there is no additional tax on accommodation.

Places to Stay

Hotel Paris International (☎ 33226, 352 Bharathiar Rd) is clearly the best choice in Karaikal. The lobby is decked out with imitation Louis XIV furniture as well as a large image of Mona Lisa. Every room is clean, modern and adorned with clichéd black and white photographs of Paris. Singles/doubles

without air-con are Rs 150/250. A double with air-con is Rs 350 and a double deluxe (somewhat bigger with even more clichéd photographs of Paris!) is Rs 400. A vegetarian restaurant is attached.

Hotel Presidency (☎ 32408, 286 Bharathiar Rd) offers doubles for Rs 100, or Rs 120 if you prefer tiles in your bathroom. An air-con double is Rs 375.

The *Government Tourist Hotel* (☎ 32621, 435 Bharathiar Rd) has double rooms with attached bath and hot water for Rs 20, and rooms for Rs 80 with air-con. (It's Rs 8 if

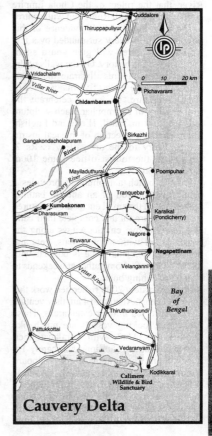

Cauvery Delta

you're a government worker, and Rs 15 with air-con if you're an MP!)

***Tourist Motel* (☎ 32757, *South Bharathiar Rd*)** has 20 double rooms ranging from Rs 100 to Rs 200 with air-con. (Their staff are keen to advise that the air-con sometimes fails to come on!)

AROUND KARAIKAL
Poompuhar

The name of this old Chola seaport has been given to the TTDC's chain of craft emporiums.

It was here, at the mouth of the Cauvery River, that the rulers of the Chola Empire conducted trade with Rome and with centres to the east. There is little evidence of this now but an art gallery surrounded by a few isolated sculptures will give you a slight inkling as to the history. On the walls of the art gallery, sculptures illustrate the *Silappathikaram*, one of the five major epics of Tamil literature. Its verses celebrate the former glory of Poompuhar. Each sculpture tells its story in Tamil, Hindi and English. There is also a selection of musical instruments. Entry to the art gallery is Rs 2, payable at the tourist office some 100m before the gallery.

On the beach a monument provides a beautiful depiction of an ancient bathing scene. Within the small enclosure sculptured women prepare for and complete their bath. The tower above enables views along the coast, dotted with fishing boats, nets and holidaymakers. This place is popular with locals, many of whom gather at weekends to watch the fishing boats.

Approximately 2000 fishermen work this stretch of coast. At around 4 am they venture 12km out to sea in their catamarans. These precarious looking vessels are much like floating logs. Made with Keralan timber, each one is about 15m long and barely 1m wide. Some fishermen attach outboard motors and hand-held sails. To see these fishermen bring their boats in through the thundering surf is an awesome spectacle. The wives of the fishermen gather the catch and take it to the wholesale markets from

where it is transported across Tamil Nadu and to other parts of India.

At the Chithrai Festival, each year on the April/May full moon, large numbers of people gather to bathe in the waters at the confluence of the Cauvery River and the sea.

While Poompuhar has a long beach, its black sands and rough surf make it unsuitable for swimming.

The only place to stay here is the ***Department of Tourism Guesthouse*** (bookings via the tourist office nearby) which offers ordinary (very basic) rooms for Rs 25 and bizarre shell-shaped concrete cottages (each with two beds) for Rs 50, or Rs 120 with air-con. The guesthouse also has a restaurant. Don't mistake it for the guesthouse by the sea – it's for government employees only. There's a quaint thatched post office here, open from 10 am to 1.30 pm and the police station's on the main (and only) drag. You can get to Poompuhar from Karaikal by train to Sirkazhi, then bus.

Tranquebar (Tharangambadi)

Fourteen kilometres north of Karaikal, Tranquebar was established by the Danish East India Company in 1620 at the invitation of the Tanjore ruler, Raghunatha Nayak, who was anxious to develop and extend trade. The **Danesborg Fort** was constructed and subsequent Danish kings dispatched administrative staff and missionaries to run the post. Churches were erected and a printing press established on which the first Tamil Bible was produced. But in 1755, rough seas destroyed much of the fort. A year later, conflict ensued between the Indians and the Danes. Heavy fines were imposed by the Tanjore rulers which resulted in Danish retaliation, with the attack on two temples. Later, in 1801, the British occupied the fort and Tranquebar came under British rule.

There is still evidence of the Danish presence in the house constructions, the Church of Zion and the New Jerusalem Church built by the Lutherans. The Danesborg Fort still looks out to sea and houses a small museum with memorabilia that includes a copy of the contract between Raghunatha Nayak and

King Christian. Entry is Rs 1. It's closed Friday. There are bus services here from all the neighbouring towns.

Tirunallar

This small village with its tiny temple is some 5km north-west of Karaikal. The temple is dedicated to the deity Sani, representative of the planet Saturn. According to legend the temple was surrounded by 13 *theerthams* (tanks), highly valued for their curative powers. Currently six tanks exist, dedicated to various deities. Each tank is believed to possess specific characteristics which affect fortunate outcomes for those who bathe within. For instance the Mandai Theertham is said to prevent adversity; and after 40 days bathing in the Vani Theertham one is said to speak in poetic tones.

It is generally believed that the influence of Saturn is negative; hence the importance in visiting and appeasing the god. Puja is held here six times a day. Hindus may enter the main shrine, but non-Hindus may wander freely around the temple precincts. Paintings on the outer wall of the main hall and shrine depict the story of King Nalla, who, beset by Saturn's evil force, was separated from his wife and overcome with depression. He travelled to this site, bathed in the waters nearby and was immediately released of his torment. Later he constructed the Nalla Theertham, which is considered to be particularly effective in ridding the unwanted effects of Saturn.

Smaller shrines are dedicated to the goddess and also the deity Vinayaka (Ganesh). Several festivals are held at the temple. Perhaps the most significant is the one which coincides with the transit of Saturn, celebrated every 2½ years.

The temple is open from 6 am to 1 pm and 6 to 9 pm. A recent visit to the temple by scantily dressed tourists caused considerable distress among the villagers who saw it as an affront to the sanctity of their temple; as a result foreigners were made less welcome. This situation seems to have abated and foreign visitors now receive a quiet acceptance or warm greeting.

Nagore (Nagur)

The village of Nagore, 12km south of Karaikal, is the burial place of the revered Muslim saint, Hazat Meeras Sultan Syed Shahabdul Hameed (1491-1570; also known as Hazat Mian). The saint is said to have treated and cured a child of the Nayak king, Shevappa Nayaka. In response the king granted an area of land at Nagore to the saint.

The *dargah* (tomb), with its beautiful domed arches, walkways and minarets, is now an important pilgrimage centre, particularly for Muslims, but also for people of all faiths. The waters of the nearby tank, Peer Kulam, are believed by many to have healing qualities. There is ample literature available on the dargah in numerous Arabic and Indian languages. Both men and women may enter and although most women are veiled this is not mandatory.

Velanganni (Vailankanni)
Tel Area Code: 04365

Velanganni, 35km south of Karaikal near the town of Nagapattinam, is the site of the famous **Roman Catholic Basilica of Our Lady of Good Health**. Constructed and renovated in many phases over several centuries, this impressive white neo-Gothic structure, with its blue (symbolic of Our Lady) trimming, dates mainly from the mid-1970s to 1980s. In 1962 it was elevated to the status of basilica during a visit by Pope John XXIII.

Three stories relating to a vision of Our Lady are connected with the site. The first dates back to the 16th century, when a shepherd carrying milk to his master's house was spellbound by an apparition of a woman and child, both with 'celestial halos'. Some years later a lame boy selling buttermilk under a banyan tree encountered the same vision and was immediately cured of his lameness. A small shrine was established and Christians and non-Christians gathered to offer prayers. The third vision took place in the 17th century when a Portuguese ship en route from China to Sri Lanka encountered a ferocious storm in the Bay of Bengal. The sailors prayed to Mary and vowed to

TAMIL NADU

build a church in her name should they happen to land safely. Following a 'miraculous' lull in the storm, they landed at Velanganni on 8 September – the feast day of the birthday of Our Lady.

Every year for nine days leading up to 8 September a festival known as the Feast of Our Lady of Good Health is held at the basilica. It draws hundreds of thousands of people (Christians as well as non-Christians) from across India. Many come seeking cures for various ailments – some place models of 'cured body parts' at the shrine. The festival includes a daily chariot procession. Instead of being pulled along by ropes, these chariots are carried by pilgrims. Some are carried by women only. Every evening of the festival, music and poetry are performed on an open stage, and the festival concludes with a special mass, conducted by the Bishop of Thanjavur.

There are many lodges and hotels in Velanganni (and many more under construction); most are within walking distance of the basilica. Accommodation, however, can be very difficult during the festival time and advance bookings are recommended.

Hotel Picnic (☎ 63510), on the main road near the basilica, offers basic but clean double rooms for Rs 140, or Rs 220 with air-con.

New Star Luxury Hotel (☎ 63527, 92 Main Rd) is a short stroll from the basilica. While this hotel is not exactly star luxury it is comfortable and friendly. Double rooms are Rs 250 for non air-con or Rs 400 with air-con. Single rooms are not available. The hotel promises 'good water not salt water' in the bathrooms.

Hotel Golden Sand (☎ 63426) is centrally located near the basilica. Inexpensive singles/doubles are available for Rs 100/170. An air-con double is Rs 450. The rooms are generous in size but they need a good clean, and if you don't mind sleeping on a cement floor, you'll find the rock-hard beds reasonable.

The Retreat (☎/fax 63534, 64 Nagapattinam Main Rd) is 1.5km from the basilica. This is the best hotel in the area, with well-appointed, clean rooms and friendly service. Double rooms and cottages are available. During high season (19 December to 16 January, 28 March to 20 June, 15 August to 15 September) a double is Rs 450, or Rs 550 with air-con. Cottages are Rs 650, or Rs 800 with air-con. Low season prices are around Rs 100 cheaper on all rooms. Credit cards are not accepted.

CALIMERE WILDLIFE & BIRD SANCTUARY
Tel Area Code: 614807

Also known as Kodikkarai, this 333 sq km coastal sanctuary is 90km south-east of Thanjavur. It sits in a wetland jutting out into the Palk Strait, which separates India and Sri Lanka by a distance of only 28km. Calimere is noted for its vast flocks of migratory waterfowl, especially the greater and lesser flamingos that congregate here every winter.

The best time to visit is between November and January when the tidal mud flats and marshes are covered with teals, shovellers, curlews, gulls, terns, plovers, sandpipers, shanks and herons. The flamingos come from Australia, Europe and Russia, gathering mainly to feed. In the early 1980s they numbered around 50,000, but recently their numbers have dwindled to around 10,000, and ornithologists from the Bombay Natural History Society are conducting research to establish reasons for the fall in numbers. There is a large and viable salt extraction industry along the coastal mud flats and environmentalists have expressed concern about its impact on the delicate ecosystem.

In the spring, a different set of birds – koels, mynas and barbets – are drawn here to the profusion of wild berries. From April to June it is unbearably hot and there's very little activity; the main rainy season is between October and December.

As well as birds, dolphins can be spotted in the early morning during the cooler months. Within the sanctuary is a wildlife area populated mainly by (endangered) blackbucks, spotted deer and wild pigs, and cows belonging to local farmers!

TAMIL NADU

The easiest way to get to Calimere is by bus (every hour for Rs 3.50) from Vedaranyam which is 12km away and the nearest town linked by frequent bus services to Nagapattinam or Thanjavur. Many travellers prefer to hire a taxi (about Rs 50) from Vedaranyam.

The sanctuary is open every day from 6 am to 6 pm. Entry is Rs 5 plus Rs 10 for a car or Rs 5 for a motorcycle. Photography is Rs 5. If you wish to shoot video you'll need special permission from the Forest Department in Chennai. Vehicles can only travel through the sanctuary during the winter season. In monsoon times you have to go by foot. If you do enter with a vehicle you can only drive through the sanctuary with a Forest Department Guide (they have limited knowledge of the flora and fauna). They don't charge anything except the usual 'small consideration to your satisfaction'. If you arrive by bus and you wish to drive around the sanctuary you'll have to hire a vehicle outside (approximately Rs 150 per hour with driver).

You don't need a guide if you walk through the sanctuary but take care when walking along the beach or paddling in the water. Human excreta litters the sand and stingrays linger, concealed in sand, in the shallows. The wildlife section at the eastern end of the bird sanctuary has a round walking track of approximately 12km. It's an easy and pleasant walk but take plenty of water and mosquito repellent.

The only accommodation within walking distance of the sanctuary is the *Forest Department Resthouse* (☎ 72424). This has four double and six single rooms. All the rooms are very basic. There are ceiling fans, and bucket water is delivered by the staff to your room, but the cost is only Rs 15 per person per night. Upstairs rooms are marginally better. The staff claim that a renovation program is due and this will fix the broken plaster and plumbing. Also upstairs is a 'museum' containing bits of skeletons as well as snakes and other creatures preserved in jars of formaldehyde. Although there's no restaurant, you can

place an order with the staff, and they will cook it for you, but the choice is extremely limited. The official line is that reservations can only be made through the Wildlife Warden in Nagapattinam (☎ 22349), but many travellers simply turn up and succeed in getting a room.

THANJAVUR (Tanjore)
Pop: 217,000 Tel Area Code: 04362
Thanjavur was the ancient capital of the Chola kings whose origins (like those of the Pallavas, Pandyas and Cheras with whom they shared the tip of the Indian Peninsula) go back to the beginning of the Christian era. Power struggles between these groups were a constant feature of their early history, with one or other gaining the ascendancy at various times. The Cholas' turn for empire building came between 850 and 1270 AD and, at the height of their power, they controlled most of the Indian Peninsula south of a line drawn between Mumbai and Puri, including parts of Sri Lanka and, for a while, the Srivijaya kingdom of the Malay Peninsula and Sumatra.

Probably the greatest Chola emperors were Raja Raja (985-1014), who was responsible for building the Brihadishwara Temple (Thanjavur's main attraction), and his son Rajendra I (1014-44), whose navy competed with the Arabs for control of the Indian Ocean trade routes and who was responsible for bringing Srivijaya under Chola control.

Thanjavur wasn't the only place to receive Chola patronage. Within easy reach of Thanjavur are numerous enormous Chola temples – the main ones are at Thiruvaiyaru, and Gangakondacholapuram and Dharasuram near Kumbakonam (for details see the Around Thanjavur and Around Kumbakonam sections). The Cholas also had a hand in building the enormous temple complex at Srirangam near Tiruchirappalli – probably India's largest.

There is some conjecture over the derivation of the name Thanjavur. It may have evolved from Tanjai, denoting beauty and lushness. Other accounts associate the name with deliverance from legendary demons who haunted the area. One such fiend was called Tanjam who, on being slain by Durga, pleaded that the site bear his name. She granted his request. Yet other accounts interpret the word as meaning refuge; Thanjavur was therefore the city of refuge from the demons.

Set on a fertile delta, agriculture is an important industry and makes Thanjavur a great place to be during Pongal (harvest) celebrations.

Thanjavur is also famous for its distinctive art style, which is usually a combination of raised and painted surfaces. Krishna is the most popular of the gods depicted, and in the Thanjavur school his skin is white, rather than the traditional blue-black.

In 1995 Thanjavur hosted the World Tamil Congress. Many hotels received a face- (and a price-) lift as a result.

Orientation

The enormous tower of the Brihadishwara Temple can be seen from most places in Thanjavur. The temple itself, between the

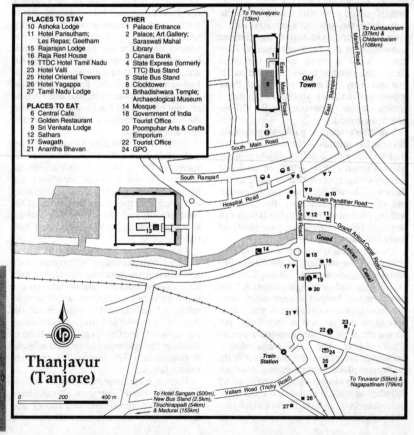

PLACES TO STAY
10 Ashoka Lodge
11 Hotel Parisutham;
     Les Repas; Geetham
15 Rajarajan Lodge
16 Raja Rest House
19 TTDC Hotel Tamil Nadu
23 Hotel Valli
25 Hotel Oriental Towers
26 Hotel Yagappa
27 Tamil Nadu Lodge

PLACES TO EAT
6 Central Cafe
7 Golden Restaurant
9 Sri Venkata Lodge
12 Sathars
17 Swagath
21 Anantha Bhavan

OTHER
1 Palace Entrance
2 Palace; Art Gallery;
    Saraswati Mahal
    Library
3 Canara Bank
4 State Express (formerly
    TTC) Bus Stand
5 State Bus Stand
8 Clocktower
13 Brihadishwara Temple;
    Archaeological Museum
14 Mosque
18 Government of India
    Tourist Office
20 Poompuhar Arts & Crafts
    Emporium
22 Tourist Office
24 GPO

To Thiruvaiyaru
(13km)

To Kumbakonam
(37km) &
Chidambaram
(106km)

Market Road

East Rampart

East Main Road

Old
Town

South Main Road

South Rampart

Hospital Road

Abraham Pandither Road

Gandhi Road

Grand Anicut Canal Road

Grand Anicut Canal

Thanjavur
(Tanjore)

0   200   400 m

To Hotel Sangam (500m),
New Bus Stand (2.5km),
Tiruchirappalli (54km)
& Madurai (155km)

Vallam Road (Trichy Road)

Train
Station

To Tiruvarur (55km) &
Nagapattinam (79km)

Grand Anicut Canal and the old town, is surrounded by fortified walls. The old town, too, used to be similarly enclosed, but most of the walls have disappeared, and winding streets and alleys, and the extensive ruins of the palace of the Nayaks of Madurai, are all that remain.

Gandhiji Rd, which runs north-south between the train station and the bus stand at the edge of the old town, has most of the hotels and restaurants, as well as the Poompuhar Arts & Crafts Emporium.

Information

The tourist office (☎ 23017), in Jawans Bhavan opposite the GPO, is open from 10 am to 5.45 pm. There's also a counter at the TTDC Hotel Tamil Nadu. The Government of India also has a small office on Gandhiji Rd.

The Canara Bank on South Main Rd changes travellers cheques. The Hotel Parisutham does this too, but at a lousy rate.

The GPO, near the train station, is open daily from 10 am to 4 pm (Sunday from noon). The telegraph office next door is open 24 hours.

Brihadishwara Temple & Fort

Built by Raja Raja in 1010, the Brihadishwara Temple is the crowning glory of Chola temple architecture. This superb and fascinating monument is one of only a handful in India with World Heritage listing and is worth a couple of visits.

The temple is dedicated to Shiva. Raja Raja was a devotee of the dancing Shiva, Nataraja, and it seems that the inspiration for the Brihadishwara Temple was conceived from his fondness for this deity. Several representations within the temple allude to this: there is the highly acclaimed bronze Nataraja, and the lingam in the sanctum has been accorded many names, all associated with Nataraja, for example, Adavallan – the skilful dancer.

Since there is no stone around Thanjavur the materials for the temple must have been transported for some distance. Constructed from a single piece of granite weighing an estimated 80 tonnes, the dome was hauled into place along a 4km earthwork ramp in a manner similar to that used for the Egyptian pyramids.

The temple is set in spacious grounds and has several pillared halls and shrines. Two-hundred-and-fifty lingams are enshrined along the outer walls. Inscriptions on the temple wall record the names of dancers, musicians and poets – a reminder of the significance of this area to the development of the arts. Within the grounds a huge Nandi, 6m long by 3m high and 2½m across, looks towards the inner sanctum. Created from a single piece of rock, it weighs 25 tonnes and is one of the largest Nandi statues in India.

Unlike most South Indian temples where the gopurams are the highest towers, here it is the 13-storey tower above the sanctum at 66m that reaches further into the sky. Its impressive gilded top is the original, presented by the king. Temple inscriptions record the presentation as occurring on the 275th day of the 25th year of his reign (although other sources cite a different year). While the inscriptions carefully record other events and contributions made to the temple, it is legend that provides the accounts of the tower – both the tower and the keystone on which it rests were donated by cowgirls. In return, they received generous grants of land from the king.

The tower contains sculptures of Hindu deities and saints. A series of particular figures have created some contention. They depict four men, in a vertical line, decreasing in size from top to bottom. The lowest in line resembles a European.

Some have speculated that the artist was representing the contemporary and succeeding dynasties from Chola, to Nayak, Maratha and finally British. Such fanciful accounts rely on the artist having clairvoyant powers. Other claims suggest that links with Europe had long been established through trade. Therefore the European figure may simply be an image drawn from the artisit's knowledge of such trade association, rather than a result of prophetic powers. Whatever the case, Europeans in bowler hats are unlikely subjects within Hindu celestial realms!

The sanctum is in two storeys and contains a 4m long lingam with a circumference of 7m, dressed in white cotton. Walls surrounding the sanctum contain large murals depicting the marriage scene and various images of Shiva as well as the 108 poses of the Bharata Natyam.

The temple now comes under the jurisdiction of the Archaeological Survey but worship there has recommenced. A sign near the entrance indicates that the hereditary trustee has extended the use of the temple. The sign reads: 'This temple has been opened to Harijans as a voluntary act of repatriation, thus hastening the process of purification that Hinduism is going through. Untouchability is a blot on Hinduism.'

Like many temples, an elephant stands at the entrance dispensing blessings for a small fee. The temple is open daily from 6 am to 1 pm and 3 to 8 pm.

The **Archaeological Museum**, on the southern side of the courtyard, has some interesting sculptures and photographs which show how the temple looked before much of the restoration work was done, as well as charts and maps detailing the history of the Chola Empire.

The museum is open daily from 9.30 am to 1 pm and 3 to 7 pm. It sells an interesting little booklet titled *Chola Temples* by C Sivaramamurti for Rs 20, (it can also be bought at Chennai's Fort St George Museum) which describes the three temples at Thanjavur, Dharasuram and Gangakondacholapuram.

Thanjavur Palace & Museums

The huge corridors, spacious halls, observation and arsenal towers and shady courtyards of this vast, labyrinthine building in the centre of the old town were constructed partly by the Nayaks of Madurai around 1550 and partly by the Marathas. Due to years of neglect many sections are in ruins, although restoration is now underway.

The poorly marked entrance to the area containing these buildings is a wide break in the eastern wall which leads past a school and a police station. The actual palace entrance is off to the left at the first junction, through the arched tunnel.

Follow the signs up to the **Royal Museum** which has an eclectic collection of regal memorabilia, most of it dating from the early 19th century when Serfoji II ruled. Exhibits include the raja's slippers, headdresses and hunting weapons. The museum is open daily from 9 am to 6 pm. Admission is Rs 1. More signs lead you from the courtyard to the magnificent **Durbar Hall**, one of two such halls in the palace where audiences were held with the king. It's unrestored but still in quite good condition.

An **art gallery** occupies the Nayak Durbar Hall. It has a superb collection of Chola bronze statues from the 9th to 12th centuries. The gallery is open from 9 am to 1 pm and 3 to 6 pm. Entry costs Rs 3. Nearby is the **Bell Tower**, reopened recently after some particularly unsympathetic restoration that does not bode well for the rest of the buildings in need of repair. It's worth the climb (Rs 2) for the views, however.

The **Saraswati Mahal Library** is next door to the gallery. Established around 1700, the library contains a collection of over 30,000 palm leaf and paper manuscripts in Indian and European languages. The library itself is closed to the public but you can visit the interesting **museum**, where there's everything from the whole of the epic *Ramayana* written on a palm leaf to a set of explicit prints of prisoners under Chinese torture. Entry is free and it's open daily (except Wednesday) from 10 am to 1 pm and 1.30 to 5.30 pm.

Places to Stay – Budget

Raja Rest House (☎ 30515), down a quiet side street off Gandhiji Rd, is the best value in town. The large, basic rooms, with bucket hot water, are arranged around three sides of a huge courtyard, and cost Rs 60/100 with bathroom and fan. The staff are very friendly.

Rajarajan Lodge (☎ 31730, 176 Gandhiji Rd) has very basic rooms for Rs 40/90 with common bathroom or Rs 50/100 with attached bathroom. The area is very noisy, and the hotel is often full.

Tamil Nadu Lodge (☎ 31088) is behind the train station, just off Trichy Rd. The rooms have a cell-like ambience but are otherwise OK and good value at Rs 65/100. However, it's somewhat inconvenient for the centre of town.

Hotel Yagappa (☎ 30421), just off Trichy Rd and near the station, has singles/doubles for Rs 150/195 in the low season and Rs 200/360 in the high season. The tariff includes tax. Its increased popularity is warranted given the hard work which has been undertaken to improve the place, and there's an enormous restaurant and a very pleasant bar.

Ashoka Lodge (☎ 30021, 93 Abraham Pandither Rd) offers airy but basic rooms for Rs 85/130 with attached bathroom. A room with five beds costs Rs 360 and an air-con double is Rs 435.

Hotel Valli (☎ 31584, MK Rd) offers clean rooms with bathroom attached from Rs 120/140, or Rs 180 for a double with TV. Air-con doubles cost Rs 320. There are also rooms with three, four and seven beds.

Railway Retiring Rooms at the station cost Rs 60 for a double, or Rs 120 with air-con. They're often full.

Places to Stay – Mid-Range & Top End

TTDC Hotel Tamil Nadu (☎ 31421, Gandhiji Rd) is a good place to stay but not the bargain it once was. Rooms in this former raja's guesthouse are spacious and clean with constant hot water in the attached bathrooms. The rooms surround a quiet leafy courtyard, and the staff are helpful. Doubles cost Rs 350, and Rs 500 with air-con. A TV in the ordinary rooms is an extra Rs 50. There is an attached restaurant, and a bar with cold beer.

Hotel Parisutham (☎ 31801; fax 30318, 55 Grand Anicut Canal Rd) is the most pleasant place to stay. It has a beautiful swimming pool, manicured lawns, two restaurants and a bar. Unfortunately a number of the balconies have recently been

enclosed to enlarge the rooms. The rooms cost US$46/86 (including breakfast).

Hotel Sangam (☎ 25151; fax 24895) is a large, flashy new hotel on Trichy Rd. Immaculate rooms (with baths and showers) cost US$45/88. There's a pool, a hall to dance in, and a multicuisine restaurant.

Hotel Oriental Towers (☎ 30724; fax 30770, 2889 Srinivasam Pillai Rd) has single/double central air-con rooms for US$37/47. It's a modern hotel that pays homage to an older style.

Places to Eat

There are plenty of simple vegetarian restaurants with thalis for Rs 20 near the bus stand and on Gandhiji Rd.

Anantha Bhavan is recommended.

Central Cafe (corner of Hospital & Gandhiji Rds) is good for snacks, but it closes at 4 pm.

Golden Restaurant (Hospital Rd) does good vegetarian meals for Rs 20.

Sri Venkata Lodge, opposite the clock tower, has good thalis for Rs 20.

Sathars is a good veg (from Rs 20) and nonveg (from Rs 40) restaurant with great service and an extensive range of dishes. It's open until midnight.

Swagath, near the roundabout on Gandhiji Rd, does nonveg food that's good value; thalis are Rs 15.

Hotel Yagappa has a large restaurant with reasonable food (eg ginger chicken is Rs 45). The bar here is a very pleasant place to drink; beers are Rs 55.

Hotel Sangam offers a wide selection in its multicuisine restaurant (sometimes with classical music).

Hotel Parisutham has the best restaurants in town – the nonveg *Les Repas* serves Indian and Chinese dishes (around Rs 60), and the *Geetham* offers vegetarian food. The bar is a popular place for a late evening beer with complimentary peanuts.

Getting There & Away

Bus The STC bus stand is fairly well organised but you may find it hard to work out the timetable if you don't read Tamil. The computerised reservation office is open from 7.30 am to 9.30 pm. There are 24 buses a day for Chennai, the fastest and most expensive being the No 323FP Bye-Pass Rider (Rs 75, 7½ hours). Other buses that can be booked here include Tirupathi (No 851, Rs 85, daily), Ooty (No 725, Rs 65) and Pondicherry (No 928, daily at midnight, 177km). There are also numerous buses passing through on their way to Tiruchirappalli and Madurai.

Most state buses now use the new bus stand, 2.5km south of the centre. Some still stop at the chaotic old state bus stand, such as those for Tiruchirappalli (Rs 9.50, 54km, 1½ hours) and Kumbakonam (37km, one hour). There are departures for both every 15 minutes.

Train To Chennai (351km), the overnight *Rameswaram Express* takes nine hours and costs Rs 108/390 in 2nd/1st class. Alternatively, and for the same prices, the *Cholan Express* takes eight hours and travels through the day. To Villupuram (for Pondicherry), the 192km trip takes six hours and costs Rs 48/239. To Tiruchirappalli (50km, one hour) it costs Rs 17/102. The trip to Kumbakonam takes one hour, and it's 2½ hours to Chidambaram.

AROUND THANJAVUR

Many of the smaller towns in the Thanjavur area are well known for their impressive Chola temples.

Thiruvaiyaru

Thirteen kilometres north of Thanjavur, this town is renowned for the saint and composer who lived here, Thyagaraja. Thyagaraja's family came from Andhra Pradesh. His first language, and many of his compositions, are therefore in Telugu. Every year an eight-day music festival is held here in his honour and people come from all over the world. Eventually a library will house his compositions as well as information about him.

The famous temple here is dedicated to Shiva and is known as Panchanatheshwara. The entrance to the inner sanctum is flanked

by several impressively sculptured guardians which increase in ferocity the closer they are to the shrine. Paintings on the wall give the history of the temple. Several small lingam shrines line the side and back halls. There is literature on the temple, available in Tamil. The temple is closed from noon to 5 pm.

Each January, at the time of the festival, accommodation is completely booked out.

Tiruvarur
Tel Area Code: 04366
Tiruvarur is the birthplace of the saint Thyagaraja (see the Thiruvaiyaru section). The Thyagararajaswami Temple at Tiruvarur, 55km from Thanjavur, is dedicated to Shiva. Set within eight hectares, the temple has large colourful gopurams at each cardinal point, and a huge temple tank just near the western tower. Shrines to Ganesh and Subrahmanya stand outside the main sanctum. The temple boasts an 807-pillared hall and the largest temple chariot in Tamil Nadu. With the deities inside it, the chariot is hauled through the streets during the 10-day Sri Thyagaraja Chithrai car festival in April/May.

The temple is 1km north of the bus stand (turn right). There are numerous cheap places to stay around the bus stand.

Lodge President (☎ 22748, 33C Thanjavur Rd) is about 500m south of the bus stand and offers basic but reasonably clean singles/doubles for Rs 60/90 with attached bathroom.

Hotel Selvies (☎ 22080, fax 22424, 1G Kattukara St) is a five minute walk from the bus stand. This hotel is clean and comfortable with friendly staff. Air-con singles/doubles are Rs 350/450 including TV. Without air-con the rooms are Rs 95/195 plus Rs 30 for a TV.

The Royal Park (☎ 21020, fax 21024) is about 1km out of town on the Bye-pass Rd. It may not have the best location, but it is certainly the best quality hotel in Tiruvarur. Singles/doubles are Rs 190/290 without air-con or Rs 400/500 with air-con. The rooms are spacious and breezy with plumbing that works. The hotel boasts two classy restaurants, the multicuisine *Golden Moments* and *The Silver Selections* with vegetarian cuisine. A bar is in progress. It's very much a male world here – women with male partners might as well be invisible, since all business and conversation is directed toward the man. Credit cards are not accepted.

Grand Anicut

Halfway between Thiruvaiyaru and Trichy is the site of Kallanai. Here the Grand Anicut Barrage, with its 30 arches of 10m each, spans the Cauvery River. The original dam was built in the 2nd century AD by the Chola king, Karikalan.

It's a pleasant place to stop, picnic, enjoy the scenery and have a coconut. Buses between Trichy and Thiruvaiyaru pass every hour.

TIRUCHIRAPPALLI (Trichy, Tiruchy)
Pop: 770,800 Tel Area Code: 0431

Trichy has a long history going back to the centuries before the Christian era when it was a Chola citadel. During the 1st millennium AD, it changed hands between the Pallavas and Pandyas many times before being taken by the Cholas in the 10th century AD. When the Chola Empire finally decayed, Trichy passed into the hands of the Vijayanagar emperors of Hampi and remained with them until their defeat, in 1565 AD, by the forces of the Deccan sultans.

The town and its most famous landmark, the Rock Fort Temple, were built by the Nayaks of Madurai. It was one of the main centres around which the wars of the Carnatic were fought in the 18th century during the British-French struggle for supremacy in India.

Maybe it's the monuments; maybe it's the good range of hotels and the excellent local bus system; somehow Trichy has a different ambience about it.

Orientation

Trichy is scattered over a considerable area. Although you will need transport to get from one part to another, most of the hotels and restaurants, the bus stand, train station,

tourist office and GPO are within a few minutes walk of each other in what is known as the junction (or cantonment) area. The Rock Fort Temple is about 2.5km north of here, near the Cauvery River. The other temples are north of the river some five to 7km away.

Information

The tourist office (☎ 460136), 1 Williams Rd, is open weekdays only. They have a free leaflet but little else. There are also branch offices at the train station and the airport.

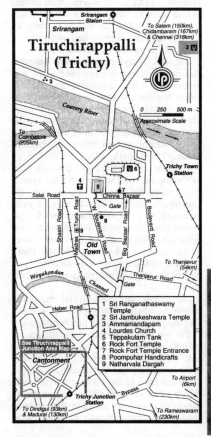

Tiruchirappalli
(Trichy)

To Salem (150km), Chidambaram (167km) & Chennai (316km)

Srirangam Station
Srirangam

Cauvery River

0   250   500 m
Approximate Scale

To Coimbatore (205km)

Trichy Town Station

Salai Road

Chinna Bazaar

Gate

Old Town

To Thanjavur (54km)

Thanjavur Road

Woyakondan

Channel

Gate

Heber Road

See Tiruchirappalli Junction Area Map
Cantonment

1 Sri Ranganathaswamy Temple
2 Sri Jambukeshwara Temple
3 Ammamandapam
4 Lourdes Church
5 Teppakulam Tank
6 Rock Fort Temple
7 Rock Fort Temple Entrance
8 Poompuhar Handicrafts
9 Natharvala Dargah

To Airport (6km)

Trichy Junction Station
To Dindigul (93km) & Madurai (130km)

Bypass

To Rameswaram (230km)

TAMIL NADU

The GPO on Dindigul Rd is open Monday to Saturday from 8 am to 7 pm.

Rock Fort Temple

The most famous landmark of this bustling town is the Rock Fort Temple, a spectacular monument perched 83m high on a massive rocky outcrop which rises abruptly from the plain to tower over the old city. This smooth rock was first hewn by the Pallavas who cut small cave temples into the southern face, but it was the Nayaks who made use of its naturally fortified position. The temple is dedicated to Vinayaka (another name for Ganesh) and there are several small shrines to him along the way, with the temple to him at the summit. On the landing halfway up there is a small pillared hall with inscriptions and some impressive sculptures.

The **Sri Thayumanaswamy Temple**, dedicated to Shiva, is also passed on the way to the top. It acquired its name from a legend about a pregnant woman: distressed and alone in her labour, she prayed for help. Shiva appeared to her in the guise of her mother and assisted her through the birth. So Shiva became known as he who became (*anavar*) mother (*thayuma*).

It's a stiff climb up the 437 stone-cut steps to the top but well worth it for the experiences along the way and the views of the countryside, the town, and the other main landmark, the Sri Ranganathaswamy Temple (Srirangam). The nearby Teppakkulam Tank is the site of the March festival where images of the deities are floated on its waters. Don't stop and look too long on the landing – you may be the target of droppings from the bats above!

Non-Hindus are not allowed into either temple but occasionally (and for a small fee) temple priests waive this regulation.

The monument is open daily from 6 am until 8 pm. Entry is Rs 1, plus Rs 10 if you have a camera (videos prohibited). The sign at the temple advises that dressing in *kaili* or *lungi* (sarong) is not allowed but it seems this is another rule which is sometimes waived. Leave your shoes at the entrance near the temple elephant, Lakshmi, who

passes each day blessing devotees in exchange for money. There's a small post office at the bottom.

Sri Ranganathaswamy Temple (Srirangam)

The superb temple complex at Srirangam, about 3km north of the Rock Fort, is situated on an island formed by two arms of the Cauvery River. For Vaishnavites this temple ranks in importance with the Venkateshwara Temple at Tirupathi.

Uncertainty surrounds its history. Legend tells of Ravana's brother, Vibhishana, who was presented with the Srirangam *vimana* (inner shrine) by Rama in appreciation of his help in war against Ravana. Vibhishana set out to return to his home in Lanka with the vimana, but upon arrival at the Cauvery River he placed the vimana on the ground. When he endeavoured to continue his journey he was unable to lift it again. He became distressed but Vishnu stated he had always wanted his sanctuary to be at this place, and in order to console Vibhishana, Vishnu promised to take a position facing Lanka. This legend has been instrumental in the development of philosophies and study in the Vishnu tradition.

The temple is mentioned in *sangam* poetry (for more information see under Madurai), but actual evidence of its existence dates from the 10th century, with inscriptions which record donations made to the temple. In the 12th century the theologist and philosopher, Ramanuja, became head of the temple school. He instituted administrative practices which continued until the 14th century Muslim invasion. With the Vijayanagar victory the temple was restored and much of the work undertaken during the 15th to 17th centuries produced the structure which exists today. Many dynasties have therefore had a hand in its construction, including the Cheras, Pandyas, Cholas, Hoysalas, Vijayanagaras and Nayaks – and work continues. The largest gopuram in the first wall on the southern side (the main entrance) was completed as recently as 1987, and now measures an astounding 73m. In

1966 the temple received assistance from UNESCO for preservation and restoration.

At some 60 hectares, the Srirangam temple with its seven concentric walls and 21 gopurams is probably the largest in India. The temple complex is very well preserved, with excellent carvings throughout and numerous shrines to various gods, with the main temple dedicated to Vishnu. Non-Hindus may go as far as the sixth wall but are not allowed into the gold-topped sanctum.

Bazaars and Brahmins' houses fill the space between the outer four walls, and you don't have to take your shoes off or deposit your bicycle until you get to the fourth wall (Rs 0.50). If you have a camera, you'll be charged Rs 10 at this point.

Just past the shoe deposit is an information centre where you buy the Rs 2 ticket to climb the wall for a panoramic view of the entire complex. A temple guide will unlock the gates and tell you what's what. It's worth engaging one of these guides (fee negotiable) as there is much to see and you could easily spend the whole day wandering around the complex.

An annual **Car Festival** is held here in January during which a decorated wooden chariot is pulled through the streets between the temple walls. The most important festival here however is the 21-day **Vaikunta Ekadasi**, or Paradise Festival, which takes place from mid-December. The celebrated Vaishnavite text, *Tiruvaimozhi*, with its 3000 hymns, is recited before an image of Vishnu. At this time the temple's northern entrance is opened and pilgrims from all over India flock in the hope of getting a touch of auspicious merit.

There's a small **museum** containing sculptures, bronze figures and plaques. The area within the fourth wall is closed daily from 10 pm to 6 am.

One kilometre south of the temple is the **Ammamandapam**, a bathing ghat for devotees.

Sri Jambukeshwara Temple

The nearby Sri Jambukeshwara Temple (also known as Tiruvanai Koil or Thirua-naikka – elephant grove) is dedicated to Shiva and Parvati, here referred to as Jumbanathar and Ahilandeswari respectively. Built around the same time as the Sri Ranganathaswamy Temple, this temple has five concentric walls and seven gopurams, with the customary decrease in size towards the sanctum. It is one of the five temples honouring the elements – the element here being water. As such, the temple is built around a Shiva lingam partly immersed in water that comes from a submerged spring in the sanctum sanctorum.

Entrance to the temple is through pleasant gardens past the elephant, Shanti. Just inside, within a pillared hall, huge yalis look down on the finely sculptured columns. An enormous statue of Kali stands here, green, menacing and ferocious with her 50 arms.

Outside there are several lingam shrines and the 'marriage tree' celebrating the union of Shiva and Parvati. There is also the small tank, Brahma Theertham, commemorating the legend that tells of how Brahma received the power of creation through the union of the two deities.

Non-Hindus are usually not allowed in the sanctum, but as often happens, the rule may be waived. A very helpful guide will show you around and advise on times to attend the numerous rituals.

The temple is open daily between 6 am and 12.30 pm and between 4 and 8.30 pm, and there's the usual Rs 10 camera fee (video Rs 125).

Lourdes Church

The church of Our Lady of Lourdes celebrates the apparitions of the young French girl, Bernadette. Completed in 1896, the cathedral is modelled on the neo-Gothic Lourdes Basilica, and its foundations were sunk 6m into solid rock. For some months leading up to January 1998, it underwent extensive renovations. Each year on 11 February, the feast of Our Lady of Lourdes, her statue is taken in procession through the streets of Trichy. People of all faiths attend the festival.

TAMIL NADU

St John's Church

Trichy also has some interesting Raj-era monuments. Built in 1812, St John's Church has louvered side doors which can be opened to turn the church into an airy pavilion. Rouse the doorkeeper to let you in. The surrounding cemetery reveals many stories.

Natharvala Dargah

This is the tomb of a popular Muslim saint, Hazrath Thable Alam Badusha, also known as Nath-her. He was born near Samarkand in 927 AD into a royal family. Like the Buddha, he renounced his royal ancestry to follow a spiritual path. He journeyed to India and reached Trichy at the age of 33, when he was the first Muslim missionary in the area. Initially he lived at the Rock Fort but moved to the site of the dargah after the land was granted to him by the king. He has numerous devotees of all faiths, who continually flock to the dargah from all around

the world. The Arcot Wallajah, Muhammed Ali (1749-95) is also buried here.

The dargah is an impressive building with a 20m-high dome with pinnacles on the dome and corners. The nearby tank is said to have curative powers. In 1998 the 1000 year anniversary of his death was celebrated with a 16-day festival and a sandal anointing. The dargah is open to people of all faiths. You may find it difficult to locate if you follow street signs: locally the Trunk Rd is known by other names. Use the Lourdes Church as your landmark (the dargah is 500m due south) and you should have no problems.

Places to Stay

Noise from the bus stand can be a significant problem in many hotels, particularly in non air-con front rooms. But accommodation in Trichy is abundant and easy to find. Most places have well-placed signs.

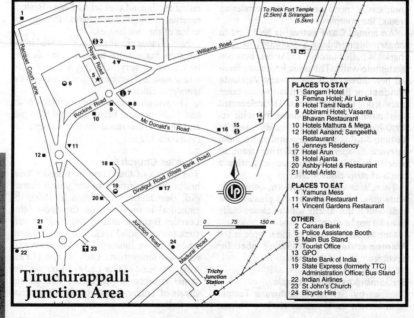

PLACES TO STAY
1 Sangam Hotel
3 Femina Hotel; Air Lanka
8 Hotel Tamil Nadu
9 Abbirami Hotel; Vasanta Bhavan Restaurant
10 Hotels Mathura & Mega
12 Hotel Aanand; Sangeetha Restaurant
16 Jenneys Residency
17 Hotel Arun
18 Hotel Ajanta
20 Ashby Hotel & Restaurant
21 Hotel Aristo

PLACES TO EAT
4 Yamuna Mess
14 Kavitha Restaurant
14 Vincent Gardens Restaurant

OTHER
2 Canara Bank
6 Police Assistance Booth
6 Main Bus Stand
7 Tourist Office
13 GPO
15 State Bank of India
19 State Express (formerly TTC) Administration Office; Bus Stand
22 Indian Airlines
23 St John's Church
24 Bicycle Hire

To Rock Fort Temple (2.5km) & Srirangam (5.5km)

Williams Road
Racquet Court Lane
Royal Road
Rockins Road
Mc Donald's Road
Dindigul Road (State Bank Road)
Junction Road
Madurai Road

Trichy Junction Station

Tiruchirappalli Junction Area

0   75   150 m

Places to Stay – Budget

Railway Retiring Rooms at the train station have dormitory beds for Rs 30 and double rooms without/with air-con for Rs 100/150.

Modern Hindu Hotel (☎ 460758) is a relatively quiet cheapie but not absolutely spotless. Singles/doubles with common bathroom are Rs 60/100, doubles/triples with bathroom attached are Rs 150/250. Note that 'brothel and bad character women are not allowed'.

Hotel Aristo (☎ 461818, 2 Dindigul Rd) is a friendly place and has been a popular choice for visitors. Now it gets mixed reports on its cleanliness. It has a laid-back atmosphere and a nice and quiet leafy garden. Singles/doubles cost Rs 100/150, quads are Rs 250 and there are also air-con double cottages at Rs 350. All the rooms have attached bathrooms and most rooms join a large shaded terrace. It's a good choice if it keeps up standards.

Hotel Arun (☎ 461421, 24 State Bank Rd) is another good place that's set back from the road, though it lacks the character of the Aristo. Singles/doubles are Rs 130/175 with bath attached. Air-con rooms are Rs 250/350. A thali in the restaurant costs Rs 11. There is also a bar.

Ashby Hotel (☎ 460652, 17A Junction Rd) is the place to go for crumbling, old-world atmosphere though it is slowly being renovated. The spacious singles/doubles all come with attached bathroom, but they're overpriced at Rs 150/270, or Rs 350/570 with air-con. There's a bar and an outdoor restaurant. One reader wrote: 'There's a stillness and sadness about the place and its staff – a memorable place to stay'.

Hotel Ajanta (☎ 460501, Junction Rd) offers good singles/doubles at Rs 165/210, or Rs 350/450 with air-con. All rooms have bath attached and the hotel has a good vegetarian restaurant.

Hotel Aanand (☎ 460545, 1 Racquet Court Lane) is one of the most attractive of the cheaper places. Rooms cost Rs 200/230, or Rs 430 for a double with air-con. All rooms have bathrooms and there is a good open-air restaurant.

Places to Stay – Mid-Range

Right outside the bus stand is a whole bunch of relatively new mid-range hotels.

Hotel Tamil Nadu (☎ 460383, McDonald's Rd) offers reasonable rooms with air-con for Rs 310/410.

Hotel Mega (☎ 463092, 8 Rockins Rd) has good doubles for Rs 170, or Rs 325/375 for a single/double with air-con.

Hotel Mathura (☎ 463737), next door to Hotel Mega, is similarly priced. Singles/doubles are Rs150/195, or Rs 350/ 420 with air-con. The rooms are clean and comfortable and the hotel has a wide range of facilities including a florist. Credit cards are accepted.

Abbirami Hotel (☎ 460001, 10 McDonald's Rd), almost opposite the Hotel Tamil Nadu, is a characterless place that has good value air-con rooms for Rs 340/390 and cheaper ordinary rooms.

Femina Hotel (☎ 461551; fax 460615, 14C Williams Rd) is a huge place offering rooms at Rs 225/350, or Rs 475/700 with air-con. There are also more expensive deluxe rooms and suites. The facilities include a rather characterless restaurant offering Indian, continental and Chinese cuisine, but no bar. There is also a Woodlands restaurant offering vegetarian lunches.

Places to Stay – Top End

Jenneys Residency (☎ 461301; fax 461451, 3/14 McDonald's Rd) is a vast place that has recently been modernised and extended. The rooms cost Rs 1350/1650; they're all air-con and the ones on the 4th and 5th floors are the best. The hotel has a restaurant, upmarket shops, a health club and a swimming pool that nonresidents can use for Rs 70 per day.

Sangam Hotel (☎ 464700, Collector's Office Rd) lacks character but has all the facilities of a four-star hotel. Rooms are US$45/88. Its restaurant is disappointing: the food is unexciting and the atmosphere is tense.

Places to Eat

Many of the hotels have attached restaurants which provide a variety of good foods.

Yamuna Mess, an open-air 'diner' on a gravel parking lot behind the Guru Hotel, is a great place for cheap eats. Here, in the evenings only, they serve a limited number of vegetarian or nonveg dishes in a casual setting. There's mellow music and friendly service.

Sangeetha Restaurant, at the Hotel Aanand, is also a good place for dinner. In the open-air restaurant most dishes (eg chilli gobi fry) are Rs 13.

Vasanta Bhavan is a very busy vegetarian restaurant at the Abbirami Hotel. Meals are Rs 15.

Vincent Gardens Restaurant is a plush place with a multicuisine menu. It has a large, pleasant garden setting.

Kavitha Restaurant does excellent, elaborate thalis for Rs 15, and has an air-con room.

The Peaks of Kunlun at Jenneys Residency gets mixed reports. It has a multicuisine menu and beer is Rs 60.

Getting There & Away

Air The Indian Airlines office (☎ 462233) is at 4A Dindigul Rd. It has flights twice a week to Chennai (US$60).

Air Lanka has a flight to Colombo on Tuesday and Sunday for Rs 1525. The airline's office (☎ 460844) is at the Femina Hotel.

Bus The STC buses use the main bus stand, although a few buses still leave from the former TTC administration office on Junction Rd.

Services to most places are frequent and tickets are sold by the conductor as soon as the bus arrives. Services include Thanjavur (Rs 10, 54km, 1½ hours, every 15 minutes) and Madurai (Rs 25, 128km, four hours, every half hour).

The STC buses can be computer-booked in advance at their offices. For Chennai the fastest bus is the Bye-Pass Rider (Rs 75, 7½ hours). Other destinations include: Bangalore (Rs 85, three daily), Coimbatore (Rs 35, twice daily), and Tirupathi via Vellore (Rs 65, 9½ hours, two daily).

Private companies such as Jenny Travels, opposite the Hotel Tamil Nadu, or KPN Travels, below the Hotel Mathura, also have superdeluxe day/night services to Chennai for Rs 100/110 and Bangalore for Rs 120/140.

Train Trichy is on the main Chennai to Madurai and Chennai to Rameswaram lines. Some trains run directly to/from Chennai while others go via Chidambaram and Thanjavur. The quickest trains to Chennai (337km, 5¼ hours) are the *Vaigai Express* and the *Pallavan Express*, which cost Rs 76/378 in 2nd/1st class. The fastest service to Madurai (155km) is on the *Vaigai Express* which leaves at 11.56 am and 5.45 pm, takes 2¼ hours and costs Rs 41/203 in 2nd/1st class. The trip to Rameswaram (265km, seven hours) costs Rs 62/312 in 2nd/1st class.

For Mamallapuram, take a Chennai train as far as Chengalpattu and a bus from there. For Mysore, take the 6 am train (No 587) to Erode Junction (four hours, Rs 25), an auto-rickshaw from Erode train station to the bus stand (Rs 35) and the 1.30 pm bus to Mysore (Rs 40, five hours).

Getting Around

To/From the Airport Into town it's Rs 160 for a taxi, Rs 60 for an auto-rickshaw.

Bus Trichy's local bus service is excellent. Take a No 7, 59, 58 or 63 bus to the airport (7km, 30 minutes). The No 1 (A or B) bus from the state bus stand plies frequently between the train station, GPO, the Rock Fort Temple, the main entrance to Sri Ranganathaswamy Temple and close to Sri Jambukeshwara Temple.

Bicycle The town lends itself well to cycling as it's dead flat. There are a couple of places on Junction Rd where you can hire bicycles for Rs 2 per hour. Note that the incredibly busy Big Bazaar Rd is a one-way road (heading north).

Shopping

There are many craft shops in and around

Trichy. Poompuhar Handicrafts is on West Boulevard Rd. A popular place, especially for quality bronzes, is Heritage Arts Emporium at 5 Amma Mandapam Rd near Cauvery River, Srirangam. This emporium is adjacent to the site of the pilgrims' riverside ritualistic bathing and cremation ceremonies.

AROUND TIRUCHIRAPPALLI
Kulittalai ·
The **Shantivanam Ashram** (Forest of Peace, ☎ 04323-3060), some 35km west of Trichy, which was established in keeping with the ideas of Father Bede Griffiths, the Benedictine priest who developed concepts around the merging of eastern and western philosophies. To get there catch the Kulittalai bus from Trichy to Thannirpalli. The trip takes about 45 minutes. Visitors are usually accommodated in dormitories, but some private accommodation is available. The ashram is popular so it's best to write first to Shantivanam Ashram, Thannirpalli, PO Kulithalai, 639 107.

Sittannavasal
Sittannavasal (Hill of the Yogis) is about 55km south of Trichy. Set within a huge hill rock, this Jain cave temple (also known as Arivarkoil) is said to contain the oldest paintings in South India. Dating from the 9th century, it is a tiny temple consisting of an outer rectangular mandapam (4m by 2m) and inner sanctum (4m by 4m) facing west. Mural paintings depict a lotus pond, swans and elephants, but they are difficult to discern now. The paintings were applied with a mixture of jaggery (palm syrup) and lime. Tiny flowers growing in the rock crevices contain colours that would have been used in the paintings. Lemongrass also grows nearby.

About 500m before the temple, a well-signposted track leads over the rock to a cave where Jain monks once lived. Their beds are carved in the rocks near inscriptions dating from the 2nd to 1st century BC. Just take the steps (some 250) to the top, then follow the iron markers to the cave.

Unfortunately the site is marred by litter and graffiti, but it is a peaceful spot overlooking a beautiful landscape. If you have an interest in ancient sites, you may wish to visit. The temple is locked, but a guide is there to unlock and show you in from 8 am to 4 pm every day. It's free if you're local; a 'small consideration' is expected if you're a foreigner. From Trichy catch the bus to Pudokkottai, and then take bus No 10, 16, 23 or 25. From the bus stop it's a further 2km walk. There are no drink or snack stands.

Southern Tamil Nadu

MADURAI
Pop: 1.23 million Tel Area Code: 0452
Madurai is an animated city packed with pilgrims, beggars, business people, bullock carts and legions of underemployed rickshaw drivers. It is one of South India's oldest cities, and has been a centre of learning and pilgrimage for centuries.

Madurai's main attraction is the famous Sri Meenakshi Temple in the heart of the old town, a riotously baroque example of Dravidian architecture with gopurams covered from top to bottom in a breathtaking profusion of multicoloured images of gods, goddesses, animals and mythical figures. The temple seethes with activity from dawn till dusk, its many shrines attracting pilgrims from every part of India and tourists from all over the world. It's been estimated that there are 10,000 visitors here on any one day!

Madurai resembles a huge, continuous bazaar crammed with shops, street markets, temples, pilgrims' *choultries* (lodgings) hotels, restaurants and small industries. Although one of the liveliest cities in the south, it's small enough not to be overwhelming and is very popular with travellers.

History
Madurai is an ancient city. Tamil and Greek documents record its existence from the 4th century BC. The city was known to the Greeks via Megasthenes, their ambassador

TAMIL NADU

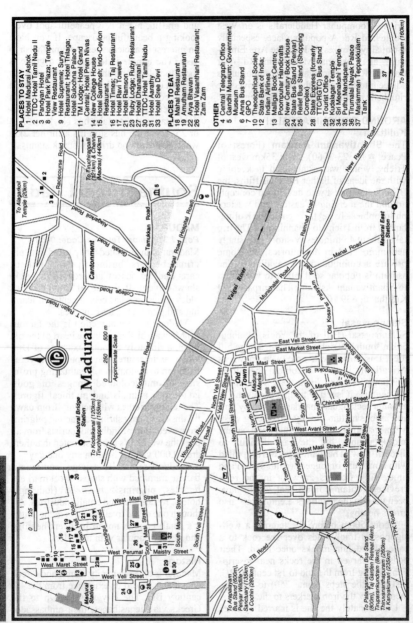

Madurai

PLACES TO STAY
1 Hotel Madurai Ashok
2 TTDC Hotel Tamil Nadu II
3 Pandyan Hotel
8 Hotel Park Plaza; Temple
  View Restaurant
9 Hotel Supreme; Surya
  Restaurant; Hotel Thilaga;
  Hotel Sulochna Palace
11 TM Lodge; Hotel Grand
  Central; Hotel Prem Nivas
14 New College House
15 Hotel Santhosh; Indo-Ceylon
  Restaurant
16 Hotel Times; Taj Restaurant
17 Hotel Ravi Towers
21 Hotel Ramson
23 Ruby Lodge; Ruby Restaurant
27 Hotel Dhanamani
30 TM-Hotel Tamil Nadu
31 Hotel Aarathy
33 Hotel Sree Devi

PLACES TO EAT
18 Mahal Restaurant
19 Amutham Restaurant
22 Arya Bhavan
26 Hotel Vasanthani Restaurant;
  Zam Zam

OTHER
4 Central Telegraph Office
5 Gandhi Museum; Government
  Museum
6 Anna Bus Stand
7 GPO
10 Theosophical Society
12 State Bank of India;
  Indian Airlines
13 Malligai Book Centre;
  Poompuhar Handicrafts
20 New Century Book House
24 State Bus Stand (Periyar)
25 Relief Bus Stand (Shopping
  Complex)
28 State Express (formerly
  TTC/RGTC) Bus Stand
29 Tourist Office
32 Kudalagar Temple
34 Sri Meenakshi Temple
35 Puthu Mandapam
36 Tirumalai Nayak Palace
37 Mariamman Teppakkulam
  Tank

to the court of Chandragupta Maurya. It was popular for trade, especially in spices. It was also the site of the sangam, or the academy of Tamil poets, and early poems celebrate Madurai and its many attributes.

In the 10th century AD, Madurai was taken by the Chola emperors. It remained in their hands until the Pandyas briefly regained their independence in the 12th century, only to lose it again in 1310 to Muslim invaders under Malik Kafur, a general in the service of the Delhi Sultanate. Here, Malik Kafur established his own dynasty until 1364 when it was overthrown by the Hindu Vijayanagar kings of Hampi. After the fall of the Vijayanagaras in 1565, the Nayaks ruled Madurai until 1781. During the reign of Tirumalai Nayak (1623-55), the bulk of the Meenakshi Temple was built, and Madurai became the cultural centre of the Tamil people, playing an important role in the development of the Tamil language.

Madurai then passed into the hands of the British East India Company, which took over the revenues of the area after the Carnatic Wars of 1781. In 1840 the company razed the fort, which had previously surrounded the city, and filled in the moat. Four broad streets – the Veli streets – were constructed on top of this fill and define the limits of the old city to this day.

Orientation

The old town, on the south bank of the Vaigai River, has most of the main points of interest, some of the transport services, mid-range and budget hotels, restaurants, the tourist office and the GPO.

On the north bank of the river in the cantonment area are top-end hotels, the Gandhi Museum and one bus stand. The Mariamman Teppakkulam Tank and temple stand on the south bank of the Vaigai, a few kilometres east of the old city.

Information

Tourist Offices The tourist office (☎ 34757), 180 West Veli St, is open weekdays from 10 am to 5.45 pm. The staff provide informa-

tion and maps and are more than willing to give advice such as the lowdown on local scams. Heed the advice given below under the Bus section, and on the notice boards around the bus stand and you should have no problems, but for further information, call in at the tourist office. There are also tourist counters at Madurai train station and the airport.

Post & Communications The post office is at the northern end of West Veli St and is open from 7 am to 7.30 pm (Sunday from 10 am to 5 pm). The poste restante counter (No 8) is open daily from 10 am to 5 pm. You can make phone calls and send faxes in the same building. There are also the usual numerous local/STD/ISD booths which offer very good service.

The central telegraph office and another post office are across the river in the Cantonment area – look for the telecommunications mast.

Bookshops Malligai Book Centre, at 11 West Veli St, opposite the train station, has a good selection of books and maps on India as well as English-language novels, academic texts and audio cassettes of Indian classical and popular music. Closer to the Sri Meenakshi Temple, the New Century Book House at 79-80 West Tower St is also well stocked with a wide range of reading matter in Tamil, Hindi and English.

A small branch of the **Theosophical Society** is located in an old house set in leafy surrounds at 97 West Perumal Maistry St. Visitors are welcome to use the quiet reading room and to browse through the small library. The society is open Tuesday to Friday from 8.30 to 10.30 am and from 3 to 6 pm. Entry is free.

Sri Meenakshi Temple

Designed in 1560 by Vishwanatha Nayak, the present temple was substantially built during the reign of Tirumalai Nayak (1623-55 AD), but its history goes back 2000 years to the time when Madurai was the capital of the

continued on page 580

Sacred Architecture

Temples

A typical South Indian Hindu temple consists of a central shrine over which rises a stepped (rather than curved) superstructure, known as a *vimana* (and which is stepped, rather than curvilinear as it is in the north), and surrounded by one or more entrance halls (*mandapams*) that lead to the shrine. South Indian temples generally have an enclosure (*prakara*) and one or more towering gates (*gopurams*).

Temples in South India evolved from shrines cut out of the rock (eg, at Badami in Karnataka) to freestanding stone structures. Temple styles changed over the centuries depending on dynastic patronage. Wooden temples built by the kings of old have long since succumbed to the elements, but their legacy lives on in the roof forms and other conventions adopted in stone buildings.

Under the Vijayanagara emperors, in response to the increasingly diverse role played by the temples in community life, temples became large city complexes containing venues for theatre, dance, public meetings and education. The temple grew larger and more complex, with artificial water tanks, columned halls ('thousand pillared halls', as they were known) and gigantic gopurams. Pillars were skilfully carved; often using mythical animals and rearing horses as motifs, eg Meenakshi Temple in Madurai, Tamil Nadu (it is speculated that the more fantastic the creature, the greater its protective powers).

The gopurams that visitors today generally associate with South Indian temples actually started to evolve from the time of the Pallavas. Under the Chola emperors they were made to literally and figuratively overshadow the vimana. The first two storeys of the gopurams are usually made of stone and the rest are made of plastered bricks, giving the whole a tapering, concave profile. During the reign of the Vijayanagara emperors the structure was covered with figurative sculpture, which became even more elaborate under the patronage successors (and former provincial governors), the Nayakas.

South India's temple pillars are intricately carved. These, pictured below, prop up the World Heritage-listed Vittala Temple, Hampi (Karnataka).

GREG ELMS

Temple Cosmology

There is a saying that if the measurement of the temple is perfect, then there will be perfection in the universe. The proportions and orientation of Hindu temples are never left to chance and conventions governing them have been handed down from ancient times. Essentially, a temple is a map of the universe. At the centre is an unadorned space, the inner shrine or (*garbhagriha*), symbolic of the 'womb-cave' from which the universe emerged. This is the *sanctum sanctorum* to which only Hindus are admitted, where the darkness is pierced only by a few lamps and by the flickering light brought in by the priest to be circled before the deity's face in the presence of devotees. Above the shrine rises a superstructure known in South India as a *vimana*, and which is representative of Mt Meru, the cosmic mountain that supports the heavens. Cave and mountain are linked by an axis that rises vertically from the shrine's icon to the finial atop the towering vimana. The simplicity of the inner shrine is in stark contrast to the light, colour and rich iconography outside it.

A temple is dedicated to a particular god or goddess. But it is more than a symbolic representation of the deity. It provides a shelter, or home, for the deity whose continuing presence is encouraged by the performance of elaborate ritual. The temple itself is therefore sacred and devotees acknowledge this by performing a clockwise circumambulation (*pradakshina*) of it, a ritual that finds architectural expression in the passageways that track round the main shrine.

PETER DAVIS

Vastu – a Concept of Harmony

Known as the science of buildings, *vastu shastra* is an ancient body of knowledge that has been applied to temple construction throughout India but especially in Tamil Nadu. The word vastu has Vedic origins and actually means *adviser to architectural, structural and technological upliftments*. The word shastra simply means system. The great sages of India are believed to have understood the intricate and symbiotic forces of the universe and how these forces shape life on earth. It is these sages who devised a system of building that would regulate

EDDIE GERALD

Perfection of proportion and orientation in Hindu temples is thought to ensure perfection in the universe. Sculpture (above), and ceiling fresco (left) at the Brihadishwara Temple, thought to be the crowning glory of Chola architecture (Thanjavur, Tamil Nadu).

the forces of nature and derive maximum advantage from them.

Through the principles of vastu shastra, architects were encouraged to study dwellings in nature. They observed for example how termites build their nests so that air flow is regulated and the temperature of the living area is maintained at around 30°C in summer and winter. The architects set down fundamental principles of design that would enable the inhabitants of a particular dwelling to enjoy wellbeing rather than incur illbeing. No major undertaking such as a temple or a palace would have been executed without first consulting the vastu.

Some of the fundamental practices of vastu include the careful selection of the site and the fixing of an auspicious date and time to commence construction (this would be determined by astrologers). There are numerous permutations and combinations when it comes to choosing a good site and a vastu practitioner will help work out the best possible set of variables. Once construction has begun, special pujas are held during specific phases. Two of the most important phases are the laying of the foundation and the installation of the main door. The specific dimensions of rooms, the angles of windows, the height of doors and the positioning of personal belongings and even the position in which you sleep can all be determined by the concepts of vastu.

To this day, when Hindu priests undergo their extensive training, they must demonstrate an awareness of the fundamental concepts of vastu shastra. However, contemporary architects with a sense of the aesthetic lament the rise of cement blocks and the disappearance of vastu shastra from modern-day knowledge.

Vastu in the bedroom

According to the principles of vastu shastra, if you sleep with your head facing north you will experience nightmares and disease. If you sleep facing east, you will experience knowledge and philosophical thought. If your head is pointing west you will be comfortable and if it is pointing south, you will experience pleasure and wealth.

A spectacular pastiche of Dravidian architecture: Sri Meenakshi Temple, Madurai.

The Sri Meenakshi Temple, Madurai

The enormously popular and powerful goddess Meenakshi (Shiva's wife) is the deity and protector of Madurai. Her temple, a spectacular pastiche of Dravidian architecture, stands in the centre of this bustling yet relaxed southern city. Its highly decorative gopurams and towers have been recently renovated and are visible from almost every point in the city.

Almost a city within a city, the temple is rectangular in shape with the *Puthu Mandapam* in the east forming a long and impressive entrance hall that leads to the eastern gopuram. All manner of business is conducted here, especially tailoring. Closer to the main part of the temple, dozens of small shops cram into crevices between statues and finely sculptured columns.

The major part of the temple, some 350 hectares, is enclosed by large walls almost forming a square. Each wall has a nine-storey-high, brightly coloured gopuram, decorated with thousands of celestial and animal figures. Within the walls, long corridors lead towards the gold-topped sanctums of the deities.

In this temple it is the custom to honour the goddess first. Most people therefore enter the temple at the south-east corner,

PETER DAVIS

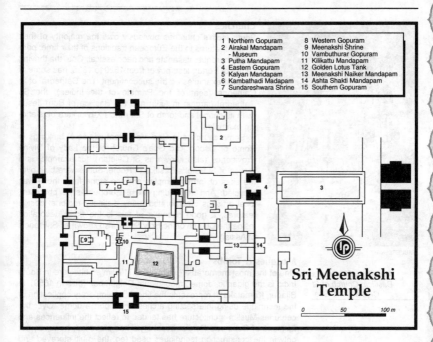

1 Northern Gopuram	8 Western Gopuram
2 Airakal Mandapam - Museum	9 Meenakshi Shrine
3 Putha Mandapam	10 Vambuthurar Gopuram
4 Eastern Gopuram	11 Kilikattu Mandapam
5 Kalyan Mandapam	12 Golden Lotus Tank
6 Kambathadi Madapam	13 Meenakshi Naiker Mandapam
7 Sundareshwara Shrine	14 Ashta Shakti Mandapam
	15 Southern Gopuram

Sri Meenakshi Temple

0   50   100 m

through the *Ashta Shakti Mandapam* and proceed directly to the Meenakshi shrine. Originally this hall was a *choultry* where pilgrims ate and rested.

A small connecting mandapam leads to the 40m-high *Meenakshi Naiker Mandapam*, which was once the stables of the temples' camels and elephants. Built in 1706, it now houses a large brass frame with 1008 oil lamps.

To the right is the *Kalyan Mandapam*. It is here that the marriage of Shiva and Meenakshi is celebrated in a spectacular festival each April/May. Directly ahead is the Golden Lotus Tank where pilgrims who believe in the sacredness of the waters descend to bathe. On the western side of the tank is the mirror chamber where, each Friday evening, images of Shiva and Meenakshi are placed on a swing and gently rocked. The walls above the tank were once adorned with fine paintings depicting Shiva's miraculous deeds around Madurai. These paintings are currently being painstakingly restored.

The path on the northern side of the tank leads directly to the tiny gopuram and into the Meenakshi shrine. To the left of the shrine is the *Kilikattu Mandapam*, a hall of intricately carved pillars.

The *Vambuthurar Gopuram*, with over 450 sculptures, marks the entrance to the Meenakshi shrine (only Hindus may enter). Within the shrine the image of the goddess is visible only in the *puja* firelight. In the north-east corner is the bed chamber, where the deities are united each evening.

A replica of St Peter's Basilica: Church of St Cajetan, Old Goa.

Churches

South India's churches obviously owe the majority of their design features to the European traditions of their time; principally baroque, Italianate and neoclassical. Goa, the thriving centre of Portuguese power from 1520 to 1835, has some of the best examples on the subcontinent. The Cathedral of St Catherine (seat of the Primate of the Indies), the Se Cathedral (largest in Asia) and the Basilica of Bom Jesus (with its chapel and tomb of St Francis Xavier) are outstanding examples.

Some churches in Goa are blatant copies of buildings in Rome or Lisbon. Old Goa's Church of the Lady of Divine Providence (also known as St Cajetan), for example, is a replica of St Peter's Basilica in Rome. Some were built over the sites of former temples and the stone from these was recycled. And in building these European-style churches, local artisans incorporated many distinctly regional design features; a good example of this is the floral decoration inside the Church of the Holy Spirit (also known as St Francis of Assisi).

Mosques & Tombs

One of the most memorable examples of Muslim architecture in South India is the gigantic, domed mausoleum Golgumbaz (built in 1659), in Bijapur, Karnataka. It represents the finest contemporary application of the technique using intersecting arches to support a dome. Over the centuries Muslim architecture has tended to reflect the influences and fashions of Delhi and Persia. Local style has prevailed, however, not only in the construction techniques used (eg, the multi-storeyed and domed royal tombs near Golconda in Andhra Pradesh), but in the use of embellishments, eg the fancy plasterwork used in the Mushiraba and Toli mosques near Hyderabad in Andhra Pradesh. In Kerala, decorative touches in mosques such as Muchchandipalli in Kozhikode echo conventions favoured in temples – although artists, forbidden in Muslim tradition to use people or animals as motifs, took to stylised flowers and complex geometrical figures.

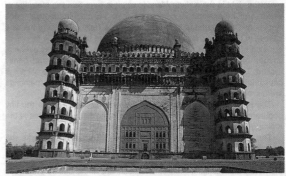

Muhammed Adil Shah's monument to himself, the massive Golgumbaz; Bijapur, Karnataka.

Synagogues

Jews first settled in Kerala nearly 2000 years ago. Although few Jews remain in the region today, at least eight synagogues still stand in Kochi. The best-known is the Pardesi Synagogue in Fort Cochin. Built in 1568, it was partly destroyed by the Portuguese in 1662 and restored in 1664. It is famous for its floor of blue-and-white Chinese tiles; the tiles themselves depict the story of a love affair between a Mandarin's daughter and a commoner. Kochi synagogues are unique in that they have two pulpits (*tebas*) – at Pardesi the second teba is on the 2nd floor.

The well-lit and famous blue-and-white tiles in the Pardesi Synagogue, Kerala, depict the story of a love affair.

GREG ELMS

continued from page 573

Pandya kings. The temple complex occupies an area of six hectares. It has 12 towers, ranging in height from 45 to 50m, the tallest of which is the southern tower. See also 'Sacred Architecture' on the preceding pages.

Depending on the time of day, you can bargain for bangles, spices or saris in the bazaar between the outer and inner eastern walls of the temple, watch pilgrims bathing in the tanks, listen to temple music in front of the Meenakshi Amman Shrine (the music is relayed through the whole complex on a PA system), or wander through the interesting, though decidedly dilapidated, museum.

This museum, known as the **Temple Art Museum**, is housed in the 1000-pillared hall. It contains friezes, beautiful stone and brass images, examples of ancient South Indian scripts, various illustrations attempting to explain the Hindu pantheon and its legends, as well as one of the best exhibits on Hindu deities anywhere. Temple structures and their relationship to human life are also illustrated. Unfortunately, many of the labels are missing. Entrance costs Rs 1, Rs 0.50 for children, plus Rs 10 for a camera. It's open from 7 am to 7 pm.

Allow yourself plenty of time to see and appreciate this temple. If you want to avoid the crowds go in the early morning or late evening and avoid holidays. Many of the priests inside are very friendly and will take the trouble to show you around and explain what's happening. Licensed guides charge negotiable fees but it will be difficult to obtain a fee below Rs 200. Assured of this fee from other travellers they'll quckly move on if you refuse their charge. There are also 'guides' who will show you around for a very reasonable fee as long as you agree to visit their tailor shop afterwards. Unless you want to shop, don't fall for the offer to take you up the tower so you can view the whole complex. Certainly you'll go up a tower – right above the local emporium!

The temple is usually open between 5 am and 12.30 pm and again between 4 and 9.30 pm. Entry is Rs 10. If you want to take photos you need to buy a permit (Rs 30), which you may be required to show inside anytime one of the priests notices your camera. Film and video are prohibited. Leave your shoes at any of the four entrances, where 'Footwear Safe Custody' stalls will mind them for a small fee.

Madurai Market

Just north of the temple, before you get to North Avani St, is the Madurai market. To stroll through the market is to see another side of this town beyond the temples , the tourists and the tailors. The produce market is a labyrinth of bustling laneways strewn with aromatic herbs which seduce your olfactory senses. Adjacent to this and upstairs in a nondescript cement building is the flower market. This is where the temple flower sellers buy their stuff. Market vendors dexterously heap mountains of marigolds and jasmine onto weighing scales. Perfumes, sometimes gentle, sometimes overpowering, waft through the thick air.

Tirumalai Nayak Palace

About 1.5km from the Meenakshi Temple, this Indo-Saracenic palace was built in 1636 by the ruler whose name it bears. It was Tirumalai's grandson who demolished much of the fine structure and removed most of the jewels and woodcarvings in order to build his own palace at Trichy (his dream was never realised). Most of what the grandson didn't touch has fallen into ruin, and the pleasure gardens and surrounding defensive wall have disappeared.

Today, only the entrance gate, main hall and dance hall remain but these are well worth seeing. Massive stone pillars support elegant cornices that give the roof of the palace a height of 20m. This rectangular courtyard is known as the Swargavilasa or 'Celestial Pavilion'. It measures 75m by 52m and it's not hard to imagine the original grandeur of the building which is regarded as one of the finest secular buildings in South India. Some historians claim that King Tirumalai engaged the assistance of an Italian architect but the evidence is disputed by historians. Many of the rooms leading from the celestial pavilion were elaborately adorned with ivory, intricate woodcarvings and priceless jewels. The queen had her own apartment leading from the west of the celestial pavilion where she would listen to music as well as literary discourses.

Many festivals revolved around the palace, including the Sceptre Festival. The king would visit the Goddess Meenakshi at the temple and, after special worship, receive the royal sceptre from her. This would then be brought to the palace by the royal elephant and, amid great ceremony, placed on the king's throne. There it would be worshipped until nightfall when it would be returned to the temple. The festival symbolised the extent to which the country was governed by Goddess Meenakshi and the king was merely her representative.

King Tirumalai may have been a strong devotee of the goddess and a lover of his subjects but he wasn't without cruelty. A popular story is told of how he was so proud of the security in his bedroom that he issued a public challenge to anyone 'having the guts to try and enter'. The challenge was taken up by a man named Kallan who made a successful night-time entry into the king's bedroom (through the roof) and promptly stole the royal jewels. Kallan gave himself up, received the promised reward and was then beheaded at the king's command.

The palace was partially restored by Lord Napier, the governor of Madras, in 1866-72, and further restoration was carried out several years ago. The palace entrance is on the far (eastern) side. It is open daily from 9 am to 1 pm and 2 to 5 pm; entry costs Rs 1.

There's a daily sound-and-light show (son et lumiere) in English at 6.30 pm and in Tamil at 8 pm. The technology consists of a few coloured lights that are switched on and off at random and an audio cassette played to maximum volume and gross distortion. The one hour show extols the virtues of King Tirumalai, particularly his passion for the arts, his victories in battle and his love of his subjects. The text, interspersed with Tamil songs, is a sort of Monty Python meets Shakespeare! If you do feel the need to see it

take plenty of mosquito repellent. Tickets cost Rs 2 to Rs 5 depending on whether you want a metal or plastic chair. A sign reads 'In case of rain or power failure the show will be cancelled – no refunds please'.

You can get to the palace on a No 11, 11A, 11B, 17 or 38 bus from the state bus stand (Shopping Complex section), or take the 20 minute walk from the Meenakshi Temple through an interesting bazaar area.

Museums
Housed in the old palace of the Rani Mangammal, the **Gandhi Museum** gives a particularly clear account of the history of the Independence of India. There are also some little-known facts about the Mahatma, although the only real piece of Gandhi memorabilia is his bloodstained *dhoti* (the cloth worn by Hindu men, draped around the waist and up between the legs) from the assassination. The grounds surrounding the museum are pleasant and relaxing and there is also a children's entertainment park.

The local **Government Museum** is in the same grounds, as is a small bookshop stocked with plenty of Gandhi reading matter.

To get there, take a No 2, 3, 4 or 23 bus from the state bus stand to the central telegraph office (look for the telecommunications mast). From there, it's 500m along a shady street. The Gandhi Museum is open daily from 10 am to 1 pm and 2 to 5.30 pm. The Government Museum keeps the same hours but closes every Friday and on the second Saturday of each month. Entry to both museums is free.

Mariamman Teppakkulam Tank
This tank, 5km east of the old city, covers an area almost equal to that of the Meenakshi Temple and is the site of the popular Teppam Festival (see the following section). For most of the year, however, it is empty save for local kids who play cricket in it. The tank was built by Tirumalai Nayak in 1646 and is connected to the Vaigai River by underground channels. The No 4 bus (Rs 2) from the state bus stand stops at the tank.

Special Events

The **Pongal** harvest festival in January is celebrated throughout India, but it is particularly significant in the Madurai area, the centre of fertile lands and abundant harvests. People flock to the temple at this time, but it is in the small villages just outside Madurai where all manner of festivities take place. If you're in a village at this time you'll no doubt be included in the celebrations.

The tourist office also runs a program for visitors to learn about the festival and witness various activities. On the last day of the festival you can take the tourist bus to the nearby village of Alanganallur for the Jallikata ('taming' of the bulls). This is good 'entertainment' if you want to witness cruelty to both people and animals.

For more information on Pongal, see the boxed text under Mamallapuram, earlier in this chapter.

Madurai celebrates 11 big annual temple festivals, with only the monsoon month, called Ani in Tamil, devoid of festivities. Timing for the festivals is based on the position of the planets, not necessarily the moon as in other rituals. The temple astrologer determines the dates. For a schedule of these, check with the tourist office.

In late January/early February the 12-day **Teppam (Float) Festival** attracts pilgrims from all over India. For this event, images of Sri Meenakshi and Sundareshwara are mounted on floats, decorated with lights and flowers, and taken to the Mariamman Teppakkulam Tank. For several days, they are pulled around the tank in a clockwise direction, then taken to the island temple in the tank's centre. On each day they circle the tank three times, twice in the morning; once in the evening. This represents three aspects in Hindu philosophy associated with the world, life and god. At the conclusion of the festival the images are returned to Madurai.

The main event is the 14-day **Chithrai Festival** (late April/early May), which celebrates the marriage of Sri Meenakshi to Sundareshwara (Shiva). The deities are wheeled around the Masi streets (the four streets surrounding the temple; see map) in huge chariots followed by thousands of devotees. The main chariot may rise to 20m high and requires some hundreds of people to haul it. The base, made from Keralan teak, is over 200 years old (except for the wheels which are new). Carpenters spend up to a week before the festival building the upper structure of the chariot, mainly from bamboo. The chariot is then decorated with brightly coloured cloths and tassels. The 6km procession of temple dignitaries, musicians and devotees takes place every morning and evening of the festival.

In the hot, still days of June people are entreated to consider their neighbours and give items, such as umbrellas or cool curd, which might provide some respite from the heat. At this time the temple observes **Vasanta**. According to the temple priests this is also known as 'the time of indecision', a time to attain balance. Images of the deities, Meenakshi and Sundareshwara, are taken each day to another temple. It's a time of vacation when the gods may 'enjoy the gentle breeze'.

The **Festival of the Cradle** occurs in July/August and is similar to the Friday evening ritual, when the deities are taken in procession to the mirror chamber. For nine days they are placed on a swing, which rocks them gently before worshipping devotees.

The 15-day 'harmony' festival **Avanimoolam** in September celebrates the coronation of Shiva. The *lila* (play) is performed where the temple priests recite the stories of Shiva and his 64 miracles, which protected the city of Madurai from adversity.

The September/October **Navratri Festival** (nine nights) is held in honour of the goddess. For Hindus the number nine is significant since it symbolises the nine planets. But it is also considered to be symbolic of the goddess; the number '9' contains every other digit, but they do not contain it. Similarly it is believed that the goddess contains all life – the entire universe.

At this festival Meenakshi is honoured in all her forms, which embody fury, compassion and wisdom. Over the nine days, nine priests chant mantras, place flowers at the feet of the goddess and pray for the well-being of the world. She is offered nine varieties of rice meals and nine varieties of flowers. The earlier practice of honouring young girls during this time was ceased by the temple in the early 1990s.

Places to Stay – Budget

In a pilgrim city of Madurai's size and importance, lots of cheap hotels offer basic accommodation. Many are just flophouses which bear the scars of previous occupants' habits, though a few places are clean and good value. These are mostly along Town Hall and Dindigul Rds.

New College House (☎ 742971, 2 Town Hall Rd) is a huge, labyrinthine place with 200 rooms. You'll almost certainly get accommodation at any hour of the day or night but the rooms are pretty basic and toilet smells permeate some of the floors. Costs are Rs 110/190/230 for ordinary singles/doubles/triples. There are more expensive deluxe and air-con rooms. A reasonable bookshop in the forecourt offers good reading material (including *Time* and *Newsweek*), as well as a wide range of Indian music cassettes.

Hotel Santhosh (☎ 543692, 7 Town Hall Rd) has very basic rooms with attached bathrooms for Rs 70/100.

Hotel Ravi Towers (☎ 741961, 9 Town Hall Rd) is a good choice, with clean rooms and quite clean sheets for Rs 125/195 with attached bath. A TV costs Rs 30 extra. There are also good air-con rooms for Rs 200/300.

Hotel Ramson (☎ 740407, 9 Permal Tank St) looks expensive but isn't at Rs 60/80 for rooms with attached bathroom. During festival time (especially Pongal in January) the hotel and environs is blasted with over-amplified music from enthusiastic revellers. In spite of this the hotel is often full.

Hotel Sree Devi (☎ 747431, 20 West Avani St) has a great view of the temple from its roof. The rooms (no singles) are spotlessly clean and start at Rs 160 for a double with bathroom. A double with air-con is Rs

400 but avoid the one with no windows. The best room is the rooftop one, where the view of the temple, including the golden dome, is spectacular. For this you'll pay Rs 600 including tax. The hotel has no restaurant but beverages and breakfast can be brought to your room.

Ruby Lodge (☎ 742253, 92 West Perumal Maistry St) has rooms with attached bathrooms (bucket showers only) for Rs 80/100. The hotel has its own pleasant outdoor restaurant and bar.

Hotel Grand Central (☎ 743940, 47 West Perumal Maistry St) is one of several hotels in this area that look more expensive than they are. It has good-sized rooms for Rs 125/175, air-con doubles for Rs 350.

Hotel Dhanamani (☎ 742701, 20 Sunnambukara St) has singles with common bath for Rs 85, singles/doubles with attached bath for Rs 95/150, and good-value air-con doubles with Star TV for Rs 250.

Hotel Times (☎ 742651, 15-16 Town Hall Rd) is clean, friendly and excellent value at Rs 120/195 for singles/doubles or Rs 350 for a double deluxe with air-con.

Railway Retiring Rooms at Madurai station are noisy and cost Rs 50/95; dorm beds are just Rs 15.

Places to Stay – Mid-Range

Hotel Aarathy (☎ 31571, 9 Perumal Koil West Mada St), just a few minutes walk from the bus stands, is a good place to stay although it lacks atmosphere. It's very popular with foreigners – you may need to book ahead. All rooms have bathrooms and cost Rs 190/270, or Rs 300/400 for air-con. The rooms are comfortable and secure, and most have a small balcony with a great view over the neighbouring temple. Rouse yourself out of bed for sunrise – it's superb! There's a pleasant open-air veg restaurant in the courtyard which is frequented daily (6 am and 4 pm) by Mahalakshmi, the temple elephant from next door.

TTDC Hotel Tamil Nadu (☎ 37471; fax 627945, West Veli St), adjacent to the tourist office, is good value. The rooms are clean and cost from Rs 150/195 with attached bath,

TAMIL NADU

Rs 260/400 with air-con and TV. There's a restaurant here serving well-priced meals and there is also a bar.

TTDC Hotel Tamil Nadu II (☎ 537461; fax 533203), across the river on Alagarkoil Rd, is nothing special. Ordinary doubles cost Rs 250, or Rs 350 with air-con (plus Rs 75 for a TV). There's also a restaurant and bar, where it's Rs 60 for a beer.

Hotel Prem Nivas (☎ 742532, 102 West Perumal Maistry St) is popular with business people and has rooms with attached bathrooms for Rs 175/250 and air-con doubles at Rs 375. Facilities are excellent and the hotel has its own air-con vegetarian restaurant.

TM Lodge (☎ 741651, 50 West Perumal Maistry St) is a reasonable place. Rooms with attached bathrooms are Rs 175/250. An air-con double with TV is Rs 375. The upper rooms are lighter and airier.

Hotel Supreme (☎ 742637, 110 West Perumal Maistry St) has doubles (no singles) at Rs 340, or Rs 580 with air-con, plus more expensive suites. Although the rooms are dark, the facilities are good and there's an excellent rooftop veg restaurant.

Hotel Thilaga (☎ 740762, 111 West Perumal Maistry St) is clean and good value. Rooms with attached bath, 24 hour hot water and TV cost Rs 150/175. Air-con doubles are Rs 310.

Hotel Sulochna Palace (☎ 741071; fax 740627, 96 West Perumal Maistry St) offers clean, comfortable rooms for Rs 280/310 without air-con or Rs 410/465 with air-con. The hotel has a rooftop vegetarian restaurant. Take plenty of insect repellent with you to this hotel; the reports are that bugs as well as travellers like the place.

Hotel Park Plaza (☎ 742112, 114 West Perumal Maistry St) is similar to the Supreme but a little smarter. It has comfortable but somewhat overpriced rooms from Rs 725/950 with central air-con and a rooftop restaurant.

Should you be overcome with a burning desire to steal the toilet, management will add Rs 2500 to your bill! The tariff includes a buffet Indian breakfast.

Places to Stay – Top End

Madurai's three top hotels are well out of the town centre.

Hotel Madurai Ashok (☎ 537531; fax 537530, Alargakoil Rd) is somewhat overpriced at Rs 1195/1800 for plain rooms but it does have a nice swimming pool (Rs 75 for nonresidents). An auto-rickshaw out here should cost no more than Rs 35, although the price generally doubles when they hear where you want to go! A taxi charges Rs 75. City buses No 2, 16 or 20 are on this route.

Pandyan Hotel (☎ 537090; fax 533424), also on Alagarkoil Rd, is a little cheaper than the Ashok, at Rs 1175/1700. It's also fully air-conditioned and has a restaurant and bar. The manicured garden offers a respite from the city chaos but there is no pool.

Taj Garden Retreat (☎ 601020), 4km south of town at Pasumalai Hill, ranks as Madurai's best (and most expensive) hotel. Rooms come in three varieties: standard – US$90/105 a single/double; old-world (part of the original colonial villa) – US$110/120; and deluxe (new cottages with private terraces and great views) – US$125/140. Facilities include a multicuisine restaurant, swimming pool (for guests only), a tennis court, gardens and a bar. Bus No 5D from the relief bus stand in Madurai stops at the main gate. From here it's still another 1.5km up the hill to the hotel (if you're walking, take the shortcut path leading off to the left about a third of the way up the road). An auto-rickshaw from town costs Rs 80, or Rs 25 from the main gate.

Places to Eat

Idli lovers love Madurai – they can get idli here all day, whereas in most towns after 10 am there's no more idli!

There are many typical South Indian vegetarian restaurants around the Meenakshi Temple and along Town Hall Rd, Dindigul Rd and West Masi St. On Town Hall Rd there are several places where you can get decent nonvegetarian food – try the ***Indo-Ceylon Restaurant*** at No 6, the ***Mahal***, which is popular with backpackers, or the ***Amutham Restaurant***, near the corner of West Masi St.

New College House has a popular vegetarian dining hall and the thalis are good value.

Arya Bhavan (corner of West Masi St & Dindigul Rd) does astoundingly large dosas.

Ruby Restaurant, next to the Ruby Lodge on West Perumal Maistry St, is the only garden restaurant in Madurai and is deservedly popular. Delicious nonveg food is served and the menu makes good reading. You could choose a mutton bullet (Rs 50), a mutton lever (Rs 20) or a chicken lollipop (Rs 45) but the tandoori items are best. You can also get a beer for Rs 50 – it's a good place for a drink, for talking, meeting other travellers and for writing letters. It stays open until after midnight.

Hotel Vasanthani (West Perumal Maistry St) is good for cheap thalis and tiffin and the upstairs section is great for watching the busy street scene.

Zam Zam, nearby, is a popular shop for sweet or savoury snacks.

Taj Restaurant (10 Town Hall Rd) offers a varied cuisine including 'continentals', puddings and peach melba!

Mahal Restaurant is a few doors along from the Taj Restaurant. It offers excellent multicuisine including 'roast lamp'. Most items are around Rs 30 (none are over Rs 60) and there's a comfortable air-con environment.

Surya Restaurant, on the roof of the Hotel Supreme, has a superb view and catches any breezes. It serves Indian, Chinese and continental vegetarian food in the evening only (5 pm to midnight) – the tandoori dishes are very good. Most items are around Rs 40. It's also open for breakfast from 6 to 11 am, and for lunch they do upmarket thalis for Rs 40.

Temple View Roof Top Restaurant, in the Hotel Park Plaza, serves nonveg dishes with the same view as the Surya, a few doors down. Chicken garlic fry is Rs 40, the tandoor chicken is especially succulent and there are good-value vegetarian dishes too.

Hotel Sulochna Palace rooftop garden restaurant at 96 West Perumal Maistry St seriously lacks atmosphere.

Taj Garden Retreat is the place to go for a splurge. There are excellent à la carte meals in the multicuisine restaurant. On Saturday and Sunday evenings there's a buffet for Rs 200.

Shopping

Madurai has long been a textile centre and the streets around the temple still teem with cloth stalls and tailors' shops. A great place to buy locally manufactured cottons as well as the batiks loved by many travellers is Puthu Mandapam, an old, stone-pillared hall just opposite the eastern entrance to Sri Meenakshi Temple. Here you'll find lines of textile stalls opposite rows of tailors, each busily treadling away and capable of whipping up a good replica of whatever you're wearing in an hour or two.

Quality, designs and prices vary greatly. Some vendors have very good quality textiles but others have limited stock of inferior quality. Touts are everywhere and of course if you accept their offers, their commissions will be added to the price of your garments.

If you want to have garments made up, it's wise to have your designs ready. It's also important to know a little about materials, quality and quantity required. Some merchants will talk you into buying way too much only to strike a deal with the tailor who makes your clothes to keep the leftovers. As always take your time, look around carefully and bargain hard before coming to an agreement. It can be great fun and very satisfying to have clothes created to your own designs and specifications.

For a good range of local crafts as well as items from other parts of India there is a Poompuhar Handicrafts shop (☎ 740517) at 12 West Veli St, just opposite the railway junction.

Close to the east gate of the temple are Madurai Gallery (☎ 627851), at 19 North Chitrai St, and Cottage Arts Emporium (☎ 623614), at 36 North Chitrai St.

All of these shops are brimming with such items as silk paintings, intricate bronzes, stone and wood carvings and even Kashmiri carpets. Prices in all these stores are fixed and an efficient shipping and air freight service is available.

TAMIL NADU

Getting There & Away

Air The Indian Airlines office (☎ 37234) is on West Veli St. There are four flights weekly to Chennai (US$70), Calicut (US$50) and Mumbai (US$150). Also, NEPC Airlines (☎ 741644) has an office in the Supreme Hotel. It flies daily except Sunday to Chennai (US$82).

Bus

Madurai has five bus stands and three of them are several kilometres from the town centre. You'll need to use either a city bus or a rickshaw to get to these terminals. Sorting out which bus leaves which terminus can be quite a task. Even the locals say it's confusing, so if you don't speak Tamil you may find it particularly confusing. For more information see the timekeeper, in the glass booth just near the Church of the Holy Redeemer. By the end of the encounter you'll probably need a holy redemption more than a timetable!

The state bus stand, Periyar, is centrally located on West Veli St. It is the principal local bus stand. It has another section, the 'relief' bus stand (also referred to as the Shopping Complex bus stand) which is situated across the street. For most places you'll pay from Rs 1.50 to Rs 2.

The STC bus stand (formerly TTC/RGTC) is next door, and is for long-distance/interstate buses. Seats on buses originating in Madurai (for details see the Bus Services from Madurai table) can be reserved in advance at the booking office (open daily from 7 am to 10 pm) and there's a timetable

in English. Plenty of other STC buses stop in Madurai on their way through and though these can't be reserved in advance, it's not usually a problem to get a seat.

The Anna bus stand, across the river to the north, services destinations to the north-east such as Thanjavur, Tiruchirappalli (Trichy), Chidambaram (Rs 40, two daily), as well as Rameswaram (Rs 25, 30 daily). If your bus terminates here, bus No 3 will take you to the state bus stand in town, or you can catch a cycle-rickshaw for Rs 15.

The dusty Arapalayam bus stand (take bus No 7A or JJ from the relief bus stand) is for points north-west including Coimbatore (Rs 29, 30 daily), Kodaikanal (Rs 18, 12 daily), Palani (Rs 16, 11 daily) and Salem (but not Bangalore – that leaves from the STC stand). During heavy monsoon rain, the road to Kodaikanal sometimes gets washed away and the buses go via Palani, adding an hour or two to the journey.

The Palanganatham bus stand to the south-west of town is for buses heading south to destinations such as Kanyakumari (Bus No 556, Rs 47, 22 daily), Tiruchendur (Bus No 403/531, Rs 25, 20 daily) and southern Kerala. Bus Nos 7, 7J and JJ7 from the relief bus stand in town will get you there.

There are several private bus companies which offer superdeluxe video buses to such places as Chennai and Bangalore. Tickets for these are sold by agencies near the state bus stand. However, *beware* of buying a ticket for any destination other than these two major cities. Many of the agencies will sell you a ticket to virtually anywhere (such

Bus Services from Madurai STC Bus Stand

Destination	Route Number	Frequency (daily)	Distance (km)	Duration (hours)	Fare (Rs)
Bangalore	846	12	450	15	103
Chennai	137, 491	32	447	10	89
Ernakulam	826	4	324	10	87
Mysore	837	2	450	12	95
Pondicherry	847	3	329	8	60
Thiruvananthapuram	865	1	305	7	58
Tirupathi		4	517	16	104

Train Services from Madurai

Destination	Train Number & Name	Departure Time	Distance (km)	Duration (hours)	Fare (Rs) (2nd/1st)
Coimbatore	6116 *Coimbatore-Rameswaram Exp*	9.45 pm	229	6.15	93/294
Chennai	6718 *Pandian Exp*	7.10 pm	490	12.00	157/531
	2636 *Vaigai Exp*	6.25 am		8.35	117/338
Rameswaram	6115 *Coimbatore-Rameswaram Exp*	6.00 am	164	5.00	24/193
Tirupathi	6799 *Madurai-Tirupathi Exp*	9.50 am	663	19.40	172/620

as Kodaikanal or Rameswaram) but you'll find yourself dumped on a state bus having paid substantially more than required. In spite of all the warnings, travellers continue to fall prey to the tricks of the agencies.

Train Madurai train station is on West Veli St, a few minutes walk from the main hotel area. The table lists the more frequent trains leaving Madurai.

If you're heading to Kollam (Quilon) in Kerala, you can take the No 721 passenger train from Madurai at 6.50 am to Virudunagar (one hour). The 6105 *Chennai-Quilon Mail* passes through Virudunagar at 9 am, reaching Kollam (225km) at 4.20 pm. The line crosses the Western Ghats through some spectacular mountain terrain, and there are some superb gopurams to be seen at Sriviliputur (between Sivakasi and Rajapalaiyam) and Sankarayinarkovil.

Getting Around

To/From the Airport The airport is 12km south of town and a taxi charges an extortionate Rs 200 to the centre. If you can find an auto-rickshaw they'll try for around Rs 100 (even Rs 150). Alternatively, bus No 10A from the state bus stand goes to the airport but don't rely on it being on schedule.

Bus Some useful local buses include No 3 to the Anna bus stand, Nos 1 and 2 to near the Gandhi Museum, and Nos 4 and 4A to Mariamman Teppakkulam Tank. All these buses depart from the Periyar state bus stand.

Auto-Rickshaw Drivers are extremely reluctant to use the meters and will quote whatever they think you will pay, but eventually they should settle on a reasonable rate.

Walking Since most of the facilities, bookshops and the temple are within a short distance of each other, one of the easiest ways to get around is to walk.

AROUND MADURAI

There are several places which may be visited from Madurai. Unless otherwise stated below, there is no accommodation at these places so day-trips from Madurai are necessary.

Alagarkoil

Twenty-one kilometres north-east of Madurai, the temple here is dedicated to the aspect of Vishnu known as Alagar, the brother of Meenakshi. Set within forested hills and a ruined fort, the temple dates from the 12th century. Ceiling paintings from the late 18th century depict stories from the *Ramayana*.

During the month of Chithrai (April-May), a festival celebrates the marriage of Meenakshi and Shiva, and a gold icon of Alagar is carried in procession from this temple to Madurai. This is representative of this deity attending his sister's wedding.

Many stories surround this festival. Perhaps the most powerful one of them is the claim that this bringing together of the deities a meeting (in auspicious circumstances, ie marriage) of two of the strands of

TAMIL NADU

Hinduism – Shaivism and Vaishnavism. The icon at this temple is made of a rare type of gold and it's believed that should it be bathed in anything other than the waters nearby (see Pazhamudhirsolai below), it will turn black.

If you are on pilgrimage or have a particular interest in ancient constructions, you will no doubt wish to visit this temple. Buses No 44 or 44D from the Periyar bus stand, will get you there for Rs 3.50.

Pazhamudhirsolai (Palamudircholai)

About 4km further up the hill, Pazhamudhir-solai ('Grove of Fruits') is a small shrine – one of the six abodes of Subrahmanya, who was the second son of Parvati and Shiva. At each of his abodes Subrahmanya expresses a different disposition. Here he is in wonderment. According to legend, it was at this place that Subrahmanya gave berries to his devotee, Avvayar. In return she sang his praises. One hundred and twenty-six steps take you up to a natural spring, Nubura Ganga, which flows near the shrine, and is said to contain high contents of copper and iron. Large numbers of people come to bathe, in the belief that the waters hold special healing qualities. Certainly they're refreshing and sweet tasting.

Just down from the shrine is a government-run conservation area for medicinal trees and plants. People come to inhale the pure air which they believe will aid health. Large signs in Tamil give information as to the purpose of this 250 hectare site with its 1800 medicinal plants. Many of the trees are marked with their Tamil as well as their botanical names. It's very pleasant to wander in the forest and bathe in the waters.

From Madurai, take bus No 44 or 44D from the Periyar bus stand to the Alagarkoil Temple and then take the van at the temple, or you can walk the 4km up to the shrine.

Pillaiyarpatti

About 50km north of Madurai this small rock-cave temple dating from the 7th century is dedicated to Bhairava, the fearful aspect of Shiva, who is depicted here with two hands

instead of the customary four. It is believed that he will destroy all evil. The temple contains a shrine with one of the largest images of Ganesh in India. People wanting a child bathe in the waters of the tank, assured that their request will be granted. The spacious setting of this temple with its attractive tank makes it a peaceful place to visit. To get there, take the Karaikudi bus from the Anna bus stand in Madurai.

Tirumayam

The small town of Tirumayam is some 75km north of Madurai (halfway between Thanjavur and Madurai), and is the site of a large fort. Constructed in 1687, and covering an area of 16 hectares, the fort was an important stronghold for early rulers of Pudukkottai and later for the British. There are two temples here: one to Shiva, and a cave temple to the reclining Vishnu.

Dindigul

Pop: 130,000 Tel Area Code: 0451

This small town is renowned for its tobacco and cotton factories and is dominated by the massive 17th century granite rock fort. The summit of this rock is nearly 400m above sea level and 90m above the Dindigul plain. Like so many Indian forts, it has been a stage for numerous battles from the time of the Madurai Nayaks through to the British who captured it in 1792.

Travellers find the township of Dindigul relaxed, peaceful and aesthetically very pleasing. Dindigul is some 65km north of Madurai. It's on a branch line that runs to Pollachi and is accessible by rail from Chennai and from Madurai.

Dindigul can also be reached by bus, direct from Madurai (Arapalayam bus stand) or from Chennai (bus No 132) via Viluppuram and Trichy.

Although it is possible to make a day visit from Madurai (buses between Dindigul and Madurai are frequent) the town offers a range of accommodation that makes an overnight stop feasible.

Hotel Anand International *(☎ 27510, 37A 3rd St, Spencer Nagar)* has air-con double rooms for Rs 250, or Rs 125 without air-con.

Dolphin Hotel (☎ *31791, 14 Chatram St*) has double air-con rooms for Rs 300 and non air-con singles/doubles for Rs 90/200

Lucky Lodge (☎ *7827, 48 Koil St*) offers basic accommodation for Rs 50.

Tiruparankundram

This rock-cut temple, 8km south of town, is another of Murugan's six abodes. It consists of long pillared halls on different levels. Off one hall to the lotus tank, young trainee priests chant in Sanskrit. At the lotus-covered tank people feed the myriad fish. The pavement stones nearby have many foot impressions. Opposite the young priests, peacocks strut their stuff, appropriately so, given that Murugan's vehicle is the peacock. The temple, which is cut into a rock almost 350m above sea level, dates from the late 8th century, but most of what is visible now was added in the 17th and 18th centuries. The temple has a constant stream of pilgrims, but particularly at the March-April festival which celebrates Murugan's coronation and marriage to Devasena.

A small bookshop sells literature in Hindi and Tamil. The temple can be reached by bus Nos 4A, 5 and 32 which leave from the state bus stand in Madurai.

RAMESWARAM

Pop: 35,750 Tel Area Code: 04573

Known as the Varanasi of the South, as well as the 'Island of Prayer', Rameswaram is a major pilgrimage centre for both Shaivites and Vaishnavites as it was here that Rama (an incarnation of Vishnu in the *Ramayana*) offered thanks to Shiva. At the town's core is the Ramanathaswamy Temple, one of the most important temples in South India.

Rameswaram is on an island in the Gulf of Mannar, connected to the mainland at Mandapam by rail, and by one of India's engineering wonders, the Indira Gandhi Bridge. The bridge took 14 years to build and was opened by Rajiv Gandhi late in 1988.

The town lies on the island's eastern side and used to be the port from which the ferry

to Talaimannar (Sri Lanka) departed before passenger services were suspended more than a decade ago. The proximity to Sri Lanka is palpable and there is a high security presence in and around the town. In spite of this Rameswaram has a decidedly laid-back atmosphere. Fishing is the main activity, and since this occurs mostly in the mornings, the afternoons are delightfully and infectiously sleepy.

Orientation & Information

If you are travelling by private vehicle to Rameswaram you'll have to pay two tolls. Before crossing the Indira Gandhi Bridge there is a toll of Rs 5/20 for motorcycles/cars, and then when you enter the town you have to pay a 'security toll' of Rs 5/10 for motorcycles/cars.

Most of the hotels and restaurants in this small and dusty town are clustered around the Ramanathaswamy Temple. The bus stand, 2km to the west, is connected by frequent shuttle buses to the town centre.

The tourist office (☎ 21371), on East Car St, near Hotel Guru, has a somewhat dated leaflet. The staff are friendly and will take the trouble to recite the history and mythology of the island. There's also a tourist counter at the train station though the opening times seem erratic. It is closed on Sunday. On the east side of the temple there's a temple information centre which sells booklets and can organise official guides.

Many travellers are attracted by the reefs off Rameswaram, but be careful of boat trips. There are no officially approved tourist boat operators, and the only way to the reef is to bargain with one of the fishing boats. Touts hang around the Hotel Tamil Nadu, promising a one hour 'luxury boat' trip with snorkel hire and a seafood meal for Rs 300. Some people pay only to find themselves on a precarious fishing vessel where the only seafood is the fly-blown leftovers of the morning catch and there is no snorkel equipment in sight. The best advice is to see the boat before you make a deal, and then bargain hard. If the boats venture too far out they will be quickly spotted (and sometimes confiscated) by the military which has the area under close surveillance.

Ramanathaswamy Temple

A fine example of late Dravidian architecture, this temple is most renowned for its magnificent corridors lined with massive sculptured pillars noted for their elaborate design, style and rich carving. Together, the four corridors span 1.2km. Most of the front pillars are cement replicas of the originals, but are tastefully rendered. Many of the rear pillars are still original and are adorned with animals, warriors and royalty in various reposes.

Legend has it that Rama sanctified this place by worshipping Shiva here after the battle of Lanka. Construction of the temple began in the 12th century AD and additions were made over the centuries by various rulers, so that today its gopuram is 53m high.

The 22 theerthams within the temple complex represent a unique feature. The waters flowing through these wells are revered by devotees who believe that each well is linked with particular powers and attributes. For example, those who bathe at the Chandra Theertham will 'acquire knowledge of the past, present and future and therefore reach the worlds they want'. Bathing at the Sarva Theertham will eradicate illness in old age, while bathing in the Kavatcha Theertham will prevent a journey to hell. Many pilgrims take time to bathe at each one of the 22 theerthams before proceeding to the inner sanctum. Only Hindus may enter the inner sanctum.

The temple is open from 5 am to noon and 4 to 10 pm. Even when the temple is closed in the afternoon, it is possible to amble through the extensive corridors, where the silence and stillness is broken only by the squawking crows and the gentle shuffling of

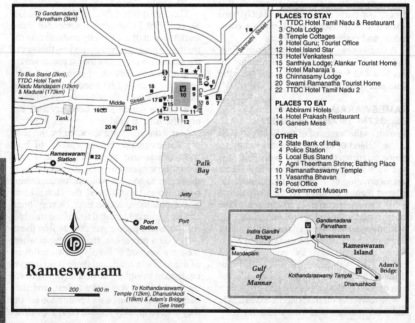

Rameswaram

To Gandamadana Parvatham (3km)

To Bus Stand (2km), TTDC Hotel Tamil Nadu Mandapam (12km) & Madurai (173km)

Middle Street

Tank

Rameswaram Station

Palk Bay

Jetty

Port Station

Port

0   200   400 m

To Kothandaraswamy Temple (12km), Dhanushkodi (18km) & Adam's Bridge (See Inset)

PLACES TO STAY
1 TTDC Hotel Tamil Nadu & Restaurant
3 Chola Lodge
8 Temple Cottages
9 Hotel Guru; Tourist Office
12 Hotel Island Star
13 Hotel Venkatesh
15 Santhiya Lodge; Alankar Tourist Home
17 Hotel Maharaja's
18 Chinnasamy Lodge
20 Swami Ramanatha Tourist Home
22 TTDC Hotel Tamil Nadu 2

PLACES TO EAT
6 Abbirami Hotels
14 Hotel Prakash Restaurant
16 Ganesh Mess

OTHER
2 State Bank of India
4 Police Station
5 Local Bus Stand
7 Agni Theertham Shrine; Bathing Place
10 Ramanathaswamy Temple
11 Vasantha Bhavan
19 Post Office
21 Government Museum

Gandamadana Parvatham

Indira Gandhi Bridge

Rameswaram

Mandapam

Rameswaram Island

Gulf of Mannar

Kothandaraswamy Temple

Dhanushkodi

Adam's Bridge

the temple elephant that is chained in the north corridor during the temple closure.

If you are staying near the temple and you fancy a sleep in, forget it. As with so many temples, excessively loud, distorted music is blasted from the temple from about 4.30 am.

Kothandaraswamy Temple & Dhanushkodi

Twelve kilometres from town, this temple was the only structure to survive the 1964 cyclone which washed the rest of the village away. Legend has it that Vibhishana, brother of Sita's kidnapper Ravana, surrendered to Rama at this spot.

Buses from the local bus stand opposite the tourist office on East Car St will bring you down there. They continue 2km beyond the temple and then it's a 4km walk through fishing communities to Dhanushkodi. Local touts offer to bring you in trucks for an exorbitant Rs 300. There's little here now but a few ruined houses (which make good sun shelters) and a lovely bathing pool. The walk right to the tip of the peninsula can be very hot but is well worth it.

Adam's Bridge

Adam's Bridge is the name given to the chain of reefs, sandbanks and islets that almost connect Sri Lanka with India. According to legend, this is the series of stepping stones used by Hanuman to follow Ravana, in his bid to rescue Sita.

Other Attractions

The **Gandamadana Parvatham**, on a hill 3km north-west of town, is a shrine containing what is believed to be Rama's footprints. Pilgrims visit here at sunrise and sunset when the view is spectacular (the shrine is closed from 11.30 am to 3.30 pm).

For a **beach**, Dhanushkodi is best. Closer to town, try the one in front of the Hotel Tamil Nadu.

Most of the time you'll have the beach to yourself as the pilgrims prefer to do their auspicious wading at **Agni Theertham**, the seashore closest to the temple.

Special Events

There are many small festivals in Rameswaram but the main ones are the Car Procession in February/March and the Holy Marriage Festival in July/August. Most of the activities revolve around the Ramanathaswamy Temple but 'once every few years' the deities are transported to Dhanushkodi. Inquire at the tourist office for festival details when you arrive.

Places to Stay

Hotels are all fairly basic, mainly geared towards pilgrims, and often completely booked out during festivals. Because of the cessation of the ferry to Sri Lanka, new hotels are virtually nonexistent and existing hotels are ageing more quickly than on the mainland.

Hotel Guru (☎ 21134, East Car St), near the tourist office, has doubles/triples for Rs 150/200. The rooms are basic and not the best value in town.

Temple Cottages (☎ 21223, Sannathi St), close to East Car St, is probably the cheapest option in town. Singles/doubles with bucket bath are Rs 30/55. This is basically a flophouse for pilgrims who are keen to wake at 4 am.

Chola Lodge (☎ 21307, North Car St) offers reasonable double rooms with attached bathroom for Rs 120. There are no singles but a family room (up to five beds) is Rs 200.

Santhiya Lodge (☎ 21329, West Car St) has rather grubby doubles from Rs 70 to Rs 110 (with bath attached). Triples are Rs 150.

Alankar Tourist Home (☎ 21216, West Car St) has basic doubles with attached bath for Rs 85.

Swami Ramanatha Tourist Home (☎ 21-217), near the museum, has clean doubles with attached shower for Rs 150. It also has quite a good display of local history and mythology near the hotel reception.

Railway Retiring Rooms are available at the train station. The rooms are large and airy, and being away from the temple are reasonably peaceful. A sign at the station promotes their recently reduced prices. Doubles/triples

TAMIL NADU

with attached bath are Rs 75/100; dorm beds are Rs 15.

Chinnasamy Lodge (☎ 21170, Middle St) has clean but basic rooms from Rs 75. The front rooms are particularly noisy.

Hotel Maharaja's (☎ 21271, 7 Middle St) is a good choice. Clean, pleasant and recently renovated doubles with attached bathroom and balcony cost Rs 200, or Rs 450 with air-con. There are no singles.

Hotel Venkatesh (☎ 21296, South Car St) has doubles/triples with attached bathroom for Rs 150/200 and four-bed rooms for Rs 300. Air-con doubles are Rs 300.

Hotel Island Star (☎ 21472, South Car St) is clean and friendly. Doubles/triples are Rs 160/260. A triple with air-con is Rs 500.

TTDC Hotel Tamil Nadu (☎ 21277) is well located, facing the sea to the north-end of town. This is a good place to stay and although prices have increased it is often booked out – reserve in advance. There are good double/triple rooms for Rs 250/300, Rs 500 for a double with air-con. There are also five and six-bed rooms which they sometimes let as dorms at Rs 45 per bed. Most of the rooms have a sea view. Guests should heed the sign 'beware of the crows' – they are particularly aggressive.

TTDC Hotel Tamil Nadu 2 (☎ 21071) is near the station and offers basic doubles for Rs 150. It is far from spotless and not as friendly as the other Hotel Tamil Nadu.

TTDC Hotel Tamil Nadu Mandapam (☎ 41512) is 12km west of Rameswaram, over the bridge. If accommodation in Rameswaram is full, this is a good alternative, more for the sandy beach than the rooms. There are basic doubles for Rs 250 in cement bunker-style cottages by the beach. A bed in the dorm is Rs 45.

Places to Eat
A number of vegetarian restaurants along West Car St serve typical South Indian thalis, many of a pretty dismal standard.

Ganesh Mess (West Car St) is clean and the thalis here are very good.

Hotel Guru (East Car St), next to the tourist office, is also a good place for a thali.

Vasantha Bhavan (East Car St) is busy, clean and efficient.

Hotel Prakash Restaurant (South Car St) has a wide range of good, cheap vegetarian dishes. Is opens in the evening only.

Abbirami Hotels (Sannathi St) also offers good cheap vegetarian cuisine.

TTDC Hotel Tamil Nadu has a popular restaurant offering reasonable veg and non-veg food, but the service is painfully slow. There's also an excellent bar with pleasant sea views.

Getting There & Away
Bus STC buses run four times daily to Madurai (Rs 32, four hours) and Kanyakumari, and three times daily to Chennai (Rs 95, 13 hours) and Trichy (273km). Local buses run to Madurai more often and take longer but are marginally cheaper. There are also buses to Pondicherry and Thanjavur via Madurai.

Train There are two express trains to/from Chennai daily – the *Sethu Express* and the *Rameswaram Express*. The 666km trip takes 15 hours and costs Rs 175/632 in 2nd/1st class. Neither of these trains go through Madurai – they take the direct route through Manamadurai and Trichy.

The direct passenger train from Madurai to Rameswaram (Rs 24/67/193, 164km, five hours) departs at 6 am and returns at 4.10 pm.

Getting Around
Town buses ply the route between the temple and the bus stand from early morning until late at night and cost Rs 1. In town, the buses stop at the west gopuram and opposite the tourist office on East Car St. Unmetered auto-rickshaws and cycle-rickshaws are available at all hours; haggle hard!

Cycling is a good way of getting around town and out to Dhanushkodi and there are many places where you can hire a bike for Rs 2 an hour.

TIRUCHENDUR
Some 50km off the main road and on the coast south of Tuticorin, this impressive

The Ayyanar Cult

An example of a local deity whose potency has survived into the 1990s is Ayyanar. Proof that his cult is still strong is to be found throughout rural south-east Tamil Nadu in the form of terracotta horses that stand guard outside the villages.

Ayyanar provides protection for the village community against natural disasters, disease and other calamities. His spirit soldiers, *veeran*, ride out at night to battle demons, and the clay horses one sees are intended as mounts for this other-world cavalry.

The intermediary between Ayyanar and his horsemen and ordinary mortals is the potter. In times of dire need, such as drought or disease, the community may group together to commission gigantic horse statues (up to 5m high). Individual supplicants who wish to call on Ayyanar's help will generally consult the potter on how to go about it, and will often commission a small horse (up to 1.5m high) to be given as an offering in thanks for the god's successful intervention.

Ayyanar's shrine is just outside the village. During festivals especially dedicated to honouring Ayyanar's benevolence, a newly-made clay horse is painted in bright colours and carried to the shrine by devotees. The potter, who becomes possessed by Ayyanar's spirit at the shrine, appeals to the god to infuse the horse with his spirit, thus making it accessible to the divine horsemen. In this state of trance the potter also answers questions and offers advice to the devotees until, suddenly, Ayyanar's spirit leaves him. At this point the ritual is over, the potter returns to his everyday work and the clay horse is left to eventually return to the earth from where it came.

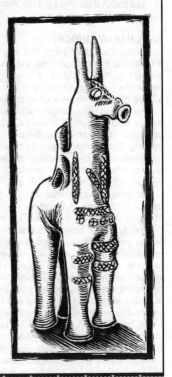

shore temple, with its 45m-high white gopuram, is one of the six abodes of Lord Murugan and is very popular with pilgrims. Dating from the 9th century, much of it was replaced early this century due to salt damage. Around the broad perimeter, fortune tellers use parrots to select the cards from which they offer their counsel.

Non-Hindus may enter the inner sanctum here for a Rs 20 donation. A priest will meet you and escort you through the puja, after which he'll promote a monthly donation plan to which you can subscribe. If you've not experienced the ceremonies of the inner sanctum, then this provides a good opportunity. Make sure you have the correct money – you won't get change! This temple is well maintained and more relaxed than many others. It's open from 5 am to 8 pm.

Hotel Tamil Nadu (☎ 42268) provides accommodation. Air-con double deluxe rooms are Rs 450, non air-con double deluxe are Rs 195, and ordinary doubles are Rs 175. There's a restaurant where you can get veg and nonveg meals from Rs 30. You can also get accommodation via the temple office.

You can get to Tiruchendur by bus from Madurai, Tuticorin or Tirunelveli; buses originate from the Palanganatham bus stand in Madurai. A train also runs the 38km from Tirunelveli.

PANCHALAMKURICHI

Originally the site of a fort, this area is now a memorial to a former king and his struggle for justice. Within a small palace **museum**, paintings depict the story of King Kattabomman who was crowned in 1790 and built a fort, Panchalamkurichi, which he named after his father. When he refused to pay taxes imposed by the British, conflict ensued. Kattabomman was betrayed by a neighbouring king, Ettapan, as well as several other of his own people. The fort was demolished by the British in 1799 and Kattabomman was subsequently captured, tried and executed. A **tomb** for 45 soldiers killed by the British is located 2km away.

In spite of the museum's inaccessibility and its gaudy paintings, the message it commemorates – justice and peace – is certainly laudable. Entrance is Rs 1. It's open from 9 am to 1 pm and 2 to 5 pm. You'll see the bright red fence long before you get here. You can catch a bus from Madurai (Palanganatham stand) to Tuticorin and then catch a city bus, No 55A for Rs 3.50. There are four per day. There are no food or drink stalls but there is clean and basic accommodation at the *Government Resthouse* for Rs 25. The resthouse has no telephone but it is directly opposite the memorial. The staff will bring basic vegetarian meals to your room.

About 40km before Panchalamkurichi, at Ettaiyapuram, is the palace of the former king, Ettapan (apparently one of Kattabomman's detractors). Although you may be tempted to visit, the palace is now in a poor state of repair. It's closed to visitors and possibly dangerous.

KANYAKUMARI (Cape Comorin)
Pop: 18,900 Tel Area Code: 04652
Kanyakumari is the 'Land's End' of the Indian subcontinent. Here, the Bay of Bengal meets the Indian Ocean and the Arabian Sea and, at Chaitrapurnima (the Tamil name for

the full moon day that generally falls in April), it is possible to enjoy the unique experience of seeing the sun set and the moon rise over the ocean simultaneously. It's a common belief that this is the only place that it is possible to observe this, but you may have similar experiences also over the rice fields throughout Tamil Nadu.

Kanyakumari is a popular pilgrimage destination and of great spiritual significance to Hindus. It is dedicated to the goddess, Devi Kanya, the Youthful Virgin, who is an incarnation of Devi, Shiva's wife. Pilgrims come here from all over the country to visit the temple and bathe in the waters which are considered to be sacred.

It's also a popular day trip for people staying at Kovalam Beach in Kerala. However, being foremost a pilgrimage town, it should not be compared with the Keralan beaches. It's a place where people fulfil their spiritual duties and this is evident in the constant chanting of the many faiths which is broadcast, like so many temple towns, throughout the area.

Orientation & Information
The temple is right on the point of Kanyakumari with all the facilities gathered around within a kilometre to the north and west. The post office is on Main Rd close to the tourist office (☎ 71276) which is open weekdays from 10 am to 5.30 pm. The train station is almost a kilometre north of the temple, while the bus stand is 500m to the west. You can change money at the Canara Bank, next to the post office. The State Bank of Travancore will also change money. There's a small branch of the government handicraft emporium, Poompuhar, just near the temple.

Kumari Amman Temple
Picturesquely situated overlooking the shore, this temple and the nearby ghat attract pilgrims from all over India to worship and to bathe.

According to legend, Devi (the goddess) did penance here to secure marriage with Shiva who was 13km away at Suchindram.

However, it was a time when the world was under the power of demons who were committing atrocities and creating much hardship throughout the universe. Vishnu advised that the Devi could save the world, but only if she remained a virgin. Her attempts for marriage were thwarted, but she singlehandedly fought and conquered the demons, so securing the freedom of the world. Subsequently, she vowed to remain a virgin *(kanya)* and continue her penance. Pilgrims see her as a protector and come to honour her sacrifice and give thanks for the safety and freedom she secured for them and their ancestors.

There are two annual temple festivals. During the May/June festivities the deity is taken in procession morning and evening for nine days, when there is a huge chariot festival. The celebrations conclude on the 10th day with a float festival.

The September/October Navratri Festival (nine nights), being the festival of the goddess, is particularly significant in Kanyakumari. It takes a somewhat different form here. The image of the deity is taken on a 4km procession to Mahadanapuram. Here the battle, where the Devi is said to have secured victory over the demons, is re-enacted.

The temple is open daily from 4.30 to 11.45 am and from 5.30 to 8.30 pm. Non-Hindus may not enter the inner sanctum, though at times this rule is waived. Men must remove their shirts, and everyone (as always) their shoes, on entering this temple. If you have a camera you may be asked to leave it at the entrance. It will be safeguarded until you return.

Gandhi Memorial

Next to the Kumari Amman Temple, this striking memorial stored the Mahatma's ashes until they were immersed in the sea. It resembles an Orissan temple and was designed so that on Gandhi's birthday (2 October), the sun's rays fall on the place where his ashes were kept. The Gandhi Memorial is open daily from 7 am to 12.30 pm and from 3 to 7 pm.

Vivekananda Puram – The Wandering Monk

This purpose-built museum (close to the tourist office) details the extensive journey across India made by the Indian philosopher, Swami Vivekananda. It is well worth a visit. The story of the wandering Swami is told through a series of 41 panels with text in English, Tamil and Hindi, as well as some fascinating archival photographs. It is often said that to know India, one must know Vivekananda.

Follow the panels around and you certainly have an idea not just of the nature of the Swami, who wanted the 'dust of India to cover his footprints', but also of the complex matrix that was, and still is, India.

The Swami encountered many significant turning points on his journey, which resulted in his synthesising the tenets of Hinduism with a strong sense of social justice and equality. Once, when seeking to share a smoke with a stranger, Vivekananda was shocked. The stranger, being an untouchable, recoiled from contact with the Swami. Vivekananda wrote 'The whole of my life I have contemplated the non-duality of the soul, and I am now thrown into the whirlpool of the caste system. How difficult it is to get over innate tendencies'.

The Wandering Monk exhibition was built by the Vivekananda Kendra, a service organisation dedicated to continuing the work and ideas of the Swami. It is open every day from 8 am to noon and 4 to 8 pm. There is also a secure cloakroom facility from 6 am to 10 pm where you can leave luggage. Entry is Rs 1. There are plenty of books available from the counter, including a complete text (with photographs) of the material on display for Rs 100.

Vivekananda Memorial

This memorial is on two rocky islands projecting from the sea about 400m offshore. Swami Vivekananda came here in 1892 and sat on the rock, meditating, before setting out as one of India's most important religious crusaders. The mandapam which stands here in his memory was built in 1970

Kanyakumari (Cape Comorin)

PLACES TO STAY
2 Vivekas Tourist Hotel
3 Vivaldi Tourist Home
4 Sankar's Guest House
6 Manickhan Tourist Home;
    Manickhan Tourist
    Restaurant
7 Hotel Sangam & Restaurant
13 Hotel Saagar
14 Gopi Nivas Lodge
15 Hotel Maadhini;
    Archana Restaurant
16 Lakshmi Tourist Home
    & Restaurant
21 TTDC Youth Hostel
22 Hotel Tamil Nadu;
    Tamil Nadu Restaurant
23 Kerala House
32 Hotel Samudra;
    Sanga Restaurant

PLACES TO EAT
11 Hotel Triveni
26 Sri Ramdev Restaurant
27 Hotel Anandha
28 Idli Shop
29 Ariya Bhavan
31 Hotel Saravana

OTHER
1 Gunganatham Temple
5 School
8 Canara Bank
9 Post Office
10 Hospital
12 Auto-rickshaw Stand
17 Vinayakar Kovil Temple
18 Police Station
19 Bus Stand
20 Lighthouse
24 Vivekananda Puram -
    The Wandering Monk
25 State Bank of Travancore
30 Tourist Office
33 Poompuhar Branch
    Emporium
34 Ghats
35 Kumari Amman Temple
36 Gandhi Memorial
37 Mandapam; Bathing Ghats
38 Vivekananda Memorial

and reflects architectural styles from all over India. The ferry to the island (half-hourly) costs Rs 6, plus a Rs 3 entry fee to the memorial, which is open from 7 to 11 am and 2 to 5 pm.

Places to Stay

Although hotels are mushrooming in Kanyakumari, demand remains high and everything is heavily booked on weekends and during festivals. Some hotels have seasonal rates so you may find that, during April/May and October to December, room

prices are 100% up on what is quoted here. Few hotels have single rooms.

Gopi Nivas Lodge has basic singles/doubles at Rs 80/100.

Hotel Saagar (☎ 71325, South Car St) is a good place with doubles (no singles) from Rs 150 to Rs 200.

TTDC Youth Hostel, at the entrance to the Hotel Tamil Nadu, charges Rs 45 per dorm bed and is rarely full.

Railway Retiring Rooms at the train station include a six-bed dorm at just Rs 15 per bed and singles/doubles for Rs 40/80.

TAMIL NADU

Vivekas Tourist Hotel (☎ 71192) has clean, colourful rooms all with bath and shower from Rs 150/200 for a double/triple.

Manickhan Tourist Home (☎ 71387) has doubles without/with a sea view for Rs 180/250.

Vivaldi Tourist Home (☎ 71972, Main Rd) is very clean and inexpensive at Rs 100/150 for a double/triple. However, you need to be a particularly slim couple to fit on the bed intended for two.

Sankar's Guest House, also in Main Rd, offers doubles/triples for Rs 190/250 in the low season.

Hotel Sangam (☎ 71351; fax 71627, Main Rd) is a little more upmarket with low season doubles at Rs 410, or Rs 520 with air-con. A room with four beds is Rs 620, or Rs 780 with air-con. The Sangam Restaurant serves a range of multicuisine dishes.

Lakshmi Tourist Home (☎ 71333, East Car St) has good doubles at Rs 250 with a sea view or Rs 900 with air-con. It also has a multicuisine restaurant.

Hotel Maadhini (☎ 71787; fax 71657, East Car St) is one of the newest hotels in town. It's a little upmarket and the balconies of the ocean-facing rooms virtually overhang the village making it fascinating for guests but probably intrusive for villagers. Watching the catamarans sail in at sunrise is a perfect way to while away the time. The rooms are airy and clean at Rs 350 for a double or Rs 450/800 for a double with ocean views without/with air-con. Rooms with three and four beds are also available. Just in case you have slept through the loud music from the nearby Catholic church the friendly staff knock on your door to let you know the sun is rising! The Archana Restaurant attached to the hotel has excellent cheap food and an open-air dining area that looks onto the hotel rather than the sea.

Kerala House (☎ 71229), on the hill just west of the temple, claims to be the southernmost house on the subcontinent. It is run by the Kerala Tourism Development Corporation and was opened in 1956. Since then it has seen many prominent visitors, including the 14th Dalai Lama. It now caters mostly

for government officials but rooms are available to travellers who are willing to apply to the Political Department of the State Secretariat in Thiruvananthapuram (Trivandrum) or who have excellent negotiating skills to practise on the hotel manager. The large double rooms with sea views and attached bath are Rs 360 to Rs 420.

Hotel Tamil Nadu (☎ 71257) has basic doubles for Rs 100 with common bath, and much better doubles with attached bath for Rs 350, or Rs 500 with air-con. Rooms are clean and most have a private balcony with great views of the Gandhi Memorial. Cottages and family rooms are also available.

Hotel Samudra (☎ 71162), near the temple, has doubles from Rs 300 to Rs 500, and a well-appointed air-con double with good views for Rs 800.

Places to Eat

Hotel Saravana, near the temple, has a well-loaded vegetarian menu, but many of the items are never available. Still, it offers South Indian and Chinese (of sorts) cuisine and is one of the town's most popular eateries. The dosas are excellent.

Hotel Triveni has basic vegetarian fare at good prices.

Hotel Anandha has basic vegetarian cuisine and is a great place for a cool drink with an ocean view.

Ariya Bhavan across the way also serves vegetarian cuisine.

Sri Ramdev Restaurant just up the road offers a mean range of North Indian vegetarian fare on its tiny open-air terrace.

Sanga Restaurant is an upmarket vegetarian place in the Hotel Samudra.

Archana Restaurant at the Hotel Maadhini has good veg and nonveg meals. The menu may offer 20 different flavours of ice cream but many are unavailable. The outdoor restaurant is open only from 7 to 10 pm; at lunchtime you'll have to go to their indoor room, which has a great ocean view.

Manickhan Tourist Home has perhaps the best nonveg restaurant in town; their vegetarian food is also excellent. However, it closes during the low season.

TAMIL NADU

The *Idli Shop*, in the row of shops leading from the temple, caters to idli addicts.

Getting There & Away
Bus The bus stand is a dusty five minute walk from the centre. It has timetables in English, restaurants and waiting rooms. The reservation office is open from 7 am to 9 pm.

STC has frequent buses to Madurai (Rs 52, 253km, six hours) and Chennai (Rs 148, 679km, 16 hours) as well as buses to Thiruvananthapuram (Trivandrum, four times daily, three hours) and Rameswaram (four times daily, nine hours).

Local buses go to Nagercoil, Padmanabhapuram (for the palace of the former rulers of Travancore – see the Around Thiruvananthapuram section in the Kerala chapter for details), Thiruvananthapuram and Kovalam, among other places.

Train The one daily passenger train to Thiruvananthapuram leaves Kanyakumari at 5 pm and does the 87km in a dazzling two hours (Rs 25 in 2nd class).

The *Kanyakumari Express* travels to Mumbai daily in just under 48 hours, departing Kanyakumari at 5 am. The 2155km trip costs Rs 341/1495 in 2nd/1st class. This train will also take you to Thiruvananthapuram and Ernakulam (eight hours).

For the real long-haulers, the weekly *Himsagar Express* runs all the way to Jammu Tawi (in Jammu & Kashmir), a distance of 3734km, taking 74 hours. It's the longest single train ride in India, and leaves from Kanyakumari on Friday at 12.50 am and from Jammu Tawi on Monday at 10.45 pm. This train also passes through Coimbatore (12 hours), Vijayawada (29 hours) and Delhi (60 hours).

Between Two Worlds
The dilemma facing many tribal groups in India is well illustrated by the circumstances of the Kanis, a nomadic tribe that has traditionally lived off the forests in the south of the Western Ghats.

Many of the Kanis are still engaged in the age-old practice of shifting cultivation. Their crops vary from bananas and tapioca to rubber and cloves. Some also maintain beehives. Ten years ago there were an estimated 64 Kanis settlements around Nagercoil in the district of Kanyakumari. Today this number has declined by one-third and their current population is estimated at 7000.

The dwindling number of settlements is attributable to increased urbanisation and the levels of resultant integration. This process has brought benefits and problems. Better education and health opportunities are indeed benefits, but at a high cost – the communities have become financially enslaved.

Before industrialisation the Kanis, like many tribal groups, thrived on a barter system. Now they are part of a monetary system and many have become trapped in a cycle of debt. They borrow money to transport crops or enhance yields. They also borrow to sustain a more materialistic lifestyle. But their ability to repay is not matched by their earning capacity. To make matters worse, intermarriage has resulted in the adoption of the customs of the plains, including the dowry system and all its expenses.

The tragedy for the Kanis is that they must now work the land harder than ever just to keep up their repayments. They can no longer afford the produce of their own labour, the land becomes exhausted and so do they. Social problems associated with kinship breakdown infiltrate what was once a harmonious community. This situation is similar to the plight of landless peasants enslaved through bonded labour in other parts of India.

Tribal welfare groups are lobbying for government intervention to prevent continued exploitation. But as long as urbanisation spreads and traditional practices disappear, the tribal people will remain vulnerable to the ways of the industrialised world.

AROUND KANYAKUMARI
Marthuval Malai (Maruda Malai, Maruntha Malai)

About 15km west of Kanyakumari near the village of Pothaiyadi the prominent mountain, Marthuval Malai, towers over its environs. In the dry season, its rocky masses and crevice structures are particularly evident. The wet season sees the abundant growth of medicinal herbs – hence the mountain's name, 'Medicine Mountain'.

Every place in Tamil Nadu has its story, but here legends, like the herbs, are prolific. There are accounts of almost every deity and how they arrived and established their abode. Each deity is designated a cave, a peak – some significant space. These legends give to the mountain a particularly awesome aura.

The most famous story is from the *Ramayana*. During the battle between Rama and the Lankan king, Ravana, Lakshman (Rama's brother) was injured by a poisoned arrow. Rama pleaded for help from the monkey god, Hanuman, who agreed to visit the sacred mountain Kailash in the Himalaya and bring back to Rama the 'medicine mountain'. He picked up the whole mountain and returned with it to Lanka. As he approached Kanyakumari part of the mountain fell away and landed in the spot now known as Marthuval Malai.

Today the mountain is inhabited by a few *sadhus* (holy men) and a priest, who share the caves with the cobras and other wildlife. Sometimes pilgrims visit. It's a hot, dusty 2000m climb along a broken path to a small temple. Travellers with a serious interest in meditation are welcome – under certain conditions. You must be fit, happy to stay in the caves with the occasional cobra and willing to assist the priest with donations for his proposed ashram.

Suchindram

This temple, 13km north-west of Kanyakumari at Suchindram, is the place where Shiva is said to have resided when the Devi came to do penance at Kanyakumari. (See the Kumari Amman Temple section, Kanyakumari.) The temple is impressive, with a large white entrance gopuram and long pillared halls. The figures on the seven storey, 40m-high gopuram depict stories from the *Ramayana* and *Mahabharata*.

While accounts vary as to when it was built, much of the temple was constructed from the 17th to 18th centuries. On the side of the long hall after the entrance, 1108 sculptured women stand, holding oil containers.

Halfway down the hall, and just outside to the right, a huge boulder contains the temple records, inscribed in three languages, Tamil, Sanskrit and Pali. At one end of the next hall, a small shrine is dedicated to Rama and Sita, the heroes of the *Ramayana*. At the other end looking back to Rama and Sita is a 6m-tall statue of their helper, Hanuman, the monkey god.

The musical hall contains pillars, similar to those in other temples, which can be struck with the fingers, hands, or a small stick to create musical sounds. Now actual instruments are used. The inner sanctum has a triple image of Shiva, Brahma and Vishnu, a major attraction for devotees of each of these deities. Non-Hindus are permitted into the inner shrine here (men must be bare from the waist up) but the process can be quite intrusive for those involved in puja, so you may prefer to decline.

The annual 10-day chariot festival commemorates the three deities Brahma, Vishnu and Shiva. Their images, each in their own chariot, are taken in procession. The procession heralds the time when the deities visit people who do not normally attend the temple. The temple is open from 3 am to 1 pm and 4 to 8 pm.

MUNDANTHURAI TIGER SANCTUARY

Mundanthurai is in the mountains near the border with Kerala. It forms an interesting landscape of rocky peaks and forested hills. Established in 1988, it extends over 840 sq km and its literature boasts of the sanctuary's pristine state and vast animal biodiversity. But large hydroelectric pipes intersect the landscape. Goats and buffalo wander freely. Seven major dams have been constructed in this area.

TAMIL NADU

As the name implies, this is principally a tiger sanctuary though it's also noted for chital, sambar and the rare lion-tailed macaque. Apparently there are 17 tigers in the reserve but tiger sightings are extremely infrequent.

There are several trekking routes ranging from seven to 24km. There are no limitations on trekking – you may go alone, or with a guide, but it may be unwise to trek here at all. The Tamil Nadu Forest Department offers a brochure with tips on how to behave when trekking, such as: '...on sight of lonely tuskers, run down hills'. If you see a tiger on your wanderings, staff advice is to ignore it. 'It's the sloth bear you have to be wary of.'

You may travel through the park in a vehicle, but you'll need to hire one (preferably a 4WD at Rs 4 per hour) since the park has no vehicles. Depending on the guard at the checkpoint you may, or may not, require a guide.

Day visitors must leave the park by 6 pm. If you want to stay you must have a permit and this is only obtainable from the Field Officer, Project Tiger, NGO 'A' Colony, Tirunelveli. Cost for the *Forest Department Resthouse* is Rs 12 per person per night. A cook will prepare meals but it is advisable to take some supplies. Aptly named Tiger Cottage, it is seriously basic.

The best time to visit is between January and March, though the sanctuary is open all year. The main rainy season is between October and December.

The closest train station is at Ambasamudram, about 25km to the north-east, and buses run from here to Papanasam (7km), the nearest village, from where you can catch another bus to the park.

KUTTRALAM (Courtallam)
Tel Area Code: 04633
About 135km north-west of Kanyakumari at the base of the Western Ghats, the village of Kuttralam is a popular health retreat for families who come to stand and bathe under waterfalls believed to be rich in minerals and containing curative qualities. Iron railings at the base of the falls offer support for those taking a shower. Men wear sarongs; women full dress. During the high season men and women are segregated in adjacent falls. It's an invigorating experience, having the full weight of a waterfall descend on your body. Try it in the early morning: it beats most hotel facilities and you'll know that you're awake. Oil massage is available, but for men only.

In the high season, June to August, the place is impossibly crowded. In the low season the falls may dry up. The area with its huge rocks, waterfalls and forest is quite scenic, but sadly, somewhat marred by the billboards right next to the falls and the vast piles of rubbish nearby.

Of the nine waterfalls, the only one in the village itself is the 60m-high **Main Falls**, a five minute walk from the bus stand. Its sheer rock face is carved with old Hindu insignia that is visible only during the dry months of January and February. Other falls, mostly accessed by shuttle buses, are up to 8km away.

Kuttralam offers only very basic lodging houses which are not good value and are usually full in 'the season'.

Hotel Tamil Nadu (☎ 22423, Tenkasi Rd) has doubles (no singles) for Rs 200 and air-con doubles for Rs 400. Prices increase by Rs 150 in the high season.

Sankar Lodge (☎ 22496) is on the main road just near the bus stand and opposite the Main Falls. It's a 15 minute walk to more robust falls. Very basic but reasonably clean singles/doubles/triples are Rs 75/150/200, all with attached bathroom.

Some people prefer to stay away from all the hype, among the rice fields in Tenkasi, 5km to the north.

Krishna Tourist Home (☎ 23125), next to the Tenkasi bus stand, has doubles for Rs 195 and some air-con rooms for Rs 450.

Hotel Anandha Classic (☎ 23303, 116-A/7 Courtallam Rd) has a similar tariff and a reasonable veg restaurant. Take plenty of insect repellent!

Tenkasi is the closest train station to Kuttralam. However the main line from Madurai to Kollam does not pass here. Catch the main train line to Shencottah (Sengottai), from where there's one express daily to take you the remaining 6km to Tenkasi. Faster and more frequent buses also ply these routes.

The Western Ghats

The mighty Western Ghats stretch about 1400km from north of Mumbai, across Maharashtra, Goa, Karnataka and Kerala, to the southernmost tip of Tamil Nadu. The hills (average elevation of 915m) are covered with tropical and temperate evergreen forest, and mixed deciduous forest, and are rarely more than 40km from the coast. The Western Ghats are the source of all major rivers in South India, including the Cauvery (aka Kaveri) and Krishna.

The Western Ghats form a vast, diverse biological and ecological haven: they are home to 27% of all flowering plants in India; 60% of all medicinal plants; a remarkable number of tribal groups; and an incredible array of endemic wildlife. The Ghats form a natural barrier between the tropical coastline and the dry Deccan Peninsula, so that, for example, Mumbai gets three times more rain than Pune, about 190km to the east. While some parts of the Western Ghats have suffered from deforestation, grazing, road construction, urban development, mining and hydroelectric dams, naturalists regard this as one of the most important pristine forest and mountain areas left in Asia.

KODAIKANAL
Pop: 31,200 Tel Area Code: 04542
On the southern crest of the Palani Hills about 120km north-west of Madurai at an altitude of 2100m, Kodaikanal – better known as Kodai – is surrounded by wooded (not so thickly any more) slopes, waterfalls and precipitous rocky outcrops. The journey up and back down again is breathtaking, although there's no toy train. In the town, there are lookouts with spectacular views of the

south. These are within easy walking distance of the town centre.

Kodai has the distinction of being the only hill station in India to be set up during the Raj by Americans, though it didn't take long before they were joined by the British. American missionaries established a school for European children here in the mid-1840s, the legacy of which is the Kodaikanal International School – one of the most prestigious private schools in the country.

Kodaikanal is not just for those who want to get away from the heat and haze of the dusty plains during the summer months, but also for those seeking a relaxing place to put their feet up for a while and do some occasional hiking in the quiet *sholas* (forests). In the surrounding hills you'll find plantations of Australian blue gums which provide the eucalyptus oil sold in Kodai's many street stalls, and unfortunately create numerous environmental problems. The rapid growth of exotic species together with rampant tourist development has resulted in local action to save Kodaikanal from the environmental disaster that has befallen Ooty (see the boxed text 'Eco Action in Kodaikanal').

Kodaikanal is the place of the Kurinji, a shrub with light, purple-blue-coloured blossoms which flowers only every 12 years (the next blossoming will be in 2004, though there are always a few whose natural clocks seem to be out of time).

This hill station is also the sometime summer retreat of Sai Baba.

April to June or August to October are certainly the best times to visit Kodaikanal. April to June is the main season. The height of the wet season is November/December. Temperatures here are mild, ranging from 11°C to 20°C in summer and 8°C to 17°C in winter.

Orientation
For a hill station, Kodai is remarkably compact. Settled on a lake, most of the accommodation and eating places are to the north-east of its shores. The main street is Bazaar Rd (Anna Salai), and the budget hotels, restaurants and the bus stand are all

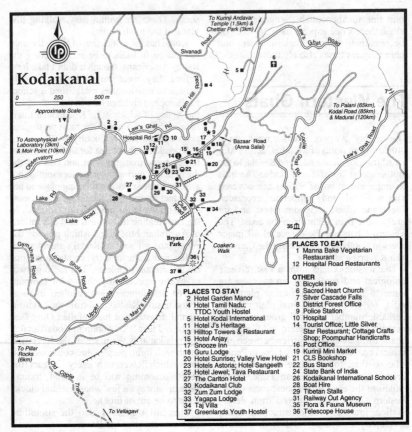

Kodaikanal

0   250   500 m
Approximate Scale

To Kurinji Andavar
Temple (1.5km) &
Chettiar Park (3km)

Sivanadi

To Astrophysical
Laboratory (3km)
& Moir Point (10km)

To Palani (65km),
Kodai Road (85km)
& Madurai (120km)

Law's Ghat Rd

Hospital Rd

Bazaar Road
(Anna Salai)

Lake Road

Bryant
Park

Coaker's
Walk

Gymkhana Road

Lower Shola Road

Upper Shola Road

St Mary's Road

To Pillar
Rocks
(6km)

Old Coolie Track

To Vellagavi

PLACES TO EAT
1 Manna Bake Vegetarian
Restaurant
12 Hospital Road Restaurants

OTHER
3 Bicycle Hire
6 Sacred Heart Church
7 Silver Cascade Falls
8 District Forest Office
9 Police Station
10 Hospital
14 Tourist Office; Little Silver
Star Restaurant; Cottage Crafts
Shop; Poompuhar Handicrafts
16 Post Office
19 Kurinji Mini Market
21 CLS Bookshop
22 Bus Stand
24 State Bank of India
26 Kodaikanal International School
28 Boat Hire
29 Tibetan Stalls
31 Railway Out Agency
35 Flora & Fauna Museum
36 Telescope House

PLACES TO STAY
2 Hotel Garden Manor
4 Hotel Tamil Nadu;
TTDC Youth Hostel
5 Hotel Kodai International
11 Hotel J's Heritage
13 Hilltop Towers & Restaurant
15 Hotel Anjay
17 Snooze Inn
18 Guru Lodge
20 Hotel Sunrise; Valley View Hotel
23 Hotels Astoria; Hotel Sangeeth
25 Hotel Jewel; Tava Restaurant
27 The Carlton Hotel
30 Kodaikanal Club
32 Zum Zum Lodge
33 Yagapa Lodge
34 Taj Villa
37 Greenlands Youth Hostel

in this area. Most, though not all, of the better hotels are some distance from the bazaar, but usually not more than about 15 minutes walk.

Information
The tourist office (☎ 41675), close to the bus stand, has little information and what material they do provide may be inaccurate. They will quote guide fees at Rs 30 per hour but their recommended guides charge way in excess of this. It seems they may be more interested in promoting their friends than

providing information! The office is open from Monday to Saturday, and they operate many local tours. If you want literature about Kodai, try the CLS Bookshop. It's opposite and a few metres down to the left.

The State Bank of India, near the post office, is the best place to cash travellers cheques. And sending mail from the post office is a breeze!

Astrophysical Laboratory
Built in 1889, this laboratory stands on the highest point in the area, 3km along Obser-

Eco Action in Kodaikanal

Less than 100 years ago the hills around Kodaikanal were covered with the thick, delicate rainforests known as *shola*. A significant feature of shola forest is the dense, leafy groundcover. The large quantity of moisture retained by the carpet is released very slowly, thus enabling the continuous flow of streams. Today, the remaining pockets of these forests are under serious threat. The enemies are rapid and unchecked tourist development, deforestation and government ineptitude.

In 1985, local concern about the threat to Kodai's unique ecosystem led to the formation of the Palani Hills Conservation Council (PHCC). The council's first significant victory was to stop the planting of exotic species such as eucalyptus. These trees, crucial to their indigenous environment, have a detrimental impact on Kodai's ecosystem. After intense lobbying by the PHCC the Ministry of Environment and Forests banned any form of commercial forestry in sensitive areas. The growing of eucalyptus plantations was taken over by farmers in the foothills as an additional revenue source.

Another successful campaign by the PHCC has been the development of a master plan for Kodai which limits the height of buildings and sets standards for waste disposal. The plan proved to be more than a paper tiger. In 1995, a hotel development (allegedly owned by a close associate of the Chief Minister) was forced by Supreme Court action to demolish five of its seven storeys. It was the efforts of the PHCC that brought the case to court.

The PHCC is continuing its battle to prevent large hotels from dumping solid waste into the lake. The lake isn't only for recreation, it's also a source of drinking water for Kodai and Palani. A major problem is the inability of existing sewerage treatment plants to deal with rapid growth. Representatives of the PHCC claim that a much improved treatment plant for Kodai has been commissioned and will be operational 'soon'.

A long-term plan of the PHCC is to have an area within the Palani Hills officially declared as a sanctuary, thus preventing any form of interference. However, a major concern of authorities is the future of the villagers who live on the edge of the shola and who make their living by gathering and selling firewood, and producing honey. Environmentalists claim that the impact of firewood collection (undertaken only by women) on the shola ecology is negligible. Others claim that the government should offer the villagers incentives to take up 'social forestry' on government land.

The ecological future of Kodaikanal remains uncertain. But whilst some people are concerned it will experience the same destiny as Ooty (where little original vegetation exists), others are more optimistic that the voice of the PHCC will eventually be heard and a sanctuary will be declared before it is too late.

The Palani Hills Conservation Council (☎ 40711) offers a range of opportunities for volunteers with specific skills and interests in conservation issues. Interested travellers should write to the President, PHCC, Amarville House, Lower Shola Rd, Kodaikanal 62410.

vatory Rd uphill from Kodai's lake. It houses a small **museum** which is open Friday from 10 am to noon and 3 to 5 pm. The buildings with the instruments are off limits. It's a hard 45 minute uphill walk pushing a bicycle, but it only takes five minutes to coast down (you'll need good brakes).

Flora & Fauna Museum

Also worth a visit is the Flora & Fauna Museum at the Sacred Heart College at Shembaganur. It's a 6km hike and all uphill on the way back. The museum is open from 10 am to noon and 3 to 5 pm; closed Sunday. Entry costs Rs 1.

Parks & Falls

Near the start of Coaker's Walk is **Bryant Park**, a botanical park laid out, landscaped and stocked over many years by the British

A Beeline to Baba

I was on the futile search for a straight answer from an Indian travel agent when Milan stormed into my life. 'Don't listen to them man' he barked in his Indian cockney accent, 'they'll rip you off man, come and see Sai Baba with me, he's a live God man'.

I didn't know Milan but I knew I couldn't let the opportunity slip. Within minutes I was hurtling south to Kodaikanal to meet …God.

On the journey Milan plied me with tales of Sai Baba: run-of-the-mill miracles, fingertips flowing with sacred ashes, his sheltering of the unloved, and his enormous band of devotees scattered around the world.

Barefoot and white-clad we headed for the ashram. We heard that only a few hundred would actually get in. Thousands of others would have to listen outside. Despite turning up three hours early, we were relegated to the queue 200m from the gate. Serious faces ahead were resigned to not getting in. The rain fell heavily. By the time the gates opened, we were saturated. Caught in the stampede, I lost Milan. The charge split and I found myself in the auditorium. People scrambled over one another to claim a place. Adept in the art of boarding Indian buses, I secured a place near the front. Within minutes the mayhem subsided. Men and women sat on opposite sides while dour looking Sai Baba acolytes stood over the crowd and sternly stared us into silence.

For the next three hours we sat and waited. Most people meditated but I couldn't take my mind off the cramp in my legs.

Half an hour before Swami was to enter, the acolytes began to sing *bhajjans*. This developed into a chanting and clapping frenzy and I was hopelessly out of sync. The singing reached a crescendo when the left door swung open, and Sai Baba glided in. A wave of awe washed over the congregation and I almost passed out. The force of energy he carried made every hair on my body stand.

Swami wore an elegant saffron robe, and while his face looked fresh and youthful his body was frail and propped up with a walking stick. People at the front lunged towards him and kissed his bare feet. His composure never faltered.

The bhajjans continued with Swami conducting. When finally he spoke he was at once passionate and calm. He spoke of our duty as human beings to hide all that is bad within us and never to let other people see anything but our inherent good. He held my attention for about 10 minutes. As he left some reached out to touch him.

That night I felt disappointed that I wasn't walking on air. I encountered a Frenchwoman who blew me away with her claim that Sai Baba was talking to me through her. 'You are right to be sceptical. Go out and seek other gurus, go all over the world and listen to them, you will come back to me but not for a long time, you will come to me when you are 34 years old and I will be waiting'.

On a street in Madurai, I decided this whole Sai Baba thing wasn't for me. I went to buy some postcards and get on with the rest of my life. I sifted through a bundle. When I came to the last one I saw Sai Baba's mischievous smile and his hands held aloft as if to say, 'What can you do. I'm everywhere'.

Martin Hughes

officer after whom it is named. At **Chettiar Park**, about 3km uphill from town near the Kurinji Andavar Temple, you may be able to see some Kurinji flowers.

There are numerous waterfalls in the area – the main one, **Silver Cascade**, is on the road up to Kodai.

Kurinji Andavar Temple

This tiny temple, 3km north-east of the lake, is dedicated to Murugan. It was constructed in 1936 by a European woman, Leelavathi Ramanathan, who converted to Hinduism. Inside the entrance are the customary planets and a statue of Ganesh flanked by two of Murugan's vehicles – peacocks. Signs near the sanctum proclaim rooms for rent! The temple is named after the Kurinji flower.

Hindus will no doubt appreciate this temple as a place for prayer and ritual. For non-Hindus, apart from the views on the other side of the gate, there is not much of interest.

Activities

Walks The views at Coaker's Walk, which has an observatory with telescope (Telescope House, entry Rs 1), and from Pillar Rocks, a 7km hike (one way), are two of the most spectacular in South India. Mist may obscure the view, but the monkeys along the way will provide ample entertainment.

For more serious trekking, head to the District Forest Office, on a winding road down (north) towards Hotel Tamil Nadu. Here you can buy a pamphlet called *Sholas For Survival*, which describes 17 local treks ranging from 8km ambles to 27km hikes. It costs Rs 15 and includes a rough map plus estimates of the time required to complete each walk and the relative degree of difficulty. This office is open weekdays from 10 am to 1 pm and 2 to 6 pm.

Cycling Although the roads are rarely flat there are some nice bike rides in the area. One reader recommended going to Moir Point (10km) via the Astrophysical Laboratory, then taking the Monnar Rd 14km to Berijam Lake passing Silent Valley and Caps Valley

Viewpoint. From December to June the Monnar Rd is closed because of the danger from fires but you can get special permission to cycle here from the District Forest Office.

Boating & Horse Riding The lake at Kodai has been wonderfully landscaped, and boats can be hired from below the Carlton Hotel, from the Kodaikanal Boat & Rowing Club (from Rs 30 for a two-seater). The tourist department also has a range of rowboats and pedal boats for rent nearby (Rs 35 for two people for 30 minutes). Around here you'll be accosted by people who want to rent you horses. They are not cheap, and you'll be quoted as much as they think you're willing to pay. The prevailing rate seems to be Rs 100 per hour and you can ride accompanied or unaccompanied. Some of the horses are in poor condition.

Places to Stay

As with the other hill stations, hotel prices in the high season (1 April to 30 June) jump by up to 300% compared to those during the rest of the year. In some cases, this is nothing but a blatant rip-off, especially at the lower end of the market. During this season, it's worth staying in a mid-range hotel since none of them hike their prices by more than 100% and some considerably less than that.

The majority of hotels here don't have single rooms and they're reluctant to discuss reductions for single occupancy in the high season. Most hotels in Kodai have a 9 or 10 am checkout time in the high season so don't get caught out. During the rest of the year it's usually, but not always, 24 hours.

And finally most hotels have carpet or some floor covering they refer to as carpet. So the visual history, so common on many hotel walls, may be missing here but it's often compensated for by an olfactory history! Such historical presentations do not usually stimulate the senses in a positive way.

Places to Stay – Budget

Greenlands Youth Hostel (☎ *41099*) has the best views of any hotel in town and it's

Looking for Mr Good Guide

Some walks around the hills are no more than a two or three hour stroll and can be completed without a guide. Other walks are more difficult and can take a full day or even several days. These walks require experience as well as good local knowledge and are best undertaken with the help of a professional guide. The problem is, how do you know a good guide when you see one? There is no easy answer to this question. The streets of Kodaikanal are full of touts claiming to be professional guides. Some who offer themselves as guides clearly are highly professional and will make your experience worthwhile. Others may have little knowledge and will take you for a ride rather than a walk.

Have a firm idea of the type of walk you want to do as well as your capability. Are you looking for something easy or strenuous? Do you want to return before nightfall or are you looking to do a two or three day hike?

Seek specific recommendations from other travellers, and if you are engaged in negotiations with a potential guide don't be shy to ask the following questions:

- Do you have any written testimonials? (These of course are easy to fabricate but they can give you a sense of who you may be talking with.)
- Can you give us an idea of the route we'll take, including the distances, grades and the type of terrain involved?
- Can you identify any potential obstacles we may encounter: river crossings, wild animals, etc?
- If we are walking for more than a day, how many hours a day will we need to walk to complete the trek?
- If we are trekking into tribal areas do you speak the language? Know the customs?
- What time can we expect to return?
- Do you have a torch (flashlight) and first aid equipment? (Trekkers should always have their own but a good guide will also have some.)
- If the guide (or the booking company) is going to supply camping equipment, can we inspect the equipment before we agree to the deal?
- If the trek includes a cook, what's on the menu and who supplies the food?
- Will there be places along the way to replenish drinking water?
- Is the price quoted per person, group, day, hour or some combination of these? Does it include meals?

It is better to travel with even a small group rather than setting out alone with a guide, and of course you should ensure that you have adequate clothing (including footwear) for variable weather. It's also a good idea if you are taking a two or three day trek to let someone know where you will be and when you expect to return.

If you are looking for a reliable guide in Kodaikanal, you may like to contact the Palani Hills Conservation Council (☎ 40711) at Amarville House on Lower Shola Rd. In Ooty, contact the Ooty Tourist Guides Association which has a small office opposite the Ooty bus stand.

where you'll find most of the budget travellers. That said, it can be suffocatingly crowded with double bunks arranged head to toe. Travellers' reports are ambiguous. Some claim that the staff are rude and indifferent. However, others say they are fine, even charming! The hostel is about to extend from 12 to 20 rooms and a common room is planned by 1999. It's about 1km from the centre, at the end of Coaker's Walk. A bed in the dorms (six to 15 beds) costs Rs 50/60 in the low/high season. There are also eight double rooms (four have fireplaces) with attached bathrooms for Rs 190 to Rs 210 in the low season and Rs 240 to Rs 250 in the high season. There's hot water from 7 to 9 am for Rs 5. Breakfast – either Indian or toasted brown bread with jam – and snacks are available.

TTDC Youth Hostel, beside the Hotel Tamil Nadu, has beds for Rs 50 but lacks atmosphere.

Guru Lodge is one of several very basic hotels strung out along the steep Bazaar Rd. Doubles are Rs 70 (Rs 160 to Rs 260 in season) with hot water for Rs 5 per bucket. Facilities are absolutely minimal – make sure they give you blankets as it gets pretty chilly here. This is not a great location.

Hotel Sunrise (☎ 40358), a few minutes walk from the bus stand, is a friendly place. There are doubles (no singles) with bathroom for Rs 150. The view from the front is excellent, and the rooms have hot water heaters which work from 6 am to 6 pm.

Zum Zum Lodge off Club Rd, has large grubby doubles for Rs 60 in the low season. It's exorbitantly overpriced in the high season. Zum Zum also has some bungalows 10 minutes walk away not far from the TV towers. The cost is Rs 80 per person. They're seriously basic and certainly not the cleanest rooms in town. The setting, however, is exquisite with splendid views into the valley. There is a cook on the premises and a kitchen for self catering. You have to make bookings for these bungalows at the Zum Zum reception.

Yagapa Lodge (☎ 41235), off Club Rd, is an excellent, peaceful place with a range of rooms. There are doubles for Rs 160 with attached bath and hot water in buckets, or Rs 200 with constant hot water. Prices double in the high season. It's a friendly hotel with good views.

Places to Stay – Mid-Range

Taj Villa (☎ 40940), off Club Rd in Coaker's Rd, is an old stone-built group of houses in its own small garden with sublime views from some rooms. Prices depend on the view. Double rooms here (no singles) cost

Rs 400 (low season) and are 'subject to hike in season'. Most of the rooms have attached bathrooms and three rooms in the older house have fireplaces. Hot water is available morning and evening.

Hotel Anjay (☎ 41089, Bazaar Rd) isn't a bad choice though it's often full. Double rooms with attached bathroom and constant hot water start at Rs 195/400 in the low/high season.

Snooze Inn (☎ 40837) has clean rooms with TV and running hot water. Economy doubles (there are no singles) cost Rs 275/500 in low/high season. Deluxe and family rooms are also available.

Hotel Sangeeth (☎ 40456) is good value at Rs 195/325 for a double in the low/high season. All the rooms have attached bathrooms with hot and cold running water, but there are no views.

Hotel Astoria (☎ 40524), next door to the Sangeeth, has ordinary/deluxe doubles at Rs 300/400 in the low season and Rs 625/800 in the high season. Its restaurant serves North and South Indian dishes.

Hotel Jewel (☎ 41029, Hospital Rd) is good value at Rs 275/300 for ordinary/deluxe doubles in the low season or Rs 450/650 in the high season. All the rooms are well furnished with wall-to-wall carpeting and colour TV.

Hotel Tamil Nadu (☎ 41336, Fern Hill Rd) is a long walk from the centre and somewhat run down. In the low/high season doubles cost Rs 250/425 and cottages are Rs 400/650. It has a restaurant and one of the few bars in Kodai.

Hilltop Towers (☎ 40413, Club Rd), opposite the Kodai International School, is a flashy place that's centrally located. The staff are keen and friendly and double rooms/suites cost Rs 400/450 in the low season and Rs 725/875 in the high season.

Hotel Garden Manor (☎ 40461, Lake Rd) lives up to its name. Set in very pleasant, terraced gardens overlooking the lake, it has spacious rooms from Rs 550 to Rs 700 (low season) and Rs 1000 to Rs 1150 (in season). Indoor and outdoor restaurants serve a variety of dishes.

TAMIL NADU

Hotel J's Heritage (☎ *41323)*, Hospital Rd, near Seven Rds is centrally situated and very good value. Low season rates start at Rs 390 for a standard double to Rs 880 for a family suite. Season rates are from Rs 750 to Rs 1550. There's a new restaurant and management promotes its fine western food – Sunday roasts and mashed potatoes. The problem is (or maybe it isn't) no one's told the chef!

Places to Stay – Top End

Kodaikanal Club (☎ *41341)* is a rather stiff place set in manicured grounds close to the lake on Club Rd. Established in 1887, this colonial-style clubhouse has a library, video room, badminton and billiard tables, four 'mud' tennis courts, a bar (with cheap beers) and a dining room. It offers 16 large double rooms for Rs 750/850 in the low/high season, plus 15% service charge. This room rate includes the obligatory temporary membership fee (Rs 50 per day which entitles you to use all the facilities), breakfast (Indian or continental) and 'bed tea' (served in your room between 6 and 7 am). The rooms are quaint and have an adjoining sitting room, bathroom, TV, heater, wicker chairs and 24 hour hot water. Don't expect to get a room here in the high season as it's booked out months ahead.

Valley View Hotel (☎ *40181)* is a large modern hotel on Post Office Rd. The rooms are well appointed and those at the front have a wonderful view of the valley. It's a bargain in the low season at Rs 350/500 for singles/doubles. High-season rates are Rs 1200/1500 but this includes all meals. There's a good vegetarian restaurant.

Hotel Kodai International (☎ *40649; fax 40753)* is overpriced and badly located. Double rooms/cottages cost Rs 990/1200 in the low season or Rs 1600/1850 in the high season.

The Carlton Hotel (☎ *40071, Lake Rd)* is Kodai's most prestigious hotel and a lovely place to stay. It has the formality associated with many of the star hotels. Overlooking the lake, this hotel used to be a colonial-style wooden structure but was completely rebuilt a few years ago and is simply magnificent. In the low season, rooms cost Rs 1590/2450 with breakfast and dinner; in the high season it's Rs 1840/3600 including all meals. There are also more expensive suites and cottages. There's an excellent restaurant and a bar.

Places to Eat

Hospital Rd is the best place for cheap restaurants and it's here that most of the travellers and students from the Kodai International School congregate. There's a whole range of different cuisines available.

Tava Restaurant, below the Hotel Jewel, offers vegetarian Indian food.

Hotel Punjab does excellent tandoori food.

Ahaar is a little vegetarian place.

Silver Inn Restaurant is a good place for breakfasts and also does pizzas and other western dishes.

Wang's Kitchen has Chinese and western food at reasonable prices.

Tibetan Brothers Restaurant is a popular place serving westernised Tibetan food.

The Royal Tibet serves veg and nonveg and is a popular place with budget travellers. It serves a range of dishes but its noodle soups make a filling meal on a cool night. Just give the coffee a miss!

Chefmaster has continental, Chinese and Keralan dishes, and also handmade chocolates!

Hot Breads pretends to be a classy bakery and coffee shop in the supermarket complex on Hospital Rd. Apple pie is Rs 25, eclairs are Rs 12.

Eco Nut, also in the supermarket complex on Hospital Rd, has a wide range of health food – brown bread, cheese, essential oils, etc. Try their Nutri Balls (Rs 10), which are a mixture of jaggery, peanuts, coconut and moong daal.

Little Silver Star is upstairs in the large building opposite the tourist office. They do probably the best tandoori chicken in Kodai – Rs 75 for half a chicken.

Manna Bake Vegetarian Restaurant is on Bear Shola Falls Rd. It's run by Israel Booshi, who doubles as a chef and an active

PETER DAVIS

PETER DAVIS

EDDIE GERALD

TERESA CANNON

EDDIE GERALD

PETER DAVIS

Tamil Nadu
Teeming with great temples and monuments (clockwise from top left): Gingee Fort; Kapaleeshwarar Temple sculpture (Chennai); a Madurai temple sculpture; Kapaleeshwarar; a Thanjavur temple fresco; Ramanathaswamy Temple sculpture (Rameswaram).

EDDIE GERALD

EDDIE GERALD

EDDIE GERALD

EDDIE GERALD

Tamil Nadu
Clockwise from top left: Brihadishwara Temple (Thanjavur); Ramanathaswamy Temple (Rameswaram); Shore Temple (Mamallapuram); Devarajaswami Temple (Kanchipuram).

environmentalist. His brown bread is legendary, as is the apple pie (Rs 15). It's open from 7.30 am until late.

Taj Villa has a new chef who is reputed to be turning out all manner of interesting dishes.

The Carlton Hotel is the place for a splurge. Here, they put on an excellent evening buffet from 7.30 to 10 pm for Rs 270 including tax. After eating you can relax in the bar.

Self Catering For food items try the small shop, *Kurinji Mini Market*, a few metres up from the post office. Kodai is a lush orchard area and, depending on the season, you'll find various fruits – pears, avocados, guavas, durians and grapefruit – in the street stalls around the bus stand.

Shopping

The Cottage Crafts Shop on Bazaar Rd opposite the post office has some excellent bits and pieces for sale. It is run by Corsock, the Coordinating Council for Social Concerns in Kodai. This organisation, staffed by volunteers, sells crafts on behalf of development groups, using the commission charged to help the needy. Corsock also runs the Goodwill Centre, Hospital Rd, which sells clothing and rents books, with the proceeds again going to indigent causes. There's a branch of Poompuhar Handicrafts just near the tourist office.

The road down to the lake (alongside the Kodaikanal Club) is lined with stalls run by Tibetans selling warm clothing, shawls and other fabrics. Their prices are very reasonable.

Getting There & Away

On arrival at Kodai you'll be overwhelmed by touts thrusting all kinds of offers for transport and accommodation your way. As always, resist the onslaught or you may find yourself settling for options that are not to your liking.

Bus Kodai's bus stand is basically a patch of dirt opposite the Hotel Astoria. State buses

run eight times a day to Madurai (Rs 20, 121km, 3½ hours), once daily to both Tiruchirappalli (197km) and Kanyakumari (356km), and twice a day to both Coimbatore (244km) and Chennai (513km, Rs 92). As well, there are more frequent buses to Palani (Rs 18, 65km, three hours), Dindigul and Kodai Road (the train station). There's also a KSRTC semideluxe bus daily to Bangalore for Rs 105 which leaves at 6 pm and takes 12 hours (480km).

Deluxe minibuses operate in the high season between Kodaikanal and Ooty, but services are suspended in the monsoon. They cost Rs 180 to Rs 220 and take all day to cover the 332km. Inquire at mid-range hotels for departure times.

Train The nearest train stations are Palani to the north (on the Coimbatore-Madurai-Rameswaram line), and Kodai Road on the Madurai-Trichy-Chennai line to the east. Both are about three hours away by bus.

There's a railway out-agency, up from the bus stand, where you can book seats on express trains to Chennai.

Getting Around

Taxis are very expensive here compared with elsewhere even though half of them stand idle most of the day. The minimum charge is Rs 50. You won't be able to haggle – there's no competition. There are no rickshaws of any description.

The stall outside the Carlton Hotel rents mountain bikes for Rs 5/40 per hour/day. The bicycle stall near the Hotel Garden Manor has ordinary bikes for Rs 20 per day (negotiable). The hills can present quite a problem but, as you'd be walking up them anyway, it's not that much extra hassle to push a bike and at least you can coast down! Check the brakes before attempting any steep descents.

AROUND KODAIKANAL
Palani

There are fine views of the plains and scattered rock outcrops on the bus ride from Kodaikanal to Palani. The hill on which the Palani temple stands appears cast into the

TAMIL NADU

centre of the landscape, isolated within an extensive flatness from the other hills, which create an almost perfect boundary.

The town's hill temple, **Malaikovil**, is dedicated to Lord Murugan. Legend says he took this abode after fleeing from his family in frustration. His mother Parvati had given him and his older brother, Ganesh, a task: whoever travelled around the entire universe and returned to her first would receive a golden mango.

Desperate to please his mother, Murugan set off on his peacock, circled the globe and returned proudly to Parvati. Ganesh, on the other hand, stood before his mother, bowed slowly and respectfully walked around her, then proclaimed 'You, dear Mother, are my universe'.

Murugan was furious when he returned to find he was not the victor. Parvati endeavoured to reassure him by teaching him the same lesson in a gentler manner. She used the words 'Pala nee' meaning 'you are the fruit'. He was not consoled, however, and he fled the family and took residence at Palani. This insightful narrative now draws thousands of people in continual pilgrimage to this site.

In the town at the bottom of the hill many pilgrims have their heads shaved as an act of humility, and give their hair in offering to the god. The hair is sold and provides income for the temple. A road circles the hill at its base. Pilgrims usually walk this road before climbing the wide 659 steps to the top. Just within the bottom entrance, a huge statue of Ganesh stands, flanked by two large five-headed cobras and decorated with marigolds. Paraffin tablets burn along the steps, pilgrims continually adding more to sustain the flame, as a symbol of their devotion. Men and women, sandal paste in hand, stand along the way, dabbing the foreheads of the devotees. The pilgrims, in their saris and dhotis, move in a mass of swaying colour and excitement up the hill towards their deity. To the side of the stairs, signs blatantly announce the temple sponsors – gone are the days of the ancient attractive inscriptions. Even the Catholic Syrian Bank sponsors Murugan.

At the top, the temple and its inner sanctum stand within a spacious area. Numerous small shrines, 2m by 3m, contain lightly hued shrines of Murugan and his family. The image of the deity within the sanctum stands just over 1m high. It is believed to be made of substances which contain miraculous powers. As such, pilgrims seek to acquire some substance (sandal paste, oil) which has touched the icon.

The views from the top are especially stunning. They extend over lush rice fields and coconut stands to the distant hills.

The temple is becoming so popular that an electric winch has been installed to carry sick and aged devotees to the top.

Many festivals are celebrated here. Some 200,000 pilgrims gather for Thai Pusam in January. At this time devotees walk and dance for days to the temple, carrying peacock feathers and playing musical instruments. Their chants become ever more exhilarated and frenetic as they approach the temple.

There are several places to stay but *Hotel Modern Home (Railway Feeder Rd)* is far enough from the centre to be reasonably peaceful. Rooms are Rs 75/95 with attached bath.

See the earlier Getting There & Away section under Kodaikanal for information on getting to Palani.

INDIRA GANDHI WILDLIFE SANCTUARY (Annamalai Wildlife Sanctuary)

This is one of three wildlife sanctuaries on the slopes of the Western Ghats along the border between Tamil Nadu and Kerala. Though recently renamed the Indira Gandhi Wildlife Sanctuary, most people still refer to it by its original name. It covers almost 1000 sq km and is home to elephants, gaur (Indian bison), tigers, panthers, spotted deer, wild boar, bears, porcupines and civet cats. The Nilgiri tahr, commonly known as the ibex, may also be spotted, as may many birds.

The sanctuary is also home to six tribal groups – the Kadars, Malai, Malasars, Eravalars, Puliyars and Muthuvars – living in 35 settlements. They have permission to stay in the sanctuary in which they scratch a precarious living through subsistence agriculture.

In the heart of this beautiful forested region the Parambikulam Aliyar Multipurpose Project involves a complex system of tunnels and canals which connect the major rivers and dams and provide water for irrigaton and energy. The question of rights to the water has been the cause of bitter disputes in the area.

Information

The first and most important aspect about Annamalai Wildlife Sanctuary is that its objective is the protection and conservation of natural flora and fauna. While visitors are not discouraged, limitations are placed on their entry: the wildlife takes priority and at least 90% of the park is closed to visitors.

Day visitors may proceed directly to the park at Top Slip, about 35km south-west of Pollachi. At Top Slip the entrance fees are Rs 5 per person, Rs 5 per still camera, Rs 50 for a movie camera, Rs 10 for cars. If you go on to Parambikulam on the Kerala side of the park you must pay Rs 25. The reception centre and most of the lodges are at Top Slip.

Unless you have accommodation you may only be in the park between 6 am and 6 pm. The infrequent buses make accessibility difficult. However, if you go by private vehicle you cannot use this in the park. You will be restricted to the tours conducted in the departmental vans which run from 8 am to 5 pm (lunch break, 1 to 3 pm). These tours take one hour, cover about 14km and cost Rs 30 per person.

Along the route you'll see two strategically placed domestic elephants. The bus will stop so you can have a better look. One of the elephants, Kalidasa (a baby, orphaned during a monsoon flood) will perform various three-legged stunts and play a mouth organ. Many tourists delight in this tragic spectacle.

If you're looking forward to an elephant ride you may be disappointed, as it may be cancelled, but you can console yourself by visiting the little museum which has several examples of stuffed elephant legs, stuffed

tigers and an elephant foetus preserved in formaldehyde!

Trekking in the park can be arranged at Top Slip. However, you must be accompanied by a guide and the maximum time is four hours for Rs 60 per person.

The sanctuary can be visited at any time of the year, but there are several factors to consider. Firstly, it's best to come on a weekday when there are staff to handle your inquiries and bookings. The time limitations for both day and residential visitors mean you are unlikely to see many, if any, wild animals. Climate wise it's best in January/February when it's cooler. However, you are more likely to see animals during the wet season – June/July and November/December. Finally, in March/April with water shortages and fire risk, the sanctuary may be closed.

Once you get through the bureaucracy and arrive at the park, it's quiet, calm, cool and green – far removed from the dust and noise of the plains. The staff are helpful and humorous. As some of them suggest, be content with the flora and the hope that, somewhere beyond it, wild animals may be living in sanctuary.

Places to Stay & Eat

Accommodation is available near Top Slip and is usually limited to one night only, with a definite maximum of three nights. All accommodation *must* be booked in advance in Pollachi at the Wildlife Warden's Office (☎ 04259-25356) on Meenkarai Rd. The office is open from 9 am to 5 pm Monday to Friday. It is therefore not possible to make accommodation bookings on weekends or holidays. Also, it cannot be assumed that your application for accommodation will be granted. Sometimes there is a screening process, where prospective visitors are interviewed to determine their suitability. Interviews are conducted from 10 am to noon. Top Slip, at 740m, can get cool at night in winter. Since the whole situation of accommodation availability and costs is currently under review it's a good idea to phone first to get the lowdown.

The accommodation near Top Slip consists

TAMIL NADU

of two dormitories, a few suites, lodges and a small house. Some places are presently closed for renovations.

Ambuli Illam, 2km from the reception centre, is the best. This has three 'suites' and costs Rs 40 per person. There's a canteen here, about the only place in the park where you'll get a half decent meal.

Hornbill House has four beds and costs Rs 240.

At Parambikulam, the very basic *rest-house* has no catering facilities and only a few 'meals' places nearby.

For day visitors, although there is food and drink available, you may wish to bring your own.

Should you get stuck in Pollachi (a likely occurrence given the erratic hours of the Wildlife Warden's Office) you could stay at *Sakthi Hotels (☎ 04259-23060, Coimbatore Rd)*. Locals will inform you that this is the choice of the stars when they come to make their movies at Top Slip. It offers doubles for Rs 225, or Rs 450 with air-con and has a large (very noisy but very good) restaurant. A cheaper option on the same road is *Ramesh Lodge*, which has doubles for Rs 125 (no singles).

Getting There & Away
Annamalai is between Palani and Coimbatore. Regular buses from both these places stop at the nearest large town, Pollachi, which is also on the Coimbatore to Dindigul train line. From Pollachi, buses leave the bus stand for Top Slip at 6 am and 3.30 pm and return at 8.30 am and 6 pm. A taxi from Pollachi is around Rs 450 one way.

COIMBATORE
Pop: 1.23 million Tel Area Code: 0422
Coimbatore is a large industrial city known as either the Manchester or the Detroit of the south for its textile manufacturing and engineering goods. It is also full of 'suitings and shirtings' shops. While the city doesn't hold any particular attraction for tourists it can make a convenient overnight stop if you're heading up to Ooty or the other Nilgiri hill stations. The streets are wide, the traffic is comparatively orderly and there is a complete range of hotels to suit all budgets.

Orientation & Information
The two main bus stands are close to each other but about 2km from the train station. Some buses from Kerala and southern Tamil Nadu arrive at a third stand, Ukkadam, south of the train station. Frequent city buses ply the route from here into town.

The GPO is open for poste restante collection from 10 am to 3 pm, Monday to Saturday. An efficient fax and email facility is available from the very cooperative staff at Best Business Centre (☎ 235538; fax 233894) in Kalingarayan St, around the corner from Zakir Hotel. Email facilities are also available at the Residency Hotel at 1076 Avinashi Rd (you don't have to be staying at the hotel).

For books try Landmark (☎ 212689) in the Lakshmi Plaza Combine, 1089 Avinashi Rd. (Don't be put off by the numerous Lakshmi complexes and all the strange numbering, just keep travelling until you're almost opposite Kamarajar Rd.) It's open Monday to Friday from 9 am to 9 pm, and weekends from noon to 7 pm.

Several places for accommodation and of interest are in Avanashi Rd (which has numerous spelling variations, including Avanasi St).

Places to Stay – Budget
Hotel Sivakami (☎ 210271, Dave & Co Lane) is friendly and helpful and has basic rooms with bathroom for Rs 120/145. There are several other similar places on this relatively peaceful street opposite the train station.

Railway Retiring Rooms at the station include doubles for Rs 120, or Rs 175 with air-con. The dorm beds (men only) are Rs 40. There is an air-con suite for Rs 300. The efficient station even has an electronic information board showing which rooms are occupied.

Hotel Shree Shakti (☎ 234225, 11/148 Sastri Rd) is a large hotel near the bus stand. Staff are friendly; rooms have a fan and bathroom and cost Rs 140/180 for singles/doubles.

Zakir Hotel *(Sastri Rd)* has rooms for Rs 80/110, and cold water only.

Sri Ganapathy Lodge *(☎ 230632, Sastri Rd)* has reasonable rooms with attached bath for Rs 125/185.

Places to Stay – Mid-Range & Top End

Hotel Blue Star *(☎ 230635, Nehru St)* has well-appointed rooms for Rs 195/270 with bathroom. The rooms out the back are quieter. There's a basement bar and both a veg and nonveg restaurant.

Hotel Tamil Nadu *(☎ 236311)*, conveniently located near the state bus stand, is surprisingly good. There are ordinary rooms for Rs 195/275 with attached bath, and air-con rooms for Rs 350/400. The deluxe rooms are somewhat overpriced given that the main difference is a piece of grotty red carpet. The ceiling fan sounds like a fire

siren and the air-con has only two settings, off or freezing. The water is hot but the taps are hotter – take care!

Hotel City Tower *(☎ 230681; fax 230103, Sivasamy Rd)* is a clean and modern place with singles/doubles for Rs 500/650, or Rs 850/950 with air-con. Although this hotel claims to be a business hotel it has no business centre or email facility and the fax 'sometimes doesn't work'. All rooms have Star TV and attached baths and the hotel has two excellent restaurants.

Nilgiri's Nest *(☎ 217247; fax 217131, 739A Avanashi Rd)* is a pleasant, well-run hotel near the racecourse. Bed and breakfast costs Rs 750/950 in comfortable air-con rooms. The hotel has the same excellent restaurant and supermarket facility as its branch in Chennai.

Hotel Surya International *(☎ 217755; fax 216110, 105 Racecourse Rd)* has luxurious standard rooms for Rs 950/1050.

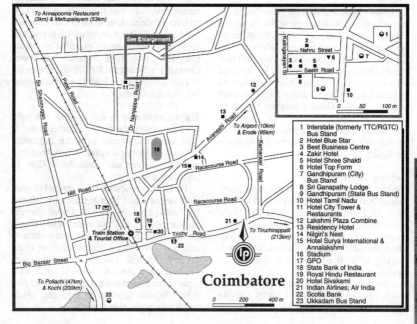

To Annapoorna Restaurant (3km) & Mettupalayam (53km)

See Enlargement

Kalingarayan St

Nehru Street
Sastri Road

St Shanmugam Road
Patel Road
Dr Nanjappa Road

To Airport (10km) & Erode (95km)

Avanashi Road

Kamaraja Road

Racecourse Road

Racecourse Road

Mill Road

Train Station & Tourist Office

Trichy Road

To Tiruchirappalli (213km)

Big Bazaar Street

To Pollachi (47km) & Kochi (200km)

Coimbatore

1 Interstate (formerly TTC/RGTC) Bus Stand
2 Hotel Blue Star
3 Best Business Centre
4 Zakir Hotel
5 Hotel Shree Shakti
6 Hotel Top Form
7 Gandhipuram (City) Bus Stand
8 Sri Ganapathy Lodge
9 Gandhipuram (State Bus Stand)
10 Hotel Tamil Nadu
11 Hotel City Tower & Restaurants
12 Lakshmi Plaza Combine
13 Residency Hotel
14 Nilgiri's Nest
15 Hotel Surya International & Annalakshmi
16 Stadium
17 GPO
18 State Bank of India
19 Royal Hindu Restaurant
20 Hotel Sivakami
21 Indian Airlines; Air India
22 Scotia Bank
23 Ukkadam Bus Stand

0   50   100 m

0   200   400 m

The Residency (☎ 201234; fax 201414, 1076 Avanashi Rd) is the newest and swishest hotel in town. Singles/doubles start at Rs 1500/1700. The hotel also has a professional business centre offering an email and fax facility. The centre is available to nonguests for the same fee as guests. The staff are still learning to become computer literate. The lobby is worth exploring for its coffee shop with tantalising goodies and a reasonable bookstore.

Places to Eat

There are numerous 'meals' restaurants in the train station area serving thalis from around Rs 20.

Royal Hindu Restaurant, just north of the train station, is a huge place offering good vegetarian meals.

Hotel Top Form on Nehru St serves non-vegetarian food at reasonable prices.

Hotel City Towers has a very pleasant rooftop restaurant, a good place for a splurge.

Annalakshmi, next to the Hotel Surya International at 106 Racecourse Rd, is the top vegetarian restaurant. Run by devotees of Shivanjali, it's an interesting place to eat and the food, though expensive, is very well prepared. There are set meals from Rs 200, and it's open daily for dinner from 6.45 to 9.45 pm and Monday to Saturday for lunch from noon to 3 pm. There's another branch in Chennai.

Annapoorna vegetarian restaurant in Mettupalayan Rd is a favourite for its thalis for Rs 25.

Getting There & Away

Air The airport is around 10km east of town. Indian Airlines (☎ 212208) and Air India (☎ 213393) offices are on Trichy Rd. There are Indian Airlines flights between Coimbatore and Mumbai (daily, US$120), Chennai (daily, US$70), Calicut (four times weekly, US$30), and Madurai (three times weekly, US$40).

Additionally, Jet Airways (☎ 212034) and Sahara Indian Airlines both fly daily to Mumbai, and Jet Airways has a daily flight to Chennai. NEPC (☎ 216741) flies to Bangalore (three times weekly, US$65).

Bus The large Gandhipuram state bus stand is well organised. Buses leave from here for destinations including Thanjavur, Trichy and Salem. Buses to Bangalore (Rs 82, 312km, nine hours, 10 daily) and Mysore (Rs 47, 205km, three times daily) can be booked at the reservation office (open from 9 am to 9 pm) on Bay 1.

Ordinary buses to Ooty (Rs 17, 90km, three hours) leave every 15 minutes from opposite the reservation office, between 4 am and 8.30 pm. Other buses leave for Chennai (15 daily, 11½ hours), Vellore and Kanchipuram.

The Ukkadam bus stand just south of the train station runs services to Pallani (every 20 minutes between 4 am and 11.30 pm), Pollachi (every three minutes from 6 am to 9 pm), Madurai (every half hour from 5.30 am to 11.30 pm) and Dindigul (seven daily).

The former TTC/RGTC bus stand on Cross Cut Rd has had many of its services transferred to the bus stands above. Most interstate services leave from or call in here.

There are also numerous long-distance 'sightseeing video buses' operated by private companies that leave from all over town. Contact a travel agent for details; one to try is HM Travels (☎ 431839) at Bharathiyar Rd, Gandhipuram.

Train Coimbatore is a major rail junction. For Ooty, catch the daily *Nilgiri Express* at 6.25 am; it connects with the miniature railway at Mettupalayam. The whole trip takes 4½ hours and costs Rs 43/204 in 2nd/1st class.

There are numerous daily trains between Coimbatore and Chennai Central (494km), the fastest being the new *Shatabdi Express* service which takes just under seven hours. Departure times are 7.25 am from Coimbatore, 3.10 pm from Chennai. Air-con chair car costs Rs 520. The *Kovai Express* takes 7½ hours and costs Rs 142/511 in 2nd/1st class. From Coimbatore it leaves at 2.20 pm; from Chennai it leaves at 6.15 am. Other trains take up to nine hours.

The *Rameswaram Express* at 11.35 pm goes daily via Madurai (Rs 56/294 in 2nd/1st class, 229km, six hours) to Rameswaram (Rs 85/435, 393km, 13 hours). The *Kanyakumari-Bangalore Express* runs daily to Bangalore (Rs 126/464, 424km, nine hours) and, in the other direction, to Kanyakumari (Rs 146/546, 514km, 12½ hours).

To the Kerala coast, the daily *West Coast Express* from Chennai Central goes to Kozhikode (Calicut) (Rs 47/235, 185km, 4½ hours) and also on to Bangalore (Rs 142/511, 504km, nine hours). The train for Pollachi leaves at 6.20 pm and costs Rs 17 (2nd class only).

There is also a superfast train from Chennai to Coimbatore (6½ hours).

Getting Around

Many buses ply between the train station and the city bus stand (also known as Gandhipuram) including bus Nos JJ, 24, 55 and 57. For the airport take No 20 from the bus stand or Nos 10 or 16 from the train station (Rs 25).

Auto-rickshaw drivers are rapacious. They'll charge Rs 25 between bus and train stations and over Rs 150 for the airport.

AROUND COIMBATORE
Black Thunder Water Theme Park

Forty kilometres from Coimbatore on the Ooty-Mettupalayam road, Black Thunder is a new 25 hectare water theme park set against the dramatic Nilgiri ranges. It offers 10 dry games and 11 water games including a large wave pool, several water slides (one for real thrillseekers), and a 1.8km meandering moat in which you can float at your leisure in a rubber dinghy.

Owned by a politician, designed by a Californian and managed by a retired and rather bored brigadier, Black Thunder claims to be India's only state-of-the-art theme park. With an entry price of Rs 200 for adults and Rs 150 for children (this includes unlimited access to all rides) it is essentially an elaborate playground for the mobile middle classes. Indeed, management policy is to exclude the 'lower classes'.

Men must wear Bermuda-style shorts (which can be hired) but women are permitted to wear what they like (most prefer full sari in the water). Some areas are designated for women and children only.

Safety measures are a priority here. More than 120 lifeguards roam the complex. The standards of hygiene are very high and the water quality is constantly monitored. The park draws its water from 16 natural wells, but the ecological impact of the discharged chlorine is mind-boggling. This aside, it can be a fun place to unwind after a hot dusty day of travelling, and parents may find it particularly attractive for their children.

The park is open every day from 10 am to 7 pm. Buses to the park from Coimbatore and Ooty are frequent. Just let the conductors know where you want to get off – they'll know! There are numerous restaurants (veg and nonveg), drink stalls and ice cream outlets within the park. Alcohol is prohibited, so is food from outside the park (visitors are searched on entry).

The park is still being developed and deluxe accommodation facilities (starting at Rs 1500) are near completion, as is a non-water area consisting of more than 200 video games.

Nilgiris

An integral part of the Western Ghats and the Nilgiri Biosphere Reserve, the Nilgiris is the oldest and second-highest mountain range in India (after the Himalaya, of course). Apparently named the Nilgiris (Blue Mountains) by local tribal people nearly 1000 years ago because of its proclivity for blue haze, it consists of 2542 sq km of rolling hills; forests which cover over half of the district, gentle and steep slopes, intriguing tribal cultures, tea plantations, lakes, and opportunities for trekking and other outdoor activities. But don't let your experiences of the capital of Ooty, and the other so-called 'hill stations', Coonoor and Kotagiri, put you off – head out into the hills as soon as you can.

TAMIL NADU

The best time to visit is winter (November to February). Try to avoid the very heavy monsoons from June to October, when about 2.5 *metres* of rain falls, and summer (March to May), when the district is chock-a-block with tourists, stretching accommodation and other facilities to breaking point.

HISTORY

The region now known as the Nilgiris featured in ancient Indian literature and its inhabitants are believed to have traded with Asian empires as far back as 3000 BC. The Nilgiris was partially ruled by the Ganga Empire in the 8th century, the Hoysalas from the first half of the 12th century and the Ummaturs in the 15th century. The area was controlled by Tipu Sultan in the late 18th century, and his quarrelling sons handed it over to the British East India Company in the early 19th century. The British, who first inhabited Coonoor and

Kotagiri, grew tea in the district from 1853. The Nilgiris has since become a favourite holiday destination for well-to-do folk from Coimbatore, Mysore and Chennai.

FLORA & FAUNA

The Nilgiris is home to ancient shola evergreen moist and mixed deciduous and southern montane forests, as well as teak trees and swamps. Cinnamon trees, orchids, rhododendron shrubs and tea plantations dot the countryside, and an extraordinary array of plants and flowers – about 40% of all Indian plant species – can be found around here.

The Nilgiris boasts an impressive array of wildlife, such as gaur; mouse deer, barking deer and sambar; four-horned antelopes; bonnet macaques; common langur; Malabar flying squirrels; rusty-spotted cats; and endangered Nilgiri tahr (see the boxed text). A small number of panthers, elephants and

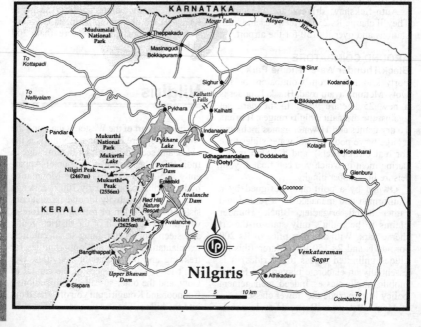

tigers inhabit pockets of Mukurthi and Mudumalai national parks. The birdlife is vast and diverse: there are cormorants, pipits, thrushes and parakeets, as well as the endemic Nilgiri verditer, Tickell's flowerpeckers and Nilgiri skylarks. Reptiles include the Nilgiri pet-viper and the King Cobra; you may also see tortoises waddling across forest paths. Some of the local fish include rainbow trout, mahseer (though not quite as big as they are in Kodagu), and Carnatic carp.

ENVIRONMENT

The environmental degradation in the Nilgiris is distressing. The capital, Ooty, is a mess, which can no longer cope with its permanent population, let alone the colossal influx of tourists each year. In the countryside, some areas have been completely deforested; smuggling of teak and poaching of tigers and elephants continue, sometimes with the connivance of forest rangers; profitable tea plantations expand indiscriminately; dams are constantly being built (there are 20 in this small district alone); unlicensed mines spring up; and there is unrestrained film production in fragile environments.

To find out how you can help, contact the following organisations in Ooty:

Hill Area Development Programme
   (☎ 43805) is a few hundred metres past the Wildlife Warden's Office. The HADP aims to 'conserve the fragile hill ecosystem' through reforestation and other conservation programs.
Nilgiri Wildlife & Environment Association
   (☎ 43968), located in a small room in the building of the District Forest Officer (North). The NWEA has a small, useful library, publishes the *Tahr* newsletter, and organises trekking for local members – but not for foreigners.
Save Nilgiris Campaign
   (☎ 43082), which produces *A Greenprint for the Nilgiris.*

BOOKS & MAPS

Try to pick up the pocket-sized booklet, *The Nilgiris* (Rs 30), compiled by the Save Nilgiris Campaign. It is a readable summary of local history, culture and attractions, and is available in Ooty. The best study about the

The Nilgiri Tahr

The Nilgiri tahr *(Hemitragus hylocrius)* is related to tahrs found in the mountains of the Himalaya and higher parts of Iran. There are only about 2000 left in the world, and 200 of them live in the Nilgiris.

Extremely shy and easily frightened, the slightest sound can result in the tahr having a heart attack, or blindly running into a vehicle or off the edge of a cliff. While technically only forest rangers and researchers are allowed into core areas of reserves which protect tahrs, such as the Mukurthi National Park in the Nilgiris, cacophonous Indian musicals are often filmed in the area!

fascinating tribal culture is *Blue Mountains Revisited*, edited by the renowned 'nilgirologist', Paul Hockings, and also available in Ooty. The *Downtown Chronicle* (Rs 10) is 'The Weekly News Magazine of the Nilgiris'. It provides the best rundown of local environmental and cultural issues, and is available in most bookshops in Ooty.

Few maps of the Nilgiris are available but the map in this guidebook should be adequate for most visitors. The Shikar Map, available at the NWEA (see the Environment section, above) is colourful and detailed, but the one from the Survey Department in Ooty is the best (see the Trekking in the Nilgiris section at the end of this chapter).

Hill Tribe Traditions

The **Toda** tribe is the oldest, highest in social hierarchy and the smallest in number of the Nilgiri hill tribes. This tribal group is distinguished by their polyandry (women can have more than one husband); distinct language; child-marriages (often at the age of two); stigma-free divorce; and cremation rituals involving the killing of buffaloes. Their social, economic and spiritual system traditionally centres on the buffalo. The buffalo and its dairy produce were all-important to the Todas, being integral to their diet, and used as currency in trade with other tribes. In exchange for buffalo produce the Todas would receive grain, tools, pots and even medical services. It was only at funeral rituals that the strictly vegetarian Todas would kill a buffalo – to provide company for the deceased. Even today, the Todas believe that the soul of the dead buffalo accompanies the soul of the deceased to heaven and that the buffalo will continue to provide milk in heaven. Milk can only be collected by sacred dairymen; buffaloes must never be touched by females. No Toda departs this earth without the most intricately embroidered shawl (see the boxed text 'Toda Shawls').

The **Badagas** are not strictly regarded as tribal people, having migrated to the Nilgiris in the wake of 15th-century Muslim invasions in the North. They brought with them communication skills and agricultural techniques, and are probably the most prosperous and numerous of the hill peoples. Their knowledge of those outside the hills enabled the Badagas to be effective representatives for the hill tribes, especially for the Todas. They often acted as referees in Toda altercations. Their agricultural produce, particularly grain, added a further dimension to the hill diet. In return they received buffalo products from the Todas. Their traditional dress is a white tunic, with a red or black shawl, and they speak a mixture of Tamil and Kannada.

The **Kota** settlements were intermingled between those of the Todas and Badagas. Considered by other tribes to be lower in status, they never entered Toda settlements, nor did the Todas

OUTDOOR ACTIVITIES
Climbing
Doddabetta The highest mountain in the Nilgiris is Doddabetta, or Big Mountain (2638m), about 10km from Ooty. It's not quite a 'mountain trek': there's a paved road to the top, where there's a telescope and a restaurant selling decent food and welcome cold drinks. There are hordes of day-trippers here, but no permit or guide is needed.

You can either walk up or down (your knees will appreciate it if you walk down), by following the Kodappamund road. On the way down from Doddabetta, ask someone official for directions to the picturesque path leading to Snowdon Peak (about 3km from Doddabetta), which offers more great views.

From Ooty, there are buses to the top of Doddabetta about every 90 minutes.

Kolari Betta Kolari Betta (2625m) is best approached from Avalanche (three to four

hours one way), but the trail is very steep at times. The peak is in the vaguely defined 'buffer zone' of the Mukurthi National Park, so you may be able to climb the peak, with permission and a guide from the WWO in Ooty.

Mukurthi Peak At the time of research, trekking in the core area of Mukurthi National Park, including Mukurthi Peak (2556m) was not allowed by the WWO in Ooty, but the following information is included in the hope that the peak will become accessible to genuine, and eco-friendly, trekkers in the future. Avoid the rain and high winds in the monsoon season (July-September), and the possible bushfires (November-February).

The various ways to the top are:

• start at any part of Portimund Dam, which is accessible by road from Ooty. From there, it's enter theirs. The Kotas are the artisans of the hill tribes: once renowned as potters, they're now better known as blacksmiths and musicians, performing especially at funerals. Due to the belief that Kota presence within the sacred space of the Toda dairy was a contaminant, Kota/Toda relations occurred outside their settlements, in neutral territory. Kota people still undertake elaborate rain-making ceremonies, in which the gods are beseeched for the monsoon. Kota men wear distinctive costumes, including a bright red cloth, during festivals; and the women have a fair say in agricultural, social, religious and domestic matters. The Kotas speak a separate dialect, comprehensible to the Todas, and worship unique deities.

The **Kurumbas** traditionally gathered products such as fruit and plants, a portion of which were supplied to the other tribes. Like all the tribes, they had secondary activities, including a little agriculture. At sowing and harvesting times, they sought the services of the Badagas, who performed rituals to secure generous yields. The Kurumbas were feared yet respected by the other tribes for their practise of witchcraft. Their services were often sought for protection from the elements and to cure illness. Unusual Karumba customs include burying the dead in a sitting position and body-piercing of children at an early age. Today the Kurumbas are predominantly labourers, and are the lowest in the contemporary social hierarchy.

The **Irulus** traditionally produced tools and gathered forest products which they converted into brooms and incense. As devotees of Vishnu they performed rituals for other tribes. Some still do this at the Rangaswami Temple, 20km north-east of Kotagiri. The Irulas are the largest tribal group in the hills (about 7000), but are low in the social hierarchy, subservient to the Todas and Badagas. The Irulas worship Vishnu, have complicated eating customs (especially during pregnancy) and unique medicinal practices, such as treating snakebite with a piece of copper. They have various religious, medicinal and domestic uses for leaves, a skill which has been of particular interest to ethnologists.

about six hours to the peak. You may be able to stay at huts near Mukurthi Lake owned by the WWO or the Nilgiri Wildlife & Environment Association in Ooty (but these are normally for members only).

- from Pandiar, the route takes about five hours, via Mukurthi Lake, and you will also need permission from the DFO (South) in Ooty.
- take a three day trek organised by Clipper Holidays for US$115 per person, all-inclusive (except transport).
- organise everything with the Red Hill Nature Resort (see under Emerald Dam in the Around Ooty section), which claims to somehow get permits when others often fail.

Nilgiri Peak A visit to Nilgiri Peak (2467m) can be combined with your Mukurthi Peak climbs, though most local trekkers used to concentrate mostly on Mukurthi. This is all academic, however, until the WWO opens this part of the Mukurthi National Park to trekkers.

Other Activities

Other leisure and adventure activities in the Nilgiris include:

Fishing
Rod or fly fishing for carp and trout is possible, with permission, at: Avalanche Dam, Emerald Dam, Ooty Lake, Upper Bhavani, Parsons Valley and Pykhara Lake. Contact the Assistant Director of Fisheries (☎ 43946), in Fishdale, not far from the bus stand in Ooty – the Assistant Director also has equipment for hire.

Paragliding
The Nilgiris is renowned for aerial sports such as hang-gliding, paragliding and parachuting. Some of the agencies listed in the Outdoor Activities around Bangalore section (see the Karnataka chapter) can arrange these activities; or contact Albatross Flying Systems (☎ 2313 or ☎ 2810), based at the 'Catwalk' shop opposite the Tandoor Mahal in Ooty. Most of the activities are located around Kalhatti. The best season is from October to March, though training courses are often held

TAMIL NADU

from March to May to coincide with the tourist season.

Rock Climbing

This is particularly good in Parsons Valley (see that section for more details). You can organise rock climbing with most agencies listed in the upcoming trekking section, or with the Youth Hostel or Sylvan Retreats & Trails in Chennai (see the Activities section in the Chennai chapter).

Trekking

Refer to the special Trekking in the Nilgiris section at the end of this chapter for details.

COONOOR
Pop: 48,000   Tel Area Code: 0423

Surrounded by tea plantations, and at an altitude of 1850m, Coonoor is the first of the three Nilgiri hill stations – Udhagamandalam (Ooty), Kotagiri and Coonoor – that you come to when leaving behind the southern plains. Like Ooty, it's on the toy train line from Mettupalayam.

Coonoor is now a bustling town where the tenacious touts, even in low season, can be overwhelming. The town appears rather squashed between the hills, and it's only after climbing up out of the busy market area with the bus and train terminals that you'll get a sense of what hill stations were originally all about. For this reason, most of the better accommodation is in Upper Coonoor.

Sim's Park

Located in Upper Coonoor and named after a former member of the Governor General's Council, this park was inaugurated in 1874. It covers 12 hectares and contains over 1000 plant species as well as many monkeys highly skilled in human interaction – watch your lunch and all your valuables. Locals carry sticks to ward them off! Magnolia, tree ferns, pines and camellia combine to make this a pleasant place to while away some time. Paths meander down to a rose garden which surrounds a lotus pond.

A fruit and vegetable show is held each May. The park is open every day from 8 am to 6.30 pm and entrance fees are Rs 5/2 for adults/children and Rs 5/25 for still camera/video.

Blue Mountain Railway

The Blue Mountain Railway was originally funded by the citizens and coffee planters of the Nilgiris. It took seven years to build, finishing in 1898. The final link was completed to Ooty 10 years later, but the railway was immediately damaged in a cyclone. Along the 45km track, there are 13 tunnels, 19 bridges and 11 stations (though not all stations may be functioning).

Quite different to the toy trains found in places like Shimla and Darjeeling in northern India, the Blue Mountain's train has a unique pinion rack system, with the locomotive pushing, rather than pulling, the carriages. Each of the three carriages has its own brakeman, who sits on a little platform and, when appropriate, waves a red or green flag.

The views of the Nilgiris (best from the left on the way up to Ooty) are spectacular, though the railway is far slower than taking the road. The train is often cancelled during or after the monsoons, and although four new locomotives have been ordered from Switzerland, the cost is prohibitive, so the future for the Blue Mountain Railway may be a bleak one.

For information on schedules, see the Getting There & Away section under Ooty leter in this chapter.

Pasteur Institute

Right opposite Sim's Park, this institute is famous for its research on treatment for rabies and production of polio vaccine. The institute was established following the death from rabies of a British colonial in 1902. A rabies vaccine had not been readily available for her treatment. Since its inception the institute has undertaken several innovative projects, especially in the area of rabies research. It also supplies vaccines for national immunisations.

Dolphin's Nose

This viewpoint is 10km from the town. The narrow road to it winds through dense forest and tea plantations, which reach deep into the valleys and are dotted with tea pickers and the occasional brightly painted shrine. From the viewpoint you enjoy a vast panorama, in which Kotagiri township and the Catherine Falls can be seen. Except for the few offers of cardamom tea, the only sound is the water crashing over the rocks in the valley floor. Regular buses leave from the bus stand.

Lamb's Rock

Some 8km from Coonoor, and on the way to Dolphin's Nose, this viewpoint is another place from which to appreciate stunning views. At the end of the road take the stone stairs to the top. You will easily find your way, so decline the persistent offers (and expense) of the guide. Regular buses leave from the bus stand.

Places to Stay & Eat

YWCA Guesthouse (☎ *34426*) in Upper Coonoor is the best budget option but it's often full: phone in advance. Open to men and women, it's a handsome old colonial house with two wooden terraces and views over Coonoor. Large, clean singles/doubles with bathroom cost Rs 190/350. There's hot water and basic food is available. To get there, take a town bus to Bedford from where it is a five minute walk.

Vivek Tourist Home (☎ *30658*), nearby, is a reasonable place. There are rooms from Rs 190/250 with attached bath, more for deluxe rooms with TV.

Sri Lakshmi Tourist Home (☎ *31022*) offers basic rooms for Rs 150/200.

Blue Hills (☎ *30103, Mount Rd*) has a good nonveg restaurant; there are also rooms here for Rs 150/300 with attached bathroom.

Hotel Tamilnadu (☎ *22813, Mount Pleasant Rd*) is OK with doubles from Rs 200/300 in the low/high season.

Taj Garden Retreat (☎ *30021*), on the hilltop, is an excellent hotel with a beautiful garden and a fine restaurant. The rooms are in cottages and cost from US$70/80 in the low season, and from US$110/120 in the high season.

(doubles only with all meals) in the high season.

Ramachandra Restaurant (*32 Mount Rd*) has very good veg and nonveg food from Rs 10. Thalis are Rs 15 and breads Rs 0.60.

Getting There & Away

Coonoor is on the toy train line between Mettupalayam (28km) and Ooty (18km) – for details see the Ooty Getting There & Away section. Buses to Kotagiri (Rs 8) leave every 15 minutes.

KOTAGIRI
Pop: 25,600 Tel Area Code: 0423

Kotagiri (Line of Houses of the Kotas) is a small, quiet village about 28km east of Ooty, at an altitude of 1950m. The oldest of the three Nilgiri hill stations, the British started building houses here in 1819. The town is dusty and uninspiring but it is not as frenetic as Ooty or Coonoor. Life is now concentrated around tea plantations, and the road from Ooty winds along hills denuded of their original cover in favour of the bright green of the tea leaves and regular Kota settlements.

From Kotagiri you can visit **Catherine Falls**, 8km away near the Mettupalayam road (the last 3km by foot only), **Elk Falls** (6km) and **Kodanad Viewpoint** (22km), where there is a panoramic view over the Coimbatore Plains, the Mysore Plateau and the eastern slopes of the Nilgiris. There is a bus to this viewpoint but its timing is somewhat erratic. A taxi will charge around Rs 200 for the return journey.

In town, there's a Women's Cooperative near Ramchand Square which sells local handicrafts including traditional Toda embroidery. A proportion of sales revenue is donated towards the welfare of the Toda people and the preservation of their culture.

Places to Stay & Eat

The wonderfully located Queenshill Guesthouse no longer accommodates tourists (it's a home for disabled children). There are a few very basic lodges in town such as the *Majestic Lodge*, the *Blue Star* and the

Hotel Ramesh Vihar. You are advised to bring your own sheets. In all, double rooms with attached bathroom start at around Rs 120. Until better accommodation is established, it is preferable to visit Kotagiri as a day trip from Ooty. There are several 'meals' restaurants. The vegetarian *Kasturi Paradise Restaurant*, diagonally opposite the Women's Cooperative, is good value. The uthappams are large and particularly tasty.

Getting There & Away

Buses stop at the edge of town, approximately 1km from the centre. From there you walk or get a taxi. Buses journey to Ooty every 40 minutes (crossing one of Tamil Nadu's highest passes) and cost Rs 10. The trip takes almost two hours. Buses to Mettupalayam leave every 30 minutes and to Coonoor every 15 minutes.

UDHAGAMANDALAM (Ooty)
Pop: 89,000 Tel Area Code: 0423

This famous hill station was founded by the British in the early part of the 19th century to serve as the summer headquarters of the Madras government. Before that time, the area was inhabited by the Todas, the tribal people whose belief systems and practices centre on the buffalo. Today only about 1500 Todas remain. You can see their shrines in various places throughout the hills.

Until about two decades ago, Ooty (altitude 2240m) resembled an unlikely combination of southern England and Australia: single-storey stone cottages, bijou fenced flower gardens, leafy, winding lanes, and tall eucalyptus stands covering the otherwise barren hilltops. The other main reminders of the British period are the stone churches, the private schools, the Ooty Club, and the terraced botanical gardens. Maharaja summer palaces hark back to yet another time.

But while parts of Ooty still exude a fading atmosphere of leafy seclusion, especially on the lake's western and southern margins, elsewhere hoteliers and real estate developers and the influx of tourist hordes

with their city habits have totally transformed it. The sewerage system is incapable of dealing with the demand placed on it. It's important to remember, should you be thinking of boating, that all this untreated filth flows directly into the lake.

In spite of this, Ooty retains a certain appeal. Life is relaxed here and the touting and haranguing, so prevalent in other areas, are much less a problem, particularly in the low season. Just a kilometre or two out of the town you are in the peace and comfort of the hills, with their superb views and welcome silence. You can find accommodation which takes advantages of these aspects. You can even stay in one of the former palaces. Ooty's a great place to escape to, particularly when the plains below are unbearably hot. The journey up on the toy train is stunning. In the winter months and during the monsoon you will need warm clothing as the overnight temperature occasionally drops to 0°C.

History

Ooty was the first established hill station in India. Before European settlement the Ooty area was predominantly Toda territory. Other tribal groups occupied some of the outlying regions. While there was interaction between the tribes each group retained its own language, customs and settlements (see the boxed text).

Over the centuries the region came under the jurisdiction of various regimes including the Hoysala rulers in the 12th century, the Vijayanagaras in the 16th century and Tipu Sultan (the Muslim ruler of Mysore) in the 17th century.

In the early 17th century (1603) the first European visited Ooty. He was a Jesuit priest named Giacome Fenicio. He spent much time documenting aspects of the tribal groups around the hills and his early accounts have proved valuable material for greater understanding and subsequent scholarship.

By the 19th century the Nilgiris came under British administration. Surveyors were sent in to map the region and assess the 'fiscal and commercial state of the British territory'.

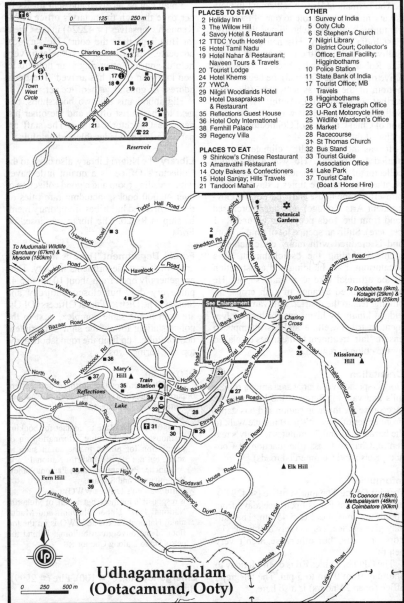

PLACES TO STAY
2 Holiday Inn
3 The Willow Hill
4 Savoy Hotel & Restaurant
12 TTDC Youth Hostel
16 Hotel Tamil Nadu
19 Hotel Nahar & Restaurant;
   Naveen Tours & Travels
20 Tourist Lodge
24 Hotel Khems
27 YWCA
29 Nilgiri Woodlands Hotel
30 Hotel Dasaprakash
   & Restaurant
35 Reflections Guest House
36 Hotel Ooty International
38 Fernhill Palace
39 Regency Villa

PLACES TO EAT
9 Shinkow's Chinese Restaurant
13 Amaravathi Restaurant
14 Ooty Bakers & Confectioners
15 Hotel Sanjay; Hills Travels
21 Tandoori Mahal

OTHER
1 Survey of India
5 Ooty Club
6 St Stephen's Church
7 Nilgiri Library
8 District Court; Collector's
   Office; Email Facility;
   Higginbothams
10 Police Station
11 State Bank of India
17 Tourist Office; MB
   Travels
18 Higginbothams
22 GPO & Telegraph Office
23 U-Rent Motorcycle Hire
25 Wildlife Wardenn's Office
26 Market
28 Racecourse
31 St Thomas Church
32 Bus Stand
33 Tourist Guide
   Association Office
34 Lake Park
37 Tourist Cafe
   (Boat & Horse Hire)

Udhagamandalam
(Ootacamund, Ooty)

0   250   500 m

The permanent British settlement in Ooty is very much attributable to one of those adventurous characters who joined the British East India Company. His name was John Sullivan. He joined the company at 15 and like Robert Clive (who became known as Clive of India, see Chennai), he began at the bottom of the heap as a 'writer' (the transcriber of accounts). Within a decade Sullivan had worked his way up to the position of Chief Collector of Coimbatore, which included the Nilgiris.

It was the cool healthy climate that appealed to Sullivan. He was a fastidious collector of meteorological data, recording weather patterns five times a day. He built himself a stone house (now part of the Government Arts College) and later purchased land from the Toda people (at around Rs 1 per acre). Sullivan spent a lot of time in Ooty and is credited with many civic achievements including the establishment of a sanatorium, road building and construction of the artificial lake as a water supply. He also introduced a range of cash crops, including tea, to the district. Sullivan has been judged kindly by historians for his involvement in tribal welfare and his attempts to ensure 'fair' treatment to the tribes displaced by the colonial regime.

Orientation

Ooty is spread over a large area among rolling hills and valleys. Between the lake and the racecourse are the train station and bus stand. From either of these it's a 10 minute walk to the bazaar area and 20 minutes to Ooty's real centre, Charing Cross (the junction of Coonoor, Kelso and Commercial roads).

Information

Tourist Office The tourist office (☎ 43977), on Commercial Rd, is open weekdays from 10 am to 1 pm and 2 to 5.45 pm. The staff may give out leaflets on Ooty and book visitors on tours, but otherwise aren't very helpful.

The GPO in Ettines Rd is open Monday to Saturday from 9 am to 5 pm. The telegraph office (open 24 hours) is also here.

Email can be received and sent for Rs 15 per page through the notary's office of Mr Kenneth Gonsalves (☎ 42224) in the Oriental Buildings near the court. He's a local advocate. His assistant, Mrs Xavier, is very helpful and will even ring your hotel to let you know an email has arrived. The email address is: gonslaw@theoffice.net.

Higginbothams has two bookshops: one next to the tourist office and the other just near the Collector's Office. The staff are particularly knowledgeable and helpful.

Library The Nilgiri Library, also close to the Collector's Office, is a quaint little haven with a reading room and a good collection of over 40,000 books, including rare titles on the Nilgiris and hill tribes. Temporary membership is Rs 20. The library is closed on Friday.

Forest Department There is a confusing array of 'forest' departments in Ooty. They are generally open from about 10 am to 5.45 pm every day, but closed Saturday and Sunday. The District Forest Officers (DFOs) are both in the same complex, next to the police station; follow the sign 'Superintendent of Police' up from the roundabout at the top of Charing Cross.

DFO (North)
(☎ 43968) covers the northern and eastern parts of the Nilgiris district, such as Coonoor, Kotagiri and Doddabetta.
DFO (South)
(☎ 44083) is the place to contact for booking resthouses and obtaining information on or permission for places in the south such as some, but not all, of Mukurthi National Park, Avalanche, Pykhara, Pandiar, Parsons Valley, Bangithappal and Sispara.
Wildlife Warden's Office (WWO)
is responsible for most, but not all, of Mukurthi National Park, Upper Bhavani, and Mudumalai National Park. The WWO is on the top floor of the olive-green building, behind the petrol station, along Coonor Rd.

Emergency Police (☎ 100), Fire (☎ 2999), Hospital (☎ 2212).

Outdoor Activities

Ooty is the place for outdoor activities. For walks see the section Around Ooty which follows. If you want a guide for walks around Ooty, you may like to contact the Ooty Tourist Guides Association. This is a nongovernment organisation and the 49 guides who claim membership have received specific training (funded by the government) in hospitality as well as knowledge of the area. The guides wear an informal uniform of a blue shirt and black trousers and they are meant to carry identity cards bearing their name, photograph and the name of the association.

The Ooty Tourist Guides Association maintains a small office opposite the bus stand. It's open every day from 7 am to 11 pm. There is no telephone at the office but you can ring the kiosk next door on ☎ 45222. The price of the guides is negotiable (around Rs 200 per day, extra if you want overnight stays).

Horse Riding Alone or with a guide, there are two choices. You can hire horses at the Tourist Cafe on the north side of the lake. The rides from here mostly consist of a circuit (up to one hour) of the lake area. Choose your animal carefully; some of these horses have clearly seen better years. Prices vary depending on season, size of the horse and mood of the guide, so haggle hard. A fair price is about Rs 100 an hour.

If you want more serious riding, horses can be booked from the reception of the Regency Villa. Each morning a pony man arrives with sturdy and spirited animals that will take you on a three hour trek through rolling hills and into a Toda village. The ride is exhilarating (not for beginners) and costs Rs 125 per hour. However, the encounter with the tribal people smacks of a beads and trinkets mentality.

Boating Rowboats can be rented from the Tourist Cafe by the lake. In the low season this is a most pleasant and peaceful way to while away time although the water is becoming heavily polluted. High season crowds can make boating somewhat tortu-

ous. Boats are available per half hour and prices start from Rs 40 for a two-seater pedal boat up to Rs 200 for a 15 seater motor boat. A deposit of Rs 60 is payable on most boats and the time period is calculated from when you purchase your ticket to when you receive your deposit so learn to be pushy! If you're stuck in a queue for more than five minutes, they'll try and sting you for an extra half hour. The best of the many entertaining signs warns people to 'Avoid dancing on the boats'.

Horse Races The season for the Ooty horse races begins on April 14 and lasts till about June. The racecourse may be rather tatty and the betting tame, but the season creates considerable entertainment.

Botanical Gardens

Established in 1848, the 22 hectares of beautifully maintained gardens include numerous mature species as well as an Italian and a Japanese garden. There is also a fossil tree trunk believed to be 20 million years old. It was the Marquis of Tweeddale who initially planned the gardens. Further development occurred under the direction of WG Ivor, a well-known horticulturist from the famous Kew Gardens in England.

The gardens have played a pivotal role in horticultural research. Each year, in the third weekend in May, the gardens host a flower show that draws visitors from around the country.

At the eastern end of the gardens is a Toda *mund* (hill) where Toda people display aspects of their traditional culture to the gawking tourists. This is now a highly commercialised show (described by one Toda activist as a human zoo). It is far removed from the reality of Toda villages deeper into the Nilgiris. The gardens are open from 8 am to 6.45 pm. Entry for children/adults is Rs 2/5. A camera is Rs 25 and a video is an astounding Rs 500.

St Stephen's Church

St Stephen's Church, on the hill in Club Rd, stands and surveys the environs of Ooty

TAMIL NADU

below. Built in 1829 and consecrated in 1830, St Stephen's is the oldest church in the Nilgiris. Its huge wooden beams came from the palace of Tipu Sultan in Srirangapatnam – hauled the 120km distance by a team of elephants. It's a quiet, peaceful place, and the attached cemetery contains the graves of many an Ooty pioneer, including John Sullivan, the founder of Ooty.

Organised Tours

The tourist office organises a couple of tours. You can go to the Mudumalai Wildlife Sanctuary via the Pykhara Dam for Rs 150 (plus Rs 30 entrance to the park) or to Coonoor taking in the Botanical Gardens, Doddabetta, Sim's Park and Dolphin's Nose for Rs 90. Naveen Tours & Travels (☎ 43747), near Hotel Nahar, and Hills Travels (☎ 42090), at Hotel Sanjay, are among several private operators who run a range of tours.

MB Travels (☎ 42604; fax 44912), adjacent to the tourist office, can organise a range of tours including camping, fishing and walking. This is also the place to go for airline reservations and confirmations.

Places to Stay

Since Ooty is a sellers' market in the high season (1 April to 15 June), hoteliers double their prices during this time. This is clearly a rip-off since prices don't necessarily equate with quality, but there are few options. Note that many hotels are fully booked in the high season and that the checkout time (usually 24 hours at hotels elsewhere) can be as early as 9 am.

If you stay in the town you'll be close to all the amenities, the noise and the pollution. Just a few kilometres out, you'll be able to enjoy the peace and solitude of the hills as well as the stunning views. As in Kodaikanal, many places have carpet which carry an olfactory history!

Places to Stay – Budget

TTDC Youth Hostel (☎ 43665, Charing Cross) offers dorm beds at Rs 80, and doubles for Rs 200/420 in the low/high season.

YWCA (☎ 42218, Ettines Rd) is reasonable value but it's often full. A dorm bed costs Rs 77 and doubles with attached bathrooms are

---

Toda Shawls

Known as the *puthikuzhi*, the traditional Toda shawl assumes a significant role in Toda culture. Embroidered exclusively by women, the shawls are made of thick white cotton about 2m by 1.5m. A large pocket is stitched into each shawl. According to anthropologists, the Todas have never engaged in the process of weaving cloth. Their tradition has been to purchase the plain cloth from the market and to dedicate many hours to embroidering the distinctive black and red designs. Although many Todas are now completely integrated into mainstream Indian society, the tradition of embroidering cloth continues in Toda villages.

The shawls are worn by both men and women (though much less often by men) and they serve many purposes. A basic shawl is for everyday use around the village. The thickness of the cloth shields against the morning and evening chill in the mountains. The same shawl may be worn in many different ways depending on the occasion. Sometimes the stripes are worn vertically, other times horizontally. On formal occasions, the shawl covers the head as well as the body. More intricate shawls are stitched for significant occasions such as weddings and births. However, the best quality shawls are reserved for funerals. During the complex rituals of a traditional Toda funeral the finest shawl is hung outside the hut where the corpse lies. Mourners touch the shawl with their forehead as they enter the hut. At a certain point in the ceremony, the shawl is taken inside the hut. A handful of leaves is placed into the pocket, and the shawl is then wrapped carefully around the corpse. For the Toda people, the shawl offers protection and security in the next life.

Rs 250 (low season) and Rs 325 (high season). There are also some quiet cottages with private bathroom which are a little cheaper and worth booking ahead. Three-course veg meals are available (Rs 65) and there is a lounge with an open fire in winter. The YWCA isn't a bad place to stay if you want to organise any trekking.

Reflections Guest House (☎ 43834, North Lake Rd) is an enjoyable place with good views over the lake and doubles at Rs 200 (Rs 300 in the high season). There are only six rooms, but all have hot water and the atmosphere is home-style. Good breakfasts and a range of snacks can be brought to your room or are served on the grassy terrace. The friendly owner, Mrs Dique, is a good source of information on the region's history.

Tourist Lodge (☎ 44357, Walsham Rd, off Commercial Rd) is cheap and very clean. Singles and doubles are Rs 100 in the low season and up to Rs 200 in season. Each room has an attached bathroom and some have a balcony overlooking an interesting streetscape. Bucket hot water is available in the morning.

Places to Stay – Mid-Range

Hotel Tamil Nadu (☎ 44370; fax 44369), on the hill above the tourist office, is a good place in this range. Set in a largish garden, doubles with attached bathroom cost Rs 400/750 in the low/high season, plus Rs 50 for a TV. Cottages are available for Rs 450/800. There's a restaurant, coffee shop and bar.

Hotel Ooty International (☎ 44423, Woodcock Rd) is about 3km from the train station and has double rooms, all with phone, from Rs 420/850 in the low/high season.

Hotel Khems (☎ 44188, Shoreham Palace Rd) is very well appointed and good value. Standard/superior doubles are Rs 500/700 (low season) and Rs 850/975 (high season). The hotel has its own restaurant. Hot water is available for three hours in the morning and evening.

Nilgiri Woodlands Hotel (☎ 42551; fax 42530, Ettines Rd) is a Raj-era hotel. Manicured gardens (with tables and chairs) offer

great views of Ooty and the dining room is cosy. All the rooms are clean but the plumbing is due for retirement. Some rooms are in the main building, and a number of detached cottages are also available. In the low season, doubles with attached bathroom cost Rs 300, cottages are Rs 550 and suites Rs 650. In the high season they range from Rs 450 to Rs 1000.

Hotel Dasaprakash (☎ 42434) is another long-established hotel, and reasonable value. Doubles with attached bathroom range from Rs 170 to Rs 460 in the low season; Rs 300 to Rs 640 in the high season.

Regency Villa (☎ 42555) is owned by the Maharaja of Mysore. Set within eight wooded hectares (along with Fernhill Palace) it is a wonderfully atmospheric place to stay, although it's getting a little shabby around the edges. There are potted plants, wicker chairs and faded photographs of the Ooty Hunt, a popular pastime of the Raj.

The best rooms are ultra spacious and have bay windows, fully tiled Victorian bathrooms (with hot water) and a sitting corner by an open fire. The manager, Mr Smith, and his staff are knowledgeable and amiable, and simple meals can be arranged in advance. In the main building doubles cost Rs 550 to Rs 900; in the cottage they're Rs 250 to Rs 550. Budget rooms, Rs 150 for doubles, are particularly good value. Prices apply to both high and low season.

Hotel Nahar (☎ 42173; fax 45173) is a huge place at Charing Cross. Carpeted doubles with attached bathroom and TV cost from Rs 600 to Rs 1000 (low season), and Rs 800 to Rs 1350 (high season). It is a 'teetotaller's paradise' and has a restaurant with multicuisine meals.

Places to Stay – Top End

Savoy Hotel (☎ 44142; fax 43318, 77 Sylks Rd) is very comfortable. Part of the Taj Group, this place has doubles for US$85 in the low season and US$130 in the high season. It has manicured lawns, clipped hedges, rooms with bathtubs, wooden furnishings, working fireplaces, a 24 hour bar and an excellent multicuisine dining room.

Fernhill Palace (☎ 43910) is still closed for renovations. Owned by the Maharaja of Mysore and managed by the Taj Group, it was built in the days when expense was of no concern and master artisans didn't command fortunes. For a small tip, the security guards will show you through the extensive ballroom. When it finally reopens (current plans are for October 1998) its prices will be similar to the Savoy and it'll probably be the best place to stay in Ooty.

The Willow Hill (☎ 42686; fax 42686, 58/1 Havelock Rd) is 3km from the station and has doubles (only) from Rs 720 to Rs 1050 and in the season from Rs 820 to Rs 1150. Suites start from Rs 1950. Most rooms have wooden floors and fine views. You can eat out on the manicured lawns or in the restaurant where (among other things) you'll be served vegetables and herbs fresh from the hotel garden.

Holiday Inn (☎ 42955) has doubles for US$70 and suites for US$158 (both seasons). It has all the facilities of a top-class hotel, including a bar, spa, gym and drivers' rest rooms.

Places to Eat
Almost all accommodation places have attached restaurants. In addition there are plenty of basic vegetarian 'meals' places on Commercial Rd and Main Bazaar.

Hotel Nahar has two veg restaurants and a popular snack bar serving ice cream and milk shakes.

Hotel Sanjay is a big, bustling place with generous servings of veg and nonveg fare.

Tandoori Mahal (Commercial Rd) has tasty veg dishes for around Rs 35 and nonveg meals for around Rs 50. The service is good, and beer – not always cold – is available (Rs 65).

Shinkow's Chinese Restaurant (also known as the Zodiac Room) at 30 Commissioner's Rd has some really good food. It's run by a Chinese family so its dishes (around Rs 50) are fairly authentic.

Hotel Dasaprakash is well known for its lunch thalis for Rs 30. People crowd in, sit in ashram-style rows and are fed huge quantities of delicious thali items.

Amaravathi, opposite the Youth Hostel, is very popular for its veg and nonveg dishes.

Savoy Hotel is the place for a splurge. Buffet lunch or dinner costs Rs 300 (plus tax) for all you can eat. The dining room is particularly atmospheric with a roaring fire that takes the chill off the cool low season nights.

Ooty Bakers & Confectioners, in the Wren Building, Charing Cross, is well worth a visit. The truly gastronomical range includes more than 20 varieties of bread, 50 types of pastry and 35 different pies (veg and nonveg). It also has croissants, strudel, eclairs and cookies.

Hot Breads is a great new place above the bakery. Small pizzas, and hot dogs cost around Rs 30 each.

Entertainment
The cinema, called Assembly Room Theatre, has low-grade but bearable English-language films every afternoon and evening.

Getting There & Away
Air Coimbatore is the closest airport to Ooty. Flight reservations and confirmations for most airlines to domestic and international destinations can be made in Ooty at MB Travels (☎ 42604; fax 44912) adjacent to the tourist office.

Bus The state bus companies all have reservation offices at the bus stand, most open daily from 9 am to 5.30 pm. Since most of the buses at the stand do not advertise their destinations in English, non-Tamil readers will have to ask a lot of questions.

There are six buses daily to Mysore (Rs 50, five hours) and many continue to Bangalore (Rs 100, eight hours). There are buses every 10 minutes to Coimbatore (Rs 18.75, three hours), every 10 to 15 minutes to Mettupalayam (Rs 13, two hours), four buses to Chennai (Rs 118, 15 hours), and also direct services to Kanyakumari (14 hours), Thanjavur (10 hours) and Tirupathi (14 hours).

Most of the private companies are clustered around Charing Cross. Their buses are a little more expensive than the state buses, but worth it.

To get to Mudumalai Wildlife Sanctuary (Rs 20, 67km, 2½ hours), take one of the Mysore buses or one of the small buses which go via the narrow and twisting Sighur Ghat road. Most of these rolling wrecks travel only as far as Masinagudi, from where there are five buses a day to Theppakadu. Buses travelling via the sanctuary sometimes ask passengers for a further Rs 30 which is the park entrance fee. Private services run to Mysore via Theppakadu for Rs 90.

Local buses leave every hour for Kotagiri (Rs 8, one to 1½ hours) and every 20 minutes to Coonoor (Rs 7, one hour). Buses to Doddabetta (Rs 10) depart about every 90 minutes.

Train The miniature railway (see the boxed text 'The Blue Mountain Railway', p 620) is the best way to get here. Departures and arrivals at Mettupalayam usually connect with those of the *Nilgiri Express* which runs between Mettupalayam and Chennai. It departs Chennai at 9 pm and arrives in Mettupalayam at 7.25 am. From Mettupalayam, it leaves at 7.25 pm.

Tickets cost Rs 163/581 in 2nd/1st class. You can catch the *Nilgiri Express* from Coimbatore at 6.25 am where there is a helpful Information Counter on platform 1. If you're catching the miniature train from Ooty, and you want a seat, be early: at least 45 minutes.

The miniature train leaves Mettupalayam for Ooty (Rs 21/150 in 2nd/1st class, 46km) at 7.45 am and arrives in Ooty at noon. From Ooty the train leaves at 3 pm. The trip down takes about 3½ hours.

During the high season, there's an extra departure in each direction daily, from Mettupalayam at 9.10 am and from Ooty at 2 pm. There are also two extra services between Ooty and Coonoor at this time – they leave Ooty daily at 9.30 am and 6 pm.

From Coimbatore there's a superfast train to Chennai (Rs 102/531 2nd/1st, 6½ hours).

The track is sometimes washed out during the monsoon or sudden landslides can occur, disrupting the service.

Getting Around

There are plenty of unmetered auto-rickshaws in Ooty, based outside the bus stand. In the high season, the drivers quote outrageous fares, even between the bus stand and Charing Cross. Haggling might get you around 20% off the first price quoted but nothing more, so it's worth walking. In the low season, fares become more reasonable. Normal taxis are also available.

You can hire a bicycle at the market but many of the roads are steep so you'll end up pushing them uphill (great on the way down though!). Motorcycles can be hired from U-Rent (☎ 4218) in the Hotel Sapphire Buildings on Ettines Rd. A 100cc machine will set you back Rs 360 per 24 hour period. This includes insurance but excludes petrol. A deposit of Rs 500 is required plus a current driving licence (a car licence will suffice). Helmets are not supplied. U-Rent is open from 9 am to 7 pm every day.

AROUND OOTY
Avalanche

Avalanche is a gorgeous area based around the huge Avalanche Dam, also known as Canada Dam, in recognition of funding provided by that country. The area is a perfect place to relax for a day or two, or as a base for **hiking** (see the Trekking section, page 634). **Fishing** in the dam for trout is allowed with a permit from the Wildlife Warden's Office in Ooty. Tiny Avalanche village (named when The Big One fell in 1823) is just a collection of forest rangers' huts, with no shops or hotels.

If you ask directions in the resthouse or village, the **trout farm**, 300m up a path from the village, is worth visiting. Incredibly, the steep slopes either side of the stream through the farm are used by elephants as corridors during their periods of migration.

Places to Stay & Eat

Just up from Avalanche village is a charming *resthouse*, built in 1852, which foreigners are allowed to use. Rooms cost Rs 75, and less salubrious dorm beds cost Rs 20 per person. Book at the DFO (South) in

Ooty. If you have a tent, you are allowed to camp on the grounds, or better, on the edge of the dam nearby. Meals are available at the resthouse.

Getting There & Away

From Ooty to Avalanche (28km), one bus leaves at 11.20 am (Rs 15, 80 minutes). It returns from Avalanche at about 1.30 pm, thereby allowing you about one hour at Avalanche – but it's worth staying longer. Chartering a jeep for a half-day return trip from Ooty costs a negotiable Rs 350, and minimises the damage to your back and neck that you might suffer if you take the bus along this rough road.

Emerald Dam

Also known as India Dam (because funding did not come from a foreign country), Emerald Dam is a charming place for short **hikes** around the lake, or to nearby Toda villages (see the trekking section below). **Fishing** for trout is possible with permission from the Assistant Director of Fisheries (see under Outdoor Activities at the beginning of the Nilgiris section).

Places to Stay The only place to stay is the *Red Hill Nature Resort* (☎ 0423-55754; fax 45117), set majestically in a tea plantation. Service, views and meals are excellent, though not cheap, for Rs 1200/1900 a single/double, including meals. You can pitch a tent on the grounds, and use their facilities, for Rs 500 per night, not including meals. Nearby, you can go for short hikes, longer treks (the managers claim to have access to restricted areas) and watch workers harvesting tea leaves. The resort is closed during the monsoons (mid-June to mid-August).

Getting There & Away From Ooty, buses leave about every 60 to 90 minutes to the village of Emerald, from where you can walk (8km) to the resort (or ring them, and they will collect you). Alternatively, two buses a day leave Ooty (currently, at 6.30 am and 4 pm), and go past the start of the 500m path up to the resort.

Parsons Valley

Parsons Valley is one more gorgeous area of rolling hills, open grasslands and pockets of forests – all wonderfully undisturbed. And, thankfully, tourists are allowed to visit, but for any **rock climbing** or **hiking** off the main road (refer to the Trekking section below), you will need to contact the DFO (South) for permission, and take a guide. However, some guides may decline to accompany you (a few tigers and panthers inhabit the area) or may insist on carrying a weapon and travelling in a vehicle as much as possible. So, be careful.

There is nowhere to stay in the area, and camping is not normally permitted. Buses leave Ooty at 10.15 am, and 12.30, 1.30 and 5 pm, but double-check these times.

MUKURTHI NATIONAL PARK

This small (79 sq km) park is tucked away in the south-west corner of the Nilgiris, and is often referred to as the Nilgiri Tahr Wildlife Sanctuary. It was established in 1982, and is home to several high peaks, such as Kolari Betta (2625m) and Mukurthi (2556m); and about 150 or so Nilgiri tahr. The headquarters of the park is the tiny village of Avalanche (see above). Refer to the Trekking section below for ideas about trekking in the region.

The park was virtually off limits to visitors at the time of research, because the diligent wildlife warden is concerned about potential damage to endangered Nilgiri tahr. This restriction may be lifted or modified, and the park may even be expanded in the future, possibly allowing trekking in the outer 'buffer zone'.

Mukurthi is mainly dry and mixed deciduous forest, and is one of the few areas in the Western Ghats with pristine shola evergreen forest. Sadly, numerous forests have been cut down and replaced with grasslands, resulting in a stark, eerie landscape.

The park is home to giant squirrels; sambar and barking deer; black-naped hares; gaur; wild boar; wild dogs; and some endangered Nilgiri tahr (see the boxed text earlier in this section). You are less likely to see wild elephants, tigers, leopards and jackals – though locals say panthers are not uncommon. Mukurthi also has plenty of kestrels, peacocks, black eagles and jungle fowl.

Visiting the Park
No hiking or camping is allowed, but if you get permission from the WWO (allow seven to 10 days), you and a guide *may* be allowed into the 'buffer zone', but not the core area. This restriction currently includes Mukurthi Peak.

The park is quite cold and wet most of the year, so be prepared: the temperature rarely rises above 20°C in summer, and about 2.5 *metres* of rain falls, mostly between April and August. In winter, mist is very common, and can make trekking difficult. The best time to visit is February to June. The only decent map is on the wall of the WWO office in Ooty.

Places to Stay & Eat
Refer to the Avalanche section above for details about staying at the forest resthouse there. Camping anywhere in the park is not currently allowed.

Getting There & Away
The best place to start an exploration is Avalanche village (see the relevant section earlier). Or you could start at Bangithappal, but buses to/from Ooty are very irregular, so you will probably need to charter a jeep.

MUDUMALAI NATIONAL PARK
Tel Area Code: 0423
On the border with Karnataka, this 322 sq km park forms part of the huge (3000 sq km) Nilgiri Biosphere Reserve (with Wayanad, Bandipur and Nagarhole national parks).

Established in 1932, Mudumalai (which means Ancient Hill Range) is easily accessible from Mysore or Ooty, so it's often overflowing with day-trippers shattering the serenity. The headquarters is the tiny village of Theppakadu in the middle of the park and on the junction of the roads to Masinagudi, Ooty and Mysore. If you come to Mudumalai with few expectations about seeing wildlife, you can still have an enjoyable time.

Orientation & Information
The entrance fee is Rs 5; it's a further Rs 5 for a still camera, and a whopping Rs 500 for a video camera. You pay this at the reception centre (☎ 56325) in Theppakadu village, or at the WWO in Ooty if you are staying overnight at the Forest Department resthouse. The centre is open every day during daylight hours, but only sells tickets for bus tours and elephant rides from 6.30 to 9 am, and 4 to 6 pm. Theppakadu also has a post and telephone office, but little else.

You can only travel around the park on an unsatisfying, 45 minute bus tour (Rs 25) run by the Forest Department. These start at about 7 am and 4 pm, and no advance bookings are possible. You are more likely to see wildlife on a morning tour, but normally only the handful of people staying in, or near, Theppakadu will bother getting up that early to fill a tour; afternoon tours always run, but are full of over-enthusiastic day-trippers. Try to get on the smaller, quieter minibus, rather than the ramshackle green truck.

While you can drive along the main road through the park, it's illegal to use vehicles for private tours. Though you may be approached to go on a private tour at night, you will be overcharged (about Rs 300 per hour per jeep), you probably won't see anything, and you must lie your way through checkpoints. Don't bother.

The best time to see wildlife is late summer (March and April), when the poor beasts struggle to find water and are forced to come closer to roads and settlements. But before you come at this time, make sure the park is open: it may be closed because of bushfires. June to September is OK, as the rains often have limited effect on the park, but the most comfortable time to visit is in winter, November to February.

Flora & Fauna
Mudumalai is mostly tropical dry and moist mixed deciduous forest, with some bamboo, sandalwood and teak. Inside the forests you

Mudumalai Wildlife Sanctuary (Central)

1	Kakkanhalla Checkpoint	11	Mountania Rest House
2	Peacock Dormitory	12	Jungle Tours & Travel
3	Rangers Office (Kargudi)	13	Wildlife Ranger Office
4	Kargudi Resthouse		(Masinagudi)
5	Park Reception Centre;	14	Police Station
	Morgan Dormitory;	15	Hotel Dreamland
	Post & Telephone Office	16	Bamboo Banks
6	Bus Stop	17	Jungle Retreat
7	Hotel Tamil Nadu	18	Blue Valley Resorts
8	Log House	19	Forest Hills Guesthouse;
9	Sylvan Lodge; TTDC		Jungle Hut Guesthouse
	Youth Hostel	20	Chital Walk (Jungle
10	Elephant Camp		Trails Lodge)

Elephant Migration Routes
Metalled Track
Salt Licks
Water Holes

may see gaur; spotted, barking and sambar deer; wild dogs; flying and Malabar squirrels (especially around the forest bungalows); common langur; and bonnet macaques (easy to spot on the bridge at Theppakadu). But without private transport (which is not allowed) you won't see sloth bears, elephants, leopards or the rare pangolins – but Mudumalai does boast one of the largest collections of wild (and domesticated) elephants in South India.

There are more than 200 species of sedentary and migratory birds, including egrets, quails, bee-eaters, owls, woodpeckers, Malabar grey hornbills, rare sirkeer cuckoos and speckled piculets. (Birdwatchers may want to pick up the handy (free) booklet, called *Birds of Mudumalai*, from the WWO office in Ooty.) Otters and crocodiles inhabit parts of the Moyar River which flows through the park, and divides Mudumalai and Bandipur National Park in Karnataka.

The reception centre in Theppakadu lists the date and location of recent sightings of the more elusive creatures, so if you are fortunate enough to spot one of these, please let them know.

Elephants A one hour ride on an elephant is good fun, and an ecologically sound way to visit the park, but you don't cover much ground. It costs Rs 25 per person, or Rs 100 per elephant. You should pre-book, especially in peak season, at the WWO office in Ooty – though if you just turn up you will probably get a ride anyway.

If you are staying in or near the park, try to see the elephants being bathed in the picturesque Moyar River. This usually takes place every day between 6 and 9 am, in front of the Hotel Tamil Nadu, or at the elephant camp. Visitors are welcome at the **elephant camp** to watch the animals being trained.

Elephants shows are run at the elephant camp at about 5.45 pm on Saturday and Sunday. The shows (Rs 20 per person) are fairly interesting, if a little tacky, but the subjugation of the elephants is a questionable practice indeed.

Hiking
Hiking in Mudumalai is not permitted, but is allowed in areas south of Masinagudi, and on the way to, but not in, the park – refer to the Trekking in the Nilgiris section below. Jungle Tours & Travel in Masinagudi, or any of the nearby hotels or resorts, can organise short hikes, and guides.

Organised Tours
Mudumalai is close enough for a day trip from Mysore or Ooty, which is what hundreds of tourists do. If you are not staying in, or near, the park, a bus tour for the day is not such a bad idea. Though the tour can be long, you will also quickly visit other scenic areas, such as Pykhara Lake and Falls and Kalhatti Falls, but you won't go on an elephant ride, or see an elephant show, in Mudumalai.

Places to Stay & Eat
A range of budgets is catered for: there are cheap forest bungalows inside the park at Theppakadu; mid-range hotels in Masinagudi (8km from Theppakadu) which are accessible to the park and Ooty by bus or jeep; and expensive resorts in Bokkapuram, three or 4km south of Masinagudi.

Bungalows *Sylvan Lodge* is superbly set along the Moyar River, in Theppakadu. The clean, simple rooms, with rustic bathrooms, are very cheap at Rs 40 a double, plus a reservation fee of Rs 2. Let staff know if you want meals (Rs 25 extra). Bookings must be made as early as possible at the WWO office in Ooty. There is a one night maximum stay, but if business is slack, and you contact the WWO at about 5 pm, you can often stay another night or two. Beds at the dormitory at the back of the lodge, or at *Morgan Dormitory*, near the park reception centre, are used if the rooms are full, and are a bargain at Rs 10 per bed.

You are unlikely to get into the nicer *Log House*, next to the Sylvan Lodge, because it's on permanent standby for VVIPs (very, *very* important people). The *Kargudi Resthouse* and *Peacock Dormitory* in Kargudi are available for the same price, but only when the other places are full.

Hotels There are two decent hotels on the main road in Masinagudi. The village has a few basic *dhabas* (truckstop-style cafes) but there's nothing to excite your taste buds.

Hotel Dreamland (☎ 56127) looks better than the outside suggests. It has clean but noisy rooms with a TV and fan for Rs 200 a double. This is certainly 'foreigner's price' but prices are negotiable, and it's far cheaper than the resorts at Bokkapuram.

Mountania Resthouse (☎ 56337) is nicer. Set in a pretty garden and away from the main road, a double room costs Rs 400, and meals (for guests only) cost from Rs 30 to Rs 40.

Hotel Tamil Nadu (☎ 56249) is a nice (if overpriced) place in a charming location. Large family rooms (with four beds) cost Rs 420; dorm beds are far better value at Rs 50 per person. The attached *restaurant* is the best place for a meal or cold drink in Theppakadu. (Please note that alcohol is banned in the park.)

TAMIL NADU

Resorts If you are staying at these places, you will need private transport between the resort and Masinagudi. You should book rooms in advance: directly, at Seagull Travels in Mysore (see that section in the Karnataka chapter for contact details), or at any major travel agency in Bangalore. There are several more 'resorts' near Bokkapuram, and others are likely to be built in the future.

Bamboo Banks (☎ *56222)* is 1.5km from Masinagudi, down a signposted turn-off to the right. One of the region's oldest private lodges, it charges Rs 770 for a single or double, not including meals.

Forest Hills Guesthouse (☎ *56216)* is a friendly, homely place. Compared to other places nearby, it's good value, and the only resort to really cater for travellers on a budget. Spacious, clean rooms cost Rs 500/650/750 for a single/double/triple, but meals are a little pricey at Rs 75/125/150 for breakfast/lunch/dinner. Follow the sign from the Jungle Hut.

Jungle Hut Guesthouse (☎ */fax 56240)* is the most expensive place, and not particularly good value: Rs 960/1080/1260, and meals are extra: Rs 90/120/150. It has a nice setting, and a small swimming pool, but not much more to justify the price.

Jungle Retreat (☎ *56470; fax 56469, email peres@giasbg01.vsnel.net.in)* is a newer place, and better value. Rooms cost Rs 780/930 for a double/triple (no singles). Buffet meals are an extra Rs 80/100/150. You can pitch a tent in the grounds, and use the facilities, for Rs 200 per tent. The wonderful outdoor bar and restaurant is probably the highlight. Follow the path for 2km from the Jungle Hut.

Chitral Walk (Jungle Trails Lodge) (☎ *56256)* has long been recognised as one of the more eco-friendly places. It is set in some genuine jungle, but make sure you book ahead to ensure that staff and food are available. Rooms are rustic, but better value at Rs 600 a double.

Getting There & Away
Bus Between Ooty and Mysore, buses leave every 20 to 30 minutes and stop at Thep-

pakadu. Along the tortuous Sighur Ghat Rd to Ooty, most public transport (Rs 18, 90 minutes) is by small minibus, but sometimes large buses inch up the hill. Most buses, however, take the longer, and less steep, road via Gudalur (Rs 21, three hours).

While buses from Ooty or Mysore race through Theppakadu, many are already bursting with people and may not stop for extra passengers. Just keep waiting. Ooty-Mysore buses can drop you off at Theppakadu, but only buses that run via Sighur Ghat stop at Masinagudi.

Jeep If you have a few extra rupees up your sleeve, or you're travelling in a small group, you may want to charter a jeep along the Sighur Ghat Rd between Ooty (or Mysore), and Masinagudi, Theppakadu or Bokkapuram. This allows you to take a leisurely trip, stop for photos, and visit Moyar Falls (if permitted) and Kalhatti Falls. From Masinagudi to Ooty a jeep costs a non-negotiable Rs 450.

Masinagudi is the nearest transport centre to the resorts in Bokkapuram. Jeeps in Masinagudi, and those owned by the resorts, will charge a hefty Rs 50 per jeep for the short trip between the resort and Masinagudi.

Getting Around
Buses run about every hour (from 6 am to 6 pm) between Theppakadu and Masinagudi. A private jeep charges Rs 50 for the same trip, and a shared taxi-jeep leaves every 20-30 minutes for Rs 6 per person. The forest rangers allow people to walk (8km) between Theppakadu and Masinagudi, but only along the main road. They do issue a warning, however: 'be careful of wild animals'.

TREKKING
The Nilgiris is the most popular area in Tamil Nadu for treksg, hikes and walks.

Enthusiasts come all the way from Chennai, and elsewhere in India, for the diverse landscape, challenging treks and peaks, mild weather, wildlife and pockets of undisturbed beauty. But there are several factors you need to take into account:

TAMIL NADU

- at the time of research, some trekking areas were off limits because of the past detrimental effects of trekking on the environment: ie in Upper Bhavani, most of Mukurthi National Park, and all of Mudumalai National Park.
- a nasty brigand called Veerappan (refer to the boxed text in the Karnataka chapter) may not still be at large, but if he is, check with the WWO before heading into the hills.
- you need permits from one of the various forest or wildlife departments (see under Forest Departments in the Ooty section) for most of the Nilgiris, including unprotected forest areas.
- leeches can be a problem in the wet, particularly in the western Nilgiris.
- unlike other areas in South India, such as Kodagu, the Nilgiris (particularly in the west) contain a lot of steep mountains and dense forests. Even experienced trekkers will need a guide most of the time.

Information

Getting decent advice and information is not easy. Don't waste your time with the tourist office in Ooty – they have no interest whatsoever in promoting local trekking. The Nilgiri Trekking Association (see under Agencies, below) is good for advice, but rarely organises local treks. The two district forest officers (DFOs) in Ooty are the best places to gather information about permits, guides, distances, forest bungalows and so on.

The booklet, *The Nilgiris*, available in major bookshops in Ooty, includes some trekking advice and routes. Though the YWCA in Ooty does not organise treks, trekking information is often pinned on the useful notice board in the main building, and it's a good place to meet other travellers wanting to share costs, guides and experiences.

Maps Better than one of the ONC or TPC maps published by the US Defense Mapping Agency Aerospace Center (not available in India), are the district maps (Rs 6) from the grandly named Office of the Assistant Director of Survey & Land Records, District Survey Unit. The office is located about 500m up a path, through the quasi-Swiss chalet at the back of the Botanical Gardens in Ooty.

Permits & Guides Just about every trekking route will require a permit. You should allow between seven and 10 days for permits to be processed, depending on the mood of the officers concerned, but bookings for bungalows can usually be arranged on the same day. The hardest part is knowing which department to contact – refer to the sections below, and Forest Departments under Ooty, for details.

If you need permission to trek, you will also need a guide; the DFOs or WWO can usually organise this. Even when permission is not required, a guide is still a good idea to show you the best trails, and facilitate visits to tribal villages. If you want a reliable guide who speaks English, the agencies listed below and the resorts, bungalows and hotels listed elsewhere in this section, will find one for about Rs 200 per day, or Rs 30 per hour. Organising one yourself for about Rs 150 per day is obviously cheaper, but the guide may not be as knowledgeable about the trails as he pretends to be.

Climate

It is vital to time your trek properly. Winter, from mid-November to mid-March, is best, though frequent mists will sometimes make trekking difficult and frustrating. Avoid the heavy rains from June to September. The rains start a few weeks earlier in the western Nilgiris, and the whole district can also be partly affected by low-level monsoons in October and November.

Accommodation & Food

You can usually stay in temples, village homes, forest bungalows or schools along the way, but guides will be able to facilitate this better than you. This means you do not have to carry a tent. There are a lot of hills in the Nilgiris, so you will soon realise the importance of carrying as little as possible.

Someone near where you stay should be able to cook a very basic, but cheap, meal, also obviating the need to carry cooking equipment. Whether you buy food along the way, or take your own, you will be expected to feed your guide and porter.

TAMIL NADU

Equipment

None of the agencies listed below has equipment for hire. If you come through Chennai or Bangalore, you can hire equipment there (refer to the separate Outdoor Activities sections under Chennai and Bangalore); otherwise you will have to bring your own camping, trekking and cooking gear.

Agencies

Most of the travel agencies in Ooty do nothing more than sell tickets for bus tours, and know nothing about trekking. And beware of agencies in Bangalore and Chennai which promise all sorts of great trekking possibilities in the Nilgiris, but will fail to deliver because of permit problems. Most resorts and hotels listed throughout the Nilgiris section can also arrange trekking.

Clipper Holidays
  (refer to Outdoor Activities around Bangalore in the Karnataka chapter) – this company runs excellent seven and eight-day treks.
Jungle Tours & Travel
  (☎ 0423-56336) Masinagudi – right on the corner in the middle of Masinagudi, this agency is fairly well informed about treks and other activities in the region, and is cheaper than anything the nearby resorts can offer.
Nilgiri Trekking Association
  (☎ 41887; fax 42883 or 41110), Kavitha Nilayam, 31-D, Bank Rd, Ooty 643 001 – the NTA is happy to offer advice and information, but, ironically, the friendly manager, NR Ayyappan, mainly organises treks to northern Himalayan regions for local members. Foreigners are allowed to join any trek that the NTA arranges, and fees are very reasonable.
Ozone
  (see Outdoor Activities around Bangalore in the Karnataka chapter) – this impressive agency runs a few seven-day treks.
Rikki Tikki Tavi
  run by Sylvan Retreats & Trails (see Activities in the Chennai chapter), this company organises some interesting seven-day treks, for an all-inclusive Rs 10,000 per person (excluding travel to/from Ooty).
Wilderness Adventures
  (☎ 0423-43057) – this local company runs reasonably priced customised treks. Though based in Lovedale, you are more likely to get hold of

staff at the 'Shacks' shop, under the Charing Cross Hotel, at Charing Cross in Ooty.
YHA
  Chennai (see Activities in the Chennai chapter) – if you're coming from Chennai, it's worth contacting the YHA beforehand. They have about 20 camp sites throughout the Nilgiris, which foreigners can use with permission. They can arrange treks from Rs 250 per person per day, including food, guide, and camping and cooking equipment.

Day Hikes

The advantage of taking a few day hikes, instead of a longer trek, is that you do not need permission or a guide for the places below, unless they are in a protected area. Camtrek also runs long, but enjoyable, day hikes among the hills surrounding Ooty, including Doddabetta.

Ooty to Mudumalai There are two steep roads down from Ooty to Mudumalai National Park: via Gudalur (67km), or along the Sighur Ghat Rd (36km). You can walk along either road for as long as you want, and shorten the trip by catching a bus some of the way, but you cannot walk into the park. The Sighur Ghat Rd is certainly shorter, but it's very narrow, so it's harder to avoid being flattened by passing trucks. The road via Gudalur is very busy, but there are two good stretches:

• from Indanagar, about 6km from Ooty, follow the road (13km) to Pykhara village. The road is reasonably flat until the last few hundred metres before this charming, hilltop village. There is no hotel in Pykhara, but you can camp somewhere discreet – but away from the Pykhara Dam, which is under military management
• the road from Pykhara village to Naduvattam (14km) is still reasonably flat, goes through tea plantations and offers awesome views of valleys and rocky outcrops. From Naduvattam, take a bus to Theppakadu.

Emerald From the tiny village of Emerald, the very pretty 8km walk to the Red Hill Nature Resort (see Emerald Dam in the Around Ooty section) offers wonderful views of tea plantations and the dam. The

Green Trekking in Tamil Nadu

Tamil Nadu's wilderness areas are already under a lot of pressure. Please think about the following tips when hiking or trekking and help preserve their beauty and fragile ecology.

Leave Nothing but Footprints

- Carry out all your rubbish. If you've carried it in you can carry it out. Don't overlook those easily forgotten items, such as silver paper, orange peel, cigarette butts and plastic wrappers. Empty packaging weighs very little anyway and should be stored in a dedicated rubbish bag. Make an effort to carry out rubbish left by others.
- Minimise the waste you must carry out by taking minimal packaging and taking no more than you will need. If you can't buy in bulk, unpack small-portion packages and combine their contents in one container before your trek. Take re-useable containers or stuff sacks.
- Don't rely on bought water in plastic bottles. Disposal of these bottles is creating a major problem, particularly in developing countries. Use iodine drops or purification tablets instead.

Dumping

- Where there is a toilet, use it; where there is none, bury your waste. Dig a small hole 15cm deep and at least 100m from any watercourse. Consider carrying a lightweight trowel for this purpose. Cover the waste with soil and a rock. Use toilet paper sparingly and bury it with the waste.

Keeping Clean

- Even if they are biodegradable, don't use detergents or toothpaste in or near watercourses. For personal washing, use biodegradable soap and a water container (or even a lightweight, portable basin) at least 50m away from the watercourse. Widely disperse the waste-water to allow the soil to filter it fully before it finally makes it back to the watercourse.
- Wash cooking utensils 50m from watercourses using a scourer such as sand instead of detergent.

Cook with Kero

- Don't depend on open fires for cooking. Cook on a light-weight kerosene, alcohol or Shellite (white gas) stove and avoid those powered by disposable butane gas canisters.

Wildlife

- Don't buy items made from endangered species.
- Do not feed the wildlife.

---

best idea is to take a bus to the path near the resort, walk down to Emerald, and catch transport back to Ooty.

The area around Emerald village and dam is ideal for day hikes, and a permit or guide is not needed – just follow any path or road. To nearby Toda settlements, you'll have to ask directions if you are hiking independently, but a guide will make it easier for you to meet the Toda people.

Theppakadu to Masinagudi Hiking in Mudumalai National Park is forbidden, but you can walk along the main road between Theppakadu and Masinagudi. Be careful: this is a national park full of wild animals. It is a pleasant 8km, but take water, a good hat and eyes in the back of your head.

Ooty to Kalhatti Falls This longish hike (14km) from Ooty finishes at the pretty

Kalhatti Falls. Though the falls are not that high (about 70m), the birdlife and butterflies can be spectacular, and if you ask directions, there is an abandoned fort to explore nearby. Take the Sighur Ghat Rd from Ooty to Mysore, and look for the turn-off. Otherwise, take a bus to Kalhatti village, and then walk about 3km from the turn-off to the falls.

Sholur-Glenmorgan-Pykhara The start and finish of this popular hike are easy to reach by bus, or chartered jeep, from Ooty. Start at Sholur; ask there for directions to Glenmorgan; keep heading in a westerly direction, until you come across the Moyar River (also known as Pykhara River, at this stage); and then follow it to Pykhara village. The trek should take about five hours.

Moyar Falls Another popular hike is to the Moyar Falls, an impressive 260m gorge on the Moyar River, sometimes known locally as the Sighur Falls. The falls are on the border between Bandipur and Mudumalai national parks, and near some hydroelectric power stations, so a guide is recommended. Just head north from the main corner in Masinagudi. Try to start and finish by noon, before the fog sets in. The falls are most impressive during or just after the monsoons, but predictably the dam upstream restricts the flow of water.

This hike can be arranged with Jungle Tours & Travel in Masinagudi (see Agencies above), or by chartering a jeep, or taking a shared taxi-jeep, along the road from Masinagudi to Moyar village (10km), and then hiking about 3km to the top of the falls. Before heading out there independently, however, check with the Wildlife Ranger Officer in Masinagudi, in case there are any restrictions.

Longer Treks If you follow the main roads, you do not need guides or permits; otherwise, allow plenty of time to arrange these treks. Alternatively, a trekking agency will deal with the paperwork.

Avalanche The dam and hills surrounding the village and resthouse at Avalanche are perfect for short hikes, or longer treks. One popular trek (24km) is between Avalanche and the northern tip of the lake at Upper Bhavani. But check with the WWO in Ooty first, because Upper Bhavani is currently off limits.

For any day hike off the main road around Avalanche, you will need a permit from the DFO (South). A guide can be arranged at the resthouse (see the Avalanche section under Around Ooty).

The road from Ooty to Avalanche is a gentle 26km, mostly downhill, but you can reduce this by taking a bus some of the way. Start at Fernhill Palace in upper Ooty, and head down the Avalanchi Rd. You don't need permission or a guide for this hike.

Ooty to Parsons Valley This gentle hike (17km) follows the main road (so no permits or guides are necessary) to Parsons Valley. Follow the South Lake Rd from Ooty – if in doubt, ask directions. You can reduce some of the trip by taking a bus.

Bangithappal to Silent Valley With permission from the DFO (South), and the Forest Department in Kerala – or, even better, organise your trek through Clipper Holidays or Ozone and let them do the legwork – you can trek for three days southwest from Bangithappal (where there is a forest resthouse), via Sispara (where there is a trekking shed), to the magnificent Silent Valley, in Kerala.

Pandiar to Avalanche This fairly gentle, six-day trek starts at Gudalur. From here, charter a jeep down the path to Pandiar (where there's a forest hut), then walk to the starting point for the climb up Nilgiri Peak (2467m). Trek to Mukurthi Peak (2556m), then pass the southern side of Mukurthi Lake. Head south through Mukurthi National Park and stay at Bangithappal (where there is a forest resthouse).

Walk around Upper Bhavani Lake and head north to Avalanche, mostly following the main road. As you will need a series of

Tamil Nadu Holidays & Festivals

January	– Pongal (Harvest Festival), Madurai; Mamallapuram Dance Festival, Mamallapuram; Temple Car Festival, Kanchipuram; Temple Car Festival, Tiruchirappalli; Thai-Pusam Festival, Palani; Thyagaraja Music Festival, Thiruvaiyaru
Jan/Feb	– Teppam (Float) Festival, Madurai
February	– Natyanjali Dance Festival, Chidambaram; Feast of Our Lady of Lourdes, Tiruchirappalli
Feb/Mar	– Masi Magham, Swamimalai
Apr/May	– Temple Car Festival, Chidambaram; Temple Car Festival, Kanchipuram; Chithrai, throughout Tamil Nadu
May/June	– Kumari Amman Temple Festival, Kanyakumari (Cape Comorin)
July/Aug	– Drowpathiamman Temple Festival of Fire, Pondicherry
September	– Feast of Our Lady of Good Health, Velanganni; **Avanimoolam**, Madurai
Sept/Oct	– Navrati, Madurai
Nov/Dec	– Karthikai Deepam Festival, Tiruvannamalai, Swamimalai
December	– Vaikunta Ekadasi (Paradise Festival), Tiruchirappalli
Dec/Jan	– Temple Car Festival, Chidambaram

permits (from the DFO (South) and the WWO), and a reliable guide, this trek is best organised with Clipper Holidays or Ozone – but even these companies may have trouble arranging permits.

Parsons Valley to Portimund Dam This trek is not normally more than one day, but you may wish to camp (subject to permission) in order to fully enjoy the tranquillity and views. From Ooty, take a bus to Parsons Valley, then ask directions (if you haven't got a guide) to Mukurthi Peak, stop at the southern tip of Mukurthi Lake, and finish at Portimund Dam. You could extend this hike to include a detour to Avalanche Dam and Kolari Betta. But a permit from the DFO (South) is required, and Mukurthi Peak is currently off limits.

North-East I This is one of the more fascinating treks, but the most difficult to organ-

ise, because of necessary permits (from the DFO (North) in Ooty). Start in Kotagiri and follow the road to Kodanad (walk or take a bus). Head north-west down to the Moyar Valley, and follow the Moyar River west to the power station near the Moyar Falls. From here look for transport to Masinagudi (you can't walk into Mudumalai National Park). This is about 25km, and will take two to three days. You can camp or stay in villages along the way.

North-East II Alternatively, start at Ebanad (accessible by bus from Ooty), and trek east to Bikkapattimund. Continue north to Sirur, and head down the valley road to Anaikkatti, then follow the road through the scrub to Sighur (also accessible by bus from Ooty). You can usually find somewhere to stay and eat at the villages along the way. This is about 25km; allow two days. Permits are also needed from the DFO (North) in Ooty.

TAMIL NADU

Andaman & Nicobar Islands

Take 300 virtually uninhabited tropical islands. Add abundant fruits, unique fauna, lush forests, deserted beaches, exquisite coral, clear water, an extraordinary history – and you have what so many travellers call a 'paradise on earth'. Indeed, for battle-scarred travellers tired of the overcrowded buses, inexplicable bureaucracy, relentless touts and nauseating pollution of the mainland, these islands can offer a perfect come-down before returning home. Island hopping is one of the favoured activities. So are snorkelling, eating, sleeping and reading. The pace is always gentle.

In tourist brochure parlance the Andaman & Nicobar Islands are 'eco-friendly emerald islands offering a dream destination'. Such accolades, however, were certainly not used during the period of British rule when the Andamans became a penal settlement. In those times the islands became widely known as Kali Pani or Black Water. The term is a poignant reference to the horrors that awaited those who were transported.

Although there can be no doubting the opportunities for relaxation and adventure that the Andaman & Nicobars offer today's traveller, the paradise is clearly lost for the islands' remaining indigenous people. As the Indian government accelerates its programs of land clearing and development, the tribal people of the Andaman & Nicobar Islands are literally struggling to survive.

Situated in the eastern part of the Bay of Bengal the islands form the peaks of a vast, submerged mountain range that extends for almost 1000km between Myanmar (Burma) and Sumatra. In fact they are much closer to Myanmar than to India, but politically the Andaman & Nicobar Islands are part of the Union Territory of India. They are linked to the mainland not through the ethnicity of their inhabitants, but through the complex confluences of colonial history.

These islands and their native inhabitants have been the focus of many anthropological

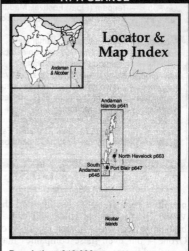

ANDAMAN & NICOBAR ISLANDS AT A GLANCE

Locator & Map Index

Andaman & Nicobar

Andaman Islands p641

North Havelock p663

South Andaman p645 • Port Blair p647

Nicobar Islands

Population: 340,000
Area: 8248 sq km on 319 islands
Capital: Port Blair
Main Languages: Hindi, Bengali, Tamil and tribal languages
Best Time to Go: mid-November to early April

Highlights
- Island hopping
- Deserted beaches
- Superb snorkelling
- Dive centres offering PADI courses

studies, including that by Radcliffe-Brown, one of the acclaimed fathers of modern anthropology. His 1922 book *The Andaman Islanders* remains an important reference for all subsequent studies.

Until the beginnings of colonial rule in India, the islands were populated mainly by

PAUL BEINSSEN

PETER DAVIS

Tamil Nadu
All God is One: a roadside poster stall (above) and a stall selling mementos of Sri Sathya Sai Baba (below).

Andaman & Nicobar Islands
The sun goes down over the idyllic Andamans (top); the Cellular Jail in the capital, Port Blair, tells a brutal history of colonial oppression (below).

Andamanese, indigenous tribes that belong to the Negrito peoples. Patterns of traditional life still remain among the Jarawa and Onge tribes who live in the interior regions of South Andaman. However, the majority of the 300,000 people on the islands are mainlanders or their descendants who live in and around the capital of Port Blair on South Andaman.

The total land area of the islands is about 8248 sq km with the Andamans clearly having the largest proportion of total land area, about 6408 sq km. Most of the Andamans are hilly and densely forested (although deforestation is now a major problem). The highest point is Saddle Peak on North Andaman which rises to 732m.

The Nicobar Islands lie south of the 10° latitude N in the Andaman Sea. The northernmost island in the Nicobar group (Car Nicobar) is approximately 200km south of Little Andaman. The indigenous people of these islands are known as the Nicobarese and are probably descended from people of Malaysia and Myanmar, as their dialects belong to the Mon-Khmer group.

Many species of flora and fauna are unique to the Andaman & Nicobar Islands, including *Diospyros marmorata* (Andaman marblewood,) *Tetrameles nudifora* (Andamanese canoe tree), *Liopeltis nicobariensis* (Nicobar stripebacked snake), and the world's largest crab, the giant robber (or coconut) crab.

Given that so many of the islands are uninhabited, opportunities for travellers to find a true escape would seem abundant. However, significant restrictions apply. The maximum period of stay for foreign visitors is 30 days. Access to the Nicobar Islands as well as some of the Andamans is denied to everyone except Indian nationals engaged in research, government business or trade. The reasons given for restricted access are that the tribal people are aggressive and/or that they require protection. The presence of an Indian naval base is never cited as a reason, but is also likely to have something to do with it. For more information on permit requirements, see the Permits section later in this chapter.

HISTORY

The name Andaman is probably derived from the Malay, Handuman, a reference to the Hindu monkey god; Nicobar is believed to mean 'Land of the Naked'.

For thousands of years prior to European contact, the tribal peoples of the Andaman & Nicobar Islands lived a subsistence life that consisted mainly of hunting, fishing and gathering. Abundant forests and oceans enabled the islanders to enjoy a good diet and good health. They used bows and spears (and later employed dogs) in their hunting. But they never made fire.

According to anthropologists, the islanders organised themselves into local groups of 20 to 50 members. Each group was associated with a traditional resource territory. Members of the local groups had equal rights to the resources within the territory and local groups could usually obtain permission to hunt or fish in neighbouring territories. A local group was made up of nuclear families plus a few independent adults.

There has been much debate within anthropological circles as to whether these groups were organised along political or linguistic lines. Radcliffe-Brown argued that there were no tribal chiefs and that leadership on the local level was informal, based on respect for the advice of older and more skilled members of the community.

The islands appeared in the 2nd century maps of the Roman geographer Ptolemy who referred to them as 'islands of cannibals'. Xuan Zang, the well-travelled 7th century Chinese Buddhist monk, also noted the existence of the islands. And the 9th century Arab traders are believed to have reported on the islands as they sailed past them on their way to the straits of Sumatra. Marco Polo dubbed the islands 'the land of the head-hunters'. The belief that Marco

---

Island Indigenes

The Andaman & Nicobar Islands' indigenous tribal people are victims of the Indian government's policy of colonisation and development. They now constitute less than 10% of the population and, in most cases, their numbers are falling. The negroid Onge, Sentinelese, Andamanese and Jarawa are all resident in the Andaman Islands. The group on the Nicobar Islands is of Mongoloid descent, and includes the Shompen and Nicobarese.

Onge An anthropological study made in the 1970s suggested that the Onge were declining because they were severely demoralised by loss of territory. Two-thirds of the Onges' island of Little Andaman was taken over by the Forest Department and 'settled' in 1977. The 100 or so remaining members of the Onge tribe are confined to a 100 sq km reserve at Dugong Creek. The Indian government has allowed further development – including the building of roads, jetties and a match factory – and has even built tin huts in an attempt to house these nomadic huntergathers.

Sentinelese The Sentinelese, unlike the other tribes in these islands, have consistently repulsed any attempts by outsiders to make contact with them. Every few years, contact parties arrive on the beaches of North Sentinel Island with gifts of coconuts, bananas, pigs and red plastic buckets, only to be showered with arrows. About 120 Sentinelese remain, and North Sentinel Island is their territory. Perhaps they understand that their only hope of survival is to avoid contact with the outside world.

Andamanese Numbering only 30, it seems impossible that the Andamanese can escape extinction. There were almost 5000 Andamanese when the British arrived in the mid-19th century.

Polo was the first western visitor to the islands is widespread. However, Radcliffe-Brown claims that the great explorer derived all his comments on the Andamans purely from hearsay and that he never actually visited them.

Colonisation of the islands began not with the spread of European power, but with the force of the Indian Marathas. In the late 17th century, the islands were annexed by the powerful Marathas whose empire swept across vast areas of India. The islands later became the base of Maratha admiral Kanhoji Angre and his efficient navy. The admiral's naval vessels had a habit of capturing British, Dutch and Portuguese merchant ships. In 1713, Angre even managed to capture the yacht of the British governor of Bombay, releasing it only after delivery of a ransom of powder and shot. Though attacked by the British and, later, by a combined British/Portuguese naval task-force, Angre remained undefeated until his death in 1729.

Throughout the 17th and 18th centuries there were numerous attempts by Europeans to establish a settlement on the Nicobar Islands. The French, Danish, Dutch, Swedish and even the Prussians had a go. The aim was always to colonise the Nicobars, 'civilise the natives' and perhaps secure whatever resources might be available. Internal squabbles, lack of provisions and the prevalence of malaria and other diseases led all the attempts to abject failure.

The islands were finally annexed by the British in the 19th century and used as a penal colony. In the early stages the convicts were drawn mostly from the ranks of 'regular thieves and criminals' on the mainland. Later on, however, the British found the remoteness of the islands very useful in quelling the dissident behaviour that threatened their own power base on the mainland.

Their friendliness to the colonisers was their undoing and, by the end of the century, most of the population had been swept away by measles, syphilis and influenza epidemics. They've been re-settled on tiny Strait Island but their decline continues.

Jarawa The 250 remaining Jarawa occupy the 750 sq km reserve on South and Middle Andaman islands. Around them, forest clearance continues at a horrific rate and the Andamans Trunk Rd runs through part of their designated territory. Settlers are encroaching on their reserve, but the Jarawa are putting up a fight, killing one or two Indians each year. In 1996 they caught five loggers, killed two of them and cut off the hands of the other three. Considering that in 1953 the Chief Commissioner requested that an armed sea plane bomb Jarawa settlements, the Jarawas' response seems comparatively more restrained than that of the Indian government. All Trunk Rd buses are now accompanied by an armed guard – though windows are still occasionally shattered by Jarawa arrows.

Shompen Only about 200 Shompen remain living in the forests on Great Nicobar. They are hunter-gatherers who have resisted integration, tending to shy away from areas occupied by Indian immigrants.

Nicobarese The 30,000 Nicobarese are the only indigenous people whose numbers are not decreasing. They are fair-complexioned horticulturalists who have been partly assimilated into contemporary Indian society. Living in village units led by a headman, they cultivate coconuts, yams and bananas, and farm pigs. The Nicobarese inhabit a number of islands in the Nicobar group, centred on Car Nicobar. The majority of Nicobarese are Christians.

And so they began to fill the jails with political prisoners who regarded themselves as freedom fighters.

Construction of the notorious Cellular Jail began in the last decade of the 19th century and was finished in 1908 (see the boxed text 'The Penal Colony' in the Port Blair section). During WWII, the islands were occupied for a time by the Japanese. While many islanders, especially local tribespeople, initiated guerrilla activities against the Japanese, some people regarded them as liberators who would undo the shackles of British colonialism. The debate on this issue still rages.

Following the end of the war the islands were incorporated into the Indian Union when Independence came to India in 1947.

Since Independence considerable development has taken place on the islands. The production of cash crops (especially timber and cocoa) and the growth of tourism may have helped offset the cost to the mainland of subsidising the islands, but there is a price to pay. In its effort to maximise island revenue, the government has largely disregarded the needs and land rights of the tribes and has encouraged massive transmigration from the mainland – mainly Tamils expelled from Sri Lanka. The population has increased from 50,000 to over 300,000 in just 20 years, and the indigenous island cultures are being swamped.

It's not only the people who have suffered in the name of development: vast tracts of forest were felled in the 1960s and 1970s. There has been some replanting of the land with economically viable timber like teak, but much of it has been turned into rubber plantations.

The Indian navy has a number of vessels that patrol the islands (gun runners and drug smugglers from other parts of Asia frequently stray into the Andaman Sea). Along with the increase in commercial shipping, these vessels have contributed to significant coral damage, thereby destabilising an already fragile ecosystem.

The political as well as the ecological future of the islands is a constant talking point among residents, tour operators and other business people. The islands may be part of the Union Territory but there is widespread support for a greater degree of autonomy. Less interference from Delhi is what many businesspeople demand. On the other hand environmentalists, people concerned with tribal welfare and some tour operators fear that more autonomy will accelerate an already unchecked level of development and result in further ecological devastation. What these people want is for Delhi to be informed and decisive on action that will bring long-term benefits to the islands.

At present, administrators are appointed from Delhi on a two-year 'hardship' posting. Some make a few nominal changes in the name of progress before they go home. Some of these 'inventive' schemes have included a velodrome (one of only four in India), a high-tech swimming pool (rarely used) and the Grand Trunk Rd (dubbed the Road to Nowhere), which cuts through a tribal reserve and links destinations already well served by sea. The islands are a paradise for the visitor, but they can be a frustrating place to live and work.

CLIMATE

There is little seasonal variation in the climate. Continual sea breezes keep temperatures within the 23°C to 31°C range and the humidity at around 80% all year. The southwest monsoons come to the islands between mid-May and June, and the north-east monsoons between November and January. The best time to visit is between mid-November and early April. December and the early part of January are the high seasons.

ENVIRONMENT & TOURISM

The Indian government continues to destructively mismanage both the tribal people and the unique ecology of the Andaman & Nicobar Islands.

The major issues which need to be addressed are the rights and privacy of the indigenous tribes, the development of controlled timber farming to halt forest clearing and preservation of the fragile ecosystems around the coral reefs.

Tourism has a potentially positive role to play in all this. There are over 250 uninhabited islands in this area, most with superb beaches and coral reefs ideal for divers. Looking to the Maldives, where a few uninhabited islands have been developed exclusively for tourism, the Indian government is considering following the same example. This could compensate for the earnings lost from reduced tree-felling and would place a value on the preservation of the environment. Anything would be preferable to the mass deforestation and decimation of tribes that is happening now. The big question with tourist development, however, relates to economic and ecological sustainability. There are disagreements about the carrying capacity of the islands as well as about the type of development that is most appropriate (see the boxed text 'The Island Economy').

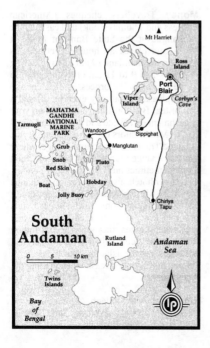

PERMITS

Foreign tourists need a permit to visit the Andaman Islands (maximum stay is 30 days from arrival). The Nicobar Islands are off limits to all except Indian nationals with special permits for research, government business or trade. The permit allows foreigners to stay in South Andaman, Middle Andaman, Little Andaman (tribal reserves on these islands are out of bounds), Bharatang, North Passage, Neil, Havelock and Long islands. On North Andaman foreigners may stay only in Diglipur.

Day trips are permitted to Ross, Viper, Cinque, Narcondam, Interview, Brother and Sister islands, but currently there are regular boats only to Ross and Viper islands. Boats are allowed to stop at volcanic Barren Island, but disembarkation is not allowed and, as yet, there are no regular services. All the islands of the Mahatma Gandhi National Marine Park are open except Boat, Hobday, Twin, Tarmugli, Malay and Pluto.

Permits are issued on arrival at the airport in Port Blair. Considerable time could be saved if the immigration authorities and Indian Airlines officials allowed the entry forms to be distributed in flight. As things stand, however, if you are a foreigner, you need to look for the man at the airport near the immigration desk. After questioning your intentions, he'll issue a green entry permit. If you lose this, your departure could be delayed.

If you arrive with an unconfirmed return flight, you'll probably initially be given a permit of only 10 to 15 days, but this can be extended to allow a 30 day stay. If there are many foreigners on the flight, the entry process can take up to one hour.

Those arriving by ship are usually required to obtain a permit before being issued with a ticket. The permit is available from the Foreigners' Registration Office in either Chennai (☎ 827 8210; Shashtri Bhavan annexe, 26 Haddows Rd) or Calcutta (☎ 033-247 3301, 237 AJC Bose Rd) – allow a couple of hours – or from any Indian embassy overseas.

If you arrive here by ship, you must immediately report to the deputy superintendent of police in Port Blair (in Aberdeen Bazaar). If you fail to do this you could encounter problems when departing since it will be difficult to prove that you have not been here longer than 30 days. Your permit will be stamped again when you depart.

PORT BLAIR
Tel Area Code: 03192

The administrative capital, Port Blair is the only town of any size on the islands. It sprawls around a harbour on the east coast of South Andaman, and has the lively air of an Indian market town. The absence of touts and beggars adds to the attraction, although if current trends continue this could soon change.

For the visitor, the infrastructure of Port Blair is surprisingly good. The roads are reasonably well maintained, passenger ferries are frequent, and the telephone system (including fax and ISD) works well. Most essentials, including bottled water and mosquito repellent, are available in the shops, and prices are only marginally higher than on the mainland. However, power and water are often restricted and the sewerage system is overstretched. Port Blair is clearly operating at capacity and further growth without infrastructure development will have disastrous effects.

Even though the Andamans are fairly close to mainland Myanmar, they still run on Indian time. This means that it's dark by 6 pm and light by 4 am.

Orientation

The town is spread over a couple of hills, but most of the hotels, the bus terminal, passenger dock and Shipping Corporation of India (SCI) office are in the main bazaar area, known as Aberdeen Bazaar. The airport is a few kilometres south of town, and the nearest beach is at Corbyn's Cove, 7km south of Aberdeen Bazaar.

Information
Tourist Offices For up-to-date information on places in the Andamans now open to foreigners, visit the Government of India

Tourist Office (☎ 33006). Open weekdays only, from 8.30 am to 5 pm, it's above Super Shoppe, a short distance from the centre of town on Junglighat Main Rd.

The Andaman & Nicobar Tourist Office (☎ 32694) is an ultramodern building which tourist officers like to call a 'tourist attraction'. It's diagonally opposite Indian Airlines. It operates from 8.30 am to 5.30 pm. The quality and accuracy of information from both these offices is variable. To some extent the staff cannot be blamed. Things are changing fast on the islands, printed schedules and prices rarely reflect current reality. However, even verbal information is often inaccurate and it pays to confirm everything, especially sailing schedules and prices.

The library, near the GPO, has a small collection of books on the history, geography, flora & fauna, and tribal people of the islands. The reference section is on the 1st floor.

Money Travellers cheques (American Express and Thomas Cook) and cash can be exchanged at the State Bank of India. It opens and closes an hour earlier than is usual on the mainland (9 am to 1 pm during the week and 9 to 11 am on Saturday). Go to the 1st floor. The process is efficient and not unpleasant; you may even be offered a cup of tea! But you'll have to insist on your encashment certificate and you'll be charged Rs 20! Most visitors use the efficient service at Island Travels, near Sampat Lodge, where you can change money daily between 2 and 4 pm (sometimes until 6 pm) except Sunday. The larger hotels also have foreign exchange facilities. Most places do not accept credit cards and though some of the larger hotels promote acceptance of credit cards, when the crunch comes, they only accept Indian cards. There is currently nowhere to get cash advances on the islands. The message is simple, take plenty of cash when visiting the Andamans.

Emergency Aberdeen Police Station (☎ 33077/32100) is next to the State Bank of India in Aberdeen Bazaar.

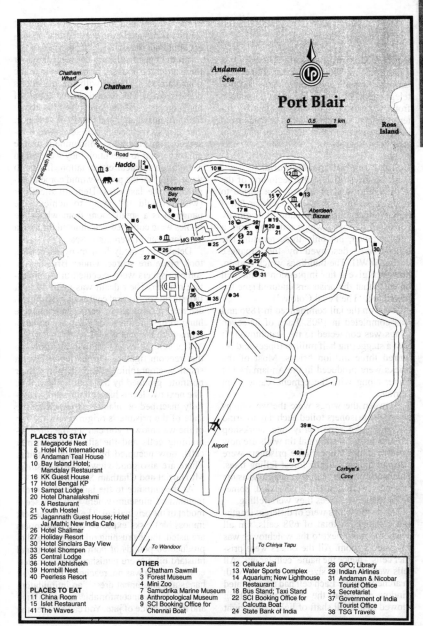

Chatham Wharf
● 1
Chatham

Foreshore Road

Peliapath Rd

Haddo ▥ 3
▥ 4
●2
▥ 10

Andaman Sea

Port Blair

0   0.5   1 km

Ross Island

Phoenix Bay Jetty

▼ 11
●5
●9
▥ 16
▥ 17
▥ 12
15 ▼
●13
14
Aberdeen Bazaar

18 ●
22 ★
23
24
●19
20
21

■6
▥ 7
8 ▥
MG Road
▥ 25

● 30

■26
■27
33 ■
32
31
26 ●
29 ●

■36
37 ●
■35
●34

● 38

Airport

To Wandoor

To Chiriya Tapu

39 ■

40 ●
41 ▼
Corbyn's Cove

PLACES TO STAY
2   Megapode Nest
5   Hotel NK International
6   Andaman Teal House
10 Bay Island Hotel;
    Mandalay Restaurant
16 KK Guest House
17 Hotel Bengal KP
19 Sampat Lodge
20 Hotel Dhanalakshmi
    & Restaurant
21 Youth Hostel
25 Jagannath Guest House; Hotel
    Jai Mathi; New India Cafe
26 Hotel Shalimar
27 Holiday Resort
30 Hotel Sinclairs Bay View
33 Hotel Shompen
35 Central Lodge
36 Hotel Abhishekh
39 Hornbill Nest
40 Peerless Resort

PLACES TO EAT
11 China Room
15 Islet Restaurant
41 The Waves

OTHER
1   Chatham Sawmill
3   Forest Museum
4   Mini Zoo
7   Samudrika Marine Museum
8   Anthropological Museum
9   SCI Booking Office for
    Chennai Boat

12 Cellular Jail
13 Water Sports Complex
14 Aquarium; New Lighthouse
    Restaurant
18 Bus Stand; Taxi Stand
22 SCI Booking Office for
    Calcutta Boat
24 State Bank of India

28 GPO; Library
29 Indian Airlines
31 Andaman & Nicobar
    Tourist Office
34 Secretariat
37 Government of India
    Tourist Office
38 TSG Travels

The GB Pant Hospital (☎ 32102) is adjacent to the Cellular Jail.

Post & Communications The GPO is 750m south of Aberdeen Bazaar. The cheapest place to send and receive faxes is at the telegraph office (fax 21318) next door, open from 10 am to 5 pm, Monday to Saturday. International telephone calls can be made from here, as well as from a number of places in Aberdeen Bazaar.

Cellular Jail National Memorial

Built by the British at the beginning of the 20th century and preserved as a shrine to India's freedom fighters, the Cellular Jail is now a major tourist attraction. It originally consisted of seven wings radiating from a central tower, but only three remain. The others were destroyed by the Japanese during WWII. The buildings which remain, however, give a fair impression of the hell on earth that the prisoners endured (see the boxed text 'The Penal Colony').

Work on the jail commenced in 1896 and was completed in 1908. Each of its seven wings was connected to the watchtower. It cost a staggering half million rupees and required three million bricks. Most of the bricks were produced in the Andamans but some, along with the cement, came from Burma.

Between the wings were the workshops where the prisoners toiled each day to grind oil and make rope. Only one workshop remains today; its original tin walls are now wooden lattice work. Some prisoners were also put to work in the forest felling trees. This work was particularly dangerous as the prisoners were constantly shackled, sometimes to the very trees they were felling.

The prison wings were of different lengths and contained a total of 698 cells. On all wings the room next to the watchtower was the guard's room. All the others were prisoner cells – hence the name 'cellular jail'. All cells were the same size – 3m by 3.5m with an arched ceiling. Each cell had a tiny grated window high on the back wall which allowed in a small shaft of light. The height

of the window and the eaves, consisting of slanted corrugated iron, ensured that prisoners could not see out.

On the outside of each cell near the door there are three hooks. The one closest to the door carried a plaque with the prisoner's name and age. The second carried details of his languages and the location of his home; the third, his charge and length of sentence. The last six cells in block seven were reserved for prisoners condemned to the gallows. Prior to execution they were given a thorough medical examination. It was to these cells that the priests would come to administer the last rites. Beneath the floor (which would fall away to achieve the hanging) is a small room from which the bodies were collected and shunted through a side fence and taken out to sea.

Details on exactly how many executions took place are scarce. Under British rule, some prisoners were executed in a clandestine manner. Their death was made to look like suicide or 'natural causes'. Under Japanese rule, records show that 87 Indians were hung in the jail, most for allegedly collaborating with the enemy.

The central tower is now a memorial to the freedom fighters. On the lower level a small photographic gallery displays their portraits, grouped by their particular crime. The next two levels have all the names carefully inscribed on plaques, grouped by the state of the prisoner's origin. From the top of the watchtower you can see the three remaining cells and the site of the former cells, now occupied by a public hospital. There are also good views of Ross Island, Mt Harriet and Chatham Sawmill.

At the entrance to the jail there's a well-maintained museum where you can see a model of the original jail. The daily (and near impossible) tasks expected of the prisoners are listed: those crushing oil were obliged to produce 30 pounds of both coconut oil and mustard oil. Severe punishment was inflicted if the quota was not reached. On one wall hangs a 'punishment dress', an intimidating and, no doubt, uncomfortable garment, huge and baggy, made of jute. You can also see the wooden number tags (which were worn around the neck), three types of fetters and a flogging stand with model in position. Prisoners were locked into the stand at their ankles, waist and wrists, and struck 40 times, 20 on each buttock.

Daily food allowance for the prisoners was two cups of boiled rice and two cups of water, one cup of each served morning and evening. The daily bath allowance was two buckets of sea water each morning.

The museum is divided into specific sections including one dedicated to the freedom fighters. The archival material here, including fading photographs and newspaper stories, is well documented.

You probably don't need a guide, but one will offer his services for Rs 30. He's knowledgeable and will provide you with extra information. The museum and jail are open daily from 9 am to noon and 2 to 5 pm; there's no entry charge.

Each evening (except Sunday) a sound & light show depicts the history of the jail and the horrendous events that took place. The story is narrated by a man who adopts the point of view of the chief witness, an old fig tree that still stands in the main forecourt. The first show, in Hindi, starts at 6 pm; the next, in English, is at 7.15 pm. Entrance is Rs 10.

Samudrika Marine Museum
Run by the navy, this interesting museum is divided into five galleries covering the history and geography of the islands, their people, marine life and archaeology. There are also good displays of shells and coral. Information boards (in English only) complement the displays, though the museum could do with a few signs informing visitors how slowly coral grows and how easily it is damaged. The large relief model of the Andaman & Nicobar Islands offers a good view of the 'big picture'. The museum opens Tuesday to Sunday from 9 am to noon and 2 to 5.30 pm; entry is Rs 10.

Aquarium
This interesting aquarium and museum (for-

merly known as the Fisheries Museum) displays some of the 350 species found in the Andaman Sea. The aquarium is open from 9 am to 1.30 pm and 2 to 5.30 pm every day except Monday, public holidays and every second Saturday. Entry is Rs 2.

Anthropological Museum
This small museum has displays of tools, dress and photographs of the indigenous tribes. The captions to some of the photos are poignant but telling. 'Why don't you leave us alone?' runs the caption under a photo of some Sentinelese people. Above the museum is a small but well-stocked library specialising in ethnographic and anthropological books and journals. Visitors are welcome to browse but material cannot be borrowed. The museum is open from 10 am to 12.30 pm and 1.30 to 4 pm daily except Sunday and declared holidays. Entry is free.

Mini Zoo & Forest Museum
The Andaman & Nicobar Islands are home to over 200 indigenous animal species found nowhere else in the world. Some can be seen at the mini zoo. These include the Nicobar green imperial pigeon and the Andaman pig, the staple diet of some tribal groups.

The zoo's saltwater crocodile breeding program has been very successful and many have been returned to the wild. Fortunately, their natural habitat is dense mangrove swamps, and there have been no reports locally of crocodiles attacking swimmers.

Some of the animals, such as the crab-eating macaque (which eats crabs only if there's no fruit around), are classified as 'Schedule 1', meaning they are highly endangered and therefore given maximum protection. As at many zoos, the animals here look jaded. Many cages are empty.

The zoo is open from 8 am to 5 pm Tuesday to Sunday; entry is Rs 0.50 for adults; Rs 0.25 for children. There's a small children's playground.

Nearby is the small Forest Museum, which has a display of locally grown woods, including *padauk*, which has both light and dark colours occurring in the same tree. The

The Penal Colony

The history of the penal colony on the Andaman Islands is a sorry tale of colonial oppression, bureaucratic ineptitude, abject cruelty, cultural displacement and untold suffering. It is also a story of courage, martyrdom and, ultimately, a triumph of the tactics of nonviolence and civil disobedience.

The colony began in 1858 with 200 convicts from India and 50 naval personnel to 'keep the convicts in check'. Some of these convicts were petty criminals; others had committed violent crimes. However, even in the early days, many of the convicts were political prisoners, arrested during the Indian Mutiny and sentenced by the British to transportation for life. This wasn't the first time that Indian prisoners had been transported abroad. The British had a habit of establishing penal settlements in many of their colonial outposts and Indian prisoners had previously been sent to Sumatra and Burma.

Within the first three months of the penal colony on the Andaman Islands, the convict population had expanded to 773. Of these, 61 died in hospital, 140 escaped never to be captured (it was assumed that escapees were either murdered by the natives or died from starvation), one of them suicided and 87 were hanged for attempting an escape. In spite of such disastrous beginnings, the penal colony continued to grow. Within 15 years, the population amounted to 8000 males, 900 females and 578 children.

During these first years the convicts endured extreme hardship. Simply depriving Hindus and Muslims of their family and religious ties would seem strong punishment. But combined with floggings, chains, rampant disease, inadequate nutrition and constant fear, it's no wonder the Indians referred to the Andaman Islands as Kali Pani, meaning Black Water, a place of no hope.

In 1872, Lord Mayo, the Viceroy and Governor General of India, was assassinated at Port Blair by a convict named Sher Ali of the radical Wahibi Muslim sect. The assassination triggered a surge of interest by the British establishment in the management of the penal colony. Reports were commissioned, VIP visits were arranged and eventually changes were made. A general relaxation of the administration resulted in improved conditions for the convicts. News of this soon reached India and the British became concerned by reports that convicts in India preferred transportation to the Andaman Islands to incarceration in an Indian jail. This resulted in tighter management of the penal settlement, a reduction in the numbers of convicts transported and, in 1896, the building of the infamous Cellular Jail.

In 1904, WRH Merk, the Superintendent of Port Blair, called upon the colonial administration to cease transportation to the Andamans. He believed that, except for a period of time in the Cellular Jail (prisoners were incarcerated even before the construction was completed in 1908), the life of the prisoners on the islands was much easier than that of prisoners in Indian jails. He claimed that the penal settlement had lost its reformative value and was therefore an unnecessary cost on the administration. Because of a shortage of space in Indian jails, the colonial administration was reluctant to agree to the cessation of transportation but it did concede that transportation would eventually be phased out.

What didn't stop, however, was the transportation of political prisoners. A second wave of such prisoners was sent to the islands in 1909. They were incarcerated at the Cellular Jail. Many of them were from the Indian intelligentsia – wealthy and educated. These prisoners were definitely not used to hard labour. Yet they were put in chains, given meagre rat-infested provisions and subjected to backbreaking work and humiliating punishments. They were allowed only three toilet breaks a day; if they could not comply with the allocated times they were flogged. One prisoner suicided; another went crazy and was eventually transferred to an asylum in Madras.

News of the treatment of political prisoners reached the Indian press and newspapers began calling for reforms. The call intensified when the press learnt of the hunger strikes among the political prisoners.

The first hunger strike was in 1912. It lasted for 72 days. Another hunger strike followed in

1914. Some hunger strikers were force-fed by the authorities. Others were transferred to the prison at Viper Island in Port Blair Harbour, an isolated place from which few would return.

The Indian press became increasingly vocal and sympathetic to the plight of the political detainees. Eventually, in 1921, the political prisoners were repatriated to Indian jails. The problem, however, did not end there.

With the intensification of political activity for Independence in the 1930s a third wave of 300 political prisoners was transported to the Andamans. It seems as if the authorities had learnt nothing from their earlier experiences of political prisoners. Once again, harsh treatment was meted out. And once again hunger strikes were staged.

The death of Mahavir Singh, a popular participant in the Lahore Conspiracy (a plan to overcome British colonial rule), gave prisoners their first martyr. The Indian press maintained its agitation for reforms. The prisoners demanded books, writing implements, the undoing of chains, reduced hard labour and social contact with other political prisoners in the jail. The authorities finally caved in and for a while conditions became almost tolerable. The prisoners even managed to produce their own hand-written magazine titled *Call* through which they commented on political and philosophical issues of the day.

The improved conditions were short-lived and many prisoners continued to suffer at the hands of cruel guards. The final turning point came with the hunger strike of 1937 involving 230 prisoners. When news of this spread throughout India, political prisoners across the nation staged a hunger strike in support. The political prisoners in Cellular Jail insisted that they were not striking for release. They were striking for civil liberties. 'Our demands are the demands of all India' they said.

In August 1937 the prisoners received a message from Mahatma Gandhi, assuring them of his support and asking them to end their hunger strike and renounce violence as a means of achieving social change. The prisoners were buoyed by the knowledge that they had widespread support in India. After a lengthy meeting they agreed to Gandhi's request and they issued a statement that read 'Violence retards rather than advances the cause of our country'.

By the end of 1937 all the political prisoners had been repatriated to India. In 1945, when the British reclaimed the islands from Japanese occupation, 40,000 other prisoners were returned to India and the penal settlement was officially disbanded.

PETER DAVIS

The Cellular Jail in Port Blair is preserved as a memorial to the Indian freedom fighters who died here.

museum is open from 8 am to noon and 2.30 to 5 pm daily except Sunday; entry is free.

Chatham Sawmill

Visiting a sawmill may not be to everyone's taste, but if you want a strong visual representation of the colonial history as well as the precarious future of the islands, this is where you'll find it. Chatham Sawmill is a government operation that happens to be the largest wood processor in Asia. It is on Chatham Island, 5km north-west of Aberdeen Bazaar.

This place will also appeal to those with a fascination for timber. The tourist literature promotes the fact that you'll see 'some of the rare species of tropical timber like padauk', although if the timbers are rare, you wonder what they're doing in a sawmill.

The mill was commenced in 1836 by the British. Its original, thick (50cm by 50cm) posts still support the huge roof. Some 2000 employees work around the clock in three shifts to mill the timber, most of which goes to the mainland.

On arrival you'll be immediately ushered to the security office where you'll be asked to sign in. You'll then be assigned a guide who speaks several languages, but little English. After showing you the fire station – huge and empty except for two motorcycles – he'll escort you through the different sections of the mill and explain the entire process.

Logs, up to 80cm wide, arrive by sea. They are mechanically hauled onto moving belts which transport them to the large sawing machines, where they are cut into 5m planks, 20cm wide and 2cm thick. Smaller pieces are also cut and the waste is sawn for firewood.

In the 'saw doctoring unit' large, Indian-made saw bands, some with 200 to 300 teeth, are sharpened on German and British machines. One British machine, some 100 years old, is still operational.

Each saw functions for two to three hours before it needs to be sharpened. Sharpening can take up to one hour. The finger test determines the degree of sharpness. Although

deforestation on the Andamans has resulted in severe logging restrictions, the sawmill continues to operate at full capacity by importing logs from Malaysia and Myanmar.

The sawmill is open from 6.30 am to 2.30 pm daily except Sunday. Entry is free; the guide will be happy to show you around 'for a small consideration'.

Water Sports Complex

At the water sports complex, by the aquarium, you can rent rowboats, windsurfing equipment and sailing dinghies.

Water-skiing costs Rs 50 for 15 minutes; windsurfing is Rs 30 for 30 minutes. You can rent snorkels here for Rs 15 per hour, but you can't take them anywhere else.

Organised Tours

A range of tours are offered by A&N Tourism at Andaman Teal House (☎ 32642); Shompen Travels (☎ 32360) in the Hotel Shompen and Island Travels (☎ 32358) in Aberdeen Bazaar. However, many tours will only take place when a minimum number of bookings have been secured. Cancellations are common and very frustrating for travellers on tight schedules.

If you're looking for deep-sea diving tours, the Samudra Centre for Ocean Appreciation & Awareness (based at Hotel Sinclairs Bay View) offers diving and camping trips from two to five days duration including all meals and equipment (see the 'Snorkelling & Diving' boxed text, opposite, for details).

KLM Tours & Travels (☎ 32111; fax 34255) is recommended for its environmental sensitivity and ability to customise an island experience for groups of from two to 50 people. The tour director has excellent local knowledge and will meet you at your hotel and take the time to discuss your needs, budget, capability, etc.

A number of the larger hotels will also organise tours around the islands. However, apart from visits to Jolly Buoy, Red Skin and Cinque Islands, independent sightseeing is easy enough.

Every afternoon at 3 pm, a boat leaves

Snorkelling & Diving

Surrounded by coral reefs and incredibly clear water, the Andaman Islands offer some of the best snorkelling and diving in the world. Marine life includes such turtle species as the olive ridley, hawksbill, green and leatherback (all of which are endangered, so must not be harassed or followed) and there are manta rays, reef sharks and thousands of such reef fish as the wrasse, trigger fish, grouper, and clown fish.

However, organised diving is still very much in its infancy here and dive centres open and close each year. Sensing that there might be money to be made from this sport, the government is keen to be involved. Its initial foray, which offered cut-price PADI courses from a centre at Wandoor, folded in 1995 but its new dive school has yet to open. When it does, the charges will probably be similar to those offered by the centres below.

At present the choice is between three dive centres. Samudra (☎ 33159; ☎ 32937; fax 32038; email: manavi_tha@hotmail.com) is very well run and based in an old Japanese bunker at the Hotel Sinclairs Bay View. It charges Rs 2000 for a couple of dives in the Port Blair area or Rs 3200 beyond (Wandoor etc). If you wish to dive in the national park itself there's an additional Rs 1000 charge (payable directly to the park). It offers the PADI Open Water course (four to five days) for Rs 14,000, and the advanced PADI course for Rs 8000. These courses lead to internationally recognised certification. It also offers a day's 'Discover Scuba Diving' for Rs 2500.

Prices are similar at the other professional outfit, Port Blair Underwater (☎ 85389, ☎ 21358; fax (040) 339 2718), which is also PADI registered. It is based at the Peerless Resort at Corbyn's Cove.

Slightly cheaper rates are available at Andaman Adventure Sports (☎/fax 30295), near the Anthropological Museum in Port Blair. It has some reasonable equipment and the owner is quite experienced, but he's not PADI registered (or recognised by any other diving organisation). The owner has experienced some recent difficulties with his business partnership which have left some travellers less than happy. This place is probably best only if you really know what you're doing.

You can rent snorkels from tour operators and hotels but these are expensive (around Rs 70 per day) and often substandard – it's best to bring your own, especially if you are travelling with children. The Jagannath Guest House rents snorkels for Rs 40.

Underwater life in the Andamans can be spectacular. In fact you don't have to incur the high cost of scuba diving, there is much to see while snorkelling. In ideal weather (clear sky and calm seas) the corals are vivid blue, pink, lilac and brown. At less than 3m you can see colourful bat, angel and butterfly fish. The vibrant, long-nosed parrotfish is also prevalent.

For tips on how to 'step lightly' while underwater, see the boxed text 'Diving' in the Lakshadweep chapter.

from the Phoenix Bay jetty for a 1½ hour harbour cruise. The trip costs Rs 20 and stops briefly at Viper Island, where the remains of the gallows tower built by the British still stand. Prior bookings are not necessary.

Tourism Festival

A 10 day Island Tourism Festival is held in Port Blair from late December to early January each year (at the time of publication there was talk about moving the festival to February but no decision has been reached). The festival is as much a commemoration of the Indian freedom fighters as it is a celebration of island culture. Leading dance groups are imported from the mainland as well as from some of the surrounding islands. The festival also gives local tourism operators an opportunity to showcase their products and espouse the rhetoric of ecotourism. One of the more bizarre aspects of the festival is the Andaman dog show.

Places to Stay

Most budget and mid-range hotels do not levy any additional taxes on their tariff. However, some top-end hotels levy a 10% service charge. Watch for checkout times, most of which are around 7 am.

Places to Stay – Budget

The **Youth Hostel** (☎ 32459) has dorm beds for Rs 30 (Rs 40 for nonmembers) and a few double rooms. There's a good restaurant for residents.

Central Lodge (☎ 33632), Middle Point, is a basic wooden building set back from the road. It's the most popular of the cheapies, with rooms from Rs 50/70 with common bath and Rs 90 for a double with bath attached. You can camp in the garden for Rs 25.

Sampat Lodge (☎ 33752), Aberdeen Bazaar, is basic but friendly with clean rooms for Rs 50/80 with a common bathroom or Rs100/150 with attached bath. The nearby **KK Guest House** is run-down and has tiny and rather drab rooms for Rs 40/70.

Hotel Bengal KP (☎ 32964) charges Rs 70/120/170 for singles/doubles/triples with attached bathroom.

Jagannath Guest House (☎ 33140) is a good choice, with spotless rooms for Rs 80/125/200, all with attached bathroom. Run by a friendly manager, it's convenient for the bus stand and Phoenix Bay jetty.

Hotel Jai Mathi (☎ 30836), near Jagannath Guest House but not quite so good, is well priced at Rs 80/110 for rooms with bathroom attached.

Places to Stay – Mid-Range

Most of the places in the mid-range bracket can be bargained down if they're not full.

Holiday Resort (☎ 30516), Prem Nagar, is fairly new, very clean and a good place to stay. Rooms are Rs 200/280, or Rs 320/380 with air-con; all rooms have bathroom attached.

Hotel Abhishekh (☎ 33565) is quite good and has clean rooms with attached bathroom for Rs 200/250/310; more for air-con. It has its own restaurant and bar but service is painfully slow.

Hotel Shalimar (☎ 33953) is on the road to Haddo. The advertised price for rooms is Rs 150/190/250 with attached bathroom, Rs 300 for an air-con double, but it might offer you a discount.

Hotel Dhanalakshmi (☎ 33953), right in Aberdeen Bazaar, has clean rooms with bathroom attached for a high Rs 200/300, or Rs 400/500 with air-con (the rooms at the back are the quietest). It also has a restaurant.

Hotel Shompen (☎ 32360; fax 32425) is overpriced at the quoted rate of Rs 350 or Rs 750 with air-con. The hotel has a restaurant and a travel agency.

Hotel NK International (☎ 33066) is convenient for the Phoenix Bay jetty, though not in a particularly attractive location. Rooms cost Rs 200/300, or Rs 300/400 with air-con.

Hornbill Nest Yatri Niwas (☎ 32018) is run by A&N Tourism. It's about 1km north of Corbyn's Cove and has sea views. This is an excellent location but the place is not particularly well run. Rooms with two/four/six beds and attached bath are Rs 250/300/400. Mosquito nets are provided. There's a basic restaurant but some dishes need to be ordered in advance.

Andaman Teal House (☎ 32642) is also run by the tourist office, but is poorly located on the road to Haddo. Doubles with attached bath cost Rs 250, or Rs 400 with air-con.

Megapode Nest (☎ 320207; fax 32702) at Haddo, on the hill above the bay, is good value at Rs 500 for a large double with attached bath, air-con and Star TV. Part of the same complex, the air-con, yurt-styled *Nicobari Cottages* are recommended. The cottages have character, good views, and cost Rs 800 for a double with attached bath.

Places to Stay – Top End
Hotel Sinclairs Bay View (☎ 32937) is on the road towards Corbyn's Cove. All rooms have a spectacular sea view and cost Rs 1045/1320, or Rs 1370/1860 with air-con and 'Sinclairs breakfast'. Although it's right on the coast there's no beach. It's a pleasant though somewhat cavernous place. The restaurant does excellent Indian dishes but the service is excruciatingly slow. The Samudra Diving Centre is based here. The Sinclairs chain of hotels has an office in Chennai (☎ (044) 852 6296; fax (044) 852 2506) through which bookings for Port Blair can be made. Major credit cards are accepted.

Peerless Resort (☎ 33462; fax 33463) at Corbyn's Cove is excellently located in a very quiet part of the island, just across the road from the beach. Air-con rooms in the main block are not particularly large and are a little overpriced at Rs 1195/2200; rooms in the very pleasant air-con cottages cost Rs 1800/2650; discounts are negotiable outside the high season. There's a bar, restaurant, foreign exchange facilities and a boat for hire. The restaurant menu is creative, particularly with its adjectives. 'Tender, fresh, coconut water' is served in less than fresh shells and the 'seasonal fruits' must be last seasons! The curries are somewhat bland. Major credit cards are accepted, but cash advances are not provided.

Bay Island Hotel (☎ 20881; fax 33389), which has sea views, is the top hotel in Port Blair. The rooms, however, don't quite rise to the heights of the aesthetics of the lobby and they are a little overpriced at Rs 2900/4300 – although this does include all meals. No single rates are available in December and January. There's an excellent restaurant and an open-air bar which is good for a quiet drink. This beautifully designed hotel is to be commended for its attempts at ecotourism. The swimming pool is filled with sea water, and guests are reminded not to waste water in bathrooms or damage coral when swimming. At the bottom of the hill, a private pier with a 'human aquarium' extends into the bay. The aquarium enables visitors to climb down into a windowed chamber to view the multicoloured fish that congregate here to be fed.

Places to Eat
Most of the hotels have restaurants, but you may have to order seafood in advance. There are numerous small restaurants in Aberdeen Bazaar.

Dhanalakshmi Restaurant (☎ 20694), in the hotel of the same name, stays open late; main dishes are around Rs 40.

New India Cafe, below Hotel Jai Mathi, does thalis for Rs 15, coconut chicken for Rs 32 and prawn dishes from Rs 34 to Rs 69. It's open early for breakfast and the coffee's good.

Islet Restaurant, near the cellular jail, offers tasty veg and nonveg dishes, and it has views of the bay. If you don't like your food heavily spiced, staff will oblige. Prices are very reasonable. Main courses are from Rs 30. Beer is Rs 65.

New Lighthouse Restaurant, beside the aquarium, gets mixed reports. It has a pleasantly cool dining area upstairs and does good fish dishes – prices vary according to the size of the fish. Its 'Fish 65' costs Rs 35.

The Waves, on Corbyn's Cove, was a good place for a drink or a meal, with tables under the coconut palms. It's currently being renovated, and promises even better service when it reopens.

China Room (☎ 30759), run by a delightful Burmese-Indian couple, is an excellent place to eat. It's really just a small outdoor area and the front room of their house, but the quality of the seafood they serve is very good. Lemon fish is Rs 60, garlic prawns Rs 80 and, given 24 hours notice, you can have Szechuan-style lobster for Rs 250 or Peking duck for Rs 200.

Mandalay Restaurant at the Bay Island Hotel is the other place for a splurge. The open-air dining area catches the breeze and has pleasant views over the bay. Main dishes are around Rs 100, prawns cost Rs 150 and a beer is Rs 100. Cheeky myna birds looking for scraps descend on tables as diners leave.

There's a good restaurant at the *Megapode Nest*, and great views over the bay. The service is quick, the menu varied and flexible. Main meals are priced from Rs 50 to Rs 70 for curries.

Getting There & Away

Air Indian Airlines (☎ 33108) has revised its Port Blair schedules yet again. Flights from Calcutta arrive at Port Blair on Tuesday, Thursday, Saturday and Sunday. These flights return to Calcutta the same day. Flights from Chennai arrive at Port Blair on Monday, Wednesday and Friday and return to Chennai the same day. The two hour flight from either Chennai or Calcutta departs around 5.30 am. The return fare to Chennai or Calcutta is US$175. The 25% youth discount is applicable on these fares. These flights can also be included on the US$500/750, two/three-week flight pass.

The Indian Airlines office is around the corner from the GPO. The staff here are very friendly, the office has a computer link and is open from 9 am to 1 pm, and 2 to 4 pm daily except Sunday.

The two hour flight to Port Blair from Chennai or Calcutta is pleasant, but securing a ticket can be difficult. Many travellers have reported major frustrations with the lateness of confirmations, despite having booked months in advance.

Part of the problem is the short runway. Indian Airlines claims that it is never really sure until the day of departure how many passengers it will be able to accommodate.

If there are empty seats on board it means the payload has been reduced to compensate for wind and other variables. If you're still on a waitlist on the day of departure, you'll probably miss out. This situation will change once extensions to the Port Blair runway are complete (see the boxed text, 'The Island Economy') but until then book your flight as far ahead as possible.

Train There are no trains on the Andaman or Nicobar Islands (a plan to construct a railway alongside the trunk road from South to North Andaman has been mercifully mothballed). There is, however, a railway reservation office where you can make bookings for mainland trains. It's near the Secretariat.

Boat There are usually two to four passages a month between Port Blair and Chennai or Calcutta on vessels operated by the Shipping Corporation of India (SCI; ☎ 33347). A ship also sails between Visakhapatnam (Andhra Pradesh) and Port Blair, but rarely more than once every two months. Contact SCI for the latest information on the erratic schedules. It's better to arrange tickets for the journey from Port Blair back to the mainland in Calcutta or Chennai. The length of journey varies depending on weather. Chennai to Port Blair is usually around 60 hours. Calcutta to Port Blair is around 56 hours and from Visakhapatnam it's around 56 hours.

The categories of accommodation available on these vessels includes deluxe Cabin (two berth), A-class cabin (usually two berth) and B-class cabin (four to six berth). Prices are Rs 3450 for deluxe, Rs 2852 for A class and Rs 2243 for B class.

Foreigners find it very difficult to secure bookings for deluxe or A Class as these are usually reserved for government VIPs. Some ships have an air-con dorm for Rs 1449. If you can get a ticket for bunk class, it costs Rs 955. Prices are the same for both the Calcutta and Chennai routes.

If you are a resident of the Andaman or Nicobar Islands, the fares will be around

40% cheaper. Food costs around Rs 100 per day and usually takes the form of thalis for breakfast, lunch and dinner, so you may want to bring something (fruit in particular) if you feel the need to supplement this repetitious diet. Although some bedding is available it is advisable to carry a sleeping sheet, especially if you are travelling bunk class.

The SCI may insist that you have a permit before selling you a ticket. However, if you do get your permit in advance, you must still register with the deputy superintendent of police on arrival in Port Blair.

The Port Blair SCI office is in Aberdeen Bazaar (☎ 33347), across the road from the Hotel Dhanalakshmi. For the Chennai boat, you may be directed to the office at Phoenix Bay. Bookings for the Calcutta boat open only a few days before the boat arrives; for the Chennai boat, you can book further in advance.

In Calcutta, the SCI office (☎ 284 2354) is on the 1st floor at 13 Strand Rd. In Chennai, the Directorate of Shipping Services (☎ 522 6873) is at Jawahar building, Rajaji Salai (opposite the Customs House). In Visakhapatnam, the office where you can find out if this route is operating is AV Bhanoji (☎ 56266), opposite the main gate at the port. Two passport-size photos and a lot of form-filling and trudging backwards and forwards between offices is required. You'll need to be organised, because bookings close four days before sailing.

The 60 hour boat trip can be hell or paradise depending on the weather, your fellow passengers and whether or not you have your sea legs. Prepare for all eventualities.

Getting Around

Port Blair has numerous taxis, three autorickshaws and no cycle-rickshaws. Taxis have meters (and charts, since the meters need recalibrating) but drivers need a lot of persuasion to use them.

From the airport, the trip to Aberdeen Bazaar should cost Rs 30 to Rs 40, and a little less to Corbyn's Cove; Rs 50 is the price that drivers quote for most local trips from hotels. If you stop them along the road

they'll charge from Rs 15 for a similar distance.

Some of the hotels offer their guests free transport to and from the airport; the tourist office airport bus will take you to any hotel in Port Blair for Rs 15.

From the bus stand in Port Blair, there are regular departures to key destinations beyond Port Blair. To Wandoor there are five buses a day. The 90 minute journey costs Rs 6. To Chirya Tapu, there's an hourly bus between 5 am and 6 pm for Rs 6. The bus to Diglipur leaves Port Blair every day (except Sunday) at 5 am. The journey is supposed to take eight hours (often it is much longer) and costs Rs 140. See the Wandoor section later, for other bus information.

Island Newspapers

Newspaper publishing is a vigorous business in the small town of Port Blair. A total of three daily, seven weekly and 11 fortnightly papers are published in various languages including English, Tamil, Hindi, and Bengali. Two of the dailies and six of the fortnightly papers are in English.

The oldest paper is the *Daily Telegrams,* which began life as a single sheet in 1926. It was started by the British mainly as a means of conveying the proceedings of the British House of Commons. Today the *Daily Telegrams* is a four page government-owned tabloid. It circulates 5000 copies in English and 1200 in Hindi. The content varies from details of local sport and government tenders to features on gun runners and conflicts between tribal people and settlers.

Competing with the *Daily Telegrams* is the *Andaman Herald Daily* which promotes itself as 'the only private daily in the islands'. The editor of this paper is a serious newshound who is not afraid to criticise the government and whose ability to sniff out a good story has resulted in many scoops.

All island papers carry the latest shipping news but there are numerous discrepancies in the published schedules.

It's best to have your own transport to explore parts of the island. You can hire bicycles in Aberdeen Bazaar for Rs 20 per day. An even better way to get around is by moped or motorcycle. Roads are not bad and certainly very quiet. TSG Travels (☎ 32894) has motorcycles (Suzuki 100s) and scooters for hire for Rs 120 per day. A deposit of Rs 1000 is required. Jagannath Guest House also has a few motorcycles for hire (Rs 120).

Private boats can be hired from the tour operators but charges are high – around Rs 10,000 per day.

AROUND PORT BLAIR
Viper Island

The moment you disembark on this island you are confronted with a sign that says 'Way to the Gallows'. This tiny island in the Port Blair harbour is further testimony to the tragic history of the region. From the sign a meandering path leads to the remains of the brick jail and the gallows. Built by the British in 1867 the structure has a curiously aesthetic appeal. The stunningly beautiful view from these gallows somehow adds weight to the sheer horror of the place. One prominent person to hang from these gallows was Sher Ali, of the radical Wahibi Muslim sect, who in 1872 assassinated Lord Mayo, the Viceroy and Governor General of India. Political prisoners who embarked on a hunger strike in the Cellular Jail were also detained here. Many of them died. Contrary to popular belief, the name Viper has nothing to do with snakes on the island. It is the name of a 19th century British trading ship that was wrecked nearby.

Unless you have access to a private boat, the best way to see Viper Island is to take the afternoon harbour cruise that departs from Phoenix Bay jetty. Some of these boats only stop at the island for 15 minutes – barely enough time to visit the gallows, let alone absorb the history. If you want more time, negotiate with the captain. Some will allow you up to an hour to meander about.

Mt Harriet & Madhuban

Mt Harriet (365m) is across the inlet, north of Port Blair. There's a nature trail up to the top and, with permission from the Forest Department, it may be possible to stay in the comfortable *Forest Guest House*. To reach Mt Harriet, take the vehicle or passenger ferry from Chatham Wharf to Bamboo Flat (Rs 1, 10 minutes). From there, a road runs 7km along the coast and up to Mt Harriet. Jeep drivers will sting you for an outrageous Rs 400 to take you to the top, wait 30 minutes and run you back down. Taxis are cheaper but still expensive (around Rs 200).

Don't be swayed by the claims from jeep drivers that ordinary taxis can't make it to the top. Taxis can and do make it to the summit! On the way up, about 500m from where the summit road begins, is the Forest Department Checkpost. Entry fee is Rs 10 per person. If you have the time and the energy try walking up (take plenty of water as there is none available along the route). The exercise is worthwhile and the walk down will certainly be easier.

To the north is Mt Harriet National Park and Madhuban, where elephants are sometimes trained for the logging camps. Madhuban is also accessible by boat; the tourist office and travel agencies arrange occasional trips.

Ross Island

A couple of kilometres east of Port Blair is Ross Island, chosen by the British for their administrative headquarters. In the early part of the 20th century there would have been manicured lawns leading up to the ballroom, umbrellas around the swimming pool and daily services in the churches. Newspapers of the day called Ross Island the 'Paris of the East'; however, the grandeur would soon crumble. In June 1941 a severe earthquake shook the islands. Some buildings were destroyed and roads were badly damaged. Six months later, after the Japanese entered WWII, the British began to evacuate Ross Island and transfer the headquarters of the penal colony to Port Blair. By the time the Japanese occupied the islands, Ross Island was almost deserted. The Japanese troops systematically dismantled many of the Ross Island buildings and used the materials for military constructions on other islands.

In 1943 the Indian National Army commander Netaji Subhash Bose stayed in the Ross Island Bungalow of the then Chief Commissioner of the Andaman Islands and hosted a dinner party for the members of the Andaman Branch of the Indian Independence League. In what remains a highly controversial act, the Japanese authorities participated in the function. Opinion remains divided over the role played by Bose in soliciting Japanese support to rid India of British domination. A somewhat portentous statue of Bose (complete with sunglasses) stands on the waterfront of Port Blair.

For a short time after the war, the British re-established themselves on Ross Island, but their settlements were only temporary. A fear that the island was sinking contributed to indecision and neglect. Today the jungle has taken over, and peacocks and spotted deer forage among the ruined buildings.

On the top of the hill stand the remains of the Anglican church, its tower strangled by roots and vines. Some of the grave sites are still visible, including one belonging to a newborn baby that died in 1863 after only 22 hours of life. The epitaph reads '… he glanced into our world to see a sample of our misery, then turned away his languid eye to drop a tear or two – and die'.

Ross Island is a distinctly eerie and rather sad place, but well worth a visit. There are ferries from Phoenix Bay jetty at 8.30 and 10 am, 12.30 and 2 pm daily except Wednesday. From Ross Island back to Port Blair, departures are at 8.45 and 10.40 am, and 12.40, 2.10 and 4.40 pm. The journey takes 20 minutes and a return ticket costs Rs 13, plus Rs 5 entry fee. You must sign in on arrival at Ross since the island is in the hands of the Indian navy. Visit the museum near the jetty before exploring the island to get an idea of how the place once looked.

Corbyn's Cove

Corbyn's Cove is the nearest beach to Port Blair. It's 7km south of the town and 4km east of the airport. The main accommodation here is the overpriced Peerless Resort.

Nearby Snake Island is surrounded by a coral reef. You can sometimes catch a ride to the island in a fishing boat, but it's inadvisable to swim out to it because of the strong current. If you do visit the islands, watch out for snakes.

It's a long, though pleasant and easy, clifftop stroll to Corbyn's Cove from Port Blair. The walk is particularly worth doing early in the morning for sunrise (you can have breakfast at Peerless Resort) or in the late afternoon for the moonrise. A taxi is about Rs 40 each way.

Sippighat Farm

On the road to Wandoor, 15km from Port Blair, is the government experimental farm, where tour groups often stop. New breeds of spices include cinnamon, pepper, nutmeg and cloves, are being tested here. The staff are particularly friendly and knowledgeable.

Wandoor

The Mahatma Gandhi National Marine Park at Wandoor covers 280 sq km and comprises 15 islands. The diverse landscape includes mangrove creeks, tropical rainforest and reefs supporting 50 types of coral. Boats leave from Wandoor village, which is 29km south-west of Port Blair, at around 10 am daily (except Monday) for visits to Jolly Buoy or Red Skin islands. Although it's well worth going along to see the coral (a few snorkels are usually available for hire), only a couple of hours are spent at the islands. It is very frustrating to get to such a stunningly beautiful place only to have to turn around and leave so soon. On Jolly Buoy, for the best coral go to the left of the landing spot, not to the right as directed. Watch out for powerful currents.

The trip costs Rs 75 (Rs 50 in the low season when boats go only as far as Red Skin). An entry permit (Rs 10) for the park must first be purchased at the kiosk by the jetty.

You can reach Wandoor by bus from Port Blair (Rs 5.50, 1½ hours) or by joining a

The Island Economy

As with many small island economies, the Andaman & Nicobar Islands face a precarious transition into the 21st century. On the surface, the economy is strong. Transport and communications seem efficient. The power is off only for a short time, water seems to flow and essential items are not significantly more expensive than on the mainland. The reality is, however, that these 'emerald islands' with their unique flora and fauna are heavily dependent on subsidies from mainland India. And in a climate of market deregulation coupled with a growing movement for independence, the vexed questions of development, sustainability and autonomy need to be addressed.

Produce from the islands includes oil from red-oil palm (used as an industrial lubricant), rice, bananas, cashew nuts, sugar, pulses, tapioca (for starch), rubber, timber, copra (from coconuts), coffee and fish. Most of the island income is derived from exporting this produce to mainland India as well as to other parts of Asia. This has to be balanced with the fact that over 60% of food consumed on the island is imported from the mainland.

Until recently, timber was one of the main income earners. However, resources are now so depleted that export earnings on timber have diminished by 50% over two years. While forestry officials claim that the reduced level of timber production is sustainable, environmentalists are calling for a total ban on the harvesting of hardwoods and other rare species.

The fishing industry has been targeted for significant development. There are 2000 registered fishermen on the islands but many of them are idle. One problem is lack of cold-storage facilities. In a joint venture with mainland companies, Andaman Fisheries is constructing new cold-storage facilities in the hope of increasing the annual harvest from a mere 26,000 tonnes to over 200,000 tonnes a year. However, cold storage requires a reliable power source, and electricity generation is a major challenge for economic growth. All the electricity on the islands is diesel generated (up to three months supply of diesel can be held at the Port Blair storage facility). At Rs 4 per kilowatt hour, island electricity is twice as expensive as electricity on the mainland.

Fresh water is another significant challenge. The islands receive 3000mm of rainfall a year but water rationing is still necessary during the dry season. Wells are not particularly successful since little water is retained in the ground. More dams are under construction and ponds are being built in remote areas. Plans to build a desalination plant have been shelved until such a plant becomes economically viable.

Sewage is another problem. The rapidly expanding population, especially around Port Blair, has placed unprecedented pressure on an already outdated system. While authorities claim the cost of a new system is prohibitive, environmentalists argue that the cost of not having one is far greater.

---

tour. There are a number of good, sandy beaches at Wandoor and some excellent snorkelling, but you should take great care not to walk on the coral exposed at low tide. Unfortunately, part of this reef has already been damaged.

Chiriya Tapu

Thirty kilometres south of Port Blair is Chiriya Tapu, a tiny fishing village with beaches and mangroves. It's possible to arrange boats from here to Cinque Island.

KLM Tours offers chartered boat trips to Cinque Island, and if you ask around the shops at Chiriya Tapu you're bound to find someone who is taking a boat out. The cost of the boat depends on the number of people, size of the vessel and your haggling skills. Prices vary from Rs 200 to Rs 800 per person. There's a beach a couple of kilometres south of Chiriya Tapu which has some of the best snorkelling in the area. There's a bus to the village every two hours from Port Blair (Rs 5.50, 1½ hours).

For many officials as well as locals, tourism is the potential golden egg. To ensure this egg will finally hatch, the airport runway is being extended so that larger aircraft can land. A customs and immigration facility is also on the drawing board. The thinking behind this is that direct flights from Thailand and possibly other parts of Asia will provide a significant boost to the island economy. Completion of these facilities is still several years away.

In the meantime tourist numbers are low. Occupancy rates of hotels average 40% during the high season and can be as low as 15% in the low season. Developers argue that this will change dramatically once the new facilities are complete and further infrastructure development has taken place.

Environmentalists claim that the projected influx from the new facilities will have a devastating impact on the fragile and unique biodiversity of the island. Strong disagreement continues over the carrying capacity of the island and the type of tourism desired. Developers employ such rhetoric as 'low-impact eco-friendly tourism' while environmentalists point to development disasters such as the cottages (for VIP use only) on Cinque Island where much of the coral was destroyed during construction.

One of the many obstacles faced by developers in their desire to expand the tourist industry is the controversial 1991 legislation on coastal zoning. Imposed by the government from Delhi, the zoning forbids the mining of sand anywhere near the island coast. Environmentalists support such restrictions but property developers claim these laws are severely retarding growth. They need sand for construction and they argue that it is not viable to import sand to the island.

Along with other entrepreneurs and free marketeers, the developers have formed a powerful lobby that may eventually succeed in persuading Delhi to at least relax if not relinquish control over the Andaman & Nicobar Islands. Most environmentalists condemn any loosening of the Delhi reins. However, they also know that central control doesn't necessarily spell conservation. Almost every week there are accusations that Delhi is ignoring and, in certain cases, actively condoning unchecked and inappropriate development.

A significant factor in the question of development is the role of the tribal communities on the island. A key recommendation of the Island Ecosystem and Sustainable Development conference held in Port Blair in 1997 states that the knowledge of the local tribal population in the utilisation of the natural resources needs to be identified and their intellectual property rights should be protected by law. There are indeed numerous examples of tribal people harvesting the natural resources in a sensitive and sustainable manner. They have been doing this for many hundreds of years.

A major concern of environmentalists is that, in the rush for the tourist dollar, such traditional ecological knowledge will be lost forever.

OTHER ISLANDS

The A&N Tourism Department has targeted half a dozen beaches for development but the tourist infrastructure is currently very limited and you shouldn't expect too much. In 1997 Bharatang (between South and Middle Andaman) and nearby North Passage were added to the list of islands fully open to visitors. Narcondam, Interview, Brother and Sister islands have just been opened for day visits only, but currently no regular boats visit these places. It's possible to charter a boat to visit volcanic Barren Island but disembarkation is not allowed.

Until the tourist complexes mooted for the islands are actually built, the only other accommodation is in *Andaman PWD (APWD) Guesthouse* or *Forest Guesthouse* (typically Rs 60 per bed in a double room). These should be reserved in advance in Port Blair, either at the APWD (☎ 30215; near Hotel Shompen) or the Forest Department in Haddo (☎ 31371).

Some people bring tents or hammocks (made up by tailors in Aberdeen Bazaar) and camp out on the beaches. In Port Blair, you can rent two-person tents for Rs 40 per day from the Andaman Teal House. Other useful items to bring include a bucket and a large knife.

If you do camp, make sure you take your rubbish out again. Fires are not allowed so bring a stove and kerosene with you. On the islands, kerosene supplies are usually reserved for locals.

Food and water on the main islands is readily available but when travelling to smaller islands you should be prepared to stock up on provisions. It's best to check with the boat or tour operator to find out what is available at your destination. As always, you should always carry water and sunscreen with you.

Neil Island

Forty kilometres north-east of Port Blair is Neil Island, which is populated by Bengali settlers. There's excellent snorkelling but some of the coral has been damaged by dynamite bombing for fish. Beaches are numbered: No 1 Beach, a 40 minute walk west of the jetty and village, is popular with campers who set up hammocks under the trees. There's a well nearby for fresh water. The snorkelling is best around the point at the far end of the beach, where you may also see very large fish. At low tide it's difficult getting over the coral into the water from the beach.

Places to Stay & Eat In the village there's a market, a few shops and a couple of basic restaurants serving dosas, fried fish, veg and rice. They often run out of mineral water and soft drinks.

Hawabill Nest Yatri Niwas offers four-bed rooms for Rs 250 and air-con doubles for Rs 400. Reserve in advance at the A&N Tourist Office in Port Blair. The *APWD Guesthouse* has just two rooms.

Getting There & Away On Wednesday and Friday at 6.30 am, ferries leave Phoenix

Bay for Neil (Rs 7/13 for deck/upper class, three hours), continuing to Havelock. Occasionally they visit Havelock first.

Havelock Island

Fifty-four kilometres north-east of Port Blair, Havelock covers 100 sq km and is inhabited by Bengali settlers. There are picture-postcard white-sand beaches, turquoise waters and good snorkelling. Although there are coral reefs, it's the marine life here – dolphins, turtles and very large fish – that make it interesting. So do the elephants that were brought to the island for work but now earn their keep from tourism.

Only the northern third of the island is settled, and each village is referred to by a number. Boats dock at the jetty at No 1; the main bazaar is a couple of kilometres south at No 3.

Having your own transport is useful – bring a bike from Port Blair or rent one for Rs 40 per day in No 3 village or from the paan shop outside the entrance to the Dolphin Yatri Niwas. A few scooters (Rs 150) are available from the Narayan paan store in No 3 village. A local bus connects the villages on an hourly circuit and also runs out to No 7 Beach. A tourist bus meets the ferry.

Places to Stay & Eat You need to make a reservation in advance at the A&N Tourist Office in Port Blair to stay in the Dolphin Yatri Niwas or the Tent Resorts.

Dolphin Yatri Niwas Complex offers pleasant accommodation in cottages beside a beautiful secluded beach (no snorkelling). Charges are Rs 200 for an ordinary double, Rs 300 for a deluxe room and Rs 800 for an air-con double, all with bath attached. Good but basic meals are served in the restaurant.

A&N Tourism's *Tent Resort*, beside No 7 Beach, has eight roomy tents (twin beds) set up under the trees. They cost Rs 100 for a double and there's a maximum stay of four days. There's a couple of toilets but no washing facilities other than the wells. Basic fish thalis (Rs 25) and drinks (tea, coffee, soft drinks and mineral water) are available.

Some people bring their own tents or hammocks and camp by the beach. The police come by occasionally to check that people aren't making fires or stripping off and indulging in 'hippy behaviour'. There's good snorkelling and the idyllic beach stretches for several kilometres. The only drawback is the sandflies, which make sunbathing an impossibility.

A second *Tent Resort* opened recently near No 5 Beach, and you can use the restaurant at the Dolphin Yatri Niwas if you stay here.

MS Guesthouse is 500m west of the jetty and has basic rooms with attached bath for Rs 100; Rs 40 for a dorm bed.

Gauranga Lodge is the green wooden building without a sign between villages Nos 1 and 3. It has doubles for Rs 45. The bathroom here contains an Indonesian-style *mandi* (water tank and scoop).

Accommodation on Havelock can be diffi-

cult for foreigners to secure, especially during election times when government officials assume the status of VIPs and book everything for themselves and their entourage.

Getting There & Away Ferries depart early in the morning usually on Tuesday, Wednesday, Friday and Saturday from the Phoenix Bay harbour in Port Blair. The four hour journey to Havelock costs Rs 7/13 on the lower/upper deck. The ferries return from Havelock to Port Blair one day later.

Long Island
This little island off the south-east coast of Middle Andaman has one small village and several sandy beaches that are perfect for camping. The only accommodation is the *Forest Resthouse*, although a *Yatri Niwas* is planned for Lalaji Bay.

On Wednesday and Saturday, the ferry from Port Blair and Havelock calls at Long Island (eight hours, Rs 9/20 for lower/upper deck) before reaching Rangat. Bicycles are the main form of transport on the island.

Middle Andaman
The Andaman Trunk Rd runs from Port Blair north to Bharatang Island and Middle Andaman, which are linked by frequent ferries. Since this road runs beside Jarawa reserves on the west coasts of South and Middle Andaman, buses carry armed guards. Having lost land to Indian settlers, the Jarawa are hostile to any outsiders and independent travel is inadvisable. If you try to take a motorcycle up here you'll probably be stopped at the checkpoint about 40km outside Port Blair, and turned back. There's tourist accommodation in Rangat and Mayabunder, but the entire island is now open to foreigners for camping.

You can get to **Rangat** from Port Blair via the Havelock, Neil or Long island ferries (Rs 12/28 for lower/upper deck, nine hours) or by bus (Rs 44, six hours). There's basic accommodation at the *Hare Krishna Lodge* and the *PWD Guesthouse*. A bus runs out to Cuthbert Bay for A&N Tourism's new *Hawksbill Nest* (Rs 75 per

Peel Island

Jetty
No 1
MS Guesthouse
PWD Guesthouse
Post Office

Gauranga Lodge
No 3

No 4
Shyam Nagar

No 5
Dolphin Yatri
No 7   Tent   Niwas Complex   Tent
Resort   No 6   Resort
Krishna Nagar

Kalapathar

**North
Havelock**

0   2   4 km

The Boy Who Fell From The Tree

In 1996, a 16 year old Jarawa boy was found semiconscious at the foot of a tree on South Andaman. He was 'picked up' by the police and taken to hospital in Port Blair. Whilst some people believe the boy fell out of the tree, others claim he was frightened out by gunshot from angry settlers. In hospital he was treated for concussion and a broken leg, and was given modern medicines, bandages and food. It didn't take long before the boy recovered and he soon became a minor celebrity at the hospital. He quickly mastered a number of Hindi words and was able to communicate with those who were helping him.

Once he was fully recovered, the authorities returned him to his village. However, within a few weeks he was back among the settlers, only this time he was not alone. He brought with him several members of his own tribe. He'd somehow convinced his people that within the settlement community, food, drink and medicine is freely available. Over the months, the boy would make several trips to the settlement areas, each time bringing new members of his tribal group in search of free food and medicine.

Local media hailed the boy's return to the settler community as a triumph of 'civilised life' over 'primitive life'. Indeed, many settlers believe that each 'contact' is a step further towards complete integration. Others, however, have expressed grave concerns for the inevitable demise of the boy and his tribe. Staff at the Anthropology Museum are especially concerned that the expectations of free food and medicine will simply exacerbate the cultural displacement and result in a destructive lifestyle, dependent on tobacco, alcohol and begging.

In their endless debate on the complex issues of appropriate development, the authorities continue to espouse the rhetoric of preservation, protection and sustainability. Meanwhile, each month, more tribal people move from a culture of independence and self-reliance into a culture of dependency.

---

bed in a four-bed dorm, Rs 400 for an aircon double). Bookings for the Hawksbill Nest must be made in advance at the tourist office in Port Blair.

Mayabunder, 71km north of Rangat, is linked by the daily bus from Port Blair (Rs 55, nine hours) and also by occasional ferries. There's an 18 bed *APWD Guesthouse* here. There's also a recently completed *Yatri Niwas* at Karmatang Bay, 10km north-east of Mayabunder. Advance bookings are advisable, through the tourist office or the APWD office in Port Blair. Accommodation is frequently booked out as government officials are given priority on bookings.

North Andaman

Diglipur is the only place on North Andaman where foreigners may spend the night. It's served by a weekly ferry from Port Blair and daily ferries from Mayabunder. There is also a bus departing at 5 am every day (except

Tuesday) from Port Blair. The fare is Rs 140 and the journey is supposed to take eight hours. Many travellers, however, report that the journey averages around 12 hours. There's a 12 bed *APWD Guesthouse*, and a recently built *Yatri Niwas*. Bookings should be made through the tourist office in Port Blair.

Cinque Island

Uninhabited North and South Cinque are part of the national park south of Wandoor. Surrounded by pristine coral reefs, they are among the most beautiful islands in the Andamans. The boats usually anchor off South Cinque and passengers transfer via dinghy to the beach. The snorkelling here is first class. Sadly, however, much of the coral close to the beach is dead and to see abundant marine life you need to swim out a few hundred metres. Various reasons are advanced for the dead coral. An unusually rough monsoon is one. Another is the destruction caused by naval boats carrying construction materials. The boats would run up onto the beach, destroying the coral in their wake. The construction materials were used to build upmarket air-con cabins on the beachfront to accommodate a Thai Princess and her entourage in 1996. A popular belief is that the visit of the princess gave the Indian authorities the excuse they needed to construct accommodation that is now used exclusively for Indian VIPs.

Unless you are a VIP, only day visits are allowed. And unless you're going on one of the day trips occasionally organised by travel agents, you need to get permission from the Forest Department.

The islands are two hours by boat from Chiriya Tapu or 3½ hours from Wandoor. The trip costs Rs 600 to Rs 800 per person depending on the vessel and the number of passengers. The advantage of departing from Wandoor is that you access the boat by a jetty. At Chiriya Tapu you join the boat via a dinghy. This is OK in the morning light, but when returning after dark it can be a little precarious climbing off the boat and then landing the dinghy close enough to the beach so that passengers don't have to negotiate rocks in the water before reaching dry ground. Another advantage of the longer trip back to Wandoor is the spectacle of the night sky and the moonlight on the mangrove swamps.

Little Andaman

The 100 remaining members of the Onge tribe are confined to a reserve in the south of this island. As the northern part of Little Andaman has been settled, and was opened to foreigners in 1997, time has probably run out for the Onge.

Ferries land at Hut Bay on the east coast. Basic supplies are available in the village 2km to the north. Another kilometre north brings you to the new *APWD Guesthouse*, which is the only accommodation (reserve bookings at the tourist office in Port Blair). Singles/doubles/triples here cost Rs 75/100/150. Just under 2km north of the guesthouse is the police station where you must register on arrival, then it's about 15km to the main beach at Butler Bay, where some people camp. The waves make this a good place for swimming but there's not much snorkelling.

The tribal reserve in the south is out of bounds to foreigners. Don't try to make contact with the Onge – you certainly won't help their cause by turning them into a tourist attraction.

Passenger boats connect Port Blair with Hut Bay (Rs 14/31 for lower/upper deck, eight hours) once or twice a week.

Language

India has no single national language. The constitution instead recognises 18 official languages, including English. The non-English varieties fall roughly into two main groups: Indic (or Indo-Aryan) and Dravidian. There were also over 1600 minor languages and dialects listed in the last census.

The native languages of the south mostly belong to the Dravidian family, although these have been influenced to varying degrees during their development by Hindi and Sanskrit. The officially recognised native languages of the south are Kannada, Konkani, Malayalam, Tamil and Telugu. As the predominant languages in specific geographic areas they have in effect been used to determine the regional boundaries for the southern states.

Major efforts have been made to promote Hindi is as the 'official' language of India, and to gradually phase out English. While Hindi is the predominant language of the north, it bears little relation to the Dravidian languages of the south; subsequently very few people in the south speak Hindi. Resistance to change has been strongest in the state of Tamil Nadu – as a result Tamil is still very much the predominant language of South India and English is still also widely spoken.

Tamil

Tamil is the official language in the South Indian state of Tamil Nadu and the Union Territory of Pondicherry. In the 1991 census of India, Tamil speakers in Tamil Nadu alone numbered around 56 million; substantial numbers of Tamil speakers can also be found in Sri Lanka and Malaysia and significant minorities in Singapore, Fiji and Mauritius. There are around 71 million speakers worldwide.

Tamil is classed as a South Dravidian language, and is one of the major Dravidian languages of South India. The exact origins of the Dravidian family are unknown but it is believed to have arrived in India's northwest around 4000 BC, gradually splitting into four branches with the passage of time. Tamil became isolated to India's south as the Indo-Aryan language varieties such as Hindi became more dominant in the north.

Along with Sanskrit, Tamil is recognised as 'one of the two classical languages of India'. It has a very rich historical tradition dating back more than 2000 years, since which time three forms have been distinguished: Old Tamil (200 BC to 700 AD), Middle Tamil (700 AD to 1600 AD) and Modern Tamil (1600 to the present).

Modern Tamil is diglossic in nature, which means it has two distinct forms: literary or classical (used mainly in writing and formal speech), and spoken (used in everyday conversation). The spoken form has a wide range of dialects, varying in social, cultural and regional dimensions. Irrespective of the differences, a common variety called Standard Spoken Tamil is widely used in mass media and by all Tamils in their day-to-day life.

Writing System & Transliteration

Tamil has its own alphabetic script which has not been included in this language guide. Our transliteration system is intended as a simplified method of representing the sounds of Tamil using the roman alphabet. As with all such systems it is not exact and should be seen only as an approximate guide to the pronunciation of the language.

Pronunciation
Vowels

The vowel system of Tamil doesn't differ greatly from that of English and shouldn't pose any real difficulties. Vowels are distinguished by length, however, and long vowels are represented in this guide by a macron (a stroke above the letter); pronounce them as you would short vowels but increase their duration.

Short		Long
a	as in 'father'	ā
e	as in 'met'	ē
i	as in 'bit'	ī
o	as in 'hot'	ō
u	as in 'boot'	ū

Vowel Combinations

ai	as in 'eye'
au	as in 'how'

Consonants

Most consonants are fairly similar to English. A few which could cause confusion are:

g	as in 'go'
k	as in 'car'
ñ	as the 'ni' in the word 'onion'; as in the Spanish 'señor'
s	as in 'sit'
zh	as the 's' in 'pleasure'

Other consonants are a little more complicated because they represent sounds not found in English. The most common variants are called 'retroflex' consonants, where the tongue is curled upwards and backwards so that the underside of the tip makes contact with the alveolar ridge (the ridge of tissue on the roof of the mouth a little behind the teeth). Retroflex consonants are represented in this guide by a dot below the letter (ḷ, ṇ and ṭ). If the lingual gymnastics prove too much you'll probably find that you can still make yourself understood by pronouncing the letter as you would in English.

Essentials

Hello.	vanakkam
Goodbye.	pōyiṭṭu varukirēn
Yes/No.	ām/illai
Please.	tayavu ceytu
Thank you.	nanri
That's fine, you're welcome.	nallatu varuka
Excuse me.	mannikkavum
Sorry/Pardon.	mannikkavum

Do you speak English?	nīnkal ānkilam pēsuvīrkalā?
How much is it?	atu evvalavu?
What's your name?	unkal peyar enna?
My name is ...	en peyar ...

Signs

ENTRANCE	vazhi/ullē
வழி/உள்ளே	
EXIT	vazhi/vezhiyē
வழி/வெளியே	
NO VACANCIES	kāli illai
காலி இல்லை	
INFORMATION	takaval
தகவல்	
OPEN	tirentullatu
திறந்துள்ளது	
CLOSED	adaikkappatullatu
அடைக்கப்பட்டுள்ளது	
PROHIBITED	anumatiyillai
அனுமதி இல்லை	
POLICE STATION	kāval nilayam
காவல் நிலையம்	
ROOMS	araikal uṇtu
அறைகள் உண்டு	
TOILETS	kazhippitam
கழிப்பிடம்	
MEN/WOMEN	ān/pen
(ஆண்/பெண்)	

Getting Around

Where is (a/the) ...?	... enkē irukkiratu?
Go straight ahead.	nērāka sellavum
Turn left/right.	valatu/itatu pakkam tirumbavum
far/near	tūram/arukil

What time does the next ... leave/arrive?	eppozhutu atutta ... varum/sellum?
boat	paṭaku
bus (city)	pēruntu (nakaram)
bus (intercity)	pēruntu (veliyūr)
tram	trām
train	rayil

I'd like a one-way/ return ticket.	enakku oru vazhi/iru vazhi ṭikkeṭ vēṇum
1st/2nd class	mutalām/irantām vakuppu
left luggage	tavara vitta sāmān
timetable	kāla attavanai
bus/trolley stop	pēruntu nilayam

train station	*rayil nilayam*
I'd like to hire ...	*enakku ... vātakaikku*
	vēnum
a car	*kāra*
bicycle	*saikkil*

Around Town

bank	*vangi*
chemist/pharmacy	*aruntukkataikkārar/*
	maruntakam
... embassy	*... tūtarakam*
my hotel	*en unavu vituti*
market	*mārkket*
newsagency	*niyūs ējensi*
post office	*tabāl nilayam*
public telephone	*potu tolaipēsi*
stationers	*elutuporul vanikar*
tourist information	*surrulā seyti totarpu*
office	*aluvalakam*
What time does it	*tirakkum/mūtum*
open/close?	*nēram enna?*

Accommodation

Do you have any	*araikal kitaikkumā?*
rooms available?	
for one/two people	*oruvar/iruvarukku*
for one/two nights	*oru/irantu iravukal*
How much is it per	*oru iravukku/oru*
night/per person?	*nabarukku evallavu?*
Is breakfast included?	*kālai sirruṇṭiyutan*
	sērttā?
hotel	*hōtal* or *vituti*
guesthouse	*viruntinar vituti*
youth hostel	*ilaiñar vituti*
camping ground	*tangumitam*

Some Useful Words

big/small	*periya/siriya*
bread	*roṭṭi*
butter	*vennai*
coffee	*kāppi*
egg	*muttai*
fruit	*pazham*
ice	*ais*
medicine	*maruntu*
milk	*pāl*
rice	*arisi*
sugar	*sakkarai*
tea	*tēnīr*
vegetables	*kāykarikal*
water	*nīr*

Times & Dates

What time is it ?	*mani ettanai ?*
day	*pakal*
night	*iravu*
week	*vāram*
month	*mātam*
year	*varutam*
today	*inru*
tomorrow	*nālai*
yesterday	*nērru*
morning	*kālai*
afternoon	*matiyam*
Monday	*tinkal*
Tuesday	*sevvāy*
Wednesday	*putan*
Thursday	*viyāzhan*
Friday	*velli*
Saturday	*sani*
Sunday	*ñāyiru*

Numbers

0	*būjyam*
1	*onru*
2	*irantu*
3	*mūnru*
4	*nānku*
5	*aintu*
6	*āru*
7	*ēzhu*
8	*ettu*
9	*onpatu*
10	*pattu*
100	*nūru*
1000	*āyiram*
2000	*irantāyiram*
100,000	*latsam*
1,000,000	*pattu latsam*
10,000,000	*kōti*

Emergencies

Help!	*utavi!*
Call a doctor!	*tāktarai kūppitavum!*
Call the police!	*pōlīsai kūppitavum!*
Leave me alone!	*ennai taniyāka*
	irukkavitu!
Go away!	*tolaintu pō!*
I'm lost.	*nān vazhi tavirivittēn*

(With thanks to ON Koul)

Kannada

Kannada (also known as Kanarese) is also a Dravidian language. It is the official language of the state of Karnataka in India's south-west, where it's spoken by around 35 million people. After Telugu and Tamil it's the third most spoken Dravidian language of South India.

The earliest known example of Kannada literature is *Kavirajamarga*, which dates back to the 9th century AD, and today the modern language is represented by a thriving tradition covering all literary genres.

Sounds in Kannada which are likely to be unfamiliar to English speakers are the retroflex consonants, represented in this guide by ḍ, ḷ, ṇ, ṣ and ṭ. A stroke over a vowel (macron) indicates a long sound. See the pronunciation guide in the Tamil section of this chapter.

Some Useful Words & Phrases

Hello.	*namaste* or *namaskāra*
Excuse me.	*kṣamisi*
Please.	*dayaviṭṭu*
Thank you.	*vandanegaḷu*
Yes/No.	*havdu/illa*
How are you?	*hēge idīri?*
Very well, thank you.	*bahaḷa oḷḷeyadu vandanegaḷu*
What's your name?	*nimma hesaru ēnu?*
My name is ...	*nanna hesaru ...*
Do you speak English?	*nīvu ingliṣ matāḍtīrā?*
I don't understand.	*nanage artha āgalla*
Where is the hotel?	*hōtel ellide?*
How far is ...?	*eṣṭu dūra?*
How do I get to ...?	*nānu allige hōgōdu hēge?*
How much?	*eṣṭu?*
This is expensive.	*idu dubāri*
Show me the menu.	*menu tōrsi*
The bill please.	*dayaviṭṭu bil koḍi*
What is the time?	*gaṇṭe eṣṭu?*
big	*dodda*
small	*cikka*
today	*ivattu*

day	*hagalu*
night	*rātri*
week	*vāra*
month	*tingalu*
year	*varṣa*
butter	*benne*
coffee	*kāfi*
egg	*motte*
fruit	*hannu*
ice	*ays*
medicine	*auṣadhi*
milk	*hālu*
rice	*akki*
sugar	*sakkare*
tea	*tī*
vegetables	*tarakāri*
water	*nīru*

Numbers

1	*ondu*
2	*eradu*
3	*mūru*
4	*nālku*
5	*aydu*
6	*āru*
7	*ēlu*
8	*entu*
9	*ombhattu*
10	*hattu*
100	*nūru*
1000	*ondu sāvira*
2000	*radu sāvira*
100,000	*lakṣa*
1,000,000	*hattu lakṣa*
10,000,000	*kōti*

Konkani

After a long and hard-fought battle Konkani was finally recognised in 1992 as the official language of the small state of Goa on India's south-west coast. Until that time argument had raged that Konkani was actually a dialect of Marathi, the official language of the much larger neighbouring state of Maharashtra.

Even though Konkani is virtually the only

universally understood language of Goa, centuries of colonial rule, significant dialectal variation and as many as five different scripts meant that defining it as an official language would always be problematic. The issue was further complicated by the varying loyalties of the high caste and predominantly Catholic and Hindu Brahmin families who spoke Portuguese, English and Konkani, and the lower caste, mainly Hindu families who tended to speak Marathi as a first language and some Konkani. Despite these obstacles Konkani went on to be added to the Indian Constitution as the country's 18th national language. In this language guide a stroke over a vowel (macron) indicates a long sound.

Some Useful Words & Phrases

Hello.	paypadta
Excuse me.	upkar korxi
Please.	upkar kor
Thank you.	dev borem korum
Yes/No.	oi/nāh
How are you?	kosso assa? (m)
	koxem assa? (f)
Very well, thank you.	bhore jaung
What's your name?	tuje nāv kide?
Do you speak	to English hulonk
English?	jhana?
I don't understand.	mhaka kay
	samzona na

Where is a hotel?	hotel khoy āsa?
How far is ...?	anig kitya phoode ...?
How do I get to ...?	maka kashe ...
	meltole?
How much?	kitke poishe laqthele?
This is expensive.	chod marog
Show me the menu.	tumcho āije meno
	kithe āsa
The bill please.	bill ād
What's the time?	vurra kitki jali?

big	hodlo
small	dhakto
today	āj
day	dees
night	racho
week	athovda
month	mohino
year	voros

butter	
coffee	
egg	
fruit	
ice	
medicine	
milk	
rice	
sugar	
tea	
vegetables	
water	udhak

Numbers

1	ek
2	don
3	tin
4	char
5	panch
6	sou
7	sat
8	att
9	nov
10	dha
20	vis
30	tis
40	chalis
50	ponnas
60	sātt
70	sottor
80	oixim
90	novodh
100	xembor
200	donshe
1000	ek hazār
2000	don hazār
100,000	lakh
10,000,000	crore

Malayalam

Like Tamil, Malayalam belongs to the Dravidian language family. Though there are obvious lexical links between the two languages, with many words sharing common roots, Malayalam includes a far greater number of borrowings from ancient Indian

Sanskrit. Its divergence from Tamil began some time after the 10th century AD, with the first official literary record of it dating back to *Ramacharitam*, a 'pattu' poem written in the late 12th century.

The modern form of the Malayalam script developed from the 16th century literary works of Tuñcatt Ezuttacchan. It's the official language in the state of Kerala on India's far south-western coast, where it's spoken by around 30 million people. Some of the sounds in Malayalam that will be unfamiliar to English speakers are the retroflex consonants, represented in this guide by ḍ, ḷ, ṇ, ṛ, ṣ and ṭ. A stroke over a vowel (macron) indicates a long sound. See the pronunciation guide in the Tamil section of this chapter.

Some Useful Words & Phrases

Hello.	*namaste*
Excuse me.	*ksamikkū*
Please.	*dayavucheytu*
Thank you.	*nanni*
Yes/No.	*ānātē/alla*
How are you?	*sukhamāṇō?*
Very well, thank you.	*sukham tanne*
What's your name?	*ninnaluṭe pēra entāṇua?*
My name is ...	*ente pēru ...*
Do you speak English?	*ninnaḷ inglīṣa samsārikkumō?*
I don't understand.	*enikka aṛiyilla*

Where is the hotel?	*hōttal eviṭeyāṇa?*
How far is ...?	*... vetra dūramāṇa?*
How do I get to ...?	*... aviṭe ennane pōkaṇam?*
How much?	*etra?*
This is expensive.	*vila kūtutal āṇa*
Show me the menu.	*menu kāṇikkū*
The bill please.	*billa tarū*
What's the time?	*mani eṭrayēyi?*

big	*valiya*
small	*cheṛiya*
today	*inna*
day	*divasam*
night	*rātṛi*
week	*ālca*
month	*māsam*
year	*vaṛsam*

butter	*venna*
coffee	*kāppi*
egg	*muṭṭa*
fruit	*palam*
ice	*ays*
medicine	*marunnu*
milk	*pāla*
rice	*ari*
sugar	*panchasāra*
tea	*cāya*
water	*veḷḷam*
vegetables	*pachakkaṛi*

Numbers

1	*onna*
2	*raṇda*
3	*mūnna*
4	*nāla*
5	*ancha*
6	*āṛa*
7	*ēla*
8	*eṭṭa*
9	*ombata*
10	*patta*
100	*nūṛa*
1000	*āyiram*
2000	*raṇdāyiram*
100,000	*lakṣam*
1,000,000	*patta lakam*
10,000,000	*kōṭi*

Telugu

Telugu is a South-East Dravidian language spoken mainly in the state of Andhra Pradesh on India's east coast; it became the state's official language in the mid-1960's. With around 70 million speakers it is the most predominant of South India's four major Dravidian languages. Its literary history dates back to the 11th century AD when the poet Nannaya produced a translation of parts of the *Mahabharata*. While Sanskrit has played a major role in Telugu literature over the centuries, there is an increasing tendency for written works to reflect the more colloquial variety of Modern Standard Telugu. Sounds used in this short phrase list which will be unfamiliar to English speakers are the retroflex consonants ḍ, ḷ, ṇ and ṭ. A stroke over a vowel (macron) indicates a long sound. See the pronunciation guide in the Tamil section of this chapter.

Some Useful Words & Phrases

Hello.	namastē or namaskāram
Excuse me.	ksamiñchaṇḍi
Please.	dayatsēsi
Thank you.	dhanyawādālu
Yes.	awunu
No.	kādu
How are you?	elā unnāru? or elā bāgunnārā?
Very well, thank you.	bāgunnānu dhanyawādālu
What's your name?	mī pēru ēmiṭi? or nī pēru ēmiṭi?
My name is ...	nā pēru ...
Do you speak English?	mīku anglam waccha?
I don't understand.	nāku artham kāwaṭamlēdu
Where is the hotel?	hōṭal ekkada undi?
How far is ...?	... enta dūram?
How do I get to ...?	... nēnu akkaḍiki weḷḷaṭam elā?
How much?	enta?
This is expensive.	idi chālā ekkuwa
The menu please.	naku paṭṭi chūpiñchaṇḍi
The bill please.	billu iwwandi
What's the time?	ganṭa enta? or ṭaym enta?

big	pedda
small	tsinna
today	īrōju or īnāḍu or nēḍu
day	pagalu
night	rātri
week	wāram
month	nela or māsam
year	ēḍu or samwatsaram
butter	wēnna
coffee	kāfī
egg	guḍḍu
fruit	paṇḍu
ice	ays or mañchugaḍḍa
medicine	awsadham or mandu
milk	pālu
rice	biyyam
sugar	chakkera or pañcadāra
tea	ṭī or tēnīru
vegetables	kūragāyalu
water	nīḷḷu

Numbers

1	okaṭi
2	reṇḍu
3	mūḍu
4	nālugu
5	aydu or ayidu
6	āru
7	ēḍu
8	enimidi
9	tommidi
10	padi
100	nūru or wanda
1000	weyyi or wēyi
2000	reṇḍuwēlu
100,000	laksa
1,000,000	padilaksalu
10,000,000	kōṭi

Glossary

adivasi – tribal person.

agarbathi – incense.

Agasti – legendary sage, highly revered in the south as he is credited with introducing Hinduism to the region as well as with developing the Tamil language.

Agni – fire, a major deity in the *Vedas*; mediator between men and the gods.

ahimsa – discipline of nonviolence, most famously practised by Mahatma Gandhi.

AIR – All India Radio, the national broadcaster.

apsaras – heavenly nymphs.

Arjuna – *Mahabharata* hero and military commander who married Krishna's sister (Subhadra), took up arms against and overcame all manner of demons, had the *Bhagavad Gita* related to him by Krishna, led Krishna's funeral ceremony at Dwarka and finally retired to the Himalaya.

Aryan – Sanskrit word for 'noble'; refers to those who migrated from Persia and settled in North India.

ashram – spiritual community or retreat.

astrology – more than mere entertainment, astrological charts are commonly consulted before any major event, for example marriage, elections, important business trips.

Auroville – an experiment in 'international living' at Pondicherry.

auto-rickshaw – small, noisy, three-wheeled, motorised contraption for transporting passengers short distances. Found throughout the country, and cheaper than taxis.

avataar – incarnation of a deity, usually Vishnu.

Ayurveda – India's ancient form of medicine; uses a combination of herbs and massage to treat a range of ailments.

Ayyanar – village guardian figure in Tamil Nadu. Votive offerings take the form of terracotta horses.

baksheesh – tip, bribe or donation (Hindi).

banyan – Indian fig tree.

basti – Jain temple.

bazaar – market area. A market town is called a bazaar.

betel – nut of the betel tree; the leaves and nut are mildly intoxicating and are chewed as a stimulant and digestive. Also called areca.

Bhagavad Gita – Song of the Divine One; Krishna's lessons to Arjuna, the main thrust of which was to emphasise the philosophy of *bhakti* (faith); part of the *Mahabharata*.

bhajjans – devotional songs.

bhakti – intense, personal devotion to god; the bhakti movement in South India rebelled against priests and the reliance on Sanskrit.

bhang – dried leaves and buds of the marijuana plant.

Bharat – Hindi for India.

Bharata Natyam – Tamil Nadu's own form of classical dance.

bidi (beedi) – small, hand-rolled cigarette; really just a rolled-up leaf.

bidri – a specialised form of handicraft found in north-east Karnataka; silver inlaid into gunmetal.

bindi – forehead mark worn by women according to marital status.

BJP – Bharatiya Janata Party (Indian People's Party). Founded in 1980. Right-wing nationalist, promotes self-reliance and Hindu revivalism. Won ruling majority power in the 1998 parliamentary elections.

Bodhisattva – one who has almost reached nirvana, but who renounces it in order to help others attain it.

Bollywood – Mumbai's huge film industry; bigger than Hollywood.

Brahmanism – early form of Hinduism which evolved from Vedism; named after the Brahmin priests and the god Brahma.

Brahmin – a member of the priest caste, the highest Hindu caste.

Buddha – Awakened One; originator of Buddhism who lived in the 5th century BC; regarded by Hindus as the ninth reincarnation of Vishnu.

burkha – one-piece garment used by Muslim women to cover them from head to toe.

cantonment – administrative and military area of a Raj-era town.

Carnatic music – South India's own form of classical music; places a heavier emphasis on song compared with its northern counterpart.

caste – one's hereditary station in life.

chaitya – Buddhist temple. Also prayer room or assembly hall.

chakra – focus of one's spiritual power; disc-like weapon of Vishnu.

Chandra – the moon, or the moon as a god.

Chandragupta – important ruler of India in the 3rd century BC.

chappals – sandals.

charas – resin of the marijuana plant; also referred to as hashish or hash.

charpoi – Indian rope bed.

chedi – *see* pagoda.

chela – pupil or follower, as George Harrison was to Ravi Shankar.

chhatri – a small, domed Mughal kiosk (literally: umbrella).

chinkara – gazelle.

chital – spotted deer.

choli – sari blouse.

choultry – *dharamsala* (pilgrim accommodation) in South India.

chowkidar – nightwatchman.

Congress (I) – Congress Party of India. Ruling part at the centre for much of post Independence. Founded 1885. Stands for democracy and secularism and, since 1991, economic liberalisation.

CPI (M) – Communist Party of India (Marxist).

CPI – Communist Party of India.

crore – 10 million.

dagoba – *see* pagoda.

Dalit – preferred term for India's casteless class; *see* Untouchable.

dargah – shrine or burial place of a Muslim saint.

darshan – offering or audience with someone; viewing of a deity.

devadasis – traditional female temple dancers; by the 16th century discredited as having more to do with prostitution than with high art.

dharma – Hindu-Buddhist moral code of behaviour.

dhirio – Goan-style bullfighting, now outlawed.

dhobi ghat – the place where clothes are washed.

dhobi, dhobi-wallah – person who washes clothes.

dhoti – like a *lungi*, but the cloth is then pulled up between the legs; mainly worn by Hindu men.

digambara – sky-clad; a Jain sect whose followers demonstrate their disdain for worldly goods by going naked.

dowry – money and goods given by a bride's parents to their son-in-law's family. Officially illegal but widely practised.

Dravidian – a member of one of the original inhabitants of India. The Dravidian languages include Tamil, Malayalam, Telugu and Kannada.

dupatta – scarf worn with a salwar kameez.

durbar – royal court; also used to describe a government.

dwarpal – doorkeeper; sculpture beside the doorways to Hindu or Buddhist shrines.

election symbols – identifying symbols for the various political parties, used because so many voters are illiterate.

Eve-teasing – sexual harassment of women.

fakir – a Muslim who has taken a vow of poverty, but also applied to sadhus and other Hindu ascetics.

Ganesh – popular god, elephant-headed; worshipped as the remover of obstacles (among other aspects).

gaur – Indian bison.

Gayatri – sacred verse of the *Rig-Veda* repeated mentally by Brahmins twice a day.

ghat – steps or landing on a river; range of hills, or road up hills.

Gonds – aboriginal Indian race, now mainly found in the jungles of central India.

goondas – ruffians or toughs. Political parties often employ gangs of goondas.

gopuram – soaring pyramidal gateway tower of a Dravidian temple.

gumbad – a dome on a tomb or mosque.
guru – teacher or holy person (in Sanskrit, literally *goe* – darkness – and *roe* – to dispel).

Hanuman – leader of the monkey army in the *Ramayana*, and devoted servant of Rama.
Hari – another name for Vishnu.
Harijan – name given by Gandhi to India's Untouchables. This term is, however, no longer acceptable. *See also Dalit* and Untouchable.
hijra – eunuch.
Hinayana – small-vehicle Buddhism.
Hindustani – North Indian classical music (South Indian classical music is called Carnatic music).
hotel – a place to eat, and sometimes a place to stay as well.
howdah – seat for carrying people on an elephant's back.

ikat – fabric tie-dyeing technique; practised in Andhra Pradesh.
IMFL – otherwise known as Indian Made Foreign Liquor.
inam – Tamil for *baksheesh*.
Indo-Saracenic – style of colonial architecture that integrated western designs with Muslim, Hindu and Jain influences.
Irulas – tribal people who live near Chennai.

Jatakas – tales from the Buddha's various lives.
jyoti lingam – the most important Shiva shrines in India, of which there are 12.

Kabaddi – known as hu-tu-tu in South India; a game of tag.
kalamkari – designs on cloth using vegetable dyes; found in Andhra Pradesh.
kambla – buffalo racing; popular in parts of Karnataka.
kameez – woman's tunic or shirt, *see also* salwar.
Kanchipuram – Tamil Nadu temple town famous for its handloomed silks.
karan – Tamil for *wallah*.
karma – principle of retributive justice for past deeds.

Kathakali – Kerala's theatrical dance/drama.
khadi – homespun cloth. Gandhi encouraged people to spin khadi rather than buy English cloth.
khan – Muslim honorific title.
kolam – traditionally a rice-paste design drawn over the threshold of a home or temple to bring good fortune and ward off bad luck. Also known as *rangoli*.
Konkani – Goa's official language
Kuchipudi – Andhra Pradesh's own classical dance form.
kumbh – pitcher or water pot.
kurta – shirt (men).

lakh – 100,000. *See also crore*.
Lakshmi (Laxmi) – Vishnu's consort, goddess of wealth; sprang forth from the ocean holding a lotus. Also referred to as Padma (lotus).
lathi – large bamboo stick; what Indian police hit you with if you get in the way of a lathi charge.
lingam – phallic symbol; symbol of Shiva.
lungi – like a sarong; usually coloured or checked.

madrasa – Islamic college.
Mahabharata – Great *Vedic* epic of the Bharata Dynasty; an epic poem, containing about 10,000 verses, describing the battle between the Pandavas and the Kauravas.
maharaja, maharana, maharao – king.
maharani – wife of a princely ruler or a ruler in her own right.
mahatma – literally: great soul.
Mahayana – greater-vehicle Buddhism.
Mahayogi – the Great Ascetic; another name for Shiva.
mahout – elephant rider/master.
maidan – open grassed area in a city.
Malayalam – official language of Kerala.
mandala – circle; symbol used in Hindu and Buddhist art to symbolise the universe.
mandapam – pillared pavilion in front of a temple.
mandir – Hindu or Jain temple.
mantra – sacred word or syllable used by Buddhists and Hindus to aid concentration; metrical psalms of praise found in the *Vedas*.

masjid – mosque. Jama Masjid is the Friday Mosque or main mosque.

mata – mother.

monsoon – rainy season.

mudra – ritual hand movements used in Hindu religious dancing.

mund – village (eg Ootacamund).

mundu – sarong-like garment worn by men in South India, especially Kerala.

Murugan – son of Shiva and popular cult deity in Tamil Nadu and Kerala.

nadi astrologers – in Chidambaram, they will tell your fortune using palm leaf manuscripts.

nadi – river.

naga – literally: serpent; naga stones depicting the spiritually potent cobra are found in rural South India.

Nandi – bull; vehicle of Shiva. Nandi's images are usually found at Shiva temples.

Nataraja – Shiva as Lord of the Dance.

Naxalites – ultra-left political movement. Began in Naxal Village, West Bengal, as a peasant rebellion. Characterised by extreme violence. Still exists in Uttar Pradesh, Bihar and Andhra Pradesh.

nirvana – the ultimate aim of Buddhists, final release from the cycle of suffering existence.

niwas – house, building

nizam – hereditary title of the rulers of Hyderabad.

NRI – Non-Resident Indian, the subcontinent's version of Overseas Chinese and of equal economic importance for modern India.

Om – sacred invocation representing the absolute essence of the divine principle. For Buddhists, if repeated often enough with complete concentration, it should lead to a state of divine emptiness.

padma – lotus.

pagoda – Buddhist religious monument composed of a solid hemisphere topped by a spire, containing relics of the Buddha; also known as a dagoba, stupa or chedi.

palanquin – box-like enclosure carried on poles on four men's shoulders; the occupant sits inside on a seat.

Pali – derived from Sanskrit; the original language in which the Buddhist scriptures were recorded. Scholars still refer to the original Pali texts.

Panchatantra – a series of traditional Hindu stories about the natural world, human behaviour and survival.

pandit – expert or wise person. Sometimes used to mean a bookworm.

Parsi – adherent of the Zoroastrian faith.

peepul – fig tree, especially a bo tree.

permit rooms – in Tamil Nadu, where alcoholic drink are served legally.

prasad – food offering.

puja – literally: respect; offering or prayers.

punkah – cloth fan, swung by pulling a cord.

raag, or raga – any of several conventional patterns of melody and rhythm that form the basis for freely interpreted compositions.

raj/Raj – rule or sovereignty/specifically, the British colonial regime in India.

raja – king.

Rama – seventh incarnation of Vishnu. His life story is the central theme of the *Ramayana*.

Ramayana – the story of Rama and Sita and their conflict with Ravana. One of India's best-known legends, it is retold in various forms throughout almost all South-East Asia.

rasa – literally flavour; the unique quality with which a skilled classical dancer imbues a performance.

rathas – 1. chariots; 2. rock-cut Dravidian temples in the style of chariots at Mamallapuram.

Rig-Veda – the original and longest of the four main *Vedas*: the sacred, pre-classical Sanskrit texts.

rishi – originally a sage to whom the hymns of the *Vedas* were revealed; these days any poet, philosopher or sage.

sadhu – ascetic, holy person, one who is trying to achieve enlightenment; usually addressed as 'swamiji' or 'babaji'.

Sai Baba – arguably India's best-known guru. His ashram in Andhra Pradesh draws hundreds of thousands of devotees annually.

Shaivaite – follower of Lord Shiva.

Shaivism – the worship of Shiva.

salwar – pyjama pants worn with a kameez or tunic top (women only).

samadhi – an ecstatic state, sometimes defined as 'ecstasy, trance, communion with God'. Also a place where a holy man has been cremated; usually venerated as a shrine.

sambar – a deer; *see also the glossary in the South Indian Food section.*

sangam – the name given to a body of Sanskrit literature written around the Middle Ages. Valuable aid to scholars of early Tamil kingdoms.

sati – from the Sanskrit, sati means *virtuous woman*; sati is the once legal and sometimes still practised Hindu custom of a widow burning herself to death on her husband's funeral pyre.

satsang – discourse by a swami or guru.

Scheduled Castes – official term for Untouchables or *Dalits*.

shakti – female energy manifest in various forms within the Hindu pantheon; can be benign or destructive.

shola – virgin forest.

sikhara – Hindu temple-spire or temple.

Shiva – the Destroyer; also the Creator, in which form he is worshipped as a *lingam* (a phallic symbol).

sudra – low Hindu caste.

Surya – the sun; a major deity in the *Vedas*.

sutra – string; a list of rules expressed in verse. Many exist, the most famous being the *Kama Sutra*.

swami – title given to initiated monks; means 'lord of the self'. A title of respect.

sweeper – lowest caste servant, who performs the most menial of tasks.

tabla – a pair of drums.

tank – reservoir.

Telugu – language of Andhra Pradesh.

Theravada – small-vehicle Buddhism.

tika – a mark devout Hindus put on their foreheads with *tika* powder.

Toda – one of India's best documented tribal peoples. Live in the Nilgiri Hills in Tamil Nadu and still preserve their animist beliefs.

tonga – two-wheeled horse or pony carriage.

Untouchable – lowest caste or 'casteless' for whom the most menial tasks are reserved. The name derives from the belief that higher castes risk defilement if they touch one. Formerly known as *Harijan*, now *Dalit*.

Upanishads – Esoteric doctrine; ancient texts forming part of the *Vedas* (although of a later date), they delve into weighty matters such as the nature of the universe and the soul.

varna – the division of society into groups with Brahmins on top and Sudras at the bottom. Within one's varna one is further defined according to one's vocational calling, or jati. This defines one's caste.

vastu shastra – India's answer to the Chinese art of divine design, feng shui.

Vedas – the Hindu sacred books; a collection of hymns composed in pre-classical Sanskrit during the 2nd millennium BC and divided into four books: *Rig-Veda, Yajur-Veda, Sama-Veda* and *Atharva-Veda*.

vimana – principal part of a Hindu temple. In South India, it's stepped as opposed to curvilinear.

veena – fretted stringed musical instrument used in classical music performances in South India.

Vindya Range – the symbolic division between North and South India.

Vishnu – the third in the Hindu trinity of gods along with Brahma and Shiva. The Preserver and Restorer, who so far has nine *avataars*: the fish Matsya; the tortoise Kurma; the wild boar Naraha; the man-lion Narasimha; the dwarf Vamana; the Brahmin Parashu-Rama; Rama (of *Ramayana* fame); Krishna; the Buddha.

wallah – man (Hindi). A useful, multipurpose suffix, eg dhobi-wallah (washerman), rickshaw-wallah (rickshaw driver), etc. *See also karan.*

yakshi – maiden.
yantra – a geometric plan thought to create energy.
yatra – pilgrimage.
yoni – vagina; fertility symbol.

zamindar – landowner.

For a glossary of food and drink terms, see the special section 'South Indian Food' in the Facts for the Visitor chapter.

Index

TEXT

Index 683

BOXED TEXT

Phrasebooks

LONELY PLANET

Phrasebooks

L onely Planet phrasebooks are packed with essential words and phrases to help travellers communicate with the locals. With colour tabs for quick reference, an extensive vocabulary and use of script, these handy pocket-sized language guides cover day-to-day travel situations.

- handy pocket-sized books
- easy to understand Pronunciation chapter
- clear & comprehensive Grammar chapter
- romanisation alongside script to allow ease of pronunciation
- script throughout so users can point to phrases for every situation
- full of cultural information and tips for the traveller

'...vital for a real DIY spirit and attitude in language learning'
— *Backpacker*

'the phrasebooks have good cultural backgrounders and offer solid advice for challenging situations in remote locations'
— *San Francisco Examiner*

Arabic (Egyptian) • Arabic (Moroccan) • Australian *(Australian English, Aboriginal and Torres Strait languages)* • Baltic States *(Estonian, Latvian, Lithuanian)* • Bengali • Brazilian • British • Burmese • Cantonese • Central Asia • Central Europe *(Czech, French, German, Hungarian, Italian, Slovak)* • Eastern Europe *(Bulgarian, Czech, Hungarian, Polish, Romanian, Slovak)* • Ethiopian (Amharic) • Fijian • French • German • Greek • Hill Tribes • Hindi/Urdu • Indonesian • Italian • Japanese • Korean • Lao • Latin American Spanish • Malay • Mandarin • Mediterranean Europe *(Albanian, Croatian, Greek, Italian, Macedonian, Maltese, Serbian, Slovene)* • Mongolian • Nepali • Papua New Guinea • Pilipino (Tagalog) • Quechua • Russian • Scandinavian Europe *(Danish, Finnish, Icelandic, Norwegian, Swedish)* • South-East Asia *(Burmese, Indonesian, Khmer, Lao, Malay, Tagalog Pilipino, Thai, Vietnamese)* • Spanish (Castilian) *(also includes Catalan, Galician and Basque)* • Sri Lanka • Swahili • Thai • Tibetan • Turkish • Ukrainian • USA *(US English, Vernacular, Native American languages, Hawaiian)* • Vietnamese • Western Europe *(Basque, Catalan, Dutch, French, German, Greek, Irish)*

LONELY PLANET JOURNEYS

JOURNEYS is a unique collection of travel writing – published by the company that understands travel better than anyone else. It is a series for anyone who has ever experienced – or dreamed of – the magical moment when they encountered a strange culture or saw a place for the first time. They are tales to read while you're planning a trip, while you're on the road or while you're in an armchair, in front of a fire.

JOURNEYS books catch the spirit of a place, illuminate a culture, recount a crazy adventure, or introduce a fascinating way of life. They always entertain, and always enrich the experience of travel.

IN RAJASTHAN
Royina Grewal

Indian writer Royina Grewal's travels in Rajasthan take her from tribal villages to flamboyant palaces. Along the way she encounters a multitude of characters: snake charmers, holy men, nomads, astrologers, dispossessed princes, reformed bandits . . . And as she draws out the rarely told stories of farmers' wives, militant maharanis and ambitious schoolgirls, the author skilfully charts the changing place of women in contemporary India. The result is a splendidly evocative mosaic of life in India's most colourful state.

Royina Grewal lives on a farm in Rajasthan, where she and her husband are working to evolve minimal-impact methods of farming. Royina has published two monographs about the need for cultural conservation and development planning. She is also the author of *Sacred Virgin*, a travel narrative about her journey along the Narmada River, which was published to wide acclaim.

SHOPPING FOR BUDDHAS
Jeff Greenwald

Here in this distant, exotic land, we were compelled to raise the art of shopping to an experience that was, on the one hand, almost Zen – and, on the other hand, tinged with desperation like shopping at Macy's or Bloomingdale's during a one-day-only White Sale.

Shopping for Buddhas is Jeff Greenwald's story of his obsessive search for the perfect Buddha statue. In the backstreets of Kathmandu, he discovers more than he bargained for . . . and his souvenir-hunting turns into an ironic metaphor for the clash between spiritual riches and material greed. Politics, religion and serious shopping collide in this witty account of an enlightening visit to Nepal.

Jeff Greenwald is also the author of *Mister Raja's Neighborhood* and *The Size of the World*. His reflections on travel, science and the global community have appeared in the *Los Angeles Times*, the *Washington Post*, *Wired* and a range of other publications. Jeff lives in Oakland, California.

LONELY PLANET TRAVEL ATLASES

Lonely Planet has long been famous for the number and quality of its guidebook maps. Now we've gone one step further and produced a handy companion series: Lonely Planet travel atlases – maps of a country produced in book form.

Unlike other maps, which look good but lead travellers astray, our travel atlases have been researched on the road by Lonely Planet's experienced team of writers. All details are carefully checked to ensure the atlas corresponds with the equivalent Lonely Planet guidebook.

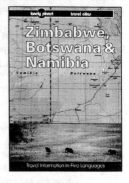

The handy atlas format means no holes, wrinkles, torn sections or constant folding and unfolding. These atlases can survive long periods on the road, unlike cumbersome fold-out maps. The comprehensive index ensures easy reference.

- full-colour throughout
- maps researched and checked by Lonely Planet authors
- place names correspond with Lonely Planet guidebooks
  – no confusing spelling differences
- legend and travelling information in English, French, German, Japanese and Spanish
- size: 230 x 160 mm

Available now:
Chile & Easter Island • Egypt • India & Bangladesh • Israel & the Palestinian Territories •Jordan, Syria & Lebanon • Kenya • Laos • Portugal • South Africa, Lesotho & Swaziland • Thailand • Turkey • Vietnam • Zimbabwe, Botswana & Namibia

---

LONELY PLANET TV SERIES & VIDEOS

Lonely Planet travel guides have been brought to life on television screens around the world. Like our guides, the programmes are based on the joy of independent travel, and look honestly at some of the most exciting, picturesque and frustrating places in the world. Each show is presented by one of three travellers from Australia, England or the USA and combines an innovative mixture of video, Super-8 film, atmospheric soundscapes and original music.

Videos of each episode – containing additional footage not shown on television – are available from good book and video shops, but the availability of individual videos varies with regional screening schedules.

Video destinations include: Alaska • American Rockies • Australia – The South-East • Baja California & the Copper Canyon • Brazil • Central Asia • Chile & Easter Island • Corsica, Sicily & Sardinia – The Mediterranean Islands • East Africa (Tanzania & Zanzibar) • Ecuador & the Galapagos Islands • Greenland & Iceland • Indonesia • Israel & the Sinai Desert • Jamaica • Japan • La Ruta Maya • Morocco • New York • North India • Pacific Islands (Fiji, Solomon Islands & Vanuatu) • South India • South West China • Turkey • Vietnam • West Africa • Zimbabwe, Botswana & Namibia

The Lonely Planet TV series is produced by:
Pilot Productions
The Old Studio
18 Middle Row
London W10 5AT UK

For video availability and ordering information contact your nearest Lonely Planet office.

Music from the TV series is available on CD & cassette.

PLANET TALK

Lonely Planet's FREE quarterly newsletter

We love hearing from you and think you'd like to hear from us.

*When...*is the right time to see reindeer in Finland?
*Where...*can you hear the best palm-wine music in Ghana?
*How...*do you get from Asunción to Areguá by steam train?
*What...*is the best way to see India?

For the answer to these and many other questions read PLANET TALK.

Every issue is packed with up-to-date travel news and advice including:

- a letter from Lonely Planet co-founders Tony and Maureen Wheeler
- go behind the scenes on the road with a Lonely Planet author
- feature article on an important and topical travel issue
- a selection of recent letters from travellers
- details on forthcoming Lonely Planet promotions
- complete list of Lonely Planet products

To join our mailing list contact any Lonely Planet office.

Also available: Lonely Planet T-shirts. 100% heavyweight cotton.

LONELY PLANET ONLINE

Get the latest travel information before you leave or while you're on the road

Whether you've just begun planning your next trip, or you're chasing down specific info on currency regulations or visa requirements, check out Lonely Planet Online for up-to-the minute travel information.

As well as travel profiles of your favourite destinations (including maps and photos), you'll find current reports from our researchers and other travellers, updates on health and visas, travel advisories, and discussion of the ecological and political issues you need to be aware of as you travel.

There's also an online travellers' forum where you can share your experience of life on the road, meet travel companions and ask other travellers for their recommendations and advice. We also have plenty of links to other online sites useful to independent travellers.

And of course we have a complete and up-to-date list of all Lonely Planet travel products including guides, phrasebooks, atlases, Journeys and videos and a simple online ordering facility if you can't find the book you want elsewhere.

www.lonelyplanet.com
or
AOL keyword: lp

LONELY PLANET

Guides by Region

Lonely Planet is known worldwide for publishing practical, reliable and no-nonsense travel information in our guides and on our Web site. The Lonely Planet list covers just about every accessible part of the world. Currently there are nine series: travel guides, shoestring guides, walking guides, city guides, phrasebooks, audio packs, travel atlases, diving and snorkeling guides and travel literature.

AFRICA Africa – the South ● Africa on a shoestring ● Arabic (Egyptian) phrasebook ● Arabic (Moroccan) phrasebook ● Cairo ● Cape Town ● Central Africa ● East Africa ● Egypt ● Egypt travel atlas ● Ethiopian (Amharic) phrasebook ● The Gambia & Senegal ● Kenya ● Kenya travel atlas ● Malawi, Mozambique & Zambia ● Morocco ● North Africa ● South Africa, Lesotho & Swaziland ● South Africa, Lesotho & Swaziland travel atlas ● Swahili phrasebook ● Tanzania, Zanzibar & Pemba ● Trekking in East Africa ● Tunisia ● West Africa ● Zimbabwe, Botswana & Namibia ● Zimbabwe, Botswana & Namibia travel atlas
Travel Literature: The Rainbird: A Central African Journey ● Songs to an African Sunset: A Zimbabwean Story ● Mali Blues: Traveling to an African Beat

AUSTRALIA & THE PACIFIC Australia ● Australian phrasebook ● Bushwalking in Australia ● Bushwalking in Papua New Guinea ● Fiji ● Fijian phrasebook ● Islands of Australia's Great Barrier Reef ● Melbourne ● Micronesia ● New Caledonia ● New South Wales & the ACT ● New Zealand ● Northern Territory ● Outback Australia ● Papua New Guinea ● Papua New Guinea (Pidgin) phrasebook ● Queensland ● Rarotonga & the Cook Islands ● Samoa ● Solomon Islands ● South Australia ● Sydney ● Tahiti & French Polynesia ● Tasmania ● Tonga ● Tramping in New Zealand ● Vanuatu ● Victoria ● Western Australia
Travel Literature: Islands in the Clouds ● Sean & David's Long Drive

CENTRAL AMERICA & THE CARIBBEAN Bahamas and Turks & Caicos ● Barcelona ● Bermuda ● Central America on a shoestring ● Costa Rica ● Cuba ● Dominican Republic & Haiti ● Eastern Caribbean ● Guatemala, Belize & Yucatán: La Ruta Maya ● Jamaica ● Mexico ● Mexico City ● Panama
Travel Literature: Green Dreams: Travels in Central America

EUROPE Amsterdam ● Andalucía ● Austria ● Baltic States phrasebook ● Barcelona ● Berlin ● Britain ● British phrasebook ● Canary Islands ● Central Europe ● Central Europe phrasebook ● Corsica ● Croatia ● Czech & Slovak Republics ● Denmark ● Dublin ● Eastern Europe ● Eastern Europe phrasebook ● Edinburgh ● Estonia, Latvia & Lithuania ● Europe ● Finland ● France ● French phrasebook ● Germany ● German phrasebook ● Greece ● Greek phrasebook ● Hungary ● Iceland, Greenland & the Faroe Islands ● Ireland ● Italian phrasebook ● Italy ● Lisbon ● London ● Mediterranean Europe ● Mediterranean Europe phrasebook ● Norway ● Paris ● Poland ● Portugal ● Portugal travel atlas ● Prague ● Provence & the Côte d'Azur ● Romania & Moldova ● Rome ● Russia, Ukraine & Belarus ● Russian phrasebook ● Scandinavian & Baltic Europe ● Scandinavian Europe phrasebook ● Scotland ● Slovenia ● Spain ● Spanish phrasebook ● St Petersburg ● Switzerland ● Trekking in Spain ● Ukrainian phrasebook ● Vienna ● Walking in Britain ● Walking in Italy ● Walking in Ireland ● Walking in Switzerland ● Western Europe ● Western Europe phrasebook
Travel Literature: The Olive Grove: Travels in Greece

INDIAN SUBCONTINENT Bangladesh ● Bengali phrasebook ● Bhutan ● Delhi ● Goa ● Hindi/Urdu phrasebook ● India ● India & Bangladesh travel atlas ● Indian Himalaya ● Karakoram Highway ● Nepal ● Nepali phrasebook ● Pakistan ● Rajasthan ● South India ● Sri Lanka ● Sri Lanka phrasebook ● Trekking in the Indian Himalaya ● Trekking in the Karakoram & Hindukush ● Trekking in the Nepal Himalaya
Travel Literature: In Rajasthan ● Shopping for Buddhas

LONELY PLANET

Mail Order

Lonely Planet products are distributed worldwide. They are also available by mail order from Lonely Planet, so if you have difficulty finding a title please write to us. North and South American residents should write to 150 Linden St, Oakland, CA 94607, USA; European and African residents should write to 10a Spring Place, London NW5 3BH, UK; and residents of other countries to PO Box 617, Hawthorn, Victoria 3122, Australia.

ISLANDS OF THE INDIAN OCEAN Madagascar & Comoros • Maldives • Mauritius, Réunion & Seychelles

MIDDLE EAST & CENTRAL ASIA Arab Gulf States • Central Asia • Central Asia phrasebook • Iran • Israel & the Palestinian Territories • Israel & the Palestinian Territories travel atlas • Istanbul • Jerusalem • Jordan & Syria • Jordan, Syria & Lebanon travel atlas • Lebanon • Middle East on a shoestring • Turkey • Turkish phrasebook • Turkey travel atlas • Yemen
Travel Literature: The Gates of Damascus • Kingdom of the Film Stars: Journey into Jordan

NORTH AMERICA Alaska • Backpacking in Alaska • Baja California • California & Nevada • Canada • Chicago • Florida • Hawaii • Honolulu • Los Angeles • Louisiana • Miami • New England USA • New Orleans • New York City • New York, New Jersey & Pennsylvania • Pacific Northwest USA • Rocky Mountain States • San Francisco • Seattle • Southwest USA • USA • USA phrasebook • Vancouver • Washington, DC & the Capital Region
Travel Literature: Drive Thru America

NORTH-EAST ASIA Beijing • Cantonese phrasebook • China • Hong Kong • Hong Kong, Macau & Guangzhou • Japan • Japanese phrasebook • Japanese audio pack • Korea • Korean phrasebook • Kyoto • Mandarin phrasebook • Mongolia • Mongolian phrasebook • North-East Asia on a shoestring • Seoul • South-West China • Taiwan • Tibet • Tibetan phrasebook • Tokyo
Travel Literature: Lost Japan

SOUTH AMERICA Argentina, Uruguay & Paraguay • Bolivia • Brazil • Brazilian phrasebook • Buenos Aires • Chile & Easter Island • Chile & Easter Island travel atlas • Colombia • Ecuador & the Galapagos Islands • Latin American Spanish phrasebook • Peru • Quechua phrasebook • Rio de Janeiro • South America on a shoestring • Trekking in the Patagonian Andes • Venezuela
Travel Literature: Full Circle: A South American Journey

SOUTH-EAST ASIA Bali & Lombok • Bangkok • Burmese phrasebook • Cambodia • Hill Tribes phrasebook • Ho Chi Minh City • Indonesia • Indonesia's Eastern Islands • Indonesian phrasebook • Indonesian audio pack • Jakarta • Java • Laos • Lao phrasebook • Laos travel atlas • Malay phrasebook • Malaysia, Singapore & Brunei • Myanmar (Burma) • Philippines • Pilipino (Tagalog) phrasebook • Singapore • South-East Asia on a shoestring • South-East Asia phrasebook • Thailand • Thailand's Islands & Beaches • Thailand travel atlas • Thai phrasebook • Thai audio pack • Vietnam • Vietnamese phrasebook • Vietnam travel atlas

ALSO AVAILABLE: Antarctica • Brief Encounters: Stories of Love, Sex & Travel • Chasing Rickshaws • Not the Only Planet: Travel Stories from Science Fiction • Travel with Children • Traveller's Tales

THE LONELY PLANET STORY

Lonely Planet published its first book in 1973 in response to the numerous 'How did you do it?' questions Maureen and Tony Wheeler were asked after driving, busing, hitching, sailing and railing their way from England to Australia.

Written at a kitchen table and hand collated, trimmed and stapled, *Across Asia on the Cheap* became an instant local bestseller, inspiring thoughts of another book.

Eighteen months in South-East Asia resulted in their second guide, *South-East Asia on a shoestring*, which they put together in a backstreet Chinese hotel in Singapore in 1975. The 'yellow bible', as it quickly became known to backpackers around the world, soon became *the* guide to the region. It has sold well over half a million copies and is now in its 9th edition, still retaining its familiar yellow cover.

Today there are over 350 titles, including travel guides, walking guides, language kits & phrasebooks, travel atlases and travel literature. The company is the largest independent travel publisher in the world. Although Lonely Planet initially specialised in guides to Asia, today there are few corners of the globe that have not been covered.

The emphasis continues to be on travel for independent travellers. Tony and Maureen still travel for several months of each year and play an active part in the writing, updating and quality control of Lonely Planet's guides.

They have been joined by over 80 authors and 200 staff at our offices in Melbourne (Australia), Oakland (USA), London (UK) and Paris (France). Travellers themselves also make a valuable contribution to the guides through the feedback we receive in thousands of letters each year and on our web site.

The people at Lonely Planet strongly believe that travellers can make a positive contribution to the countries they visit, both through their appreciation of the countries' culture, wildlife and natural features, and through the money they spend. In addition, the company makes a direct contribution to the countries and regions it covers. Since 1986 a percentage of the income from each book has been donated to ventures such as famine relief in Africa; aid projects in India; agricultural projects in Central America; Greenpeace's efforts to halt French nuclear testing in the Pacific; and Amnesty International.

'I hope we send people out with the right attitude about travel. You realise when you travel that there are so many different perspectives about the world, so we hope these books will make people more interested in what they see. Guidebooks can't really guide people. All you can do is point them in the right direction.'

– Tony Wheeler

LONELY PLANET PUBLICATIONS

Australia
PO Box 617, Hawthorn 3122, Victoria
tel: (03) 9819 1877 fax: (03) 9819 6459
e-mail: talk2us@lonelyplanet.com.au

USA
150 Linden St
Oakland, CA 94607
tel: (510) 893 8555 TOLL FREE: 800 275-8555
fax: (510) 893 8572
e-mail: info@lonelyplanet.com

UK
10a Spring Place,
London NW5 3BH
tel: (0171) 428 4800 fax: (0171) 428 4828
e-mail: go@lonelyplanet.co.uk

France:
1 rue du Dahomey, 75011 Paris
tel: 01 55 25 33 00 fax: 01 55 25 33 01
e-mail: bip@lonelyplanet.fr

World Wide Web: http://www.lonelyplanet.com
or *AOL keyword: lp*